International Investment Banking   20

International Labor Relations   35

International Marketing Mix   32

International Public Affairs   42

International Risk Management   12

International Taxation   24

International Trade in Service   14

International Transportation   11

Legal Aspects of International Investment   25

Legal Aspects of International Lending   27

Legal Aspects of International Trade   26

Management of the International Marketing Function   33

Marketing Research in the International Environment   29

Multinational Corporation   16

Offshore Sourcing, Subcontracting and Manufacturing   38

Organization Design   39

Political Environment of Multinational Corporations   7

Research, Development and Technology Transfer   36

Sources of Information on International Business   A

State Trading   15

System of International Payments   3

Trade Blocs and Common Markets   4

Trade Financing   13

Transfer of Proprietary Technology to Developing Countries   37

HANDBOOK OF
INTERNATIONAL BUSINESS

HANDBOOK OF INTERNATIONAL BUSINESS

Edited by

INGO WALTER

New York University

Associate Editor

TRACY MURRAY

University of Arkansas

1807 1982

A Ronald Press Publication

JOHN WILEY & SONS

New York · Chichester · Brisbane · Toronto · Singapore

Library of Congress Cataloging in Publication Data:

Main entry under title:

Handbook of international business.

    "A Ronald Press publication."
    Appendices (   ) A. Sources of information on
international business/Betty Jane Punnett—B. A
bibliography of international business/Thomas N.
Gladwin.
    Includes index.
    1. International business enterprises—Management—
Handbooks, manuals, etc. I. Walter, Ingo. II. Murray,
Tracy.

HD62.4.H36   658'.049   81-21960
ISBN 0-471-07949-9   AACR2

Printed in the United States of America

10 9 8 7 6 5 4 3 2

PREFACE

Up to now, there has been no comprehensive reference work on international business for the nonspecialist—the executive, accountant, banker, or lawyer who may be fully familiar with particular markets or functions but needs a ready source of clear, concise, and up-to-date information on related dimensions. The *Handbook of International Business* is intended to fill this need.

The *Handbook* is divided into six parts dealing, respectively, with dimensions of the international business environment, problems of international trade, aspects of international finance, legal issues in international business, international marketing, and management of international operations. We have sought uniform coverage of the external setting, internal operations, and interactions of the firm with the outside environment. Each section is written by a highly respected authority, with heavy stress on clarity of exposition and organization.

The book can be used in several ways. Key words, concepts, or institutions can be found through the index to focus specifically on user requirements. Alternatively, individual sections may be read in their entirety in order to develop a thorough acquaintance with a major subject area in international business. Finally, the major sections of the *Handbook* may be read completely, as a textbook for the material covered. The last use will necessarily involve some repetition, but the different perspectives offered by each author will add to the insights obtained.

Readers will note that most sections of the *Handbook* are followed by comprehensive bibliographies. These can be useful as guides to further reading and additional information on the subjects covered. There is also a guide to international business services (Appendix A) and a listing of "classic" reference works (Appendix B) which can be used in building a core library on the subject.

We, as editors, naturally owe our complete gratitude to the authors of the various sections of the *Handbook*. Our job was to design the volume, select authors, encourage, cajole, nag, and finally edit the results. But credit for substance clearly belongs to the individual authors.

We would particularly like to honor Professor Wilson E. Schmidt, who passed away tragically shortly after completing his section of the *Handbook*, having just taken up his new position as U.S. Executive Director of the World Bank.

INGO WALTER
TRACY MURRAY

New York, New York
Fayetteville, Arkansas
February 1982

CONTENTS

PART 1 THE ENVIRONMENT OF INTERNATIONAL BUSINESS

1 The Fundamentals of International Trade and Investment
THOMAS A. PUGEL

2 The Balance of Payments
DAVID T. DEVLIN

3 The System of International Payments
HOLGER L. ENGBERG

4 Trade Blocs and Common Markets
PETER W. WOOD
ROBERT F. ELLIOTT

5 International Economic Institutions and Negotiations
WILSON E. SCHMIDT
TRACY MURRAY

6 Formation of International Economic Policy
CHARLES R. JOHNSTON JR.

7 The Political Environment of Multinational Corporations
DAVID H. BLAKE

PART 2 INTERNATIONAL TRADE

8 Export Development: Basic Principles and Methods
AMICUS MOST

9 Impediments to International Trade
WENDY TAKACS

10 Government Aids and Services
JONATHAN C. MENES

11 International Transportation
H. PETER GRAY

12 International Risk Management
G. FREDERICK RICHARDSON

13 Trade Financing
MAXIMO ENG

14 International Trade in Service
H. PETER GRAY

15 State Trading
JOSEF BRADA

PART 3 INTERNATIONAL FINANCE

16 The Multinational Corporation
THOMAS G. PARRY

17 Forecasting Exchange Rates
CLAS G. WIHLBORG

18 International Financial Markets
HARVEY A. PONIACHEK

19 International Commercial Banking
FRANCIS A. LEES

20 International Investment Banking
EDWARD B. FLOWERS

21 Country-Risk Assessment
INGO WALTER

22 Comparative Accounting Systems
KONRAD W. KUBIN

23 Accounting for Multinational Operations
FREDERICK D. S. CHOI

24 International Taxation
LOWELL DWORIN

PART 4 LEGAL ASPECTS OF INTERNATIONAL BUSINESS

25 Legal Aspects of International Investment
U. P. TOEPKE

26 Legal Aspects of International Trade
MORTON POMERANZ

27 Legal Aspects of International Lending
    MICHAEL GRUSON

28 Codes of Conduct
    SOTIRIOS MOUSOURIS

PART 5 INTERNATIONAL MARKETING

29 Marketing Research in the International Environment
    SUSAN P. DOUGLAS
    C. SAMUEL CRAIG

30 Information for International Marketing Decisions
    SUSAN P. DOUGLAS
    C. SAMUEL CRAIG

31 Entering International Markets
    FRANKLIN R. ROOT

32 International Marketing Mix
    SAMUEL RABINO

33 Management of the International Marketing Function
    KENNETH D. WEISS

PART 6 MANAGEMENT OF INTERNATIONAL OPERATIONS

34 International Financial Management
    JAMES L. BURTLE

35 International Labor Relations
    DUANE KUJAWA

36 Research, Development and Technology Transfer
    A. J. PRASAD

37 Transfer of Proprietary Technology to Developing Countries
    WALTER A. CHUDSON

38 Offshore Sourcing, Subcontracting and Manufacturing
    RICHARD MOXON

39 Organization Design
    STANLEY M. DAVIS

40 International Corporate Planning
    MICHAEL Z. BROOKE

41   Conflict Management in International Business
THOMAS N. GLADWIN

42   International Public Affairs
JEAN BODDEWYN

APPENDIXES

A   Sources of Information on International Business
BETTY JANE PUNNETT

B   A Bibliography of International Business
THOMAS N. GLADWIN

INDEX

CONTRIBUTORS

DAVID H. BLAKE is Dean of the College of Business Administration at Northeastern University in Boston, Massachusetts. With an A.B. from Dartmouth College, an M.B.A. from the University of Pittsburgh, and a Ph.D. in 1968 in international politics from Rutgers University, Dean Blake has researched and published in the fields of corporate strategy, the management of public affairs, and the international political economy. Among other books, he has written *Managing the External Relations of Multinational Corporations, The Social and Economic Impacts of Transnational Corporations: Case Studies of the U.S. Paper Industry in Brazil* (with Robert Driscoll), and *The Politics of Global Economic Relations* (with Robert S. Walters). He was vice-president of the Academy of International Business from 1979 to 1980. Dean Blake has consulted widely with corporations and other agencies on the management of external affairs and the development of international corporate strategy.

JEAN BODDEWYN is Professor of International Business and Coordinator of International Business Programs at Baruch College, City University of New York. He holds a Commercial Engineer degree from the University of Louvain (Belgium), an M.B.A. from the University of Oregon, and a Ph.D. in Business Administration from the University of Washington (Seattle). His teaching centers on international business, management, and marketing; while his present research interests and consulting activities deal with international business-government relations, corporate external affairs, disinvestments, and advertising. Major publications include *Comparative Management and Marketing* (1969)*, World Business Systems and Environments* (co-author, 1972)*, Public Policy Toward Retailing: An International Symposium* (co-editor and co-author, 1972)*, Western European Policies Toward U.S. Investors* (1974), *International Business-Government Communications* (co-author, 1975)*, European Industrial Managers: West and East* (editor, 1976), *International Divestment: A Survey of Corporate Experience* (1976), *Multinational Government Relations: An Action Guide for Corporate Management* (1977), and *Comparison Advertising: A Worldwide Study* (1978). He is a member of the Academy of International Business, International Studies Association, and the Academy of Management. He is also the author of a series of international surveys of advertising regulations, conducted for the International Advertising Association.

JOSEF C. BRADA is Associate Professor of Economics at Arizona State University. He received his B.S. and M.A. degrees from Tufts University and his Ph.D. from the University of Minnesota in 1971. Dr. Brada is the author or editor of three books and over 50 articles on the Soviet and East European economies and on East–West economic relations. Since 1977 he has also served as the editor of the *Bulletin of the Association for Comparative Economic Studies*. Dr. Brada has served as a consultant on East–West trade to industry, government, and international organizations.

MICHAEL Z. BROOKE is Visiting Professor at the School of Business, Queen's University, Kingston, Ontario, where he teaches international business and business policy. He began research into international strategies in 1963, and his first book on this subject—*The Strategy of Multinational Enterprise*, written in collaboration with H. Lee Remmers (professor at the European Institute of Business Administration, INSEAD, Fontainebleau)—was published in 1970. Since then he has published five more books, including a major bibliography, as well as over 100 articles and papers. In 1970 he founded the International Business Unit in the University of Manchester Institute of Science and Technology, which conducts research and teaching as well as bibliographical and consultancy work on all aspects of international business. Michael Brooke has lectured or conducted seminars in fourteen different countries and in fifteen states of the United States.

JAMES BURTLE is managing editor of the International Country Risk Guide, a publication of International Reports, New York. The risk guide, an advisory service for leading companies and financial institutions world-wide, establishes risk ratings for 90 countries based on political evaluations and analysis of economic and financial data. Before joining International Reports, Mr. Burtle was vice-president in the economics department of W. R. Grace and Company 1958–1980. At W. R. Grace one of his main concerns was as adviser to the Grace treasury department on foreign exchange operations. While at Grace he also maintained a foreign exchange advisory service for 12 major U.S. companies. Prior to joining W. R. Grace he was a member of the economics division of the International Labor Office in Geneva, Switzerland. He is a graduate of the University of Chicago with B.A. and M.A. degrees in economics. Mr. Burtle is co-author with the late Sidney Rolfe of *The Great Wheel, The International Monetary System* (1975). He has written numerous articles on international economics and finance for scholarly and financial publications. Mr. Burtle has had adjunct teaching positions at Columbia University, New York University, and other universities and is now Adjunct Professor of International Finance at Montclair State College. He has been a director of Predex Corporation (exchange rate forecasting) and a member of the Advisory Committee to the U.S. Office of Management and the Budget on the presentation of U.S. Balance of Payments Statistics. He has testified before the Senate Banking Committee on international monetary reform and the operation of foreign exchange markets.

FREDERICK D. S. CHOI (Ph.D., University of Washington, 1972) is Professor of Accounting at New York University. He has served on the faculties of the University of Hawaii, University of Washington, Cranfield School of Management (England), Japan–America Institute of Management Science, and as a member of the First American Visiting Team to establish the National Center for Industrial Science and Technology Management Development in the Peoples Republic of China. Dr. Choi is co-author of *An Introduction to Multinational Accounting* and *Essentials of Multinational Accounting: An Anthology* and is a frequent journal contributor on the subjects of international accounting and finance. On several editorial boards, he has consulted with both private and public organizations including Business International, the U.S. Department of Commerce, the United Nations, and major international public accounting firms. He is also a frequent lecturer in executive development programs in the United States and abroad.

WALTER A. CHUDSON is a consulting economist in New York. He was Senior Adviser (1973–1979) at the United Nations Centre on Transnational Corporations. He also served as Visiting Professor at the School of Advanced International Studies, Johns Hopkins University, 1980. He received his Ph.D. in economics at Columbia University in 1942, and his M.A. at Oxford University in 1936, where he was a Rhodes Scholar. Dr. Chudson also served as Professor of International Business, Graduate School of Business, Columbia University from 1967 to 1970, and as Economist, United Nations Secretariat, from 1946 to 1979. In addition, he taught at Yale University, the University of Oregon, and the New School for Social Research, and was a research associate at the National Bureau of Economic Research from 1939 to 1941. He has advised governments in Latin America, Africa, and Asia.

C. SAMUEL CRAIG is Associate Professor of Marketing at New York University's Graduate School of Business Administration. He has taught at the Ohio State University, College of Administrative Sciences, and Cornell University, Graduate School of Business Administration. He received a B.A. from Westminster College in 1965, an M.S. from the University of Rhode Island in 1967, and a Ph.D. from the Ohio State University in 1971. Dr. Craig has done considerable work in the areas of advertising, assessing communication effectiveness, the diffusion of innovation, and marketing of energy conservation. He worked for IBM's Data Processing Division and currently is a consultant to a number of major corporations. Dr. Craig is author or co-author of over 50 articles and technical papers and is on the editorial boards of the *Journal of Marketing Research* and the *Journal of Retailing*. He is co-author of *Consumer Behavior: An Information Processing Perspective* (1982) and is working on *International Marketing Research* (with Susan Douglas).

STANLEY DAVIS' interests span three areas: organizational behavior, international management, and management policy. He completed his B.A. at Brandeis University and holds his M.A. and Ph. D. in sociology from Washington University. He served for a number of years on the faculty of the Harvard Graduate School of Business Administration and more recently was Professor of Management at Columbia University. The author of several books, including *Matrix* (with Paul Lawrence) and *Managing and Organizing Multinational Corporations,* he also contributes regularly to scholarly journals. Professor Davis has extensive consulting experience and has conducted corporate executive and continuing education programs as well.

DAVID T. DEVLIN, currently working in Nairobi, Kenya, is in charge of cross-border exposure lending by Citibank in sub-Sahara Africa, and also coordinates Citibank's business relations with commercial and central banks in the region. After joining Citibank's Economics Department as vice-president in 1973, he transferred to the International Banking Group. He joined the newly formed Government/Public-Sector Unit based in New York; the unit coordinated Citibank's worldwide lending and other business with governments. During this period, he also was on a number of advisory committees to the U.S. Treasury Department. From 1969 to 1973, Dr. Devlin was chief of the balance-of-payments division in the Bureau of Economic

Analysis, U.S. Department of Commerce and later associate director of BEA for international analysis, in charge of both the Balance-of-Payments Division and the Direct-Investment Division. During this period, he was also on the advisory committee for balance-of-payments statistics of the IMF, which led to the fourth edition of their *Balance of Payments Manual*. He also received a Department of Commerce gold medal for work on balance of payments and direct investment. He has written and edited numerous articles in the *Survey of Current Business*. From 1962 to 1969 he was with the Federal Reserve Bank of New York, as an economist and as chief of the Balance-of-Payments Division. Dr. Devlin received his Ph.D. from Columbia University in 1968, a B.A. in 1956, and a B.S. (civil engineering) in 1957 from Lehigh University.

SUSAN DOUGLAS is currently Professor of Marketing and International Business at the Graduate School of Business Administration of New York University. Previously, she was a member of the faculty at the Centre d'Enseignement Superieur des Affaires at Jouy-en-Josas, France, and was Professor of Management (Associated) at the European Institute of Advanced Studies in Management in Brussels. She received a B.A. and an M.A. from the University of Manchester in the United Kingdom, graduated from the Institute des Sciences Politiques, Paris, in 1963, and obtained a Ph.D. from the Wharton School of the University of Pennsylvania in 1969. Other teaching experience includes the University of Louvain, Belgium, the University of the Witwatersrand, Johannesburg, and the Tatung Institute of Technology, Taipei, Taiwan. Her principal areas of research are cross-national consumer behavior, international market research, and strategic planning for multinational markets. She has published extensively in these areas in leading journals in the United States and Europe, including the *Journal of Marketing*, the *Journal of Consumer Behavior*, and *European Research*. Recent publications include "Measure Unreliability: A Hidden Threat to Cross-National Research" (with Harry Davis and Alvin Silk, 1981) and "International Portfolio Strategy: The Challenge of the 80s" (with Yoram Wind, 1981). She is currently collaborating on a monograph on International Marketing Research with C. Samuel Craig. She has served as consultant to a number of companies in the United States, Europe, and the Far East, including Robinson Associates in Philadelphia, S.A.E.D.E.C. in Paris, Canadean in London, and Tatung Industries in Taiwan. She has held research grants from the Marketing Science Institute, in Cambridge, the U.S. Department of Agriculture, and the Delegation Generale des Récherches en Sciences Sociales, Paris.

LOWELL DWORIN has a Ph.D. in physics from Columbia University and a Ph.D. in business administration from the University of Michigan. He is an Assistant Professor in the College of Business Administration of The University of Texas at Austin, where he teaches courses in taxation in the Master of Professional Accountancy program. Among the courses he has taught are Multinational Taxation, Taxation of Partnerships and Corporations Filing Consolidated Returns, and Oil and Gas Taxation. He is engaged in a study of the taxation of international oil and gas exploration and production for the U.S. Department of the Treasury. His earlier work for the Treasury Department and the Bureau of Business Research at the University of Texas at Austin dealt with the taxation of deep-sea mining and the relationship between manufacturing investment and employment in Texas and national economic conditions. He is a member of the editorial board of *The Accounting Review*.

ROBERT ELLIOTT is a lecturer in Political Economy at the University of Aberdeen, Scotland. Since 1976 he has also been Visiting Associate Professor at the Graduate Business School of New York University and the Department of Economics at Stanford University, California. He is a graduate of the University of Oxford and obtained an M.A. in Labour Economics from Leeds University. Mr. Elliott's principal research areas include international economic integration in Western Europe, and a wide range of issues within the areas of wage bargaining and wage inflation. He has contributed papers to both professional journals and books in these fields, and to date he is the author or editor of three books. Within these areas, he has served as a consultant to both private corporations and government agencies.

MAXIMO ENG is Professor of Economics and Finance at the Graduate Division, College of Business Administration, St. John's University, New York. He was formerly a member of the international banking staff at Citibank. He has served as consulting editor for the Intercontinental Publications, Inc. Dr. Eng has published a number of books and articles on overseas banking, international lending, and international financial markets. He received his M.B.A. and Ph.D. from the Graduate School of Business Administration, New York University.

HOLGER L. ENGBERG is Associate Professor of Finance and International Business at the Graduate School of Business Administration of New York University. He previously taught at Columbia University and at The University of Ghana in West Africa. He received his M.A. in economics from the University of Copenhagen and his Ph.D. degree from Columbia University. Dr. Engberg's principal areas of research include financial institutions and markets in the context of developing countries, with specific reference to Africa. He has published papers and articles in professional journals and books in this and related fields. He is currently a sectional editor of the Journal of International Business Studies. He has been a business economist and served as a consultant to a number of organizations in Africa as well as in the United States. He is currently a consultant to the Nigerian Stock Exchange, Lagos.

EDWARD B. FLOWERS is currently Assistant Professor of Economics and Finance in the College of Business Administration of St. John's University, New York. In 1975, Professor Flowers received his Ph.D. in International Business from Georgia State University, and, one year later, won the National Dissertation Award of the Academy of International Business for his Ph.D. dissertation, "Oligopolistic Reaction in European Direct Investment in the United States." An article based on this dissertation was subsequently published in the *Journal of International Business Studies* in 1977. Professor Flowers has also served as a Foreign Policy Officer for the Office of the Assistant Secretary for International Affairs of the U.S. Treasury Department, Washington, D.C.

THOMAS N. GLADWIN is Associate Professor of Management and International Business at the Graduate School of Business Administration of New York University. He received a Ph.D. in Business Administration from the University of Michigan in 1975. He is the author of numerous books and articles in the fields of conflict management and international business, including *Multinationals Under Fire: Lessons in the Management of Conflict,* written with Ingo Walter (1980). Dr. Gladwin directs the Multinational Energy-Environment Conflict Project at N.Y.U., is a member of the Editoral Board of *The Journal of International Business Studies,* and has served as a consultant to AMAX, IBM, General Electric, the E.P.A., and O.E.C.D.

H. PETER GRAY, born in Cheltenham, England, obtained an undergraduate degree at Cambridge University in 1949 and a Ph.D. in economics at the University of California, Berkeley, in 1963. He has been a fellow at the Brookings Institution, a visiting professor at Thammasat University, Bangkok, a professor at Wayne State University in Detroit and is currently professor of economics and chairman at Douglass College, Rutgers University. He has written five books: *International Travel: International Trade* (1970), *The Economics of Business Investment Abroad* (1972), *An Aggregate Theory of International Payments Adjustment* (1974), *A Generalized Theory of International Trade* (1976), and *International Trade, Investment and Payments* (1979) and has written more than fifty articles and notes in scholarly journals.

MICHAEL GRUSON is a member of the New York Bar and since 1973 a partner of the law firm Shearman & Sterling, New York. His principal areas of practice include banking law and financings, such as international loan transactions, project financings, and public offerings.

Dr. Gruson received his legal education in Germany (University of Mainz, LL.B. 1962; Freie Universität, Berlin, Dr. iur. 1966) and in the United States (Columbia University, M.C.L. 1963; LL.B. 1965). He is a member of the faculty of a seminar on Legal Aspects of International Business Transactions, which is conducted annually by the University of Illinois for Latin American public-sector attorneys.

He has published a book, *Die Bedürfniskompetenz* (Berlin, 1967), which deals with legislative jurisdiction of the federal parliament under the German constitution. In addition he has published a number of articles in professional journals. His recent articles are "The New Co-Determination Law in Germany" (with W. Meilicke, 1977), "Nonbanking Activities of Foreign Banks Operating in the United States" (with J. Weld, 1980), "Issuance of Securities by Foreign Banks and the Investment Company Act of 1940" (with P. Jackson, 1980), and "Governing Law Clauses in Commercial Agreements—New York's Approach" (1979).

CHARLES R. JOHNSTON, JR., is a partner in the Washington, D.C., law firm of Webster, Johnston, McGeorge & Davidson and a professional lecturer in law at the National Law Center, George Washington University. Mr. Johnston formerly served as Trade Counsel for the U.S. Senate Committee on Finance where he advised Republican senators on the committee and their staffs on international trade issues. Prior to his service in the Senate, Mr. Johnston served as counsel to a commissioner at the U.S. International Trade Commission. Mr. Johnston is the author and editor of *Law and Policy of Intergovernmental Primary Commodity Agreements* (1976) and has published articles, notes, and book reviews in various legal periodicals. A graduate of Ohio University and the California Western School of Law, Mr. Johnston received his Diploma in International Law from Cambridge University, England. He also attended the Hague Academy of International Law in the Netherlands.

KONRAD W. KUBIN is Associate Professor of Accounting at Virginia Polytechnic Institute and State University. He studied in three countries and received his Certificate of Candidacy (B.S. equivalent) from Erlangen-Nürnberg University, his M.B.A. from the University of Colorado, and in 1972 his Ph.D. from the University of Washington. At Virginia Tech Dr. Kubin was instrumental in developing a graduate course in international accounting. He has delivered and published numerous papers on international accounting in the United States as well as abroad, has been a member of the American Accounting Association's International Accounting Committee, and currently serves as an officer of its International Section. Dr. Kubin is a CPA in the Commonwealth of Virginia. His business experience includes working for three years for a German public accounting firm and serving as a consultant to a "Big 8" CPA firm in France, Belgium, and Germany. He also was a Visiting Exchange Professor at the Politechnika Warszawska and the Oskar Lange Academy of Economics in Wrocław, Poland. He is a former recipient of a Fulbright Grant and received the 1979 Outstanding Faculty Vice President Award from Beta Alpha Psi, national honorary and professional accounting fraternity.

DUANE KUJAWA (Ph.D., Business Administration, University of Michigan, 1970) is Professor of International Business, School of Business Administration, University of Miami, Coral Gables. He has researched and published considerably on industrial relations and employment issues related to multinational enterprise. Publications include *International Labor Relations Management in the Automotive Industry: A Comparative Study of Chrysler, Ford and General Motors* (1971), *Management and Employment Practices of Foreign Direct Investors in the United States* (1976), *Employment Effects of Multinational Enterprises: A United States Case Study* (1980), *Production Strategies and Practices of Foreign Multinationals in the United States* (1981), and "Foreign Sourcing Decisions and the Duty to Bargain Under the NLRA" (1972). Dr. Kujawa has lectured extensively in the United States at universities, before professional associations, and in executive development programs. Additionally, he has traveled and taught in West Germany, Venezuela, Colombia, and throughout Central America. Consultancies have included government agencies, international organizations, academic institutions, and corporations.

FRANCIS A. LEES is Professor of Economics and Finance and Chairman of Department at St. Johns University. He taught at Fordham University from 1956 to 1960 and at the University of Maryland in 1955. He received his A.B. from Brooklyn College, his M.A. from St. Louis University, and his Ph.D. degree in 1961 from New York University. Dr. Lees' principal areas of research include international finance, international banking, and international economic relationships. He has published papers in professional journals in these fields and is the author of eight books and monographs including two published by The Conference Board. His most recent book is *International Lending, Risk and the Euromarkets* (1979). At the present time his research interests focus on international banking and financial risk faced by corporate borrowers. He has served as a consultant to The Conference Board, New York Clearing House Association, New York State Education Department, Central Bank for Cooperatives, Royal Commission on Electric Power (Toronto), Point of Purchase Advertising Institute, and University of the State of New York. Dr. Lees served in the U.S. Army from 1953 to 1956.

JONATHAN C. MENES has been the Director of the Office of Export Planning and Evaluation in the International Trade Administration of the Department of Commerce since 1978. He has been responsible for the development and operation of a system for the planning and evaluation of ITA's worldwide export assistance programs.

Other responsibilities include operation of a global market research program and the identification and analysis of industries to be targeted for export assistance. In 1980 he managed and coordinated the preparation of the Export Promotion section of the "Report of the President on Export Promotion Functions and Potential Export Disincentives." Mr. Menes began his government career in 1966 as a Foreign Service Officer and served in Paris and in Washington in the Bureau of Economic and Business Affairs of the State Department. He joined the Department of Commerce in 1971 as an international economist. He has served as a member of the policy development staff of the Secretary of Commerce and as Director of the Applied Research Division in the Bureau of International Economic Policy and Research, specializing in the quantitative analysis of the relationships between the domestic economy and international trade. He has authored numerous staff studies on international trade topics and has presented papers on import forecasting models and on the Balance of Payments and Direct Foreign Investment. Mr. Menes received his undergraduate degree from Tufts University in Medford, Massachusetts in 1964 and his M.S. with a specialization in International Economics from the London School of Economics in 1966. He is a member of the American and Southern Economic Associations.

AMICUS MOST is retired Professor of International Trade, having taught at Pace University Graduate Business College and Graduate Business School of New York University. He also lectured and taught at universities throughout the world including World Trade Institute of New York; University of Tel Aviv in Israel; Chung-Ung University in Korea; University of Edinburgh; and many others. He was also the Director of the Institute of International Business at Pace Graduate School. For 15 years he served with the U.S. State Department's Agency for International Development (AID) as adviser in over 40 countries, residing in Korea, Guatemala, and Indonesia. He was director of A.I.D.'s Export Development Assistance Office. For five years he was consultant for the United Nations in Export Development in Indonesia, Philippines, Mexico, Southeast Asia, and Iran. He has worked in India, Pakistan, Nepal, Venezuela, Central America, and other countries. He also spent three years with the Marshall Plan as Industry Chief in France, Italy, and Germany. Professor Most is known as a leading expert in trade development, has written a number of books on the subject, and has lectured widely. Prior to and between his government assignments, he was engaged in private business for many years. He has been Executive Vice President of New Haven Clock and Watch Co. and Parkway Foundry Corp. (subsidiary of Neptune Metri Co.) and of Roman Bronze Works (subsidiary of General Bronze Corp). He has also been in the construction business. He studied engineering at Cornell University, Class of 1926, and in 1969 received a Honorary Doctor's Degree from Chung-Ung University of Seoul, Korea. He has been honored by the governments of Korea, the City of Berlin, and the Confinindustry of Italy, and various trade associations in Korea. He was appointed by the Governor of New York to the Housing Advisory Committee of the State Commission Against Discrimination. He is a member of the Academy of International Business, the Society for International Development, the Asia Society, and many other technical and international interest organizations.

SOTIRIOS G. MOUSOURIS is Assistant Director of the Policy Analysis Division, at present Officer-in-Charge of that Division at the United Nations Centre on Transnational Corporations (UNCTC). Since the establishment of the UNCTC in 1975 as

Deputy to the Director of the Policy Analysis Division, Dr. Mousouris has been supervising research on the economic, political, legal, and social aspects of transnational corporation activities, and since 1977 has been serving as Secretary to the Intergovernmental Working Group on a Code of Conduct. Before the establishment of UNCTC he was involved in the work of the United Nations on transnational corporations. He was a main author of the study *Transnational Corporations in World Development: A Re-examination* and served as Deputy Secretary of the Group of Eminent Persons, consisting of 20 high-level experts who first studied the impact of transnational corporations on world development and international relations. He joined the United Nations in 1966 as Economic Officer in the Department of Economic and Social Affairs where he dealt with issues of international trade, finance, investment, and regional integration. He served for a year on a team working in Africa which prepared a plan of economic cooperation among 14 West African countries. Dr. Mousouris received diplomas in law and in economic and political sciences from the University of Athens and practiced law for two years before resuming graduate studies in the United States where he obtained an M.A. in Economics from Boston University and a Ph.D. from Harvard Business School in 1966. He has published a number of articles on theoretical aspects of international trade, on economic development, and on codes of conduct relating to transnational corporations. He is the editor of the *CTC REPORTER,* a biannual publication of the UNCTC.

RICHARD W. MOXON is Associate Professor of International Business at the University of Washington. He earned his Doctor of Business Administration degree from Harvard University in 1973. He has been a Fulbright scholar while teaching in Colombia, and has also taught in France and Nicaragua. His publications include *Offshore Production in the Less Developed Countries—A Case Study of Multinationality in the Electronics Industry,* and a number of articles on technology transfer and foreign investment in developing countries.

TRACY MURRAY received a Ph.D. from Michigan State University in 1969 and is now Phillips Petroleum Company Distinguished Professor of International Economics and Business, University of Arkansas. His past positions include Economic Affairs Officer, U.N. Conference on Trade and Development (UNCTAD), 1971–1973; Associate Professor, Graduate School of Business Administration, New York University, 1974–1978; and economic consultant to the Organization of American States (1977 to present), Executive Office of the White House (USTR) (1979), U.N. Industrial Development Organization (1981), U.N. Conference on Trade and Development (UNCTAD) (1975, 1979, 1981), Government of Colombia (1980, 1981), and Government of Argentina (1980). He received an IBM Post-Doctoral Fellowship for International Business Studies (1976) and American Participant Lecture Grants to the Philippines, Hong Kong, Singapore, Indonesia, Papua–New Guinea, India, Egypt, West Germany, Malta, Yugoslavia, Colombia, Argentina, and Brazil. Dr. Murray has published various articles, including "Alternative Forms of Protection Against Market Disruption" (with W. Schmidt and I. Walter 1978), "Quantitative Restrictions, LDC Exports, and the GATT" (with I. Walter, 1977), "MFN Tariff Reductions and Developing Country Trade Benefits Under the GSP" (with R. E. Baldwin, 1977), and a book, *Trade Preferences for Developing Countries* (1977).

THOMAS PARRY is Associate Professor of Economics at The University of New South Wales in Sydney, Australia. He previously taught at the University of Reading and New York University Graduate School of Business Administration in 1978. He received his B.Ec and M.Ec. degrees from The University of Sydney and his Ph.D. degree from The University of London (London School of Economics) in 1975. Dr. Parry's principal areas of research include industry economics, international economics, international technology transfer, and the economics of multinational corporate operations. He has published papers in professional journals in these fields and is the author or editor of several books and monographs. His recent book in the area of multinational corporations is *The Multinational Enterprise: International Investment and Host-Country Impacts* (1980). At the present time his research interests focus on technology transfer via multinational corporations and structural adjustment in open economies. Dr. Parry has served as a consultant to the United Nations Centre on Transnational Corporations in New York, the Economic and Social Commission for Asia and the Pacific in Bangkok, and several Australian Government agencies and private corporations. He has held research awards from the Bank of England, Social Science Research Council, Reserve Bank of Australia, Australian Research Grants Commission, and the Australia-Japan Foundation.

MORTON POMERANZ is a graduate of Columbia College and earned an LL.B. (J.D.) from Columbia Law School in 1945. Since February 1, 1980, Mr. Pomeranz has been in private law practice in Washington, D.C. He is counsel to the firm of Gage, Tucker and vom Baur, where he specializes in international trade and investment matters. Before moving to private practice, he served 14 years with the President's Special Representative for Trade Negotiations. For much of this time he was Executive Secretary of the Trade Expansion Act Advisory Committee and of the Trade Executive Committee. He was Acting General Counsel for the Office of the Special Trade Representative during the trade bill hearings of 1970. He then served as Senior Industrial Adviser and Chairman of the Section 301 Committee. In these capacities he has played a senior staff role in the major trade developments of the period. Mr. Pomeranz has been a key U.S. adviser to every major tariff and trade negotiation since 1959. Immediately prior to joining the Office of the Special Trade Representative he was International Activities Assistant in the Office of the Secretary of the Interior where, as a part of his duties, he represented that Department on the interagency committees charged with developing U.S. foreign economic, tariff, and trade policies. In 1961, he accompanied Secretary of the Interior Stewart Udall (as his adviser) to the first meeting of the U.S.-Japan Cabinet Committee on Trade and Economic Affairs in Tokyo. More than ten years of his career were devoted to serving the Bureau of Foreign Commerce of the Department of Commerce, first as Legal Consultant to the American Republics Division and later as Foreign Trade and Tax Specialist to the Bureau. He has also served in Latin America as a Vice Consul in the Foreign Service of the United States. He is a member of the Bar of New York State and of the District of Columbia. The American Bar Association named him chairman of its subcommittee on Latin American Law, a function he fulfilled for five consecutive terms. He is also a member of the American Society of International Law. He has lectured and is the author or co-author of a number of books, monographs, and articles on foreign trade and on Latin American law, taxation, and foreign investment. Mr. Pomeranz was, in recent years, the U.S. negotiator in resolving a number of bilateral trade problems with one or another of our principal trading partners. He has served as U.S. Delegate or adviser to numerous international conferences on trade and economic affairs.

HARVEY A. PONIACHEK is Vice President and Senior International Economist at Bank of America, New York, and Adjunct Associate Professor of Economics at Pace University Graduate School of Business. Dr. Poniachek has been with the Bank of America since 1973—engaged in money and foreign exchange markets, strategic planning and banking studies, and responsible for the Europe, Middle East, and Africa economic desk. In 1980 he was a visiting economist at Bank of America's European headquarters in London for six months. Dr. Poniachek conducted major research studies on a broad spectrum of topics, including the Eurocurrency market and the foreign exchange system, international banking and the payments system, regional economies, international trade finance and foreign direct investment. He has gained extensive expertise in the banking industry and is a member of Bank of America's Task Force Committee on Same-Day Settlement and the Hudson Institute study on the future of the financial services industry. Harvey Poniachek received a Ph.D. degree in 1977 from the State University of New York at Albany; he has also studied at New York University. He has published in professional journals and is the author of *Monetary Independence Under Flexible Exchange Rates* (1979) and *International Economic and Financial Relations in a Changing Global Environment* (1982). He is also the author of Bank of America's publication "Direct Investment from Abroad" (1981).

A. J. PRASAD is the Chief Executive and President of Hyderabad Batteries Ltd., India, a manufacturer of specialized batteries. From 1977 he has been teaching courses on international business during the summers at New York University. He has previously taught at the Graduate School of Business of Columbia University and at the Administrative Staff College of India. He has a B.S. in Science and in Engineering from India, an M.B.A. from the Sloan School of Management at MIT, and his Ph.D. from Columbia University. Dr. Prasad's principal interests are technology policy and development. He has published papers on export of technology from India and is the author of a book on Technology Policy for Industry. His recent book in technology transfer and economic development (with Robert Hawkins) is being published by the JAI Press in 1982. Dr. Prasad has served as a consultant to UNCTAD on the subject of the electronics industry in developing countries, and to several Indian companies before his career as an entrepreneur. He has also conducted research for ESCAP on the regulation of transnational corporations.

THOMAS A. PUGEL is an Associate Professor of Economics and International Business at New York University Graduate School of Business Administration. He received a B.A. in economics from Michigan State University and a Ph.D. in economics from Harvard University. His research interests include industrial organization, international trade, and international taxation. He is the author of *International Market Linkages and U.S. Manufacturing*. He received the Danielian Award in International Economics from the Department of Economics at Harvard University in 1975.

BETTY JANE PUNNETT is a Ph.D. candidate in International Management at the Graduate School of Business Administration of New York University. She received her B.A. in 1968 from McGill University and her M.B.A. in 1975 from Marist College. Ms. Punnett spent several years, prior to receiving her M.B.A., working in the Caribbean, then worked with a New York based firm that operates assembly factories in South America and the Caribbean. Immediately prior to attending New York University she taught Management and Organization Behavior at the State University of New York at Plattsburgh. Her major research interests focus on cross–cultural management and the problems of cultural differences. She is actively engaged in research aimed at relating value differences among cultures to differences in organization behavior. In addition she serves as a management consultant for the Small Business Administration.

SAMUEL RABINO is an assistant professor of marketing at Boston University. His consulting and research interests lie in the areas of product development, testing advertising copies for European advertisers marketing in the United States, and developing export-promotion programs for the federal government. He received his M.B.A. and Ph.D. degrees from New York University.

G. FREDERICK RICHARDSON is Assistant Professor of Marketing and International Business at the School of Business Administration of Gonzaga University in Spokane, Washington. He received a J.D. degree from Columbia University School of Law and was admitted to the New York Bar in 1949. He received his Ph.D. degree in 1979 from the Graduate School of Business Administration of New York University. From 1950 to 1979 he was employed by American International Group, Inc., in New York, Havana, Bermuda, Caracas, and Guatemala, in various capacities including Manager for Central America, Panama, Ecuador, and Bolivia, President of La Seguridad de Centroamerica, Cia. De Seguros, S.A., Deputy Regional Manager for Latin America, Director of Manpower Planning, and Deputy Regional Manager for Europe.

FRANKLIN R. ROOT is Professor of International Business and Management and Director of International Business Programs at the Wharton School. A graduate of Trinity College, he has an M.B.A. from the Wharton School and a Ph.D. from the University of Pennsylvania. Professor Root has lectured in several countries in the fields of international business and economics. He has served on the faculties of the University of Maryland (1950–1955), the Copenhagen School of Economics and Business Administration (1963–1964), and the Naval War College (1967–1968). During the summer of 1970, he was Regional Advisor on Export Promotion for the Economic Commission for Latin America in Santiago, Chile. Professor Root has engaged in extensive consulting with business and government agencies. He has published over 50 articles and has written two books: *Strategic Planning for Export Marketing* and *International Trade and Investment* (Fourth Edition). A third book, *Foreign Market Entry Strategies,* will be published in 1982. Professor Root conducts executive seminars throughout the United States and abroad on foreign market entry strategies and political risk management. He is currently President of the Academy of International Business.

WILSON E. SCHMIDT was executive director designate at the World Bank and Professor of Economics, Virginia Polytechnic Institute and State University at his death in 1981. He received his Ph.D. from the University of Virginia in 1952. He served as Deputy Assistant Secretary, U.S. Treasury, 1970–1972; Member, Shadow Open Market Committee; Member, International Monetary Working Group, The Atlantic Council of the United States; Member, Foreign Portfolio Investment Survey

Advisory Committee, U.S. Treasury; Adjunct Scholar, American Enterprise Institute; Advisor, International Institute for Economic Growth; Member, Advisory Committee on Balance of Payments Statistics Presentation, Office of Management and Budget; Vice Chairman, President's Advisory Committee on International Investment; Trustee, Institute for International Economic Studies. Publications include *The U.S. Balance of Payments and the Sinking Dollar* (1979) and *Rethinking the Multilateral Development Banks* (1979).

WENDY TAKACS is Assistant Professor of Economics at the University of Maryland–Baltimore County and Professorial Lecturer at the School of Advanced International Studies, Johns Hopkins University. A former research fellow in the Brookings Institution Foreign Policy Studies Program, she also served on the staffs of the International Finance Division, Board of Governors of the Federal Reserve System, the International Monetary Fund, the Foreign Agricultural Service of U.S. Department of Agriculture, and the President's Commission on International Trade and Investment Policy. She is the author of articles on international trade policy and empirical estimation of trade flows.

UTZ TOEPKE is an international attorney admitted to practice law in New York and West Germany, presently of counsel to the New York law firm of Schwartz, Klink and Schreiber. Formerly he was Senior Attorney-International Law, IBM Corp., where he has served in various capacities in both domestic and overseas legal operations. He is also Adjunct Professor of International Business at the Graduate School of Business Administration of New York University. Dr. Toepke received his Abitur in 1961 from the Johanneum Lüneburg in West Germany and his degrees of Referendar (LL.B.) and Doctor of Laws from Hamburg University, School of Law, in 1965 and 1967, respectively. In 1970 he received the degree of Assessor (LL.M.) from the Ministry of Justice in Munich, and in 1977 he passed the New York State Bar Examination. Dr. Toepke's principal areas of practice and research are international commercial law and litigation, international antitrust, and in particular the law of the European Common Market. He has published several papers related to these areas in both German and American professional journals and commentaries. At present, he is working on a comprehensive review of the antitrust case law as established in the EEC by the European Court of Justice and the Commission of the European Communities since 1965. In 1966/67, Dr. Toepke held a research grant from the Volkswagen Stiftung and the German Academic Exchange Service (DAAD), which led to a research sabbatical at Yale Law School in 1966 and resulted in the publication of his doctoral thesis, *State Supervision of Charitable Trusts, Endowments, and Fiduciary Funds in German and Anglo-American Law* in Hamburg in 1967.

INGO WALTER is Professor of Economics and Finance and Chairman of International Business at the Graduate School of Business Administration of New York University. From 1971 to 1979 he served as Associate Dean for Academic Affairs of the School. He previously taught at the University of Missouri–St. Louis, where he was Chairman of the Department of Economics from 1967 to 1970. He received his A.B. and M.S. degrees from Lehigh University and his Ph.D. degree in 1966 from New York University. Dr. Walter's principal areas of research include international trade policy, international banking, environmental economics, and economics of multinational corporate operations. He has published papers in professional journals in these fields and is the author or editor of a dozen books, including a widely used textbook. One of his recent books is *Multinationals Under Fire: Lessons in the Management of Conflict* (with Thomas N. Gladwin, 1980), which deals with non-market factors affecting foreign direct investment. At the present time, his research interests focus on the international banking industry and risk elements relating to international trade and capital flows. He has served as a consultant to a number of U.N. agencies, the U.S. Department of Commerce, Environmental Protection Agency, National Academy of Sciences, Ford Foundation, and other institutions, as well as private firms such as the General Electric Company, IBM Corporation, Citibank, Chemical Bank, and Morgan Guaranty Trust Company. Dr. Walter has held research grants from the Ford, Rockefeller, National Science, General Electric, and Alcoa foundations, among others.

KENNETH D. WEISS is Senior Trainer, export development and trade promotion, for the World Trade Institute in New York. He has previously held positions as trade-promotion training officer for the United Nations in Africa, foreign-trade information adviser to the government of Honduras, marketing-development adviser in Colombia for the Council of the Americas, and project coordinator in South Korea for the International Marketing Institute. He has also taught international business and marketing at Laredo State University in Texas, operated an export-management company, and done independent consulting. Mr. Weiss received an M.B.A. degree from Stanford University in 1965 and is now enrolled in the Doctor of Professional Studies program of Pace University. He is a member of Beta Gamma Sigma, scholastic honorary society, and was awarded a life membership in Alpha Kappa Psi, professional business fraternity. He received special training in export promotion from the U.S. Department of Commerce and the International Trade Center (UNCTAD/GATT) in Geneva. Mr. Weiss has written several magazine articles and business cases and has lectured on export promotion in more than 20 countries. He is conversant in English, French, and Spanish.

CLAS WIHLBORG is Associate Professor of Finance and International Business at the Graduate School of Business Administration of New York University. He received his Ph.D. in economics from Princeton University in 1977. Dr. Wihlborg's principal areas of research include international finance and monetary economics and the economics of common property resources. He has published papers in professional journals in these fields and is the editor of *Exchange Risk and Exposure* (with Richard M. Levich, 1980). At the present time his research interests focus on the transmission of disturbances between the real and financial sectors via the exchange rate, and on the economics of exposure management for multinational corporations.

PETER WOOD is a lecturer in the Department of Political Economy at the University of Aberdeen. He was awarded an M.A. by the University of Glasgow in 1975 and from 1975 to 1977 carried out research at the University of Oxford. In Spring 1980 he was Visiting Professor at the University of Gdansk, Poland. Mr. Wood's main research interests concern the economics of the European Community, public expenditure economics, and regional economics. At present he is particularly concerned with the trade and industry policies of the EEC and with public expenditure on education in Scotland. Dr. Wood has acted as a consultant to the OECD and also to governmental and private organizations.

PART 1

THE ENVIRONMENT OF INTERNATIONAL BUSINESS

THE FUNDAMENTALS OF INTERNATIONAL TRADE AND INVESTMENT

CONTENTS

REASONS FOR INTERNATIONAL TRADE 3

Law of Comparative Advantage 3
  Heckscher-Ohlin theory 4
  Differences in the technology available 4
  Economies of scale 4
Consumer Preferences and Product Differentiation 4
Transport Costs: A Natural Impediment to Trade 5
Gains from Trade 5

PROTECTIONISM 5

Tariffs and Nontariff Barriers to Import 5
The Optimum Tariff 6
The Domestic Politics of Protection 6
  Lobbying in favor of free trade 6
  Lobbying in favor of protection 7
  The infant-industry argument 7
  The national defense argument 7
The Effective Rate of Protection 7
Subsidies and Countervailing Duties 7

ROLE OF EXCHANGE RATES 8

Exchange-Rate Regimes 8
  Floating exchange rate 8
  Fixed exchange rate 9
  Exchange control 9
  Exchange-rate changes 9
  The current system 9
Spot Rates and Forward Rates 10
Speculation 10
  Methods of speculation 10
  Stabilizing or destabilizing speculation 11
Exchange Rates in Relation to the Macroeconomy 11
  The Keynesian approach 11
  The Monetary approach 12

INTERNATIONAL INVESTMENT 12

Growth, Investment, and Saving 12
Risk and Return in International Investment 12
International Portfolio Investment 13
Eurocurrency Market 13
Foreign Direct Investment 13

SOURCES AND SUGGESTED REFERENCES 14

THE FUNDAMENTALS OF INTERNATIONAL TRADE AND INVESTMENT

Thomas A. Pugel

International business includes in its domain most aspects of domestic business operations and certain features of the international environment that have no counterpart domestically. This chapter describes some of these special features of international trade and investment. The chapter is an introduction to such issues as the reasons for international trade in goods and services, the gains accruing to countries that participate in international trade, the reasons for and effects of protectionist impediments to trade, the role of exchange rates, and the importance of international financial investment. Many of the issues introduced in this chapter are discussed in more detail in subsequent chapters.

REASONS FOR INTERNATIONAL TRADE

The volume of international trade has been growing more quickly than the volume of world production since World War II. Economists and other observers have proposed a variety of reasons that countries would trade with each other. The reasons generally focus on fundamental differences in supply and demand between countries. The role of governments is usually ignored. After the fundamental reasons are discussed, the role of governments, especially in providing protection from imports or subsidies to local production or export, is added.

The reasons for trade can be divided into those that focus on supply differences between countries and those that focus on the role of demand patterns. Differences in supply are captured in the various bases of comparative cost advantages. The role of demand is most pronounced in the theory that focuses on the importance of consumer preferences and differentiated products.

LAW OF COMPARATIVE ADVANTAGE. The *law of comparative advantage* was first formulated in the nineteenth century by David Ricardo, building on work by Adam Smith. The law states that production will be located where it is relatively cheapest. According to the law of comparative advantage, a country will specialize in producing and will export those goods that it can produce cheaply relative to the costs of producing the goods in foreign countries and will import those goods that it could produce only at relatively high cost. Countries specialize somewhat in producing various goods and then trade among themselves to satisfy local consumption demands.

The initial applications of the law of comparative advantage focused on the importance of climate and the availability of natural resources as the basis for trade. Portugal would be expected to export wine to England, and to pay for the wine England might export cloth to Portugal. Zambia would be expected to export copper ore, and the United States to export wheat.

Heckscher-Ohlin Theory. Modern applications of the law of comparative advantage find the basis for trade in differences in the availability of factors of production, such as land, labor, and capital. Factors that are relatively abundant in one country should tend to be relatively cheap in that country. Goods that use these abundant factors should then be relatively cheap to produce in that country. A modern statement of the law of comparative advantage is the *Heckscher-Ohlin theory*: a country tends to export those goods that are produced with relatively intensive use of those factors of production that are found in abundance in that country relative to other countries. Goods that require relatively intensive use of relatively scarce factors are imported.

Although modern theories often consider the most important productive factors to be capital and labor, empirical studies indicate that the availability of skilled labor, as distinguished from unskilled labor, appears to be the most important factor in explaining observed patterns of trade. The United States tends to export goods intensive in the use of skilled labor and to import goods intensive in unskilled labor. The availability of land and the climate also determine the comparative advantage of a country, along with the availability of natural resources.

Differences in the Technology Available. A further refinement of the law of comparative advantage is based upon the observation that differences between countries in the costs of producing a good can also arise because of differences in the availability of technology. For instance, immediately after the development of the black and white television set, the United States was the only country with access to this technology. The United States soon became an exporter of sets. Over time the production technology became available in foreign countries, the basis for comparative advantage shifted, and the United States became a net importer of sets. This process of dynamic comparative advantage based on new technologies is called the *product-life-cycle theory of trade*. Closely related is the technological-gap theory.

Economies of Scale. A final refinement of the law of comparative advantage is based upon the importance of *economies of scale* in some industries. Where scale economies are important, the lowest unit costs are likely to be achieved by the largest producers. These producers are also likely to be exporters, especially to smaller markets that cannot support producers of minimum efficient scale. Countries in which the large producers exist then have comparative advantage in these products. For instance, the United States is a leading exporter of aircraft in large part because economies of scale require centralized production to achieve low unit costs. U.S. comparative advantage in aircraft is also based on intensive use of skilled labor in the production process.

CONSUMER PREFERENCES AND PRODUCT DIFFERENTIATION. Although the law of comparative advantage explains many of the observed patterns of international trade, a major portion of trade seems inconsistent with the "law." For instance, the United States both exports and imports significant numbers of automobiles. This aspect of international trade is often called two-way trade or *intraindustry trade*. Intraindustry trade appears to account for the large volumes of international trade in manufactured products that exist between the developed countries.

The basis for most intraindustry trade is found in the nature of *consumer preferences* and the existence of *differentiated products*. Although local producers may satisfy most local consumers with the products offered, some consumers in each country prefer imported varieties, because of physical differences or differences in image or perceptions. Local producers both export to satisfy segments of foreign demand and face import competition in some parts of the local market. Intraindustry trade is the result.

TRANSPORT COSTS: A NATURAL IMPEDIMENT TO TRADE. International trade generally incurs a cost not borne by purely domestic commerce: the cost of international freight and insurance. Even for easily transported products, this cost can easily reach 5–10 percent of the value if the products are shipped across an ocean, and for bulky or perishable items may equal or exceed the value of the products shipped. Because transport costs raise the price of imports, they tend to reduce the volume of trade, and to act as a natural impediment to international trade.

GAINS FROM TRADE. The *gains from trade* depend upon the basis for the trade. Where trade is based upon production specialization in countries according to the law of comparative advantage, the gains from trade are due to the benefits to consumers (or industrial users) of purchasing low-priced imports and the benefits to export producers of a wider market for their products and favorable international prices. Where trade is based upon consumer preferences and the existence of differentiated products, the gains from trade accrue as the benefits to consumers of an increased variety of products from which to choose. An additional benefit to consumers in this latter case may also accrue if the market power of local firms is reduced and imports make pricing and other aspects of market conduct more competitive.

The gains accruing to a country from international trade depend on two factors: the country's *terms of trade* and the volume of trade that occurs. The terms of trade can be thought of as the purchasing power of a country's exports on international markets, and the phrase is defined formally as the price (index) of a standard unit of exports relative to the price (index) of a standard unit of imports.

As a country's terms of trade improve, the purchasing power of its exported products increases. The welfare of the country increases because the same volume of exports buys a larger volume of imports. On the other hand, given the terms of trade, a larger volume of trade indicates a greater gain from trade for the country.

PROTECTIONISM

TARIFFS AND NONTARIFF BARRIERS TO IMPORT. In addition to transport costs, a natural impediment to trade, national governments create or condone various forms of artificial barriers to trade. In many cases these artificial barriers are designed to protect local producers from import competition. A common form of protection is the *tariff*, a tax levied on imports. All other forms of protecion are called nontariff barriers (NTBs). A well-known nontariff barrier is the quota, a quantitative limit on allowable imports. Other nontariff barriers are generally more subtle, and include "voluntary" export restraints (VERs), orderly marketing arrangements (OMAs), discriminatory practices in government procurement, discriminatory effects of technical standards, and arbitrary valuations by the customs authorities.

THE OPTIMUM TARIFF.   The government of a country may be able to increase the country's gains from trade by reducing a country's willingness to trade, as perceived by other countries. For instance, the country could raise its level of tariffs. To prevent their share of the market from falling too much, foreign countries would lower the prices of their exports. The terms of trade of the first country would then improve, as the purchasing power of her exports rose. The improvement in the terms of trade tends to increase the gains from trade, but the reduction in the volume of trade tends to reduce the gains. A level of tariff rates, called the *optimum tariff,* exists where the net improvement in the gains from trade is the largest.

In practice, countries seldom, if ever, attempt to impose an optimum tariff, in large part because such an optimum would be difficult to determine and because the country could end up a net loser if other countries retaliated with optimum tariffs of their own.

Several countries use taxes on exports to accomplish much the same result. For instance, the Brazilian tax on coffee exports is designed to improve the Brazilian terms of trade. The gains from this improvement more than offset losses due to the lower volume of coffee exports. In the same way, the pricing of oil by OPEC involves royalty taxes that may approximate optimum export taxes.

THE DOMESTIC POLITICS OF PROTECTION.   The imposition of tariffs and nontariff barriers to imports is seldom based on international considerations such as the optimum tariff. Indeed, international efforts are generally aimed toward avoiding the escalation of protectionism and retaliation. The *General Agreement on Tariffs and Trade* (GATT) has sponsored several rounds of multilateral tariff reductions. The most recent round, the Tokyo Round, also developed a set of codes to control nontariff barriers.

The imposition of tariffs and nontariff barriers is generally the outcome of a domestic political process in which protectionist lobbying vies with free-trade lobbying.

Lobbying in Favor of Free Trade.   The free-trade lobbyists are generally representatives of export-oriented producers, multinational enterprises, and the distributors of imported goods. Export-oriented producers favor free trade in large part because they fear foreign retaliation that would reduce their export market. Multinational enterprises often favor free trade because they desire freedom from government restrictions on their flexibility to optimize their international operations. The stake of the distributors is obvious, and they can be thought of as representing the interests of the ultimate consumers and users of imported products. Household consumers especially seldom find it worthwhile to organize a lobbying effort because of the high costs involved relative to the low individual benefits to be derived.

The free-trade lobbyists have powerful and correct economic arguments on their side: Protection permits domestic production that is inefficient by world standards, and domestic consumers and users bear the burden of paying for the inefficiency. In addition, the inefficient allocation of resources due to protection tends to reduce the rate of economic growth of the country.

Lobbying in Favor of Protection. The lobbyists for protection are generally the representatives of the import-competing industries. Although the country as a whole gains from free trade, factors employed in these industries may suffer losses. For labor employed in these industries, protection can be used to avoid the costs of transitional unemployment due to increased import penetration of the domestic market. Further, labor may also avoid decreases in real income that would otherwise be necessary to avoid unemployment or to acquire alternative employment. For the owners of capital or land employed in these industries, protection can be used to avoid capital losses on their assets due to a reduction in expected future profitability because of increased import competition.

The Infant-Industry Argument. The need to develop specific industries is often offered as an argument in favor of protection, especially by developing countries. In some cases these industries are considered prestigious and are thus supported on grounds of national pride. In other cases the argument of the infant industry may be applied. Temporary protection of an industry that is initially inefficient by world standards may be justified economically if the industry is expected to "grow up" to become internationally competitive. The protection then can be removed. Of course such an argument is subject to misuse and may justifiably be greeted with skepticism.

The National Defense Argument. Another argument in favor of protection is based upon the need to provide for the national defense. The output of certain industries is deemed to be critical to national security and must be available immediately in case of emergency. Protection of the industries from import competition may then be necessary, even in peacetime, to assure adequate domestic production capacity. However, as with the Infant-Industry Argument, the National Defense Argument is misused. In addition, alternatives such as stockpiling or subsidies to domestic producers may achieve the goal of providing for the national defense at a lower economic cost to the nation.

THE EFFECTIVE RATE OF PROTECTION. A tariff on goods that compete with the output of a domestic firm offers protection to the firm. But tariffs on material inputs raise the costs of production of this firm and tend to reduce its competitiveness. The net protective impact of the entire tariff system on the firm is summarized in the *effective rate of protection*. The effective rate of protection is essentially the difference between the tariff on imports that compete with the firm's output and a weighted average of the tariffs on material inputs, where the weights represent the importance of each material input to the value of the final output. For instance, the effective rate of protection of a producer of women's blouses is increased by a tariff on the import of women's blouses but decreased by any tariff on the type of cloth used by the firm to produce blouses and, to a lesser extent, by any tariffs on the types of buttons used. Thus a firm can be expected to lobby against tariffs on goods that are inputs into its production processes.

The effective rate of protection can also be calculated to include the impact of existing nontariff barriers to import and the impact of specialized taxes.

SUBSIDIES AND COUNTERVAILING DUTIES. National governments also offer a variety of explicit or implicit subsidies to domestic production or to exports. Most subsidies affect to some extent the pattern of international trade.

An export subsidy tends to increase the exports of the subsidizing country. The increased imports in other countries tend to reduce their own domestic production and to reduce their imports from nonsubsidizing third countries. A subsidy to domestic production may have similar effects if the good is exported by the subsidizing country. It may also reduce imports into the subsidizing country, as the domestically produced, subsidized goods become artificially more competitive.

According to generally accepted international agreements, subsidies to domestic production are a legitimate form of domestic policy but should not have a serious adverse effect on the production or trade of other countries. Export subsidies are generally prohibited, except for limited use by developing countries or in trade in agricultural products.

A country whose industry is harmed by imports subsidized by the producing country is permitted to impose *countervailing duties*. The countervailing duties are taxes on these imports to offset the effects of the foreign subsidies. The countervailing duties should be temporary in the sense that they should cease if the foreign subsidy is ended or if injury to the domestic industry is no longer likely.

ROLE OF EXCHANGE RATES

An *exchange rate* is the price of one currency stated in terms of another currency. For instance, the price of the dollar can be stated as two Deutsche Marks per dollar. The price of the Deutsche Mark (DM) is the reciprocal of this, or 50 cents. The fact that any rate of exchange between two currencies can be stated in two ways is potentially troublesome. Recently, common practice has developed to quote all currencies other than the U.S. dollar, British pound, and Canadian dollar as units of foreign currency per U.S. dollar. The values of the British pound and the Canadian dollar are, however, stated in U.S. dollars. Currencies are traded for each other in the *foreign-exchange market,* which is really a group of banks and brokers tied to each other by telecommunications.

Cross-exchange rates generally remain in line with each other, so there are no opportunities for arbitrage profits. For instance, if the dollar is valued at DM2 and the pound at $2, then the Deutsche Mark is priced at £0.25, or the pound at DM4.

A major use of the exchange rate is to translate prices of goods, services, or assets stated in one currency into prices stated in another currency. If the price of a bushel of wheat is $4, and the exchange rate is DM2/$, the price of the bushel of wheat could also be quoted as DM8.

EXCHANGE-RATE REGIMES.   The national government usually decides the method by which the value of the exchange rate is determined. The major distinction is between a *floating rate* and a *fixed rate*.

Floating Exchange Rate.   In the absence of government intervention, the value of the exchange rate is determined by the interaction of supply and demand for the two currencies in the foreign-exchange market. The exchange rate is then determined by private traders (exporters, importers, investors, borrowers, speculators, etc.) in a perfectly *flexible* or *floating-rate system*. Even in a floating-rate system, governments may choose to influence the exchange rate, for instance by purchasing or selling local currency in exchange for foreign currency. Such action by the government or its central bank is called *intervention*. For example, if the U.S. government wishes to stop or slow the decline in the exchange value of the dollar, it could intervene by purchasing dollars in the foreign exchange market. The extra demand for the dollar would tend to stabilize its value. A floating-rate system with significant government intervention is often referred to as a *managed float* or a *dirty float*.

Fixed Exchange Rate.   Another exchange rate regime is a *fixed-rate system* in which governments state a central rate or par value for each currency. The governments or central banks then must be ready to intervene to protect the fixed rate if the exchange rate threatens to move outside of a narrow band centered on the fixed rate. For instance, if the fixed rate is $2.40 per pound, and the band is plus or minus 2 percent, a central bank must sell pounds (and buy dollars) if the actual exchange rate moves to $2.448. Selling pounds prevents their value from rising any further. If the rate falls to $2.352, a central bank must buy pounds (and sell dollars) to prop up the value of the pound. It is of no consequence to the exchange market which central bank actually intervenes. The way the fixed-rate system in existence until 1971 worked, however, the Federal Reserve Board of the United States almost never intervened. Rather, a foreign central bank, such as the Bank of London, would do so.

Fixed-rate systems may differ by their degree of fixity. At the one extreme, fixed rates may be stated to be immutable. At another extreme, fixed rates may be changed frequently, perhaps almost monthly, as is done in some developing countries. This is called a *crawling peg,* and operates almost like a managed float. In between is the *adjustable peg*, in which fixed rates may be changed only infrequently. The Bretton Woods system of fixed rates, in existence from World War II to 1971, was an adjustable-peg system in which the fixed rate, or peg, could be changed only in the face of fundamental disequilibrium.

Exchange Control.   In addition to direct intervention in the exchange market, governments often attempt to protect the exchange value of their currencies in other ways. The government could use *exchange controls* to ration out the available supply of foreign exchange according to some set of priorities. Developing countries especially use exchange control to suppress the excess demand for foreign currencies. Multiple exchange rates may be used to favor certain types of international transactions and penalize others. Import protection and export subsidies can also be used to alter supply and demand in the foreign-exchange market.

Exchange-Rate Changes.   Specific terminology applies to exchange-rate changes, depending on the exchange-rate regime. Under a floating-rate system, an increase in the value of a currency is called an *appreciation* and a decrease is called a *depreciation*. For instance, if the Deutsche Mark goes from $2 to $2.01, the Deutsche Mark has appreciated (and the dollar has depreciated).

Under a fixed-rate system, the changes are typically large and abrupt. If the value of the currency increases, the event is called a *revaluation,* and if the value decreases, a *devaluation*. In 1967, the exchange rate of the British pound was changed from $2.80 to $2.40, a devaluation of the pound.

The Current System.   The exchange system operating today is a mixture of the various types described above, with a few unusual arrangements as well. The general form of the system is a set of blocs of currencies, members of each set fixed among themselves, and each bloc floating against the other blocs. The float is heavily managed by government intervention. The blocs are generally identified by their dominant currency. A U.S. dollar bloc exists, with many currencies tied to the dollar either by an adjustable peg or a crawling peg. The currencies of the members of the European Economic Community (except the United Kingdom) form a bloc called the European Monetary System, whose dominant currency is the Deutsche Mark. Several currencies, such as the Canadian dollar, basically float alone. Several countries choose to fix their currencies to a weighted average value of a market basket of currencies, where the weights sometimes represent the importance of particular foreign countries as trading partners.

SPOT RATES AND FORWARD RATES.   Discussion of exchange rates to this point has been about *spot exchange rates,* the exchange rates applicable to an immediate (actually one or two days hence) exchange. Contracts often call for future payment in foreign currency, however, and the value of this payment obligation stated in local currency is not known if the future value of the spot exchange rate is uncertain.

The *exchange-rate risk* due to the uncertainty of future spot rates can be eliminated by *hedging.* Hedging is the act of acquiring assets (or liabilities) denominated in foreign currencies to offset liabilities (or assets) denominated in this currency. By balancing assets and liabilities denominated in this foreign currency, exchange-rate exposure is reduced or eliminated.

A generally low-cost method of hedging is available in the forward foreign-exchange market. In the forward market, contracts are traded for future exchange of currencies at a price agreed upon and fixed today. Common maturities for a forward contract are 30, 60, and 90 days. For instance, a producer in the United States has contracted to buy a machine from a West German firm, delivery and payment to be effected in 60 days, at a price of DM200,000. The buyer in the United States may not be willing to gamble on the spot exchange rate between dollars and Deutsche Marks existing in 60 days. To hedge the Deutsche Mark liability, the U.S. producer would enter into a forward contract to buy DM200,000 in 60 days at a price of DM2.5/$. This price is called a *forward exchange rate*. The U.S. producer is now assured that the machine will cost exactly $80,000. The hedge has eliminated exposure to exchange rate risk.

SPECULATION.   The act of acquiring exposure to exchange rate risk, often to seek a profit, is called *speculation*. Indeed, any individual whose assets and liabilities in a foreign currency do not exactly offset each other can be said to be speculating, at least "passively."

Methods of Speculation.   The active speculator in the foreign-exchange markets is betting on the uncertain future value of the spot exchange rate. There are several ways to speculate; two are noted here.

The speculator could speculate using the forward exchange market. The speculator must develop a guess as to the spot rate of a currency in the future and compare this to the current forward rate for the currency. If the expected future spot value of the currency is greater than its current forward value, the speculator should consider speculating in favor of the currency forward. Whether to speculate or not depends on whether the expected return compensates sufficiently for the riskiness of such a position. If it does, the speculator would buy the currency forward, in the hope that upon receipt he could sell it off at the higher future spot rate and thereby earn a profit.

The speculator could also speculate on the future spot rate of a foreign currency using the current spot rate and investing in short-term assets denominated in the foreign currency. Speculation in this case would be profitable if the yield on the foreign asset, inclusive of the expected gain or loss on the currency exchange (buying the foreign currency at the spot rate now, and selling it at maturity at the spot rate existing in the future), exceeds the yield obtainable on comparable assets denominated in the local currency. Again, the speculation would occur only if the expected net return compensated sufficiently for the risks involved.

Stabilizing or Destabilizing Speculation. Theoretically, speculation can be characterized as *stabilizing* or *destabilizing*. The act of speculating alters supply-and-demand relationships in the exchange markets and thus creates pressures for exchange-rate changes. If these changes are consistent with underlying economic conditions, the speculation is termed stabilizing. If the changes are not consistent, the speculation is called destabilizing. Central bankers live in fear of destabilizing speculation, perhaps due to "bandwagon" effects. In practice, it is very difficult to identify destabilizing speculation, because agreement on the meaning of the underlying economic conditions is not easily achieved.

EXCHANGE RATES IN RELATION TO THE MACROECONOMY. *Inflation* and *unemployment* are generally considered to be the two main concerns of macroeconomics. The government has two types of domestic policies to affect the macroeconomy: *fiscal policy,* covering government spending and taxation, and *monetary policy,* covering the money supply and interest rates. In an international setting the government has a third policy tool, the exchange rate, and a third concern, the international balance of payments.

The interactions among policies and the behaviors of the various participants in the economy are complex and often controversial. Thus this short survey can only give a flavor of the relationships between the exchange rate and the macroeconomy. Most of the discussion below is based upon a modern interpretation of the Keynesian view of the macroeconomy. A short section describing an increasingly popular alternative view, the monetary approach, is also presented.

The Keynesian Approach. A significant change in the exchange rate is likely to affect the domestic macroeconomy. Consider a case in which the local currency (call it the dollar) suffers a general depreciation of its value relative to foreign currencies. Such a depreciation could be the result of government policy (a particular case would be a devaluation under a system of fixed exchange rates).

According to a *Keynesian approach* to depreciation, the initial effects of the depreciation are changes in the prices of internationally traded goods and services. With the dollar worth less in terms of foreign currency, the dollar prices of imports tend to rise (to yield the same foreign currency revenues to the foreign sellers). Domestic buyers see the higher dollar prices of imports and tend to switch their spending toward local products, whose prices now are relatively more competitive. Demand for locally produced goods rises, so that domestic production and real gross national product (GNP) rise. The rise of production reduces the rate of domestic unemployment.

Pricing of local exports is also affected. Foreign currency prices of exports can be lowered and still yield the same revenue in dollars. Local exports are more price-competitive in foreign markets, and the quantity exported increases. Again domestic production and real GNP rise, and domestic unemployment falls.

However, the generally welcome decrease in unemployment is not without its cost. The dollar prices of imports rise, and this directly tends to increase the price level or rate of domestic inflation. Domestic products that compete with imports also tend to rise in price, perhaps because of the increased demand for them. Workers see the prices of the goods they consume rising, and demand higher wages to protect their real income. As wages rise, costs rise, and further increases in the prices of goods and services are justified. The wage-price spiral escalates and gains a new twist. In an international setting the spiral becomes a *vicious cycle* of depreciation and inflation.

The effect of an appreciation of the local currency follows a similar chain of reasoning, but of course all the results are opposite. Thus a *virtuous cycle* of appreciation and low inflation can also occur.

The Monetary Approach.   The *monetary approach* offers an important alternative to the Keynesian approach to effects of the exchange rate. According to the monetary approach, the exchange rate is generally not a separate policy tool of the government, but rather reflects the monetary policy followed by the government. If the government follows a loose monetary policy (relative to the policies followed in foreign countries), the domestic money supply grows quickly, and the inflation rate of the country is high. In order to maintain the competitiveness of the country's goods and services in international markets, the exchange-rate value of the local currency must depreciate to offset the relatively rapid rise in the local currency price of these goods and services. Of course, relatively tight monetary policy would tend to result in low domestic inflation and an appreciating currency.

INTERNATIONAL INVESTMENT

GROWTH, INVESTMENT, AND SAVING.   *Economic growth*, the steady rise in real income per person, depends in part on amassing real capital such as buildings, plants, machinery, and other equipment. The process of *real-capital formation* requires financing, and this is the role of *financial investment*. The borrower and lender in a financial transaction can meet almost directly in the financial markets, or the matching of savers with borrowers can be effected through intermediaries such as banks.

The supply of financing depends on *saving*. Financial capital resulting from saving is used in the socially best way if it is channeled into its most-productive or highest-yielding uses. Within a country the allocation is among industries and individual firms in those industries.

Optimal use of financial capital may also require international reallocations. The international flow of capital is desirable to equalize rates of return among various uses in various countries.

RISK AND RETURN IN INTERNATIONAL INVESTMENT.   In addition to seeking high return on a financial investment, the degree of risk is also an important consideration in the investment decision. For a local investor, then, foreign investments may be desirable because their combination of returns and risks are useful in building an optimal portfolio. International investment becomes a vehicle with which to diversify a portfolio to achieve lower total risk without sacrificing returns, or to achieve a higher return without increasing risk, or to achieve some desirable intermediate result.

Certain sources of risk attach to international financial investment that do not arise in domestic financial investment. The most obvious one is exchange-rate risk, the possibility that the currency in which the asset is denominated might depreciate unexpectedly. A second special source of risk is called *country risk* and refers to the possibility that a foreign government would limit or prevent the payment of interest or repayment of principal for either political or economic reasons. This would occur, for instance, if the government refused to permit the exchange of its currency into the investor's home currency.

INTERNATIONAL PORTFOLIO INVESTMENT. There are basically two forms of international investment, and they are distinguished by whether the investor does or does not have or establish control of the foreign borrower. If no control is established, the transaction is termed a *portfolio investment*. Purchases of small quantities of foreign stocks and bonds are portfolio investments. A distinction in portfolio investment is often made between short-term investment (instruments with a maturity of one year or less) and long-term investment. Further, the portfolio investment may be either covered or uncovered. A *covered investment* involves the acquisition of a forward exchange contract to assure the rate at which the principal and yield can be converted back into local currency. The covered investment thus is hedged and is not subject to exchange-rate risk as the maturity date approaches. An uncovered portfolio investment is subject to exchange-rate risk and therefore is speculative, unless it is offset by some other liability denominated in the foreign currency.

EUROCURRENCY MARKET. Portfolio investment often moves through intermediaries. Perhaps the most important type of intermediary active in international investment is the set of banks dealing in Eurocurrencies. The *Eurocurrency market,* or Eurodollar market, although Euromarks and other Eurocurrencies also exist, is formed by a group of banks and their affiliates who are willing to accept time deposits (not demand deposits) and to make loans in currencies other than the currency of the country in which the bank or affiliate is physically located. Eurocurrency banking activity exists basically because it is unregulated. Eurocurrency banking activities are not subject to cost-raising regulations such as reserve requirements, so that the Eurocurrency banks can operate on relatively small spreads between the rates at which they borrow and the rates at which they lend. The Eurocurrency banks thus can compete successfully for business by offering slightly higher rates on time deposits, charging slightly lower rates on loans, or both.

FOREIGN DIRECT INVESTMENT. Foreign direct investment differs from portfolio investment in that management control resides in the investor lender. If both lender and borrower are incorporated, the lender is often the parent corporation and the borrower its foreign subsidiary or affiliate. As a system they form a *multinational* or *transnational corporation.*

No precise amount of equity can be quoted as establishing control. Certainly if the parent owns more than 50 percent of the subsidiary, control exists. For statistical purposes, control is often assumed even if the parent owns as little as 10 percent of the equity.

Horizontal foreign direct investment is often distinguished from vertical foreign direct investment. In horizontal investment the subsidiary performs the same functions as the parent, but in a different country, at least for some of the products sold. For instance, the European operations of the U.S. automobile companies historically have been horizontal, although this is changing. The European subsidiaries designed, produced, and marketed automobiles, so their operations were similar in nature to the operations of the U.S. parents.

Vertical foreign direct investment involves specialization of the parent and its subsidiaries in various stages of production. One important form of vertical investment is backward to secure sources of supply of natural resources. For instance, the U.S. aluminum companies own subsidiaries that mine bauxite ore. The bauxite is often shipped to the parent or to another subsidiary for refining. Another important form of vertical foreign direct investment involves the location of the labor-intensive stages of production in developing countries offering low-cost labor. For instance, semiconductor chips are made in the United States and then are shipped for assembly to subsidiaries in Taiwan, Hong Kong, Mexico, and other developing countries. The assemblies are returned to the U.S. parents for final testing and sale. Vertical foreign direct investment generally is based upon exploiting the comparative cost advantages of the countries involved, according to the technology of each production stage.

Foreign direct investment is important to economic growth because it generally involves more than the international flow of financial capital. Financial capital is only a small part of the package of resources that are transferred internationally by foreign direct investment. The resources transferred usually include technology, marketing skills, and management skills, in addition to financial capital. At the same time, national governments have also identified certain costs of foreign direct investment, and regulation of the activities of multinational corporations by national governments has increased greatly over the past decade.

SOURCES AND SUGGESTED REFERENCES

Additional information and discussion of these topics can be found in any textbook on international economics. Among these are the following:

Kindleberger, C., and P. Lindert. *International Economics,* 6th ed. Homewood, IL: Richard D. Irwin, 1978.

Kreinin, M.E. *International Economics: A Policy Approach,* 2nd ed. New York: Harcourt Brace Jovanovich, 1977.

Richardson, J.D., *Understanding International Economics,* Boston: Little Brown, 1980.

Walter, I. and K. Areskoug, *International Economics,* 3rd ed. New York: Wiley, 1981.

A good description of the Eurocurrency market is found in:

Dufey, G., and I.H. Giddy, *The International Money Market.* Englewood Cliffs, NJ: Prentice-Hall, 1978.

THE BALANCE OF PAYMENTS

CONTENTS

WHAT IT'S ABOUT   3

Definition   3
  Goods, services, and income   3
  Unrequited transfers   3
  Capital   7
  Reserves   7
Double Entry Accounting   7
Data   7
Valuation and Timing   7
Currency   8
Overall Balances and Exchange Rates   8
Authorities and Practice   8

IMF PRESENTATION   9

Organizing the Figures   9
Trade Balance   9
Current Balances (A)   10
  Balance goods, services, and income   10
  Current account excluding official
  transfers   10
  Current account   12
Basic Balance (A plus B)   12
  Direct investment   13
  Portfolio capital   13
  Other long-term capital   13
Overall Balance A through D   13
  Exceptional financing   13
  Liabilities to official foreigners   14
Overall Balance A through E   14

Overall Balance A through F: Official
Settlements   14
Overall Balance A through G: Change
in Reserves   14
  Reserves   14

**POLICY ISSUES OF OVERALL
BALANCES**   15

Controversy   15
Macroeconomic Policy and Balances   15
IMF Approach   16
Various U.S. Approaches   16
  Liquidity balance   17
  Official settlements balance   17
  Additional balances   18
  No balances   18
Monetarist Approach   18
  Central bank balance sheet   19
  Monetary balance   19
  Monetary balance of reserve currency   20

**HOW TO USE BALANCE-OF-
PAYMENTS STATISTICS**   21

Clear Presentation of Data   21
Interpreting the Pressures   21
Closed Economies   22

**SOURCES AND SUGGESTED
REFERENCES**   22

THE BALANCE OF PAYMENTS

David T. Devlin

WHAT IT'S ABOUT

DEFINITION. According to the International Monetary Fund (IMF):

> The balance of payments is a statistical statement for a given period showing (a) transactions in goods, services, and income between an economy and the rest of the world, (b) changes of ownership and other changes in that economy's monetary gold, special drawing rights (SDRs), and claims on and liabilities to the rest of the world, and (c) unrequited transfers and counterpart entries that are needed to balance, in the accounting sense, any entries for the foregoing transactions and changes which are not mutually offsetting.

INTERNATIONAL MONETARY FUND, 1977

It is a fairly esoteric subject. If you want to understand it, you must first get the accounting straight and then the definitions of the various balances. After that, you can talk about what it all means.

Broadly speaking, there are four major categories of flows as follows.

Goods, Services, and Income. Physical goods are imported into and exported from a country; exports include reexports that are first imported. Services include tourists' spending in the country (an import of a service) and the country's tourists' spending abroad (an export of a service), shipping, insurance, and other transportation fees paid to or received from foreigners, as well as many miscellaneous service-fee types of payments and receipts (see Exhibit 1). Income paid to or received from foreigners, often called factor income, includes earnings (including reinvested earnings) on direct investment, portfolio investment (stocks and bonds), and interest on other assets or liabilities. This is the "real" side of the balance of payments.

Unrequited Transfers. Unrequited transfers are essentially financial gifts from the home economy to foreigners (a debit) or from foreigners to the home economy (a credit). For instance, if the U.S. government gives wheat to a developing country, the wheat shows up in U.S. exports of goods (credit), but it is offset by an equal debit under unrequited transfers. Major categories of such transfers (often without a counterpart in goods or services) are workers' (abroad) remittances, migrants' transfers, other private transfers, and various types of official transfers.

EXHIBIT 1   DETAILED PRESENTATION OF BALANCE OF PAYMENTS

CURRENT ACCOUNT

Goods, Services, and Income

Total Credit
Total Debit
1. Merchandise: exports f.o.b.
2. Merchandise: imports f.o.b.
3. Shipment: credit
4. Shipment: debit
5. Passenger services: credit
6. Passenger services: debit
7. Other transportation: credit
8. Other transportation: debit
9. Travel: credit
10. Travel: debit
11. Reinvested earnings on direct investment abroad
12. Reinvested earnings on direct investment in (reporting economy)
13. Other direct-investment income: credit
14. Other direct-investment income: debit
15. Other investment income of resident official, incl. interofficial: credit
16. Other investment income of resident official, incl. interofficial: debit
17. Other investment income of foreign official, excl. interofficial: credit
18. Other investment income of foreign official, excl. interofficial: debit
19. Other investment income: credit
20. Other investment income: debit
21. Interofficial, n.i.e.: credit
22. Interofficial, n.i.e.: debit
23. Other resident official, n.i.e.: credit
24. Other resident official, n.i.e.: debit
25. Other foreign official, n.i.e.: credit
26. Other foreign official, n.i.e.: debit
27. Labor income, n.i.e.: credit
28. Labor income, n.i.e.: debit
29. Property income, n.i.e.: credit
30. Property income, n.i.e.: debit
31. Other goods, services, and income: credit
32. Other goods, services, and income: debit

UNREQUITED TRANSFERS

Total Credit
Total Debit
33. Migrants' transfers: credit
34. Migrants' transfers: debit
35. Workers' remittances: credit
36. Workers' remittances: debit
37. Other private transfers: credit
38. Other private transfers: debit
39. Interofficial transfers: credit
40. Interofficial transfers: debit
41. Other transfers of resident official: credit
42. Other transfers of resident official: debit
43. Other transfers of foreign official: credit
44. Other transfers of foreign official: debit

EXHIBIT 1   CONTINUED

CAPITAL ACCOUNT

Capital, Excluding Reserves

Direct investment abroad

45. Equity capital
46. Reinvestment of earnings
47. Other long-term capital
48. Short-term capital

Direct investment in (reporting economy)

49. Equity capital
50. Reinvestment of earnings
51. Other long-term capital
52. Short-term capital

Portfolio investment

Public Sector Bonds
53. Assets
54. Liabilities constituting foreign authorities' reserves
55. Other liabilities
Other Bonds
56. Assets
57. Liabilities constituting foreign authorities' reserves
58. Other liabilities
Corporate Equities
59. Assets
60. Liabilities constituting foreign authorities' reserves
61. Other liabilities

Other long-term capital of resident official sector

62. Drawings on loans extended
63. Repayments on loans extended
64. Other assets
65. Liabilities constituting foreign authorities' reserves
66. Drawings on other loans received
67. Repayments on other loans received
68. Other liabilities

Other long-term capital of deposit money banks

69. Drawings on loans extended
70. Repayments on loans extended
71. Other assets
72. Liabilities constituting foreign authorities' reserves denominated in national currency
73. Liabilities constituting foreign authorities' reserves denominated in foreign currency
74. Drawings on other loans received
75. Repayments on other loans received
76. Other liabilities

Other long-term capital of other sectors

77. Drawings on loans extended
78. Repayments on loans extended
79. Other assets
80. Liabilities constituting foreign authorities' reserves
81. Drawings on other loans received
82. Repayments on other loans received
83. Other liabilities

EXHIBIT 1   CONTINUED

Other short-term capital of resident official sector

84. Loans extended
85. Other assets
86. Liabilities constituting foreign authorities' reserves
87. Other loans received
88. Other liabilities

Other short-term capital of deposit money banks

89. Assets
90. Liabilites constituting foreign authorities' reserves denominated in national currency
91. Liabilities constituting foreign authorities' reserves denominated in foreign currency
92. Other liabilities

Other short-term capital of other sectors

93. Loans extended
94. Other assets
95. Liabilites constituting foreign authorities' reserves
96. Other loans received
97. Other liabilities

Reserves

Monetary gold
98. Total change in holdings
99. Counterpart to monetization/demonetization
100. Counterpart to valuation changes

Special drawing rights (items 101–103)

101. Total change in holdings
102. Counterpart to allocation/cancellation
103. Counterpart to valuation changes[a]

Reserve position in the Fund (items 104 and 105)

104. Total change in holdings
105. Counterpart to valuation changes[a]

Foreign-exchange assets

106. Total change in holdings
107. Counterpart to valuation changes

Other claims

108. Total change in holdings
109. Counterpart to valuation changes

Use of Fund credit (items 110 and 111)

110. Total change in holdings
111. Counterpart to valuation changes[a]

NET ERRORS AND OMISSIONS (item 112)

Source.   IMF, *Balance of Payments Year Book.*
[a]Not applicable to a statement expressed in SDRs.

Capital.   Here we are dealing with transactions resulting in changes in claims and liabilities of residents on foreigners, aside from the special kind of claims and liabilities defined as reserves as discussed below. Major types are (1) direct-investment flows where the resident (or foreigner) has or obtains an ownership-equity relation with the investment entity abroad (or in the home country), (2) portfolio investment in bonds or stocks where there is insufficient ownership to be considered direct investment, and (3) other long-term and short-term claims and liabilities, usually broken down according to whether the resident is the official sector, deposit money bank, or other sector.

Reserves.   Reserves comprise gold, SDRs, reserve position in the IMF, foreign-exchange assets, certain other claims, and, on the liability side, changes in use of IMF credit. These are usually assets or liabilities of the central bank (sometimes the finance ministry), which can be used by the authorities to finance imbalances from the other accounts in the balance of payments.

DOUBLE ENTRY ACCOUNTING.   The balance of payments is a double entry accounting system in that there are two equal and opposite entries for each transaction. For instance, an export is shown in export of goods (credit) and the financing of it as an increase in claims abroad of, say, the exporter (a debit) if he finances it, or an increase in reserves of the central bank (also a debit), if the exporter is paid cash in foreign currency and he turns the proceeds over to the central bank to get local currency. Thus in principle the algebraic sum of all entries in the balance of payments, including reserves, is zero.

DATA.   In practice, different sides of the same transaction are collected by different reporting systems, and the statistical system inevitably misses some of the data. Thus in adding up all the debits and credits, there is an imbalance that is shown as errors and omissions.

It is important to remember that the balance of payments can only be compiled if the necessary reporting systems are in place to identify the transactions. No country has a perfect reporting system, nor should it, as it would be too expensive and would interfere excessively with the privacy of its citizens. Even in countries with total foreign-exchange controls, black-market transactions usually escape the statistical net and show up in errors and omissions. What is required is a reporting system sufficient to get shifts in the major flows and keep errors and omissions reasonably small and not too volatile.

The major reporting systems usually include (1) *merchandise trade*: customs documents and/or bank reports from an exchange control system; (2) *tourism*: statistical samples of travelers' expenses; (3) *other services and transfers*: special reports to a central statistical bureau; (4) *government merchandise, services, income, and capital*: data reported directly from government accounts; (5) *banking systems*: regular reports to a central bank of capital flows; (6) *direct investment*: special reports to a central statistical bureau or central bank; (7) *portfolio investment*: usually reports from financial intermediaries that do transactions, occasionally benchmark surveys of holders; (8) *reserve movements*: reports from a central bank's own accounts.

VALUATION AND TIMING.   In principle, although it is often difficult in practice, both sides of a transaction should be reported as equal in value and at the same time.

The convention is that valuation should be the market value or its closest approximation. Timing for merchandise should be when change of ownership takes place, with a simultaneous capital transaction. Timing for services is usually tied to the payment for the services.

Note that capital flows are entered into the accounts at the value of the transaction that takes place. Later changes in the values of assets and liabilities are not balance-of-payments flows. For instance, 100 shares of a foreign equity stock may be purchased for $50, and a capital outflow of $5000 would be shown. If the value of that stock then rises to $75, the value of the holding rises to $7500, but the $2500 increase in value is not a balance-of-payments flow. Such valuation changes, however, do affect the investment position (outstanding external assets minus liabilities).

An exception is made to this principle, however, in the case of reserves. For instance, changes in official foreign-exchange assets have two components: line 106 Exhibit 1, which is the total change in the value of the assets from end period to end period and an offsetting counterpart, line 107, which reflects how much of the change was caused by changes in valuation of outstanding assets, rather than purchases or sales of foreign exchange by the central bank. The sum of the two lines thus reflects only purchases and sales of foreign exchange by the central bank and this treatment is consistent with the treatment of other capital flows.

CURRENCY.   The balance of payments is often expressed in the local currency as a unit of account, but often in SDRs or dollars. Of course claims and liabilities may be denominated in any of many foreign currencies, but they are converted to the unit of account used.

OVERALL BALANCES AND EXCHANGE RATES.   The first question most people have about an actual balance of payments is whether it is in deficit (implying bad) or surplus (good). To answer that, one must define one or more overall balances, and there is considerable disagreement on that. But inextricably tied to the whole issue of balance-of-payments analysis is exchange-rate policy. Thinking about it in a simple way, central banks maintain fixed (or moving) targets for their exchange rates by buying or selling foreign currencies against their own currencies, thus increasing or decreasing their reserves. If a currency is under pressure and the central bank is losing reserves, it can only continue as long as it has reserves. When they run out, the exchange rate tends to move to the market rate (aside from rates established by fiat). If the overall balance is measured simply by the change in reserves, the overall balance is at this point in zero balance with all other items in the accounts netting out to zero.

Note that if the central bank has a fixed exchange-rate target, all of the pressure on exchange rates shows up as a change in reserves. If the central bank has a moving target, then part of the pressure shows up as change in the exchange rate and the rest as a change in reserves. As is discussed below, the matter is much more complicated in practice.

AUTHORITIES AND PRACTICE.   Each country compiles and publishes its balance of payments in whatever way it wants. The major international standard is set by the IMF, currently as defined in its *Balance of Payments Manual*, fourth edition, 1977. In addition, the IMF collects and publishes balance of payments statistics from all member countries in its *Balance of Payments Yearbook,* in which the country data is organized, as closely as possible, in the format they recommend.

After going through their presentation, we will consider other approaches.

IMF PRESENTATION

ORGANIZING THE FIGURES.   As we saw in Exhibit 1, balance-of-payments flows are broken down into 112 categories, roughly grouped under (1) goods, services, and income, (2) unrequited transfers, (3) capital, and (4) reserves, as well as the residual errors and omissions. However, such a mass of figures is hard to use for purposes of analyzing the evolution of a country's external position. In Exhibit 2, the mass of numbers is organized and condensed into a more useful "aggregated presentation."

The basic idea is that certain types of transactions that have similar economic characteristics are grouped and then arranged in the table from top to bottom with balances shown at various points summing the inflows and outflows above the line where the balance is drawn. Thus netting merchandise exports and imports one gets a trade balance; adding in services, income, and transfers one gets the current account. Looking at it the other way, the current account is "financed' by all the items below the line, namely, items B through H. Moving down, another balance is drawn for the sum of A plus B and is financed by the rest. This is the basic logic of any balance-of-payments presentation.

In other approaches the entries are shown in different order, and lines are drawn at different places. Sometimes only one overall balance is shown, as if that were the only one of importance. This is usually a mistake.

TRADE BALANCE.   This is the most commonly used balance. It usually comes out monthly and is the earliest figure published in any given period for any of the balance-of-payments transactions. It is given wide publicity, so much so that many people think it is the same as the balance of payments. It is not.

The balance of payments requires that merchandise exports and merchandise imports be reported f.o.b. (free on board but excluding cost of insurance and freight). Often the earliest reports of the trade balance, compiled from customs figures, give exports f.o.b. but imports c.i.f. (covered for insurance and freight). Normally, in the balance-of-payments tabulation, insurance and freight paid to foreigners on imports are reported under their appropriate service categories and are excluded from the value of merchandise imports. Furthermore, some of the insurance and freight paid on imports is paid to nationals of the importing country and is not a balance-of-payments entry at all. Only payments to foreigners count.

Consistency in the balance of payments requires that both the exports (or imports) entry and the corresponding capital entry (payment for the merchandise) be entered at the same time, and the usual convention is that this is done when ownership of the merchandise changes. When merchandise figures are based on customs data, they are usually recorded when the goods enter or leave the country and/or possession changes, whereas the capital is more often reported when ownership changes. This causes errors and omissions.

In some countries, customs data are not used for tracking merchandise exports and imports; rather, reports from banks as required under a foreign-exchange control program are used. In this case, the goods are not reported when they change pos-

EXHIBIT 2 AGGREGATED PRESENTATION AT BALANCE OF PAYMENTS

Aggregated Presentation	Detailed Presentation	
A. Current Account, excl. Group F	Current Account	
Merchandise: exports f.o.b.	Goods, services, and income	1–32[a]
Merchandise: imports f.o.b.		
Trade balance		
Other goods, services, and income: credit		
Other goods, services, and income: debit		
Total: goods, services, and income		
Private unrequited transfers	Unrequited transfers	33–44
Total, excl. official unrequited transfers		
Official unrequited transfers		
	Capital Account	
B. Direct Investment and Other Long-Term Capital, excl. Groups F through H		
Direct investment	Direct investment abroad	45–48
	Direct investment in (reporting economy)	49–52
Portfolio investment	Portfolio investment	53, 55, 56, 58, 59, 61
Other long-term capital		
Resident official sector	Other long-term capital of resident official sector	62–64, 66–68
Deposit money banks	Other long-term capital of deposit money banks	69–71, 74–76
Other sectors	Other long-term capital of other sectors	77–79, 81–83
Total, Groups A plus B		
C. Other Short-Term Capital, excl. Groups F through H		
Resident official sector	Other short-term capital of resident official sector	84, 85, 87, 88
Deposit money banks	Short-term capital of deposit money banks	89, 92
Other sectors	Other short-term capital of other sectors	93, 94, 96, 97
D. Net Errors and Omissions	Net Errors and Omissions	112
Total, Groups A through D		
E. Counterpart Items	Reserves—counterpart components	
Monetization/demonetization of gold		99, 100, 102, 103[b], 105[b], 107, 109, 111[b]
Allocation/cancellation of SDRs		
Valuation changes in reserves		
Total, Groups A through E		
F. Exceptional Financing[c]	(included wherever classified)	

EXHIBIT 2   CONTINUED

Aggregated Presentation	Detailed Presentation	
G. Liabilities Constituting Foreign Authorities' Reserves	(listed in numerical order among the other components, above)	54, 57, 60, 65, 72, 73, 80, 86, 90, 91, 95
Total, Groups A through G		
H. Total Change in Reserves	Reserves—excluding counterparts	
Monetary gold	Monetary gold	98
SDRs	Special drawing rights	101
Reserve position in the Fund	Reserve position in the Fund	104
Foreign exchange assets	Foreign-exchange assets	106
Other claims	Other claims	108
Use of Fund credit	Use of Fund credit	110

Source.   IMF, *Balance of Payments Yearbook.*
*a*Numbers in third column are component numbers.
*b*Not applicable to a statement expressed in SDRs.
*c*Details of this group will be provided in separate lines.

session or ownership but tend to be reported when they are paid for or when certain documents are filled out, possibly causing errors and omissions. Such vagaries complicate analysis.

For analytical purposes, one should not take the trade balance out of context of the whole of the balance of payments, even though in most countries trade flows are large compared with capital flows.

CURRENT BALANCES (A).   Below the trade balance are a number of balances of interest.

Balance Goods, Services, and Income.   Adding to the trade balance the credits and debits reflecting other goods, services, and income, one gets total goods, services, and income. This is often called net exports of goods and services. It is roughly equivalent to the external sector of the national accounts, although there are often small technical differences in actual figures published by national authorities. In developing countries, investment in the national accounts usually exceeds savings. This resource gap is reflected in a deficit in net exports of goods and services. The deficit, in turn, is financed by a net overall inflow of unrequited transfers, capital, and change in reserves.

Current Account Excluding Official Transfers.   If one adds to the above balance on goods, services, and income the net flow of private unrequited transfers, one gets the balance on current account excluding official transfers. This is sometimes called the balance on goods, services, and remittances. This balance is often used by the World Bank, the IMF, and development agencies when discussing the aid needs of developing countries. Private transfers that are above the line are considered an autonomous flow, similar to earnings on service exports. Furthermore, the difference between official transfers or grants and very soft loans often is not very substantial in an economic sense. Such soft loans necessarily go below the line. On the other hand, some of the official transfers are simply the financial counterparts of goods given without charge to developing countries by developed countries, suggesting that both sides of the transaction should be netted above the line.

Current Account.   Adding official transfers to the current account excluding official transfers naturally gives the current account. If the current account is in deficit, a country's net external liabilities increase, including all capital and reserve flows. If the current account is in surplus, then its net external assets increase. This concept (or sometimes the previous one) is useful in analyzing the total international flow of funds. At least in principle, if one group of countries, such as OPEC, is in current-account surplus, then by definition the rest of the world must be in current-account deficit. Similarly, the increase in net assets of the surplus countries is matched by the increase in net liabilities of the deficit countries. The efficiency of this international flow of funds has occasionally caused great concern.

Even aside from the OPEC issue, developed countries in the past often had current-account surpluses and developing countries, deficits. The associated flow of funds from developed to developing countries finances the resource gap of the latter and thus helps their development.

Note that one thinks of a balance such as the current account in two ways: (1) in terms of the items contributing to it, above the line, and (2) in terms of the items below it that finance it. This is not to say that the items above the line determine its size in an economic sense independently of the financing items below the line. In fact, both tend to be determined simultaneously. A current-account deficit cannot be run unless it is financed. If there is no inflow of financing for a potential deficit, then exports or imports or transfers will change so that the deficit disappears.

BASIC BALANCE (A PLUS B).   Adding net long-term capital flows to the current account produces what is often called the basic balance and the IMF calls Total, Groups A plus B. Long-term capital is classified as direct investment, portfolio investment, and other long-term capital, usually breaking out that of the resident official sector and of deposit money banks.

Note that the direct and portfolio classifications reflect types of transactions, the first involving some element of control of a foreign enterprise and the second a type of instrument (bonds and stocks) bought or sold where control is not an element. Other long-term capital of the resident official sector reflects transactions leading to increases or decreases in both external claims and liabilities of the sector. All of these types are net in two senses. They include the net change in assets over the period (or on liabilities) even if assets go up and down a couple of times, and they include both assets of residents and liabilities of residents (assets of foreigners). An increase in assets abroad is an outflow, or debit, and an increase in liabilities to foreigners is an inflow, or credit. This concept is also used for change in reserves.

For analytical purposes the basic balance was used more frequently in the past than now. Analytical use of the basic balance was based on the idea that a current-account deficit, needed for development for instance, should be financed by net inflows of longer-term capital, with temporary inflows and outflows of more volatile short-term capital washing out over the longer term. In this sense, policy makers might aim for equilibrium in the basic balance over the business cycle. This idea has some merit, but in practice the business cycle is only one of a number of factors to consider, and long-term flows are often as volatile, sometimes more so, as shorter-term flows. Furthermore, long-term flows are usually based on initial maturity, rather than current maturity. Thus, if a foreign 20-year bond is bought by a resident when it has only six months before maturity, it is a long-term, not a short-term capital outflow.

Direct Investment. The IMF manual defines direct investment as follows:

> Direct investment refers to investment that is made to acquire a lasting interest in an enterprise operating in an economy other than that of the investor, the investor's purpose being to have an effective voice in the management of the enterprise. The foreign entity or group of associated entities that makes the investment is termed the direct investor. The unincorporated or incorporated enterprise—a branch or subsidiary, respectively—in which direct investment is made is referred to as a direct investment enterprise.

Usually this criterion is satisfied when foreign ownership is concentrated in the hands of one investor or group of associates and they own at least 25 percent of the equity, but sometimes as little as 10 percent is used as the criterion for significant control. Even if one investor or group owns less than 10 percent, if various foreigners own, say, more than 50 percent, that too is classified as direct investment.

Direct investment capital includes all flows—equity, reinvested earnings, other long-term and short-term flows—between the foreign direct investor and the direct investment enterprise in the host country, but not that from other foreigners; this is classified as portfolio or "other," depending upon the type of flow.

Portfolio Capital. This includes all purchases (inflow) or sales (outflow) by foreigners of domestic stocks and bonds and purchases by residents of foreign stocks and bonds.

Other Long-Term Capital. This includes foreign long-term borrowing of official entities in the country, net amortization of old loans, as well as net lending abroad by official entities. It also includes long-term capital transactions of deposit money banks and other sectors of the economy. It excludes long-term capital classified in other accounts.

OVERALL BALANCE A THROUGH D. Adding short-term capital (C) and errors and omissions (D) to the basic balance gives one version of an overall balance. Note that only the short-term capital not included in other capital categories is included here. This short-term capital is usually broken down by changes in assets and liabilities of the resident official sector, resident deposit money banks, and other sectors.

The meaning of this balance can best be understood in terms of the items that finance it: total change in reserves (H) adjusted for counterpart items (E) (essentially valuation changes, allocations of SDRs, and monetization of gold) plus exceptional financing (F) plus changes in liabilities constituting foreign authorities· reserves (G).

Exceptional Financing. These are transactions arranged by the authorities of the country to make up for a surplus or deficit in the other items of the balance of payments. They are sometimes called "compensatory official financing." Balance-of-payments loans to a country in order to finance an identified deficit are of this type. Sometimes such loans by banks or official agencies supplement financing provided by the IMF, which is listed under reserves. Buildups or reductions of external arrearages by a country also fall in this category. Since such transactions require judgments of intent, they are sometimes difficult to identify.

Liabilities to Official Foreigners.   Changes in liabilities constituting foreign authorities' reserves is an item that applies only to countries whose currency is used as a reserve currency. The idea is that when a foreign central bank accumulates, say, dollars in its reserves through intervention in the exchange market, this purchase of dollars not only prevents its own currency from appreciating but the dollar from falling. Thus it is in some sense financing not only the surplus of the country in question, but also what could be thought of as a deficit of the United States, and the United States would recognize the deficit by showing such increases in liabilities to official foreigners. This approach also helps to make deficits and surpluses in various countries around the world symmetrically defined so they add up to zero.

OVERALL BALANCE A THROUGH E.   The only change from the preceding balance is that reserve counterpart items are above the line, so that one is looking at a balance financed by the total change in reserves including valuation and other such items, as well as exceptional financing and liabilities in official reserves.

OVERALL BALANCE A THROUGH F: OFFICIAL SETTLEMENTS.   Here the only change from the preceding balance is that exceptional financing is above the line, in effect ignoring whether the deficit has been affected by compensatory financing. Since defining which transactions are and which are not exceptional financing is very judgmental, some analysts prefer to ignore them.

This balance is virtually identical to what used to be called the *official reserve transactions balance*, or official settlements balance as used by the United States. The United States does not use it now, although it can be constructed from published data. It was discontinued to avoid misunderstanding, on the basis that in a world of more-or-less-floating exchange rates, accumulation of dollar reserves by foreign central banks is voluntary and may be a free choice for investment purposes. Of course to the extent that countries accept the key currency role of other countries, there is nothing particularly wrong about a United States deficit due to such use of its currency.

OVERALL BALANCE A THROUGH G: CHANGE IN RESERVES.   This balance also puts changes in liabilities to foreign officials above the line and is financed by changes in reserves. For countries whose currency is not used as a reserve currency, this and the preceding balance are identical.

Reserves.   These are defined by the IMF as follows:

> Reserves is singled out as a category because the kind of capital that it is designed to comprise can perform a distinctive and important function in the context of an economy's international transaction. The category may be described as the monetary gold, special drawing rights (SDRs) in the Fund, reserve position in the Fund, use of Fund credit, and existing claims on non-residents that are available to the central authorities either to

finance payments imbalances directly or to manage the size of such imbalances by intervening to influence the exchange rate for the national currency.

For an asset to be considered a reserve asset it must have two qualities: It should (1) be under the effective control of the authorities and (2) be available for use, which means in part that it should be liquid. Control of the authorities is interpreted quite strictly and literally, although it does not absolutely require ownership. The manual notes, "For instance, private deposit money banks may sometimes be allowed to hold legal title to foreign assets but may be permitted to deal in them only on the terms specified by the authorities or only with their express approval; such assets would still be subject to the authorities· direct and effective control." As with other capital, an increase in reserves (assets abroad) is shown as a debit (an outflow).

POLICY ISSUES OF OVERALL BALANCES

CONTROVERSY.   There has been a surprising amount of controversy, both in the United States and in the international community, concerning the proper presentation and interpretation of balance-of-payments statistics. See for example, symposium papers edited by Stern, *et al.*, 1977.

The symposium was held in Princeton, N.J., in 1977 to discuss the situation following a change in the official U.S. balance of payments presentation in which all balances below the current account were eliminated. The June 1976 *Survey of Current Business* gives the "Report of the Advisory Committee on the Presentation of Balance of Payments Statistics." A number of discussants in the symposium concluded that further changes in the presentation were likely.

Earlier discussions were reflected in the 1964 Bernstein Committee Report; its recommendations were implemented in the June 1965 *Survey of Current Business*. There was also a further revision in the presentation in June 1971.

MACROECONOMIC POLICY AND BALANCES.   Why all the concern for the balance-of-payments presentation? In essence, the balance of payments measures the financial interaction between a country and the rest of the world. The relationship is complicated, so one organizes the data to show balances. And although it is probably a mistake, public attention tends to focus on some overall balance as the measure of whether the country is doing all right or not. Grossly, the judgment tends to be that a deficit is bad and a surplus good.

The issues involved are not trivial. The balance of payments is determined by the whole spectrum of macroeconomic policies of the home country compared to the policies of the rest of the world. Budget surpluses and deficits influence real growth and inflation, in concert with credit creation by the central bank. This is turn influences monetary growth and interest rates. Gains and losses of reserve by the central bank, reflecting balance-of-payments pressures, in turn affect monetary growth. Such intervention in the exchange market reflects exchange-rate policy. Trade, services, and capital flows in turn are affected by real growth, inflation, interest rates, exchange rates, monetary growth, and so forth.

Thus if one uses the wrong measure of the overall balance or interprets it improperly, one could be lead to conclude, perhaps erroneously, that major shifts in macroeconomic policies were required. Changes in exchange rates are major shocks for a country, as are smaller budget deficits or slower credit creation and are only made after exhausting political and technical debates. Also shocking are the impositions of various types of exchange controls that are sometimes used in lieu of major policy changes.

The problem is compounded further by the lack of agreement among authorities on a clear and understandable theory of what determines the balance of payments, much less how to measure it. If there were such a measurable concept, one could always go out and get the data. Furthermore, the international institutional environment changes, fixed to more-or-less-floating exchange rates, the abandonment of gold, the rise of the SDR and the Deutsche Mark as key currencies, and the enormous OPEC surplus, to mention a few. An overall balance appropriate for one environment may not be appropriate for another.

IMF APPROACH. The IMF *Manual* and *Yearbook* presentation is a quite reasonable approach to this complexity. In part, the approach reflects a rough consensus among expert opinion and national balance-of-payments compliers from member countries. However, reflecting such a consensus it tends to be formalistic and avoids strong positions on principle and theory. Rather, it focuses on pragmatic judgments of what goes where.

The IMF balance reflecting the total change in reserves (A through G) is one that most analysts would look at in any case. Foreign-exchange assets are used to intervene in the foreign-exchange market and to affect the value of the domestic currency against others. If these assets continually decline, then some change in policy, perhaps exchange-rate policy, is required. SDR holdings and IMF reserve position are easily available sources of foreign exchange, monetary gold somewhat less so because the price is so volatile.

Use of Fund credit is another matter. If a member borrows from the Fund, his foreign-exchange assets go up simultaneously with liabilities under use of Fund credit with no change in reserves. However, Fund credit gets bigger and is given for longer periods. In some ways this situation resembles exceptional financing more than a reserve item.

The balance financed by reserves and liabilities constituting foreign authorities' reserves (A through F) is also of interest for a key currency country. An increase in such liabilities is not necessarily bad, however, as long as the world accepts the key currency role, so one would always be careful to look at the breakdown of the financing of this balance.

The balance with exception financing, also below the line (A through E) likewise gives interesting and important information that would be missed if one focused only on the reserve (A through G) or the official balance (A through F).

Thus the IMF presentation focuses attention on a useful array of information in a clear manner. It allows the analyst to sort through the real, capital, and financing flows, to see their relationships and interactions, and to make up his or her own mind what situations are sustainable and what situations require policy changes, based on personal theories of how it all works.

VARIOUS U.S. APPROACHES. Until the early 1960's, official U.S. balance-of-payments presentations tended to focus almost exclusively on the liquidity balance as the overall balance. In 1965 the official balance was added, and in June 1971 a number of other overall or central balances were added. In June 1976 all overall balances below the current account were abolished. (See earlier references.)

Liquidity Balance.   The liquidity balance was developed to reflect the dominant key currency role of the dollar in the postwar world. The key concept was that the balance was financed by changes not only in U.S. reserves (mostly gold), but also by changes in U.S. liquid liabilities to foreigners, both private and official. All other capital flows were above the line of the liquidity balance. Liquid liabilities included U.S. short-term money market instruments, treasury bills, deposits at U.S. commercial banks and various other short-term instruments. They did not include other short-term liabilities to foreigners reported by the U.S. government or nonbanks.

Whereas liquid liabilities to private foreigners were shown separately from those to official foreigners (essentially central banks), both counted below the line. The idea was that anytime private foreigners lost confidence in the dollar they could sell the dollars to foreign central banks. Thus private liquid-dollar holdings were a potential threat to the stability of the system. Under the system then prevailing, foreign official holders of dollars could turn their dollars in to the United States in exchange for gold. U.S. gold was the basis for the whole system in this sense, with official dollars an immediate possible claim, and private liquid dollars a second potential pressure.

Focusing attention on this balance meant that U.S. monetary and other policies should attempt to prevent too large a deficit in the liquidity balance. If the deficit were too large, the system would break down as private foreigners turned dollars into foreign central banks and the central banks in turn demanded gold. The United States had only a limited amount of gold, and liquid liabilities were much larger than the U.S. gold stock valued at $35 per ounce. To change the price of gold would have violated the trust implied by the role of the dollar.

Official Settlements Balance.   This balance was introduced because it focused on the change in reserves and only the change in liabilities to foreign official agencies. (Most liabilities to foreign official agencies were liquid, so that wasn't much of an issue.) The argument was that private liquid-dollar holdings were held mostly for transaction reasons reflecting the role of the dollar in financing international trade and that the threat of them all being turned into foreign central banks was remote. Furthermore, they could not be turned in to the United States for gold, so there was no direct claim on the gold.

In addition, gains and losses of dollars (as well as gold) by foreign central banks was a good measure of the pressure on the fixed-exchange-rate system that prevailed. To the extent that foreign central banks gained dollars and showed a surplus and the United States showed a corresponding deficit in the official balance through the increase in liabilities, this was a measure of the imbalances and pressures in the system, and this was what policy should focus on.

Furthermore, whereas the statistical measurement of changes in liabilities to official foreigners was fairly straightforward, and they mostly tended to keep their dollars in very liquid form in any case, defining what was liquid and what was not liquid for foreign private dollar holdings was very imprecise. And this was important because private foreigners held dollar assets that reflected the full spectrum of liquidity.

Additional Balances. In the 1971 presentation, the official balance was retained (with small changes in definition), the basic balance was added, and the net liquidity balance was substituted for the liquidity balance. The net liquidity balance was defined very similarly to the liquidity balance except that it included below the line not only reserves and U.S. liquid liabilities to foreigners, but also U.S. liquid claims on foreigners. This implies that the liquidity position of the United States, like that of a bank, should take into account liquid claims to offset liquid liabilities.

In effect, a large array of balances was drawn, similar (but not identical) to the presentation now used by the IMF. (The IMF does not use the concept of liquidity, and they have an extraordinary financing category.) This presentation, however, emphasized the statistical and conceptual weaknesses of all of the overall balances shown, noting that any one single balance was inadequate for any serious purpose. In part this reflected the ambiguity of the prevailing international financial system.

The United States was still formally on the gold standard, and there was still a general commitment to fixed rates. But it was general knowledge that foreign official agencies were discouraged from trying to convert dollars into gold, such conversion being the basis of the system. There was a large array of control mechanisms to support the U.S. external position. And more flexibility in exchange rates was considered by many a more viable option. In such an environment, there was no clear policy focus for an overall balance that could be a useful measurement of policy targets.

No Balances. By June 1976, when most of the balances were eliminated, the ambiguity of the earlier period had been resolved. Gold was not bought or sold by the United States at a fixed price. Exchange rates were more or less floating, OPEC was accumulating a large surplus that showed up, in part, as increases in U.S. liabilities to official foreigners but could not be thought of in the same way as exchange market intervention by, say Germany, to hold the mark-dollar rate. The significance of all balances was significantly reduced.

MONETARIST APPROACH. It is clear from the preceding discussion that to focus heavily on any one overall balance or even a few, it is necessary that one has a coherent theory of the factors determining the balance of payments and an institutional framework for the international monetary system to which policy is in some sense committed. If one doesn't care about the exchange rate, the overall balance of payments has little interest.

One such theoretical approach is gaining support: the monetary approach to the balance of payments. Some of the key concepts are as follows: (1) the exchange rate is basically a monetary phenomenon, reflecting the rates of exchange between the home currency and the currencies of the rest of the world; (2) if there is an excess supply of or demand for the home currency to the extent that this excess is not met by the central bank losing or gaining reserves, the exchange rate will change to eliminate the excess; (3) through the central bank balance sheet, changes in domestic credit and net foreign assets (part of which is reserves) are related to changes in the monetary base, and thus the money supply; (4) domestic credit creation is related to fiscal policy (financing budget surpluses and deficits); and (5) growth in the money supply is related to nominal GNP, and thus to real growth and inflation (see, for instance, Frenkel and Johnson, 1976, or the IMF's *Monetary Approach*, 1977).

Central Bank Balance Sheet.   The balance sheet of a central bank can be consolidated into the following format:

Assets	Liabilities
D	MB
F	

Assume for the moment that the country's currency is not held in foreign reserves. MB is the monetary base, central bank liabilities to the banking system (the reserves of commercial banks including currency in their vaults and deposits at the central bank), and currency in circulation outside banks.

F is net foreign assets, the central bank assets in foreign currencies, monetary gold, SDRs, and reserve position in the IMF minus similar foreign liabilities.

D is net domestic credit, which is everything else in the balance sheet of the central bank including capital, reserves, and so forth.

Since this is a balance sheet, by definition the change in D plus the change in F equals the change in MB. D can be thought of as domestic credit policy, and F as exchange-rate policy; together they determine MB. If the multiplier is reasonably stable or predictable, changes in MB determine changes in the money supply. MB times the multiplier equals M_1 or M_2 and so forth. Furthermore, if velocity V is stable or predictable, $M \times V =$ GNP. Reflecting various lags and interreactions, growth of money determines growth of GNP and how much of that is real growth or inflation.

D reflects credit policy. If the central bank finances a government budget deficit (or lends to the private sector), then D rises. If F does not change, then MB rises by the same amount as D.

F is the proxy for exchange-market intervention to influence the exchange rate. If the central bank borrows foreign currency and puts the proceeds in reserves, then both foreign assets and liabilities rise by equal amounts with no change in F. If the central bank sells foreign exchange for local currency to support the exchange rate, then F declines. When F declines and there is no change in D, MB must decline.

This simplified tautology of the central-bank balance sheet conveniently pulls together most of the major macroeconomic policy variables of an economy. It relates budget, credit, monetary, and exchange-rate policies. It also provides a focus for measuring the overall balance of payments. Essentially, the financing of the overall balance of payments would be measured by the change in F.

Monetary Balance.   This concept is not much different from the IMFs balance H, total change in reserves, as long as it is the central bank that holds the country's foreign exchange and claims on and liabilities to the IMF. It does exclude "other claims" (see Exhibit 2) held by the banking system or government.

This approach to measuring the overall balance of payments has the advantage of relating the overall balance to exchange-rate, credit, and monetary policy in a firm way, but it forces one to put above the line changes in foreign assets and liabilities that are not those of the central bank. The IMF, on the other hand, tries to focus more clearly on changes in foreign assets and liabilities that affect the exchange rate directly, whether they are on the central-bank balance sheet or not, but loses the clear interaction with credit and monetary policy. Another difference is that all increases in foreign-currency liabilities of the central bank affect F negatively. In the IMF balance total, Group A through G equals H, increases in liabilities to the IMF alone count negatively as a change in reserves; some, but not all, of the other increases in foreign-currency liabilities of the central bank would go into "exceptional financing."

Although one must accept one approach or the other in drawing the bottom overall balance, one can construct a series of balances using the monetary approach that results in roughly the same kind of display of information as does the IMF approach. Still excluding the problems of reserve currencies, the balances would be as follows:

Balance A through E (essentially the same as IMF through counterpart items)

Exceptional financing plus items counted as reserves but not on central-bank balance sheet

Balance after exceptional financing

Change in F (financing)

Essentially, one moves items defined as change in reserves by the IMF but not on the central-bank balance sheet into exceptional financing. Note that all central-bank foreign assets and liabilities are included in F and excluded from capital flows above the balance A through E. For instance, if the central bank borrows long term from other than the IMF, it might be counted as long-term capital inflows in the IMF presentation (possibly as exception financing), but the logic of the monetarist approach compels it to be included in F.

Monetary Balance of Reserve Currency. So far we have put aside the case where the currency of the country is held in the reserves of foreign central banks. The IMF term is "liabilities constituting foreign authorities· reserves."

Such liabilities may be those of the central bank, the commercial banks, or of the government (U.S. Treasury bills for instance). Only the first would be on the balance sheet of the central bank. They could be included as a separate category FF of foreign liabilities in domestic currency as below:

Assets	Liabilities
D	MB
F	
FF	

The lowest overall balance would then be measured by F through FF. But the rest of the liabilities would have to be shown in a category such as G ("other" liabilities constituting foreign authorities· reserves) used by the IMF.

Another approach (with some interest even if the currency is not a reserve currency) is that in which the above balance sheet would include not only assets and liabilities of the central bank, but a consolidated balance sheet of the banking system where MB would be the money supply of the country, F foreign-currency claims and liabilities of the banking system, and FF local-currency liabilities to foreign monetary authorities. One would then draw an overall balance financed by F through FF of the banking system and then, lower down, an overall balance financed by F through

FF of the central bank alone. Liabilities to foreign monetary authorities outside the banking system would be shown as a special entry (*G*) above those balances as is done by the IMF for all such liabilities.

HOW TO USE BALANCE-OF-PAYMENTS STATISTICS

CLEAR PRESENTATION OF DATA.   As must be clear from the previous discussion, there is no single overall balance that tells you everything you want to know about the balance of payments. The best that can be hoped for is an array of clearly defined figures in a reasonable order with balances drawn at appropriate places. Movements in reserves, as defined by the IMF, are of much interest, as are the changes in net foreign assets of the central bank to relate such changes to credit and monetary policy and their interactions with exchange-rate policy. For reserve currencies, liabilities to foreign official agencies are also important. A breakout of exceptional financing is also necessary to understand special actions taken by the authorities to shield their reserves.

Other balances, such as the current account and those above it, also have their uses.

When reading a balance-of-payments statement of an individual country, it is necessary to understand the terminology and presentation. In many cases they differ significantly from the IMF standard. One often has to dig to unearth exceptional financing, arrearages, and so forth that give quite a different meaning to movements in reserves.

In addition, one must read the figure on the level of reserves with great care. Reported reserves are not always available to defend the currency because they are tied up as compensating balances, or are allocated for defense or other special purposes. On the other hand, the definition of reserves may be too conservative and may exclude assets that are quite liquid and could easily be counted as reserves. Comparison of reserves with the central-bank balance sheet is often helpful. In this way one often can also identify offsetting liabilities to the reserve assets.

INTERPRETING THE PRESSURES.   When analyzing the balance of payments it is well to look at the figures for at least the last three to four years. What is of most interest is which way they are moving. Are exports growing or stagnant? Is the trade balance and/or current account deteriorating? What is the structure of the capital flows financing the current account? Are there big unsustainable shifts in short-term flows?

Most important is to keep in mind what one is looking for in the context of institutional setting in which the country is operating. If the country is on a fixed peg against the SDR and the balance of payments starts to deteriorate, then one might be concerned that eventually the currency would be devalued. Deterioration would be indicated by an increasing deficit in the current account, at first financed by short-term capital flows, exceptional financing such as balance-of-payments loans, and perhaps a buildup of arrearages, and eventually a decline of reserves.

Behind such pressures are usually excessively expansionary fiscal and monetary policies—a large and growing budget deficit, financed in large part by credit from the central bank. Such credit expansion ($+D$) is partly offset by loss of reserves ($-F$). On balance, monetary growth ($+MB$) is excessive and inflation accelerates. The excessive inflation compared to the rest of the world when the country has fixed exchange rates tends to discourage exports, encourage imports, and leads to a deteriorating current account. Exceptional financing protects reserves temporarily, but unless the basic policies are shifted, reserves eventually run down and the exchange is devalued.

Where internal inflation is likely to remain high compared to the rest of the world, it is usually better to continually depreciate the exchange rate to offset the excessive inflation and thus avoid deterioration of the current account.

CLOSED ECONOMIES.   The more open an economy to the outside world, the more sensitive movements of goods, services, and capital are to relative prices, interest rates, growth, and so forth. But in varying degrees, many economies are closed in the sense that residents are not allowed to hold foreign currencies, exports are state controlled, imports strictly rationed, external borrowing controlled by the government, and so forth. The most perfect examples of closed economies are some of the Eastern bloc countries. Developing countries run the spectrum from closed to open.

In such closed economies, excessive budget deficits and credit creation can be bottled up within the economy and the balance of payments isolated to a greater or lesser extent from such pressures. Analysis of the balance of payments then tends to become an exercise in understanding the management of the external flows by the government. Even then, relative prices and exchange rates have some impact, and an inappropriate exchange rate makes such management much more difficult.

In closed economies, internal prices are often also controlled. This means that if the current account deficit is too large and exports are stagnant, it is not enough to devalue the currency. For instance, if the major export crop is sold to the government at a fixed price and that price is not increased with a devaluation, then producers have little incentive to increase production. Thus analysis of and policy for balance of payments in such circumstances must reach deep into the administration of the country's economy.

SOURCES AND SUGGESTED REFERENCES

Berstein Committee Report. *Review Committee for Balance of Payments Statistics,* Washington, D.C.: U.S. Government Printing Office, 1964.

Delvin, D.T. "The U.S. Balance of Payments: Revised Presentation," *Survey of Current Business,* Vol. 51, No. 6 (1971).

Frenkel, J.A. and H.G. Johnson. *Monetary Approach to the Balance of Payments,* London: Allen & Unwin, 1976.

International Monetary Fund. *Balance of Payments Manual,* 4th ed., Washington, D.C.: IMF, 1977.

International Monetary Fund. *Monetary Approach to the Balance of Payments: A Collection of Research Papers by Members of the Staff of the IMF,* Washington, D.C.: IMF, 1977.

Stern, R.M., Schwartz, Triffin, Berstein and Lederer. *The Presentation of the U.S. Balance of Payments: A Symposium,* Princeton University Essay in International Finance, No. 123 (1977).

SECTION **3**

THE SYSTEM OF INTERNATIONAL PAYMENTS

CONTENTS

INTERVENTION   4

INTERNATIONAL RESERVES   4

Foreign-Exchange Reserves   5
Special Drawing Rights   5
Reserve Position   6
Gold   6
Adequacy of International Reserves   7

THE INTERNATIONAL MONETARY
FUND   7

Basic Credit Facilities   8
Special Credit Facilities   9

DEVELOPMENT OF THE PAYMENTS
SYSTEM   10

THE EUROPEAN MONETARY SYSTEM   12

Credit Facilities   13

SOURCES AND SUGGESTED
REFERENCES   13

THE SYSTEM OF INTERNATIONAL PAYMENTS

Holger L. Engberg

The international payments system, as it exists in the early 1980s, is a hybrid of pegged and floating *exchange rates*, official *reserve assets* issued by national and international entities, and all shades of currency *convertibility*.

Most member countries of the International Monetary Fund (IMF or simply the Fund) follow fixed exchange-rate practices: More than 90 of the 141 members define the international value of their currencies in terms of either one major world currency or a *composite*, or *basket*, of currencies. Most currencies pegged to another currency are pegged to the U.S. dollar, which implies a joint float with the dollar against other currencies.

The member countries of the European Economic Community (EEC) (with the notable exception of Britain) maintain common margins of exchange-rate fluctuations and are consequently floating jointly in a *bloc* arrangement against other currencies, including the dollar. Some major currencies, such as the U.S. dollar, the pound sterling, the Japanese yen, and the Canadian dollar, are floating independently. No currency has been pegged to gold since the official price of gold was abolished in 1978.

Countries that define their currencies in terms of a composite, or basket, of currencies use either the special drawing right (SDR), which consists of five major currencies (see below), or a "homemade" basket that more closely reflects the currency composition of the country's international trade. Most of these countries are less developed countries that seek to minimize the fluctuations in the external values of their currencies. It is believed that such fluctuations, by increasing uncertainty, have adverse effects on their trade and domestic price stability and tend to frustrate economic decision making. By pegging their exchange rates to currency baskets, rather than to a single currency such as the U.S. dollar or the pound sterling, they may avoid some of the real economic costs associated with the fluctuations in the value of an independently floating world currency.

The EEC countries, forming a bloc (the European currency snake), are linked together in a parity grid permitting exchange fluctuations within upper and lower limits around the central rates. Each member also has a fixed central rate against the European currency unit, or the ECU, which in itself is a basket currency made up of snippets of the member currencies plus the pound sterling. The ECU is issued by the European Monetary Cooperation Fund against deposits of gold and dollar reserves by countries participating in the European Monetary System (EMS); it is an international reserve asset and is expected to be increasingly used as an international unit of account (the EMS is described in greater detail below).

INTERVENTION

The independently floating currencies, as well as the European currency snake, are not freely floating. National monetary authorities or central banks *intervene* in the foreign-exchange markets by selling foreign exchange against their own currencies when there is an excess demand for foreign exchange, and depreciation (an increase in local-currency price of foreign exchange) is deemed undesirable; and by buying foreign exchange in order to avoid an appreciation. Through such intervention the monetary authority *manages* the exchange rate, and the floating is often referred to as "dirty" floating.

Central-bank intervention is resorted to in order to smooth out short-term and random fluctuations in the exchange rate (to maintain "orderly market conditions"), or to prevent a change in the exchange rate that, in the opinion of the central bank, is not justified by fundamental economic forces. It is of critical importance for successful intervention that the central bank is able to distinguish reversible short-term disturbances from fundamental changes in the economic variables.

Central banks are also known occasionally to intervene in the foreign-exchange markets for other reasons than to smooth out random fluctuations and counter reversible changes. For example, intervention may be undertaken in order to gain international reserves, or to prevent an appreciation of the currency, (a decrease in the domestic-currency price of foreign exchange), which may adversely affect the country's export industries and its import-competing industries. Likewise, the monetary authority may deliberately reinforce, and thus overshoot, a downward pressure (depreciation) on its currency by buying foreign exchange in order to stimulate the domestic economy through increased exports. Such manipulation of the exchange rate is considered "illegitimate" under the surveillance provisions of the IMF (see below), but it is difficult to detect.

Exchange rates are affected not only by central-bank intervention, which may not necessarily lead to greater stability, but also by shifts in expectations about future exchange-rate movements and consequent speculative activities in the foreign-exchange markets. For example, in the 1970s the major exchange markets went through periods of increasing volatility that could not always be explained by developments in underlying economic forces, but rather was caused by institutional speculation. If holders of a currency expect the currency to depreciate, perhaps because an increasing rate of inflation is expected, and if these holders therefore sell the currency against other currencies or against commodities, such as gold, then the expectations may become self-fulfilling and the currency may depreciate, unless the central bank is able to launch a massive defense by selling large amounts of foreign reserves to supply the excess demand of the speculators for foreign exchange.

INTERNATIONAL RESERVES

When national monetary authorities intervene in the exchange markets in order to achieve an exchange rate consistent with their macroeconomic objectives, the result is a change in the country's *official reserve assets,* which are the ultimate means of making international payments. A country can use these reserve assets to finance a temporary imbalance in its international transactions and thereby avoid, or postpone, corrective policies such as an exchange-rate modification or the use of monetary and fiscal policy tools to affect domestic economic variables.

If the imbalance in international transactions is an excess demand for foreign exchange to pay for imports of goods and services and for foreign securities, the official reserve assets decline; and if the amount of reserve assets held by the central bank is inadequate to bridge the gap between the demand for and supply of foreign exchange at the target foreign-exchange price, the country may have access to various sources of borrowing the needed reserve assets. The provision of international reserves, and their distribution among countries, is therefore an important feature of the international payments system, and it is intimately linked to the monetary and exchange-rate policies that countries wish to pursue.

International reserve assets consist of official holdings of convertible foreign currencies, SDRs, and the reserve position or reserve tranche in the IMF.

FOREIGN-EXCHANGE RESERVES.   Official foreign-exchange reserves have consistently been the principal reserve assets since World War II and have in recent years represented about 90 percent of the total amount of international reserves. The largest component of these official holdings of convertible currencies consists of dollar-denominated assets, that is, short-term dollar claims that foreign central banks hold in the form of U.S. Treasury securities, commercial-bank certificates of deposit, commercial and finance paper, Eurodollar deposits, and similar obligations, as well as demand deposits. Thus the U.S. dollar remains the world's principal reserve, or key currency.

Most of the increase in total international liquidity in the postwar period was due to an increase in foreign official holdings of U.S. dollar claims. This pattern began to change in the late 1970s, as more national monetary authorities diversified their foreign-exchange portfolios and increased both the absolute and relative amounts of reserve assets denominated in Deutsche Marks, Swiss francs, and Japanese yen, as well as in the new European currency unit, the ECU. However, dollar-denominated claims still represent nearly two thirds of total official holdings of foreign exchange.

SPECIAL DRAWING RIGHTS.   This international reserve asset was created by the IMF in 1969 to supplement the existing reserve assets. The SDR is international money created by fiat under a convention entered into by member countries of the Fund. Its acceptability derives from this international convention, which specifies the obligation of the participants to accept it (up to three times the original allocations). When SDRs are created, they represent unconditional reserve assets; they are not repayable but may be canceled in the remote event that the Fund deems existing reserve assets to be excessive.

The SDR was first valued in terms of the U.S. dollar. This method was changed in 1974, when its valuation was based on a basket of 16 currencies, including the U.S. dollar, to provide a greater degree of stability. However, the relatively large number of currencies in the reference basket prevented a wider use of the SDR as a unit of account, and in early 1981 the basket was simplified to five currencies: the U.S. dollar, the Deutsche Mark, the French franc, the Japanese yen, and the pound sterling. The original weights were 42 percent for the dollar, 19 percent for the Deutsche Mark, and 13 percent each for the three other currencies. Since the daily calculation of the value of the SDR in terms of the U.S. dollar is based on specified quantities of each currency, the percentage share of each currency included changes as the exchange rates among the five currencies change. In mid-1981, the U.S. dollar value of one SDR was about $1.28.

The first allocations of SDRs, totaling SDR9.3 billion, were distributed to IMF member countries in proportion to their quotas (see below) in the years 1970–1972. Further allocations of SDR4 billion were made for each of the years 1979–1981. The total number of SDRs outstanding after the second round of allocations was SDR21.4 billion (about $25 billion), amounting to about 6 percent of world international reserves.

A member country with holdings of SDRs in excess of its total allocations earns net interest on the excess, and members with SDR holdings below their allocations pay charges at the same rate on their net use of SDRs. In mid-1981, the interest rate on the SDR was increased from 80 to 100 percent of a combined weighted interest rate, calculated as an average of interest rates on specified short-term money-market instruments in the five countries whose currencies make up the SDR basket. The Fund raised the interest rate on the SDR in order to enhance the substitutability of the SDR (and thus its use) with other reserve assets.

SDRs are used to an increasing extent in transactions among official holders and between the IMF and its members. For example, central banks use SDRs to acquire foreign currencies for intervention purposes from other central banks, either directly or through the agency of the IMF. Financial obligations to the Fund and other parties may be settled in SDRs. Swap arrangements and forward operations in SDRs are used increasingly. A dozen countries or so define the international value of their currencies in SDRs, which are also used as a unit of account not only by the IMF and other international and regional organizations, such as the Arab Monetary Fund and the Nordic Investment Bank, but also as the *numéraire* by Eurobond issues and other private financial instruments, including syndicated Euro-currency credits. A number of commercial banks accept deposits and issue time certificates of deposits (CDs) denominated in SDRs. The CDs can be traded in a secondary market formed by a group of banks. The simplification of the SDR basket in 1981 paved the way for a wider use of the SDR as a unit of account by private financial institutions, which now can more easily cover SDR liabilities by offsetting claims denominated in the five reference currencies.

RESERVE POSITION.   The third component of international reserves is the reserve position (reserve tranche) in the IMF. This is the difference between a member's quota (see below) and the Fund's holdings of that member's currency. The reserve tranche is available to the member country virtually on demand; it is similar to a checking account at the IMF, ready for use at any time, and it is therefore included in the total of international reserve assets.

GOLD.   Gold is no longer counted as part of the world's reserve assets. The Fund has attempted to *demonetize* gold, that is, to gradually reduce the role of gold in the international monetary system, by abolishing the official price of gold and the use of gold as a currency peg.

However, national monetary authorities still hold very large quantities of gold in their vaults; in fact, the *market* value of gold held by central banks and other official holders far exceeded the total of international reserve assets, as defined above, in

1981. Some central banks periodically revalue their gold holdings at market price, whereas the United States uses the fixed price of $42.22 per ounce established in 1973. The position of gold in the international monetary system is still uncertain; it remains to be seen whether gold will be completely demonetized or phased back into the international payments system.

ADEQUACY OF INTERNATIONAL RESERVES.   Official reserve assets are the ultimate means of making international payments and are needed by central banks for intervention in the exchange markets to maintain desired exchange rates. This raises the question of whether existing international reserve assets, and their growth, are adequate for the national monetary authorities to pursue their intervention goals.

If there were no intervention in the exchange markets, there would be no need for reserve assets. When in such a situation an excess demand for foreign exchange developed in a country's exchange market, the local currency would depreciate until enough supplies of foreign exchange were attracted into the market. However, no nation is willing to leave the international value of its currency solely to be determined by market forces, and reserves are therefore needed.

One measure of adequacy of international liquidity used by the IMF is to relate reserve assets to annual merchandise imports. This ratio has been declining, with a few interruptions, for most countries since the late 1950s. However, the ratio of *owned* reserve assets to specific uses of foreign exchange, such as merchandise imports, has become less relevant as more *borrowing* facilities have been developed by the IMF. In addition, high rates of domestic credit expansion in the major financial centers, such as New York and London, have been accompanied by high rates of expansion of credit to a large number of countries, including many of the non-oil less developed countries, which face a perennial international liquidity shortage. The facilities of the Eurocurrency markets, the opening of national credit markets for foreign bonds and other debt issues, and the broadening of credit arrangements between central banks have all contributed to a high elasticity of supply of international liquidity.

Although global reserves and their growth may be adequate, the distribution of reserves and the terms at which reserves can be acquired may be unsatisfactory for many countries, in particular the non-oil less developed countries. These are subject to greater payments imbalances and variability of export earnings than are the more-diversified industrial countries, and therefore need greater amounts of reserve assets. Moreover, most of these developing countries do not have ready access to borrowing facilities outside the IMF.

THE INTERNATIONAL MONETARY FUND

The IMF has been the centerpiece of the world payments system since World War II. It was created under the Bretton Woods Agreement of July 1944, which also established the International Bank for Reconstruction and Development, now called the World Bank. The Fund was given jurisdiction over exchange rates, multilateral payments, and the balance-of-payments policies of member countries, whereas the Bank was to lend long-term capital for development purposes. Membership in the Fund is a prerequisite for membership in the World Bank, and the two organizations have maintained close working relationships throughout the years.

The Fund consists of a pool of national currencies and SDRs that have been contributed by the member countries in proportion to their quotas. The size of a *quota* reflects the member's economic size relative to the total membership of the Fund. The quota system has been revised several times, and individual member quotas have been changed as the economic power of nations changed relative to each other, but the largest quota by far is still that of the United States (SDR 12.6 billion or 20.8 percent of the total). The quotas determine the voting power of members, their access to the Fund's financial resources, and their share in allocations of SDRs.

The resources of the IMF have been augmented through periodic increases in quotas and by additions of the quotas of new members. Fund membership has risen from 35 countries in 1945 to 141 members in 1981, when total resources were SDR 60.7 billion, or about $70 billion. In addition, the Fund may supplement its resources by borrowing needed currencies from member countries under a network of borrowing agreements, including the *General Agreements to Borrow* (GAB). Under this arrangement, 10 major industrial countries, the Group of Ten, plus Switzerland stand ready to lend to the Fund to meet the balance-of-payments requirements of any one of them, permitting a maximum credit to the Fund equivalent to about SDR 6.8 billion in lenders' currencies. The Fund has also supplemented its resources by borrowing from member countries whose balance of payments and international reserve positions are sufficiently strong to enable them to make medium-term arrangements with the Fund. For example, in 1981 the Saudi Arabian Monetary Agency (SAMA) made a loan commitment to the Fund of SDR 4 billion a year for 3 years, with an estimated average maturity of 5½–years and at an interest rate based on an average of government bond yields in the five countries whose currencies constitute the components of the SDR "basket." The Fund has negotiated similar arrangements with other countries and official institutions, and has also explored the possibility of raising funds in private capital markets by issuing negotiable notes and certificates.

BASIC CREDIT FACILITIES. When a member borrows from, or *draws* on, the Fund to meet balance-of-payments needs, it uses its own currency to purchase the currencies of other members or to acquire SDRs. Thus borrowing (drawing) results in an increase in the Fund's holdings of that member's currency and a decrease in the holdings of the currencies of other members. No change takes place in the total of reserve assets, but the composition of the Fund's resources changes, and the Fund may at certain times experience a shortage of some currencies. The borrowing arrangements mentioned above were created in part to help meet such possible shortages.

Member access to the Fund's resources is limited in various ways. Drawings, that is, purchases of other currencies, are virtually automatic and unconditional as long as they do not cause the Fund's holdings of the borrowing member's currency to exceed the member's quota. This is the earlier-mentioned reserve position or *reserve tranche*, which is the difference between the member's quota and the Fund's holdings of the member's currency.

Drawings in the subsequent *credit tranches* are subject to increasing *conditionality;* as a minimum the member must show the Fund that it is making reasonable efforts to deal with its balance-of-payments difficulties. If more-substantial Fund assistance is needed, relative to the size of the member's quota, the Fund is likely to require agreement with the member on a more specific program regarding domestic credit expansion, government financing, external borrowing, and trade and payments restrictions. Each member has (since 1981) an overall annual access to Fund resources of up to 150 percent of its quota or up to 450 percent over a 3-year period. A member's cumulative access, net of scheduled repayments, is up to 600 percent of its quota. These limits do not take into account borrowings under the compensatory and buffer stock financing facilities (see below), and they are not entirely inflexible; in some cases, member countries are able to borrow larger amounts than the limits would normally allow.

Drawings are generally made under lines of credit, or *standby arrangements*, which ensure a member access to the Fund's resources up to a specified amount for a period of 1–3 years. Repayment is made in the form of *repurchase* of the member country's currency from the Fund within 3–5 years (up to 10 years under the extended facility). Thus the IMF provides credit facilities to help members finance temporary and cyclical balance-of-payments deficits while domestic economic policies are being pursued to correct the imbalances. If a more fundamental or structural imbalance has developed in a member's external transactions, perhaps because of a persistent deterioration in its terms of trade, that cannot be remedied by the use of monetary, fiscal, and exchange-rate policies, then the member may turn to the World Bank for long-term assistance.

SPECIAL CREDIT FACILITIES.   A number of facilities in addition to the credit tranches have been developed over the years, specifically designed for the large number of less developed countries that are now members of the IMF. They make it possible for these countries to borrow far in excess of the regular scale of Fund assistance.

Compensatory financing is available to members experiencing payments difficulties caused by temporary declines in export earnings attributable to circumstances largely beyond their control, such as falling commodity prices in the world markets or bad weather and draught. This facility, which permits a member to borrow up to 100 percent of its quota, was first introduced in 1963 and has been used extensively by developing countries greatly dependent on export revenue from the sale of one or a few primary commodities.

Buffer-stock financing was established in 1969 to help members in balance-of-payments difficulties finance their contributions to international buffer-stock arrangements maintained to stabilize world markets for commodities, such as those for cocoa, sugar, and tin.

The extended facility was created in 1974 for countries that need Fund assistance for longer periods and in amounts larger than those available under the credit-tranche policy. Repayment can be made over as long as 10 years, and interest is the same as that charged for use of the credit tranches. Arrangements for extended assistance have been made for substantial amounts but only for a relatively small number of developing countries.

Temporary credit facilities have been established to meet particular needs, such as the *oil facility*, under which members could borrow to meet balance-of-payments needs resulting from higher oil prices in 1974 and 1975. A *trust fund* provides additional balance-of-payments assistance on concessional terms to less developed countries. Its resources are derived mainly from the profits realized on the sale of one sixth of the Fund's gold for the benefit of less-developed member countries. These sales of 25 million ounces, and another 25 million ounces distributed among members, out of the Fund's holdings of approximately 150 million ounces of gold were part of the efforts in the late 1970s to gradually reduce the monetary role of gold.

The *supplementary financing facility*, also called the "Witteveen facility" after the then-managing director of the Fund, was established in 1978 with SDR 7.8 billion raised from financial institutions, mostly central banks, in 14 oil-producing and industrial countries, including the United States. Its purpose was to assist members with economies suffering from serious balance-of-payments deficits that require larger resources, relative to the quota, than are available under the regular facilities.

Since it supplements other borrowing, it effectively carries the usual conditionality; and the charges levied by the Fund on the amounts borrowed are tied to the market rate for U.S. government securities. Consequently, this facility was used very little by member countries, mostly developing countries, that are eligible, until it was made more attractive by the establishment of a *subsidy account,* amounting to SDR 1 billion. This helped reduce the cost of using the supplementary financing facility for low-income developing member countries, and its resources were exhausted by April 1981. However, the Fund was able to continue to provide supplementary assistance, under its *enlarged access policy,* by arranging additional borrowing from institutions in industrialized and oil-producing countries, including the Saudi Arabian Monetary Agency (see above).

DEVELOPMENT OF THE PAYMENTS SYSTEM

The world payments system, since it was founded by the Bretton Woods Agreement in 1944 and until its demise in 1971, was anchored to the basic principles of international economic cooperation, free multilateral trade, currency convertibility, and freedom from direct control. It recognized that responsibility for balance-of-payments imbalances rested on both surplus and deficit countries, that is, that a surplus represents an imbalance that has to be dealt with by appropriate policy measures, just as a deficit represents an imbalance. It was also assumed that domestic economic policy tools would be used by countries to correct the external imbalance.

The three main thrusts of the IMF were fixed, but adjustable, exchange rates; a multilateral payments system with freedom of international payments; and provision of adequate international reserve assets to enable members to maintain fixed exchange rates without resorting to trade and payments controls.

Member exchange rates were fixed at a par value, defined in terms of U.S. dollars and therefore in gold, since the dollar was defined in gold, and the dollar was freely convertible into gold. To permit the exchange market to absorb small and random shifts in demand and supply conditions, a band of one percent above and below the par value was maintained within which the exchange rate was allowed to fluctuate. A change in the par value could take place only if a member's balance of payments was in "fundamental disequilibrium," and then only with the concurrence of the Fund. The concept of fundamental disequilibrium was never defined by the Fund, but it was sometimes interpreted as a persistent balance-of-payments imbalance that could not be corrected by the use of domestic economic policies without incurring severe and unacceptable social and political costs.

Throughout the period of the Bretton Woods system, the doctrine of fixed exchange rates was breached in numerous ways. Several currencies were floated for extended periods of time (for example, the French franc and the Canadian dollar), and systems of multiple exchange rates were widespread, particularly in Latin America. In contrast, some major currencies were maintained at their par values at considerable intervention costs, when fundamental economic conditions dictated a change. Par values tended to become sticky when considerable political significance was attached to them and governments committed themselves to defend them "at all costs."

The system of fixed exchange rates came under increasing attacks in the late 1960s. The linchpin of the system was the U.S. dollar, as a reference and reserve currency, and its convertibility into gold. The world's need for an ever-increasing supply of international liquidity in the 1950s and 1960s had been met primarily by the deficits in the U.S. balance of payments; as these deficits grew larger, however, and surplus countries accumulated substantial dollar balances, doubts were raised about the continued convertibility of the dollar into gold. The postwar Bretton Woods system of fixed exchange rates finally broke down in August 1971 when the United States announced an unprecedented series of measures, including cessation of official gold sales and no intervention to maintain fixed exchange rates. This meant that the U.S. dollar was no longer convertible into gold and that the dollar was left free to float. Although in subsequent months attempts were made to return to a modified fixed-exchange-rate system, a new regime of floating rates had in effect been established.

The IMF was the custodian of the Bretton Woods payments system and indeed persistently and strongly defended the "fixed but adjustable" exchange-rate regime, even after its effective demise in 1971. Nevertheless, the Fund has survived and even flourished as a central policy-making and operating institution. After the energy-price increases in the mid-1970s and the resulting large-scale shifts in balance-of-payments positions, it became clear that international financial cooperation was essential in a world of *managed* floating, and that there was no real alternative to the Fund as a truly international institution.

The Fund had already over many years developed a *consultation* procedure involving *annual* appraisals of each member country's economic and financial situation and policies. These consultations give the Fund considerable leverage in dealing with individual members, and the recommendations resulting from the consultations are usually accepted by the members and often lead to appropriate policy changes.

The Fund has further leverage in dealing with those members that need access to its resources, since it has the power to deny assistance, and this power has been used both directly and as a threat. For example, France was denied the right of using the Fund's resources for five years (1949–1954) as a punishment for establishing a free exchange market in addition to the official market, contrary to the Fund articles of agreement, which then required the maintenance of exchange rates within narrow limits. In the extreme, the Fund may expel a member country that fails to cooperate, and this power was used once, when the membership of Czechoslovakia was terminated in 1953.

In addition to its annual consultations, the Fund has been given the responsibility of *continuous surveillance* over member countries' exchange policies. Under the articles of agreement, amended in 1978, member countries are prohibited from "manipulating" their exchange rates to prevent effective balance-of-payments adjustment or to gain competitive advantage over other members; and they are required to intervene in the exchange market to counter "disorderly conditions" caused by, for example, speculative short-term capital movements. The Fund has designed a series of indicators to help identify inappropriate exchange-rate policies. These indicators include protracted large-scale intervention in one direction in the exchange market; a high level of official or semiofficial borrowing or lending for balance-of-payments purposes; various kinds of restrictions or incentives affecting the balance of payments; and exchange-rate behavior that appears to be unrelated to underlying economic and financial conditions.

With this surveillance responsibility, and with the power to *initiate* high-level discussions with members who may appear to be violating the exchange-rate principles agreed on by the collective membership, the Fund is firmly placed in the center of the international payments system. However, the effectiveness of the Fund to influence economic-policy decisions made by its sovereign members is limited. On one hand, more than two thirds of its members are non-oil less developed countries for which the Fund is the "lender of last resort." These countries may, and some do, consider the consultations and the Fund's insistence on conditionality in connection with the use of credit tranches and other facilities infringements of their national sovereignty, but few have refused to comply with the Fund for any length of time. On the other hand, its effectiveness to influence economic-policy decisions is limited when dealing with those members who have little or no need for the Fund's resources or who are participating in a powerful currency bloc, such as the European Monetary System. In such cases the Fund is constrained to rely on negotiation and persuasion.

THE EUROPEAN MONETARY SYSTEM

The European Monetary System (EMS), which became operational in March 1979, is designed to develop into a full-fledged monetary system embracing the members of the European Economic Community (EEC) and is part of the European integration movement. It has established a new multinational reserve asset, the European currency unit (ECU), which in many respects is similar to, and eventually may compete with, the Special Drawing Right (SDR) created by the International Monetary Fund.

The seven European currencies (Belgian/Luxembourg franc, Danish krone, Deutsche Mark, French franc, Italian lira, Irish pound, and Netherlands guilder, but not yet the pound sterling) are linked together in a *grid* of 21 bilateral central exchange rates with agreed margins of fluctuations of plus or minus 2¼ percent (± 6 percent in the case of the Italian lira). These are the limits at which central-bank intervention in the exchange market is obligatory. Thus the grid is a continuation of the European currency snake introduced in 1972, when the European governments decided that wide fluctuations of their currencies against each other would destroy any hopes of closer monetary harmonization. Eventually the agreed margins of plus or minus 2¼ percent may be narrowed as the EMS members move toward monetary integration.

In addition, each currency participating in the EMS has a central rate in terms of the ECU, which is a basket of fixed amounts of eight currencies: the seven currencies listed above, plus the pound sterling. The weights are given in units of national currencies; for example, the basket contains 83 German pfennigs, 1.15 French francs, and so forth. The weights will therefore change over time as the values of the eight currencies change against each other; but the approximate weight of the Deutsche Mark, the most important currency in the basket, is one third, compared to about one fifth for the French franc and one seventh for the pound sterling. In mid-1981, one ECU was equivalent to about $1.18 (U.S.) or SDR1.03.

The linkage to the ECU serves as an early-warning device that signals whether a currency diverges from the average of the others in the ECU basket. When a currency crosses its "divergence threshold" (about 0.7 percent above or below its central rate with the ECU, adjusted for the currency's weight in the ECU basket), the relevant monetary authority is expected to take measures to correct the situation, either through exchange-market intervention and interest-rate policy, or through a change in the central rate. The ECU linkage with its divergence indicator is sometimes referred to as the "rattlesnake."

The ECU is more than just a unit of account but has become an international reserve asset. Members of the EMS have deposited with the *European Monetary Cooperation Fund* (EMCF), which was established in 1973, 20 percent of their gold and dollar reserves, adjusted every three months, against the issue of ECU, which are then held as official reserves and can be used to settle claims between EMS central banks. The ECU issued against gold add to total world liquidity, since national gold reserves are no longer counted as official reserves; whereas the ECU issued against dollars merely change the composition, and not the size, of such reserves. The gold deposits against ECU are valued at an average market price; hence gold has regained a partial foothold in the international payments system, as official reserves change when the market price of gold changes. The ECU now accounts for 15 percent of the world's official foreign-exchange reserves, more than the Deutsche Mark or any other single currency except the dollar. Eventually it is intended that the EMCF will issue ECU against not only dollars and gold but national currencies, greatly increasing the EMS countries' international liquidity.

CREDIT FACILITIES. Complementing the resources of the IMF, various credit facilities are available to the full-scale members of the EMS, coordinated under the aegis of the EMCF. A *very short-term financing facility* for the financing of exchange-market intervention provides mutual credit lines for unlimited amounts by the participating central banks. These loans have to be repaid within 45 days after the month in which intervention was made, but can be extended by 3 months.

In addition, *short-term monetary support* of up to 9 months is granted to central banks for the financing of temporary balance-of-payments deficits. These credits are granted without "conditionality," but they do trigger consultations with the appropriate EEC bodies, such as the Committee of Central Bank Governors, the Monetary Committee, the Economic Policy Committee, or the Council of Ministers, which meet regularly. It is expected that successive consultations in these bodies, with increasingly political involvement, will result in a convergence of monetary and other economic policies among the EMS members. The short-term monetary support is available under a borrowing ceiling or "debtor quota," which, however, may be extended; and each country's commitment is limited to a "credit quota," which is twice as high as the borrowing ceiling, to safeguard the viability of the system under varying distributions of payments imbalances among member countries. For example, the "debtor quota" of France, Germany, and Britain is ECU1,740 million (about $2.1 billion) each, whereas the "credit quota" for these same countries is ECU 3,480 million (about $4.1 billion) each.

Beyond short-term credits, the EMS provides for *medium-term financial assistance* to any member country in serious balance-of-payments difficulties with credits extended for two to five years, but subject to economic policy conditions (conditionality) to be laid down by the EEC Council of Ministers. The short-term monetary support and the medium-term financial assistance together make available about ECU25 billion ($30 billion) of additional balance-of-payments assistance to the members of the EMS.

The EMS, with its grid of bilateral exchange rates, linkages with the ECU, usage of the ECU as a reserve asset and *numéraire,* and with its large short-term and medium-term credit facilities, was designed to enhance the integration of EEC economic policies and to progressively narrow the margins of fluctuation of the EEC currencies against each other, thus promoting currency integration. Additionally, it has become an increasing concern, as the EEC has expanded, to strengthen the economic potential of the poorer countries of the EEC. The EMS is also seen as part of that effort.

SOURCES AND SUGGESTED REFERENCES

Gold, J. *Conditionality.* IMF Pamphlet Series No. 31. Washington, D.C.: International Monetary Fund, 1980.

Gold, J. *Financial Assistance by the International Monetary Fund: Law and Practice.* IMF Pamphlet Series No. 27. Washington, D.C.: International Monetary Fund, 1979.

IMF. *Annual Report.* Washington, D.C.: International Monetary Fund, issued annually.

IMF. *IMF Survey.* Washington, D.C.: International Monetary Fund, issued bi-monthly.

Southard, J., F.A. *The Evolution of the International Monetary Fund.* Essays in International Finance No. 135. Princeton: Princeton University International Finance Section, 1979.

de Vries, T. *On the Meaning and Future of the European Monetary System.* Essays in International Finance No. 138. Princeton: Princeton University International Finance Section, 1980.

TRADING BLOCS AND COMMON MARKETS

CONTENTS

ECONOMIC INTEGRATION
CONCEPTS   3

The Economic Case for Integration   3
  The basic model   3
  Large trading blocs   5
  Specific arguments for less developed
  countries   6
  Arguments for communist countries   7
Levels of Economic Integration   8

THE EUROPEAN COMMUNITY   10

The Institutions of the European
Community   10
  European Coal and Steel Community   10
  European Economic Community   10
The Structure of the Economies   13
Development of the Customs Union   15
Progress Toward Economic Union   16
  Competition policy   16
  Regional policy   17
  The Common Agricultural Policy   18
Monetary Union and Fiscal
Harmonization   20
  Monetary union   20
  Fiscal harmonization   22
External Relations   23
Measuring the Progress of Economic
Integration   23

THE EUROPEAN FREE TRADE AREA   24

ECONOMIC INTEGRATION IN
COMMUNIST COUNTRIES   25

The Structure of the Council for Mutual
Economic Assistance   25

The Impact of the Council for Mutual
Economic Assistance   27
  Trade   27
  Rationalization of production   28
  Labor flows   29
  External relations   29
  Convergence   30

INTEGRATION AMONG LESS
DEVELOPED COUNTRIES   30

General Situation   30
Latin America   31
  Latin American Free Trade Area and
  Latin American Integration
  Association   31
  Central American Common Market   32
  Caribbean Community   33
  Progress toward integration   33
Africa   34
  East African Community   35
  Economic Community of West
  African States   36
  Effects of African integration   36
Asia   37

ECONOMIC VERSUS POLITICAL
INTEGRATION   37

THE FUTURE OF REGIONAL
ECONOMIC BLOCS   40

SOURCES AND SUGGESTED
REFERENCES   42

Additional References   44

TRADING BLOCS AND COMMON MARKETS

Peter W. Wood
Robert F. Elliott

The formation and development of trading blocs and common markets are part of the process of international economic integration. Integration involves the development of links through trade and the movement of factors of production between national economies and thus leads to mutual economic interdependence among nations. In the broadest terms, then, economic integration can be regarded as the unification of separate economies into an international economy in which the fortunes and economic experience of each nation depend on developments in the body as a whole. In market economies, economic integration will tend to occur spontaneously under the influence of market forces, but the direction and pace of integration can be affected by trading agreements. Attempts to promote economic integration through the creation of trading agreements are to be found among Western industrialized nations, communist economies, and less developed countries. However, a distinctive rationale for the formation of a trading bloc exists in each of these three broad cases and corresponds to a distinctive concept of economic integration.

ECONOMIC INTEGRATION CONCEPTS

THE ECONOMIC CASE FOR INTEGRATION. The simplest economic argument for integration arises from the so-called *theory of customs unions* pioneered by Jacob Viner (1953). Prior to Viner's work, economists had favored customs unions as a step toward free trade.

The Basic Model. Orthodox economic theory teaches that, under certain restrictive conditions, free trade improves resource allocation and leads to potential gains in welfare. Customs unions were regarded as a stage in this process. Viner demonstrated that a customs union could improve or worsen resource allocation depending on the relative strengths of *trade creation* and *trade diversion*. This distinction can be made clear by a simple example. Consider country A, which provides its own supplies of good X at a cost of $1 per unit. In country B a unit of X can be produced at 90 cents, but A levies a tariff of 20 cents on X. In consequence B cannot compete in A's market. If A and B form a customs union and abolish tariffs, consumers in A will obtain good X at a price of 90 cents, while production will be concentrated in the more efficient production source—country B. This is trade creation. However, suppose that a third country, C, exists with a production cost of 75 cents per unit. Prior to formation of the union, C supplied A's market at a price of $75 + 20 = 95$ cents. After formation of a union between A and B, C was displaced from the market by B. In this case a low-cost producer is replaced by a higher-cost producer—this is trade diversion. Although the consumers in country A are obtaining the good at a lower price, the country as a whole is worse off as it has lost the tariff revenue of 20 cents per unit. Viner's analysis indicates that customs unions will be beneficial if trade creation exceeds trade diversion. This is most likely to take place when countries have similar industrial structures with industries which are competitive with one another. Such a situation gives the greatest scope for the elimination of inefficient tariff-protected industries. Further, the larger the area of the union, the more likely it is to be trade creating, since more of each nation's trading partners will fall within the area of free trade.

Viner's original analysis was subject to some further development which argued that even a trade-diverting customs union could increase economic welfare if imports from the partner country (say B in the example above) replaced still higher cost production by domestic firms in addition to displacing the original lowest cost source of imports. However, it has been convincingly demonstrated by H. G. Johnson (1974), that if we confine the term "trade diversion" to the replacement of a lower cost by a higher cost producer and the term "trade creation" to the replacement of higher cost by lower cost production, Viner's conclusions stand. Thus we may state unequivocally that the balance of costs and benefits from customs union formation will depend upon the balance between trade diversion and trade creation.

Since trade diversion is the result of the existence of barriers against imports from third countries, it follows that the introduction of universal free trade would result in only trade creation. Clearly this is a preferred solution, and consequently the formation of a customs union must be recognized as an inferior or "second-best" alternative to universal free trade. We must, however, note that in a world characterised by government intervention and distorting effects on markets, free trade may not be feasible. It has been argued that distortions in other markets and constraints on policy choice may be such that a customs union is superior to simple trade liberalization in terms of economic efficiency—as indicated by the so-called theory of second best. However, Cooper and Massell (1972), have demonstrated that a policy of nondiscriminatory tariff reduction will be superior to the formation of a customs union even where free trade is not the best policy. Essentially this is because with a nondiscriminatory tariff reduction no problem of trade diversion arises and imports still yield tariff revenue, whereas a customs union would lead to a diversion of trade to the (tariff-free) partner and thus to a loss of tariff revenue. Even if it is desired to reorient trade toward specific partners for political reasons, a discriminatory tariff policy which gives greater tariff reductions to the preferred partners is superior to a customs union, since some tariff revenue is still generated with the former policy. The customs union emerges as the optimal second best policy only if (1) a specific reorientation of trade is desired and (2) international agreements such as the General Agreement on Tariffs and Trade (GATT) exclude the use of discriminatory tariffs except for customs unions and free trade areas.

The very early attempts to estimate the value of the resource allocation effects of customs union formation invariably produced results which suggested that these gains were extremely modest. The work of P.J. Verdoorn indicated a gain to the original six members of the European Economic Community (EEC) amounting to around 0.005 percent of their combined national income. This was presented and discussed by T. Scitovsky (1957) who stated "Verdoorn's figures are probably underestimated, but, if by way of correction, we should raise them five or even twenty-five fold, that would still leave unchanged our basic conclusion that the gain from increased intra-European specialisation is likely to be insignificant." More recently Waelbroeck (1978) concluded that "the welfare significance of the EEC appears less than that of the Concorde aeroplane"!

Large Trading Blocs.   There are, however, other sources of advantage in economic union. For large trading blocs, the reduction of demand for imports from outside the bloc caused by the imposition of a common tariff may produce a fall in the price of imports from nonbloc countries and thus cause an improvement in the bloc's terms of trade. This gain, unlike the gains from trade in general, is obtained at the expense of nonbloc members. The gain can be obtained only where the bloc is sufficiently large to affect world prices and where appropriate external tariff policies are adopted.

Quite apart from these essentially static effects, attention has also been drawn to the potential dynamic benefits of economic integration. A number of arguments exist on this. First and most commonly it has been argued that segmentation of markets in Europe prevented European national producers from reaping economies of scale. The creation of larger markets would enable economies of scale to be reaped. This argument ignores the fact that European industries compete in world as well as domestic markets and begs the question of why such economies of scale would not be exploited by exporting firms. However, as Waelbroeck (1978) emphasizes, firms may be inhibited from attempting to penetrate foreign markets for fear that successful market penetration will provoke the imposition of trade barriers by the importing nation. Second, therefore, formal integration will reduce the fear of discriminatory policies and thus reduce the risk involved in exporting. Third, Waelbroeck (1978) also suggests that by increasing the extent of the market, integration may reduce the degree of monopoly and increase the level of competition (as indicated by numbers of competing firms). In this way, prices will be brought closer to marginal costs, production increased, and firms induced to produce at a level of output involving near-minimum average costs. In this vein Scitovsky (1957) argued that integration in Europe would create a more competitive atmosphere in which the less energetic economies (notably France) would be stimulated by vigorous competition from Germany. The subsequent history of the French economy may be regarded as providing some support for this thesis. In contrast the British experience since Britain's accession to the EEC suggests that dynamism is not always contagious and that psychological or sociological barriers to growth can be persistent. A fourth dynamic argument in the European context is that integration, by creating larger markets and transnational collaboration, will foster technological development and the flow of technology within the bloc. A review of these issues by Elliott and Wood (1981) indicates that European levels of technology have risen during the period since the EEC's formation, but that by no means all of this can be attributed to the dynamic effects of the EEC. Fifth and finally, it is now recognized that under some circumstances an increase in industrial output resulting from customs union formation may be counted a gain even if "home" production is more costly than importation. This apparent paradox arises from the possibility that a country or society may have a preference for industrial production—that is, industrial production (compared with other economic activities) may be regarded as a "public good." However, this argument is most often deployed in relation to less developed countries.

For the advanced industrial countries of Europe, opinion remains divided over the benefits of formal integration. The static effects are evidently trivial whereas the dynamic effects, being difficult to quantify, remain an area of contention. The relatively rapid growth experienced by some European economies in the 1950s and 1960s cannot be taken as proof of dynamic benefits of integration. This view has been put by Södersten (1971): "By a coincidence in time, the effects of European economic integration were taken to be much more splendid than they actually were. The last few years have also demonstrated that economic integration does not guarantee rapid economic growth unless other factors are also favourable."

Specific Arguments for Less Developed Countries. In less developed countries (LDCs), integration is generally seen not as an end product of economic development but as a stage and instrument in the process of development. The objective of international economic integration in LDCs is usually to create a reasonably large, protected market within the bloc in the hope that this will stimulate "domestic" production of import substitutes and create profitable opportunities for investment—including foreign investment. Thus the LDC concept of the role of integration is essentially a development of the *infant industry* argument for protection, but one which recognizes that scale economies may exist that cannot be exploited within the domestic market.

The economic argument for integration among the economies of LDCs thus owes even less to static trade theory than is the case in developed countries. Given that the objective of integration is to provide protected markets upon which domestic industries may develop, trade diversion is, as Willmore (1970) states, not to be regarded as an unfortunate side effect but rather as an integral part of the process. Trade diversion will lead to a short-run economic loss, as indicated in the static theory, but this is regarded as the price to be paid for establishing industries that will be competitive at a world level in the future. The argument put forward in the European context that economies of scale can be exploited by export industries without integration schemes has less force in LDCs since one is considering industries that scarcely exist and are deemed to require protection during the "infant" phase. Integration then becomes simply a technique for combining protection with economies of scale. The adoption of interventionist policies such as the direction of investment into agreed sectors and the formation of joint enterprises is generally justified on the grounds that market forces are poorly developed in the LDC economies and operate too slowly or fail to produce the desired effects.

The economic case for integration in LDCs may be criticized on the same grounds as infant-industry protection is criticized. Thus it can be argued that protection of an industry is as likely to inhibit its development through lack of competition as it is to stimulate it. Furthermore, it is generally accepted that product subsidies provide a superior method for supporting a developing industry than the creation of a protected market, though it must be recognized that tariffs may be easier to administer than a system of subsidies. Finally, a straightforward economic argument in favor of the integration-protection policy would require that the returns from the protected industries once they had become world-competitive were sufficiently great to offset the losses experienced during the period of protection. The returns include not only direct profits but potential benefits to the economy through the creation of an industrialized and dynamic sector. However, even this requirement for an excess of financial benefit over cost must be modified if the existence of an industrial sector assumes the qualities of a public good. Thus the citizens or leaders of a country may prefer to develop an industrial sector, say for reasons of prestige, even if this involves a loss of output and income. The possibility that this preference exists must be borne in mind if the process of integration in LDCs is to be correctly understood and analyzed.

Arguments for Communist Countries. The concepts of trade creation and trade diversion are of very little relevance to the economic case for integration under communism. This follows from the fact that international trade under communism is carried out through state monopolies in accordance with physical planning decisions using prices which bear no real relation to costs of production. Furthermore, the Marxist theory of trade rejects the argument of orthodox economic theory that free trade is beneficial.

In communist countries, economic integration has been seen as a means to the creation of a "socialist international division of labor." The objectives of the communist concept of integration are, according to Ellman (1979) to "maximise the gains from economies of scale, specialisation and participation in the international division of labour. Economic integration takes such forms as trade, industrial co-operation, movement of labour, technical and scientific co-operation, energy integration, the financing of investment, the creation and operation of socialist common enterprises, and plan co-ordination." In a number of respects, the first sentence describes the desired outcome of integration in market economies. The important difference is that whereas in a market economy these effects would be expected to flow from the operation of market forces in a suitable environment, all integration in socialist countries requires deliberate positive steps. Thus in the West, integration is seen as an omnipresent latent force whereas in communist countries it is, as with all economic policy, a politically chosen course of action. Because of this, socialist integration requires the creation of institutions which will undertake the tasks left to the price mechanism in market economies. For example, a major stated objective of the Council for Mutual Economic Assistance (COMECON) has been the creation of a system for arriving .at international exchange prices that reflect conditions of production in socialist economies. In Marxist terms these prices would allow for "equivalent exchange" free from the allegedly exploitative elements of capitalist market prices. As yet the COMECON countries have been unable to arrive at a basis for calculation of such prices, and world prices continue to be used in COMECON trade. Similarly, relatively little progress has been made in calculating profitability indexes that, it was hoped, would indicate which products each country should specialize in and trade. In general there has been a conflict in socialist discussions of integration between those favoring immediate resource allocation efficiency and those favoring a longer term equalization of levels of development. The socialist theory of integration thus is incomplete in that it lacks clear agreement on mechanisms of trade and exchange, and because there are unresolved disputes between productive efficiency and equality of development.

Whereas the exploitation of market opportunities provides the motive force of integration in free-enterprise economies, such considerations are virtually irrelevant in the case of communist economies. In a communist country, foreign enterprises, whether state owned or not, do not enjoy free access to the market. The barrier to access is not created by tariffs or quotas but by the fact that communist countries carry out almost all of their trade through state-controlled export-import monopolies. In a few cases, enterprises are allowed to trade directly with foreign firms. This state monopoly is generally justified in terms of the Marxist theory of trade, which argues that free trade between an advanced Western country and a less-advanced communist country will lead to the exploitation of the latter by the former. The form of foreign-trade mechanism rationalized in terms of East-West relations continues to influence trade within the communist bloc.

LEVELS OF ECONOMIC INTEGRATION. At the highest level, international economic integration, as conceived in market economies, involves a process by which distinct national economies become interconnected and interdependent so that there is free movement of goods and factors of production. In this way, it is argued, resources will be most productively allocated and the total output of the integrated area will be greater than that which would be obtained by the constituent parts. Even in the relatively highly developed EEC, however, integration falls far short of the ideal outlined above. The removal of formal impediments to trade in the form of quotas and tariffs leaves other trade barriers such as national safety standards and product specifications. Free movement of labor is impeded by language differences, professional accreditation, and other restrictive practices while barriers to capital movement are only gradually being eliminated. Thus in analyzing integration in market economies, one is dealing with degrees of integration rather than with a completed process.

A useful distinction in the analysis of integration has been introduced by Tinbergen (1965), who distinguishes between *positive integration* and *negative integration*. Negative integration refers to the removal of barriers to trade such as when quotas are lifted or tariffs eliminated. With the barriers removed, the process of integration is left to the forces of the market. Positive integration involves the creation of new, supranational institutions. These institutions may exist to facilitate the operation of the market, as with a body dealing with harmonization of product standards, or may pursue policies such as public investment on a transnational basis. In market economies, notably in the EEC, policies of both negative and positive integration have been pursued. Negative integration policies may be regarded as the essential step in market integration, whereas the highest levels of complete integration will require the implementation of positive policies.

For market economies a straightforward typology of integration agreement exists. At the simplest level, integration may be restricted to free intragroup trade in a single commodity or commodity group; this was the case with the European Coal and Steel Community (ECSC). A more-common arrangement is the *free trade area*, in which members abolish formal impediments to trade in all products or a specified group of products within the area whereas each member retains an independent policy with regard to countries outside the area. Free-trade area agreements also contain provisions relating to the country of origin of products. These provisions restrict free trade to goods which are produced within the member states thus preventing "outside" producers from evading tariff barriers by bringing their products through the member state with the lowest external tariff. The free-trade area can be regarded as the basic form of negative integration. Examples of free trade areas include the European Free Trade Area (EFTA) and, in its initial form, the Latin American Free Trade Area (LAFTA). A *customs union* is distinguished from a free trade area by the fact that members harmonize their tariff policies toward nonmembers. Unlike the free trade area, where external policy remains independent, the members of a customs union adopt a common tariff on imports from nonmembers. The trade arrangement within the EEC is of this form.

The establishment of a *common market* takes us beyond the realm of free movement of goods in that free movement of factors of production is established. Thus a common market may be regarded as a customs union within which the free movement of labor and capital is permitted. The common market is the most developed stage of negative integration in that its establishment is achieved by the removal of impediments, although in practice the promotion of, for example, factor mobility may require positive steps such as the creation of new institutions.

Integration agreements cannot proceed beyond the common market level without the adoption of a positive integration strategy. An *economic union* adds to the structure of a common market the unification of fiscal and monetary policies. In general, unification of fiscal policies means the harmonization of taxes and subsidies throughout the bloc. The object of this process is to promote efficient resource allocation through market forces by eliminating discriminatory policies. Monetary integration requires fixed exchange rates and free convertibility of currencies between the members of the union as well as free movement of capital within the union. Because convertibility of currency is essential for a customs union whereas capital movement is free in a common market, the distinctive element in *monetary union* is the maintenance of constant exchange rates. Given free convertibility and the absence of exchange controls, the maintenance of a constant exchange rate will require members of the union to harmonize their rates of monetary expansion. Consequently, entrance into a monetary union requires a nation to relinquish an independent monetary policy. The objective of monetary union is to improve resource allocation by permitting and encouraging the free movement of capital. It is also sometimes argued that the creation of a monetary union enables countries to offer one another mutual support when in balance-of-payments difficulties. At its highest level, economic union would involve the abolition of national currencies and the adoption of a common currency by all members. Beyond economic union lies complete *political integration* with the creation of a new unitary state. It may be argued that complete economic union with genuinely unified economic policies would require political union.

The levels of integration described above represent only a typology of arrangements. As El-Agraa (1980) points out, these levels "should not be confused as stages in a process leading to a complete political union. They can be ultimate objectives in their own right as is the case in EFTA, the Central American Common Market (CACM), the East African Common Market (EACM), etc. Moreover, none of the existing arrangements falls neatly into any of these types." The latter point is well illustrated in the case of the EEC, which is a full customs union, a well developed common market, a partly developed economic union, and weakly politically integrated. Among market economies, integration schemes will generally be characterized by partial negative and positive integration.

Among LDCs, the typology of integration schemes given above is partially appropriate in that the initial stages have corresponded to free-trade areas and customs unions. However, subsequent developments such as *complementarity agreements* and schemes for *joint enterprises* fit less well into the above categories. The level of formal integration among LDCs may thus be characterized to some extent within the above scheme but other critera—such as numbers of joint enterprises—will also be relevant. The typology is least appropriate in the case of communist countries. Given the role of state trade monopolies and the absence of a price mechanism in foreign trade, the stages corresponding to negative integration are irrelevant. The level of formal integration in socialist countries could be measured in terms of the extent to which national economic plans are integrated and the numbers of cooperative projects undertaken. The point is made by Dell (1963) that "the concept of a common market can be applied to these communist countries only in a special sense if at all. We may say, perhaps, that a common market would exist between two or more such countries if, for the purpose of their economic planning they treated their combined area as a single unit."

THE EUROPEAN COMMUNITY

THE INSTITUTIONS OF THE EUROPEAN COMMUNITY.   The European Community (EC) represents the most developed form of economic and political integration existing at this time, and it will be discussed in some detail.

The EC comprises three separate entities, each of which was created by its own treaty but which are now amalgamated. The first, the European Coal and Steel Community (ECSC), was set up by the Treaty of Paris in 1951, and is valid for 50 years; the second and third, the European Economic Community (EEC) and the Atomic Energy Community (Euratom) are of unlimited duration and were both established by treaties signed in Rome in 1957. These treaties subsequently have been amended and supplemented as the EC has evolved. The totality of these documents together with the legislative acts to which they give rise and the case law of the Court of Justice of the European Communities may be viewed as the constitution of the Community. Significantly, this constitution and the legislation take precedence over national decisions. In 1981, 10 countries in Western Europe comprised the EC: Belgium, Denmark, France, West Germany, Greece, The Netherlands, Ireland, Italy, Luxembourg, and the United Kingdom.

European Coal and Steel Community.   The ECSC provides for a single authority controlling development of the coal and steel industries. Originally it appeared attractive for it offered the economic advantages of a large unified market, which seemed essential to these industries, and the political advantage of integrating and controlling some of the essential materials for warfare. Most recently the authority has presided over the planned rundown of the European steelmaking capacity, a process that has been marked by bitter controversy between member states and the blatant flaunting of the authority's directives by some member countries.

The original six signatories to the Treaty of Paris were Belgium, France, The Netherlands, Italy, Luxembourg, and West Germany, the founding members of the EEC. These were expanded to include Britain, Ireland and Denmark, on their accession to the EEC in 1973, and Greece in 1981.

European Economic Community.   Article 3 of the Treaty of Rome, *European Economic Treaties*, 1977) details the principal objectives of the EEC, which involve elements of both positive and negative integration. The principal elements of negative integration were

1. "The elimination as between Member States of customs duties and of quantitative restrictions in regard to the import and export of goods as well as all other measures having equivalent effect." In turn this necessitated:
2. "The establishment of a common customs tariff and of a common commercial policy towards third countries."
3. A further 'negative' feature was "the abolition, as between Member States, of obstacles to freedom of movement for persons, services and capital"; the remaining objectives were essentially positive in nature, involving
4. "the establishment of a common policy in the sphere of agriculture;
5. the adoption of a common policy in the sphere of transport;
6. the establishment of a system ensuring that competition in the common market is not distorted;
7. the application of procedures by which the economic policies of Member States can be co-ordinated and disequilibria in their balance of payments can be remedied;
8. the approximation of the laws of Member States to the extent required for proper functioning of the common market;
9. the creation of a European Social Fund in order to improve the possibilities of employment for workers and to contribute to the raising of their standard of living;
10. the establishment of a European Investment Bank to facilitate the economic expansion of the Community by opening up fresh resources; and
11. the association of overseas countries and territories with a view to increasing trade and to promoting jointly economic and social development."

Many of these original aims have now been achieved, but subsequent issues have emerged that are not covered by the treaty. Thus as time passes and the treaty recedes into history, it becomes increasingly less useful as a guide to policy. In turn policy is increasingly determined and shaped by political processes reflecting both national and Community political structures. Hence it becomes increasingly important to understand the basic political and institutional structure of the Community in order to understand present policy. The key institutions of the EC are the Commission of the European Communities, the Council of Ministers, and the European Parliament. These institutions, however, do not coexist in harmony one with another, and the early life of the EC was marked by tensions between the Council and the Commission. In the future these may be superseded by still more significant rivalries between the Parliament and the Council.

The Commission is essentially the civil service of the EC which at the time of writing is headed by a single President of the Commission supported by 13 commissioners, each with responsibility for one or more major areas of Community policy. The commission staff itself is organised into general directorates each corresponding to the main areas of Community policy.

The general directorates and commissioners are responsible for both the administration of existing policies and the initiation of new proposals. The Treaty of Rome increasingly provides no clear guide on major policy issues, and this gives considerable power to the Commission. Indeed in the early and mid-1960s it pursued the cause of integration with considerable enthusiasm. More recently the Commission has become cautious in this respect, as first the council and later the parliament, to which it is ultimately accountable, have sought to constrain its initiatives in some of the more controversial areas. Nevertheless, since in addition to being both an administrator and an initiator of policy the Commission is also charged with representing the Community interest (i.e., mediating between the pursuit of national self interest by member states), it is quite unlike any other national or international bureaucracy.

The Council of Ministers consists of the representatives of member governments and therefore comprises the government ministers responsible for the issue under discussion. The presidency of the council is held by each member state in turn for a six-month period and the chairmanship of several Community committees alters accordingly. The council is served by its own secretariat and a Council of Permanent Representatives (Coreper), comprised of senior officials and specialists who prepare the meetings and handle business between council meetings. Ministers can attend only parttime to council business, and they handle the most sensitive and political of issues. Frequently they feel obliged to refer back to their respective domestic cabinets before reaching decisions, and as a result the time lag in reaching policy decisions at this level has become serious. Moreover, these lags will be magnified as the Community is enlarged still further. Proposals for reverting to majority voting in the council have been put forward as a means of overcoming these deficiencies. However, until a much deeper unanimity of interest and purpose emerges between member states, it is unlikely that there will be any significant developments on this issue.

Direct elections to the European Parliament took place for the first time in June 1979. This was a unique event in international affairs, for it represented the first truly international election. It was initially thought that the election would legitimize the parliament and strengthen its hand in dealing with the Council of Ministers and Commission. Indeed, this may be the eventual outcome but at the time of writing the authority of the parliament appears less than that of either the Commission or Council of Ministers and certainly less than the respective national parliaments. The initial 410 European Members of Parliament (EMPs) represent constituencies of markedly different sizes and were elected as a result of a very low turnout in some member states. Accordingly this has done much to undermine the authority of the first supranational parliament.

The major formal power of the parliament lies in its ability to dismiss the Commission but since it has no powers to appoint a successor this is essentially a fairly negative weapon. Indeed the parliament has few formal powers established in the Treaty of Rome, and those it does have it has wrested from the Council of Ministers. At the time of writing the most important of these was control over the discretionary element of the budget which it has used to express dissatisfaction at the arrangements for agricultural support in the EEC. In 1979 it did this by failing to agree on the budget for the Common Agricultural Policy. Again, however, this power is essentially negative for it can only modify components of the budget with the Council's approval and in the final analysis only reject the draft budget and demand a new one.

The powers of the parliament will expand only as they are won from the Council of Ministers and Commission, and to do this it must rely heavily on the moral authority invested in it by the direct elections. To the extent that the first of these was less than an unqualified success, the accretion of power to the parliament is likely to be a slow process.

Other Community institutions abound to support the work of the EC. The Court of Justice of the European Communities exists to ensure the observance of the growing body of Community rules by states, firms, and individuals. Community rules continue to operate alongside national rules, and the process of incorporating Community law into different legal systems is necessarily a slow one. States agreed in the Treaty of Rome to abide by the judgments of the court and in practice have been found to do so thereby strengthening its authority.

The Economic and Social Committee exists to represent the various categories of economic and social activities that exist in the Community. It serves in an advisory capacity and is composed of representatives of employers, trade unions, and members representing the general interest. It is usually consulted on major acts of policy and is entitled to initiate discussions on items it believes to be important.

The European Investment Bank has three main fields of operation: first, to aid regional development; second, to assist projects of common interest to members where other financial means are lacking; and finally, to assist with projects made necessary by the creation of a common market that similarly fail to attract normal financial support. Nonetheless the Bank is charged with operating under normal financial criteria, and its capital comes from members states and is raised in the normal manner from financial markets.

THE STRUCTURE OF THE ECONOMIES.   The EC is one of the world's largest markets; the population of 259 million in 1977 was larger than that of the United States (217 million) and the Soviet Union (about 250 million) and over twice that of Japan. Taking the population of the 10 together with those of the two countries expected to join the Community in the early 1980s, Portugal and Spain, the population was almost 315 million. However, this gap may narrow as the annual average rate of growth of population in the Community over the period 1964–1974 was 0.7 percent compared with 1.2 percent in Japan and 1 percent in the United States.

In 1977 the Gross Domestic Product (GDP) of the then nine Community members was below that of the United States ($1879 billion). Accordingly, per capita GDP was still considerably higher in the United States ($8667 compared with $6096 in the Community). Of course there were considerable variations within the EC ranging from Denmark, with the highest per capita GDP ($9020) to Ireland with the lowest (just $2813) (see Exhibit 1). On average the Community experienced a much higher growth rate than did the United States over the period 1965–1975, 3.6 and 0.9 percent per annum respectively, but once again there was considerable variation in the experience of individual member states. Over this period the Netherlands experienced the fastest growth rate with an average of 4.1 percent per annum while Luxembourg and the United Kingdom experienced the lowest, 1.3 and 2.3 percent respectively. Output per worker-hour grew more rapidly than GDP in all countries, reflecting the sharp fall in hours worked per employee throughout the EC. In Italy it grew at an annual average rate of 7.8 percent over the period—over three times that of the United States, although still far short of the 10.1 percent achieved by Japan. In general, output per worker-hour grew at around 5 percent over this period, although again it was lower in the United Kingdom where it was 2.3 percent.

The structure of output and employment differs significantly between the various EC countries. The proportion employed in agriculture is by far the smallest in the

EXHIBIT 1   THE EUROPEAN COMMUNITY: KEY STATISTICS

	Population (millions) 1977	GDP (billions US dollars) 1977	GDP (per capita US dollars) 1977	Growth Rate Annual GDP % 1965–1975	Growth Rate Output per Man-Hour % 1960–1973
Belgium	9.8	7.9	8,061	3.8	5.4
Denmark	5.1	4.6	9,020	2.7	5.0
France	53.1	38.1	7,175	4.0	5.5
West Germany	61.4	51.6	8,404	3.8	5.5
Ireland	3.2	0.9	2,813	4.0	—
Italy	56.4	19.6	3,475	4.0	7.8
Luxembourg	0.4	0.3	7,500	1.3	a
Netherlands	13.9	10.6	7,626	4.1	—
United Kingdom	55.9	24.4	4,365	2.3	3.4
EC total	259.2	158.0	6,096	3.6	—
Greece	9.0	2.6	2,889	5.3	—
Portugal	9.8	1.6	1,633	—	—
Spain	36.7	11.6	3,161	2.0	—
The 12 Total	314.7	173.8	5,523	3.5	—
United States	216.8	187.9	8,667	0.9	2.3
Japan	113.9	69.4	6,093	7.3	10.1

Source. Eurostat, Statistical Office of the European Communities.
[a]See figure for Belgium, which together with Luxembourg forms BLEU.

United Kingdom, in contrast, almost a quarter of all employment was to be found in this sector in Ireland. Upon the accession of Portugal and Spain, as well as Greece, the balance of the EC will change dramatically, for these countries are still heavily dependent on agriculture for employment. In contrast, the maturer economies of Belgium, the United Kingdom, Denmark, and the Netherlands have around 60 percent of total employment in the service sector, and in recent years this proportion has been growing. The share of industry in employment has been falling in all of the nine pre-1981 member states with the exception of Ireland. In this respect Ireland is similar to Greece, Portugal, and Spain, which may be similarly characterized as industrializing nations.

Government plays a significant role in the economies of the EC. Quite apart from the usual responsibilities for managing the economy, all the governments are also involved in the production and marketing of a whole range of goods and services that in many other countries are provided by the private sector. Thus the revenues they raise by selling the output, or taxing, borrowing, and printing money are much larger than elsewhere. As a result they have a powerful impact on the development of the economy. Exhibit 2 provides some indication of the size of government involvement by detailing their direct expenditures as a percentage of GDP in 1977. However, insofar as this omits the further role of government in transferring incomes

EXHIBIT 2   FOREIGN TRADE AND THE GOVERNMENT SECTOR 1977

	Foreign Trade Sector[a] (% of GDP)	Current Government Expenditure (% of GDP)
Belgium	47.4[b]	43.5
Denmark	25.4	42.8
France	17.6	40.4
West Germany	21.2	41.3
Ireland	52.1	43.3
Italy	23.7	42.5
Luxembourg	47.4[b]	44.4
Netherlands	42.0	52.3
United Kingdom	24.8	41.5
Greece	18.2	29.0
Portugal	21.4	31.1
Spain	12.1	23.4
Japan	10.9	22.3
United States	7.2	32.6

Source. El-Agraa, 1980.
[a](Exports + Imports)/2.
[b]Belgium and Luxembourg are counted together as BLEU.

between individuals through taxes and welfare payments, it clearly understates the magnitude of government involvement. Even without this, the proportions revealed are substantial being everywhere in excess of 40 percent and as high as 52.3 percent in the Netherlands. In this respect the nine are once again quite unlike either the new candidates for membership of the EC or the United States and Japan.

The economies of the EC are quite unlike those of the United States and Japan in another important respect for they are far more "open" than either of these. In the case of Ireland, foreign trade accounts for over half the GDP whereas in Belgium, Luxembourg, and the Netherlands, well over 40 percent of the GDP is directly involved in foreign trade.

Thus in general the EC economies are far more heavily dependent on the vagaries of world trade than are the economies of Japan and the United States, and they are also all subject to much greater direct involvement by government than either of these two economies. In these respects, therefore, the economies of the EC appear relatively homogeneous, but as other statistics have revealed, this is far from the truth. The growth rates of productivity, output per worker-hour, and in particular GDP, showed considerable variations between member states over recent years, and the structure of employment, and accordingly output, differ substantially among the preexisting nine. Moreover, with the accession of the new states this heterogeneity will be exaggerated and as such will place a considerable strain on the existing institutions of the EC.

DEVELOPMENT OF THE CUSTOMS UNION.   Article 13 of the Treaty of Rome called for the abolition during the transition period of all customs duties on members' imports from each other. This, together with the establishment of a Common External Tariff (CET), was to be accomplished in full by the end of 1969, but in fact both were completed ahead of schedule by July 1968. Adoption of the CET on industrial products had been achieved in three stages in 1961, 1963 and 1968 while adoption of the tariffs on agricultural products was similarly accomplished in 1962, 1966, and 1968. Intra-area tariffs on industrial products were reduced more gradually with a series of eight successive 10 percent reductions between 1959 and 1966 followed by a 5 percent reduction in 1967 and the final 15 percent in 1968. Following the accession of Denmark, Ireland, and the United Kingdom in 1973, intra-area tariffs in the enlarged community were reduced by 20 percent each year between 1973 and 1977, and the CET was adopted in four stages of first 40 percent and subsequently 20 percent between 1974 and 1977. Thus in the original six the customs union had been achieved by July 1968 and in the enlarged Community by January 1, 1977.

Although Article 3 of the Treaty calls for "the elimination as between member states of customs duties and of quantitative restrictions in regard to the import and export of goods as well as all other measures having equivalent effect," substantial nontariff barriers remain as major impediments to genuinely free trade between member states. Such barriers always have the most laudable of motives—to protect the consumer and to standardize and improve quality—but in extreme cases they completely deny imports any access to the markets in question. The Commission has attempted to *harmonize* legislation in member states to eliminate such practices, and an elaborate complaints procedure has been established to deal with firms' and customers' complaints about such protective measures.

Of major concern in this area is the continuing practice in most member states of awarding most public or semipublic supply and works contracts to national firms. Total public contracts in member states range from around 7 to 11 percent of GDP, and thus substantial sums are involved. The EC has issued a series of directives—an order issued by the Council that is binding in its objective but which allows states to achieve this in their own ways—forbidding such practices, but since a number of major sectors (transport, telecommunications, water and energy production and distribution) are still not covered by Community rules, the directives have a limited impact. Elimination of nontariff barriers has therefore proved a slow and laborious task which is still far from complete.

PROGRESS TOWARD ECONOMIC UNION.   Steps beyond the creation of a common market have involved the development of a competition policy and a regional policy, although perhaps the greatest progress has been achieved in developing a common market in agricultural produce.

Competition Policy.   Competition policy in the EEC is essentially pragmatic, attempting to balance the twin aims of the development of a single market and the promotion of efficiency through competition with full realization of any potential economies of scale. At times this policy may also conflict with regional policy which provides government aid to depressed industries and sectors. Thus while a substantial body of case law has been promulgated by both the Commission and the Court of Justice, this is considerably more flexible than the "fixed-rules" of U.S. antitrust policy.

EEC competition regulations apply only to those situations where trade between community members is affected, and thus actions having a purely domestic effect in a member state or having an effect outside the EEC are excluded. On the other hand, companies incorporated outside the EEC and taking actions outside the EEC that have effects within it are included. Thus in the case of multinationals incorporated outside the Community but with subsidiaries operating inside the Community, the Commission and Court of Justice have ruled that in the case of "restrictive practices" parent companies are responsible for the actions of their legal independent subsidiaries. Also in the case of "dominant market positions," the world position of the parent company is to be taken into account.

In contrast to U.S. antitrust legislation, Community and national policies differentiate between "good" and "bad" cartels. Thus if benefits accrue from *restrictive practices*, these are not contrary to the Treaty and it has been the view of the Commission that a wide range of patent licensing arrangements and agency agreements do not merit prohibition. In a number of cases, ownership of a patent has been suggested to promote economic progress by allowing mass production at low cost whereas exclusive territorial rights have been permitted where the product concerned required a highly technical and relatively expensive support network. The Commission has in fact gone so far as to suggest that not only did it recognize that cooperation between large firms could be economically advantageous, but that it had a duty to facilitate cooperation among small and medium sized companies. In contrast to this otherwise fairly permissive approach by the Commission and Court of Justice, they have in general taken a very firm stand against price-fixing cartels, and in a number of cases fairly heavy fines have been levied.

The Treaty of Rome prohibits any actions which take improper advantage of a *dominant position*. Dominance can derive from a combination of several factors and applies to situations in addition to those where an undertaking dominates through sheer size alone. Thus where an undertaking has the power to behave to an appreciable extent independently of its competitors and customers, or where because of situations of shortage (e.g. the recent oil crisis) customers' dependence on the output of the undertaking is increased and this potential is exploited, action may be taken. On the other hand the Community is relatively powerless to prohibit mergers for reasons of dominance, for it is extremely unlikely that the act of merging will in itself lead to abuse of the dominant position. Only if subsequent to the merger the firm abuses its dominant position will action be taken, and this is of course irrelevant to the merger per se.

Substantial state aid to declining industries and regions was a feature in most EC countries during the 1970s. In particular members competed one with another through grants and tax concessions to attract foreign investors, and in most cases the Commission was powerless to act. Aid that distorts trade between member states is prohibited but aid to underdeveloped or declining regions and hence industries is essential if the basic aims for which the Community was established are to be realized. Thus the Commission requires prior notification of all new or modified aid to industries and regions and approves only that which "does not change trading conditions to such a degree as would be contrary to the common interest." In practice this has proved difficult to implement.

Regional Policy. In a number of important respects, joining a customs union places each country in the position of a single region rather than a full independent sovereign state. Upon joining, the power to impose tariffs and quotas disappears, and as monetary integration proceeds, the power to vary exchange rates is removed. Thus if the larger market results in increased specialization and the exploitation of economies of scale, there may be a tendency for the decline of certain areas to accelerate. Indeed, this may be exaggerated if there are any centripetal tendencies. It could be, therefore, that the creation of the EEC will tend to increase the disparities between the main regions in the Community, although to the extent that the creation of such a body results in higher growth rates it may increase the resources that can be concentrated on these areas to offset these developments.

Evidence presented by Nevin (1980) for the peripheral regions of the original six over the period 1958 to 1972 suggested that income differentials have in general narrowed. In the peripheral regions of France, per capita incomes rose from 83.5 percent of the national average in 1958 to 84.5 percent in 1972, in Germany they rose from 89.5 percent to 93.3 percent, in Italy from 73 percent to 76.8 percent over the same period. Nonetheless, there were declines in the relative incomes of some of the regions over part of the period, and the narrowing of the gaps has been relatively slow. Most important, these figures ignore the substantial differences that exist between the average levels of income in *different* countries, and thus whereas in the "poorest" region of Germany, Schleswig-Holstein, average income was 106 percent of the EEC average, in southern Italy it was only 45 percent in 1972. Certainly progress toward economic integration would not appear to have aggravated the "regional problem" but neither has it disposed of it.

The Treaty of Rome made provision for "aid intended to promote the economic development of regions where the standard of living is abnormally low or where there exists serious underemployment" (Article 92, Section 3(a), Treaty setting up the European Economic Community, Rome, 25 March 1957, HMSO). However although recognizing the problem, the treaty laid down no specific guidelines. Accordingly, for the first 20 years of the life of the Community there was no effective regional policy, and the matter was left in the hands of individual governments. Indeed, regional policy was in some sense against the spirit of the EEC, for it involved support for particular regions and industries, whereas the ethos of the Community was the commitment to competition and the belief that prima facie all state aid to industry was an interference with this. Nonetheless, throughout the first 20 years a broad consensus emerged that agreed both that there was a need for a regional policy and that the regions requiring assistance could be identified by the following characteristics: first, by a relatively low level of income; second, by an above average level of unemployment; and finally, by an excessive tendency toward population migration.

Matters came to a head in the mid-1970s. The recession of this period bore unevenly on the different member states and regions and tended to exaggerate regional differences. Moreover, one of the new members, Britain, had always pursued an active regional policy and insisted that the EEC do the same. Most important, the proposals for monetary union, if realized, would have further exaggerated regional disparities, and for this reason firm proposals for a regional policy were adopted by the Council in 1975. The European Regional Development Fund (ERDF) was established to provide up to 50 percent of the cost of projects submitted by member governments. However, the resources devoted to this fund were small, less than 5 percent of the total community budget in 1978, and funds were initially allocated to each country on a quota basis. Thus the allocation of funds bore little resemblance to the demand for such finance, and recent proposals to modify these have yet to have any substantial impact. EEC regional policy serves as little more than a supplement to the various regional policies of the member states and in large part appears to have been used by governments as a way of recovering part of the cost of projects that would have been undertaken in any event.

The Common Agricultural Policy.   The single most important and controversial of all the Community's policies is the CAP. The policy aims among other things to create a common market in agricultural produce and to ensure stability of supply of agricultural products together with a guarantee of a "fair standard of living" to those engaged in agriculture. Farmers' incomes are supported by a series of protective measures which ensure that produce is sold on domestic markets at prices which are effectively isolated from cheaper and potentially competing world imports.

Each year a *target price* is established for most major agricultural products. The price is established with regard to several criteria, one of which is the regional market in the EEC in which the product in question is in shortest supply. A *threshold price* for imports of this product into the EEC is then calculated by deducting from the target price the transport costs that would be incurred in transporting the product from the port of entry to a wholesaler for the relevant regional market. To the extent that the threshold price thus calculated is found to be above the world price for this product, a *variable import levy* is imposed to ensure that imports cannot be sold more cheaply than the domestic product.

Import levies would clearly be unnecessary if the world price were above the target price (under these circumstances an export tax would be imposed to prevent the export of community produce), but in practice this has all too rarely been the case. Moreover, the target prices and their associated intervention prices are so high that they frequently result in large surpluses, and support buying of these becomes necessary. For the purposes of support buying, a third basic price—the *intervention price*—is established slightly below the target price, and national intervention agencies then buy at this price all produce of appropriate quality which is offered to them. The resulting stockpiles of surplus products have variously been described as "butter mountains" and "olive oil lakes." Furthermore, since the world price is usually below the EEC intervention price, exporters are also subsidized by the difference between these two prices, in order that they may sell abroad.

These institutional agricultural prices are now established in terms of the basic unit of account employed by the EEC, the European Currency Unit (see the section on monetary union below for a detailed exposition), and thus when a member state devalues (revalues) or its currency depreciates (appreciates) relative to that of its partners, its farm prices expressed in terms of the national currency should rise (fall). In the early 1970s the currencies of the member states began to diverge as the world moved to a system of floating exchange rates, but member countries were not always willing to change their farm prices in the manner implied by the movement of their national currencies. In particular, countries which devalued were reluctant, for domestic political reasons, to increase domestic farm prices, and by failing to do so they had effectively destroyed one of the basic aims of the CAP—the establishment of a uniform set of agricultural prices for all member states.

In fact, the country which had failed to increase its farm prices in line with the devaluation of its currency could now export agricultural produce to other members of the Community at lower prices. To prevent this development and to ensure that other member states could continue to export at no disadvantage *monetary compensation amounts* (MCAs) were introduced. These were a series of border taxes and subsidies which taxed the exports of the country which had devalued but failed to raise its domestic farm prices and subsidized the exports of other member states to this country. Effectively this amounted to operating a system of multiple exchange rates with one set of rates for agricultural produce—which came to be known as *green rates*—and one for all other products. Recently countries have sought to eliminate MCAs by bringing their green rates into line with the rates of their currencies as given on the foreign exchange markets.

Of course the introduction of MCAs, which are financed from the EEC budget, effectively increased the cost of the CAP over and above that already required for support buying. Moreover, since in many products there are substantial surpluses, the magnitude of support buying is considerable. In 1979 it was estimated that the total cost of the CAP, which is financed through the European Agricultural Guidance and Guarantee Fund (FEOGA), amounted to $14.6 billion, which in turn accounted for 70 percent of the total EEC budget.

It is interesting to note that in recent years the main beneficiaries of payments from FEOGA have been the Northern European countries and in particular, Germany. In part this is due to increased efficiency of German agriculture, which has boosted German output, but by far the largest part is due to the coverage of the CAP and the existence of MCAs. Of total FEOGA expenditures 35 percent go on dairy products alone, of which Germany is a substantial producer, while in general the CAP is biased toward the type of products produced in northern Europe. Thus as Yoa-Su Hu (1979) detailed, in April 1978 Germany accounted for 73 percent of the Community's butter stocks and 67 percent of the total skimmed milk powder stocks. MCAs have added to the problems for in the early and mid 1970s Germany refused to revalue the "green Deutsche Mark"; that is, to cut farm prices when expressed in her domestic currency. Thus the "artificially" high domestic prices for agricultural produce further encouraged output of the German agricultural sector.

To the extent, therefore, that MCAs are being phased out, this will remove some of these distortions, but in general Germany has proved reluctant to do just this. At the time of writing it is therefore widely predicted that the EEC is heading for a crisis over the issue of the CAP. It is forecast that by 1981/82 the expenditures from FEOGA will have exhausted the whole of the EEC budget and that as a result a new system of agricultural support will have to be devised. The accession of Greece, and later Spain and Portugal, in the early 1980s could further exacerbate these problems, for the high CAP prices will encourage further production of certain Mediterranean products, which will merely add to surpluses. Thus it is unlikely that the CAP will continue in its present form for many more years, yet the form of its successor is difficult to predict.

MONETARY UNION AND FISCAL HARMONIZATION. Further progress toward economic union has recently been taken with steps toward monetary union and fiscal harmonization.

Monetary Union.   While the Treaty of Rome offers no specific proposals on *monetary integration*, it is clear that this is an essential step on the road toward economic union. Moreover, since this is a stage which will in general follow the creation of a customs union, interest in the issue did not occur on a wide scale until the 1970s. Early proposals contained in the *Werner Report* (1970) envisaged the establishment of a *European Monetary Union* (EMU) by stages. This would begin with the elimination of fluctuations between the exchange rates of member states and proceed through the creation of a single currency and the coordination and complete harmonization of monetary policies. At that time it was envisaged that complete monetary integration would have been achieved by 1980, but in fact with the monetary upheavals and oil crises of the mid-1970s, this timetable had to be abandoned.

Perhaps the only substantial achievement of the early 1970s was the *European Currency Snake*. This arrangement fixed the margins within which the cross-rates between any two currencies could diverge to within ±2.25 percent. Thus the maximum by which the currencies of any two member states could diverge one from another, if one moved to the top of the range and the other to the bottom, would be by a full 4.5 percent. Central banks in practice intervened to ensure that currencies did not move outside these upper and lower limits using the U.S. dollar but this had the unfortunate side effect of further destabilizing the dollar. The arrangement was instituted in early 1972 and included the existing six EEC countries plus two of the intending members, Britain and Denmark, together with the Scandinavian countries, and, effectively, Austria. In fact Britain, France, and Italy found it extremely difficult to maintain these parities, and all dropped out at a fairly early stage, so that by early 1978 the snake members numbered only West Germany, Denmark, Norway, and the Benelux countries. Nonetheless the snake formed an essential element of the next stage of monetary integration.

Following initiatives by the Commission which found support from France and Germany, the Council of Ministers adopted a resolution proposing the establishment of a *European Monetary System* (EMS) in December 1978, the essential elements of which were as follows:

1. The revitalization of the snake to include France, Italy, and Ireland with a wider margin of fluctuation permitted for Italy (6 percent). Thus the new arrangements have become known as the *boa* to reflect the slightly wider margin that will be tolerated.

2. The creation of a *European Currency Unit* (ECU), which is intended eventually to become an international reserve asset and hence used to settle debts between member countries. The ECU is the old *European Unit of Account* which was used for accounting purposes only. It is a "basket" currency made up of portions of each national currency, the size of each portion being determined by the relative importance of each economy, (at the time of writing the size of each country's GDP in 1974).

3. The creation of a *European Monetary Fund* (EMF), which is responsible for short-term financing arrangements to ensure that currencies remain within the permitted margins of fluctuation. To equip the EMF for this purpose, countries have transferred 20 percent of their gold and dollar holdings to the EMF in exchange for an equivalent issue of ECUs. In addition the EMF will be responsible for providing medium-term loan facilities for balance of payments assistance. The next stage, the complete transfer of foreign exchange reserves to the EMF, was originally planned for 1981, but at the time of writing this has been deferred.

At the end of 1980 the then nine members of the EEC with the exception of Britain were members of the EMS, although Britain had cooperated in the creation of the

EMF by accomplishing the necessary transfer of reserves, and sterling was a component of the ECU.

The existence of both the boa and the ECU involves two permitted margins of fluctuation between any two currencies. The boa limits fluctuations between member countries' currencies and also effectively limits fluctuation between their currencies and the ECU. However, because each currency is part of the ECU, when a currency moves it pulls the ECU in the same direction and by so doing reduces the change in its ECU rate (although it should be noted that because each currency has a different weight in the ECU these margins are much larger for some states than others). Thus if the Deutsche Mark moves, it pulls the ECU by one third of that amount in the same direction, for it makes up one third of the weight of the ECU. To allow for this, each currency has a permitted margin of fluctuation around the ECU and these will be narrower for the Deutsche Mark than say for the Irish punt. Effectively, the ECU provides a set of much tighter margins than those which are given by the limits on bilateral currency movements contained within the boa, and these have been viewed as "divergence indicators," which reveal which individual currency is causing the trouble and hence where action should be taken.

The EEC has clearly embarked on only the first stage of monetary integration. There is no single central bank and no single currency, although the ECU may eventually fulfill this latter role. More immediately, to the extent that the ECU becomes established as a means of payment in international transactions, this will relieve the pressure on the dollar and reduce the currency instabilities that were so much a feature of the 1970s.

Fiscal Harmonization.   As the early theoretical discussion revealed, a monetary union is unlikely to be accepted without an adequate regional policy, and it is also unlikely to be attained without the harmonization of fiscal policies between member states. The Treaty of Rome specifically calls for the harmonization of indirect taxes since, with the removal of tariffs, these would remain as the main source of intra-EEC trade distortion. Some progress has been made along these lines with the adoption by all member states of the value added tax (VAT) as the appropriate form of turnover tax but considerable differences still exist in its operation. In 1977 the standard rate of VAT varied from 20 percent in Ireland to 8 percent in the United Kingdom and the increased rate from 12.5 percent in the United Kingdom to 35–40 percent in Italy. Moreover, the range of commodities subject to the different tax rates and indeed those exempt from VAT altogether varied between member states.

Even more substantial differences emerge with other forms of taxation. Thus in 1977 the rate of corporation tax varied from 37 percent in Denmark to 56 percent in West Germany, and countries used different methods of calculating the tax and permitted different exemptions. Social security contributions and income and wealth taxes also varied substantially between member states with social security contributions accounting for almost 42 percent of total revenues raised from taxation in France in 1977 compared with only 1.2 percent in Denmark in that same year. Corresponding to this was the fact that Denmark raised 57 percent of its tax revenues from taxes on income and wealth whereas France raised only 21.3 percent from this source in 1977. Moreover, the total tax burden was substantially lower in France than in most other EEC countries. Thus while some moves toward harmonizing the types of taxes in operation in the EEC have been made, their incidence and coverage still diverge substantially and fiscal harmonization has as yet hardly begun.

EXTERNAL RELATIONS.   The commercial policy of the EEC is based on

> uniformly established principles particularly in regard to tariff amendments, to the con-
> clusion of tariffs and trade agreements, to the establishment of uniform practice as
> regards measures of liberalisation, to export policy and to commercial protective mea-
> sures including measures to be taken in cases of dumping or subsidies.

TREATY OF ROME, EUROPEAN ECONOMIC TREATIES, ARTICLE 113

Accordingly, the EEC negotiated as a single unit in the Kennedy and Tokyo rounds
of negotiations under GATT.

Quite apart from this general posture, the EEC has also agreed to the signing of
special *association treaties* with those non-European countries and territories that
once had special relations with the nine. Such association granted preferential access
to one another's markets and provided EEC aid toward capital investment in these
countries. These agreements have been signed with a large number of countries in
the Mediterranean region, the Middle East, the Maghreb and Africa although the
Lomé Conventions of 1975 and 1979 make further provision for developing countries.
The Lomé Conventions provide for duty-free access, on a nonreciprocal basis, for
exports from in excess of 50 African, Caribbean, and Pacific countries (*A.C.P. countries*) of manufactured goods and tropical agricultural products. Provision is also
made for a revenue stabilization scheme (*STABEX*) which guarantees these states
a specific level of income on certain exports to the EEC. The Convention also
provides for wide ranging development assistance and replaces the preexisting
Yaounde Conventions and Arusha Agreement, which were negotiated with a smaller
number of African states. Aside from this the *Generalised System of Preferences*
(GSP) provides for duty-free access for the manufctured exports of over 90 LDCs.
Finally, *most-favored-nation* treatment has been accorded to a number of countries
that do not fall within the above schemes.

MEASURING THE PROGRESS OF ECONOMIC INTEGRATION.   During the first stage
of the creation of the EEC, the abolition of tariffs and quantitative restrictions on
intra-area trade was accompanied by a rapid growth of trade between the six. Between
1959 and 1971 intra-area trade increased nearly sixfold compared with a fourfold
increase in the total imports and exports of these countries. As a result the share of
intra-EEC trade rose from one-third to one-half of total trade over this period. But
to what extent does the increase in intra-EEC trade represent trade creation as
opposed to trade diversion?

Balassa (1974) suggested that under the assumption that the historical relationship
of imports to GNP would have remained unchanged, a rise in the ratio of total imports
to GNP represents trade creation whereas a decrease in the ratio of extra-area imports
to GNP represents trade diversion. Applying this methodology to the 1959–1970
period, he showed that the volume of imports into EEC countries rose at an annual
average rate of 11.3 percent compared with 9.6 percent over the period 1953–1959,
essentially a pre-EEC period. Over these same periods national income growth rates
rose only slightly, from 5.4 percent to 5.5 percent per annum, with the result that
by 1970 total imports exceeded the imports that would have been projected on the
basis of the relationships in the earlier period by $11.3 billion. The volume of extra-
area imports also rose at a rate of 8.9 percent per annum over the period 1959–1970

but only slightly exceeded the rate of 8.3 percent in the earlier period. Balassa concluded that these results show the preponderance of trade creation over trade diversion as a result of the establishment of the EEC.

There is, however, evidence of a trend in import consumption relationships within the EEC, and the methodology of Balassa is therefore open to objection. Neglect of the trend overstates trade creation and understates trade diversion, and attempts have therefore been made to adjust these calculations to take account of this. Even so, it remains extremely difficult to adjust for the several other developments in the international economy which could affect the growth of trade during the periods under study. The relaxation of restrictions on convertibility and the easing of exchange controls over the period 1953–1960 will have done much to increase the volume of trade over this period while more recently the general reductions in tariffs under GATT will have had similar effect. Similarly, it is impossible to estimate the effects of the rival trade bloc EFTA which was set up specifically to counteract the possible damaging effects of the EEC, and few studies take adequate account of the changes in membership of these two organizations.

A useful survey of these various methodologies is contained in a recent study by Mayes (1978). Measuring the simple effects, he concluded that the trade creation effects of the enlargement of the EEC and of free-trade arrangements between EFTA and the EEC dominate the trade diversion resulting from these developments. Thus despite the methodological difficulties associated with these estimates, there appears to be broad agreement that trade creation dominates trade diversion. Nonetheless, these simple static effects are of relatively trivial magnitude, and it is therefore as a result of the dynamic effects that the chief benefits of integration arise.

THE EUROPEAN FREE TRADE AREA

Established in 1960, EFTA was conceived to counteract the possibly damaging effects of the EEC and was never more than a simple free-trade area. At its peak, before the defection of the United Kingdom and Denmark to the EEC, full membership of EFTA numbered seven countries in Western Europe, each of whom had considered, but rejected, membership of the EEC. Denmark had strong trading ties with the United Kingdom and therefore, as with membership of the EEC, followed her lead. Sweden, Switzerland, and Austria rejected the supranational emphasis of the EEC and, with Sweden and Denmark opting out, Norway followed suit and Finland gained associate membership. Portugal was the final member and had joined EFTA because at that time she proved politically unacceptable to the EEC.

The Stockholm Convention of 1959, which had proposed the establishment of EFTA, limited the application of free trade to industrial products. Since there was no common external tariff, as there would have been in a customs union, special provisions had to be made for ascertaining and assigning the origin of goods traded in EFTA. Were such provisions not made, exporters from outside would obviously send their goods to the member countries with the lowest tariffs for transfer to high tariff areas.

Tariffs on trade in manufactured goods between member countries were completely abolished in a number of stages between 1960 and 1966. A year later, tariffs had also been abolished between Finland and other EFTA countries. More recently, following the entry of the United Kingdom and Denmark into the EEC in 1973, the tariffs on trade in manufactured goods between the nine countries of the EEC and the seven countries of EFTA (Iceland, which had joined EFTA in 1970, and Finland make up the numbers) were abolished completely in July 1977. The maximum differences in tariffs between the two trading blocs in Western Europe occurred in 1967–1968. At that time the CET of the EEC was approximately 11.5 percent on manufactures while the most-favored-nation tariffs the EEC enjoyed with EFTA ranged from 18 percent in the case of Austria to 4.5 percent for Norway and Switzerland. The abolition of the tariffs between the EEC and EFTA in 1977 means that Western Europe is now the world's largest free-trade area in industrial products.

During the early years of the creation of EFTA and the EEC intra-area trade rose fastest in EFTA despite the more disadvantageous geographical dispersion of EFTA members around the periphery of the EEC. Taking the period 1953–1958 to represent the pre-EEC and pre-EFTA periods and 1958–1965 to represent the immediate postcreation period, the increase in the growth in the imports and exports of EFTA outstripped that of the EEC. Over the period 1958–1965, the rate of increase of imports from other member countries of EFTA more than doubled to a compound rate of 11.3 percent per annum from 5.5 percent per annum in the earlier period. The rate of increase of EEC imports from other member countries also rose following the formation of the EEC but in this case it was less dramatic involving an increase from an annual compound rate of 12.2 percent to 17 percent.

Similarly, EFTA exports to EFTA countries more than doubled, increasing from 5.4 percent per annum to 11.5 percent while EEC exports to other EEC members rose from an annual rate of 12.3 percent to 17.1 percent. Thus the creation of trading blocs in Europe appears to have provided a stimulus to intra-area trade as the earlier studies suggested, and on this evidence EFTA appears to have been the more successful of the two—though EFTA started from a lower growth rate.

ECONOMIC INTEGRATION IN COMMUNIST COUNTRIES

THE STRUCTURE OF THE COUNCIL FOR MUTUAL ECONOMIC ASSISTANCE.
Membership of the Council for Mutual Economic Assistance (CMEA) also known as COMECON, consists of the Soviet Union, Bulgaria, Cuba, Czechoslovakia, the German Democratic Republic (GDR), Hungary, Mongolia, Poland, Rumania, and Vietnam. It thus involves all of the world's communist countries with the exceptions of China, Albania, Yugoslavaia, and Cambodia, although the development of economic integration has been confined to the European members of COMECON and the Soviet Union. The role of the non-European members of COMECON has essentially been that of aid recipients.

COMECON was established in 1949, in response to disagreements between the Soviet Union and the Western powers over the Marshall Plan for economic recovery and the formation by 16 Western countries of the Organisation for European Economic Co-operation (later to be the Organisation for Economic Co-operation and Development—OECD). COMECON was formed to promote economic cooperation and to encourage technical exchange and mutual assistance among socialist states. A conference of the member states, known as the Session of the Council, was established and a small permanent secretariat set up in Moscow.

COMECON existed at a very low level of activity until 1956, when 12 standing commissions, each concerned with a major industrial sector, were set up. These commissions were purely mechanisms for discussion and the exchange of information. The first multilateral COMECON treaty was established in 1957 with an agreement to clear intrabloc foreign trade balances through the Soviet State Bank, although in practice this scheme failed.

The COMECON charter was adopted in Sofia in 1960, and a "statement of principles" was issued in 1962. These documents emphasized the benefits of cooperation and coordination and called for the creation of an international socialist division of labor with the objective of gaining economies of scale and of specialization. However, the charter also stated that COMECON decisions must be unanimous, at least among the parties affected by a decision and thus the organization was to involve no supranational powers such as those enjoyed by the EEC. In consequence, from an early stage there arose a conflict between the desire to coordinate and rationalize the economic plans of members and the claims of national sovereignty.

The period to 1964 saw the creation of independent agencies dealing with coordination in particular industries, but the most significant development was a further attempt to promote multilateral trade through the creation of a mechanism for clearance of balance-of-payments accounts. A bank, the International Bank for Economic Co-operation (IBEC), was set up; through it all intra-COMECON trade was to be financed. Balances of trade were recorded in a new currency, transferable rubles, which were transferable in the sense that a surplus in trade with one country could be used to offset a deficit with another.

Soviet economists have claimed (Bogomolov, 1978) that the transferable ruble has become a "collective currency" but this instrument is no more than a limited unit of account. Quite simply, the transferable ruble failed because it could not be readily converted into goods, for each country's foreign trade was largely determined within its economic plan. A country with a surplus of transferable rubles was therefore unlikely to find any goods available for unplanned purchase. The problem has been described as *commodity inconvertibility* and as a result of the failure of the transferable ruble, a certain amount of intra-COMECON trade has been settled using convertible Western or "hard" currencies.

Following the Bucharest meeting of COMECON in 1971, a "Comprehensive Program for the Extension and Improvement of Collaboration and the Development of Socialist Integration" was adopted. The comprehensive program covered an extremely wide range of economic activity and contained a great variety of bilateral and multilateral planning and investment agreements. The plan also projected intra-COMECON trade to grow faster than total trade. The intention of making the transferable ruble convertible within the bloc was also stated—though this would do nothing to solve the problem of commodity inconvertibility explained above. New committees were established to promote cooperation in scientific research and in planning. This latter committee was to promote bilateral and multilateral agreements at the stage when national economic plans were drawn up. In the financial sector, the most substantive proposals were an extension of the activities of IBEC and the creation of an International Investment Bank (IIB). Of the IIB's capital, 30 percent was in convertible or hard currency and it could raise funds outside the bloc. The IIB was established to finance investment projects of common interest, but the major impediment to the Bank's operations has been the problem of commodity inconvertibility. The creation of a fund did nothing to ensure that resources would be available for purchase, since the transfer of commodities between nations required appropriate decisions in national plans.

Despite the rather negative initial reasons for COMECON formation, there have been repeated attempts since the mid 1950s to make the institution a more effective integrating force. However, these attempts have repeatedly been faced with the inherent conflict between integration and national sovereignty as seen by socialist states. There has been a pronounced reluctance on the part of several states, most notably Rumania, to yield authority to any supranational planning body, and there have been parallel disagreements over the principles upon which coordinated investment and specialization should proceed. Consequently, COMECON contains no genuinely supranational commissions or organizations, and virtually all decisions still require unanimity—at least among affected parties.

In the absence of integration by market forces, the progress of economic integration is determined by governmental decisions. Thus the difficulties of obtaining unanimity in COMECON are a major constraint on socialist integration. In the place of supranational authorities, attempts have been made to bind the COMECON economies together by a web of bilateral and (to a lesser extent) multilateral agreements on specific projects and sectors. Indeed, COMECON's most important function has probably been to facilitate such agreements.

The absence of market forces and the problem of commodity inconvertibility exert a strong influence on COMECON developments. Surpluses of transferable rubles cannot be spent freely on imports from other bloc members (far less on imports from the West), and thus countries aim to balance trade with each partner on a bilateral basis. Occasionally, more complex triangular deals are set up, but these solutions reduce intra-COMECON trade to the level of barter and must be regarded as a source of inefficiency. Further, the role of IBEC and the activities of the IIB are constrained by the problem of ensuring that plans will make available goods to match flows of finance.

Despite frequently repeated statements of intent, the COMECON nations have as yet failed to establish a "socialist pricing system" for intrabloc trade. Until 1976, COMECON trade prices were based on the average of world prices in the previous five-year period. Since 1976, prices have been altered annually to allow for inflation in world markets.

THE IMPACT OF THE COUNCIL FOR MUTUAL ECONOMIC ASSISTANCE. The formation of COMECON has had a mild impact on trade between member countries but as yet few of the other features of economic integration are in evidence.

Trade.   Prior to World War II, trade among the countries which were later to form COMECON was negligible. The Soviet Union, in line with the Stalinist model of "socialism in one country" engaged in very limited and highly controlled trade whereas the other European COMECON nations traded on a large scale with Germany and only to a limited extent with each other. In the years immediately after the war, the establishment of communist governments in Eastern European countries and the development of the Cold War led to a reorientation of Eastern European trade toward the Soviet Union. It may be argued that for these nations the Soviet Union filled the vacuum left by Germany.

Evidence of growth in trade following the formation of COMECON is given in Exhibit 3. Particularly in comparison with the prewar position, these figures indicate a very considerable redirection of trade. Ellman (1979) has argued that "a major aspect of CMEA integration is the co-ordination of the trade plans of the member

EXHIBIT 3   GROWTH OF COMECON TRADE

Year	Intra-COMECON Exports as a Percentage of All COMECON Exports
1948	44
1950	60
1955	60
1960	61
1965	62
1970	62
1974	56

Source.   Ellman, 1970.

states. This has facilitated a substantial increase in trade." However, the role of COMECON in this process is open to question, for as Exhibit 3 indicates, the major reorientation of trade took place prior to 1955—that is, during the period when COMECON was least active. Indeed, Holzman (1976) concluded that "the increase could not be attributed to any special form of collaboration or integration as a result of CMEA. Rather it simply represented the natural increase in trade to be expected as the various Soviet bloc nations recovered from the war." Thus although COMECON may have facilitated intrabloc trade, it cannot be regarded as the basic cause of the reorientation of socialist bloc trade.

The absence of both market forces and a supranational planning authority suggests that COMECON institutions can have only a very limited impact on trade flows while the inconvertibility of COMECON currencies, basically the commodity inconvertibility problem, represents a substantial barrier to intrabloc trade. Corresponding to "hard" and "soft" (i.e., COMECON) currencies are hard and soft goods. Since hard currencies may be freely spent on world markets, COMECON states will have a preference for exporting goods to Western countries. Consequently only those goods unacceptable to Western markets (i.e., soft goods) will be freely available within the bloc. For additional details see Section 15, State Trading.

Rationalization of Production.   Although in market economies it is expected that changes in the structure of production will follow the development of trade, this has been a specific objective of COMECON since the mid 1950s. Rationalization to obtain economies of scale and avoid wasteful duplication can be accomplished through joint investment programs, joint research programs, and specialization agreements. All such agreements require the coordination of national economic plans.

A number of large-scale investment projects have been carried through, notably an electricity grid, which enables generating capacity to be shared, and an oil pipeline. Industrial plants and mining complexes have also been established as collaborative ventures. In these cases the contributing nations receive a share of the output as their return on their investment. Joint investment also takes the form of common enterprises—often on a bilateral basis.

While some steps have been made toward specialization (see Bogomolov, 1980), the process has not been without difficulties. In general, there was strong resistance from Bulgaria and Rumania (the relatively less developed states) to any specialization plans which would limit their own industrialization programs. It is difficult to assess the scope of specialization and joint investments, due to the absence of comprehensive figures, though it has been claimed (Bogomolov, 1980) that 1700 engineering products are covered by multilateral agreements. However, Ellman (1979) has observed that "CMEA integration is notable for its lack of component specialisation" and that "specialisation appears to be largely confined to . . . the range of final products."

Proposals for the exchange of scientific knowledge and technology transfer were the subject of the initial COMECON agreement and it was stated that scientific documents would be exchanged without charge while exchanges of personnel would be encouraged. COMECON officials argue that this has been an important aspect of the organization and Kaser (1967) stated "The interchange of expertise has unquestionably been one of COMECON's most successful objectives." However, there are difficulties in judging the validity of this argument, for statistics detailing the number of exchanges say nothing about the quality of those exchanges. Further, Holzman (1976) quotes COMECON sources admitting that COMECON technical cooperation lags behind that in the West and the continued interest of COMECON nations in importing Western technology suggests that intra-COMECON flows have not proved as fruitful as hoped. Nevertheless, joint R&D programs exist and are being developed in a number of industries.

Labor Flows. In market economies, integration is generally conceived as involving not only trade and specialization but also the movement of factors of production. Movements of capital and knowledge in COMECON depend principally upon the investment projects and exchanges discussed above, whereas flows of labor within COMECON are extremely small. The immobility of labor is a consequence of three features of communist society. First, the absence of free movement of persons over all frontiers rules out the possibility of individuals moving spontaneously in response to any market signals which might be instituted. Second, there are certain ideological objections to labor mobility as a "capitalist" phenomenon, which discourage plans for exchanges of workers. Finally, there are difficulties in determining payment to the "home" nation. Socialist countries generally demand compensation for the loss of even supernumerary workers. Disagreements over payment inhibit mobility.

External Relations. COMECON countries compare their own absence of tariff barriers favorably with the protectionism of the EEC, United States, and Japan. Bogomolov (1980) argues that COMECON is "not fenced off from third countries by discriminatory barriers." However, since foreign producers have no free access to communist countries' markets, and since trade is quantitatively controlled by state agencies, tariffs are of no relevance whatsoever. It is through quantitative restrictions that communist countries "protect" home producers from foreign competition. This dichotomy of systems has created trading difficulties for COMECON countries in negotiating favorable tariff treatment from market economies. Essentially, reciprocal tariff cuts by communist countries are worthless, since such tariffs are redundant. These difficulties have mainly been resolved though not on a COMECON-wide basis. Certain countries have joined GATT, though the Soviet Union has preferred bilateral arrangements.

EXHIBIT 4   NATIONAL INCOME PER CAPITA IN COMECON COUNTRIES[a]

Country	1950	1970
Bulgaria	0.6	0.8
Hungary	1.2	0.9
German Democratic Republic	1.3	1.3
Poland	1.1	0.8
Rumania	0.5	0.8
Soviet Union	1.0	1.0
Czechoslovakia	1.6	1.2

Source.   Holzman, 1976.
[a]Soviet Union = 1.

Convergence.   Equalization of levels of development is a basic aim of the COMECON agreement. Severe difficulties arise in measuring levels of development in communist countries, although Exhibit 4 provides some indication of the extent to which equalization has occurred. From this it emerges that the least developed communist economies have experienced the greatest growth over the period 1950–1970, although it is not evident that this is the outcome of COMECON integration policy. Indeed, Holzman (1976) argues that "equalization has taken place, however, not primarily as a result of CMEA integration . . . but primarily because growth of GNP among capitalist and socialist nations alike appears to be related to rates of investment, levels of development and other such factors." Clearly COMECON cannot be regarded as a successful vehicle for the realization of socialist economic integration. However, it has made a transition over its history from a minor forum for the discussion and encouragement of small bilateral trades to a body coordinating joint investment, specialization, and cooperation on a wide basis. Future development of COMECON will require a successful resolution of the conflict between national sovereignty and supranational rationalization and the creation of more effective trade mechanisms.

INTEGRATION AMONG LESS DEVELOPED COUNTRIES

GENERAL SITUATION.   Although the trade blocs of Europe are the most economically significant regional groupings, the majority of integration schemes (both realized and potential) are to be found among less developed countries (LDCs). In fact, within LDCs, integration schemes have been almost entirely confined to Latin America and Africa; within Asia such schemes have, as yet, come to very little. The number of schemes which are, or have been, in operation should not be regarded as an indicator of the success of LDC integration. Salgado (1979) describes the current position concisely when he pointed out that, with two exceptions, "all the other integration groupings in the developing world today are in a state of stagnation and conflict . . . or have deviated from their objectives and can no longer be regarded as integration programmes."

Characteristically, the integration schemes of LDCs have begun as negative integration. The economic theory of customs unions suggests that the gains from such negative integration will be greatest when the countries forming the trade bloc carry out a large amount of trade with one another prior to formation of the bloc. In fact, the vast majority of LDCs forming trade blocs typically undertook most of their trade with third countries (usually those of the industrial world). However, it may be argued that the preexisting trade pattern is irrelevant to integration among LDCs, since for these countries economic integration is part of a development strategy which aims to create a new structure of production. On this argument, the greatest gains may result from schemes of positive integration: those involving joint projects and the promotion of development. Positive policies of coordinated planning have, however, been inhibited by differences of political and economic systems, problems of sovereignty, and differences in levels of economic development between partner countries.

LATIN AMERICA.   Integration schemes for South and Central America were actively encouraged by the United Nations Economic Commission for Latin America, generally known by its Spanish acronym, CEPAL. Three main groupings exist within this area. The largest and oldest grouping was LAFTA, formed in 1960 and comprising Mexico and all the countries of mainland South America with the exception of the Guianas. In August 1980, LAFTA was wound up and the same group of countries signed a treaty to establish the Latin American Integration Association (LAIA). This new organization has similar aims to LAFTA but is said to aim at greater flexibility. A subgrouping, known as the Andean group, comprising Bolivia, Peru, Columbia, Ecuador, and Venezuela, was established within LAFTA and continues to function. Within the LAIA steps have been taken to set up a subgrouping, the Amazon Pact, comprising Brazil, Venezuela, Colombia, Ecuador, Peru, and Bolivia. The Central American Common Market (CACM), also dating from 1960, consists of Costa Rica, El Salvador, Guatemala, Honduras, and Nicaragua. Finally, the Caribbean Free Trade Area (CARIFTA) was formed in 1968 and in 1973 became the Caribbean Community (CARICOM) composed of Antigua, Barbados, Belize, Dominica, Grenada, Guyana, Jamaica, Monserrat, St. Kitts-Nevis-Anguilla, St. Lucia, St. Vincent, and Trinidad and Tobago. A subgrouping known as the East Caribbean Common Market exists within CARICOM.

Latin American Free Trade Area and Latin American Integration Association.   LAFTA was created by the Montevideo Treaty of 1960, which established an executive committee and a secretariat. As its name would suggest, LAFTA's main objective was the elimination of barriers to trade between member countries. A phased program of tariff reductions aimed to arrive at the creation of free-trade zone by 1973. Escape clauses were included in the agreement to allow for balance of payments disequilibria and threats to "vital" sectors of national economies. The agreement also included a pledge to move toward a common external trade policy and coordination of industrial development by sectors. Although the first few years of LAFTA's life saw a large number of tariff reductions, these were not evenly spread among partner countries, and progress was slower than that envisaged in the original agreement. By 1969 the establishment of the free trade zone had been postponed till 1980 and the agreed rate of tariff reduction slowed. Subsequently, these revised targets were not achieved.

So far as positive integration policies are concerned, LAFTA's achievement was very small. The Inter-American Development Bank provided funds for projects in border areas, and a few complementarity agreements promoting integration of certain industries were signed. Nevertheless, by the early 1970s progress had come to a halt and in 1979 Salgado (1979) stated, LAFTA "has continued to function in a languid fashion still applying the system of concessions which had been arrived at when it came to a halt." Dissatisfaction with the virtually moribund state of LAFTA led, in 1980, to the establishment of LAFTA's successor the LAIA. As with LAFTA, the objective of the LAIA is to establish a common market within Latin America, but it is as yet too early to assess the chances of success. Certainly, the LAIA's first task will be to preserve and restore vigour to the agreements reached under LAFTA rather than to promote new agreements.

The Andean group was formed in 1969 partly in response to the slow progress of LAFTA and partly as a response to the perceived power, within the larger group, of Brazil, Argentina, and Mexico. As well as a phased program of tariff reduction and the eventual adoption of a common external tariff, the group adopted from the outset positive integration policies of sectoral industrial cooperation and policy harmonization. Bolivia and Ecuador, the least developed group members, received special treatment under the agreement. This last provision is an important one, as it is widely believed in Latin America that, as Beautell (1976) says, "There is a natural tendency for the least-developed countries to become the losers in integration processes."

The withdrawal of Chile halted the progress of the group between 1975 and 1977 and despite giving explicit attention to the distribution of benefits from integration, the pact has not been able to avoid serious disputes over the different needs and objectives of partners. As Vargas-Hidalgo (1979) documented, this has led to non-compliance in decisions by members, but despite this the group continues to function, if under stress.

The Amazon Pact was first proposed by Brazil in 1977 but held its inaugural meeting in October 1980. Its objectives include coordinated regional development programs—especially in relation to the use of the Amazon River—the settlement of territorial disputes, and joint programs in research, transport, and health. It is possible that trade agreements may also emerge.

Central American Common Market. The Managua Treaty of 1960, which established the CACM, was the outcome of 10 years of work toward integration. Under this treaty, free intraregional trade was granted to a wide range of products at once and restrictions on all but a few (though very important) products were removed within a few years. Within a year, a secretariat (SIECA), a clearinghouse, and the Central American Bank for Economic Integration (CABEI) had been set up. The plans involved positive as well as negative integration, and since 1958 a scheme had existed to develop *integration industries*. Such industries would have a semimonopoly status within the group and would form the basis of new industrialization, which would be spread "fairly" throughout the common market.

Good progress was made throughout the 1960s with the elimination of restrictions on trade amounting to about 80 percent of intrabloc commerce and the establishment of uniform external tariffs on many goods. Indeed according to Cohen and Rosenthal (1977), "The Central American Programme has done better, in a very short space of time, than any other sub-regional integration movement in the developing world." Progress in industrialization had, however, been less than originally hoped—being limited to marginal improvements in the existing structure—while rather extreme differences emerged at the end of the decade with military conflict between El Salvador and Honduras. According to Grunwald *et al.* (1972) several important problems emerged to set against the successes in trade liberalization. These problems included "the 'unequal' participation of the least developed countries, Honduras and Nicaragua; the stagnation of regional, industrial policy; the high level of protection against the rest of the world; the absence of co-ordination in the agricultural sectors." Failure to resolve these problems, particularly those of "equality in development," contributed to the stagnation of the CACM in the 1970s. Indeed ground was lost as countries turned toward import substitution policies.

Caribbean Community. CARICOM, a rather small and peripheral grouping, was formed in 1973 from CARIFTA. The original CARIFTA agreement essentially envisaged a slow process of trade liberalization on selected products, although one positive measure—the creation of the Caribbean Development Bank in 1969—was taken. The transition from CARIFTA to CARICOM involved a broadening of the scope of cooperation to include coordination of development policies, planning, and trade relations with third countries. CARICOM absorbed some preexisting organizations, notably in the area of common services, but the most unusual feature of the CARICOM agreement lay in its proposals to coordinate the foreign policies of most member states. The subgrouping, the East Caribbean Common Market, contains the less developed members of CARICOM.

CARICOM has suffered from tensions caused by ideological differences among partners and by the relative dominance of Trinidad and Tobago. Despite some achievements, by the latter part of 1979 the future of the group was in doubt, largely because of disappointment with the pace of industrial development promoted by integration. Moreover, this disappointment was heightened by the variations in both the levels of development and development potential of partner countries.

Progress Toward Integration. As the previous section suggests, the 1960s were a period of relative progress in Latin American integration, whereas in the 1970s the processes were generally stagnated. Perhaps the most tangible effects have been in progress toward trade liberalization, and Exhibit 5 indicates that the formation of trading blocs was in general followed by a reorientation of commerce toward intrabloc trade. CACM's intrabloc trade growth has been by far the most spectacular, though the figure of 25.6 percent is low by Western European standards. Willmore (1976) indicates that the CACM has led to the replacement of imports of nondurable consumer goods by "local" production (trade diversion) while leading to increased

EXHIBIT 5   INTRABLOC TRADE IN LATIN AMERICA

Group	Intrabloc Trade (% of all bloc trade)			
	1960	1970	1972	1974
LAFTA	7.7	10.2	10.7	9.7
Andean group	1.5	2.7	3.6	3.4
CACM	7.5	26.9	22.5	25.6
CARICOM	4.8	8.1	10.2	7.1

Source. Robson, 1980.

imports of intermediate goods from outside the bloc (trade creation). For the other Latin American groupings, relative growth of intrabloc trade has been much more modest and has, in the 1970s, displayed a tendency toward relative decline. Trade ratios are far from being perfect indicators of integration, but they do cast sufficient light for the conclusion to be reached that, with the modest exception of the CACM, trade integration in Latin America has achieved very limited results.

In LDCs, however, trade does not represent the major aim of integration. Rather, the intention is to promote industrial development on a regional basis; but progress in this area has been disappointing. As Beautell (1976) pointed out, "Free trade spreads day by day without the need for any sort of additional regulation whatever, whereas the development of programmed industries is bogged down in interminable negotiations." Industrial cooperation has been inhibited by problems both of negotiation and implementation. Governments have been unwilling to accept decisions that would harm their own industries. Even where agreements could be reached, market forces have not always led to even development. In LAFTA, the larger countries were, according to Salgado (1979), "the only countries capable of taking advantage of the complementarity agreements, which constituted the system set up for negotiating integration industry." Similarly in the CACM, Cohen and Rosenthal (1977) stated, "Investments encouraged by the expanded market were channelled towards the areas or countries which had the biggest market and the best developed physical and human infrastructure." The tendency for development to be uneven and the apparent inability of "corrective" mechanisms to offset this trend has contributed to the "crisis" of Latin American integration. The Andean group, from the outset, gave explicit attention to "positive" policies but even here, as Cohen and Rosenthal (1979) observed, "Joint programming has in fact been applied only to a few projects or sub-branches of industry." The failure of positive integration creates serious problems for Latin America; Robson (1980) argues that in the absence of effective cooperation there will be "an intense and unprofitable competition for foreign capital and technology, producing a proliferation of competing plants each operating at excess capacity."

AFRICA. Eight integration groupings have been in operation in Africa during the 1970s. Exhibit 6 provides a summary account of the structure of these groups along with their dates of origin. The Arab Council of Economic Unity has been included under Africa, although not all of its members are African. Although numerous, not all of the groupings are of major significance, and several are moribund. The West African Economic Community (CEAO) has generally failed to put into effect the mechanisms of integration for which it was established. However, with the exception of Mauritania and Mali, the CEAO states are part of a monetary union which shares a central bank and is assisted by France. The Central African Customs and Economic Union (UDEAC) although still in existence has had a limited scope and its agreements have not always been complied with. The Southern African Customs Union is dominated by South Africa and exists simply to facilitate trade. Economic cooperation rather than integration is the purpose of the Arab Economic Unity Council while its projected offspring, the Arab Common Market, has not materialized. The two integration groupings of greatest significance in Africa are the now-defunct East African Community (EAC) and the developing Economic Community of West African States (ECOWAS).

EXHIBIT 6   INTEGRATION GROUPINGS IN AFRICA

Group	Members	Origin
Arab Economic Unity Council (CAEU)	United Arab Emirates, Iraq, Jordan, Kuwait, Morocco, Mauritania, Egypt, Libya, Syria, Yemen (Arab Republic), Yemen Democratic Republic, Sudan, Somalia	1964
Central African Customs Union (UDEAC)	Congo, Gabon, Central African Republic, Cameroon	1966
East African Community (EAC)	Kenya, Tanzania, Uganda	1967
Economic Community of West African States (ECOWAS)	Upper Volta, Benin, Ivory Coast, Gambia, Ghana, Guinea, Guinea-Bissau, Liberia, Mali, Mauritania, Niger, Nigeria, Senegal, Sierra Leone, Togo	1975
Communaute de l'Afrique de l'Ouest (CEAO)	Ivory Coast, Mali, Mauritania, Niger, Senegal, Upper Volta	1974
Southern African Customs Union	South Africa, Botswana, Lesotho, Swaziland	1969
Economic Community of the Countries of the Great Lakes (CEPGL)	Zaire, Rwanda, Burundi	1976
Mano River Union (MRU)	Liberia, Sierra Leone	1973

East African Community.   Until its demise in 1978, the EAC was the most developed and most effective of African integration groupings. Although the Community was established by treaty in 1967, the history of East African integration goes back at least to the formation of the Kenya-Uganda customs union in 1917 and Tanganyika (later Tanzania) joined this union in 1949.

As British colonies the three partners were highly integrated and shared common services including railways, ports, postal services, currency, courts, airways, customs, and excise. Following independence an *East African Common Services Organization* (EASCO) was set up to administer the majority of the shared services. However disagreements arose within the arrangements, particularly in that the two other countries resented the economic dominance of Kenya. The Kampala Agreement of 1964 introduced trade barriers within the bloc and created a policy of planned industrial location. Shortly afterward it was announced that the countries would issue their own currencies. Concern over incipient disintegration led to the establishment of the Philip Commission, the report of which led to the 1967 treaty. This treaty called for the elimination of trade quotas though restrictions were allowed on certain products. A *transfer tax* was introduced which was effectively a tariff which a country could impose on imports from a partner with which it had a trade deficit. The East African Development Bank (EADB) was established with the requirement that it was to favor Tanzania and Uganda in its investment policy and the headquarters of the shared services were reallocated to new locations on a more "even" basis. Since the treaty introduced some new restrictions, it is possible to see it, in Hazelwood's words (Hazelwood, 1979), "Not as a stride forward in co-operation but as a stage in a process of disintegration."

For the first few years after the 1967 treaty, the arrangements worked fairly well. However, following the rise to power in Uganda of Idi Amin, the Community's highest body—the Authority—ceased to meet. Other tensions arose and contributed to disintegration. These included resentment based on the belief that Kenya benefited disproportionately from the common services; the state control of foreign trade by Tanzania, which was regarded as creating trade barriers; the failure to establish any regional planning agency; and balance-of-payments difficulties. In Hazelwood's view (Hazelwood, 1979), the combination of these forces and a lack of political will to support the group led to its collapse in 1977. The group broke up with considerable acrimony.

Economic Community of West African States.   The treaty establishing ECOWAS was signed in 1975, and although its secretariat was set up in 1977, the group is still in the early stages of formation. ECOWAS includes countries joined in the CEAO and the Mano River Union (MRU). The main objectives of the group are elimination of intrabloc trade barriers, adoption of a common external tariff and commercial policy, free movement of factors of production, establishment of a cooperation fund, and harmonization of agricultural, industrial, and monetary policies. The major economies of ECOWAS participate in the West African Clearing House. According to Osagie (1979), this agency aims to restore monetary sovereignty to those countries whose monetary arrangements are closely linked to France, to promote a degree of currency convertibility, and thus to encourage liberalized trade and monetary co-operation. Although it is too early to judge ECOWAS's prospects, it is at present the only African integration movement making identifiable progress.

Effects of African Integration.   The data of Exhibit 7 clearly indicate that integration schemes in Africa cannot be regarded as having led to a striking growth in intrabloc trade. Indeed there are pronounced contrary trends in evidence in the 1970s—particularly in the CEAO. The history of the EAC reveals the familiar problem of differential development with the relative concentration of benefits in the most developed and most dynamic economy. Although it is far too early to judge the success of ECOWAS, integration movements elsewhere in Africa have failed to overcome problems of heterogeneity in partners. There has been an unwillingness to live with the consequences of market forces and an inability to agree on viable planning mechanisms for modification of market forces.

EXHIBIT 7   INTRABLOC TRADE IN AFRICA

| | Intrabloc Trade (% of all bloc trade) | | | |
Group	1960	1970	1972	1974
EAC	14.1	16.9	13.7	13.9
UDEAC	1.7	7.5	8.9	7.4
CEAO	2.4	9.1	8.4	4.3

Source.   Robson, 1980.

Finally, we must note that Africa is involved in an intercontinental integration system in that most African countries south of the Sahara are linked with the EEC through the Lomé Conventions of 1975 and 1979. The agreement covers trade, financial aid, and technical assistance. According to Olofin (1978), this link with the EEC may pull against or even dominate intra-African integration.

ASIA.   No fully developed trade blocs or common markets exist in Asia, although some minor sectoral cooperation was undertaken by Iran, Pakistan, and Turkey through the organization Regional Co-operation for Development (RCD). A more significant grouping is the Association of Southeast Asian Nations (ASEAN), comprising Indonesia, Malaysia, the Philippines, Singapore, and Thailand. The group, established in 1967, consists of four primary exporters and one manufacturing entrepôt center (Singapore). For the first nine years of its existence, ASEAN was stagnant, but in 1976 a treaty was signed in Bali setting out ASEAN's objectives as mutual assistance, industrial cooperation, preferential trading agreements, and cooperation in trade dealings with third parties. A secretariat was set up in Jakarta, but trade liberalization has so far been slow and on a product-by-product basis. As Exhibit 8 shows, intra-ASEAN trade is small, though it is too early yet to judge what effect trade liberalization will exert. Joint industrial projects are at a very early stage, though a urea plant planned by Indonesia has been " adopted" by ASEAN. As Arndt and Garnvat (1979) stated, industrial projects tend to be viable on the basis of the domestic market or on the basis of exports to worldwide markets with only a few projects of such a size as to benefit from preferential access to an ASEAN-wide market.

ECONOMIC VERSUS POLITICAL INTEGRATION

The relationship between political and economic integration is complex. In theory, at least, each could proceed in the absence of the other, though it is difficult to conceive of political integration that does not lead to, or involve, economic integration. On the other hand, economic integration can proceed, at least to some extent, without political integration. The forces of competition left unfettered in the world economy would concentrate production along lines of comparative advantage and

EXHIBIT 8   INTRAGROUP TRADE IN ASEAN

Year	Intra-ASEAN Trade (% of All ASEAN Trade)
1960	21.7
1970	14.8
1972	14.5
1974	11.3
1977[a]	16.2

Source.   Robson, 1980; Business Asia, 1978.
[a]Figures for 1977 include reexports from Singapore. These are excluded from the earlier figures.

lead to increasing specialization and trade flows between nations. In the absence of barriers to trade erected by political decisions, factor flows would ensure that the earnings of the inputs to the production process would tend to equality at the margin. Of course this would not mean that pecuniary incomes would tend to equality throughout the world, for there are many nonpecuniary elements within the notion of factor earnings. Nor would factor earnings tend to equality on a per capita basis, for difference in the productivity of individuals would undoubtedly remain. Nevertheless, the forces of competition left unhindered by political decisions would in themselves promote greater economic integration.

However, the process of commercial integration described above may be encouraged by political initiatives. The creation of a free-trade area or trade bloc can, by removing trade barriers, liberate market forces. Thus to the extent that an absence of political integration is expressed in policies of autarchy or isolationism, this absence can impede economic integration. Even so, considerable economic integration is possible between states which undertake no more than the negative integration steps involved in removing trade barriers.

In contrast to simple reliance on market forces, positive integration requires the creation of common institutions and policies. Such positive initiatives may be viewed as taking one of two forms. They may take the form of intergovernmental initiatives promoting collaboration on specific projects to foster economic integration by rationalizing production along desired lines. Such initiatives have been described as *intergovernmentalism* by Nau (1974). Clearly these initiatives are likely to be restricted to those industries in which the government has a direct stake and can therefore realize its ambitions immediately—collaboration on aerospace projects in Europe is an example of this. On the other hand, positive initiatives may take the form of establishing common, but general, institutions which create the climate within which private enterprises are encouraged to rationalize production along the desired lines. Such are the initiatives to remove impediments to factor mobility and to introduce monetary union or fiscal harmonization. These have been described by Nau as *supranationalism*, for they effectively reduce the sovereignty of each participating state. Indeed, the extent to which the sovereignty of each state should be challenged by establishing common political institutions has been a central point of conflict in trade blocs in all parts of the world and under all economic systems. In general, the pursuit of economic growth and efficiency has been a major imperative of supranationalist policies—though it must be noted that the European Community owed much of its early development to considerations of politics and defense. The intergovernmentalist approach has at times been directed toward economic ends, but its reliance on political will rather than economic forces has, notably in the case of Concorde, led to outcomes which can scarcely be regarded as economically rational.

Advocates of supranationalism have also argued that the creation of supranational institutions would reduce the ability of national governments to follow economically damaging macroeconomic policies. Thus the establishment of a common currency overnight has been advocated by those who believe that the gradual steps toward monetary union in the EEC permit too much discretion to national governments, who continue to delude themselves that they can choose between different levels of inflation and unemployment. While different currencies remain, governments continue to intervene in foreign exchange markets and continue to pursue different monetary policies. More seriously, by deluding themselves that by manipulating these monetary variables they can affect real variables, output and unemployment, they fail to concentrate their attentions where they are urgently needed in improving the underlying productivity of the economy. A common currency would take discretion out of the hands of governments and subject them to the authority of a single, nonpolitical, central bank.

It is questionable whether the harmonization of economic policy described in the previous paragraph could long continue in the absence of fundamental political integration. So long as national governments remain the highest level of genuine political power, there will be a tendency for countries to withdraw from cooperation in times of perceived disharmony of interests. The creation of the directly elected European parliament may be seen as a short step along the road to high-level political integration. A substantial increase in its powers would represent a political parallel to, and concomitant of, a major economic initiative such as the creation of a common currency.

Contradictions between the claims of national sovereignty and the economic benefits of integration have been nowhere more in evidence than among the members of the communist trade bloc COMECON. Fears of domination by the Soviet Union have led to the insistence that all important decisions must be taken by a unanimous vote of all members. For similar reasons there has been a marked reluctance to establish genuinely supranational bodies. Thus the process of integration has effectively become ossified in communist countries, for it is only through political integration that they can move forward. In the absence of market forces, the normal process of commercial integration will not occur and integration will only take place as a result of political decisions either of an intergovernmental or supranational type. Supranationalism has clearly been ruled out, and therefore the little integration that has occurred has resulted from intergovernmental collaboration on specific projects. Further progress would seem to depend on either the moves to supranationalism, a most unlikely course, or, ironically, as greater play is given to the rule of market forces, integration through normal commercial pressures.

The very limited success achieved by integration schemes among LDCs has been largely confined to those effects consequent upon the operation of market forces. When schemes, notably those in Latin America, have sought to move beyond influencing the pattern of trade toward more positive policies, tensions and disparity of interests have become evident. The purpose of integration in these areas has been to promote industrial development, but this has required agreement on the nature and location of projects. Perhaps the most successful example of integration within the LDCs was the EAC, but this was precisely because considerations of sovereignty were of no importance when the original structure was established. Decisions about the creation of supranational bodies and the nature and the location of integrated projects were all taken by a supreme supranational authority, the British, for the Community was a product of the Empire. Once these nations gained independence, issues of sovereignty became paramount and resulted in the steady disintegration of the Community.

The EC represents the supreme attempt at both political and economic integration and at least at its inception combined appreciation of the economic benefits from this process with a strong political will toward creating a supranational body. Perhaps this latter can be only clearly understood by realizing the context within which the idea of the EEC was conceived: postwar Europe, and the overriding desire to ensure that continental Europe was never again plunged into war. However, as these memories have faded among the founder members, let alone the new members, such overriding concerns have become less and less significant. The result has been that at a fairly early stage in the life of the EC issues of national sovereignty once again assumed paramount importance. Thus the Council of Ministers was and remains the supreme decision making authority, and these ministers are in turn then responsible to their national parliaments. Voting in the Council of Ministers is still essentially unanimous, and proposals for majority voting have been deferred. The powers of the European Parliament, a truly supranational body, are limited and appear unlikely to be increased substantially in the near future. The Council of Ministers will become a truly supranational body only when the practice of majority voting is adopted, and this would appear to be the next step on the road to integration within the EC.

The major recent political and economic initiatives within the EC, direct elections and moves toward monetary union, respectively, serve to highlight the interrelatedness of the processes of political and economic integration. Thus the European Parliament is unlikely to have its powers extended much further into areas such as health or education without any additional source of revenue (at present the budget's own funds arise from a share of VAT, import duties, and agricultural levies), for its expenditures on agriculture and the small regional and social funds exhaust this already. Further powers to tax and raise revenues are unlikely to be granted to any significant degree, for these will begin to impinge on the ability of governments to use fiscal policy as a method of controlling the economy. Equally, the progress toward monetary union and, more importantly in this context, fiscal integration are opposed, for again these reduce the discretion of national governments. (It is, of course, precisely those who believe that in reality fiscal and monetary manipulations have little real impact who are most eager to see such powers handed over to some supranational political body.) Thus the distinction between economic and political integration is in many ways false. Only at the earlier stage of negative integration are political considerations relatively minor. At each later stage, political and economic considerations are involved and although it has been argued that there are distinct political and economic paths to integration, in reality this is not so. Moves toward economic union involve considerations of national sovereignty which are unlikely to be overlooked, whereas creation of supranational political bodies requires considerations of the revenue-raising and expenditure functions of these bodies. Not surprisingly, therefore, once we move toward positive integration, the simple distinction breaks down.

THE FUTURE OF REGIONAL ECONOMIC BLOCS

The process of economic integration represents a direct challenge to the idea of national sovereignty. During the 1970s nations became increasingly reluctant to surrender their sovereignty in all but the most trivial areas, and thus the process of integration was slowed. At the start of the decade, considerable progress had been made toward integration in several areas of the world, but the last half of the period witnessed something of a retreat from this. The world recession was largely to blame, for it gave rise to a growth in protectionist sentiment, and at the start of the 1980s these sentiments have not weakened. Indeed, if anything, they have strengthened, as unemployment in the industrialized West continues to grow. It is widely accepted that the problems of slower growth and higher unemployment will be a feature of much of the 1980s and as a result it is difficult to believe that protectionist sentiments will abate. Further progress on the road toward economic integration is therefore difficult to envisage—indeed the decade may well see a weakening of the associations that already exist.

Among Western industrialized nations the process of negative integration is now largely complete. Thus the Kennedy and Tokyo Rounds of tariff reductions under the auspices of GATT and the further reductions in tariffs between EFTA and the EEC have largely eliminated the necessity to negotiate regional free trade areas among industrialized nations. However, there is no reason why integration should stop at this level and in one area at least, the EEC, there is the declared intention of proceeding much further. The EEC is already in the process of expanding its membership from 10 to 12 and it is currently embarked on the road to full economic union. Furthermore, it has already taken the first steps on the road to political union with the direct election of a supranational parliament. Thus it is tempting to conclude that in Western Europe, if nowhere else, integration will advance rapidly during the 1980s. However, there are reasons for believing that further progress will be much slower and more painful than is generally recognized.

Although at the time of writing Greece has just entered the EEC, the timetable for the accession of Spain and Portugal is being deferred. The new members will increase the diversity of living standards and rates of economic growth in the EEC, and much of their agricultural output of Mediterranean produce and some of their industrial output (e.g., steel and shipbuilding) will merely add to the surpluses that already exist in the Community. Initial attempts to rationalize production in those areas between the new and existing members have already provoked serious controversy.

In fact even among the existing members, the EEC has approached what may be regarded as the most difficult stage of integration. The EEC has successfully completed almost all those steps that we have described as negative integration, and it is now engaged in establishing those common institutions that are essential to political and economic union. Thus it is engaged in the process of establishing a central bank, moving toward fixed exchange rates, and effectively surrendering monetary control to a supranational body. The proposed fiscal harmonization involves surrendering control of the instruments of revenue raising that in the past have also been manipulated in attempts to manage the economy. Similarly, the creation of a regional fund, the strengthening of the social fund, the continuance of some form of agricultural support, together with any new responsibilities (for example, education, health, and transport) that may be given to a supranational body imply a reduction in the freedom of national governments to vary public expenditures.

These economic developments and the probable consequences of the creation of a fledgling European Parliament which is eager to gain new powers and express its independence from narrow chauvinist considerations mean that the EC is now at the stage at which the principle of national sovereignty is most clearly challenged. It is precisely because the behavior of the member states provides little indication that they are willing to surrender sovereignty on any but the most-trivial issues that further progress toward integration is likely to be extremely slow. Furthermore, to the extent that the Community becomes less and not more homogeneous during the 1980s, as growth rates continue to diverge and new members are eventually admitted, these problems will be exacerbated.

Among LDCs the imperative of national sovereignty has more often than not been stronger than the lure of gains from cooperation. Thus there are few reasons for optimism that trade blocs among the LDCs will develop to any significant degree over the next decade—the best prospects appear to lie with ECOWAS and the LAIA. The LDCs have failed to establish any consensus as to which projects should be the subject of collaboration and where to site common facilities. In most cases the size of the market, even after the creation of the trade bloc, is sufficient to support only one of each major type of industrial project, and inevitably, therefore, these decisions are surrounded by political controversy. In common with COMECON, integration in the LDCs is very much an outcome of a political process as market forces are effectively damped over a very wide range of economic activity. To place the question of integration firmly on the political stage does not help in newly independent African states where considerations of sovereignty are paramount nor in COMECON, where fears of domination by one member override other considerations. Moreover, when the static gains from integration are shown to be relatively trivial, with the major benefits arising from the dynamic effects, it is difficult for the economist to convince politicians of the desirability of integration policies. Thus as the process of integration proceeded in several areas of the world during the 1970s, it represented an increasing challenge to national sovereignty, which governments proved reluctant to relinquish.

Overriding these considerations, however, a new phenomenon emerged during the 1970s, the full impact of which for the process of integration is only now being realized. The advent of the energy crisis in the 1970s resulted in a slowdown in the rate of growth of all non-oil-producing nations. International competition intensified, and it became widely accepted that if countries were to sustain their previous rates of growth of output, they would only be able to do so at the expense of the slower growth of others. Thus the strategy of industrialization leading to rapid growth, which had been a principal motive for the creation of trade blocs in the LDCs, appeared much more difficult and indeed less feasible.

The less favorable trading climate of recent years has increased the disagreements between LDCs about the appropriate strategies to adopt and has led to a retreat into protectionism on the part of many. In the industrialized West, a similar increase in protectionist sentiment is evident and this is nowhere more apparent than in the least-successful industrial nations. It therefore seems possible that the 1980s could witness a retreat from the level of free trade realized during the 1970s. Of course it is always possible that this retreat will take place within the existing trading blocs, as, for example, the EEC as a whole erects tariff barriers against Japanese goods, but this implies a unanimity of interest within the EEC which in general does not exist. Far from exhibiting such unanimity, recent years have revealed the EEC to be torn by dissension and this suggests that those protectionist measures which are introduced will largely be introduced at the level of the nation state, thus further prejudicing the process of integration.

SOURCES AND SUGGESTED REFERENCES

Arndt, H.W., and H.R., Garnvat. "ASEAN and the Industrialisation of East Asia," *Journal of Common Market Studies*, Vol. XVII, No. 3 (1979), pp 191–212.

Balassa, B. "Trade Creation and Trade Diversion in the European Common Market: An Appraisal of the Evidence," *Manchester School*, Vol. XLII (1974), pp 93–135.

Beautell, L.B. "Notes on Integration," *CEPAL Review*, First Half (1976), pp 195–207.

Bogomolov, I. "Integration by Market Forces and through Planning," in F. Machlup, ed. *Economic Integration, Worldwide, Regional, Sectoral.* London: Macmillan, 1980.

Business Asia, September 8, 1978.

Cohen, I., and G. Rosenthal. "Reflections on the Conceptual Framework of Central American Integration," *CEPAL Review*, First Half (1977), pp 21–48.

Cooper, C.A., and B.F. Massell. "A New Look at Customs Union Theory," *Economic Journal*, Vol 75 (1965), pp 742–747.

Dell, S. *Trade Blocs and Common Markets.* London: Constable, 1963.

El-Agraa, A.M. *The Economics of the European Community.* Oxford: Philip Allan, 1980.

Elliott, R.F., and P.W. Wood. "Technology Transfer in European Economic Integration," in R. Hawkins and A.J. Prasad, eds. *Research in International Business and Finance*, Vol. 2. Greenwich, CT: JAI Press, 1981.

Ellman, M. *Socialist Planning.* Cambridge: Cambridge University Press, 1979.

European Economic Treaties, 3rd ed. London: Sweet and Maxwell, 1977.

Grunwald, J., M.S. Wionczek and M. Carnay. *"Latin American Economic Integration and US Policy.* Washington D.C.: *Brookings Institution,* 1972.

Hawkins, R., and A.J. Prasad. *Research in International Business and Finance*, Vol. 2, Greenwich, CT: JAI Press, 1981.

Hazelwood, A. "The End of the East African Community," *Journal of Common Market Studies*, Vol. XVIII, No. 1 (1979), pp 40–58.

Holzman, F.D. *International Trade under Communism.* New York: Basic Books, 1976.

Hu, Y.S. "German Agricultural Power: the Impact on France and Britain." *The World Today*, Vol. 35, (1979), pp 453–461.

Johnson, H.G. "Trade Diverting Customs Unions: a Comment," *Economic Journal*, Vol. 84 (1974), pp 618–621.

Kaser, M. COMECON 2nd ed. London: Oxford University Press, 1967.

Machlup, F. *Economic Integration, Worldwide, Regional, Sectoral.* London: Macmillan, 1978.

Mayes, D.G. "The Effects of Economic Integration on Trade," *Journal of Common Market Studies*, Vol. XVII, No. 1 (1978), pp 1–25.

Nau, H.R. *National Politics and International Technology: Nuclear Reactor Developments in Western Europe.* Baltimore: Johns Hopkins University Press, 1974.

Nevin, E. "Regional Policy," in A.M. El-Agraa. *The Economics of the European Community.* Oxford: Philip Allan, 1980

Olofin, S. "ECOWAS and the Lomé Convention," *Journal of Common Market Studies*, Vol. XVI, No. 1 (1977), pp 53–72.

Osagie, E. "West African Clearing House, West African Unit of Account and Pressures for Monetary Integration," *Journal of Common Market Studies*, Vol. XVII, No. 3 (1979), pp 227–235.

Robson, P. *The Economics of International Integration.* London: Allen and Unwin, 1980.

Salgado, G. "The Latin American Regional Market: The Project and the Reality," *CEPAL Review*, April (1979), pp 85–132.

Scitovsky, T. *Economic Theory and West European Integration.* London: Allen and Unwin, 1957.

Södersten, B. *International Economics.* London: Macmillan, 1971.

Tinbergen, J. *International Economic Integration* 2nd ed. Amsterdam: Elsevier, 1965.

Vargas-Hidalgo R. "The Crisis of the Andean Pact," *Journal of Common Market Studies*, Vol. XVII, No. 3 (1979), pp 213–226.

Viner, J. *The Customs Union Issue*. New York: Carnegie Endowment for International Peace, 1953.

Waelbroeck, J. "Measuring the Degree of Progress of Economic Integration," in F. Machlup, ed. *Economic Integration, Worldwide, Regional, Sectoral*. London: Macmillan, 1980.

Werner Report. "Report to the Council and Commission on the Realisation by Stages of Economic and Monetary Union in the Community," *Bulletin of European Community*, Vol. III, suppl. (1970).

Willmore, L.N. "Trade Creation, Trade Diversion and Effective Protection in the Central American Common Market", *Journal of Development Studies*, Vol. XII, No. 4 (1976), pp 396–414.

ADDITIONAL REFERENCES

Aamo, S.B. "The Achievements of EFTA: 20 Years of Trade Co-operation," *EFTA Bulletin*, Vol. XXI, No. 3 (1980), pp 9–14.

Chernick, S. *The Commonwealth Caribbean: The Integration Experience*. Baltimore: Johns Hopkins University Press, 1979.

Coffey, P. *Europe and Money*. London: Macmillan, 1977.

Commission of the European Communities. *Report of the Study Group on The Role of Public Finance in European Integration*, Vols. 1 and 11, Brussels: Office for Official Publications of the EC, 1977.

Coombes, D. *The Future of the European Parliament*, Studies in European Politics, No. 1, London: Policy Studies Institute, 1979.

Drew, J. *Doing Business in the European Community*. London: Butterworths, 1979.

EFTA Secretariat. "EFTA—Past and Future," *EFTA Bulletin*, Vol XXI, No. 4 (1980), pp 11–14.

El-Agraa, A.M. ed. *International Economic Integration*. London: Macmillan, 1981.

El-Agraa, A.M. and A.J. Jones, *The Theory of Customs Unions*. Oxford: Philip Allan, 1980.

Georgakopoulos, T.A. "Greece and the EEC," *Three Banks Review*, No. 128 (1980), pp 38–50.

Haas, E.B. *The Obsolescence of Regional Integration Theory*, Research Series No. 25, Institute of International Studies. Berkeley: University of California, 1975.

Hermen, V. and J. Lodge. *The European Parliament and the European Community*. London: Macmillan, 1978.

Kruse, D. *Monetary Integration in Western Europe: EMU, EMS and Beyond*. London: Butterworths, 1980.

Machlup, F. *A History of Thought on Economic Integration*. London: Macmillan, 1977.

Tsoukalis, L. *The Politics and Economics of European Monetary Integration*. London: Allen and Unwin, 1977.

UNCTAD. *Economic Co-operation and Integration among Developing Countries*, Vols. 1 & 11, Geneva: United Nations, 1976.

Wionczek, M.S. *Economic Co-operation in Latin America, Africa and Asia*. Cambridge: MIT Press, 1969.

SECTION **5**

THE INTERNATIONAL
ECONOMIC INSTITUTIONS

CONTENTS

**THE MULTILATERAL DEVELOPMENT
BANKS**   4

The International Bank for
Reconstruction and Development   5
   Early history   5
   Structure   5
   Loan policies and procedures   6
   Projects and sectors   7
   Aid coordination   7
   Finance   7
The International Development
Association   8
   Early history   8
   Structure   9
   Finance   9
   Loan policies and procedures   9
The International Finance Corporation   9
   Structure   9
   Lending and investing policies   9

**THE INTERNATIONAL MONETARY
FUND**   10

Early Features   11
Subsequent Changes   11
Special Drawing Rights   11
Floating   12
Structure   13
Loan Policies and Procedures   13
   Quotas   13
   Conditionality   14
Surveillance   16

**THE BANK FOR INTERNATIONAL
SETTLEMENTS**   16

**THE GENERAL AGREEMENT ON
TARIFFS AND TRADE**   17

GATT Principles and Rules   18
   Nondiscrimination   18
   Quantitative restrictions   20
   Fair-trading rules   21
   Dispute settlements   22
The GATT in Operation   22
Emerging Issues   24
   Nontariff barriers   24
   Industrial restructuring   25
   Exchange rates   26

**THE ORGANIZATION FOR
ECONOMIC COOPERATION AND
DEVELOPMENT**   26

Origins   26
Stated Purposes   27
Structure   27
Activities   27

**THE U.N. CONFERENCE ON TRADE
AND DEVELOPMENT**   28

**SOURCES AND SUGGESTED
REFERENCES**   29

THE INTERNATIONAL ECONOMIC INSTITUTIONS

Wilson E. Schmidt and Tracy Murray

The U.S. government belongs to 77 international organizations and seven international financial institutions, all of which have three or more member governments.

Only nine of these organizations are chiefly political or military in character. (See the Department of State's annual *United States Contributions to International Organizations* for a brief description of each.) The rest provide services, many of which are analogous to services provided by local, state, and federal governments, except that their provision is determined internationally. With few exceptions the problems and opportunities that justify government intervention on the national or local scene also exist at the international level and thereby justify international cooperation among governments. Thus the problem of garbage disposal is not greatly different in principle from the problem of an oil spill on the beach of one country by a tanker flying the flag of another country. The imperfections in national capital markets used to justify national credit institutions such as the Federal Home Loan Bank find their analogy in the international capital market justifying the various international financial institutions. Just as state and national governments regulate industries and employment to prevent what is perceived as excessive competition, so the International Air Transport Association was employed by national governments to regulate international air fares and the Bureau of International Exhibitions established rules that restricted competition among nation states in the provision of world fairs. The nations of the world have many common property resources that are jointly used, such as the oceans and their resources, and the air. Because they are not owned by any nation, no one nation has an interest in protecting them from overharvesting or abuse.

State governments issue fishing licenses to prevent excessive fishing, which otherwise would occur because no one owns the fish in a stream. Similarly, a number of nations established the International Whaling Commission to seek to regulate the harvesting of whales. Another common property resource is the radio-wave spectrum, which has to be allocated among nations; this is done under the auspices of the International Telecommunications Union.

There is of course no world government with the power to tax and to enforce its decisions. But numerous functions of a world government are performed through separate international institutions by means of voluntary cooperation among member states, which tax their own citizens to finance these international activities and enforce the international rules to the extent that the national governments perceive them to be beneficial. The willingness of governments to participate varies enormously, depending presumably on their perceptions of the benefits and costs. It is hardly surprising that virtually all countries of the world are members of the Universal Postal Union, which provides common rules for the exchange of mail among national post offices, whereas only 20 countries contribute to the expense of the North Atlantic Ice Patrol, which warns against icebergs for the benefit of the ships owned by the participating nations as well as others. Similarly, it is hardly surprising that virtually all nations' governments are members of the International Civil Aviation Organization, which provides a common set of rules and standards for international aviation, whereas only 19 nations, the major users of the North Atlantic routes, contribute to the financing of joint air navigation, meteorological facilities, and communications aids located in Greenland and Iceland under the umbrella of that organization.

The degree of participation depends on more than the perceived benefits because, in the absence of a world government with the power to coerce, free riding is possible. Thus 14 nations jointly finance the maintenance of two lighthouses (a natural governmental function) in the Red Sea, but their shipping makes up only about half the tonnage through the Suez Canal.

We cannot hope to review all of these institutions. Rather, we will focus on those that traditionally have caught interest, in particular, the following:

Multilateral development banks, institutions that provide economic development finance.

The International Monetary Fund, the institution that deals with monetary relations among countries, including provisions for financing balance-of-payments difficulties.

The Bank for International Settlements, an influential bank for European central banks.

The General Agreement on Tariffs and Trade, the major institution dealing with the rules governing international trade and the resolution of disputes.

The Organization for Economic Cooperation and Development, an influential organization for intergovernmental discussions of economic and social issues among the industrial countries of Western Europe, North America, Japan, Australia, and New Zealand.

The U.N. Conference on Trade and Development, an organization to promote economic development of the developing countries through North–South discussions.

THE MULTILATERAL DEVELOPMENT BANKS

The World Bank is composed of three institutions: the International Bank for Reconstruction and Development (IBRD), the International Development Association (IDA), and the International Finance Corporation (IFC). As the name implies, these institutions operate worldwide. In addition there are four regionally oriented banks: the Inter-American Development Bank (IDB), the Asian Development Bank (ADB), the African Development Bank (AfDB), and the Caribbean Development Bank (CarDB).

They are all owned by national governments and now chiefly make loans for the economic development of their members, except those that are already developed.

THE INTERNATIONAL BANK FOR RECONSTRUCTION AND DEVELOPMENT. The International Bank for Reconstruction and Development (IBRD) is the oldest and largest of the multilateral development banks. It has set patterns for the regional banks in structure, operations, and policies.

Early History. Early in World War II, financial experts of the Allied nations believed that some form of international cooperation would be necessary to cope with the monetary and financial difficulties of the postwar period. After some preliminary meetings, the 44 Allied nations convened the U.N. Monetary and Financial Conference at Bretton Woods, New Hampshire, in July 1944. The conference produced charters, called articles of agreement, for two institutions: the International Monetary Fund (IMF) and the IBRD. These articles of agreement came in force on December 27, 1945, when 28 nations signed them. The IBRD began operations on June 25, 1946.

Although reconstruction of the war-torn nations was one of the original objectives of the IBRD, it quickly became apparent that its resources were miniscule compared to the task of reconstruction. Though the IBRD did make $500 million in reconstruction loans to four European nations, after the advent of the Marshall Plan in 1948, it shifted to development lending.

Structure. As of 1980, the IBRD had 135 members. Each member government receives 250 votes plus one vote for each share of stock held in the bank. The amount of stock is determined by the member government's subscription at one share (and thus one vote) per $100,000.

Any country can join the IBRD, though its admission is conditional on membership in the IMF and must be approved by the board of governors, consisting of usually very high level officials from each member government. The board of governors meets annually, and every other meeting is held in Washington, D.C., the headquarters of the bank.

The governors have delegated their powers, with the exception of certain key decisions, to a board of executive directors, who are resident in Washington and meet at least once a week. Five of the executive directors are appointed by the five leading stockholders, namely the United States, the United Kingdom, the Federal Republic of Germany, France, and Japan. The United States has slightly more than 20 percent of the votes. There is no veto. In fact, the top five countries combined do not have a majority of the votes. Each of the 15 other executive directors are elected by separate groups of countries, and each casts the entire votes of all the countries he represents without splitting. In fact, there is very little voting in the IBRD. As Zamora (1980) states, ". . . in many international economic organizations (including the World Bank, the International Monetary Fund, and the regional development banks, all of which have carefully devised weighted voting procedures) a formal vote, either in the Board of Directors or in the Board of Governors, is a relatively rare occurrence; most decisions are made by a form of consensus, or 'sense of meeting.' "

As of 1980, the IBRD had a staff of approximately 5000, headed by a president. Since the outset there has been informal agreement that the president shall be an

American. The executive directors of the bank choose the president, who is responsible for the organization, appointment, and dismissal of officers and staff. Only the president can propose loans.

The subscriptions of member countries are determined by the economic and financial strengths of the members and are linked to the members' quotas in the IMF. Upon joining, the member pays 1 percent of its subscription in dollars or gold, which is freely usable by the bank, and 9 percent in its own currency, which only can be used by the bank with the permission of the member. The remaining 90 percent is not paid, but can be called by the bank to meet its obligations arising out of its borrowings or guarantees.

The IBRD is a specialized agency of the United Nations. But the agreement providing for that status, according to the World Bank (1976), ". . . explicitly recognized the operational independence of the Bank from the political bodies of the U.N." The bank's annual report is submitted to the U.N. Economic and Social Council. It has both formal and informal working relationships with a number of U.N. specialized agencies. Thus it has formal cooperative arrangements with the Food and Agricultural Organization, the World Health Organization, and the U.N. Industrial Development Organization, for example, in which it shares the cost of professional staff engaged in the identification and preparation of projects for IBRD financing.

Loan Policies and Procedures.   Except in special circumstances, an IBRD loan must be for a specific project in a member country or in a territory under the administration of a member. A project must be technically, financially, and economically sound and of high priority for the economic development of the country to qualify for a loan. The bank must be satisfied that it will be well managed, both in construction and after completion. There must be a reasonable assurance that the loan will be repaid. The borrower must not be able to obtain finance on reasonable terms from others. The bank lends only to national governments or to public or private organizations that can obtain guarantees for repayment from their national governments. There are no political criteria per se in the selection of projects or countries, though the political situation has impinged indirectly through its effect on the criteria stated above.

Project selection by the IBRD occurs in the context of a comprehensive review of the structure and prospects of the local economy. Bank missions examine the country's agricultural, mineral, industrial, and human resources, its basic facilities, its infrastructures such as transport and electric power, the quality and education of its civil service, and its external and internal finances. To this overview, are added special studies of particular sectors such as agriculture, transport, and so forth. Then come the project studies, which may be suggested by the member government, by a bank mission, or by the various organizations in the United Nations with which it has relations.

The bank usually provides only the foreign-exchange costs of the project. It requires international competitive bidding, though limited preferences are given to manufacturers in the borrowing country, to member countries that have joined the borrowing country in a preferential tariff arrangement, and to contractors in very low income countries.

In the years prior to 1980, the IBRD has on occasion provided financing for local costs, in effect buying the currency of the borrowing country. In addition, the bank occasionally provided program, as distinct from project, financing. Thus loans to expand education need not be tied to specific projects (e.g., a building), and because their foreign-exchange contents would be low, local-cost financing would be provided. In 1980 there appeared to be a distinct shift toward nonproject, local-cost financing with the adoption of a policy of structural-adjustment lending in face of enlarged current-account deficits attributable to higher oil prices and slower growth in the advanced countries. As the bank explained (World Bank, 1980), "Structural adjustment lending was seen as one response in an effort to help supplement, with longer term finance, the relatively short-term finance available from commercial banks and the resources available from the IMF in order that the current account deficits of many developing countries do not become so large as to jeopardize seriously the implementation of current investment programs and foreign exchange producing activities." Although its articles of agreement permit the IBRD to issue guarantees of obligations issued by others, this technique has been used very little because it was thought that the interest cost to the borrower would be higher than if the bank issued its own bonds and then made direct loans.

The bank charges interest only on the disbursed position of the loan plus a small commitment fee on the undisbursed amounts.

Projects and Sectors. Until about 1972 the emphasis of the bank's lending was on infrastructures, namely transportation (roads, railways, ports, air facilities, and pipelines) and public utilities (electricity generation, telecommunications, water supply, and sewerage). Since the early 1970s it has increased the share of projects that are destined to help the very poorest segments of members' populations, and this has meant a substantial increase in the relative share of agricultural projects in its portfolio. This has been part of a shift to "new style" projects such as agricultural credit, new settlements, rural training, visiting and extension services, and so forth (see Hurni, 1980).

The sectors covered by bank loans in recent years have been categorized by the bank as follows: agricultural and rural development, development finance companies, education, energy, industry, nonproject, population, health and nutrition, small-scale enterprise, telecommunications, tourism, transportation, urbanization, water supply, and sewerage.

Aid Coordination. Occasionally the IBRD will seek to increase the effectiveness of aid coming to a country from many sources by organizing and chairing an aid-coordination group consisting of all the donors to a country, including the regional banks and the countries providing bilateral assistance. This tends to improve the quality of information available to the donors and the bank, permits the bank and other members to put pressure on donors whose terms of assistance seem to be too harsh, and provides an opportunity to mitigate the effects of the tied procurement policies under bilateral aid in which the donor insists that its aid be spent in the donor nation by allocating projects to the cheapest source.

Finance. The IBRD has financed the loans it has made primarily by issuing its own general obligations in the private marketplace and to official institutions such as central banks. When the bank opened operations, the only capital market open to it was the United States. In the 1960s and 1970s, as the international capital markets developed and spread, it widened its borrowing considerably, so that in March 1978, some 90 countries held its obligations. In many of the countries, it is given preferential access to the capital market over other nonresident borrowers. Its obligations are exempt from withholding taxes in member countries and exempt from tax in the case of nonresidents.

The bank's obligations carry a triple A rating around the world. This is partly attributable to the callable-capital feature of the bank's capital structure under which member governments are obligated to pay the appropriate portion of the uncalled-capital subscription to the bank in the event of default by the bank on its obligations. But other factors are also involved. The articles of agreement restrict its loans to a total equal to its subscribed capital, surplus, and reserves, making it one of the most conservative lending institutions in the world. It has about 1900 separate loans to 122 different countries; the highly diversified nature of its portfolio reduces the risk for any given return, making its obligations more attractive (see Schmidt, 1979). It takes no foreign-exchange risk on its borrowings because it lends the currencies it borrows, and the borrowers repay in the currency they have borrowed; that would not be the case if the bank received repayment in a currency different from that which it borrowed. It has never had a default on its loans. If a member is 30 days late in its interest or amortization payments to the bank, that event becomes highly visible, for all of the member governments are informed automatically. It refuses to reschedule the interest and amortization payments by members in debt difficulty.

The interest rate it charges on its loans does not vary among countries at a given point in time and is based on its cost of funds, which, since it pays no dividends, is somewhat lower than it otherwise would be. It has made a profit every year since 1948.

THE INTERNATIONAL DEVELOPMENT ASSOCIATION.   The International Development Association (IDA) provides loans called credits on very cheap terms (0.75 percent) for very long periods (50 years). The credits are repaid, after a 10-year grace period, at a rate of 1 percent for 10 years and then 3 percent for the remaining 30 years.

Early History.   In the late 1950s the U.S. government sold large amounts of agricultural commodities to less developed countries in exchange for their local currencies, for which the United States had no or little use. The accumulated currencies became a source of tension between the U.S. government and the recipient of U.S. agricultural products. Senator John Monroney of Oklahoma began to look about for ways to dispose of the currencies, hitting upon the notion that they could be given to some international institution. At the same time, a number of the less developed countries were pressing the advanced nations to establish an aid institution under the auspices of the United Nations. Monroney's proposal made little sense, because the foreign currencies did not reflect real resources, since they were not freely convertible into other currencies to buy goods and services. But in response to the pressure built up for his proposal and in response to the less developed countries' demands, the United States pushed for the establishment of a soft-loan affiliate administered, not by the United Nations, but by the safer hands of the World Bank. IDA was established in 1960. The rationale was that very poor countries needed cheap credit and that some countries' balances of payments were in such poor shape that they could not stand the IBRD's harder terms.

Structure.   Some countries that are members of the IBRD have chosen not to join IDA, as joint membership is not required. The voting power in IDA is tied, as with the IBRD, to subscriptions and contributions, though with a slight twist such that the richer countries have less voting strength than their contributions, whereas the smallest have more. Although IDA is an organization that is separate legally from the IBRD, the executive directors, officers, and staff of the IBRD administer it. For this service, the IBRD charges IDA a fee.

Finance.   Unlike the IBRD, given its soft terms, IDA cannot be a self-sustaining organization. Resources are obtained in a number of ways. The members are divided into Part I (richer) and Part II (poorer) countries. The subscriptions of Part I countries are entirely paid into IDA and are completely freely usable by IDA. Part II countries pay only 10 percent of their subscriptions in freely usable currencies; the remaining 90 percent consists of their own currencies, which may not be used by IDA without the individual members' permissions. At the time of its organization, it was expected that the members would replenish the funds of IDA with additional transfers to it from time to time. Voting power within IDA is a function in part of the size of the contributions a member makes to the replenishment. In the past, these replenishments have been negotiated by governments, but delays in obtaining ultimate approval of the negotiated sums have caused slowdowns in IDA lending. Still another source of funds is transfers from the profits of the IBRD. Finally, small sums are obtained from the service charge of 0.75 percent.

Loan Policies and Procedures.   IDA credits are restricted to the poorest members, with those with more than a certain gross national product per head being excluded. There are no other differences in the lending criteria under IDA and the IBRD.

THE INTERNATIONAL FINANCE CORPORATION.   The International Finance Corporation (IFC) was established in 1956 as an affiliate of the World Bank to make loans to private enterprises in the less developed countries.

   The U.S. government acceded to pressures from the less developed countries to establish the IFC because it was the less costly and more conservative of the proposals (Mason and Asher, 1973).

Structure.   The IFC has 113 members. Any country may join the IFC, but the country must also be a member of the IBRD and gain the approval of the IFC's board of governors.

   Although the IFC has a separate board, the member states are represented on the board by the same people who are members of the IBRD board of governors. The directors of the IFC fulfill the same functions as they do in the IBRD.

   As of 1980, the IFC had a staff of 360. The president is chosen by the board of directors. In the past the president of the IBRD and the IFC have been the same person.

Lending and Investing Policies.   In 1962, the IFC articles of agreement were amended to allow it to make equity investments.

   Through 1980, about 15 percent of its gross commitments were in the form of equity investments; the remainder were loans at commercial rates of interest. Unlike the IBRD, the IFC cannot receive any guarantee of repayment from the governments of the countries in which it operates. It will not invest in a company against the government's wishes.

The IFC normally does not take a controlling interest in an enterprise nor does it take a seat on the board, because it prefers to attract private capital and cannot involve itself in the management of the company according to its charter. Nonetheless, there are periodic checks on the performance of the enterprise receiving IFC funds, including quarterly reports.

Three criteria must be met with respect to IFC loans and investments. The project must have a reasonable prospect of a profit, as this is the only way the IFC can get its money back. The IFC has made a net profit in each year of its existence. In addition it must benefit the economic development of the host country. Thus land-speculation schemes and enterprises that produce luxury consumer goods are ruled out. The IFC will not provide funds if it believes that sufficient private capital is available.

The IFC provides funds both to entirely new enterprises and for the expansion of existing ones, approximately half and half. The funds do not go through governments. Unlike commercial banks, the IFC provides substantial amounts of technical assistance in designing projects and promoting them. Of course prospective clients may initiate a contact. It also provides technical and financial assistance for the development of local capital markets.

After an enterprise matures, the IFC sells off its equity holdings in order to revolve its funds to still other enterprises. It will not sell its shares to new investors to whom the existing owners have valid objections.

The largest part of IFC funds have gone into manufacturing activities. Some have gone into local development banks, which lend or invest them to small or medium-sized firms in the private sector.

A company does not need to be purely private to qualify for IFC monies.

In addition to its being paid in capital and the proceeds of its equity sales and repaid loans, the IFC borrows funds from the IBRD. The IFC reimburses the IBRD for certain administrative services and uses the various studies made by that institution.

THE INTERNATIONAL MONETARY FUND

In his authoritative history of the post-World War II international financial system, Solomon (1977) succinctly summarizes the genesis of the International Monetary Fund (IMF): "Those responsible for designing the IMF had aimed at establishing a system of multilateral trade and payments compatible with the maintenance of high levels of income and employment. Consistent with this purpose, they wanted to prevent a repetition of the so-called beggar-thy-neighbor policies of the 1930's, when countries used trade restrictions, subsidies, and competitive depreciation of exchange rates [the reduction by one nation of the price in foreign currency of its money] in attempts to solve domestic unemployment problems by increasing their trade surpluses—thereby shifting their domestic problems to other countries."

EARLY FEATURES.   The main features of the new organization were as follows:

1. It was to be a permanent organization to promote consultation and collaboration among member governments on international monetary problems.
2. Each member would establish, with IMF approval, a par value for its currency in terms of gold and the dollar and would maintain the market exchange rate for its currency within 1 percent of that par value by buying and selling dollars in exchange for its own. For its part, the United States would not buy and sell foreign currencies in exchange for dollars to stabilize its exchange rate, but would freely buy and sell gold at a fixed price in terms of dollars to achieve that purpose. In that fashion, gold, the dollar, and foreign currencies were to be firmly linked in price.
3. Member governments would change the par values of their currencies only after receiving IMF approval. Such approval would only be given if the member's balance of payments were in "fundamental disequilibrium"—a term that was not defined in the articles of agreement and was never officially defined. Temporary and cyclical imbalances in the international payments of a country were to be financed by using reserves of foreign currencies or gold held by the country or by borrowing from the IMF rather than changing exchange rates. The IMF would have funds from the initial contributions of the members.
4. Currencies would be convertible in the sense that countries would redeem balances of their currencies obtained by others. Restrictions on current transactions, that is, on payments for goods and services as distinct from capital movements, would be removed. Restrictions that discriminated among countries were to be eliminated. However, if a country's currency became scarce in the IMF, the latter could authorize discriminatory exchange controls on current-account purchases from the scarce-currency country.

With the exception of the "scarce currency" clause, the world's international financial system developed very much like this outline until the early 1970s. When the IMF opened its doors for business in March 1947, exchange and trade restrictions were widespread and, except for the U.S. dollar, the Canadian dollar, and several central American currencies, all currencies were inconvertible because many members were suffering from wartime destruction and a chronic dollar shortage. But in 1958, 15 Western European nations were able to declare their currencies convertible. By 1965 discriminatory exchange restrictions had largely been wiped out, restrictions on both current and capital transactions had been greatly reduced, and the vast majority of members had agreed par values or fixed exchange rates.

SUBSEQUENT CHANGES.   Subsequently, two important changes in the system as originally envisaged took place. One was the introduction of the special drawing right (SDR) and the other was the shift away from fixed exchange rates, a big change in the way the system operated.

SPECIAL DRAWING RIGHTS.   In 1969 the articles of agreement of the IMF were amended to establish the SDR account. The SDR has euphemistically been called "paper gold," whereas in fact it is on computer tape. Starting in 1970 the IMF has periodically created SDRs, which have been allocated to members. The members then have employed their SDRs to buy each other's currencies to settle international transactions and to make payments to the IMF. When a member holds more SDRs than its cumulative allocations, it receives interest on them, whereas a member who holds less than its cumulative allocations is charged interest. As of 1981, the value of the SDR is determined by the weighted average of five major currencies. In 1978 the members agreed to the objective of making the SDR "... the principal reserve asset in the international monetary system" (Article XXII).

The genesis of the SDR lay in the mounting concerns in the mid-1960s over the functioning of the international financial system, first with respect to the adequacy of the liquidity of the system (see Triffin, 1960). The problem as perceived was that "... no adequate provision existed for enlarging the supply of world reserves [for the settlement of international transactions] to keep pace with the expansion in international trade and investment" (IMF 1980). The gold supply was barely increasing. Most of the increase in the supply of world reserves was coming, in the late 1950s and the 1960s, from an increase in U.S. liabilities to foreign central banks as they bought excess supplies of dollars resulting from continuing American balance-of-payments deficits. As the United States had only a finite amount of gold, the American deficits could not continue forever to supply the needed liquidity. Furthermore, as American liabilities mounted, there was fear that there would be a run on the dollar that would force suspension of its convertibility into gold, which was then perceived as the basis for the par-value system. In short, the second problem that developed was confidence in the system.

The third difficulty lay in the absence of adequate balance-of-payments adjustments as evidenced by persistent American deficits and persistent German and Japanese surpluses in their balance of payments. The industrial countries were too reluctant to adjust through demand management or par-value changes, so that disequilibrium persisted, marked by occasional par-value adjustments that were too long delayed. This gave rise to large movements of speculative funds whose owners knew that a given weak currency could go only in one direction, namely down, thereby affording the speculators rich opportunities for gain at little cost and low risk.

FLOATING. Finally the so-called Bretton Woods system collapsed, the process beginning with President Nixon's decision in August 1971 to refuse to buy and sell gold at a fixed price. There followed a period in which foreign governments sought to keep exchange rates stable at appreciated levels for their currencies, but in March 1973 those efforts failed, and the system of generalized floating exchange rates began. This subsequently led to another amendment of the IMF articles of agreement, which among other things allowed a member to choose any exchange-rate system it wanted. The IMF could go back to the par-value system but only with 85 percent of the votes, giving the United States an effective veto. Members agreed to "... avoid manipulating exchange rates or the international monetary system in order to prevent effective balance of payments adjustment or to gain an unfair competitive advantage over other members ..." (Article IV, IMF articles of agreement). The IMF was charged with exercising "firm surveillance over the exchange-rate policies of members ..." The role of gold was greatly diminished in the IMF, a large part of its holdings being sold off.

STRUCTURE.   As of 1980, the IMF had 140 members. Each member government receives 250 votes plus one vote for each SDR 100,000 of quota. The number of votes provided to each member is a function of its quota. At the Bretton Woods conference in 1944, the formula for the determination of quotas took into account national income, international reserves, imports, export variability, and the ratio of exports to national income. This was subsequently modified to give smaller countries a larger share of the total vote. Each country is obliged to provide the IMF with international reserves equal to 25 percent of its quota. Quotas are reviewed at intervals of not more than five years. In addition, under the General Arrangement to Borrow (1962) the IMF has borrowed resources from the governments of the leading financial countries. As of 1980 the IMF had never borrowed on the open market.

Any country can join the IMF, though its admission must be approved by the board of governors, consisting usually of the ministers of finance and/or the chief officers of the central banks of the member governments. The board of governors meets annually, and every other meeting is held in Washington, D.C., the headquarters of the IMF.

The governors have delegated their powers, with the exception of certain key decisions, to a board of executive directors, who are resident in Washington and who meet at least once a week. As of 1980, there were 21 executive directors. One each is appointed by the United States, the United Kingdom, the Federal Republic of Germany, and Japan, and one by the two largest creditors of the IMF in the most recent 2-year period, if not included among the first five. The remaining 15 are elected by groupings of other members. The United States has slightly less than 20 percent of the votes. There is no formal veto, except that certain key decisions require an 85 percent vote. A formal vote of the executive directors or board of governors is rare.

As of 1980 the IMF had a staff of approximately 1500, headed by the managing director. Since the outset there has been informal agreement that the managing director shall be a European. The executive directors choose the managing director. The IMF is a specialized agency of the United Nations.

LOAN POLICIES AND PROCEDURES.   The IMF provides temporary funding to its members for balance-of-payments problems.

Quotas.   The size of a member's quota in the IMF governs the rate at which it can draw on the resources of the IMF. Each member contributes 25 percent of its quota upon joining the IMF in international reserves and the remainder in its own currency.

Technically, the IMF does not make loans. Rather, a country needing help obtains foreign currencies or SDRs from the IMF in exchange for its own currency. These are called *drawings*.

For many years, total drawings by an individual member were limited to 125 percent of its quota, that is, the point at which the IMF's holdings of its currency equalled 200 percent of its quota. Recently, the purchase limit was raised to 200 percent, that is, the point at which the IMF holdings of the member's currency reach 275 percent of the member's quota.

The member drawing on the IMF must represent that it has a balance-of-payments problem. The problem must be temporary, that is, not fundamental. The funds normally must be repaid within three to five years if they are drawn from the general resources of the IMF.

A drawing may occur under either a direct purchase, in which case the member expects to draw the full amount after approval, or under a standby arrangement, in which case the member draws from time to time during the period of the standby arrangement.

Conditionality. Quotas are divided into tranches. The first tranche is equal to 25 percent of the member's quota and is called the *reserve tranche*. The remaining tranches, each equal to 25 percent, are called *credit tranches* to indicate that the member is drawing more than the original amount of reserves it contributed.

In principal, IMF drawings are designed to give a country time to adjust its balance of payments through corrective action. To that end, the IMF permits drawings subject to conditions.

These conditions vary with the level of the IMF holdings of the member's currency. With regard to a drawing in the reserve tranche, the member is given "the overwhelming benefit of the doubt"; it is given "liberal treatment in the first credit tranche" but there are "more rigorous expectations for corrective action" in the subsequent tranches, according to its longtime deputy managing director (Southard, 1977).

In the first credit-tranche drawing, the member is expected to show that it is making reasonable efforts to solve its balance-of-payments problem. "In practice, this criterion has often meant that, when differences of judgement arise, the member receives the benefit of the doubt" (IMF, 1980).

Drawings in the higher credit tranches are always made under a standby agreement, so that funds are made available at specified intervals in the period of the standby agreement. The member's right to draw under the standby agreement is always subject to its observance of certain key policy indicators agreed on in advance.

Along with the standby agreement, the minister of finance and/or governor of the central bank sign a letter of intent in which the member quantifies what it plans to do. These become the performance criteria.

Typically, the performance criteria are worked out by a mission from the IMF to the country with top officials of the government. "The program is not dictated by the Fund, but the Fund has the duty to determine whether or not support of a program with its resources would be consistent with the Articles and with the policies of the Fund," according to the IMF's longtime general counsel (Gold, 1979).

One performance criterion that is always employed is a limit on the expansion of credit by the central bank or the banking system. This stems from the fact that balance-of-payments problems almost always reflect excessive demand in the country. By restraining excessive demand, the demand for imports is slowed and the balance-of-payments problem is eased.

Another performance criterion in constant use is a prohibition on the introduction or intensification of multiple-exchange-rates practices (the country has several different exchange rates for different types of transactions) and restrictions on payments and transfers for current transactions or restrictions on trade.

The member's problems may stem in part from excessive borrowing abroad, which leads to burdensome interest and amortization payments. In that event, limits on the amount and maturities of further borrowing may be employed as a performance criterion.

Inasmuch as a member's cost and price levels help to determine its competitiveness in world markets, its exchange rate may have to be adjusted to reduce the value of its currency in terms of foreign currencies. In order to insure that the member does not use its international reserves to support an overvalued currency (which stimulates imports and impedes exports), the performance criteria may include a minimum level for the foreign-exchange reserves of the member.

The foregoing performance criteria concern essentially macroeconomic variables. In exceptional cases, they may include individual prices that bear significantly upon the public finances and on trade. For example, there may be heavy subsidies to food that put the budget in serious deficit, thereby causing inflation.

Decisions on how credit should be allocated, where public spending should be cut, and what taxes should be increased are left to the member government. To do otherwise would involve the IMF in determining the appropriate distribution of the burden of adjustment among sectors within the member country, a determination that no sovereign country will permit.

According to Southard, failure to live up to the performance criteria may lead only to expressions of regret on both sides. On the other hand, the country may be quietly told that it should not seek access to additional IMF resources unless it can demonstrate stronger ability to perform. He writes, "Men and countries are fallible, and on very many occasions the Fund has given a country a second or even a third chance if support for a new action program seemed to be worth the gamble" (Southard, 1977).

The amounts that a member may draw from the IMF are higher than those discussed above under certain schemes because outstanding drawings under the regular scheme are not counted.

In 1963 a *compensatory financing facility* was created within the IMF to provide funds to members—particularly primary-product-producing countries—having balance-of-payments difficulties due to shortfalls in their export proceeds that are "temporary and largely attributable to circumstances beyond the member's control," according to Goreux (1980). To qualify, an absolute decline in export earnings is not required, only a decline in their rate of growth. Under this facility, members may draw up to 100 percent of their quotas. The drawings are repaid in the 3 to 5 years following the drawing. As the export shortfall is temporary and not attributable to the actions of the member, no performance criteria are required.

In 1969 a *buffer-stock financing facility* was established in the IMF. If a member contributes to the financing of a buffer stock, which buys and sells a commodity to reduce its price fluctuations, and if that member faces balance-of-payments difficulties, it may draw up to 50 percent of its quota from the IMF to help in financing its contributions to the buffer stock.

In 1974 an *extended facility* was agreed upon in the IMF. It seeks to provide funds to members in larger amounts and for longer time periods than available under the credit-tranche policies. This facility is aimed at members whose payments difficulties stem from structural maladjustments if they are planning to try to correct them. Drawings of up to 140 percent of the member's quota are permitted. Repayments are made over a 4–10-year period.

Finally, in 1979 a *supplementary financing facility* was organized to meet the needs of members whose balance-of-payments deficits were large in relation to their quotas. The funds for this facility are borrowed from 14 nations. The IMF borrows at market rates of interest to obtain these funds and therefore charges the members who borrow under this facility higher rates of interest than the IMF normally charges.

SURVEILLANCE.   In 1978 the IMF articles of agreement were amended to require the IMF to "exercise firm surveillance over the exchange rate policies of members . . ." Governments, through their central banks, often seek to change the levels of their exchange rates by buying or selling foreign currencies. The principles adopted by the executive directors were as follows (IMF, 1977):

> A member shall avoid manipulating exchange rates or the international monetary system in order to prevent effective balance-of-payments adjustment or to gain an unfair competitive advantage over other members.
>
> A member should intervene in the exchange market if necessary to counter disorderly conditions that may be characterized inter alia by disruptive short-term movements in the exchange value of its currency.
>
> Members should take into account in their intervention policies the interest of other members, including those of the countries in whose currencies they intervene.

Members are required to consult with the IMF regularly, in principle on an annual basis. These consultations afford the IMF an opportunity to review each member's economic and financial position and its policies. They facilitate the consideration of any subsequent requests for drawings. And they give the member an opportunity to complain to the IMF about the behavior of other members.

Between annual consultations, if the managing director considers that some modification in a member's exchange-rate policies or the behavior of its exchange rate is important or has important effects on other members, he can initiate an informal and confidential discussion with the members.

It is impossible to say how effective the surveillance and consultation process is. As Southard (1977) notes, ". . . in practice the Fund has no formal sanctions that it can use to force members to comply with Fund policy or to take corrective monetary, exchange, or economic action. It can set conditions for the use of its resources only for deficit countries that need the resources. With surplus countries, the Fund must rely on suasion applied during the course of consultations and on the organized opinion of the Executive Board." Solomon (1977) repeats a statement of Paul Volcker, the under secretary of the treasury for monetary affairs, to the effect that ". . . when disagreement arose between the IMF and member countries on the need for policy changes, if the country was small, it fell into line; if it was large, the IMF fell into line; if several large countries were involved, the IMF disappeared."

THE BANK FOR INTERNATIONAL SETTLEMENTS

The Bank for International Settlements (BIS) is a bank for European central banks.
   It was formed in 1930 by the major European central banks (Auboin, 1955). Its broad purpose was to promote cooperation among its member central banks. At the

time, its particular purpose was to serve as a trustee and agent in the payment of German reparations arising from World War I.

After World War II the BIS served as the bank for settling transactions among the Western European central banks (the Intra-European Payments Scheme and subsequently the European Payments Union).

As of 1980 it was still serving its German reparations functions. In addition, it serves as agent for the European Monetary Cooperation Fund, which administers settlements among the members of the European Monetary System, a system by which most of the Western European members maintain narrowly fixed exchange rates among themselves.

During the bulk of the post-World War II period, the BIS served as the site of monthly meetings of the central banks of the advanced countries, including the United States, though the latter never joined (Coombs, 1976).

The BIS collects important data on the size of the Eurocurrency markets, which are published, and data on central-bank intervention in the foreign-exchange market, which are made available to the central banks of the advanced countries.

The BIS annual report, which is released in June, is widely noted and influential for its review of the international financial system. Interestingly, unlike the situation in other international economic institutions, the report is not passed upon by the board of directors or the membership but is an independent report of the managing director.

THE GENERAL AGREEMENT ON TARIFFS AND TRADE

The origin of the General Agreement on Tariffs and Trade (GATT) can be attributed to U.S. diplomatic efforts to create a postwar economic environment based on the principles of free and nondiscriminatory trade among nations. In the simplest sense, all nontariff barriers to trade were to be abolished, and tariffs were to be reduced through international negotiations. To accomplish this, the United States envisaged the GATT to contain explicit rules governing international trade that all members would voluntarily obey.

The principles and rules were originally contained in the Havana Charter for an International Trade Organization of the United Nations (the so-called ITO). However, because of reasons to be discussed below, the ITO was never ratified. This failure to ratify the ITO left a void that was filled by a general agreement that had been drawn up in 1947 to contain the results of a tariff conference presumed to be the first in a series of such conferences under the ITO. In order to assure that tariff concessions would not be negated by other restrictions on trade, this agreement contained a number of rules governing international trade that were contained in the ITO charter. Because there was no international trade organization, this general agreement became the basis for the creation of an international institution, with secretariat, to provide a forum for discussing and resolving trade issues among nations.

The primary reason for the failure of the ITO to be ratified is that the United States pressured for an institution based on explicit rules (or laws) rather than on procedures for the resolution of conflicts (see Dam, 1970). Obviously it is extremely difficult to specify explicit rules to which countries with very different economic problems can agree.

Some of the problems were the following:

Postwar balance-of-payments deficits resulted in many countries being unwilling to abolish import quotas.

The U.S. agricultural interests were unwilling to abolish those import quotas that were needed to support domestic farm prices at levels above world prices.

The United Kingdom insisted on continuing the Commonwealth preference arrangement whereby Commonwealth countries discriminate in favor of one another.

In order to arrive at a document that all member countries could abide by, the ITO contained a number of exceptions to the general principles. Because of these compromises, a free-trade principle was often followed by a trade-restriction loophole. Such compromises by the United States and the international prestige of the United States led to general acceptance of the ITO abroad; however, concern for the loopholes raised sufficient apprehensions at home that President Truman decided in 1950 not to seek ratification by the U.S. Congress.

GATT PRINCIPLES AND RULES.   The principles and rules of the GATT are contained in some 38 articles containing numerous phrases that defy comprehension by the educated layman. In order to understand fully the meaning of some articles it is often more necessary to recognize the importance of what is not contained therein. The areas of agreement among nations are clearly stated; areas of disagreement are omitted or stated in legalistic generalities that can be bent to fit any interpretation. A comprehensive examination of the GATT articles is contained in Jackson's *World Trade and the Law of GATT* (1969). What follows will be a general layman's description of the major principles and rules, and exceptions, of the GATT. The presentation will be organized to facilitate understanding rather than to treat the articles in order. Moreover, the content of the 38 articles will be grouped into four substantive topic areas with only the highlights being discussed here. The four areas are (1) nondiscrimination, (2) elimination of quantitative restrictions, (3) fair-trading rules, and (4) dispute settlements. These areas will be treated in turn.

Nondiscrimination.   The primary objective of the GATT was to create fair and equitable trading relationships among the nations of the world. Given this objective it is not surprising that the first article was devoted to the principle of nondiscrimination. Following historical custom, nondiscrimination was defined in terms of "general most-favored-nation treatment," which stated in simplified form is as follows:

> Exports from one member country to another shall be admitted under conditions not less favorable than those accorded to exports from the most favored nation, and thus, since exports from all member countries enjoy access identical to that accorded the most favored nation, they all enjoy identical treatment—i.e., none are discriminated against.

Under Article I, such most-favored-nation treatment shall be accorded with respect to customs duties, charges of any kind imposed on imports or exports, international transfer payments, methods of levying duties, and with respect to rules, regulations, and formalities governing imports and exports.

Thus under the most-favored-nation principle, imports from any source country will be treated equally, provided only that the source country accept the obligations of the GATT as a party to the agreement (called contracting parties). In practice, countries that are not formal contracting parties often enjoy full most-favored-nation treatment under bilateral trade agreements. Under U.S. law, countries that do not enjoy most-favored-nation treatment are communist countries (other than Poland and Romania) (U.S. International Trade Commission, 1976). China has also been granted most-favored-nation treatment under a recent trade agreement.

This most-favored-nation principle requires governments to treat all foreign goods equally (i.e., all exports by contracting parties or countries accorded most-favored-nation treatment under bilateral trade agreements). The next issue concerns the extent to which a government may favor domestic goods over foreign goods. Obviously the existence of tariffs is evidence that the international community accepts the concept of discrimination in favor of domestic goods. At the same time the call for the abolishment of quantitative restrictions demonstrates the feeling that limits should be placed on the extent of this national preference. For example, a purely internal tax could provide protection for local goods if it were applied in a discriminatory fashion; regulations to safeguard the health, safety, and environment of the population could similarly discriminate against imports; government purchasing could be administered to favor domestic firms.

This issue is treated in several articles, and the general principle is set forth in Article III. In essence, this article calls for *national treatment* with respect to matters under government control such as taxation and regulations—because of an inability of nations to agree, this principle was not to be applied to government purchasing or state trading. National treatment means that imported goods are to be accorded the same treatment as goods of local origin.

It is recognized that sovereign nations have legitimate rights to establish regulations to protect the health, safety, and environment of their populations. National treatment means that these regulations shall not be specified or administered in a manner designed to discriminate against foreign goods. Obviously governments will introduce regulations to solve local problems, and different governments will face different problems. Thus regulations will differ, and these differences will have trade impacts. The national-treatment principle is violated only when the *intent* of these differing regulations is to favor local goods. Such trade-distorting effects of differing national health, safety, and environmental regulations can be reduced by international negotiations to harmonize regulations across countries, that is, by negotiating international standards.

The taxation issue is much more complex. Fair and equitable trading rules mean that goods should compete in world markets on the basis of production costs and product characteristics such as quality. However, if countries have different taxes on products, the tax rates could significantly affect price competitiveness. Moreover, a country whose products are not competitive could alter its tax rates to improve the price competitiveness of its products, thereby causing injury to more-efficient producers in other countries. National treatment in this area is designed to permit nations to establish tax rates to achieve domestic objectives but to administer the taxes in a manner that does not favor local goods over foreign goods in the local market or in foreign markets. The potential trade-distorting effect was minimized through the application of the principle of taxation at destination, not at origin. Thus all products are taxed only once; local and foreign goods are taxed by the consuming country at rates applicable to local products. This is accomplished through *border tax adjustments*. Product taxes (called indirect taxes as opposed to direct taxes on income or profits) are rebated to producers when goods are exported; and such taxes are assessed on imports (as well as tariffs). As a result, local and foreign goods compete on the basis of production costs and product characteristics in the importing country, since both products face the same tax rate (excluding only tariffs).

Under GATT rules, border tax adjustments are not to be granted to offset the price effects of direct taxes. This practice tends to place countries that utilize direct taxes (in comparison to indirect taxes) at a competitive disadvantage. (For a discussion of this complicated issue see Dam, 1970.)

Exceptions to the principle of national treatment are recognized in the area of government procurement and state trading. Likewise, exceptions to the most-favored-nation principle of nondiscrimination are permitted for countries belonging to trading blocs such as a customs union (e.g., the European Economic Community) or free-trade area (e.g., the European Free Trade Area). A customs union is a group of countries that have eliminated restrictions on trade among themselves but have established uniform tariffs on imports from nonmembers. A free-trade area differs only in that each member country applies its own tariffs on imports from nonmembers. In both cases, member countries discriminate in favor of member countries and against nonmembers. A third exception to the most-favored-nation principle permits countries to grant preferential treatment in favor of developing countries. (See Section 4 of the *Handbook* for a discussion of trading blocs; trading preferences in favor of developing countries are examined in Murray, 1977.)

Quantitative Restrictions.   Right from the beginning, the United States sought the abolishment of quotas that limit imports to a predetermined quantity. Quotas are an effective trade-restricting mechanism and are easily understood by all traders. However, it is literally impossible to administer quotas in any manner other than a discriminatory manner. Thus the call for the abolishment of quotas.

In the main, quotas have been phased out, with three major exceptions. First, Article XII permits the use of quotas by countries facing balance-of-payments difficulties. Countries invoking Article XII are to apply such quotas on a most-favored-nation basis to the maximum extent possible.

The second major exception deals with trade in agricultural products. The developed countries typically have farm-income support programs that operate by maintaining farm prices above world prices. In order to accomplish this, the domestic market must be separated from world markets. The United States separates these markets by the use of import quotas. The European Community uses a system of variable levies. A variable levy is simply a tax on imports (like a tariff) that is adjusted daily to assure that import prices (inclusive of the variable levy) are maintained above a minimal target price for local farm products.

The third exception is governed by the GATT Long Term Arrangement Regarding International Trade in Cotton Textiles of 1962 [subsequently renewed and expanded to the current Multifiber Arrangement (MFA)]. Under this arrangement, countries whose markets for textiles and apparel are disrupted by imports can negotiate "orderly marketing agreements" (previously called "voluntary export restraint agreements") with selected exporting countries, whereby the exporting country limits its exports to the importing country (see Dam, 1970, Chapter 17).

The orderly marketing agreements that the United States has recently negotiated with Japan, Korea, and Taiwan covering color televisions, with Korea and Taiwan covering footwear, and with Japan covering automobiles are essentially outside the scope of the GATT. Instead they fall under the import-relief provision of U.S. law (see Section 26 of the *Handbook*).

Fair-Trading Rules. Fair-trading rules are designed to prevent "unfair trading practices" of governments, exporters, or importers that give products from one country a competitive advantage over products from another country. The unfair practices of major concern involve governmental subsidies and dumping practices by commercial entities. Unfair trade practices of lesser concern include patent infringement, nonmarket pricing of socialist countries, and export restrictions on critical raw materials. Other unfair trade practices such as discriminatory health, safety, or environment standards, customs valuation, and so on are essentially covered by the national-treatment principle. The following discussion will concentrate on subsidies and dumping practices.

Subsidies can be used by governments to affect international trade in three ways. Subsidies granted to domestic producers can enable them to gain a competitive advantage over imports. Subsidies granted to exporters (whether or not granted if the product is sold in the domestic market) enable them to gain a competitive advantage over domestic producers in the importing country. And subsidies enable exporters in the subsidizing country to gain a competitive advantage in third-country markets over exporters from nonsubsidizing countries. These trade-distorting effects can cause economic injury to producers and workers in firms that are otherwise economically viable and efficient.

The GATT recognizes these adverse effects but also recognizes that sovereign nations can use subsidies to achieve important domestic economic objectives. Thus under the GATT, subsidy practices are not "illegal" per se, but only if they cause injury to producers and/or workers in a trading partner. In such cases the GATT aims at remedying the situation. If subsidies stimulate exports that cause injury to import-competing firms in the importing country, the GATT authorizes the importing country to levy a *countervailing duty* sufficient to offset the price effect of the subsidy. However, in the case of subsidies that reduce exports to the subsidizing country or that divert trade to a third country, the injured country has no unilateral remedy available other than to introduce competitive subsidies of its own, that is, to counter an unfair practice with an unfair practice. In these latter cases, the remedy must come from consultations with the subsidizing country with the aim of eliminating the injurious effects of the subsidy.

Dumping practices can have trade impacts similar to the effects of subsidies. And the remedies are similarly the introduction of an offsetting antidumping duty or international consultations. The major distinction between these practices is that dumping is defined to be selling in the foreign market at prices below fair value. Theoretically, dumping is considered to be a specific action of a firm to increase the firm's market share, to sell off excess inventories, or to take advantage of profit-maximizing price-discriminatory opportunities. In practice, however, the dumping issue is often concerned with government firms that benefit from the government's willingness to underwrite firm losses in order to maintain high levels of employment (e.g., British Steel). Antidumping and countervailing duties are treated in Dam (1970)

Chapter 10; for a more legalistic treatment see Jackson (1969), Chapters 15 and 16. U.S. law regarding these issues is contained in the Trade Act of 1974, Title III and the Trade Agreements Act of 1979, Title I.

Dispute Settlements.   Two major problems that confront the GATT, as well as all other international organizations, is how to achieve a system in which the parties to the agreement reasonably comply with their obligations under the agreement and, in cases where disagreements do occur, how to resolve disputes. Disputes arise from a number of sources, including differences in national interpretation of the rules of the GATT, which are typically written in general statements; inconsistencies between national laws and GATT rules; and cases in which national governments are forced by domestic political pressure to introduce trade policies that are in violation of GATT rules.

The intention of the dispute-settlements process is to resolve disputes either by the elimination of the "illegal" trade practice or by steps taken to eliminate the injurious effect of the practice. In almost all cases in which a dispute is successfully resolved, the solution comes through bilateral discussions between the disputing countries. The GATT contribution to this settlements process is primarily coercion by "pointing a finger" at the country engaging in the "illegal" practice rather than the authorization or introduction of sanctions against the country. After all, GATT has no police force, jails, or ability to levy fines against countries that fail (or refuse) to honor their obligations under the agreement. In the final analysis, all disputes are resolved voluntarily.

Nevertheless, within the GATT there is a semiformal dispute-settlements process that consists of four stages, roughly defined as follows:

1. One contracting party initiates a complaint against a specific practice of another contracting party.
2. The GATT appoints a panel (or working party) to investigate the issue with the view of determining if the specified practice is in fact contrary to the rules of the GATT agreement.
3. The panel reports its findings to the GATT; the GATT as a whole reviews the panel's findings.
4. In cases in which the panel's findings are with the complainant, the GATT "points a finger" at the country in violation of GATT rules with a view toward resolving the conflict. At the extreme, the GATT may authorize the complainant to retaliate against the other country. Retaliation takes the form of the suspension of a GATT concession or a GATT obligation with respect to the country in violation of GATT rules.

Throughout these four stages, however, the two countries involved in the dispute are encouraged to resolve the dispute through bilateral consultations. And in almost all cases the dispute is resolved prior to the final stage; seldom is retaliation used to resolve GATT disputes.

THE GATT IN OPERATION.   Even though the GATT rules of today are almost identical to those of four decades ago, the GATT is a living agreement. The objective of the GATT was, and is today, to liberalize trade for the mutual benefit of all nations.

The liberalization has come as a result of reductions in tariff rates, modifications in national laws to bring trading practices more into conformity with the GATT principles, and occasional modifications in the GATT rules themselves. In general, these steps have steadily liberalized international trade, with only a few incidents of regressions toward protectionism.

The major successes toward liberalizing trade have come out of the seven "rounds" of tariff negotiations (called conferences), the most recent of which is the Tokyo Round of Multilateral Trade Negotiations, which occurred during 1973–1978. The reasons for successes in the tariff area are partly historical and partly pragmatic. When the GATT was initiated, tariff rates were very high as a result of governments' attempting to generate employment through import restrictions to alleviate the economic hardships of the Great Depression. These policies did reduce imports, but since one country's imports are another country's exports, exports and export jobs also were reduced. Thus these "beggar-thy-neighbor" policies simply traded export jobs (generally high-wage jobs) for import-competing jobs (generally low-wage jobs), thereby beggaring all trading partners. A major aim of the GATT was to reverse these policies through negotiations, whereby all countries would simultaneously lower tariff rates.

The pragmatic attractiveness of tariff negotiations was their simplicity. Exporters, importers, and governmental officials all understood clearly what tariffs are and how they affected trade flows. Further, since the rates were so high to begin with, even significant reductions in the levels would have minor impacts on trade flows. Finally, it was easy for government negotiators to justify the net benefits to their domestic constituencies by highlighting the concessions granted by trading partners on products of export interest to domestic exporters.

This resulted in a negotiation process based on the principle of *reciprocity*. Reciprocity is not defined or otherwise incorporated into the GATT in any formal way. Instead it is a pragmatic procedure whereby countries determine the package of concessions they are willing to grant (i.e., the list of products subject to tariff reductions and the respective magnitude of the particular reductions) by comparing it to the packages of concessions granted by trading partners. Each country attempts to obtain deep tariff cuts from the major importing countries on products of export interest while granting small tariff cuts on import-sensitive products. Since all countries make similar self-interest reciprocity calculations, it is anticipated that when all is said and done (during several years of haggling) the total package will provide an equitable sharing in the gains from expanded international trade.

Unfortunately, this concept of reciprocity soon came into conflict with the most-favored-nation principle of nondiscrimination. Since any tariff cut granted by a contracting party would apply to all other contracting parties, whether or not they granted a concession in return, countries had an incentive to become *free riders* and not grant any concessions. This problem was minimized by the "principal supplier" rule, namely that negotiations for a tariff cut would always include reciprocal concessions by the principal suppliers (the largest exporters) of the product. Thus only minor suppliers could be free riders. Another technique to further reduce the free-rider problem is to define products for tariff purposes very narrowly, thereby reducing the number of countries that are interested in the product. But these techniques turned the GATT tariff conferences into a series of bilateral negotiations on narrow issues.

The outgrowth of these approaches produced tariff schedules that are very complex and often irrational. For example, the tariff schedules of the United States contain some 10,000 different product categories for the determination of the rate of duty; included in these categories are roughly 3500 textile and apparel items yet only six items covering "aircraft, spacecraft, and parts thereof" (U.S. International Trade Commission, 1976). In addition, the principal supplier rule concentrated all negotiating attention on the largest trading countries. Not only were the smaller countries free riders, but they were de facto excluded from the negotiations, as their requests for concessions were ignored. This ultimately led the developing countries to reject the GATT as a forum for discussing their trade problems; they instead turned to the United Nations, which created the U.N. Conference on Trade and Development (UNCTAD) to fill this void.

During the Kennedy Round (1962–1967) the bilateral principal-supplier technique of negotiation was abandoned in favor of an across-the-board approach, whereby every country was called upon to reduce all tariff rates by 50 percent. This certainly simplified the negotiating process, but did not eliminate controversy or difficulty. In the first place, all countries faced intense import competition in certain sectors and were unwilling to cut tariffs on selected products. It was soon recognized that this across-the-board approach could not work unless countries could exclude selected products from the general 50-percent-cut rule. Thus attention turned away from the principal supplier and toward the negotiation of "exceptions lists." The difficulties came from (1) purely domestic negotiations, in which country negotiators faced the import-competing industries' lobby pressure to exclude their product, and (2) making the reciprocity calculations to assure all contracting parties that an equitable sharing of the gains from trade would result.

As a result of the seven tariff rounds, tariff rates have been reduced to rather low levels (averaging less than 10 percent for the industrial countries). These reductions have contributed to a massive increase in world trade though, of course, other factors have also contributed. But as a consequence, there have been instances in which rapidly growing imports have displaced domestic output, causing serious injury to domestic producers and workers. Such possibilities were forseen by the original drafters of the GATT, who provided an *escape clause,* Article XIX. To paraphrase, if a concession (or GATT obligation) results in import injury to a domestic industry, the importing country may remedy the injury by withdrawing or modifying the concession, for example, by reintroducing the preconcession tariff rate. Under normal procedures, escape-clause action must be applied in a nondiscriminatory manner. In cases where the escape-clause action results in the withdrawal of a concession, compensation must be "paid" to those contracting parties that had previously granted a reciprocal concession; compensation takes the form of an alternative concession. (For a detailed treatment see Jackson, 1969, Chapter 23.)

EMERGING ISSUES.   With the success of the tariff conferences, tariffs are now quite low and no longer considered the major barrier to trade. Attention is increasingly turned to other issues such as nontariff barriers to trade, industrial restructuring, and the effects of changing exchange rates. These issues have not been fully resolved to date.

Nontariff Barriers.   During the Tokyo Round, major negotiating effort was expended to resolve disputes on such nontariff barriers as subsidies (and the application of countervailing and antidumping duties), government purchasing preferences for domestic firms, import licensing, customs valuation, and health, safety, and technical standards. The approach was to negotiate codes of conduct governing these practices.

At this point, significant disagreement still exists, to the point that not all contracting parties are willing to abide by the codes that are in force. Consequently, the provisions of the existing codes only apply to signatories of the codes, with a different list for each code.

To generalize, the codes provide the following:

Government policies to benefit domestic industries should be designed so as not to injure industries in other countries.

Government purchasing practices should conform to the principle of national treatment.

Government regulations governing international trade should not constitute a barrier to trade in their own right.

All nontariff measures should be applied in a nondiscriminatory manner.

These codes are contained in *Agreements Reached in the Tokyo Round of the Multilateral Trade Negotiations* (1979).

Industrial Restructuring. Industrial restructuring is the current term to describe adjustments that a country makes to bring its economic structure into conformity with the dictates of international comparative advantage. With the rapid growth in the newly industrializing countries (so-called NICs), the massive jump in oil prices, and worldwide inflation, the pattern of comparative advantage is changing much more rapidly than before. Such changes are associated with surges in imports of particular products that cause serious injury to import-competing producers and workers. Such injury brings intense political pressure for the government to introduce policies to avoid this injury, that is, to restrict imports. But since the injury is not due to a GATT concession or obligation, remedies for this import injury do not come under the escape clause. Instead, such remedies would give rise to cries of "protectionism" and would lead to a GATT conflict.

Such a conflict occurred in the early 1960s regarding trade in cotton textiles; it was resolved by a GATT arrangement that provided for bilateral "voluntary export-restraint agreements" to be negotiated between the importing and exporting countries. Since the early case involved powerful importing countries and weak exporting countries, the GATT arrangement was accepted. More recently, this precedent was used to justify "orderly marketing agreements" (which are the same as voluntary export-restraint agreements, which are in fact involuntary export quotas) regarding trade in shoes, color television sets, textiles (U.S. exports to the United Kingdom), steel, and automobiles, to name a few of the major cases.

These emerging conflicts have led to pressure to modify the GATT escape clause; the objective of these efforts is to negotiate a new GATT *safeguard mechanism*. The major controversy in these negotiations is between the developed countries and the developing countries over the concept of selectivity, that is, limiting imports from major suppliers only. The latter feel that a new safeguard would be used by the developed countries against the emerging export potential of the developing countries. The import-impacted countries, on the other hand, argue that a new safeguard is needed to protect the export markets of the minor suppliers, who will suffer whenever escape-clause action is applied on an most-favored-nation basis. The second element of controversy concerns the duration of permitted import limitations. The proponents of a new safeguard argue that temporary protection is justified to reduce the costs of adjustments, since slower and orderly adjustment is cheaper than rapid and disorderly adjustment. The opponents argue instead that temporary and declining protection somehow seems to always end up as permanent and increasing protection, citing the Multifibre Agreement as evidence.

No agreement has been reached to date; current indications are that no agreement is in the offing.

Exchange Rates.   Exchange-rate matters are considered under the competence of the IMF. Within the GATT the concern is the effect of exchange-rate changes on the concept of reciprocity. A country that grants a concession in return for a concession may find that the concession gained is subsequently taken away by a depreciation of the trading partner's currency.

If future exchange-rate policies of countries are adjusted to balance the balance of payments, protective policies will not influence the magnitude of trade, but only the structure of trade, that is, trade policies will influence which products are imported and which are exported. And changes in trade policies will influence the trade pattern of trading partners.

A future issue that is just beginning to come before the GATT is the problem of export financing by government financing agencies such as the U.S. Export-Import Bank. The problem is that many countries are attempting to stimulate exports by granting foreign importers especially favorable credit conditions, that is, below market rates of interest and extremely long maturities. The effect of such competitive financing "wars" is to distort trade to third countries. Thus traditional remedies against export subsidies (which such financing practices amount to) are not applicable. This issue will have to be resolved through international negotiations and could very likely take the form of a code of conduct governing export credits.

THE ORGANIZATION FOR ECONOMIC COOPERATION AND DEVELOPMENT

The Organization for Economic Cooperation and Development (OECD) is an organization that provides for intergovernmental discussion among 24 industrial countries in the fields of economic and social policy. The subject matter is extremely diverse.

ORIGINS.   In 1947 Europe was in economic chaos as a result of the destruction of war and the continuation of governmental controls. A serious shortage of dollars prevailed in Europe to pay for needed imports. Although the U.S. government had anticipated these problems by providing a large loan to the British government in 1946 and through its participation in the U.N. Relief and Rehabilitation Administration, the United States subsequently deemed these inadequate. The secretary of state, General George C. Marshall, in 1947 challenged the European governments (including those of Eastern Europe) to cooperate in the resolution of their economic problems in exchange for dollars (the Marshall Plan). To divide up the proffered resources and to coordinate their programs, the Western European governments formed the Organization for European Economic Cooperation (OEEC), which subsequently became the OECD.

One of the major accomplishments of the OEEC was the reciprocal reduction of quantitative import restrictions among themselves through the Intra-European Payments Scheme, which permitted partial settlements of imbalances in their payments among themselves (1949). This was followed (1950) by the establishment of the European Payments Union, which provided for multilateral clearing of such imbalances.

The cooperation established among Western European nations through the OEEC undoubtedly laid the basis for the eventual establishment of the European Economic Community.

The OEEC might have been abandoned in 1952, the end of the Marshall Plan, but there remained considerable opportunities for trade liberalization among the member governments (Western Europe had divided into the European Community and the European Free Trade Association), and thus it was continued until 1961, when the original 18 OEEC countries, Canada, and the United States formed the OECD, joined later (1964) by Japan.

STATED PURPOSES. The OECD was formed in 1960 ". . . to achieve the highest sustainable economic growth and employment and a rising standard of living in member countries, while maintaining financial stability, and thus to contribute to the development of the world economy; to contribute to sound economic expansion in member as well as nonmember countries in the process of economic development; and to contribute to the expansion of world trade on a multilateral, nondiscriminatory basis in accordance with international obligations" (OECD, 1980).

STRUCTURE. The OECD today (1980) is essentially a forum where the representation of member governments can talk about their common problems, common either among themselves or vis à vis the rest (underdeveloped) of the world. Not surprisingly, the OECD is therefore a collection of committees, expert groups, and working parties.

The central body is the council, which is composed of the permanent representatives of the member governments to the OECD and which guides the operations of the organization.

There are specialized committees that deal with general problem areas: development assistance, industry, agriculture and fisheries, trade, energy, manpower and social affairs, science, education, and various financial and fiscal matters. Many of the committees have expert groups or working groups to deal with specific problems (in all about 200 as of 1980).

In addition, the OECD contains several semiautonomous bodies, more-limited membership activities, and specially financed projects. These include the Nuclear Energy Agency, which was formed in 1958 to deal with problems of nuclear energy; the Development Center (1962), which does research on the problems of less developed countries; the Center for Educational Research and Innovation (1968); the Road Research Program (1968); and the International Energy Agency (1974), under whose auspices an agreement for sharing oil among the members was worked out.

Supporting this complex organization is a secretariat of 1700 professional economists and other experts. The secretariat is headed by a secretary-general, who is appointed for a term of 5 years by the members.

ACTIVITIES. The secretariat provides a data bank for members and, where appropriate, the public. It collects information from member governments and processes it for comparability. Its compilations of national income, trade, economic indicators, and financial stastics are probably the best known of the publicly disseminated data.

However, it provides much more detailed data. For example, the annual report of the Development Assistance Committee provides the only comprehensive report on flows of grants, loans, and investments from the richer to the poorer countries.

The secretariat uses its vast statistical resources to make semiannual short-term (12–18 months) forecasts of the key economic variables of each of its members. These are published in its biannual *Economic Outlook*. They merit special attention because an effort is made to take account of the interactions among countries.

In addition, an annual review of economic policy in each member government is done by the secretariat; it is published after a review by the member country and other governments.

Occasionally, the OECD will appoint a group of independent experts from outside the secretariat to examine a particular situation and publish the results. In 1971, for example, Jean Rey headed a group to report on the relations between trade, investment, and monetary policy after the Brettons Woods (fixed exchange rate) system had broken down.

THE U.N. CONFERENCE ON TRADE AND DEVELOPMENT

The U.N. Conference on Trade and Development (UNCTAD) was created in 1964 as a permanent organ of the General Assembly as the brainchild of Raul Prebisch, its first secretary-general. The creation of UNCTAD, however, also reflects the serious dissatisfaction of the developing countries with the GATT as an institution to assist them in solving their trade problems. The failure of the GATT in this area is often attributed to the principle of reciprocity, which is used in all GATT negotiations. Since the developing countries experience serious foreign-exchange shortages, they have little capacity for granting concessions in trade negotiations; therefore, they have had little success in obtaining concessions from the developed countries on products of export interest to them.

The developing countries charge that the GATT is ruled on the basis of economic power rather than any equitable voting system, and that this economic power has been used to their disadvantage. On the other hand, since UNCTAD is also an international organization with agreements enforced only by voluntary compliance, the voting majority of the developing countries is impotent.

Nevertheless, UNCTAD has proved to be a useful organization for the developing countries if one does not judge its effectiveness in comparison with purely national bodies. The major work of UNCTAD is structured into a number of permanent committees with specific charges, as follows:

Committee on Commodities is concerned with stable prices and export earnings for developing-country exports of primary commodities.

Committee on Manufactures has produced the generalized system of (tariff) preferences (GSP) under which exports of most manufactured industrial products from developing to developed countries receive duty-free treatment. This committee also deals with nontariff measures and restrictive business practices by multinational corporations, and a semiautonomous body deals with the transfer of technology.

Committee on Shipping attempts to improve shipping schedules and pricing to the benefit of developing countries (this is an issue that is not treated in the GATT).

Committee on Invisibles and Financing also deals with issues outside the scope of the GATT including development finance, tourism, insurance, and so forth.

Much of the work of UNCTAD actually occurs in *ad hoc* working groups, often such groups meet periodically and achieve progress slowly over time. Though somewhat dated, an excellent treatment of the work of UNCTAD is contained in Gosovic (1972).

SOURCES AND SUGGESTED REFERENCES

Sources

Agreements Reached in the Tokyo Round of the Multilateral Trade Negotiations. Message From the President of the United States. House Document No. 96-153, Part 1 (96th Congress, First Session).

Auboin, R. *The Bank for International Settlements.* Princeton: Princeton University International Finance Section, May 1955.

Coombs, C. *The Area of International Finance.* New York: Wiley, 1976.

Dam, K.W. *The GATT: Law and International Economic Organization.* Chicago: University of Chicago Press, 1970.

Goreux, L. *Compensatory Financing Facility.* Washington, D.C.: International Monetary Fund, 1980.

Gosovic, B. *UNCTAD: Conflict and Compromise.* Leiden: Sijthoff, 1972.

Gold, J. *Conditionality.* Washington, D.C.: International Monetary Fund, 1979.

IMF. *IMF Survey: Supplement on the Fund.* Washington, D.C.: International Monetary Fund, September 30, 1980.

IMF. *IMF Survey.* Washington, D.C.: International Monetary Fund, May 2, 1977.

Hurni, B.S. *The Lending Policy of the World Bank in the 1970's.* Boulder, CO.: Westview Press, 1980.

Jackson, J.H. *World Trade and the Law of GATT.* New York: Bobbs-Merrill, 1969.

Mason, E.S., and R.E. Asher. *The World Bank Since Bretton Woods.* Washington, D.C.: Brookings Institution, 1973.

Murray, T. *Trade Preferences for Developing Countries.* London: Macmillan, 1977.

OECD. *Activities of the OECD, 1979.* Paris: OECD, 1980.

Solomon, R. *The International Monetary System, 1945–76.* New York: Harper and Row, 1977.

Southard, F. *The Evolution of the International Monetary Fund.* Princeton: Princeton University International Finance Section, 1977.

Schmidt, W. "Rethinking the Multilateral Development Banks," *Policy Review,* Vol. XXI (1979), pp. 55–86.

Triffin, R. *Gold and the Dollar Crises.* New Haven: Yale University Press, 1960.

U.S. International Trade Commission. *Tariff Schedules of the United States Annotated (1976)* as amended. Washington, D.C.: USITC Publication 749, 1976.

World Bank. *Questions and Answers.* Washington, D.C.: World Bank, March 1976.

World Bank. *Annual Report.* Washington, D.C.: World Bank, 1980.

Zamora, S.A. "Voting in International Economic Organizations," *The American Journal of International Law,* Vol. LXXIV (1980), p. 568.

Suggested References

Curzon, G. *Multilateral Commercial Diplomacy*. London: Michael Joseph, 1965.

Dam, K. W. *The GATT: Law and International Economic Organization*. Chicago: University of Chicago Press, 1970.

Department of State. *U.S. Contributions to International Organization*. Washington, D.C.: U.S. Government Printing Office, 1978.

de Vries, M. G. *The International Monetary Fund, 1966–71*, Vols. I and II. Washington: The International Monetary Fund, 1976.

Gilbert, M. *Quest for World Monetary Order*. New York: Wiley, 1980.

Horsefield, J. K. *The International Monetary Fund, 1945–65*. Vols. I–III. Washington: International Monetary Fund, 1969.

Hudec, R. E. *The GATT Legal System and World Trade Diplomacy*. New York: Praeger, 1975.

Jackson, J. H . *World Trade and the Law of GATT*. New York: Bobbs-Merrill, 1969.

Jacobsson, E. E. *A Life for Sound Money*, Oxford: Clarendon Press, 1979.

Williamson, J. *The Failure of World Monetary Problems, 1971–74*. New York: New York University Press, 1977.

SECTION **6**

FORMATION OF INTERNATIONAL ECONOMIC POLICY

CONTENTS

ECONOMIC AND LEGAL PRINCIPLES	4	Treasury Department	11
		Labor Department	11
Economic	4	Defense Department	11
Legal	5	Agriculture Department	11
OBJECTIVE AND EFFECTS	5	Justice Department	11
		Eeport-Import Bank	12
THE FORUM	7	Federal Trade Commission	12
		International Trade Commission	12
Office of the U.S. Trade		Securities and Exchange Commission	12
Representative	11		
Commerce Department	11	SOURCES AND SUGGESTED	
State Department	11	REFERENCES	12

FORMATION OF INTERNATIONAL ECONOMIC POLICY

Charles R. Johnston, Jr.

For the individual concerned with international business transactions, the formation of international economic policy is a particularly valuable subject to understand. Knowing why a given policy exists and how it is established allows one to conduct international business with a greater degree of confidence and control. It also permits a better sense of the predictable and unpredictable events that both short- and long-term business planning require.

There are three general factors that govern the formation of international economic policy:

1. Economic and legal principles that serve as fundamental considerations in international economic relations.
2. The objectives and effects of the policy.
3. The infrastructure and operational dynamics of the forum in which the policy is formed.

Before these factors are discussed, however, the parameters of this section must be outlined.

Policy is a word used in many different contexts. For the purposes of this section, policy is treated as a defined, predetermined course of conduct that is selected to guide present and future decisions. Policy should not, as is too often the case, be confused with the transactional instruments that carry out a policy. The instruments may change, but the policy can remain the same. This distinction is exemplified in the international business setting by the policy of many countries to maintain or establish production capacity in specific "vital" industries, such as steel. The instruments by which that policy is carried out may include government subsidies or other forms of government support. One might argue that the use of subsidies when the government seeks to support an industry is a policy in and of itself. But the commitment to use subsidies rather than, for example, imposing higher tariffs, may simply be a method by which a liberal trade policy is implemented. Such a policy would encourage trade flows by, among other things, not raising tariff barriers. The use of subsidies, therefore, would be the most appropriate *instrument* to accomplish both policies: that is, establishing a vital industry and encouraging trade flows.

The preceding discussion of the differentiation between policy and policy instruments demonstrates the complexity of analyzing the formation of international economic policy. What is policy, as opposed to the transactional instrument to carry out the policy? Are there overlapping or conflicting policies? These are questions that must be addressed when policy analysis is conducted. If the instrument is the focal point of analysis rather than the underlying policy, or if the policy is not considered in the context of other interrelated policies, the analysis will be misplaced and misleading.

The complexity of analysis is further exacerbated by the international character of economic-policy formation. In reality, international economic policy has both an international and a domestic perspective. The truly international side of such policy formation takes place at the international level, where all countries treat each other, at least formally, as equals. This level produces policy that is multilateral and "public" in perspective, with the agreement and consensus of all parties being sought before the policy becomes effective among them. The domestic side of international economic policy treats policy in a more unilateral manner. Thus from this perspective international economic policy dictates how an individual government will treat international economic issues, in relation to both the way it relates to other governments and how its citizens will participate in international transactions. Examples of the two levels are embodied in the U.N. Charter on Economic Rights and Duties and the U.S. Export Administration Act. The charter states what its signatories agree should be international economic policy. The Export Administration Act is a unilateral legislative decision made by the U.S. government that expresses its policy on the regulation of exports and the method by which that policy will be carried out.

Taking the above-mentioned conditions into account, the balance of this section will now turn to a review of the three governing factors influencing the formation of international economic policy.

ECONOMIC AND LEGAL PRINCIPLES

ECONOMIC.   International economic policy in the current global setting is founded upon economic principles and theories generally advanced by the schools of classical political economy (eighteenth century) and socialism (nineteenth century).

Classical political economy espouses a doctrine of utilizing a free market and private investment in capital to generate and distribute wealth on the most efficient and progressive basis. It was from this school of economic theory that David Ricardo in 1817 enunciated his principle of comparative advantage, on which the policy of free trade and the current international trade infrastructure are based. Ricardo's principle teaches that a country has a comparative advantage in the production of those goods that it can produce *relatively* more efficiently than other goods. Thus regardless of the general level of the country's productivity or labor costs relative to those of other countries, it should produce for export those goods in which it has the greatest competitive advantage and import those goods in which it has the greatest competitive disadvantage. Ricardo's principle is conditioned upon the assumption that there is a free market in operation; that is, no government intervention that would have an unnatural effect on the laws of supply and demand.

The economic school of socialism, on the other hand, emphasizes the labor theory of value and discounts capitalism as well as the free-market principle as means by which wealth should be created and distributed. This school prefers a state-controlled economy in which the factors of production are owned and managed by the public authority for the general benefit of the populace.

International economic policy in today's global setting is a composite of these two schools of economic thought—and is characterized as *postcapitalist political economy*. This composite is reflected in both international and domestic economic policies. Notwithstanding their merging in current political economic practice, the two schools still serve as basic sources upon which the formation of economic policy is based.

LEGAL.   Transactions and relations among governments and citizens in international affairs require predictability and security in order for them to continue on a rational basis. Policy formation in international economic affairs is heavily reliant upon this predictability and security. To achieve the environment in which interaction can take place based on certain assumptions, nations have, by consensus, adopted a set of rules that generally govern international relations. The cornerstone of these rules is the recognition of the nation state and the supremacy, or sovereignty, of its civil authority. Thus in accordance with the concept of sovereignty, sovereigns (i.e., national governments) agree not to intervene in their counterparts' domestic affairs without approval. Moreover, sovereigns adhere to the doctrine of equality among states, which means all sovereign states enjoy equal rights and obligations in their international relations.

A consequence of the concept of sovereignty is the legal principle known as *jurisdiction*. By exercising its jurisdiction, the government of the sovereign state asserts the authority to regulate transactions within its boundaries, activities of its citizens, and in some circumstances, activities outside its boundaries that threaten its security as a state or its governmental functions.

Jurisdiction, however, is limited in light of the doctrine of equality of states. Thus the principle of sovereign immunity generally provides that no state may be subject to the jurisdiction of another state's courts, and that the courts of one state may not question the validity of the official acts of another sovereign insofar as those acts purport to take effect within the latter's jurisdiction. The "official" acts qualification is worthy of note because it serves as a delimitation of the extent of sovereign immunity. Thus a state's public acts are immune from jurisdiction (*jure imperu)*, whereas its private or commercial acts are not (*jure gestionis*). This means that if a government is involved in a venture for strictly commercial purposes, it could be subject to the jurisdiction of another country's courts, notwithstanding the sovereign-immunity principle.

OBJECTIVE AND EFFECTS

The formation of international economic policy at either the international or the domestic level is clearly subject to the objective sought to be achieved by implementing the policy. In a broad context, the national and international objectives of international economic policy are founded upon the economic principles mentioned earlier, which in different ways focus on the creation and distribution of wealth. These economic principles give rise to one of the most difficult policy issues confronting governments: balancing, on the one hand, the pursuit of economic efficiency and a minimum concentration of power in a free market setting against, on the other hand, the restriction of international transactions for the purpose of furthering interests that, for various social or political reasons, require shelter from competition.

The creation and distribution of wealth, however, have not been the exclusive goals of international economic policy following World War II. For many countries, and for most multilateral organizations established after the war, a primary objective of their international economic policy has been the maintenance of world peace while at the same time promoting economic development. This objective, which served as the driving motivation for the establishment of the United Nations, the General Agreement on Tariffs and Trade (GATT) and several other post-World War II multilateral institutions, is explained as follows:

> The fundamental choice is whether countries will struggle against each other for wealth and power, or work together for security and mutual advantage. . . . The experience of cooperation in the task of earning a living promotes both the habit and the techniques of common effort and helps make permanent the mutual confidence on which peace depends. U.S. PROPOSALS FOR A DRAFT CHARTER FOR AN INTERNATIONAL TRADE ORGANIZATION (1946).

The objective of international economic cooperation, however, becomes more difficult as economies become increasingly interdependent. Shifts in economic and political strengths between countries test the system by which the interdependence is promoted. The more closely distinct political entities relate on an economic basis, the more likely friction will develop when one party does not cooperate on a basis required by the other. This is particularly true when the parties (i.e., countries) are equals in a formal sense and consider their authority and control over their domestic economic matters to be virtually inviolate.

As Richart N. Cooper (1967) pointed out, achieving national economic goals is made much more difficult when a country becomes increasingly interdependent with others. First, the number and magnitude of disturbances affecting a country's balance of payments is increased. Second, national authorities are restrained in taking actions to reach national goals. Third, the adjustments necessary for integration may hurt some sectors of a national economy more than is necessary. Finally, Cooper noted, the system of international agreements accompanying interdependence reduces the number of policy instruments available to national governments for use in achieving their national economic goals.

The global trade environment, reflecting the trend toward further interdependence, often seems to be more confrontational than cooperative. The current emphasis on national security as an objective of international economic policy is a manifestation of this confrontational environment. However, the confrontations are vented in multilateral and national institutions and guided by rules that have been designed to reconcile these confrontations on a political and economic, rather than military, basis. The results may not be as timely or responsive as we would like, but the global framework for economic problem-solving certainly helps promote rational solutions to the far-reaching economic questions confronting the world as national economies become more closely intertwined.

The primary objectives of the creation of wealth and peace permeate virtually all of international economic policy. There are other objectives, however, that might be considered components or factors in the formula for wealth or peace. These factors appear on a recurring basis in national documents, such as our Declaration of Independence, and international documents, such as the U.N. Charter of Economic Rights and Duties of States or the U.N. Charter for an International Trade Organization. The factors are full employment, adequate access to supplies and resources, diversification of the national economy, rising living standards for the country's citizens, and improved terms of trade for the products that the country exports. Other objectives are also relevant factors in the formation of international economic policy, but unlike the recurring objectives mentioned above, the importance of these other, more detailed, objectives varies depending on the relative development of the nation's economy and the political/economic principles of its government. Such objectives include preserving the environment and natural resources, maintaining national security and a positive military posture, and promoting human rights.

Clearly the more objectives a country tries to balance and incorporate in its international economic policy, the more difficulty it will have formulating and implementing the policy. The protracted difficulties inherent in forming international economic policy that attempts to incorporate numerous, and at times varying, objectives is exemplified in the potential effects that the policy can have. John Jackson, in his text *Legal Problems of International Economic Relations* (1977), lists the following effects that should be considered when trade restraints are undertaken for policy reasons:

1. The protective effect.
2. The consumption effect.
3. The revenue effect.
4. The redistribution effect.
5. The terms-of-trade effect.
6. The competitive effect.
7. The income effect.
8. The balance-of-payments effect.

Jackson comments on their impact in the context of varying policy interests:

> A [trade restraint] can be analyzed from the standpoint of a plant, industry, region, factor of production, country, or the world, and one interest's meat may be another's poison. In particular, an interference is likely to alter trade, prices, output, and consumption, and to reallocate resources, change factor proportions, redistribute income, change employment, and alter the balance of payments.

THE FORUM

The principles, objectives, and effects discussed above are basic considerations in the formation of international economic policy. These components, however, are ultimately subject to the operational and political dynamics of the forum in which the policy is formulated and enunciated. The members of the forum, their de facto and *de jure* relationships, their subjective attitudes on the basic principles and objectives, the interests and influences of their constituencies, and the interests of the forum as an entity all affect the strength with which the principles and objectives are communicated and consolidated within the forum for the purpose of establishing an international economic policy. Thus the variance of these factors dictates that international economic policy statements emerging from, for example, the United Nations will differ in scope and effect from those emanating from the Conference of Non-Aligned Countries. Similarly, international economic policy formed at the national level will be different from that formed at the international level, and policy will also differ between nations, notwithstanding the attempt and stated purpose of most international economic organizations to coordinate the international economic policies of their members. The same dichotomy appears in federal systems of government in which the federal government seeks to coordinate and rationalize, when possible, the economic policies of the state governments, which may indirectly or directly affect the federal government's international economic policy.

Making an orderly analysis of the policy-formation process in a given forum requires a firm understanding of the organizational infrastructure of the forum that applies to the given policy-formation process. Using the forum of the U.S. government as an example, the impact that the organizational infrastructure has on policy formation becomes evident. As I.M. Destler states in his book *Making Foreign Economic Policy* (1980):

> Substantive complexity brings with it organizational complexity. Tensions among domestic and international objectives are hardly new to U.S. experience, but their apparent increase both offers evidence that domestic-international interdependence may be growing and illuminates the problem in American policy management that results.

The organizational complexity to which Destler refers is increasingly evident in the trade-policy area and has been recognized both in the congressional and executive branches as well as by private-sector interests. Recently the government has taken action to consolidate and coordinate the trade-policy functions within the executive branch. The balance of this section describes these recent actions, which serve as excellent examples of the importance organization has in the formation and implementation of international economic policy.

In recognition of the growing impact that international economic relations had on domestic interests, Section 135 of the Trade Act of 1974 established an institutional framework to ensure that representatives of the private sector had the opportunity to make known to the U.S. trade negotiators their views regarding negotiation objectives and bargaining positions in the Tokyo Round of multilateral trade negotiations. The mechanism also permitted the designated private-sector representatives to be informed of developments during the course of the trade negotiations.

The actual structure sanctioned in the Trade Act consisted of the following committees:

1. The Advisory Commitee for Trade Negotiations (ACTN) consisting of representatives from government, labor, industry, agriculture, service industries, consumer interests, and the general public. The U.S. Trade Representative served as its chairman.
2. Three Policy Advisory Committees for industry, labor, and agriculture.

3. Forty-one industry-, labor-, and agriculture-sector technical advisory committees.

Section 135 also provided exemptions from antitrust and other restricted activities specified in the Federal Advisory Committee Act (P.L. 92-463).

In actual application, many participants saw the mechanism serving more as an information-distribution tool than as a policy-making process. Some even argued that it was used as a compromising device to neutralize private-sector opposition to the trade negotiations.

Notwithstanding the problems that some parties had with the process, Section 1103 of the Trade Agreements Act of 1979 continued the private-sector-advisory-committee mechanism. The basic committee structure remains intact, with the U.S. Trade Representative managing the committees jointly with the Departments of Agriculture, Commerce, and Labor. Section 1103 also amends the original format in order to

1. Broaden the mandate of the advisory committees to include support of implementation of trade agreements and other trade-policy activities.

2. Provide complete discretion for the President to establish general policy advisory committees "on an appropriate basis." This contemplates advisory committees for agriculture, industry, labor, *and services.*

3. Provide for committee reports to the President, Congress, and the U.S. Trade Representative regarding the operation and effect on U.S. economic interests of new trade agreements.

4. Provide, to the extent practicable, that advisory committee members be informed and consulted before and during any negotiations and be permitted to participate in international meetings to the extent that the head of the U.S. delegation deems appropriate. Private-sector advisers, however, are not permitted to speak on behalf of the United States.

5. Add to advisory-committee exemptions by excusing committee members from the financial and other reporting requirements of Title XVIII of the Food and Agriculture Act of 1977.

The Trade Agreements Act of 1979, which President Carter called "the most important and far-reaching piece of trade legislation in the history of the United States," also served as the necessary catalyst for an executive-branch reorganization intended to improve its trade-policy and administrative functions. The events leading to the reorganization reveal why it took its ultimate form.

In 1977 certain senators were becoming aware of private-sector complaints regarding the complexity and seeming lack of direction of the trade-policy infrastructure of the executive branch. A few years earlier, in 1974, the Commission on the Organization of the Government for the Conduct of Foreign Policy had reported that centralization and coordination of executive-branch functions in the area of international economic policy was necessary. Intertwined with the congressional attention to the trade-policy dilemma were growing concerns by certain private-sector interests, and consequently certain members of Congress, that Treasury Department enforcement of the antidumping and countervailing-duty laws was inadequate and even biased in favor of importing interests. This, in turn, was interpreted as undermining the policy that Congress, with its authority to regulate imports and exports, had expressed legislatively. The Commerce, State, and Defense departments were also coming under fire at this time for the drawn-out, arbitrary, and confused manner in which applications for validated export licenses for high-technology goods were being (or not being) processed. Finally, the overwhelming trade deficit drew attention to the meager export financing the Export-Import Bank was providing in contrast to its foreign counterparts and the decreasing share of world export markets held by U.S. producers. By the close of 1979, Congress had reacted to this scenario by amending the Export-Import Bank Act to permit more-generous export financing, and amending the antidumping, countervailing-duty, and export-administration procedures to clarify and expedite actions under those laws. At the same time, however, support for a major reorganization of the executive-branch trade infrastructure had swelled both in Congress and in the private sector. There was general dissatisfaction with the process of trade-policy formation and implementation, and the legislative actions just mentioned were not enough to curb the momentum.

With the passage of the Trade Agreements Act of 1979, major congressional proponents of reorganization, led by Senators William Roth, Jr., and Abraham Ribicoff, pushed for a concomitant reorganization. The President's private-sector Advisory Committee for Trade Negotiations echoed the call for a new infrastructure.

Executive Order 12188 (January 2, 1980) reflected a measured step in the direction of consolidation and coordination of trade policy and enforcement. Rather than establishing a new department for international trade (an idea that lost some power in the light of the problems of the new Department of Energy and the creation of a Department of Education), the President opted for a plan pushed by the Office of Management and Budget. That plan sought to strengthen the Special Trade Representative's office in the trade-policy sphere and to transfer the enforcement of countervailing-duty and antidumping laws to the Commerce Department. In addition, Foreign Service officers stationed overseas for the purpose of promoting U.S. exports would also be transferred out of the "political" State Department to the "commercial" Commerce Department.

The reorganization accomplished essentially two things. It placed the U.S. Trade Representative in the chief role as adviser to the President on trade-policy issues, thereby reducing the formal authority the Departments of State and Treasury had exercised in this area. Secondly, it upgraded the Department of Commerce's role in export promotion and import regulation by consolidating those functions within that agency.

Some commentators, however, feel that many problem areas remain that further reorganization will have to address. For example, the overlap of the Office of the U.S. Trade Representative and Commerce Department in the area of import regulation and its policy implications may cause continued confusion. Another problem may arise when the Office of the U.S. Trade Representative attempts to formulate an informed policy on a specific subject and finds that it must assign a substantial portion of the work to agencies, such as the State Department, that had been exorcised from the lead policy-formation position. The inexorable "turf fights" will likely continue. These and other foreseen problems cause the continued discussion of further consolidation of trade-policy authority or at least trade-policy coordination within the executive branch.

There follows a list of various executive departments and agencies and their relevant trade authorities in the wake of the 1980 reorganization, pending further consolidation:

Office of the U.S. Trade Representative. Has general responsibility to formulate trade policy, negotiate trade agreements, and serve as the chief representative of the United States in discussions with foreign entities in GATT, the United Nations Conference on Trade and Development (UNCTAD), the Organization for Economic Cooperation and Development (OECD), or other forums where trade or commodity issues, including East-West trade, are primary issues under consideration; conducts investigations and appropriate dispute-settlement procedures for unfair trade practices having an adverse effect on U.S. commerce or actions violating a trade agreement (19 USC 2411); administers the Generalized System of Preferences (19 USC 2461); and chairs the Trade Policy Committee (19 USC 1872).

Commerce Department. Promotes exports, through, for example, the Foreign Service Act of 1946, as amended (22 USC 801 et seq.); regulates exports, through the Export Administration Act, as amended (50 USC app. 2401); conducts investigations regarding imports threatening national security (19 USC 1862); administers the antidumping and countervailing-duty laws (19 USC 1673 and 1671); administers the trade-adjustment-assistance program for firms (19 USC 2341); monitors effects of imports of textiles on U.S. industry; with Department of the Interior, administers quotas on watch imports from U.S. territories, with Departments of Treasury and Health and Human Services, administers the laws authorizing duty-free entry of imports of scientific and technical equipment by nonprofit institutions; administers the Foreign Trade Zone Law (19 USC 81 *a–u*); and Bureau of the Census compiles trade statistics (13 USC 301).

State Department. Registers and licenses exports on the U.S. Munitions List (22 CFR pt. 121; 22 USC 1934).

Treasury Department. Administers embargoes and monitors foreign-asset controls through various regulations pursuant to the Trading with the Enemy Act [50 USC app. 5(b)] and the International Emergency Economic Powers Act (50 USC 1701); also is responsible for the administration of various foreign-exchange, banking, and tax laws affecting international monetary affairs and foreign direct investment; Customs Service is part of the Department.

Labor Department. Administers worker-trade-adjustment-assistance program (19 USC 2271).

Defense Department. Participates in clearing items for export license under the Export Administration and Munitions Control laws.

Agriculture Department. Participates in the administration of Section 22 import restrictions under the Agriculture Adjustment Act of 1933, as amended (7 USC 624); Commodity Credit Corporation administers food exports under P.L. 480 (Agricultural Trade Development and Assistance Act of 1954, as amended); administers foreign-service activities under the Agricultural Trade Act of 1978; restricts agricultural imports to the terms of agricultural marketing orders (7 USC 608E); participates in administration of the Meat Import Law (7 USC 1202 note); and promotes export generally (7 USC 612c).

Justice Department. Enforces antitrust violations in foreign commerce that have an effect on the U.S. market (e.g., Sherman Antitrust Act, 15 USC 1–7); enforces

Wilson Tariff Act, which prohibits anticompetitive behavior in the importation of goods into the United States (15 USC 8); may enforce Antidumping Act of 1916 (15 USC 72); is partially responsible for enforcement of the Foreign Corrupt Practices Act (15 USC 78 *dd*–1 and *dd*–2, 78 *m*(*b*) and 78 *ff*); and enforces Clayton Antitrust Act (15 USC 12).

Export-Import Bank.   Provides direct financing, loan guarantees, and insurance generally for foreign buyers purchasing U.S. goods (12 USC 635*h*).

Federal Trade Commission.   Enforces Federal Trade Commission Act, which declares unlawful unfair methods of competition in commerce among the states and with foreign countries (15 USC 41–58); enforces Clayton Act Section 2 which prohibits price discrimination, particularly regarding payment of commissions overseas (15 USC 12); administers anti-trust exemptions for export trade associations under the Webb-Pomerene Act (15 USC 62).

International Trade Commission.   Conducts injury portion of investigations under the antidumping and countervailing-duty laws; recommends import relief from increasing imports under Section 201 of the Trade Act of 1974 (19 USC 2251); provides relief from unfair import trade practices under Section 337 of the Tariff Act of 1930 (19 USC 1337); recommends import relief from imports from communist countries under Section 406 of the Trade Act of 1974 (19 USC 2436); conducts investigations regarding impact of imports on agricultural-price-support programs under Section 22 of the Agricultural Adjustment Act; provides the President with probable-economic-effect advice regarding coverage of specified articles under the Generalized System of Preferences (GSP); compiles the Tariff Schedules of the United States; provides advice to the President regarding the economic impact of trade retaliation or proposed trade agreements; and conducts general studies regarding trade at request of Congress or the President.

Securities and Exchange Commission.   Enforces in part, the Foreign Corrupt Practices Act; enforces antifraud provisions of the securities laws applied extraterritorially [15 USC 77*q*(*a*), 78 *j*(*b*), 78 (*o*) (*c*) (1)].

SOURCES AND SUGGESTED REFERENCES

Cooper, R.N. "National Economic Policy in an Interdependent World Economy," *Yale Law Journal,* Vol. LXXVI (1967), p. 1273.

Department of State, *U.S. Proposals for a Draft Charter for an International Trade Organization,* Washington, D.C.: State Department, Pub. No. 2411, 1946, pp. 1–2.

Destler, I.M. *Making Foreign Economic Policy,* Washington D.C.: Brookings Institution, 1980, p. 6.

Jackson, J. *Legal Problems of International Economic Relations,* St. Paul: West, 1977, p. 9.

Johnston, C.R. "Statement," *U.S. Trade Policy: Hearings Before the Subcomm. on Trade of the House Comm. on Ways and Means,* 96th Cong., 2d Sess., Serial 96–119 (1980), p. 604.

Kapp, K.W. and L.L. Kapp, eds. *History of Economic Thought.* New York: Barnes & Noble, 1949.

THE POLITICAL ENVIRONMENTS OF MULTINATIONAL CORPORATIONS

CONTENTS

THE NATURE OF THE POLITICAL
ENVIRONMENT   3

The Multiplicity of Political
Environments   3
  Many governments   3
  Nongovernment actors and the
  political process   3
  Uniqueness of a corporation's
  environment   4
  The issue context   4
Opportunities, Challenges, and
Problems   4

LEVELS OF THE POLITICAL
ENVIRONMENT   4

State of Origin   4
Host States   5
Regional Organizations   6
Functional Organizations   7
International Organizations   7

STATES OF ORIGIN: CONCERNS
AND POLICIES   8

Economic Factors   8
Trade-union concerns and policies   8
Concerns of competing firms   9
  Protection of the national economy   9
Political Factors   10
  Foreign-policy issues   10
  Proper behavior   10
  Issues of national jurisdiction   11

HOST STATE: CONCERNS AND
POLICIES   11

Ownership and Control   11
Financial Flows and Balance of
Payments   11
Employment Security and Labor
Matters   12
Impact of Technology   12
Information and Disclosure   13
Overly Effective Competitor   13
Exploitation of Natural Resources   13
Transborder Data Flows   13
Neo-Imperialism   14
MNC Benefits and Host-State
Incentives   14

MNC–HOST-STATE RELATIONS   14

Conflict and Cooperation   14
  The power balance   14
Changing Requirements   15
  The obsolescing bargain   16
  Limits to greater host-country control   16
  Regional cooperation by states   17

THE INTERNATIONAL POLITICAL
ENVIRONMENT   18

Rationale for International Political
Activities   18
International Governmental Actions   18
  The Organization for Economic
  Cooperation and Development   18
  The United Nations   18
Trade Unions and Nongovernmental
Organizations   19
International Law   20

CONCLUSION   20

THE POLITICAL ENVIRONMENTS OF MULTINATIONAL CORPORATIONS

David H. Blake

THE NATURE OF THE POLITICAL ENVIRONMENT

The political context is critical for firms engaged in international business activities. In some situations it presents substantial business opportunities for companies; in others it can create significant obstacles for corporate strategy and headaches for managers. More generally, though, it is an important component of the overall context within which international business is pursued. This chapter will examine the concept of the political environment for multinational corporations and will identify the different levels at which political environments exist. Critical issues in these political environments will be discussed.

THE MULTIPLICITY OF POLITICAL ENVIRONMENTS. To understand the importance and the nature of the political environment, it is necessary to recognize and accept the fact that there are multiple political environments. For this reason the plural form is used in the title of this chapter. The multiplicity of the environments stems from many different factors.

Many Governments. First, international business activity intersects a number of different political entities. There are municipal and provincial governments, regions within individual countries, such as the Northeast region of Brazil, specific countries (more than 160 of them), regional organizations such as the Andean Group that are composed of a number of countries, functional international organizations such as the Organization of Petroleum Exporting Countries (OPEC), and international institutions such as the United Nations.

Nongovernment Actors and the Political Process. Also shaping the political environment are hundreds and in some cases thousands of nongovernmental interest groups at each of the above levels that engage in political activity to advance their particular views. These views encompass everything from the basic role of private enterprise to the encouragement of disadvantaged groups to protection of the indigenous culture. The successes and failures of such efforts constitute a part of the corporation's political environment. Moreover, the involvement of groups in the political process and the nature of that process itself establish the political context within which international business activity is pursued. In sum, the political environment for international business is far more than the pronouncements and decisions of official government bodies. It is also the social and political activities by which issues are defined, expressed, and pursued in a society.

Uniqueness of a Corporation's Environment.   Adding to the complexity of the political environment is the fact that the meaning and impact of the environments found in a specific country vary with the company or business activity. A company engaged in the extraction of raw materials will find a different political environment from that of a high-technology, capital-intensive company, which in turn will encounter an environment different from that of a labor-intensive, intermediate-goods industry. In addition, within each industry category the managerial style and past history of individual companies will have helped to develop a political environment that is unique to the specific company. Some companies are viewed very positively; others have negative reputations that last well beyond the initial events causing these negative views.

The Issue Context.   The political environment for a specific company often depends upon the particular issues of importance to the political entity at a given point in time. For example, a company that engages in substantial importing of nonessential materials into Brazil, a country struggling to overcome its huge balance-of-payments deficit, will face a very different environment from that of a company that has a positive impact on Brazil's balance of payments. The substance of the issues of concern and the particular timing of the corporation's impact on those issues are important determinants of the company's political environment. A number of the more critical issues are discussed below.

OPPORTUNITIES, CHALLENGES, AND PROBLEMS.   The political environments of corporations are too often assumed to be negative or hostile in character. Indeed, often that is the case. However, the political environment can also present opportunities and challenges that alert managers can take advantage of to further the interests of their company and the relevant political units. For example, a region of a country with severe unemployment problems can be well served by a company that is able to generate new employment and stimulate and assist supplier industries. The opportunities possible in the political environment are sometimes embodied in a package of host-government incentives designed to attract foreign investment in order to further objectives determined by the political process. In addition, creative analysis and understanding of the complex political environment will often lead to the identification of new opportunities for conducting business in ways that will serve the goals of various political entities and create a positive environment for business operations.

LEVELS OF THE POLITICAL ENVIRONMENT

STATE OF ORIGIN.   The most dominant (though certainly not the only or the oldest) mode of political organization in the world is the nation state. These political and territorial entities are the major vehicles for the development and enforcement of rules governing the behavior of citizens and of institutions in each country.

All international business activity originates in a state or, in a few cases, a combination of several states (for example the Dutch-British multinational corporations Unilever and Royal Dutch Shell). Trade, licensing, direct foreign investment, or other forms of international business begin in a state that is often referred to as the home country or parent state. Parent states have the sovereign power to control the nature and effects of international business activity originating therein, though the degree to which the power is exercised varies widely. How, when, and why parent states engage in such activity depends upon the mix of political interest groups, their specific concerns about international business activity, and their relative influence on the governmental policy-making process.

Of course the parent-state political environment is not limited to the actions of the government. The nongovernmental activities of private groups can have a major impact on international commerce as well. This is more likely to occur in those countries in which there is a tradition of direct interest-group pressure on corporate structures, so that managers are forced to pay attention to the needs and concerns of these groups. For example, trade unions in Europe have attempted to influence the actions of companies in their international business activities. In the United States, the so-called Sullivan Principles regarding the activities of the subsidiaries of U.S. firms in South Africa have no official governmental backing, but nonetheless are an important part of the parent-state environment for U.S. firms.

This latter example illustrates the fact that the parent-state environment is concerned not only with business activities that affect the home country but sometimes also with the impact of companies on foreign or host-country environments. This results in an interesting political, philosophical, and jurisdictional situation in which a home country seeks to control the behavior of firms in their foreign operations, sometimes in disregard of host-country wishes. In subsequent sections, this jurisdictional conflict will be addressed, as will the substance of the concerns evidenced in the home-country environment.

HOST STATES. Host states are all the other countries in which the company's activities take place. A firm in Brazil exports shoes to the United States and Europe. In this case, Brazil is the parent country and the others are host countries. Licenses from Siemens in West Germany to other firms in various Latin American countries exhibit a similar kind of relationship. In a sense, host countries are the recipients of the international business activity emanating from a parent state.

Note that these labels are generic and reflect an international business relationship—not a characteristic of a particular state. Thus an individual country like France, South Korea, or the United States is a host state when the recipient of international trade and investment activities and a parent state when it is the origin of such activities. As a result, the policies of states will frequently reflect both host- and parent-country concerns. For example, at the same time that the Japanese government is promoting exports and other foreign business activities of its corporations, it has carefully controlled access to its own home markets by companies from other countries.

The host-country environment is frequently composed of a confusing mixture of governmental authorities. Non-U.S. multinational corporations (MNCs) are often overwhelmed by the many governmental authorities in the United States with which they must deal in order to build and operate a plant. There are the multiple parts of the federal government, including myriad regulatory agencies; a similar structure is likely to exist at the state level. Then at the local and county level, the foreign investor is confronted with many overlapping government units from municipal governments to sewage authorities to school boards to environmental protection agencies. Not only is there often little contact and coordination among these government units at different levels, but even within a single slice of the multitiered structure, coordination and consistency are often lacking. Many other countries present similar degrees of confusion to international business. Although the central government may have formal sovereignty, the politics of the situation are such that the capital's authority does not reach to certain areas of the countryside.

As in the parent-country context, nongovernmental interests also have the ability to shape the host-country environment. Trade unions, single-issue interest groups, ideological groups, ethnic groups, and many others sometimes do contribute to an environment to which international business must adapt. Although lacking the authoritative sovereign power of government, these nongovernmental groups may be just as important in certain areas. As an example, the clergy and organized religion may have significant influence on the political environment within which business is conducted in Brazil, El Salvador, and other Latin American countries.

Recognizing the complexity of the host-state environment, managers of international business firms need to adopt procedures that will enable them to determine the relevant environment for their particular business. In addition, strategies should be developed and implemented that facilitate the effective management of relations with the host country. Policies supportive of these efforts are examined in the last section of this chapter.

REGIONAL ORGANIZATIONS.   Nations have joined together to form regional economic and political groups that are designed to enhance the economic and political welfare of their members. In some cases these organizations have been formed for positive internal reasons. In other situations they have developed to protect the members against some external force. Most regional organizations have emerged to serve both functions. The European Economic Community (EEC) now comprises 10 countries that have collaborated to develop common policies on a number of economic, social, and political issues. Some of these have direct relevance for international business activities. A cornerstone of the EEC is the set of tariff and nontariff barriers that have been erected against imports from other countries. Also, the EEC has promulgated an EEC company law and other rules that affect how multinational corporations are able to conduct business within the Common Market.

The EEC is the most highly developed regional organization, with a legislature, a large bureaucracy, and an executive branch. Other regional groupings in Europe provide judicial functions, and still others such as the Iron and Steel Community, embrace a more specialized segment of European industry. Some of the same political characteristics of governments at the state level exist in the EEC too.

There are many other regional governmental organizations. Some of them are the Andean Group (Bolivia, Colombia, Ecuador, Peru, Venezuela), the Association of Southeast Asian Nations (Indonesia, Malaysia, the Philippines, Singapore, Thailand), the Latin American Free Trade Association, various U.N.-sponsored regional organizations, and others.

The actual workings and effectiveness of regional organizations vary greatly. Yet they promise to be an important component of the economic and political environment within which international business is pursued. In any case, many of these organizations are important sources of information, provide the potential for cooperative efforts within the group to foster foreign investment and international business, and may have concerns and regulations that must be considered by international business.

In addition to governmental regional organizations, nongovernmental regional organizations also have an important, though usually specialized, impact on international business. These organizations are often regional counterparts to those found at the national level. There are regional labor organizations, the most well developed of these coinciding with the EEC or the European region. For example, the European Metalworkers Federation has held sessions with several multinational corporations including Philips to discuss areas of concern. Some of the same political groups active in states have organized loose confederations to advance their effectiveness on the regional level as well as at the national level.

FUNCTIONAL ORGANIZATIONS. Similar to regional organizations, functional groupings represent combinations of governments along a dimension other than geography. The most well known of these organizations is OPEC, which brings together most of the petroleum-producing countries. It has succeeded in dramatically increasing revenues from the export of petroleum and has emerged as a major economic and political force with impact throughout the world.

There are other cartel organizations for countries producing commodities. None has been as successful as OPEC, but they too have had important impacts. Cartels have been formed for bauxite, iron ore, phosphorus, sugar, coffee, and other commodities.

An interesting result has been the development of countervailing organizations in response to the formation of producer cartels. A less formal, more fluid, and far less effective group of petroleum consuming countries was formed to deal with OPEC in the 1970s. Similar organizations of governments and private corporations have emerged in response to the development of other commodity cartels.

Another functional organization of substantial importance is the Organization for Economic Cooperation and Development (OECD). Twenty-four states belong to the OECD, and for the most part they represent the more-wealthy nonsocialist countries. The OECD secretariat produces many useful studies of economic conditions in member countries and in the world. It has also promulgated a set of investment guidelines for multinational companies that was endorsed in 1976 by the representatives of member governments. This will be discussed in greater depth in the next section.

Nongovernmental functional groups have evolved to represent labor and business interests in the OECD. Formal advisory councils have been established to provide information to the OECD in its deliberations.

The developing countries are not without their own organizations either. The U.N. Conference on Trade and Development (UNCTAD) represents in a continuing way the interests of developing countries. Although part of the U.N. family of organizations, UNCTAD is mentioned here because of its important role in promoting the views of the developing countries.

INTERNATIONAL ORGANIZATIONS. A number of governmental and nongovernmental institutions at the international level have significant impact on international business activities. Other chapters in this *Handbook* have discussed the General

Agreement on Tariffs and Trade (GATT), the International Monetary Fund (IMF), the World Bank, and the International Labor Organization (ILO) and the important roles they have in the global economic and business system.

The United Nations has developed a significant interest in transnational corporations. The Centre on Transnational Corporations, a part of the U.N. bureaucracy, has been established to perform three major functions with regard to transnational firms. First, it serves as an information-gathering and data center for studies and reports on the activities of these firms and their effects on states. Second, it has developed a consultation service that can be used by countries in their deliberations and negotiations with these enterprises. Third, the Centre has been charged with developing a code of conduct for transnational corporations, host states, and parent states. Although the Centre is designated specifically to be concerned with direct foreign investment, other units of the United Nations are also interested in this phenomenon. The importance of the United Nations and its related organizations for international business will grow.

Again, international nongovernmental groups have emerged to influence the political environment in which multinational corporations operate. The reasoning is obvious: As business is increasingly conducted internationally, various groups affected by or otherwise interested in their activities seek to develop a corresponding international presence. Thus single-interest groups, broad political coalitions, and economic groups like unions have slowly but gradually expanded their sphere of influence to the international level. Few are as well organized or globally strong as business interests, but it is inevitable that there will be increased international political activity in response to the internationalism of business.

STATES OF ORIGIN: CONCERNS AND POLICIES

ECONOMIC FACTORS.   Some of the concerns of parent states and the policies designed to alleviate these concerns are primarily economic. However, economic issues as discussed below often advance to the status of major national issues through the activities of interest groups using political strategies to pursue their interests.

Trade-Union Concerns and Policies.   Trade unions in the United States, the United Kingdom, Germany, Sweden, and other advanced industrial states are concerned about the impact of their own multinational companies on domestic unemployment. They fear that much of the investment overseas is investment lost to the parent state with negligible benefits and substantial costs to the parent-state economy. The argument is that if the money invested overseas were invested at home, unemployment would be reduced.

Trade unions are convinced that foreign investment creates unemployment, or at least results in lost job opportunities. The AFL-CIO in the United States identified three ways in which jobs are "exported." First, export-oriented jobs are lost because previous export markets are served by overseas production. Automotive manufacturing facilities in host countries serve that market and often third-country markets, taking away the jobs from parent-state workers who otherwise would have been employed to make cars for export.

Second, trade unions allege that serious unemployment problems are caused when MNCs locate production in other countries and then import the finished product into the parent state. Television sets made by U.S. firms in other countries but imported into the United States result in jobs for non-American workers but few or none for Americans. Finally, the MNC is able to shorten or "telescope" the time from technological innovation to use by workers in the plants of the company anywhere in the world. New techniques or products developed in the R&D laboratories of a Swedish firm can be made available immediately to workers employed by the MNC in plants in other countries. Since the technology is immediately available, the Swedish workers are competing with workers in other countries on the basis of the cost of labor. Workers in the more-advanced industrial and high-wage states will lose jobs to workers in countries where wage rates are substantially lower.

As a result of these concerns, trade unions have pressed for, and some governments have agreed to, reduction or elimination of the "advantages" to MNCs. Swedish firms investing overseas must receive approval from an agency that examines the potential effects on employment in Sweden. Volkswagen had to assure German workers that no reduction in employment would occur as a result of that company's decision to manufacture in the United States. In the United States, trade unions have attempted to make the tax treatment of overseas earnings and payments for foreign taxes less supportive of foreign investment. Moreover, protectionist legislation has been introduced to reduce the flow of goods manufactured in lower-wage countries by a country's own MNCs.

Concerns of Competing Firms.   Competitor firms sometimes charge that the internationalism of MNCs provide them with "unfair" advantages not available to strictly domestic firms. The MNC has a larger potential market, which may result in economies of scale in the manufacturing and marketing of the product. Unit costs of goods produced or services offered can be reduced as overhead such as research and development and various management services can be spread over a larger number of operations. Activities in other countries may enable the company to weather more effectively economic downturns in one state while business is good in other countries. In addition, the MNC is usually able to take better advantage of nonparent-state sources of supply and financing. These and other factors make MNCs formidable competition for domestic companies. Indeed, some studies have shown that MNCs achieve a higher rate of return than purely domestic companies in the same industry.

The concerns of competitors may be exacerbated by parent-state government support that provides incentives and subsidies for MNCs. These may range from government-sponsored market-research efforts to tax incentives to spur investment such as tax deferrals or tax credits to active support of government officials on behalf of their MNCs—incentives that are not available to firms limited to domestic activities. As a result of these concerns, competitors of the MNCs sometimes seek to reduce or have eliminated the "advantages" that they see accruing to international firms.

Protection of the National Economy.   Parent-state governments and various pressure groups influence the environment of MNCs in order to protect domestic economic values. Balance-of-payments concerns can lead to currency regulations designed to reduce the outflow of funds, to establish new investment, or to pay for imported goods. Similarly, governments are often subject to pressure from managers and workers in marginal industries to provide them with protection against foreign competitors and against national companies with an international strength. Indeed, parent-state concerns about foreign investment are often linked with policies designed to protect domestic industries from foreign-trade competition. In short, trade, monetary, and investment policy are sometimes implemented in ways that directly affect the ability of multinational companies to pursue business ventures in other countries.

As a corollary to these concerns, the parent state's vision and philosophy of noncompetitive business practices or antitrust activities sometimes leads to the establishment of policies to prevent such practices. In the United States, the activities of foreign subsidiaries of U.S. firms are subject to the antitrust provisions of U.S. law when it is felt that such activities might be in restraint of trade. Thus the efforts of the government of the United Kingdom to bring about a merger between a British subsidiary of a U.S. firm and a British firm ran afoul of the U.S. antitrust law.

POLITICAL FACTORS.   Although the line between political and economic factors is blurred, nonetheless, predominantly political concerns have led parent states to seek to control the activities of their own multinational corporations.

Foreign-Policy Issues.   Some countries, as parent states, seek to advance foreign-policy objectives through the control of the activities of their own multinational corporations. A number of countries have established limits on the conduct of business, trade or investment with certain "unfriendly" countries. This may be a selective or blanket prohibition, depending upon the particular product or service. A number of countries asked their companies to suspend dealings with Iran after the taking of the U.S. diplomatic hostages in 1979. At other times, racist, dictatorial, or antagonistic regimes have been the target of such prohibitions.

The "Trading with the Enemy" Act passed by the U.S. Congress in the heyday of the Cold War proscribes U.S. companies *and their foreign subsidiaries* from trading with specific "enemy" countries in certain identified goods. The U.N. boycott against Rhodesia was supported by many governments around the world. The United States specifically prohibits its companies from compliance with the Arab-led boycott of Israel. Transgressions are clearly detailed and penalties rather severe.

On the other hand, some parent-state governments are also active supporters of the foreign activities of their MNCs. Economic incentives may be offered and government protection provided to help assure the success of one's own multinationals. France, Italy, and Japan urged greater activity on the part of their petroleum firms in response to the rise of OPEC, the higher prices for petroleum, and the insecurity of the source of supply.

Proper Behavior.   A number of countries have identified proper or appropriate behavior, which their international firms are expected to follow. Sweden, Canada, and Japan have developed such statements at one time or another, though the impact of such efforts is questionable. The United States through its Overseas Private Investment Corporation (OPIC) can withhold payments for clients if it is deemed that the company acted in an inappropriate fashion. In 1977 the United States enacted the Foreign Corrupt Practices Act, which imposed severe penalties on firms that made payments to officials of other countries in the attempt to secure business.

On the nongovernmental level, pressure groups in several countries have expressed concern about the practices of multinationals and their host-government partners. In the United States, many major multinational corporations have been faced with stockholder resolutions chastising the company for pursuing business opportunities in certain countries whose governments are thought to be undesirable.

Issues of National Jurisdiction. An unresolved, yet rather critical, question is whether the parent or host state has ultimate jurisdiction over the multinational corporation and its foreign subsidiaries. Canada and the United States have had several disputes over whether Canadian subsidiaries of U.S. firms must respond to the dictates of the U.S. government when they have been expressly prohibited from doing so by Canada. Most recently the uranium-cartel situation brought this issue to the forefront in relations between Canada and the United States. The international manager needs to be alert to these potential conflicts.

HOST STATE: CONCERNS AND POLICIES

OWNERSHIP AND CONTROL. Who controls the subsidiary? To whose set of objectives and concerns is it responsive? How can the host state influence the policies and actions of a subsidiary of a multinational corporation? These questions are at the core of this vital area of concern. For economic and political reasons, many host states (and nongovernmental groups within host states) fear that they are host to firms that are not responsive to their interests. Significant and potentially damaging decisions are thought to be made at headquarters in another country by people with little or no loyalty to the host state.

In response, countries have devised many rules and regulations seeking to increase their influence in decision making in the subsidiary. They include the following:

1. Mandatory-local-ownership provisions in which local share varies from a minority to a majority position (100 percent local ownership represents a nationalized situation).
2. Insistence that local citizens hold responsible managerial positions by designating certain positions that must be held by local citizens or by establishing limits on value of salaries that may be paid to expatriate managers.
3. Establishment of rules that carefully delimit the subsidiary's ability to operate. Instead of requiring local decision makers, governmental policies are established that perforce restrict managerial freedom.

FINANCIAL FLOWS AND BALANCE OF PAYMENTS. Host countries in a serious balance-of-payments-deficit situation may impose regulations to insure a greater contribution to a surplus by subsidiaries of multinationals. Some of the most frequent methods are

1. Restrictions on profit repatriation.
2. Restrictions on payments to the parent for licenses, royalties, and management fees.
3. Prohibition against local borrowing, thereby forcing companies to bring in additional capital.
4. Imposition of barriers to imports and incentives or requirements for exports.
5. Increasing requirements for local sourcing of components (local-content regulations).

EMPLOYMENT SECURITY AND LABOR MATTERS.   The subsidiary of a multinational corporation is thought to be more mobile than a domestic firm. In general, it can more readily reduce or shut down operations in response to better economic opportunities elsewhere. For example, if the labor-relations climate becomes unattractive or wage rates too high, it is thought that the subsidiary of a multinational corporation is more likely to move to a production site located in another country than is a domestic firm. In addition, multinationals are charged both with paying overly low wages and with establishing high wage rates that attract the best employees, thereby creating disadvantages for local industry and contributing to wage inflation. Also, trade unions often feel that the international nature of the multinational corporation gives it an unfair advantage in industrial-relations matters.

Labor-related responses are

1. Requirements for consultation with workers prior to major production decisions.
2. Extremely large severance-pay provisions, making it very costly to close down operations.
3. Minimum-wage requirements.
4. Wage controls.
5. Incentives/demands that funds be contributed to a national training system.
6. National-union collaboration with the unions associated with the same MNC in other countries.
7. Cooperation with union representing workers at parent-company operations.

IMPACT OF TECHNOLOGY.   Like many of these concerns, the issue of technology transfer has several different components. The technology transferred by multinationals is sometimes thought to be outmoded, and host countries may therefore be paying high prices for out-of-date technology. Indeed, some companies have been charged with using payments for technology as a means of circumventing restrictions on profit repatriation. There is also concern that subsidiaries in host states are not able to make the most of the technology ostensibly purchased because of restrictions imposed by the parent company.

Another concern is that the host state may become merely the consumer of technology developed elsewhere, with the result that local research and development efforts atrophy through lack of funds and scientific personnel. A fourth concern is that the technology brought to the host country may be too advanced, that is a capital-intensive technology introduced in countries that need more labor-intensive practices. The best and the latest may be "inappropriate" given the unemployment problems faced by the host state.

Some of the responses to these technology concerns are

1. Technology review boards that review applications for the transfer of technology.
2. Determination of "fair market value" for technology that is transferred.
3. Prohibitions against payments by subsidiaries to parent companies or other subsidiaries for technology.
4. Disallowing restrictions on the use of the technology.

5. Encouragement/insistence that the subsidiary undertake some research and development in the host country.

INFORMATION AND DISCLOSURE. Because of the complexity of the activities and financial statements of multinational corporations, some host countries have found it difficult to obtain needed information. There is special concern about transfer-pricing issues, corporate profitability, tax liability and payments, and matters related to wage rates and employment practices. Consequently, some countries are seeking to specify more precisely the information desired of multinationals. Even then, the suspicions caused by corporate complexity, reluctance to reveal proprietary information, and the general foreignness of the multinational linger on.

OVERLY EFFECTIVE COMPETITOR. The size, wealth, and internationalism of multinational corporations sometimes result in these foreign firms dominating important segments of the host-country market. This tends to be especially true in the high-technology industries or in those where there are particular advantages to an international structure. Some countries are not bothered by the success of multinationals headquartered in another state. Others are concerned because they see domestic markets absorbed by the export firms, foreign markets lost, and a general dependence upon foreign firms in an industry critical for national defense or economic growth.

In response to such concerns, host states have developed a number of different policies:

1. Barriers to entry designed to keep out foreign competition.
2. Demands for local participation.
3. Discriminatory government purchases aimed against the multinationals.
4. Formation of a "domestic" competitor with government backing that receives subsidies to compete more effectively against foreign firms.

EXPLOITATION OF NATURAL RESOURCES. For years host countries felt that foreign firms took advantage of host-country weaknesses and paid low prices for the natural resources, earnings from which were critical to the host state's economy. OPEC has changed this with petroleum, but some countries still feel that they are too dependent upon multinational extractive companies to mine and refine the ore and to market the product. As a result host countries have

1. Formed producer cartels.
2. Nationalized ownership and organized management contract arrangements.
3. Controlled production to reduce supply and increase prices.
4. Increased taxes and royalties on companies.
5. Established their own refineries and other downstream business activities.

TRANSBORDER DATA FLOWS. Of increasing importance, particularly among the European countries, is the concern that multinationals have large data banks containing information about their citizens that could be abused. As companies develop more-sophisticated information about employees and customers, host-country efforts to restrict and regulate the use and transfer of this data will have important impacts on how multinational companies pursue business on an international basis.

NEO-IMPERIALISM.   Many host states fear the imperialistic nature of multinational corporations and their parent governments. Multinationals have been charged with meddling in the internal affairs of host governments, establishing alliances with oppressive regimes, using their parent states to apply governmental pressure on hosts, serving as agents of imperialism, destroying the indigenous culture through mass-marketing techniques, and exacerbating the inequitable distribution of wealth in host countries. Each of these matters is complex and also critical. In their complexity and the fervor with which some persons subscribe to these views, they provide an important part of the political environment within which international business operates. Indeed, this basic ideological suspicion and antipathy toward the multinational corporation may be the chief motivating force behind some efforts to restrict and even eliminate direct foreign investment.

MNC BENEFITS AND HOST-STATE INCENTIVES.   The importance of this ideological antagonism should not be underestimated, but equally important is the fact that all but a handful of countries are eager to attract foreign investment and offer substantial incentives to such firms. Indeed, at times potential host countries compete vigorously with each other to lure foreign investment and the benefits that result. As a consequence, managers of corporations may be able to identify specific ways in which the efforts of their companies can serve to advance the interests of the host states and receive host-state support to do so. Thus the political environments in host countries are often characterized by ambivalent feelings about the multinationals. Management of such firms must be prepared to accept these mixed signals, respond to major host-country concerns, and implement strategies that recognize business opportunities in the environment but pursue them in ways that are cognizant of the issues discussed above.

MNC–HOST-STATE RELATIONS

CONFLICT AND COOPERATION.   Inherent in the relationship between multinational corporations and host states are the seeds of both conflict and cooperation. Cooperation is called for, since both parties seek the benefits to be achieved from such a relationship. Conflict results when the objectives of each are somewhat contradictory or the means to achieve the objectives are thought to damage the interests of the other. The host country wants the benefits of technology transfer, industrial development, increased standard of living, new investment, expanded employment, balance-of-payments surpluses, and many other items. Multinationals want expanded markets, increased profit opportunity, additional resources (natural and human), reduced production and transportation costs, market or production advantages over competitors, and other similar factors. The precise nature of the relationship depends upon the country and the company, particular issues of importance at that time, and all the other elements that constitute the environment for a multinational corporation. This makes it difficult to generalize, but some general propositions can contribute to an understanding of this relationship.

The Power Balance.   A "balance sheet" of the elements of power available to multinationals and host states can help to identify the strengths and weaknesses of each in the relationship.

The following items are on the *host country* side of the ledger:

1. Ultimate sovereign power, including ability to nationalize.
2. Legislative, administrative, and regulatory power to establish conditions under which multinationals can operate.
3. Rationale for foreign investment in that country including markets, natural resources, and cheap factors of production, including labor.
4. Competition among firms for access to these attractions.
5. "Unbundling," or the ability to obtain benefits of foreign investments from many different sources (e.g., capital from Germany, technology from United States, international marketing network from Japan, construction from South Korea) instead of from a single multinational corporation.

On the *multinational corporation* side of the ledger are these items:

1. Withdrawal of investment from host country.
2. Refusal to invest more.
3. Control of the delivery of the benefits sought by the host state from foreign investment (e.g., industrial development, employment, technology, increased exports, etc.).
4. The international advantages embodied in the multinational corporation including the international marketing network and the multistate location of various aspects of the production function—both of which are difficult for a host country to reproduce.*
5. Potential for parent-state pressure on the host country.
6. Inhospitable actions by host states frightening off other foreign investment.
7. The linkage between the international credit network centered around the International Monetary Fund and the positive treatment of foreign investment.

Both the host state and the multinational corporation have in their control an ultimate weapon that will in the process of its use destroy the relationship between the two. The ability to nationalize and the ability to withdraw give each side the power unilaterally to end the relationship. But at a substantial cost. Consequently, the conflicts between host states and MNCs most often are pursued in the realm of negotiation, bargaining, and compromise. The objective is to develop a relationship that will allow each party to have "sufficient" benefits to offset the costs of the relationship. A key challenge to the management of multinationals is to manage relations with host countries in ways that result in satisfactory relationships being maintained.

---

*For example, a company can organize its production so that the manufacturing occurring in any single state is only a part of the overall process, with no state having a potential stranglehold over the entire process. The production operation in a specific state is valuable only as it is integrated by the multinational corporation into the overall production network.

CHANGING REQUIREMENTS.   The host country's definition of benefits and costs and its determination of what are acceptable conditions for foreign investment are political processes; thus these conditions are likely to change periodically and to lack clarity and precision. The ambiguous and sometimes contradictory nature of the rules and regulations for multinational corporations is a result of the contradictions that often exist within political systems. The need to appease the interests of different political groups frequently results in a patchwork of policies that can confuse the manager. It helps somewhat to understand that this is not just host-country obstreperousness or inefficiency, but rather the natural result of the pushes and pulls of interest groups promoting their views.

Change, too, is a natural outgrowth of complex political systems. New governments supported by somewhat different coalitions of groups often have slightly different views of the treatment that should be accorded foreign investment. Of course radical shifts in government may result in drastic shifts in the policies toward foreign investment, but the latter does not always follow the former.

The Obsolescing Bargain.   A host state may seek to alter the conditions for investment because it feels that its bargaining position has become stronger. The reasons for such a shift are varied, but an important one is the stage of the investment. Early in the life of any investment, the risk of failure is borne by the multinational firm. For example, the quality of the ore may make mining and refining too expensive; the workers may not be able to adapt to new machinery and production processes and may therefore manufacture products of low quality; the marketing and distribution problems encountered may make the investment unprofitable until complex social and environmental problems are overcome. Consequently, the terms for that investment offered by the host country may be supportive of the firm, providing numerous incentives. However, once the corporation has overcome the risk and is looking forward to a long uninterrupted flow of profits, the host country may seek to change the terms to provide more benefits to the host at the expense of the corporation. This is possible because the host country no longer needs to woo the foreign investor, and the corporation has already absorbed and overcome the business risks associated with a new venture. This relationship is pictured in Exhibit 1. After the risk has been overcome and the company foresees a vigorous flow of profits, the host country is more able to change the conditions of investment by insisting upon a greater return for itself. The company is likely to accede as long as it can still predict a satisfactory flow of profits.

Limits to Greater Host-Country Control.   There are many factors that interrupt the inevitable progression of greater host-country controls as described above. A critical one is the attractiveness of the host state as a place to pursue business. A country that has a small market, few natural resources, and an inadequate supply of inexpensive labor does not have much to offer a multinational firm. Should such a country try to impose substantially greater demands on the foreign investor, it is likely that the corporation will not find it worthwhile to put up with the increased costs of doing business and may therefore withdraw. On the other hand, a country that offers a growing and large market, important resources, and a good manufacturing base will be in a better position to increase its returns on the foreign investment. Brazil is an

EXHIBIT 1   THE "OBSOLESCING BARGAIN"*

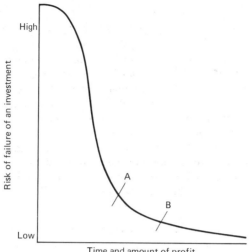

*The period from A to B is the time in which the host country will most likely seek to increase its return from foreign investment. Derived from Raymond Vernon, *Storm Over the Multinationals,* (Cambridge, Mass.: Harvard University Press, 1977), p. 151.

example of the latter type of country. Paraguay or Bolivia might be examples of the former. Any firm can go through the calculations to determine at what point its projected returns from the investment are insufficient in the light of the added costs of operating in a more stringent host-country environment.

Regional Cooperation by States.   One response of host countries with inadequate resources to offer multinational firms is to join with other neighboring states to form a larger market or resource base for these firms. By providing a more attractive environment, the group of countries may be successful in obtaining a greater amount of foreign investment. The great surge of U.S. investment in Europe took place in response to the formation of the European Common Market. Some regional groupings hope that the attractions will be enough to offset more-stringent regulations regarding the conduct of these firms within their member countries.

Thus the Andean Group of countries—Bolivia, Colombia, Ecuador, Peru, and Venezuela—have restrictions on matters such as amount of foreign ownership, profit repatriation, and payments for royalties and licenses for those firms that take advantage of the common-market character of the group. The ASEAN countries of Indonesia, Malaysia, Philippines, Singapore, and Thailand are similarly seeking to offer an expanded market and resource base to multinationals, though their conditions are not nearly as stringent as those of the Andean Group. Managers of multinationals will want to be aware of the opportunities and challenges offered by these regional groups.

THE INTERNATIONAL POLITICAL ENVIRONMENT

RATIONALE FOR INTERNATIONAL POLITICAL ACTIVITIES.   National governments and home- and host-state interest groups have attempted to develop international strategies to meet more effectively the challenges of multinational corporations. The rationale behind such efforts is to develop a countervailing strength to the internationalism of the firms. National governments and most interest groups are limited in their ability to exert influence on corporations beyond the boundaries of a particular state. Yet the internationalism of many corporations often means that key decision makers are located in foreign countries beyond the reach of state-bound interest groups or governments. In addition the multinational nature of the business frequently means that the corporations are not dependent solely upon operations in any one state. Thus most pressure tactics that impose economic burdens on only one part of the enterprise will have limited impact on the enterprise as a whole.

INTERNATIONAL GOVERNMENTAL ACTIONS.   There are various international governmental organizations that are contributing to the international political environment of multinational corporations.

The Organization for Economic Cooperation and Development.   In 1976 this organization of wealthy market-economy countries developed and passed a set of voluntary guidelines for foreign investment. These guidelines, subscribed to by all member governments, include items on disclosure of information, competition, financing, taxation, employment and industrial relations, and science and technology.

Subsequent to the initial promulgation of the guidelines, the actions of a few MNCs have led to the implementation of a procedure to monitor the conformance of multinationals to the guidelines. In addition, specific companies have been pressured to behave more appropriately by governments and trade unions through the OECD mechanism. Moreover, a number of European countries have incorporated the guidelines into national law.

Recently the OECD has developed guidelines governing the protection of privacy and transborder flows of personal data. These guidelines support the free flow of information but raise important issues about accuracy and the ability to correct inaccurate information, privacy, and full disclosure as to the use of this information. This international action has been buttressed by legislative requirements by host governments.

The United Nations.   The United Nations and its many family organizations have been actively engaged in the multinational corporation issue since the mid-seventies. Through the Centre on Transnational Corporations, data has been gathered on the activities and impact of MNCs, assistance has been offered to developing countries regarding contracts with these firms, and work is proceeding on the development of a code of conduct that is supposed to apply to corporations and home and host governments. The Centre has become the central locus of U.N. activity regarding MNCs, but significant efforts have also been undertaken elsewhere within the U.N. framework. A few of these are

1. UNCTAD is conducting studies of individual industries to support its attempts to develop codes of conduct for technology transfer and restrictive business practices.

2. The World Health Organization (WHO) is concentrating on the infant-baby-formula industry.

3. The ILO has developed a set of guidelines regarding working conditions in MNCs.

4. The World Intellectual Property Organization (WIPO) is seeking to reduce the protection to companies and their industrial properties as afforded by existing patent laws.

5. The Economic and Social Council (ECOSOC) is working in the area of consumer-protection regulations.

At the international level, and particularly within the United Nations, the debate between the North and South, the have and the have-not nations, been vigorously pursued. Since the multinational is perceived to be a major instrument in this struggle over the global allocation of resources, frequent attempts will be made in the United Nations and elsewhere to harness and restrict the activities of these firms. Many of these efforts may be unenforceable, but even so, these attempts and the emotion and suspicion behind them will create substantial political problems for multinationals at the national and international level.

TRADE UNIONS AND NONGOVERNMENT ORGANIZATIONS. The trade union is one of the most-active nongovernmental international organizations, and a major vehicle for these activities on behalf of workers is the *international trade secretariats*. International trade secretariats are organized by broad industry types and have affiliated to them national unions from around the world. (There are communist-oriented trade secretariats, confessional (religious) ones, and socialist-oriented ones, which are the most significant.) For example the International Metalworkers Federation, headquartered in Geneva, Switzerland, has affiliate national unions located in most countries of the noncommunist world in steelmaking, the automobile industry, electrical and electronics industries, and many other industries. Other major international trade secretariats are concerned with the chemical and petroleum industries, food and tobacco processors, lumber and woodworking, telephone and telegraph, mining, and others.

One of the major functions of the most aggressive of the international trade secretariats is to enable their member unions to develop an international presence in response to multinational companies. The companies have international activities, with decisions made in the great headquarter cities that affect workers all over the globe. Consequently, the rationale goes, the unions themselves need to establish an international dimension also.

To accomplish this, a variety of cooperative efforts have been undertaken. Some of these are

1. International support for a national union in its confrontations with a multinational corporation. Such support may take the form of money, pressure on headquarters and subsidiary executives, and the provision of advice and counsel.

2. Actions expressing international solidarity, which include a refusal to work overtime to take up the production slack caused by a strike elsewhere in the network, a refusal to handle goods produced by strikebreakers, and the organization of boycotts.

3. Collaboration and cooperation, which ranges from exchanging information to coordinating strategies to presenting (rarely) a united front to an employer.

In some international trade secretariats, these efforts have been given institutional life through the creation of continuing world company councils, which periodically bring together representatives of affiliate unions associated with a specific multinational company. Particularly in the auto, electrical and electronics equipment, food, chemical, and petroleum industries world company councils have been formed. In these instances the unions are seeking to overcome the perceived disadvantages of being national organizations representing people who work for international firms.

There are other nongovernmental actors of growing importance. International cooperation among environmental groups is increasing in recognition of the international nature of ecology. Groups espousing particular political ideologies on a global basis exist, and more narrowly focused single-interest groups are developing an international network. Terrorist groups also have moved beyond the confines of single states. Although many of these types of groups are not major factors nor focused specifically on multinationals, they do exist and do represent part of the international political environment. Indeed, in response to the internationalization of the economy, there is a slight trend toward the internationalization of political activity.

INTERNATIONAL LAW. This is too technical a subject for this section, but it also plays an important and probably emerging part in the international political environment. Moreover, there are increased efforts to establish institutions that will assist in the arbitration or settlement of international investment disputes, although the use of these is still rare.

In short, the essence of the international political environment is that many governmental and nongovernmental institutions are seeking to have an international countervailing power in response to the multinational firm. For the most part, national institutions can affect only that piece of the corporation that neatly fits into their particular national boundaries. But functionally and geographically, multinationals exist and operate over many sovereign jurisdictions. Just as interest groups and governments at the national level engage in extensive political activity regarding corporations, so too international political efforts are developing to undertake similar activities for the multinational firm. The emergence of international governmental institutions, international interest groups, and international cooperation among national groups emphasizes the need for managers of corporations to attend to the international political environment.

CONCLUSION

The political environments of multinational corporations present complex challenges to management. The multiple levels of political activity, the many governmental and nongovernmental groups, the susceptibility to change, and the lack of clarity in process and direction combine to create problems that managers frequently do not confront in more traditional areas of business. Yet it is not only possible but necessary for managers of MNCs to manage creatively relationships with the political environments.

Management of these relations is possible because certain aspects of the relationship are predictable. Some of them are the following:

1. The social and political processes by which issues evolve and governmental and nongovernmental groups become involved can often be understood and therefore are somewhat predictable.

2. In host countries and parent countries, there are many elements of an MNC's political environment that are eager to obtain the benefits that result from foreign investment.

3. Usually management can foresee or predict how its actions are going to affect and be perceived by important elements of the company's environment.

This predictability suggests that there is an opportunity to manage relationships proactively instead of merely responding to external events under the control of others. Subsequent sections will discuss more specifically how MNCs can and do manage these relationships.

PART 2

INTERNATIONAL TRADE

EXPORT DEVELOPMENT: BASIC PRINCIPLES AND METHODS

CONTENTS

IMPLEMENTING THE ELEMENTS OF A PROGRAM   5

Desire To Export   5
Entrepreneurial Community   6
Organization   6

Economic Studies   7
Export Financing   7
Incentives   8
Product Selection   9
Export Promotion   10
Support Institutions   12
Training   12

EXPORT DEVELOPMENT: BASIC PRINCIPLES AND METHODS

Amicus Most

There has been a mounting appreciation in almost every developing country of the need for increasing and diversifying exports. There have been many success stories and many failures in the efforts at trade development; numerous methods were tried, some were discarded and some successful. We will attempt here to summarize some results of this experience. It is only in recent years that most developing countries have begun to think in terms of a national strategy, with systematic plans and consciously selected methods for developing the processes necessary to increase trade. Taiwan, South Korea, Hong Kong, Singapore, Mexico, and Israel are examples of successes based on overall planning developed some years ago, and we believe this approach should be more widely adopted.

It is clear that overall economic growth rates are affected by export growth. It has also become clear that in terms of quantities of foreign exchange supplied, foreign trade is more important than aid to developing countries; also, trade receipts are usually available for use without conditions or restrictions. A central feature of development is an increase in imports; foreign-exchange earnings are needed to pay for important inputs of technical know-how and for investments in modern equipment and machinery. Economic growth often requires large inputs of imported raw materials or consumer goods as well. Almost every developing country is, therefore, seeking sources of foreign exchange, and those with balance-of-payments deficits are under special pressure to do so.

More and more countries are engaged in organized, but not always well-planned, export activities. Export organizations, private and public, have been widely established; incentive measures of various kinds have been adopted, financing plans created, and market-research-promotion efforts developed. In these and other ways growing interest is demonstrated. New international organizations have been created to assist in this effort. In the U.N. family, the International Trade Center (ITC) in Geneva and the U.N. Industrial Development Organization (UNIDO) are actively promoting export programs. The Organization of American States (OAS) has established the Inter-American Export Promotion Center (CIPE) as its export development arm. New training schools and programs are being developed. Bilateral assistance is being given to these programs by a number of developed countries, including Sweden, Canada, Great Britain, and the United States. AID has established an Export Development Assistance office in Washington to assist in programs throughout the world, and such assistance has been extended in Korea, Central America, India, Colombia, and many other countries throughout the world.

A program of export development is of course conditioned by the history, economics, geography, climate, natural resources, traditions, and political factors in each country. Nevertheless, certain general patterns may be applicable in whole or in part to others. It seems increasingly evident that the major export success stories have not been accidents, but are the result of planned government programs, and that a set of principles and methods can be described that will provide guidelines for other countries. In simplified terms, any program should contain the following basic elements:

1. *Desire to export.*   A national sense of the necessity for export development and a willingness to do something about it are basic requirements, and can be stimulated if desirable.

2. *Entrepreneurial community.*   There must be an entrepreneurial and trading community interested in and capable of developing and marketing the necessary manufacturing and agricultural output. If such a community is weak, there should be evidence that it can be strengthened, or if it is nonexistent, that it can be created. Positive steps should be taken to develop such a community where necessary.

3. *Organization.*   An organizational structure is needed that can mobilize and activate all the related sectors, including the economic ministries, government and quasi-public support institutions, banks, and educational institutions, along with the trading and producing community, private and public.

4. *Economic studies.*   Initial studies must be made of the economic conditions and requirements for a program; these should include a prognosis of the potential export growth rate and the establishment of priorities to channel the resources needed to create this growth rate.

5. *Export financing.*   Short-term working capital and longer-term investments for export-oriented production are necessary. Government programs to expand loan capability and provide capital to exporters on concessional terms are usually needed.

6. *Incentives.*   A broad program of economic-incentive measures and a removal of disincentives will motivate the private and producing sector to engage in export trade. These should include comprehensive measures for the removal or remission of inhibiting taxes and procedural barriers, the creation of credit and export insurance support, and the development or strengthening of promotional and support institutions.

7. *Product selection.*   Based on defined criteria and the nation's comparative advantages, products should be selected that are already exportable or can be made exportable and that can meet the competitive requirements in the available international markets.

8. *Export promotion.*   International export-promotion programs and organizations are necessary for what may be broadly defined as the "selling" process.

9. *Support institutions.*   Such institutions are private and public organizations and facilities that assist the production and trading community. They might

include, but are not limited to, such activities as technical assistance, quality control and inspection, productivity aids, product standardization, market research and promotion, export insurance, transportation facilities, testing and product-development laboratories, dispute arbitration, and so forth.

10. *Training.*   Training of personnel at all levels will be required to carry out the program.

IMPLEMENTING THE ELEMENTS OF A PROGRAM

In developing exports it is important to have a complete national strategy and program. Bits and pieces of a program, which in themselves can be productive, may be useless or inadequate when they are treated as the major effort. Because export development programs have been spreading so fast, some of the directors of export programs may lack training or understanding of some elements of their programs. They may, therefore, select the more obvious and known concepts rather than try to develop a complete strategy. They frequently look to the developed countries for advice and guidance, but unfortunately these advisers in many cases reflect the conditions in their own countries. The U.S. and European countries do not have "a development problem"; in their approach to exports, they are engaged less in working out new products for foreign markets than in promoting the sales of products they already have. The developing countries have to create the products before they can be sold. Yet too often they emphasize promotional activities, even when these activities are premature or only a small part of the total program they should be undertaking. Although it is important to work out a complete export program, one cannot always wait for its logical, step-by-step development. If an individual product meets international standards and a market is found, it should be pushed without waiting for the whole program. Success stories are important, and one should take advantage of opportunities as they present themselves. Thus the strategies must be both comprehensive and well thought out, and also flexible and adaptable to local situations that may appear.

Below is a discussion of each of the program elements listed above, some of which are treated more fully in other sections of the Handbook.

DESIRE TO EXPORT.   Pressure to export may be created by economic necessity, e.g., an unfavorable balance of payments or a decline in world prices for a commodity such as coffee or sugar, or by a strong developmental requirement for foreign exchange that impels policy makers to recognize the necessity for large-scale increases in exports. The desire to export does not automatically create the steps needed to carry out a program or knowledge of how a program should be developed. But it remains an essential ingredient. If the desire, specific or vague, is present and has a sound economic base, then it is possible to create the requisite "export atmosphere." In order to build up this desire in countries where exporting of nontraditional products is relatively unfamiliar, a certain amount of education of the public and influential leaders and groups will be justified and indeed necessary, so that they themselves will create and implement a strategy and program. For example, it may be useful in some countries to initiate an "export drive," to have the president or prime minister and other leading personalities make inspirational speeches to selected groups and localities, and to organize systematic publicity to follow. But it will not be sufficient to "wave the flag" and appeal to patriotic endeavor unless the other elements in the program are undertaken.

ENTREPRENEURIAL COMMUNITY. The core group of potential exporters often consists of those businessmen who are already traders. This group can also include those now engaged in manufacturing for domestic use, or indeed any persons who have the ability and imagination to engage in new and expanding activities. In Central America, for example, the trading community in nontraditional products was typically engaged in importing, because there has been very little export of such products, and these importers with considerable experience in international trade may be the natural candidates for export activity. Honduras in 1969 curtailed its imports, and facing a loss of income, the local importers of nontraditional products—represented by the chamber of commerce—became very interested in the possibility of becoming exporters; they took specific steps in that direction. In other situations, it may be other groups. Governments can do much to stimulate and guide the development of their entrepreneurial communities, not only by the control of entry into exporting or other activities through licensing, but also through influence on the availability of finance and its terms and conditions, through allocation of import licenses and other permits, through training facilities, and so forth. Governments should try to encourage a wide spectrum of potential entrepreneurs, including the existing large international trading companies, to embark on the untried overseas expansion the country needs, rather than limit the privileges to the established interests.

ORGANIZATION. A massive export-development program affects almost every part of the economy. A method must be found that will involve every economic ministry and quasi-government agency, the universities, the financial community, and all pertinent elements of the industrial and agricultural business community, and that can bring them together—preferably into a single organization that can plan, coordinate, activate, and direct the entire program. In many countries, the writer has observed the establishment of a top-level export committee composed almost exclusively of government and/or banking officials. These committees may achieve some limited successes, but they will face difficulties and frustrations because they do not actively enlist the private business community in the decision-making process. In other cases there is a tendency to form a small bureaucratic agency within the ministry of economics or industry, or as part of a financial institution, which is outside the mainstream of economic life. Even when the membership of an export-development committee includes the important officials of both public and private organizations, it does not necessarily serve its intended purpose. What is essential is a conscious and continuing effort to get their active participation and mutual support in the tasks that must be done.

In each country or area the form of an export commission will be influenced by local political and economic forces. Ideally such a commission should be independent, though it might be under the general supervision of one of the ministries or banks. It should serve primarily in an advisory, rather than executive, capacity, but contain within its membership the leading elements of the private and public decision-making establishment. It should be assisted by a small permanent staff that will maintain a flow of communication among the commission's members and subcommittees, keep its records, and transmit its decisions to government and financial institutions for implementation. Cross-section subcommittees, involving in each instance the private and public organizations and individuals involved in a specific problem or product area, could be established. Within the appropriate government ministries, commodity chiefs might be appointed, each of whom will work with a related private industry or agricultural group.

Whatever detailed form of organization is used, the objective should be to create an export "atmosphere" and a dynamic approach. One way to reach this goal is to try to involve as many as possible of the export community in the day-to-day decision processes and activities, a method that requires a high level of cooperative spirit that is often very difficult to achieve and maintain. Antagonisms between the private and public sectors and bureaucratic rivalries and desires to keep all activities under their control all tend to frustrate the widely inclusive type of organization. Nevertheless, it is this writer's belief—reinforced by the successful experience in South Korea—that this approach is feasible, and that in the long run it can bring about a more enduring result than would a more narrowly based or exclusively governmental form of organization.

ECONOMIC STUDIES.   A program could be launched without any prior economic studies, but it would be difficult to proceed very far. An initial study should primarily determine realistic levels of export increases and the resources necessary to achieve these growth rates. Export development requires medium- and long-term capital to go into many industrial, agricultural, and extractive activities; short-term credit financing is also needed, and financing is necessary to develop physical and institutional infrastructures. Besides considering the sources of the financial resources needed to achieve growth targets, the study should also concern itself with monetary stabilization and how this affects potential exports. Priorities should be established, and a determination of how far it may be necessary to draw resources from other programs. In conjunction with the fiscal and monetary policies to emerge from such a study, related policies governing trade controls and exchange rates must be recognized as very important in the success of any export program.

Such an initial economic study cannot be very definitive, since it must be based on results of an incentive program yet to be tried and estimates of which products can be exported. However, exact figures are not necessary; trends and educated guesswork are sufficient for this purpose. The main point is that an export program cannot be developed in a vacuum, or separated from other aspects of economic planning, so goals and targets are required—even though they will be changed as the program develops.

EXPORT FINANCING.   In an all-inclusive program for export expansion, short-term financing must be made available quickly and at internationally competitive interest rates. If new products and new companies and traders are to be encouraged, special measures of attractive financing must be made available. It is not sufficient that this financing be part of a general credit structure. In addition to being made available, it should be spelled out and handled in such a way that the export community can understand what kinds of loans can be had and where this credit is available. Traders (who may also be producers) need short-term credit as a major tool in their operations. Quick borrowing against foreign orders, letters of credit, inventories, bills of lading, and other export paper must be easily available. In order to generate this credit where sales are made on a credit basis (which is particularly prevalent in consumer-goods exports), export insurance—although not essential—can be very helpful.

In South Korea, for example, where general interest rates for business loans ranged between 16 percent and 28 percent in 1965, the Bank of Korea made it possible to give short-term credit to exporters against letters of credit at 6 ½ percent interest. In order to make certain that this would not become an incentive to delay deliveries, regulations required a jump to 20 percent if delivery was not made on the contracted delivery date. This is one example of the many methods of providing incentives to desired actions through terms of finance.

In addition to short-term credit, preexport working capital is essential in order to develop the agricultural crops and manufactured inventories in advance of sales. In long-range capital investments, the type of financing pertinent to exports does not necessarily differ from other development financing. However, priorities can be given in development financing based on a specific new export industry and commitments to engage in this business. It is also possible through financing measures to make it unprofitable *not* to export. A company, for example, desiring to expand its plant might be given financing with a firm commitment to export all or part of its new production for a given period, even if this has to be done at a loss in the initial stages, provided that there is a real possibility for future exports without loss.

INCENTIVES.   Every successful export program has as one of its major elements a set of incentive measures that will motivate the potential export community to look upon this activity as more desirable than other activities in which they are engaged. "Incentives" here include both positive measures and the removal of disincentives or barriers that inhibit exporting. Incentives may include tax and other financial measures, and the establishment of support institutions. They would also include removal of such barriers as unnecessary procedures, difficulties in obtaining credit, lack of marketing knowledge, and so forth. The writer's philosophy concerning the nature of incentives may be stated as follows:

1. Although all incentives are a form of subsidy, these should not become merely gifts for particular producers; they should be generalized, designed to create efficiency, and easy to remove when their need disappears. Where protectionist measures or subsidies create inefficient industries, as often happens, they impose a drain on the rest of the economy to support the protected sector. Some input of resources is necessary for incentives, but methods can be found to minimize the drain on the national budget.

2. As much as possible, incentive benefits should be limited to the increased sales of items now being exported or to new exports of nontraditional products. The purpose is to expand exports, that is, to stimulate exports that would not otherwise occur, not to create an extra bonus for already-existing exports. A second reason why tax incentives or removal of tax disincentives should be limited to new or expanded exports is that these do not reduce existing government resources. Subsidies or tax rebates related to established export products clearly sacrifice existing budget revenues; but where a new export is stimulated, what is lost to the budget is only a possible new revenue, one that might not have appeared without the stimulus. Indeed, if new export activities generate new incomes, hence new tax revenues of other kinds, the incentive scheme may be self-financing on balance.

3. Tariff protection should be limited as far as possible. Import substitution is in theory a proper way to reduce the foreign-exchange requirements; however,

it often results in high-cost industries that attract funds away from export activities to products for domestic use, and acts as a brake on export expansion. Tariffs also become politically difficult to remove.

4. A wide variety of incentives should be developed that are applicable to many situations. They should be constantly reviewed, and changed as required.

PRODUCT SELECTION.   One of the first and often one of the weakest steps in any program should be to make a detailed product analysis of a country's exportable items that have competitive advantages in world markets. Product identification requires a high degree of expert knowledge. Most people engaged in directing export development are generalists. Production for export is related to the possible markets for very specific products; general market information is useful, but does not give sufficient information to the producer of a particular product. A manufacturer needs to know not only that there is a market for his type of product in a particular country, but also that his specific product meets the market requirements in price, terms of sale, delivery time, quality, quantity, design, and packaging. Too often product lists are developed by production people with little knowledge of the market, or by market people with little knowledge of local production facilities and capacities. There is no use producing for an overseas market that does not exist; yet it happens again and again. Product development must be accompanied by specific market research; and because of the specialized knowledge required, this research must be selective.

Since it is generally impossible to exploit all possibilities, it is necessary to establish a list of priorities and a set of criteria for selecting products, for both short-range and long-range development. For the short run, items already being produced should be examined. In most developing countries the selection criteria would include the following: (1) high labor content; (2) products for which labor could be trained quickly; (3) utilization of any existing idle capacity; (4) small investments; (5) utilization of native raw materials; and (6) availability of international markets.

There is a widespread misconception that low-priced consumer articles represent the best possibility for export development from less developed countries. Although there are some possibilities in the initial stages, this is a poor area for competitive growth. Cheap items are often produced in developed countries with highly sophisticated automatic, big-scale machinery, so that their labor content is small and the comparative advantage of low-cost labor is lost.

There is a strong belief that because of the inferior quality of goods produced in the less developed countries, other less developed countries are a prime market for these products. This is undoubtedly true where "free trade" common markets exist, and the establishment or liberalization of a common-market arrangement can result in large increases in trade among the countries involved in these pacts. The Central American Common Market, even with its many problems, is an outstanding example. Other regional market arrangements now being developed, such as the Andean Pact and Latin American Free Trade Area (LAFTA) in Latin America, comparable groupings in Africa, and the Association of Southeast Asian Nations (ASEAN) in Asia, could eventually bring similar results and should be encouraged. Where no such arrangements exist, there are traditional markets, particularly for familiar products in neighboring countries, and these will no doubt expand and diversify with the progress of development and rising incomes. Nevertheless, the largest and fastest-growing markets for exports of developing countries appear to be, for the immediate future at least, in the industrial countries. Developing-country exports to the developed countries are about four times as large as those to other developing countries; and since the former had an annual growth rate slightly higher than the latter, even when petroleum was excluded, the absolute growth in exports to developed-country markets was also about four times as great. This difference in growth values can largely be explained by three factors: (1) the considerable potential import demand resulting from the higher income levels and larger absolute growth of incomes in the developed countries; (2) the high level of tariff protection that the developing countries have generally erected, particularly for products that other developing countries produce; and (3) the trade structures (finance, shipping, insurance, etc.) that have traditionally directed developing-country trade toward the developed countries to the detriment of intra-developing-country trade.

Product development, although basically guided by economic criteria, must be flexible and dynamic. In determining the list of product priorities and product selection, allowance must be made for opportunities of convenience and accidental or unusual growth possibilities. If a market for a specific item develops, it should not be held up because it does not fit the established criteria or growth pattern. For example, Korea has developed a substantial market for plywood in the United States. Korea has had no timber growth for many years; it is far removed from both sources of supply and markets; plywood manufacturing is a capital-intensive industry, and its quality demands training of skillful engineers and labor. By any normal economic criteria, this would not have been selected as a product to develop for exporting; nevertheless, for almost accidental reasons, it has been a major success.

EXPORT PROMOTION.   Although some countries overemphasize export promotion before they have products available for export, this does not mean that such activities are unimportant. Export promotion and selling are essential parts of any export program. Promotion requires a professional staff; it cannot be left to amateurs or political appointees with little or no training or experience. Unfortunately, commercial attachés are often in the latter category. In addition, export promotion is an expensive activity and may bring no immediate income return.

It is important to distinguish between the job of promotion agencies and that of the sales organization of a private company or state enterprise. Although there may be some overlapping, it is generally unwise for a promotion agency to be directly involved in sales activities. A sales agency will understandably wish to promote profitable items and will, therefore, concentrate on the best items already being marketed. A promotion agency, on the other hand, will attempt to develop markets for new items and to make wide contacts with the market, will undertake general promotion activities, and will do a considerable amount of market research. Its initial task will be that of market research. It will be engaged in broad market studies, but more important, it will place great emphasis on determining and reporting the requirements of the marketplace for the specific items being produced in the home country. This activity will simultaneously develop market contacts that can result in actual sales.

A country embarking on an export-development program must determine which markets can bring the best immediate results. It must establish representation in these markets and supply adequate staff, facilities, and budgets to make these services productive and useful. It is often wiser to have a limited number of overseas offices adequately financed and staffed, rather than a great many, none of which have sufficient assets to fulfill their tasks. Since most developing countries can only afford small overseas offices, the staff must be jacks-of-all-trades. They must understand market structure, public relations, advertising, how to and how not to entertain, what kind of samples and displays are required, and so forth. They will be furnishing the home office and home producers with detailed information on products, will often be required to settle disputes, and must educate home office and producers to the methods and ideas of business practices in the market countries. Although it is very desirable to employ in each of these offices a native of the market country, cost factors often prevent this. This poses an added burden to the knowledge and skills of the staff. Since maintaining offices is expensive, the staff must be few, but for this reason they must have sufficient funds to do considerable traveling in the host country.

The field offices require a home office to back them up and transmit the information to and from the local producers. They also have to supply general information to both the government agencies and the private sector and advise on government measures required to assist the export process. When potential buyers visit their country, the domestic offices must be prepared to help these buyers to locate the products and supply the information required. They should maintain a display center of products available in that country. They may wish to publish a news bulletin or magazine for overseas and home consumption.

There is always a great pressure to enter all types of national and international fairs. Although certain fairs may have political or cultural importance to a country, they do not always assist in trade development. Fairs have to be carefully selected, and exhibits should be based on products available for sale and impact on the market. Similarly, the idea of sending out missions to promote a country's products has great glamour and appeal, but must be treated with caution. One of the reasons for the Japanese success, to be sure, was that thousands of its people went out as individuals and in groups to study markets, production methods, and so forth, throughout the world. Bringing missions to the home country is equally important. But we must caution against costly boondoggle missions that have no specific relationship to the general program or the specific products and problems of the home country.

One of the useful tools in export development is an exporter's "service" agency in the home country for individual businessmen who are or wish to be involved in exporting activities. It gives them necessary information, helps solve their problems, makes contact with the government or financial institution on their behalf, and generally acts to smooth the way for a businessman—giving him a sense of personal relationship with the government and banks. This is especially valuable for small or new industries. Although this type of work goes beyond promotional activities, it well might be part of the task of the home office of a promotion agency.

There are various ways of financing export promotion. Most countries give direct governmental budgetary support to this activity. In other instances this support comes from the central bank, or from some combination of business organizations, banks and government. Small fees can be charged for some services such as subscriptions to newsletters, advertising, payment for displays, and so forth; but such fees will not cover all the costs of the organization. Some countries support this activity through direct taxes on exports and imports. For example, Hong Kong charges 0.5 percent taxes on exports and 0.5 percent on imports for a promotional fund. Colombia charges 1 ½ percent on all imports, and finds this revenue sufficient not only for promotional purposes, but also to finance all types of export activities including direct financing and loans for export development. An arbitrary figure, of say 1 percent of proposed export targets, might be established as a basis for the cost of promotion—a small cost if the services bring results.

This short statement cannot give all the details of an adequate export promotion organization. Studies of activities in this field by Japan (JETRO), Korea (KOTRA), Israel, Ireland, Mexico, and Colombia are recommended.

SUPPORT INSTITUTIONS. Many of the backup institutions required for an export program are expensive to create and operate. Certain activities, such as product development, quality control, quality inspection, standardization, export promotion, and market research, require direct budgetary support. A limited number of activities can be partly or wholly self-financed; these include export insurance, export inspection, industrial parks and free-trade zones, market news and information, and several others. International assistance agencies can be called upon for help. Countries should select and give priority to the activities they can afford, and then develop new ones as exports increase. It is better to have a few adequate facilities than many inefficient ones.

In specific problem areas, it is sometimes possible to have the industries involved finance their own technical institutional assistance. Customers can often play a vital role, particularly in technical assistance. For example, it was possible to interest an American shoe importer in three emerging Korean shoe-manufacturing companies. These companies had potential, but were not able to meet the quality and style requirements of the American buyer. The importer supplied two full-time technicians for one year to assist these companies, with an agreement for exclusive U.S. representation. Subsequently the company purchased large volumes from the three Korean companies. Many buying organizations and traders use the expert knowledge that their buyers have, and will give technical assistance to future sellers. Travel for the purpose of visiting customer countries is extremely helpful.

TRAINING. There is a dearth of the trained middle- and top-level personnel required to carry on the various phases of export development. This is true of the local managerial staff and also of advisers from the developed countries. Competent people in the field of trade are giving valuable assistance in many countries to these programs; but many of them have background in promotion without sufficient training or knowledge in development, and they need additional training in this field.

A number of international centers are giving short-term training courses. The International Trade Center in Geneva, the Inter-American Export Promotion Center in Bogotá, the International Marketing Institute at Cambridge, Massachusetts, the World Trade Institute (World Trade Center) in New York, and CICOM in Rio de Janeiro are conducting international training programs. Universities in many countries are developing their own training facilities. Obviously only a few individuals can be sent overseas; most of the training must take place at home or in neighboring countries. As the needs for personnel in a country's emerging export program increase, consideration should be given to establishing local training centers. Returnees from international training and guest instructors should be part of the teaching staffs. Training and teaching staffs should include theoreticians and economists and also people experienced in the practical day-to-day aspects of the problems to be encountered.

Training seminars and conferences are helpful, and they are taking on a very prominent role as part of the tendency to develop small portions of programs. These are an attractive type of activity and comparatively easy to organize; but in the opinion of this writer, there has been overemphasis on them. Training courses should grow out of a basic export program and be related to activities going on or being planned. Trainees should have specific activities with which they can be associated upon the completion of their training programs. Seminars and conferences, likewise, should be as much as possible oriented to specific problems and to problems in the countries in which they are held. In specialized activities such as export promotion and product identification, training should be done by professionals who also have a clear understanding of the problems in the developing countries. Fortunately, as more knowledge and experience are gained, more and more of the current training programs and activities are fulfilling these requirements; but many programs will require examination and lack relationship to the home problems.

In this connection, a great deal more attention than is generally devoted should be given to the study of "business anthropology," that is, to the understanding of the business cultures of other countries. It is essential that to do business in other societies than one's own requires an understanding in depth of the histories, habits, customs, mores, politics, religions, and languages of the "foreign" countries. This should include the special problems in multinational, multireligious and multiethnic countries.

In conclusion, there are many facets of export programs that I have been unable to discuss, for it would take a large volume to describe them all. I have spoken of the value of an overall strategy and program, but it might be well to repeat that no specific blueprint can be applied in all situations. Export programs must be varied and developed according to the conditions of individual countries, but in each case a general strategy, intelligently applied, is almost essential. Finally, outside assistance can be extremely useful, but no program can succeed without the desire and will of the local community to undertake the work required.

IMPEDIMENTS TO INTERNATIONAL TRADE

CONTENTS

TRADE BARRIERS: PRO AND CON	3
Motivations for Trade Barriers	3
Arguments Against Protection	4
INTERNATIONAL AGREEMENTS REGARDING TRADE IMPEDIMENTS	5
DIRECT IMPEDIMENTS TO TRADE	6
Tariffs and Export Taxes	7
Quantitative Restrictions	8
Import and Export Licensing	10
Antidumping Duties	10
Countervailing Duties	11
Other Direct Trade Barriers	12
Payments Restrictions	14
Escape Clause or Safeguard Actions	14
INDIRECT IMPEDIMENTS TO TRADE	15
Standards	15
Government Aids to Domestic Industries or Groups	17
Government Procurement Practices	18
Customs Valuation and Classification	18
SOURCES AND SUGGESTED REFERENCES	19

IMPEDIMENTS TO INTERNATIONAL TRADE

Wendy E. Takacs

TRADE BARRIERS: PRO AND CON

MOTIVATIONS FOR TRADE BARRIERS.   Countries set up barriers to trade on the import and the export side for a variety of reasons. Import and export duties constitute a source of *government revenue*. In industrialized nations import and export taxes are a minor source of revenue, but in many developing countries with less-developed fiscal systems, taxes on trade provide a major share of tax earnings. Governments also use trade barriers to foster industrial development by protecting newly developed *infant industries*. High tariffs in less developed countries are designed in part to protect fledgling industries from competition from established firms in industrialized nations. Similarly, industrialized nations often desire to protect older, established industries, such as textiles, footwear, and steel, that find it difficult to compete with low-cost exports from newly industrializing nations. The protection can be temporary, designed to give the import-competing industry time to adjust to new conditions, or it can turn out to be lasting. Countries also often protect basic industries such as steel, shipbuilding, agriculture, textiles, or footwear on *national security* grounds. The argument put forth is that these industries cannot be allowed to be driven out of business by import competition because their presence would be essential in case of national emergency or war. Maintaining *employment* is another motivation for import restrictions. Trade barriers proliferated in the 1930s as governments attempted to maintain domestic employment despite the worldwide depression. Countries encountering *balance-of-payments* problems are often tempted to impose import restrictions to limit imports and reduce trade deficits. *Unfair trade practices* on the part of foreign suppliers also prompt corrective measures in the importing country in the form of restrictions on the importation of the unfairly priced or produced item.

Countries may impose barriers to exports as well as barriers to imports. *Inflation* or *shortages of supply* are the primary motivations for restricting exports. If exporting a product is prohibited, limited, or discouraged, this will increase the supply available domestically and thus lower the price of the product or at least reduce the upward pressure on prices. *National-security* or *political* considerations may also play a part in export restrictions, as governments attempt to deny critical materials or technology to enemy or rival countries.

Finally, a country may impose an import or export restriction to influence its *terms of trade*, the ratio of its export prices to its import prices. Import restrictions reduce the demand on the world market for the goods the country imports and thus tend to drive down their prices. Export restrictions reduce the supply of the goods the country exports and thus tend to increase their prices. So if a country is important enough economically to influence the prices of its import or export goods, it can improve its situation by making the goods it sells more expensive relative to the goods it buys.

ARGUMENTS AGAINST PROTECTION. The arguments against protection are based on the economic loss to the country that occurs when the patterns of production and consumption are distorted by trade barriers. On the consumption side, consumers have to pay higher prices for imported goods and for similar products produced at home as well, because the prices of domestic substitutes will be bid up as consumers switch from the now-more-expensive imports. Domestic producers expand their production in response to higher prices, but the increased domestic output is produced at a higher cost than that at which the goods could have been obtained from abroad. Import barriers thus result in a transfer of money (or economic welfare) from consumers to producers in the form of higher profits and to the government in the form of tariff revenue if the restriction is a tariff. There is a net loss to the economy as well, because trade restrictions encourage comparatively high-cost domestic production in lieu of lower-cost imports and force consumers to pay higher prices.

Numerous studies have attacked the problem of measuring the *cost of protection*, that is, the value of the loss to society attributable to existing tariffs and other trade barriers, or, equivalently, the benefits that would be created by the reduction or removal of existing trade barriers.

Leamer and Stern (1970) summarized the early attempts. More recently Magee (1972) estimated that the average annual cost to the United States of U.S. import restrictions as of 1971 was $3.3–$5 billion. A number of studies have estimated the impact of proposed tariff reductions negotiated during the Tokyo Round of trade negotiations, completed in 1979. Cline *et al.* (1978) estimated that the annual gain for the United States from a 60 percent tariff cut would be approximately $1 billion. Studies of the cost of protecting particular industries also reveal the potentially high costs of protection. In a study of U.S. trade restrictions on CB radios, sugar, non-rubber footwear, textiles, and color televisions, Morkre and Tarr (1980) concluded: "The overwhelming result of these case studies is . . . that the costs of protection invariably exceed the benefits. In some cases, witness footwear and CB's, the costs are 25 or more times the benefits."

As noted at the beginning of this section, governments impose trade barriers for a variety of reasons or, to put the matter a different way, to achieve various objectives. Whereas imposing a trade barrier may attain the objective, it will also impose costs upon the country. A sizable literature has addressed the question of whether a trade barrier is the best-possible policy tool to achieve the desired goal, or whether some other policy tool could achieve the same goal at a lower cost. As a general principle, Bhagwati (1971) has shown that to achieve a given objective, the best policy tool is the one that affects the target variable most directly.

The *infant-industry* and *national-security* arguments for trade restrictions actually boil down to arguments for maintaining or encouraging a minimum level of production in an industry. However, a tariff or other import restriction is not the best policy to achieve the goal of preserving or encouraging the industry, because a *direct subsidy* to the industry can achieve the same goal at lower cost. The tariff imposes an additional cost upon consumers by increasing the price of the product, which the direct subsidy to the industry does not. In addition, from the point of view of national-public-policy formulation, the direct subsidy is highly visible and thus less likely to be continued when encouraging production is no longer justifiable on infant-industry or national-security grounds. Simply stockpiling strategic goods also may be a preferable alternative to a trade restriction. At times efforts to promote national security by protecting domestic industries have been counterproductive, such as, for example, the U.S. import quotas on petroleum products, which encouraged the depletion of domestic petroleum reserves in peacetime.

The *employment* and *balance-of-payments* arguments for import restrictions, and the *inflation* arguments for export controls also can be countered on the grounds that trade restrictions are not the proper policy tools to use to correct the problem at hand. Macroeconomic policy measures, that is, fiscal, monetary, and/or exchange-rate policy measures, are directed at these aggregate measures of economic activity and are thus the appropriate tools to use in these instances. In any event, the use of import restrictions to promote domestic employment was attempted on a massive scale during the 1930s and proved to be counterproductive. Competing imports were reduced, but exports fell as well because of falling activity levels abroad and retaliation on the part of trading partners.

The *optimum tariff* argument is one case in which a trade restriction may be the appropriate policy strictly from nationalistic point of view. A tariff that improves the *terms of trade* will still result in distortions to production and consumption that impose costs upon the economy. The *optimum tariff* is the tariff rate that balances the benefits of the terms-of-trade improvement against the costs of resource misallocation and leaves the country as well off as possible. The optimum-tariff argument for increased protection is only valid if the country is large enough to influence world market prices, if the tariff is not retaliated against by trading partners, and if the country's tariff level is currently below the optimal tariff rate. Even under these conditions, the tariff can only be justified from a national, not from a global, perspective. (See Johnson, 1968)

INTERNATIONAL AGREEMENTS REGARDING TRADE IMPEDIMENTS

The generally accepted international "rules and regulations" concerning trade impediments are found in the *General Agreement on Tariffs and Trade* (GATT). GATT is essentially a trade agreement adhered to by almost all major trading nations. The purpose of the agreement is to promote a free, open, nondiscriminatory trading system. In the world trading system envisioned by the framers of GATT, tariffs were to be the only trade barriers, and these were to be lowered through successive rounds of tariff negotiations. Thus GATT includes a general *prohibition against quantitative restrictions*, except for balance-of-payments reasons or in conjunction with agricultural programs (Articles XI and XII). Imported goods are to be accorded *national treatment*, that is, they are to receive the same treatment with respect to internal taxes and regulations as domestically produced goods. Each contracting party to GATT is to apply trade restrictions in a nondiscriminatory manner, so imports from all countries adhering to the agreement would be treated identically. The basis of the nondiscriminatory system under GATT is the *most-favored-nation* principle for the application of tariffs. When a country extends most-favored-nation (nondiscriminatory) tariff treatment to another country, it charges a tariff on imports from that country equal to the tariff rate it charges the "most-favored-nation," that is, the lowest tariff it charges on imports from any source. Most-favored-nation treatment is not universal. The United States, for example, does not extend this treatment to 17 communist-controlled countries and territories; thus imports from these countries are subject to higher rates of duty. The fourth major feature of GATT is the principle of *reciprocity*. Negotiated tariff reductions are to be reciprocal, with each nation reducing its import restrictions in exchange for reductions in the import restrictions of its trading partners.

Although more narrow than GATT itself, a network of bilateral and multilateral treaties also contributes to the legal framework for world trading arrangements. Some of these treaties create preferential trading arrangements among the signatory countries. Preferential trading arrangements depart from the general principle of nondiscrimination but are permitted under certain GATT provisions or have been sanctioned by specific GATT waivers.

Some preferential arrangements are attempts to achieve higher degrees of *economic integration* among the countries involved. When several countries form a *free-trade area*, they grant duty-free access to imports from other members of the group, but maintain tariffs on imports from nonmembers. The Latin American Free Trade Area (LAFTA) and the European Free Trade Area (EFTA) are examples of free-trade areas. To form a *customs union*, the member countries eliminate barriers to trade among themselves and, in addition, form a *common external tariff* with respect to nonmembers. An even more ambitious attempt at integration is the *common market*, in which the countries not only form a customs union, but also allow the free movement of labor and capital among the participating nations and coordinate economic and social policies. The formation of the *European Economic Community* (EEC) is as yet the most important, most ambitious, and most successful attempt at economic integration among nations. A second major deviation from most-favored-nation practice is the *generalized system of preferences* (GSP) under which many less developed countries receive preferential tariff treatment from industrialized nations. The exact product coverage, eligibility criteria, and administrative details differ among the industrial countries granting preferences, but in general exports of manufactured goods from less developed countries enter duty-free or at reduced tariff rates. The intent of the GSP is to encourage exports of manufactured products from developing countries to promote industrialization and reduce their dependence upon exports of raw materials and agricultural products. Evaluations of the contribution of the GSP to achieving this goal, however, have been somewhat pessimistic. (See, for example, Murray, 1977, and U.S. International Trade Commission, 1978, *Study of the Effects*.)

Narrower preferential agreements have specified special treatment or special arrangements regarding trade in particular commodities. For example, the *Canadian-American Automobile Agreement* provides for duty-free treatment of shipments of motor vehicles and parts between the United States and Canada.

DIRECT IMPEDIMENTS TO TRADE

The instruments used to restrict or limit trade are so numerous that it is difficult to formulate a classification scheme into which the myriad types of government policy measures affecting international trade fall neatly. The traditional approach is to distinguish between *tariff barriers* and *nontariff barriers*. According to this classification system, a nontariff barrier is any government action other than a tariff that distorts trade flows. The disadvantage of this system is that many trade barriers that are essentially "tarifflike" in their impact, such as antidumping and countervailing duties, fall under the rubric of "nontariff barriers." An alternative approach, used here, is to distinguish between direct impediments to trade, that is, measures or restrictions that affect trade flows directly, and indirect impediments to trade, or government policies directed at other objectives, which nonetheless have an impact on the flow of traded goods.

TARIFFS AND EXPORT TAXES. A tariff, or import duty, is simply a tax imposed upon a good when it enters the country through customs. Tariffs can be *ad valorem*, a percentage of the value of the shipment (such as the 3.5 percent U.S. duty on sewing machines or the 2.9 percent duty on automobiles); or *specific*, a certain amount per unit imported (such as the 1-cent per pound U.S. duty on condensed milk, the 6-cent per gallon duty on beer, or the $1.75 per gallon duty on rum); or *compound*, including both *ad valorem* and specific components (such as the duty on watch movements of 57 cents each plus 8.5 percent *ad valorem* plus 3½ cents per jewel, or the duty on fresh mushrooms of 5 cents per pound plus 25 percent *ad valorem*). Specific and compound duties can be converted to *ad valorem* equivalents if the price of the imported good is known (see U.S. International Trade Commission, 1978, *Conversion*.) The major difference between specific and *ad valorem* tariffs arises because the *ad valorem* equivalent of specific tariffs automatically decreases as the price of the good rises, as has occurred over time due to worldwide inflationary pressures.

Taxes can also be placed on exports of a product. Although export taxes are unconstitutional in the United States, they have served as an important source of revenue in other countries.

Tariffs have been important historically both as a source of government revenue and as a means of protecting domestic industries from the competition of lower-cost imports. During the postwar period, tariff rates in industrial countries have been lowered through successive rounds of tariff negotiations held under GATT auspices. The most important of these were the Dillon Round (1960–1962), the Kennedy Round (1962–1967), and most recently the Tokyo Round of Multilateral Trade Negotiations (MTN) (1975–1979). The average U.S. tariff rate, measured as the ratio of duties collected to the value of total dutiable imports, reached 59 percent in 1933, but fell to just over 5 percent by 1977. Agreements reached in the Tokyo Round negotiations will lower the average tariff rate still further.

The imposition of a tariff or an increase in the tariff rate directly increases the cost of the imported good to the importer, thereby increasing the price of the good in the importing country. Identical products and close substitutes produced domestically will also increase in price as consumers switch from higher-priced imports to domestically produced goods. Imports will fall, both because consumers will demand a smaller quantity at a higher price and because domestic production will be stimulated by higher prices and profitability. If the country imposing or increasing the tariff is large relative to the world market for the imported good, the price of the good in the world market will fall because of reduced demand.

A modern refinement of tariff theory has shown that the impact of a country's tariff structure on the pattern of production will be determined by the *effective rate of protection*, rather than the nominal rate. The concept of the effective rate of protection is based on the observation that a firm will benefit from a tariff on the product it produces, but tariffs on inputs into the firm's production process put it at a cost disadvantage and reduce profitability. For example, producers of leather gloves benefit from a tariff on leather gloves but are hurt by a tariff on leather. Automobile companies benefit from tariffs on automobiles but are disadvantaged by restrictions on steel imports.

Calculation of the effective rate of protection measures the protective effect of the entire tariff structure on a productive activity by taking into account the tariff rates on all of the inputs as well as the tariff rate on the final product. Formally, it measures the percentage by which a country's tariff structure raises the value added in a particular production activity above what the value added would be in a free-trade situation (see Grubel, 1971). Balassa (1965) has shown that the effective rates of protection for manufactured goods in industrial countries generally exceed the nominal rates because tariff rates on manufactured final products exceed the tariff rates on imported inputs.

QUANTITATIVE RESTRICTIONS. A *quantitative restriction*, or quota, imposes a limit on the quantity of a good that may be imported into, or exported from, a country during a specified period of time. An *embargo*, which prohibits trade in a particular product or with a particular country, is simply a special case of a quantitative restriction, with the quota limit set at zero. *Global quotas* limit imports or exports without regard to the country of origin or destination. More often, however, import quotas are divided up among the exporting countries, with separate subquotas for imports from each supplying country. For example, the United States limits imports of cheeses with a system of import quotas. The quota of cheddar cheese for 1980 was approximately 10.4 million pounds, with individual country quotas of approximately 2.7 million pounds from Australia, 6.8 million pounds from New Zealand, and so forth.

Quantitative restrictions date back at least to a 1463 English embargo on imports of manufactured goods, but governments only began to resort to quantitative controls on a large scale during World War I. These were gradually eliminated during the 1920s, only to be followed by more severe and widespread restrictions designed to protect domestic economic activity during the 1930s. Many developing countries still rely on import quotas for both balance-of-payments and protective purposes, but in the industrialized nations their use is limited mainly to controlling trade in sensitive product lines.

The *impact of a quota* on imports or exports is similar to, but may not be identical to, the impact of an import tariff or export tax. An import quota that is actually restrictive (that is, the quota limit is lower than what the level of imports would be in the absence of the quota) increases the price of the imported product and domestic substitutes within the protected market. The price increases because the quota restricts import supply. The exact size of the price increase depends upon the size of the quota, the extent to which producers of like or similar goods are encouraged by higher prices to increase output, and the extent to which consumers react to higher prices by cutting back on purchases.

Both import quotas and tariffs restrict imports, but the *impact of a quota and a tariff can differ*. Once imports reach the quota ceiling, there is no possibility of increased imports, even if conditions change drastically in the domestic or foreign markets. This implies that there will be a much higher degree of certainty about the level of imports with a quota than with a tariff. Moreover, price fluctuations in the world market will not be transmitted into the domestic economy if imports are limited by quota, whereas they would be with a tariff. Likewise, even drastic price increases at home will not lead to increases in imports. Thus an import quota may allow a domestic monopolist to raise prices without fear of competition from increased imports, which implies that a quota may allow a domestic producer with market power to more fully exploit his monopoly position, whereas a tariff would not. Also, with a tariff the difference between the price of the product in the importing country and the export price goes to the government in the form of tariff revenue. An import quota will tend to increase the domestic price above the price of the product in the world market, but the "windfall profit" implicit in the price difference does not necessarily accrue to the government. If the government auctions off import permits, it may be able to capture part or all of the implicit revenue. If not, the windfall profit may go to importers or exporters, depending upon the relative degree of market power on the importing and exporting side.

A particular type of quantitative restriction that has become increasingly important during the past two decades is the so-called *voluntary export restraint* (VER) or *orderly marketing agreement* (OMA). An exporting country threatened with import restrictions on the part of a major trading partner may "voluntarily" limit its exports of a particular product to that importing country. For example, Japan and the members of the European Economic Community agreed to restrain their exports of steel-mill products to the United States from 1969 through 1974 to forestall unilaterally imposed U. S. import restrictions on steel. South Korea and Taiwan likewise limit their exports of nonrubber footwear to the United States, and Japan, South Korea, and Taiwan restrain color television exports to the United States.

Like unilaterally imposed import quotas, VERs and OMAs restrict import supply and drive up prices. C. Fred Bergsten (1975, "On the Nonequivalence") has pointed out that VERs appear more diplomatic than unilaterally imposed quotas, are more flexible, and are less likely to invite retaliation. VERs and OMAs differ from import quotas in that they are normally negotiated with only the most important supplying countries or with those countries whose exports are growing most rapidly. VERs and OMAs thus may be less restrictive than global import quotas because increased exports from countries left out of the agreements may to some extent offset the cutback in exports from restraining countries (Takacs, 1978). On the other hand, VERs and OMAs can be more restrictive than import quotas because the export restrictions are administered in the exporting country, which invites monopolization of exporting, and thus cutbacks in supply in an attempt to drive up prices (Murray *et al.*, 1978).

Export quotas are sometimes used to relieve domestic shortages of supply of important commodities, to alleviate domestic inflationary pressures, or to keep the price of a good high in the world market by restricting supply. Limiting exports increases the quantity available domestically, while reducing the supply on the world market. Thus restricting exports will put downward pressure on the price of the product at home at the same time that it tends to increase the price in the world market. The United States, for example, limited exports of soybeans and iron and steel scrap during 1973 as an anti-inflationary measure. Supplying countries participating in commodity agreements designed to stabilize commodity prices often agree to limit exports by way of export quotas. The International Sugar Agreement is an attempt to stabilize world-market sugar prices that operates by way of export quotas imposed by the major sugar exporters.

IMPORT AND EXPORT LICENSING.   Many countries employ *import licensing* and/ or *export licensing* systems, under which importers or exporters must obtain a license from the appropriate government agency before they may import or export a good. Licensing systems are normally used to administer quantitative restrictions. "Automatic" licensing systems are also used, ostensibly only for statistical purposes. However, to the extent that obtaining the license imposes costs upon traders, or to the extent that the licensing system could be used to limit trade, even automatic licensing can act as an impediment to trade.

Realizing that licensing regulations are potentially severe trade restrictions, the countries participating in the Tokyo Round of trade negotiations reached an agreement that establishes general principles to ensure that licensing procedures do not become unduly restrictive. The agreement provides for publishing relevant laws and procedures and making forms and procedures as simple as possible. It was also agreed that where automatic licensing systems are used they are not to be administered in a way that would restrict imports, and that where nonautomatic licensing systems are used the number of licenses to be issued must be public and interested parties must be informed of their allocations.

The United States uses import license systems in conjunction with import-quota programs. For example, cheese importers must obtain an import license from the Department of Agriculture. On the export side, all items exported from the United States are subject to an export license. The majority of items can be exported under a *general license*, which means that it is not necessary to submit a formal application or receive written authorization to ship these products. But for reasons of short supply, strategic significance, or foreign policy, the United States controls exports of some commodities, such as certain chemicals, plastics, electronic and communication equipment, and scarce materials such as petroleum. To export these commodities the exporter must obtain a *validated export license* from the Office of Export Administration in Washington.

ANTIDUMPING DUTIES.   *Dumping* is said to occur when a foreign producer prices an imported good at "less than fair value." As Wares (1977) explains, "Economists define dumping as price discrimination in international trade; that is, the sale of like goods at different prices in two or more national markets. This general definition encompasses both price discrimination between the producer's home market and foreign markets and between export markets alone." In recent practice, the definition of dumping has been extended to include sales below the full cost of production, including a reasonable profit.

The motivations behind dumping are varied. Foreign producers may find market conditions different in their home markets and the international market, and may find it more profitable to price discriminate. Alternatively, they may be attempting to make inroads into a new market abroad, drive a competitor out of business in the importing country (so-called *predatory dumping*) or simply get rid of surplus inventory without cutting prices at home (so-called *distress dumping*).

Whatever the motive behind dumping, importing countries respond to dumping by imposing antidumping duties. In general, antidumping duties counteract the dumping by imposing an extra duty on the dumped merchandise equal to the difference between the price of the imported good and the price charged for the same good in the home market of the exporting country, or the difference between the import price and the full cost of production. The so-called *trigger-price mechanism* for steel products instituted by the Treasury Department in December 1977 was essentially a fast-track antidumping procedure. The Treasury Department calculated the cost of production of steel products in Japan (the lowest-cost source). Any imports below these trigger prices were then subject to an antidumping investigation.

In the United States, import-competing industries may petition for antidumping duties if they feel imports are being dumped in the U.S. market. The two-stage procedure, as modified by the Trade Agreements Act of 1979, is outlined in Exhibit 1. First the Department of Commerce must decide whether dumping has in fact occurred. Second, the *International Trade Commission* (ITC) must investigate whether a domestic industry in the United States has been injured by importation of the dumped merchandise. The ITC (formerly the Tariff Commission) is made up of six commissioners, no more than three of which may be from one political party, appointed by the President for a term of nine years. If the ITC decides that the dumping has injured a domestic industry, then antidumping duties are imposed. In response to complaints from industry that the dumping cases were so time consuming that the remedy was ineffective, Congress imposed time limits on each stage of the procedure in 1974; these were further shortened in 1979.

COUNTERVAILING DUTIES. A countervailing duty is an extra charge imposed on imports that have received a "bounty or grant" in the exporting country. Countervailing duties, like antidumping duties, are designed to counteract "unfair" competition in international trade. Whereas antidumping duties are directed against less-than-fair-value sales by foreign exporters, countervailing duties are, in practice, directed against export subsidy practices of foreign governments. Countervailing duty investigations are therefore often more diplomatically sensitive than antidumping investigations since what is "investigated" is in essence the policy of another government.

Governments may subsidize exports for a variety of reasons. Agricultural exports are often subsidized to dispose of surpluses resulting from domestic agricultural-support programs. Export subsidies are used to encourage exports for balance-of-payments reasons. Some developing countries subsidize exports of manufactured goods to encourage industrialization and growth and diversify the composition of exports.

A countervailing duty neutralizes the effect of the subsidy by imposing an extra import duty equal to the amount of the subsidy. An export subsidy appropriately countervailed then in effect is simply a transfer of revenue from the coffers of the government of the exporting country to the government of the importing country. In the United States, the *procedure* in countervailing duty cases involves the Department of Commerce and the ITC. The Department of Commerce must determine that the exports in question have benefited from a "bounty or grant," and the ITC must determine that a domestic industry is being injured as a result. This procedure is illustrated in Exhibit 2. The requirement that a domestic industry be injured was added by the Trade Agreements Act of 1979, which implements the Agreement on Subsidies and Countervailing Measures reached in the MTN. Previously, no injury test was required in countervailing duty cases unless the imported good was free of duty in the tariff schedules.

EXHIBIT 1 ANTIDUMPING DUTY PROCEDURE

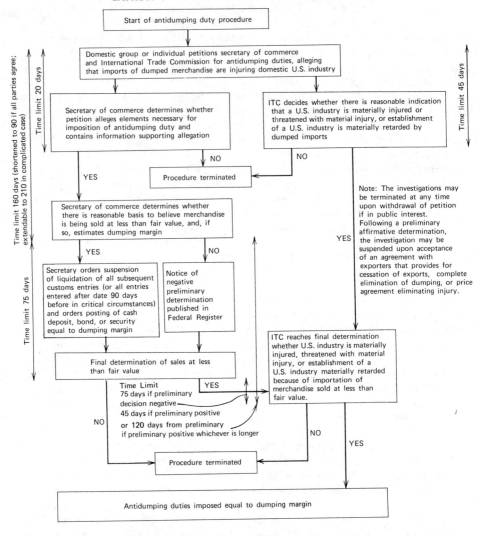

OTHER DIRECT TRADE BARRIERS. There are a number of other trade barriers that are special applications of tariffs or quotas, or combinations of tariffs and quotas. A *variable levy* is a tariff in which the rate charged depends upon the price of the imported good. The best example is the operation of the variable-levy system on imports of agricultural products into the EEC. Minimum prices are set for agricultural goods within the EEC. A variable levy, or duty, on imports is imposed equal to the difference between the minimum price and the price of the imported good. This has the effect of raising the price of imports up to the minimum price of the product within the EEC, whatever its price in the world market.

EXHIBIT 2   COUNTERVAILING DUTY PROCEDURE

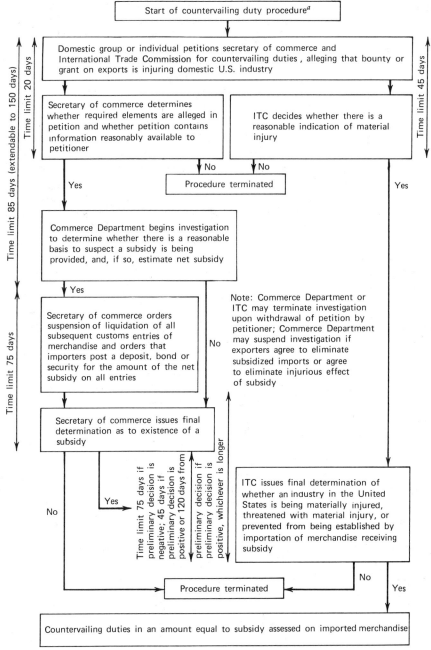

Start of countervailing duty procedure[a]

Domestic group or individual petitions secretary of commerce and International Trade Commission for countervailing duties , alleging that bounty or grant on exports is injuring domestic U.S. industry

Secretary of commerce determines whether required elements are alleged in petition and whether petition contains information reasonably available to petitioner

ITC decides whether there is a reasonable indication of material injury

No   No

Procedure terminated

Yes   Yes

Commerce Department begins investigation to determine whether there is a reasonable basis to suspect a subsidy is being provided, and, if so, estimate net subsidy

Yes

Secretary of commerce orders suspension of liquidation of all subsequent customs entries of merchandise and orders that importers post a deposit, bond or security for the amount of the net subsidy on all entries

No

Note: Commerce Department or ITC may terminate investigation upon withdrawal of petition by petitioner; Commerce Department may suspend investigation if exporters agree to eliminate subsidized imports or agree to eliminate injurious effect of subsidy

Secretary of commerce issues final determination as to existence of a subsidy

No   Yes

Time limit 75 days if preliminary decision is negative; 45 days if preliminary decision is positive or 120 days from preliminary decision if preliminary decision is positive, whichever is longer

ITC issues final determination of whether an industry in the United States is being materially injured, threatened with material injury, or prevented from being established by importation of merchandise receiving subsidy

No   Yes

Procedure terminated

Countervailing duties in an amount equal to subsidy assessed on imported merchandise

Time limit 20 days

Time limit 45 days

Time limit 85 days (extendable to 150 days)

Time limit 75 days

[a]For imports of dutiable articles from countries adhering to the GATT agreement on subsidies and countervailing measures and nondutiable imports from all sources. A countervailing duty can be levied on dutiable imports from countries not adhering to the GATT agreement on subsidies and countervailing measures without an injury determination by the ITC.

Another variant on the theme of tariffs and quotas is the *tariff-quota*. This trade impediment combines features of both a tariff and a quantitative restriction. A given tariff rate is charged on imports up to a certain amount (the quota limit). Imports over and above the limit may still enter the country, but are charged at a higher rate. A tariff-quota of this type was used to limit imports of stainless steel flatware into the United States. A tariff-quota that is restrictive enough to cause the higher tariff rate to come into effect will raise the price of the product in the importing country by the amount of the higher tariff rate (Pearson, 1979).

PAYMENTS RESTRICTIONS.   In addition to tariffs, quantitative restrictions, or other measures that limit imports, regulations pertaining to obtaining foreign exchange to pay for imports, or requirements concerning conversion of foreign-exchange earnings into domestic currency can act as trade barriers (see International Monetary Fund, 1979).

Many countries, primarily developing countries, employ various types of *exchange control*. All foreign exchange to pay for imports must be obtained from the central bank or authorized banks. Likewise, any foreign exchange earned by exporters must be surrendered to the authorities to convert it into domestic currency. These restrictions can act as trade impediments if foreign exchange is not made available for some transactions that are considered nonessential, such as imports of luxury or consumer goods.

Use of *multiple exchange rates* in conjunction with exchange control is another way of influencing trade flows through the payments system. The exchange rate used by the authorities to convert domestic currency into foreign currency differs, depending upon the type of transaction. The exchange rate (price of foreign currency in terms of domestic currency) is lower for goods considered essential and higher for luxury, or nonessential, goods. On the export side, the exchange rate is higher for foreign exchange earned on exports the government wants to encourage and lower for exports that the government wants to discourage or tax. A system of multiple exchange rates can have essentially the same impact as a system of import tariffs and export taxes on the goods themselves.

Yet another method of controlling trade is to require *prior import deposits* on shipments of imported goods. Under such a scheme, a certain percentage of the value of import shipments must be kept on deposit in interest-free accounts for a period of time. This effectively makes imports more expensive because of the loss of interest earnings and the difficulty of obtaining liquid funds in times of tight credit conditions.

ESCAPE CLAUSE OR SAFEGUARD ACTIONS.   *Escape-clause* or *safeguard* measures hark back to provisions of commercial treaties that allowed the signatories to rescind the provisions of the agreements if increased imports due to concessions seriously injured a domestic industry. GATT includes such a provision in Article XIX, which states:

> If, as a result of unforeseen developments and of the effect of the obligations incurred by a contracting party under this Agreement, including tariff concessions, any product is being imported into the territory of that contracting party in such increased quantities and under such conditions as to cause or threaten serious injury to domestic producers in that territory of like or directly competitive products, the contracting party shall be

free, in respect of such product, and to that extent and for such time as may be necessary to prevent or remedy such injury, to suspend the obligation in whole or in part or to withdraw or modify the concession.

In the United States the Trade Act of 1974 liberalized the criteria for the application of the escape clause by eliminating the necessary link between an increase in imports and a prior trade concession. As the legislation now stands, a firm, industry association, or trade union can petition for temporary protection. The escape clause (Section 201) procedure is outlined in Exhibit 3. The ITC first considers the case to determine (1) if imports have increased, (2) if the domestic industry has been seriously injured, and (3) if imports are a substantial cause of the injury. If the ITC finds that increased imports are a substantial cause of injury (or threat thereof) to a U.S. industry, it recommends a remedy to the President, such as an increased tariff, a quantitative restriction, a tariff-quota, or the provision of adjustment assistance to workers and/or firms. The President may implement the recommendation of the ITC, provide no relief, or choose a different remedy. The President has tended to choose adjustment assistance or negotiation of orderly marketing agreements (See Adams and Dirlam, 1977). The protection provided under the escape clause provisions is expressly temporary and limited. The remedies are for a period not to exceed five years (renewable for three more years at a level no more restrictive than the end of the first period). Tariffs may not be increased by more than 50 percent *ad valorem*, and quantitative restrictions may not reduce imports below the level in the most-recent representative period.

INDIRECT IMPEDIMENTS TO TRADE

Tariffs, quantitative restrictions, and the other restrictions and regulations used to limit trade are relatively straightforward. Their impact on trade flows, although at times difficult to estimate exactly, is at least conceptually direct and straightforward.

As government intervention in all aspects of economic life increased in the market-oriented economies of the West, it became evident that all government policies and programs that affect the economy also affect, and potentially distort, international trade flows. Krauss refers to the myriad ways in which "the totality of government intervention in the private economy affects international trade" as "the new protectionism" (Krauss, 1978). Government-mandated product standards, government aids to particular sectors, indeed, even the government's own purchasing decisions can, and do, distort the pattern of international trade.

STANDARDS.   To protect the health and safety of the population, governments often require that products sold within their territories meet certain minimum standards. For example, in the United States, high-pressure vessels must be approved by the American Society of Mechanical Engineers; meat products must be packaged in plants inspected and approved by the U.S. Department of Agriculture; certain foodstuffs must be labeled to indicate content. U.S. government regulations require that all imported automobiles meet U.S. emission, safety, and fuel-economy standards. Few other countries have emission standards, and no other country has fleet fuel-economy standards.

EXHIBIT 3   ESCAPE-CLAUSE PROCEDURE

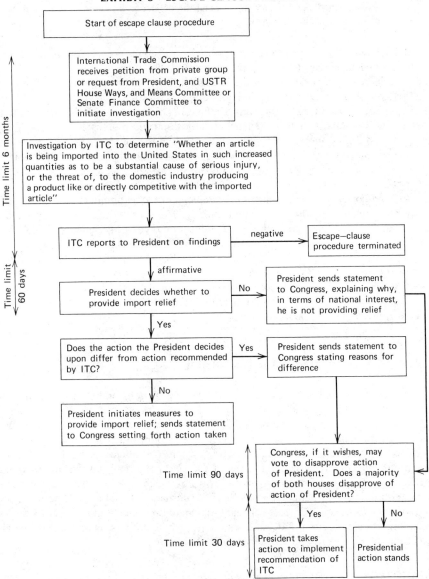

Source. Trade Act of 1974 PL 93-618, January 3, 1975, Section 201 of Tariff Act of 1930, amended.

These regulations are directed at domestic health, safety, and conservation objectives but can serve as *technical barriers to trade*, operating to make imports unavailable or effectively more expensive. If imported goods are barred from tests or procedures to certify that products meet the required standards, then imports will be barred from the market entirely. If requirements are not made public, are changed capriciously, or differ widely among countries, trade becomes riskier, and economies of large-scale production for export may be lost.

The issues surrounding standards are particularly thorny and difficult to negotiate. A certain technical requirement may pose a significant barrier to trade and harm the interests of a country's trading partners. Yet governments impose standards to achieve important domestic goals, so negotiations threaten to impinge on national sovereignty. Despite the difficulties involved, as part of the Tokyo Round of multilateral negotiations the participating countries attempted to reach agreements to mitigate the effects of these technical barriers to trade. The agreement reached in these negotiations is designed to minimize the possibility of discrimination against imports when governments impose product standards. First of all, it was agreed that any procedures to be followed to certify that products meet the required standards be open to imported as well as domestic goods. Secondly, the nations agreed that whenever possible domestic product standards should conform to existing international product standards.

GOVERNMENT AIDS TO DOMESTIC INDUSTRIES OR GROUPS. Governments undertake a wide variety of programs intended to improve or maintain the standard of living of particular groups, promote certain industries, or encourage the development of particular regions within the country. *Low-interest loans* to particular industries, *direct subsidies* to production, *infrastructure investment, investment grants, wage subsidies,* labor *training programs*, special *tax allowances*, and *government-sponsored research and development* all operate to reduce costs in particular economic activities. These programs thus in effect operate, to a greater or lesser degree, to subsidize domestic production and either encourage exports or discourage imports.

The European Community directly subsidizes coal production; in the United States the oil depletion allowance greatly reduces the tax liability of petroleum producers, and investment tax credits subsidize the acquisition of capital facilities. A number of industrial countries aid their electronics industries through grants, participating directly in the industry, and providing low-interest loans and tax incentives. Because of their link to national defense, shipping and shipbuilding industries are major recipients of government aids, particularly investment grants, preferential credit rates, tax exemptions and premiums for breaking up ships that are to be retired. (For details on various countries' policies see U.S. Tariff Commission, 1974, and Baldwin, 1970.)

Although the *GATT provisions* against export subsidies on nonprimary products are quite clear, GATT takes a weaker and more ambiguous stand on domestic subsidies. GATT permits "the payment of subsidies exclusively to domestic producers" (Article III) but requires that the country notify GATT about the extent, nature, impact, and reasons for the subsidy. If the interests of another contracting party are prejudiced by the subsidy, "the contracting party granting the subsidy shall, upon request, discuss . . . the possibility of limiting the subsidization" (Article XVII, see Contracting Parties to the GATT, 1969.)

Government price-support programs for particular products often have a direct impact on trade flows, because trade barriers must be imposed to keep imports from undermining the effectiveness of the program. Import quotas on certain agricultural products in the United States and the variable levies on agricultural imports into the European Community are both outgrowths of the domestic agricultural price-support programs.

GOVERNMENT PROCUREMENT PRACTICES. Governments, state and local as well as federal, are important consumers of goods and services. Government purchases constitute a lucrative potential market for foreign as well as domestic suppliers, but most governments favor domestic over foreign suppliers through a variety of regulations, practices, and procedures. Discrimination against foreign suppliers can be as open as the U.S. Buy American Act of 1933, which specifies that government agencies must procure goods from domestic sources unless the goods are to be used outside the United States, are unavailable in sufficient quality or quantity in the United States, or are "unreasonably costly." The exact margin of preference given to domestic suppliers before their products are considered "unreasonably costly" has varied over the years. In general, domestic suppliers are extended a 6 percent differential (increased to 12 percent for small businesses or labor-surplus areas) and a 50 percent differential for Department of Defense procurements. Domestic bids may be accepted even if they exceed foreign bids by more than this margin to protect national security or when domestic production is in the public interest.

In Europe and Japan, laws specifically favoring domestic producers are less common. However, lack of publicity in bid solicitation, failure to disclose the exact criteria for awarding contracts, covert discrimination, and inadequate time to prepare bids all can operate to the disadvantage of foreign suppliers.

Discrimination against foreign suppliers is expressly allowed by GATT and is not considered a violation of the national-treatment provision. Nonetheless, concern over the distorting effect of government procurement practices on trade flows prompted the nations participating in the Tokyo Round to include discussions on government procurement practices. The agreement reached sets forth rules on the drafting of the specifications for goods to be purchased, the advertising of prospective purchases, the time allowed for the submission of bids, qualifications of suppliers, opening and evaluation of bids, awarding of contracts, and hearing and reviewing protests. Signatories of the agreement agree to make their procurement regulations consistent with the agreement and to publish their regulations and all bid opportunities. This agreement is limited in scope in that it does not cover all contracts by all government agencies, but it constitutes a first step toward discouraging international discrimination in government purchasing.

For the United States, the Trade Agreements Act of 1979, which implements the agreements reached in the MTN, grants the President authority (as of January 1, 1981) to waive the provision of the Buy American Act for countries who grant reciprocal treatment for U.S. companies bidding on their government contracts.

CUSTOMS VALUATION AND CLASSIFICATION. The administrative procedures involved with clearing goods through customs can be as important an impediment to trade as the tariff rates themselves. Classification systems, valuation rules, discretionary power of customs officials, documentation requirements, consular formalities, and other government regulations all can create great uncertainty or impose substantial costs upon traders.

Where *ad valorem* duties are imposed, the method of determining the value of the goods is as crucial in determining the amount of duty ultimately paid as the tariff rate itself. Difficulties arise because of differences in valuation practices among countries. Most European countries and Japan adhere to the *Brussels Definition of Value*, or the cost of the goods delivered to the buyer at the place of importation or as the result of an open-market sale between independent buyers and sellers. This is equivalent to the *c.i.f.* value, or the value of the goods including the cost of the goods in the exporting country, marine or other freight insurance, and transportation costs (hence cost, insurance, freight). The valuation method used by the United States varies among products. For most U.S. imports, duties are assessed on the value of the good upon exportation, or the *f.o.b.* (free on board) value. A notable exception is the *american selling price* valuation method for benzenoid chemicals, certain rubber-soled footwear, certain wool knit gloves, and canned clams. These items are valued for customs purposes on the basis of the (higher) price of competing U.S. products. Many other countries, especially developing countries, use arbitrary "official" prices or "minimum" prices for valuation purposes.

Differences in customs classification systems among countries also pose problems for traders. The United States and Canada are the only two major trading nations that do not use the *Brussels Tariff Nomenclature* (BTN) to classify products for customs purposes.

Differences in classification systems create uncertainty for traders about exactly how their goods will be classified, and thus how much duty must be paid.

The importance of classification matters is illustrated by the controversy surrounding the classification of imported truck cabs and chassis in the U.S. tariff schedules. As of 1980, trucks were dutiable at 25 percent *ad valorem*, but the rate of duty for cabs and chassis for trucks was 4 percent *ad valorem*. As a result, cabs and chassis were imported separately and assembled in the United States. In 1980 the Treasury Department announced that imported lightweight cab/chassis would be reclassified as trucks, thus dutiable at the 25 percent rate.

An agreement reached on customs valuation matters during the Tokyo Round standardizes internationally the methods used to determine the value of imports dutiable on an *ad valorem* basis. The agreement specifies the transaction value of the imported merchandise as the primary method of valuation, with alternative valuation methods to be used only in specific conditions that allow the transaction value to be rejected as the appropriate valuation method. For the United States, the major impact of the agreement will be the elimination of the controversial american selling price valuation method.

SOURCES AND SUGGESTED REFERENCES

Adams, W., and J.B. Dirlam. "Import Competition and the Trade Act of 1974: A Case Study of Section 201 and Its Interpretation by the International Trade Commission," *Indiana Law Journal*, Vol. 52, No. 3 (1977), pp. 535–599.

Balassa, B. *Trade Liberalization among Industrial Countries: Objectives and Alternatives*, New York: McGraw-Hill, 1967.

Balassa, B. "Tariff Protection in Industrial Countries: An Evaluation," *Journal of Political Economy*, Vol. LXXIII, No. 6 (1965), pp. 573–594.

Baldwin, R.E. *Nontariff Distortions of International Trade*. Washington, D.C.: Brookings Institution, 1970.

Bergsten, C.F. "On the Nonequivalence of Import Quotas and 'Voluntary' Export Restraints," in Bergsten, C.F., ed. *Toward a New World Trade Policy: The Maidenhead Papers*. Lexington, MA: Lexington Books, 1975.

Baldwin, R.E., and J.D. Richardson, *International Trade and Finance: Readings*. 2nd ed. Boston: Little Brown, 1981.

Bhagwati, J.N. "The Generalized Theory of Distortions and Welfare," in Bhagwati *et al*. ed. *Trade, the Balance of Payments and Growth: Papers in International Economics in Honor of Charles P. Kindleberger*. Amsterdam: North-Holland, 1971.

Caves, R.E., and R.W. Jones. *World Trade and Payments: An Introduction*. Boston: Little, Brown, 1977.

Cline, W.R., N. Kawanabe, T.O.M. Kronsjö, and T. Williams. *Trade Negotiations in the Tokyo Round*. Washington, D.C.: Brookings Institution, 1978, p. 86.

Contracting Parties to the General Agreement on Tariffs and Trade. *Basic Instruments and Selected Documents. Vol. IV. Text of the General Agreement*. Geneva: GATT, 1969.

Corden, W.M. *The Theory of Protection*. London: Oxford University Press, 1971.

Corden, W.M. *Trade Policy and Economic Welfare*. London: Oxford University Press, 1974.

Dobson, J.M. *Two Centuries of Tariffs*. Washington, D.C.: U.S. Government Printing Office, 1976.

Grubel, H.G. "Effective Tariff Protection: A Non-Specialist Introduction to the Theory, Policy Implications, and Controversies," in H.G. Grubel and H.G. Johnson, eds. *Effective Tariff Protection*. Geneva: GATT and Graduate Institute of International Studies, 1971.

International Monetary Fund. *Annual Report on Exchange Arrangements and Exchange Restrictions*. Washington, D.C.: International Monetary Fund, 1979.

Johnson, H.G. *Aspects of the Theory of Tariffs*. London: Allen and Unwin, 1971.

Johnson, H.G. "The Gain from Exploiting Monopoly or Monopsony Power in International Trade," *Economica*, N.S. Vol. XXXV, No. 138 (1968), pp. 151–156, reprinted in *Aspects of the Theory of Tariffs*.

Krauss, M.B. *The New Protectionism: The Welfare State and International Trade*. New York: New York University Press, 1978.

Leamer, E.E., and R.M. Stern. *Quantitative International Economics*. Boston: Allyn and Bacon, 1970.

Magee, S.P. "The Welfare Effects of Restrictions on U.S. Trade," *Brookings Report on Economic Activity*, No. 3 (1972).

Meade, J.E. *Trade and Welfare*, London: Oxford University Press, 1955.

Metzger, S.D. *Lowering Nontariff Barriers: U.S. Law, Practice and Negotiating Objectives*. Washington, D.C.: Brookings Institution, 1974.

Morkre, M.E., and D.G. Tarr. *The Effects of Restrictions on United States Imports: Five Case Studies and Theory*. Staff Report, Bureau of Economics, Washington, D.C.: U.S. Government Printing Office, Federal Trade Commission, 1980.

Murray, T. *Trade Preferences for Developing Countries*. New York: Wiley, 1977.

Murray, T., W. Schmidt, and I. Walter. "Alternative Forms of Protection Against Market Disruption," *Kyklos*, Vol. XXXI (1978), pp. 624–637.

Pearson, C. "Protection by Tariff Quota: Case Study of Stainless Steel Flatware," *Journal of World Trade Law*, Vol. XIII, No. 4 (1979), pp. 311–321.

Richardson, J.D. *Understanding International Economics*, Boston: Little, Brown, 1980.

Stern, R.M. "Tariffs and Other Measures of Trade Control: A Survey of Recent Developments," *Journal of Economic Literature*, Vol. XI, (1973), pp. 857–888.

Takacs, W. "The Nonequivalence of Tariffs, Import Quotas, and Voluntary Export Restraints," *Journal of International Economics*, Vol. VIII (1978), pp. 565–573.

U.S. Congress. House. *Trade Agreement Act of 1979 Report*. House Report No. 96–317, July 3, 1979. Washington, D.C.: U.S. Government Printing Office.

U.S. Congress. House. *Agreements Reached in the Tokyo Round of the Multilateral Trade Negotiations*, 96th Congress, 1st Session House Document 96–153, Part I. Washington, D.C.: U.S. Government Printing Office, 1979.

U.S. International Trade Commission. *The History and Current Status of the Multifiber Arrangement*. Washington, D.C.: USITC Publication 850, 1978.

U.S. International Trade Commission. *Conversion of Specific and Compound Rates of Duty to Ad Valorem Rates*. Washington, D.C.: USITC Publication 896, July 1978.

U.S. International Trade Commission. *Study of the Effects of the Generalized System of Preferences on U.S. Trade in the Program's First Year of Operation, 1976*. Washington, D.C.: USITC Staff Study No. 12, March 1978.

U.S. International Trade Commission. *Summary of Statutory Provisions Related to Import Relief*. Washington, D.C.: USITC Publication 1057, April 1980.

U.S. Tariff Commission. *Trade Barriers; Part II, Nontariff Trade Barriers*. Washington, D.C.: USITC Publication 665, April 1974.

Walter, I. and K. Areskoug. *International Economics*, 3rd ed. New York: Wiley, 1981.

Wares, W.A. *The Theory of Dumping and American Commercial Policy*, Lexington, MA: D.C. Heath, 1977.

SECTION **10**

GOVERNMENT AIDS AND SERVICES

CONTENTS

ASSISTANCE PROVIDED BY THE U.S. DEPARTMENT OF COMMERCE 3

How It Is Organized 3
  U.S. Commercial Service 4
  Foreign Commercial Service 4
  Export Development 4
  East-West Trade 5
Counseling and Assistance 5
  Country specific 5
  Tailored Export Marketing Plans Services 5
  Seminars, workshops, and conferences 6
  Trade complaints 6
  Major projects 6
Commercial Intelligence and Marketing Information 7
  Commercial intelligence: Finding buyers and agents 7
  Trade opportunities 7
  Locating an agent 8
  World traders data report 9
  Worldwide information trading system 9
Overseas Promotions 9
  Exhibitions and trade fairs 9
  Trade missions 10
  Product-marketing service 11
  Foreign buyers 11
  New product information service 11
Other DOC assistance programs and services 11
  Multilateral trade negotiations 11
  Investment assistance 12

SMALL BUSINESS ADMINISTRATION 12

Counseling and Information 12

Small Business Institute/Small Business Development Center Program 12
Call Contract Program 12
Export Workshops and Conferences 13
Revolving Line of Credit Program 13
Other Loan Programs 13

DEPARTMENT OF AGRICULTURE 13

Cooperator Program 13
Trade Exhibits and Promotions 13
Trade Opportunity Referral Service 14
New Products Testing System 14
Export Incentive Program 14
Cooperation with State Departments of Agriculture 14
Commodity Programs 14
Export Credit and Foreign Assistance Programs 15

FINANCIAL SERVICES AND AIDS 15

Export Finance 15
  Short-term programs (to 180 days) 15
  Medium-term programs (180 days to 5 years) 16
  Long-term programs (over 5 years) 16
  Small business activities 17
  Agricultural export programs 17
Other Ex-Im Activities 17
Overseas Private Investment Corporation 17
  Project financing 18
  Insurance protection 18
  Feasibility studies 18
  Bid, performance, and advance-payment guarantees 18
Tax Incentives 20
  DISC provisions 20
  Recent legislative changes 20

10 · 2 GOVERNMENT AIDS AND SERVICES

International Development and
Cooperation Agency   21
   Trade and Development Program   21
   Agency for International Development   21

APPENDIX A: KEY CONTACTS   **21**

**APPENDIX B: REFERENCES AND
PUBLICATIONS**   **23**

GOVERNMENT AIDS AND SERVICES

Jonathan C. Menes

The federal government provides a variety of aids and services to assist and encourage U.S. exporters. The U.S. Department of Commerce is the principal agency of the federal government charged with promoting U.S. exports of manufactured goods and services. For agricultural products the Department of Agriculture has the principal responsibility. In the financial area the Export-Import Bank is the principal source of assistance. In addition there are other agencies, for example, the Small Business Administration (SBA), whose primary missions are not export expansion, but who nonetheless provide assistance to exporters.

Although a degree of coordination exists among agencies and their field offices, no one-stop shop exists for exporter assistance. It is frequently necessary for the individual or company seeking export services to contact a number of different agencies and offices in order to find the desired assistance. In addition, since much of the export information available within the government has not been automated, numerous inquiries may be necessary before the desired information is found. Thus patience and persistence is very important.

ASSISTANCE PROVIDED BY THE U.S. DEPARTMENT OF COMMERCE

Services and assistance provided by ITA fall into three areas: (1) business counseling and assistance; (2) commercial intelligence and marketing information and (3) overseas promotion. Many of the services offered by DOC involve fees. Where significant, these are noted, but a potential user should verify the current fees, since they are subject to change.

HOW IT IS ORGANIZED.   To make effective use of U.S. Department of Commerce (DOC) services, a knowledge of DOC's organizational structure as it pertains to export assistance is essential. The International Trade Administration (ITA) of the Department of Commerce is charged with the responsibility for expanding U.S. exports. Those units within ITA having direct responsibilities for export assistances services are

- United States Commercial Service
- United States Foreign Commercial Service
- Export Development
- East-West Trade

U.S. Commercial Service.   The Commerce Department's district-office network in the United States, now named the United States Commercial Service (USCS), is the domestic field arm of ITA's export-promotion activities. There are 47 district offices and 12 branch offices (see Appendix A) that serve as contact points for businesses seeking information on international trade subjects. Key functions of the USCS are to

- provide personal assistance to U.S. companies that have questions or problems regarding exports.
- serve as first point of contact for American exporters seeking assistance through ITA's worldwide network of commercial services.
- provide counseling for businesses seeking to enter exporting or expand their current efforts.
- organize and sponsor seminars, conferences, and workshops on business developments, international marketing, and related business subjects.
- provide advice to exporters on regulatory and procedural matters involving export controls and licenses and, in some authorized offices, issue licenses to exporters.

Foreign Commercial Service.   Since early 1980 U.S. commercial attachés and staff in the leading overseas markets have been part of the Commerce Department. The Foreign Commercial Service (FCS) is represented in 65 countries. In other parts of the world foreign service officers of the Department of State continue to provide commercial services. Among the more-important functions of the FCS are to

- counsel and support visiting U.S. businesspeople.
- gather and transmit commercial intelligence and marketing data to the United States.
- assist in the operation of promotional activities in support of U.S. products such as trade fairs and trade missions.

Obtaining the assistance of the foreign commercial service is normally accomplished through a USCS district office or the Washington staff. It is particularly important if a visit is planned to notify the FCS in advance. State and Commerce Departments both publish booklets listing key staff overseas (see Appendix B).

Export Development.   Export-assistance programs are developed and operated out of Washington by the Export Development (ED) unit. Although access to most of the programs operated by ED are available through the USCS, offices in ED can provide more in-depth counseling and assistance, particularly on questions or problems relating to specific overseas markets and export events.

East-West Trade.   The EWT unit parallels ED for exporter assistance but is limited to communist nations.

COUNSELING AND ASSISTANCE.   For an individual unfamiliar with government services for exporters, and particularly DOC services, the first place to start is a USCS district office. USCS trade specialists can explain in detail the available exporter services and accept applications for a variety of assistance services. The district offices have available most of the DOC publications of interest to an exporter.

A major function of the trade specialists in the district offices is providing advice and guidance on getting started in exporting. They can provide advice and guidance on the mechanics of exporting, including export financing and documentation, as well as helping to identify markets and buyers overseas. A limited number of district offices are equipped with computer terminals that provide immediate access to a variety of marketing information and trade leads. Where district offices cannot supply the desired information, they usually can refer the requester to the appropriate office or individual in Washington. The counseling as such is free; however, many of the ITA services available through the USCS do involve charges. In addition, where a computer terminal exists, retrievals must be paid for.

At DOC in Washington, a number of offices provide a variety of counseling services. For general inquiries the business-counseling staff provides assistance of the same type available from district offices. Staff members also refer inquiries to the more-specialized units in ED as necessary and will set special appointment schedules for business callers with other offices.

Country Specific.   Counseling that relates to a specific overseas market is provided by the trade specialists of the Office of Country Marketing. A country officer exists for every noncommunist nation. For communist countries the Office of East-West Country Affairs provides equivalent services. The country specialists are the principal source of information on economic and business conditions for specific countries. They are also a primary source of advice on marketing, including local business practices and laws, tariffs, and trade regulations. In addition to providing counseling on purely export-promotion matters, the country specialists should also be consulted when export-related problems arise with respect to a specific foreign country.

The *Trade Advisory Center* has been established to serve as a central point of contact for any problems or questions arising as a result of the multilateral trade agreements. This unit provides general information on the agreements and acts as a referral to other offices that can deal with the specific problems as well as a source of general information about the agreements.

In addition to offices already noted, there are a number of other offices and staffs in ED that can provide counseling and information beyond that which is available from published sources. A district-office trade specialist should be able to identify these units as necessary.

Tailored Export Marketing Plans Services.   A structured form of counseling is provided in the form of Tailored Export Marketing Plans Services (TEMPS). A TEMP is an export work plan and timetable to guide a firm through the fundamentals of exporting. Each TEMP is developed after consultation with the individual firm's management and provides information specific to that company's products. Currently

DOC is capable of producing approximately 100 TEMP's per year. In addition, TEMPs are also programmed for selected industry segments and made available to all interested firms. A substantial fee is charged for the individual TEMPS service. Firms interested should contact the district office. It is recommended that an interested firm examine an already completed TEMP to determine if the information and program would be of benefit to them. In many instances the marketing data contained in the TEMP is already available at a minimal cost. The TEMP alleviates the need for a major search or research effort to find the information, however.

Seminars, Workshops, and Conferences.   DOC and other agencies such as the Export-Import Bank hold many seminars throughout the United States. A number of general "how-to-export seminars" are held each year in different parts of the country. In addition, country-specific seminars focusing on a region or specific market and seminars keyed to a particular industry are programmed. There have been small-business seminars conducted jointly by DOC, SBA, and the Ex-Im Bank. Specialized conferences and workshops are also held. These have included conferences to match up smaller companies with export-management companies (EMCs). A schedule and details on upcoming seminars and conferences can be obtained from the local district office.

Trade Complaints.   This program facilitates the amicable settlement of commercial disputes involving U.S. exporters. Complaints are brought to the program staff by U.S. sellers or foreign purchasers. The program does not take sides in these disputes; rather, it uses the offices of the FCS and USCS to informally encourage both parties to establish or resume direct negotiations. Interested business persons should contact ED's business counseling staff or the USCS.

Major Projects.   This program assists U.S. industry to bid successfully on major international construction or infrastructure projects and on major product-sales opportunities. The program staff monitors foreign tenders, consultancy and product-sales contracts, and strategic system sales. Through the FCS, officers abroad and through private sources, the program staff gathers and disseminates information to U.S. firms interested in particular opportunities.

The program staff also plays a facilitative role on projects in which problems arise. The staff coordinates U.S. government support to insure that American firms receive fair treatment in bidding on projects. Such support usually takes the form of official representations to foreign buyers of major projects on behalf of all U.S. firms bidding on each project. The staff is also responsible for qualifying U.S. firms to bid on procurements by the North Atlantic Treaty Organization. No fees are charged for any of these services. Interested persons should contact the Major Projects Division.

An *export-information reference room* is maintained at DOC in Washington. This room is a centralized source of information on projects being considered for financing by development banks as well as "early warning cables" from foreign-service posts on major projects developing worldwide. This material is available for review on a personal-visit basis. A central information file on all project awards for prime contracts in international markets is also under development. This file is being established to assist U.S. companies interested in pursuing subcontractor/subsupplier opportunities. In addition to major project information, this reference room also contains a wide variety of publications, both government and private, relating to exporting.

COMMERCIAL INTELLIGENCE AND MARKETING INFORMATION.   DOC produces and collects from other foreign and domestic sources a vast amount of information concerning exporting and overseas markets. This information is made available both as received from the FCS and in specialized publications. The information available includes broad economic analyses of foreign economies, specialized studies of markets for specific products, and foreign business practices.

DOC conducts a *market research* program to develop detailed information on foreign markets. This information, most of which is generated through contracts with private market-research firms, is published in the form of country surveys for specific industries or product areas. The program is known as the Global Market Surveys. Some 70–100 new country surveys are produced each year. In addition, country sectoral studies, which cover virtually all significant industries for a particular country, are published on an occasional basis.

DOC also publishes a number of booklets and brochures to assist companies in exporting. A detailed list of publications is contained in Appendix B.

Through DOC, extensive *U.S. and foreign trade statistics* are available. This data can be extremely useful in assessing foreign market potential. The Census Bureau collects and publishes a large number of data series on U.S. exports and imports. The more-popular publications are available at libraries and district offices. The *Trade Reference Room* at DOC in Washington has a comprehensive collection of the census publications, including unlisted special computer runs. In addition to U.S. trade statistics, DOC maintains a library of reference materials on other countries export and import statistics is available in the *Foreign Trade Refernce Room.*

No central index of export information currently exists. Some partial indexes are available, including several on computerized data bases. A USCS district office is a good place to start in searching for export information.

Commercial Intelligence: Finding Buyers and Agents.   A long-established and extremely useful service of DOC is providing U.S. firms with information on specific overseas trade opportunities and obtaining foreign representation. Information and applications for these programs can be obtained from a USCS district office, and by writing to the export communications section of ITA, Washington, D.C.

Trade Opportunities.   The FCS collects information overseas on specific trade opportunities. These can be for immediate sales or representation. The sales opportunities include both private and government purchases. This information is cabled to Washington and is available to U.S. firms through the Trade Opportunity Program (TOP) in two ways: a notice service and a bulletin service. For the notice service, firms complete a form indicating the Standard Industrial Classification (SIC) product codes and countries they are interested in. This information is placed in the computer, and incoming opportunities are matched to the companies' interests. Firms pay in advance for a fixed number of opportunities. The bulletin is published once a week and contains all opportunities that have come in since the previous bulletin.

The notice service offers the advantage of speed, since the computer prints out notices in mailgram form for immediate transmittal to the subscriber firm. The bulletin, since it is published weekly, increases the delay in receiving the information. If the firm is interested merely in seeing the types of opportunities coming in, in order to gain a sense of the market, the bulletin is quite adequate and cheaper. If, however, firms are anxious to follow up on specific opportunities, the notice service is preferable. It can be useful to subscribe to the bulletin in addition to the notice service. Because of the difficulty in coding products, an opportunity may be missed if only the notice service is used. The bulletin provides a double check. The TOP program is also used for transmitting opportunities arising from *foreign government procurements*. Firms wishing to learn of foreign government procurements that have been opened up to U.S. companies as a result of the Multilateral Trade Agreements can obtain these as part of their normal subscription to the TOP program.

Locating an Agent.   For a firm seeking a foreign agent or representative, there are two principal ways in which DOC can be of assistance. One is to utilize the Foreign Traders Index, which is a data base of foreign representatives and buyers. A second is to request an agent distributor service (ADS), which provides for a specific search for a potential agent or representative by the FCS.

The *Export Contact List Service,* which provides information on more than 138,000 foreign importing firms, agents, representatives, distributors, and manufacturers, is stored on a central computer file known as the Foreign Traders Index. Information from this file can be obtained in three basic formats. (1) The Export Mailing List Service (EMLS) provides a customized retrieval against the computer file. Retrievals can be in the form of either mailing labels or a standard computer printout. The requesting firm needs to provide information about product areas and countries. At certain district offices, the Lockheed Dialogue system can be used to make the retrievals on an immediate basis. (2) Preprinted trade lists are also available. A number of lists have been developed for a variety of product areas. The index of currently available trade lists is available from DOC district offices. (3) The complete Foreign Traders Index computer file can be purchased, so that users can make their own retrievals.

Choosing among the various alternatives is primarily a question of cost versus convenience. The preprinted lists are very inexpensive and are available without delay, but are not usually detailed to the companies' specific product areas. The EMLS provides a detailed list, but at a significantly higher cost, and usually takes several weeks to be prepared. Accessing the Foreign Traders Index through private data-base services such as DIALOG offers both customized lists and rapid turnaround, but is usually considerably more expensive than the other alternatives. Purchase of the complete Foreign Traders Index table would probably only be cost effective for organizations making secondary distributions.

The *Agent Distributor Service* program assists U.S. companies to obtain foreign market representation by identifying firms in the selected country or countries that indicate an interest in handling the specific products.

The U.S. company's proposal is presented to potential agents or distributors by a U.S. foreign service officer in person or by telephone. Companies need to submit catalogs and other descriptive material to assist potential agents/distributors to fully assess the product. It is suggested that c.i.f. quotations (or price lists) can be included as a guide in determining price competitiveness.

The advantage of an ADS search over the export mailing lists is that the firms identified have been contacted and have indicated an interest in representing the requesting firm. There are several disadvantages. The ADS program is considerably more expensive. Each ADS search costs $90. A second disadvantage is that it usually takes several months, since company literature must be mailed to the foreign service. Whatever type of service is used to identify potential agents, a trip overseas may be necessary in order to make final arrangements. Before a trip is made to find a foreign agent, it would be wise to either write to potential agents identified from the Foreign Traders Index or to request an ADS search several months before departure.

World Traders Data Report. The WTDR service provides a data and credit report on foreign firms with an assessment by a U.S. FCS officer. This service can be used to provide information on potential agents or representatives identified by an ADS search or mailing lists. The service is used in conjunction with extensions of credit for export sales, and the report will serve as the second credit report required by the Foreign Credit Insurance Association (FCIA) for an export guarantee. The current fee is $40. A WTDR can be requested through a district office or directly from the Office of Trade Information Services in Washington.

Worldwide Information Trading System. DOC is now developing a computerized data-base system that will link the commercial attachés with the Washington staff with the district offices and will provide instantaneous communication and retrieval of export-related information. In addition to containing marketing information, the system will permit U.S. firms to register as U.S. suppliers, so that potential buyers can directly contact potential U.S. sellers. Currently this system is in the pilot stage and is available in five district offices in the United States. The system is due to expand in 1982. It is recommended that companies seeking more information ask their local district offices about the availability of the Worldwide Information Trading System (WITS).

OVERSEAS PROMOTIONS. A variety of assistance programs exist to help U.S. companies promote their products or services overseas and to make direct contact with agents and buyers. The overseas promotional vehicles offered by DOC are of two basic types: exhibitions and missions. The schedule of upcoming DOC-sponsored promotional events is published in the *Overseas Export Promotions Calendar,* which is available from any USCS district office or the Export Communication Section, Washington. For all DOC promotional services, the normal rule is that the products to be sold must be manufactured in the United States with at least 50 percent U.S. content.

Exhibitions and Trade Fairs. A number of different types of exhibit activities are offered through DOC, ranging from major trade fairs to catalog shows. Exhibitions are typically utilized by companies to acquire representation in a market and to expose their products to determine market interest as well as to make sales. It has generally been the philosophy of DOC that immediate sales at the exhibition are not the principal goal of its exhibition activity, which is to help firms obtain representation if new to market and to help firms already in the market to increase their share or introduce new products. It is important in making a decision on going overseas to consider carefully the firm's marketing strategy and how that fair would fit into it.

The major exhibit activity is through DOC-sponsored exhibits in existing *international trade fairs* and *solo fairs* organized either in temporary space or within permanent DOC exhibit facilities. DOC has fixed exhibit facilities capable of mounting exhibitions in three locations around the world. With few exceptions, solo exhibitions are usually organized around a product theme and in the case of international trade fairs DOC sponsored participation is undertaken only at fairs having a specific industry theme. The only exception occurs where U.S. participation is organized locally by the FCS and U.S. participants are drawn from companies already represented in the market.

For major exhibitions DOC provides a wide variety of *services to a participating U.S. company*. For an international trade fair, the U.S. participant can rely upon DOC to make all arrangements with show promoters. DOC will design and construct a U.S. pavillion and the individual booths for each exhibitor. Shipment of the products to the exhibit is faciliated by DOC's New York shipping office. Essentially all the U.S. firm must do is to provide products for display, technical and promotional literature, and a qualified represenative to staff the booth. One of the most-important services provided by DOC is market promotion. The DOC exhibit staff conducts a market promotion and publicity campaign prior to the exhibit to identify and attract to the exhibit potential customers and agents for each exhibitor. For solo exhibits, the services are roughly equivalent. DOC services can be extremely useful for a firm with relatively limited experience overseas. Exhibit services are not inexpensive, however. Participation in a major trade exhibit sponsored by DOC can be expensive. *Required participation contributions* vary from event to event, depending on location. In 1981 the average required contribution was $3500, but ran as high as $7000 for several events in the Middle East. Travel costs for the company representatives attending the exhibit are, of course, additional.

In addition to alleviating the need for the participating company to make arrangements directly with fair authorities, DOC exhibitions can offer some other benefits. For some international trade fairs, DOC-sponsored participation is sometimes the only access, because space in the fairs is booked way in advance. In some parts of the world, particularly the Middle East, the DOC-sponsored exhibit may be the only promotional activity available. The *market launch* service, which is new and not available in all countries, provides lower-cost, no-frills assistance to U.S. firms that wish to participate in existing international trade fairs. Unlike the regular trade-fair program, where a U.S. DOC pavillion is set up, and considerable assistance is given in the design and construction of exhibit booths, in this program DOC acts only as a conduit for financial, transportation, and exhibit arrangements between U.S. companies and overseas trade-fair managers and organizers. This program is still in the pilot stage.

For companies already in the market, DOC through its ED offices overseas can in some locations help organize what is known as *business-sponsored promotions*. Essentially, DOC makes its exhibit space overseas available to a company at a relatively small fee to help it exhibit its products. In this case DOC does not organize the exhibit or provide promotional assistance. Normally local agents or representatives of the U.S. company make the appropriate arrangements.

Overseas promotional exposure and sales leads can be obtained at a lower cost through *catalog* and *video/catalog exhibitions*. As the names imply, no equipment is exhibited, and the firm participating in the catalog show does not send a representative. The exhibition is supported by FCS officers as well as a U.S. industry expert selected by DOC.

Video/catalog exhibitions are sales exhibits based on sound and color videotape presentations and a display of company catalogs. Twenty to 30 U.S. firms in a particular product area provide audiovisual materials and scripts highlighting the features, applications, and benefits of one or more related products; these are then edited and produced in videotape form. A U.S. industry expert is present at the show to explain the products and assist potential buyers and representatives. Typically a video/catalog exhibition or a catalog show is staged in three to four overseas market locations.

Trade Missions.   The trade missions is the other principal export-promotion vehicle. These are organized in a number of different ways. The principal types are: DOC-sponsored, industry-organized government-approved (IOGA) and seminar missions. Virtually all *DOC-sponsored missions* are organized on a vertical, that is, industry or end-user basis. Experience has shown that vertical missions tend to be more effective, with a limited number of products all sharing some similar characteristics or end-users. This type of organization makes it easier for overseas commercial officers to develop appointments and meetings with potential buyers, agents, and government officials in foreign markets.

In conjunction with the commercial attachés in each country market, DOC organizes a series of meetings and separate appointments for participants in the mission with potential agents, representatives, and buyers, and in some cases with government officials. The types of appointments are dependent on the firms' needs and the nature of the market.

The *industry organized government-approved trade missions* are generally similar, except that the impetus for the mission comes from industry-sector groups, state development agencies, and chambers of commerce. These organizations select the members and the locations to be visited. When approved by DOC, assistance in facilitating the mission is provided by Washington and overseas by the staff.

Trade missions can be useful vehicles for penetrating new markets or expanding existing ones, particularly when dealing with products that are not easily transportable or lend themselves to trade fairs, for example, very large construction equipment and chemicals. Also, because of the affiliation with the U.S. government and the U.S. embassy, the missions frequently can provide access to decision makers in the business community and government that otherwise could not be reached. In certain cases, high-level U.S.-government officials will travel with the mission to provide additional exposure and access.

A somewhat different type of mission is the *seminar mission*. These missions are designed principally to facilitate the sale of sophisticated technologies and products abroad. They combine a generic discussion of a given product or technology with private appointments to assist each company in marketing its product. These types of missions are particularly useful in creating a demand for a product where it doesn't already exist. Thus the benefits can be of a longer-term variety, as opposed to more-immediate sales that might be obtained in a market where technology is already known and a market exists.

The schedule of DOC-sponsored overseas promotional events is usually available at least a year in advance. The selection of events is based on a detailed analysis of major markets around the world and the potential for U.S. exports to each market. Market research is usually conducted in advance to provide analysis of the market. This research is provided to potential participants. Specific questions about events should be directed to the industry participation division of the Office of Export Promotion. (For a communist country the appropriate unit is the Trade Promotions Division.) A company with specific questions about a particular market or promotional event may also want to speak with the appropriate country specialists in the Office of Country Marketing.

Product-Marketing Service.   Not specifically an exhibition but a useful service is the product-marketing service, which can provide business executives with office space for up to five days, free local phone service, access to telecommunications, audiovisual equipment, market briefings, and lists of key business prospects. Assistance is also available in obtaining secretarial and interpreter services at the U.S. companies' expense. It is only available at selected locations in the world where space is available. Again arrangements should be made through DOC's district offices or through the Office of Export Promotion in Washington.

Foreign Buyers.   Exposing products to foreign buyers can also be done through participation in trade fairs held in the United States. To facilitate this process, DOC assists in bringing foreign buyers to the United States. Interested trade-fair-organizing authorities should contact the Foreign Buyer Division.

New Product Information Service.   A very inexpensive way to obtain overseas exposure for new U.S.-made products is through the New Product Information Service (NPIS). The U.S. company submits promotional product descriptions to DOC. In turn this information is published in DOC publication *Commercial News USA,* which is distributed to 240 foreign-service posts. In many embassies portions of *Commercial News USA* are translated into the local language. For further information, contact a district office or the Export Communications Section in Washington, D.C.

OTHER DOC ASSISTANCE PROGRAMS AND SERVICES

Multilateral Trade Negotiations.   The Multilateral Trade Negotiations (MTN), or the Tokyo Round, was the latest round of trade negotiations held under the auspices of the General Agreement on Tariffs and Trade (GATT). As a result of the negotiations, agreements were signed. DOC is the principal source of assistance in taking advantage of these agreements.

The *Trade Advisory Center* in ITA is a central contact point to which inquiries and problems regarding the MTN agreements can be directed. The center has available pamphlets that briefly describe the codes and their principal benefits for U.S. firms. The center is also publishing a series of booklets giving a more extensive discussion of the codes. Both the pamphlets and booklets should be available at USCS district offices. Where the center cannot answer a question itself, it will make referrals to the appropriate office.

A key agreement reached in the MTN was the Code on *Foreign Government Procurement,* which opens to U.S. firms for the first time government procurements in other major industrial nations. The code allows for two basic types of procurements, open and selective. In both cases the government making the procurement must follow specified procedures to ensure that foreign companies have an equal opportunity. The FCS sends back by cable a notice of each foreign-government tender notice. These are disseminated to the U.S. business community through the TOP program and are also published in summary form in *Commerce Business Daily.* Firms wishing to receive these notices should subscribe to the TOP notice or bulletin service. It is important to note that the code does not require more than 30 days between publication of the tender notice and the closing of bidding. In addition to cabling the tender notices, the commercial service also ships to Washington the complete tender documents. These can be obtained through a private reproduction service.

Investment Assistance. DOC provides some limited assistance in facilitating investment and licensing in the United States and overseas. These programs are carried out by the Investment Advisory Staff in ED.

Foreign-Investment Facilitation. Counseling and information is available to U.S. firms seeking to invest overseas, in particular to establish licensing and joint-venture arrangements. In addition to providing information on foreign investment regulations, laws, and taxes, the investment staff publishes and disseminates information on special foreign licensing and joint-venture and investment proposals. Almost all of these opportunities are published in *Business America.*

The *Invest in the U.S.A.* program offers several types of assistance to facilitate investment in the United States. These include (1) arranging contacts between foreign investors and the National Association of State Development Agencies, individual state-agency banks, firms, and individuals, and (2) providing guidance to interested foreign manufacturers on U.S. business conditions and laws.

SMALL BUSINESS ADMINISTRATION

The Small Business Administration (SBA) offers through its 110 field offices various programs and services to assist prospective or current small exporters. The extent to which these services are available varies among SBA field offices. Eligibility for certain of the SBA programs and services is dependent upon the size of the business. The definition of a "small business" varies by industry, and a local SBA office should be consulted. SBA's programs and services are provided at no charge to small businesses. SBA offers a variety of programs to assist small businesses to expand into exporting.

COUNSELING AND INFORMATION. Members of the Service Corps of Retired Executives (SCORE) and the Active Corps of Executives (ACE), who have had many years of practical experience in international trade, are available to help the small-business entrepreneur make a preliminary assessment of his/her export potential. These volunteers can help a small business to identify managerial, financial, or technical problems. There are presently over 675 such business executives who are available to assist the small-business exporter.

SMALL BUSINESS INSTITUTE/SMALL BUSINESS DEVELOPMENT CENTER PROGRAM. In the SBI program, senior and graduate-level students of international business are made available to provide overseas marketing assistance to small businesses. Students from over 450 colleges and universities cooperate with SBA district offices to provide in-depth and long-term counseling to small businesses in their areas. At a limited number of small-business-development centers located within certain state colleges and private universities, additional export counseling and assistance is offered through international trade centers. These centers currently exist at Rutgers University, the University of Georgia, the University of Alabama, the University of Wisconsin, and Washington State University.

CALL CONTRACT PROGRAM. This program provides small exporters with sophisticated market information and production technology to identify and service overseas markets. This specialized export assistance is provided by professional management and technical consultants.

EXPORT WORKSHOPS AND CONFERENCES. Export workshops are conducted periodically in cities across the country under the cosponsorship of SBA district offices, DOC, and other agencies and institutions concerned with international trade. Workshops principally focus on the mechanics of exporting.

REVOLVING LINE OF CREDIT PROGRAM. This is a pilot program designed specifically for small firms engaged in exporting. Using SBA's guaranteed-authority plan, the program can provide additional support to finance small-business exports through a group of selected banks in four states: California, Illinois, New York, and Texas. Under the current pilot plan, SBA guarantees repayment to the participating private-sector lender of 90 percent of export revolving-line-of-credit loans used to perform export sales contracts.

OTHER LOAN PROGRAMS. Primarily through its regular business loan guarantee program, SBA can assist a bank in providing to an exporter the funds necessary to purchase machinery or supplies to manufacturers or to sell products overseas or for working capital. However, the supply of available direct loan funds is very limited.

DEPARTMENT OF AGRICULTURE

The export promotion activities of the U.S. Department of Agriculture (USDA) are intended to develop, maintain, and expand foreign markets for U.S. agricultural commodities. The Foreign Agricultural Service (FAS) carries out these efforts through its network of agricultural counselors, attachés, and trade officers stationed overseas at about 70 American embassies and eight trade offices. This overseas staff is supported by a backup team of commodity analysts, marketing specialists, and negotiators in Washington, D.C.

FAS representatives can provide information and advice to U.S. businessmen on a variety of subjects affecting international sales of agricultural commodities, including U.S.- and foreign-trade data, foreign competition, marketing intelligence, transportation and contract information, and promotion techniques. FAS has several services to help develop export opportunities.

COOPERATOR PROGRAM. The agricultural export development program overseas is carried out in cooperation with more than 50 agriculturally oriented, nonprofit commodity associations known as market development cooperators. These cooperators represent approximately 3.5 million farmers, 1500 U.S. cooperatives, and more than 7000 processors and handlers. The cooperators work with an estimated 1600 foreign firms and trade associations in 80 foreign markets. Cooperator activities are carried out under contractual agreements with FAS. Promotional activities are proposed in annual marketing plans, developed by the cooperator, and submitted to FAS for approval. These projects include technical trade servicing, joint promotional efforts with the foreign customer, and trade and consumer press contacts and advertising.

TRADE EXHIBITS AND PROMOTIONS. FAS participates in exhibitions aimed directly at specific, targeted decisionmakers in the food trade. Promotional activities include participating in international and FAS-sponsored trade shows, agent food exhibits, agricultural attaché product displays, point-of-purchase (POP) promotions, livestock shows, and sales teams. Exhibit fees for participating companies cover exhibit space, facilities, and various trade relations services. Exhibitors are responsible for providing the product and full-time representation at some of the shows.

TRADE OPPORTUNITY REFERRAL SERVICE. This three-part system provides a fast link between foreign buyers and domestic sellers of U.S. food and agricultural products. It consists of (1) a computerized direct-mail service for established food and agricultural export firms interested in trade leads and other export information for one or more specific items. Foreign buyers contact USDA representatives overseas about products they wish to purchase. This information is cabled to Washington and mailed directly to U.S. suppliers; (2) *Export Briefs,* a weekly trade bulletin for export agents, trade associations, and companies interested in export opportunities for all food and agricultural items. This bulletin provides trade leads, news of upcoming trade shows, and other foreign trade developments; (3) a monthly newsletter that enables U.S. producers, particularly new exporters or exporters with new-to-market products, to publicize their products with foreign buyers. This monthly release is sent to USDA representatives overseas who distribute it to interested foreign firms.

NEW PRODUCTS TESTING SYSTEM. The new products testing system helps locate overseas markets for food products and determine if they meet specifications necessary for overseas sales. The system consists of label clearance and/or taste testing. For a $5.00 fee per label per country, label(s) will be forwarded to USDA representatives overseas for clearance by the foreign government. Firms are then notified of the results of the evaluation and what changes, if any, would be necessary for products to enter the market. Firms can arrange for products that meet entry requirements to be taste-tested by a consumer or marketing panel to determine how well it would be received in a foreign country. The cost of the service in each country ranges from $50 to $200 per product.

EXPORT INCENTIVE PROGRAM. The EIP program is designed to assist private U.S. firms in promoting their branded products overseas. Under the program, FAS reimburses firms for a portion of their export promotion expenditures, which is determined by the level of exports and promotional activities. Approval of a program is based on certain criteria, such as the probable success in maintaining or increasing consumption of U.S. products, long-range contribution to U.S. agriculture, and competition in the export markets. The program features such products as nuts, fresh fruits and vegetables, wines, and some canned and frozen fruits and vegetables.

COOPERATION WITH STATE DEPARTMENTS OF AGRICULTURE. FAS has developed working relationships with every state department of Agriculture. These states and their regional organizations have committed manpower and funds to joint promotional activities overseas. A major function of the state representatives has been to provide a further link between FAS and potential food exporters, to assist in carrying out selected exhibitions, and to perform selected market surveys.

COMMODITY PROGRAMS. Through this section of FAS, data relating to foreign demand, production and supply, and distribution of agricultural commodities can be obtained. The data is collected from overseas field reports, special field studies conducted in Washington, and from various other sources. Advanced economic analyses are conducted to produce short-term commodity forecasts, commodity status summaries, and market potential guidance on a country and commodity basis. In addition, FAS uses remote sensing data and data processing technology to analyze satellite, weather, and other data.

EXPORT CREDIT AND FOREIGN ASSISTANCE PROGRAMS.   FAS also is responsible for administering USDA's export credit programs and foreign assistance. The Public Law 480 Program (also called the Food for Peace Program) and the Commodity Credit Corporation (CCC) Export Credit Sales Program allow FAS to provide concessional and commercial financing for agricultural products purchased by some countries. P.L. 480 is aimed at long-range improvement in the economies of developing countries. CCC offers protection for U.S. exporters against payment defaults by foreign buyers. Private channels of trade are used to the fullest extent possible. Purchases are made from U.S. exporters and interest charges are usually negotiated by the buyer with U.S. banks.

Many of the above USDA programs are provided free of charge to U.S. agricultural producers and exporters. Interested individuals or companies seeking more information should contact the Foreign Agricultural Service, U.S. Department of Agriculture.

FINANCIAL SERVICES AND AIDS

EXPORT FINANCE.   The *Export-Import Bank* of the United States, which is an independent U.S. government agency, plays a key role in the financing of U.S. exports. Export-Import operations can be conveniently divided into three areas: short, medium, and long term.

Short-Term Programs (To 180 Days).   The short-term programs are based exclusively on the Export Credit Insurance program that Ex-Im Bank operates through the Foreign Credit Insurance Association (FCIA). FCIA is a private association made up of leading American insurance companies. Such insurance permits an exporter to obtain or offer better financing in certain cases. Exporters or banks seeking to use these programs should work directly with FCIA insurance brokers.

The *FCIA* Ex-Im short-term credit insurance is available in several different forms. There is a *short-term comprehensive policy,* which covers both political and commercial credit risks. The comprehensive policy permits the exporter to obtain coverage automatically on individual transactions based on the exporter's own credit decisions up to a discretionary limit. Beyond that the exporter must contact FCIA for approval. The comprehensive policy covers up to 90 percent of commercial credit risks and 100 percent of political risks for sales on terms up to 180 days. The terms are slightly different for agricultural commodities. These short-term policies are also issued to banks to assist them in financing export sales and are able to commit FCIA and Ex-Im on short-term transactions up to $200,000. A short-term political-risk policy is also available. FCIA insurance is on a whole turnover basis. That is, the exporter must insure all short-term risks and not simply selected sales.

FICA also offers a *master policy* that covers both short- and medium-term credit sales with repayment periods up to 5 years. The policy can cover sales to end-users, dealers, or distributors. To reduce paperwork and premium, the exporter assumes first losses up to a stated deductible, with losses thereafter from FCIA's account.

Services.   FCIA also offers a policy covering the exporters' services performed by U.S. personnel. This policy is available in either short or medium terms and covers contract billings in the same way that the short- or medium-term policies cover the sale of tangible goods.

Medium-Term Programs (180 Days to 5 Years)

FCIA Medium-Term Policies.   FCIA offers *single-buyer policies,* which provide medium-term coverage for exports on a buyer-by-buyer basis. These can cover separate sales or credit lines covering repetitive sales to a specific customer.

For exporters who sell to overseas dealers and distributors, a combination short- and medium-term insurance policy is available. This type of policy can cover inventory financing as well as receivables financing. Master policies as were described in the previous section are also available. In addition, there are other specialized types of coverage offered through FCIA for preshipment coverage and consignment sales.

Commercial Bank Guarantee Program.   Under this program, Ex-Im offers protection against commercial and political risks on debt obligations acquired by banks from U.S. exporters. Ex-Im Bank has established relationships with almost 300 American commercial banks engaged in financing medium-term U.S. capital equipment exports. U.S. commercial banks can obtain authority from Ex-Im Bank to make commitments without obtaining prior approval.

Discount Loan Program.   Ex-Im provides support to U.S. commercial banks in offering fixed-rate medium-term credits by extending a loans against a bank's purchase of a foreign obligation. Ex-Im will also agree to purchase foreign obligations from U.S. banks.

Information on these Ex-Im programs is available from the Office of the Vice President for Export Credits and Guarantees.

Long-Term Programs (Over 5 Years).   Long-term programs are designed to facilitate the export of U.S. capital equipment, and frequently involve major projects or large-scale installations warranting long repayment terms. Ex-Im Bank financing can be in the form of either a direct credit to an overseas buyer or a financial guarantee to elicit long-term private-sector lending. In many cases these two types of assistance are blended together. Ex-Im normally expects that private financing will be sought for each transaction, and Ex-Im will not become involved until efforts to obtain private credits are undertaken. The degree to which Ex-Im participates varies widely, depending on competitive conditions in the capital market. Normally Ex-Im involvement, including both loan and guarantee, runs between 30 percent and 85 percent of the U.S. cost of the transaction.

Ex-Im is required to find a reasonable assurance of repayment, and often requires a repayment guarantee by a financial organization in the buyer's country in order to assure payment.

Applications.   There is no standard application for direct loan of financial guarantees. Organizations seeking to make application should write directly on their letterheads to Ex-Im Bank describing the nature of the financial request. Bank responses to requests for assistance can take three forms, depending on the stage of negotiations. In a *letter of interest,* the bank does not provide specific terms of its possible involvement, but it will generally advise whether or not it would consider financing the type of product or project in the particular country. A preliminary commitment will outline amount, terms, and conditions of the financial assistance that it is prepared to offer. Unlike the final application, which must be submitted by the overseas buyer, applications for *preliminary commitments* may be submitted by the overseas buyer, U.S. exporter, or U.S. or foreign bank involved in the transaction. The final application for a loan and guarantee must be submitted by the prospective borrower/ lender. For additional information contact the senior vice president for direct credits.

Small Business Activities.   Ex-Im and FCIA offer a short-term insurance policy specifically to meet the needs of small-business exporters. This policy is available to firms with a net worth of $2 million or less who have not previously used Ex-Im or FCIA programs. For medium-term financing, Ex-Im Bank offers coverage similar to that offered under the short-term policy. Ex-Im has made some modifications to its guarantee program in order to make it appeal to a broader range of banks in providing sufficient incentives to finance small-business transactions. In addition to its financing activities, the Ex-Im Bank provides a hotline, which is designed to specifically help answer questions of small-business exporters concerning export and financing of goods or sales to foreign countries. The toll-free number is 800-424-5201. Export-Import Bank also cooperates with other government agencies in providing seminars and conferences to help the smaller firms learn how to export and finance their exports.

Agricultural Export Programs.   Export-Import Bank also provides assistance to help U.S.-farm-product exports. Ex-Im and FCIA short-term commercial- and political-risk insurance is available. In addition, a program has been developed with USDA's Commodity Credit Corporation to support exports of storage and processing facilities to facilitate the export of U.S. farm products.

OTHER EX-IM ACTIVITIES.   The *Contractors Guarantee Program* designed for U.S. constructors engaged in overseas construction projects was previously operated by the Overseas Private Investment Corporation. It covers four types of losses: inconvertibility, confiscation, war risks, and disputes.

Ex-Im also offers risk coverage on the *leasing* of American capital equipment overseas on medium- and long-term payout arrangements.

Ex-Im will support U.S. firms undertaking *feasibility studies* for overseas projects. FCIA, commercial bank, and the Cooperative Financing Facility programs are available. Only the U.S. cost of such studies is eligible for financial coverage.

Ex-Im's Office of Public Affairs conducts *briefings* at the bank's headquarters to familiarize exporters with Ex-Im's four programs. Both 1-day and 2-day programs are offered.

OVERSEAS PRIVATE INVESTMENT CORPORATION.   The Overseas Private Investment Corporation (OPIC) is an independent, self-sustaining government corporation that operates as a component of the International Development Cooperation Agency (IDCA). OPIC offers U.S. investors in over 90 developing countries coverage against the political risks of expropriation, inconvertibility of currency, and loss arising from war, revolution, and insurrection. This insurance is available for conventional equity and debt and for arrangements such as licensing and service contracts. Bilateral agreements between OPIC and host governments form the basis for providing these facilities and for subrogation of rights should a claim be paid. OPIC recently implemented an insurance program for bids, advance payments, and performance bonds related to construction projects.

In its finance program, OPIC makes direct loans and guarantees loans against both commercial and political risk. OPIC loans are available to help finance projects that involve significant U.S. equity participations. OPIC also offers preinvestment assistance, such as partial feasibility funding, investment brokering between U.S. investors and potential host countries, and sponsorship of investment missions to developing countries. OPIC maintains special-sector programs for mineral and energy investment; food production, processing, and distribution; and U.S. small businesses and cooperatives to facilitate their entry into international markets.

Project Financing. OPIC can provide medium- and long-term funds for project financing. OPIC commitments cannot exceed 50 percent for start-up projects and 75 percent for expansions of existing businesses. It can participate through direct loans, which usually range from $200,000 to $3 million, and loan guarantees up to a maximum of $50 million for any one project made by private U.S. financial institutions.

Insurance Protection. OPIC can provide political-risk insurance to cover (1) currency inconvertibility, (2) expropriation, and (3) loss or damage caused by war, revolution, or insurrection. Foreign government approval is required.

Feasibility Studies. OPIC can provide cost-sharing with a U.S. firm to determine the feasibility of an investment opportunity identified by the firm. The maximum OPIC participation is $50,000.

Bid, Performance, and Advance-Payment Guarantees. Engineering and construction contractors can obtain insurance for irrevocable standby letters of credit, which are required by many countries as bid, performance, and advance-payment guarantees. OPIC insures U.S. contractors against losses caused by arbitrary drawings and thus enables U.S. engineering and construction companies to meet third-country competition in overseas markets. This program also offers insurance to nonservice contractors and supliers who are required to post unconditional bond guarantees for their exports. This insurance removes a competitive disadvantage that U.S. exporters faced against other-country exporters whose governments provide protection from loss due to arbitrary drawings against these bonds.

OPIC analyzes the potential competitive impact of each insurance and finance project it supports on the level of U.S. exports and U.S. employment. Consequently, the foreign-investment projects selectively encouraged by OPIC result in U.S. export benefits, primarily as a result of purchases of U.S. machinery and equipment to construct the facilities, and continuing purchases of U.S. raw materials and farm product, semifinished goods, and spare parts required by these projects. Some OPIC projects are specifically designed to facilitate increased levels of U.S. exports, including bulk transshipment facilities, flour mills, foreign construction contracts, and distributorships for U.S.-made heavy equipment.

Businesses should contact OPIC directly for more information and application details.

TAX INCENTIVES. The domestic international sales corporation (DISC) is a form of organization that provides a tax incentive for exports. Through its use, companies incorporated in the United States and engaged almost exclusively in the export of U.S. products are allowed to defer payment of federal income taxes on one half of their export profits. It was enacted into law as part of the Revenue Act of 1971, and is contained in Sections 991 through 997 of the Internal Revenue Code.

DISC Provisions. To qualify as a DISC, a company must be incorporated in the United States, meet certain minimal organizational requirements, derive at least 95 percent of its receipts from qualifying export sales, leases, or rental transactions, and show that 95 percent of its assets are export related. Qualified receipts include those derived from architectural and engineering services, services "related and subsidiary" to the sale of export property, managerial services provided to another DISC, and certain receipts from export finance, as well as income derived from the sale, lease, or rental of export property.

A DISC can function as a principal, buying or selling on its own account, or as a commission agent. It may be related to a manufacturing parent, or be an independent merchant or broker. Special intercompany pricing rules on transactions between a DISC and its parent allow a larger profit to the DISC than would normally be permitted under the "arm's-length" pricing rules of the Internal Revenue Code.

The DISC provisions allow qualified companies to retain, free of current income-tax liability, up to one half of their annual income. Such income is not taxed until distributed, provided it is used in certain export-development activities. The remaining half of a DISC's annual income must be "passed through" to the shareholders on a current basis, and these prorated amounts are taxable as part of the shareholders' income. In cases in which DISCs are owned by corporations, which is the most frequent case, the intercorporate dividend deduction does not apply on the distributions.

The DISC's tax-deferred earnings retained by the DISC can be (1) invested in its export business to build up inventories or provide office and warehouse facilities, (2) used to extend financing to its foreign customers, and (3) invested in certain Export-Import Bank obligations or in loans to related or unrelated U.S. producers for export.

Recent Legislative Changes. The Tax Reduction Act of 1975 and the Tax Reform Act of 1976 have somewhat narrowed eligibility criteria and the scope of DISC benefits. The former disqualifies exports of raw material and energy resources, the extraction of which is subject to percentage depletion, unless at least half of the value of the export is due to postextraction U.S. processing or manufacturing. It also denies benefits to exports of products declared in short domestic supply under the Export Administration Act.

The Tax Reform Act of 1976 reduces the DISC deferral on exports of military property to one half of that usually allowed. It also provides that DISC earning in excess of $100,000 may take advantage of the standard 50 percent deferral only to the extent that the value of its exports in the tax year reported exceeds 67 percent of its previous average annual base-period exports. Until 1980 the base period comprised the 4 years from 1972 through 1975. For 1980 and each successive tax year, the 4-year base period progresses annually by one year.

Additional information on establishing a DISC is available from the Foreign Business Practices Division of ITA in the Department of Commerce.

INTERNATIONAL DEVELOPMENT AND COOPERATION AGENCY

Trade and Development Program. This program, which succeeds a previous reimbursable development program administered by the Agency for International Development, supports feasibility studies for projects that can be financed by developing countries and undertaken by U.S. private industry or government agencies. Preproject planning studies are carried out by U.S. firms and, in some cases, other U.S. government agencies.

Detailed information is available from the Trade and Development Program, IDCA.

Agency for International Development. A.I.D. assists U.S. firms by publishing a variety of memos and bulletins concerning A.I.D.-financed commodity purchases. Information is provided on procurements as well as on subjects of general value to suppliers and shippers. Potential suppliers are also encouraged by A.I.D. to send copies of catalogs, brochures, price lists, and other descriptive materials to selected U.S. A.I.D. missions overseas for their catalog librairies. For more information on A.I.D. financed procurements and to be included on A.I.D.'s mailing list, contact the Office of Business Relations (also known as the Office of Small Business.), A.I.D.

APPENDIX A: KEY CONTACTS

International Trade Administration
U.S. Department of Commerce
14th & Consititution Avenue, N.W.
Washington, D.C. 20230
  Office of Country Marketing
  Room 3202
  202/377-5341
  Office of Export Marketing Assistance
  Room 4009
  202/377-5455

    Export Communications Section
    Room 3056
    202/377-5133

    Major Projects Division
    Room 3413
    202/377-5225

    Export Reference Room
    Room 1326
    202/377-4225

  Business Counseling
  Room 2015B
  202/377-2107

  Office of Trade Information
    Services
  Room 4205
  202/377-5719

  Office of Export Promotion
  Room 4001
  202/377-4231

  Market Research Division
  Office of Export Planning &
    Evaluation
  Room 4002
  202/377-5037

  Director-General
  U.S. Foreign Commercial Service
  Room 7099-C
  202/377-5777

Office of East-West Country
  Affairs
Room 4816
202/377-2076

Trade Reference Room
Room 2314
202/377-2185

Deputy Assistant Secretary
U.S. Commercial Service
Room 4808
202/377-3641

District Offices are located in:

Birmingham, AL
Anchorage, AK
Phoenix, AZ
Little Rock, AR
Los Angeles, CA
San Francisco, CA
Denver, CO
Hartford, CT
Miami, FL
Atlanta, GA
Savannah, GA
Honolulu, HI
Chicago, IL
Indianapolis, IN
Des Moines, IA
Louisville, KY
New Orleans, LA
Augusta, ME
Baltimore, MD
Boston, MA
Detroit, MI
Minneapolis, MN
Jackson, MS
St. Louis, MO
Kansas City, MO
Omaha, NE
Reno, NV
Newark,NJ
Albuquerque, NM
Buffalo, NY
New York, NY
Greensboro, NC
Cincinnati, OH
Cleveland, OH
Oklahoma City, OK
Portland, OR

Philadelphia, PA
Pittsburgh, PA
San Juan, PR
Providence, RI
Columbia, SC
Memphis, TN
Dallas, TX
Houston, TX
Salt Lake City, UT
Richmond, VA
Seattle, WA
Charleston, WV
Milwaukee, WI
Cheyenne, WY

Export-Import Bank
811 Vermont Avenue, N.W.
Washington, D.C. 20571

Office of Public Affairs
202/566-8990

Office of Exporter Insurance
202/566-8955

Office of Exporter Credits and
  Guarantees
202/566-8819

Office of Direct Credits and
  Financial Guarantees
202/566-8187

Small Business Hotline
800/424-5201

Foreign Credit Insurance
  Association

New York (Head Office)
One World Trade Center—9th
  Floor
New York, New York 10048
212/432-6311
Telex: 127561

Other Offices in:

Atlanta
Chicago
Cleveland
Detroit
Houston
Los Angeles
Milwaukee
Washington

Small Business Administration
1441 "L" Street, N.W.
Washington, D.C. 20416

Office of International Trade
Small Business Administration
Room 602-G
Washington, D.C. 20416
202/653-6544

Overseas Private Investment
Corporation

Information Officer
OPIC
1129 20th Street, N.W.
Washington, D.C. 20527
202/653-2800

Small Business Information
800/424-OPIC

International Development and
Cooperation Agency (IDCA)

The Director
Trade & Development Program
U.S. IDCA
Washington, D.C. 20523
703/235-1800

Office of Business Relations
A.I.D.
Washington, D.C. 20523
703/235-9155

U.S. Department of Agriculture
Foreign Agricultural Service
14th & Independence Avenue, S.W.
Washington, D.C. 20250

Export Trade Services Division
Room 4945-S
202/447-6343

Information Services Staff
Room 5918–S
202/447-3448

APPENDIX B: REFERENCES AND PUBLICATIONS

The Federal Government, especially the Department of Commerce, publishes a wide variety of booklets, pamphlets, and brochures on international commerce, particularly exporting. There are, however, few reference sources to U.S. government services and aids for international business. Most agencies publish pamphlets that describe programs, but comprehensive and detailed guides to the operation and use of programs are usually not available. The publications that are listed below include both those intended to describe the services available, as well as those intended to provide information as an end in itself. Unless otherwise noted the publications cited can be obtained from the U.S. Government Printing Office. Sample copies of most of the DOC publications and many of the other publications are available from USCS district offices.

Report of the President on Export Promotion Functions and Potential Export Disincentives.   This report, which was transmitted to Congress in September 1980 together with a detailed review of programs and disincentives, is the most comprehensive review available on government assistance activities. As a guidebook or reference for business its utility may be limited, but it does provide insight into the overall strategies and objectives of the various programs.

DEPARTMENT OF COMMERCE

Overseas Business Reports.   OBR's are country specific pamphlets issued in three basic series. *Marketing In* covers the selected country's trade patterns, industry trends, distribution channels, transportation facilities, trade regulations, and prospects for U.S. products, *Market Profile* provides an economic digest for countries in a particular region and covers foreign trade investment, financing, the economy, and natural resources, *World Trade Outlook* gives a twice-a-year analysis of U.S. export prospects to all major trading countries. In addition, special reports are issued from time to time. OBR's are available on a subscription basis ($40/year) and are sold individually. About 60 reports are issued each year.

Foreign Economic Trends.   FETs are prepared by U.S. economic and commercial officers overseas and provide a 5–15 page summary of current business and economic developments and the latest economic indicators. They are prepared for 100 countries each year. Available by subscription ($50) and by single copy.

Basic Guide to Exporting.   This 68 page pamphlet is intended principally for new or inexperienced exporters. It covers all the basic elements of exports including both market identification and documents and finance.

Business America.   This is an International Trade Administration biweekly publication containing articles relating to international trade. It is a good source of information on ITA programs and publications. It is available by subscription ($40).

Market Research.   DOC produced research is available in several different formats. "Global Market Surveys" (GMS) is a subscription series currently covering 10 target industries. Approximately 5–8 country surveys are issued per target industry each year. To register write to the Office of Export Planning, Room 4002, U.S. Department of Commerce, Washington, D.C. 20230. The country surveys are available individually from the Government Printing Office (GPO). Country sector studies when produced are also available from the GPO. The original research is available from the National Technical Information Service. An index of international market research is also available from the GPO.

Census Trade Statistics.   Census publishes a variety of export and import statistics. The "Guide to U.S. Trade Statistics" provides descriptions of the various reports both published and unpublished that are available.

International Economic Indicators.   This is a quarterly compendium of economic and trade data for leading exporting countries including the United States. Available by subscription ($10/year).

Foreign Business Practices: Materials on Practical Aspects of Exporting, International Licensing, and Investing.   This is a compendium of articles and studies by the Foreign Business Practices Division covering legal or tax related export topics including: Webb-Pomerene, DISC, industrial property rights, and carnets. It is available from GPO. This office also has available a study, "Current Developments in Product Liability Affecting International Commerce." This can be obtained directly from the Foreign Business Practices, Room 4204, U.S. Department of Commerce 20230.

The following publications are available from the Export Communication Section, Room 3056, U.S. Department of Commerce, Washington, D.C. 20230.

A Business Guide to the Association of Southeast Asian Nations

A Guide for Business—U.S. Commercial Service Offices and the Foreign Commercial Service Posts

A Guide to Financing Exports

An Introduction to Contract Procedures in the Near East and North Africa

Attracting Foreign Investment to the U.S.: A Guide for Government

Business Guide to the Near East and North Africa

Doing Business With NATO

Doing Business With PEMEX

European Trade Fairs: A Guide for U.S. Exporters

Export Information Services for U.S. Business Firms

Export Management Company (EMC) Directory

Foreign Investment and Licensing Checklist for U.S. Firms

Foreign Investment Organizations Assist U.S. Firms

German Trade Fairs: A Handbook for American Exporters

How to Get the Most From Overseas Exhibitions

International Marketing News Memo

Invest in U.S.A.: A Guide for the Foreign Investor

Obtain Tax Deferral Through a Domestic International Sales Corporation (DISC)

Sources of Information on U.S. Firms: A Guide for International Traders

U.S. Trade Center Facilities Abroad

U.S. Trade Opportunities Resulting from the MTN Agreement on Tariff Cuts

Overseas Export Promotion Calendar

U.S. Foreign Buyer Shows and Major Trade Exhibitions, 1981-82

Program Brochures.   For virtually every ITA trade assistance program a descriptive pamphlet is available.

DEPARTMENT OF AGRICULTURE

Foreign Agricultural Service.   Publishes program brochures covering the Foreign Agriculture Service overseas, overseas trade offices, PL. 480 program, Commercial Export Financing for products and Sales Aids for Food Exporters. These brochures are available from Information Services Staff, FAS.

Export Briefs.   Weekly listing of Trade Opportunities and foreign trade developments. Available from Export Trade Services Division, FAS.

Food and Agricultural Export Director.   Lists key contacts export business. Available from Information Services Staff, FAS.

Foreign Agricultural Reports.   Reports covering production, trade and their specialized topics for major world commodity groups. Also Weekly Roundup of World Production and Trade and Monthly World Crop Production report. Available from Information Services Staff, FAS.

Foreign Agricultural Trade of the United States.   Monthly statistical and analytical review of U.S. agricultural trade. Available from Economics, Statistics, and Cooperative Services Division of Information, U.S. Department of Agriculture, Washington, D.C. 20250.

SMALL BUSINESS

Export Marketing Guide for Smaller Firms.   An 84 page guidebook on how to get started in exporting published by the SBA. Includes references on both government and nongovernment publications and services.

The Small Business Market in the World.   This pamphlet describes international trade services available from Ex-Im Bank, Department of Commerce, U.S. SBA, and OPIC. It is geared to small business needs. Available from any of the above agencies.

FINANCE

Export-Import Bank.   Publishes a 45-page guide to its programs. It is available from Office of Public Affairs, Export-Import Bank of the United States.

FCIA.   Brochures describing FCIA services are available from FCIA, New York.

OPIC.   Publishes a number of pamphlets including a "Finance Handbook" and an "Investment Insurance Handbook." Both handbooks are around 20 pages and provide details of OPIC programs. OPIC also publishes a newsletter. These publications are available from the Office of Public Affairs.

SECTION **11**

INTERNATIONAL TRANSPORTATION

CONTENTS

MARITIME TRANSPORTATION	3	Administration	12
The Broad Categories	3	**THE MECHANICS OF SHIPPING**	12
Cargo liners	3		
Liner rates	4	Finding a Shipper	12
Tramps	5	The Paperwork	13
Bulk carriers	6	**AIR CARGO**	14
Containerization	6		
Other forms of intermodal		General Information	14
transportation	7	Air Carrier Organization	15
Future Prospects	7	Cargo Rates	16
		Ground Support Services	17
THE U.S. MERCHANT MARINE	9	Future Prospects	17
Economic Support	9	**SOURCES AND SUGGESTED**	
Flags of Convenience	11	**REFERENCES**	18

INTERNATIONAL TRANSPORTATION

H. Peter Gray

International transportation takes place when goods are carried across national boundaries. In the United States, international transportation is conducted by ocean-going vessels or aircraft for all countries with the exceptions of Canada and Mexico. These countries have road and rail links to the United States in addition to the maritime and air connections. This section will devote itself virtually exclusively to the subject of transportation to and from nations outside the North American continent, on the grounds that the procedures for land transportation to Canada and Mexico by train or by truck are very similar to domestic-transportation procedures for sending a cargo from Schnectady to Sacramento. Common carriers that provide domestic transportation will be able to provide the international services as well. The only important distinction lies in the need for additional documentation for customs purposes and in the complexities of conversion of one national currency into another.

Strictly, it would be possible to include passenger transportation under this heading, but passenger transportation is more appropriately considered together with tourism in Section 14—International Trade in Services.

MARITIME TRANSPORTATION

THE BROAD CATEGORIES. International (freight) transportation involves several distinct types of oceangoing vessels and services as well as air-cargo services. The three most important types of oceangoing services are (1) cargo liners, which carry general cargo over predetermined routes with schedules times of departure and arrival; (2) tramp (or irregular) ships, which carry cargoes when and where the need arises; (3) and bulk carriers, which are usually owned or chartered by large corporations and used for transportation of basic commodities. Bulk carriers are dominated by tankers. Each category of service has its own distinctive features—particularly with respect to the price charged. This variation in pricing derives, in part, from the peculiarities of the markets served but also from the organization of the shipping lines engaged in the particular service.

Cargo Liners. A cargo liner has a scheduled itinerary in much the same way as a passenger liner (which is, in fact, usually a combination ship carrying some commercial cargo in addition to its passengers). Because of its committed schedule, a liner cannot guarantee to use all of its carrying capacity on any single voyage. Another problem faced by cargo liners is that the cargoes they carry may be very bulky for their weight. The liner can, therefore, be filled by volume before it reaches its weight capacity. Rates are charged by weight or by volume according to which is the more expensive; the volume unit is called a measurement ton and comprises 40 cubic feet. Cargo liners offer a relatively assured date of delivery of cargoes shipped, greater speed of transportation than tramps and they usually dock at parts with good facilities, including storage and cargo-handling equipment. Cargo liners carry what is referred to as general cargo; general cargo covers a wide range of individual goods but usually comprises manufactures and other goods of relatively high value. Liner charges are the highest of any category of oceangoing carrier. Daniel Marx, Jr. (1953), has identified three kinds of costs incurred by a maritime carrier: (1) commodity costs, which are variable costs and are directly allocable to a particular cargo; (2) vessel expenses, which are the joint costs of running the ship over a particular route and which must be distributed over the whole cargo carried; and (3) overhead costs. Commodity costs include such items as cargo loading and unloading expenses; these tend to be high for cargo liners because of the importance of the ports served by liners and because of the dockside facilities supplied. General cargo, by definition, does not lend itself to bulk handling. Vessel expenses are also likely to be higher for liner cargoes because of the possibility of a lower capactiy-utilization rate that follows from maintaining a prepublished sailing schedule and the high costs of services in major ports. Finally, overhead costs tend to be higher for liners because of the liners' greater speed and more modern equipment and because liners tend to be the newest ships used in the carriage of general cargo. Old liners often become tramps. It is not possible to allocate the vessel expenses or the overhead costs to individual cargoes except arbitrarily. Therefore, freight rates charged by liners are determined in advance and discriminate among types of cargoes shipped.

Liner Rates.   Rates charged for transportation by liners are predominantly determined by producers' associations known as *shipping conferences*. Because the members of a conference usually comprise all of the major suppliers of scheduled services along a trade route, the rates have monopolistic overtones, and conferences have been accused of many antisocial pricing practices and cartellike tactics. But the monopoly powers of a shipping conference (there is one conference for each major trade route) are not complete, since it is extremely difficult for a conference to prevent nonconference competition on its route. Similarly, shippers have ways to evade any monopolistic and extortionate set of freight rates—by chartering a tramp or by shipping by a different route. Samuel A. Lawrence (1969) has summarized the many studies of the conference system as indicating that there are risks that conferences may abuse their power, but that industrial stability, including rate stability, mandates the cooperation of shipping lines in rate-fixing. For this reason, shipping conferences are exempt from the antitrust provisions of the Sherman Act (except in cases of blatantly antisocial behavior). There is, however, a clear recognition that conferences will attempt to discriminate among shippers according to what each individual category of traffic will bear, so that individual shippers taking the same amount of a ship's capacity on a single voyage can be charged quite different freight rates. This capability is limited by the sheer detail involved and by the inability of conferences to determine in any scientific way exactly what each category of cargo will, in fact, bear. When the overall level of cargo-liner rates is adjusted in response to changes in the level of business, rates change quite slowly. Rates are particularly slow to decline. This is shown, albeit in an inflationary period, in Exhibit 1, which gives a comparison of liner and tramp rates (in index form) for the years 1976–1978. Tramp rates are more volatile than liner rates, particularly so when rates decline. It is, of course, the ability of large shippers to divert potential liner traffic to tramps when liner rates are relatively high that restricts the monopoly power of the liner conferences.

In recent years, cargo liners have undergone a technical revolution in the form of the introduction of *container ships*. These innovations are considered later.

Tramps.   Tramp steamers have no regular routes or schedules but respond to known seasonal patterns of commodity movement or to instructions from their owners. On occasion they are hired out (chartered) to a private shipper, but frequently they are used to move raw materials that provide *seasonal* cargoes. This is a service that lacks any element of monopoly, and rates are highly competitive. This higher degree of competition explains the much greater volatility of tramp rates than liner rates. To the extent that the availability of tramps limits the monopoly power of the conferences, it is the differential between tramp and liner rates that determines the willingness of large shippers to charter tramps. Of course the advantage of liner shipping is that there is no need to have shipments of the size that will fill a ship. When tramps are chartered by firms that ordinarily ship on liners, the costs of the tramp increase if all of its capacity is not filled. Tramps are relatively small. When liner rates are high, conferences are themselves able to charter tramps to add to their own capacities. In so doing, they will tend to raise the costs of charter and to keep the rate differential within a narrower range. Because of their general-purpose role,

EXHIBIT 1   LINER- AND TRAMP-RATE INDICES, 1976–1978[a]

Month	1976[b]		1977[b]		1978[b]	
	Liner	Tramp	Liner	Tramp	Liner	Tramp
January	208	129	224	135	237	134
February	208	118	225	136	241	133
March	214	121	226	135	241	134
April	214	129	229	132	242	135
May	215	134	229	129	242	148
June	214	136	228	131	241	138
July	213	138	230	132	241	137
August	214	138	231	129	241	140
September	218	141	231	131	241	141
October	219	143	232	134	242	142
November	219	143	233	136	242	149
December	219	140	233	134	242	150

Source.   OECD, 1978.
[a]The tramp-rate index is a "voyage-charter index" computed by *Norwegian Shipping News*. The liner-freight index is published by Bundesministerium für Verkehr, Hamburg.
[b]Base years: liner index, 1965; tramp index, June 1965 to June 1966.

tramps are built on a general-purpose design, able to accommodate nearly all kinds of cargo.

Bulk Carriers. This kind of ship is usually owned or chartered on a long-term contract (more than five years) by a nonmaritime corporation for its own purposes. Some may be available for single-voyage charters (like tramps). Oil companies transporting crude or refined petroleum products from their own docks in a producing country to their own docks in an importing nation are typical of bulk-carrier users. Steel corporations and aluminum refiners use bulk carriers for the transportation of iron ore and bauxite in much the same way. Dry carriers used to be tramps hired on long-term charter, but since 1960 the bulk carriers have become increasingly designed and built for the one type of cargo for which they were intended, and the dock facilities have been tailored to the ship design. The result of these innovations is that transportation by bulk carrier is extremely efficient both in operating costs per ton of cargo and in terms of cargo handling and turnaround time in port. The epitome of bulk carriers in these respects is the so-called supertanker.

CONTAINERIZATION. The traditional design of vessels employed in the transportation of general cargo is a breakbulk ship. Breakbulk ships have two or more cargo decks as well as their own cranes and cargo-handling equipment on deck. In many respects, breakbulk liners are merely faster and more sophisticated tramps. Ships of this design are self-sufficient in handling cargoes of a wide variety of shapes and sizes and rely minimally on the equipment available in the port. They are, therefore, able to deliver goods to ports in developing countries as well as to port terminals on well-established liner routes. The benefits of adaptability enjoyed by breakbulk ships are countered by the slowness of loading and unloading cargoes with the inherent costs of extra berth charges and slow turnaround.

 This type of ship is in the process of being superseded by *container ships*. Containerization is a mode of transportation by which general cargoes (transported on cargo liners) can achieve some of the economies of handling that specialized facilities and ship design accord to bulk cargoes. Goods are shipped in containers of standard sizes. The biggest is 40 by 8 by 8 feet, but the capacity of a container ship is reported in terms of 20-foot equivalent units (TEUs). In addition to the savings in commodity costs from easier handling and in vessel costs from quicker turnaround, the shipper gains from reduced pilferage and reduced breakage. The container is packed at the shipper's place of business and sealed, transported on a flatbed truck, to the dock where it is picked up by a gantry crane and loaded as a single unit. On arrival in the foreign port, it is unloaded in the same way and, except for customs, travels as a sealed and single unit to the recipient's warehouse. This type of transportation is particularly suited to large-scale, multinational business that combines foreign and domestic production or foreign production and domestic sales; such a firm will need to ship large amounts of goods regularly from one subsidiary to another. Handling facilities and container design can be standardized within the multinational corporation and containers used to capacity in both directions. The growth of containerized cargo tonnage is shown in Exhibit 2. The tonnage has increased by more than 200 percent from 1970 to 1976 (the latest year for which data are available).

 Many shipping corporations combine breakbulk and container capacity on the same ship, and this combination offers a compromise between flexibility and speed of cargo-handling. The decision to utilize container ships, partial container ships, or to rely purely on breakbulk ships is very sensitive to the routes being served. The

EXHIBIT 2   COMMERCIAL CONTAINERIZED CARGO ON U.S. ROUTES,
1970–1976

Year	Total (long tons)	U.S. Share (%)	Inbound (long tons)	U.S. Share (%)	Outbound (long tons)	U.S. Share (%)
1976	25,688	36.3	12,814	36.3	12,874	36.0
1975	21,326	41.0	10,112	43.3	11,214	38.9
1974	20,819	42.3	10,190	43.0	10,629	41.7
1973	17,487	38.5	8,705	39.5	8,782	37.5
1972	12,077	37.3	6,684	39.0	5,391	35.2
1971[a]	8,346	41.2	4,655	45.1	3,691	36.3
1970	7,704	45.7	4,275	48.8	3,428	41.7

Source.   U.S. Department of Commerce, 1979, *Containerized Cargo.*
[a]Longshore Strike.

greater the volume of cargoes comprising standard manufactured products, the more likely is the route to rely heavily on containerization. The route between the East Coast ports of the United States and Europe is served predominantly by container ships. On other routes between manufacturing countries, containerization is important and growing, whereas routes involving developing countries usually make only limited use of container ships. But traffic on these routes is expected to come to rely increasingly heavily on containerization.

Other Forms of Intermodal Transportation.   Container ships are the one way in which a cargo can be shipped on different modes of transportation without massive handling. Container ships are the dominant, but not the only, form of intermodal transport. Both of the other forms require ships designed to suit the particular type of traffic and handling, and both attempt to achieve the economies of handling that containers offer. The first type of ship is a roll-on/roll-off ship (known as a Ro/Ro ship in contrast to a container ship, which is sometimes referred to as a Lo/Lo—an acronym for lift-on/lift-off). A Ro/Ro ship has its containers delivered directly into the cargo space by truck, the truck simply deposits its trailer and drives off. The other type of intermodal transportation is a lighter-aboard ship (LASH), which lies offshore and receives a cargo of barges. The barges (lighters) are lifted on by means of a crane and effectively constitute containers for cargo brought to the port by river instead of by road. LASH is likely to remain in service for a narrow range of specialized cargoes, and Ro/Ro ships are particulary suited to shipments of motor vehicles.

FUTURE PROSPECTS.   The merchant marine industy is still evolving technologically to the concept of containerization, and this mode of transportation can be expected to increase steadily in importance in the future. On well-developed routes, such as the North Atlantic, containerization is virtually fully developed and is unlikely to increase its share of general cargo significantly. Other routes involving developed nations at least at one end currently enjoy partially developed containerization, and containerization on these routes can be expected to expand. Finally, there are certain routes in which containerization is still dominated by breakbulk vessels and in which the potential for growth of containerization is substantial. Probably the main bottleneck handicapping the growth of containerization will not be vessel capacity so much as the development of port facilities. With engrained institutional opposition to mechanization either by strongly entrenched longshoremen or by national governments seeking to employ surplus labor, the capacity to handle container ships may increase less quickly than the potential demand for such services. If vessels are held up in ports awaiting their turns to use gantry facilities, the advantages of containerization in terms of quick turnaround time will be nullified.

Supertankers probably represent a maximum size for bulk carriers, but the average size of bulk carriers, with attendant economies, will probably increase. Dry bulk carriers can increase in size, and supertankers can increase their share of total tanker tonnage. Given the political as well as the economic uncertainties that surround the international petroleum industry, any forecast of increases in tanker tonnage is likely to founder. Much will depend upon the volume of international trade in petroleum products and this, in turn, depends upon the ability of the United States to reduce its dependence on foreign oil and on the degree to which oil-importing developing countries continue to import oil financed by balance-of-payments loans from the developed world.

The final identifiable and important source of change in merchant marine activity is the movement by the poor nations to use their combined political power through the United Nations Conference on Trade and Development (UNCTAD) to command a larger share of world tonnage. At the end of 1975, the fleets of poor nations (excluding those countries that offer flags of convenience) amounted to 20 million gross tons of a world fleet of 345 million gross tons. The developed world had 200 million gross tons registered under its flags, and flags of convenience accounted for another 95 million tons. The tanker tonnage of the UNCTAD bloc was 6 out of a total of 160 million.

Through the UNCTAD Secretariat, the developing nations (excluding flag-of-convenience nations) call for the following measures:

1. Recognition that poor nations should be able to share equally in the transportation of cargoes outbound from and inbound to their countries.

2. Recognition that poor countries, because of the low wages that their labor commands, have a potential cost advantage in the provision of maritime transportation.

3. Elimination of flags of convenience, since this type of registry allows developed nations to retain control of large merchant fleets without the involvement of the other developing nations.

4. Institution of a formula that 40 percent of traffic would be carried by ships of the importing country, 40 percent by the exporting country, and only 20 percent would be available for third-country vessels.

The effects of such action, if it could be enforced, would be to remove the dominance of such traditional maritime powers as Greece, Norway, and the United Kingdom. The merchant marine of these countries has traditionally carried global cargoes far in excess of the direct involvement of these countries in global international trade. Flags-of-convenience vessels play much the same role for bulk cargoes that the traditional maritime powers do for general cargoes.

These targets were agreed to at UNCTAD V in Manila in 1979. But, like many of the UNCTAD goals and resolutions, they tend to neglect the problems of adjustment that the changes would impose on the developed world. Four problems that the UNCTAD program does not face up to are as follows:

1. There is the problem of bringing about change. The developed and the flag-of-convenience nations understandably prefer the *status quo* and have the established positions. Change will therefore be brought about, if at all, by political means rather than through the exercise of cost advantages.

2. Many of the poor nations supporting the UNCTAD policies do not have an oceangoing maritime tradition and cannot be expected to build up a reservoir of nationals with broad experience in less than a generation.

3. The 40-40-20 division would seriously restrict competition and would preclude the most efficient supplier of the service winning a large share of the world trade.

4. It is not clear that the merchant marine is necessarily a good investment for many developing nations. The provision of merchant marine services will earn and save foreign exchange, but foreign-exchange gains may not be positive. Ships must be bought from abroad, in the early years officers will be foreign nationals who will require that their salaries be paid in hard currency, imports of port services will be sharply increased as own-flag vessels dock in foreign ports, and current exports of port services will be lost as own-flag vessels replace foreign-flag ships.

Nonetheless, the Manila position does contain a basic truth: Some (even many) poor, labor-surplus countries could benefit from an expansion of their merchant tonnage, and the existing conditions impose tremendous difficulties for these countries to expand their oceangoing fleets.

THE U.S. MERCHANT MARINE

ECONOMIC SUPPORT. Maritime transportation takes place on the "high seas" beyond national boundaries and legal jurisdiction. This geographic feature of the international transportation industry means that national governments are unable to use traditional methods of protecting their merchant marines from cheaper foreign competition. When a nation wishes to protect, say, its high-cost steel industry from foreign imports, it has a wide variety of protectionist devices at its disposal. The most-common means of protectionism is the tariff, which is a (discriminatory) tax levied on imports but not on home-produced goods. This has the effect of increasing the relative cost of imports and enables the domestic industry to sell at a higher, cost-covering price and to enjoy a larger share of the domestic market. Another important means of protection is the quota, which limits the number of imports that can be brought into the country during a calendar year. This mechanism restricts the quantitative severity of foreign competition and allows domestic suppliers to sell at prices that cover their own costs. Both forms of protection are capable of leaving to the domestic industry a share of the domestic market that is deemed adequate for national purposes. In the case of the merchant marine, the argument for protection is "national defense." The United States chooses to protect its shipbuilding industry on the same grounds. The geographic factor requires that the United States supply this protection by subsidy and not by tariff or quota, so that instead of penalizing the consumer of the good (through higher market prices), the government pays out tax revenues from the general fund. Both the shipbuilding subsidy and the subsidy of the costs of operation are designed to equalize U.S. costs with the prevailing world prices. The original legislation authorizing these subsidies was passed in 1936 in the depths of the Depression, when protectionism of all forms was widespread. The laws affecting economic support for the merchant marine are amended every 10 years or so. President Carter sent a package of new proposals for the government support of the merchant marine to the Congress in 1979. These measures died with the end of the 96th Congress. A summary of these measures is given in the annual report of the Maritime Administration for 1979 (U.S. Department of Commerce, 1979, *Marad*).

Because of high wages (relative to foreign standards), the U.S. merchant marine would have priced itself out of world markets if it were not for governmental subsidy. The *operating differential subsidy* is calculated to be the sum of money by which the "fair and reasonable" costs of operation of a U.S.-flag vessel with a crew of U.S. citizens exceeds the "fair and reasonable" cost of operating the same vessel under a foreign flag. The operating subsidy is available only on ships built in American shipyards (and in this way reinforces the shipbuilding subsidy). It is reserved for cargo liners serving "essential routes." The reason for the restriction of the subsidy to cargo liners is that higher conference rates on liner traffic are likely to reduce the subsidy rate required to keep U.S.-flag ships operating at a reasonable rate of return, and the cargo liners are more-up-to-date vessels with better wartime potential (including speed). By virtue of the subsidy, the U.S.-flag fleet manages to retain better than 25 percent of total liner traffic on routes inbound to and outbound from the United States. The U.S.-flag fleet carried only 5 percent of the country's total ocean-borne trade in 1975.

The discrepancy between the costs of operation on U.S.-flag and foreign-flag ships is so large that it is essentially true to say that there would be a negligible amount of U.S.-flag liner capacity were it not for the subsidy. As a rough estimate, it can be reckoned that foreign-crew costs are about 30 percent of American-crew costs. Moreover, the subsidy program as it exists gives shipowners no incentive to keep wage costs down, since the government pays the "additional wages." In 1975, 190 ships received operating differential subsidies in the amount of $237.4 million. In 1979, 177 ships received subsidies of $290.5 million. (Subsidy costs are made public by the Maritime Administration in its annual report.[1])

In addition to subsidies paid to cargo liners on essential routes, the United States acts to preserve the existence of a small fleet of U.S.-flag tramps by earmarking certain government cargoes for U.S.-flag ships and paying rates well above those obtainable in the open market. These cargo-preference (or flag-discrimination) laws control the shipments of U.S. government cargoes whether they be military, food shipments under P.L. 480 or "aid" cargoes.

A final means of supporting the existence of a U.S.-flag fleet is the reservation of coastal traffic between U.S. ports for U.S.-flag ships. Since service on these routes is not subject to international competition, shipping corporations can charge rates that will cover their relatively high costs. These protected operations are important for the United States since they include such ocean voyages as those from the mainland to Alaska, Hawaii, and Puerto Rico, as well as voyages between the East and West coasts and the Gulf and East Coast ports. In 1979, 229 vessels operated in this trade. The recent growth of Alaskan oil output has surpassed the availability of Jones Act tankers,[2] and four subsidized supertankers were granted permission to enter the Alaskan/Californian trade for periods of not more than six months in any calendar year. While employed in these trades, the supertankers receive no operating differential subsidy and must repay pro rata amounts of the construction subsidy received.

The side effect of the reservation of domestic offshore and coastwise trades for high-cost U.S.-flag vessels has severe ramifications for certain parts of the nation and for certain industries. There is no question but that the cost of goods in Alaska, Hawaii, and Puerto Rico is higher because of this restriction, and the temptation of merchants in these areas to import goods from abroad is greater because of the differential in shipping costs. The Jones Act can also affect industries; a clear example of this existed when lumber from Oregon was being undercut in price in East Coast ports by lumber from British Columbia, despite the fact that the Canadian lumber cost more in Vancouver than did its equivalent in Portland.

FLAGS OF CONVENIENCE.   These are also called *flags of necessity*. Multinational corporations, particularly those using bulk carriers, prefer to have operational control over a substantial part of their shipping tonnage. For these vessels to be registered under the U.S. flag involves significant costs (since only cargo liners are eligible for the operating differential subsidy). The large corporations have registered their ships under the flag of nations that offer registration with maritime laws favorable to foreign ownership. Strictly, a flag of convenience is a flag of registry of a nation that sets out to attract absentee ownership shipping by the passage of special legislation. The purpose of this legislation is that registration fees and tax receipts form a valuable source of foreign (hard) currency, and they offer employment outlets for their own citizens. The creation of this type of registry has made real shipping capital much more mobile among nations than it could otherwise be expected to be.

Three nations, Panama, Liberia, and Honduras, are of particular importance to the United States, since their maritime laws expressly allow American owners of ships to commit these ships to the service of the U.S. government in times of military need.[3] These ships are described as being under "effective U.S. control." In this way, the defense capability of the U.S. merchant marine far exceeds that which might be deduced from an examination of the tonnage registered under the U.S. flag.

At the end of 1975, there were 739 vessels owned by U.S. corporations and registered under foreign flags. Liberia accounted for 384 of these vessels and almost two thirds of the total deadweight tonnage. Most of the foreign-flag-registered vessels were tankers (523), and 271 of these were registered in Liberia. Another 77 were registered in Panama and 72 in the United Kingdom (where costs are competitive). The Liberian-registered tankers accounted for almost two thirds of the deadweight tons of foreign-registered tankers.

In comparison with the U.S.-flag fleet, foreign-flag registry of U.S.-owned vessels was 30 percent greater in terms of number of vessels, and 300 percent greater in tonnage. This discrepancy is due in large part to the difference in the size of ships registered abroad and in the United States: the average tanker of U.S. registry was 37,900 deadweight tonnage, and foreign-registered bulk carriers averaged 52,000 deadweight tonnage (taken from U.S. Department of Commerce, 1977, *Foreign Flag Merchant Ships* as of December 31, 1975). The discrepancies in the average size of tankers in the "two fleets" makes economic sense in terms of the route structure: In 1975 most U.S.-flag tankers were involved in coastal traffic—mainly from the Gulf to the East Coast ports. Only since the completion of the Alaska Pipeline and the Valdez terminal would large tankers be economical in the protected domestic offshore and coastwise trades.

The United States is not the only nation whose owners take advantage of flags of convenience, and therefore it would be misleading to imagine that all PanLibHon ships are under "effective U.S. control." For owners of most other nationalities, the advantages of a flag of convenience is not any difference in operating costs but rather in tax savings.

ADMINISTRATION.   The U.S. merchant marine owes its existence to government subsidy and cargo-preference laws, but it pays dearly for that succor. The industry is the concern of almost every agency of government—to a greater or lesser degree—and although some bureaus or agencies are concerned only in service roles, it is extremely difficult for the industry to accomplish much without expending large amounts of effort on governmental liaison. The primary responsibility for supervision lies in the Maritime Administration (Marad). It is still a part of the Department of Commerce despite the recent creation of a Department of Transportation. In addition to the important tasks of researching, calculating, and disbursing the capital and operating differential subsidies, Marad is required to promote the industry's prosperity, to conduct research, and to oversee the many different aspects of regulation that Congress has legislated. It is a small bureau and has suffered from too rapid a rate of turnover of politically appointed executive personnel for efficient operation.

Following Samuel A. Lawrence (1966), it is possible to identify four types of governmental involvement. The most numerous are the agencies that supply technical services. The second type consists of agencies in charge of the shipment of government-owned or government-financed cargoes play an important role in determining the quantity of government aid directed to the industry and to the division of that aid within different branches. The Defense Department (through the Military Sea Transport Service), the Department of Agriculture (for P.L. 480 shipments), and the Agency for International Development are the most important. Frequently, these agencies are more concerned with their own purposes than with maximizing the benefit accruing to the merchant marine. The third type is that of the regulator; for international commerce it consists preeminently of the Federal Maritime Board, which was instituted expressly to prevent undue exploitation by the conferences of their potential economic power. Finally, there is a group of agencies that is interested in the viability of the merchant marine. Here the Department of Commerce and Defense are preeminent.

In addition to agencies involved in enforcing the policies of the U.S. government, there are congressional committees and subcommittees that, together with the executive branch, are responsible for policy formulation.

The complexity of the administration functions of the different agencies and the lack of common interest among them means that the government's policies are contradictory and have weakened the industry's ability to respond to public needs.

THE MECHANICS OF SHIPPING

FINDING A SHIPPER.   Provided that the volume to be shipped is either large or regularly scheduled, finding a shipper is not difficult. The U.S. Maritime Administration is charged with the task, among many others, of promoting the use of the U.S. merchant marine. It maintains market-development offices in 10 major cities in the nation, including Atlanta, Chicago, Cleveland, Houston, Long Beach, New

York, and San Francisco. The Maritime Administration also publishes small brochures for the benefit of potential shippers: These brochures contain the names of the major U.S.-flag shipping corporations, the routes they serve, and the types of services provided, as well as their addresses and telephone numbers. The shipping lines are essentially wholesale operations dealing in fairly large shipments. They maintain sales staffs and will provide all the information that a shipper might need (with the exception of how to ship outside of a conference). Provided that the shipment is suitable for a cargo liner, there is no need to indulge in comparison shopping because of the conference rate structure. There are nonconference ships that will ship general cargo, but a firm without experience in oceanborne shipping will probably do well to make use of the more-orthodox methods. When some experience has been gained, and if the volume of shipments merits the effort, nonconference lines can be investigated.

When the cargo is not large enough to warrant the smallest service of a shipping line, the sales force will probably refer the would-be shipper to a retail-level shipping agent or shipping service. This arrangement will take a great deal of burdensome detail from the shoulders of the occasional shipper, but it may not guarantee rapid delivery. Corporations that are shipping goods in large volume may find the chartering of a ship economical when tramp rates are low. The main market for such a charter is the Baltic Exchange in London, England.

THE PAPERWORK.   Standard procedures have developed over the years that reduce the commercial risk to which a shipper is exposed. The procedures involve the retention of legal title to the cargo until the buyer has made a binding commitment to pay.

When goods are shipped, they are itemized on a *bill of lading*, which when signed by the carrier (the transportation company) acknowledges receipt of the goods. A second copy of the bill of lading is sent to the exporter's agent in the foreign port. The agent will endorse the bill of lading to the importer, thereby transferring ownership of and access to the goods, when payment is assured. Payment can be made in cash in the importer's currency (at the going rate of exchange), but this is unlikely. Usually, payment will be made by the importer issuing a *bill of exchange*, which is a formal acknowledgment of the debt (and is in many ways equivalent to writing a check). The bill of exchange undertakes to pay the money due (the invoiced amount) but does not ensure that there is enough money in the bank to cover the sum due. The bill of exchange fulfills two purposes: It acknowledges the indebtedness, and it instructs someone (the drawee) to make payment to the exporter (the payee) and to charge the payment to the credit of the importer (the maker of the bill). Usually, but not always, the drawee is the importer's bank, in which case the bill is virtually identical to a check. If the bill of exchange is due when presented (a so-called sight draft), the bank or drawee pays the funds, and the transaction is completed. The risk of the exporter has been kept to a minimum, since the exporter retains title to the goods themselves until the moment that the buyer undertakes payment. If the buyer had gone bankrupt while the goods were in transit, the exporter could cut his losses by selling them by auction or finding another buyer.

It is usual for large international orders to give the importer a period of grace before paying. The exporter extends credit to the importer for, say, 90 days so that payment is due 90 days after the bill of exchange is issued. It must be issued when the goods arrive (to acknowledge the debt and to obtain the endorsement of the bill of lading authorizing release of the goods to the importer). The bill then becomes a postdated check (if drawn on a bank). The exporter has to wait 90 days before the money becomes available and runs the risk of the firm's bankruptcy or insolvency in the interim. There is a way for the exporter to receive almost all of the money immediately: The bill of exchange can be discounted. But there is another problem: The open market for bills of this kind will only function well if the debtor (the maker of the bill) has a national credit rating. A small firm may have excellent credentials that are simply not known, and the costs of confirming them would be too great. In that event, the small firm can pay a fee to have its own commercial bank countersign the bill of exchange. By this process, the bank assumes responsibility for the debt, and its credit substitutes for that of the (unknown) importer. A countersigned bill is "accepted" and the bill becomes a *banker's acceptance*. Ordinarily, the original agreement between buyer and seller will specify if the importer is responsible for having the bill of exchange countersigned.

AIR CARGO

GENERAL INFORMATION.   Transportation of goods by air is relatively expensive per ton-mile. For most of the traffic on international routes, the comparison of freight costs for air cargo is with maritime transportation. Sea transportation, even allowing for inland transportation by truck or rail, is far cheaper. It is also far slower. The major categories of goods to be transported by air cargo are likely to be those with high value per unit of weight or bulk. The Air Transport Association lists the "major commodities moving in air freight" as follows:

Wearing apparel
Electronic/electric equipment
Machinery and parts
Printed matter
Cut flowers and nursery stock
Auto parts and accessories
Entertainment goods such as records and tapes
Fruits and vegetables
Photographic equipment, parts and film
Pharmaceuticals, drugs, and medicines
Food preparations
Chemicals
Footwear
Animals
Sporting goods
Tools and hardware
Electronic data storage/processing machines

This listing does not distinguish between international and domestic freight, but both categories of air cargo have been growing rapidly in the last 20 years (see Exhibit 3).

EXHIBIT 3   AIR FREIGHT CARGOES, 1954–1978 (in millions of tonne-kilometers)

Year	International	Domestic	Total
1954	405	695	1,100
1959	840	1,090	1,930
1964	2,140	1,790	3,930
1969	3,900	5,860	9,760
1973	9,850	5,731	15,581
1975	11,460	5,795	17,255
1977	14,400	6,620	21,020

Source. IATA, *World Air Transport Statistics* (Montreal, various issues).

Lewis M. Schneider (1963) has identified three categories of air cargoes:

1. Emergency traffic
2. Routine perishable traffic
3. Routine surface-divertible traffic

These categories are clearly not limited to an analysis of domestic cargoes.

Air cargo has a clear competitive edge in the shipment of goods for which delivery time is of the essence. This is particularly true with international shipments out of the North American continent. The declared value of the goods shipped may have little relevance to the benefit to be derived at their destination—particularly when production processes are immobilized for need of a spare part on one machine in a complex linkage. All emergency cargoes will be shipped by air.

The second group consists of goods that owe their markets to their ability to reach their destinations quickly. Perishables (fruit and flowers) may owe their international markets to the existence of air-freight services. Some printed matter, particularly news-related and topic magazines, will have the same urgency. Shipment of these goods is unlikely to be sensitive to differences in costs of shipment between a fast and a slow means of transportation—the slow transportation is simply not viable.

The third group consists of those items for which an argument can be made for fast shipment by an expensive means but for which the slower transportation is a realistic alternative. Shipment of these goods will be especially sensitive to relative costs (including insurance, handling, and financing costs). The reduced time spent in transit will reduce the costs of financing appreciably in times of high interest rates.

It may be possible to add a fourth category: goods destined for places not served by surface transportation. Increasingly in the modern, technologically advanced world, resources are being developed in places not served by surface transportation.

The obvious relationship between high value per unit weight and air shipment is confirmed by one estimate of international shipments to and from the United States. International air cargoes to and from the United States make up 0.5 percent of international shipments by weight but 10 percent by value.

AIR CARRIER ORGANIZATION.   The majority of air cargo is carried by combination aircraft, which carry cargo to supplement the revenues earned by carriage of passengers on scheduled services. William E. O'Connor (1978) points out that the cargo compartment in a Boeing 747 on a passenger flight holds nearly as much cargo as a Boeing 707 devoted wholly to cargo. Thus the main carriers of air cargo are the well-known passenger airlines, and a shipper needs merely to know which passenger airline services the required destination in order to identify a suitable freight carrier. In addition to the passenger lines, there are two important all-cargo carriers: The Flying Tiger Line has transpacific routes, and Seaboard World Airlines is primarily a transatlantic carrier. Although the identity between passenger airline and freight service holds true on a country basis at the present time, a new degree of flexibility is beginning to emerge in air-cargo shipments. It is now possible that there will be cargo service between pairs of cities in different countries that do not enjoy direct passenger linkage.

In addition to combination aircraft, there are aircraft that are simple freighters. These are mainly aircraft that have been adapted from passenger service and, in some cases, can be equipped to handle both passengers and freight on an exclusive basis. These are known as convertible aircraft. More important is the emergence of freighters that are designed for the carriage of cargo from inception. These are called uncompromised cargo aircraft. The advantage of such aircraft is that most shipments of cargo have large bulk relative to their weight, and a Boeing 747F will generally be filled to capacity ("cube out") at about 40 percent of its weight capacity. Uncompromised cargo aircraft will be designed to be wide and square to reduce the likelihood of cubing out and will feature large doors for the easy trans-shipment of goods. Commercial use of uncompromised aircraft is likely to grow with the growth of air freight. But because of the smaller numbers of such aircraft, design and production costs are likely to be higher, and they lack the versatility of convertible aircraft. Uncompromised aircraft are used mainly by the military.

CARGO RATES.   The prices of international air cargo services are set by agreement between the governments of origin and destination. Usually these agreements are negotiated under the auspices of the International Air Transport Association and follow the rules that determine international passenger air fares. Prices are rigid, and virtually no price competition exists among carriers. The only basis for competition is the quality of service, which will include advice on problems of documentation in the different countries.

Similar to the situation with maritime transportation, large shippers can charter an air freighter and in this way escape from the rate schedule. Charters can be hired from either scheduled airlines or supplemental carriers. Scheduled carriers have traditionally shown a lack of eagerness to charter aircraft; supplemental carriers that are limited to charter activities are generally more likely to be receptive to inquiries. The potential saving in costs depends upon the quantity of goods to be shipped as well as the difference between scheduled freight rates and charter costs. The more nearly the capacity of the chartered aircraft can be filled (the higher the load factor), the more substantial the gain from chartering will be likely to be.

Containerization is making gains in the air cargo markets and offers a means of reducing the costs of transportation. Carriers will provide additional discounts when cargoes are containerized. Containers are standardized by airline agreement and are owned either by the carrier or the shipper. Containers are contoured to fit different types of equipment. O'Connor (1978) has summarized the mutual advantages: "The advantages to the airlines may be summarized as cost savings on labor, faster turn-around time on aircraft, better utilization of the space within aircraft, reduction in theft and damage, space saving at terminals, and resultant lower rates which, in turn, will help develop air cargo traffic. Shippers benefit primarily from the rate discounts but also may benefit from reduced damage and theft."

GROUND SUPPORT SERVICES. Getting shipments from one airport to another is only a small part of the task of shipping a good from its origin to its destination. The ground support services are vital. These services are usually subject to regulation by "ministries of transportation" and the carriers themselves seek to disassociate themselves from this part of the service. This is understandable, because it is a completely different type of operation, involving a great deal of small-scale business.

Carriers must use terminals in which air freight is assembled and to which it is taken from the incoming aircraft. Schneider (1973) pointed out that "the terminal problem . . . is that it represents a buffer between a capital-intensive, carefully planned system of aircraft operations and a fragmented, chaotic conglomeration of private and common carriers for the most part delivering mountains of packages in relatively small vehicles." The terminals at airports tend to be high cost relative to truck terminals, and, partly because of the high values of air cargoes, have serious problems of theft and pilferage.

To get the cargo to and from the terminal, the shipper has three separate options. The first is to use his own trucks. This option will only be cost-efficient if the firm is shipping goods by air on a regular basis so that its drivers have a familiarity with, and understanding of, terminal procedures. The second option is to have the carrier arrange pickup and delivery, which will involve transferring the instructions to a licensed, local trucking firm. The final option is to use the services of an air-freight forwarder, who is to the air-cargo business what the wholesale travel agent is to tourism. Air-freight forwarders assemble small shipments into larger lots and obtain lower rates from carriers by shipping larger lots. The saving on freight costs enables them to supply some services to the shipper without charge. The problem with air-freight forwarders is that their margin relies on the existence of other goods going to the same destination, and there is always a danger of delay as the forwarder awaits these other goods.

FUTURE PROSPECTS. The future of air cargo is likely to be quite sensitive to the rate of increase of fuel costs. Air transportation costs are dominated by the costs of fuel, and therefore the rates will tend to move parallel to the price of fuel. But the effect of fuel costs will affect the rate of growth of air cargo rather than bringing on a serious decline in volume: Industry has become too used to relying on air cargo for emergency traffic, and established markets built on air shipments of routine perishable traffic will not lightly be relinquished. There is the possibility of technological improvements in terms of aircraft design and improved ground support services.

NOTES

1. For an authoritative description of the subsidies, see U.S. Department of Commerce, Maritime Administration, *Maritime Subsidies 1976*, Washington, D.C., 1977, pp. 131–133.

2. The Jones Act is the name of the legislation reserving domestic offshore and coastwise trades for U.S.-flag ships. The generic name for such laws is *cabotage laws*. The practice of reserving coastal trade for domestic-flag vessels is virtually universal.

3. The expression *PanLibHon* is a shorthand for registries that are used by ships under "effective U.S. control": in fact, Honduras is no longer quantitatively significant.

SOURCES AND SUGGESTED REFERENCES

Air Cargo Magazine

Cook, J.C. *International Air Cargo Strategy*, New York: Air Cargo Magazine, 1973.

Gibney, R.F. *Containerization Year Book, 1978*, London: Containerization International, 1978.

International Air Transport Association. *World Air Transport Statistics, 1978*, Montreal: IATA, 1979.

Journal of Air Law and Commerce

Laing, E.T. "Shipping Freight Rates for Developing Countries: Who Ultimately Pays?" *Journal of Transportation Economics and Policy*, Vol. XI, (1977).

Lawrence, S.A. *United States Merchant Shipping Policies and Politics*. Washington, D.C.: Brookings Institution, 1966.

Marx, D. *International Shipping Cartels*. Princeton: Princeton University Press, 1953.

O'Connor, W.E. *An Introduction to Airline Economics*. New York: Praeger, 1978.

Organization for Economic Co-operation and Development. *Maritime Transport, 1978*. Paris: OECD, 1979.

Rapping, L.A. "Overhauling the Nation's Maritime Policy," *Challenge*, Vol. IX, (1966).

Schneider, L.M. *The Future of the U.S. Domestic Air Freight Industry*. Boston: Harvard Graduate School of Business Administration, 1973.

Sturmey, S.G. "National Shipping Policies," *Journal of Industrial Economics*, Vol. XIV, (1965).

U.S. Department of Commerce, Maritime Administration. *Containerized Cargo Statistics, Calendar Year, 1976*. Washington, D.C.: Dept. of Commerce, 1979.

————. *Foreign Flag Merchant Ships Owned by U.S. Parent Companies*. Washington, D.C.: Dept. of Commerce, 1977.

————. *Marad*. Washington, D.C.: Dept. of Commerce, various years.

————. *Maritime Subsidies, 1976*. Washington, D.C.: Dept. of Commerce, 1977.

SECTION **12**

INTERNATIONAL RISK MANAGEMENT

CONTENTS

THE INSURANCE RESPONSIBILITY 3
RISK MANAGEMENT 3
PROBABILITY, RISK, AND PERIL 4
LOW-RISK ITEMS 4
HIGH-RISK ITEMS 5
ASSESSING CONSEQUENCES OF OCCURRENCE OF PERILS 6
MANAGING THE RISK 9
KINDS OF COVERAGE 10

Property Insurance 10
Liability Insurance 12
Fidelity Insurance 12
Surety Bonds 12

INSURANCE CONSIDERATIONS OTHER THAN RISK 15
PERSONNEL INSURANCE 16
AMOUNTS OF INSURANCE TO BUY 18
ADMITTED INSURANCE 19
INTERNATIONAL INSURANCE MARKETS 21

INTERNATIONAL RISK MANAGEMENT

G. Frederick Richardson

THE INSURANCE RESPONSIBILITY

The international business executive usually is involved in a smaller operation than his or her counterpart in the domestic market. Because of its smaller size, the international operation offers less opportunity for specialization. The international business executive therefore has broader responsibilities than does a domestic colleague; this is particularly true of firms that have grown large in the United States and only then begun to test the international market.

The international businessman may not be expert in all these responsibilities, but expert or not, he may be reponsible for insurance. This chapter is written on the assumption that he has no more than the usual passing acquaintance with insurance domestically.

RISK MANAGEMENT

International insurance is best managed as part of the broader concept of international risk management. Risk-management analysis enables the international manager to determine whether he needs insurance, and if so, what kind and how much.

The most useful starting point of risk-management analysis is the projected future profit-and-loss statement, that is to say, the budget.

The budget is a statement of income and expenses that are thought to be highly probable, and that result from foreseeable events, such as sales of products and services; payments of salaries, rent, and fuel bills; purchases of raw materials; payment of taxes, and the like. The manager makes subjective judgment of the probability of the event and the resulting monetary effect. He makes a subjective determination of the threshold of probability that an event and its monetary effect must have to warrant inclusion in the budget. For example, the manager must weigh the probability of getting a certain major new customer, perhaps, and the amount of income he can earn from that customer in order to prepare the income budget. He makes a similar judgment with respect to events causing expense, such as purchase of goods and services.

Perils such as fire, automobile collision, industrial accidents, and many others, are also events that can affect the budget. They are subject to the same kind of evaluation of probability of occurrence and of monetary effect on the profit-and-loss statement in order to determine whether they should be included in the budget and for what amounts.

PROBABILITY, RISK, AND PERIL

Probability is well understood to mean the degree of likelihood or certainty that an event will occur. It is a statistical concept. It is often expressed mathematically on a scale of zero to one. *Zero* represents the lowest possible likelihood that an event will occur, that is to say, there is an infinitesimally small likelihood of occurrence. At the upper end of the scale, *one* represents the highest probability of occurrence, namely, certainty that the event will occur.

Risk is a less-precisely understood term, because of the variety of ways in which it is used in common parlance. In risk-management analysis, it is used in a special sense to mean the difference between the statistically probable effect and the actual effect. For example, the history of 1,000 factories may show that 10 of them will experience fires with damage in varying amounts, averaging $50,000. All of this may be expressed, perhaps, in the statement that factories have a statistical probability of .01 of experiencing every year a fire causing damage of $50,000. This statement is of little use to the manager, since the probability of occurrence of the event is so low that he will not feel justified in budgeting $50,000 or any other figure. Yet if the event does occur, his operation may incur an unbudgeted loss of an amount ranging from trivially small to the total loss of his factory. The difference between the actual loss that may occur and the statistically probable loss is the "risk," as we use the term here. We have postulated a case of low probability and high risk.

In contrast, the history of operation of 1,000 motorcycles may show that there is an annual probability of .99 that each one will experience a collision causing damage requiring $500 to repair. This probability of the event is high, so the manager would wish to budget some value for it. The $500 difference between the statistically expected value of the loss and the depreciated value of the motorcycle, perhaps $1,000, would be the largest possible loss in the worst case. It is small. The manager might then choose to budget the probable loss of $500. This is a case of high probability and low risk. The risk manager would reason that the enterprise is not exposed to the *risk* of losing $500 because of collision of each motorcycle that is operates, rather it is exposed to the near *certainty* of such loss.

We will use the term *peril* to mean an event that could cause damage to the international manager's operation, perhaps a fire, a war, the failure of a customer to pay his bill, and the like.

LOW-RISK ITEMS

Items of low risk and correspondingly high certainty should be budgeted just as the manager budgets all such items. Thus the hypothetical case of highly probable repair expenses resulting from collision damage to motorcycles should be budgeted just as the manager would budget a salary expense, and for the same reason, namely, the high probability of occurrence of the expense.

Historical insurance-premium expenses should be examined lest they mask expenses of the above nature. It is possible that some low-risk (high probability) perils are insured, and that the cost of loss is paid directly by the insurance company, thus not appearing on the assured's books. The insurance premium for such costs would normally be greater, perhaps by 50 percent or more, than the direct costs themselves, because the insurance company, knowing that the occurrence of these perils is highly probable, must charge enough to pay them and to cover its overhead, sales expense, and profit as well. It is more economical for the operator to retain such risks for his own account rather than to insure them. For example, if his operation in a Latin American country included 50 bill collectors using company motorcycles to make their rounds, and if he observed that nearly every year there was one accident resulting in the death of the collector and the total loss of the motorcycle, he would view the consequences as being of high certainty (low risk) and would thus expense directly the death payments due under the labor law and the value of the motorcycle, rather than insure them. He might also reduce these costs and benefit the collectors by instituting a safety program, which would be another way of managing risk. However, he would weigh the cost of the program against the benefits, which might be negligible if the collectors felt that their courage and skill made safety rules inapplicable to them.

Nevertheless, laws may require that some low-risk items be insured. Let us look at the case of a sizable labor force. There may be a sufficiently high probability of claims resulting from industrial accidents to warrant inclusion in the budget of an estimate of their cost. However, in those countries where workmen's compensation insurance is a compulsory legal requirement, the operator has no choice but to insure the peril. Even so, it is sometimes possible for the international manager to negotiate a workmen's compensation policy satisfying legal requirements, with a deductible for the highly probably (low risk) claims volume and thus enjoy a premium saving. In that case, the insurance company insures the claims volume that exceeds the deductible. The outcome is that the insurance company covers the low-probability (i.e., high risk) consequences of the peril, at an appropriately low premium based upon the low statistical probability, plus its expenses and profit loading, and the operator budgets and covers directly the high-probability consequences of the peril at their direct cost. The insurance premium is included in the budget just as any other highly probable expense.

HIGH-RISK ITEMS

The next step in international risk management is to determine those perils whose probability of occurrence is low, but whose cost if they do occur may be higher than the manager is willing to accept without budgeting. These perils are essentially the same as those involved in a domestic operation, with the addition of those to which the operation may be exposed because of its international or foreign nature. These may be inconvertibility of currency, change in exchange rates, embargoes or hostilities between the firm's home country and that of its foreign operation, and others. There is also the possibility of new geographic risks because of the foreign operation. For example, a manufacturer in Nebraska will not be concerned about the possibility of a tidal wave, yet this is a peril commonly insured by owners of property along coastal areas.

Some perils may be considered peculiar to specific foreign areas but not to the United States, simply because Americans associate them with those areas only. Kidnapping for ransom by terrorist groups is one, revolution is another, confiscation of property by the government or nationalization are others. Kidnapping, revolution, and government confiscation however, have all occurred in the United States. The peril that a foreign debtor docs not pay his account is not different, essentially, from the peril of a domestic debtor not paying his account. The consequences of these may all be more difficult for the international manager to handle, however, because of their occurrence in a foreign country. On the other hand, some perils may be easier to cope with for that reason, the peril of lawsuit being an example.

The determination of perils that may affect an international manager's operation is, therefore, a process much like that applicable to a domestic operation. Its difficulty lies in the fact that it requires listing perils whose probability of occurence is small; thus they do not come readily to mind. It is easy to list those of relatively frequent occurrence, such as automobile accidents, or the familiar peril of fire. However, there have been other perils that have had serious effects on business, or could have had such effects, but which are far from the average businessman's mind until they occur, when it is too late to insure them. For example, in recent years deaths due to the previously unidentified "Legionnaire's disease" affecting guests in a Philadelphia hotel resulted in a loss of clientele such that the hotel corporation could no longer continue in business. More recently, the Mount St. Helens volcanic eruption caused substantial loss to tourist and other industries in Washington State. In 1908 a meteor struck an area in Siberia, fortunately uninhabited, leveling and searing trees in an area of 20 to 30 miles diameter. These are examples of perils whose occurrence is low in probability but whose consequences were, or could have been, extremely damaging. They illustrate the wide-ranging thoroughness and imagination with which an international manager should examine the possible perils that could affect his operation.

Useful ways to make as complete a list of perils as possible are to consult insurance brokers, to consult checklists, to consult an engineer who knows the manager's industry, to consult colleagues, to read newspapers and magazines, to inspect the operation and its surroundings, and to examine the operation's processes from all inputs to all outputs. It may be helpful to list perils according to their causes; a checklist is suggested in Exhibit 1.

It is helpful to list all the places where the operation is performed, where its inputs come from and its outputs go to, in case they suggest perils to which the operation is exposed.

ASSESSING CONSEQUENCES OF OCCURRENCE OF PERILS

Once the manager has completed the list of perils to which his business is exposed that are of sufficiently high risk so that he does not feel justified in budgeting them, then he should assess the consequences of their occurrence and its impact on his profit-and-loss statement.

Direct damage of goods, buildings, machinery, and machine parts are measured by the value of the item—but what value? In what currency? Book value is usually

EXHIBIT 1 PERILS CHECKLIST

Perils Caused by Nonhuman Factors	Perils Caused by One's Own Personnel	Perils Caused by Other People
Windstorm Lightning Flood Rain Hail Snow Severe cold Severe heat Drought Earthquake Landslide Land subsidence Tidal wave Transportation: sea, air, and land Volcanic eruption Meteor Sickness	Incorrect operation or maintenance, causing fire, smoke, explosion, or other injury to one's own people or goods or those of others. Lawsuits caused by operations or conditions failing to meet legal standards of care, including collision of vehicles, vessels, and aircraft, defective design or manufacture, malpractice, defamation, pollution, release of harmful substances. Strike.	Fire, smoke, explosion, pollution, release of harmful substances, collision with vehicles or falling or thrown objects. War, revolution, civil disturbance, stoppage of supplies or services, misplacement or other loss of goods held by others, noncompliance with contract, injury or damage to customers, failure to pay debts, change in laws, confiscation, change in exchange rates, inconvertibility of currency.

derived from historical cost less depreciation permitted by local tax laws. In a foreign operation, books are generally required by law to be kept in the local currency. However, assets such as machinery may have been bought from another country with foreign currency. Rates of inflation and currency exchange are different and constantly changing all over the world. The value resulting from depreciated cost is likely to differ importantly from the monetary effect upon the profit-and-loss statement of loss or damage to the property. Valuation will be discussed later in this chapter. Our purpose here is to suggest that the task of assessing the consequences of direct damage should not be viewed simplistically.

The *indirect* results of damage to property can be far more serious than is generally realized. In less sophisticated areas of the world, local managers frequently fail to recognize the effects of business interruption. If the international manager is responsible for supervising operations headed by local managers, he should guard against the advice, "It's not necessary to insure against business interruption here. Nobody does it." In fact, its effect is as devastating in an unsophisticated country as in any other, and if not provided for, it can drive a company into dissolution.

The typical indirect result of damage to property is interruption of business pending repair or replacement of the damaged property. This usually causes loss of income to cover profits and continuing and sometimes new expenses. Employees may become surplus during the business interruption. However, labor laws in many countries require substantial severance pay to discharged employees, so the company may find it expensive either to keep them on the payroll or to discharge them. Cessation of operations may result in the loss of clientele, and it takes time to rebuild the business. If goods are in the process of shipment to an overseas location that has been destroyed by fire, the international manager may be unable to reverse the transit and may be obliged to pay for the goods, for their freight and insurance costs and customs duties, and then may have no ready place to store them at their destination nor any ready way of using them or selling them. Resolving this problem can be expensive, perhaps involving a sacrifice sale of the goods.

Another class of consequences consists of litigation for damages due to various forms of negligent operation or improper activity. It is not necessary that the defendant have actually committed any negligent or improper activity; it is only necessary that the plaintiff allege it. There are probably no people in the world as litigious as those of the United States, nor are judgments so high elsewhere. Consequently, the international manager may be told that his firm's overseas operation does not act in a negligent way; that if negligent, it is not likely to be sued; that if sued, its defense will be successful; and finally, that if it loses, the judgment will be small. There may be a good deal of truth to all of these statements, except, perhaps, the first. However, that is why a liability-insurance premium should be low; it is not a reason for omitting to insure or for insuring to low limits. Lawsuits do occur, and many international managers feel that their firms, being foreign, are more likely to lose a lawsuit then would a local defendant. Meanwhile, judgments are steadily rising in most, if not all parts of the world, although in many countries they have a long way to go to reach American levels.

When assessing consequences of a lawsuit, the international manager should bear in mind that in many countries whose law derives from the Napoleonic Code, the plaintiff is permitted to begin a lawsuit by attaching the defendant's property. This is in contrast to Anglo-Saxon common law countries, where generally the plaintiff seeking an order of attachment has to make a strong showing that the defendant is about to leave the jurisdiction of the court or to remove the property therefrom. It is an interesting experience for an international manager to receive his first knowledge of a claim in the form of a notification that his firm has been sued, its inventory attached, and its bank accounts frozen, including, perhaps, the payroll account on the eve of payday. International managers are often ill prepared for this, lacking a prearranged plan of response.

Similarly, it is common that in case of an automobile accident involving personal injury to an occupant of the other car, the driver of the first car is arrested. The arrest is not so much punishment for a traffic violation as it is a device to guarantee the availability of the defendant to respond for damages if he is found to be at fault.

The consequences of destruction of records may be difficulty in collecting receivables or inability to prove that a payable has been paid. It should also be borne in mind that in countries with exchange control, it is usually necessary to be able to show evidence of registry of import of capital if it is desired to reexport the capital later on, or to export dividends. It may be impossible to get a copy from the government in case of loss of the original, issued, perhaps, many years back. Furthermore, countries that do not have exchange control today, and therefore no mechanism for registering the foreign origin of capital funds, may impose exchange control in the future, and call upon established foreign enterprises to produce evidence of the foreign source of their local investment, perhaps made many years ago. Loss of records, therefore, can have effects extending beyond those that would be expected in the United States.

The consequences of crime to the victim company are much the same all over the world. However, the consequences of embezzlement are probably underestimated in many parts of the world, particularly those with less sophistication. The common error is to believe that the worst consequences are the loss of exposed cash or a small part of inventory embezzled by a low-level employee. In fact, embezzlement is often by well-known and trusted employees, who are able to embezzle because they are trusted. The defalcation frequently goes on for years before discovery, and the accumulation of values embezzled can be astonishingly high.

The consequences of perils assumed by contract can be a Pandora's box. Many firms have no program of recording and reviewing these for risk management purposes, and no one really knows what guarantees and hold-harmless agreements have been given in the course of many years of business.

The listed peril *change in laws* is intended to suggest a variety of possibilities such as nationalization, devaluation, and other acts of government that may affect the firm's profit-and-loss statement.

MANAGING THE RISK

Once the list of perils is complete, the international manager should consider how to cope with the possibility of their occurrences. Generally the responses are to minimize the consequences, or to transfer them to another firm or insurance company. The specific methods vary with the circumstances of each peril and each business. Some examples are discussed below.

Cessation of vital supplies can stop an industrial process and cause loss of profits and goodwill, and the imposition of penalties. If the manager has access to alternate suppliers, it may be enough merely to identify the peril and note that shifting to an alternate supplier will solve the problem. Lack of alternate sources of supply, however, may require the manager to insure the risk. For example, producers of aluminum require electricity as a vital supply and may be dependent on only one source of electric power, which may be owned by the government or a private generating plant. Sudden interruption of power may result in the solidifying of the molten aluminum in the potlines. The solid aluminum then has to be chipped from the pots, a process that is expensive and takes a long time, during which profits are lost due to cessation of production, and expenses are incurred either to maintain employees or to lay them off. When there is no alternate source of electric power, the aluminum company is likely to insure against the consequences of interruption of its electric power supply.

Breakage of a vital machine part can similarly cause loss beyond the value of the part, by interrupting a business operation. Some firms minimize the consequences of loss by identifying these key parts and keeping spares on hand. This is particularly important if the spares can be obtained only from another country, with possible delays in their import because of the necessity of obtaining import permits and the possibility that the parts may have to be fabricated to order. The practice of keeping vital spares may be coupled with business interruption insurance as a backup protection, in which case the insurance should be less expensive than if no spares were kept.

Many firms have a system of duplicate-record storage at a location separate from that of the originals, as a precaution against damage by fire, sabotage, earthquake, war, and the like. Firms with duplicate records outside Nicaragua found them helpful when the originals in Managua were destroyed by fires following the 1972 earthquake. Foreign firms in Cuba that did not have duplicate records outside Cuba found themselves put to considerable expense and inconvenience when Fidel Castro nationalized their Cuban offices. The records were there, intact, but the firms no longer had access to them.

Various types of safety programs, of engineering measures, of controls, guards, audits, and the like, can reduce the probability of different types of losses, their severity if they occur, and the price of insurance if the peril is insured. A perfectly peril-free operation is likely to produce nothing, however, and the international manager will wish to weigh the costs of protective measures against their benefits. These costs and benefits may be other than the immediately measurable financial ones. For example, some safety programs may be so onerous that the employees refuse to follow them, some may yield morale benefits by reduction of accidents, and all of these may have indirect effects upon the operation.

In most cases, the international manager will find that the most practical way to handle the peril is to insure it.

KINDS OF COVERAGE

The kinds of insurance coverage that the international manager will buy will be those that cover those perils affecting his operation whose consequences he cannot reasonably budget because their occurrence is of low probability but high risk.

He will insure those perils whose insurance is compulsory under local laws, typically automobile liability insurance and workmen's compensation insurance.

Some perils may be impossible to insure. War and revolution occurring on land are examples, since insurance companies do not insure against them because the accumulation of claims would be too great a burden for their financial resources. The international manager must make such plans as he can for those contingencies. It is also possible that the insurance market will not wish to provide an insurance program exactly like that desired by the international manager or recommended by his insurance broker, as respects some perils, limits, and deductibles. One of the purposes of shopping among different insurance companies is to find one with the desired product flexibility.

PROPERTY INSURANCE.   The basic property-insurance policy is the fire policy, which is usually extended to cover windstorm, earthquake, riot, vandalism, collision by vehicles and aircraft, and other miscellaneous perils. Much has been made earlier in this chapter of the advisability of insuring against remote and unlikely perils whose occurrence, nevertheless, could be devastating to a business enterprise. This is not always easy to do. The international manager and his insurance broker may not think of them; indeed, we are referring to those perils that are unusual rather than those commonly thought of. Some insurance companies may have barriers against departure from tradition, or may be inhibited by internal contractual limitations or those of supervisory authorities who may not authorize unique coverages. However, some professional insurance brokerage firms and insurance companies of the sort that specialize in international business pride themselves on their ability to obtain and provide special coverages, and may, for example, be able to provide so-called all-risk insurance, which is beginning to be written in the United States.

All-risk coverage does carry some exclusions, but it removes from the international manager the burden of listing remote and unlikely occurrences, and puts on the insurance company the burden of listing those perils that it wishes to exclude, which are thus brought specifically to the attention of the international manager.

The insurance manager must consider the adequacy of the description of the property to be insured. He will have to list the property and its location in order to know himself what he wants covered and the values for which it is to be covered, and also to enable the insurance company to price the insurance. Nevertheless, if he can obtain an extremely broad description in the policy, it will relieve him from the possibility of an uninsured loss should he have made an error or failed to keep his list up to date. Such a failure is possible as business changes. For example, overflow inventory may be stored temporarily in a rented warehouse, or property belonging to a third party may be temporarily held by the assured. A good insurance broker will attend to matters of this nature; however, in many cases the international manager does not have freedom to choose his insurance broker or insurance company, being obliged to use those that his head office has chosen for its domestic operation, for reasons that may be appropriate for the domestic operation but not for the foreign operation.

The consequences of damage to insured property are typically the damage itself and interruption of business due to inability to use the damaged property until repaired or replaced. The manager should consider carefully the consequences of damage and interruption of business for his particular operation, since many situations are unique.

Valuation of these consequences is worth special attention by the international manager, because it is likely to be more complex in his case. A common approach is to insure direct damage for book value of the property. This may be sometimes appropriate for raw materials and manufactured goods whose book value has been calculated both recently and correctly. However, often the only recorded value of the goods is in the assured's local books overseas, which are kept in local currency. In a country with galloping inflation, the time between establishing the original book value and the replacement of the property after a loss may well be enough that the original insured values are inadequate.

Some countries provide indexing formulas, but the index rate is sometimes substantially different from the true inflation rate. If it is necessary to replace damaged material by imports, it is necessary to consider the exchange rate in the valuation. Some countries have more than one exchange rate, with a two-tier or multiple-tier exchange system, and the manager will presumably keep this in mind for those valuations. The international manager may wish to work out with the insurance company some formula or procedure for maintaining the adequacy of insured values.

In the case of capital assets that have been on the books for some time, some assureds cover them for book value. Although some countries with a history of hyperinflation provide for tax-free revaluation of assets, this may be infrequent and unrealistic. Book value—historical cost less depreciation permitted by the tax authorities—is likely to be inadequate. If the capital asset is machinery, frequently it has been imported. The valuation may depend on current value in the country of manufacture and the applicable exchange rate. Thus valuation is a task requiring some thought and consultation with the insurance company. In practice, this is often not undertaken until a claim occurs, when differences of opinion may result in conflict.

Business interruption poses a different type of valuation problem; the task is to foresee correctly the duration of an interruption, the elements of resulting loss, and their cost. This is made more difficult in the international field because of uncertainties introduced when repair or replacement of damaged property must be obtained in countries other than the one where the loss occurred. This may introduce a delay that is long or difficult to calculate. Some managers keep on hand vital spares to reduce this delay.

Some countries levy a tax on insurance-loss payments, amounting to a percentage of the payments. The payment then falls short of being complete reimbursement to the assured by the amount of that tax, unless the international manager has thought to include it in the valuation formula.

LIABILITY INSURANCE.   Liability-insurance forms vary more widely around the world than do fire-insurance forms. Liability insurance is more developed in the United States than in other countries; thus the United States is an excellent market in which to obtain such coverage, and the international manager is likely to be most comfortable with an American firm.

The principal hazard to guard against is the temptation to insure for low limits because foreigners are less litigious than Americans and foreign judgments lower than in the United States. These facts do not justify low limits so much as they justify low prices for high limits. The assured cannot safely rely on the judgments always being low. There have been cases of injury to Americans overseas who have obtained a local judgment in their favor and used this as the basis for a successful lawsuit against the assured or the assured's parent organization in the United States, for sums exceeding policy limits. Also, the low judgments in nonindustrialized economies are typical of injuries caused by local citizens to other local citizens whose earning power is low. One cannot be sure that the judgment would be as low if the injury were caused by a foreign corporation or subsidiary, particularly if it were caused to a citizen whose earning power was high.

FIDELITY INSURANCE.   The risk of embezzlement may be greater in international operations than in the United States because the international operations are typically smaller, so that it is more difficult to maintain the same degree of checks and controls that would exist in the home office. In some cases pay levels overseas are less than in the United States, so that the temptation to embezzle is greater. Some modes of operation differ from those in the United States and thus present problems of control for which the American international manager may not be prepared. In many countries debtors do not respond to bills sent by mail, and it is the custom to collect accounts receivable by sending a collector to visit the debtor and solicit payment. Payment may often be in cash, against tender of a presigned receipt that the collector carries with him. Several visits may be necessary to effect one collection. This system is difficult to control, and the collector is usually at a low level of remuneration. He is subject to robbery, and the system lends itself to petty defalcation. Indeed, the probability of loss is high enough so that the international manager may feel that he should buy fidelity insurance with a deductible to exclude predictable losses.

SURETY BONDS.   Surety bonds are guarantees that a person or corporation, called the principal, will perform an obligation due to another person or corporation, called the obligee. They are issued by a surety, which is a specialized surety company, or an insurance company.

Surety bonds are used in a wide variety of situations and with a variety of names for specific situations. A customs bond, for example, guarantees that an importer will pay the customs duty assessed on an import. It may be permitted in some countries as a device to permit passage of imported goods through customs without prior payment of duty. A release-of-attachment bond guarantees that the defendant will pay the judgment if the plaintiff wins the lawsuit, and is a device to permit the release of the defendant's property that has been attached by the plaintiff.

Other forms of surety bonds that international managers are most likely to encounter are the bid bond, the performance or supply bond, and the maintenance bond.

The bid bond guarantees that if the bidding firm is successful in a bidding situation, it will execute the contract for which it has bid and will provide a performance or supply bond. Sometimes when sealed bids are opened, the winning bid is so very much lower than the others as to suggest that the bidder has made an error in computation. The bidder may then wish to limit his loss by refusing to sign the contract. The bid bond is designed to protect the obligee in that circumstance. It will be apparent that what will protect the obligee is a payment in the amount of the difference between the lowest bid and the next lowest bid.

The performance bond guarantees that the principal will perform the contract that it has executed. The name *performance bond* is typically used to designate those bonds guaranteeing contracts for the construction of buildings, plants, highways, bridges, dams, and the like. If, however, performance of the contract requires the supply and perhaps the installation of manufactured goods or the supply of commodities, the name *supply bond* is used for the corresponding guarantee. It is apparent that protection to the obligee in case of default by the principal may be either payment of whatever sum is necessary so that the obligee may get someone else to complete or perform the defaulted contract, or it may be completion of the contract by the surety. The cost of either of these alternatives depends on the nature of the default. If the contract is nearly completed before default, the cost of final completion is low. However, if very little has been done on the contract or if the work done or the goods supplied are seriously defective, the work may have to be done all over again, or entirely new goods submitted. In that case, the cost could be high.

If the principal must guarantee the work or the goods, and if this guarantee must be secured by a surety bond, that bond is called a *maintenance bond*. In case of failure of the work or goods within the guarantee or maintenance period, the obligee would be protected by repair or replacement of the defective work or good, or payment of the cost of repair or replacement.

The international manager will find that in most parts of the world it does not occur to the parties to a guarantee that it may be issued by an insurance company, this being customary only in the case of insurance companies in the United States and a handful of other countries. In most parts of the world, business custom is that banks issue guarantees. It may be to the international manager's benefit to provide guarantees from American insurance companies rather than banks for the reasons stated below.

Guarantors, whether insurance companies or banks, do not expect their principals to default, causing the guarantors to absorb the cost of making good their guarantees. Consequently, the guarantors go to a good deal of effort to make sure that they guarantee only those principals who can be expected to comply with their obligations, and they take appropriate measures to secure themselves.

Banks typically equate their guarantees with letters of credit, and often issue them in that form. A letter of credit is a document usually used for other purposes, such as payment in import-export transactions, and provides for payment of the face amount of the instrument against shipping or other appropriate documents. The bank may, and frequently does, protect itself by collateralizing a portion of the principal's assets. The risk to the international manager when his firm is principal is that the bank may pay under the letter of credit, perhaps to its full face amount, upon receipt of documents from the obligee certifying to a default. If the obligee is a government entity, which is a frequent case, the documents will have an official character. The bank will seek to make itself whole from the principal, probably beginning with the principal's collateralized assets. This may not seem troublesome during the euphoria when the principal has just succeeded in obtaining what appears to be a profitable contract with the obligee and when the guarantee is obtained from the bank and the parties are confident that there will be no difficulties between principal and obligee. It may be distressing later, however, if a dispute develops between principal and obligee and the obligee then demands, and the bank pays, the full amount of the guarantee, which may be far in excess of the amount needed to protect the obligee. Indeed, if the obligee's claim is not justified, the principal may feel that no payment at all was in order. In those countries where the use of bank guarantees is a common business practice, obligees are sometimes inclined to treat them as customary letters of credit and to demand full payment without regard to the niceties of the actual amount of damages that they may feel they have suffered.

An American insurance company issuing a surety bond operates in accordance with American surety custom. It may or may not collateralize assets of the principal, being less likely to do so than a bank, although it will require a written guarantee from the principal to hold it, the surety, harmless in case of payment. Nevertheless, in case of claim, the American insurance company will normally resist payment if unjustified and litigate the question of liability and amount if necessary. It will obtain completion of the guaranteed obligation in the least-expensive manner possible. This may even take the form of guaranteeing loans to the principal, who may be on the brink of default because of unexpectedly high expenses and consequent insufficiency of funds to complete the contract. In such a case, dispute with the obligee is avoided, and the obligee may not need to know that there was a problem.

The international manager when faced with a requirement for a guarantee should be careful about the source of the guarantee that he provides and the manner of operation of the guarantor in case of claim; he may regret it if he indulges a feeling of confidence that no dispute will arise between principal and obligee. It is precisely because of the possibility of dispute that the obligee requires the principal to give a guarantee. A guarantee is by no means an empty formality.

It should be understood that not all defaults necessarily involve disputes. The parties may be in agreement on the fact of default and the amount of damage caused thereby. However, in case of dispute between principal and obligee, the American insurance company traditionally considers itself a partner in interest with its client principal, and this reflects itself in claim handling. The bank is more likely to be concerned with the correctness of documents accompanying the demand for payment, and to treat the payment of claim more in the nature of a financial transaction without regard to the details of the dispute between the principal and obligee. This may be discussed between the international manager and the bank, and resolved prior to issuance of the guarantee, in those cases in which a bank guarantee seems more desirable to the international manager.

Pricing of bank guarantees and insurance-company surety bonds is often on different bases, and the international manager will want to compare these.

The international manager may find that it takes more time than he expects to obtain a surety bond from an insurance company. This may be particularly true if the American insurance company considers that the financial worth of the principal does not justify the bond, as is often the case with a small overseas subsidiary. In that case the surety is likely to require the counterguarantee of the parent company, which may take unexpected time. It is beneficial to the international manager who expects to be faced with the necessity for a guarantee to make arrangements for it well in advance of the date when it must be submitted.

INSURANCE CONSIDERATIONS OTHER THAN RISK

The international-risk manager will probably buy insurance for considerations other than the problem of nonbudgetable risk alone. These considerations include compliance with the law where compulsory insurance is required, even if a determinable volume of loss is nearly certain, as we have seen. Other considerations are various kinds of services.

In those countries where it is customary to jail the driver of an automobile involved in an automobile accident causing personal injury, the international manager will find it helpful to buy automobile liability insurance from an insurer that moves to extricate its clients from jail as quickly as possible. Such a company has claims adjusters who know their way around the police courts, having performed that function for their company's clients innumerable times. The release of its clients from jail is usually tied to a rapid claims settlement with the injured party. In contrast, if the international manager relies on his corporate lawyer, the latter is apt to be out of his milieu, to operate with less deftness and speed, and with less expertise in settling automobile liability claims, and he may be expected to charge a fee for his services.

In many countries the law stipulates that in case of fire the owner of the premises is presumed to have committed arson unless he proves to the contrary. This is less ominous than it sounds, and does not result in automatic jailing as in the case of an automobile accident involving injury. It results in placing the burden of proof of innocence upon the owner, or, in the case of a corporation, upon its representative, the manager. This is routinely discharged by a hearing in a police or other court, where the manager is usually able to prove his innocence without great difficulty. It is helpful to the international manager to deal with an insurance company that will help him through this process.

Another service provided by insurance companies is the assumption of responsibility for economical handling of liability claims small and predictable enough so that the assured need not insure them from a risk-management standpoint. As long as these claims remain small, there is no problem if the international manager elects to handle them without insurance. However, it sometimes happens that a small claim escalates into a big one, meriting treatment quite different from that accorded when it was thought to be small. In that case, the insurance company may deny liability for the larger claim, alleging that the international manager's handling of the claim when it was thought to be small has prejudiced the insurance company's ability to defend the case. The international manager should consult with his insurer to determine how this problem is best solved. It may be that the insurance company should handle all claims, both small and big, to avoid the possibility of its criticizing the manager for his handling of small claims.

Similar reasoning would suggest that perhaps the insurer should handle all workmen's compensation claims. It should be borne in mind that although it is common for national law to require that employees be covered for industrial accidents at the cost of the employer, there are many countries where this is legally the direct obligation of the employer, it being the latter's option whether to insure that obligation or not. Therefore, the employer must take a position on this point in those countries.

PERSONNEL INSURANCE

Personnel insurance is another kind of service that is of sufficient importance to warrant special attention, even though it does not cover perils to the employer.

Employees are subject to certain perils whose coverage by the employer may be part of normal market remuneration, or, if not customary, may nevertheless, be desirable from management's viewpoint in order to improve employee relations.

In many countries, the government operates a social security program, for which it usually taxes the employer, and sometimes the employee. Although Social Security in the United States implies old-age pensions, this is often not the case in other countries. Social security may provide any or all of the following benefits: medical care and disability pay for industrial injuries and illness, for nonindustrial injuries and illness, for maternity, indemnity to surviving family upon death of an employee, and old-age pensions.

Where the social security system provides medical care, it is often under conditions and of a quality such that executive-level personnel and their families prefer not to use it. If, then, they use private medical services they must pay for these and are exposed to the possibility of high costs for serious medical problems. Therefore, they would be interested in some form of medical-expense insurance such as hospitalization and major-medical insurance. However, they may not expect it if it is not a local market custom.

Old-age pensions are inadequate in some countries, because of lack of funds in the social security's pension fund. This may result in failure to increase pensions in countries with high inflation rates, where the purchasing power of pension levels established in earlier years may have eroded to the point where it is scarcely worth filing application for the pension. The pension problem is further complicated by the fact that it is usually payable locally and in local currency. Although this is satisfactory to persons residing in that country during their retirement, it is unsatisfactory for foreigners who may be expected to reside elsewhere during their retirement.

The international manager should be familiar with the employee designations described below, as they are involved in employee-benefit decisions. An international operation conducted outside the country of the home office may have the following categories of employees: local nationals, home-country nationals, and third-country nationals. Local nationals usually expect the normal remuneration programs of their local labor markets. These may not involve privately insured employee benefit plans if those benefits are not customary or are provided by the government social security program.

Home-country nationals usually expect the employee benefits of their home labor market. If the home country is the United States, the home-country nationals typically expect those medical insurance, life insurance, and pension programs that they would receive in the United States. They will usually hold to these expectations even if the local social security provides some of these benefits, and indeed the quality of some of the social security benefits in some countries is unsatisfactory.

There is a growing group of third-country nationals in international business, persons who are neither citizens of the local country nor of the home country. They do not necessarily have the expectations of the local labor market nor of the home-country labor market, and it is impractical to construct separate employee benefit programs for each third-country nationality. Third-country nationals are typically of a senior-technical or executive-level category and will not be satisfied with those government social security benefits that are inadequate or of poor quality.

With respect to local social security pensions, both classes of expatriates, the home-country and third-country nationals, may have worked for one employer in several countries in the course of an international business career. They may have accumulated social security pension benefits in several countries, each payable in its own local currency, some with exchange-control restrictions, and some requiring collection to be effected locally. Such pensions are of no practical use to the employee, who may not reside in any of these countries and certainly cannot reside in all of them during his retirement. An American can enroll in the U.S. Social Security program, and his home office can maintain contributions for him while he works in another country, but similar arrangements are often not possible for third-country nationals.

Senior local nationals, home-country nationals, and third-country nationals are usually all of executive or near-executive level. The international manager may find that to provide them with different employee-benefit programs according to nationality rather than to level of responsibility could cause disaffection, especially if the home-country national level is higher than that of the other two. Therefore, he may find it advisable to provide all three categories with privately insured employee-benefit programs based on those of the home country, with eligibility to the programs based on the level of responsibility of the employee. It is, of course, unlikely that the manager would import expatriates for low-level jobs.

At least one of the American international insurance companies can provide pension programs such that contributions can be made by the employer in many of the countries where the employee works, in the local currency and with the tax deductibility provided by local law, yet the program permits the ultimate pension eligibility to accumulate throughout the employee's transfers from country to country, and upon retirement pays him elsewhere in another currency, typically that of the home country.

A different service that may be required of the insurance company is the furnishing of voluntary workmen's compensation insurance benefits. It may be that the American employee of an oil-well drilling company, for example, considers the benefits required by local law in a foreign country to be less than those of a typical United States jurisdiction, or he may simply not know what the foreign benefits are and may not wish to have to review them for adequacy in each country, nor to have his benefits vary as a result of his transfers from country to country. Therefore, it is not uncommon to provide expatriate workmen with the voluntary workmen's compensation insurance of a jurisdiction whose benefits are adequate.

AMOUNTS OF INSURANCE TO BUY

The purpose of buying insurance can be fully served only if the upper policy limits are adequate. Therefore, in the case of property insurance, the international manager will seek to buy insurance for limits adequate to cover the cost of damage to property, interruption to business, and any other consequences that he may foresee from property damage. In the case of liability insurance, however, there is no upper limit of possible loss as in the case of property insurance. The consequences of an alleged negligent act can be astonishingly and unexpectedly extensive. However, the probability of a claim reaching increasingly higher limits becomes ever smaller, decreasing at a more rapid rate than that of the increase in limits. Therefore, higher limits cost proportionately less than lower limits, and extremely high limits are proportionately extremely inexpensive. It is good strategy, therefore, to buy limits comfortably and amply above the highest liability claim that may be expected in the worst circumstances.

In the case of automobile liability insurance, some countries require coverage without limit, and the policies issued in those countries provide unlimited automobile liability insurance.

The criteria for the lower limits of insurance are different. The lower limits are the deductible amounts of any claim, which are for the account of the assured rather than the insurance company. Of course in the case of compulsory insurance the law may not permit a deductible, in which case the lower limit is zero—that is to say, there is no deductible and the insurance company's liability begins with the first penny of loss. In the case of liability insurance it is not uncommon to avoid deductibles in order that all claims should come to the attention of the insurance company. However, in the case of property insurance, such as automobile "own damage" insurance covering against collision and other perils to the insured vehicle, and also in the cases of cargo insurance and fire or all-risk insurance covering property other than cargo, a deductible may be an appropriate strategy, permitting a saving in insurance premiums.

One of the criteria for a deductible is high probability of loss, mentioned earlier in this chapter. If the international manager considers a loss figure sufficiently probable so that he feels justified in budgeting it, he should not insure it, because the cost of insurance will normally exceed the loss figure by the amount of the insurance company's other expenses and profit. This analysis refers to an annual budget, therefore the deductible mentioned would be an annual deductible applicable to the total of losses in the year, not to a deductible applicable to each individual claim, providing always that the insurance company is willing to insure on such a basis.

The other criterion for a deductible is that variation that the manager is prepared to accept in his annual budget. Unexpected variations in expenses, especially in sales volume, can cause the year-end profit-and-loss figure to vary from the budgeted figure. The manager usually has an appreciation of the amount of variation that will be accepted by his superiors without difficulty, beyond which unhappiness will occur. It would be inconsistent and needlessly expensive to buy certainty against the effects of various perils for amounts below that threshold. For example, if the international manager operates a one-man sales office for high-cost products that are infrequently purchased, such as major machinery or construction projects, sales may vary by hundreds of thousands of dollars from one year to the next. It would seem strange, then, to worry about the variation in the annual profit-and-loss statement resulting from the possible total loss by collison of a $6000 company car. If the manager's superiors will accept that view, he may retain a certain amount of risk in the form of a higher annual deductible and enjoy the consequent premium savings.

ADMITTED INSURANCE

The international manager should acquaint himself with the concept of admitted insurance and some of its implications.

Admitted insurance is a technical term meaning insurance issued by a company licensed to operate in the jurisdiction where it is "admitted." Thus, admitted insurance in Brazil is insurance issued by a company, Brazilian or foreign, that is licensed by the Brazilian authorities to operate in Brazil.

A great many countries have laws prohibiting the *purchase* of nonadmitted insurance, that is, insurance issued by companies that are not admitted in the jurisdiction. An even-larger number of countries have laws prohibiting the *sale* of nonadmitted insurance, but that is the problem of the insurance company, not of the client, hence it will not be discussed here. We will explore further the concept of admitted insurance from the purchaser's viewpoint.

It is worth noting, by comparison, that the United States generally does not legislate against the *purchase* of nonadmitted insurance. If a U.S. owner wishes to insure his home or factory against the peril of fire with, say, a European insurance company that is not licensed to operate in his state or in any of the United States, he is legally free to do so. Since the European company, lacking a license in the United States, is not permitted to have an office nor an agent in the United States, the client may encounter practical problems in making the purchase. He might have to make it by mail, or while on a trip to Europe. Indeed, it is not uncommon for foreigners living in countries with exchange control and serious inflation to take advantage of a trip to the United States to buy U.S.-dollar life insurance from American companies that are nonadmitted in the assured's own country. However, the likelihood of an American buying a nonadmitted policy is generally remote because of the limited advantages that it offers and the practical difficulties involved.

There are two exceptions to the foregoing paragraph. First, where insurance is compulsory, nonadmitted insurance is not considered to meet the compulsory requirement. Thus a New York State resident cannot comply with its compulsory automobile-liability-insurance law by buying a French automobile-liability-insurance policy while on a vacation trip in Paris. Second, there are so-called surplus-line laws in the United States permitting surplus-line insurance brokers to buy nonadmitted insurance in cases where the United States market is unwilling or unable to insure certain risks. Americans do buy this insurance because the presence of these brokers in the United States makes it feasible for them to do so. Similar laws exist in other countries, although it is rare that circumstances exist permitting their use.

Let us now turn to the case of the international manager. It is both easy and, perhaps, tempting for him to buy nonadmitted insurance. If he has a sales subsidiary in Peru, for example, with employees, an office, warehouse, inventory, and vehicles all located in Peru, he will need to insure them. Meanwhile, the United States home office that employs him has its traditional American insurer, which will often be willing to include coverage of the small Peruvian sales operation along with its coverage of the much-larger American operation, for a low premium, which the home office would, perhaps, charge to its Peruvian subsidiary. Indeed, the home office may do just that, and press its international manager to accept the premium charge. However, such insurance is not admitted in Peru, because the American insurer is not licensed to operate in Peru. Peruvian laws, like those of many countries, impose penalties on buyers of nonadmitted insurance.

In this situation, some firms have sought to conceal the nonadmitted insurance from the authorities. This incurs several hazards, all of which have occurred in practice. One is that the local personnel may be careless and divulge the clandestine insurance, perhaps in response to the importunities of a local insurance agent seeking to make a sale. If, however, the nonadmitted insurance is kept as a purely home-office coverage, not divulged to the local manager, he may buy legal insurance locally, thus duplicating the United States coverage. In case of loss, the nonadmitted insurer is not equipped with claims adjusters who know the local language and are able to operate legally in the country. In case of claims payments, the client has a problem in booking the inflow of money. It is necessary to show a source of the inflow and a reason for it. It may be shown as a contribution to capital from the parent company, but if so, problems may arise with admissibility and registry of capital and the share allocable to any local joint venturer. Meanwhile, the local subsidiary cannot pay nor take an income-tax deduction for the premium for a nonadmitted policy. This must be paid by the U.S. parent company, which then may be faced with an American income-tax problem if it seeks to charge overseas expenses in its American tax return, since the U.S. tax authorities may then require it to include overseas income as well.

In contrast, an admitted policy overseas causes no income-tax problem in the United States. It creates no risk of legal violation in the country where it is admitted. It permits deduction of the insurance premium in the local tax return and payment of insurance-premium expenses out of local funds, which is usually desirable when there are exchange-control restrictions or taxes on the remittance of profits. An admitted policy permits local service by the insurance company, which is a convenience in routine adjustments of the details of the policies to conform to varying current conditions and of vital importance in case of an insurance claim. Only admitted policies will satisfy local legal requirements for compulsory insurance.

Admitted policies do bring their own problems to international managers, but these have been solved by some American insurance companies specializing in the foreign field. In most countries the policies will be in the local language, which, if not English, sometimes cannot be read by the international manager, and rarely by his head office. In most countries the policy forms differ from the American forms. In the countries that formerly formed the British Empire and in other countries where the British pioneered in the insurance industry, the forms are derived from standard British forms, although the language may be that used locally. In the former French colonies, the language and policy forms are usually French. Other countries have their own forms in their own languages. There is a surprising amount of traditionalism with respect to insurance-policy forms in many countries. Thus it is common enough that the international manager cannot buy locally the broad coverages or full limits or level of deductible that he wishes.

Transportation or cargo insurance is generally a worldwide exception to the foregoing. Buyers and sellers across national boundaries are usually able to specify whether the seller or the buyer of goods shall buy insurance to cover the perils of transportation. Nevertheless, in countries where admitted insurance laws prevail, the buyer of cargo insurance must buy it from admitted insurers. Some countries do not leave open the choice of whether the buyer or seller of goods shall insure the transportation perils. Instead, they require that the importer of goods insures them. They may, however, not specify a required coverage; thus the importer may be able to satisfy the requirement by buying the narrowest and least-expensive transportation insurance (so-called free-of-particular-average coverage), so that the exporter, if desired, can afford to insure with a broader, all-risk coverage in his own insurance market.

The problems of language and form presented by admitted policies have been solved by some American insurance companies, which provide locally admitted policies through locally admitted branches or subsidiaries, or through friendly local companies, and at the same time provide the parent company in the United States with an American policy in English, on a familiar form, covering the differences between the desired coverage and that of the local admitted policy. This American policy is, of course, nonadmitted with respect to the international manager's foreign operation, and must be paid for by the parent company, but its cost is low, and it is seldom required to pay a claim because its coverage is for fringe perils while the principal perils are covered and charged for under the locally admitted policy. The American policy serves as a security backup in case the local admitted policy is inadequate.

INTERNATIONAL INSURANCE MARKETS

Those countries that formerly had large colonial empires developed insurance companies that followed their empires. Thus British insurance companies and Lloyd's agents followed the British flag, and French companies followed the French flag. The British, in particular, became active in insurance in other countries as well.

Within Britain there are two insurance markets, the Lloyd's market and the companies market. The latter is a market of insurance companies much as exists in the United States and many other countries. Lloyd's, however, is a market in the more traditional sense of one place, a room in a building, where many buyers and sellers come together to do business. The insurers are individuals, called *names.* Each is pledged to the full amount of his net worth to guarantee his obligations. The names join together, still as individuals, in syndicates that employ skilled insurers, called *underwriters,* to represent them in their sales of insurance. The individual names authorize the underwriter to commit themselves for only small amounts on any one risk, so that the total commitment of all the names in a syndicate is often insufficient to cover an industrial risk. Therefore, it is necessary to accumulate the total obligations of many syndicates to cover such risks. The buyers are insurance brokers who buy, and thus accumulate, the obligations of as many syndicates as may be necessary, on behalf of their clients.

Many of these clients are foreign, and Lloyd's has a large international premium volume. Lloyd's is located in London, and its insurance policies are contracted and issued there, being sent by mail to clients who are located abroad. For routine risks, various syndicates may authorize a correspondent overseas to commit them on certain classes of risk. Claims settlement is usually handled by mail submission of claims supported by reports prepared by local Lloyd's claims agents, following which the amount of the claim is remitted by mail from London. In recent decades insurance laws in many countries have become increasingly sophisticated, requiring insurers to have a fully authorized local representative in the country and a deposit of funds to guarantee insurance obligations, to issue policies in the local language, and to keep local books. Lloyd's has generally not met these requirements, and has thus withdrawn from one country after another the authority given to local agents to commit it on certain risks or even to negotiate a commitment with Lloyd's underwriters in London. Where Lloyd's has withdrawn, it is, of course, not licensed to operate, and cannot provide admitted policies whose premiums can be taken as income-tax deductions by local insurance customers. The strengths of Lloyd's are its reputation for meeting its obligations and its flexibility to providing special insurance coverages to meet the special needs of individual clients.

Local insurance industries have gradually grown up in the less industrialized countries. Usually these are extremely small relative to those of the industrialized countries, and the participation of an individual insurance company is, of course, for an even-smaller volume. To give an idea of scale, the total annual premium of a small American city may be several times as large as the total annual premium of a country in Central America.

In the smaller economies of the less industrialized nations, the local insurance companies lack the large number of clients necessary to give them a spread of risk. Many policies represent individually an undesirable vulnerability to a larger loss than the financial resources of the company can support. In response to this situation, local companies rely heavily on reinsurance, which is merely insurance that one insurance company buys from another, covering its insurance exposures in order to reduce its vulnerability to excessive loss resulting from those exposures. The amount of reinsurance purchased is astonishingly large to those not acquainted with operations in those countries. Although it may be small in the case of automobile insurance, where individual policy limits in such countries are low, in fire insurance it is not unusual to find that well over 90 percent of total fire-insurance premiums are reinsured into foreign reinsurance markets such as those of Lloyd's, Switzerland, the United States, and others. In such cases the local insurance companies become similar in many respects to insurance agents, bearing almost no insurance risk themselves and being heavily dependent on the foreign reinsurers for the ability to pay local claims. Because of this dependence on others, they have a limited flexibility in providing special policy texts designed for the special wants of some individual clients.

In some countries, concern at the loss of foreign exchange to foreign reinsurers has resulted in legislation to establish local government-owned and government-operated reinsurers, with whom local insurance companies are obliged to place all their reinsurance. These government reinsurers, by virtue of their monopoly of the supply of reinsurance to the local insurance industry, exercise a great deal of control over the latter. They can and do establish price levels and standard policy forms, and intervene in claims settlements. The international manager is likely to find, if he buys insurance locally in these markets, that he has less bargaining power both in buying insurance and in resolving any disagreements over claims than he would in a country with a free reinsurance market, because the insurance company has so little autonomy and so little flexibility. Insurance executives in countries with free reinsurance markets comment that the insurance industry in countries where the government monopolizes reinsurance is slow in providing modern insurance developments to the public.

The international manager has two choices to make when buying insurance, aside from the many choices involving coverage. He must make a choice of insurance broker or agent, and of insurance company.

Local people, whether brokers, agents, or insurers, tend to be knowledgeable about local markets, local nuances and considerations. Some buyers feel that buying from local suppliers enhances their local image. However, purely local suppliers are unable to furnish services suitable for the complexity of an operation involving more than one country. Nor is insurance important in affecting image. It is too small a part of a firm's input and is as near to invisible as any input can be.

Credit is a more important factor. Sometimes local banks require a borrower to buy insurance from an affiliated bank as a condition to obtaining a loan. If this occurs, it constitutes an additional cost of credit. The cost lies most heavily in the possibility of insufficiency in the insurance program, which may not be apparent until a loss occurs. Also, insurance sold in this manner is under no pressure to be competitive in price.

Insurance programs and the fine print of policies are sufficiently technical so that an insurance manager would be best served to employ the services of an international insurance broker. In most countries the insurance *agent* represents only one insurance company, not several as in the United States, and therefore cannot serve customers as well as an insurance *broker,* who is a professional buyer for his customers. To serve an international manager, the broker must have his own international expertise, or be able to obtain it. At this writing, the principal, if not the only, international insurance brokers are American and British. The British tend to function internationally in Europe and former British colonies, where they have no language problems and can buy from familiar British insurers. The American international brokers function in countries where their American clients generate sufficient business to justify a local insurance brokerage branch or subsidiary. The account executives at these local offices of international insurance brokers know the local laws, customs, and nuances as well as purely local brokers. In the less industrialized countries, the account executives at the local office of an international broker often have considerably more professional expertise as well as understanding of the customs and requirements of the international manager's home country than would a purely local broker.

The American insurance market consists of a vast number of insurance companies. This market is by far the largest in the world, producing nearly 50 percent of the world's insurance premium. It is a truly immense market; consequently, most American insurance companies are oriented to the American market only, serving it in fashion of a mass market. Insurance companies that are important in the American market, therefore, often do not claim to be able to serve international customers, or may merely include coverage of their customers' international operations with coverage of their domestic operations without regard to inability to furnish admitted policies and local service.

A few American insurance companies have specialized in international business, and some that do not specialize in it have set up international departments. These operate in different ways. Some have their own branches or subsidiaries abroad. This control enables them to provide American-style service to customers abroad. Others have arrangements with local insurance companies either as correspondents or through minority shareholding. In these cases the lack of ownership control results in service and style of dealing with the international customer that is more likely to be that of a local insurance company. It behooves the international manager to investigate the type of foreign organization of the American international insurer from whom he proposes to buy. A feature of international insurance in the American international insurance market is that it can be bought locally by the international manager overseas from the local branch of the American international insurance company, or it can be bought in the United States. American international insurers, through their offices all over the world, are knowledgeable about requirements and conditions in those countries and thus can provide the necessary expertise for those countries where international insurance brokers do not operate.

TRADE FINANCING

CONTENTS

FINANCING INTERNATIONAL TRADE 3

Evolution of Trade Financing 3
Growth and Importance of International
Trade and Trade Financing 4
Strategy for Trade Financing 5
  Recognition of realities 5
  Who will bear the credit risk? 5
  Currency of invoice 5

THE PAYMENT PROCESS 6

Critical Factors Affecting the Payment
Process 6
The Methods of Payment 6
  Payment in advance 7
  Open account 7
  Consignment 8
  Documentary draft for collection 8
  Letter of credit 8

EXPORT DRAFTS AND LETTERS OF
CREDIT 10

Types of Drafts 10
Types of Letters of Credit 10
  Confirmed irrevocable letter of credit 10
  Uncomfirmed irrevocable letter of
  credit 10
  Revocable letter of credit 10
  Revolving letter of credit 10
  Transferable letter of credit 10
  Back-to-back letter of credit 10
  Red-clause letter of credit 11
  Authority to purchase 11
  Letter of credit for financing third-
  country transactions 11
  Export Letter of Credit 11

IMPORT LETTERS OF CREDIT 15

Distinction Between Import and Export
Letters of Credit 15
Import Letter of Credit—Procedure 15
  Applications 15

Letter-of-credit contents 15
Advice to beneficiary 19
Amendments 19
Presentation and checking of
documents 19
Payment and refinancing 21

ACCEPTANCES 21

Types of Bankers Acceptance
Transactions 21
  Exportations from the United States 21
  Importations into the United States 23
  Shipments within the United States 23
  Storage within the United States or
  overseas 24
  The creation of dollar exchange 24
Advantages of Acceptance Financing 24
Bankers Acceptance Market 24

FOREIGN EXCHANGE 25

Importance of Foreign Exchange in
International Trade 25
Foreign-Currency Letters of Credit 25
Foreign Exchange and Other Methods
of Payments 26
Foreign-Exchange Control 26

OFFICIAL AGENCIES 27

U.S. Official Agencies 27
  The Export-Import Bank of the
  United States 27
  Commodity Credit Corporation 28
  Overseas Private Investment
  Corporation 28
International Institutions 28
Official Agencies in Foreign Countries 29

SOURCES AND SUGGESTED
REFERENCES 29

TRADE FINANCING

Maximo Eng

FINANCING INTERNATIONAL TRADE

EVOLUTION OF TRADE FINANCING. International traders have for many centuries (probably since the Romans invented the draft or bill of exchange) relied on financial houses and commercial banks to finance their imports and exports. But changing circumstances have required new concepts, methods, techniques, and instruments in the financing process. During the seventeenth and eighteenth centuries, mercantilists understood that the changes in ratios of gold and silver would affect not only their profits, but also their government policies on flow of specie between nations. After the Industrial Revolution, the theory of comparative advantage has commanded international trade and trade financing, since it involves the entire economic process from natural and human resources to consumption. In the nineteenth and the first half of the twentieth centuries, national protective measures were adopted by many nations in order to safeguard primarily their domestic industries and employment. Restrictive measures, such as tariff and exchange control, have significant effects on strategies and methods of trade financing. After the World War II, international trade as well as its financing have become important parts of national economic development. Furthermore, the emergence of multinational enterprises and the Eurocurrency markets in the 1960s has complicated the trade-financing process. The changes in political, economic, and financial forces in the 1970s have basically restructured the international trading relations and trade-financing competition. For example, the adoption of floating exchange rates from fixed exchange rates since 1973, the surprising oil-price increases since 1974, and the greater participation of nations in international trade including the non-market-economy countries have intensified the international "trade war" and trade-financing competition among government financial agencies.

Confronted with all these major evolutionary, or revolutionary forces, international traders must be keenly aware of the fact that the purpose of international trade involves not only a firm's profits but also national trade policy and global interactions. Goods in trade are not only diversified or differentiated products but also involve "package" arrangements between the trading parties. The market structure is no more a pure "free competition" but involves various segments (monopoly, oligopoly, monopolistic, etc.). Institutions servicing trade financing and insurance are covered not only by private organizations but also by national and international official agencies. For these reasons, the concept, process, methods, and techniques of trade financing will post challenges to serious international traders, financial experts, and official decision makers in the 1980s.

GROWTH AND IMPORTANCE OF INTERNATIONAL TRADE AND TRADE FINANC-ING.   International trade plays different roles in different countries, but trade financing is important to any country. In 1979, according to *International Financial Statistics* published by the International Monetary Fund, international trade (imports and exports) accounted for about 40 percent of total trade in the United Kingdom, 40 percent in West Germany, 90 percent in the Netherlands, 25 percent in Japan, and 16 percent in the United States. Increasing world trade competition and oil prices in the 1970s have intensified trade-financing competition among international commercial banks as well as government financial agencies. The last part of this section will discuss these official institutions.

In the United States, the growth of international trade and trade financing in the past two decades has been more impressive than the growth of the gross national product (GNP). As shown in Exhibit 1, during the periods 1960–1970 and 1970–1979, U.S. international trade grew from 240 percent to 373 percent and dollar bankers acceptances surged from 250 percent to 543 percent, while U.S. GNP only increased from 94 percent to 140 percent. It was argued that the higher the base amount was in 1960, the lower the growth rate became afterward. Moreover, the higher prices of exporting commodities, especially oil, have bolstered the dollar volumes of international trade and trade financing. Obviously the rapid growth of dollar bankers acceptances reflected not only the growth of U.S. international trade from 4.7 percent of its GNP in 1960 to 16.4 percent in 1979, but also the liquidity squeeze of working capital in American firms in the 1970s.

By looking at the ratios of international trade as percentage of GNP, and bankers acceptances as percentage of trade, there is room for the United States to improve its trade in the international trading community. The bankers acceptance is an important type of international trade-financing instrument, but it only accounted for

EXHIBIT 1   GROWTH OF THE U.S. ECONOMY, INTERNATIONAL TRADE, AND THE USE OF DOLLAR BANKERS ACCEPTANCES, 1960–1979 (BILLIONS OF DOLLARS)

	1960	1970	1979	Growth Rate 1960–70 (percent)	Growth Rate 1970–79 (percent)
Gross national product	506	982	2,368	94	140
International trade (imports and exports)	24	82	388	240	373
Dollar bankers acceptances	2	7	45	250	543
International trade as % of GNP	4.7	8.3	16.4		
Bankers acceptances as % of trade	8.8	8.5	11.6		

Source.   U.S. Department of Commerce and *Federal Reserve Bulletin,* various issues.

11.6 percent of U.S. international trade in 1979. This means that although this important trade-financing instrument can continue to grow, other trade-financing instruments, such as the sight draft, collection, or factoring, may be further employed by U.S. exporters in the 1980s.

STRATEGY FOR TRADE FINANCING. Since trade financing involves the entire process of natural resources, production, transportation, and the delivery of goods from seller (exporter) in one country to the buyer (importer) in another country, strategy for trade financing must be considered in connection with the following factors: (1) recognition of realities, (2) question of who will bear the credit risk, and (3) currency of invoice.

Recognition of Realities. First, the nature of the product must be recognized. Durable products such as machinery usually require long-term financing, whereas seasonal products such as fruits and Christmas trees need short-term financing. Second, market conditions in connection with business cycles or new products may favor either the exporter or importer, depending on the demand elasticity of the product in question. Third, the kind of relations between exporter and importer should be considered if trade financing may be needed. For example, affiliates of multinational corporations may use "open account" financing, whereas the lack of confidence between two trading parties normally requires a confirmed letter of credit from a commercial bank. Fourth, the availability of financing services to trading parties would certainly affect the cost and means of financing. Fifth, locations of trading parties affecting transportation and risk in transit and, sixth, local government regulations definitely have vital effects on the way of financing. For example, the requirements for government inspection of products make deferred payment the only desirable means.

Who Will Bear the Credit Risk? Once the situations are clear, questions continue to be raised. Trade financing is not needed under barter agreement. The risk of trade financing is born by the exporter if he promises to ship and deliver the product to the importer and receives payment only after the importer sells the product. This is commonly called *consignment*. On the other hand, the importer bears the credit risk if he advances the entire amount to the exporter before the delivery of the merchandise. This may happen if the exporter lacks financial means and the importer expects his potential profit would justify the risk. In modern international trade, the environment is complex and trade financing is available in most countries. Credit risk is usually shifted from the trading parties to a third party—a private or government financial institution. These include commercial banks, factors, merchant houses, commission agents, trade associations, Export-Import Banks of the United States, and so forth. Obviously whereas private institutions take credit risks for fees, official institutions bear the credit risk primarily for national or international trade policies; for example, to improve the balance of payments.

Currency of Invoice. Foreign-exchange risk is a permanent problem in international trade because it affects costs and profits of both exporter and importer. Normally traders would prefer a key and stable currency commonly acceptable to both parties. At the present, the U.S. dollar, British pound, Deutsche Mark, and Japanese yen are popular in international transactions. But under the floating exchange rates in effect since 1973, currency fluctuations may change the cost-price-profit relations from the moment of production to payment. This problem will be discussed in detail.

THE PAYMENT PROCESS

Since the basic purpose of international trade is for the exporter to get paid as invoiced and the importer to obtain the merchandise as ordered, the payment process must satisfy both parties. To achieve these purposes, two aspects must be recognized: (1) critical factors affecting the payment process, and (2) methods of payment.

CRITICAL FACTORS AFFECTING THE PAYMENT PROCESS.   The nature of the merchandise, the business relationship between importer and exporter, and the possible risks involved in the shipment of the merchandise are critical factors affecting the payment process. The nature of the merchandise determines the price and terms of payment. High-value or perishable goods normally require special payments arrangements, such as advance payment or inspection after arrival of the merchandise. Business relationships between importer and exporter determine the confidence level of both sides; therefore, they influence the payment methods. Multinational affiliates shipping raw materials or merchandise to each other on the open-account basis are typical examples. However, the most-important factors affecting the payment process are probably the anticipated risks in the transactional process. These include distance risk, currency risk, and institutional risk. Distance risk relates to the time and method of shipment of the merchandise. Besides increasing transportation insurance, long distances may affect the quality of merchandise shipped, especially that of perishable and fragile goods. Currency risk is the most well known factor in trade financing, since it affects costs and profits in accounting statements. Changing exchange rates between the two currencies of the importing and exporting countries has vital effects on costs and profits of the two trading parties. Institutional risk refers to political and social problems that may disrupt the payment process, such as political unrest, social commotion, or changes in government policies and regulations. In a broad sense, institutional risk may also include problems associated with international institutional changes, such as sudden changes in oil prices or international tariff agreements.

Within this frame of reference, the appropriate method of payment should be selected.

THE METHODS OF PAYMENT.   Ideally, international traders should recognize both the conceptual and practical aspects of the payment process. As shown in Exhibit 2, the payment process basically involves multiple relationships between the exporter and the importer, their respective banks, national regulations, and international agreements. In case of acceptance financing, the investor comes into the play, since the bankers acceptance market would affect trade-financing methods. For example, the lack of a bankers acceptance market in the United States before the passage of the Federal Reserve Act in 1913 affected time-draft financing except that handled by the British banks. The overview of payment relationships is important since the payment process, simple or complex, must follow these paths one way or another. There are several commonly used methods of payment that require different payment processes in international trade. They are payment in advance, open account, consignment, collection, and letter of credit.

EXHIBIT 2   OVERVIEW OF PAYMENTS RELATIONSHIPS

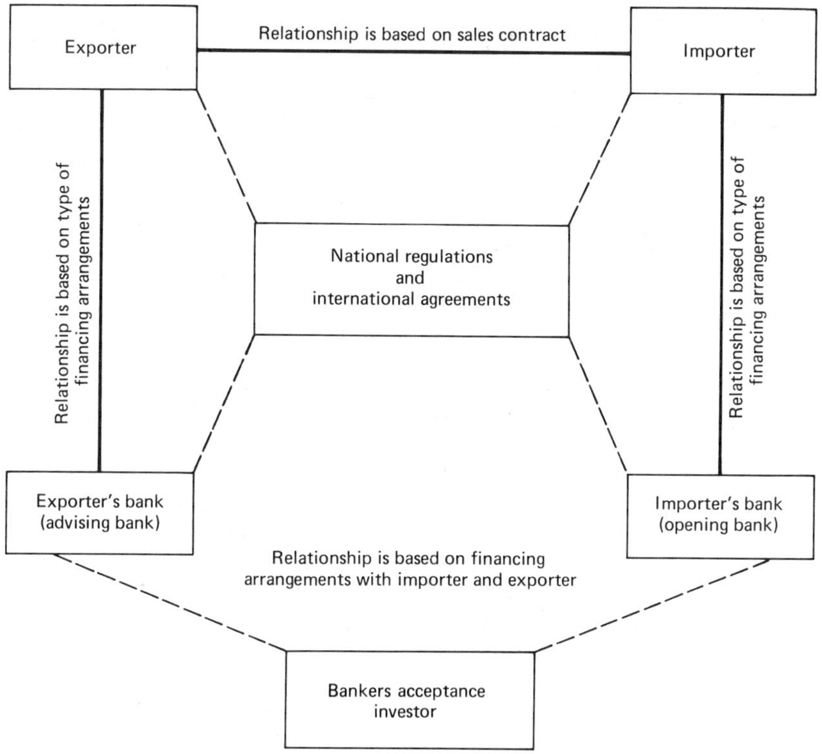

Payment in Advance.   Payment in advance to the exporter could be made by the importer, importer's bank, or exporter's bank. In the first case, the importer must pay for the goods at the time he places the order with the exporter. This method is rarely encountered in foreign trade except when the importer's credit standing is unsatisfactory or unknown. The exporter receives payment before he ships the goods, and the importer assumes all risks. If the goods are delayed or of inferior quality, the importer's last resort is to take legal action on the basis of the sales contract unless the exporter makes a satisfactory adjustment. In the second case, the payment is made in advance by the importer's bank in accordance with a letter of credit requested by the importer. The exporter is authorized to draw drafts upon a designed bank in his location and the proceeds are deducted when the goods are shipped and documents are presented to the importer's bank in good order. Sometime the importer is required to put up a certain amount (margin) before the bank releases the documents to him. In the third case, the exporter obtains funds from his bank upon the presentation of his documents evidencing the shipment of the merchandise. The bank may discount the draft drawn by the exporter with recourse or the exporter can sell the bankers acceptance in the money market at a discount. The funds are recovered by the final payments from the importer through his bank.

Open Account.   This method of payment is frequently used in domestic trade but rarely used in foreign trade except when goods are shipped to a foreign branch or subsidiary of a company—normally a multinational. Selling on open account means selling on credit terms arranged between exporter and importer. Should the importer default, the legal procedures abroad to enforce payment under an open-account arragement are more difficult than the legal procedures to enforce payment for collection. Furthermore, experienced U.S. exporters know that under foreign-exchange controls, many foreign countries give priorities of foreign-exchange allocation to their importers for collection over open account.

Consignment.   Under a consignment contract, the exporter ships the goods to the importer, but the exporter still retains the title of the goods until the importer has sold them to a third party and has paid the exporter (consignor). Under this arrangement, the exporter runs considerable risk, since he cannot get paid until the merchandise is sold. He takes this route of payment normally under the circumstances that the importer is his branch or affiliate or the marketability of the goods (say, a new product) cannot be limited by time. If the consignee defaults, laws in foreign countries are difficult to enforce payment.

Documentary Draft for Collection.   This means that the exporter, after shipping his goods to the importer, presents a draft and documents to his bank, which, in turn, forwards them to the importer's bank for collection. The exporter is guaranteed that the goods will be paid for before the documents are handed over to the importer. The importer is also guaranteed that the goods have been shipped in order before he pays for them. This payment method is popular because it satisfies both exporter and importer. Furthermore, this payment method is less expensive than a letter of credit. From the standpoint of credit risk to the exporter, ranging from highest to lowest, the methods are consignment, open account, document collection, letter of credit, and payment in advance. Collection stands in the middle. It is estimated that the amount of U.S. exports made on a letter-of-credit basis is about equal to the amount made on a collection basis.

Documentary-draft collection may be either a *document against payment* draft (D/P) or a *document against acceptance* draft (D/A). The exporter retains control of the goods until the importer pays or accepts the draft. Upon receipt of payment from the importer, the importer's bank follows the instructions of the exporter (see Exhibit 3) and remits the funds to the exporter's bank, which in turn makes them available to the exporter. Banks in this case do not finance the trade but simply earn commissions.

Letter of Credit.   A letter of credit (L/C) is a written undertaking, or obligation, of a bank, made at the request of its customer (importer), to honor an exporter's drafts or other demands for payment upon compliance with conditions specified in the letter of credit. When a letter of credit is issued by the importer's bank, it assumes the payment responsibility for the importer. The L/C is immediately forwarded to a foreign correspondent bank or its own branch, which in turn forwards the L/C to the exporter (beneficiary). With the use of a letter of credit, importer and exporter do not communicate directly. This is in contrast to the relationship inherent in a sales contract as illustrated in Exhibit 1. The banks are positioned as intermediaries between importer and exporter, performing various functions on their behalf. The letter of credit is classified operationally as either an import or export credit, depending on who the bank's customer is. In the case of an import credit, the importer in the

EXHIBIT 3   COLLECTION FORM

Item 801399(FOB615*(L)7-77)

TO:

Citibank, N.A.
WCG COLLECTION OPERATIONS
111 WALL STREET, NEW YORK, N. Y. 10015

1

COLLECTING
BANK

(IF BLANK,
YOUR CORRES-
PONDENT)

DATE _____

WE ENCLOSE THE FOLLOWING ITEM FOR ☐ COLLECTION AND ☐ AN ADVANCE   CREDIT TO OUR ACCOUNT NUMBER _____

☐ REMITTANCE TO US BY CHECK

¹ SUBJECT TO UNIFORM RULES FOR THE COLLECTION OF COMMERCIAL PAPER (**1967** REVISION) INTERNATIONAL CHAMBER OF COMMERCE, BROCHURE NO. 254.

DRAWERS REFERENCE NUMBER	DATE OF DRAFT	TENOR	AMOUNT

DRAWER

DRAWEE

ADDRESS

BILLS OF LADING ORIG.	DUP.	PARCEL POST RECEIPTS	INSUR. CERT'S.	INVOICES	CONSULAR INVOICES	PACKING LISTS	WEIGHT CERT'S.	CERT'S. OF ORIGIN	OTHER DOCUMENTS

DELIVER DOCUMENTS AGAINST	ACCEPTANCE	PAYMENT	YOUR CHARGES	DRAWEE'S EXPENSE	DRAWER'S EXPENSE
ADVISE BY CABLE	NON—ACCEPTANCE	NON—PAYMENT	MAIL DOCUMENTS	DRAWEE'S EXPENSE	DRAWER'S EXPENSE
REMIT PROCEEDS BY CABLE	DRAWEE'S EXPENSE	DRAWER'S EXPENSE	FOREIGN BANK CHARGES	DRAWEE'S EXPENSE	DRAWER'S EXPENSE
REMIT PROCEEDS BY AIRMAIL			WAIVE CHARGES IF REFUSED		
PROTEST	NON—ACCEPTANCE	NON—PAYMENT	DO NOT WAIVE CHARGES		
DO NOT PROTEST			HOLD FOR ARRIVAL OF MERCHANDISE		

IF DOLLAR EXCHANGE IS NOT IMMEDIATELY AVAILABLE AT MATURITY (OR ON PRESENTATION IF DRAWN AT SIGHT) AND IT IS NECESSARY TO PROVISIONALLY ACCEPT LOCAL CURRENCY PENDING AVAILABILITY OF DOLLAR EXCHANGE, IT MUST BE DISTINCTLY UNDERSTOOD THAT THE DRAWEE SHALL REMAIN LIABLE FOR ALL EXCHANGE DIFFERENCES. AT TIME OF DEPOSIT OF LOCAL CURRENCY OBTAIN FROM DRAWEES THEIR WRITTEN UNDERTAKING TO BE RESPONSIBLE FOR ANY EXCHANGE DIFFERENCES. THE DRAFT MUST NOT BE SURRENDERED TO DRAWEES UNTIL FINAL PAYMENT FOR FACE AMOUNT IN U.S. DOLLAR EXCHANGE.

ALLOW A DISCOUNT OF   IF PAID

COLLECT INTEREST AT THE RATE OF   % FROM

IN CASE OF NEED REFER TO		WHO IS EMPOWERED BY US: TO ACT FULLY ON OUR BEHALF I.E. AUTHORIZE REDUCTIONS, EXTENSIONS, FREE DELIVERY, WAIVING OF PROTESTS ETC.	WHO MAY ASSIST IN OBTAINING ACCEPTANCE OR PAYMENT OF DRAFT, AS DRAWN, BUT IS NOT TO ALTER ITS TERMS IN ANY WAY.

OTHER INSTRUCTIONS

_____
AUTHORIZED SIGNATURE

$ _____   DATE _____ NO. _____

_____ DAYS AFTER   of this SOLE BILL OF EXCHANGE

pay to the order of **Citibank, N.A.**

Value received and charge the same to account of

To _____

SOLE BILL OF EXCHANGE

United States opens a letter of credit in a U.S. bank, whereas with an export credit, an opening bank in a foreign country on behalf of its customer (importer) sends its letter of credit to a U.S. bank, which in turn forwards the L/C to its U.S. exporter. In the first case, the U.S. bank is *active* in opening import credits. In the second case, the U.S. bank is *reactive* in advising, confirming, and negotiating export credits. Because of the complexity of documentation and possible misinterpretation of documents, the International Chamber of Commerce has set a worldwide standard, *Uniform Customs and Practice for Documentary Credits* (1974) to settle documentary disputes in international trade.

Basically, there are three types of payment under a letter of credit: sight draft, time draft, and deferred payment. When the exporter presents the documents together with a sight draft as stipulated in the letter of credit to the opening bank, the exporter has to be paid on demand. Under the time letter of credit, the exporter presents the required documents together with a time draft, 30 days, 60 days, or 90 days, to the opening bank, which, if no discrepancy is found in the documents, accepts the draft for payment at maturity. This is called bankers acceptance. If the exporter needs the money right away, he can ask the opening bank to discount the draft or sell the draft in the open market at a low rate of discount. Under a deferred payment, the exporter effects shipment but does not get paid immediately. The payment is made by the opening bank at a specified time, when all stipulated conditions in the letter of credit are met. A typical example is a shipment of food or drugs to the United States that must be inspected and approved by the U.S. Food and Drug Administration. Pending approval, the documents are normally released by the opening bank to the importer against a trust receipt. That means the bank still owns the merchandise. Once it is advised that the merchandise is approved by the government agency, the bank pays the exporter, charges the importer's account, and transfers the title of the merchandise to the importer.

Since the commercial letter of credit plays a major role in trade financing, a further analysis follows.

EXPORT DRAFTS AND LETTERS OF CREDIT

TYPES OF DRAFTS.   Basically, there are two types of drafts in relation to export letters of credit. One is the sight draft and the other is the time draft. If a letter of credit stipulates that the sight draft must be accompanied by certain documents, the amount in the draft is paid at sight immediately if all required credit terms are complied with. However, if a time draft is required—30 days, 60 days, 90 days, or 180 days—the presented draft is not paid until maturity, unless the exporter asks the paying bank to discount it. Whether the time draft will be discounted or not or who will absorb the discount charges depends on the agreement between the exporter and importer. In any event, the time draft must be accepted by the exporter's bank if it is a confirmed letter of credit. Otherwise the time draft will be forwarded to the importer's bank, or the opening bank, to accept, and the disposal of such an accepted draft is subject to the instructions of the exporter. This process is called bankers acceptance financing and will be discussed later in detail.

TYPES OF LETTERS OF CREDIT.   The following types of letters of credit are commonly used in export and import trade financing.

Confirmed Irrevocable Letter of Credit.   This type of credit is issued by the importer's bank and confirmed by a bank in the exporter's country. The importer's bank commits itself irrevocably to pay the exporter's draft and the confirming bank (the exporter's bank) adds its undertaking to this commitment and assumes the responsibility to pay the exporter's draft, provided all conditions stated in the letter of credit are met. This type of letter of credit gives the exporter the greatest protection, since he has the commitment of two banks to make payment. The confirming bank will pay even if the issuing (or opening bank) cannot or will not honor the draft for any reason whatsoever.

Unconfirmed Irrevocable Letter of Credit.   This type of credit differs from the one just mentioned in one important aspect; that is, the advising bank (the exporter's bank) is under no obligation to pay such a draft. Payment is the sole responsibility of the issuing bank (the importer's bank). The advising bank may or may not negotiate the exporter's draft depending on the degree of political and financial risk anticipated in the issuing bank's country and the credit standing of the issuing bank.

Revocable Letter of Credit.   This type of credit is issued by the importer's bank and advised by an exporter's bank, but the importer's bank (the issuing bank) may amend or cancel the credit at any time without approval by the exporter (beneficiary). For this reason, this type of letter of credit gives the exporter no protection prior to negotiation of his draft.

Revolving Letter of Credit.   When an exporter and importer agree that goods will be shipped on a continuing basis, it may be desirable to establish one letter of credit to handle the shipments as they occur rather than to establish individual letters of credit for each shipment. One letter of credit to finance multiple shipments over an extended period of time is called a *revolving* credit. Revolving credit can be *cumulative* or *noncumulative*. The former means that a revolving credit becomes reavailable for future shipments if the amount or quantity has completed in accordance with the credit terms. If the terms do not specify cumulative, the letter of credit is considered noncumulative and will terminate upon failure of the exporter to ship during any prescribed period unless the importer amends the terms.

Transferable Letter of Credit.   If the credit is transferable, the beneficiary (exporter) may request the advising or opening bank to make the credit available to one or more secondary beneficiaries up to the total value of the original credit instrument. This type of credit is issued mostly when the exporter acts as a middleman who intends to make profit between the original amount of the credit and the total amount he assigns to the secondary beneficiaries. In other cases, the exporter may not have enough goods to meet the credit requirement and has to transfer a part to another manufacturer(s). In either case, negotiation of draft and documents must be through the advising and the opening bank on the basis of the original letter of credit.

Back-to-Back Letter of Credit.   This type of credit shows that an exporter has an irrevocable letter of credit in his favor. He wants to use the instrument as a financing basis for having a bank (normally the same advising bank) open a similar irrevocable letter of credit in favor of the ultimate supplier or manufacturer. The existence of two letters of credit to finance the same shipment in this manner is called back-to-back credit. The second credit is similar to the first except that the amount may be lower and the presentation of documents would be earlier in order to allow time for substitution of invoices, since the beneficiary wants to earn the price differentials between the two credits. This arrangement gives substantial protection to the supplier, since he is guaranteed by the first credit. However, the opening of the second credit based solely on the existence of the first credit may involve considerable risk to the opening bank.

Red-Clause Letter of Credit.   This instrument is similar to a normal letter of credit except that a clause is printed or typed in the instrument in red ink authorizing the advising bank to make clean advances to the exporter. The red-clause type of credit originated in connection with the China fur trade. When documents were finally submitted, the advances were deducted from the proceeds. At present, this type of credit is used for a buying company's agent in the exporting country. Obviously the importer bears all risk—financial risk and currency risk—since he extends an unsecured loan to the exporter in local currency before receiving his merchandise and pricing his product. Therefore, this type of credit is used only where there is a close business relationship between the importer and the exporter.

Authority to Purchase.   This type of credit is used principally by the Far Eastern banks. The opening bank usually instructs the advising bank to purchase the exporter's draft at face value. Under an authority to purchase (A/P), draft is drawn on the buyer with or without recourse. Therefore, the advising (negotiating) bank must be aware of the fact that negotiation of the draft without the assurance of the importer is highly risky. On the other hand, if the draft is presented by the exporter with recourse, that means the negotiating bank can recover the amount previously made from the exporter, should the importer or opening bank refuse to honor the draft.

Letter of Credit for Financing Third-Country Transactions.   With this type of credit, a procedure similar to that used with other types of credit is followed, except the exporter and importer are outside the country of the advising (negotiating) bank. For example, a Brazilian bank on behalf of its domestic importer requests a U.S. bank in New York to advise a Japanese exporter in Tokyo that an export from Japan to Brazil may be payable in U.S. dollars. The American confirming bank pays the sight draft to the Japanese exporter when it is presented together with all required documents. This type of credit or practice has been very popular after World War II, since the U.S. dollar is a key currency in international transactions.

EXPORT LETTER OF CREDIT.   As Exhibit 4 illustrates, L.B. Importer Company in Brazil arranges to purchase 500 television sets from H.K. Exporter Corporation in New York City. On the basis of the contract, both importer and exporter agree that the shipment will be financed by a letter of credit confirmed and payable at sight for $25,000. L.B. Company asks its bank, Banco de Sugar Loaf, Rio de Janeiro, Brazil, to open an irrevocable straight credit payable at Citibank, N.A., New York, with the credit to be confirmed by that bank. Upon receiving instructions from its Brazilian correspondent bank, Citibank issues a confirmed irrevocable straight credit to the beneficiary, H.K. Exporter Corporation.

   After receiving the letter of credit, the exporter should carefully review the following points in the credit instrument:

EXHIBIT 4   EXPORT LETTER OF CREDIT

Citibank, N.A.

CABLE ADDRESS "CITIBANK"   111 WALL STREET, NEW YORK, NY 10015

Confirmed Irrevocable Straight Credit   DATE: May 13, 19--
   MAIL TO:
                                        MAIL

H. K. EXPORTER CORPORATION   All drafts drawn must be marked:
1000 BROAD STREET   CITIBANK Ref. No.: 20020000
NEW YORK, NY 10005   E2125 Opener's Rerference No:
                                                                   315

Dear Sirs: (Export)

   We are instructed by:

BANCO DE SUGAR LOAF
RIO DE JANEIRO, BRAZIL

to advise you they have opened their irrevocable Credit in your favor for the account
of L.B. IMPORTER COMPANY for a sum or sums not exceeding a total of U.S. $25,000.00
available by your drafts at SIGHT on us subject to the following:

   Expiration Date: July 21, 19--
   Trans shipment not allowed.
   Partial shipment not allowed.
   Ship from: NEW YORK
   Ship to: BRAZIL
   Latest shipping date: July 14, 19--

and accompanied by the following documents:

1.FULL SET ON BOARD OCEAN BILLS OF LADING ISSUED TO ORDER BLANK ENDORSED NOTIFY
BRAZILIAN IMPORTER.

2.CONSULAR INVOICE.

3.FULL SET NEGOTIABLE MARINE INSURANCE CERTIFICATE INCLUDING WAR RISKS.

4.COMMERCIAL INVOICE IN TRIPLICATE STATING THAT IT COVERS: "500 TELEVISION SETS."

   This letter is to accompany all draft(s) and documents. When presenting your
draft(s) and documents or when communicating with us please make reference to our
reference number shown above.
   The above-named opener of the credit engages with you that each draft drawn
under and in compliance with the terms of the credit will be duly honored on
delivery of documents as specified if presented at this office on or before the
expiration date.
   We confirm the credit and hereby undertake to honor each draft drawn and presented
as specified in the above referenced credit.
   The credit is subject to the Uniform Customs and Practice for Documentary Credits
(1974 Revision), International Chamber of Commerce - PUBLICATION 290.

                                        Yours very truly

Source. Leonard A. Back. *Introduction to Commercial Letter of Credit,* Citibank, N.A.
1976, p. 21.

1. The name and address must be correct.

2. The credit amount must be sufficient to cover the shipment agreed on in the sales contract, especially if freight and insurance charges are to be paid by the exporter.

3. The documents required must be obtainable and in accordance with the sales contract.

4. The points of shipment and destination of the merchandise must be correctly stated.

5. The shipping date must allow sufficient time to dispatch the goods from the supplier's warehouse to the shipping point as required by the credit.

6. The expiration of the credit must allow sufficient time for the presentation of the draft and required documents at the banking office where the credit expires.

7. The description of the merchandise and any specifications must be agreeable with the terms of sales.

If the exporter finds any discrepancies between the letter of credit and the sales contract or any terms that would cause misunderstanding or problems, the exporter should contact the issuing bank (Citibank, in this case) and the importer for an adequate amendment before the shipment is made. Satisfaction must be obtained by both importer and exporter through direct or indirect communication in order to avoid any misunderstanding, especially under extraordinary circumstances, such as drastic changes in market conditions or outbreak of war.

If H.K. Exporter Corporation ships the goods before July 14 and presents the documents required before July 21 to Citibank for payment, the bank will examine the documents and pay the sight draft (see Exhibit 5) in the amount of $25,000 if all documents are in order. In turn, Citibank in New York will forward the documents to the Brazilian bank, which will release the documents to the Brazilian importer and obtain payment from him.

Caution must be taken by the exporter in preparation of draft and documents since any discrepancies between the documents presented and the conditions stipulated in the letter of credit (for example, if the bills of lading is not marked "on board," or if the insurance policy or certificate bears a date later than the date

EXHIBIT 5   SIGHT DRAFT

Item 160499 (SF 1468(L) Rev. 11-79)   New York, NY   July 15, 19____   1-8 / 210

At sight
——————— DAYS AFTER ———————

PAY TO THE ORDER OF _____ Citibank, N.A. ------------------------------------ $25,000.00 _____

_____ *******Twenty Five Thousand and no/100************************** DOLLARS

FOR VALUE RECEIVED AND CHARGE TO ACCOUNT OF CITIBANK LETTER OF CREDIT NO. _____

Citibank, N.A.
111 WALL STREET
NEW YORK, N. Y. 10043   SPECIMEN

                                        H.K. Exporter Corporation

⑆021000089⑆ 03152325⑈

on the bills of lading) may cause delay or rejection of payment by the negotiating bank. If problems are serious ones, the beneficiary (exporter) may have to communicate directly with the importer and request the needed amendment of the credit, or make concessions to importer.

IMPORT LETTERS OF CREDIT

DISTINCTION BETWEEN IMPORT AND EXPORT LETTERS OF CREDIT.   Commercial banks usually distinguish between and handle separately import and export letters of credit. A commercial bank, on the application of the importer, may issue a commercial letter of credit in favor of an exporter located abroad. This is termed an import letter of credit. The principal function of the importer's bank is to open, to issue the letter of credit, and to carry the main responsibility for payment to the exporter. An export letter of credit is one issued by a foreign bank in favor of a domestic exporter for the account of an importer abroad (see Exhibit 4). In export credit, the exporter's (seller's) bank performs the function of advising, confirming, and negotiating the letter of credit and carries the main responsibility for payment to the exporter.

The types of draft for import and export are essentially the same depending on the terms being used in the credit. Following is an illustration of an import letter of credit.

IMPORT LETTER OF CREDIT—PROCEDURE

Application.   As shown in Exhibit 6, An Import Corporation in New York requests Citibank to open a letter of credit for An Export Corporation in Kowloon, Hong Kong, in the amount of $10,000 covering a shipment of parkas from Hong Kong to New York. The draft will be paid at sight in New York. It is important that the application of opening a letter of credit be in conformity with the underlying sales contract, and the instruction to the opening bank must be clear with respect to the type of credit, amount, draft tenure, required documents, shipping date, expiration date, beneficiary, and so forth. Upon receiving the application, the opening bank usually checks the credit line of the applicant, determines whether cash security is necessary, and scrutinizes the contents of the application to see whether they generally are consistent with national and international legal requirements. If the application is satisfactory to both sides, the importer and the opening bank sign an agreement to open a letter of credit.

Letter-of-Credit Contents.   An import letter of credit must be written and signed by an authorized person of the opening bank (see Exhibit 7) and mailed to the advising bank in the location of the exporter. In case of expediency, a letter of credit may be advised by cable or telex to the foreign bank and confirmed in writing shortly afterward. In general, a letter of credit must contain the following information:

1.   Names of the importer (account party) and exporter (beneficiary).
2.   Name of advising bank and address.
3.   Place and date of issuance.

EXHIBIT 6 APPLICATION FOR COMMERCIAL LETTER OF CREDIT

Citibank, N.A.
LETTER OF CREDIT OPERATION
111 WALL STREET, NEW YORK, N.Y. 10043

APPLICATION AND AGREEMENT FOR
COMMERCIAL LETTER OF CREDIT

of Citibank, N.A.   CREDIT NUMBER OF ADVISING BANK

──────── ADVISING BANK ────────

Citibank, N.A.
P.O.Box 18
Hongkong, Hongkong

An Import Corporation
New York
New York   A P P L I C A N T

──── BY ORDER OF ────

──────── BENEFICIARY ────────

An Export Corporation
Kowloon, Hongkong

AMOUNT

U.S.$10,000.00
────── EXPIRY ──────
DATE IN   May 25, (current year)
Hongkong   FOR NEGOTIATION

SUBJECT TO THE FOLLOWING TERMS AND CONDITIONS, PLEASE ISSUE AND TRANSMIT BY THE METHOD INDICATED HEREIN BELOW YOUR IRREVOCABLE LETTER OF CREDIT (HEREINAFTER CALLED THE "CREDIT") TO BE AVAILABLE BY THE BENEFICIARY'S DRAFT(S):

DRAWN AT ☒ SIGHT   ☐ _____ DAYS SIGHT ☐ _____ DAYS DATE (Drafts to be dated same date as Bill of Lading) ☐ _____ (Other)

DRAWN ON ☒ Citibank, N.A. New York, N. Y. FOR 100 % INVOICE COST

DRAWN ON ☐ _____ FOR _____ % INVOICE COST
(Overseas Bank if "Credit" in Foreign Currency)

FOR DRAFTS ON TERM BASIS, DISCOUNT CHARGES FOR ☐ SHIPPERS ☐ BUYERS ACCOUNT

ACCOMPANIED BY THE FOLLOWING DOCUMENTS WHICH ARE INDICATED BY "X".

☒ COMMERCIAL INVOICE — ORIGINAL AND 2 COPIES

☒ CUSTOMS INVOICE — ORIGINAL AND _____ COPIES

☐ INSURANCE POLICY AND/OR CERTIFICATE (TO BE EFFECTED BY SHIPPER, UNLESS OTHERWISE INDICATED BELOW)

☐ INSURANCE TO INCLUDE WAR RISK

☐ AIR WAYBILL CONSIGNED TO _____ DATED LATEST: _____ 19 _____

☒ Full set
☐ ON BOARD ORIGINAL OCEAN BILL OF LADING OR CONTAINER BILL OF LADING OR BILL OF LADING BEARING CONTAINER ENDORSEMENT (IF MORE THAN ONE ORIGINAL HAS BEEN ISSUED, ALL ORIGINALS ARE REQUIRED)

ISSUED TO ORDER OF: Citibank, N.A.

MARKED: NOTIFY Applicant

MARKED: FREIGHT ☐ COLLECT ☐ PAID   DATED LATEST: May 10, _____ 19 (current year)

☐ OTHER DOCUMENTS _____

COVERING: MERCHANDISE DESCRIBED IN THE INVOICE(S) AS:

Parkas

TERMS: ☐ FAS _____ ☒ FOB Hongkong ☐ C & F _____ ☐ CIF _____ ☐ C & I _____
Location   Location   Location   Location   Location

SHIPMENT FROM: Hongkong

TO: New York

PARTIAL SHIPMENTS ☐ PERMITTED ☐ PROHIBITED

TRANSHIPMENTS ☐ PERMITTED ☐ PROHIBITED

☒ DRAFT(S) AND DOCUMENTS MUST BE PRESENTED TO NEGOTIATING OR PAYING BANK WITHIN 15 DAYS AFTER THE DATE OF ISSUANCE OF THE BILL(S) OF LADING OR OTHER SHIPPING DOCUMENTS BUT PRIOR TO EXPIRY OF LETTER OF CREDIT.

☒ INSURANCE EFFECTED BY APPLICANT.

TRANSMISSION BY: ☐ CABLE (Full Details) ☐ SHORT CABLE (Full Details to follow by Air Mail) ☒ AIR MAIL THROUGH YOUR CORRESPONDENT, OR DIRECTLY TO:

Advising Bank _____ SUBJECT TO THE TERMS AND CONDITIONS SHOWN HEREON. IN THE EVENT THE CREDIT IS DENOMINATED IN OTHER THAT U.S. DOLLARS, DRAFTS MAY BE DRAWN AT YOUR OPTION ON YOU OR YOUR CORRESPONDENT.

WE HEREBY CERTIFY THAT TRANSACTIONS IN THE MERCHANDISE COVERED BY THIS APPLICATION ARE NOT PROHIBITED UNDER THE FOREIGN ASSETS CONTROL REGULATIONS OF THE UNITED STATES TREASURY DEPARTMENT AND THAT ANY IMPORTATION COVERED BY THIS APPLICATION CONFORMS IN EVERY RESPECT WITH ALL EXISTING UNITED STATES GOVERNMENT REGULATIONS.

ALL DRAFTS AND DOCUMENTS LISTED HEREIN ARE TO BE FORWARDED BY NEGOTIATING BANK TO Citibank, N.A. NEW YORK, N. Y. BY AIR MAIL IN A SINGLE MAILING.

SHIPPING DOCUMENTS FOR CUSTOM HOUSE ENTRY ARE TO BE SENT BY YOU TO Applicant _____ (Name)

_____ (Address)

_____ January 15, _____ 19 (current year
(Place and Date)

Item 305508(COM 513(L)Rev. 1-78)

13 · 16

EXHIBIT 6 CONTINUED

In consideration of your issuing the Credit, substantially according to the Application appearing on the reverse side hereof or as attached thereto and initialed on behalf of the undersigned, the undersigned hereby (jointly and severally) agree(s) as follows:

1. To pay you on demand, at your Head Office and in the United States currency, the amount of each draft (whether SIGHT or TIME) which may be drawn IN UNITED STATES CURRENCY under the Credit, or purport to be so drawn; also, in any event and without demand, to effect such payment with respect to each such TIME draft sufficiently in advance of its maturity date to enable you to arrange (in the usual course of the mails) for cover to reach the place where such time draft is payable not later than ONE (1) business day prior to its maturity, it being understood that you will notify the undersigned of the amount and date of maturity of each such time draft.

2. To pay you on demand, at your Head Office and in United States currency, the equivalent (at your then selling rate for cable transfers to the place where and in the currency in which such draft is payable) of the amount of each draft (whether SIGHT or TIME) which may be drawn IN OTHER THAN UNITED STATES CURRENCY under the Credit, or purport to be so drawn; also, in any event and without demand, to effect such payment with respect to each TIME draft sufficiently in advence of its maturity date to enable you to arrange (in the usual course of the mails) for cover to reach the place where such time draft is payable not later than ONE (1) business day prior to its maturity, or, at your option, to provide you then with the amount of currency in which such time draft is payable in such form and manner as shall be acceptable to you, it being understood that (i) you will notify the undersigned of the amount and date of maturity of each such time draft (ii) the undersigned will comply with any and all governmental exchange regulations now or hereafter applicable to any foreign exchange provided you pursuant to this paragraph, and will indemnify and hold you harmless from any failure so to comply.

3. In the event of any U.S. Currency draft(s) being drawn by the undersigned on you for the purpose of refinancing any obligation(s) set forth in "1" and "2" hereof and such draft(s) being accepted by you (at your option), the undersigned will pay you on demand, but in any event not later than ONE(1) business day prior to its maturity, the amount of each such acceptance. It is understood that each amount which may become due and payable to you under this agreement, may, in your discretion and if not otherwise paid, be charged by you to any available funds then held by you for the account of the undersigned.

4. That, if the aforesaid Application requests the inclusion in the Credit of any provision for Clean Advance(s) to the beneficiary, you may place in the Credit such a provision in that respect as you may deem appropriate, under which any bank entitled to negotiate drafts under the Credit, acting in its discretion in each instance and upon the request and receipt in writing from the beneficiary, may make any one or more Clean Advances at any time on or prior to the date by which bills of exchange are to be negotiated under the Credit. The aggregate of such advance(s) shall in no event be more than the amount specified in the Application for Clean Advances, and in no event shall any such advance exceed the amount remaining available under the Credit at the time of the advance. While it is expected by the undersigned that each such advance will be repaid to the bank(s) that made the advance(s) by the beneficiary from the proceeds of any draft(s) drawn under the Credit, should any such advance(s) not be thus repaid, the undersigned will on demand pay you the amount(s) thereof as if such advance(s) were evidenced by draft(s) drawn under the Credit, together with interest on each such amount for the period that the same shall have been outstanding at such rate as you may find at the time of demand to be payable. It is understood that neither you or any bank(s) which makes such advance(s) shall be obligated to inquire into the use that may be made thereof by the beneficiary and that you and each such bank shall be without liability for any wrongful use that may be made by the beneficiary of any funds so advanced.

5. To pay you on demand, with respect to the Credit, a commission at such rate as you may determine to be proper, and any and all charges and expenses which may be paid or incurred by you in connection with the Credit, together with interest where chargeable.

6. That, except as instructions may be given you by the undersigned in writing expressly to the contrary with regard to, and prior to the opening of, the Credit: (a) you and/or any of your correspondents may receive and accept as "Bills of Lading" relative to the Credit any document(s) issued or purporting to be issued by or on behalf of any carrier which acknowledge(s) receipt of property for transportation, whatever the specific provisions of such document(s), the date of each document shall be deemed the date of shipment of the property mentioned therein, and any such bill of lading issued by or on behalf of an ocean carrier may be accepted by you as an "Ocean bill of lading" whether or not the entire transportation is by water; (b) part shipment(s), and/or shipment(s) in excess of the quantity called for in the Credit may be made and you may honor the relative drafts, the liability of the undersigned to reimburse you for payments made or obligations incurred on such drafts being limited to the amount of the Credit; (c) if the Credit specifies shipments in installments within stated periods, and the shipper fails to ship in any designated period, the Credit shall not be available for that or any subsequent installment(s); (d) you and/or any of your correspondents may receive and accept as documents of insurance under the Credits either insurance policies or insurance certificates which need not be for an amount of insurance greater than the amount paid by you under or relative to the Credit, and (e) you and/or any of your correspondents may receive, accept or pay as complying with the terms of the Credit, any drafts or other documents, otherwise in order, which may be signed by, or issued to, the administrator or executor of, or the trustee in bankruptcy of, or the receiver for any of the property of the party in whose name the Credit provides that any drafts or other documents should be drawn or issued.

7. To procure promptly any essential import, export or other licenses for the import, export or shipping of any and all property shipped under or pursuant to or in connection with the Credit and to comply with any and all foreign and domestic governmental regulations in regard to the shipment of any and all such property or the financing thereof and to furnish such certificates in that respect as you may at any time(s) require, and to keep the property covered by insurance satisfactory to you, issued by insurers acceptable to you, and to assign the policies or certificates of insurance to you, or to make the loss or adjustment, if any, payable to you, at your option, and to furnish you, if demanded, with evidence of acceptance by the insurers to such assignment.

8. That, as security for any and all obligations and/or liabilities of the undersigned hereunder, and also for any and all other obligations and/or liabilities, absolute or contingent, due or to become due, which are now, or may at any time(s) hereafter be owing by the undersigned to you, the undersigned hereby recognize(s) and admit(s) your ownership in and unqualified right to the possession and disposal of any and all shipping documents, warehouse receipts, policies or certificates of insurance and other documents accompanying or relative to drafts drawn under the Credit and in and to any and all property shipped under or pursuant to or in connection with the Credit, or in any way relative thereto or to any of the drafts drawn thereunder (whether or not such documents, goods or other property be released to or upon the order of the undersigned on trust or bailee receipt), and in and to the proceeds of each and all of the foregoing, until such time as all the obligations and/or liabilities of the undersigned to you at any time existing under or pursuant to this Application and Agreement, or the Credit herein referred to, or any other obligations or liabilities of the undersigned to you, now existing or hereafter arising, have been fully paid and discharged. That all or any of such property and/or documents, and the proceeds thereof, coming into your possession, or that of any of your correspondents, may be held and disposed of by you as hereinafter provided, it being understood that the receipt by you, or by any of your correspondents, at any time of other security of whatsoever nature, including cash, shall not be deemed as a waiver of any of your rights or powers hereunder. Insofar as any property and/or documents, which may be held by you, or for your account, as collateral hereunder, may be released by you to or upon the order of the undersigned in trust, the undersigned will sign and deliver to you on demand such form(s) of trust receipt or other form(s) of security agreement and/or Statement(s) of Trust Receipt Financing and/or Financing Statement(s) as may be satisfactory to you, and will pay any relative filing fees, it being understood that your rights as specified herein or therein shall be in furtherance of and/or in addition to, but not in limitation of, your rights under any applicable law. Upon any transfer, sale, delivery, surrender or endorsement of any bill of lading, warehouse receipt or other document at any time(s) held by you, or held for your account by any of your correspondents, relative to any draft(s) accepted by you in reliance hereon, the undersigned will indemnify and hold you harmless from and against each and every claim, demand, action or suit which may arise against you, or any such correspondent(s), by reason thereof. You may file a Financing Statement, at your option, without the signature of the undersigned with regard to any of the above described property.

9. To pledge, and do(es) hereby pledge, to you as security for any and all of the obligations and/or liabilities of the undersigned hereinbefore or hereinafter referred to, now or hereafter existing, any and all property of the undersigned now or at any time(s) hereafter in your possession or control, or that of any third party acting in your behalf, whether for the express purpose of being used by you as collateral security or for safekeeping or for any other or different purpose, including such property as may be in transit by mail or carrier to or from you, a lien and security interest being hereby given you upon and in any and all such property for the aggregate amount of any and all such obligations and/or liabilities; and the undersigned hereby authorize(s) you, at your option, at any time(s), whether or not the property then held by you as security hereunder is deemed by you to be adequate, to appropriate and apply upon any and all of the said obligations and/or liabilities, whether or not then due, any and all moneys now or hereafter with you on deposit or otherwise to the credit of or belonging to the undersigned and/or, in your discretion, to hold any such moneys as security for any such obligations or liabilities until the exact amount thereof, if any, shall have been definitely ascertained by you. Your rights, liens and security interests hereunder shall continue unimpaired, and the undersigned shall be and remain obligated in accordance with the terms and provisions hereof notwithstanding, the release or substitution of any property which may be held as collateral hereunder at any time(s) or of any rights or interests therein, or any delay, extension of time, renewal, compromise or other indulgence granted by you in reference to any of the aforesaid obligations and/or liabilities, or any promissory note, draft, bill or exchange or other instrument given you in connection with any of the aforesaid obligations and/or liabilities, the undersigned hereby waiving notice of any such delay, extension, release, substitution, renewal, compromise, or other indulgence, and hereby consenting to be bound thereby as fully and effectually as if the undersigned has expressly agreed thereto in advance.

10. At any time and from time to time, on demand, to deliver, convey, transfer, or assign to you, as security for any and all of the obligations and/or liabilities of the undersigned hereunder, and also for any and all other obligations and/or liabilities, absolute or contingent, due or to become due, which are now, or may at any time hereafter, be owing by the undersigned to you, additional security of a value and character satisfactory to you, or to make such cash payment(s) as you may require.

EXHIBIT 6 CONTINUED

11. You are hereby authorized, at your option and without any obligation to do so, to transfer to and/or register in the name(s) of your nominee(s) all or any part of the property which may be held by you as security at any time(s) hereunder, and to do so before or after the maturity of any of the said obligations and/or liabilities and with or without notice to the undersigned.

12. Upon the non-performance of any of the promises to pay herein above set forth, or upon the non-payment of any of the other obligations or liabilities abovementioned, or upon the failure of the undersigned forthwith, with or without notice, to furnish satisfactory additional collateral or to make payments on account as hereinbefore agreed, or to perform or comply with any of the other terms or provisions of this Application and Agreement, or in the event of death, failure in business, dissolutions or termination of existence of the undersigned, or in case any petition in bankruptcy should be filed by or against the undersigned, or any proceedings in bankruptcy, or under laws or regulations of any jurisdiction relating to the relief of debtors, should be commenced for the relief or readjustment of any indebtedness of the undersigned, either through reorganization, composition, extension or otherwise, or if the undersigned should make an assignment for the benefit of creditors or take advantage of any insolvency law, or if a receiver of any property of the undersigned should be appointed at any time, or in the event of any seizure, vesting or intervention by or under authority of a Government by which the management of the undersigned is displaced or its authority in the control of its business is curtailed, or if any funds or other property of the undersigned which may be in, or come into, your possession or control, or that of any third party acting in your behalf as aforesaid, should be attached or distrained or should be or become subject to any mandatory order of court or other legal process, then, or at any time after the happening of any such event, any or all of the aforesaid obligations and/or liabilities of the undersigned shall, at your option, become due and payable immediately, without demand or notice; and full power and authority are hereby given you to sell, assign, and deliver all or any of the property herein-before referred to, at any broker's board, or at public or private sale, at your option, either for cash or on credit or for future delivery, without assumption of any credit risk, and without either demand, advertisement, or notice of any kind, all of which are hereby expressly waived. At any sale hereunder, you may, in your discretion, purchase the whole or any part of the property sold, free from any right of redemption on the part of the under-signed all such rights being also hereby waived and released. In event of any sale or other disposition of any property aforesaid, after deducting all costs or expenses of every kind for care, safekeeping, collection, sale, delivery or otherwise, you may apply the residue of the proceeds of the sale(s) or other disposition thereof, to the payment or reduction, either in whole or in part, of all or any of the aforesaid obligations and/or obligations and/or liabilities, whether or not then due, making proper allowance for interest on obligations or liabilities not then due, and return the overplus, if any, to the under-signed (or the one(s) of us whose property may have yielded the overplus); all without prejudice to your rights as against the undersigned with respect to any and all amounts which may be or remain unpaid on any of the aforesaid obligations and/or liabilities at any time(s), provided, however, that where the provisions of the Uniform Commercial Code of any jurisdiction apply to such a default, you shall have in lieu of the foregoing all of the rights and remedies provided to a secured party by such Uniform Commercial Code as in effect at that time, and in addition to such rights and remedies, the under-signed further agrees that (1) in the event that notice is required to be given for any purchase, written notice mailed to the undersigned at the mailing address given above three days prior to the date of public sale of the property subject to the lien and security interest created herein or prior to the date after which private sale or any other disposition of said property will be made shall constitute reasonable notice, but notice given in any other reasonable manner or at any other reasonable time shall be sufficient, (2) in the event of sale or other disposition of such property, you may apply the proceeds of any such sale or disposition to the satisfaction of your reasonable attorneys' fees, legal expenses and other costs and expenses incurred in connection with your re-taking, holding, preparing for sale, and selling of the property, and (3) without precluding any other methods of sale, the sale of property shall have been made in a commercially reasonable manner if conducted in conformity with reasonable commercial practices of banks disposing of similar property, but in any event you may sell at your option on such terms as you may choose without assuming any credit risk and without any obligation to advertise.

13. That neither you nor any of your correspondents shall be responsible for; (a) the use which may be made of the Credit or for any acts or omissions of the beneficiary(ies) in connection therewith; (b) the existence, character, quality, quantity, condition, packing, value or delivery of the property purporting to be represented by documents; (c) any difference in character, quality, quantity, condition, or value of the property from that expressed in documents; (d) the validity, sufficiency or genuineness of documents, or of any endorsement(s) thereon, even if such documents should in fact prove to be in any or all respects invalid, insufficient, fraudulent or forged; (d) the time, place, manner or order in which shipment is made; (f) partial or incomplete shipment, or failure of omission to ship any or all of the property referred to in the Credit; (g) the character, adequacy, validity or genuineness of any insurance; (h) the solvency or responsibility of any insurer, or for any other risk connected with insurance; (i) any deviation from instructions, delay, default or fraud by the shipper and/or any other(s) in connection with the property or the shipping thereof; (j) the solvency, responsibility or relationship to the property or any party issuing any documents in connection with the property; (k) delay in arrival, or failure to arrive, of either the property or any of the documents relating thereto; (l) delay in giving, or failure to give, notice of arrival or any other notice; (m) any breach of contract between the shipper(s) or vendor(s) and the consignee(s) or buyer(s); (n) failure of any draft to bear any reference or adequate reference to the Credit, or failure of documents to accompany any draft at negotiation, or failure of any person to surrender or to take up the Credit or to send forward documents apart from drafts as required by the terms of the Credit, each of which provisions, if contained in the Credit itself, it is agreed may be waived by you, or (o) errors, omissions, interruptions or delays in transmission or delivery of any messages, by mail, cable, telegraph, wireless or otherwise whether or not they may be in cipher; (p) failure of any document to conform to, or to be presented under, the Credit in any instance where the undersigned or its agent, upon request, has received documents and/or property represented thereby or therein. That you shall not be responsible for any act, error, neglect or default, omission, insolvency or failure in business of any of your correspondents, and that the happening of any one or more of the contingencies referred to in the preceding sentence shall not affect, impair or prevent the vesting of any of your rights or powers hereunder. In furtherance and extension and not in limitation of the specific provisions hereinbefore set forth, it is hereby further agreed that any action, inaction or omission taken or suffered by you, or by any of your correspondents, under or in connection with the Credit or the relative drafts, documents or property, if in good faith, and in conformity with such foreign or domestic laws, customs or regulations as you or any of your correspondents may deem to be applicable thereto, shall be binding upon the undersigned and shall not place you or any of your correspondents under any resulting liability to the undersigned.

14. The word "property" as used herein includes goods and merchandise, as well as any and all documents relative thereto; also, securities, funds, choses in action, and any and all other forms of property, whether real, personal or mixed and any right or interest of the undersigned therein or thereto.

15. That in the event of any change or modification with respect to: (a) the amount or duration of the Credit; (b) the time or place of shipment of any relative property; (c) the drawing, negotiation, presentation, acceptance, or maturity of any drafts, acceptances or other documents, or (d) any of the other terms or provisions of the Credit, such being done at the request of the undersigned, this Agreement shall be binding upon the undersigned in all respects with regard to the Credit so changed or modified, inclusive of any action taken by you or any of your correspondents relative thereto.

16. That you may assign or transfer this Application and Agreement, or any instrument(s) evidencing all or any of the aforesaid obligations and/or liabilities, and may deliver all or any of the property then held as security therefor, to the transferee(s), who shall thereupon become vested with all the powers and; rights in respect thereto given you herein or in the instrument(s) transferred, and you shall thereafter be forever relieved and fully discharged from any liability or responsibility with respect thereto, but you shall retain all rights and powers hereby given with respect to any and all instrument(s), rights or property not so transferred.

17. No delay on your part in exercising any power of sale or any other rights or options hereunder, and no notice or demand, which may be given to or made upon the undersigned by you with respect to any power of sale or other right or option hereunder, shall constitute a waiver thereof, or limit or impair your right to take any action or to exercise any power of sale, or any other rights or options hereunder, without notice or demand, or prejudice your rights as against the undersigned in any respect.

18. That, except as otherwise expressly provided in this Application and Agreement or as you and the undersigned may otherwise expressly agree with regard to, and prior to your issuance of, the Credit, the "Uniform Customs and Practice for Documentary Credits (1974 Revision), International Chamber of Commerce Publication No. 290" shall in all respects be deemed a part hereof as fully as if incorporated herein and shall apply to the Credit.

19. This Application and Agreement shall be binding upon the undersigned, the heirs, executors, administrators, successors and assigns of the under-signed, and shall insure to the benefit of, and be enforceable by, you, your successors, transferees and assigns. If this Application and Agreement should be terminated or revoked by operation of laws as to the undersigned, the undersigned will indemnify and save you harmless from any loss which may be suffered or incurred by you in acting hereunder prior to the receipt by you, or your successors, transferees or assigns, of notice in writing of such termination or revocation. If this Application and Agreement is executed by two or more parties, they shall be severally liable hereunder, and the word "undersigned" wherever used herein shall be construed to refer to each of such parties separately, all in the same manner and with the same effect as if each of them had signed separate instruments; and in any such case, this Application and Agreement shall not be revoked or impaired as to any one or more of such parties by the death of any of the others or by the revocation or release of any obligations hereunder of any one or more of such other parties. Furthermore, this Application and Agreement shall be deemed to be made under and shall be governed by the laws of the State of New York in all respects, including matters of construction, validity and performance, and none of its terms or provisions may be waived, altered, modified or amended except in writing duly signed for and on your behalf.

Very truly yours,

____

Applicant's Authorized Signature Registered With Us

NOTE: To be signed for and on behalf of the applicant by a duly authorized Officer or Representative

EXHIBIT 6   CONTINUED

FOR BANK USE ONLY

☐ SIGNATURE VERIFIED   ☐ APPROVAL FOR AUTOMATIC REFINANCING

☐ CREDIT RISK APPROVAL   ☐ PRIOR ACCOUNT MANAGER APPROVAL FOR REFINANCING

CUSTOMER'S ACCOUNT NUMBER _____ EXPENSE CODE _____

FOR NEW CUSTOMERS IN ADDITION TO ABOVE, ACCOUNT MANAGER MUST SUPPLY S.I.C. NUMBER _____

_____   _____

4. The tenure of the draft (sight or time).

5. A general description of merchandise. Sometimes special description is required, such as quantity, specification, and packing method.

6. The name of the bank on which drafts may be drawn.

7. The maximum amount up to which the beneficiary may draw.

8. A list of the documents that must accompany the draft.

9. The latest shipping date.

10. The expiration of the credit.

11. The type of credit—revocable, irrevocable, confirming, transferable, etc.

12. Statement about who will pay the charges, such as ocean freight, insurance, discount charges, etc.

Advice to Beneficiary.   The opening bank usually sends the original letter of credit to the beneficiary through an advising bank, which may be a branch or correspondent bank of the opening bank. The advising bank may or may not add its confirmation to the credit depending on the request of the opening bank. Once the beneficiary receives the irrevocable letter of credit, the liability of the issuing bank to pay when the required documents are properly presented is established.

Amendments.   It is not unusual that the beneficiary requests the buyer (importer) to amend the letter of credit for certain reasons, such as a workers' strike, which may require an extension of the shipping date; prolonged bad weather, which may delay shipment of the merchandise; or sudden changes in prices of raw material or fuel used in the manufacturing process, which may require an adjustment of the price of the final product. The amendment of credit has to be authorized by the buyer and issued by the issuing bank to the beneficiary through the same channel.

Presentation and Checking of Documents.   As soon as the beneficiary ships the merchandise, he presents all required documents with the draft to the advising and negotiating bank, which, except for a confirming credit, usually forwards all documents to the opening bank for payment. The documentary-payment section of the opening bank examines the documents in detail to make sure that they comply with the terms of the credit. Several key points are considered important in the examination process: clean on-board bills of lading, risk coverage in the insurance certificate, approval of inspection certificate, verification of certificate of origin, description of merchandise in commercial invoice, consular invoice for tariff purposes,

EXHIBIT 7   IMPORT LETTER OF CREDIT

ORIGINAL

Citibank, N.A.

WORLD CORPORATION GROUP
LETTER OF CREDIT OPERATIONS
P.O. BOX 2006 GRAND CENTRAL STATION
NEW YORK, NEW YORK 10017

JANUARY 18, (CURRENT YEAR)

AN EXPORT CORPORATION
KOWLOON, HONGKONG

ADVISING BANK INSTRUCTIONS:
DELIVER ORIGINAL TO BENEFICIARY
COPY FOR YOUR FILES

CITIBANK, N.A.
P.O. BOX 18
HONGKONG

REF: IRREVOCABLE DOCUMENTARY LETTER OF CREDIT WCG-C00000A.

GENTLEMEN:
     BY ORDER OF OUR CLIENT, AN IMPORT CORPORATION, NEW YORK, N.Y. WE HEREBY OPEN
OUR DOCUMENTARY LETTER OF CREDIT NO. WCG-C00000A, IN YOUR FAVOR, FOR THE AMOUNT
TEN THOUSAND AND 00/100 U.S. DOLLARS $10,000.00 U.S. DOLLARS AVAILABLE BY
NEGOTIATION OF YOUR DRAFTS AT SIGHT DRAWN ON US MARKED "DRAWN UNDER
DOCUMENTARY CREDIT NO. WCG-C00000A OF CITIBANK, N.A., NEW YORK" ACCOMPANIED
BY THE FOLLOWING DOCUMENTS NEGOTIATED ON OR BEFORE MAY 25, (CURRENT YEAR).

1. SPECIAL CUSTOMS INVOICE.
2. COMMERCIAL INVOICE IN TRIPLICATE STATING THAT IT COVERS: PARKAS FOB HONGKONG.
3. FULL SET ORIGINAL CLEAN ON BOARD OCEAN BILLS OF LADING EVIDENCING SHIPMENT TO
NEW YORK FROM HONGKONG DRAWN TO THE ORDER OF CITIBANK, N.A. MARKED NOTIFY:
BUYER TO BE DATED NOT LATER THAN MAY 10, (CURRENT YEAR).
INSURANCE TO BE EFFECTED BY BUYER.
DRAFT (S) ARE TO BE FOR 100% OF INVOICE VALUE.
ALL DRAFTS AND DOCUMENTS TO US BY THE NEGOTIATING BANK IN ONE AIRMAIL.
DOCUMENTS MUST BE PRESENTED FOR NEGOTIATION WITHIN 15 DAYS AFTER BILL OF LADING
DATE.

     WE HEREBY ENGAGE WITH DRAWERS AND/OR BONA FIDE HOLDERS THAT DRAFTS DRAWN
AND NEGOTIATED IN CONFORMITY WITH THE TERMS OF THIS CREDIT WILL BE DULY HONORED
ON PRESENTATION AND THAT DRAFTS ACCEPTED WITHIN THE TERMS OF THIS CREDIT WILL BE
HONORED AT MATURITY.

     THE AMOUNT OF EACH DRAFT MUST BE ENDORSED ON THE REVERSE OF THIS CREDIT BY
THE NEGOTIATING BANK.

     THIS LETTER OF CREDIT IS SUBJECT TO THE UNIFORM CUSTOMS AND PRACTICE FOR
DOCUMENTARY CREDITS (1974 REVISION), INTERNATIONAL CHAMBER OF COMMERCE
BROCHURE NO. 290.

VERY TRULY YOURS,

ITEM 823930 (LC6/2"REV 9/76)

negotiating and shipping date, and amount and tenure on the draft. Should any
discrepancies occur between the documents and letter of credit, the issuing bank
immediately tells the buyer (importer) that remedial actions must be made. Four
alternative actions may be taken: (1) the discrepancy may be waived by the importer
if it is a minor one; (2) corrections of discrepancies may be needed from the beneficiary if they are serious; (3) a letter of indemnity may be given by the negotiating

bank stating that the draft can be paid with recourse to the exporter; and (4) the exporter may request the opening bank to present the documents to the importer on a collection basis. If the importer refuses to accept the merchandise, the exporter may suffer losses.

Payment and Refinancing. At best, all documents and drafts are in compliance with the credit terms, or the discrepancies are straightened out by both importer and exporter. Then the issuing bank finally pays the amount stipulated in the credit to the exporter (usually credit to the account of the negotiating bank for the exporter's account). At the same time, the issuing bank sends the documents to the importer and charges his account accordingly.

In case the importer does not have enough funds in the opening bank, he may request the bank to make a loan to cover the entire amount and use the newly received merchandise as collateral. He will pay back the bank when the merchandise is liquidated.

ACCEPTANCES

An acceptance is a time draft that has been accepted and signed by the drawee for payment at maturity. If a time draft is accepted by a buyer of merchandise, it is called a trade acceptance. If a time draft is accepted by a bank, it is called a bankers acceptance. There is no doubt that a draft accepted by a reputable bank enjoys higher credit standing than a draft accepted by a firm, since the bank will meet its obligation at maturity, and a firm in a foreign country may not comply with its obligation. Moreover, acceptance instruments usually involve the laws of the country where they are issued. Since bankers acceptance plays an important role in international trade, its functions in trade financing, its advantages from the drawer's standpoint, and its importance in the money market are discussed below.

TYPES OF BANKERS ACCEPTANCE TRANSACTIONS. Bankers acceptances in the United States were originally governed by Regulation C of the Federal Reserve Act of 1913. This regulation was amended on April 1, 1974, covering bankers acceptances of two major categories—those "eligible for discount" and those "eligible for purchase." Acceptances that are eligible for discount are defined in Federal Reserve Regulation A and enjoy the best discount rates in the bankers-acceptance market. Acceptances eligible for purchase are defined in the Federal Reserve Open Market Committee, effective April 1, 1974. In general, the regulations now provide that the member banks may accept drafts maturing in not more than nine months covering the following transactions:

Exportations from the United States.

Importations to the United States.

Shipments within the United States.

Storage within the United States or overseas.

The creation of dollar exchange.

Exportations From the United States. Exhibits 8 and 9 illustrate that the beneficiary under the letter of credit presents documents and a time draft (90 days) to the

EXHIBIT 8   EXPORT CREDIT–ACCEPTANCE FINANCING

Citibank, N.A.

CABLE ADDRESS "CITIBANK"   111 WALL STREET, NEW YORK, NY. 1001

Confirmed Irrevocable Straight Credit   DATE: May 3, 19--

MAIL TO: MAIL

A MISSOURI CORPORATION   All drafts drawn must be marked:
100 BROADWAY   CITIBANK Ref. No.: 30030029
ST. LOUIS, MO 80020   E2125   Opener's Reference No:
                                                                        1500

Dear Sirs: Export Credit - Acceptance Financing

  We are instructed by:

A GERMAN BANK
FRANKFURT, GERMANY

to advise you they have opened their Irrevocable Credit in your favor for the
account of A GERMAN IMPORTER for a sum or sums not exceeding a total of
U.S. $11,091.00 available by your drafts at 90 DAYS SIGHT on us subject to
the following:

    Expiration Date: August 30, 19--
    Trans shipment not allowed.
    Ship from: U.S.A. PORT
    Ship to: BREMEN
    Latest shipping date: August 15, 19--

and accompanied by the following documents:

1. ORIGINAL ON BOARD OCEAN BILLS OF LADING ISSUED TO ORDER BLANK ENDORSED,
   MARKED FREIGHT PAYABLE AT DESTINATION.

2. PACKING LIST.

3. INSPECTION CERTIFICATE ISSUED BY CARGO SUPERINTENDENCE CO., INC.

4. SIGNED COMMERCIAL INVOICE IN TRIPLICATE STATING THAT IT COVERS WINDOW
   SCREENING.

    This letter is to accompany all drafts(s) and documents. When presenting your
draft(s) and documents or when communicating with us please make reference to
our reference number shown above.
    The above-named opener of the credit engages with you that each draft drawn
under and in compliance with the terms of the credit will be dully honored on
delivery of documents as specified if presented at this office on or before the
expiration date.
    We confirm the credit and hereby undertake to honor each draft drawn and
presented as specified in the above referenced credit.
    The credit is subject to the Unform Customs and Practice for Documentary
Credits (1974 Revision), International Chamber of Commerce - PUBLICATION 290.

                                              Yours very truly

                                              _____

EXHIBIT 9   BANKERS ACCEPTANCE

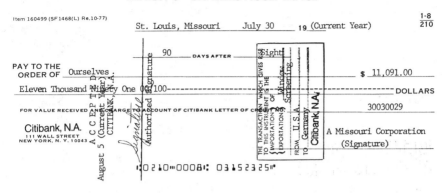

negotiating bank in New York. Upon examination of the documents, following a procedure similar to that followed with the sight draft as explained previously, Citibank would place its acceptance as well as its eligibility stamp on the time draft, and forward the documents to the opening bank in the foreign country.

The bankers acceptance would be returned to the beneficiary (exporter) and he would present it to Citibank on maturity for payment of the face amount. The exporter also could request Citibank to discount the time draft and credit the net proceeds to his account; this means Citibank would buy his acceptance less discount. The third alternative would be for the exporter to sell this accepted draft to any bank or firm dealing in the purchase of bankers acceptances. In any event, the exporter could obtain funds immediately after presentation of documents without waiting for 90 days. On the other hand, the importer would not be required to pay the accepted draft until maturity.

Importations Into the United States.   The import letter of credit illustrated previously could be changed to acceptance financing only by changing the words from "your draft at SIGHT" to "your draft at 90 DAYS SIGHT." This means that the importer's bank would accept the time draft presented by the exporter after examination of his documents. The bank would forward the documents to the importer in order to obtain the goods and would charge the importer's account on the maturity of the time draft drawn by the overseas exporter-beneficiary on the U.S. bank. The bankers acceptance could be returned to the exporter, discounted and the proceeds credited to his account, or simply held by the importer's bank until maturity, depending on the exporter-beneficiary's instructions.

Even under the sight draft, the imported goods can be refinanced by bankers acceptance if the importer needs such financing. In this case, the importer draws a time draft on his bank for the agreed-upon terms, say 60 days after sight. His bank, after accepting it, discounts the acceptance and credits the proceeds to the importer's account. This kind of refinancing is intended to help the importer when imported goods are to be packed, distributed, and processed before actual sale is realized by the importer.

Shipments Within the United States.   Domestic trade is rarely financed by bankers acceptances, since most domestic shipments are made on open-account terms or documentary-draft collection. It is used only in cases such as the sale by a Pacific Coast wine grower to a distributor in New York; the distributor expected to sell the wine and collect funds within a certain time, say 90 days, after shipment. For domestic shipments, Federal Reserve regulations require that the bank that accepts the draft must have the documents of title to the shipment in its possession at the time of acceptance.

Storage Within the United States or Overseas.   A merchant who wishes to finance the storage of goods by way of acceptances submits to his bank a warehouse receipt conveying title to the goods, together with a time draft. The bank accepts and discounts the draft, crediting the net proceeds to the merchant. Bankers acceptances eligible for discount created to finance the storage of goods must cover merchandise defined as a ''readily marketable staple.'' The regulations require that the accepting bank remain secured throughout the life of the acceptance for storage transactions. When goods are stored abroad, sometimes it may be difficult to obtain title documents that could qualify the transaction for acceptance financing.

The Creation of Dollar Exchange.   Some foreign countries rely on one or a number of crops for their foreign-exchange earnings. A shortage of foreign exchange may occur before the start of the season. To overcome this shortage temporarily, banks in the exporting countries may draw U.S. dollar drafts on U.S. banks, which accept the drafts, discount them, and credit the net proceeds to the foreign banks. After a few months, these agricultural countries export their crops and liquidate the bankers acceptances. The creation of dollar-exchange acceptances is permitted by the Federal Reserve regulations for a short duration. Recently this type of acceptance has been less important, since many former agricultural countries have diversified their agricultural as well as industrial products. Brazil is a case in point.

ADVANTAGES OF ACCEPTANCE FINANCING.   There are several advantages to using acceptance financing. First, the use of the bankers acceptance allows the exporter to receive immediate payment for his goods through the sale of the bankers acceptance, whereas the buyer abroad need not make payment until the acceptance matures. Second, the use of bankers acceptances permits the importer to receive his goods shipped from abroad and make payment only after he sells the goods. Third, commercial banks often prefer to finance trade transactions of a self-liquidating nature, since the accepting bank does not pay out any funds and its liquid assets are not affected. Fourth, acceptance financing is especially attractive during periods of tight liquidity. The drawer of the draft receives funds by selling the acceptance in the market and attracts other investors into the financing of foreign trade. Fifth, there may be cost advantages in acceptance financing. Firms that do not qualify for bank loans at the prime rate may qualify as acceptance borrowers. The discount rate for bankers acceptances is usually below the prevailing prime rate for bank loans. Furthermore, the acceptance agreement usually requires no compensating balance, whereas a commercial bank loan usually does.

BANKERS ACCEPTANCE MARKET.   Bank acceptances are important not only for trade financing, but also for domestic and international capital mobility as reflected in the bankers acceptance market. Participants in the market are importers and exporters, commercial banks, acceptance dealers, individual investors (domestic and foreign), and central banks. Importers and exporters are major borrowers in the market since they use the funds for financing their international transactions. Commercial banks are acceptors guaranteeing payments at maturities; they earn commission charges and sometimes discount charges if they discount and buy the drafts for their own portfolios. Under Federal Reserve Regulation A, commercial banks could use the eligible acceptances for rediscount at the federal discount window. However, a bank's acceptances must not exceed 50 percent of its capital and surplus, and a bank may not accept any one customer to 10 percent of its capital and surplus.

Investors of bankers acceptances include dealers, individuals, commercial banks, and central banks at home and abroad since the instruments are safe, liquid, and have higher yields than U.S. Treasury bills. For this reason, the acceptance market stimulates short-term-fund flows between nations. New York and London are particularly important for this short-term market.

FOREIGN EXCHANGE

IMPORTANCE OF FOREIGN EXCHANGE IN INTERNATIONAL TRADE.   In international commerce, payment for goods and services usually involves the currencies of exporter's and importer's countries. There would be no problem if the money of an exporter's country could always be bought and sold at a fixed and invariable price compared with the money of an importer's country. Unfortunately, the modern currency system is a complex one, especially after 1973, when all major currencies began to float. That means that the value of one currency is determined by the supply and demand for that currency in the international exchange market. The supply and demand for a currency basically depend on the imports and exports of the country as well as the inflow and outflow of capital from that country. Sections 3 and 10 of this *Handbook* provide more detail on this subject.

From an international trader's standpoint, currency risk is one of the biggest problems, since fluctuations in currency value affect his cost and profit. For example, prices of imported raw materials from foreign countries may change if the currency of the exporter's country vis-à-vis the currency of the importer's country fluctuates in the foreign-exchange market. Changes in prices of imported raw materials automatically affect the price and profit of the final product. In order to minimize the currency risk in international trade transactions, importer and exporter usually prefer to use a currency of stable value, even if it is not their own. The popularity of the British pound sterling before World War II and of the U.S. dollar in the postwar era is a typical example. In the 1970s and early 1980s, the Japanese yen and German Deutsche Mark have also been important in trade transactions, since Japan and Germany are strong exporting countries and the values of their currencies have generally shown upward movements in the foreign-exchange market.

FOREIGN-CURRENCY LETTERS OF CREDIT.   Since exporter and importer want to protect their profits and avoid currency risk, they usually shift the foreign-exchange risk to commercial banks. If the U.S. importer arranges to establish a letter of credit in the exporter's country, the payment to such an exporter will be effected in his own currency by a designated overseas paying bank in the exporter's country. Upon receiving the documents from the U.S. opening bank, the U.S. importer is required to supply U.S. dollars equal to the amount of foreign currency paid by the overseas bank, if the documents are in compliance with the terms in the letter of credit. The conversion of U.S. dollar to foreign currency on the same day is usually based on the exchange rates of the two currencies on the same day; it is called the spot rate. Actually, the opening bank just sells the foreign exchange to the importer at the spot rate and credits the foreign-exchange account of the overseas bank. Since the rate of exchange differential between the time the importer arranges to open the credit and the date of actual payment affects the amount of his U.S. dollars, the U.S. importer can eliminate any unfavorable exchange risk by arranging with his bank at the time of the opening of the letter of credit to execute a forward exchange contract. Thus the importer knows the exact cost in dollars to him in time for the actual payment, and any exchange risk is assumed by his bank.

On the contrary, if the U.S. exporter receives an export letter of credit from an advising bank in a foreign currency rather than U.S. dollars, he may arrange with the advising/negotiating bank to sell the foreign currency to be realized upon payment. In this case, the risk of exchange is assumed by the exporter, since the conversion of foreign currency into U.S. dollars will be effected at the rate of exchange on the day (spot rate) the exporter executes the exchange contract with his bank. If the foreign currency is weak, there will be a downward movement in the exchange rate, which may result in losses to the exporter. If the foreign currency is strong, an upward movement in rates may result in a good profit. To avoid the risk of foreign-currency devaluation on the date of transaction, the exporter should consider borrowing the same foreign currency for the tenure of the outstanding transaction and selling the loan proceeds spot for his own currency. At the time of payment by the foreign bank, receipt of foreign currency will repay the borrowing. By immediately selling the loan proceeds spot at the outset for the exporter's own currency and placing them on time deposit, the ensuring interest yield will reduce the gross borrowing expense. This is called a hedging operation in the foreign-exchange market.

FOREIGN EXCHANGE AND OTHER METHODS OF PAYMENTS.   Under foreign-currency letters of credit, exchange risk could be shifted to commercial banks with fees. However, other methods of payment, such as cash in advance, open account, collection, consignment, and deferred payment, may involve currency risk directly with either the exporter or importer, depending on what currency the exporter invoices to the importer. To the importer, no currency risk is involved if any of the above-mentioned payments are made in his currency by the exporter. On the contrary, if any of these payments are made in the exporter's currency, the exchange risk is completely shifted to the importer, since the foreign-exchange rate may fluctuate in the future, when the payment is made. For this reason, exporter and importer usually agree to invoice in a strong and stable currency, even a third country's currency. That is why a key currency, such as the U.S. dollar, has been widely used in international payments.

FOREIGN-EXCHANGE CONTROL.   Government control and intervention in national foreign-exchange markets has been a fact of life after World War II. Fortunately, the current trends seem to be less government control and more central-bank intervention because of the adoption of floating exchange rates. According to the *Foreign Exchange Regulations* published annually by the International Monetary Fund, the popular methods of foreign-exchange control used by its member nations (about 140) are licensing, quotas, multiple exchange rates, and capital restrictions. These controls have profound effects on trade financing, methods of payment, and currency risk. Licensing means allocation of limited foreign-exchange resources to a nation's importers and exporters. Quotas on the quantity of merchandise to be imported and exported not only affect the supply and demand for such merchandise but also influence the foreign-exchange market. Multiple exchange rates have been used by some countries, such as Brazil and Colombia, for encouraging certain exports and limiting certain imports. Capital restriction is primarily intended to regulate the capital inflow and outflow of a nation to other nations, but it affects exchange rates of that currency as well; therefore, it affects the payment process in international trade with the country concerned. Japan is a case in point.

Central-bank interventions in national foreign exchange have been frequently used by the major-currency countries, such as the United States, the United Kingdom, West Germany, and Japan. The prime purpose of the interventions is to stabilize their foreign-currency markets, especially the value of their respective currencies. In the private sector, foreign-currency futures and the Eurocurrency markets have been important alternatives to hedge currency fluctuations and to assist short-term trade financing.

OFFICIAL AGENCIES

U.S. OFFICIAL AGENCIES

The Export-Import Bank of the United States. The Export-Import Bank is an independent U.S. government agency, and has been an important source of export financing for short-term, medium-term, and long-term programs. It was created in 1934 by presidential executive order and has operated on a statutory basis since 1945 with passage of the Export-Import Bank Act. Its charter has been renewed periodically, most recently in late 1978, when it received a new five-year mandate.

The bank has three major functions: (1) direct loans to exporters or importers; (2) assistance to commercial banks and other financial institutions that are supporting export sales; and (3) export credit insurance and guarantees. Its financial services support a broad cross section of products and projects. Application for loans and guarantees may be made by letter. A request for information prior to application, sometime with the assistance of commercial banks, is advisable.

The Export-Import Bank's support for short-term (up to 180 days) export sales rests exclusively with the export-insurance program that it operates jointly with the Foreign Credit Insurance Association (FCIA), which includes about 50 leading American insurance companies. FCIA was founded in 1961 and offers a variety of short- and medium-term policies covering commercial and political risk from 90 percent to 100 percent.

Closely associated with the Export-Import Bank in some of its direct loan operations is the Private Export Funding Corporation (PEFCO). Established in 1970 on the initiative of the Bankers Association for Foreign Trade, PEFCO is a private company owned by U.S. commercial banks and major industrial corporations. PEFCO was organized as a supplemental lending source and extends medium- and long-term loans for overseas purchases of American capital goods such as power plants, aircraft, mining projects, industrial installations, communication facilities, and railroad equipment. All PEFCO loans are covered by an unconditional Eximbank guarantee on both principal and interest.

Commodity Credit Corporation.   The Commodity Credit Corporation (CCC) is an agency of the U.S. government under the administration of the Department of Agriculture. CCC conducts four programs in connection with foreign trade: (1) dollar financing generally up to 12 months, sometime up to 36 months; (2) sales of surplus agricultural commodities against local currencies; (3) sales of surplus commodities under long-term supply contracts; and (4) barter transactions. Goods eligible for financing under the programs must come from private stocks of surplus agricultural commodities and must be in compliance with the list of commodities announced by the CCC on a monthly basis. Although the commodities financed come from surplus stock, all sales under the programs are made through private U.S. exporters.

Overseas Private Investment Corporation.   OPIC was formed in 1971 to take over a number of programs previously offered through the Agency for International Development (AID). OPIC is wholly owned by the U.S. Treasury Department with the objective of stimulating and facilitating U.S. private equity and loan investments in friendly developing countries. Their programs also promote world trade, since U.S. private investments abroad mostly involve U.S. exports of capital goods, especially in cases of project financing in those countries. OPIC provides investment-guarantee programs covering inconvertibility of currency, expropriation of property, and other political risks such as war and revolution. It charges low fees for insurance. It should also be noted that AID is under the administration of the U.S. State Department sponsoring the foreign-aid program. Exporters interested in the program should inquire directly or through commercial banks, which issue letters of credit to beneficiary-exporters and receive reimbursements from AID after shipment of merchandise.

INTERNATIONAL INSTITUTIONS.   International trade financing has been indirectly helped by the establishment of various international financial institutions after World War II. The International Monetary Fund (IMF), established in 1944, is intended to stabilize the exchange rates of its members' currencies and to extend loans to member nations if they have a "temporary disequilibrium" in trade deficits. Its functions are important to traders in terms of currency value and a nation's credit standing. The International Bank for Reconstruction and Development (the World Bank), established in 1945, makes loans to member countries for roads, power plants, steel mills, irrigation projects, and so forth. The suppliers of these projects get built-in export financing. Two other financial organizations belong to the World Bank group and play supplemental roles in financing economic developments of less developed countries. One is the International Development Association (IDA), which makes low-interest and long-term loans to the poorest nations, which may repay the loans in local currencies; another is the International Finance Corporation (IFC), which makes direct investments and loans to individual productive private businesses. These private businesses may use IFC financing for resource exploration and new ventures that, one way of another, would help international trade. Regional development banks such as the Inter-American Development Bank, European Investment Bank, Asian Development Bank, and African Development Bank all are designed to foster economic development of their respective member countries, including stimulation of regional trade.

OFFICIAL AGENCIES IN FOREIGN COUNTRIES.   National policy to assist exports as a means of earning foreign exchange and gaining domestic employment has gradually developed in the past 60 years. The United Kingdom formed the Export Credit Guarantee Department (ECGD) in 1919. In 1946 France established the Compagnie Française pour l'Assurance du Commerce Exterieur (COFACE), which provides insurance for export risk, and the Banque Française pour le Commerce Exterieur (BFCE), which plays a central role in mobilizing the necessary finance. In 1952 West Germany formed the Ausfuhrkredit (AKA), which is a consortium comprising all German commercial banks for medium- and long-term export financing with a special rediscount facility provided by the Bundesbank. In 1962 the German government commissioned two private concerns, Hermes and Treuarbeit, to provide official export credit insurance. Japan established the Export-Import Bank of Japan in 1951 to accommodate medium- and long-export financing, but export insurance covering commercial and political risks is provided by the Export Insurance Division of the Ministry of International Trade and Industry.

Besides the major trading countries, many other developed countries such as Sweden and Holland, as well as many developing countries such as Brazil and India, also established official agencies to finance and insure their exports during the 1960s and 1970s. Furthermore, many state trading companies in centrally planned countries and oil-producing countries have exercised even stronger policies in international trade financing. In the 1980s, competition among national agencies for financing exports will be keen, since every nation would like to boost its exports for the purposes of economic growth, domestic employment, and the strengthening of balance-of-payments positions. Moreover, if interest rates remain at the current high levels resulting from worldwide inflation, trade-financing subsidies may lead to cutthroat competition, which would eventually hurt, not help, international trade in the years ahead.

SOURCES AND SUGGESTED REFERENCES

Back. L.A. *Introduction to Commercial Letters of Credit,* New York: Citibank, N.A., 1976.

Chase World Information Corporation. *Methods of Export Financing,* 2nd ed., New York: Chase World Information Corporation, 1976.

Eng, M. "Structural Changes in International Banking," *Atlanta Economic Review,* Vol. XXVIII, No. 5 (1978), pp. 49–54.

Export-Import Bank of the United States. *Financing for American Exports,* Washington, D.C.: Export-Import Bank of the United States, 1980.

Federal Reserve Bank of New York. "Trading in the Bankers Acceptances: A View from the Acceptance Desk of the Federal Reserve Bank of New York," *Monthly Review,* Vol. LVIII, No. 2 (1976).

International Chamber of Commerce. *Uniform Customs and Practice for Documentary Credits,* Publication No. 290, Paris: ICC, 1974.

International Monetary Fund. *Foreign Exchange Regulations,* Washington, D.C.: International Monetary Fund, 1980.

Jonnard, C.M. *Exporter's Financial and Marketing Handbook,* Park Ridge, NJ: Noyes Data Corporation, 1975.

McKinnon, R.I. *Money in International Exchange,* New York: Oxford University Press, 1979.

Organization for Economic Cooperation and Development. *The Export Credit Financing Systems in OECD Member Countries,* Paris: OECD, 1976.

Pratt, P. *A Handbook on Financing U.S. Exports,* 3rd Ed. Washington, D.C.: Machinery and Allied Products Institute, 1979.

Schneider, G.W. *Export-Import Financing,* New York: Ronald Press, 1974.

SECTION **14**

INTERNATIONAL TRADE IN SERVICES

CONTENTS

Definitions	3	PASSENGER TRANSPORTATION	15
Factor services and nonfactor services	3	Causation	15
The importance of trade in services	5	International regulation	16
The Broad Categories	5	Route Authorization	16
Tourism	6	National Carriers	17
Transportation	6	Scheduled and Nonscheduled Airlines	18
Royalties	6		
Entertainment	6	TECHNOLOGY TRADE	18
Other private services	7	Definitions	18
Miscellaneous government services	7	Determinants	19
Causation	7	Impediments to Technology Trade	20
Coverage	8		
		ENTERTAINMENT AND EDUCATION	21
TOURISM	8	Types of Transaction	21
Definition	8	Summary	22
Economics	9		
Determinants	11		
Specialty Tourism Markets	13	SOURCES AND SUGGESTED	
Government Impediments	14	REFERENCES	22
The Tourism Business	14		

INTERNATIONAL TRADE IN SERVICES

H. Peter Gray

DEFINITIONS. International trade in services takes place when resources belonging to one country are used to provide intangible goods for the residents of a second country. The category of *services* embraces everything other than tangible commodities. In Great Britain, international trade in services is commonly referred to as invisible trade.

Factor Services and Nonfactor Services. The general category of international trade in services contains two distinct types of transaction. Since this section of the-*Handbook* is primarily concerned with nonfactor services, it is useful to identify the two categories. International trade in factor services takes place when resources belonging to a nation are relocated in a foreign nation and provide services (output) there. Payments are then sent back to the nation of origin. These are factor services, and the name derives from the practice of economists of referring to productive resources as *factors of production*. Payments (for the local use of factors of production) that are sent back to the country of origin are *factor services*. These comprise remittances to families by migrant workers or guest workers and funds taken home with them when they leave the country of employment. Similarly, payments of dividends and interest from one country to another are factor services in the sense that the factors of production are located in the country in which the good is produced and consumed. The most obvious example of this kind of transaction is the remittance of profits from a foreign subsidiary of a multinational to the parent corporation.

These payments for factor services can be important elements in the balance of payments of individual countries. The United States is a major recipient of factor services in the form of income on U.S. assets abroad. In 1979, net receipts on assets abroad amounted to approximately $32.5 billion (see Exhibit 1). Of this sum, only $17.8 billion is repatriated, and the balance is reinvested abroad. Other countries, particularly poorer countries, rely heavily on receipts of factor services from people who are working abroad on a temporary basis. These include migrant workers whose work is seasonal and mainly agricultural as well as guest workers who work steadily for protracted periods before returning home. For example, Pakistan's receipts of factor service payments amounted to one third of total current earnings of foreign exchange in 1977. Greece, Turkey, and Yugoslavia count factor service receipts as important components of their total foreign-exchange earnings.

EXHIBIT 1 U.S. RECEIPTS AND PAYMENTS ON FACTOR AND NONFACTOR SERVICES, 1979 (millions of dollars)[a]

Category	Receipts	Payments
Direct defense expenditures[b]	—	8,469
Travel	8,335	9,413
Passenger fares	2,156	3,100
Other transportation	9,793	10,466
Fees and royalties from affiliated foreigners	5,042	471
Fees and royalties from unaffiliated foreigners	1,150	235
Other private services	4,291	2,779
Government miscellaneous services	522	1,714
Receipts of income on U.S. assets abroad and payments of income on foreign assets in the U.S.[c]		
Direct investment	37,815	6,033
(of which reinvested earnings)	(18,414)	(3,730)
Other private receipts and payments	25,861	16,361
Government receipts and payments	2,294	11,066
Private remittances and other transfers (net)[c]	—	955

Source. U.S. Department of Commerce. *Survey of Current Business,* June, 1980, pp. 32–33.
[a]Detailed descriptions of the components of each category can be obtained from the *Survey of Current Business,* June 1978, Part II, pp, 8–12.
[b]"Direct defense expenditures" involves payments made by the U.S. military overseas including expenditures by members of the armed services and their dependents.
[c]Net receipts of income on assets abroad and that part of private remittances that relates to migrant workers' remittances make up factor services.

Nonfactor services comprise intangible goods produced outside of the country in which the good is consumed or used. The definition "everything other than tangible goods" has a residual quality. The category embraces a very large number of different kinds of transactions. A 1980 U.S. government document (relating to an inquiry on the quality of U.S. data on nonfactor services currently collected) listed the following subsectors:

1. Accounting
2. Banking
3. Consultants
4. Construction engineering
5. Data processing and transborder data flows
6. Education
7. Employment
8. Franchising
9. Health
10. Hotels/motels
11. Tourism
12. Insurance and reinsurance

13. Leasing & motion pictures
14. Transportation and other business
15. Professional and technical services fields

As can be seen from Exhibit 1, which provides the best data available for publication from the U.S. Department of Commerce, the data on some activities are scarce to the point of invisibility. Many of the categories overlap with others, and for some activities, there is little hope that data can be collected for a reasonable outlay of dollars and effort.

International trade in nonfactor services does involve transactions in commodities to a minor degree. Examples are the purchases of commodities for consumption by tourists and commodities to take home as gifts and mementoes. Similarly, ships and aircraft take on food and fuel in foreign ports.

The Importance of Trade in Services. Traditionally, analysts of international trade have concerned themselves almost exclusively with trade in commodities. But international trade in services is quantitatively important. In the United States in 1979, international trade in both factor and nonfactor services accounted for 31.7 percent of international trade in commodities (excluding defense spending and commodities exports financed under military grants). The percentage is higher for receipts than for payments. When dividend and interest payments are omitted, the ratio falls to 15 percent. In several European countries, the ratio is significantly higher.

A basic distinction between trade in services and trade in commodities lies in the way in which the different kinds of goods are made available to the buyer. Commodities are purchased in one country and the goods are shipped to foreign ports. When services are traded, the national space of one of the trading partners is usually penetrated by a foreign person or resource. For example, transportation services involve the penetration of national space by foreign ships and aircraft and their crews. When tourism or travel is the service being provided, the foreign consumer comes to the country providing the service. When technological knowledge is licensed, foreign knowledge is transferred to the importing country; to the degree that technology licensing requires that consultants and technicians accompany the technology to make the licensees familiar with it, the analogy is even more exact.

The particular character of services has one important implication. In comparison with the reliability of data reported on trade in commodities, the reliability of data on the value of international trade in services is poor. Except for such commodity-related items as payments for merchant shipping, data on international trade in services, for those categories for which they exist, are derived from sampling procedures of varying degrees of sophistication and modernity. Even among those categories of invisible trade on which data are generated, there are frequently sizable gaps in the coverage. Published data probably provide reasonably accurate orders of magnitude with consistent built-in biases but nothing more.

THE BROAD CATEGORIES. International trade in services comprises a very large number of categories. But since any economic phenomenon derives its importance from its value, it is possible to restrict serious analysis to a few broad groups: tourism, transportation, technological know-how, entertainment, and financial services. The latter category is covered in detail in Sections 12, 13, 20, and 21 of this *Handbook* and is not considered further here.

Tourism. Tourism is used here as an all-embracing term meaning foreign travel regardless of purpose. Reported expenditures on tourism include all expenditures in a foreign country by a resident of another country. The visit may be an organized tour, an individual tour, a one-stop pleasure visit, a business trip, or an educational, or even health-related visit. The designation *foreign-travel expenditures* is more appropriate.

Transportation. Transportation is fairly self-explanatory. A nation uses services provided by a foreign nation whenever it imports a good that is transported by a ship registered under a foreign flag. By the same token, the carriage of other countries' imports on a ship of its own registry earns money from foreigners. The same distinctions apply to passenger traffic. Expenditures of this kind are substantially offset by carriers' expenditures in foreign ports. When a ship visits a foreign port, it incurs pilot's fees and charges for use of the berth. It must refuel and reprovision, and its crew must be afforded some free time ashore. With the possible exception of crew's expenditures, aircraft incur equivalent costs.

It is important to distinguish clearly between freight transportation and passenger transportation. Nowadays, most goods are shipped by sea, and people travel by air. This is not exclusively so. The important distinction is that passenger transportation tends to involve a higher percentage of transportation expenditures relative to the value of the imports than does freight. For passengers the value of the imports is the value of services purchased in foreign countries; To avail themselves of these services, passengers are obliged to travel in both directions (in contrast to goods) and passengers require quick and comfortable transportation. Freight transportation is described in Section 11.

Royalties. Technological know-how enters into international trade in services in two major ways: by the licensing of technology to a foreign corporation, and by giving advice to foreign firms. The first is paid for by *royalties* and the second by *management fees*. Frequently the two are combined, as when a firm licenses a foreigner to use a process developed by the licensing firm, and, to assist the foreign firm in utilizing the technology for which it will be paying, the licensing firm sends over a group of experts (production engineers) to assist the licensees in mastering the new technology. On occasion, foreign firms wish to avail themselves of managerial know-how or professional assistance quite separately from any licensing arrangement. For these services, foreigners will visit the firm and provide services for which fees are charged (in addition to the living expenses of the visitors, but these are domestic or internal expenditures in the country of the importer). The third element in this category is the processing and analysis in one country of data collected in, and referring to, residents of another country. This so-called *transborder data flow*-business has recently become a matter of concern and legislation in many countries.

Entertainment. Entertainment covers a variety of quite distinctive activities: renting movies and television programs from foreign producers; reproduction of records (discs) and tapes; and publication in one country of books and magazine articles written abroad, so that fees for publication rights or royalties are paid to foreigners. This group of activities clearly includes educational topics as well as items designed purely for diversion.

There is a paucity of data about many subcategoreis of the last two items because of the proprietary nature of the transaction. Gross data are reported for international accounting purposes, but the information is frequently given to the data-collecting agency of a government under the veil of confidentiality. Trade in technological services is conducted between two firms and details are frequently suppressed if the transaction is part of a package designed to facilitate one corporations's ability to bypass currency regulations in the paying nation. When the two firms are part of the same multinational corporation, the confidentiality aspects become even harder to disentangle.

Other Private Services.   This category is clearly the residual. It includes such items as foreign-contract operations of construction, engineering, consulting, and other technical-services companies; international cable, radio, telephone, and satellite services; expenditures in the host country of foreign embassies, consulates, and registered agents of foreign governments; international reinsurance transactions and film rentals; and, in the words of the Department of Commerce, "Various other receipts and payments."

Miscellaneous Government Services.   Governments, no less than the private sector, conduct trade in services with foreigners. This subcategory reports on those transactions. The expenditures are predominantly the expenditures abroad of nonmilitary government agencies such as embassies and consulates. The category also includes the expenditures of their staffs and dependents for goods and services purchased while on foreign duty. Receipts are governmental receipts from private foreigners as well as from foreign governments. In the United States, these include not only the receipts for the standard government agencies but also such items as fees received by the Panama Canal Company, the National Aeronautics and Space Administration, and the U.S. Postal Service.

Because the expenditures in a country of foreign embassies on food and provisions are made to private-sector supplies, whereas expenditures by home-government agencies located abroad are made by government, there is a tendency for this category to show an excess of payments over receipts. Expenditures abroad by government agencies and personnel are entered in this account whereas their counterpart expenditures by foreign governments are reported under "other private services."

When a nation maintains armed forces in foreign countries, the local expenditures of those personnel are invisible imports. These expenditures also include the expenditures of the military units themselves on local purchases. Normally, any armaments purchased are considered imports of commodities and are considered to be imported physically into the home country (as commodities) and shipped back to foreign-based units.

CAUSATION.   International trade in services takes place because foreigners can supply a service more cheaply than domestic suppliers or because domestic producers are not in a position to offer the particular service in question. International trade in services depends to an important degree on the availability of a particular asset or resource in the supplier nation.

When both nations possess similar or identical resources and can both supply the service in question, the decision to buy from a foreign source depends upon any difference in costs and in perceived value. The question of perceived value derives from the fact that in many cases, and particularly in tourism, the service provided by foreigners is not identical with that supplied by domestic producers. The individual tastes of the purchasers become important in distinguishing between the relative value of service provided by competing suppliers.

When a nation does not possess a particular resource it cannot supply the associated service. Thus, to license computer technology from I.B.M., a foreign firm must pay royalties to a U.S. corporation. To see the Eiffel Tower, a person must go to Paris. The decision to indulge in international trade in services of this kind does not offer any choice among different nations and depends essentially on the intensity of the demand for the particular country-specific service.

International trade in services depends directly upon the availability of service-specific assets in different countries and on the money costs of the cooperating factors of production. Like international trade in commodities, trade in services takes place when the service is available from abroad more cheaply than an identical service can be obtained at home. A distinction between commodity trade and trade in services is the greater degree of individuality that exists in services. Services supplied by or from different countries are usually competing substitutes rather than identical products. For this reason, tastes qualify the role of prices as the determining factor.

COVERAGE.   This section considers four major categories of international trade in services in order:

1. Tourism
2. Passenger transportation
3. Technology trade
4. Entertainment and education

Financial services and freight transportation are the subject matter of separate sections in the *Handbook*.

Each of the four categories of international trade in services will be explained in terms of the reasons for its existence and the sensitivity of the volume of trade to different determinants. Impediments imposed by governments in the various areas will be summarized. The practical aspects of each category will be reviewed where general principles can be evolved.

TOURISM

DEFINITION.   The tourism committee of the Organization for Economic Co-operation and Development (OECD) defines a tourist as "any person visiting a country, other than that in which he usually resides, for a period of at least 24 hours." The following are considered tourists:

1. Persons traveling for pleasure, for domestic reasons, for health, and so forth.
2. Persons traveling to meetings, or in a representative capacity of any kind (scientific, administrative, diplomatic, religious, athletic, and so forth).
3. Persons traveling for business reasons.
4. Persons arriving in the course of a sea cruise, even when they stay less than 24 hours.

Explicitly excluded from the definition are persons arriving to take up employment; persons coming to establish residence; students registered in schools or colleges; residents in a frontier zone and those who live in one country and work in an adjoining one; and through travelers even if their stay exceeds 24 hours.

For practical purposes, it is useful to divide tourists into two groups: those traveling for pleasure or personal reasons (motivations 1 and 4), and those traveling for representative reasons (2 and 3). Even then there will be overlapping cases: Many business persons manage to "sneak in" a couple of days sightseeing when in an unexplored locale, and many scientists have been known to extend a visit to a conference by a day or two or to interrupt a homeward journey for pleasure.

Pleasure travelers can be subcategorized again by motivation since there are two quite different kinds of pleasure travel: wanderlust and sunlust (or resort tourism). Gray (1970) points out that the two quite different kinds of tourism give rise to quite different kinds of tourism business. *Wanderlust tourism* involves seeing new things and experiencing new cultural ambiances; *resort tourism* means going to a resort and doing at the resort things that one can do at home. Wanderlust essentially involves "foreignness," whereas resorts tend to cater to the yearning for luxury, but otherwise cater to the domestic tastes of the visitors. (National dishes may be served but these are usually adulterated in order not to risk offending foreign palates.) Wanderlust travelers may stop at many places on a single vacation whereas resort tourists probably make only one stop. Resorts are especially built for the tourist trade in places with climatic and other attributes (relative to the residence of the tourist). Wanderlust travel does generate demand for hotel space near points of interest and in cities, but the city hotels serve business and domestic visitors as well as pleasure travelers. With the exception of hotels at sites near particular landmarks (such as at Agra, Giza, Siem Reap), wanderlust facilities are part of the day-to-day living of the residents of the country providing the service.

In a country that is as large and as varied as the United States, people can indulge in wanderlust or sunlust without going abroad. This is in contrast to Denmark, for example, where the national attributes are fairly standard throughout and where sunlust in the winter mandates foreign travel. In the United States in 1978, domestic travel is estimated (by the U.S. Travel Data Center) to be between 11 and 12 times more important than international travel ($140.7 billion for domestic travel compared to $12.6 billion for international travel).

ECONOMICS. Except for any contribution to national pride as the attributes of a nation are shown to foreigners, tourism is a purely commercial business. It may have its educational benefits for the tourists, but selling tourist services to foreigners is a means of making a living and of earning foreign exchange. As such, there is a good deal of competition among national tourism industries and among different locales within individual nations. Some of the appeal of different places lies in the quality of their offerings and the intensity of the desires of travelers to visit such places. But like other forms of international trade, price or cost is important and the tourist will be sensitive to cost.

Tourism may be distinguished from trade in other forms of services and commodities by its great dependence on the availability of particular kinds of resources in the exporting country. Inputs into the production of transportation and manufacturing are (potentially) available in all countries; where the technology is not immediately available it can be transferred within a multinational corporation or through licensing. Tourism relies on immobile resources such as ski slopes or beaches with warm, shark-free seas for resort tourism, or cultural distinctiveness and buildings and sites of historical interest for wanderlust travelers. As a general rule, the types of resources that serve as a basis for resort tourism are less distinctive than the historical/cultural aspects of different cities and nations. Price competition among resorts and resort-oriented national tourism industries is likely to be more severe than among wanderlust attractions. Costs for the traveler include travel costs as well as local costs. Geographic proximity to important tourist-originating markets (Japan, Europe, and North America) adds value to a natural resource. A warm, sandy beach in the Bahamas is more valuable than one of similar inherent quality located in Colombia, Venezuela, or Chile.

In contrast to the lack of distinctiveness of resort tourism, wanderlust tourism is frequently quite individualistic, and the price sensitivity of demand is likely to be secondary to the intensity of the desire to visit the individual country or attraction. This intensity may be expected to reach its peak for pilgrimages: the pilgrimage of Moslems to Mecca (the Hajj), and of Catholics to Rome in Holy Years. But even when the intent of travel is less serious, a great deal of inflexibility in the choice of the locale may remain. The Taj Mahal, the Pyramids, and Angkor Wat are all unique, and each monument reaches the height of impressiveness in its own individual right. The ambiances of New York, London, Paris, and Rome are all quite distinct. Cost considerations may preclude the satisfaction of a lifelong desire to travel to a particular spot, but if that journey is canceled, the funds may be spent on nontouristic activities. Within a region, there is probably greater substitutability in response to cost differences: An itinerary can be changed to spend longer in relatively cheap places and to limit the time spent in high-cost cities. Exhibit 2 shows the share of U.S. travel receipts and expenditures enjoyed by different countries.

EXHIBIT 2   U.S. INTERNATIONAL TRAVEL PATTERNS (millions of dollars)[a]

	1970		1979	
	Receipts	Expenditures	Receipts	Expenditures
Total	2,331	3,980	8,335	9,413
Canada	859	1,018	2,002	1,599
Mexico	583	778	1,869	2,460
(Mexico border area)	(520)	(463)	(1,160)	(1,291)
Western Europe	318	1,310	1,667	2,842
United Kingdom	51	293	375	826
France	39	160	180	355
Italy	29	172	84	300
Switzerland	14	108	[b]	158
Germany	67	148	440	283
Caribbean and Central America	170	390	375	1,019
South America	164	90	793	288
Japan	101	97	699	142

Source.   U.S. Department of Commerce. *Survey of Current Business*, May 1980, p. 31.
[a]Not including transportation.
[b]Not available.

Tourism can be an extremely important source of foreign exchange for some developing nations. Because they may have a combination of highly suitable natural resources, low wage scales, and an ability to attract foreign capital in the tourism industry, developing nations find tourism to be an important contributor to the balance of payments and, in this way, a vital component of their economic development strategy. One important aspect of sales of tourism services to foreigners is that the natural resources that form the basis for the tourism industry are so scarce (in terms of a combination of quality and location) that they can generate a higher than average profit rate. In a purely decentralized economy, the surplus accrues to the owners of the natural resource. If the resource is a climate or a coastline, it is "owned" by the state, but the state is unable to charge for it in any straightforward way, and the surplus will accrue to owners of nearby privately owned assets—particularly hotels. If the hotel chains are foreign-owned, there may be a potential conflict over the division of any surplus among the private-sector owners, the state, and the workers in the industry as each group tries to acquire the surplus. To the extent that the surplus accrues to nearby property, it enhances the capital value of that asset. Developing nations also find tourism to be a very important source of employment where local labor supplies cannot be utilized in other ways. Tourism does produce a great deal of *employment*, and it has a particularly valuable characteristic in that many of the skilled tasks in tourism can be learned on the job.

DETERMINANTS. Given that the definition of tourism is all-embracing and includes business and representative travel as well as pleasure travel, any explanation of the factors affecting the total volume of tourism will be quite general. Most studies are concerned with the way in which tourism patterns change through time in response to changes in underlying situations, and stress the roles of levels of prosperity (or national income) and relative prices at home and abroad.

The basic underlying pattern is for the developed nations of the world to exchange an important proportion of tourism expenditures among themselves. In 1978, according to the International Monetary Fund (*Yearbook* 1972–1978 and *Supplement*, 1979) industrial countries accounted for 76.7 percent of the expenditures and received 65 percent of the payments. These figures relate merely to expenditures made in foreign countries and do not include international transportation. The United States alone generated 12.3 percent of global tourism expenditures and received 10.7 of total receipts. Much of this can be explained by business travel, which is likely to take place predominantly among industrial nations. The other factor is that the many industrial nations contain wanderlust attractions. Paris, Rome, New York, and London are located in industrial nations, but they remain centers of culture and foreign ambiance, and foreigners are quite naturally interested in seeing and enjoying their amenities. The nations that are net recipients of tourism are the developed countries in the northern Mediterranean and some non-oil-developing countries. The attractions in most of these countries are oriented toward resort tourism. Egypt, Greece, and Kenya will rely heavily on wanderlust, but even in these countries, there is likely to be an element of resort tourism combining with the wanderlust industry. Non-oil-developing nations received, net, 9.6 percent of global expenditures of $45,600 million in 1977. Similarly, industrial countries can provide resort tourism, as Japanese visitors to Hawaii, European visitors to Florida, and northern European visitors to the Riviera attest. Global patterns of tourism are summarized in Exhibit 3.

EXHIBIT 3   GLOBAL PATTERNS OF TOURISM, 1977 (millions of SDRs)

Region or Country	Receipts	Expenditures	Balance
World	45,677	45,514	—
Industrial countries	29,763	34,903	−5,140
United States	5,281	6,383	−1,102
Japan	383	1,843	−1,460
France	3,758	3,363	−395
Italy	4,074	2,101	+1,973
United Kingdom	3,256	1,645	+1,611
West Germany	3,287	9,272	−5,985
Other developed areas	6,199	2,530	+3,669
Greece	839	140	+699
Portugal	345	116	+229
Spain	3,531	454	+3,077
Oil-exporting countries	1,672	3,972	−2,300
Non-oil-developing nations	7,943	4,009	+3,934
Bahamas	349	47	+302
Egypt	624	147	+477
Israel	394	158	+236
Thailand	193	134	+59
Tunisia	287	54	+233

Source.   International Monetary Fund, 1978.

Once the pattern of tourism expenditures among nations has been established, it is reasonable to expect that its growth and year-to-year variations will depend directly upon such economic phenomena as levels of prosperity and relative costs. This has certainly been borne out, but some of the estimates are imperfect because it is not possible to differentiate between the effects of increases in affluence and improvements and cost reductions in international air travel. Similarly, the data do not permit an accurate estimation of changes in relative costs. Gray (1970) was the first to provide satisfactory estimates of the relative importance of affluence and prices in the level of foreign-travel expenditures. He separated travel from the United States to Mexico and Canada from travel to Europe and found that travel to both North American neighbors was quite sensitive to changes in income. Travel expenditures in Canada and Mexico by U.S. residents, deflated for any inflation, tended to vary proportionately by about twice as much as income. Thus a 10 percent increase in income would lead to a 20 percent increase in expenditures in those countries. Travel expenditures to Canada also reacted to changes in the rate of exchange—a devaluation of the currency augmenting sales of travel services to foreigners. Travel to overseas countries proved to be even more sensitive to changes in American prosperity, reacting to changes in per capita income by a factor of about five. Gray's results reflect the time period covered in his analysis (1950–1969). The period probably tended to exaggerate the sensitivity of travel expenditures abroad to income. During these 19 years, air travel made great technical strides, and the introduction of jet aircraft greatly reduced the time involved in a transatlantic flight as well as reducing the cost of the fare. Business travel was also increasing rapidly over this period as many large American corporations established foreign subsidiaries in Europe. A final factor was the gradual trend toward overvaluation of the U.S. dollar during the period, so that Americans were enjoying foreign travel services at something less than their real cost.

More-recent tests show that the sensitivity of U.S. foreign expenditures on travel services to income has tended to decline slightly. Using data from 1960 through 1978, Jane Sneddon Little (1980) showed that travel to France, Italy, and Canada no longer shows sensitivity to changes in U.S. per capita income. Of course, this may be due to the very high level of imports—possibly approaching saturation—in these countries prior to 1960. Total U.S. expenditures are shown to be sensitive to changes in American affluence: A change of $10 in American per capita income (adjusted for inflation) leads to a change in foreign travel expenditures of approximately $17.5. Travel to Canada appears to have been very sensitive to changes in the exchange rate between the Canadian and U.S. dollars and to changes in the cost of living. Little's results do seem to confirm the idea that tourists are discriminating among nations by cost, since the sensitivity of expenditures in individual countries to changes in relative costs (including exchange-rate changes) is much greater than it is for the pattern of total expenditures.

One problem with analyses of this kind is the existence of special events that cannot be completely allowed for. Thus, Canadian results were affected by the Expo in 1967 and the Olympic Games in 1976. French expenditures were affected by the political riots in Paris in 1967–1968.

Data supporting the logic of the argument that lower travel fares increase tourism are scarce. This scarcity does not impugn the obvious relationship but tends, instead, to qualify results obtained by tests of this kind.

The sensitivity of tourism to cost factors is borne out by the steady increases in foreign travel expenditures in the United States by Europeans. Between 1978 and 1979, foreign-travel expenditures in the United States increased by 18.8 percent. This was a period of particular weakness of the U.S. dollar and made travel to the United States by people from European industrial nations and Japan very attractive.

SPECIALTY TOURISM MARKETS.   Most national markets are identifiable within the broad distinction of wanderlust and resort tourism. Certain special areas carry on quite thriving businesses by catering to particular sports and pastimes. In Nepal and northern Pakistan, backpacking is a major industry. Switzerland and India feature mountaineering as an attraction to skilled climbers. The Bahamas have developed gambling as a special attraction on Grand Bahama Island. Thailand and Taiwan cater to the market for sex. Many areas cater to specialist pursuits such as diving. Markets such as these are generally advertised within magazines catering to the potential clientele rather than advertised in general tourism-promotion campaigns.

It is possible to regard cruises as a specialty market, although cruises represent, in reality, merely wanderlust using the liner as a hotel. Currently transatlantic crossings are made more and more to resemble cruises than mere oceanborne transportation. This accounts for Cunard's slogan "Getting there is half the fun." Despite the demise of the fleet of transatlantic liners, cruises are still a flourishing business in Europe and in the Caribbean. In 1975, 750,000 Americans were passengers on cruise ships. Although most of these were relatively local voyages to Bermuda or the Caribbean from New York, or to Alaska from Los Angeles (via Vancouver), the cruise business has managed to survive in the face of severe competition from aircraft. It has declined slowly since 1975.

GOVERNMENT IMPEDIMENTS.   Many nations restrict the ability of their citizens to travel abroad. Most of these restrictions derive from economic rather than political concerns. The most common method is to restrict the availability of foreign money to travelers, allowing them a mere pittance to spend abroad. The motivation here is to preserve foreign exchange for more-serious needs than mere pleasure time spent in a foreign country. Developing nations tend to impose these restrictions steadily through time, since a shortage of foreign exchange is chronic in developing nations. Developed nations tend to keep the legislative power in reserve for use during a period of especial weakness of the national currency. Business travel is usually considered to be an acceptable use of foreign exchange that is made available for this purpose.

The imposition of restrictions on the availability of foreign exchange for travel has unfortunate discriminatory overtones, and its effectiveness as a means of saving foreign exchange is not beyond question. When foreign-exchange restrictions are imposed on people, the ability to circumvent the regulations is not evenly distributed. Businesspersons and the rich are usually much better prepared to have funds available to them abroad and, in this way, to be able to bypass the restrictions. Funds are usually made available to businesses more easily than to pleasure travelers, and business travelers have the ability to use corporate resources abroad if need be. People with family or property located abroad can also escape the stringency of foreign-exchange restrictions. But even the poorer travelers are unlikely to forego foreign travel over a period of years in consequence of the travel restrictions. First, restrictions apply only to funds spent abroad and not to the costs of transportation, and, second, holidays are often postponed rather than canceled. The net result of this tendency to postpone means that when travel restrictions are imposed in a period of financial crisis lasting, say, two or three years, the release of the restrictions is accompanied by what the British call a floodgates effect. Postrestriction foreign travel surges to catch up with holidays postponed during the period of limited availability of foreign exchange.

THE TOURISM BUSINESS.   One important characteristic of nearly all branches of the tourism industry is its reliance upon fixed capacity. Hotels, restaurants, and all means of transportation have given capacities. If the beds, chairs or seats are not filled at any particular time, the capacity is completely wasted. This type of production of services has particular economic implications that affect marketing strategies. The behavior pattern is similar to that of an electric utility with spare capacity: When the choice is between letting capacity go to waste and selling it for less than the average cost of the capacity, suppliers are willing to recognize that the cost of the potentially wasted capacity is virtually zero and to offer bargain prices to utilize it.

Advertising expenditures are high in order to promote the sale of existing capacity. Recognition that profit margins can be enhanced by selling potentially wasted capacity at significantly less than average cost leads to severe price competition. But no business can operate for long if its average revenue fails to cover its average costs, and tourism firms have to ensure that any sales made at below-average cost are balanced by sales made at above-average cost. This leads to the segmentation of the tourist market. Tourists are divided into different groups according to perceived price sensitivity: Those who will pay full fare are charged full fare and those who will respond to cut-price offers are charged low prices. The problem is to prevent the person who would pay full fare from taking advantage of cut-price offers. Because businesspersons are seen as price insensitive and pleasure travelers to be more price sensitive, cut-price offers usually require several weeks of advanced reservation on the presumption that businesspersons will not be able to plan their commitments a long time in advance. Market segmentation also underlies the practice of offering sizable variation in rates according to the seasonal-demand pressures.

The emphasis of tourism suppliers on capacity utilization rates underlies the modern emphasis on the organized group tour. The organized tour has a natural appeal for unsophisticated travelers and particularly for those unfamiliar with the languages of the countries to be visited. But it also offers price advantages in comparison with the same "package" arranged on an individual basis. Travel agents earn their income by fees paid to them by the seller of the tourism service: They are able to arrange individual tours at no cost to the tourist. They are the retail arm of the industry. Wholesalers provide group packages. The ability of the wholesaler to price a group package competitively and still to meet the retailer's commission and overhead costs lies in the wholesalers' ability to wring lower prices from hotels and airlines in return for a guarantee of a large number of people. This group reservation provides the supplier with some minimum rate of capacity utilization, and the supplier will compete for sales of this kind.

PASSENGER TRANSPORTATION

CAUSATION.   With the exception of cruise travel, and to a lesser degree transatlantic liners, international travel is merely a means to an end: It offers no inherent satisfaction. People travel to reach a destination and seek to arrive there by minimizing some combination of cost and discomfort. There is a tendency in the United States to think of international travel almost exclusively in terms of air travel. This is misleading, since travel to contiguous countries can be, and is, conducted by passenger car, bus, and train. In Europe, where the distance between cities tends to be less, air travel is far less important. For long distances, air travel dominates international travel. In 1977, 434,000 million passenger miles were flown by scheduled airlines, according to data provided by the International Air Transport Association.

The desire to travel is an indirect desire—the result of a desire or need to be somewhere else for either business or pleasurable reasons. Because of the indirect quality of the demand for air travel, it follows that the number of potential passengers depends upon circumstances largely outside the control of the international airlines. With the exception of any ability to attract business away from ground transportation or actually to induce someone to travel by lowering fares, airlines compete among themselves for a given volume of business. A second important feature of airline operation (and profitability) is the need for carriers to use as much of their available scheduled capacity as possible. Unused space is potential revenue lost forever, because the additional costs of carrying an extra passenger are negligible. As a result of this characteristic, airlines adopt the same marketing strategy as hotels and try to discriminate among passengers by means of market segmentation. This practice is endemic to the tourism industry, but it is not inherently exploitative since it may enable a service to be offered that could not cover its cost if market segmentation were not practised. For a lucid description of the mechanics of market segmentation, see Phillips, 1965, pp.310-312. It also has the problem that some persons who have an urgent need to travel find ways to take advantage of the subsidized rates.

International Regulation.   The fact that airline profits are very sensitive to capacity-utilization rates (load factors) can lead to cutthroat competition among airlines as they progressively try to reduce all prices and particularly to broaden the coverage of the subsidized fares, so that an excessive number of "urgent travelers" fly at subsidized rates. Under these conditions of competition, many airlines are forced out of business, and the stronger carriers survive and make a satisfactory profit. To prevent this kind of excessive competition with all that such conditions might entail for the shaving of costs on such vital aspects as aircraft maintenance, the airlines combined to form a supervisory body that would oversee the setting of fares as well as ensuring that the industry would obey reasonable safety standards. This body is the *International Air Transport Association* (IATA). Its operations are described by O'Connor (1978), and its pricing practices are examined in detail by Straszheim (1969), who concludes that "the IATA fare structure does not conform to rational pricing," but "neither IATA as a rate-making body nor its administrative procedures should be held primarily accountable." Although IATA does have cartel-like over-tones in the sense that it involves price-setting and even market-sharing arrangements, these attributes were built into the system, not by the airlines, which are the ostensible members of IATA, but by the governments in the process of agreeing to the exchange of routes. The fact that the governments are, commonly, the owners of the national international air carriers is more than a coincidence.

ROUTE AUTHORIZATION.   One of the fundamental aspects of international air travel is the penetration of national space by foreign aircraft. At the 1944 Chicago Conference, which shaped the international airline industry in the postwar world, the Five Freedoms were promulgated so that airlines could fly and land freely without prior consent. The complicated question (the Fifth Freedom) was the degree to which an airline flying from its country of origin to a destination country could stop and pick up and discharge passengers and cargo at intermediate points. The Fifth Freedom would allow aircraft to conduct such operations freely, subject only to the requirement that through traffic from origin to destination and back was sufficient to make the service economically viable.

The idea of an open exchange of routes was voted down by the participating nations, and they voted to exchange routes by specific negotiation between pairs of nations. This decision made national governments an integral part of the international air transportation business, and the role is enhanced by the fact that nearly all international airlines are government-owned and government-operated or government-subsidized.

The exchange of routes came to be patterned after the first bilateral agreement of its kind reached between the United Kingdom and the United States in Bermuda in 1946. The main clauses of the Bermuda Agreement were as follows:

1.   Routes are to be exchanged, and the exchange shall be negotiated between governments.

2.   There shall be no restrictions placed on the frequency of the scheduled services nor any other limitations on the capacity offered on the agreed route.

3. Fifth Freedom traffic shall be negotiated between governments subject to the proviso that the capacity operated shall be related to

   a. traffic requirements between the country of origin and the country of ultimate destination of the traffic;

   b. the requirements of through-airline operation; and

   c. the traffic requirements of the area through which the airline passes after taking account of local and regional services.

4. Rates are to be controlled.

The key conditions were the second and the fourth clauses. No capacity limitations were to be imposed, but fare tariffs had to have the approval of both governments. In many "Bermudas" between pairs of European nations, capacity was to be predetermined by governments as were prices.

The actual setting of the fares was accomplished under the auspices of IATA. This process required unanimous approval of the schedule of fares by all members of the regional conference. The unanimity rule has resulted in periods of so-called open rates, when no officially agreed upon rate structure existed. These periods took place most frequently when technological breakthroughs were tending to reduce costs for efficient carriers with modern equipment in periods when excess capacity was common.

In 1976 a second Bermuda Agreement was signed between the United Kingdom and the United States. It calls for preconsultation on schedules and capacity, and if governments do not agree, then the matter goes to "consultation," where the two governments attempt to achieve an agreement. O'Connor (1978) describes the new agreement as saying to the international airlines: "Decide what you'd like your frequencies and capacity to be, but remember that before you operate them the foreign government has a right to challenge them." The trend seems to be toward greater, rather than less, governmental control.

NATIONAL CARRIERS. National carriers do earn foreign exchange for the country or at least save it being paid to other nations' carriers, but there is no evidence that national carriers are always a good investment from the point of view of the owning nations. International air transportation is a highly technological industry, and the aircraft are manufactured only in technologically advanced nations. Other nations must import the capital equipment. These foreign-exchange costs and the foreign and domestic costs of operations can mean that the existence of a national carrier is an expensive luxury. This situation is likely to apply particularly to the national airlines of the poorer nations, for which countries it serves mainly as a boost to the national image and the stature of politicians. In poor countries, national airlines use up scarce technicians and absorb many hours of highly paid and skilled civil servants at international conferences. If, in addition, the operations of the airlines themselves are not efficient, their cost structures can result in certain routes having excessively high fares as governments seek to reduce the need for subsidy by maintaining high fare levels.

On the other hand, some airlines are efficiently run irrespective of the national income of the owning nation and earn a satisfactory return on invested capital. Where the nation has a thriving tourism business, an international carrier should be a good investment, since the market will be large enough to allow the airline to achieve a satisfactory rate of capacity utilization. The airline's promotional and fare policies can be integrated with those of the tourist industry, and presence at international fare-setting conferences will allow the nation to ensure that its tourist destinations are not put at a cost-disadvantage.

SCHEDULED AND NONSCHEDULED AIRLINES.   Scheduled airlines are those that publish and maintain departure schedules. Nonscheduled airlines are those that fly aircraft over routes at the instigation of the traveler. The services for which so-called non-scheds are best known are charter services. On the main international routes, non-scheds have provided severe price competition for the scheduled airlines and have exerted downward pressure on prices and fares. The charters could be assured of a high load factor and could offer prices well below those permitted to scheduled airlines in the 1960s and early 1970s. Chartered airlines still do an important amount of business (particularly in Europe, where fares tend to be higher and where group tours combine resort vacations with charter travel), but they became less important on major routes as the scheduled airlines increased their market segmentation. Scheduled airlines will also provide charters, on occasion, but frequently they are using their equipment so tightly that they cannot find an aircraft available.

TECHNOLOGY TRADE

DEFINITIONS.   Technology trade comprises three kinds of transactions that give rise to nonfactor payments: the use in a country of proprietary technology owned by a foreign resident; the provision of consultancy and technical services; and transborder data analysis.

When a citizen of one (home) country (usually a corporation) owns a piece of technology for which no substitute is available in a foreign country, the foreign country can acquire that technology in one of two ways. The knowledge can be utilized by a subsidiary of the owner of the technology, in which event a multinational corporation will have established a subsidiary. Alternatively, the technology can be made available to a local firm in the foreign country by a *licensing agreement*. It is probable that a licensing agreement with a specified rate of payment will be established for both possibilities. The owner of the technology will receive a royalty at a specified price per unit manufactured and sold. The rates may vary but probably will not; they are likely to be lower for the subsidiary corporation only if it is wholly owned. When a licensing arrangement is worked out with an unaffiliated foreign corporation, the licensor will frequently restrict the area in which the end product can be sold in order to avoid competition between the licensee and the licensor in third countries. As can be seen from Exhibit 1, the U.S. international accounts distinguish between payments made to and received from affiliated and nonaffiliated foreign firms.

The provision of technical services, including managerial and engineering consultancy, also distinguishes between affiliated and unaffiliated foreign firms. Frequently the provision of technical consultancy is associated with the transfer of technology under a licensing arrangement or with the institution of sales and distribution arrangements. The sale of straightforward managerial consulting does take place, but these services tend to be less important. A distinctive branch of international trade in technological services is the administration and development of public services in the newly rich oil-exporting countries. Nigeria, for example, has employed the India Railway to develop its railroad, KLM to upgrade its airline's reservations systems, and ITT to set up a modern communications network.

Transborder data flow analyses involve the transmission of information on markets and people in one country to a second country for analysis. Usually the country in which the analysis is performed has a technological lead in data processing (often from the availability of ultralarge computers). Frequently these analyses are merely a special kind of production sharing within a multinational corporation. There is no reliable data on the value of transborder-data-flow analyses, but a crude estimate given by the Canadian Department of Communications puts the 1978 value of Canadian imports from the United States at between $200 and $300 million.

DETERMINANTS. When an industrial nation holds a technological lead in one activity, it is quite likely to be laggard in another sector. A nation is likely, therefore, to be simultaneously an exporter and an importer of technology. This simultaneity can occur within a single industry, as different corporations have different emphases and technological achievements. One of the important aspects of technology trade is the degree to which such trade (and its consequences) results from trade within multinational corporations or between arm's-length participants (licensing.) Several factors affect this decision. The first question is whether the owner of the technology is big enough and well enough supplied with managerial talent to be able to create a foreign subsidiary. The second factor is the perceived risk (of exporporiation, for example) of acquiring real assets (a production subsidiary) in a foreign country. Only if the corporation and the prospective host country both satisfy the necessary standards will foreign investment be a realistic alternative.

If those standards are met, there is a natural predilection in this modern age for establishing foreign subsidiaries in preference to licensing. Multinational corporations are capable of generating cost-reducing efficiencies by operating several national units under the control of a single, cohesive management: flexibility in production planning and better production/sales relationships are two aspects of these efficiency gains. In contradistinction, licensing arrangements have several disadvantages. The agreements are costly to negotiate and to renegotiate but when the technology is expected to be a one-shot item (as distinct from a forerunner of succeeding waves of innovation emanating from the first seminal idea), licensing is a more probable way of using the technology in a foreign market. The most important aspect of the licensing/foreign-investment decision is which set of arrangements best allows control over the proprietary knowledge to be retained. Technology is the return on expenditure on research and development, and any corporation will attempt to ensure that it gets full payment for that investment. Stephen Magee (1977) stressed this need to appropriate the return due on earlier investment in research and development and allocates to that factor, the crucial role in the foreign-investment decision. If the knowledge is not patentable, it must be safeguarded either within a foreign subsidiary or the know-how will not be exploited abroad. Certainly the retention of the proprietary aspect of the knowledge is of primary importance, since its loss could endanger the owner's home market position as well as any returns earned in foreign markets. Licensing will, therefore, only be used where patent protection exists and is enforceable.

The provision of management consultancy services will ordinarily take place between nations with significant disparities in managerial know-how. Corporations in developing or poor nations may use the services of management-consultant firms located in industrial nations. Normally, sheer managerial know-how—unconnected with the manufacture or sale abroad of a specific, technology-intensive product—is not a service in which one developed country can be expected to have a sizeable advantage over another. Even if small advantages exist, they are likely to be neutralized by the impact of cultural differences on managerial practices.

IMPEDIMENTS TO TECHNOLOGY TRADE.   Impediments to technology trade usually manifest themselves originally in the readiness (or lack of it) of a sovereign nation to allow a multinational to establish a subsidiary within its boundaries or to permit one of its own firms to undertake a commitment to pay out foreign exchange for the use of licensed technology. The host nation, particularly a developing or semideveloped nation, will retain control mainly by virtue of its control over the use of foreign exchange. Royalty agreements almost invariably need governmental approval in developing nations. In practice, the payments of royalties for the use of technology and for management-consultancy services are usually accorded more-favorable access to foreign exchange than are the profits of foreign subsidiaries. More importantly, royalties and fees are costs for firms, and profits are taxed. (This tax aspect explains why most multinationals will charge royalties at the full rate to their own wholly owned subsidiaries.) Frequently profits are taxed at differential rates according to whether they are reinvested in the host country or repatriated to the parent concern.

The most-serious impediments to technology trade pertain to transborder-data-flow analyses. Many European nations are leaders in the passage of legislation prohibiting the transmission of data out of their countries. Developing nations are beginning to follow their lead. The European laws prohibit the transfer of data across national boundaries unless assurance is provided by the laws of the receiving country that the data will be protected from possible abuses. In this context, protection means legislation similar to their own. There are several reasons underlying the passage of this kind of legislation: Some are economic and other social. The most important are lost opportunities for employment and the failure to establish a modern industry, balance-of-trade concerns, fear of loss of access to national data, cultural infringement and social vulnerability. The economic reasons are self-evident. The social reasons derive from a fear that national data in the hands of foreigners could lead to a weakening of the national defense capability, that citizens might be identified to third nonfriendly nations, and that foreign high-powered marketing techniques that are ''culturally repugnant'' might be based on the transferred data. Modern societies rely heavily on computerized data analysis, and a country can perceive itself as socially vulnerable according to the degree to which data pertaining to it are handled by computers in another country.

Although legislation limiting the flow of data across national boundaries can have potentially serious effects on any independent firms that may provide the data analysis, the major impact is likely to be felt by multinational corporations. The ability of these giant corporations to plan the integration of production (particularly) and sales on a worldwide basis will be seriously impaired if not destroyed. The efficiency gains that derive from the multinational corporate form could be drastically reduced. Moreover, if the intent of the European and developing nations is primarily one of economic protection, the passage of ''protective legislation'' by the United States would probably be countered by further legislation. In all cases such as these it is virtually impossible to determine the degree to which mercantilist, economic protectionism is masquerading under the more elevated guise of "social concern."

ENTERTAINMENT AND EDUCATION

TYPES OF TRANSACTION.   Little is reported on the volume of international trade in this category of services. Such transactions on which coverage exists are reported under "other private services." Some data included in this category are provided to the U.S. government, at least, on the promise that they will not be individually identifiable. Moreover, given the multinational character of many of the major entities in the publishing and entertainment worlds, many transactions are likely to be *intracorporate* and therefore more difficult to identify.

This category includes authors' royalties for books published, for plays produced, and for music performed abroad. The books, at least, can be either educational or entertaining. The big item in this category is television programs and movies, and, to a somewhat lesser degree, royalties on recordings.

The movie industry is particularly interesting since it set the pattern that many other businesses in this category have followed. Despite producing a tangible product, the industry chose to rent, rather than to sell, that product in order to retain copyright over the contents of the canister of film. The television industry has retained the practice.

The net earnings of the movie and television industries are rental fees acquired from foreigners less rental fees paid to foreign companies. But there is a further ingredient. When a film company goes on location abroad, it reports its payments to foreign photographers, actors, and extras as purchases of foreign services, together with any expenses incurred by the company or by its American staff. What is reported to the U.S. government is the total contribution of the industry to the American international accounts.

The products of all movie and television industries are discriminated against abroad. This discrimination, usually in favor of a home industry but on occasion enforced simply for the preservation of scarce foreign exchange, takes many forms. Among developed nations, the most usual forms are screen quotas on the showing of foreign programs, and discriminatory taxes. In some countries, there is a government monopoly over trade in film, and still other countries enforce local work requirements. As in the case of transborder-data-flow analyses, it is impossible to separate out the narrow economic protective arrangements from those designed to preserve the home industry as a contributor to the nation's culture and cultural heritage.

When actors visit a foreign country and are permitted to perform, their earnings, net of local expenditures, constitute factor-service payments. The degree to which authors' and composers' royalties are paid depends upon the actual distribution arrangements. If the foreign author's book is produced abroad and imported, there is no international trade in services. Trade in services takes place only if a book by a foreign author is produced locally and the author paid a royalty by the local printer. Arrangements such as these are normally screened by governments in developing countries insofar as they entail a commitment to pay out foreign exchange.

SUMMARY.   International trade in the categories of service considered in this section of the *Handbook* suffer from a lack of reliable data on their importance. With the possible exception of tourism and passenger transportation, the many different types of activity that fall under "international trade in services" have been neglected and do not receive adequate statistical reporting. It is quite likely that many of the activities are simply of insufficient quantitative importance to warrant the costs of data generation. Although an awareness of manifold impediments to international trade in services exists, the many impeded activities are possibly all so small that great efforts to negotiate away the impediments may not be worthwhile. There is an obvious danger: There is a lack of firm ground in an argument that the impediments are not worth removing because of the lack of size of the activities when no reliable data on the size of the activities exist. But international trade in services is by its very nature less tangible or more slippery than international trade in commodities and, for this reason alone, less easily subject to the removal of impediments.

SOURCES AND SUGGESTED REFERENCES

Annals of Tourism Research.

Bryden, J. M. *Tourism and Development.* Cambridge: Cambridge University Press, 1973.

Gray, H. P. *International Travel: International Trade.* Lexington, MA: Lexington Books, 1970.

Griffiths, B. *Invisible Barriers to Invisible Trade.* London: Macmillan, 1975.

International Air Transport Association. *World Air Transport Statistics, 1978.* Montreal: IATA, 1979.

International Monetary Fund. *Balance of Payments Yearbook.* Washington, D.C.: IMF, 1972-1978.

International Monetary Fund. *Balance of Payments Yearbook. Supplement .* Washington, D.C.: IMF, 1978.

International Monetary Fund. *Balance of Payments Yearbook. Supplement.* Washington, D.C.: IMF, 1979.

Little, J. S. "International Travel in the U.S. Balance of Payments," *New England Economic Review,* May/June 1980, pp. 42-55.

Magee, S. "Multinational Corporations, the Industry Technology Cycle and Development," *Journal of World Trade Law,* Vol. XI (1977), pp. 297-321.

McIntosh, R. W. *Tourism: Principles, Practices, Philosophies.* Columbus, OH: Battelle, 1972.

O'Connor, W. E. *An Introduction to Airline Economics.* New York: Praeger, 1978.

Phillips, Jr., C. F. *The Economics of Regulation.* Homewood, IL: Richard B. Irwin, 1965.

Straszheim, M. E. *The International Airline Industry.* Washington, D.C.: Brookings Institution, 1969.

U.S. Department of Commerce. *Survey of Current Business.* Washington, D.C.: U.S. Department of Commerce, May and June 1980.

SECTION **15**

STATE TRADING

CONTENTS

THE NATURE AND EXTENT OF
STATE TRADING   3

Definition of State Trading   3
Extent of State Trading   3

ORGANIZATION OF STATE TRADING
IN MARKET ECONOMIES   4

Direct Sales and Purchases by the State   4
    Arms sales   4
    Government import monopolies   4
    Government procurement   4
    Price preferences in government
    purchasing   5
    Miscellaneous government
    restrictions in favor of domestic
    suppliers   5
Sales and Purchases by State-Owned or
State-Controlled Companies   6
    Corporations implementing
    government functions   6
    State-owned businesses   6
    State trading companies   7
State Marketing Boards   7
    Marketing boards in exporting
    countries   8
    Marketing boards in importing
    countries   8

OBJECTIVES AND ECONOMIC
CONSEQUENCES OF STATE TRADING   8

External Objectives of State Trading   8
    Improvements in international
    bargaining power and terms of trade   9
    Export expansion   9
    Fulfillment of international obligations   9
    Linking of trade with politics   10
Domestic Objectives of State Trading   10
    Protection of domestic industry   10
    Price and distribution policies   10
    Government revenue   10
    Health and public security   10

Economic Consequences of State
Trading   11
    State trading as a trade restriction   11
    Discrimination   11
    Bilateralism   11
    Monopolization of markets   12
    Inefficiency   12

LEGAL ASPECTS OF STATE TRADING   12

State Trading and Commercial Law   12
    Immunity from taxation   12
    Immunity from regulation   14
    Immunity from the jurisdiction of
    courts   14
State Trading and International
Organizations   14
    State trading and GATT   15
    GATT and centrally planned
    economies   16
    State trading and the European
    Community   16
    State trading and EFTA   16

THE ORGANIZATION OF ECONOMIC
ACTIVITY IN COMMUNIST
COUNTRIES   17

The State and the Communist Party   17
    The Communist party   17
    The government   17
Organization of Industry   17
The Organization of Agriculture   18
Planning and Plan Implementation   18
    Plan construction   19
    Reforms in the economic mechanism   19
    Managerial incentives   20
Money, Banking, and Prices   20
    The banking system   20
    Prices   20

FOREIGN TRADE IN THE CENTRALLY PLANNED ECONOMY   21

The Organization of Foreign Trade   21
  The ministry of foreign trade   21
  Foreign-trade organizations   21
  The foreign-trade bank   22
Convertibility, Exchange Rates, and Price Equalization   22
The Planning of Trade Flows   23

TRADE AMONG COMMUNIST COUNTRIES   23

The Council for Mutual Economic Assistance   23
  The organization of the CMEA   23
  Plan coordination in the CMEA   24
Economic Integration in the CMEA   24
  Specialization agreements   24
  International economic organizations   25
  Large-scale international projects   25
Foreign-Trade Prices in the CMEA   25
  Hard goods and soft goods   25
International Monetary Relations in the CMEA   26
  The intra-CMEA payments system   26
  Convertible currency trade within the CMEA   26
  Capital flows in the CMEA   26

THE POLITICAL ECONOMY OF TRADE WITH COMMUNIST COUNTRIES   27

Policy Objectives in East-West Trade   27
  Economic warfare   27
  Linkage of trade and politics   27
  Reinforcement of mutual dependencies   27
Export Controls   28
The Export Administration Act   28
  General license for exports   28
  Validated licenses for exports   28
  Transactions subject to licensing   28
International Restrictions on Exports   29
COCOM   29
Import certificate/delivery verification   29
Credit Restrictions   30
  Johnson Debt Default Act   30
  Export-Import Bank   30
  Commodity Credit Corporation   31
  Overseas Private Investment Corporation   31
Credit Availability in Other Western Countries   31
  Official credit supports   31

The Berne Union   31
Borrowings in the Eurodollar market   31
Convertible-currency debts of the Communist countries   32
Import Restrictions   32
  U.S. restrictions   32
  Import restrictions in Western European countries   32
Dumping   33
  Bilateral treaties   33
  The GATT solution   33
  United States market disruption and antidumping regulations for Communist countries   33

COMMERCIAL TRANSACTIONS BETWEEN THE EAST AND THE WEST   34

Trade Transactions with Planned Economies   34
  Trade decision makers in planned economies   34
  Building markets in communist countries   35
Negotiations   36
Contracts   36
  Choice of law and arbitration   36
  Delivery   37
  Force majeure   37
  Export licenses   37
  Inspection, testing, and guarantees   37
  Penalties   37
  Contract compliance   38
Payments in East-West Trade   38
  Letters of credit   38
  Switch transactions   38
  Barter and counterpurchase agreements   38
The Transfer of Technology   39
  Scientific cooperation agreements   39
  Licensing   39
Industrial Cooperation and Joint Ventures   40
  Licenses and turnkey plants   40
  Subcontracting   40
  Coproduction and specialization   40
Foreign Direct Investment Between Capitalist and Communist Countries   41
  Joint ventures   41
  Tripartite joint ventures   41
  Communist investments in the West   41

SOURCES AND SUGGESTED REFERENCES   42

Additional References   45

STATE TRADING

Josef C. Brada

THE NATURE AND EXTENT OF STATE TRADING

DEFINITION OF STATE TRADING. A definition of state trading consistent with international usage as contained in the Havana Charter is that state trading consists of those international transactions wherein a state or state-controlled enterprise receives or passes title to the goods traded. This definition includes transactions undertaken between an organ of government and foreign persons, as might occur in the purchase abroad of provisions for an embassy or state-to-state transactions, such as the sale of arms and munitions by one government to another. It also explicitly includes transactions undertaken by corporations if those corporations are owned or controlled by the government, as are the foreign-trade corporations of the centrally planned economies of Eastern Europe. This definition of state trading has been criticized as being too narrow in two respects. Allen (1959) argues that the definition of state trading should be extended to those situations where foreign transactions are in the hands of private individuals whose freedom of choice is so circumscribed by government restrictions that they cannot but make decisions that reflect the wishes of the government. Viner (1944) argues that cases where foreign trade is in the hands of private individuals but the domestic market for the commodity is monopsonized, monopolized, or otherwise strongly influenced by the government also effectively constitute state trading. Such a broadening of the definition of state trading would have an important impact on the assessment of the extent of state trading in international trade. For example, the export of grain from the United States would be considered state trading under the broader definition but not under the narrow one. This is because the United States government negotiates the terms of the transaction with the foreign buyer, but in most cases it leaves the execution of the transaction to private traders.

EXTENT OF STATE TRADING. In view of the lack of a precise boundary between state trading and private transactions, any attempt to give a quantitative estimate of the importance of state trading in world trade must be viewed as tentative and highly dependent on the precise definition of state trading employed. Kostecki ("State Trading," 1978) estimated that between 20 and 25 percent of the world's trade was carried out by means of state trading in the 1970s. He further reported that in the developed market economies, state trading was not the predominant means of carrying out foreign trade. Nevertheless, state trading accounted for from 3 to 25 percent of either the exports or imports of a sample of developed market economies in the 1970s. Among the developing countries, state trading is much more prevalent, accounting for from 10 percent of Brazilian foreign trade to 90–100 percent of Egyptian trade. In the centrally planned communist countries, foreign trade is a monopoly of the state, and virtually all foreign-trade transactions are carried out by means of state trading.

Although examples of state-traded commodities range from handicraft items to sophisticated military hardware, there are a number of commodity groups in which state trading is relatively extensive. Among these are arms and munitions, international transportation, agricultural commodities (especially grains), and petroleum.

ORGANIZATION OF STATE TRADING IN MARKET ECONOMIES

DIRECT SALES AND PURCHASES BY THE STATE. In all market economies, the government plays a significant role both as the purchaser of goods and services and as their supplier. The economic role of the state in international trade is quite similar.

Arms Sales. The U.S. Arms Control and Disarmament Agency (1974) reported that "virtually all conventional arms transfers are transacted on a government to government basis or are otherwise controlled by governments." Exports of arms from the United States are governed by the International Security Assistance and Arms Export Control Act. The act subjects private arms exports to licensing by the Department of State and prohibits private sales in excess of $25 million unless destined for member countries of NATO, Australia, Japan, or New Zealand or unless they are part of an approved coproduction scheme. Consequently the bulk of arms exports from the United States is carried out by the Department of Defense, which either sells arms from its own stocks or takes title to arms and munitions from U.S. arms contractors and resells them to foreign governments. The U.S. Senate Banking Committee (1978) reported that the Department of Defense accounted for about 90 percent of U.S. arms exports in the 1970s. The governments of other industrialized countries are similarly involved in arms sales.

The direct involvement of the government in the arms trade reflects the unique characteristics of such transactions. First, the export of arms and services has an important effect on national security, both by assuring the military strength of allies and by denying military supplies to enemies. Arms sales also play an important role in diplomatic relations between states. Finally, the technological complexity of modern weapons often creates a need for extensive training of the military personnel of the receiving country by the armed forces of the exporting country, thus creating a need for extensive government-to-government arrangements.

Government Import Monopolies. Occasionally government organs are charged with the responsibility for importing goods for resale to domestic users. Domestic sales may be made by private retailers who purchase the commodity from the government or by the importing agency. In Japan, for example, government ministries have a monopoly on the importation of alcohol and of opium for medical purposes.

Government Procurement. In market economies, government purchases of goods and services account for 15–40 percent of GNP. Thus the government is potentially a large purchaser of imported goods. However, in the procurement of goods, many governments discriminate against foreign suppliers according to Baldwin (1970).

One form of discrimination is the use of selective or single tenders or of negotiated contracts. Although in the United States public bidding is commonplace, many other countries restrict the number of firms invited to bid on government contracts. For example Dam (1970) reported that only 1 percent of government contracts in the United Kingdom was open to public bidding.

Under selective or single tenders, the government does not advertise for bids. Rather a preselected firm or group of firms is invited to submit bids. Since foreign firms are less likely to be known to government officials or to be on the list of vendors from which the government seeks bids, they tend to be excluded from government contracts. Public bidding, although having the potential of giving foreign vendors equal access to government contracts, can be subverted by the government's failure to advertise widely for bids or by the imposition of very short deadlines for the submission of bids.

Price Preferences in Government Purchasing.   Many governments have formal or informal decision rules for the evaluation of bids that favor domestic vendors in the letting of government contracts. The U.S. Senate Committee on Finance (1973) reported that one common discriminatory mechanism is the price preference for domestic bidders. With such a mechanism, domestic bidders are selected over foreign bidders unless the foreign bid is lower by some minimum percentage of the price than the domestic bid. Examples of preferences currently in force are 6 percent in the United States (50 percent for Department of Defense contracts), 15 percent in Norway, and 8 percent in Greece. Some countries impose additional preferences if domestic bidders are from regions of high unemployment or are small businesses. It should be noted that such preferences are often the minimum that must be accorded to domestic producers, and government agencies may impose higher preferences. On the positive side, most preference legislation permits preferences to be waived if such waiver is in the public interest.

Miscellaneous Government Restrictions in Favor of Domestic Suppliers.
Governments also employ a variety of nonprice restrictions against foreign bidders. Among these are the following:

1. Residence requirements that permit only residents to bid on government contracts.
2. Use of administrative discretion to disallow foreign bids.
3. Exclusion of foreigners from bidding on projects in certain sectors of the economy.
4. Quotas that reserve a certain percentage of government contracts to domestic suppliers.
5. Domestic content requirements that specify a certain percentage of domestic content for government contracts or that specify that certain inputs must be of domestic origin.
6. Use of specifications and standards that are more difficult or expensive for foreign firms to meet.

SALES AND PURCHASES BY STATE-OWNED OR STATE-CONTROLLED COMPANIES. In many market economies government enterprise accounts for a significant proportion of domestic economic activity and foreign trade. States have two principal motives for organizing state-owned economic activities in the corporate form rather than through direct government activity. One motive is to impose accountability on the managers of such enterprises by giving them some degree of financial and decision-making autonomy. The second is to place the state on a more equal footing with other market participants, since corporate entities are more easily sued than are governments.

Corporations Implementing Government Functions. Some government corporations are established to provide goods or services that would not be supplied by private firms or would be supplied on terms other than those desired by the government. Consequently the policy decision of the government to provide such goods or services entails the creation of a government corporation. The provision of international credit and credit guarantees by the Export-Import Bank of the United States and by its counterparts in other industrialized countries is one example of obvious relevance to international trade. Another example is the sale of foreign exchange and precious metals by central banks where such banks are in fact corporate entities.

Corporations formed to implement government policy do not attempt to operate on a profit-maximizing basis even though businesslike procedures may be employed. Rather they are often run at a loss so that objectives such as export promotion, exchange stability, and so forth may be met.

State-Owned Businesses. Governments also own or control enterprises that produce goods and services in direct competition with private firms. Nationalized firms, such as Renault in France and British Leyland Inc. in the United Kingdom are two examples in the automobile industry. National enterprises are particularly common in international transportation and communications. Many airlines are government owned, as are shipping companies in developed and, according to Strange and Holland (1976), increasingly in developing countries.

State-owned corporations constituted to engage in business are much more likely to base decisions on profit maximization and commercial principles employed by privately owned competitors than are state corporations charged with implementing state policy. Nevertheless, both in their import and export activities such corporations may distort international trade in the following ways:

1. Government firms may have a competitive advantage due to the waiver of tax or tariff payments to the government.

2. Government firms may have access to government loans or subsidies not available to private firms.

3. Government firms may follow goals such as export promotion or import substitution, maintenance of high employment, national technical or economic prestige, and so forth at the expense of profit maximization.

4. Government firms may discriminate against foreign customers or foreign suppliers of inputs.

5. Government procurement policies may favor state-owned firms.

State Trading Companies. A special type of government business is the state trading company that produces nothing, but merely acts as an importer or exporter under government ownership or control. Often such trading companies have a monopoly over trade in a commodity, but even if they do not, it may be assumed that their decisions have significant impact on the behavior of competing private traders.

State trading companies organized mainly for the importation of goods may be divided into two categories. Some operate so as to assure the domestic supply of vital goods at favorable prices. Examples of such companies drawn from a compilation for the U.S. Senate Committee on Finance (Subcommittee on International Trade, (1971), include companies for the importation of fishing tackle and pharmaceuticals in Norway and petroleum and petroleum products in Brazil, Sri Lanka, and Finland. Other import monopolies exist as part of a state monopoly designed to limit the use or consumption of harmful substances. Tobacco, alcohol, and matches are common examples of such commodities.

Trading companies engaged in exporting may usefully be divided into two categories. One category consists of those firms exporting the output of indigenous producers. An objective of such companies may be export promotion in situations where domestic producers are unlikely to be able to export on their own account. An apt example is a trading company organized by the Indian government to export Indian handicrafts. Other export monopolies aim at restricting exports to keep international prices high. Finally, the export monopoly may be established as an alternate to an export tariff by buying at low prices from domestic producers and selling at high prices abroad.

The second category of state trading company is the national petroleum or mineral company. In some cases these companies actually produce output and thus should be classified as state businesses. However, many such companies lack the technical knowledge and marketing network to exploit and export domestic resources. A common solution is to form a partnership with a multinational firm whereby the state company receives part or all of the output and then sells it to the multinational. Adeniji (1977) gives some examples of such arrangements with reference to Nigeria. As the technical and commercial skills of such state firms increase, it is likely that they will evolve into true state businesses.

STATE MARKETING BOARDS. A unique form of state trading company is the marketing board. Such boards are most frequently encountered in trade in agricultural commodities, although they are also employed to trade in raw materials. Some boards, such as the Federal Wheat Administration of Switzerland, are organs of the state. Others take a corporate form with either the state or, less frequently, an organization of producers as owner. In all cases the ultimate authority rests with the government and is usually exercised by the ministry for agriculture or analogous organ.

Marketing boards have two common objectives. The first is to assure stable markets and adequate domestic supplies of food and, in the case of exporting countries, to dispose of exportable surpluses on the most favorable of terms. The second objective of marketing boards is to employ international markets to support domestic agricultural policies. Warley (1976) concluded that "the core of agricultural policy in most countries is the redistribution of income toward farmers by bolstering the price of products they produce."

Marketing Boards in Exporting Countries.   Government policies designed to maintain artificially high prices for agricultural products in exporting countries, stimulate domestic production, reduce domestic consumption, and increase exportable surpluses. In many cases, however, such exportable surpluses cannot be sold abroad by private sellers because the domestic price is higher than the international price. Consequently the state marketing board purchases the commodity at the higher domestic prices and sells it on the world market at the lower international price. Thus, for example, the Australian Wheat Board generally sells wheat to domestic users at higher prices than those charged foreign purchasers, according to the International Wheat Council (1970). Losses thus incurred by the board are subsidized by the government. The objective of the board is to manage domestic stocks and international sales so as to dispose of surpluses on the most favorable terms.

Although by the very nature of agricultural policies marketing boards generally sell for less abroad than at home, circumstances may cause them to reverse such a policy. For example, international prices rose above support prices for wheat in Australia and Canada in 1973. According to Grennes *et al.* (1978) the marketing boards in those two countries chose to stabilize the domestic market by selling wheat to domestic users at prices 40–50 percent lower than prices charged to foreigners.

Marketing boards are also employed to implement exporting countries' commitments under international commodity agreements. In such agreements, members agree to limit their exports so as to support the international price. Kravis (1968) and Kofi (1977) illustrate the possibilities for employing marketing boards to meet the needs of members of such agreements.

Marketing Boards in Importing Countries.   Marketing boards in importing countries seek to assure stable supplies of agricultural products, hopefully at favorable terms by means of bulk buying, and to support domestic agricultural policy. Since, as in exporting countries, the objective of agricultural policy is to keep prices high, the benefits of low international prices (and of any international market power possessed by the marketing board) are not passed on to consumers. Instead, the marketing board sells only enough to meet domestic needs at the government's support price.

In certain circumstances, government policy may call for marketing boards to subsidize the importation of agricultural commodities. The Swiss Federal Wheat Administration has followed a policy of low prices for imports of grain in order to keep food costs low. In most countries, however, subsidization was a temporary phenomenon of the early 1970s, when international prices of many agricultural staples rose above support levels. Grennes *et al.* (1978) reported that the Japan Food Agency responded to such an increase in the price of grain by subsidizing grain imports. Such pro-import policies are, however, to be viewed as temporary expedients in most importing countries.

OBJECTIVES AND ECONOMIC CONSEQUENCES OF STATE TRADING

EXTERNAL OBJECTIVES OF STATE TRADING.   Governments may engage in state trading either because it can achieve improvements in the conduct of international trade and in the gains to the nation from such trade or because they desire outcomes that could not be achieved by private traders. In a number of cases the same objectives could be achieved by the imposition of tariffs and quotas whereas in others the objectives of the state can only be met by means of state trading.

Improvements in International Bargaining Power and Terms of Trade. When a state monopolizes the trade in a particular commodity, it may hope to improve the nation's gains from trade. By controlling the volume of imports or exports of a commodity, the state hopes to influence international prices in such a way as to raise the price of exportables or to lower the price of imports. Second, because the state is a bulk buyer or seller it may hope to obtain terms on its transactions that would not be available to private firms. In particular, the state may hope to obtain better prices, longer-term contracts, and priority in access to supplies. Finally, by acting as the sole buyer or seller the state may hope to discriminate among foreign markets. Acting as a seller, for example, the state would charge higher prices on those markets where demand is inelastic and lower prices on markets where demand is elastic. Private traders, on the other hand would, through competition, equalize prices in all markets. Although the first of these objectives could be met by general tariffs or quantitative restrictions on trade, the latter two objectives could not.

Export Expansion. State involvement in trade for purposes of export promotion exists for two purposes. The first consists of the use of state trading to expand exports beyond the volume that private profit maximization would achieve. The establishment of export-import banks and similar institutions is an example of such an impulse.

It is, however, difficult to draw the line between such mercantilistic impulses and legitimate efforts on the part of the state to correct market failures that lead private traders to trade amounts that are suboptimal from a social standpoint. In some cases, cartelization of international markets may limit the access of domestic producers to international markets, and the power of the state may be effective in obtaining access to such markets. An example of such state involvement is provided by Strange and Holland (1976), who report the international shipping conferences may not operate in Brazil unless the Brazilian national shipping company is a full member. A more common form of market failure, particularly in developing countries, is the existence of many small producers. Since, according to the evidence of Seev Hirsh and Zvi Adar and others, large firms are better able to bear the risks and costs of exporting than small firms, the volume of trade may be suboptimal unless the government establishes a trading corporation to assume the risks and high overhead that would be too expensive for small independent producers.

Fulfillment of International Obligations. States may wish to exercise direct control over foreign trade flows to better fulfill their international obligations. One example is the establishment of state trading companies to organize the importation of goods obtained through foreign assistance or relief programs. Many countries participate in commodity agreements that are implemented by assigning members export quotas. Under such circumstances the government may view a state trading company as preferable to quantitative controls such as export licenses. Finally, a number of countries, particularly developed ones, have organized state trading companies in order to facilitate their trade with the communist countries.

Linking of Trade with Politics.   States may seek to link trade with politics in two ways. The first is to use trade as a device to aid in the achievement of their foreign-policy objectives. Examples include discriminatory selling or buying in order to strengthen the economies of allies or to create dependence on the home country's markets or exports among potential allies. Similarly, enemies may be weakened by the denial of markets, by a refusal to sell strategic goods, or by preemptive purchases of such goods on international markets. Alternatively, states may alter their foreign policies in the hopes that other countires will view such changes with favor and consequently be more willing to engage in trade.

A second political goal of state trading is to reduce the power of foreigners over a country's economy or foreign trade. National oil companies are an obvious example of such efforts.

DOMESTIC OBJECTIVES OF STATE TRADING.   Even if a country is so small that it can influence neither international prices nor the behavior of other states by its trading policies, it may nevertheless engage in state trading in order to fulfill domestic goals.

Protection of Domestic Industry.   State trading can be employed to protect domestic industry from foreign competition in a number of ways. Government procurement, to the extent that it discriminates against foreign vendors, affords protection to domestic firms. Similarly, state trading companies, often acting on behalf of domestic state monopolies, may limit purchases from abroad, impose excessive markups, and limit the amount of promotion given to goods of foreign origin. Acheson (1977) gives a penetrating analysis of such practices in the case of the Ontario Liquor Control Board. Finally, state companies may be subject to pressure from government officials in their procurement of inputs.

Price and Distribution Policies.   The role of state marketing boards in supporting government policies regarding agricultural prices has already been discussed. Government distribution of agricultural imports and of goods such as pharmaceuticals may also seek to insure that certain basic needs are met for all members of society.

Government Revenue.   When large differences exist between international and domestic prices, traders are able to earn large profits. Such profits could be taxed away or eliminated by the use of appropriate tariffs. However, the state may also choose to establish a state trading company in order to obtain the revenues directly.

Health and Public Security.   State trading in both harmful and beneficial drugs, alcoholic beverages, tobacco, and so forth, exists for two broad reasons. The first is that the state wishes to exercise control over all aspects of the distribution of these commodities, including imports or exports. Alternatively, the state may feel that private decisions, for example in the importation of alcohol, lead to a socially undesirable volume of imports or that trading in such socially undesirable commodities should not be a source of private gain.

Public-security considerations are most obvious in the case of arms and munitions, where the state seeks to maintain a total monopoly over the use of such implements, although such considerations also play a role in trade in nuclear fuels and explosives.

ECONOMIC CONSEQUENCES OF STATE TRADING. Except in those cases discussed above where state trading is employed to overcome market imperfections, state trading tends to distort international trade flows and thus to reduce international welfare. In some cases, state trading has effects similar to those of tariffs and quantitative restrictions. However, some of the consequences of state trading cannot be duplicated by means of tariffs and nontariff restrictions.

State Trading as a Trade Restriction. Ideally, free trade would result in the equalization of prices worldwide and a maximization of world welfare. To the extent that state trading leads to a divergence between foreign and domestic prices, it reduces world welfare in much the same way as does the use of quotas, tariffs, and subsidies. Exhibit 1 gives the equivalances between these more traditional tools of commercial policy and state trading.

It should also be recognized that state trading can improve the welfare of the country much as can an "optimal" tariff or quota. In each case the objective is to restrict trade in such a way as to yield an improvement in the terms of trade for the home country. Indeed, a state-trading country may have an advantage over countries using tariffs and quotas for such a purpose. Unlike tariffs and quotas, the decisions of a state trading organization are not open to public scrutiny and thus are less likely to invite retaliation from other countries.

Discrimination. State trading organizations can discriminate among buyers and sellers in three ways. The first form of discrimination is a distinction between foreign and domestic purchasers of the same good or service. Peston *et al.* (1977) argue that a state trading company, such as an international airline, should charge a price equal to marginal cost for home-country residents but should charge foreigners a price that equates marginal revenue and marginal cost, thus maximizing the subsidy granted to residents by discriminating against foreigners.

Another form of discrimination is that between one country and another. If such discrimination is carried out for political reasons, then both national and world economic welfare must fall to the extent that discrimination leads the state trading company to sell at lower or buy at higher prices than necessary.

Discrimination among foreigners may, however, have a purely economic basis. If the state trading company can exercise some market power and if national markets are separated, then the profits of the trading company and the national advantage will be maximized by means of discrimination. The state trading company would wish to charge prices that equate marginal revenue in each foreign country with the marginal cost of production and to purchase so as to equate the marginal cost of imports from each country. The benefits of such discrimination are not available to a country with a single tariff, as the discrimination would be eliminated by competition among private traders. Consequently, by being able to discriminate in this rational way, state trading benefits the nation more than do tariffs and quotas. However, it must be borne in mind that such gains come only at the expense of a decline in world welfare and in the efficiency with which resources are allocated.

Bilateralism. State trading organization often bilateralize trade because of government concern over the balance of trade. Thus state trading companies may wish to offset purchases of imports with equivalent sales of exports as part of a single

EXHIBIT 1 EQUIVALANCES BETWEEN STATE TRADING AND TARIFFS AND QUANTITATIVE RESTRICTIONS

Consequence of State Trading	Commercial Policy Equivalent	Domestic Production	Domestic Consumption	Imports
Imports		Change in Activity Relative to Free Trade		
Domestic price > international price	Tariff or quota on imports	Increase	Decrease	Decrease
Domestic price < international price	Subsidy on imports	Decrease	Increase	Increase
Exports		Change in Activity Relative to Free Trade		
Domestic price > international price	Subsidy on exports	Increase	Decrease	Increase
Domestic price < international price	Tariff or quota on exports	Decrease	Increase	Decrease

transaction, effectively reducing trade to barter. Such practices impose losses on both the participants and on third parties. The participants lose because the prices and quantities required to balance imports and exports may be suboptimal. Third parties lose because they are excluded from the transaction even though they might be willing to offer more-attractive terms.

Monopolization of Markets.   There is a widespread belief that state-trading countries have important advantages over countries that conduct their trade through private traders. Warley (1976) and Vernon (1974) give examples of such a view in two very different situations. As a consequence of this belief, it is to be expected that state trading by one country will be followed by the introduction of state trading by competitors, and eventually by countries that face the state traders from the other side of the market. Thus a market with a large number of private participants is replaced by one with a few large participants, most of whom may have significant noneconomic motives.

The international grain market is one example of such a situation. Australia, Canada, and the United States account for 75 percent of world wheat exports. Each of these countries uses either marketing boards or government control to manage wheat exports. On the other side of the market are the marketing boards of the importing nations. Although scholars disagree whether the market price is controlled by the sellers, as Alouze *et al.* (1978) feel or by the buyers, as Carter and Schmitz (1979) argue, it is amply evident that the market is not characterized by free competition.

Inefficiency.   A good deal of research in industrial organization suggests that public enterprise is less efficient than private enterprise. In the case of state trading, there is little hard evidence beyond a study of Indonesian public and private firms by Funkhouser and MacAvoy (1979). They find that both state trading companies and state enterprises producing goods and services for international consumption were less efficient than comparable private firms. If this evidence can be extended to other countries, then state trading imposes a deadweight loss on those countries that choose to employ it.

LEGAL ASPECTS OF STATE TRADING

STATE TRADING AND COMMERCIAL LAW.   When the state engages in international trade, either directly or through a state corporation, it may enjoy certain immunities that either give it a competitive edge over private competitors or provide its acts with protection not available to private firms. According to Setser (1959) these immunities may be classified as immunity from taxation, from regulatory laws, and from the jurisdiction of the courts.

Immunity from Taxation.   Although practice varies from country to country and sometimes within a country, state-trading activities are often exempt from some or all of the taxes and duties imposed on private traders. In the United States, instrumentalities of the federal government are exempt from state taxes; in Canada they are exempt from provincial property taxes. The tendency to exempt government corporations from taxation is most prevalent in common law countries. In continental

Europe the tendency is to treat public and private enterprise alike for tax purposes. Obviously, to the extent that state enterprises go untaxed, they will have a competitive edge over private rivals.

Immunity from Regulation.   Within their home countries, state trading organizations may be exempt from laws and regulations governing private firms. Among such exemptions might be those from antitrust policies, from regulations over business operations, and from various trade and foreign-exchange restrictions. In most industrialized countries the tendency is to subject government enterprises to the same rules that apply to private firms, with the exception of antitrust laws. In the United States, government instrumentalities are exempt from regulations applying to private persons unless there is legislative intent to do so. To the extent that such exemptions make the execution of trade cheaper or more expeditious for state traders than for private individuals, the competitive position of private traders is injured.

Immunity from the Jurisdiction of Courts.   Perhaps the most troublesome form of immunity enjoyed by state-trading activities is their relative immunity from the jurisdiction of courts both within their home countries and abroad. This immunity rests on the doctrine of sovereign immunity, which generally protects a sovereign from suit. Progress in bringing state-trading activities under the jurisdiction of the courts has come from the recognition that state acts may be divided into two categories. The first category consists of those acts in which the government acts in its capacity as sovereign (*iure imperii*). In these acts the state is, under the doctrine, immune from suit. However, the state may also act in the capacity of a private person (*iure gestiones*), in which case the tendency is to treat such state acts in the same way as the acts of private persons.

Setser (1979) reported that among West European states "liability for contract seems universally accepted" and state enterprises can be sued either in civil or administrative courts, though the ease of access to legal remedies does differ from country to country.

Courts in the United States have in the past tended to take a broad or "absolute" view of the doctrine of sovereign immunity, according to Kintner and Griffin (1977). The Foreign Sovereign Immunities Act of 1976 specifically brings the commercial dealings of foreign governments, if performed in the United States or having a direct effect on the United States, under the jurisdiction of United States courts.

Although this act has gone some way toward clarifying the legal status of state trading, the U.S. Department of Justice (1976) pointed out that a gray area exists between private and public acts of state.

Somewhat less well defined by legislation and precedent are two other defenses that might be raised by state trading companies: the act of state doctrine and cases in which a party's acts are compelled by a private sovereign. Kintner and Griffin's survey would seem to suggest that some progress is being made in this area, though Pisar (1970) suggests that both doctrines are open to abuse by state trading organizations and their governments.

STATE TRADING AND INTERNATIONAL ORGANIZATIONS.   International organizations such as the General Agreement on Tariffs and Trade (GATT), the European Community (EC), and the European Free Trade Area (EFTA) have as their objective the liberalization of trade by means of the reduction of trade barriers and the equalization of market opportunities between foreign and domestic firms. State trading poses a number of problems for these organizations. First, state trading organizations are trade barriers; second, they possess the power to discriminate between foreign and home-country residents, and among foreigners; and third, they do not respond to changes in the rules of the game in the same way that private traders do. Consequently, international efforts at trade liberalization have had to develop special rules to deal with state trading by market and nonmarket economies.

State Trading and GATT.   The basic principle behind GATT is to expand international trade through negotiated reductions in tariff and nontariff barriers. These reductions are to be applied to other countries on a nondiscriminatory basis through the application of most-favored-nation principle.

As Gupta (1974) concluded, state trading by its very nature is inconsistent with the straightforward application of GATT principles. There are three fundamental inconsistencies. The first is that unlike private traders, state trading organizations will not necessarily respond to a reduction in trade barriers such as tariffs by increasing the volume of trade. The state trader may offset the reduction in tariffs by refusing to increase the volume of imports by administrative fiat, by offsetting the reduction in tariffs by an increase in its markups on imports, and by discriminating against foreign products in its marketing procedures. Second, to the extent that the state trader has a monopoly, and thus some market power, it is likely to use that market power to discriminate among foreign markets in order to maximize its profits. Finally, state trading organizations, by selling imported inputs at prices below those of the world market, can provide protection in excess of that provided by tariffs to domestic industries that utilize such inputs.

To deal with these problems GATT contains the following provisions:

1. Article II-4 requires that state import monopolies shall not operate in such a way as to provide protection to domestic industry above the degree of protection provided by the tariff schedule. This would seem to preclude both excessive markups on imports and the subsidization of imports.
2. Article III-8(a) exempts government procurement of goods from equal treatment provisions of Article III. Goods so exempted must not be for resale or for use by the government in the production for commercial sale of goods or services. Most governments have tended to interpret "production for commercial sale" as narrowly as possible and thus to maximize the discrimination against foreign vendors of such goods.
3. Article XI-2 exempts agricultural products from the prohibition on quantitative restrictions and thus establishes a basis for the use of such restrictions by state marketing boards.
4. Article XVIII deals entirely with state trading. Paragraph 1(a) requires that state trading organizations act in a nondiscriminatory way. This is interpreted in 1(b) to mean that they should take only commercial criteria into account in their decisions. This means that irrational discrimination, buying or selling at the least-profitable prices, is prohibited. However, state trading organizations may discriminate among markets in such a way as to maximize their profits. Paragraph 2 requires that those goods exempted under Article III-8(a) be accorded "fair and equitable treatment" in trade with other contracting

parties. Such treatment presumably falls short of nondiscriminaiton. Paragraph 4 requires parties to report on products that they state trade. This provision has been rendered nugatory by the capricious interpretation of state trading by many parties to GATT. Paragraph 4 also requires contracting parties to disclose details about import markup of state trading enterprises at the request of other contracting parties.

An addendum to Article XVIII subjects marketing boards to the provisions of this article.

5. Articles XX and XXI provide general and security exceptions to the agreement and thus constitute a further basis for uncontrolled state trading particularly in fissionable materials, arms, and munitions.

GATT and Centrally Planned Economies.   A particularly difficult problem for GATT is the participation of the centrally planned communist countries. Since their import decisions are made by state organs, often on the basis of the plan rather than on the basis of price comparisons, the ability of these countries to offer nondiscriminatory treatment and the benefits of tariff reductions to the contracting parties is problematic.

Czechoslovakia joined GATT at its formation whereas Hungary, Poland, and Romania have joined more recently. After what Kostecki (Kostecki, *East-West Trade*, 1978) describes as complex negotiations, GATT agreed that under the Hungarian economic system, tariffs had a significant-enough role, and trading organizations sufficient freedom of choice to enable Hungary to participate in GATT on essentially the same basis as market economies. For Poland and Romania, however, special rules had to be developed. Poland agreed to increase imports from the contracting parties at 7 percent per year; Romania at a rate equal to the five-year plan rate for total imports.

State Trading and the European Community.   The Treaty of Rome, which lays the foundation for the EC is much more ambitious in its approach to the elimination of state trading than GATT. This is understandable, since the degree of economic integration and thus the elimination of trade barriers sought by members of the EC is much greater than that sought by the parties to GATT. Article 37(1) of the Treaty of Rome states that "member states shall progressively adjust any state monopolies of a commercial character in such a manner as will ensure the exclusion, at the date of expiry of the transitional period, of all discrimination between the nations of member states." In a tacit acknowledgment of the inherently discriminatory nature of state trading, the Commission (the EC's executive body) has stated that the most effective solution would be the elimination of state trading.

The EC has also acted to eliminate discrimination against suppliers from other EC countries in bidding for government contracts. A distinction is made between public works and government supply, with some discrimination in favor of domestic vendors allowed in the latter.

State Trading and EFTA.   Article XIV of the Stockholm Convention establishing EFTA also calls for a greater access of EFTA member countries' firms to government contracts. Specifically it calls for the use of public tenders that are to be adequately publicized and that give foreign firms sufficient time to place bids. If selective tenders are employed, equal opportunity is to be given to firms in all EFTA countries. Such tenders are to be used only in exceptional circumstances.

THE ORGANIZATION OF ECONOMIC ACTIVITY IN COMMUNIST COUNTRIES

THE STATE AND THE COMMUNIST PARTY. Communist countries are one-party states with the Communist party having a monopoly over political activity. This monopoly creates a unique relationship between the party and the government. Thus writing about the Soviet Union, Hough and Fainsod (1980) state that "the communist party is clearly the dominant institution . . . The active participants in the political process are . . . almost all party members, and the ultimate policymaking organs . . . are . . . party bodies." In a simplified sense, then, the party makes policy and the government implements it. Any understanding of economic decision making in communist countries thus requires a knowledge of both the party and the government.

The Communist Party. The Communist party strives to be an elite rather than a mass-participation party. Candidates for membership are screened, and members may be expelled if their performance is lacking. The basic unit of organization is the cell. Cells are organized in places of employment (factories, institutes, etc.) of sufficient size. The cells elect representatives to the party congress, which in theory is the most powerful organ of the party.

Because party congresses meet infrequently, policymaking devolves to the Central Committee, the Politburo, and the party secretary. Details regarding the size and name of these organs differ from country to country. Current information is available from Starr (*Communist Regimes*, 1980, and *Yearbook*, 1980). As Hough and Fainsod observe (1980), "The real cabinet of the Soviet political system is the party Politbureau, the real parliament is the Central Committee, and the real prime minister is the party General Secretary."

The Government. Although there is greater intercountry variance in government organization than in party organization, government organs tend to parallel those of the party. A legislature that meets infrequently elects a council of ministers, president, and/or premier. Party policy is transmitted to the government mainly by the dual membership of individuals in party decision-making organs and in the government bureaucracy. As Hough and Fainsod (1980) point out, "The leading officials of the [Soviet] government agencies are members not only of the party but of the leading party organs as well. Five of the fourteen voting members of the party Politburo in May 1978 were officials of the Council of Ministers, while nearly all of the ministers were members or candidate members of the party Central Committee."

ORGANIZATION OF INDUSTRY. The organization of economic activity displays even greater variety than does the political organization. However, with the exception of Yugoslavia, the major differences are to be found in the relative importance of the plan and market in regulating economic activity and in the decision making and financial autonomy of enterprises. Yugoslavia is unique in two ways. First, social ownership of the means of production is implemented by vesting workers at individual enterprises or enterprise subunits with the rights of ownership, including the rights to manage and to receive the profits of the enterprise. Second, markets are utilized to allocate inputs, outputs, and capital.

In the other socialist countries, social ownership of the means of production is realized, in industry and in services, through state ownership. The basic unit of organization is the enterprise, which is managed by a state-appointed manager and is subject to financial accountability in its operations. Enterprises may be grouped into trusts or combines in order to facilitate the coordination of their activities. In the late 1960s and early 1970s new forms of organization, variously called associations, large economic organizations, or centrals, were introduced in the Soviet Union and a number of the East European countries. Associations are groupings of enterprises, trusts, and combines operated by an independent management that has latitude to distribute resources and tasks among the constituent units. Associations also have responsibilities for carrying on appropriate research-and-development activities and in some cases for the execution of foreign-trade transactions.

All enterprises in a given branch of industry are controlled by their branch ministry. The ministry is responsible for the development of its particular industrial sector and for the operations of the enterprises and associations subject to it. The ministry allocates resources and output goals to the associations and enterprises and allocates goals for the collection and distribution of their output to the rest of the economy. Inputs are distributed through ministry and national wholesale or supply organizations on the basis of the economic plan. Consumer goods are sold to the retail network, which sells them to consumers at controlled prices.

THE ORGANIZATION OF AGRICULTURE.   In agriculture there are three types of organization. Least common, except in Poland, are privately owned and operated farms. The collective farm is the most common form of agricultural organization. Members of collective farms jointly own the means of production and share in the profits of the collective according to the quality and quantity of labor that they contribute. Members are also permitted to grow crops and raise animals on so-called private plots. State farms, which tend to be larger than collectives, operate on the same ownership basis as industrial enterprises. The state owns the means of production and the state farm pays workers a stipulated wage. Collective and state farms are assigned output targets and sell their output to the state at fixed prices; it is subsequently distributed to the population through the retail network. The output from private plots is sold on free markets at market clearing prices.

PLANNING AND PLAN IMPLEMENTATION.   Economic activity in the communist countries is governed by plans, whose purpose is to translate the policy of the communist party into purposeful and coordinated activity by workers, managers, enterprises, and the government. Nove (1977) stresses the need to distinguish between the long-term 15-year and 5-year plans and the annual plans. The long-run plans are perspective in nature, indicating the desired rates of growth of aggregate and sectoral outputs, investment, employment, and productivity as well as of foreign trade and consumption. In recent years these long-term plans, according to Ellman (1979) have also included programs for the solution of interindustry and regional problems.

The annual plan, in contrast, is operational, in that it not only describes the evolution of economic activity over the course of the year, but also contains the detailed instructions to economic organizations regarding the level and disposition of their outputs and the volume and source of their inputs. The major exceptions in this regard are Hungary and Yugoslavia, where annual plans are indicative rather than obligatory in nature.

Plan Construction.   Plan construction is the responsibility of the state planning committee (SPC), which is attached to the council of ministers. The SPC monitors economic performance and provides evaluations of future policy options to the party and government. Based on this information, the leadership develops economic goals for the future. At the same time, enterprises and associations are formulating their own plans, consisting of combinations of inputs and outputs, which are aggregated and modified by their branch ministries and passed on to the SPC. The SPC issues a draft plan, which is sent to the branch ministries, which disaggregate it and send plans to their subordinate enterprises. A period of bargaining then ensues, with subordinates seeking more inputs or easier output goals from supervisors, and supervisors seeking to apportion goals and resources among subordinates in such a way as to meet the more-aggregate plans facing the supervisors. At the end of the bargaining period, the SPC reaggregates what they hope is a consistent plan; the plan is then enacted as law.

The task of the SPC is twofold. First, it must advise policy makers about the courses of action open to them and the tradeoffs between various goals. Second, it must strive to transform these goals into plans that make maximum use of productive resources while taking cognizance of capacity constraints, and it must do so within the framework of a consistent plan. Plan consistency both in the aggregate and at the level of individual enterprise requires that the demand for inputs required for the planned level of outputs be consistent with the supply actually available. The principal means for insuring that supply meets demand is the method of materials balances, which is employed for several hundred of the most important commodities such as coal and steel. Each balance lists sources of supply such as domestic production, imports, and inventory decumulation. Against these supplies are ranked the uses: exports, sales to consumers, accumulation of stocks, and the requirements of other industries. This last category is disaggregated by using industries and is usually calculated by means of coefficients that relate input usage to the output of the consuming industry. Although practive varies from country to country, plan consistency tends to be subverted by plan tautness or overfull-employment planning, by the failure to recalculate materials balance to account for the secondary and tertiary effects on demand of an increase in production of an industry, and by the inability of planners to induce managers to reveal the true relationship between inputs and outputs.

Reforms in the Economic Mechanism.   In the late 1960s a movement toward the reform of the economic mechanism was evident in a number of the East European countries and in the Soviet Union. According to Bornstein (1977), these reforms involved a variety of changes in the economic mechanism. Chief among these were greater enterprise autonomy in setting production goals, stress on market prices as guides for decision making by producers, and the substitution of profit for output as the principal success indicator for firms. Only in Hungary and to a much smaller degree in Poland have these reform measures survived the 1970s with much vigor. Under the Hungarian new economic mechanism, enterprises choose their own output goals, suppliers of inputs, and customers. Although the government disposes of powerful macroeconomic tools, including control over a part of investment, the plan is merely indicative rather than binding on enterprises. Most prices respond to market forces and are linked to foreign market prices as well. In the other countries, reforms were abolished in the 1970s in response to external and domestic events, but the pressures for developing mechanisms that will promote greater efficiency and technological progress remain.

Managerial Incentives. In all communist economies except Hungary and Yugoslavia, enterprise compliance with the plan is induced by a system of annual and quarterly bonuses for managers and workers. Bonuses are contingent on the fulfillment of a battery of indicators, the most important of which are the fulfillment of the output plan and profitability. That this system leads to disfunctional behavior on the part of enterprise managers is widely recognized by communist observers and by Western scholars such as Berliner (1980) and Granick (1975). Among the problems created by managerial response to the bonus system are as follows:

1. Stress of quantity over quality.
2. Resistance to innovation and risk taking.
3. Tendency to overstate input needs and to understate productive potential.
4. Avoidance of excessive plan overfulfillment so that future targets grow at moderate rate.

MONEY, BANKING, AND PRICES. In a centrally planned economy there are two types of money: cash and enterprise deposits. Cash is used by households as a store of wealth and for transactions between households and the state sector, as well as among households. Enterprises use cash only to pay wages. All other enterprise transactions are made by means of drafts drawn against accounts that all enterprises must maintain with the state bank. This system of drafts enables the bank to monitor the compliance of the enterprises with the plan and to prevent illegal or nonplanned transactions, since each draft must be accompanied by a document attesting to the transaction's consistency with the enterprise's plan.

The Banking System. According to Garvy (1977), the most important banking institution in centrally planned economies is the state bank. It is the bank of issue; it holds government and enterprise deposits; and it is the sole source of short-term and in some countries, long-term credit to enterprises. Government investment funds are channeled to industry and agriculture through specialized investment banks or more frequently through the state bank. Household savings are serviced through a savings bank, although this bank merely deposits its funds with the state bank. Finally, with the exception of Hungary, a foreign-trade bank is employed to carry out transactions with foreigners and to manage foreign-exchange reserves.

Although reforms in the 1960s and 1970s increased the role of credit in regulating enterprise activity, credit and credit creation remain subordinate to the physical plan. Thus the state bank automatically issues short-term credit to facilitate interenterprise transactions consistent with the plan. The principal change has been to require enterprises to pay interest on, and to repay funds allocated to them for, long-term investments.

Prices. The emphasis on the physical allocation of goods by the plan reduces not only the role of money but that of prices as well. A prime objective of policy has been to maintain stable prices, though the reforms of the 1970s and inflationary pressures from abroad have tended to produce greater price flexibility or at least volatility.

For manufactured goods, there are three types of prices. Interenterprise transactions take place at wholesale prices. In most countries, these are set equal to the average variable cost plus a charge equal to some percentage of the capital cost. Averages are taken over the appropriate sector of industry, and thus some firms may earn a profit while others sustain losses. Commodities are sold to consumers at retail prices. These are equal to the wholesale price plus markups for the retail network and a sales tax called the turnover tax. This tax, which is a major source of government revenue, is levied on goods at nonuniform rates designed in part to influence consumption in socially desirable directions. In general these prices tend to be relatively uniform both among enterprises and regions of the country. One exception is in prices paid to natural-resource producers, who face widely differing costs of production and consequently receive differentiated prices.

Agricultural goods produced by collectives are sold to the state at established procurement prices. These goods are sold through state stores at fixed prices, with staples such as bread often sold below cost. The output of private plots is sold at peasant markets at uncontrolled prices.

FOREIGN TRADE IN THE CENTRALLY PLANNED ECONOMY

THE ORGANIZATION OF FOREIGN TRADE. In the communist countries, international trade is a monopoly of the state. Problems encountered in the organization and execution of trade activities include the need to mesh trade flows with the domestic plan, with the plans of other communist countries, and with the world market. Trade organizations must be devised to facilitate this coordinating function, to serve as an effective bridge between market and planned economies, and to maximize the benefits from trade and technology transfer while minimizing the adverse effects on the domestic economy of fluctuations in international markets.

The Ministry of Foreign Trade. The state's monopoly over foreign trade is exercised through the ministry of foreign trade (MFT). The MFT does not directly engage in foreign-trade transactions. Rather it sets policy for foreign-trade transactions, negotiates trade agreements with foreign countries, and supervises the execution of the foreign-trade plan. According to Gruzinov (1979) and Quigley (1976), the MFT has a number of departments, some dealing with specific geographic regions (eg., Africa), with functional areas (eg., legal), and with products (eg., raw materials).

Foreign-Trade Organizations. Foreign-trade transactions are carried out by foreign-trade organizations (FTOs). FTOs are corporations established under the ownership of the MFT or more recently under the ownership of the associations or enterprises whose products the FTO trades. Each FTO is specialized along product lines, and in general there is no overlap between the products traded by two FTOs. Each communist country publishes a guide to the FTOs and the products they are empowered to purchase and sell. In addition to FTOs that trade commodities, each country has FTOs that specialize in the provision of services such as insurance, transportation, and advertising. Each FTO is responsible for the fulfillment of its import and export plan, including the letting and evaluation or tendering of bids, and the negotiation and signing of contracts.

According to the United Nations Economic Commission for Europe (1973), in the late 1960s and early 1970s a number of the East European nations reformed their trade organizations. Operating control and ownership of the FTOs was taken away from the MFT, whose role was restricted to general policy making and supervision. The FTOs were handed over to the branch ministries or associations whose products they traded. According to Brada and Jackson (1978), the objective of this reform was to give domestic producers greater contact with the world market and to give them a financial stake in the success of their goods on export markets. Although these reforms have been partly dismantled in recent years, and the MFT's authority has been reasserted, some elements of the reforms, as well as the conditions that led to their enactment in the first place, remain.

The Foreign-Trade Bank.   Although the FTOs acquire title to goods that are imported or to be exported, they neither make nor receive payments in foreign exchange. Such transactions between a communist country and foreigners are carried out by the foreign-trade bank (FTB). This separation of functions between the FTB, the FTO, and the domestic supplier of exports or purchaser of imports leads to a complex network of financial transactions.

In the case of an export transaction, the FTO purchases the commodity from the domestic supplier. Under the classic Soviet system it pays the supplier the domestic wholesale price. Under the reforms enacted in some countries, the supplier receives the price for which the commodity is sold abroad. The foreign-currency price is converted into domestic currency at either a commercial rate of exchange or the commercial rate with some industry-specific adjustment. The FTO turns the buyer's letter of credit over to the FTB for collection, and receives domestic currency in return. For payment to the FTO, foreign exchange is converted into domestic currency at either the official or commercial rate, with some industry-specific adjustment possibly employed.

Import transactions follow a similar pattern. The FTO contracts with a foreign exporter, and sells the goods to the domestic user either at the domestic wholesale price or at the foreign price converted into domestic currency by means of a commercial exchange rate and possibly with an industry-specific adjustment. The FTO then pays the FTB the requisite amount of domestic currency, and the FTB pays the Western exporter in convertible currency.

CONVERTIBILITY, EXCHANGE RATES, AND PRICE EQUALIZATION.   Internationally, the currencies of the communist countries are inconvertible both in the traditional financial sense and also in a special sense called commodity inconvertibility. Since the state determines the types and quantities of goods to be exported as well as the terms on which they are to be offered, a foreign holder of a communist country's currency cannot know in advance what goods his financial claim can be used to purchase.

As shown in the preceding section, under the Soviet system, there is no connection between the domestic price charged to buyers of imports and that paid to suppliers of imports. Therefore, any responses to foreign market developments must be made by the plan rather than through the automatic responses of exporters and importers. As a result, the exchange rate may be set at a nonequilibrium rate, since the rate at which foreign prices are converted into domestic prices has no effect on trade decisions. Thus for example, it may be desirable to export goods whose domestic price is higher than the world market price (evaluated at the official rate of exchange) or to import goods that at the official rate cost more abroad than domestically. Such transactions of course impose losses on FTOs, which are then covered by the price-equilization fund or foreign-trade subsidy. Under the reformed system, the exchange rate and the comparison of foreign and domestic prices are critical in trade decisions, though there has been a tendency in many countries to subsidize imports in the face of rapid international inflation.

THE PLANNING OF TRADE FLOWS.   Since planning in the communist countries entails the allocation of inputs and outputs by the plan, foreign-trade flows must be an integral part of both annual and five-year plans. Therefore, the construction of foreign-trade plans follows that of the national plan. Enterprises and associations may, on their own or in conjunction with the state committee charged with the supervision of scientific progress, request imports of technology, equipment, or other imported inputs. Similarly, they may wish to provide goods for export. These plans are aggregated by the ministries and passed on to the state planning commission. Simultaneously FTOs prepare trade plans based on their assessment of international market conditions and on the basis of long-term commitments in force with other communist countries. Such plans are disaggregated by both commodities and by markets. The MFT aggregates and adjusts these plans and transmits them to the state planning commission. The commission reconciles and adjusts the plan as required; subsequently it becomes law. Although trade is thus planned, it is necessary to recognize that planners may anticipate a certain amount of unplanned trade to overcome unexpected domestic shortages, to take advantage of unanticipated output surpluses, or to benefit from unforeseen market opportunities.

TRADE AMONG COMMUNIST COUNTRIES

THE COUNCIL FOR MUTUAL ECONOMIC ASSISTANCE.   Although the communist countries share similar ideologies and economic institutions, and to a lesser extent, similar goals, they have had to devote considerable effort to the development of institutions that facilitate commercial relations among them. The most important of these institutions is the Council for Mutual Economic Assistance (CMEA or CO-MECON). Kaser (1967) finds that, although the CMEA was organized in 1949, it did not play an active role in promoting trade and specialization among its members until the late 1950s.

Current CMEA members are the six communist countries of Eastern Europe (Bulgaria, Czechoslovakia, the German Democratic Republic, Hungary, Poland and Rumania), Cuba, Mongolia, the Soviet Union, and Vietnam.

The Organization of the CMEA.   The CMEA apparatus consists of the Council and the Executive Committee, which are deliberative organs; and standing commissions and the Secretariat, which provide staff support for CMEA activities. The Council is the supreme decision-making body, but its powers are severely limited. First, its decisions must be based on the unanimous agreement of all members, which makes decisions on substantive issues difficult to achieve. This problem is only partly mitigated by the "interested party" principle that permits some members to reach accord on matters of mutual interest without requiring the assent of nonparticipating CMEA members. A more serious limitation on the Council's power is that it can only render advisory opinions on substantive issues; final decisions are only reached after discussion by the party leaders of the member countries.

Standing commissions deal with functional areas of mutual interest, such as statistics, finance, et cetera, and with specific sectors of the CMEA economy such as chemicals, ferrous metallurgy, et cetera, where efforts are made to coordinate national investment strategies and to promote standardization and specialization.

Plan Coordination in the CMEA. In trade between two planned economies, each transaction must be planned by both the exporter and the importer. As a result, the planning of trade requires bilateral negotiations with each communist trade partner so that each will include the desired transactions in their plans. This of course results in a complex procedure in which the domestic plan and a multitude of bilateral trade plans have to be adjusted to take into account both the interactions between trade and domestic resource flows and the trade opportunities available with each communist partner. In general the bilateral negotiations result in five-year plans that deal with broad aggregates and with critical commodities such as oil and steel. Annual trade plans are much more detailed in their descriptions of commodities to be traded and transaction prices.

The CMEA has played a role in aiding members to negotiate trade agreements. The five-year planning cycles for CMEA members have been synchronized, and the CMEA attempts to promote the exchange of information about prospective plan decisions and sectoral development strategies. However, CMEA has no power to impose on its members either the coordination of economic activity or the coordination of trade decisions.

ECONOMIC INTEGRATION IN THE CMEA. The inability of the CMEA to impose supranational plan coordination on its members has hampered integration, and, in the view of some observers such as Holzman (1976), economic progress of member countries. Members perceive that the supranational coordination of five-year plans would eliminate domestic control over the pattern of economic development. Although CMEA members have promulgated two documents (the Basic Principles of 1962 and the Complex Program of 1971) that attempt to develop the basis for greater intra-CMEA trade and plan coordination, the CMEA has not been able to eliminate the opposition of some members, most notably Rumania, to the supranational coordination of plans. As a result, coordination and integration have been implemented by voluntary means and at a cautious pace.

Specialization Agreements. Under voluntary agreements for specialization, CMEA member countries are assigned responsibilities for the development of products or branches of industry to the point where they can supply the needs of all CMEA members. The objective is thus to coordinate investment and production to take advantage of economies of scale and serial production and to improve technological standards by focusing research efforts on narrower areas of inquiry in each country. Although Levcik and Stankovsky (1979) reported that such specialization accounted for a growing proportion of intra-CMEA trade in 1973 and 1974, problems continue to exist, as some countries refuse to relinquish domestic production while those that are given specialization positions may have difficulty in initiating production.

International Economic Organizations. One genuinely supranational economic organization employed among some CMEA countries is the international economic organization (IEO). Membership in an IEO is voluntary. Those countries that choose to participate form a multinational management organization that coordinates the production and investment decisions for a product or branch of industry in the participating country. The decisions of the IEO are binding on member countries and are taken to optimize the utilization of capacity in those countries. Among sectors where IEOs have been formed are ferrous metals (Intermetal), rollar bearings (Interbearing), and electric motors.

Large-Scale International Projects. A form of economic integration that has taken on greater significance in recent years is the cooperative development of natural resources or productive resources in one CMEA country utilizing resources contributed in part by other CMEA members. When the project is completed, the investing countries are repaid by deliveries of the output of the project. The Orenburg natural gas pipeline, bringing natural gas from fields in the Soviet Union to Eastern Europe, is one example of such a project. The Eastern European members of the CMEA have contributed resources and funds for the construction of the pipeline and for the purchase of the pumping equipment. They will be repaid by deliveries of natural gas when the project is completed.

FOREIGN-TRADE PRICES IN THE CMEA. The domestic price structures of the CMEA countries reflect neither costs of production nor supply-demand equilibria. Similarly, the official rates of exchange reflect neither purchasing power parity nor equilibrium in the balance of payments. Thus domestic price structures cannot serve as the basis for intra-CMEA trade prices. The effect of a lack of a basis for intra-CMEA prices is only partially offset by the fact that trade flows are planned and that trade transactions are negotiated on a country-to-country basis.

Lacking the means to develop independent intra-CMEA prices, CMEA has adopted world market prices as the basis for intra-CMEA trade. Until the oil crisis of 1973, intra-CMEA prices were fixed for a five-year period coinciding with the five-year plan period, and they were based on an average of world market prices for the preceding five-year period. As oil and raw-materials prices in world markets rose rapidly since 1973, the effect of such a pricing rule on CMEA raw-materials exporters (and particularly on the Soviet Union) led to a change in the price formulation rules in 1975. The revised rules call for annual changes in intra-CMEA prices based on a moving average of world prices for the past five or fewer years. Thus as Western prices change, CMEA prices will react more rapidly than in the past.

Hard Goods and Soft Goods. The use of world prices in intra-CMEA trade would pose no problems if factor endowments and consumption patterns within CMEA were identical with those of the rest of the world. However, because this condition does not hold, certain goods on the CMEA market are in excess demand, others in excess supply. The former have been dubbed hard goods, the latter, soft goods. Hard goods include fuels, raw materials, agricultural products, and commodities produced utilizing Western technology or components. In general these goods can be sold easily on Western markets at world market prices. Soft goods, consisting of standardized machinery and equipment and consumer manufactures, on the other hand, can only be sold on Western markets at significant discounts from world market prices because of deficiencies in quality, packaging, or promotion.

Each CMEA country has an incentive to dispose of its hard goods in world markets for convertible currency and to sell as much of its available supply of soft goods on the CMEA market. As a result, van Brabant (1973) reported that in their bilateral trade negotiations CMEA countries increasingly seek to balance exports of hard goods against imports of hard goods and imports of soft goods against like quantities of exports. The Soviet Union has assumed the task of being the main net exporter of fuels and raw materials within CMEA; this promotes CMEA economic integration and provides political leverage for the Soviet Union.

INTERNATIONAL MONETARY RELATIONS IN THE CMEA.   The inconvertibility of CMEA currencies has forced CMEA countries to develop special means for settling international transactions. A rather unsatisfactory solution has been the tendency for each CMEA country to insure that its trade with every other CMEA country is bilaterally balanced each year. In this way, trade was carried out on what was, in essence, a barter basis. Such a basis, however, was inimical to the expansion of intra-CMEA trade and investments.

The Intra-CMEA Payments System.   Payments between CMEA member countries are cleared through the International Bank for Economic Co-operation and Development (IBEC), which was founded in 1964. Payments are made in transferable rubles. The transferable ruble is a unit of account with gold content equal to that of the Soviet ruble. Transferable rubles are, however, not convertible into gold, into the national currencies of IBEC members, nor into convertible currencies. Each member country maintains a transferable ruble account with IBEC and uses this account to settle trade transactions with other IBEC members. IBEC may also extend short-term credits to members in transferable rubles or in convertible currencies.

It was hoped that the introduction of payments by means of transferable rubles would multilateralize intra-CMEA trade. This, however, has not occurred. As Brainard (1980) notes, the transferable ruble suffers from both of the defects of the national currencies of the CMEA member countries: financial inconvertibiltiy and commodity inconvertibiltiy. Consequently IBEC members continue to avoid accumulating transferable ruble balances of dubious value by bilaterally balancing their trade.

Convertible Currency Trade within The CMEA.   A relatively recent development in intra-CMEA trade is transactions that are denominated in, and paid for with, convertible currencies such as the U.S. dollar. Transactions cleared in this way include above-plan deliveries of hard goods such as petroleum, and goods produced in CMEA countries but entailing significant convertible currency expenditures for components or licenses. The volume of trade cleared in convertible currencies is uncertain; Kohn and Lang (1977) estimated that such trade accounts for 5–25 percent of total intra-CMEA trade.

Capital Flows in the CMEA.   The shortcomings of the transferable ruble as a medium of exchange and store of value have also hampered capital flows within the CMEA. In 1970 the International Investment Bank (IIB) was established. One of the objectives of the bank was to make long-term loans to its members in transferable rubles and convertible currencies. Of particular interest to the IIB are loans for projects of interest to several members. Thus for example, the IIB has supported major CMEA-wide development projects such as the Orenburg gas pipeline. The IIB has also made convertible currency loans to the foreign-trade banks of CMEA members to finance their East-West trade activities. In addition to the convertible currencies subscribed by the member countries, both the IIB and IBEC have borrowed convertible currencies on the Eurodollar market to meet their lending requirements.

THE POLITICAL ECONOMY OF TRADE WITH COMMUNIST COUNTRIES

POLICY OBJECTIVES IN EAST-WEST TRADE.   During the post-World War II period, an adversary relationship has existed between many of the communist countries and the United States and its allies. As a result, Western policies toward trade between the two blocs has been formulated to meet a variety of often-conflicting economic and political objectives.

Economic Warfare.   An important component of Western policy toward East-West trade has been the desire to limit the contribution that such trade makes to the military and economic potential of the communist countries. Efforts to restrict both exports of strategic goods and the extension of credits to communist countries are examples of such policies.

Western countries have also sought to protect themselves against potential economic warfare by the communist countries. Import restrictions were enacted to protect Western markets against dumping, disruption, and exploitation by the communist countries. More recently the increased volume of East-West trade has engendered concerns about excessive dependence of Western exporters on communist markets or of Western economies on critical supplies from communist sources. The large convertible currency debts of the CMEA member countries and the possible effects of defaults on the international financial system have also became sources of concern.

Linkage of Trade and Politics.   The willingness to trade and to extend credit has been employed by Western countries to influence the cohesion of the communist countries. The United States has extended favorable trade treatment to Poland, Rumania, and the Peoples Republic of China in part as a response to their independence of Soviet policy.

The United States has also sought to link East-West trade policies with the domestic or foreign policies of communist countries. The embargo on exports of grain to the Soviet Union in the wake of Soviet intervention in Afghanistan is one such example. The linking of most-favored-nation status and U.S. Export-Import Bank financing to Soviet emigration policy is an example of linkages between trade and domestic policy for the Soviet Union.

Reinforcement of Mutual Dependencies.   Although trade warfare and linkages suggest restrictions on East-West trade, policy makers have recognized that the expansion of trade with the communist countries might improve relations between the two blocs. The development of mutual interdependencies, greater mutual understanding and contacts, and the increased affluence of communist countries as a result of greater trade should serve to develop a commonality of interests and reduce the possibility of hostilities between East and West.

EXPORT CONTROLS.   To prevent the export of advanced technology and equipment to the communist countries, the United States and other Western countries have developed a system of controls over such exports. In order for such a system to be effective, it is first necessary to identify goods of strategic significance, a matter that Mountain (1978) indicates is quite complex. Moreover, unless the embargo is total, choices must be made between the gains from trade to the exporter and the gains in the strategic capability of the importer. Second, a system must be devised to coordinate the embargo policies of all suppliers of a particular technology and to insure that exports of embargoed goods to friendly countries are not reexported to communist countries.

THE EXPORT ADMINISTRATION ACT.   Legislative authority to regulate exports from the United States is provided in the Export Administration Act. The provisions of this act are administered by the Office of Export Administration (OEA) of the U.S. Department of Commerce. In addition to the controls maintained by the OEA, other agencies of government administer controls over such items as arms and munitions, atomic-energy materials, natural gas, and electricity.

General License for Exports.   Although all exports from the United States require an export license, many commodities may be exported under a so-called general license. The exporter of goods covered by a general license does not need to request permission to export. According to the OEA (U.S. Department of Commerce, 1978), several types of general licenses exist. Under one type of general license, a commodity may be exported to any destination in any quantity. In other cases, the general license applies only to exports to certain countries; for other destinations (usually communist countries) the general license does not apply. Finally, some general licenses permit exports to communist countries only if the value of the shipment is less than a stated amount.

Validated Licenses for Exports.   Goods that do not qualify for a general license may be exported only if the OEA issues a validated license. In order to obtain such a license, an application must be submitted to the OEA. If the exporter is not subject to U.S. jurisdiction, he must appoint an agent to act for him in filing the application. Applications for validated licenses are considered in the first instance by the OEA.

In addition, other government departments (State and Defense) and agencies may provide inputs into the decision process as, ultimately, may the President. According to the OEA (U.S. Department of Commerce, 1978), among the criteria considered in the issuance of a validated license are the potential military uses of the commodity or technology, whether the technology can be extracted by the purchaser, the contribution that the transaction might make to the military potential of the purchaser, whether or not the commodity can be diverted from civilian to military applications, and whether or not there are sources of supply other than the United States.

If the commodity for which a validated license is to be issued is subject to international export controls established by the Coordinating Committee (COCOM), the application must be submitted to that organization by the U.S. government.

Transactions Subject to Licensing.   According to the OEA (U.S. Department of Commerce, 1978), licensing requirements extend to the following:

1. Exports of commodities and technical data from the United States.
2. Reexports of U.S.-origin commodities and technical data from a foreign destination to another foreign destination.
3. U.S.-origin parts and components used in a foreign country to manufacture a foreign end product for export.
4. In some instances, the foreign-produced direct product of U.S.-origin technical data."

Licensing controls thus extend to the foreign affiliates of U.S. firms and to foreign-owned and foreign-located firms to the extent that these employ restricted U.S. technology or components. This implicit extraterritoriality of the licensing mechanism has caused some friction between the United States and other Western governments, with American firms and their foreign affiliates caught in the middle, according to Behrman (1970).

To determine whether a particular transaction requires a validated license, exporters should consult the Commodity-Control List of the Export Administration Regulations. For each commodity, the list gives the country groups for which validated licenses are required and, if applicable, the maximum value of transactions to such countries that may be exported under general license. The stringency of licensing requirements varies from one communist country to another. Exports to Rumania and Poland are treated relatively liberally, whereas North Korea, Vietnam, Cambodia and Cuba are subject to the most-stringent restrictions. Restrictions on exports to the remaining communist countries fall between these two extremes.

INTERNATIONAL RESTRICTIONS ON EXPORTS.   Although other Western countries instituted export controls over shipments to communist countries at about the same time as did the United States, it was soon recognized that some coordination of national policies as well as some measures to prevent circumvention of the controls by the diversion of goods from their rightful destinations was necessary.

COCOM.   In 1949 the NATO countries excluding Iceland, and later joined by Japan, organized an informal organization to coordinate national export-control programs. This organization consisted of a policy-making Consultative Committee whose acronym, COCOM, gave the organization its name, and a secretariat whose tasks were to draw up a list of goods that members would not export to communist countries and to implement COCOM policies. Each member of COCOM is free to establish an export-control list more restrictive than the common list to which all members agree, but in practice only the United States does so to any significant degree. Moreover, since COCOM is a voluntary organization, its decisions are not binding on member countries. COCOM members wishing to export goods on the COCOM list to communist countries may request COCOM approval for the transaction.

Import Certificate/Delivery Verification.   In order to prevent the diversion of stategic goods to the communist countries, the COCOM countries have established a system of import certificates and delivery verification (IC/DV). The commodity-control list indicates which commodities are subject to IC/DV requirements. American exporters of such goods must secure an import certificate and may be required to provide an official delivery verification to the Office of Export Control. For shipments to nonmembers of COCOM, exportees must submit a "statement by ultimate consignee and purchaser" to the Office of Export Control.

CREDIT RESTRICTIONS.   The United States has maintained restrictions over credits to communist countries. There has been some international coordination of such credit restrictions.

Johnson Debt Default Act.   The Johnson Debt Default Act, as amended, prohibits loans to, or purchases of, securities of foreign governments in default of debts to the United States. Countries that are members of the International Monetary Fund (IMF) and the International Bank for Reconstruction and Development (IBRD) are exempt from the provisions of the act. Of the major communist countries, Albania and Bulgaria are not in default of debts to the United States, and Rumania and Yugoslavia are members of the IMF and the IBRD.

Although the Johnson Debt Default Act thus prevents American banks from extending loans to most communist governments, the act is sufficiently narrow to enable American banks to take an active part in East-West finance. First of all, the act has been interpreted as not prohibiting the extension of credit for export financing so long as the credit is comparable to that usually employed in similar transactions. Thus according to Porter (1976), suppliers' and buyers' credits, barter arrangements, and the deferral of payment pending the development of earnings are all transactions in which American banks and firms may participate.

More important, the act does not apply to transactions undertaken by foreign affiliates of American firms if such transactions are financed wholly outside the United States. Similarly, foreign subsidiaries and branches of American banks are free to lend to communist countries money that they have raised overseas. In this way many American banks have participated in Eurodollar loans to communist countries.

Finally, the act specifically exempts loans by public corporations from its provisions. Thus loans by the Commodity Credit Corporation and the Export-Import Bank are acceptable as are private loans in which the Export-Import Bank participates.

Export-Import Bank.   Although the Export-Import Bank was originally established to facilitate trade between the United States and the Soviet Union during the post-World War II period, there has been a good deal of hostility to the use of the bank for financing East-West trade. According to Marer (1975) the difficulty is that the bank supports exports by offering financing at below-market rates. Although this is viewed as a subsidy for the seller when exports go to Western countries, in East-West transactions such rates are perceived by many as a subsidy to the Eastern European importer.

Under the Trade Act of 1974 the Export-Import Bank cannot make loans to nonmarket economies to which the United States has not extended MFN treatment and which do not grant their residents freedom of emigration. Thus the bank is currently constrained to lending to Hungary, Poland, and Rumania. The bank's credit-guarantee programs are similarly constrained. For the communist countries where Export-Import Bank participation is permitted, Porter (1976) reported that the bank guarantees loans, makes direct loans to communist foreign-trade banks to finance imports from the United States, and lends to U.S. banks to support exports under the Cooperative Credit Facility.

Export-Import Bank participation in East-West transactions is important for two reasons. First, Export-Import Bank participation reduces the interest cost to the buyer, making U.S. credit terms competitive with officially supported export credits of other Western countries. Second, loans guaranteed by the Export-Import Bank do not count against the participating commercial bank's country's legal lending limit.

Commodity Credit Corporation. The Commodity Credit Corporation (CCC) is a government corporation that finances the export of agricultural commodities. It is subject to the same country restrictions as the Export-Import Bank. Moreover, commodities that are eligible for CCC loans vary over time, and therefore exporters interested in utilizing CCC credits should first consult the corporation.

Overseas Private Investment Corporation. Insurance of American investments in Rumania is eligible for OPIC programs. These involve both insurance against political risks and default and the provision of long-term credit. It is likely that investments in the People's Republic of China will also become eligible for OPIC guarantees in the future.

CREDIT AVAILABILITY IN OTHER WESTERN COUNTRIES. Credit for the financing of East-West trade is much more readily available in other industrialized Western countries than it is in the United States. Although this tends to put American exporters and American financial institutions at a competitive disadvantage, two points should be borne in mind. First, American banks are able to participate in the financing of East-West transactions through their overseas branches. These are subject to host-country rather than U.S. restrictions. Second, American firms may be able to take advantage of foreign export-credit-support programs through their foreign affiliates.

Official Credit Supports. All the major industrialized countries maintain government credit-support and credit-guarantee programs for export transactions. In general these services as described by Porter (1976) and Wolf (1975) are similar to those offered by the U.S. Export-Import Bank. However, unlike the United States, other Western countries impose no broad restrictions against the use of these programs for the support of East-West transactions. American firms can take advantage of such credit programs by sourcing shipments to communist countries from affiliates in Western Europe or Japan.

The Berne Union. The International Union of Credit and Investment Insurers, commonly called the Berne Union, was established to coordinate the official export-credit programs in the Western countries. In the 1950s and 1960 the United States sought to maintain a limit of five years on the duration of credits to communist countries by Berne Union members. Although such a prohibition proved impossible to maintain through the 1960s, Western governments continue to use the Union to exchange information about prospective credits.

Borrowings In the Eurodollar Market. The Eastern European countries, the Soviet Union, and the two CMEA banks became active borrowers in the Eurodollar market in 1960s and particularly in the 1970s. The bulk of this borrowing has consisted of three-to-five-year credits, although Hungary has secured longer-term loans in the

Eurobond market. In the late 1960s and early 1970s, the CMEA countries were seen as attractive borrowers, with low levels of debt, good international payments records, and stable economies. However, the rapid increase in their indebtedness and the delayed effect of the energy crisis on the communist countries has tarnished their credit ratings to some extent.

Convertible-Currency Debts of the Communist Countries.   The total amount of Soviet and Eastern European debt to the West is not known with absolute precision because the communist countries, excepting Hungary, publish only balance-of-trade data. However, Western estimates agree sufficiently to provide a general view of the situation. Gross convertible-currency debt of the six Eastern European CMEA members in 1979 was close to $70 billion dollars and for the Soviet Union about $17 billion, according to the CIA (1980). About 20 percent of this debt was in the form of government IMF and World Bank credits, 80 percent private commercial debt. The accumulation of debt has been particularly troublesome for Poland, both because its volume, some $20 billion, and its short maturity had by 1979 pushed Poland's ratio of debt service to exports to over .9. In contrast to the rapid growth of debt among the CMEA countries in the 1970s, the People's Republic of China maintained a very conservative policy toward foreign credits.

IMPORT RESTRICTIONS.   Restrictions against goods of communist origin spring from two motives. The first is economic warfare. The denial of access to Western markets reduces the ability of the communist countries to earn convertible currency and worsens their terms of trade. The second motive is the protection of domestic and international markets from the effects of communist trade policies. Because communist trade is a state monopoly, trade decisions may be made for political motives or may make use of the state monopoly to exploit Western markets or injure Western producers by means of dumping.

U.S. Restrictions.   The principal barrier against imports of communist goods to the United States is the lack of most-favored-nation treatment for such goods; thus tariffs charged on imports are much higher than those facing most-favored-nation exporters. Only Poland and Yugoslavia have been accorded the type of treatment granted to noncommunist countries, whereas Rumania and Hungary are accorded most-favored-nation status under the provisions of Section 402 of the Trade Act of 1979. Under this act, most-favored-nation status is contingent on a satisfactory review of the communist country's emigration policies each year. As a developing country, Rumania is also eligible for lower tariffs under the generalized system of preferences.

Import Restrictions in Western European Countries.   Other industrialized countries grant the communist countries most-favored-nation treatment. However, most of the Western European countries have employed a system of quotas against communist goods in order to protect domestic markets. These quotas were substantially liberalized in the 1960s and 1970s, although they continue to be a sore point in relations between Eastern and Western Europe. The European Community has also imposed special restrictions on agricultural imports from CMEA countries. An anomalous situation in East-West European trade is the trade between the Federal Republic of Germany and the German Democratic Republic. It is the position of the Federal Republic that its trade with the German Democratic Republic is not international trade. Thus goods from the German Democratic Republic enter the Federal Republic without payment of tariffs.

DUMPING   Dumping by communist countries has been a serious concern for Western countries. The state monopoly over trade makes dumping likely for two reasons. First, the state is better able to bear the economic losses entailed in dumping in order to attain political or commercial objectives than is a private firm. Second, dumping may occur for commercial purposes. FTOs may dump in order to meet export plans, or the state's need for critical imports may induce it to dump in order to earn the necessary foreign exchange.

Dumping, or selling below cost or the domestic selling price, is difficult to discover in the case of a planned economy. Domestic prices are arbitrarily set, as is the exchange rate. Thus a comparison of domestic prices or costs of production to prices obtained on foreign markets cannot reveal whether a communist country is dumping. Consequently, Western policy makers have had to seek workable, though admittedly imperfect, alternative solutions to the dumping problem.

Bilateral Treaties.   In many of the commercial treaties negotiated between communist and Western countries, the communist party agrees to withdraw from the Western partner's market any goods that the Western partner alleges are disrupting domestic markets. Such a clause was included in the ill-fated trade agreement between the United States and the Soviet Union negotiated in the early 1970s.

The GATT Solution.   In order to provide for the participation of communist countries in GATT, Article VI was modified to define normal value, the price floor for exports, as either the price on the importer's domestic market or the prices of similar goods offered by other countries.

United States Market Disruption and Antidumping Regulations for Communist Countries.   Section 406 of the Trade Act of 1974 provides for protection against market disruption by the exports of nonmarket economies. Disruption occurs if there is a rapid increase in imports that is a significant cause of material injury to domestic producers. In such situations, the International Trade Commission must hold a hearing to determine the facts and submit a recommendation to the President. If the recommendation is positive, the President has two months to determine which remedy to apply. The provisions of the Trade Act differ from GATT provisions for the use of the escape clause against market disruption.

The Antidumping Act of 1921 as amended, the Antidumping Act of 1916, and Section 321 of the Trade Act of 1974 apply to antidumping procedures against communist countries. Under the Act of 1921, special levies may be imposed on imports if (1) the Treasury Department determines that they are, or are likely to be, sold at less than fair value (LTFV), and (2) the International Trade Commission finds that the domestic industry is suffering, or is likely to suffer, injury. A good is sold at LTFV if its price in the United States is (1) less than the price in the exporter's home market, or if such is not available then (2) less than the price charged by the exporter in other countries. If neither criterion can be used, then the Treasury Department must establish a constructed value based on foreign costs of production.

Since all three of these methods are difficult to apply or irrelevant in the case of communist countries, the Treasury Department has developed special methods that are codified in Section 321 of the Trade Act of 1974. Communist country exports are sold at LTFV if their price is less than:

1. The "exfactory" price charged to domestic consumers by a selected firm in a market economy; or
2. The export price of a selected firm from a market economy to either the United States or third countries; or
3. The constructed value in a selected market economy; or
4. The price of similar products manufactured in the United States.

Treasury Department practice with respect to choice of market economies to be employed in such comparisons and the possibility for adjusting costs for differences in levels of development and resource endowment are currently in flux.

COMMERCIAL TRANSACTIONS BETWEEN THE EAST AND THE WEST

TRADE TRANSACTIONS WITH PLANNED ECONOMIES. Since the trade flows of the communist countries are planned, a Western firm wishing to buy or sell products in such a country must accomplish two objectives. The first is to get the product it seeks to buy or sell included in the foreign-trade plan. The second objective is to reach an acceptable commercial contract with the relevant FTO so that the Western firm will be the partner chosen to implement that portion of the trade plan. Achieving these objectives is a complex and time-consuming procedure. In the short run, the Western firm can only hope to compete for contracts for goods that are already in a communist country's trade plan. Larger transactions must await the drafting of the next annual or five-year plan, and may require up to several years of preliminary contacts and up to six months of intense negotiations. The length of the negotiations is directly related to the size of the contract and inversely to the urgency of the Eastern European country's needs.

Trade Decision Makers in Planned Economies. Marketing in communist countries is different from marketing in market economies, because the ultimate users or suppliers of traded goods, be they consumers, retailers, or producing enterprises, do not make foreign-trade decisions. Such decisions are the responsibility of the FTOs. Consequently a Western firm seeking to trade with a communist country must first contact the FTO competent to trade the products in which the firm has an interest. The FTO's response will depend on whether or not the indicated commodities are in its trade plan and on the characteristics of the Western firm. Of importance to FTOs are the Western firm's size, reputation, the technological level and quality of its products, and its ability and willingness to meet the commercial needs of the FTO.

Although contacts with FTOs are necessary in order to purchase or sell goods already in the foreign-trade plan, they are not sufficient to induce planners to include the Western firm's products in future trade plans. Such decisions can be influenced only through contacts with end users: enterprises and associations, branch ministries, and, in the case of technology, the agency responsible for scientific and technological progress, such as the State Committee for Science and Technology in the Soviet

Union. Although these end users do not make determinations on which goods to import or which firm's products to purchase, they do submit import plans to their branch ministry or establish plan goals for technological advance. These decisions create a potential market for the Western firm's products. Similarly, although Western firms importing from communist countries deal with FTOs, contacts with the producing enterprise may make both buyer and producer aware of potential problems and opportunities. In all cases, business protocol in the planned economies indicates that end users or suppliers be approached through the auspices of the appropriate FTO or through the local chamber of commerce.

Building Markets in Communist Countries. Personal visits to FTOs and to end users, particularly by high-level corporate officials, are an important way of demonstrating the firm's interest in developing trade relations. However, such visits are expensive and may not be justified by market expectations. Correspondence with FTOs and end users is inexpensive and may be a useful way of disseminating information about the Western firm and its products. However, in some communist countries attitudes toward replying to business correspondence are casual at best.

Advertising in the communist countries exists, and the Western firm may wish to attempt to utilize it to reach potential end users and decision makers. Advertising to households is neither feasible nor appropriate, since they do not make import decisions. However, advertising in technical journals read by FTO personnel, enterprise managers, engineers, and designers is useful particularly if the material is factual and specific. In most communist countries there is an FTO that specializes in aiding Western firms mount advertising campaigns.

Technical seminars and presentations by company personnel, although expensive, have a good reputation for drawing the interest of decision makers in the communist countries. A number of formats are available. Presentations can be organized by a single firm, or several firms may join together to present a wider-ranging seminar. Such presentations can be organized with the cooperation of the FTO that deals in the products being displayed and possibly with that of the research institute attached to the appropriate branch ministry or association. Alternatively the services of the U.S. Department of Commerce or of an FTO that specializes in aiding Western firms with such programs may be utilized.

Even more expensive than a seminar is a display at one of the trade fairs staged by many communist countries. Among the better known annual fairs are those held in Canton, China, Brno, Czechoslovakia, and Poznan, Poland. These are large, general-purpose exhibitions of goods and machinery and are attended not only by managers, engineers, and trade officials from the host country but from other countries as well. In addition to these general fairs a number of more-specialized fairs, devoted to one, or at most several, branches of industry also exist. In all cases, arrangements to participate at such fairs must be made well in advance, and the exhibitor should be certain to assemble a delegation with ample technical expertise. In some cases exhibitors have succeeded in selling machinery and equipment exhibited at the fair to the host country.

Western firms wishing to keep expenses low may choose to employ an agent to represent them. Such agents may be either Westerners who represent Western firms in one or several communist countries, or residents of the communist country. In the latter case the Western firm must obtain such an agent from an agency, usually under the control of the ministry of foreign trade, which provides representation services to foreign firms. Many communist countries also permit Western firms to establish representative offices in their countries. Such offices require appreciable paperwork and expense to establish and tend to have high operating costs for office space (usually a hotel room) and for services. Only firms with a long and successful record of dealings in a communist country should seek (or will be granted) permission to establish such offices.

NEGOTIATIONS.   Once a decision has been made to include goods or equipment in the import plan, the end user and the branch ministry draw up the technical specifications. The responsibility for choosing a supplier and for negotiating a contract lies with the FTO. The negotiator is generally required to obtain a minimum of three bids and to demonstrate some success in improving the terms of the transaction in the course of negotiations.

The first phase of negotiations deals with technical aspects. Communist negotiators often request more technical documentation than is common in negotiations between Western firms. In some cases this is because both the FTO and end user are sufficiently unfamiliar with what is available from the West or what their actual needs are, so early negotiations are little more than window-shopping expeditions.

When the FTO is satisfied that the Western firm is able to meet the technical requirements established for the transaction, negotiations of the commercial terms begin. In addition to the standard criteria of price, quality, performance, and delivery and credit conditions, communist negotiators may have to take into account special instructions from the ministry of foreign trade. These may involve directives or de facto changes in exchange rates to favor exporters from one Western country over those from another for balance-of-payments or political reasons. With the exception of Hungary, tariffs and the supplier's ability to qualify for most-favored-nation tariff treatment should not be important decision variables.

All those who have studied communist negotiating tactics, including the Central Intelligence Agency (1979) Gorlin (1979), and Stowell (1975) agree that the aims and negotiating techniques of communist negotiators differ from those of their Western counterparts both because of the constraints under which communist negotiators must operate and from a desire to maximize the gains from any transaction. In particular, East-West negotiations tend to be prolonged, and thus costly, to the Western firm and characterized by tactics such as trying to outwait the Western firm, playing off one Western firm against another, and changes in the makeup of the communist negotiating team.

CONTRACTS.   FTOs generally base their contract negotiations on standard contracts that they have drawn up for transactions with Western firms. Experience indicates that the terms of such contracts are subject to negotiation, and because the Western firm will be expected to adhere to the letter of the written contract, it should exercise care in drafting mutually acceptable contract terms.

Standard contracts differ both among countries and among FTOs within a country. Nevertheless, there are some common features of standard contracts that Western legal experts such as Pisar, (1970), and the contributors to Starr (1974) suggest should receive special attention from Western negotiators.

Choice of Law and Arbitration.   Under the standard contract, the communist country's laws apply, and conflict is to be resolved through arbitration before an arbitral court established by the country's chamber of commerce. Western firms may wish to have third-country law apply and arrange for arbitration before a tribunal in a third country.

Delivery.   Most communist countries maintain a merchant marine and in order to conserve convertible currency prefer to purchase f.o.b. and utilize their own ships. Sellers should specify their responsibilities for dockside storage and liability for late delivery if occasioned by the buyer's vessel.

Force Majeure.   Standard contracts take a relatively narrow view of what constitutes *force majeure*—acts of state and acts of nature beyond the communist party's control—in importing and a broad view when exporting. The communist buyer is also given broad powers to cancel the contract if *force majeure* is invoked for a sufficient length of time.

Export Licenses.   Responsibility for obtaining the necessary export licenses lies with the seller. Western firms should make the validity of the contract contingent on their ability to procure such licenses to avoid penalties in cases where licenses requests are denied or excessively delayed. This is particularly relevant for firms exporting from the United States, where licensing requirements are more stringent. In the case of communist country exports, the existence of a state monopoly over trade makes the license issue problematic.

Inspection, Testing, and Guarantees.   Communist countries often require that the buyer's agent be able to visit the seller's plant to conduct inspections and tests. The seller must provide the necessary test equipment and documents. Although the inspector may hold up shipment of defective goods, his approval does not relieve the seller of liability for defects. The Western firm may wish to limit access of such agents to those parts of the plant where the goods they are to inspect are assembled, to provide for the protection of industrial secrets; the tests to be carried out should also be specified. The seller should also recognize that equipment that meets such inspections and satisfies the standards of the buyer may also have to meet general codes and standards in force for such equipment in the importing country.

FTOs request guarantees from the seller regarding the workmanship, materials, and technical standards of the goods purchased. In addition FTOs often request guarantees that imported equipment will produce output of the quality and quantity specified. Before agreeing to such a performance guarantee, the seller should evaluate the potential effects of abuse, improper installation or maintenance, poorly trained labor, or inferior inputs on the performance of the equipment being sold.

Penalties.   Pisar (1970) points out that Western firms are breach oriented in their approach to the drafting of East-West trade contracts, whereas the FTOs are performance oriented. That is to say, above all the FTO seeks to insure that all provisions of the contract are fulfilled. Heavy penalties are sought for late delivery and for failure of the equipment to operate as promised. These penalties are imposed, as Pisar notes, "for deterrence rather than liquidated damages," since in an economic environment where success is judged by the fulfillment of the national plan, the failure of one vital element may have ramifications well beyond the loss of output of the enterprise dependent on the imported goods.

Contract Compliance.   FTOs have a reputation for interpreting contracts literally, complying with them as exactly as possible and expecting their Western partners to do likewise. Pisar (1970) admits that in communist compliance with foreign-trade contracts, "performance is not impeccable. Errors . . . are encountered here no less than elsewhere. . . . However, the essential thing to bear in mind is that wherever fault is found, it is generally attributable to inefficiency of methods rather than to premeditated breach."

PAYMENTS IN EAST-WEST TRADE.   The financing of East-West trade is a combination of the traditional methods of international finance and techniques unique to East-West trade. The latter have been developed primarily to overcome the obstacles created by the inconvertibility of communist currencies and the perennial convertible-currency shortages of the communist countries.

Letters of Credit.   The most common form of payment in East-West trade transactions is the irrevocable letter of credit. In general, communist foreign-trade banks will accept unconfirmed letters of credit only from major Western banks; letters of credit issued by other banks will be accepted if confirmed by a major Western bank. Because of their excellent payments reputation, most foreign-trade banks refuse the additional expense of having their letters of credit confirmed. Cash against documents and open account are relatively rare in East-West transactions and are utilized only after the parties have established a long and satisfactory business relationship.

Switch Transactions.   One way of overcoming a shortage of convertible currency in a communist country is to employ switch trading to transform the communist country's surplus holdings of inconvertible currencies into a convertible currency acceptable to the Western seller. Surpluses of inconvertible currencies may accumulate, for example, where a communist country has a bilateral clearing account with a developing country. If it runs a trade surplus with the developing country it accumulates a surplus in its clearing account of, say, "Polish-Angolan clearing dollars." Poland may not wish to purchase Angolan goods with these clearing dollars. Instead it may offer to pay a Western supplier with these clearing dollars. If the Western firm agrees, it may either use the clearing dollars to purchase Angolan goods or sell the clearing dollars at a discount to a switch house or dealer located in the West. The Western firm thus receives convertible currency and the switch house can utilize the clearing dollars to purchase Angolan goods. Such transactions are likely to decline over time because many CMEA countries are eliminating their bilateral clearing accounts with the developing countries.

Barter and Counterpurchase Agreements.   Because communist countries are not very effective at marketing their exports in the West, they try to pass this task on to the Western firms. In barter transactions, the Western firm accepts goods offered by the FTO as partial or total payment for the goods sold to the communist country. In contrast to barter, which is a short-term transaction, counterpurchase agreements are of a longer term and involve the extension of credit. An example of a counterpurchase agreement would be the construction of a turnkey plant by a Western firm in a communist country. The construction of the plant would be financed by credits from a Western bank. The Western firm would agree to purchase some of the output of the plant over a period of years, thus assuring the communist country of convertible currency earnings with which to repay the loan.

In a survey of such practices in the trade of Eastern European countries Matheson *et al.* (1977) cite four factors that motivate communist planners to seek such arrangements. First, they are viewed as promoting exports and thus helping to alleviate balance-of-payments difficulties. Second, they are seen as helping the long-range penetration of Western markets. Third, because the Western firm is committed to a fixed value of purchases, foreign-trade planners are able to forecast convertible currency receipts with greater certainty. Finally, because the Western firm is to receive the output of the project, it is likely to have a greater interest in seeing that the project is successfully implemented and that the technology is updated as needed.

There are, of course, disadvantages to such arrangements. Western firms often resist them, refusing to undertake the risk of committing themselves to large future purchases of products whose markets may be cyclical in nature and whose quality may not be acceptable to Western buyers. Eastern European experts have also recognized that barter may result in the dumping of the bartered goods on the Western markets with attendant damage to the commercial reputation of the communist country and possibly at the expense of communist exports of the same goods through normal trade channels. Nevertheless, given the balance-of-payments problems that plague communist countries, it is likely that Western firms will continue to face pressures for such transactions.

THE TRANSFER OF TECHNOLOGY. Among market economies, international trade in commodities has increasingly been supplemented by transfers of technology and by direct foreign investment. The evolution of these new forms of international commerce in East-West trade has been hampered by systemic differences between market and communist countries, and only recently have they begun to play an important role as institutional innovation and policy changes on both sides have begun to facilitate such nontraditional commerce.

Scientific Cooperation Agreements. According to Wiczynski (1976), communist countries have signed a number of agreements with Western governments to promote cooperation in research on scientific problems of common interest. Since the bulk of research and development in market economies is carried out by the private sector, such government-to-government agreements serve as the framework for cooperation agreements between communist governments and western firms. The United States has signed several such agreements with the Soviet Union and one with Poland, and within the framework of these agreements, a number of American firms have negotiated cooperation agreements with the Soviet State Committee for Science and Technology. The objective of such aggreements is to exchange information and coordinate research on topics of mutual interest. Useful results may then be utilized by both parties. Theriot's (1976) survey of the experiences of American firms indicated rather mixed results. Some firms felt that such agreements had been worthwhile, either in terms of information received or sales of technology and equipment resulting from cooperation. Other firms, however, expressed dissatisfaction with Soviet contributions to the cooperative effort.

Licensing. The transfer of technology between market and communist economies began to take on importance in the 1960s. Prior to that time, as Sutton (1973) documents, communist countries tended to copy Western equipment and processes rather than pay for them. Copying and reverse-engineering, however, became increasingly difficult, and the communist countries came to recognize that utilization of the know-how of the innovating firm was necessary for the mastery of new industrial processes. Consequently as the contributors to Starr (1974) indicate, laws for the protection of Western industrial property were enacted, a number of communist countries acceded to the Paris Convention, and special FTOs for buying and selling licenses were established.

Although systematic data on license transactions are not available, figures cited by Hanson (1977-1978) and Wilczynski (1976) suggest that CMEA royalty payments in the 1970s were about $500 million per year. There is also a smaller reverse flow of licenses from communist countries to the developed-market economies according to Kiser (1976).

Among the problems surrounding the use of licenses as a mechanism for the transfer of technology to communist countries are the length of time required to negotiate a license transaction and subsequently to put the information thus acquired into use. In a number of cases, Western firms have sold obsolete technology or failed to provide updates on technology licensed to communist countries. Such difficulties are further exacerbated by the fact that communist enterprises rarely undertake any efforts to improve or update technology obtained under license.

INDUSTRIAL COOPERATION AND JOINT VENTURES. Although resources and technology can be transferred through trade in machinery and equipment and through the sale of licenses, neither of these methods creates a lasting relationship between the Western and communist firms. Such long-term relationships are recognized by both sides as valuable in expanding markets and business opportunities and in providing for the continuing exchange of technology and managerial expertise.

Licenses and Turnkey Plants. One form of industrial cooperation involves the sale of licenses and/or industrial installations to communist countries. However, the Western firm is less interested in benefiting through the sale of its technology and equipment than in establishing a low-cost and reliable source of supply of a product that it wishes to sell in Western markets.

Subcontracting. Western firms often supply communist firms with specifications, components, and machinery that enable the communist firm to supply the Western firm with a specified volume of product.

Coproduction and Specialization. More-intimate and higher forms of cooperation are arrangements in which the Western and communist partners intimately link their production. In specialization agreements each partner may produce a segment of a product line. The partners then exchange output with each other so that each is able to market a full product line.

In coproduction agreements each partner produces part of the final product, with components then swapped between the two partners. In many such cooperative undertakings there is a transfer of technology and know-how from the Western firm to the communist partner. Cooperation in production is usually accompanied by an agreement on marketing the finished product. The Western firm generally takes responsibility for marketing the output of the cooperation in Western markets. The communist partner may gain exclusive or nonexclusive rights to the CMEA market and possibly to some developing-country markets.

A survey of the participation of American firms in industrial cooperation by Marer and his associates for the United States Commerce Department (Marer *et al.* 1976 and surveys of the experiences of Western European firms by Levcik and Stankovsky (1979) and McMillan (1977) indicate that industrial cooperation has grown rapidly in the 1970s. Western firms find both that it is a useful way of penetrating communist markets and that their communist partners represent an inexpensive means of developing a stable and low-cost source of supply. On the communist side, cooperation is seen as an attractive way of obtaining Western technology on a continuing basis, penetrating Western markets, and gaining the ability to produce goods that will be in demand by both domestic users and other communist countries.

FOREIGN DIRECT INVESTMENT BETWEEN CAPITALIST AND COMMUNIST COUN-TRIES. Because the private ownership of the means of production is prohibited in communist countries, direct investment by Western firms in communist countries is rare. Communist countries may, of course, own commercial concerns in market economies. However, their domestic needs for capital have kept such investments at modest levels.

Joint Ventures. Joint ventures have been permitted since the 1970s in Yugoslavia, Rumania, and Hungary. More recently Bulgaria, Poland and the People's Republic of China have enacted joint-venture legislation, although in these countries there is little experience to date from which to draw any useful conclusions. In a joint venture the Western firm is able to contribute up to 49 percent of the capital toward the establishment of a productive unit. This investment gives the Western firm a right to share in the management and profits of the venture.

In all countries, the accounts of the venture are denominated in a convertible currency, and the Western firm's profits may be repatriated only to the extent that the venture is able to earn convertible currencies through exports. The venture is administered by a management council on which both partners are represented, although in Yugoslavia, the workers' council of the venture is, by law, the ultimate authority.

Tripartite Joint Ventures. In a number of cases, socialist countries have joined with Western firms to construct and operate a production facility jointly owned with a developing country, which is the host for the project. Although these ventures are viewed with enthusiasm by some observers, there are few examples of such ventures available for analysis, and consequently little is known about their operations and record of success.

Communist Investments in the West. Surveys of communist country investments in the west by the Central Intelligence Agency (1977) and by McMillan (1979) indicate that the CMEA countries have numerous investments in both developed and developing market economies. McMillan estimates that there were 359 CMEA-country-owned firms in developed market countries and 185 CMEA-owned firms in developing countries. Investments in developed countries primarily take the form of marketing organizations for the sale of goods and services (such as marine transport) from the investing country. The Soviet Union also has an extensive network of commercial banks in Europe, the Middle East, and Asia. CMEA-owned enterprises in the developing countries engaged mainly in manufacturing, assembly, and raw-materials extraction and processing.

SOURCES AND SUGGESTED REFERENCES

Acheson, K. "Revenue vs. Protection: The Pricing of Wine by the Liquor Control Board of Ontario," *Canadian Journal of Economics*, Vol. X, No. 2 (1977), pp. 246-262.

Adeniji, K. "State Participation in the Nigerian Petroleum Industry," *Journal of World Trade Law*, Vol. XI, No. 2 (1977), pp. 156-179.

Allen, R. L. "State Trading and Economic Warfare," *Law and Contemporary Problems*, Vol. XXIV, No. 2 (1959), pp.257-258.

Alouze, C. M., A. S. Watson, and N. H. Sturges, "Oligopoly in the World Wheat Market," *American Journal of Agricultural Economics*, Vol. LX (1978), pp. 178-85.

Baldwin, R. E. *Nontariff Distortions of International Trade*. Washington, D.C.: Brookings Institution, 1970.

Behrman, N.*National Interests and the Multinational Enterprise*. Englewood Cliffs, N.J.: Prentice-Hall, 1970.

Berliner, J. *The Innovation Decision in Soviet Industry*. Cambridge: MIT Press, 1980.

Bornstein, M. "Economic Reform in East Europe," in Joint Economic Committee, U.S. Congress. *East European Economies Post-Helsinki*. Washington, D.C.: U.S. Government Printing Office, 1977.

van Brabant, M. M. P. *Bilateralism and Structural Bilateralism in the CMEA*. Rotterdam: Rotterdam University Press, 1973.

Brada, J. C. and M. R. Jackson. "The Organization of Foreign Trade Under Capitalism and Socialism," *Journal of Comparative Economics*, Vol. II, No. 4 (1978), pp. 313-316.

Brainard, L. J. "The CMEA Financial System and Economic Integration," in P. Marer and J. M. Montias, eds. *East European Integration and East-West Trade*. Bloomington: Indiana University Press, 1980.

Carter, C. and A. Schmitz. "Import Tariffs and Price Formation in the World Wheat Market," *American Journal of Agricultural Economics*, Vol. LXI (1979), pp.217-252.

Central Intelligence Agency. *Soviet Strategy and Tactics in Economic and Commercial Negotiations with the United States*. Washington, D.C.: Central Intelligence Agency, 1979.

Central Intelligency Agency. *Soviet Commercial Operations in the West*. Washington, D.C.: Central Intelligence Agency, 1977.

Central Intelligence Agency. *Estimating Soviet and East European Hard Currency Debt*. Washington, D.C.: Central Intelligence Agency, 1980.

Dam, K. W. *The GATT-Law and International Economic Organization*. Chicago: University of Chicago Press, 1970.

Ellman, M. *Socialist Planning*. London: Cambridge University Press, 1979.

Funkhouser, R. and P. MacAvoy. "A Sample of Observations on Comparative Prices in Public and Private Enterprises," *Journal of Public Economics*, Vol. XI, No. 4 (1979), pp. 353-368.

Garvy, G. *Money, Financial Flows, and Credit in the Soviet Union*. Cambridge: Ballinger, 1977.

Gorlin, A. C. "The Soviet Negotiating Style in East-West Commercial Negotiations." *ACES Bulletin*, Vol. XXI, No. 3-4 (1979) pp. 384-396.

Granick, D. *Enterprise Guidance in Eastern Europe*. Princeton: Princeton University Press, 1975.

Grennes, T., P. Johnson, and M. Thursby. *The Economics of World Grain Trade*. New York: Praeger, 1978.

Gruzinov, V. P. *The USSR's Management of Foreign Trade*. White Plains, NY: M. E. Sharpe, 1979.

Gupta, R. R. "GATT and State Trading," *Journal of World Trade Law*, Vol. VIII, No. 1 (1974), p. 78.

Hanson, P. "Technology Transfer to the U.S.S.R.," *Survey*, Vol. XXIII, No. 2 (1977-78), p. 91.

Hirsch, S. and Z. Adar. "Firm Size and Export Performance," *World Development*, Vol. II, No. 7 (1974), pp.41-46.

Holzman, F. D. *International Trade Under Communism*. New York: Basic Books, 1976.

Hough, J. F. and M. Fainsod. *How the Soviet Union is Governed*. Cambridge: Harvard University Press, 1980.

International Wheat Council. *Trends and Problems in the World Grain Economy*. London: International Wheat Council, 1970.

Kaser, M. *COMECON*, 2nd ed. London: Oxford University Press, 1967.

Kintner, E. W. and J. P. Griffin. "Jurisdiction Over Foreign Commerce Under the Sherman Antitrust Act," *Boston College Industrial and Commerical Law Review*, Vol. XVII, No. 2 (1977), pp. 227-229.

Kiser, J. W. "Technology Transfer is Not a One Way Street," *Foreign Policy*, No. XXIII, (1976), pp. 314.

Kofi, T. "The International Cocoa Agreements." *Journal of World Trade Law*, Vol. 11, No. 1 (1977), pp. 37-52.

Kohn, M. J. and N. R. Lang. "The Intra-CMEA Foreign Trade System: Major Changes, Little Reform," in Joint Economic Committee, U.S. Congress. *East European Economies Post-Helsinki*. Washington, D.C.: U.S. Government Printing Office, 1977.

Kostecki, M. M. "State Trading in Industrialized and Developing Countries," *Journal of World Trade Law*, Vol. XII, No. 3 (1978), pp. 191-193.

Kostecki, M. M. *East-West Trade and the GATT System*. New York: St. Martins Press, 1978.

Kravis, I. "International Commodity Agreements to Promote Aid and Efficiency," *Canadian Journal of Economics*, Vol. I, No. 2 (1968), pp. 219-231.

Levcik, F. and J. Stankovsky. *Industrial Cooperation Between East and West*. White Plains, NY: M. E. Sharpe, 1979.

Marer, P., ed. *U. S. Financing of East-West Trade*. Bloomington, IN: International Development Research Center, 1975.

Marer, P., J. Holt, and J. Miller. *The U.S. Perspective on East-West Industrial Cooperation*. Bloomington: Indiana University for the U.S. Department of Commerce, 1976.

Matheson, J., P. McCartney, and S. Flanders, "Countertrade Practices in Eastern Europe," in Joint Economic Committee, U.S. Congress. *East European Economies Post-Helsinki*. Washington, D.C.: U. S. Government Printing Office, 1977.

McMillan, C. "Forms and Dimensions of East-West Inter-firm Cooperation," in C. J. Saunders, ed. *East-West Cooperation in Business: Inter-firm Studies*: Vienna: Springer Verlag, 1977.

McMillan, C. "Growth of External Investments by the Comecon Countries," *The World Economy*, Vol. II, No. 3 (1979), pp. 419-441.

Mountain, M. J. "Technology Exports and National Security," *Foreign Policy*, No. XXXII (1978), pp. 257-269.

Nove, A. *The Soviet Economic System*. London: Allen and Unwin, 1977.

Peston, M. H., E. Katz, and H.S.E. Gravelle. "Public Sector Pricing with Foreign Demand," *Applied Economics*, Vol. VIII, No. 1 (1977), pp. 1-10.

Pisar, S. *Coexistence and Commerce*. New York: McGraw-Hill, 1970.

Porter, S. F. *East-West Trade Financing*. Washington, D.C.: U.S. Department of Commerce, 1976.

Quigley, J. *The Soviet Foreign Trade Monopoly: Institutions and Laws*. Columbus: Ohio State University Press, 1976.

Setser, V. G. "The Immunities of the State and Government Economic Activities,"*Law and Contemporary Problems*, Vol. XXIV, No. 2 (1959), pp. 285-315.

Starr, R. F. *Communist Regimes in East Europe*, 3rd ed. Stanford: Hoover Institution Press, 1980.

Starr, R. F. ed. *Yearbook on International Communist Affairs*. Stanford: Hoover Institution Press, 1980.

Starr, R. ed. *East-West Business Transactions*. New York: Praeger, 1974.

Stowell, C. E. *Soviet Industrial Import Priorities*. New York: Praeger, 1975.

Strange, S. and R. Holland. "International Shipping and the Developing Countries," *World Development*, Vol. IV, No. 3 (1976), pp. 241-251.

Sutton, A. C. *Western Technology and Soviet Economic Development, 1945 to 1965*. Stanford: Stanford University Press, 1973.

Theriot, L. H. "U.S. Governmental and Private Industry Cooperation with the Soviet Union in the Fields of Science and Technology," in Joint Economic Committee, U.S. Congress. *Soviet Economy in a New Perspective*. Washington, D.C.: U.S. Government Printing Office, 1976.

U. N. Economic Commission for Europe. "Recent Changes in the Organization of Foreign Trade in the Centrally Planned Economies," *U. N. Economic Bulletin for Europe*, Vol. XXIV, No. 1 (1973), pp. 36-49.

U. S. Arms Control and Disarmament Agency. *The International Transfer of Conventional Arms*. Washington, D.C.: U.S. Government Printing Office, 1974.

U.S. Department of Commerce, Office of Export Administration. *A Summary of U.S. Export Administration Regulations*. Washington, D.C.: U.S. Department of Commerce, 1978.

U.S. Department of Justice. *Antitrust Guide for International Operations*. Washington, D.C.: Department of Justice, 1976.

U.S. Senate Committee on Banking, Housing, and Urban Affairs. *Financing of Foreign Military Sales through the Federal Financing Bank*. Washington, D.C.: U.S. Government Printing Office, 1978.

U.S. Senate Committee on Finance. *Discriminatory Government Procurement Practices*. Washington, D.C.: U.S. Government Printing Office, 1973.

U.S. Senate Subcommittee on International Trade of the Committee on Finance. *World Trade and Investment Issues*. Washington, D.C.: U.S. Government Printing Office, 1971.

Vernon, R. "Apparatchiks and Entrepreneurs: U.S.-Soviet Economic Relations," *Foreign Affairs*, Vol. LII, No. 3 (1974), pp. 280-296.

Viner, J. *Trade Relations Between Free-Market and Controlled Economies*. Geneva: League of Nations, 1944.

Warley, T. K. "Western Trade in Agricultural Products," in A. Shonfield, ed. *International Economic Relations of the Western World, 1959-1971*. London: Oxford University Press, 1976.

Wiczynski, J. *The Multinationals and East-West Relations*. Boulder, CO: Westview Press, 1976.

Wolf, T. A. "East-West Trade Credit Policy: A Comparative Analysis," in P. Marer, ed. *U.S. Financing of East-West Trade*. Bloomington, In: International Development Research Center, 1975.

ADDITIONAL REFERENCES

Goldman, M. I. *Detente and Dollars*. New York: Basic Books, 1975.

Leng, S. ed. *Post-Mao China and U.S.-China Trade*. Charlottesville: University of Virginia Press, 1977.

U.S. Congress, Joint Economic Committee. *East European Economies Post-Helsinki*. Washington, D.C.: U.S. Government Printing Office, 1977.

U.S. Congress, Joint Economic Committee. *Chinese Economy Post-Mao*. Washington, D.C.: U.S. Government Printing Office, 1978.

U.S. Congress, Joint Economic Committee. *Soviet Economy in a Time of Change*. Washington, D.C.: U.S. Government Printing Office, 1979.

PART 3

INTERNATIONAL FINANCE

FOREIGN DIRECT INVESTMENT AND THE MULTINATIONAL CORPORATION

CONTENTS

DEFINITION—NATURE OF THE BEAST   3

ORGANIZATIONAL STRUCTURE   6

COMPETITIVE STRENGTHS   7

HOME-COUNTRY IMPACTS   8

HOST-COUNTRY IMPACTS   11

SOURCES AND SUGGESTED REFERENCES   15

FOREIGN DIRECT INVESTMENT AND THE MULTINATIONAL CORPORATION

Thomas G. Parry

One of the most significant international developments of the post-World War II period has involved the increasing operation of enterprises across national boundaries. These operations have extended beyond simple trading-enterprise activites to encompass the movement of labor, capital, management, finance, and "know-how" within structures bounded by what have become known as *international, transnational* or *multinational* enterprises. The significance of multinational enterprises (MNEs) transcends the economic, political, and cultural realms of the "global village."

Inevitably, a form of organization as highly visible as the MNE has generated strong perceptions and reactions. As Raymond Vernon of the Harvard Business School, one of the leading students of the MNE, has stated:

> The multinational enterprise has come to be seen as the embodiment of almost anything disconcerting about modern industrial society. . . . Certain attributes of multinational enterprises would be singled out for that dubious distinction.

VERNON, 1977

This section sets out some of the existing evidence on and prevailing perceptions of the MNE, its attributes and impacts.

DEFINITION—NATURE OF THE BEAST

A useful working definition of a multinational enterprise is a corporate structure "where operations are in two or more countries on such a scale that growth and success depend on more than one nation, and where major decisions are made on the basis of global alternatives" (Parry, 1973)

There are two elements to this definition of a multinational enterprise:

1. A structural involvement in more than one market, with a "significant" proportion of enterprise operations based in more than one nation.

2. An organizational commitment to decision making on the basis of global resources available to, and global opportunities facing, the enterprise.

Obviously a structural measure of multinationality *alone* will not provide a great deal of information about the nature of organization and control that characterizes the MNE proper. Nevertheless, information about the nature of multicountry operations provides a first indication of the extent of the MNE form of enterprise operations in the international economy.

Recent U.N. data provides an indication of the importance, at least in simple aggregate numbers, of the MNE in the modern-day economy. Exhibit 1 presents data on the number of firms with one or more foreign affiliates, by number of host countries, for 1973. The total number of firms with one or more foreign affiliates was 9481, with the large proportion of these firms based in the United States and the European Economic Community (notably, the United Kingdom, France, and West Germany). The United Nations has estimated that the affiliates of all industrial MNEs in the world economy in 1976 accounted for some $670 billion of sales (excluding intrafirm

EXHIBIT 1   FIRMS WITH ONE OR MORE FOREIGN AFFILIATES BY THE NUMBER OF HOST COUNTRIES, 1973

Number of Host Countries	Number of Firms Based in			Total	
	European Economic Community	United States	Other countries	Number	Percentage of Grand Total
1	1807	1136	1312	4255	44.9
2	783	334	383	1500	15.8
3	454	206	197	857	9.0
4	293	140	111	544	5.7
5	232	95	82	409	4.3
6	144	88	51	283	3.0
7	128	75	31	234	2.5
8	92	45	32	169	1.8
9	78	56	29	163	1.7
10	54	44	17	115	1.2
11	45	37	22	104	1.1
12	41	37	14	92	1.0
13	34	22	12	60	0.7
14	43	26	12	81	0.9
15	29	25	11	65	0.7
16	23	17	5	45	0.5
17	20	14	8	42	0.4
18	11	25	5	41	0.4
19	26	14	5	45	0.5
20	22	18	5	45	0.5
>20	173	113	38	324	3.4
Grand total	4532	2567	2382	9481	100.0
Percentage	47.8	27.1	25.1	100.0	

Source. U.N. Commission on Transnational Corporations, 1978.

sales). To put this value in perspective, it should be noted that the 1976 value of the GNP in the United States was some $1706 billion. Further, the stock of direct investment abroad of the developed market economies, commonly associated with the extent of "MNE" operations, has been growing from $105 billion in 1967 to $259 billion in 1975 and an estimated $287 billion in 1976.

Contemporary views of foreign direct investment, particularly associated with its corresponding international institution, the MNE, treat such investment as a package of resource transfers across countries *within* the enterprise. The resource transfers essentially encompass capital, technology, management, finance, and marketing access and expertise. Thus foreign direct investment involves considerably more than just the financial flows tied to private international capital movements. Indeed, as discussed below, much of the competitive advantage that underlies the MNE is tied to one or more of these "resources."

John Dunning (1970) has distinguished between different types of MNE activity according to the direction of market involvement. Thus Dunning distinguishes between backward vertical operations, involving seizing and exploiting raw materials; forward vertical operations, involving selling to foreign markets; and horizontal operations, involving integration of global units along lines of international specialization within the MNE. This last form of MNE operation includes the controversial "off-shore" activities of MNEs, discussed below.

The traditional view of the potential role of foreign direct investment, and hence the MNE, is reflected in the notion of the foreign-direct-investment package associated with the operations of MNEs. Although a commonly accepted view of at least the potential role of foreign direct investment in the 1960s, this view of the development inputs associated with the MNE has not been without criticism. The nature of the potentially available alternative forms of the package has changed during the 1970s, with relevance for the activities of MNEs in developing nations. In particular, the question of the potential for "unbundling" the package traditionally associated with private foreign-direct-investment operations has assumed considerable importance in a policy context, not only for developing host nations, but also for some more-advanced nations.

Although there are now a variety of possible operational as well as ownership arrangements associated with the activities of MNEs, the elements of the package remain much the same. These basically involve access to financial capital, management and related personnel skills, technology, and markets and marketing channels associated with the corporation itself. Whether it is individual elements of this package or the entire package that host nations wish to acquire, there are a number of options involving the best way of obtaining the elements of the traditional foreign-direct-investment package from the point of view of maximizing net benefits for the host nation itself.

The basic areas of MNE involvement are broadly associated with *vertical* and *horizontal* types of market commitment. Historically, the most important form of foreign direct investment has been raw-material extraction and the export of essentially unprocessed raw materials by MNEs. Although the traditional forms of ownership and involvement in raw-material ownership and extraction have undoubtedly changed during the 1970s, and will most likely continue to evolve through the 1980s, there is still a significant interest in the raw-material sector of developing countries by MNEs.

In addition, MNEs have been involved in import-replacing activities in the manufacturing sectors of many nations, playing an important role in industrialization. Import-replacing activities have essentially been directed toward servicing the host-economy market itself.

In addition, MNEs have become involved, particularly in a number of the more-advanced yet relatively low-labor-cost countries (such as Taiwan, Singapore, Hong Kong, Mexico, and Brazil, for example), in the manufacture for export of both traditional and "new" consumer goods. These export activities have mainly been based in the so-called off-shore, technologically standarized manufacturing activities. Recently there has been a new development in the export activities of MNEs in developing nations. The establishment of export-processing zones and a switch from import-replacing activities to export markets has been taking place in certain countries and certain sectors in the late 1970s.

ORGANIZATIONAL STRUCTURE

Broadly speaking, there are two main types of organizational structures that characterize the operation of modern MNEs. First, MNEs may operate along geographic lines. Hence control is exercised *across functions* by area. For example, a number of MNEs operate one global and several regional headquarters that exercise control over all activities along geographic lines. Secondly, MNEs can operate according to a product-line or function structure. In the case of product-line forms of organization, product divisions exercise control *across countries* within that division. Similarly, functional structures, which may exist with either regional or product structures, are characterized by centralized control across both regions and products within a particular functional category. For example, research and development may be structured along functional lines across all products and all regions in the form of a centralized global activity.

Obviously, these broad types of organizational structure need not be mutually exclusive. Indeed, one suspects that individual MNEs are evolving particular organizational forms that reflect their own historical experiences and managerial styles. A combination of geographic-, product-, and function-based organizational structures is certainly common in the actual operations of MNEs.

The principal purpose of an organization structure at the level of the enterprise is to facilitate effective communication and control. For the internationally operating MNE, the organizational goal is the same, but the tasks of that organization are more complex. *Communication*, requiring two-way flows of information, and *control*, involving diverse operational constraints, across national boundaries require special organizational focus. The appropriate form will depend not only on the nature of the enterprise and its management but also on the particular countries, and hence environments, in which the MNE operates.

Given that the MNE seeks to maximize some objective function or functions, and that its operation involves activities across several national markets, the elements of potential conflict between the corporation and the nation become clear. Indeed, the likely costs as well as benefits associated with the operation of MNEs in different countries—both home and host—arise from the very nature of the MNE and its underlying strengths and *raison d'être*: corporate organization and operation based on global choices and resources. It is the global basis of decision making that results in the inherent tendency of many MNEs to shift decision-making power away from the nationally operating enterprises. When the global objectives of the MNE differ from the perceived goals of the nation, then the problems of conflict arise.

The conflict is essentially one of "national interest" versus various extranational considerations. An example of this might be the ability of the MNE to distort prices involved in interaffiliate transfers, discussed below. Possible tax-revenue losses by national governments as one result of these distortions, however "rational" they are for the MNE in the pursuit of its objectives, are the result of the shift in the locus of decision making. Another issue along the same lines concerns the location of new (and, indeed, existing) employment opportunities generated by multinational-firm activities.

COMPETITIVE STRENGTHS

The potential advantages and disadvantages of MNEs for both home and host countries derive from the underlying strengths of this form of enterprise. In general, MNEs are seen to possess certain advantages relative to national enterprises. In particular, MNEs have advantages in technology, diversity, financial resources, and, perhaps reflecting a variety of influences, size or scale of operations across national boundaries.

On the one hand, the competitive strengths of MNEs are embodied in the foreign-direct-investment package of "benefits" for the host country. The package of "product, technology, management, capital, and market access" is a potential source of growth, development of domestic industries, increased employment, and access to technology.

On the other hand, the competitive strengths of the MNE may lead to a dominant market position in either home or host country, or both. It is the power base of the MNE in its global operations, together with specific competitive strengths, that often manifests itself in the exercise of monopoly power vis-à-vis national firms and the nation. To the extent that monopoly power is exploited, any benefits to the nation of the foreign-direct-investment package may be eroded or redistributed in favor of the enterprise.

There is evidence to support this monopoly-power view of MNE international direct investment. Some analyses have emphasized the "bandwagon" behavior of MNE direct investment undertaken by international oligopolists. A study by Knickerbocker (1973) provides an elaborate demonstration of bandwagon entry characteristics of U.S. multinationals as international oligopolists.

Some specific features of MNE subsidiaries relate to monopolistic or oligopolistic *structures*. The evidence regarding the relative size of MNE affiliates in host economies, as one indicator of potential monopoly power, seems reasonably conclusive. The affiliates of U.S. enterprises in both developed and developing countries do seem to be significantly larger than domestically owned alternatives.

With regard to the concentration of activity of the MNE, there is also evidence consistent with the imperfect-competition view of international investment. Countries with significant penetration by MNEs, particularly in manufacturing and mining, usually find a high degree of concentration in certain sectors of the economy by foreign MNEs. In particular, MNE affiliates tend to concentrate in high-growth, high-technology, and export-oriented sectors of the economy. The structure of those host industries in which MNEs cluster also tends to be highly concentrated, perhaps reflecting the structure of the home-country industry. Even if the host industry structure is not highly concentrated, one may still argue that the MNE affiliate's market power lies in being part of a wider, global network with access to those resources not available to local firms.

There is also considerable evidence that imperfect competition is associated with technological advantage in international investment. Advantages in technology, as measured by R&D expenditures on personnel, appear to be an important part of both international trade and international investment by U.S. manufacturing MNEs. There appear also to be connections between technology creation, again measured by R&D, and the industrial composition of U.S. direct investment in Europe and elsewhere.

The technological basis of MNE advantages, as a specific type of market imperfection, generates special features in the structure-conduct-performance linkages within host industries. Vernon (1974) distinguishes between innovation-based and mature oligopolies in terms of the advantages each exploits. The innovation-based international oligopolist possesses advantages in introducing new products into world markets and in differentiating old products. Advantages of know-how are embodied in science-based and marketing-based international operations.

With time, these innovation-based MNEs, or at least certain activities undertaken by them, undergo transition to become "mature oligopolies," in which international market positions are grounded in the more-traditional forms of oligopoly collusion and entry barriers. Certain allegations about MNE conduct and impact on the industry structure in the host country are primarily related to the technology associated with the MNE. One involves the suitability of technology for the host industries; another concerns the monopoly power associated with proprietary technology. What does seem likely is that when the technology or know-how associated with the MNE is standardized, that is, approaches the nature of a public good, the problems inherent in the MNE–host-country relationship are quite different.

If technology is one of the main elements in the foreign-direct-investment package, it is important to assess the net benefits to host countries associated with the entry of science-based MNEs that provide access to technology.

The MNE does provide a highly sophisticated mechanism for technology transfer. The economies of centralized R&D, together with the available financial resources, provide considerable scope for the MNE to develop technology and to use it on a global basis. The foreign affiliate that is a branch of a highly integrated MNE may well have access to the latest technology through its parent, and this method far exceeds in efficiency alternative channels for importing technology. However, the conditions attached to that parent technology may entail the exploitation of monopoly power, with overall net costs. Certainly the organizational features of the MNE indicate the relative ease with which technology is freely transferred, though the operational objectives of the firm raise a number of potential difficulties for the host nation.

The nature of the *conduct* or behavior of the MNE related to technology transfer also affects the benefits or costs to the host country. Fundamental to any assessment of technology associated with MNE operations are the terms and costs applied to the proprietary technology of the MNE. According to the recent U.N. study (United Nations, 1978), the concentration of existing know-how and technological advances in MNEs is a major source of their monopoly power. In particular, the creation of monopoly rights over proprietary technology, reinforced by existing patent laws, provides a potentially powerful basis for maximizing the MNEs' share in host-market operations. The problem is especially difficult since the R&D commitments of MNEs are normally grounded in the expectation of monopoly rents from the new products and processes that result.

The exercise of monopoly power related to proprietary technology may be manifested in transfer-pricing practices and various restrictive conditions imposed on the use of technology. The evidence assembled for Colombia highlights some of the problems. Vaitsos' (1974) classic study argues that the resource transfer embodied in direct foreign investment by the MNE takes place in a package of collective inputs. The degree of indivisibility of these collective inputs, particularly with regard to the technology element, creates the monopoly power of the MNE.

If technology is embodied and the market for it imperfect, MNEs can exercise considerable monopoly power within host nations. This problem may be compounded by the relative bargaining power of host nations vis-à-vis the MNE, as well as inappropriate government policies that actually validate and reinforce the MNEs' monopoly power. According to Colombian evidence, there was indeed significant overpricing in certain sectors of industry through the transfer-pricing practices of MNEs tie-in clauses placing restrictive requirements on subsidiary purchasing policies and export franchises and related restrictive conditions on the use of the technology and know-how provided by the MNE.

HOME-COUNTRY IMPACTS

Concern with the MNE has circumscribed a large range of issues relevant to both home and host countries and cutting across economic, political, and social boundaries. For the home country, interest in the MNE, in the early days confined to a noninstitutional concern with private-direct-investment *outflows*, has evolved from an initial preoccupation with balance-of-payments effects. Thus, for example, the 1960s U.S. restrictions associated with private investments abroad were designed to improve what was feared to be a negative impact on that home-country's balance of payments. Essentially, the balance-of-payments effects are seen to consist of a series of ''initial'' and ''continuing'' flows that either have a favorable or unfavorable impact on the home-country's balance of payments. For example, initial capital outflows may be partly compensated for by sales of home-country equipment required in setting up foreign-investment plants. Similarly, any displacement of home-country exports as a result of foreign-affiliate production has to be set against exports generated in the form of direct input requirements of the subsidiary, which are supplied by the parent, as well as indirect export creation for the home country generally, associated with specific foreign-affiliate operations. Another potentially important contribution to the home-country balance of payments, apart from the more-obvious direct payment of profits and dividends on the investment (which may not be generated for some period of time), are the service fees associated with management and technology often provided by the parent firm to the subsidiary.

Although specific interest in possible net balance-of-payments effects associated with private direct investment has become relatively unimportant in the post-Bretton Woods era of flexible exchange rates and overall macromanagement of the external sector, a number of the issues related to these effects are still of some concern. Perhaps the most important has been the interest in the so-called runaway industry form of off-shore foreign direct investment, which has relevance not only for the pattern of trade flows of the home country, but also for domestic employment and capital creation in the home country. Indeed, in the early 1970s this employment issue became the most contentious home-country concern in the United States, with the unsuccessful attempt to restrict investment and technology outflows through the proposed Hartke-Burke legislation.

The home-country-jobs argument suggests that the off-shore production by foreign affiliates for the home market as well as for third countries occurs at the expense of home-country domestic production and, hence, home-country employment. Implicit in this argument is the assumption that off-shore activity does in fact displace home-country production (and employment) in the home-country market itself, as well as in third-country markets. What is ignored is the fact that very often the choice is not simply between off-shore or home-country production. In many cases the move to off-shore production is required to maintain cost-competitiveness vis-à-vis production in other locations—competing in both the home market itself as well as in other foreign markets. In this type of off-shore involvement, the alternative is often the loss of home-country production to other sources of supply. Furthermore, off-shore production can generate secondary production activity in the home market through the provision by home-country firms of both direct and indirect inputs to foreign-affiliate production. Such secondary effects may have employment consequences for the home country, perhaps requiring some structural adaptation to changed production patterns, though these may not necessarily be different from the adjustment requirements that are associated with changing trade patterns *per se*.

Other issues with specific home-country relevance include the taxation of MNE profits, and general income-distribution effects. Basically, the concern over the taxation of foreign-sourced income involves a consideration of whether or not tax rules discriminate in favor of overseas operations, and whether or not devices such as financial manipulation and transfer pricing are used to shift the burden of taxation between the different countries in which the MNE operates. These issues have been examined by the Brookings Institution (Bergsten, *et al.*, 1978). It seems reasonable to accept the view that most *home* countries do have sufficiently sophisticated taxation and customs authorities, which scrutinize the tax incidence of MNE operations. There are possibly problems in the areas of intrafirm services' transactions, where arm's-length prices are difficult to establish, and in the day-to-day financial practices of MNEs in dealing with foreign-exchange transactions. With regard to discriminating in favor of foreign-source income, recent changes in the U.S. practice of reporting foreign profits (F.A.S.B. 8) and proposed changes in the taxation of foreign-source income demonstrate some ways in which the home country is able to modify fiscal instruments in accordance with desired objectives in this area.

Perhaps more controversial are the attempts by some home countries to impose sociopolitical constraints on the foreign operations of nationally based firms. The earlier and more familiar example of this has been the U.S. "trading with the enemy" provisions that were commonly imposed on foreign affiliates (though there is reason to believe that in some cases foreign affiliates were used to getting around trading-with-the-enemy provisions). As the restricted countries get smaller in number this issue become less of a problem, though it does reveal one aspect of the conflict of sovereignty in the intercountry operations of MNEs.

What has become more common is the attempt by some home countries, most notably the United States, to impose "good behavior" requirements in various areas of corporate activity. Most noticeable among these are the areas of "human rights" and "questionable payments." With regard to human rights, it seems that the most home-country pressure has come not from governments as such, but rather from various pressure groups within the home country. Thus shareholder groups and various religious/political organizations have had a degree of success in influencing the corporate decisions of certain U.S. MNEs in their operations in countries like South Africa. At the government level, the human-rights issue presumably accounts for the official ban on commercial relations with Uganda, which, although small in terms of MNE interests, does demonstrate the way in which the freedom of action of the MNE is constrained by the home-country response to social and political perceptions.

Following the revelation of significant bribes paid out by a number of U.S. MNEs in their dealings in various overseas countries, the U.S. government has imposed a set of rules and requirements that forbid these so-called "questionable" payments. It is perhaps interesting that the U.S. government is imposing a set of business-ethics value judgments on its home-based MNEs that are not in fact appropriate in a large number of countries in which these firms operate, the "questionable payment" is often an accepted part of business activity in many countries. Nevertheless, the home-country-imposed business ethic may be placing severe constraints on the freedom of action of U.S. MNEs that may not be imposed on the MNEs of other home countries nor especially relevant to various host countries' objectives.

HOST-COUNTRY IMPACTS

Many of the home-country-related issues emerge in the outlook of countries that are host to MNEs. Thus balance-of-payments concerns similarly enter into the policy thinking of a number of host countries. The host-country tries to secure a favorable balance-of-payments impact from private foreign direct investment. On the one hand, this requires some contribution on capital account from private direct investment as well as a matching of the servicing outflows associated with profits, fees, and royalties with some favorable trade-flow impacts such as import replacement and new export generation. The less-developed host country in particular, often sees foreign private direct investment through the MNE in terms of easing the foreign-exchange gap that, together with other input shortages, constrains the development goals of the country. Although the balance-of-payments question seems much less a concern to home countries and for the same reason (post-Bretton Woods changes in both the international financial system and in modern macromanagement) of less concern to the developed host countries (such as the United Kingdom, France, Australia, Canada, etc.), there is still interest in the balance-of-payments impact in the less developed country that is host to the MNE.

The interaction of the MNE and the host nation has led to allegations of a number of "harmonies" and "tensions." These in fact represent extensions of the earlier cost-benefit debate over foreign direct investment, taking explicit account of the relevant foreign-investment institution—the MNE. The "effects of interaction" are in fact the effects of foreign ownership of domestic firms on national economies and societies, and are the results of the very nature of the MNE: corporate decisions made in varying degrees on the basis of global alternatives facing the integrated parts of the firm. The effects of interaction are not so much brought about by a conspiracy by the firm as by the global perspective of the firm.

One source of tension, specifically a result of the behavior of the MNE, involves the existence of restrictive export franchises imposed on national subsidiaries. It is often claimed, with varying degrees of empirical support, that subsidiaries are not permitted to export, or can export only to designated markets. The argument implicitly assumes that the subsidiary has the potential to export and that export franchises impose a real restriction on the subsidiary's export potential. The restrictive export franchise is allegedly designed to protect different subsidiaries' market from competition by other subsidiaries. Distortions may arise where one national subsidiary is prevented from exporting where, if the market were operating without such restrictions, that subsidiary would service the relevant market.

Another major problem area involves MNE subsidiaries' imports from overseas affiliates. It is often claimed that the pricing of MNE intrafirm goods and factor flows has adverse effects on the host country's balance of payments. In fact, the manipulation of these prices has important income-distribution effects where factor returns are distorted and where tax payments are potentially avoided.

In addition to minimizing global tax outlays, the MNE can use transfer prices as a means of getting profits out of a country where there are controls over income repatriation, or where the existence of minority shareholders in one subsidiary encourages higher charges in order to maximise the MNE's share of profits. Although many countries have tax authorities capable of minimizing distortions in interaffiliate pricing, this is complicated by the difficulty of establishing arms-length relationships, especially for intangible service fees such as those for management and technology. Where, as in the less developed nations, the proper tax administration does not exist, the problems of interaffiliate price manipulation are substantially greater. The implications for national policy go beyond any possible balance-of-payments effects of inflated trade prices to more-important questions of distortions in income distribution through factor-price manipulation and the optimal taxation of foreign investment, an issue of some importance given the potential benefits of this taxation.

Other features of interaffiliate trade raise questions about the use and development of national resources by the MNE where such development is seen as desirable in some sense by the host-country government. To a large extent, the resource-use issue is tied up with the question of the centralization of decision making within the MNE. It is often claimed that centralized decision making results in an import propensity of subsidiaries to the neglect of domestic sources of supply, failure to fully develop domestic management and other skills, and finally, the import of technology and centralization of R&D to the neglect of domestic R&D. Centralization in all these cases may be fully consistent with the firm's global profit maximization. The conflict, however, occurs between one nation's perceived interests (whether "right" or not) and the MNE's preferred behavior. The supposed import bias of the subsidiary limits the development of domestic production and service industries because of restrictions on the sources from which the subsidiary may buy, particularly because of requirements to buy parts, equipment, and services from the parent and affiliates abroad.

The real question is whether the fact of external control involved in the centralization of decision making in the parent leads to discrimination against domestic sources of supply. Once again, the conflict between the nation and the MNE involves the tendency of the firm to use least-cost sources, whereas the nation often encourages the development of domestic supply capacity without regard to short-run efficiency considerations.

The MNE may not, however, be using the most-efficient supply sources: Where artificial barriers to trade influence the initial establishment of a subsidiary, there is good reason to expect substantial domestic content despite higher costs. Similarly, transport costs and significant differences in the market requirements of the subsidiary (including domestic-content policies of certain host countries) will influence the amount of local content. The overall purchasing behavior of any one subsidiary at one time will be the result of a number of considerations. It is reasonable to expect that the extent to which a subsidiary relies on imports will depend on the suitability, availability, and cost of domestic sources. Unfortunately, however, the experience of developing nations especially points to a lack of capacity to sustain domestic sources, and the free import by the subsidiary of production inputs is severely constrained by the nation's concern (whether a misplaced concern or not) with the balance of payments. Further, the tariff policies of some of the more-developed countries, designed to stimulate the development and use of domestic resources, often work counter to any tendency of the MNE to more-efficient (or least cost) resource use.

Closely related to the alleged import bias of the MNE subsidiary is the alleged bias against domestic management and technology. Critics argue that the MNE will centralize research-and-development facilities (though not necessarily in the parent country) and will control the size and purpose of any R&D activity undertaken by the subsidiary. In addition, management personnel are often from the parent organization, and little attempt is made to train indigenous personnel. This behavior, it is alleged, inhibits the development of domestic technology and technical, scientific, and management skills within the host country. In the final analysis, it is not unreasonable to expect the firm to base decisions on the suitability of domestic personnel and institutions.

Another important effect of MNE interaction with the host nation is its impact on the structure and performance of the industries in which the MNE operates. The impact of the MNE on industrial structure is often identified with the level of industry concentration in host countries. But the issues go beyond just seller concentration. There is no conclusive evidence about how MNE entry does in fact affect seller concentration.

On the one hand, Vernon (1972) argues that the "mature oligopolies" are becoming less concentrated in global markets because the overall world market is growing and the number of new enterprises entering international markets is increasing. The evidence to support this proposition is especially apparent in the automobile, petroleum, aluminium-smelting, and pulp-and-paper industries. On the other hand, there is some presumption that in certain individual host nations, the MNE raises seller concentration.

There is also considerable interest in the inherent efficiency of the actual plant associated with MNE entry, not only from the point of view of the suitability of embodied technology, but also from the point of view of the direct effect on host industry structure. A number of studies have pointed to the inefficient industry structure created by the entry of internationally competing oligopolists behind tariff walls, especially in the smaller developed and developing markets.

The combination of almost any actual or potential barrier to trade with the oligopolistic nature of most of the industries in which foreign investment is important tends to produce a great proliferation of small-scale foreign units, without any real prospect of rationalization or consolidation. *If the units were domestically owned, one would expect market forces to bring about consolidation over a period*; when they are owned by large internationally competing corporations, this is highly unlikely.

D.T. BRASH, 1970

The large MNE with global financial resources and a commitment to individual market positions can resist normal market forces. This is especially true whenever market forces are themselves weakened by tariff distortions that present an obstacle to competitive rationalization that might otherwise occur.

There is also a case for supposing that MNE entry compounds the problems of industry fragmentation, especially in the case of international oligopolistic rivalry of MNEs. Inappropriate plant size is certainly possible, particularly behind protectionist barriers, but the crowding practices of MNEs can also lead to or compound excessive industry fragmentation. Of course, it is not always the case that the MNE entrant will introduce an inappropriate plant associated with higher unit costs and/or excess capacity. There is some evidence from the experience of foreign investment in the Australian chemical industry that the MNE entrant, even with *existing* tariff protection, will undertake some adaptation of derivative technology to install a smaller-scale, near-optimum-size plant with comparable unit costs and little if any excess operating capacity (Parry, 1980).

The operations of the MNE in the host country can also have an effect on industry structure through their influence on barriers to entry. In the first place, it is often only the MNE that can overcome existing barriers to entry in host industries. The suggestion is that the MNE has the necessary resources to overcome barriers to entry whereas indigenous firms do not. In particular, where existing industry entry barriers are characterized by large economies of scale, product differentiation, or advanced technology, the MNE is more likely to be able to enter the industry successfully. This is because of its usually assumed advantages, discussed above, in exploiting international production based on such industry characteristics. Thus MNE entry that overcomes existing barriers and breaks down established, highly concentrated structures can have a significant, favorable effect on competitive structure in the host industry.

However, just as the MNE can reasonably be assumed to have access to various advantages enabling it to overcome barriers to entry in host industries, the MNE may well create additional, or compound existing, barriers to entry. Further, if the MNE entrants force out established marginal firms and/or stimulate mergers or takeovers among established firms, then the end result may well entail an increase in concentration, particularly if the surviving MNE affiliates establish higher entry barriers. The apparent ability of the MNE in exploiting scale economies, product differentiation, marketing advantages, technological advances, and vertical integration economies suggests that MNEs have the potential to create significant entry barriers.

Paradoxically, it is because of its competitive ability that the MNE may limit overall competition in an industry. Because of special advantages related to global operations, the MNE can limit the development of indigenous firms, effectively curtailing competition. The activities of MNEs in the electrical-equipment industry have been reasonably well documented and highlight the ways in which international cartels as well as various market-power positions have impeded the development of indigenous industry in several host countries. In the main, the monopoly power of MNEs has been used in the form of predatory practices against indigenous firms.

In these circumstances, the effective market power of MNEs means that the host-country government is unable to rely on any effective competitive or countervailing pressures to determine the host-country share of gains from MNE activities. Indeed, host governments are increasingly relying on case-by-case bargaining with MNEs over the share of rents. The policy responses, especially those of developing host countries, will increasingly need to take account of the market-power implications of MNE operations in terms of the broad issue of the distribution of total gains associated with the activities of the multinational enterprise.

SOURCES AND SUGGESTED REFERENCES

Bergsten, C.F., *et al. American Multinationals and American Interests.* Washington, D.C.: Brookings Institution, 1978.

Brash, D.T. "Australia as Host to the International Corporation," in C.P. Kindleberger (ed.), *The International Corporation.* Cambridge: MIT Press, 1970.

Dunning, J. "The Multinational Enterprise," *Lloyds Bank Review*, Vol. 97, (1970), pp. 19–36.

Gladwin, T. N. and I. Walter, *Multinationals Under Fire: Lessons in the Management of Conflict.* New York: Wiley, 1980.

Knickerbocker, F. T. *Oligopolistic Reaction and Multinational Enterprise.* Cambridge: Harvard University Graduate School of Business Administration, 1973

Parry, T. G. "The International Firm and National Economic Policy." *Economic Journal*, Vol. 83, December 1973, pp. 1201ff.

Parry, T.G., *The Multinational Enterprise: International Investment and Host Country Impacts.* Greenwich, CN: JAI Press, 1980.

U.N. Commission on Transnational Corporations, *Transnational Corporations in World Development.* New York: U.N. Economic and Social Council, E/C 1038, March 1978, p. 211.

Vaitsos, C. *International Income Distribution and Transnational Enterprises.* Oxford: Oxford University Press, 1974.

Vernon, R. *Restrictive Business Practices: The Operation of Multinational United States Enterprises in Developing Countries.* New York: United Nations, 1972.

Vernon, R. "The Location of Economic Activity." In J.H. Dunning (ed.), *Economic Analysis and the Multinational Enterprise.* London: Allen & Unwin, 1974.

Vernon, R. *Storm over the Multinationals.* Cambridge: Harvard University Press, 1977.

SECTION **17**

FORECASTING EXCHANGE RATES

CONTENTS

IS EXCHANGE-RATE FORECASTING
NEEDED?   4

Goods Markets and the Irrelevance of
the Exchange Rate   4
Financial Markets and the Irrelevance
of Forecasting   5
Empirical Evidence on Arbitrage   5
Conclusions: What Should be Forecast?   9
  Forecasting needs for the long run   10
  Forecasting needs for the short run   10
  Forecasting needs for the very short
  run   11

DETERMINANTS OF THE EXCHANGE
RATE—ELEMENTARY THEORY   12

The Long-Run-Purchasing-Power-Parity   12
The Short-Run-Real-Exchange-Rate
Changes   14
The Very Short Run   16

The Role of Governments   17

FORECASTING METHODS   19

Description and Evaluation of Forecasts   19
The Forward Rate and Relative Interest
Rates   20
Time-Series Analysis   21
Econometric Models   22
Leading Variables   22
Foreign-Exchange Advisory Services   23

SOURCES OF INFORMATION   24

MANAGEMENT CONSIDERATIONS   25

General Conclusions for Forecasting   25
Treatment of Uncertainty—Hedging and
Covering   25

SOURCES AND SUGGESTED
REFERENCES   27

FORECASTING EXCHANGE RATES

Clas Wihlborg

Professional investment may be likened to those newspaper competitions in which the competitors have to pick out the six prettiest faces from a hundred photographs, the prize being awarded to the competitor whose choice most nearly corresponds to the average preferences of the competitors as a whole; so that each competitor has to pick, not those faces which he himself finds prettiest, but those which he thinks likeliest to catch the fancy of the other competitors.

(JOHN MAYNARD KEYNES, *The General Theory of Employment, Interest and Money*, p. 156)

The quote from the British economist John Maynard Keynes illustrates well the difficulties of forecasting exchange rates and making profits on the choice of currency denomination of investments and borrowing. Keynes was very successful in financial markets by applying his principle. However, its application demands an in-depth understanding of the determinants of future prices and the functioning of the markets. For each market participant earning above-average profits, there must be another market participant earning below-average profits, or losses.

This chapter should provide guidance for *what* to forecast, *when* to forecast, and *how* to forecast for a firm with foreign projects, foreign trade, or foreign borrowing.

The question of *what* to forecast is raised, because the exchange rate itself is irrelevant for the firm under certain conditions. Instead the exchange rate's deviation from the value it would have achieved under those conditions is the interesting variable. Also, estimates of the market's expectation of the future rate can often be observed in the market, in which case it is the future deviations from this value that are of interest.

The question of *when* to forecast is related to the quality of the observable estimate of the future rate. The forecaster must be able to do better than this estimate in order to invest resources in forecasting. Before investing in forecasting ability, the forecastor must be able to evaluate the potential and costs of alternative forecasting methods. In other words, it is necessary to know *how* to obtain a forecast.

The first part of this section describes the conditions under which the exchange rate is irrelevant and illustrates the relevant variables to forecast over the long run, the short run, and the very short run. The long run is defined as above one or two years, the short run ranges from three months to one or two years, and the very short run ranges from the day-to-day horizon up to three months.

"Determinants of the Exchange Rate—Elementary Theory" summarizes modern theories of exchange-rate determination over the different time horizons and "Forecasting Methods" describes and compares alternative methods for obtaining forecasts with respect to cost and quality.

"Sources of Information" lists different sources of historical information about the variables of relevance for exchange-rate determination.

Finally, "Management Considerations" draws some conclusions with respect to forecasting and financial management under uncertainty about the future exchange rate.

No distinction is drawn between more-or-less-flexible or fixed exchange rates. Most of the arguments are valid under any regime. A separate section in "The Role of Governments" contains a discussion about how government behavior in foreign-exchange and other markets could affect the forecasting of exchange rates by making the "long run" shorter or the "short run" longer.

The references at the end include books or articles that contain valuable summaries of the topics discussed.

IS EXCHANGE-RATE FORECASTING NEEDED?

It is not obvious that exchange rates should or need be forecast, even when a firm is heavily involved in international operations. The exchange rate simply does not matter under certain conditions in international goods and financial markets. The understanding of these conditions, even if unrealistic, provides insight into what variables need be forecasted.

There are two conditions under which the exchange-rate forecast is superfluous. First, when goods markets are in equilibrium with purchasing-power parity, the exchange rate is irrelevant. Second, when the interest-rate differential reflects the best-available information on the expected rate of change of the exchange rate, no gain can be made by forecasting, even if the exchange rate is of relevance. We shall explore the two conditions in greater detail.

GOODS MARKETS AND THE IRRELEVANCE OF THE EXCHANGE RATE. Since the exchange rate formally is a price of one kind of money in terms of another, it is intuitively reasonable that changes in the exchange rate *need* not matter economically—in real terms. This is in fact the case when purchasing-power parity (PPP) holds. Then the exchange rate's movements offset movements in two countries' relative price levels. In other words, the exchange rate only translates one unit of account into another.

The implications of PPP are far reaching. If PPP holds, the firm need not worry about exchange-rate changes, since any unanticipated fluctuations would correspond to changes in at least one country's price level. *Exchange risk* would *not exist*, only uncertainty about inflation rates. Also, *exchange rates need not be forecasted.*

PPP is not sufficient to make currency denominations of contracts irrelevant, however, because the firm may suffer losses on assets or liabilities in a currency when there are unanticipated changes in the *price level* in the contract currency. Thus the firm needs to be concerned about inflation in contract currencies when contracts are set in *nominal terms.* Naturally this is true whether the currency denomination is domestic or foreign.

Inflation is also irrelevant under certain conditions. Changes in a country's price level are irrelevant for the firm when *contracts* are specified in *real terms and* when *inflation is independent of relative prices* among commodities. Assets on which the return is indexed to the price level are perfect examples, of course. The returns on physical assets such as buildings or machinery in a country are also independent of inflation, when prices (in terms of other goods) of the services or products that are produced by the assets are independent of inflation.

The arguments above illustrate the conditions under which *inflation and exchange rates* are of no economic consequence—when the firm need forecast only future *relative prices* among commodities when evaluating a project in any country. Thus only conventional business risk matters.

It is important to note that the conditions above are fairly strict. It was mentioned that inflation must be independent of relative prices and that the exchange-rate changes must reflect relative inflation rates. In addition, tax payments in real terms must be independent of the inflation rate. This is *not* true in countries where depreciation allowances are based on historical costs (see Hong, 1977). Naturally the firm's concern must be the real value of the firm's profit stream as opposed to nominal profits. The fact that accounting is performed in nominal prices may cause "money-illusion" in the stock market. Firms could then be induced to be more concerned with accounting numbers than with economic values. On the other hand, each firm could inform the market about the economic implications of published figures.

FINANCIAL MARKETS AND THE IRRELEVANCE OF FORECASTING. Explicit forecasting of the future exchange rate is naturally only profitable if there is no easily available market price that incorporates the best-possible forecast. Many economists argue that relative interest rates and the forward rate reflect all available information about the future. Then firms or investors need only study the interest rate differential on identical assets in two currencies in order to obtain the optimal forecast. Alternatively, the forward exchange rate provides the same information.

Note that forecasting can be irrelevant even if the exchange rate matters for the profit of the firm. The irrelevance implies only that the firm cannot hope to gain anything by investing or borrowing in one currency instead of another.

The conditions under which there are no gains to be made by attempting to forecast the exchange rate in order to obtain a favorable currency position are strict. For all available information to be incorporated in interest rates and forward rates, the small part of the market participants that have access to the best information must have *unlimited* access to arbitrage funds and they must *not* be *averse to risk* for the arbitrage process to function perfectly. There are profit opportunities for individuals or firms with good information and with little risk aversion, if one of the above conditions does not hold.

EMPIRICAL EVIDENCE ON ARBITRAGE. Exhibits 1 and 2 illustrate the exchange-rate developments of the United Kingdom and West Germany relative to the United States, the time paths of the relative consumer price indices in dollars, and the time paths of relative unit labor costs in dollars. Purchasing-power parity in terms of consumer price indices and unit labor costs, respectively, holds at index 100. The diagrams cover the period 1973–1977.

Exhibit 3 shows the rates of change of deviations from PPP over quarters and years, measured on an annual basis for the same currencies as Exhibits 1 and 2. PPP is here measured for wholesale price indexes.

EXHIBIT 1   RELATIVE UNIT LABOR COSTS IN
DOLLARS (ULC$_1$/ULC$_2$), RELATIVE CONSUMER
PRICES IN DOLLARS (CP$_1$/CP$_2$) AND RELATIVE
EXCHANGE RATE (e). UNITED KINGDOM
RELATIVE TO THE UNITED STATES

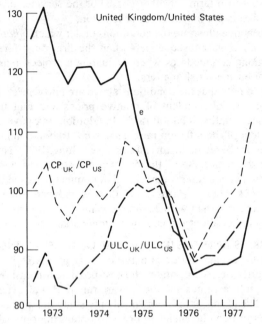

It is clear that PPP does not hold statistically among consumer and wholesale price indexes for the period, though yearly changes in the deviations are much smaller than the quarterly. This should not be taken to mean that PPP does not hold over *any* time horizon. Statistical measures of price indexes are very unreliable over all time horizons. Over the long term, relative price changes in countries with different taste patterns will cause deviations from PPP in a statistical sense. The economic conditions for the irrelevance of the exchange rate and the inflation rates is only that identical goods cost the same in two countries and that relative price changes are independent of the exchange rate and the inflation rate. At some point, the statistical errors in the estimates of PPP—increasing with time—will dominate the economic deviations—decreasing with time.

The very short term deviations from PPP may also be exaggerated because prices on many goods with fixed list prices fluctuate in the short term in the form of rebates, credit terms, and the like. Nevertheless, there is little doubt that nontraded goods and imperfect international competition may cause substantial deviations from PPP over periods up to one or two years. We can therefore be sure that the exchange rate matters over these time horizons.

Empirical evidence on any interdependence between inflation rates and relative price changes within countries is harder to come by. There are increasing indications

EXHIBIT 2   RELATIVE UNIT LABOR COSTS IN
DOLLARS (ULC_1/ULC_2), RELATIVE CONSUMER
PRICES IN DOLLARS (CP_1/CP_2) AND
EXCHANGE RATE (e). WEST GERMANY
RELATIVE TO THE UNITED STATES

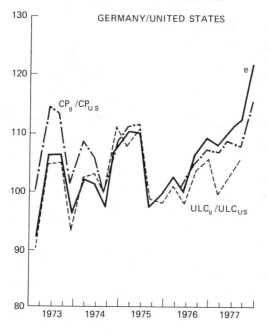

that the volatility of relative prices increases with inflation (Wachtel and Cukierman, 1980) but this need not imply any correlation.

The figures above provide some lead with respect to the important relationship between labor costs, inflation, and exchange-rate changes. Relative unit labor cost is an important variable for the relative profitability of investments in different countries. We saw in Exhibits 1 and 2 the relative unit labor costs in dollars between the United States and the United Kingdom and between the United States and West Germany. These figures for the United Kingdom follow a different pattern from that of deviations from PPP, indicating that wage costs do not rise or fall perfectly with inflation in all the countries. One can trace temporary co-movements between the relative inflation rates and relative unit labor costs in the United Kingdom and the United States whereas the relative unit labor costs between the United States and Germany seem to follow deviations from PPP and the exchange rate. The latter indicates that price levels and nominal wages followed each other well in West Germany and the United States. Nevertheless, we can see that yearlong or longer profit opportunities may occur as a result of wage developments that differ from the general inflation rates. Thus nonneutral inflation rates as well as nonneutral exchange rates affect firms over nonnegligible periods of time.

We turn now to empirical evidence on arbitrage conditions in international finan-

EXHIBIT 3 ANNUAL PERCENTAGE RATES OF CHANGE IN THE DEVIATION FROM WHOLESALE-PRICE PPP FOR THE UNITED STATES, THE UNITED KINGDOM, AND WEST GERMANY OVER QUARTERS AND YEARS, 1967-1976. (a) UNITED STATES AND WEST GERMANY; (b) UNITED STATES AND THE UNITED KINGDOM; (c) UNITED KINGDOM AND WEST GERMANY

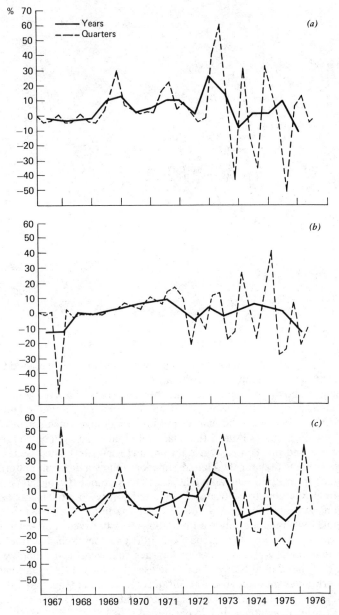

Source. Clas Wihlborg, *Currency Risks in International Financial Markets*, Princeton Study in International Finance, No. 44, December, 1978.

cial markets. The first important observation is that *interest-rate parity holds in forward markets among the major currencies represented in Euromarkets* (see, e.g., Frenkel and Levich, 1975, and Kohlhagen, 1978). The forward markets in other currencies are not sufficiently well developed to test, but it is safe to assume that temporary deviations occur. This is the case, for example, for Sweden, where parity relative to the Eurodollar is violated for periods up to a couple of months (see Sveriges Riksbanks *Förvaltningsberättelse*, the yearly report by the Swedish Central Bank). The implications for forecasting is first that forward rates *or* interest rates are not unbiased estimates of the future spot rate among most minor currencies. In fact, it is most likely that neither of the two is unbiased. Second, forward rates *and* interest rates *could* be, but *need not* be, unbiased estimates for the major currencies. Interest-rate parity is not a sufficient condition for perfect arbitrage in international financial markets.

It is naturally difficult to test whether the forward rate or the interest-rate differential is equal to the best-available forecast of the exchange rate. Measures of the expectations of the most well informed market participants are necessary. A number of indirect tests have been performed, however, First, Giddy and Dufey (1975), Levich (1979), Poole (1967), and others have studied whether daily fluctuations are serially correlated, since this may imply profit opportunities. The tests show mixed evidence for the random-walk hypothesis—that the spot exchange rate is the best forecast of the future exchange rate. These tests are typically very short run, because they can not be performed over time horizons, when fundamental determinants are likely to change, without a detailed model.

Levich (1980) conducted another kind of indirect study of profit opportunities over different periods by tracing the performance of the forecasts of foreign-exchange advisory services relative to the forward rate. There is evidence that some services are able to outperform the forward rate consistently, indicating profit opportunities of having access to superior information (or judgment). However, it still remains to show that *one* foreign-exchange advisory service can outperform the forward rates among the major currencies consistently over long periods. If not, the firm or individual must know when to substitute one advisory service for another. Naturally this presumes the access to superior information by the firm itself.

Under some conditions it is possible to make predictions that are superior to the forward rate even without access to superior information. Specifically, it was mentioned above that arbitrageurs will not necessarily push the forward rate to the expected future spot rate when they are risk averse and/or when the supply of arbitrage funds is limited.

CONCLUSIONS: WHAT SHOULD BE FORECAST.   The discussion of the relevance of the exchange rate can now be summarized as follows:

1.   Exchange-rate changes may have real effects on the firm, independent of inflation rates, up to at least periods of one year.

2.   Inflation or deflation in the currency of denomination of a fixed-price contract (accompanied by exchange-rate changes) leads to gains or losses on contracts that are fixed in nominal terms. This consideration gains in importance with the length of the contract periods.

3.   Inflation affects the real return on physical assets when the tax liability of the firm depends on historical costs, and when some relative prices depend on the rate of inflation.

These conclusions imply that the firm needs estimates of *future deviations from purchasing-power parity* and *inflation rates* to be able to forecast the real value of cash flows that are fixed in nominal terms. In other words, exchange rates *and* price levels need to be forecast. *Forecasts of the deviations from PPP suffice* when nominally fixed contracts play minor roles. Forecasts of *levels* of exchange rates and price levels *may be unnecessary* if deviations from PPP can be forecast directly.

The conclusions of the discussion of arbitrage conditions in financial markets are as follows:

1. The forward rate and the interest-rate differential for *major currencies* can normally be outperformed only by the forecaster who holds *superior information or judgment* about future determinants of the exchange rate.

2. The investors or borrowers with *less* risk aversion than those that last entered the market (the marginal market participant) may gain by forecasting even when their available information is not superior to the information held by the marginal market participant.

3. The exchange rate expectation for currencies without well-developed financial markets are less well reflected in relative interest rates and forward rates. This increases the value of separate forecasts.

Forecasting Needs for the Long Run. Forecasting needs for the long run (above two years) would mostly be needed for long-term project analysis and long-term financing. Purchasing-power parity is usually a reasonable approximation for periods above two years. Only *inflation forecasts* are then needed, and only for fixed-price contacts. Naturally, the exchange rate may deviate temporarily from parity in both directions, but such deviations are likely to cancel out over periods above two years for major currencies (compare Exhibits 1 and 2). Therefore, it is only the firm with a relatively short pay-off period (high cost of capital) that needs to be concerned about possible deviations over the short term when making cash-flow estimates.

We have also seen that inflation does not affect the real value of the firm if its market prices *relative to other prices are independent* of the average price level and if depreciation allowances based on historical costs play a minor role. The firm can evaluate cash flows at a constant price level under these circumstances and need only forecast how its input and output prices are going to develop relative to each other and substitutable commodities. Heavy disturbances and government actions may slow down the adjustment process. This seems to have happened during 1977 and 1978, when the dollar remained undervalued relative to other major currencies for longer than two years. We shall discuss this further in "The Role of Government." Similarly, central banks defend a disequilibrium exchange rate much longer during a pegged system than during a flexible regime. This happened during the late 1960s and the early 1970s while the Bretton Woods system was breaking down. Accordingly, the validity of the long-term relationship could differ among countries with different degrees of commitment to an exchange rate.

Forecasting Needs for the Short Run. The short run means here periods from a quarter of a year up to one or two years, or the period over which long-run relationships should hold for a particular pair of countries.

It follows from the discussion above that the firm should *concentrate on the forecasting of deviations from PPP* (the real exchange rate) over the short run. The reason is not only that this is the variable that is of real significance but that the deviations may many times be easier to forecast. The long-run relationship (PPP) can be described as a trend line, describing the *scale* of nominal magnitudes (the relative units of account), whereas the short-run forecasting problem involves the estimation of deviations from the trend. Such deviations can be viewed as temporary *overvaluations and undervaluations* of an exchange rate due to factors that will be discussed below.

The firm that faces decisions about the currency in which to borrow or about whether to cover a foreign currency position must evaluate effective interest costs, including exchange rate changes. The main concern in these situations is to evaluate whether the interest rate differential over- or underestimates the expected rate of change of the exchange rate, and whether the forward rate is higher or lower than the expected future spot rate. The actual rate of change of the exchange rate does not matter for these financial decisions, assuming that the firm wishes to borrow at the lowest cost.

The deviations from PPP or the real exchange rate can be forecast as the difference between the expected rate of change of the exchange rate and the change in relative price levels. This may be the most practical procedure when the forward rate provides a reasonably unbiased forecast. However, when the forward rate is biased or does not exist, and when inflation forecasts are uncertain, it may be easier to forecast deviations from purchasing-power parity directly from economic and political observations, since the variables that determine the deviations are likely to be separable from those that determine the trend (compare "Determinents of the Exchange Rate—Elementary Theory").

Statistical problems provide another reason for forecasting deviations from PPP rather than the levels of exchange rates and inflation rates. More specifically, consumer and wholesale price indexes that can be used for forecasting are often not the most-relevant measures of price-level developments. It is *economic* deviations rather than the often-exaggerated statistical deviations that are of interest to the firm. These economic deviations may be more correctly forecast directly rather then by using forecasts of price indices that could misrepresent inflationary developments. Similarly, it could be easier to forecast whether interest rates and forward rate overestimates or underestimates the future exchange rate in order to obtain exact numerical forecasts. Government policies with respect to interest rates could provide important insight, for example.

Forecasting Needs for the Very Short Run. The very short run is defined as any time horizon between a day and a quarter. Shorter periods are hardly relevant for firms and individuals except those directly involved in market making.

The very short run is characterized by negligible changes in the price levels and large fluctuations in the exchange rate (measured as annual rates of change). Accordingly, the changes in the exchange rates correspond almost perfectly to changes in the *real* exchange rate—deviations from PPP. The exception occurs for or between countries with hyperinflation like many Latin American countries in the 1970s. The long-term and short-term relationships can be expected to hold over much shorter time periods for these countries (Frenkel, 1977, provides empirical evidence for this hypothesis with reference to the German hyperinflation in the 1920s).

The volatility of the exchange rate over the very short run under flexible exchange rates has induced a number of tests of the random-walk hypothesis (compare section below) and of the forward rate as the best available predictor. The empirical evidence referred to above suggested that the forward rate may often, but need not be, the best-available forecast. In any case, the major concern for the forecaster should again be *the development of the exchange rate relative to the forward rate rather than relative to the current spot rate*. Even though it may many times suffice to *forecast the bias of the forward rate* in its prediction of the future spot rate, it does not follow that this forecasting task is an easy one. However, Levich's (1980) empirical evidence suggests that many foreign-exchange advisory services have been able to predict the bias sufficiently consistently for the user of the forecasts to make profits although the mean square error of the actual forecasts was larger than the forward rate's.

DETERMINANTS OF THE EXCHANGE RATE—ELEMENTARY THEORY

The exchange rate is a price of one currency (money) in terms of another. Thus we would expect that relative supplies and demands for money in two countries would be important building blocks in a model of exchange-rate determination. It is true that this view gives us substantial insight into the factors determining the exchange rate. For example, the exchange rate is a relative price of financial assets, like prices of equity in stock markets, and depends therefore on *expectations* about the future. However, the supplies and demands for money are determined by a number of factors some of which are stock variables—they can be defined at a certain point in time, like wealth—whereas others are flow variables—they must be defined over a certain time horizon, like yearly production. Moreover, an individual's demand for a stock of money at an instant is certainly related to the flow of, for example, consumption over some period in addition to expectations about the future rate of return or loss on holdings of money. Thus the demands and supplies of money—and the exchange rate—depend on a combination of interrelated stock, flow, and expectations variables. The relative importance of different variables must be related to the time horizon over which we are looking. With this introduction, we shall look briefly at modern theories of exchange-rate determination over different time periods.

THE LONG-RUN PPP.   The PPP theory of the exchange rate exists in a multitude of formulations. The *absolute* version considers the relationship between price levels at points in time. Taxes, tariffs, transport costs, and the like, make it difficult to implement tests of this version of the theory. Instead we shall be concerned with the *relative* PPP theory which says that the *rate of change* of the exchange rate reflects different inflation rates in two countries.

The PPP theory has also been developed for different kinds of price levels. There are consumer price levels, wholesale price levels, producer price levels, factor price levels, and price levels referring to parts of different aggregates. Since the demand for money should be related to the level of prices on the purchased bundle of goods and services, we shall discuss the theory for *consumer price levels*. We would ideally like price levels that correctly reflect changes in people's welfare at a certain nominal income, but such "economic" price levels can not be constructed.

The PPP theory in its relative version for consumer price levels says simply that the *rate of change of the exchange rate is equal to the percentage change in the ratio of price indexes*. One explanation is that commodity arbitrage among countries will make the exchange rate adjust in this way, provided that the exchange rate is the less rigid variable. Although all goods are not in international trade, PPP should hold, because, the prices of non-traded goods must follow traded-goods prices as long as taste and production patterns do not change.

The above explanation of the theory indicates that the exchange rate need *not* reflect PPP, if taste and technology induce different developments of the relative price between traded and nontraded goods in two countries. Empirical evidence substantiates this. Isard (1978) showed that there were deviations from consumer-price-index parity over the period 1950–1970 for most industrialized countries. For example, the ratio of the exchange rate to the relative price index for United States and Germany was .72 in 1950 and .87 in 1970. Other countries show similar though smaller deviations.

The conclusion from this is that the *PPP theory does not hold perfectly for available price indexes*. Thus the forecasting of exchange rates by the forecasting of relative inflation rates is likely to be misleading. Still, PPP in an *economic sense* may hold for an individual, when comparing exchange-rate developments with the development of the relative price level in terms of *the individual's own* consumption bundle. Thus the long-run neutrality of the exchange rate may hold better for an individual or a firm than the available data actually shows.

The factor-price version of the PPP theory should also be mentioned here. It says that the exchange rate should move so as to offset changes in the ratio of factor prices. If factor costs (estimated in a common currency) grow faster in one country than another, the first country's competitive position deteriorates. This may be reflected in the current account and unemployed resources—market disequilibria.

Most often the factor-cost version is expressed in terms of labor costs. Unit labor costs expressed in terms of a common currency should move together for labor markets to be in equilibrium. This theory suffers from a number of difficulties, as it presumes identical capital-labor ratios in all countries for a certain sector. Also, when we aggregate over all sectors, the average unit labor cost depends on the relative sizes of different sectors in each country. Thus changing structures may account for statistical deviations from parity even when there is cost parity for each sector.

The unit-labor-cost parity is probably a weaker long-run condition than consumer-price parity, because labor markets adjust slower than commodity markets (compare this with empirical evidence in "Is Exchange-Rate Forecasting Needed?"). Nevertheless, the empirical evidence shows that substantial short-term deviations from unit-labor-cost parity tend to reverse themselves within the time span we call the short run here. However, it is well known that countries have suffered from substantial labor-market disequilibria over much longer periods.

An additional weakness of the purchasing-power-parity theory for forecasting purposes should be mentioned. The economic reason for the exchange rate to adjust to prices and factor costs rests on the presumption that exchange rates are more flexible. However, central banks rarely allow complete flexibility but peg the exchange rate or manage the float (dirty float). Then the market pressures could work to restore parity by adjustments of prices and factor costs instead. In this case, the exchange rate must be used to forecast these other variables. Evidently government behavior is crucial for the direction of causality and the forecast. We shall return to this point later.

The conclusion of this section is that purchasing-power parity for consumer price indexes is probably the best forecast for the long run without detailed forecasts of consumption patterns and relative price changes. This is a qualitative forecast, however. The *statistical problems* of measuring actual price levels indicate that it may be better to estimate future cash flows for long-term projects at constant price levels and simply neglect inflation. Then it suffices to forecast real exchange-rate changes—deviations from purchasing-power parity. Again it should be mentioned that this is only valid when contracts are not fixed in nominal magnitudes and when the effects of inflation are negligible. Also it is important to obtain an estimate of the *time horizon* over which commodity and labor-market disequilibriums correct themselves. Government behavior and the magnitude of disturbances are important for this consideration.

THE SHORT-RUN-REAL-EXCHANGE-RATE CHANGES. Theories of exchange-rate determinations over the short run are generally concerned with deviations from PPP—the real exchange rate. The exceptions are monetarist models that are based on PPP. The models that are summarized here refer solely to recently developed explanations of "real" exchange-rate changes. Thus any forecast of the actual exchange rate would have to be based on the above long-term models in addition to those presented below.

Two papers by Kouri (1976) and Dornbusch (1976) formulate the main ingredients of modern exchange-rate theory. Many other authors have developed the models further, but these two articles provide the basis for this section.

Recent exchange-rate theory stresses the distinction between flow and stock equilibria. Flow equilibrium holds in the long run and implies that goods and wealth are not reallocated among countries. It is characterized by current-account balance and PPP. Stock equilibrium holds in asset markets in the short run and determines relative interest rates and the exchange rate.

A common story of adjustments after a shift in demands or supplies for a country's financial assets is as follows. At *constant nominal rates of interest and expectations*, an increased supply or decreased demand for domestic money or bonds leads to a sudden depreciation of the real exchange rate until outstanding supplies are willingly held. The depreciation will slowly induce a current-account surplus. This corresponds to increased holdings of foreign-currency assets by domestic residents. The exchange rate *appreciates* over time with the accumulation of foreign-currency assets, since these will not be willingly held unless the foreign currency depreciates. The process goes on until the current account is in balance at the original exchange rate and the initially desired portfolio shift has occurred.

The above model illustrates that an expansive monetary policy and an expansive fiscal policy both lead to a depreciation at *constant interest rates*. However, interest rates need not be pegged by the central bank. Then the expansive fiscal policy would lead to a higher interest rate that could increase the demand for domestic currency assets so that the sudden depreciation would not occur. However, the expansive fiscal policy is likely to increase aggregate demand so that the current account goes into a deficit. The corresponding capital-account surplus that must occur under flexible rates can only be realized if foreigners are induced to hold an increasing amount of domestic assets. Therefore the exchange rate is likely to depreciate as long as the current-account deficit persists, though the initial effect of the fiscal policy shift is uncertain.

The discussion of fiscal policy leads us to disturbances in the markets for commodities and services. Any factor causing a current-account deficit causes a process of depreciation while the deficit remains. The exchange rate depreciates until it has induced an increase in the demand and the supply of domestic goods of such a magnitude that the current account is in balance.

The factors that can cause a deficit in the current account are many. They involve either a decrease in domestic production or an increase in the domestic demand for all goods, or both. This follows from the identity that exports minus imports is equal to aggregate supply minus aggregate demand. Examples of real economic disturbances that *could* cause a current-account deficit are an increase in unit labor costs due to wage increases, productivity decreases, and a deterioration in the terms of trade. In these cases, aggregate supply will fall below aggregate demand if labor markets also do not adjust immediately because, for example, nominal wages are rigid and labor is immobile between sectors. Correspondingly, the exchange rate will not induce the necessary adjustments unless the same conditions hold, but continue to depreciate if, for example, nominal wages increase along with the depreciations. The adjustment to a new equilibrium depends crucially on the time it takes for supplies and demands to react to changes in relative prices induced by the exchange-rate changes. Estimates vary between quarters and a couple of years.

Shifts in expenditure and borrowing patterns may similarly trigger a process of depreciation. Increased consumption and/or investments, based on net borrowing abroad, pushes the current account into a deficit and the capital account into a surplus. However, if the central bank allows the real rate of interest to increase, other expenditures would be squeezed out and the current account could remain in balance.

Expectations have hardly been mentioned so far. They have been assumed to be stationary. In other words, the developments above take place only when the disturbances are *unanticipated*. The view of the exchange rate as a financial variable makes it clear, however, that the demands for assets of different currency denominations depends crucially on *expectations about the future exchange rate*. Thus, a depreciation occurs not only when the above disturbances take place but *starts when the disturbances are anticipated* and only obtains the full effect at the time the actual disturbances occur. Modeling exchange-rate determination involves, therefore, the modeling of expectations formation to a very large extent.

The implications of the role of expectations for forecasting are fundamental. *Forecasting the exchange rate involves not only forecasting the actual disturbances. Information must be obtained on other market participants' expectations about future disturbances as well as their exchange-rate model.* The observed exchange rate at a point in time incorporates the average market expectations about future economic disturbances and the effect they will have on the exchange rate. Thus, it is not always helpful to have only a "correct" model of exchange-rate determination, because other people's models will temporarily affect the path of adjustments.

The discussion of the short-run exchange-rate determination can now be summarized. Exhibit 4 shows factors that will induce a depreciation of the real exchange rate, everything else being constant. Note that the disturbances are not always independent. Also, it is assumed that foreign variables remain constant. Naturally foreign disturbances of the same kinds and domestic disturbances with the opposite signs induce appreciations of the domestic currency. The disturbances listed under 1 in Exhibit 4 are self-correcting in the sense that the real exchange rate appreciates

EXHIBIT 4   FACTORS INDUCING DEPRECIATION OF THE REAL EXCHANGE RATE

Sudden Depreciations Follow After	A Process of Depreciation May Follow After
Unanticipated disturbances such as:	Unanticipated disturbances such as:
Monetary expansion	Fiscal expansion with flexible interest rate
Fiscal expansion at pegged interest rate	Increased aggregate demand with net foreign
Portfolio shifts out of domestic currency	borrowing
assets	Decreased aggregate supply
Lowering of interest-rate target	(Increased wage costs)
Shifts in anticipations about the above	(Decreased productivity)
disturbances	Shifts in anticipations about the above
	disturbances

back to its PPP value by the real effects that occur as a result of the depreciation.

The disturbances listed under 2a correspond to deviations from some version of PPP that orginate in other variables than the exchange rate. The exchange-rate adjustment causes a return to the long-run equilibrium. Note also that the exchange-rate effects depend in all cases on some *price rigidity*. Interest rates, commodity prices, or nominal wages must be rigid after the initial disturbance for the exchange-rate effect to occur *and* for the exchange rate to induce the adjustments back to equilibrium.

The conclusion with respect to forecasting real exchange-rate changes is that *the observed exchange rate is the best forecast of the present value of the future exchange rate, unless the forecaster has superior information—he or she must be able to anticipate disturbances that are unanticipated by the market as a whole.*

THE VERY SHORT RUN.   The short-run model presented above provides the necessary ingredients for the understanding of the very-short-run behavior of the exchange rates. Time periods below a quarter can here be characterized as short enough for the accumulation of assets (the flow effects above) of different currency denominations not to impact significantly on the relative supply of assets. Disregarding the flow of assets among investors in different countries, the exchange rate and/or interest rates must always adjust to make the outstanding supplies willingly held. This willingness to hold assets of different currency denominations should depend primarily on *relative expected rates of return* and on *relative riskiness*. Therefore, the exchange rate in the very short run must be determined by these two factors and possibly on *relative supplies*.

The relative riskiness and the relative supplies are irrelevant for the exchange rate when there are a sufficient number of "risk neutral" market participants in the markets—traders who base their investment decision solely on expected rates of return—and when these traders have unlimited supplies of funds for arbitrage purposes. These conditions ensure that the observed exchange rate always is equal to the present value of the expected future spot rate. Then there is no risk premium and the relative supplies do not matter, because the traders are willing to purchase whatever amount is supplied of a currency as soon as there is an expected profit opportunity.

The conditions under which the observed spot rate is equal to the present value of the future spot rate correspond to the conditions under which the observed exchange rate contains the best-available information about the future exchange rate. This information about the determinants of the exchange rate is then incorporated in the observed rate. The forward rate, which reflects interest-rate differentials, becomes the best-available forecast of the future exchange rate. *Actual outcomes must then be randomly distributed around the forward rates.*

This view of the exchange rate determination would lead us to expect a substantial degree of random fluctuations in the exchange rate, because new information, which by definition is random, should be reflected immediately and fully in the exchange rate. Nonrandomness would occur only as a result of the spot rate approaching the forward rate as time passes without revisions of the anticipated rate.

It should be noted that the extreme random-walk hypothesis is disputed and basically nontestable. We noted previously, however, that some recent evidence points to bias of the forward rate as a predictor. The discussion here shows that *risk aversion, limited supply of arbitrage funds of traders, or nonaccess to (or disregard of) the best-available information by the traders are each sufficient* to explain that the forward rate is a biased predictor. These conditions leave room for attempts to model and forecast short-run exchange-rate changes, based on supply and demand factors, but the empirical evidence leaves no doubt that the very large part of daily, weekly, and monthly fluctions are random and depend on news "hitting" the market. Empirical evidence on the volatility of daily exchange rate changes is provided by Levich (1981).

Finally, the randomness of the exchange rate is a characteristic of highly efficient foreign-exchange markets under flexible rates. The less developed a country's financial markets are, the more limited is the supply of arbitrage funds, and, therefore, the greater is the scope for modeling and forecasting the exchange rate even for the very short run.

THE ROLE OF GOVERNMENTS.   Government and central-bank policies are of great relevance for the modeling and the forecasting of exchange rates and deserve separate treatment, although the above theories should, in principle, hold under any exchange-rate regime. The reason for stressing the role of governments is that their monetary and fiscal policies and anticipations about these are among the major determinants of the exchange rate. Thus predicting government behavior is crucial for forecasting the exchange rate. More interesting is that governments can affect the *adjustment process* in financial, commodity, and labor markets by their policies. They may do this by holding policy targets for monetary and fiscal policies that differ from the tendencies of the market. Also they may impose quantitative controls that affect the functioning of the market and therefore the relevance of the above models. These two issues will be addressed here.

We shall first note that the forecasting of government behavior is as superfluous as the forecasting of other determinants of the exchange rate when markets are so efficient that unbiased forward rates exist for all time horizons.

Government-policy targets that differ from the tendencies of the market could be extremely important for the forecasting of exchange rates over the short run, as well as for the time span over which the above short run factors are at work. The intervention in foreign-exchange markets provides the most obvious example. It is common that central banks stick to a pegged rate, although it has become clear to most market participants that the rate is not viable. At the same time nominal rates may be pegged so that the forward rate becomes "locked in" at a level far apart from the forecasts of most observers. These conditions characterized long periods during the late 1960s and early 1970s, when large adjustments were made at times. The adjustments were often made months or quarters after it had become a safe bet to forecast an adjustment. In other words, forecasts that were different from the forward rate were highly successful. In fact, forward markets nearly disappeared for some currencies. Private arbitrageurs could move funds aggressively into for example, Deutsche Marks, with central banks purchasing the weak currencies. Once the adjustments were made, central banks realized losses and private market participants realized gains.

There is little doubt that the adjustments towards the long-run equilibrium were delayed by years by the central-bank policies during the late 1960s. Thus real exchange rates went far out of line and the most important forecasting task was how long central banks would keep on intervening to sustain an unrealistically pegged rate.

Black (1980) showed that the management of the dirty float during the 1970s has been characterized by similar behavior, though to a lesser extent. Many times, when substantial exchange-rate changes would have occurred during a clean float, central banks have intervened to hold on to an exchange-rate target only to let go of it after some time. At the same time, nominal interest rates have not been allowed to adjust to reflect exchange-rate expectations, with the consequence that forward rates at times should have been biased predictors. It seems however, as if central banks' policies have changed during the late 1970s. Specifically, money-supply targets have been substituted for exchange-rate and interest-rate targets in many countries.

The second area in which governments' price targets may prolong the adjustment process is labor-market policies. For example, a government may pursue a full-employment policy, when nominal wage increases or a fall in productivity otherwise would have caused unemployment and an adjustment of wages. A depreciation and price inflation could follow, but if the government's employment commitment is strong, labor can obtain compensation for the fall in real wages. Thus real-wage flexibility becomes low, so that adjustments of relative unit labor costs becomes extremely slow. The country may find itself with continuing and increasing inflation and depreciation of its currency without any substantial impact on the real disequilibrium. England has found itself in this situation during large parts of the 1970s.

The other kind of government policies of importance for the adjustment process is *direct regulation*. Most obvious in this connection is exchange controls on financial-capital flows, but import licensing and price and wage controls are also important.

Most countries impose controls on the private activity in foreign-exchange markets. The measures may range from "voluntary" agreements on limits to banks' foreign-exchange exposures to direct regulation of exports and imports. All these measures have in common that quantity adjustments to incentives are slowed down. The financial-arbitrage activities become less efficient, with the result that there is more room for relative interest rates and the forward rate to deviate from the expected future spot rate. In other words, the time horizon, over which the very short run model above is valid, shrinks, leaving more room for explicit modeling of exchange-rate movements.

Controls on trade flows, as in many developing countries, may also have the effect of prolonging market adjustments in commodity markets, with the result that deviations from the long-run equilibrium could be sustained longer than otherwise.

Domestic price and wage controls often go hand in hand with labor-market policies in countries with substantial inflation. Their effects in this context could be that exchange-rate changes take longer to be reflected in domestic prices. Thus demand and supply adjustments after exchange-rate changes take time with the result that deviations from the long-run equilibria are prolonged.

In conclusion, government behavior is important for exchange-rate modeling and forecasting, not only because monetary and fiscal policies contribute to exchange-rate changes, *but also for assessing the values of the different kinds of exchange-rate models and the value of forecasting over different horizons.* Price targets with respect to the exchange rate, commodity prices, and wages may make the above short-run model of deviations from PPP valid for periods above two years and thus make forecasts of deviations from PPP more important. Government activities in the form of direct regulations may have the same impact, but could also hamper the functioning of international financial markets. The consequence of this is that forward rates become less-effective predictors of the forward rate, and the short-run model above becomes valid over the very short run, too. The value of forecasting increases over the very short run (weeks) as well as over periods of several years in extreme cases.

FORECASTING METHODS

This section deals with different kinds of forecasting methods that are available to a firm. The relative accuracy and costs are discussed. The following alternatives are treated here:

1. The forward rate and relative interest rates.
2. Time-series analysis of historical developments.
3. Econometric modeling.
4. Leading variables.
5. Advisory services.

Before discussing the forecasting methods, different kinds of forecasts and the evaluation of forecasts will be described.

DESCRIPTION AND EVALUATION OF FORECASTS. Forecasts may take many different forms depending on the method of forecasting. Naturally, the desired form of a forecast depends on the purpose of it as well as on costs of obtaining it.

A point forecast for a certain date is a forecast of an actual price at a future date (e.g., $3.00/£ for January 1, 1984). It gives the impression of exactness though the uncertainty usually is considerable. Accordingly, a point forecast can be accompanied by a likely *range* or a *standard deviation* for the same date in the future. A range is a simple measure of uncertainty and describes subjectively evaluated maxima and minima (e.g., $2.90/£ - $3.10/£ for January 1, 1984).

A standard deviation is a somewhat more sophisticated measure of uncertainty and describes a band within which the exchange rate is going to fall with a probability of, for example, 95 percent according to the forecasters (e.g., a standard deviation of $.10/£ in the above example implies that the 95 percent probability range is $2.95/£ - $3.05/£).

A point forecast can be useful for making financial, purchasing, or sales decisions with respect to a specific future date.

The quality of a borrowing or covering decision depends on the outcome of the exchange rate *relative to* the forward rate or the interest rate differential rather than the exact outcome. It may therefore be more desirable to limit the forecast to *the future spot rate relative to the forward rate or relative to the expected rate implied by the interest rate differential*. Such forecasts could be cheaper to form. The range or the standard deviation of a point forecast may contain the forward rate and therefore offer little guidance for a financial decision. However, a point forecast combined with a standard deviation contains implicitly the probability that the future spot rate will exceed the forward rate.

An even simpler forecast can be stated in the form of *direction of change*. However, such a forecast is not useful for financial decisions unless the forward rate is equal to the spot rate at the time the forecast is made. On the other hand, this is the easist forecast to make by judgment alone.

Many forecasting methods cannot produce forecasts for specific dates but only for *averages over periods*. For example, a point forecast of $3.00/£ could be the expected average rate during the month of January 1984, the first quarter of 1984, or even the expected average for the entire year. It is nonsensical to make a forecast for a specific date far into the future. Most forecasting models are based on averages of historical data over months or quarters and can produce forecasts only in the form of such averages. Nevertheless, the forecast may be presented in the form of a point forecast for a specific date. It is impossible to produce meaningful average forecasts for periods that are shorter than a month. Even this may be overly optimistic. The impression of exactness of a point forecast should not fool the user. It is unnecessary to have specific dates forecasts for many purposes, such as cash flow analysis of foreign projects.

The *evaluation* of forecasts depends naturally on the form that they take. Directional forecasts relative to the spot rate as well as relative to the forward rate can be evaluated by the *proportion of forecasts showing the correct direction*. Alternatively, one can measure the *profits that would have resulted from relying on the forecast relative to the profits of alternative strategies*.

Point forecasts make it possible to estimate the *mean squared error* of the forecast. This is a good measure of the degree of exactness of the forecasts but it need not be a good measure of the profitability of relying on the forecasts since the point forecast can be near the outcome but still on the wrong side of the forward rate. Levich (1980) shows that the forward rate is better than most advisory services in terms of mean squared errors. However, he also shows that relying on the forward rate would have been less profitable historically than relying on some of the advisory services for covering decisions.

THE FORWARD RATE AND RELATIVE INTEREST RATES.   The forward rate is naturally the cheapest available forecast of the exchange rate. Its accuracy relative to other forecasting methods was discussed above. It was argued that the forward rate does not represent the ideal forecast for all countries and all time horizons. First, forward markets are well developed only for the major currencies. Second, they tend to become thin for periods longer than a year for all currencies. Third, there is limited evidence that forward rates can be outperformed for considerable lengths of time even for the major currencies. It should be stressed again, however, that an alternative forecast in cases where well-developed forward markets exist presumes either superior information or judgment about future disturbances and their effects or less risk aversion than the marginal participant in the forward markets.

The forecast contained in the forward rate for relatively long periods, say from six months to two years, is not necessarily the most interesting from a firm's perspective, since many times it is changes in the *real* exchange rate (deviations from PPP) that are of concern. Then inflation rates must be forecast in addition to the future exchange rate.

In conclusion, the forward rate is hard to beat and is a cheap forecast of the future exchange rate as well as of deviations from PPP for the major currencies for the very short run or for periods when the price level is stable.

TIME-SERIES ANALYSIS. Many economic variables develop over time in such a way that the historic development provides a guide to the future course. The exchange rate between two countries could behave in this way over time when inflation rates differ. A trend forecast would in this case only concern nominal exchange-rate changes and not deviations from PPP. A more interesting issue is whether the real changes—changes in the very short run or the short run—show any such "autocorrelation" over time. It would be a sign of inefficiencies in the foreign-exchange markets, and the forward rate would be biased, if this were the case. The reason is that historical exchange rates could not be a guide to the future when the best-available information is contained in the spot exchange rate.

Giddy and Dufey (1975) conducted time-series tests on the daily exchange rates of Canada, France, and the United Kingdom relative to the dollar. The tests were performed on data for the flexible period up to October 1974. The results showed that there is *some* autocorrelation of daily exchange rates, but the predictive power of the tests is extremely low.

Time-series forecasts were also compared to other forecasts for different time horizons up to 90 days. The time-series forecasts are consistently worse than those provided by so-called martingales or submartingales. The former implies a pure random walk, whereas the submartingale is a random walk around the forecast implied by relative interest rates. When interest-rate parity holds, this is equivalent to the forward rate.

These negative results for the time-series forecast do not rule out their use at all times. They may be valuable, for example, when substantial government intervention is suspected because government targets may make the autocorrelation of exchange rates relatively high. The time series forecast could also be more valid for longer-term inflationary developments and therefore for *long run* exchange-rate changes. There is no empirical evidence to substantiate these hypotheses, however.

In conclusion, it seems as if time-series analysis could be useful for forecasting only under special conditions. It cannot beat relative interest rates and the forward rate in the very short run for major currencies. Only when governments induce trends in economic variables and when financial markets are not well developed, could time-series analysis be superior to the use of observed interest rates and forward rates.

The techniques of time-series forecasting should be commented upon. It is a relatively cheap econometric method. A regression on historical data with different weights is run. Forecasts are updated as new data are observed. A major problem is naturally to assign the weights to data of different ages. Fairly sophisticated models, *ARMA* and *ARIMA*, have been designed for this purpose. Most major textbooks on econometrics describe these methods. The *Box-Jenkins* technique for regression analysis, also described in most textbooks, is a popular and powerful technique that can be applied on ARIMA models. Naturally, simpler time-series models like moving averages and exponential smoothing can be used for forecasting purposes, though these models are less powerful than ARIMA.

ECONOMETRIC MODELS.   Econometric modeling of exchange rates range from large simultaneous multiequation interdependent structures to simple one-equation systems. The largest model heretofore has been developed at the Federal Reserve Board. It is a quarterly five-country model (plus the rest of the world) with about 30 equations for each county, including commodity, labor and financial markets (see Berner *et al.*, 1976). Naturally the building of such a model is extremely costly, and the continuous use of it for forecasting purposes involves updating not only of data but of essential parts as well.

On the other extreme are simple monetarist one-equation models. Since these models are based on the assumption that PPP holds and that financial markets are efficient; they do not provide an alternative to the forward rate. These models are estimated for the purpose of explaining, but not necessarily forecasting, exchange rates.

In between these extremes there are a number of efforts at econometric modeling of exchange rates. Helliwell (1969), Herring and Marston (1977) and Artus (1976) provide examples.

Most of the models referred to are structural models, that is, their main purpose is *not* to obtain efficient forecasts but to test exchange-rate theories. The main problem for forecasting purposes is to describe expectation formation and government behavior. Many of these models treat the latter as exogenous, whereas a forecasting model must include a formulation for the government's reaction to different disturbances. It is naturally a very difficult task to achieve general formulations for government behavior as well as for expectations formation.

Econometric models explicitly for forecasting purposes have been developed by a number of advisory services. These models need not be structurally correct, but it is instead important that they capture variables that systematically lead exchange-rate changes. The task of developing, changing, and running large models is naturally enormous and can only be worthwhile if they consistently outperform the forward rate or other more-simplistic forecasting methods. The empirical evidence for these forecasting services is mixed (see section on forecasting services) but it is clear that it is a formidable and expensive task with an uncertain outcome for an individual firm to attempt to construct its own large-scale model.

LEADING VARIABLES.   A simple and inexpensive method that can be used to complement and evaluate the forward rate and relative interest rates as predictors, is to study variables that tend to indicate changes in exchange rates before they occur (leading variables). Naturally this implies that the observer has some more-or-less-explicit exchange-rate model in the background. This kind of forecasting is probably done in more or less sophisticated a manner by all forecasters.

A large number of variables can be thought of as leading variables for different time horizons. For example, the theory in "Determinants of the Exchange Rate" suggests that long-lasting deviations from PPP cannot be sustained—the exchange rate must adjust. Similarly, relatively fast increases in unit labor costs often proceed adjustments of pegged rates. Over shorter time periods the forecaster could ask: How have monetary aggregates developed, and does it seem as if the exchange rate has not adjusted sufficiently? Current-account developments and changes in exchange reserves are also variables that often are mentioned as leading variables. It is necessary to be very careful with the use of these indicators, because the exchange rate and the mentioned variables may be interdependent and the order of changes that occur depend on a number of economic circumstances. Therefore, it takes a trained eye with an overview of economic developments and a good grasp of exchange-rate determination to use this forecasting technique successfully.

Forecasting by leading variables can of course be performed by econometric techniques as well. The forecaster who attempts to obtain exact estimates of the future rate can use regression equations of the conventional kind. *Factor and discriminant analysis* has also been attempted. These methods—explained in econometric textbooks—involve the search for the variables that take on certain values at the time the exchange rate changes in certain ways.

Discriminant analysis is used for prediction by classifying observations into groups, such as depreciation or appreciation. Then one studies the "classificatory power" of different variables—the extent to which other variables take on certain values when the target variable falls in the different classifications. Folks and Stansell (1975) used this method successfully to predict large exchange-rate movements for a number of countries in 1971–1972. They developed a discriminant function on observations drawn on an earlier period. The variables that were most powerful in discriminating between countries with more than 5 percent depreciation over a two-year period and those outside this group were the change in the price index, the growth of reserves, a variable indicating the debt-service burden, the ratio of exports to imports, and the central bank's discount rate.

There are naturally serious drawbacks to discriminant analysis. It cannot be used to obtain exact and continous forecasts, and it is not based on structural relationships. Therefore, the classificatory power that is found during one period could be coincidental.

Leading-variables observation in general may be a valuable complement to other forecasts. Especially with respect to deviations from PPP in different versions, this technique could be successful, because such deviations imply that there are market pressures to restore equilibrium.

FOREIGN-EXCHANGE ADVISORY SERVICES. There are now a large number of firms specializing in forecasting and a number of large banks and brokerage firms in the United States have set up departments for the forecasting of exchange rates. Most of these firms and banks sell not only forecasts but a whole range of advisory services for the international firm.

The subscription fee for obtaining the full services of a forecasting firm is now (1981) about $10,000 per year. This may sound like a high figure, but it is small for the firm that is heavily involved in international trade. The service need not beat the forward rate by many points continuously for the fee to pay off.

Most forecasting services provide biweekly or monthly direct forcasts for time horizons ranging from a month up to one or two years, normally for 11 major currencies. Judgmental evaluations of economic developments with respect to the exchange rate can be obtained for shorter and longer terms. It is now possible to purchase regular forecasts for 40 countries.

The techniques used by forecasting services can be all combinations of the highly intuitive and the technically sophisticated models. Some services rely on large-scale econometric models and other rely only on the observation and evaluation of economic developments.

The quality of the forecasts supplied by private forecasting services is very low in absolute terms (all forecasts are), and some services have been able to predict better than the forward rate consistently over several years. However, there is not one service that has been clearly and consistently superior over all time horizons or for all currencies. There is no doubt, however, that many services are able to say whether the forward rate will exaggerate or underestimate the future spot rate and be right more than 50 percent of the time. The problem for the customer is to evaluate when and for which currency to employ a particular forecasting service, or whether to purchase several forecasts and employ a weighted average. In summary, it takes expertise to derive benefits that exceed the costs of forecasting services.

SOURCES OF INFORMATION

International Financial Statistics, published by the *International Monetary Fund* is a monthly publication with historical *monthly, quarterly, and yearly* data on nearly all relevant financial and real variables of relevance for forecasting.

Main Economic Indicators, published by the OECD (Organization for Economic Cooperation and Development) contains similar data for the OECD countries.

Many banks publish limited financial data for many countries coupled with analysis in the form of biweekly or monthly newsletters as part of their foreign-exchange advisory services. Harris Bank in Chicago collects and makes available for subscription a very complete set of *weekly* financial data, covering spot exchange rates, forward rates, and Euromarket interest rates over different maturities for nine currencies. The Morgan Guarantee Trust Company in New York publishes *World Financial Markets.* This contains monthly data and analysis of developments in the international money and bond markets in North America, Europe, and Asia.

The central banks of most countries publish annual reports containing statistics and often English summaries. The U. S. Federal Reserve Board also has a quarterly journal, the *Federal Reserve Bulletin,* with a statistical appendix on a large amount of national and international financial and banking data. The *Bank of England Quarterly* is the corresponding British publication, and the German Central Bank (Deutsche Bundesbank) prints quarterly, largely statistical publications. Data on international trade can be found in the *United Nations' Monthly Bulletin of Statistics* and *Directions of Trade.* Detailed national-accounts-data for the United States is published in the *Survey of Current Business* by the Department of Commerce. The *U.S. Treasury Bulletin* (quarterly) and publications by the regional *Federal Reserve Banks* are additional sources of national and international financial data.

Finally, *Annual Report on Exchange Arrangements and Exchange Restrictions* lists and describes all exchange controls imposed by members of the International Monetary Fund. It is published by this organization.

MANAGEMENT CONSIDERATIONS

GENERAL CONCLUSIONS FOR FORECASTING.   It is obviously impossible to summarize the whole discussion about the forecasting of exchange rates by a simple recommendation on how to go about it and what sources to use. It is clear that the forward rate and relative interest rates can be outperformed as predictors of the exchange rate, but the manager must ask: At what costs and what can be gained? It takes the continuous use of substantial human resources to predict better than the forward rate consistently. Forecasts by foreign-exchange advisory services are certainly cheaper and seem to perform well for many currencies, but the optimal use of these services also demands additional time for evaluation and choice. Naturally the more time and resources a firm spends and the more alternative methods for forecasting that are compared, the better a forecast could become. However, most of the fluctuations in exchange rates during the flexible regime have been unanticipated. In other words, *all* forecasts have been *bad* forecasts, and the gains that can be made relative to the forward rate are marginal for the major currencies. Nevertheless, such marginal improvements may be worthwhile for large firms with large international transactions.

It should also be noted that even if the exchange rate could be forecast well by the forward rate, the firm may need additional forecast capability for price levels in order to be able to assess the "real exchange rate"—deviations from PPP—over different time horizons. This is the variable that matters for the return on foreign projects, equity, and other investments that are not defined in nominal terms.

TREATMENT OF UNCERTAINITY—HEDGING AND COVERING.   Once a forecast of the future development has been obtained, there is still considerable uncertainty about the forecasts. What should the firm do in face of this uncertainty? The answer to this question depends on the risk attitude of the firm, the time horizon of the cash flow, and on the forecast rate itself.

The time horizon is important because uncertainty about the exchange rate need not be of any major concern if it is believed that prices at home or abroad can be adjusted or will adjust in the market. This has been discussed in connection with the relevance of the exchange rate. A few examples could add clarity to the argument. First, a firm with a production subsidiary in Brazil need not worry about long-term depreciations of the *cruzeiro*, if it can raise its output prices there correspondingly. Second, a firm that has borrowed long term in Swiss *francs* need not worry about long-term appreciations of the currency if this appreciation depends on inflation in the United States, because the larger amount of dollars that are needed to pay back the loan is worth less in terms of purchasing power. Third, the importer with trade credits need not worry about exchange-rate developments *if* the goods are held in inventories and the sale prices in the United States can be adjusted to compensate for exchange-rate changes. The implication of this discussion is again that it is mainly "real" exchange-rate uncertainty against which the firm potentially needs to cover. This kind of uncertainty is of major importance in the short run (up to one or two years). Thus the fact that forward markets do not exist for the long maturities is of no real concern. Locking in the exchange rate for the long term would expose firms to other risks.

Uncertainty about the inflation rate could of course be a major consideration for long-term financial loans or investments. However, this kind of uncertainty exists for domestic as well as for foreign loans and could be decreased by shortening the loan periods or by making the interest rate flexible or renegotiable.

The risk attitude of the firm should depend on whether the stock market puts a premium on the firm with a low variance in its profits. There is some dispute about this, which we cannot cover here. The risk-*neutral* firm strives to maximize the *expected return* in investments without considering the variance. (The expected return naturally contains an evaluation of the probabilities of different exchange-rate changes. Once the expected return is estimated, the decisions are based *only* on this value).

The behavior of the risk-neutral firm would be characterized by a reluctance to pay transactions costs for reducing uncertainty. Therefore, such a firm would *never hedge or cover* accounts payable or receivables when the forward rate is equal to the expected future spot rate, because no gain can be expected by such a transaction. The *risk-averse firm*, on the other hand, would *always cover* short-term payables and receivables when the forward rate is equal to the expected future spot rate (unless the transactions costs are so high that the firm's risk aversion does not motivate the outlays).

The argument above is, of course, valid also for covers and hedges taken in money markets (a loan is taken in the currency with an expected positive cash flow, transferred to the home currency and invested in the money market) as long as interest-rate parity holds—the forward rate reflects the interest-rate differential.

The simple rules above, always cover or never cover, cannot be recommended when financial and exchange markets are less efficient. The firm can then obtain forecasts of the future exchange rate that deviates from the forward rate or relative interest rates. The deviation from interest-rate parity for the forward rate is less interesting, since it only affects the choice of forward cover versus money-market cover. When the expected future spot rate is not equal to the forward rate it may pay for the risk-neutral firm to use the forward markets (though we should not call it cover or hedge) because the value of a future payable in a foreign currency may be worth more translated at the forward rate than at the expected future spot rate. The risk-neutral firm would naturally always choose the most advantageous rate.

The risk-averse firm may choose *not* to cover when the forward rate is such that the firm expects a higher domestic currency value when the payable is translated at the future spot rate. Naturally the degree of risk aversion and the difference between the forward rate and the expected future spot rate will determine whether to cover or whether to take the risk of leaving a foreign-currency position open.

The terms *hedging* and *covering* are often used interchangeably. However, cover should refer to the taking of a position in forward or money markets that makes the value of a *future cash flow* certain in terms of the domestic currency. In other words, cash flows are covered. Hedging, on the other hand, refers to the taking of a position in forward or money markets in order to offset potential gains or losses on foreign-currency assets or liabilities. Thus hedging implies that the firm may realize a gain (loss) on the forward contract against an unrealized loss (gain) in the value of an asset. Accordingly, balance-sheet or translation exposures are hedged. Hedging of translation exposures has been used with two different meanings in the literature. Sometimes (and correctly) it stands for the *locking in* of the firm's accounting value at a certain date (see, e.g., the introductory chapter in Levich and Wihlborg, 1980).

The locked-in value includes translation losses/gains *and* the realized gain/loss on the forward contract. This kind of hedging would naturally only be done by the risk-averse firm that is concerned about fluctuations in its accounting net worth.

The second use of the term *hedging* is used in some textbooks like Aliber (1979) and Rodriguez and Carter (1976); firms can take positions in the forward markets on which they expect to realize gains that are equal in size to an expected translation loss. This operation presumes a forecast of the future exchange rate to calculate the expected translation loss. Also, the forward rate must differ from the expected future spot rate for the operation to be feasible. Otherwise it is impossible to make a gain on the forward market transaction. Naturally, this kind of hedging is highly speculative and may expose the firm substantially to potential economic losses. The closer the expected future rate is to the forward rate, the larger the forward transaction must be to obtain an expected gain of a certain size. No risk-averse firm would undertake such "hedging" operations unless the forward-rate bias is expected to be substantial. The risk-neutral firm could be willing to undertake such risky operations, but there is no economic reason to limit the forward contract to the implied size if the firm has trust in its forecast.

SOURCES AND SUGGESTED REFERENCES

Aliber, R. Z. *Exchange Risk and Corporate International Finance*. London: Macmillan, 1978.

Artus, J. R. "Exchange Rate Stability and Managed Floating: The German Experience," International Monetary Fund, *Staff Papers*, Vol. XXIV (1976), pp. 312–333.

Artus, J. R. and J. H. Young. "Fixed and Flexible Rates: A renewal of the Debate," International Monetary Fund, *Staff Papers,* Vol. XXVI (1978), pp. 324–355.

Berner, R., P. Clark, H. Howe, S. Kwack and G. Stevens. *Modeling the International Influences on the U.S. Economy: A Multi-Country Approach*, International Finance Division, Discussion Paper No. 93. Washington, D.C.: Federal Reserve Board.

Black, S. W. *Flexible Exchange Rates and National Economic Policies*. New Haven: Yale University Press, 1977.

———. "Central Bank Intervention and the Stability of Exchange Rates," in R. M. Levich and C. G. Wihlborg, eds. *Exchange Risk and Exposure*. Lexington, MA: Lexington Books, D.C. Heath, 1980.

Dornbusch, R. "Expectations and Exchange Rate Dynamics," *Journal of Political Economy*, Vol. 84 (1976), pp. 1161–1176.

Eiteman, D. K., and A. I. Stonehill. *Multinational Business Finance*, Reading, MA: Addison-Wesley, 1979.

Folks, W. R., and S. R. Stansell. "The Use of Discriminant Analysis in Forecasting Exchange Rate Movements," *Journal of International Business Studies*, Vol. 6 (Spring 1975), pp. 32–50.

Frenkel, J. A. "The Forward Exchange Rate, Expectations and the Demand for Money: The German Hyperinflation," *American Economic Review*, Vol. 67 (September 1977), pp. 653–670.

Frenkel, J. A., and R. M. Levich. "Covered Interest Arbitrage: Unexploited Profits?" *Journal of Political Economy*, Vol. 83 (April 1975), pp. 325–338.

Giddy, I. M., and G. Dufey. "The Random Behavior of Flexible Exchange Rates: Implications for Forecasting," *Journal of International Business Studies*, Vol. 6 (Spring 1975), pp. 1–31.

Officer, L. M. "The Purchasing Power Parity Theory of Exchange Rates: A Review Article," IMF *Staff Papers*, Vol. XXIII (1976), pp. 1–60.

Helliwell, J. "A Structrual Model of the Foreign Exchange Market," *Canadian Journal of Economics*, Vol. 17 (1969), pp. 90–105.

Herin, J., A. Lindbeck, and J. Myhrman. *Flexible Exchange Rates and Stabilization Policies*. London: Macmillan, 1977.

Herring, R. J., and R. C. Marston. *National Monetary Policies and International Financial Markets*. Amsterdam: North Holland, 1977.

Hong, H. "Inflation and the Market Value of the Firm: Theory and Tests," *Journal of Finance*, Vol. 32 (1977), pp. 1031–1048.

Isard, P. *Exchange Rate Determination: A Survey of Popular Views and Recent Models*, Princeton Study in International Finance, No. 42 (1978).

Jacque, L. L. *Management of Foreign Exchange Risk*, Lexington, MA: Lexington Books, D. C. Heath, 1978.

Kohlhagen, S. W. *The Behavior of Foreign Exchange Markets—A Critical Survey of the Empirical Literature*, Monograph Series in Finance and Economics, No. 3, New York: New York University, 1978.

Kouri, P. J. K. "The Exchange Rate and the Balance of Payments in the Short Run and the Long Run," *Scandinavian Journal of Economics*, No. 2, Vol. 78 (1976), 148–170.

Levich, R. M. "Further Results on the Efficiency of Markets for Foreign Exchange," *Management Exchange Rate Flexibility*, Federal Reserve Bank of Boston, No. 20 (1979).

———. "Analyzing the Accuracy of Foreign Exchange Advisory Services: Theory and Evidence," in R. M. Levich and C. G. Wihlborg, eds. *Exchange Risk and Exposure*. Lexington, MA: Lexington Books, D. C. Heath, 1980.

———. "An Examination of Overshooting Behavior in the Foreign Exchange Market." Occasional Paper, Study Group on the Foreign Exchange Markets of the Group of Thirty, May (1981).

Levich, R. M., and C. G. Wihlborg. *Exchange Risk and Exposure*, Lexington, MA: Lexington Books, D. C. Heath, 1980.

McKinnon, R. *Money in International Exchange, The Convertible Currency System*, Oxford: Oxford University Press, 1979.

Poole, W. "Speculative Prices as Random Walks: An Analysis of Ten Time Series of Flexible Exchange Rates," *Southern Economic Journal*, Vol. 43 (1976), pp. 468–478.

Rodriguez, R. M., and E. E. Carter. *International Financial Management*, 1st ed. Englewood Cliffs, NJ: Prentice-Hall, 1976.

Schadler, S. "Sources of Exchange Rate Variability: Theory and Empirical Evidence," IMF *Staff Papers*, Vol. XXV (1977), pp. 253–296.

Sveriges Riksbank. *Forvaltningsberattelse*, Stockholm, 1980.

Wachtel, P., and A. Cukierman. "Differential Inflationary Expectations and the Variability of the Rate of Inflation: Some Theory and Evidence," *American Economic Review*, Vol. 69 (1979), pp. 595–609.

Wihlborg, C. G. *Currency Risks in International Financial Markets*, Princeton Study in International Finance, No. 44. (1978).

———. "Currency Exposure Taxonomy and Theory," in R. M. Levich and C. G. Wihlborg, eds. *Exchange Risk and Exposure*. Lexington, MA: Lexington Books, D. C. Heath, 1980.

SECTION **18**

INTERNATIONAL FINANCIAL MARKETS

CONTENTS

THE FRAMEWORK OF THE
INTERNATIONAL FINANCIAL MARKET   3

THE NEW INTERNATIONAL
MONETARY SYSTEM   6

Exchange-Rate Regime   7
The Role of Gold in the International
Monetary System   8
Promotion of the Special Drawing
Rights to Become the Principal
International Reserve Asset   10
Foreign-Exchange Arrangements   11
Multiple Currency Practices, Bilateral
Payment Arrangements, and Capital
Controls   16
International Reserves and Liquidity   16

THE FOREIGN-EXCHANGE MARKET   21

Types of Foreign-Exchange
Transactions   21
Foreign-Exchange Markets and Trading   25
Futures Trading in Foreign Exchange   34
The Role of the Foreign-Exchange Rate   34
Foreign-Exchange Determination   35
Experience with Floating Exchange
Rates   38
Foreign-Exchange Management and
Intervention   39

THE EUROCURRENCY MARKET   42

Definition   42
Factors Affecting the Market's Growth
and Development   44

The Effect of Terminating the U.S.
Balance-of-Payments Controls   48
Characteristics   49
Functions   54
The Theoretical Interpretations of the
Eurocurrency Market   61
International Interest Rates   64
International Financial Centers   66

INTERNATIONAL BANKING
FACILITIES IN THE UNITED STATES   69

Financial Markets' Banking
Environment   70
The Payments system   71
EUROCURRENCY LENDING   72

Market Size and Characteristics   72
Syndicated Loans   73
Recycling OPEC's Surpluses   87

THE INTERNATIONAL BOND MARKET   87

Definitions   87
The Emergence of the Eurobond
Market   90
Eurobond-Market Characteristics   92
Foreign-Bond-Market Characteristics   94

CONTROL OF THE EUROCURRENCY
MARKET   95

SUMMARY AND PROSPECTS   99

NOTES AND SOURCES   100

INTERNATIONAL FINANCIAL MARKETS

Harvey A. Poniachek

THE FRAMEWORK OF THE INTERNATIONAL FINANCIAL MARKET

In the last two decades the international financial market has grown rapidly, has become large, efficient, and competitive, and has gained in breadth, depth, and resiliency. It has developed a unique institutional setup, with markets and participants throughout the world.

In the 1960s and early 1970s the rapid expansion of world trade and multinational corporations' activities, combined with the imposition of regulatory restrictions in many countries, provided a strong impetus for the expansion of the international financial market. The market's structure and operations were largely affected by the regulatory environments and economic developments around the world, which in turn shaped the evolution of the instruments, regulations, and performance.

The market is in a continuous state of evolution, and in recent years it has experienced profound changes, which have been induced by changes in (1) the global monetary system, (2) the institutional and regulatory environment, and (3) global patterns of the flow of funds, resulting from the emergence of OPEC's surpluses.

The international financial market, which is part of and operates within the international monetary system, comprises the foreign-exchange market, the Eurocurrency market, and the international bond market. The market both competes with and functions as a complement to the national financial markets in many respects.

The international financial market, particularly its money and credit or capital sectors (i.e., the Eurocurrency and international bond markets), has many linkages with the domestic financial markets in many countries, which, in turn, have contributed to international economic and financial integration. The increased integration of the world economy has helped to improve the global allocation of capital funds and productive resources.

In the foreign-exchange markets, national monies are exchanged for each other. The operation of these markets is largely affected by the international monetary system, particularly the exchange regime, which is established by the Articles of Agreement of the International Monetary Fund (IMF or the Fund). In the Eurocurrency and international bond markets—the markets for money, credit, and capital—funds denominated in foreign currencies are deposited, lent, and borrowed, and international bonds are issued.

The distinction between international money markets and international credit or capital markets is arbitrary and is based on the length of maturity. Accordingly, transactions for maturities of up to 12 months are classified as money-market activities, whereas transactions beyond 12 months constitute credit or capital transactions.

In this section I pursue an integrated approach to the international monetary system and financial market and provide an analytical framework for its analysis. Methodologically, I survey and analyze the international financial markets within the broader context of the international monetary system. I discuss the size, structure, and operation of the international financial market and analyze the role and operation of the various markets and the issues of regulation and control. More specifically, I discuss the following aspects (1) purpose/goals, (2) factors affecting growth, (3) institutions, participants, and instruments, (4) flow of funds and interest rate, and (5) regulations and controls.

The global monetary system sets the stage for and affects the environment of the international financial markets. It determines the exchange-rate arrangements and affects the balance-of-payments adjustments and flow of funds. Therefore, the international monetary system and foreign-exchange arrangements are discussed.

The market for foreign-exchange facilitates the exchange of different national monies across national borders, and it is part of the international-payments mechanism. The exchange rate is a key price, particularly for very open economies and for firms and individuals involved in international business. Since early 1973 the world has operated under a hybrid exchange-rate system: The major currencies are floating and have no central par values; some currencies are floating in terms of a specially designed basket of currencies of the special drawing right (SDR), and some have fixed rates in terms of a major currency.

The international money market includes the Eurocurrency market, of which the major sector is the Eurodollar market, and its linkages with other sectors of national financial markets. The Eurocurrency market is an international financial market for bank deposits and loans denominated in foreign currency. The market is parallel to and interdependent with the traditional international domestic capital markets, and it is closely linked to the corresponding national markets.

The Eurocurrency market differs from both the traditional international and domestic capital markets in regulation, institutional structure, interest-rate determination, the flow of funds, and lending and borrowing practices.

The debate over the nature of the Eurocurrency market and the policy implications arising from its operation continues. The growth of the Eurocurrency market represents an efficient financial intermediation on a worldwide scale, whereby international liquidity is to some degree created through maturity transformation and global credit distribution. The market has not created, as it is alleged, excessive domestic liquidity through the money and credit multiple mechanism, but instead has contributed to a more efficient distribution of world credits and has induced capital mobility and movements.

The Eurocurrency market's growth and expansion depends in part on its competitiveness, relative to the respective domestic markets, which in turn is derived from differences in the regulatory environments (reserve requirements; ceilings on interest payments; and fiscal incentive, particularly tax) and operational efficiencies (economies of scale). On the other hand, the Eurocurrency market's growth is also affected by demand for its services.

The Eurocurrency market is closely interdependent with the foreign-exchange market, (almost all Eurobanks also deal in foreign exchange), but the two markets are distinct in function. The Eurocurrency market is a market for credit, in which deposits are accepted and loans are granted, usually in the same currency. In contrast, the foreign-exchange market does not constitute part of the international money or credit market.

The international bond market—the long-term capital market—is composed of foreign and Eurobond sectors. Like the Eurocurrency market, the Eurobond sector is not subject to various national regulations, and it extends throughout the world. Its existence depends on its competitiveness and attractiveness to borrowers and investors. Interest rates on Eurobonds are normally closely related to those prevailing in the national domestic markets, unless exchange controls or other factors inhibit arbitrage.

The international money and capital market has an independent international interest-rate structure, but it mirrors the interest rates in the correspondent national financial markets, and it is greatly affected by them.

The theoretical interpretations of the Eurocurrency market vary considerably, and have different implications concerning the market's control. The theory of international financial intermediation, rather than the money and credit multiplier model, seems to be the most appropriate for the Eurocurrency market. In this context, the market is a substitute for, rather than a supplement to, domestic financial markets.

The Euromarkets are frequently alleged to cause inflation through excessive monetary creation and to threaten the stability of the international financial system. While the debate about the need for controlling the Euromarkets continues, some controls are nevertheless forthcoming. Initial international agreement on international banking supervision has been reached, but formal regulation of their activities has not been agreed upon. The most likely developments in the medium term are agreement on reserve requirements and prudential controls in the form of maximum capital-to-assets or capital-to-deposits ratios, liquidity ratios, or credit ceilings.

The outlook for the international financial market is dominated by several factors: (1) evolution toward a multiple-currency international reserve system and regional currency blocs, and the reemergence of gold as a reserve asset; (2) changes in regulations in the major countries; (3) development of new payment systems and procedures; (4) increased international and regional interdependence of financial markets, and the need for their coordinated control and supervision; and (5) cyclical and structural economic trends of which some are characterized by large non-OPEC LDC's balance-of-payments deficits, growing external financial requirements and debt burden.

The above trends could: (1) diminish the significance of the U.S. dollar in the long run; (2) modify the relative competitive position of the major international financial centers and affect the location of transactions; (3) improve the efficiency of the international payments system; (4) increase the likelihood of control and supervision over Eurobanks, and have a tendency toward standardization of supervision across national borders, partly in an effort to eliminate competitive advantages originating from diversity in national regulations (in this context, the American attempt to restore international financial competitive equality provided an impetus for the adoption of the 1978 International Banking Act and for the establishment of offshore banking facilities in the United States); (5) contribute to balance-of-payments disequilibrium and mounting external debt of less developed countries, requiring continuous recycling by Eurobanks. However, commercial banks reduced capacity to recycle OPEC's surpluses (because of decreased risk of international lending, prudent behavior, and regulatory requirements) could reduce their capacity to perform this vital function. Under this circumstance, there is a likelihood that reduced access of less developed countries to financial markets could increase the risk of widespread default.

The rest of this chapter is organized in seven sections as follows:

"The New International Monetary System" reviews and analyzes the international monetary system, with emphasis on the main factors affecting the international monetary system (i.e., foreign-exchange arrangements, international liquidity, etc.).

"The Foreign-Exchange Market" is devoted to the foreign-exchange market. It reviews the various foreign-exchange instruments, trading, and markets, and examines the role of foreign exchange in the economy and its determination. Finally, the experience under the flexible exchange rate and currency management are examined.

"The Eurocurrency Market" provides a thorough analysis of the Eurocurrency market, international financial centers and the international interest-rate structure.

"Eurocurrency Lending" deals with Eurocurrency lending, particularly the loan-syndication market.

"The International Bond Market" analyzes alternative sources of credit and capital through international bonds.

"Control of the Eurocurrency Market" examines some of the proposals for controlling the market and the evolution of control over the Eurobanks.

"Summary and Prospects" provides a brief conclusion of the major issues dealt with in this chapter and outlines some of the anticipated trends and prospects of the market.

THE NEW INTERNATIONAL MONETARY SYSTEM

As a result of unprecedented disturbances in the world economy, the international monetary system has undergone profound changes in the last decade. The foreign-exchange regime of the Bretton Woods system was abandoned and a hybrid international monetary system evolved. The world monetary relations are currently conducted in the context of a heterogeneous system, characterized by both flexible and fixed exchange rates; this system is often described as the widespread floating of currencies. The system is still in a state of evolution without strictly defined rules of behavior, and three regional monetary blocs and a multiple reserve system—along the U.S. dollar, the European currencies, and the Japanese yen—are emerging.

The IMF's Articles of Agreement are the central legal framework of the international monetary system. They provide the basis for consistent purposes and principles together with rights and obligations accepted by all member countries. The second amendment of the Articles of Agreement entered into force on April 1, 1978.

The most-important modifications of the articles deal with the exchange arrangements, gold, and SDRs. The amended articles give legal recognition to a (new) system comprising a multiplicity of exchange-rate practices that represent a complete departure from the central feature of the Bretton Woods articles, but they provide procedures for a possible future return to a par-value system. Although the new system gives member countries a free choice in the exchange arrangements that they may adopt and allows a rather loose concept of exchange discipline, it emphasizes underlying domestic economic and financial policies and conditions as the source of currency stability. Therefore, it puts more of the burden on domestic policies for the maintenance of balance-of-payments adjustment and exchange-rate stability than the par-value system did. In addition, the articles give the IMF powers of surveillance over exchange-rate policies to ensure that no country manipulates exchange rates.

The monetary agreements embodied in the second amendment reflect both the profound changes that occurred in the global economic environment in recent years and the compromise on international monetary reform. The new system, unlike the original Bretton Woods system, allows a greater degree of flexibility in members' behavior and permits international monetary relations to evolve through time. In essence, the new monetary system represents only a phase of international monetary evolution and reform rather than a complete reform, and it allows the existing rules and regulations to evolve further in the future.

There is controversy about whether the second amendment of the IMF's Articles of Agreement does establish a new international monetary system or instead only legalizes the existing practices and policies that had emerged over the years by incorporation into the articles. Regardless of this controversy and even though the monetary relations are still evolving, the system provides a substantial improvement over the original Bretton Woods system in terms of all three major problem areas of the international monetary system—adjustment, liquidity, and confidence.

EXCHANGE-RATE REGIME.   The second amendment of the IMF's Articles of Agreement gives legal validity to a new system of multiple exchange-rate practices by allowing members to choose their exchange arrangements. According to Article IV Section 2(b), exchange arrangements may include "(i) the maintenance by a member of a value for its currency in terms of the special drawing right or another denominator, other than gold, selected by the member, or (ii) cooperative arrangements by which members maintain the value of their currencies in relation to the value of the currency or currencies of other members, or (iii) other exchange arrangements of a member's choice."

Each member is required to notify the IMF of the exchange arrangements it applies and of any subsequent changes it intends to adopt in its exchange regime. Although members are free to apply the exchange arrangements of their choice, they are subject at all times to general obligations and surveillance by the IMF. Moreover, each member is required to seek to promote exchange stability by pursuing orderly economic and financial conditions and to avoid manipulating exchange rates or the international monetary system. In essence, the system gives members freedom of choice in foreign-exchange arrangements but not freedom of behavior, and it emphasizes internal economic conditions, rather than exchange discipline, as the source of currency stability.

The IMF is required to oversee the international monetary system in order to ensure its effective operation, and the observance by each member of its obligations.

Accordingly, the principles and procedures for surveillance over exchange-rate policies went into effect under the second amendment.

The IMF exercises firm surveillance over the exchange-rate policies of its members. The principles and procedures for surveillance may be modified from time to time according to experience and the circumstances of the international monetary system, but they must be consistent with the pursuit of orderly domestic economic and price stability, social and political conditions, and the freedom of members to choose their exchange arrangements. These principles must respect the domestic social and political policies of members, and in applying them the IMF must pay due regard to the circumstances of members. To assist the IMF in fulfilling this objective, each member is required to provide it with the information necessary for such surveillance and, when necessary, to consult with it on the exchange-rate policy.

Since exchange rates are affected by a wide spectrum of factors, and since governments differ in their views about how their economies work and in their domestic policy objectives, the range of these factors makes it difficult to determine whether a country's exchange rate is inappropriate. Because of these problems, it is widely agreed that surveillance should focus on identifying observed policy actions rather than on motives.

THE ROLE OF GOLD IN THE INTERNATIONAL MONETARY SYSTEM. Gold had a central role in the post-World War II monetary system of the Bretton Woods System, but the second amendment of the IMF's Articles of Agreement introduces many changes designed to achieve a gradual reduction of the role of gold (and reserve currencies) in the international monetary system, and to make the SDR the principal reserve asset.[1]

The most-important changes in the amended articles are removing gold as the common denominator of the exchange rate and the SDR; abolishing the official gold price of 35 SDRs per ounce; abandoning any obligation to pay in gold by members to the IMF and by the IMF to members; allowing monetary authorities of member countries to deal in gold among themselves or in the free market at market-related prices; and agreeing to permit the disposal of some IMF gold holdings.

One sixth of the original IMF gold holdings (or 25 million ounces) was sold through the IMF Trust Fund to the private market, and the profit (i.e., the difference between the selling price and the official price) was distributed among the neediest of the least developed countries. The sale was through public auctions over the four-year period that ended on May 7, 1980.

Another sixth of the IMF's original holdings was almost entirely sold (restituted) to the member countries at the official price. The rest of the Fund's 100 million ounces of gold is to be held by it until its disposition is determined by an 85 percent majority of the total voting power.

Although the formal role of gold in the international monetary system has been diminished and the present IMF arrangements, to a large extent, demonetize it *de jure,* demonetization de facto will not be accomplished, because gold continues to be held as an official reserve asset by member countries. In addition, the IMF Articles of Agreement allow central banks to trade gold among themselves at market prices, which may thereby reverse the de facto demonetization that occurred in August 1971, monetize new gold, and give gold a higher degree of liquidity than it had before.

Although the termination of gold transactions between the IMF and its members and the disposal of one third (and perhaps ultimately all) of the gold originally held by the Fund are major steps in reducing the monetary role of gold, the acquisition by countries of the gold sold by the Fund increases their gold reserves and enhances its role in the system, rather than diminishing it.

The degree of gold demonetization, as it is now reflected in the IMF's Articles of Agreement, had to be compromised during the negotiations on monetary reform. In the real world, however, the decade-old efforts to demonetize gold have been only partially successful, and it remains a significant component of central banks' reserves.

Despite its diminished role and its immobile and not very productive nature, gold is presently a highly desired asset, and it has again achieved enhanced status in financial markets. Valuation of official gold holdings at market prices is spreading, and gold's reemerging monetary role is now well under way.

The threefold increase in the market price of gold (and the value of officially held gold reserves) in the past year provides a strong impetus to those who would like to see it offically enhanced in the international monetary system.

Despite the high price of gold and the freedom to trade in it by the monetary authorities, it is doubtful whether gold will be widely used in international settlements, although central banks of small countries may sell some as a last resort in case of severe balance-of-payments problems when access to alternative credit is not available.

Therefore, in practice the valuation of official gold holdings at market prices and the higher reserve-adequacy ratios are expected to have little effect on financial behavior and balance-of-payments financing methods and to produce little benefit to the countries involved.

Higher valuations are inconsistent with the idea that the SDR should have an enhanced role in the international monetary system and should become a crucial element in liquidity control. A drastic reduction in the role of reserve currencies, particularly the dollar, is crucial in making SDRs the main reserve asset. (The consolidation of official foreign-exchange holdings by exchanging them against SDRs was proposed in the form of a substitution account, which was rejected. This account would have enabled official holders of dollars to exchange them at the IMF for SDR-denominated assets, and then to have the reserve-currency countries redeem the currencies by issuing long-term instruments to the Fund. The capabilities of this account would have been rather limited, and at best it could have provided a vehicle to diversify only some international currency holdings.)

Whatever benefits are to be derived from higher gold prices, they are unequally distributed. The main beneficiaries are the industrial countries, whereas the less developed countries could be aversely affected. Hence the latter's interest should be in promoting gold demonetization, further allocation of SDRs, expansion of IMF credit lines, and creation of a more efficient mechanism for transfer of resources.

The official attitude toward the role of gold in the monetary system is inconsistent among the foreign countries, particularly between the United States and Western Europe. Although they all act within the legal context of the IMF Articles of Agreement, their behavior and intent differ substantially. Evidence of the increased significance of gold is reflected in the role of gold in the structure and operation of the European Monetary System (EMS), official gold valuation procedures, official acquisition/liquidation of gold holdings, and government and official attitudes.

Evidence of creeping remonetization is reflected in the design of the EMS, whereby in March 1979, eight countries participating in the EMS (Belgium, Denmark, France, Germany, Ireland, Italy, Luxembourg, and the Netherlands) were issued

SDR14 billion European currency units (ECUs) against their deposit with the European Monetary Cooperation Fund (EMCF) of gold and U.S. dollars. In July 1979, the United Kingdom was also issued ECUs against its deposit with EMCF of gold and U.S. dollars. For these countries, reserves deposited with the EMCF are excluded from their official reserve holdings, but all ECU holdings are included in the foreign exchange.

Pooling reserve currencies and gold, against which ECUs were issued, implies a strong monetization of gold as well as an enhancement of the dollar, two assets of monetary significance which the IMF attempts to reduce.

The EMS has effectively monetized gold at approximately the market price and given it an enhanced monetary role. It provided for the conversion of some official gold reserves of its eight member countries and the United Kingdom into ECUs. The idea behind the plan was provided by Italy and France, the most gold-conscious countries of the EEC.

Several major countries are now valuing their official gold stocks at or near the market price. Among them are Austria, France, Italy, the Netherlands, Switzerland, and West Germany. In the past official gold reserves have been sold in the market only by countries in need of balance-of-payments financing, for example, Portugal, Zaire, and India.

In the mid-1970s, Italy used official gold valued at 80 percent of market value, to back up a big balance-of-payments loan from West Germany. The increased use of gold as collateral in transactions among central banks, at or near market prices, or for official settlements among central banks, would remonetize official gold holdings.

The IMF and the U.S. Treasury gold auctions are in line with their policy designed to demonetize gold in the system. The sale of U.S. gold to the private market started in 1975 to keep Americans from going abroad to buy gold when the prohibition against domestic gold ownership was removed. In the past 2 years the sales of U.S. gold were intended to help reduce the trade deficit and assist the dollar. U.S. gold auctions have presently been suspended.

The Japanese government has reportedly arranged for the purchase of gold by Japanese industry, allegedly for stockpiling purposes, but these holdings can be monetized when needed.

PROMOTION OF THE SPECIAL DRAWING RIGHTS TO BECOME THE PRINCIPAL INTERNATIONAL RESERVE ASSET. The Special Drawing Right (SDR) is a basket of currencies with each component (as well as the basket itself), determined at spot exchange rates. Since January 1, 1981, it is based on a basket five currencies instead of the 16 in the basket that was in effect from mid-1978 to the end of 1980. This will simplify and enhance its attractiveness.

In the new basket, the currency weights are based on international trade statistics for the 5 year period, 1975–1979, and on other considerations (e.g., international investment and finance) as follows: U.S. dollar, 42 percent; Deutsche mark, 19 percent; British pound, 13 percent; Japanese yen, 13 percent; and French franc, 13 percent.

Presently, the role of the SDR is rather limited, confined to an official reserve status, and accounts for a very small proportion of total global reserve. Commercial SDR-denominated transactions are conducted, however, on a limited scale, and no transactions between governments and the private sector occur.

The objective of the changes in the characteristics and expansion of the possible uses of SDR is to become the principal reserve asset of the international monetary system. Recent changes include the increase in its holdings and uses; the abrogation of the reconstitution requirement; the adoption of a simplified valuation system for the SDR; and the increases in interest rates paid by the IMF to members on their holdings of SDRs. Some of the most important changes that were introduced at the time of the amended Articles of Agreement and more recently are as follows:

1. The amended Articles of Agreement require the value of the IMF's assets to be expressed and the currency holdings in the General Resources Account to be maintained in terms of SDRs.

2. The IMF is authorized to allocate SDRs to members that participate in the Special Drawing Rights Department when the world's need for additional liquidity arises.

3. The use of SDRs has been broadened by allowing participants to enter into transactions that include swap arrangements, spot and forward activities, loans, pledges, and donations by agreement, without the necessity of decisions by the IMF.

4. The IMF may authorize transactions in SDRs between participants that are not otherwise provided for by the Articles, subject to appropriate safeguards.

5. The IMF has raised (to eight) the number of institutions other than national treasuries, central banks, and the Fund, that can hold SDRs.

6. The valuation of the SDR was simplified by reducing the size of the basket on which it is valued from 16 currencies to the 5 currencies that are most widely used in international trade, investment, and finance.

7. The interest rate paid by the IMF to members on their holdings of SDRs was increased from 80 percent to 100 percent of the weighted rate in the markets of the five countries whose currencies are included in the SDR valuation basket. This change should make the SDR more competitive with other reserve assets. The weighting system or basket used to determine the value of and interest rate of the SDR is now identical.

8. The Fund decided in principle to abrogate the requirement that members maintain, over time, a minimum average level of SDR holdings.

These changes, particularly in the simplified valuation and the increase in interest rate, should induce the private use of the SDR by making the currency composition of the basket more stable, and easier for market participants to cover exchange risks involved in SDR-denominated transactions.

FOREIGN-EXCHANGE ARRANGEMENTS. Some countries continuously adopt new exchange arrangements or modify their existing ones. These changes reflect the trend observed in recent years to adopt exchange practices best suited to each country's institutional circumstances and individual policies. Most of these changes consist of the abandonment of a pegged exchange rate in favor of a more flexible exchange regime. In recent years, there has been a reduction in the number of countries maintaining a fixed exchange rate.[3]

Increased flexibility in exchange arrangements has involved the use of wider margins in the pegging of a currency to a composite of other currencies. In addition, several countries have begun to declare official market exchange rates for up to 1 year in advance, based primarily on anticipated variations in inflation rates at home and abroad. (Between January 1, 1979, and March 31, 1980, 22 members adopted new exchange arrangements. In addition, there were numerous exchange-rate actions that did not involve changes in members' exchange arrangements.)

Since the breakdown of the Bretton Woods system of fixed exchange rates in early 1973, countries have adopted a broad spectrum of exchange-rate practices, ranging from independent floating rates with relatively little intervention to the maintenance of a fixed exchange rate in terms of a single currency. Although the heterogeneity of exchange-rate practices makes it difficult to define precisely the present exchange regime, it has come to be known as the system of widespread floating of currencies. The second amendment of the IMF's Articles of Agreement legalized the status quo of the wide spectrum of existing exchange arrangements and in effect gave legal validity to a (new) system comprising multiple exchange-rate practices.

A country that adopts a floating exchange rate either can float independently or in a group, or can let its currency crawl; whereas a country that adopts a fixed exchange rate can peg its currency rate either to a single foreign currency (e.g., U.S. dollar, British pound, French franc) or in terms of a basket of foreign currencies (e.g., SDR, or a composite of currencies of countries with which trade is the most significant).

At the end of March 1980, the currencies of 59 members were pegged to a single currency; 41 were to the U.S. dollar, 14 to the French franc, 2 to the South African rand, and 1 each to the pound sterling and Spanish peseta.[4] Fourteen currencies were pegged to the SDR, whereas another 20 maintained a fixed relationship between their currencies and another currency basket. Three members were adjusting their exchange rates at relatively short, irregular intervals according to a set of indicators; 8 members were maintaining cooperative exchange arrangements within the European Monetary System; and 35 were maintaining other, more-flexible, exchange arrangements (see Exhibit 1).

The major industrial countries' currencies (including such currencies as the Canadian dollar, the Japanese yen, the British pound, and the U.S. dollar) float independently on the exchange markets, and their exchange rates are essentially determined daily by market forces of supply and demand. The monetary authorities of each country intervene, to varying degrees, in their respective foreign-exchange markets in order to maintain orderly conditions. The balance-of-payments adjustment mechanism thus operates through both exchange-rate variations and changes in official reserves.

Since March 1979, eight European countries (Belgium, Denmark, France, Germany, Luxembourg, Italy, Ireland, and the Netherlands) have participated in the European Monetary System. They float jointly against other currencies and peg their currencies to each other within a band of 2.25 percent between the central cross rates (Italy 6.0 percent). Their internal pegging is accomplished by multiple currency intervention.

As Exhibit 1 shows, three countries (Brazil, Colombia and Portugal) pursued policies of frequent minidevaluation relative to the major currencies (mainly the dollar) to which they were pegged, in order to compensate for the differences in the rates of inflation at home and abroad.

Many of the less developed countries peg their exchange rates to the currencies of their major trading partners and fluctuate along with them, whereas some of the less developed countries' currencies are pegged to a weighted basket of major cur-

EXHIBIT 1 EXCHANGE RATES AND EXCHANGE ARRANGEMENTS, MARCH 31, 1980

Member (currency)	Exchange Rate Maintained Against[h]	Exchange Rate[a]	Exchange Rate Otherwise Determined[b,c]
Afghanistan (Afghani)			
Algeria (dinar)[d]	bskt	3.9595	43.50
Argentina (peso)			1747.5
Australia (dollar)			0.923276
Austria (schilling)	bskt	13.908	
Bahamas (dollar)[d]	$	1.00	
Bahrain (dinar)			0.3775
Bangladesh (taka)[d]	bskt	16.0198	
Barbados (dollar)[d]	$	2.00	
Belgium (franc)[d]			31.17[e]
Benin (franc)	F	50.00	
Bolivia (peso)			24.51
Botswana (pula)[d]	$	0.788705	
Brazil (cruzeiro)[d]			46.60[f]
Burma (kyat)	SDR	8.50847	6.80036
Burundi (franc)	$	90.00	
Cameroon (franc)	F	50.00	
Canada (dollar)			1.1914
Cape Verde (escudo)	bskt	41.5541	
Central African Republic (franc)	F	50.00	
Chad (franc)	F	50.00	
Chile (peso)	$	39.00	
China, Rep. (new Taiwan dollar)			36.06
Colombia (peso)[d]	F		45.60[f]
Comoros (franc)	F	50.00	
Iran (rial)			70.475
Iraq (dinar)	$	0.295314	
Ireland (pound)			0.515996[e]
Israel (shekel)			4.1478
Italy (lira)[d]			898.25[e]
Ivory Coast (franc)	F	50.00	
Jamaica (dollar)	$	1.78142	
Japan (yen)			249.70
Jordan (dinar)	SDR	0.387	0.309308
Kampuchea, Democratic (riel)[e]			31.17[e]
Kenya (shilling)[d]	SDR	9.66	7.72071
Korea (won)	bskt	0.27606	589.00
Kuwait (dinar)			
Lao People's Dem. Rep. (new kip)[d]	$	10.00	
Lebanon (pound)			3.41725
Lesotho (maloti)[d]	R	1.00	
Liberia (dollar)	$	1.00	
Libya (dinar)	$	0.296053	
Luxembourg (franc)[d]			31.17[e]
Madagascar (franc)	F	50.00	
Malawi (kwacha)	SDR	1.05407	0.842461
Malaysia (ringgit)	bskt	2.2778	
Maldives (rupee)[d]			7.55
Mali (franc)	F	100.00	
Malta (pound)	bskt	0.36361	
Solomon Islands (dollar)	bskt	0.872661	
Somalia (shilling)[d]	$	6.2950	
South Africa (rand)[d]			0.809389
Spain (peseta)			72.30
Sri Lanka (rupee)			16.375
Sudan (pound)	$	0.50	
Suriname (guilder)	$	1.785	
Swaziland (lilangeni)[d]	R	1.00	
Sweden (krona)	bskt	4.4569	
Syrian Arab Rep. (pound)[d]	$	3.925	
Tanzania (shilling)	bskt	8.23561	
Thailand (baht)	bskt	20.425	
Togo (franc)	F	50.00	
Trinidad and Tobago (dollar)	$	2.409	
Tunisia (dinar)	bskt	0.41771	
Turkey (lira)[d]			70.70
Uganda (shilling)	SDR	9.66	7.72071
United Arab Emirates (dirham)			3.736
United Kingdom (pound)			0.46151
United States (dollar)			1.00
Upper Volta (franc)	F	50.00	
Uruguay (new peso)[d]			8.648

EXHIBIT 1 CONTINUED

Member (currency)	Exchange Rate Maintained Against[h]	Exchange Rate[a]	Exchange Rate Otherwise Determined[b,c]
Congo (franc)	F	50.00	
Costa Rica (colon)	$	8.57	
Cyprus (pound)	bskt	0.370989	
Denmark (krone)			6.026[e]
Djibouti (franc)	$	178.16	
Dominica (East Caribbean dollar)	$	2.70	
Dominican Rep. (peso)[d]	$	1.00	
Ecuador (sucre)[d]	$	25.00	
Egypt (pound)[d]	$	0.70	
El Salvador (colon)	$	2.50	
Equatorial Guinea (ekuele)[d]	P	1.00	
Ethiopia (birr)[d]	$	2.07	
Fiji (dollar)	bskt	0.859697	
Finland (markka)	bskt	3.886	
France (franc)	bskt		4.4785[e]
Gabon (franc)	F	50.00	
Gambia, The (dalasi)	£	4.00	
Germany, Fed. Rep. (Deutsche Mark)[d]			1.9419[e]
Ghana (cedi)[d]			2.75
Mauritania (ouguiya)	bskt		7.99246
Mauritius (rupee)[d]	SDR	10.00	
Mexico (peso)			22.8514
Morocco (dirham)[d]	bskt	4.0922	
Nepal (rupee)[d]	$	12.00	
Netherlands (guilder)			2.127[e]
New Zealand (dollar)	$		1.06033
Nicaragua (cordoba)[d]	$	10.00	
Niger (franc)	F	50.00	
Nigeria (naira)			0.641026
Norway (krone)	bskt	5.17	
Oman (rial Omani)	$	0.3454	
Pakistan (rupee)	$	9.90	
Panama (balboa)	$	1.00	
Papua New Guinea (kina)	bskt	0.707914	
Paraguay (guarani)[d]	$	126.00	
Peru (sol)[d]			267.029
Philippines (peso)			7.4285
Portugal (escudo)			51.12[f]
Qatar (riyal)			3.6775
Venezuela (bolivar)[d]	$	4.2925	2.12885
Viet Nam (dong)[d]	SDR	2.66358	
Western Samoa (tala)[d]			0.9481
Yemen Arab Rep. (rial)[d]	$	4.5625	
Yemen, People's Dem. Rep. (dinar)	$	0.345395	
Yugoslavia (dinar)	SDR	3.80952	19.10455
Zaire (zaire)[d]			3.04475
Zambia (kwacha)	SDR	0.976311	0.780312

Country (currency)	Symbol	Rate[a]	Market rate[b]
Greece (drachma)			41.894
Grenada (East Caribbean dollar)[d]	$	2.70	
Guatemala (quetzal)	$	1.00	
Guinea (syli)	SDR	24.6853	19.7296
Guinea-Bissau (peso)	SDR	44.00	35.1668
Guyana (dollar)	$	2.55	
Haiti (gourde)	$	5.00	
Honduras (lempira)	$	2.00	
Iceland (krona)			429.15
India (rupee)			8.23796
Indonesia (rupiah)			629.00
Romania (leu)[d]	$	12.00	
Rwanda (franc)	$	92.84	
St. Lucia (East Caribbean dollar)	$	2.70	
Saint Vincent (East Caribbean dollar)	$	2.70	
São Tomé and Principe (dobra)	SDR	45.25	36.1659
Saudi Arabia (riyal)			3.325
Senegal (franc)	F	50.00	
Seychelles (rupee)	SDR	8.3197	6.64948
Sierra Leone (leone)[d]	SDR	1.36693	1.09251
Singapore (dollar)	bskt	2.27	

Source. IMF Survey, April 21, 1980.

[a] Rates as notified to the Fund and in terms of currency units per unit listed; rates determined by baskets of currencies are in currency units per U.S. dollar.

[b] Market rates in currency units per U.S. dollar.

[c] Under this heading are listed those members that describe their exchange-rate arrangements as floating independently or as adjusting according to a set of indicators (see footnote f), and certain other members whose exchange arrangements are not otherwise described in this table. In addition, U.S. dollar quotations are given for the currencies that are pegged to the SDR and for those that participate in the European Monetary System (see footnote g).

[d] Member maintains multiple currency practices and/or dual exchange market. A description of the member's exchange market. A description of the member's exchange arrangements as of December 31, 1978, is given in the *Annual Report on Exchange Arrangements and Exchange Restrictions, 1979.*

[e] Belgium, Denmark, France, Germany, Ireland, Italy, Luxembourg, and the Netherlands are participating in the exchange rate and intervention mechanism of the European Monetary System and maintain maximum margins of 2.25 percent (in the case of the Italian lira, 6 percent) for exchange rates in transactions in the official markets between their currencies and those of the other countries in this group. No announced margins are observed for other currencies.

[f] Exchange rates adjusted according to a set of indicators.

[g] Information on exchange arrangements not available.

[h] Exchange rate symbols:

$	U.S. dollar	R	South African rand
£	pound sterling	SDR	special drawing right
F	French franc	bskt	currency basket other than SDR
P	Spanish peseta		

rencies, such as SDRs, or an especially constructed basket. In most of the developing countries, however, international transactions are subject to various exchange controls.

In terms of the number of countries in the various categories of exchange arrangements, the majority of the IMF members are classified as having pegged rates, which makes the system look closer to a fixed-rate system than to a floating-exchange-rate system. However, most of the major currencies float independently, float jointly, or crawl, which implies that even currencies that peg their exchange rates against major floating currencies or weighted baskets are subject to fluctuations.

In addition, the significance of the various exchange arrangements is reflected by the extent to which foreign trade is transacted through them. On this ground, it seems that four fifths of all exports of IMF members is transacted by members who do not peg their currencies, whereas the balance is carried out by members who are classified as having pegged their exchange rates.

MULTIPLE CURRENCY PRACTICES, BILATERAL PAYMENT ARRANGEMENTS, AND CAPITAL CONTROLS.   In recent years measures were taken in a number of countries to abolish or simplify multiple currency practices and unify existing dual exchange-rate arrangements. By definition, a multiple currency practice arises when the authorities create a spread of more than 2 percent between the buying and selling rates for spot exchange transactions, or create a difference of more than 1 percent between spot exchange rates for different types of transactions (i.e., special exchange-rate regime for some or all capital transactions and/or some or all invisibles, import rate(s) different from export rate(s), more than one rate for imports, and more than one rate for exports.[5])

In addition, there was a further reduction in the number of bilateral payments arrangements both among Fund members and between members and nonmembers. The number of bilateral arrangements among members declined from 95 in 1964 to about 44 at the end of 1978. The number of bilateral payments arrangements maintained by Fund members with nonmembers has also declined substantially over this period from 227 in 1964 to about 123 in early 1980. Over the period 1964–1978, the overall number of bilateral payments arrangements with both members and nonmembers declined by 46 percent (from 322 in 1964 to 167 in early 1980[6]).

Capital controls are implemented in various forms, some implicit, others explicit. According to the IMF definition,[7] the following types of controls are the most common:

1. Restrictions on payments in respect to current transactions.
2. Restrictions on payments in respect to capital transactions.
3. Prescription of currency.
4. Bilateral payments arrangements with members.
5. Bilateral payments arrangements with nonmembers.
6. Import surcharges.
7. Advance import deposits.
8. Required surrender of export proceeds.

INTERNATIONAL RESERVES AND LIQUIDITY.   The international reserves of a country are composed of monetary authorities' holdings of SDRs, reserve position in the

IMF, foreign exchange, gold, and, since 1979, ECUs. There are five ways by which international reserves may be created:

1. New SDR allocation by the IMF.
2. Increased reserve position in the IMF through expansion of quotas and Fund's use of countries' currencies.
3. Increased foreign exchange through international borrowing, particularly from the Eurocurrency markets, through an autonomous capital inflow of reserve currencies and through intervention in the foreign-exchange markets.
4. Purchases of nonmonetary gold by monetary authorities, thereby monetizing it, or by valuing official gold holdings at or near market price.
5. Creation and distribution of ECUs by the EMS.

See Exhibit 2 for changes in global reserves, 1977–1979.

Although the term *international reserves* usually refers to actual official holdings, a country's international liquidity includes both its official international reserves, its ability to borrow from financial markets, and conditional borrowing available at the IMF.

The distinction between changes in official monetary reserves, changes in foreign investment, and international liquidity has diminished for three main reasons: relatively easy access to, and widespread use of the Eurocurrency market; international borrowing; and the increased financial significance of the Organization of Petroleum Exporting Countries (OPEC).

This development has had several effects. It reduced the optimum level of reserves and diminished the link between a country's reserve position and its willingness and ability to run balance-of-payments deficits; it made necessary a revision of the concept and estimation of reserve adequacy whereby access to international capital markets and use of borrowings have to be considered.

International reserves are liquid assets that are immediately available (for liquidation at or near market price) to smooth out fluctuations in foreign-exchange earnings needed to finance imports of goods and services and cover temporary balance-of-payments deficits. Although gold has conspicuously lacked this liquidity characteristic since August 1971, this has changed recently. The high price of gold and freedom to trade gold by monetary authorities could increase its liquidity and monetary role.

Monetary authorities who value their gold holdings at market-related prices cannot be sure that in case of need they can liquidate their gold at those prices. The effective gold holding at lqiuidation might, depending on market conditions, be below the market price, but above the the official price.

Central banks could jointly support and stabilize (but not fix) the gold price, thereby increasing its degree of stability and making it more liquid and attractive.

Priced at 35 SDRs per ounce, official gold holdings amount to 32 billion SDRs, or about 11 percent of total global reserves.[7] Valued at 500 SDRs per ounce (about the average price that prevailed in 1980) gold amounts to 460 billion SDRs, or 53 percent of total reserves, about twice the world's currency reserves of 260 billion SDRs. Official gold holdings can increase by monetary authorities' acquisition of nonmonetary gold and its remonetization or by valuation of existing stocks at or near market prices.

Higher gold prices and official gold valuation at market prices could affect the global distribution and the nominal level of international reserves. Accordingly, re-

EXHIBIT 2 CHANGES IN GLOBAL RESERVES, 1977–1979

Areas and Periods	Gold (millions of ounces)	Gold (billions of U.S. dollars)ᵃ	Foreign Exchange	IMF Reserve Positions	SDRs	ECUs	Non-gold Total
			(billions of U.S. dollars)				
Group of ten countries and Switzerland							
1977	7.5	26.4	34.2	1.1	-0.2		35.1
1978	3.2	51.5	35.6	-2.6	-0.1		32.9
1979	-95.0	199.3	-30.4	-2.3	3.7	41.2	12.2
Amounts outstanding at end-1979	140.1	388.1	109.7	9.0	11.2	41.2	171.1
Other developed countries							
1977	-5.4	2.0	1.7	—	-0.1		1.6
1978	-1.3	5.3	9.9	0.3	0.3		10.5
1979	0.5	27.1	0.9	-0.1	0.2	0.7	1.7
Amounts outstanding at end-1979	90.7	47.5	33.0	1.3	1.2	0.7	36.2
Developing countries other than oil-exporting countries							
1977	2.4	2.0	10.8	0.1	—		10.9
1978	2.9	3.9	13.7	0.4	0.3		14.4
1979	2.1	17.7	7.6	0.3	1.2		9.1

Amounts outstanding at end-1979	57.8	30.3	68.0	1.2	2.6		71.8
Total oil-importing countries							
1977	4.5	30.4	46.7	1.2	– 0.3		47.6
1978	4.8	60.7	59.2	– 1.9	0.5		57.8
1979	– 92.4	244.1	– 21.9	– 2.1	5.1	41.9	23.0
Amounts outstanding at end-1979	889.2	465.9	210.7	11.5	15.0	41.9	279.1
Oil-exporting countries							
1977	– 2.6	0.7	10.6	0.2	0.1		10.9
1978	1.9	2.6	– 14.5	– 0.8	0.2		– 15.1
1979	0.3	11.1	15.4	– 1.8	0.8		14.4
Amounts outstanding at end-1979	37.2	19.5	70.5	4.0	1.4		75.9
All countries							
1977	1.9	31.1	57.3	1.4	– 0.2		58.5
1978	6.7	63.3	44.7	– 2.7	0.7		42.7
1979	– 92.1	255.2	– 6.5	– 3.9	5.9	41.9	37.4
Amounts outstanding at end-1979	926.4	485.4	281.2	15.5	16.4	41.9	355.0

Source. Bank for International Settlements. *Fiftieth Annual Report.* April–March, Basle, Switzerland, June 1980.

^aGold reserves valued at market prices.

serve distribution could shift in favor of the industrial countries that possess 83 percent of total official gold (the Western European countries, Canada, and the United States), but away from the less developed countries, which hold only 6 percent of the total.

With official gold holdings valued at current market prices, the major industrial countries gain 17 percent of total international reserves. Among the industrial countries, the major gainers are the United States, with an increase of 12 percentage points, France, 2 percent; Switzerland, 2.5 percent; and Italy, 1 percent. OPEC is losing about 9 percent, and non-OPEC less developed countries some 8 percent of their reserves.

The redistribution of nominal international reserves toward the industrial countries but away from non-OPEC less developed countries could have only a relatively small adverse effect on the latter, unless official gold valuation and use of collateral borrowings and settlements proliferate.

The reserve-adequacy criterion is used to determine whether official gold valuation at market prices will create excessive international reserves. The narrowly defined international reserve adequacy—measured in terms of the ratio of international reserves to annual imports and expressed in a percentage—shows that (with gold valued at 35 SDRs per ounce) global reserve adequacy deteriorated over an extended period of time.

Between 1972 and 1979 the reserve adequacy for all countries declined from about 38 percent to 27 percent; the ratio for OPEC declined from 79 percent to 74 percent; and non-OPEC less developed countries' reserve adequacy ratio declined from 37 percent to 33 percent.[8]

When official gold holdings are valued at market prices (500 SDRs per ounce) estimates show that the reserve adequacy ratio for all countries improved from about 45 percent in 1972 to 81 percent in 1979; the ratio for the industrial countries went up from 46 percent to 68 percent; OPEC's ratio increased from 87 percent to 96 percent; and non-OPEC less developed countries' ratio increased from about 40 percent to 48 percent.

Hence a valuation of official gold holdings improves substantially the global reserve adequacy. The main gains, however, are for the industrial countries, and the least gains for the non-OPEC less developed countries.

Estimates based on actual official-reserve data reported in the IMF publication, *International Financial Statistics,* show that the sharp decline in the reserves-to-imports ratios is most pronounced in the industrial countries. This suggests a greater utilization of the international financial market for borrowings and a lesser reliance upon economization of international reserves.

The relatively higher ratios observed in the non-OPEC less developed countries resulted from their deliberate policies of maintaining higher reserves, despite their high opportunity cost, in order to improve their creditworthiness. (In addition, since most of OPEC's reserves could be considered investments or idle balances, rather than international reserves in the usual sense, their exclusion from the present definition of global reserves capable of supporting economic expansion is warranted, thereby further diminishing global reserve adequacy.)

The above estimates indicate that contrary to the widespread belief, international reserves have contracted in recent years, and oil-importing countries, with a few exceptions, are in a less comfortable reserve position.

The valuation of gold at the market price overstates reserves, but it is probably closer to economic reality than valuation at the official price. The proper economic evaluation of international reserves requires that gold be valued at a price somewhat below its market price but above the official price.

Although gold reserves valued at market prices would create excessive reserve ratios compared with the historical record of the 1970s, this analysis is oversimplified. It erroneously assigns the same liquidity characteristics to the various components of international reserves.

It was suggested that the most useful role for officially held gold could be in easing some of the problems of official balance-of-payments settlements, particularly those involving recycling of OPEC's surpluses. Since the monetary authorities of some major OPEC countries have reportedly become significant gold buyers, this could provide an important alternative channel of financing their large surpluses, if it ever becomes feasible, thereby making gold a part of the petrodollar recycling process.

Willingness by OPEC and non-OPEC countries to settle some of their international transactions in gold could reduce, to some extent, the intermediation through, and burden of, the international banking system, whose capacity to continue recycling indefinitely is questionable. OPEC's acquisitions of gold through official settlements could be held as investments rather than official monetary reserves, thereby further demonetizing gold and reducing total international reserves.

Other key currencies (Deutsche Mark, Japanese yen, Swiss franc) and the emergence of intervention and portfolio considerations affect the currency composition (as well as trade patterns) of international reserve assets. The bulk of international reserve and international financial assets are denominated in dollars, and the dollar's value determines the value of those holdings. The desire to minimize exchange-rate losses has contributed in recent years to currency diversification by official and private foreign-exchange holders.

Central banks play a major role in the foreign-exchange market through their holdings of foreign-exchange reserves. The process of exchange diversification could have profound effects on future developments in the foreign-exchange markets and could encourage the evolution of a multiple-reserve currency system. This trend is an inevitable development, which reflects the changing distribution of global economic power and the consequent responsibilities accompanying it. Indeed, the monetary authorities of the major currencies are now more willing to assume a relatively larger key-currency role. In a multicurrency reserve system, there is an important role for artificial units (e.g., the ECU, SDR, etc.). In this context a dollar substitution account could be beneficial. Important steps have recently been taken to enhance the SDR, but its development into a fully accepted reserve asset and unit of account will take a long time.

THE FOREIGN-EXCHANGE MARKET

TYPES OF FOREIGN-EXCHANGE TRANSACTIONS. There are three types of foreign-exchange transactions: spot, forward, and swap. In spot transactions, the most common in the foreign-exchange market, currencies are bought or sold for immediate delivery. In practice, however, to allow for paperwork to be processed, settlement or value date is usually two business days after the transaction is originated. Exchange transactions for next-day value, one business day after the transaction is originated, are conducted for spot Canadian dollar against U.S. dollar transactions in North

America. Trading for "value today" requires an adjustment of the spot rate to reflect the interest-rate differential between the two currencies involved for the two days between today and the value day for spot transactions.[9]

Foreign-exchange rates are quoted in terms of the buying, or the bid, rate and the selling, or the offer, rate. Accordingly, quotes are stated with two numbers; the first indicates the price at which the trader is willing to purchase the foreign currency in terms of local currency; the second shows the price at which the trader is willing to sell the foreign currency in terms of local currency. The difference between the buying and selling rates is the spread. The spread fluctuates according to the stability in the market, the currency involved, the location of the market, and the volume of transactions in a particular currency. Higher spreads are caused by greater uncertainty, low volumes of trade, and a relatively small market. Conversely, narrower spreads occur with stable conditions, a high volume of trade, and an actively traded currency.

Spot exchange rates can be quoted in terms of (1) the number of foreign units to 1 local unit (i.e., the European method) and (2) the number of local units to 1 or 100 units of foreign currency (i.e., the U.S. method). In London, sterling against foreign currencies is quoted according to the European method. In New York the dollar against foreign currencies used to be quoted in U.S. terms, but in mid-1978 the European method of quotations was adopted, except for sterling quotations.

In the forward exchange market, currencies are bought or sold now for future delivery (i.e., value dates are more than 2 days in the future). A forward exchange contract is an agreement to deliver a specified amount of one currency for a predetermined amount of another currency at a given rate at an agreed time. Hence although payment is in the future, the exchange rate is agreed upon in the present. Each maturity has a specific exchange rate that almost always differs from today's spot exchange rate.

Forward transactions are usually for one month or a multiple thereof from the spot value date at the time of the transaction. Forward exchange rates are normally quoted with a buying and a selling rate for periods of 1, 2, 3, 6, 9, and 12 months for the major trading currencies. Up to these maturities the market is very active, and trading does not lead to wide exchange-rate fluctuations. Beyond these maturities the market is "thin," and trading usually leads to wide exchange-rate fluctuations.

At a higher cost, contracts can be arranged for a specific date in the future that does not indicate a number of full months, that is, an odd date. Forward deals are usually for a year or less, but banks occasionally provide for much longer periods.

When the forward exchange rate is higher than the current spot rate, the currency is trading at a premium for that forward maturity. If the forward rate is below the spot rate, then the currency is trading at a discount.

Forward-exchange-rate quotations are made in three different ways: (1) in terms of discounts or premiums expressed in points; the forward rate is calculated by subtracting or adding the points from or to the spot rate; (2) in terms of outright forward buying and selling rates, derived by subtracting the corresponding points from the spot buying and selling rates; and (3) in terms of the forward discounts or premiums expressed in percentages, which should be converted into points and the forward rates are determined by subtracting or adding them to the spot rates.

Under ideal market conditions the forward discount or premium on a currency in terms of another is determined by and related to the difference in interest rates that prevail in the two countries (i.e., the forward market is determined by international interest-rate differentials). Accordingly, the currency of the higher-interest-rate country is at a discount in terms of the currency of the lower-interest-rate country, whereas, the currency of the lower-interest-rate country is at a premium in terms of the higher-interest-rate currency.

The forward contract is the most important device among the various methods that are available for eliminating exchange risk that arises because of future foreign-exchange-rate fluctuations. The demand for forward transactions arises because of fluctuations in exchange rates and the need to reduce the risk of an exchange-rate appreciation or depreciation. In addition, forward exchange contracts allow determination of the exact value of an international transaction that is scheduled in the future, thereby assisting in corporate business planning.

The activities of arbitrageurs ensure a simultaneous process of rate determination in foreign exchange and money markets, whereby the interest-rate differential is just offset by the discount or premium on forward exchange. This is the point at which *interest parity* holds, or at which the covered interest differential—the nominal interest-rate differential adjusted for the forward premium or discount—is zero. In this case, the forward exchange rate is also said to be at interest parity, whereby the interest differential and the forward discount or premium, expressed in percent per annum, are equal.

Large deviations between domestic interest-rate differentials and forward-exchange-rate discounts or premiums are usually evident when exchange rates are under pressure and speculation is rampant. In practice, interest parity is seldom achieved in domestic markets and deviations from interest-rate parity are common because (1) exchange restrictions may impede the flow of arbitrage funds; (2) the cost of transacting foreign exchange and securities is not a negligible factor and it reduces capital mobility and movements; (3) there is a commercial and country risk of default; and (4) because of the above factors the supply of arbitrage funds is limited, that is, not infinitely elastic. Interest parity is more likely attained in the offshore Eurocurrency market because of the absence of restrictions and the resulting high mobility of funds from one Eurocurrency to another (see Exhibit 3 for Eurocurrency interest rates and forward discounts and premiums for the corresponding currencies).

The relationship between the interest-rate differential and the exchange rate is expressed by the following equation:

$$\text{forward exchange rate} = \text{spot exchange rate} \times \text{interest rate differential} \times \frac{\text{lifetime}}{\text{number of days}}$$

Besides forward exchange contracts, the alternative methods of reducing foreign = exchange risk are (1) the use of currency composites (e.g., SDR, ECUs, etc.); (2) leads and lags, by speeding up or delaying payments and receipts proceeds from international transactions; (3) matching income and outlays; (4) changing the currencies in which transactions are invoiced; and (5) the most direct competitor of the forward contract is the use of spot exchange transactions coupled with money-market deposits.[10]

A swap transaction is one in which a currency is bought and sold simultaneously, but the delivery dates for the purchase and sale are different. In a swap transaction, the amount purchased always equals the amount sold, and the bank's net exchange

EXHIBIT 3   EUROCURRENCY INTEREST RATES, EXCHANGE RATES, AND FORWARD DISCOUNT/PREMIUM POINTS

DEPOSIT RATES AT ANNUALIZED RATES[a]

	1 Month 215/210	2 Months 370/365	3 Months 484/479	6 Months 760/750	12 Months 1060/1030
Dol	20.40–.50	20.10–.20	19.50–.60	17.90–.00	16.17–.27
Hfl	9.45–9.65	9.85–.05	10.05–.25	10.10–.30	10.35–.55
Bff	11.90–.15	12.60–.85	12.80–.05	12.85–.10	13.00–.25
Stg	14.35–.60	14.80–.05	14.65–.90	14.70–.90	14.40–.60
Dnk	10.05–.15	10.05–.15	10.00–.10	9.75–9.85	9.50–9.60
Sfr	6.50–6.65	6.40–6.55	6.45–6.60	6.40–6.55	6.30–6.45
Ffr	11.35–.60	11.65–.90	12.00–.25	12.60–.85	13.25–.50
Yen	10.45–.70	10.50–.75	10.60–.85	10.40–.65	10.05–.35

EXCHANGE RATES VIS-A-VIS THE U.S. DOLLAR[b]

	Spot	1 Month	2 Months	3 Months	6 Months	12 Months
Stg	2.3428/38	123/130	203/210	272/282	365/375	385/400
Dmk	1.9585/95	188/178	335/325	455/440	760/735	1160/1120
Sfr	1.7685/95	219/211	397/386	550/542	955/940	1520/1490
Hfl	2.1225/40	215/200	370/355	485/470	765/745	1060/1035
Ffr	4.5325/40	375/355	620/600	815/785	1090/1040	1100/1000
Yen	207.65/85	195/185	340/325	450/435	725/705	1200/1100
Lit	927/929	450/300	450/300	450/300	100/400	2100/2600
Fbc	31.47/49	25/23	42/40	52/49	78/70	90/80
Hks	5.1300/20	160/130	160/130	200/170	400/300	700/300
Iep	1.8995/15	115/125	170/180	225/235	300/315	160/190

Source: Reuter LTD, Dec. 8, 1980.
[a]Quoted by Netherlandse Credietbank, NV, Amsterdam, on December 8, 1980, at 14:13 GMT.
[b]Quoted by Barclays Bank International, London, on December 8, 1980, at 14:15 GMT. Sterling is quoted as U.S. dollars per pound sterling.

position remains unchanged. If there is a change in the spot rate of the currencies, there will not be a foreign-exchange gain or loss as a result of a swap transaction.

The swap rate is the difference between the spot exchange rate and a related forward exchange rate expressed on an annual percentage basis in terms of *forward discount* if the forward rate is lower than the spot rate and *forward premium* if the forward rate is higher than the spot rate. This rate is the link between the spot rate and the forward rate or the link between two forward rates for two different maturity dates. This link is directly related to the interest-rate differential between the two relevant currencies. Swap rates are not true exchange rates and may not be reciprocated to change the terms in which they are expressed. These rates may be determined by several factors that affect both spot and forward exchange rates.

The two value dates in a swap transaction can be any pair of future dates. However, in practice, markets exist only for a limited number of standard maturities—that is, exactly 1 week, 1 month, 2 months, and so on—are called *even* dates. Maturities, such as 1 month and 6 days, are called *odd* dates. Active trading in the interbank market is usually limited to even dates for maturities longer than a week. A common swap transaction is called a *spot against forward swap,* in which the trader buys or sells a currency for the ordinary spot value date and simultaneously sells or buys it back for a value date a week, a month, or 3 months later. Another type of swap transaction is called a *tomorrow-next swap* or a *rollover,* in which the dealer buys or sells a currency for value the next business day and simultaneously sells or buys it back for value the day after. Yet a more elaborate type of swap is called a *forward-forward;* the dealer buys or sells a currency for one future date and sells or buys it back for another future date.

Banks conduct swap transactions among themselves and with some of their corporate customers. The parties to the contract do not incur any foreign-exchange-rate risk since the bank contracts are both to pay and to receive the same amount of currency at specified rates. A swap transaction which can be considered as if it were a simultaneous borrowing and lending operation, provides several functions: (1) it allows the use of a currency for a period in exchange for another currency that isn't needed during that time; (2) it offers an attractive investment vehicle for temporarily excess funds of corporations; and (3) it provides a mechanism for a bank to accommodate the outright forward transactions conducted with customers or to bridge gaps in the maturity structure of its outstanding spot and forward contracts.

Covered interest-rate differential is the difference between interest rates on comparable financial instruments in two different currencies, adjusted for the relevant swap rate. A covered interest-rate differential implies that the interest obtainable on the foreign currency investment is without exchange risk. Uncovered interest arbitrage occurs when an investor transfers funds from one currency to another and ignores the fact that currencies with high interest rates tend to be prone to devaluation.

Arbitraging involves the simultaneous buying and selling of currencies to take advantage of a price and yield differential in the market. A trader or investor may compare the premium or discount with current money-market interest rates in different currencies to determine whether profitable investment opportunities exist. If the interest differential in favor of a given currency is higher (lower) than the discount in the forward market on that currency, then there is an incentive to swap one currency for another, invest the funds in the high-(low-) interest-rate currency, and cover the investment in the forward market.

Hence whether or not it is profitable to move short-term funds from one market to another depends not only on the nominal interest rate that might be gained by so doing, but also on the relation of the two currencies in the spot and forward markets. The comparison between covered and uncovered yield differentials determines which one the investor will choose. Covered interest arbitrage is a transaction in which an investor transfers funds and takes out a corresponding forward contract that guarantees against exchange risk. (A more refined method of determining the costs and benefits of moving funds internationally would have to consider foreign-exchange-rate margins between buying and selling rates and interest-rate margins between ask and bid rates, as well as transactions costs. In practice, such cost factors are likely to represent important barriers to covered arbitrage operations.)

FOREIGN-EXCHANGE MARKETS AND TRADING. The global market for foreign exchange consists of numerous domestic markets that are closely interdependent through arbitrage and an efficient communication network. The market has acquired breadth, depth, and resilience from (1) a wider spectrum of participants, currencies, and types of transactions, combined with (2) the ability to absorb large transactions without excessive price movements, and (3) the ability to recover quickly from a price distortion resulting from a large transaction.

Banks and brokers in each country constitute a market for foreign exchange in which individuals, corporations, banks, and brokers buy and sell currencies. Currency trading in each country is conducted through the intermediation of foreign-exchange brokers, who match currency bids and offers of banks and also trade directly among themselves internationally. Banks in each country and throughout the world are linked by telephone, telex, and the Reuter Monitor. The latter is a telecommunication system that allows market participants to display the exchange rates at which they deal and to transmit other news and market information. All subscribers have their own monitor and access to the price information that is provided. Through the Reuter Monitor and other means of rapid communication, there is quicker and wider dissemination of exchange-rate information and quotations. This in turn contributes to a worldwide market with narrower spreads to nonbank participants.

The foreign-exchange market for any currency consists of all the financial centers around the world (e.g., London, New York, etc.) where the currency is traded. However, local banks often benefit from closer access to national money markets, and they usually have an advantage in trading their national currency, although this advantage is not absolute.

Although the market is global, the exchange market in each country has its own identity and institutional and regulatory framework. An efficient communication system can substitute for participants' need to convene in a specific location (bourse). Indeed, the British-American type of market is based on communication networks, whereas the European approach remains traditional, based on the physical meeting of the participants, usually at the bourse. Daily meetings take place in some markets such as those in Frankfurt, Paris, and so forth, where representatives of commercial banks and the central bank meet and determine a rate, known as the *fixing rate*. In those countries, the posted fixing rate serves as a guide for pricing small-to-medium-sized transactions between banks and their customers. Among major industrial countries, Japan, Germany, France, Italy, and the Scandinavian and the Benelux countries have a daily fixing. The United Kingdom, Switzerland, Canada, and the United States do not.[11]

Foreign exchange is traded in a 24-hour market. As the market in the Far East closes, trading in Middle Eastern financial centers has been going on for a couple of hours, and the trading day in Europe is just beginning. At noon in London, the New York market is opening; as London closes, the market in San Francisco opens and trades with the East Coast of the United States and the Far East as well.

Banks, including central banks, dominate the foreign-exchange market, and 90 percent of foreign-exchange trading is interbank trading. Nonbank participants in foreign-exchange trading include commodities dealers (45 percent of total nonbank trading), multinational corporations (30 percent) nonbank financial institutions (10 percent) and oil corporations (10 percent).[12]

The foreign-exchange market performs three major functions: (1) It is part of the international payments system and provides a mechanism for exchange or transfer of the national money of one country into the money of another country, thereby facilitating international trade; (2) it assists in supplying short-term credits through the Eurocurrency market and swap arrangements; and (3) it provides forward exchange instruments for hedging against exchange risk.

Foreign exchange trading expanded sharply under the floating-exchange-rate system, and the number of banks participating in the market increased significantly as they entered the market to service their corporate clients. Increased hedging by companies of the flow of funds and increased matching of currency assets and liabilities was accompanied by the entrance of new corporate participants into the market. In addition, to some extent, the growth of spot and forward business resulted from the increase in Eurocurrency lending and speculative activity.

The demand for a particular currency in the foreign-exchange market depends on the need of participants to settle international transactions involving current-account and capital transactions of each country or third countries. The major determinants for a currency choice in trade contracts are (1) exchange-rate stability, (2) financial expediency, and (3) tradition and habit in commodity-market trading.[13]

Evidence shows that the pattern in the use of various currencies in global trade is as follows: (1) exports of industrial commodities tend to be denominated in the currency of the exporting country; (2) trade in raw materials tends to be quoted and denominated in dollars; (3) when export invoicing is not in the country's currency, the importing country's currency or the dollar is usually used, although the former has first preference; and (4) the existence of forward markets is a precondition for the use of that currency in trade contracts.[14]

The dollar is used in 52 percent of world exports, whereas the U.S. share of global trade is about 12 percent, which implies that 40 percent of world trade is denominated in dollars as a third currency. In 1977 the German and Swiss trade share were 11 percent and 1.5 percent respectively, but about 3 percent and 0.5 percent of world exports were contracted in Deutsche Marks and Swiss francs respectively as third currencies. Thus there is no use of the Deutsche Mark for third-country trade, but the Swiss franc is widely used. The use of other currencies as third currencies is negligible. These proportions of third-country uses in global trade are similar to those of the Eurocurrency market, where the dollar consists of some 75 percent of the market.[15]

The daily average volume of worldwide foreign-exchange trading, defined as dollar turnover of all purchases, spot, forward and swap contracts, was estimated at $103 billion in 1977, or $26 billion for the whole year. (World trade during the year was about $1.15 trillion.[16] See Exhibit 4 for global currency trading.)

Foreign-exchange trading is composed of spot, outright forward, and swap transactions. The latter are almost entirely interbank dealings. Although most commercial banks handle foreign-exchange transactions for their clients, many banks also act as money-makers, with each prepared to deal with other banks at any time. This activity constitutes the interbank market, where portfolio positions are adjusted and exchange rates are determined.

The most-important exchange markets are located in London, New York, Paris, Frankfurt, Amsterdam, Milan, Zurich, Toronto, Brussels, Bahrain, and Tokyo. There are significant differences among various markets in size and type of transactions.

As Exhibit 4 shows, some 90 percent of all foreign-exchange activity consists of interbank trading for speculative and arbitrage purposes among a few currencies. The bulk of trading is through the dollar, which remains the dominant currency through which foreign-exchange transactions are executed. Nondollar trading is dominated by the Deutsche Mark, the pound sterling, and the Swiss franc, which far exceeds their proportionate role in international trade and investment. Their main properties are well-developed markets and wide institutional support, combined with relative freedom from exchange controls.

EXHIBIT 4 WORLDWIDE FOREIGN-EXCHANGE TRADING

Daily Average Foreign-Exchange Turnover
Spot and Forward
($ billions equivalent)

Market[a]	1973	1979
Frankfurt	19–20	15
London	4–5	10–12
Zurich	5–6	5
Paris	1	3–4
Total	29–32	33–36

Interbank Turnover as a Proportion of Total
Spot and Forward Turnover, 1979

Market	Percentage[b]
London	90
Frankfurt	75–90
Zurich	90[c]
Paris	85–90

Proportion of Foreign-Exchange Transactions via
the Dollar in the First Instance, 1979[d]

Market	Percentage
London	99
Frankfurt	90
Zurich	95–99
Paris	60[e]

Source: The Group of Thirty. *Foreign Exchange Market Under Floating Rates.* New York: Group of Thirty, p. 80.

[a]Central bank estimates in each center.

[b]*Source.* Central bank estimates.

[c]In Zurich the proportion is estimated at 80 to 85 percent excluding interbank deposit business between Swiss banks, which is conducted through the dollar in the absence of a domestic money market.

[d]Central bank estimates.

[e]In Paris, about 15 percent of turnover is in Deutsche Marks, about 10 percent each in Swiss francs and sterling and the residual 5 percent in other currencies. The proportion going through the dollar has declined from about 80 percent in 1970.

New York is the largest and fastest-growing foreign-exchange market, in which a great number of currencies are traded; about half a dozen major currencies account for the bulk of the volume. A 1980 survey of the Federal Reserve Bank of New York[17] showed that gross currency transactions by 90 banking institutions in the United States foreign-exchange market amounted to an average $23 billion each business day in March, or $491 billion for the whole month, nearly five times greater than average gross daily turnover in April 1977. After adjusting for double-counting, average daily gross turnover was $18 billion. Gross transactions by 11 foreign-exchange brokers averaged $8.5 billion per day. The remaining section examines the New York exchange market based on the above survey.

The survey showed that the relative significance of foreign currencies has changed since 1977 (see Exhibit 5). Trading in Deutsche Marks has expanded and continued to dominate market activity, accounting for about 32 percent of the transactions by the banking institutions in spot, forward, and swap contracts, up from 25 percent in 1977. The role of the pound sterling as a key currency has been enhanced, and it has become the second most actively traded currency, accounting for about 23 percent of gross turnover, up from 17 percent in 1977. The Canadian dollar, which had been the second most actively traded currency in 1977, moved into third place, accounting for 12 percent of the total turnover. Economic and financial independence placed the Canadian dollar in a special position in the U.S. foreign-exchange market. Most dealing in Canadian dollars is concentrated in North America, whereas trading of Canadian dollars in European and Asian financial centers is relatively less active.

A major change in the trading pattern of the Japanese yen occurred as a result of liberalization of exchange restrictions and its internationalization trend. The yen moved to fourth place, accounting for 10.2 percent of the total, up from seventh place, with 5.3 percent, in 1977. The Swiss franc was fifth, with 10.1 percent, down from fourth place in 1977, with 13.8 percent.

A large volume of transactions is denominated in French francs; the franc ranks sixth, with 6.8 percent of total volume, up from 6.3 percent in 1977. The Dutch guilder is an important trading currency, ranking seventh, with some 2 percent of the total, down from 5.7 percent in 1977. Other currencies are not heavily traded in the U.S. market, and most banks usually limit their operations to handling the commercial needs of their corporate customers.

At brokerage firms, Deutsche Marks accounted for nearly 28 percent of March 1980 transactions, about the same as in April 1977; the British pound was the second most actively traded currency, accounting for 22.7 percent of turnover; the Japanese yen was third, accounting for 13.7 percent of total transactions; the Canadian dollar was fourth, accounting for 11.4 percent; the Swiss franc was fifth, with 7.9 percent; and the French franc was sixth, with 7.3 percent.

During March 1980, 64 percent of all foreign-exchange trading was in spot contracts, up from 55 percent in 1977, generally for delivery in 2 days; 30 percent was in swap contracts, down from 40 percent in 1977; and the remaining 6 percent of total turnover was in outright forward contracts.

About 8 percent of the 1980 total turnover reported by the 90 banking institutions was with nonbank customers, and the remaining 92 percent was reported between banks, about the same as in April 1977. About 43 percent of the March 1980 nonbank business took place in the forward market, 36 percent in spot contracts, and 21 percent in swap contracts. The turnover in the forward market is now only slightly higher than it was in 1973; its increase has been much less than the growth in spot

EXHIBIT 5a DISTRIBUTION OF FOREIGN-EXCHANGE TURNOVER REPORTED BY BANKS (TOP) AND REPORTED BY BROKERS IN MARCH 1980 (BOTTOM).

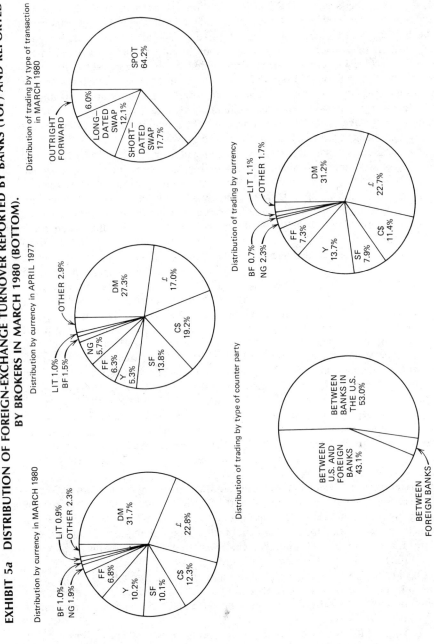

Source. Federal Reserve Bank of New York. *1980 Foreign Exchange Survey,* No. 1371. New York: FRBNY, 1980.

[a]Because of rounding errors, some totals may not sum to 100 percent.

EXHIBIT 5b GROWTH IN FOREIGN-EXCHANGE TURNOVER AMONG U.S. BANKS APRIL 1977 TO MARCH 1980

Currency	Institutions Represented on Both Surveys			All Institutions Represented on Each Survey		
	April 1977 ($ billions)	March 1980 ($ billions)	Change (%)	April 1977 ($ billions)	March 1980 ($ billions)	Change (%)
Deutsche Mark	28.7	92.6	+222.6	29.0	155.9	+437.6
British pound	17.4	77.4	+344.8	18.1	112.1	+519.3
Canadian dollar	18.1	39.1	+116.0	20.4	60.5	+196.6
Japanese yen	5.6	30.5	+444.6	5.7	50.1	+778.9
Swiss franc	14.6	43.0	+194.5	14.6	49.7	+240.4
French franc	6.6	21.4	+224.2	6.7	33.6	+401.5
Dutch guilder	6.0	9.0	+ 50.0	6.0	9.3	+ 55.0
Belgian franc	1.5	4.3	+186.7	1.6	5.1	+218.8
Italian lira	1.2	3.1	+158.3	1.2	4.2	+250.0
All other	3.0	5.5	+ 83.3	3.1	10.8	+248.4
All currencies	102.7	325.9	+217.3	106.4	491.3	+361.7
Sample Size	41	41	—	44	90	—

Source. Federal Reserve Bank of New York. *1980 Foreign Exchange Survey*, No. 1371. New York: FRBNY, 1980.

EXHIBIT 5c FOREIGN-EXCHANGE TURNOVER SURVEY OF 90 BANKS IN THE UNITED STATES, MARCH 1980
(MILLIONS OF U.S. DOLLARS EQUIVALENT)

Type of Transaction	Deutsche Mark	British Pound	Swiss Franc	Japanese Yen	Canadian Dollar	French Franc	Dutch Guilder	Belgian Franc	Italian Lira	All Other	All Currencies
Outright spot transactions											
Interbank											
Through brokers	55,520	39,135	16,367	16,810	12,858	13,246	4,142	1,278	1,127	2,007	162,490
Direct, with											
Banks in the U.S.	28,091	11,765	6,347	4,827	5,360	3,874	640	488	241	759	62,392
Banks abroad	21,553	13,274	10,591	5,059	15,204	3,472	1,610	1,080	839	2,793	75,475
Customer											
Nonfinancial institutions	2,431	2,827	859	544	2,518	776	130	142	135	450	10,812
Financial institutions	1,011	1,386	509	202	803	226	95	8	10	46	4,296
Swap transactions											
Interbank											
Short-dated (1 week or less)	22,296	17,591	8,099	11,838	11,132	6,066	1,743	1,399	990	1,756	82,910
Long-dated	16,168	15,226	3,539	7,137	6,096	4,044	484	336	402	1,421	54,853
Customer											
Nonfinancial institutions											
Short-dated	481	1,439	215	57	732	101	12	36	11	20	3,104
Long-dated	697	1,555	261	164	636	104	21	21	26	87	3,572
Financial institutions											
Short-dated	152	225	44	188	227	1	3	—	—	46	886
Long-dated	117	315	108	159	237	52	21	20	—	106	1,135
Outright forward transactions											
Interbank	3,852	2,744	869	1,118	746	887	182	203	224	729	11,554
Customer											
Nonfinancial institutions	2,036	2,553	614	1,165	2,341	751	229	90	190	514	10,483
Financial institutions	134	244	91	68	440	34	13	12	8	55	1,099
Arbitrage members of currency futures exchange	1,333	1,785	1,176	750	1,211	2	—	—	—	5	6,262
Total outright spot transactions	108,606	68,387	34,673	27,442	36,743	21,594	6,617	2,996	2,352	6,055	315,465
Total swap transactions	39,911	36,351	12,266	19,543	19,060	10,368	2,284	1,812	1,429	3,436	146,460
Total outright forward transactions	7,355	7,326	2,750	3,101	4,738	1,674	424	305	422	1,303	29,398
Total interbank	147,480	99,735	45,812	46,789	51,396	31,589	8,801	4,784	3,823	9,465	449,674
Total customer	8,392	12,239	3,877	3,297	9,145	2,047	524	329	380	1,329	41,649
Total turnover	155,872	112,064	49,689	50,086	60,541	33,636	9,325	5,113	4,203	10,794	491,323

EXHIBIT 5d FOREIGN EXCHANGE TURNOVER OF BROKERS IN THE UNITED STATES, MARCH, 1980 (MILLIONS OF U.S. DOLLARS EQUIVALENT)

Type of Transaction	Deutsche Mark	British Pound	Swiss Franc	Japanese Yen	Canadian Dollar	French Franc	Dutch Guilder	Belgian Franc	Italian Lira	All Other	All Currencies
Outright spot transactions											
Between banks in the U.S.	22,308	12,671	6,019	7,202	3,894	3,966	1,856	446	415	911	59,688
Between banks abroad	661	336	a	a	1,523	112	2	1	9	9	2,767
Between a bank in the U.S. and a bank abroad	15,940	11,498	3,915a	4,058a	4,314	5,518	1,649	319	374	730	48,201
Swap transactions											
Between banks in the U.S.											
Short-dated (1 week or less)	7,827	3,060	2,037	6,130	1,772	1,431	a	a	444	298	23,497
Long-dated	3,032	2,450	638	1,719	799	838	296a	264b	72	124	9,734
Between banks abroad											
Short-dated	a	a	25	a	1,443	a	—	—	—	—	2,474
Long-dated	134a	1,818a	—	149a	577	48	8	—	—	—	1,728
Between a bank in the U.S. and a bank abroad											
Short-dated	3,058	4,453	a	2,948	3,521	469	a	a	a	373	16,525
Long-dated	2,451	2,335	1,389a	1,717	2,086	547	369a	293a	554a	92	10,130
Outright forward transactions											
Between banks in the U.S.	a	522	a	a	a	—	—	—	—	468	1,386
Between banks abroad	a	—	a	a	a	—	—	—	—	—	—
Between a bank in the U.S. and a bank abroad	38a	1,189	25a	439a	422a	—	—	—	—	128	1,845
Total outright spot transactions	38,909	24,505	9,934	11,260	9,731	9,596	3,507	766	798	1,650	110,656
Total swap transactions	16,502	14,116	4,089	12,663	10,198	3,333	673	557	1,070	887	64,088
Total outright forward transactions	38	1,711	25	439	422	—	—	—	—	596	3,231
Between U.S. banks	33,201	18,703	8,709	15,337	6,526	6,235	2,152	710	931	1,801	94,305
Between foreign banks	795	2,154	46	242	3,543	160	10	1	9	9	6,969
Between U.S. and foreign banks	21,453	19,475	5,293	8,783	10,282	6,534	2,018	612	928	1,323	76,701
Total turnover	55,449	40,332	14,048	24,362	20,351	12,929	4,180	1,323	1,868	3,133	177,975

Source. Federal Reserve Bank of New York. *1980 Foreign Exchange Survey,* No. 1371. New York, FRBNY, 1980.

a In order to protect the confidentiality of individual respondent's data, amounts in this category are consolidated with the category immediately below. Therefore, individual figures in certain rows and columns will not add to totals and subtotals. All row and column totals and subtotals reflect the data prior to these adjustments.
b Consolidated total as indicated above.

exchange transactions or in the value of total international transactions. This is explained partly by the fact that part of the increased need for forward cover has been handled through alternative methods. In addition, most countries regulate forward transactions in order to deter speculation, thereby reducing the number of forward contracts. Finally, 15 percent of the trading reported with nonbanks was with arbitrage members of currency-futures exchanges. The survey of brokerage firms shows that 53 percent of the transactions reported by brokers were between two U.S. banks and 47 percent between a U.S. bank and a foreign bank, or between two foreign banks.

FUTURES TRADING IN FOREIGN EXCHANGE.   Trading in foreign exchange "futures" (forward) contracts for standardized currency amounts, and maturities not tailored to the exact requirements of individual parties or selected value dates, has been conducted in the International Monetary Market (IMM) in Chicago since 1972, and in the Commodity Exchange (COMEX) in New York City since 1980. Regulated by the Commodities Futures Trading Commission, the markets provide an alternative method for hedging foreign-currency positions as well as for speculation.

Future foreign-exchange contracts are usually settled before the value dates by payment or receipt of the difference between the contract and present prices rather than by actual delivery of the currency traded. Daily limits are placed on the allowed exchange fluctuations, that is, on the increases or decreases in the prices of foreign currencies from one day to the next. Buyers and sellers pay brokerage fees on transactions; the fees actually replace the spread between buying and selling rates, and they are required to establish a margin or security deposit for each contract bought or sold. After a transaction has been arranged, the buyer and seller each make a separate contract with each other.

THE ROLE OF THE FOREIGN-EXCHANGE RATE.   Foreign-exchange-rate considerations play a significant role in financial management of international business. Exchange rates are the prices of one country's money in terms of other countries' money. Through exchange rates, domestic prices are effectively translated into foreign prices, and vice versa. Close links exist between exchange rates and key economic variables (i.e., inflation, interest rates, capital flows, the balance of payments, etc.), and, depending on the openness of the economy, the exchange rate could become a key price that affects a wide range of economic activity.

The exchange rate affects prices and costs, particularly of tradable goods, and plays a significant role in the economy. The immediate effect of a currency depreciation is to increase the prices of imports to domestic buyers and to reduce the prices of exports to foreign buyers. Changes in relative prices promote domestic balance-of-payments adjustments along the lines of traditional analysis. A devaluation-induced increase in the domestic price levels reduces the country's real-income thereby gradually reducing domestic demand. The contractionary effect results in lower import demand and reduced demand for domestically produced goods, releasing some of these goods for the export market.

The exchange rate has an important, but by no means decisive, role toward the solution of balance-of-payments problems. Often exchange-rate changes are not very effective in promoting balance-of-payments problems. Often exchange-rate changes are not very effective in promoting balance-of-payments adjustments, since domestic developments neutralize these changes. Reasonable domestic policies are the essential prerequisities on which exchange-rate policy can be solidly based. To treat the exchange rate as a panacea and to neglect or play down the necessity for responsible monetary, fiscal, and income policies would be naive. Exchange-rate changes must be accompanied by appropriate fiscal and monetary policies if they are to be effective. Otherwise a depreciation can be inflationary. In the short run, depreciation usually worsens the trade balance through the *J*-curve effect, that is, the terms of trade initially worsen and exports decline, whereas imports may increase. Normally the favorable effects of currency change take some time to become effective.

The impact of exchange-rate movements on domestic prices, production, and employment depends on the state of the economy. When the economy is at full capacity, currency depreciation could be inflationary, thereby diminishing international competitiveness that might have resulted from the initial exchange-rate decline.

FOREIGN-EXCHANGE DETERMINATION. Each country has as many foreign-exchange rates or bilateral rates as there are currencies, and these exchange rates in turn imply cross rates between the other currencies, that is, the rate of one foreign currency against another foreign currency. Exchange rates are also expressed in terms of weighted baskets or composites (ECUs, SDRs).[18]

There are different views of the process of exchange-rate determination that reflect different theories. Although there is no generally accepted theory or model of exchange-rate determination, there are three main approaches that provide a general framework for analysis of exchange rates: (1) the income-expenditure theory, (2) the monetarist theory, and (3) the portfolio theory. Additional or alternative theories or hypotheses are either derived from or based on the above approaches, or are formulated in a reduced form, usually based on a single or many variable(s) or factor(s) explaining exchange-rate behavior.

The approach based on the traditional Keynesian income-expenditure theory considers foreign-exchange rates as prices that clear the international supply of, and demand for, goods (and in turn foreign exchange) in a process that simultaneously determines many other variables in the economy. In the Keynesian model, there are two links between the international trade and the foreign-exchange rate. One is the income effect, where the dominant influence flows from the international trade balance to the exchange rate; the other is the relative-price effect, where the influence is exerted from the exchange rate to international trade. A reduction in income and, subsequently demand for imports, will improve the international trade balance and lead to an exchange-rate appreciation; and, in turn, to changes in relative prices, substitution of exports for imports, and an improvement in the international trade balance. In the short run, the income effect generally dominates the substitution effect, because it normally takes longer for prices than for income to affect international trade flows.

Deteriorating trade (or current account) deficits (i.e., excess supply of domestic exchange) are likely to lead to exchange-rate depreciation, whereas improving conditions have an opposite effect. An excess supply of the currency would depreciate the exchange rate, whereas excess demand would appreciate the exchange rate. In a sense, the exchange market is always in equilibrium; supply and demand are always matched off at a going price.

An alternative and new approach of exchange-rate determination is based on the asset market or monetary theory of exchange rates, which emphasizes the role of markets for money and securities in the determination of exchange rates. This theory views the exchange rate as a relative price of two national assets or monies; the equilibrium exchange rate is attained when the existing stock of the two monies is willingly held. The exchange rate is seen as endogenously determined by stock equilibrium conditions in markets for national monies, that is, by current and past relative supplies of national monies.

In this context, the exchange rate clears the market by balancing foreign demand for domestic financial assets and domestic demand for foreign financial assets, either through a change in international reserves or a change in the exchange rate. The monetary authorities can affect the foreign-exchange market by altering relative money-stock growth rates and relative rates of return on financial assets. However, the exchange rate is not purely a monetary phenomenon, but is affected in part by real factors of the demand for money.

The monetary approach to exchange-rate determination involves several assertions:[19] (1) exchange-rate fluctuations are largely explained in terms of variations in the relative supplies of national money stocks and the latter could be used to forecast exchange rates; (2) in the long run, the domestic inflation rate is a monetary phenomenon, and the relative national price levels are dominant factors in determining the exchange rate between two currencies, that is, the purchasing power parity; and (3) in the short run, the exchange rate is determined by the supply of and demand for financial assets, because they adjust more quickly to a monetary disturbance than does the goods market.

The purchasing-power parity (PPP) theorey maintains that free international trade equalizes prices of tradable goods in different countries, so a product will sell for the same price in common currency in all countries (its price should change by the same proportion across countries at current exchange rates). Different rates of changes in prices must eventually induce offsetting exchange-rate changes in order to restore approximate price equality. Underlying the PPP theory is the assertion that any divergence of the exchange rate from its equilibrium level will set in force corrective forces designed to restore equilibrium; which may however, take time.

The PPP theory has several versions; the absolute version maintains that the foreign-exchange rate between any two countries should equal the ratio of their general price levels. The relative PPP version asserts that the exchange rate between any two countries should be a constant multiple of the ratio of their general price indexes. Equivalently, the percentage changes in their exchange rate should equal percentage changes in their ratio of price indexes. Mathematically, the PPP theorem can be stated as follows:

rate of change of the exchange rate = rate of change in relative price levels

or

expected rate of change of the exchange rate = expected inflation-rate differential

Evidence shows that disparities between relative prices and exchange rates exist in the short run, but the theorem holds over the long run. The usefulness of the PPP model to estimate divergences between the actual exchange rate and the long-term equilibrium rate depends on (1) the choice of a base period, (2) the choice of the relevant price indexes, and (3) the projection of the price indexes for the forecast period.[20]

Monetary models of exchange-rate determination hypothesize that the foreign-exchange markets are efficient markets in which present spot exchange rates fully reflect the available information. The efficient-market hypothesis asserts that market participants operate in such a way that the spot exchange rate normally reflects all available information to them that could be potentially beneficial in earning excess profits.

The weak efficient-market hypothesis asserts that historical foreign-exchange rates convey no information that could help a market participant profit (beyond earning a competitive risk premium) by speculating on future exchange-rates. Present exchange rates contain all the information that history provides about what future exchange rates are likely to be.[21] Traders' and speculators' activities ensure that exchange rates fluctuate in anticipation of future demand and supply, rather than in reaction to present demand and supply. However, since new information arrives randomly, exchange rates are likely, according to this hypothesis, to fluctuate randomly. Analysis of future demand and supply is of no use in predicting exchange-rate changes unless the analyst is convinced of his ability to forecast changes in future demand and supply faster than or more accurately than the market can.[22]

The evidence is inconclusive about whether or not the foreign-exchange markets have been efficient during the current floating era. Most research into forward market efficiency has found the forward rate to be a poor but unbiased predictor of the future spot rate.

The asset-market approach is mainly relevant for countries that have highly developed capital and money markets and where exchange restrictions do not impede substantial arbitrage between domestic and foreign assets. In countries where the likelihood of such arbitrage is limited or nonexistent, the exchange rate is determined mainly by supply and demand in goods markets and by official exchange intervention.[23]

The portfolio approach combines both the income-expenditure and monetary approaches and considers exchange-rate determination as a simultaneous process of adjustments induced by monetary and real factors. The exchange rate is determined by supply and demand for goods (i.e., trade-balance equilibrium) and financial assets (i.e., equilibrium in the capital account). The portfolio model shifts the emphasis from the goods market and the current account to the bond market and capital account as the major determinants of the exchange rate. Since asset markets adjust more quickly than goods markets, the exchange rate in the short run is determined in the asset market. The exchange rate may (in the short run) be inconsistent with both goods- and bond-market equilibriums, but in the long run, both markets must be in equilibrium at the same exchange rate.[24]

As indicated above, there are a number of additional approaches to exchange-rate determination that are based on technical properties of the foreign-exchange market, rather than complete theories. In a sense they are subsets of the three main theoretical approaches discussed above. These hypotheses are (1) the forward-exchange-rate theory, (2) the speculative theory, and (3) the expectation theory.

Covered interest arbitrage will eliminate any covered interest-rate differentials between equivalent-interest-bearing assets denominated in different currencies, and interest-rate parity will prevail. Otherwise, traders would have opportunities to make profits by moving funds from one currency to the other.

In practice, interest rates, forward and spot exchange rates are determined simultaneously, along with relative interest-rate differentials between countries. However, for analytical purposes, the interest parity condition can be viewed as an explanation of the spot rate, given interest rates and the forward rate; an explanation of the forward rate, given interest rates and the spot rate; or an explanation of the interest differential, given spot and forward rates.

The forward-exchange theory does not provide an adequate framework for explaining exchange rate determination and behavior. Indeed, empirical evidence shows that forward rates are not satisfactory predictors of future spot rates in a floating-rate system. (The efficient-foreign-exchange-market theory does not apply to the ability of the forward exchange rate to predict future spots.)

The speculative hypothesis of exchange-rate determination asserts that participants may move into a currency on the basis of fundamental economic conditions, but the market thereafter reflects a self-sustaining speculative activity. Speculative leads and lags are also very common; importers who expect the domestic currency to devalue speed up debt settlements and exporters delay remittances of sales proceeds. These activities could create pressure that could lead to a depreciation.

The large fluctuations of exchange rates that occurred under the present exchange regime were to some extent speculative. Such views are short lived, because a revision in expectations of future exchange rates can quickly change the balance of supply and demand in foreign-exchange markets.

An integrated exchange-rate model assumes relationships among exchange rates, interest rates, and relative prices. Accordingly, in equilibrium under perfect conditions, interest rates, prices, and forward and spot exchange rates are interdependent in such a manner that the PPP, interest-rate parity, and the expectations of the forward exchange rate are maintained.

EXPERIENCE WITH FLOATING EXCHANGE RATES.   The foreign-exchange markets have been characterized by considerable volatility and uncertainty since the adoption of floating rates in 1973. Divergent economic performance of the major countries and currency diversification contributed to unsettled conditions that can be measured by several criteria. First, exchange-rate movements were at times far greater than the corresponding movements in domestic price levels. Markets at times overreacted to changing circumstances and moved exchange rates beyond underlying equilibrium levels (i.e., overshoot). Second, exchange markets have not always been reasonably accurate in anticipating short- or medium-term trends in the exchange-rate movements.

There are substantial economic costs when exchange rates fluctuate widely over the short run: (1) Transaction costs associated with covered interest arbitrage increase compared with the previous periods, and (2) market quotations or spreads (the difference between the bid and offer quotations) widen, reflecting the higher risk involved in doing business at that time. The greater the risk preceived, the wider the bid–offer spread.

The floating exchange rates often require substantial official exchange-rate intervention to create more-stable conditions. Opponents of flexible rates argue that the instability of floating rates contributes to poor economic performance in the world, whereas proponents maintain that the volatility and instability of exchange rates are primarily symptoms of the instability of the underlying economic and financial fundamentals.

Floating exchange rates did not solve the underlying international financial problems that led to their adoption, nor did they completely free countries from the effects of those problems. The evidence to date shows that despite substantial nominal as well as real exchange-rate movements, large balance-of-payments imbalances persist. The recent experience has consequently raised some doubts about the efficiency of the flexible-exchange-rate system in facilitating international adjustments. It seems, however, that the limited impact of the recent exchange-rate changes on the balance-of-payments adjustment mechanism is attributable to three main factors: the inadequate application of domestic policies; short- and medium-term lags in the balance-of-payments adjustment mechanism; and divergent cyclical trends in the major industrial economies. Exchange-rate changes can induce a balance-of-payments adjustment over a short- and medium-term period only if domestic policies are applied in the same direction. In the absence of appropriate domestic policies, currency adjustment fails to improve the balance of payments, and in some cases it can even aggravate the rate of inflation through a vicious cycle.

Relative price changes brought by exchange-rate movements have a strong effect on the volume of foreign trade, but only after a considerable time lag. The evidence suggests that divergent cyclical economic trends have had a larger effect on the current-account performance than changes in nominal or real exchange rates. Hence exchange-rate movements have been offset by inadequate domestic policies, by lagged responses—both short- and medium-term—to relative price changes, and by divergent cyclical developments in different countries.

FOREIGN-EXCHANGE MANAGEMENT AND INTERVENTION. Since March 1973 the exchange-rate system has been floating, but managed to varying degrees by the monetary authorities, both through direct and indirect intervention. Different countries attach varying degrees of importance to exchange-rate stability and, in turn, exercise different exchange-rate policies. These diverging policies stem, in part, from differences among countries in the degree of their openness (i.e., relative share of imports in GNP), which affects the importance of the exchange rate as a price that influences the economy.

There are three main ways to intervene in the foreign-exchange market: (1) to prevent disorderly markets, (2) to lean against the wind, and (3) to establish either a moving or fixed exchanged-rate target. Exchange-rate management may involve intervention by the central bank or monetary authorities in the foreign-exchange market, official or quasi-official borrowing or lending, various forms of controls on foreign transactions and payments, or indirect intervention through monetary and fiscal policy measures. Intervention through the purchase and sale of foreign exchange is most common. Domestic money-market conditions and interest rates exert major influences on the exchange market through their effects on short-term capital flows.

Intervention is likely to occur when disorderly market conditions develop. The market becomes extremely asymmetrical, large exchange-rate movements take place on little trading volume, and traders are unwilling to make quotations for certain currencies; or there is a sudden widening in bid–offer quotations for a given currency and a tendency for rate movements to accumulate in one direction which would indicate that traders are unwilling to acquire a given currency. Disorderly markets could move exchange rates out of line with underlying economic trends in such a manner that exchange-rate fluctuations were not based on underlying economic conditions, thus impeding normal commercial and financial transactions.

The case for intervention becomes stronger, the greater are the potential costs of wide exchange-rate fluctuations. Exchange management is necessary if the free market forces could lead in the short run to excessive fluctuations.

Some countries intervene in the exchange market to offset the effects of secular or fundamental exchange movements by "leaning against the wind," that is, intervening when currency rates are compatible with fundamental trends. Sometimes intervention has broad macroeconomic objectives designed to achieve growth targets, price stability, and a balance-of-payments equilibrium. The authorities may seek to resist appreciation in order to avoid an erosion of their exporters' positions in world markets, or they may seek to resist depreciation to avoid the inflationary consequences of higher import prices.

Yet in other cases the authorities are committed to intervene in their exchange markets under international or regional agreements, for example, within the European Monetary System. The latter is a regional fixed, but adjustable, exchange-rate system that floats against the currencies of the rest of the world. Members of the EMS have central cross-exchange rates and intervene to maintain the fixed parities. Intervention is conducted in dollars and each other's currencies.

Intervention seeks to reduce the expected variance and volatility of exchange rates. Exchange-rate-intervention targets may be stated in terms of bilateral rates, effective or weighted-average rates, or in relation to predetermined central rates. Intervention requires that the monetary authorities act as sellers (or buyers) of foreign exchange and buyers (or sellers) of domestic currency. When a foreign central bank intervenes by selling, say, dollars and buying domestic currency, it finances the dollar sales from its international-reserve holdings or obtains the funds by borrowing from a variety of sources: from private financial institutions, from official institutions (e.g., IMF), or under swap networks (e.g., Federal Reserve, the EMS). In contrast, when a central bank intervenes by buying foreign currency (e.g., dollars) and selling its own currency, it creates domestic liquidity.

In the case of the United States, almost all the Federal Reserve System borrowing for intervention has been through the swap network. This network enables the United States and other participating countries to acquire foreign currencies needed for market intervention. It is a set of short-term reciprocal currency agreements of $30 billion that the Federal Reserve maintains with 14 foreign central banks and the Bank for International Settlements (BIS). Each agreement allows the Federal Reserve and the foreign bank short-term access to the other's currency up to a specified limit. The agreements establishing swap arrangements are limited to 1 year, but have been renewed annually, by mutual consent, for additional 1-year periods. Since 1973 the Federal Reserve and other central banks have often used the swap arrangement to finance exchange-market intervention[25] (see Exhibit 6).

The U.S. Treasury Department has also established temporary swap lines to facilitate operations of the Exchange Stabilization Fund (ESF), and it may intervene with the Federal Reserve in the exchange market. The Treasury Department can also obtain foreign exchange by borrowing from the International Monetary Fund, by selling foreign-denominated securities, and by selling gold and Special Drawing Rights.

U.S. intervention is conducted on a day-to-day basis by officers at the foreign-exchange desk at the Federal Reserve Bank of New York, under authorization and a directive from the Federal Open Market Committee (FOMC), which consults closely with the U.S. Treasury Department. Intervention is conducted indirectly through the brokers' market through commercial bank agents, and directly through dealing with commercial banks.

The techniques of central-bank foreign-exchange intervention vary from country

EXHIBIT 6   FEDERAL RESERVE RECIPROCAL CURRENCY ARRANGEMENTS
(MILLIONS OF DOLLARS EQUIVALENT)

Foreign Bank	Amount of Facility January 1, 1979	Increase Effective August 17, 1979	Amount of Facility January 31, 1980
Austrian National Bank	250		250
National Bank of Belgium	1,000		1,000
Bank of Canada	2,000		2,000
National Bank of Denmark	250		250
Bank of England	3,000		3,000
Bank of France	2,000		2,000
German Federal Bank	6,000		6,000
Bank of Italy	3,000		3,000
Bank of Japan	5,000		5,000
Bank of Mexico	360	340	700
Netherlands Bank	500		500
Bank of Norway	250		250
Bank of Sweden	300		300
Swiss National Bank	4,000		4,000
Bank for International Statements: Swiss francs-dollars	600		600
Other authorized European currencies-dollars	1,250		1,250
Total	29,760	340	30,100

Source.   FRBNY. *Quarterly Review* Vol. V, No. 1 (1980), p. 38.

to country, according to the institutional setup. In countries where foreign-exchange brokers operate, some central banks actively participate and intervene in the brokers' market while others may trade directly with commercial banks. Some central banks approach the brokers' market indirectly through a commercial bank that acts as agent in order to conceal their operation.

U.S. intervention is conducted mainly through the swap system, under which drawings can only be upon mutual consent. The Federal Reserve gives the foreign central bank a dollar account equal to the size of the intervention and receives sufficient foreign exchange to cover its dollar purchases. The foreign bank's dollars are then invested in a nonnegotiable U.S. Treasury certificate or indebtedness until the swap is retired. Usually initiated by telephone and followed by an exchange of cables specifying terms and conditions, a drawing consists of a spot and a forward foreign-exchange transaction. For example, the Federal Reserve Bank of New York, which acts on behalf of the Federal Reserve system, sells dollars spot for the currency of the foreign central bank. It simultaneously contracts to purchase the dollars forward for the same amount of foreign currency on or before the maturity date 3 months later. Drawings under the swap arrangements may be rolled over for additional 3-month periods by mutual agreement. Borrowings mature by repurchasing the foreign banks dollars.

There is evidence that active management of an exchange-rate policy does not necessarily ensure exchange-rate stability or a desired exchange level; the management becomes more effective if it is accompanied by fiscal and monetary measures. This is shown by a brief highlight of U.S. intervention in the late 1970s and in early 1980. The experience reviewed below also indicates that intervention is often a combination of direct and indirect measures.

Following a period of strong pressure on the U.S. dollar in foreign-exchange markets, the Federal Reserve Board and the U.S. Treasury Department announced on November 1, 1978, a program to defend the dollar. The program included (1) an increase in the Federal Reserves's discount rate, (2) an imposition of reserve requirements on large time deposits, and (3) an expansion of U.S. intervention capabilities in the foreign-exchange markets by an increase in the size of the Federal Reserve's swap network with several key central banks and by the Treasury Department's use of some reserves from the IMF. In addition, the Treasury Department announced increases in the volume of monthly gold sales, which began in May 1978. The U.S. authorities followed up the announcements by intervening massively in the New York market.

In October 1979, the U.S. Treasury Department announced that future gold auctions would not follow a regular monthly pattern and that future sales would be subject to variations in amounts and dates. In addition, the Treasury Department announced two new issues of treasury notes denominated in Deutsche Marks to be offered in the German market in November 1979 and January 1980. In March 1980, President Carter announced an anti-inflationary program that included extremely tight monetary policy.

THE EUROCURRENCY MARKET

DEFINITION. Eurocurrencies or Eurocurrency deposits (and loans) are bank deposits (and loans) denominated in currencies other than those of the countries in which the issuing banks are located, and the Eurocurrency market is the market for these deposits and loans. For instance, a Eurodollar deposit is a (time) deposit denominated in dollars in a bank outside the United States (and a Eurodollar loan is a dollar-denominated loan issued by a bank located outside the United States). Likewise, Euro-Deutsche Mark deposits (and loans) and Euro-Swiss franc deposits (and loans) are Deutsche Mark and Swiss franc denominated deposits (and loans) made outside Germany and Switzerland respectively.

The Eurocurrency market comprises Eurobanks that are located worldwide, not necessarily in a geographically defined area. Despite the domestic connotation, the market is not necessarily located in Europe. Whereas the main market is located there, rapidly growing Eurocurrency markets exist in Canada, Japan, the Bahamas, Cayman Islands, Panama, Hong Kong, Singapore, and Bahrain.

Eurocurrency deposits are created when a domestic or a foreign holder of domestic demand deposits denominated in domestic currency places them on deposit offshore. For instance, a Eurodollar deposit arises when the owner of a dollar-denominated deposit in the United States deposits it abroad in a foreign bank (or in a U.S. foreign branch). Although the latter receives title or ownership of the original deposit and it issues a claim (deposit) against itself denominated in dollars, the dollars are never physically removed from the United States. Therefore, the creation of Eurodollars or Eurocurrencies involves only the transfer of ownership from domestic to foreign holders, but not the physical removal of domestic money to foreign countries. The Eurocurrency deposits are usually in the form of large short-term time deposits, including negotiable certificates of deposit (CDs), which are issued to banks and nonbanks, resident and nonresident. All Eurocurrency transactions are unsecured credits. Business in the Eurocurrency market is conducted in large sums; the common unit for Eurodollar transactions is $1 million, although smaller amounts of $200,000–$250,000 can be found. The funds offered on the market range in maturity from 24 hours to several years in the case of medium-term loans.

A Eurocurrency does not necessarily involve a foreign-exchange transaction. Instead it involves a transaction in a foreign currency, that is, a deposit and loan made and repaid in the same currency. However, the transfer of a Eurodeposit is often accompanied by a foreign-exchange transaction, in which the proceeds are switched into some other currency. Therefore, the Eurocurrency market should be considered part of the money market instead of the foreign-exchange market.

The Eurocurrency market constitutes a money market that is parallel to the respective domestic money markets and provides services that compete with and complement those markets. Apart from their location, Eurocurrency deposits (and loans) are essentially identical in characteristics to the deposits (and loans) of a bank in the corresponding domestic market. Accordingly, Eurodollars or, say, Euro-Deutsche Mark deposits (or loans) are not special types of dollars or Deutsche Mark instruments, and there is nothing to distinguish them from ordinary dollars or Deutsche Mark deposits (or loans) when they are used for spending purposes.

The Eurocurrency banks are not subject to disadvantaged domestic banking regulations (i.e., reserve requirements and interest-rate restrictions) and benefit from various fiscal incentives (low tax rates) and economies of scale. These factors give Eurobanks a competitive advantage over their domestic counterparts, and enable them to attract business from domestic banks by offering better terms to both borrowers and lenders (i.e., higher deposit rates and lower lending rates than the corresponding domestic rates). The margin between deposit and lending rates is narrower than that in the corresponding domestic money market.

Transactions in the Eurocurrency market involve substantial interbank deposits.

For example, a European bank holding a deposit in a U.S. bank may make a Eurodollar deposit with another European bank, which in turn may deposit the proceeds with another bank, and so on. Each redeposit transfers ownership of the original deposit at the U.S. bank and creates new Eurodollar-deposit liabilities on the books of the foreign banks involved. The total Eurodollars so created may be several times the amount of the original claim on the U.S. bank.

FACTORS AFFECTING THE MARKET'S GROWTH AND DEVELOPMENT. The fundamental impetus to the emergence of the Eurocurrency market was primarily Eurobanks' ability to avoid numerous costs and restrictions that existed in the domestic market, combined with demand for an efficient offshore financial service. The market offers the possibility of obtaining and employing funds that are not subject to additional costs and regulatory restrictions applicable in the various countries (i.e., monetary policy, specifically in the form of reserve requirements; interest payments and interest-rate ceilings; and capital controls and higher tax rates). Hence the cost-benefit associated with avoiding reserve requirements, interest-rate restrictions, and higher tax rates, the consequent interest advantage shared between the Eurobanks, depositors, and borrowers, and freedom from foreign-exchange restrictions contributed to the development of the Eurocurrency market.

The origin of the Eurocurrency market in its present form is traced back to the early 1950s, when the Eastern bloc countries, particularly the Soviet Union, sought after World War II to deposit their dollar assets outside the United States to avoid the risk of a seizure of their funds by the United States in case of an aggravation of East-West relations. Accordingly, they transferred their dollar assets from United States to European banks. This move set the initial stage for the creation of the Eurodollar market. Later they were gradually joined by U.S. multinational corporations, individuals, and other governments with sizeable dollar holdings that for a variety of reasons wished to keep their holdings outside the United States.

The preconditions for proper functioning of the Eurocurrency market (or any other external financial market) are (1) freedom from foreign-exchange controls; (2) ability to offer competitive deposits and loan rates; and (3) demand for offshore financial services. These conditions did not exist until the post-World War II recovery of the global economy and the restoration of convertibility of major European currencies in 1958.

A combination of several major events provided further impetus for the vigorous development of the Euromarket: (1) the pound sterling crisis of 1957, (2) the introduction in 1958 of convertibility for Europe's major currencies, (3) substantial U.S. balance-of-payments deficits, which led to U.S. monetary and balance-of-payments controls, and (4) various balance-of-payments policies in the industrial countries.

Historically, in the postwar period, European governments tightly controlled private transactions on current and capital accounts, particularly in U.S. dollars. But as intra-European payments were progressively liberalized, London provided sterling finance for many European corporations that were engaged in European trade as well as for its ex-colonies. However, in 1957 the British government curbed the use of sterling for the finance of non-sterling-zone trade, in order to protect the external value of the pound sterling. In addition, tight monetary conditions, in the form of direct ceilings on bank lending, were also imposed. Sterling balances held by non residents in non-United Kingdom banks were exempted from these restrictions. Consequently, a market in Eurosterling balances developed as an alternative source of financing foreign trade.

The United Kingdom's exchange restrictions resulted in a shift away from financing third-country trade with sterling (and diminished Eurosterling credit and deposit activities in London) and encouraged the use of dollars for this purpose. This strengthened significantly the role of the U.S. dollar as an international currency and provided an impetus for the expansion of transactions in Eurodollars. The most convenient method to obtain dollar balances was to offer a sufficiently high interest rates to attract such balances to London. The Western European return in 1958 to full currency convertibility set the stage for the development of markets in Eurocurrency deposits alongside the Eurodollars, which continued to dominate the scene.

Markets in Euro-Deutsche Marks and Euro-Swiss francs developed when the monetary authorities of West Germany and Switzerland placed ceilings on the interest rates that could be paid on nonresident bank deposits in an effort to discourage speculative inflows of short-term funds. Individuals and corporations that wished to hold blances in these currencies found that the banks outside West Germany and Switzerland were willing to pay rates of interest in excess of those permitted by these national monetary authorities or offered by their national banking cartels.

The Euromarket received further stimulus from substantial U.S. balance-of-payments deficits during the 1960s. This, in turn, contributed to the fast growth of the market by expanding the dollar liquidity. The evolution of the markets has also been promoted by balance-of-payments controls in other major industrial countries (West Germany, Japan, and Switzerland), which introduced defensive measures designed to neutralize large capital inflows. These measures provided further support to the growth of the Euromarket by recycling international funds from national markets toward the Euromarket.

The relative freedom of U.S. foreign trade and monetary policy in the 1950s and the early 1960s, in contrast with European exchange controls and tight domestic financial conditions, plus the return to convertibility of the major West European countries in 1958, all stimulated the growth and development of the United States as the world's banker. This, in turn, benefited the New York banks, which became active in the new market by financing third-country trade.

Relatively large and persistent balance-of-payments deficits led to the impositions of U.S. capital controls, which were in effect from 1963 to 1973 and consisted of (1) the Interest Equalization Tax (IET), (2) the Foreign Direct Investment Program (FDIP), and (3) the Voluntary Foreign Credit Restraint (VFCR) program. These controls blocked foreign borrowers and U.S. multinational corporations from the U.S. money markets and drove them into the Eurocurrency market.

The rapid expansion in the 1960s and early 1970s of international activities of U.S. corporations and the sharp growth of world trade generated a strong demand for international finance and banking services. However, the imposition of U.S. capital controls and the existing monetary constraints prevented the U.S. banks from providing these services out of their U.S. offices. To accommodate their corporate customers, American banks established a network of foreign branches for the purpose of tapping foreign sources of funds and setting up loan placements and financial services facilities. By branching overseas and by undertaking an ever-increasing role in the international credit market, U.S. banks were able to overcome the unfavorable regulatory environment that had been imposed on them. This, in turn, stimulated the growth of the Eurocurrency market and increased the internationalization of the world's financial markets.

The U.S. government introduced the IET in 1963 to discourage long-term U.S.

investments in foreign securities. The IET imposed a tax on yields of foreign securities, thereby reducing their effective return and attractiveness to U.S. investors. Consequently, foreign financing in the U.S. capital market became more expensive, and this drove foreigners out of the U.S. capital markets toward the Eurocurrency and Eurobond markets. Underwriting international bond activities on the New York capital market came to a virtual halt, and the markets moved to Europe and developed there. As a result, long term U.S. bank loans to foreigners promptly spurted, and the IET was amended to cover those loans as well.

Further growth of the Euromarkets was stimulated by the FDIP, which was initiated as a voluntary program in 1964 and made mandatory in 1968. Accordingly, U.S. corporations were limited in the amount of foreign direct investment abroad, that is, limited in their foreign subsidiaries or in new ventures, either financed with funds (dollars) raised in the United States or out of foreign earnings. In addition, foreign affiliates of U.S. corporations were required to remit a specific share of their annual earnings. This policy forced U.S. corporations that expanded abroad to raise loans and credits outside the United States.

Early in 1965, the Federal Reserve Board introduced the VFCR as a part of a comprehensive effort to improve the U.S. balance-of-payments problem. The program was designed to limit the amount of foreign credit that U.S. banks and nonbank financial institutions could extend abroad, by requiring U.S. banks' head offices to limit their domestic-based foreign lending to ceilings that reflected their historical foreign-credit levels. The program severely curtailed the capacity of home offices of U.S. banks to meet the financial needs of their large corporate customers located abroad. In addition, the Commerce Department asked U.S. corporations' foreign subsidiaries to follow the VFCR program, thereby forcing them into the Eurocurrency market.

In the beginning of 1968, the Office of Foreign Direct Investment (OFDI) regulations went into effect, initiating mandatory compliance with the voluntary regulations governing the international financial transactions of nonfinancial organizations. The OFDI regulations have served to increase demands for Eurodollars. The overall limitations were based on a share of the total credit each bank extended in 1964.

In addition to capital controls, the Federal Reserve Systems' Regulations Q and D played a significant role in the Eurodollar development and provided a strong stimulative impact on the growth of the market. These regulations increased the cost of funds and reduced the banks' ability to compete with foreign banks. These factors induced, to a large part, the establishment of overseas branches of U.S. banks and, in turn, promoted the growth of the Eurocurrency market in order to secure funds exempted from these limitations.

Regulation Q establishes a ceiling on interest rates on time deposits in the United States and forbids member banks to pay interest on deposits with maturities of less than 30 days. Regulation Q was originally designed to protect savings-and-loan associations from excessive competition from commercial banks. The thrift institutions were considered the weaker institutions and supposedly deserved this competitive edge to allow them to continue to channel most of their resources into long-term home mortgages.

By contrast, the Euromarket interest rates are determined by market forces of supply and demand, which are free of any national regulations. Therefore, the Eurocurrency market provided an alternative to U.S. investors by offering higher interest rates than those prevailing domestically. However, U.S. banks, overseas branches are not subject to Regulation Q.

However, since the 1960s Regulation Q constrained banks from attracting additional deposits and making additional loans during periods of tight money. U.S. banks gained access through their overseas branches to funds that they were precluded by various regulations from acquiring directly from foreign depositors. The Eurodollar banks' ability to offer higher rates than the banks in the United States greatly increased their attractiveness to investors, particularly when domestic money rates were above Regulation Q ceilings.

On several occasions, as the level of U.S. interest rates rose, member banks experienced a runoff in deposits at domestic offices due to their inability to compete effectively for domestic funds. Consequently, they turned to their foreign branches, which were not subject to interest-rate ceilings and thus were able to compete for funds. Deposits received at overseas branches were transferred back to the United States for use by the domestic offices. Effective in September 1969, the Federal Reserve Board imposed a 10 percent marginal reserve requirement on any increase in the net liabilities of U.S. offices of member banks to their overseas branches above their May 1969 levels, thus reducing the attractiveness of Eurodollar funds.

Regulation Q was modified on several occasions: (1) In 1962 it was suspended on deposits of foreign official agencies, thereby permitting U.S. banks to compete with the Eurodollar market for the dollar deposits of foreign central banks; (2) in June 1970 the interest-rate ceiling on large negotiable CDs with maturities of 30 to 89 days was suspended, thereby reducing the impetus for Eurocurrency growth; and (3) in May 1973 Regulation Q was suspended for all categories of large CDs, thereby further reducing the impetus for Eurocurrency growth. (The Monetary Control Act of 1980 provides for the gradual phase-out over 6 years and the ultimate elimination of all limitations on the maximum rates of interest and dividends that may be payable on deposits and accounts by depository institutions.)

Deposits at U.S. commercial banks, members of the Federal Reserve System, for less than 30 days were classified until recently as demand deposits, subject to Regulation D reserve requirements. (The Monetary Control Act of 1980 modified Regulation D. It defines a new type of time deposit with a minimum maturity of 14 days, to help improve the ability of domestic banks to compete with Eurocurrency markets.) Reserve requirements increase the effective cost of funds. Eurobanks, as well as foreign branches of U.S. banks, are not subject to Regulation D, and this amounts to a substantial cost savings on their sources of funds. Hence Eurobanks are able, on the one hand, to bid for funds by offering competitive rates and maturities tailored to depositors' needs, and, on the other hand, to relend or offer these funds at slightly higher rates. Consequently, Eurocurrency deposit rates are normally higher and loan rates are lower than those in the domestic market for the corresponding currency. For instance, the Eurodollar rate is largely affected by U.S. interest rates, and it moves jointly with it.

In summary, in the 1960s and early 1970s capital controls and monetary policies sharply curtailed the ability of banks in the U.S. to lend abroad. These regulations drove U.S. corporations to the Eurodollar market, not only to finance their capital expenditures abroad but also to cover the required repatriation of foreign earnings.

Hence the imposition of various U.S. capital controls in the 1960s combined with the spectacular expansion of U.S. multinational corporations were the major factors behind the growth of the Euromarkets. In January 1974, the VFCR program, the

OFDI program, and the IET were terminated. The removal of these controls initially had negatively affected the Eurocurrency market, but have reinforced New York's position. Future modification of Regulations Q and D could probably continue to produce a less favorable operating environment for the Eurocurrency market.

THE EFFECT OF TERMINATING THE U.S. BALANCE-OF-PAYMENTS CONTROLS. The termination of the balance-of-payments programs in January 1974, has (1) increased the significance of New York as a leading financial center, (2) reduced for several years the growth rate of the Eurocurrency market, and (3) stimulated a gradual change in the geographic location of the market, with centers outside Europe assuming greater importance. These developments are reflected in the increased activities of U.S. banks vis-à-vis the rest of the world as well as changes in the geographic trends and activities of the Eurocurrency market.

A revival of international lending by U.S. banks started in 1974, following the abolition of balance-of-payments restrictions. In addition, a growing portion of U.S. banks' lending was channeled through the Caribbean area and other branches of the Eurocurrency market. After a long period of stagnation in U.S. foreign-bank lending, short-term lending in 1974 almost doubled from the previous year, whereas long-term loans expanded by 20 percent. In the period 1974–1979, long- and short-term loans expanded by an average annual rate of 37 percent, compared to 20 percent in the previous four years.

Furthermore, with the abolition of capital controls, the United States became once again an attractive market for foreign bonds. In 1979 the total value of the foreign bonds issued in the United States was $4.6 billion or 25 percent of the aggregate world market.

Since the removal of the balance-of-payments programs, New York has become a very attractive site for agencies and branches of foreign banks, and their number and assets expanded very steeply in the past four years. At the end of 1980, foreign agencies and branches in New York reached 143, compared with 79 in 1973 and 56 in 1969. Hence the cumulative growth rate in 1974–1980 was over 80 percent, compared with over 40 percent in 1969–1973; and their total assets reached about $113 billion in 1980, compared with $21 billion in 1973, a cumulative increase of 438 percent, compared with 100 percent in the previous four years.

The removal of controls in 1974 slowed down considerably the Eurocurrency activities, as reflected by balance-sheet totals of foreign branches of U.S. banks, which, in turn, slowed down the growth rate of the Eurocurrency market. In 1974–1979 the Eurocurrency market, narrowly defined, expanded at an annual average of 23 percent, compared with 36 percent in 1970–1973 and 46 percent in 1966–1969. At its broadest definition, the market has shown a similar trend.

Between 1974 and 1979, the average annual growth rate of U.S. foreign branches was 33 percent, down from over 35 percent in 1970–1973. The slowdown in London was particularly noticed, with growth averaging 21 percent in 1974–1979, compared with 35 percent in 1970–1973.

Although U.S. activities in the Bahamas and Cayman Islands in 1974–1979 were growing somewhat more slowly, they have expanded at an annual average rate of 60 percent, compared with 67 percent in 1970–1973. Yet U.S. activities in the Bahamas and Cayman Islands expanded over three folds faster than the rate in the United Kingdom (see Exhibit 7c).

Despite the removal of several of the factors that contributed to the growth and development of the Eurocurrency market, the latter still contains several characteristics that make it unique and advantageous: (1) U.S. overseas branches are not subject to Regulation D member-bank reserve requirements or to fees of the Federal Deposit Insurance Corporation; (2) funds acquired by foreign branches of U.S. banks are not subject to Regulation Q; and (3) the market could continue to benefit from the geographic, political, and structural advantages, that is, different time zones, lower tax rates, and its wholesale nature.

By eliminating additional restrictions, and by allowing operations of International Banking Facilities (IBFs), the stage has now been set for the further emergence of the United States (particularly New York City) as a leading traditional and Eurocurrency financial market. This occurs against the background of diminished attractiveness of competing markets in Western Europe.

CHARACTERISTICS. The Eurocurrency market centers in London and it is composed of additional financial centers in Western Europe, the Caribbean, Asia, and Canada. According to the Bank for International Settlements, the narrow definition of the Eurocurrency market (or Eurocurrency aggregate) includes the external assets or liabilities denominated in foreign currencies of banks in 12 reporting European countries: Austria, 2.7 percent of the market in 1979; Belgium (6.5 percent); Luxembourg (11.4 percent); Denmark (0.5 percent); France (15 percent); Germany (3.5 percent); Ireland (0.3 percent); Italy (5.3 percent); the Netherlands (6.7 percent); Sweden (1.2 percent); Switzerland (4.6 percent); and the United Kingdom (42.3 percent).

There has been a secular change in the currency composition of the Eurocurrency market. The U.S. dollar in 1979 accounted for 68 percent of all foreign liabilities of European banks, down from 78 percent in 1970. In addition, the domestic-currency components of all foreign assets of European banks amounted to 18 percent of their total international portfolios, up from 11 percent in 1970.

The gross size of the Eurocurrency market, measured in terms of the external liabilities of banks in Group of Ten countries and Switzerland, Austria, Denmark, and Ireland and of the branches of U.S. banks in the offshore centers of the Caribbean and Far East reached a total of $1120 billion in 1979. The gross size includes the total foreign-currency liabilities of banks in the above countries vis-à-vis banks and nonbank residents and nonresidents, outside and within the reporting area.

The narrowly defined Eurocurrency market—defined in terms of the total assets or liabilities of the reporting European area—reached $666 billion at the end of December 1979 (30.4 percent above the level of the previous year), of which $437 billion, or 66 percent, was denominated in U.S. dollars and $229 billion, or 34 percent, was denominated in European currencies (Deutsche Mark, 19.2 percent; Swiss franc, 6.1 percent; pound sterling, 2.3 percent; Dutch guilders, 1.3 percent; French franc, 1.7 percent; and other currencies, 3.8 percent). Following the U.S. dollar, the Deutsche Mark was the second most significant currency in the market, amounting to some $128 billion, or over 19 percent of the entire market.

The broadest definition of the gross Eurocurrency market measures the external assets or liabilities denominated in foreign currencies of banks in the reporting European countries, the United States, Canada, and Japan, as well as the foreign branches of U.S. banks in the Caribbean and the Far East. This market reached about $874 billion in December 1979 (30 percent above the level of the previous year); the 12 reporting European countries accounted for 75 percent, and the Caribbean, 15 percent—the second largest center, after London (see Exhibit 7a–7f).

The estimated sources and uses of the Eurocurrency market show the volume of new funds intermediated in the market. This aggregate is also known as the net size of the Eurocurrency market, since it excludes interbank deposits in the reporting area, but makes allowance for the banks' use of foreign-currency funds for domestic lending.[27] All net foreign-currency deposits within the European reporting area plus payments by outside banks are counted as sources of funds to the market. Similarly, all net foreign-currency loans to nonbanks plus deposits made in banks outside this inner circle are counted as uses of Eurocurrency resources. This market reached $475 billion in December 1979 (see Exhibit 8).

Suppliers of funds to the Euromarket are commercial banks, central banks, governments, international monetary institutions, nonfinancial institutions, and individual investors. Borrowers of funds in the market include commercial banks, securities brokers and dealers, governmental agencies, international corporations, exporters, and importers. Data show that in December 1979 OPEC was a net supplier of funds. It provided $81 billion (or about 17 percent of the total resources) compared with 7.6 percent in 1973, and it used about $30 billion (or 6.4 percent) of the total uses, compared with 2.5 percent in 1973. Non-OPEC less developed countries used some $50 billion, or 10 percent, of total uses, and supplied $55 billion, compared with $16 billion in uses and sources (or 8.9 percent) in 1974.

There are two fundamental questions regarding the Eurocurrency market and the conventional definition of national money stock: Is Eurocurrency money? And whose money is it? All concepts of the U.S. and European money stock exclude Eurocurrency deposits. However, a case can be made for treating them as money on the grounds that these deposits fit into a broad definition of money.[28]

The bulk of Eurocurrency liabilities are time deposits that are excluded from narrowly defined domestic money supplies. Regardless of maturity date and unlike demand deposits in domestic currency, the Eurocurrency deposits cannot be used directly as payment mediums. Hence Eurocurrency deposits do not constitute money in its narrowly defined sense of *a means of payment* and cannot be compared with the narrowly defined money stock M1.

In fact, the same qualification about the degree of near money of domestic time and savings deposits and money-market paper applies to Eurocurrency deposits. These assets have to be liquidated first to facilitate a payment. Eurodollars have to be converted into a demand deposit with a bank in the United States to facilitate a payment. (These characteristics make Eurocurrency deposits more likely candidates for inclusion in the broader monetary aggregates such as M2 and M3 than in M1.)

Moreover, national money supply usually excludes all interbank deposits, the bulk of the Eurocurrency market. A large portion of the net market size is already counted in some countries' domestic money supplies. Thus there is substantial overlap between net Eurocurrency liabilities and domestic monetary aggregates. The only portion of the net size of the Eurocurrency market that does not overlap national money supplies and is strictly comparable with them is the nonbank portion. The net size of the market as measured by Eurobanks' liabilities to nonbanks was about $150 billion at the end of 1979.

In summary, whether the Eurocurrency market consists of banks or of financial

EXHIBIT 7a THE EUROCURRENCY MARKET (BILLIONS OF U.S. DOLLARS)

	Eurodollars		Eurocurrencies		Eurocurrency Market Narrowly Defined[a]		Canada, Japan, and U.S.		Offshore Branches of U.S. Banks[c]		Eurocurrency Market Broadly Defined[d]	
	Level	Growth Rate (%)	Level	Growth Rate (%)	Level	Growth Rate (%)	U.S. $	Others[b]	U.S. $	Others	Level	Growth Rate (%)
1964	9.65		2.57		12.22		4.97	0.67			17.86	
1965	11.39	18.02	2.82	9.72	14.21	16.28	4.92	0.67			19.80	10.08
1966	14.77	29.67	3.57	26.59	18.34	29.06	4.70	0.64			23.68	19.60
1967	19.12	29.45	4.15	16.24	22.27	21.42	5.86	0.83			26.96	22.30
1968	26.87	40.53	6.84	64.81	33.71	51.36	6.96	0.97			41.66	48.85
1969	46.20	71.93	10.52	53.80	56.72	66.25	8.05	1.09	3.04		68.90	65.39
1970	58.70	27.05	16.59	57.69	75.29	32.73	10.05	1.37	4.81		91.52	32.83
1971	70.82	20.64	26.97	62.56	97.79	29.88	12.33	1.68	8.49		120.29	31.44
1972	96.73	36.75	35.20	30.51	131.93	34.91	15.03	2.05	13.09		162.10	34.07
1973	130.47	34.88	60.96	73.18	191.43	45.09	25.61	3.49	23.13	6.47	250.13	54.30
1974	156.18	19.70	64.75	6.21	220.93	15.41	34.05	4.75	30.24	10.45	300.42	20.10
1975	189.47	21.09	69.20	6.87	256.67	17.22	35.90	4.90	40.87	10.68	346.12	15.21
1976	230.04	20.41	80.61	16.49	310.65	20.99	36.76	5.02	59.94	15.77	428.19	23.69
1977	272.88	18.62	110.56	37.15	383.44	23.43	35.86	3.99	73.02	19.19	515.54	20.40
1978	348.59	38.22	162.22	28.92	510.81	33.22	49.83	5.17	87.28	20.30	673.39	30.61
1979	436.60	41.42	229.42	30.64	666.02	30.38	72.07	6.65	104.61	24.20	873.55	29.72

Source. Bank for International Settlements. Variorus *Annual Reports* BIS: Basle, Switzerland, 1969.

[a]As measured by the external assets or liabilities of eight reporting European countries: Belgium-Luxembourg, France, Germany, Italy, Netherlands, Sweden, Switzerland, and the United Kingdom. Since 1978 Austria, Denmark, and Ireland have also been included.

[b]The distribution between the U.S. dollar and other currencies was estimated.

[c]Offshore branches of U.S. banks in the Bahamas, Cayman Islands, Panama, Hong Kong, and Singapore.

[d]Includes the narrowly defined market plus Canada, Japan, the U.S., and offshore branches of U.S. banks.

EXHIBIT 7b EXTERNAL ASSETS AND LIABILITIES OF BANKS IN INDIVIDUAL REPORTING COUNTRIES AND OF CERTAIN OFFSHORE BRANCHES OF U.S. BANKS (MILLIONS OF U.S. DOLLARS)

			1977 Dec.	1978 Dec.	1979 March	1979 June	1979 Sept.	1979 Dec.
Austria	Assets	Domestic currency	1,950	2,930	3,090	3,350	3,910	4,160
		U.S. dollars	3,870	4,460	5,010	5,910	5,890	6,610
		Other foreign currencies	3,570	5,120	4,550	5,880	6,770	7,130
	Liabilities	Domestic currency	540	830	820	850	1,010	1,090
		U.S. dollars	4,320	5,300	5,190	5,830	5,940	6,870
		Other foreign currencies	5,380	7,490	7,080	8,710	9,640	11,040
Belgium	Assets	Domestic currency	2,470	2,800	2,870	2,970	3,230	3,330
		U.S. dollars	14,260	18,550	19,490	20,100	22,860	23,310
		Other foreign currencies	8,650	13,230	13,790	14,340	15,630	16,380
	Liabilities	Domestic currency	3,790	4,730	5,720	5,280	5,590	6,590
		U.S. dollars	13,080	18,040	18,900	19,450	21,620	22,200
		Other foreign currencies	10,450	15,500	16,570	18,060	20,390	21,350
Luxembourg	Assets	Domestic currency	710	1,050	990	1,090	1,420	1,400
		U.S. dollars	18,820	22,040	23,010	24,450	25,460	29,300
		Other foreign currencies	25,220	36,300	38,100	42,030	46,660	50,100
	Liabilities	Domestic currency	570	730	860	790	910	1,030
		U.S. dollars	18,680	24,400	25,450	28,590	28,760	32,950
		Other foreign currencies	23,260	30,080	31,560	33,910	39,350	42,680
Denmark	Assets	Domestic currency	90	90	140	190	290	150
		U.S. dollars	1,420	1,640	1,590	1,620	1,650	1,860
		Other foreign currencies	640	1,200	1,230	1,420	1,650	1,960
	Liabilities	Domestic currency	260	390	380	370	390	410
		U.S. dollars	840	1,500	1,530	1,280	1,230	1,900
		Other foreign currencies	530	860	890	1,110	1,310	1,420
France	Assets	Domestic currency	11,450	18,200	18,100	19,280	21,410	23,180
		U.S. dollars	45,160	60,210	53,230	57,730	61,080	71,740
		Other foreign currencies	17,050	20,570	21,110	22,750	26,180	28,700
	Liabilities	Domestic currency	4,220	5,700	5,760	5,820	6,060	6,610
		U.S. dollars	44,430	53,160	46,190	49,220	52,010	61,100
		Other foreign currencies	18,540	25,630	26,650	29,490	34,600	38,500
Germany	Assets	Domestic currency	31,450	40,340	40,190	42,630	43,490	47,620
		U.S. dollars	12,710	14,720	13,360	13,790	14,100	14,360
		Other foreign currencies	4,570	6,050	6,150	6,310	7,160	7,350
	Liabilities	Domestic currency	24,330	40,220	37,250	41,320	45,830	54,330
		U.S. dollars	12,380	14,510	13,350	13,690	14,760	16,430
		Other foreign currencies	2,850	4,370	4,180	4,370	6,860	7,000
Ireland	Assets	Domestic currency	—	—	—	—	—	—
		U.S. dollars	710	400	330	390	380	380
		Other foreign currencies	830	1,110	660	670	820	1,280
	Liabilities	Domestic currency	—	—	—	—	—	—
		U.S. dollars	800	550	540	480	640	740
		Other foreign currencies	890	1,260	910	860	1,030	1,470
Italy	Assets	Domestic currency	300	590	610	600	770	1,320
		U.S. dollars	11,480	17,380	10,440	11,740	11,480	21,190
		Other foreign currencies	3,300	4,780	4,550	5,680	6,400	7,130
	Liabilities	Domestic currency	1,540	2,010	2,010	2,420	2,730	2,900
		U.S. dollars	17,010	21,840	15,700	17,010	15,640	25,400
		Other foreign currencies	4,510	5,960	6,200	8,260	8,800	9,850
Netherlands	Assets	Domestic currency	5,240	8,490	9,210	9,640	10,460	11,390
		U.S. dollars	15,150	19,470	18,210	20,460	20,380	23,010
		Other foreign currencies	12,030	17,090	16,690	18,110	20,170	21,470
	Liabilities	Domestic currency	5,100	7,930	8,700	8,650	9,070	10,860
		U.S. dollars	15,460	20,710	18,820	19,920	20,980	23,320
		Other foreign currencies	10,010	14,840	15,330	18,050	19,640	21,270

			1977 Dec.	1978 Dec.	1979 March	1979 June	1979 Sept.	1979 Dec.
Sweden	Assets	Domestic currency	930	860	1,060	1,210	1,100	1,030
		U.S. dollars	1,970	2,160	2,260	2,380	2,570	2,950
		Other foreign currencies	1,210	1,230	1,410	1,530	1,570	1,830
	Liabilities	Domestic currency	580	700	730	860	950	900
		U.S. dollars	2,120	2,790	3,470	3,740	4,130	4,620
		Other foreign currencies	1,290	1,730	2,200	2,600	2,740	3,190
Switzerland	Assets	Domestic currency	14,500	19,290	21,430	24,430	27,720	27,170
		U.S. dollars	17,070	21,580	20,660	20,860	21,840	21,510
		Other foreign currencies	5,940	9,830	9,810	9,140	10,140	10,390
	Liabilities	Domestic currency	5,650	6,820	6,390	6,830	7,290	7,440
		U.S. dollars	13,130	18,540	17,040	18,440	18,980	21,110
		Other foreign currencies	4,880	8,330	8,030	7,900	9,100	9,670
United Kingdom	Assets	Domestic currency	12,230	14,740	14,870	15,140	15,480	15,490
		U.S. dollars	125,810	156,910	159,610	171,620	196,500	211,760
		Other foreign currencies	33,400	45,940	44,290	49,840	56,010	58,240
	Liabilities	Domestic currency	11,100	11,950	13,280	14,680	16,040	19,230
		U.S. dollars	136,590	167,250	170,370	182,280	207,730	219,980
		Other foreign currencies	34,770	46,170	46,290	52,110	58,580	61,980
Total for European reporting countries	Assets	Domestic currency	81,320	109,380	112,560	120,530	129,280	136,240
		U.S. dollars	268,430	339,520	327,200	351,050	384,190	427,980
		Other foreign currencies	116,410	162,450	162,340	177,700	199,160	211,960
	Liabilities	Domestic currency	57,680	82,010	81,900	87,870	95,870	111,390
		U.S. dollars	278,840	348,590	336,550	359,930	392,420	436,620
		Other foreign currencies	117,360	162,220	165,890	185,430	212,040	229,420
Canada	Assets	Domestic currency	430	480	500	570	570	580
		U.S. dollars	16,480	20,430	20,780	21,450	22,820	22,990
		Other foreign currencies	1,240	1,460	1,380	1,830	2,000	2,030
	Liabilities	Domestic currency	2,180	2,620	2,640	2,860	3,000	3,080
		U.S. dollars	15,860	21,340	23,260	25,380	26,270	28,170
		Other foreign currencies	840	1,010	910	1,400	1,550	1,560
Japan	Assets	Domestic currency	3,550	7,970	8,720	9,490	10,260	11,350
		U.S. dollars	15,930	22,520	24,950	24,120	31,290	30,350
		Other foreign currencies	2,220	3,200	2,960	3,460	3,460	3,730
	Liabilities	Domestic currency	4,110	8,690	7,170	5,380	5,130	3,820
		U.S. dollars	23,360	28,490	30,900	31,980	41,910	43,900
		Other foreign currencies	1,110	1,830	1,730	2,340	3,400	2,770
United States[a]	Assets	Domestic currency	90,210	115,370	108,350	115,070	127,250	133,590
		Foreign currencies	2,350	3,500	2,590	2,520	2,610	2,440
	Liabilities	Domestic currency	77,940	89,910	96,820	110,690	122,980	128,540
		Foreign currencies	920	2,240	1,780	1,960	2,320	2,320
Offshore branches of U.S. banks	Assets	Foreign currencies[a]	91,090	106,520	111,130	118,570	128,590	127,670
	Liabilities	Foreign currencies[c]	91,660	107,480	112,260	118,300	128,960	128,820

Source. Bank for International Settlements. *Fiftieth Annual Report* BIS: Basle, Switzerland, June 1980.

[a]As of December 1978 the figures for banks in the United States exclude all custody items except negotiable U.S. bank certificates of deposit held on behalf of nonresidents. Previously the only custody items excluded were nonresident holdings of Treasury bills and certificates. On the old basis the figures for December 1978 were domestic currency assets, $126,540 million; foreign currency assets, $3,870 million; liabilities, $99,000 million and $2,490 million respectively.

[b]Offshore branches of U.S. banks in the Bahamas, Cayman Islands, Panama, Hong Kong, and Singapore.

[c]Including negligible amounts in domestic currencies.

EXHIBIT 7c   FOREIGN BRANCHES OF U.S. BANKS BALANCE SHEET DATA

	1973		1979		1980		
	Total ($ billions)	Percentage of Total	Total ($ billions)	Percentage of Total	Total ($ billions)	Percentage of Total	Growth Rate 1973–1980
Total assets	121.9	100.0	364.2	100.0	376.6	100.0	209.9
United Kingdom	61.7	50.7	130.9	35.9	376.6	36.9	125.4
Bahamas and Caymans	23.8	19.5	108.9	29.9	115.4	30.6	385.3
Total liabilities	121.9	100.0	364.2	100.0	376.6	100.0	209.1
United Kingdom	61.7	50.7	130.9	35.9	139.1	36.9	125.3
Bahamas and Caymans	23.8	19.5	108.9	29.9	115.4	30.6	385.3

intermediaries that do not create money but only increase the efficiency with which it is used, they offer assets that are near money.

FUNCTIONS.   The Eurocurrency market is primarily an international interbank deposit market, through which the world's major banks (1) adjust their overall liquidity positions in both domestic and foreign currencies by bidding for (borrowing) and offering (lending, deposit) excess balances, (2) conduct foreign-exchange hedging and arbitrage operations, and (3) recycle or intermediate funds through bank loans and international bond issuing, from surplus to deficit countries.

Eurocurrency business is conducted vis-à-vis financial and nonfinancial entities, but interbank transactions account for the bulk (75 percent and 85 percent respectively) of the market's assets and liabilities. The interbank market allows banks to adjust their liquidity positions to some degree in an analogous manner to the interbank Federal Funds market in the United States, and provides a mechanism by interbank lending and borrowing to obtain foreign exchange to cover forward foreign-exchange commitments and to conduct covered interest-rate arbitrage.

Eurobanks are able to improve their liquidity positions by borrowing Eurocurrency funds and relending them in the form of Eurocurrency deposits at call or for several days. In countries where national capital markets are imperfect, domestic banks may find that they can best adjust their reserve positions in the national currency by Eurocurrency transactions.

The Eurocurrency market is closely linked to the foreign-exchange market, and in some respects it can be considered an integral part of it. Although Eurobanks also deal in foreign exchange, the two markets are distinct in function. In the foreign-exchange market one currency is exchanged for another, but in the Eurocurrency market deposits and loans are usually made in the same currency. The Euromarkets enhance substitutability among currencies and link foreign-exchange markets (forward and spot) closely to domestic markets.

Eurocurrency transactions are often linked with foreign-exchange activities because (1) many of them occur solely for the sake of swapping funds into the local currency or into a third currency; (2) they often form part of arbitrage activity that can only be conducted in the foreign-exchange market; and (3) their activities lead to a considerable amount of various foreign-exchange transactions.

For instance, Eurobanks in temporary need of, say, Deutsche Marks may prefer to borrow them in the form of Euro-Deutsche Mark deposits rather than buying them

EXHIBIT 7d EXTERNAL POSITIONS, IN DOMESTIC AND FOREIGN CURRENCIES, OF BANKS IN THE REPORTING AREA AND OF CERTAIN OFFSHORE BRANCHES OF U.S. BANKS^{a,b} (BILLIONS OF U.S. DOLLARS)

	1977 Dec.	1978 Dec. I	1978 Dec. II	1979 March	1979 June	1979 Sept.	1979 Dec.
Banks' claims on:							
Group of Ten countries and Switzerland, Austria, Denmark, and Ireland	349.9	472.7	466.9	457.2	490.3	546.7	587.9
of which: Reporting European area	268.6	362.8	359.9	339.7	363.1	394.2	437.5
United States	39.8	53.0	53.0	62.0	70.9	86.7	81.9
Canada	11.9	17.9	15.9	16.6	16.8	18.0	19.2
Japan	29.6	39.0	38.1	38.9	39.5	47.8	49.3
Offshore banking centers^c	98.9	123.8	123.5	121.6	132.9	147.7	155.6
Other countries in Western Europe	40.8	50.7	50.4	49.6	52.4	56.1	58.7
Australia, New Zealand, and South Africa	14.7	13.8	13.5	13.0	13.8	13.9	13.7
Eastern Europe	38.3	47.6	47.5	47.0	49.5	52.8	55.9
Oil-exporting countries	39.1	57.2	56.4	55.5	57.7	62.5	64.1
Non-oil exporting countries	98.7	123.4	121.7	127.1	136.6	146.6	158.8
of which: Latin America^d	65.9	80.8	79.9	82.8	88.4	94.7	103.5
Middle East	5.2	6.6	6.5	6.4	7.3	7.4	8.2
Other Asia	20.5	24.8	24.3	26.5	29.3	31.7	33.1
Other Africa	7.1	11.2	11.0	11.4	11.6	12.8	14.0
Unallocated^e	9.3	15.1	12.9	12.4	13.2	15.2	16.2
Total	689.7	904.3	892.8	883.4	946.4	1,041.5	1,110.9
Banks' liabilities to:							
Group of Ten countries and Switzerland, Austria, Denmark, and Ireland	408.5	539.1	533.5	527.5	576.6	635.8	685.9
of which: Reporting European area	314.5	409.6	404.4	395.4	436.0	473.4	528.3
United States	74.1	101.9	101.9	100.9	110.1	126.0	123.8
Canada	12.6	15.8	15.7	17.0	17.2	17.8	17.8
Japan	7.3	11.8	11.5	14.2	13.3	18.6	16.0
Offshore banking centers^c	71.5	97.2	96.9	104.0	115.5	131.1	139.2
Other countries in Western Europe	25.7	35.8	35.4	34.9	37.8	41.4	42.5
Australia, New Zealand, and South Africa	2.4	2.7	2.7	3.2	3.6	3.6	3.6
Eastern Europe	8.4	10.7	10.6	9.4	9.9	12.6	15.4
Oil-exporting countries	77.9	83.9	82.5	84.4	87.3	106.9	120.3
Non-oil developing countries	62.0	78.0	77.1	79.9	83.9	87.3	90.3
of which: Latin America^d	25.2	33.9	33.2	34.1	35.4	36.7	38.4
Middle East	10.0	13.8	13.8	14.0	15.2	15.3	16.0
Other Asia	20.1	22.9	22.7	24.5	25.6	26.7	26.6
Other Africa	6.7	7.4	7.4	7.3	7.7	8.6	9.3
Unallocated^e	15.6	18.4	17.7	18.5	18.9	17.1	23.2
Total	672.0	865.8	856.4	861.8	933.5	1,035.8	1,120.4

Source. Bank for International Settlements. *Fiftieth Annual Report,* BIS: Basle, Switzerland, June 1980.

^{a}The figures in this table are partly based on estimates.
As of December 11, 1978, the figures for banks in the United States exclude all custody items except negotiable U.S. bank certificates of deposit held on behalf of nonresidents. Previously the only custody items excluded were nonresident holdings oif Treasury bills and certificates.

^{b}The offshore branches of U.S. banks whose external positions are included in the figures are those located in the Bahamas, Cayman Islands, Panama, Hong Kong, and Singapore.

^{c}Bahamas, Barbados, Bermuda, Cayman Islands, Hong Kong, Lebanon, Liberia, Netherlands Antilles, New Hebrides, Panama, Singapore, and other British West Indies.

^{d}Including those countries in the Caribbean area that cannot be considered as offshore banking centres.

^{e}Including international institutions other than the BIS.

EXHIBIT 7e   CURRENCY STRUCTURE OF THE EUROMARKET: EXTERNAL ASSETS IN FOREIGN CURRENCIES OF REPORTING EUROPEAN BANKS (QUARTERLY AMOUNTS OUTSTANDING).

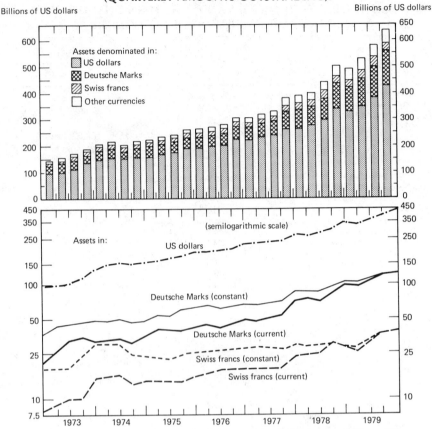

Source. BIS. *Annual Report,* Basel: Bank for International Settlement, 1980, p. 121.
[a]At constant end-December 1979 exchange rates.

EXHIBIT 7f   THE CURRENCY COMPOSITION OF THE EUROCURRENCY MARKET (PERCENT OF NARROWLY DEFINED MARKET)[a]

Currency	1972	1979
Dollar	73.3	65.6
Deutsche mark	14.8	19.2
Swiss franc	6.7	6.1
Sterling	1.7	2.3
Dutch guilder	1.0	1.3
French franc	0.8	1.7
Others	1.7	3.8

Source. Calculated from Bank for International Settlements. *Fiftieth Annual Report.* April 1979–March 1980. B.I.S.: Basle, Switzerland, June, 1980.
[a]The dollar show of the broadly defined worldwide market was 73 percent at the end of 1979.

or obtaining them through swap transactions. Conversely, mismatched maturity dates of Eurocurrency deposits may be more conveniently rectified with the aid of swap or uncovered spot transactions instead of Eurocurrency transactions.

The linkage of the Eurocurrency market with foreign-exchange markets is reflected in a large share of foreign-exchange contracts that have Eurodeposit counterparts. A Eurodollar claim on, say, a London bank has an exchange rate that is exactly one-to-one with a dollar deposit located in the United States, say in New York. Transactions in foreign deposits often serve as alternatives to foreign-exchange transactions. To the extent that the foreign-exchange markets do not fully accommodate forward hedgers, the balance will be covered in the Eurocurrency market by simultaneously borrowing in one currency, covering in the spot market, and lending in other currencies.

The Eurocurrency market performs the enormous task of recycling funds from surplus to deficit countries and financing balance-of-payments deficits, particularly in the aftermath of the oil crisis. Eurobank lending in 1979 amounted to $70 billion, whereas Eurobond issuing was about $15 billion.

The market mobilizes funds from surplus sectors on a worldwide basis and enables large-scale projects to be financed that otherwise would not have been undertaken. By channeling funds to countries with a higher-than-average growth performance, the level of world income has been higher because a larger proportion of the world's investible funds has been provided to these countries.

Like domestic bank deposits, Eurocurrency deposits are usually in the form of interest-bearing time deposits that are issued by banks to banks and nonbanks, residents and nonresidents, and their maturities are accommodated to depositors' needs. Exhibit 9 shows the maturity profile of the Eurocurrency market in London (the London market accounts for about half the entire market). The standard maturities are similar to those of the forward exchange market. It is possible, however, to obtain quotations for almost any date up to 12 months. As of February 1980, about 70 percent of the deposits matured in less than 3 months. About 22 percent of the deposits matured in less than 8 days, over 19 percent matured between 8 days and 1 month, and over 28 percent matured between one and three months. In addition, about 18 percent matured between three and six months, over 7 percent matured between 6 months and 1 year, and about 5 percent had a maturity of 1 year or more.

The degree of transformation conducted by the Eurocurrency market is reflected by several indexes: (1) the ratio of transformation (i.e., the ratio of each net position in absolute terms to the sum of total foreign-currency assets and liabilities), (2) the maturity profile of assets and liabilities (i.e., percentage of each maturity category to the sum of total assets and liabilities), and (3) the net credit creation measured by assigning various coefficients of liquidity to both assets and liabilities based on maturities (e.g., 10 to cash, 9 to time deposits up to one month, etc.).

The evidence shows that the maturity structure of interbank activity is highly balanced and a relatively small amount of transformation is undertaken in trading among Eurobanks. Over 70 percent of total liabilities mature in less than three months, whereas some 65 percent of the assets mature in less than three months.

Substantial transformation occurs vis-à-vis the nonbank sector. The data show that the average term to maturity of loans to nonbanks (assets) exceeds that of deposits (liabilities). Whereas 77 percent and 90 percent of total liabilities mature within three and six months respectively, 57 percent and 63 percent of claims mature within one year and over and six months to several years respectively.

EXHIBIT 8 ESTIMATED SOURCES AND USES OF EUROCURRENCY FUNDS (BILLIONS OF U.S. DOLLARS)[a]

End of Month	Reporting European Area Total[b]	of which Nonbank[c]	United States	Canada and Japan	Other Developed Countries	Eastern Europe[d]	Offshore Banking Centers[e]	Oil-Exporting Countries[f]	Developing Countries	Unallocated[g]	Total
					USES						
1977 December	110.4	77.3	21.3	18.7	30.8	25.7	43.9	15.7	30.3	3.2	300.0
1978 March	115.6	80.3	18.5	20.4	31.9	27.0	43.4	17.8	31.8	3.6	310.0
June	117.8	82.3	19.6	20.8	31.9	28.5	44.6	18.6	33.7	3.5	319.0
September	127.0	87.0	22.0	21.8	32.9	31.2	51.5	21.0	36.6	4.0	348.0
December 1	136.0	92.0	24.6	24.6	34.7	31.4	55.0	24.3	40.1	4.3	375.0
December 11	139.5	94.5	24.6	24.6	34.7	31.4	55.0	24.3	40.1	2.8	377.0
1979 March	141.8	96.2	25.6	26.3	34.0	30.9	53.2	24.2	44.5	3.5	384.0
June	147.5	100.9	29.1	27.5	36.1	32.6	58.6	26.3	48.7	3.6	410.0
September	160.0	105.2	34.0	32.4	38.2	34.5	66.1	29.4	51.1	4.3	450.0
December	171.3	111.3	36.7	33.0	40.5	36.0	67.5	30.4	55.1	4.5	475.0
					SOURCES						
1977 December	117.3	56.0	25.4	8.4	18.8	7.0	33.4	54.5	29.6	5.6	300.0
1978 March	123.2	58.6	26.9	9.6	20.0	6.6	33.9	54.5	31.3	4.0	310.0
June	131.0	62.1	26.5	9.7	21.6	6.9	35.5	51.4	33.1	3.3	319.0
September	140.5	66.3	29.1	11.3	25.2	7.7	39.7	52.6	37.3	4.6	348.0
December 1	142.5	70.1	37.0	13.0	26.2	8.8	45.4	54.7	39.8	7.6	375.0
December 11	144.5	70.1	37.0	13.0	26.2	8.8	45.4	54.7	39.8	7.6	377.0

1979 March	150.5	73.1	36.4	13.3	26.0	7.7	43.7	56.3	42.4	7.7	384.0
June	163.0	81.4	41.0	13.9	28.1	7.8	45.5	58.6	44.6	7.5	410.0
September	167.5	87.0	50.0	15.2	30.9	10.4	49.0	73.2	46.3	7.5	450.0
December	174.0	93.0	50.5	15.2	31.7	13.0	52.8	81.0	47.8	9.0	475.0

Source. Bank for International Settlements. *Fiftieth Annual Report.* B.I.S.: Basle, Switzerland, March 1980.

[a] As of June 1979 a change has been made in estimating procedures, insofar as the partial netting-out of interbank assets and liabilities, previously limited to the growth of the reporting European banks' positions within their own area, has been extended to cover their positions vis-à-vis the United States, Canada, Japan, and the offshore centers. This change has become necessary as a result of the very rapid growth of such positions, which suggests that the figures have been inflated to a substantial extent by circular flows of interbank funds between the reporting European area and these other market centers.

[b] Includes (a) under "Uses," the banks' conversions from foreign currency into domestic currency and foreign currency funds supplied by the reporting banks to the commercial banks of the country of issue of the currency in question (such as Deutsche Mark funds deposited with German banks); (b) under "Sources," deposits by official monetary institutions of the reporting area, the banks' conversions from domestic into foreign currency and foreign currency funds obtained by the reporting banks from the banks in the country of issue of the currency in question (such as funds received in Deutsche Mark from German banks).

[c] On the sources side including trustee funds to the extent that they are transmitted by the Swiss banks to the other banks within the reporting area and to the extent that they are not reported by the Swiss banks themselves as liabilities vis-à-vis nonbanks outside the reporting area.

[d] Excluding positions of banks located in the Federal Republic of Germany vis-à-vis the German Democratic Republic.

[e] Bahamas, Barbados, Bermuda, Cayman Islands, Hong Kong, Lebanon, Liberia, Netherlands Antilles, New Hebrides, Panama, Singapore, other British West Indies.

[f] Algeria, Bahrain, Brunei, Ecuador, Gabon, Indonesia, Iran, Iraq, Kuwait, Libya, Nigeria, Oman, Qatar, Saudi Arabia, Trinidad and Tobago, United Arab Emirates, Venezuela.

[g] Including positions vis-à-vis international institutions other than the BIS.

EXHIBIT 9 MATURITY PROFILE AND TRANSFORMATION OF EUROCURRENCY LIABILITIES AND CLAIMS OF ALL BANKS IN THE LONDON MARKET AS OF FEBRUARY 20, 1980

Maturity	Total		Interbank		Nonbanks	
	Liabilities (% of total)	Claims (% of total)	Liabilities (% of total)	Claims (% of total)	Liabilities (% of total)	Claims (% of total)
Less than 8 days	21.9[a]	16.9	22.8	19.6	31.7	8.9
8 days to less than 1 month	19.4	16.0	19.2	18.4	21.6	8.6
1 month to less than 3 months	28.1	23.0	28.5	26.8	23.9	11.2
3 months to less than 6 months	18.4	15.8	19.2	18.3	12.9	8.2
6 months to less than 1 year	7.3	7.0	7.0	7.3	5.7	5.9
1 year to less than 3 years	3.2	6.7	2.2	4.5	1.9	13.5
3 years and over	1.7	14.6	1.3	5.1	2.2	43.7
Total	100.0	100.0	100.0	100.0	100.0	100.0

Source. Percentages were calculated from Bank of England. *Bank of England Quarterly Bulletin*, Vol. XX, No. 2 (1980), Table 13.
[a]Figures rounded to the nearest tenth.

Hence there is a significant amount of transformation vis-à-vis the nonbank sector, and it occurs primarily in the form of medium-term loans, which accounted for 57 percent (or over $53 billion) of all bank assets in February 1980.

Transactions in the Eurocurrency market involve substantial interbank deposits. For example, a European bank holding a deposit in a U.S. bank may make a Eurodollar deposit with another European bank, which in turn may deposit the proceeds with another bank, and so on. Active wholesale Eurocurrency markets exist for most major currencies. This interbank transaction may continue through several banks, which function as intermediaries between the original depositor and the ultimate borrower. Each depositing bank charges a small profit or spread above the London Interbank Offering Rate (LIBOR). The margins usually range from one thirty-second to one-fourth of 1 percent for prime means. The lending bank typically uses a broker, who disguises the names of the potential transactors until the deal is near conclusion in order to secure the best offer of an interbank-deposit rate of interest.

THE THEORETICAL INTERPRETATIONS OF THE EUROCURRENCY MARKET. The theoretical interpretation of the credit-creating potential of the Euromarket is a controversial issue that arises from the diversity of the theoretical interpretations of the market's growth and mechanism. The competing hypotheses or interpretations of the Eurocurrency may be classified in terms of (1) the money-and-credit-multiplier model, (2) the nonbank financial intermediaries, and (3) supply and demand of the Eurocurrency markets.[29]

The rapid growth of the Eurocurrency market is often explained in the context of a multiple credit-and-deposit-expansion mechanism, similar to that which prevails in a national commercial banking system. This hypothesis is based on (1) the observation of the rapid growth of the Eurocurrency market on the basis of a very small fraction of assets held by the Eurobanks as demand deposits with the issuing countries' banking systems, and (2) the observation that, to some degree, Eurocurrencies are money or near money, and as is in a domestic commercial banking system are created through a money-and-credit-multiplier mechanism. (The domestic money multiplier relates some monetary aggregate, say, M1A or M2B to a monetary base, which consists of currency plus reserves of the banking system held with the central bank. The domestic-multiplier mechanism explains how the banking system as a whole can create credit and deposits as a multiple of an initial increase in the monetary base. There are, however, numerous leakages (e.g., cash held by the public) which drain cash out of the banking system and reduces the credit multiplier.)

The concept of a Eurocurrency multiplier is essentially similar to that of the commerical-bank credit-creative multiplier mechanism. Just as in the domestic banking system, Eurocurrencies are loaned, redeposited, and loaned again. Thus lending institutions multiply an initial quantity of primary deposits or reserves into a larger final quantity of deposits, as the primary deposits are lent out to nonbank borrowers, who in turn redeposit some of the proceeds with Eurobanks. There is some "leakage" from this system, that is, some of the money loaned is not redeposited in the Euromarket, thereby reducing the multiplier effects.

Accordingly, an initial "reserve" injection into the Eurobanking system could, through the chain of lending and depositing in the market, expand credit by some multiple of the initial cash added. This interpretation, though inappropriate, serves as a basis for many of the exaggerated estimates of the Euromarket's potential credit creation.

Within the general context of the multiplier mechanism, there are various applications to the Eurocurrency market. Some consider the credit creation of the Eurobanks in the context of a multi-stage banking system, in isolation or in a global context.[30]

Empirical verification of the multiplier model identifies a reserve base for the Eurodollar market and relates it to the volume of outstanding Eurodollar liabilities to obtain a multiplier. These measures are arbitrary and the very high figures obtained in some studies are distorted by the use of a very small base (some portion of foreign banks' holdings of demand deposits in the United States) and a very large total for Eurodollar deposits (the gross or net size of the Eurodollar market or Eurocurrency market rather than liabilities to the nonbank public).

Based on the above approach, a multiple expansion mechanism of money and credit in the Eurocurrency market was estimated. For the reporting European area, I define the liabilities denominated in domestic currencies as the monetary base on which Eurocurrency deposits are expanded. In the case of the United States, I define the external liabilities denominated in dollars as the monetary base for the multiple expansion of the Eurodollar market. The monetary base for the Eurocurrency market was equivalent to about $127.90 billion of European currencies in December 1980, whereas the total external liabilities generated by the market and denominated in those currencies reached $252.10 billion. In this case, the multiplier was 1.97, whereas in the case of the Eurodollar deposits (base $197.95 billion, total deposits $548.40 billion) the multiplier was 3.71. The average multiplier for both segments of the market was 2.90. Finally, empirical evidence shows that the above multipliers or ratios remain virtually unchanged over the past 4 years.

Applications of the commercial bank deposit and credit multiplier model is inappropriate for several reasons. First, only in a system where the liabilities of the financial intermediaries also serve as the means of payment can there be multiple expansion of money and credit. Second, Eurocurrency deposits are not money since they do not serve as a means of payment. They are near money and function as a short-term store of value fitted into broadly defined money concepts.

There is a growing consensus that Eurobanks create very little additional money or credit for the nonbank public. Accordingly, some studies suggest that between 1968 and 1972 the Eurodollar multiplier was 1.4 at the maximum. Alternative estimates for the period 1968–1972 show that the multiplier would have been 0.63 in the absence of central-bank deposits and that it could have been as high as 1.4 on the basis of an admittedly very high estimate of the central-bank redeposit ratio. More recent work produced a range of estimates of the multiplier including central-bank deposits with 1.05 as the best guess.[31]

Since Eurobanks' deposits do not serve as a medium of exchange, and they do not hold stable or fixed ratios of reserves to deposits, since they are not subject to reserve requirements, there is no clearly defined base money for Eurobanks; the Eurobanks are more like nonbank financial intermediaries than like commercial banks. This alternative interpretation of the Eurocurrency market, known as the Yale or portfolio approach, treats it as a system not of credit creation but of efficient global credit distribution, which gives no basis for concern about its deposit-creating potential. The market operates as an efficient intermediary linking various national financial markets. The value of the Yale multiplier applicable to a shift in asset preferences will be between zero and one.[32]

Although no multiple credit creation takes place in the Euromarket, the market still exerts an expansionary impact by changing the liquidity of the nonbank public, by modifying the maturity structure of the nonbank public's assets and liabilities (i.e., by providing nonbanks with short-term assets for relatively longer-term debt). Creation of net liquidity by the nonbank sector requires that assets and liabilities be "mismatched" in the sense that the banks "borrow short" in order to "lend long." This is positive maturity transformation. If funds are matched for each maturity, there is no net liquidity creation, and the balance sheet is perfectly matched. If the banks borrow long in order to lend short, that is, with negative maturity transformation, net liquidity of the nonbanks is reduced. Since the typical U.S. commercial bank is engaged in positive maturity transformation, the question is whether the typical Eurobank behaves in the same way and, if so, to what extent.[33]

The net-liquidity effects brought by maturity transformation can be analyzed by the volume of various bank assets and liabilities, the maturity with the shortest term being considered the closest to money and thus assigned the highest weight. To quantify aggregate net liquidity, we have to assign weights to different assets and liabilities intended to reflect the degree of their "moneyness." Assessment of such weights will depend on one's view about the macroeconomic system. The traditional money-supply theory assumes that currency and deposits (either including or excluding time deposits) have liquidity one, whereas bank claims (except reserves) have liquidity zero. While the weight for M1 is unity, there is a marked fall in the weights beyond M2, and there is a large difference in the weights assigned to demand deposits and, say, treasury bills. The degree of maturity transformation performed is then derived by summing the banks' maturity-weighted liabilities to nonbanks and subtracting its total maturity-weighted claims on nonbanks. A positive number reflects that the banks are borrowing short to lend long. The bigger the number, the greater the degree of positive maturity transformation occurring.

International financial intermediation is in principle similar to the process that occurs within a domestic financial system by banks and nonbank institutions. This process facilitates maturity, risk, and liquidity transformation. (In this context, the Eurocurrency market may be analogous to a system of domestic nonbank intermediaries such as savings banks rather than commercial banks. Hence money creation in the Eurocurrency market cannot occur any more than it can in the domestic savings-and-loan system.) The Eurocurrency markets perform an entrepôt or financial-intermediation function by channeling funds from surplus to deficit countries and sectors. Since 1974, the market has provided a major channel for recycling OPEC surpluses, thereby enabling OPEC countries to avoid country, currency, and maturity risks.

It has been argued that the size of the Eurocurrency market is demand-determined, and the market has an infinite capacity for expanding in response to an increase in the demand for loans. This also implies that there is no upper limit on the Eurodollar multiplier. Under this assumption, Eurobanks can attract deposits that have a high interest elasticity in unlimited quantity at rising interest rates to satify any increase in the demand for credit, and the shift of deposits to Eurobanks does not destroy liquidity elsewhere.[34] The most significant demand factor in recent years has been the sharp rise in balance-of-payments disequilibriums. Thus, in turn, has expanded the demand for balance-of-payments financing.

It is often argued that the Eurocurrency market draws its supply of funds from the U.S. balance-of-payments deficit, the OPEC surplus, or similar sources. From this it is sometimes concluded that the market is supply determined. On the supply side, the following factors can explain the market's growth:

1. Willingness and ability of banks to increase the volume of funds they intermediate. Banks' capacity to accept Eurodeposits and extend loans is limited by their capital. There are prudent, and sometimes regulatory, limits on the relationship between banks' assets or liabilities and their capital.
2. Sufficient profitability, i.e., satisfactory return on capital and assets necessary to provide a basis for future capital growth.
3. Credit limitation. Creditworthiness of potential borrowers.

The Eurocurrency market exists largely because of its competitiveness, which is derived from its freedom from regulatory practices of national monetary authorities, and a more profitable nature of the wholesale market. Banks are able to offer higher rates of interest to depositors and lower lending rates to borrowers than prevail in domestic money markets. This competitive edge is derived from freedom from a number of regulatory practices of national monetary authorities.

INTERNATIONAL INTEREST RATES. The Eurocurrency market has developed an international interest-rate structure that is determined mainly by the corresponding interest rates in each country's currency. Although Euromarket interest rates are dominated by domestic rates, to some degree, they also influence these rates. Interest rates in national markets and the corresponding Eurocurrency sectors are closely linked and may be largely determined by the degree of capital controls and the degree of freedom for arbitrage and capital flows (see Exhibit 10).

The interest-rate structures for equal maturities in the Eurocurrency market and the corresponding national market are closely linked, but rate differentials exist because of reserve requirements on domestic deposits and higher operating costs. Accordingly, the Eurocurrency market offers higher deposit rates and lower loan rates.

Under free-market conditions, arbitrage keeps interest rates in the domestic market and the corresponding Eurocurrency market closely linked. The Euromarket rate can fall to a level at which it becomes profitable to place funds in the domestic market. Below that level the rate is unlikely to fall as long as arbitrage activity continues. Similarly, the Euromarket cannot rise vis-à-vis the corresponding domestic market beyond the level at which it becomes profitable to move funds from the domestic to the Eurocurrency market.

There are close relationships between Euromarket interest rates and the corresponding national rates and spot and forward foreign-exchange rates. In general, spot exchange rates, forward discounts or premiums, and Eurocurrency interest-rate differentials are determined simultaneously in such a way as to ensure that the interest-rate differential will be equal to the discount or premium on the forward exchange rate.

For instance, although Eurodollar rates are influenced by interest rates in the United States, they reflect a different interest-rate structure from that prevailing in the American market. The different exists because of reserve requirements and FDIC fees on U.S. deposits of member banks. But both interest-rate structures are closely linked. For instance, at times three-month Eurodollar rates may move more in line

EXHIBIT 10a   EUROCURRENCY DEPOSIT RATES (PRIME BANKS' BID RATES IN LONDON, AT OR NEAR END OF MONTH)

	1977	1978	1979	1980							
	Dec.	Dec.	Dec.	March	April	May	June	July	Aug.	Sept.	Oct.
Eurodollar	7.12	10.62	14.00	19.25	12.25	9.37	9.50	9.12	10.50	12.50	13.25
Overnight											
Seven-day fixed	6.31	10.62	14.00	19.37	12.75	9.50	9.50	9.25	10.62	12.50	13.50
One month	6.87	11.00	14.37	19.25	14.25	9.87	9.50	9.50	11.19	13.19	14.50
Three months	7.19	11.69	14.44	19.69	14.37	10.12	9.75	9.81	12.25	13.81	15.37
Six months	7.50	12.31	14.44	19.56	13.69	10.25	9.94	10.06	12.50	13.94	14.87
Twelve months	7.67	12.00	12.87	18.00	12.75	10.25	9.87	10.19	12.50	13.69	14.12
Euro-Deutsche mark											
One month	2.19	3.19	8.50	8.94	9.06	9.37	9.50	8.69	8.62	8.87	8.81
Three months	2.50	3.31	8.56	9.69	9.06	9.37	9.37	8.25	8.50	8.87	8.94
Six months	2.81	3.69	8.56	10.06	9.00	9.00	8.81	7.81	8.31	8.87	8.81
Twelve months	3.06	3.81	8.12	10.00	8.69	8.50	8.19	7.75	8.12	8.69	8.56
Euro-Swiss franc											
One month	1.31	—.06	5.19	5.87	5.25	5.56	5.62	5.06	6.00	5.25	4.12
Three months	1.37	0.00	5.75	7.12	6.12	5.37	5.69	5.12	5.87	5.75	5.44
Six months	1.87	0.12	5.87	7.50	6.25	5.37	5.69	5.25	5.75	5.75	5.12
Twelve months	2.25	0.62	5.56	7.00	5.62	5.25	5.12	5.00	5.50	5.62	5.37
Euro-sterling											
One month	6.50	12.00	16.75	18.00	17.25	17.00	17.37	16.87	16.75	16.25	17.00
Three months	6.62	12.62	16.75	18.25	17.25	16.75	16.75	15.62	16.62	15.87	16.75
Six months	7.12	13.25	16.75	18.37	16.37	16.12	15.25	14.25	16.25	15.00	16.12
Twelve months	7.37	13.00	15.25	17.50	15.37	14.75	14.00	13.25	15.12	14.37	15.00
Euro-French franc											
One month	12.25	10.50	13.87	13.37	12.50	12.31	12.25	12.37	12.00	11.62	11.00
Three months	13.25	9.87	14.00	14.12	12.75	12.50	12.25	12.12	12.12	12.06	11.31
Six months	14.00	9.87	14.12	14.50	12.87	12.62	12.25	12.00	12.37	12.56	12.00
Twelve months	13.25	10.25	13.75	14.87	13.00	12.75	12.25	11.94	12.62	12.81	12.62
Euroyen											
One month	0.62	—.69	7.62	15.00	11.50	12.62	13.00	12.87	11.62	12.50	10.00
Three months	1.81	0.62	8.31	15.50	12.50	12.25	12.25	12.25	11.62	12.25	9.62
Six months	2.75	1.87	8.62	15.00	11.37	11.37	11.12	11.37	11.12	11.50	9.12
Twelve months	3.25	2.19	7.94	13.62	10.37	10.25	9.37	9.75	9.75	10.50	9.00

Source. Morgan Guaranty. *World Financial Markets.* New York: Morgan Guarantee Trust Company, 1980.

with three-month U.S. CD rates, which would indicate that the CD arbitrage channel has become the most active one; at other times U.S. nonbank borrower arbitrage on a three-month basis may become more important, which would affect the CD differential between the U.S. and the Eurodollar market.

The above interest-rate relationship is also observed in other sectors of the Eurocurrency market. For instance, in Germany where there are no impediments to international interest arbitrage, Euro-Deutsche Mark rates are unlikely to rise above domestic interbank market rates. However, they may decline below those rates because of the cost effect of minimum-reserve requirements on nonresident deposits. The higher the reserve ratios, the wider will Euro-Deutsche Mark rates deviate from domestic interbank rates. Thus as long as Euro-Deutsche Mark rates are in line with domestic interbank rates, the differential between domestic money-market interest rates in Germany and the United States will determine the swap rate and the uncovered differential between Eurodollar and Euro-Deutsche Mark rates. However, as Euro-Deutsche Mark rates decline below the domestic rates, the swap rate will then determine the uncovered interest-rate differential.

EXHIBIT 10*b*   DAY-TO-DAY MONEY RATES (MONTHLY AVERAGES)

	1977	1978	1979	1980							
	Dec.	Dec.	Dec.	March	April	May	June	July	Aug.	Sept.	Oct.
United States	6.56	10.03	13.78	17.19	17.61	10.98	9.47	9.03	9.61	10.87	12.81
Japan	5.01	4.57	8.02	10.73	12.21	12.56	12.62	12.68	12.11	11.40	11.00
United Kingdom	4.81	10.00	14.87	15.00	16.06	15.90	14.06	15.06	14.87	14.90	15.00
France	9.30	6.67	12.17	12.96	12.40	12.61	12.43	12.04	11.32	11.37	n.a.
Germany	3.24	3.61	9.15	8.65	9.06	9.80	10.04	9.81	8.95	9.28	8.98
Switzerland	0.85	0.00	1.25	1.75	2.75	4.00	3.75	2.50	6.50	2.00	0.87

Source. Morgan Guaranty. *World Financial Markets.* New York: Morgan Guarantee Trust Company, *November 1980.*

The Euromarket provides an efficient mechanism for almost perfect covered-interest-rate arbitrage. Hence under normal conditions, covered interest differentials are reduced or nonexistent, that is, there is no scope for making profits by borrowing one currency for investment in another on a covered basis. This implies that interest-rate differentials between the different Eurocurrencies should correspond to the swap rates between the respective currencies (i.e., the difference between spot and forward exchange rates expressed on an annual percentage basis).

The equilibrium between interest rates on different Eurocurrencies and the corresponding swap rates is brought about by a continuous process of arbitrage by the Euromarket operators. When interest-rate parity does not hold exactly, discrepancies will be particularly great when there are large movements in relative rates and prices.

Although interest rates and swap rates may temporarily get out of line, market participants will discover any incentives for covered-interest-rate arbitrage opportunities, thereby rectifying the disequilibrium in the market. The cost of foreign-exchange transactions may, however, be considerable barrier to covered-interest-rate-arbitrage operations within the Euromarket; thereby allowing an attractive covered interest rate differential to persist for a while. Sometimes investors would be better off if they stayed in their positions rather than switching into another one on a covered basis, while in other instances borrowers of a specific currency are better off if they borrow the desired currency directly rather than borrowing the other currency on a swap basis.

INTERNATIONAL FINANCIAL CENTERS.   The international financial market is composed of international financial centers, entrepôt capital markets, and offshore centers. An international financial center may provide several services, of which the following are usually conducted by the domestic financial market:

1. Traditional international financial transactions between foreign and domestic entities. These transactions include clearing of international payments, foreign-exchange transaction, short-term credit supply, and so forth.

2. Facilitation of financial transactions between foreign entities. This is defined as entrepôt finance services (or offshore banking), in which the financial center merely intermediates by providing banking services to foreigners.

3. Offshore banking. The distinction between major international financial centers (e.g., London, New York) and offshore centers (e.g., Bahamas, Lux-

embourg, Singapore, etc.) is to some extent an arbitary one. For example, New York offers many of the same advantages for Eurocurrency business, in terms of freedom from reserve requirements and interest withholding taxes, that the Bahamas does.

A financial center (e.g., London, New York, etc.) has a highly developed commercial infrastructure and a great concentration of financial institutions where the national or regional financial transactions are conducted. Prior to the emergence of the Eurocurrency markets, international financial centers provided the traditional international banking services (loans, foreign-exchange transactions, letters of credit, and underwriting of international securities).

With development of the Euromarket, entrepôt and offshore financial transactions became significant. Entrepôt financial centers provide the services of their domestic financial institutions to both domestic and foreign entities, and may or may not be capital exporters.

Offshore centers may be of two types, either *shell* or *functional.* A shell center acts as a location of record, but little or no actual banking transactions are carried out there, whereas a functional center is one at which financial transactions are conducted. Functional centers serve as significant links between Eurocurrency markets, helping to intermediate funds around the world, from major international financial centers to end users. Shell centers are commonly used by international banks and nonbanks to minimize taxes and other costs.[35]

Offshore banking centers attract international banking business (nonresident, foreign-currency denominated assets, and liabilities) by reducing or eliminating restrictions on operations as well as lowering taxes and other levies. Over 15 centers qualify under this definition (see Exhibit 11). More specifically, the following five advantages of offshore centers can be observed:

1. Absence of central-bank regulations, particularly absence of reserve requirements on Eurocurrency deposits.
2. Absence of restrictions on interest paid on deposits.
3. Fiscal incentives. Taxes and levies on offshore business are actually nonexistent, in sharp contrast to the situation at domestic locations, and license fees are usually low.
4. Local capital requirements are low or nonexistent and entry is relatively easy.
5. Offshore centers allow a reduction of country risk.

The Asian and North American currency markets are of particular interest. The Asian currency market is the pool of dollars and other foreign-currency-denominated assets and liabilities of banks located in Asia. The market was created in Singapore in 1968, when the government licensed a branch of Bank of America to establish a special international department to handle transactions of nonresidents. All banks that were granted such licenses were required to set up a special account for nonresident transactions, namely the Asian Currency Unit (ACU). Banks that operate in this market receive fiscal incentives and exemptions from various bank restrictions.[36]

EXHIBIT 11   OFFSHORE BANKING CENTERS

	Number of Offshore Banks
Anguilla	100
Bahamas	263
Bahrain	37
Cayman Islands	260
Hong Kong	74
Jersey	33
Lebanon	78
Luxembourg	92
Netherlands Antilles	43
New Hebrides	13
Panama	66
Philippines	17
Seychelles	1
Singapore	66
United Arab Emirates	55

Source. International Monetary Fund. *Finance & Development,* Vol. XVI, No. 4 (1979), p. 46.

The Asian currency market developed vigorously in Singapore and Hong Kong, growing from $0.1 billion in 1968 to over $50 billion at the end of 1979. The market performs several functions:

1. It intermediates between Asian and Eurocurrency markets and within Asia.
2. It provides arbitrage facilities.
3. It is a channel for funds flowing into Asian projects and mobilizes funds for the region.

The growth of North American Eurocurrency market (see Exhibit 7) has been influenced by the same general factors that affected the Eurocurrency market and other offshore centers. An additional consideration is that the Caribbean shell branches operate during the same hours as their parents and other U.S. banks on the East Coast.

Most Caribbean branches are shell branches managed and staffed at the head office of the parent rather than locally. Loans and deposits are negotiated at non-Caribbean centers (e.g., New York, San Francisco, etc.) but are booked at the Caribbean branches particularly for tax considerations. The increasing importance of these centers has led to slower growth in Euromarket transactions in London.

During the 1970s an increasing share of business has been captured by various offshore banking centers. The volume of business transacted through offshore centers has increased with the growth of Eurocurrency, and by 1979 it accounted for some 12 percent of the global Euromarket. The striking increase in the importance of offshore centers largely reflects the advantages they offer vis-à-vis more traditional centers. Host countries' benefits from offshore banking are salaries, other expenditures and fees, and profit on taxes.

INTERNATIONAL BANKING FACILITIES IN THE UNITED STATES

The plan for the establishment of International Banking Facilities or free monetary zones in the United States was approved by the Board of Governors of the Federal Reserve in June 1981 effective December 3, 1981. Accordingly, IBFs may be established by United States depository institutions, by Edge and Agreement Corporations and by the United States branches and agencies of foreign banks. An institution is not required to establish a separate organizational structure for an IBF. It is contemplated that an IBF would be operated primarily as a recordkeeping entity similar to an offshore shell branch.

The Board of Governors of the Federal Reserve System has amended its regulations regarding reserve requirements and payment of interest on deposits to permit the establishment of IBFs in the United States. The IBF's state and city tax treatment varies among the various states, but they might ultimately be exempt from those taxes, thus benefiting from lower effective tax rate and greater competitiveness. (IBFs in New York will benefit from a gradual phase out of state and city tax over a 5-year period.)

In May 1979 New York became the first state to adopt legislation that would allow the establishment of IBFs in New York City. Since then many other states have expressed interest in this type of banking and adopted similar legislation.

IBFs can accept deposits exempted from reserve requirements (Reserve D) and interest rate restrictions (Regulation Q) can make loans to foreign borrowers. These activities may be denominated in United States dollars and/or in foreign currencies.

More specifically, subject to restrictions concerning eligible holders of deposits and loans, maturity and size of deposits and loans, IBFs may conduct the following transactions:

1. Accept deposits from and make loans to bank and nonbank customers located abroad only if that supports the customers non-U.S. operations.

2. Extend credit to other IBFs, or to an IBF parent institution in the United States. (However, funds received by United States offices of IBFs parent institutions will be subject to reserve requirement on Eurocurrency liabilities.)

3. Offer to foreign nonbank residents time deposits with a minimum maturity, or required notice period prior to withdrawal, of 2 business days. Such deposit accounts require minimum deposits and withdrawals of $100,000.

4. Offer time deposits to foreign offices of U.S. depository institutions or foreign banks, to other IBFs or to the parent institution of an IBF with a minimum 1 day (overnight) maturity.

The IBFs will eliminate some of the disadvantages in the regulatory and tax environments that currently prevail in New York City as well as in other financial centers in the United States vis-à-vis the Eurocurrency market, and will enhance the international competitive position of banking institutions in the United States. However, the Federal Reserve Board has introduced several restrictions designed to reduce the likelihood that these facilities will circumvent interest rate restrictions or reserve requirements, and reduce the effectiveness of monetary policy. These measures will not allow the IBFs to enjoy the full advantages that offshore Eurocurrency centers have.

FINANCIAL MARKETS' BANKING ENVIRONMENT. The London banking environment could deteriorate due to regulatory developments in both the United Kingdom and the United States. Britian's proposals for monetary and prudential controls could make operations in London more costly and less competitive. Against this background, the Federal Reserve's decision to allow International Banking Facilities (IBFs) in the United States could make the latter more attractive. Both developments could reinforce each other and result in Eurocurrency business shifting away from London to New York as well as to other markets.

The British proposals have been presented in four papers: (1) The Green Paper on Monetary Control; (2) The Measurement of Capital; (3) Foreign Currency Exposure; and (4) the Measurement of Liquidity. United Kingdom branches of foreign banks will also be subject to the requirements.

Britian's proposals for monetary and prudential controls could make operations in London more costly and less competitive. The Bank of England maintains that the proposed controls are not designed to adversely affect the Eurocurrency market in London but to rather contribute to the market's stability. According to the Bank's Governor there are two reasons for control and supervision: (1) there is a need to introduce more effective supervision over a wider range of financial institutions than had previously been the case, thereby promoting greater stability; and (2) there is the obligation of the United Kingdom to give statutory effect to the principle established by the first (December 1977) European Directives on Credit Institutions.

The authorities strong vested interest in the continuance of London as a major international financial center is, to some extent, compromised by the need to follow the directives of the European Community on coordination of banking legislation and cooperation. It is assessed that if the proposed controls are enacted they could lead to a substantial erosion of London's position as the world's leading banking center by inducing banks to conduct business in other international centers to the detriment of London and to the British balance of payments.

Moreover, the elimination of Regulations D and Q entirely could be crucial for Eurodollar development, because these regulations were an important part of the environment in which the Eurocurrency market developed, and they have continued to act as buffers between the United States domestic and Eurodollar markets interest-rate structures. Currently, the monetary effectiveness of these regulations is being questioned, and efforts are being made for their amendment. Indeed, the Monetary Control Act of 1980 calls for the gradual elimination of Regulation Q over a 6-year period.

The elimination of Regulation D reserve requirements is the more remote possibility, since the Federal Reserve continues to support the concept of reserve requirements for all type of deposits. In fact, while the Monetary Control Act of 1980 provides for a gradual reduction in reserve requirement ratios, the application of Regulation D has been expanded from member banks of the Federal Reserve System toward the entire banking system. This is despite the Hunt Commission's recommendation that reserve requirements on time and savings deposits be abolished, since open-market operations should be adequate for controlling the money supply.

The IBFs could transform the geographic composition of U.S. Eurocurrency business, and perhaps radically affect the geography of the entire international banking activities and the world's flow of funds. They could turn New York into a leading Eurocurrency center that will constitute a threat to several Eurocurrency centers, particularly those that are in the same time zone as New York (Caribbean, Panama) and those that are heavily used by the U.S. (Caribbean, Panama, and London). Although London is presently the leading Eurocurrency center and the main location of the American Eurocurrency activities, it would probably suffer by the IBFs because of an outflow of U.S. business. About 40 percent of London's Eurocurrency activity is generated by U.S. banks; this accounts for 33 percent of U.S. Eurocurrency activity, compared with 31 percent of U.S. Eurocurrency activity in the Caribbean. However, the time zone will still give Europe a comparative advantage over the U.S. by allowing it to deal with the Far East in the morning and the U.S. in the afternoon. Moreover, certain offshore centers have more than tax advantages over New York, for example, Bahrain, Singapore, and Hong Kong, which in addition benefit from being on the spot for Middle East and Far East business. Preliminary forecasts suggest that by the end of this decade, the business volume of the New York City banks could equal those of London.

While conditions have improved for the New York market, the London banking environment could deteriorate due to unfavorable regulatory developments. The deterioration in the London banking environment and the improvement in New York's position could shift Eurocurrency business from London to other locations, particularly New York City (as well as other cities in the United States).

THE PAYMENTS SYSTEM.   The bulk of Eurocurrency payments are settled through book entries in correspondent bank accounts in the countries where the particular currency is the legal tender, and, to a lesser extent, through branch networks, rather than through the central banks' clearing and settlement facilities. The final net–net sums are settled through the central banks.

International transactions denominated in dollars are cleared in the United States through the New York CHIPS, SWIFT, The Fedwire, and proprietary communication networks of the major banks with their main international branches. Dollar clearings are performed for a variety of transactions, including payments for foreign trade in goods and services; direct and portfolio investment; Eurodollar market activity; and foreign exchange and arbitrage transactions. The daily volume of the CHIPS system is presently about $200 billion. A substantial amount of international payments is settled through book entries in correspondent-bank accounts.

New developments in the international payments system, both in terms of operating procedures and the development of new systems, could improve efficient and have significant effects on the operation of the banking industry and international cash management.

Starting October 1, 1981, the CHIPS system settlement will be on a 1-day value date basis, the same as the Fedwire and in line with practices in the rest of the world. This will eliminate overnight and overweekend arbitrage between U.S. money markets and the Eurodollar market. The $200 billion daily clearing through the CHIPS system is facilitated through three main mechanisms: (1) working balances of foreign banks held with U.S. correspondent banks, particularly in New York; (2) daylight overdrafts; and (3) matching of payments and receipts.

The adoption of same-day settlement reduces the risk of overnight overdraft and default, however, daylight overdraft has expanded significantly. Working balances maintained with U.S. correspondent banks (i.e., demand deposits) amount to some

$23 billion or 1/9 of CHIPS' clearings. Alternatively, CHIPS clearings are 9-fold the working balances maintained with U.S. banks.

It is possible to arrange for delivery beyond the customary settlement date, subject to negotiation. There is no regular forward market in Eurocurrency deposits (not even Eurodollars). Such deals, which in fact, amount to deferred loans of Eurodollars, can be arranged, even though such transactions are not very frequent.

In addition to the above changes, modification in the structure of the system is also underway. For instance, a proposal by the Bank of England to set up a wholesale dollar clearing system in London was discussed during 1980. The proposal calls for the establishment of a central facility in London where dollar payments would be exchanged between participants each working day to a given cut-off time. Items eligible for exchange would be dollar payments made between participating banks in London, and capable of being netted out and settled in London. The London clearing house will transmit the net settlements instructions to New York, through SWIFT and/or the Federal Reserve Bank, for ultimate settlement.

The creation of this system could significantly affect the pattern of dollar balances, whereby smaller working balances will be held by overseas banks with their New York correspondents. The major disadvantage of the proposed system is the risk of exposure to clearing default by participants, settling and non-settling, as well as to their correspondents. (In the CHIPS system, credit exposure can be large, and individual banks, often relatively small, experience high daylight clearing liabilities). If credit exposures cannot be avoided to the maximum extent, then wholesale London dollar clearing would merely have the effect of transferring to London credit risk which New York banks are now confronting. This position is unlikely to be supported by the large banks in London, while most American banks there oppose or have no interest in it.

SWIFT provides an electronic communication system designed to transmit instructions speedily and efficiently. In the medium and long term, additional developments could occur in SWIFT, which operates in over 20 countries through the world and serves some 800 major banks. It is becoming the major impetus behind the standardization of the international operations of banks around the world. As SWIFT transactions grow, pressure will build for it to add a net settlement mechanism or multiple mechanisms in countries that have high transactions in foreign currencies, including dollars. The development of a central Eurocurrency settlement mechanism would require the cooperation of central banks or multilateral institutions (e.g., the BIS), in order to reduce the enormous credit risk involved. Such a development is, however, unlikely to occur in the near future.

EUROCURRENCY LENDING

MARKET SIZE AND CHARACTERISTICS.   The international market for bank loans, or syndicated medium-term Eurocurrency bank-loan market, emerged in the late 1960s and developed rapidly in the 1970s to become the most important source of international bank credit and balance-of-payments financing. Loans expanded from about $5 billion in 1970 to $70 billion in 1979, providing more than half of the medium- and long-term borrowing in international capital markets (international bonds account for almost one fifth, and the balance is supplied by individual banks, unpublicized, and for shorter maturity than syndicated loans). Syndicated Eurocurrency loans involve the making of bank loans or extending of credits by a group, or syndicate, of international banks, with each bank providing a part of the loan.

The syndicated loan market is a relatively small segment of the Eurocurrency market and bank lending as a whole, although it has grown rapidly. Outstanding loans, about $150 billion in December 1979, represent about one third of the net total of Eurocurrency claims outstanding in the European area. These loans have become a significant activity and source of income for international commercial banks.

In the aftermath of the sharp oil-price increases and the consequent worldwide balance-of-payments disequilibriums, the need for large balance-of-payments financing generated growing demand for Eurocredits. The Eurocurrency market has performed an enormous task of recycling OPEC surpluses, channeling them to oil-importing countries (in the form of deposits and loans) to finance balance-of-payments deficits.

Borrowing in the Eurocurrency loan market by country, type of borrower, purpose of the borrower, currency denomination, type of credit, maturity, and interest rates and spreads is detailed in Exhibits 12–14.[37]

In 1979 non-OPEC less developed countries borrowed over $42 billion, or 62 percent of total Eurocurrency borrowing in the international capital market. The second-largest major borrowers were the industrial countries ($19 billion, 25 percent); third, centrally planned economies ($7 billion, 10 percent); fourth, OPEC ($1 billion, 1.5 percent).

Borrowers in the market are mainly government agencies, corporations, and utilities, as well as natural-resource-development projects. Syndicated loans to sovereign states have been used principally to finance balance-of-payments deficits, even if development projects have often been the declared purpose. In 1979 borrowing in the international capital markets by central governments accounted for 16.9 percent of the total; other borrowers were state and local governments (2.6 percent), public nonfinancial entities (32.6 percent), private nonfinancial entities (19.6 percent), banks (9.8 percent), central banks (3.23 percent), other public financial institutions (12.7 percent), and other private financial institutions (2.1 percent).

Borrowers classified by purpose of the borrower were as follows in 1979: bank and finance (28 percent); transport (8 percent); public utilities (18 percent); petroleum and natural gas (10 percent); natural resources (3 percent); industry (13 percent); and general purpose (20 percent).

The majority of syndicated credits are denominated in dollars, but loans in other currencies are also available. U.S.-dollar-denominated Eurocurrency credit accounted for 95.3 percent of the total in 1979, followed by the Deutsche Mark (2.4 percent), pound sterling (1 percent), and Saudi Arabia riyal (0.4 percent).

SYNDICATED LOANS. The most common type of syndicated loan is a term loan (90 percent of all loans in 1979) under which the funds can be drawn down by a borrower within a specified period (the drawdown period) after the loan agreement has been signed and repayment is usually to an amortization schedule, which can begin anytime starting from drawdown, but generally not later than the first 5 or 6 years of the loan. Another type of loan, less frequently used, is a revolving-credit (0.7 percent of total Eurocurrency loans in 1979) where the borrower is given a line of credit that can be drawn down and repaid with more flexibility than the term loan. This is similar to the term loan, but the borrower must pay a fee for the undrawn portion of the credit line. A combination of term loan and revolving-credit facility is also available, along with other variations tailored to the borrower's requirements.

EXHIBIT 12a BORROWING IN INTERNATIONAL CAPITAL MARKETS BY TYPE OF LOAN, CATEGORY OF BORROWING COUNTRY AND BORROWING COUNTRY, 1976 TO 1979
(MILLIONS OF U.S. DOLLARS OR EQUIVALENT)

Category of Borrowing Country	Foreign Bonds			International Bonds			Total Bonds			Eurocurrency Credits	Total Bonds and Credits
	Public	Private	Total	Public	Private	Total	Public	Private	Total		
Industrialized											
1976	4,945.1	7,381.5	12,326.6	9,205.4	1,598.2	10,803.6	14,150.5	8,979.7	23,130.2	7,434.9	30,565.1
1977	4,662.2	5,153.7	9,815.9	10,673.9	2,302.9	12,976.8	15,336.1	7,456.6	22,792.7	11,055.1	33,847.8
1978	8,172.7	4,536.9	12,709.6	7,566.7	2,123.8	9,690.5	15,739.4	6,660.7	22,400.1	31,343.5	53,743.6
1979	6,147.1	5,359.7	11,506.8	10,885.8	1,651.6	12,537.4	17,032.9	7,011.3	24,044.2	18,807.2	42,851.4
Developing											
1976	700.6	318.9	1,019.5	1,123.5	193.2	1,316.7	1,824.1	512.1	2,336.2	18,131.4	20,467.6
1977	1,226.4	723.0	1,949.4	2,405.2	401.3	2,806.5	3,631.6	1,124.3	4,755.9	20,145.2	24,901.1
1978	1,459.8	1,306.0	2,765.8	2,408.5	916.6	3,325.1	3,868.3	2,222.6	6,090.9	38,276.2	44,367.1
1979	1,182.0	842.9	2,024.9	1,742.3	246.9	1,989.2	2,924.3	1,089.8	4,014.1	42,356.7	46,370.8
Oil exporting											
1976	—	—	—	—	—	—	—	—	—	243.6	243.6
1977	—	—	—	9.9	42.2	52.1	9.9	42.2	52.1	1,572.6	1,624.7
1978	—	—	—	25.0	36.6	61.6	25.0	36.6	61.6	1,347.1	1,408.7
1979	—	14.7	14.7	—	—	—	—	14.7	14.7	799.0	813.7

Centrally planned											
1976	—	—	—	47.0	25.0	72.0	47.0	25.0	72.0	2,371.4	2,443.4
1977	—	6.3	6.3	93.5	155.7	249.2	93.5	162.0	255.5	2,691.0	2,946.5
1978	—	—	—	30.0	—	30.0	30.0	—	30.0	3,702.1	3,732.1
1979	18.1	—	18.1	30.0	—	30.0	48.1	—	48.1	7,231.1	7,279.2
International organizations											
1976	3,220.5	1,972.1	5,192.6	1,174.6	1,888.6	3,063.2	4,395.1	3,860.7	8,255.8	377.0	8,632.8
1977	2,966.3	1,782.1	4,748.4	1,549.7	861.9	2,411.6	4,516.0	2,644.0	7,160.0	197.0	7,357.0
1978	2,638.7	3,067.3	5,706.0	1,528.8	1,189.8	2,718.6	4,167.5	4,257.1	8,424.6	181.7	8,606.3
1979	2,785.0	2,912.2	5,697.2	1,724.4	1,101.5	2,825.9	4,509.4	4,013.7	8,523.1	310.0	8,833.1
Others											
1976	165.0	239.6	404.6	112.3	—	112.3	277.3	239.6	516.9	388.6	905.5
1977	56.9	33.3	90.2	702.9	337.1	1,040.0	759.8	370.4	1,130.2	97.0	1,227.2
1978	141.3	53.9	195.2	132.2	43.4	175.6	273.5	97.3	370.8	220.0	590.8
1979	117.2	16.3	133.5	225.8	118.0	343.8	343.0	134.3	477.3	186.2	663.5
All categories											
1976	9,031.2	9,912.1	18,943.3	11,662.8	3,705.0	15,367.8	20,694.0	13,617.1	34,311.1	28,703.3	63,014.4
1977	8,911.8	7,698.4	16,610.2	15,425.2	4,058.9	19,484.1	24,337.0	11,757.3	36,094.3	34,185.3	70,279.6
1978	12,412.5	8,964.1	21,376.6	11,666.2	4,273.6	15,939.8	24,078.7	13,237.7	37,316.4	73,723.5	111,039.9
1979	10,249.4	9,131.1	19,380.5	14,608.3	3,118.0	17,726.3	24,857.7	12,249.1	37,106.8	68,891.2	105,998.0

Source. World Bank. *Borrowing in International Capital Markets.* Washington, D.C.: World Bank, 1980.

EXHIBIT 12b EUROCURRENCY BANK CREDITS
(PUBLICLY ANNOUNCED IN PERIOD, IN MILLIONS OF DOLLARS)

	1977	1978	1979	1980 (January–November)
Industrial countries	17,205	28,952	27,248	30,652
Australia	360	212	941	2,475
Canada	3,292	5,075	1,845	1,677
Denmark	868	2,242	1,205	1,359
Finland	314	550	92	1,040
France	2,325	1,915	2,955	1,745
Greece	204	509	1,010	1,291
Ireland	440	616	687	237
Italy	1,024	2,485	3,708	6,144
Norway	182	1,517	935	665
Spain	1,973	2,426	4,184	4,070
Sweden	1,446	1,872	1,263	1,720
United Kingdom	1,992	3,899	795	1,410
United States	826	1,206	2,348	2,349
Other[a]	1,959	3,798	5,280	4,470
Developing countries	20,986	37,290	47,964	32,507
Non-OPEC countries	13,504	26,892	35,411	22,003
Argentina	849	1,461	2,965	2,376
Brazil	2,814	5,634	6,278	4,007
Chile	591	1,045	867	1,024
Korea	1,265	2,651	3,258	1,705
Malaysia	212	858	1,168	—
Mexico	2,727	7,250	8,243	5,521
Morocco	797	605	500	400
Peru	189	—	596	460
Philippines	698	2,073	2,067	856
Taiwan	524	255	1,063	280
Other[b]	2,838	5,060	8,406	5,374
Opec countries	7,481	10,398	12,553	10,504
Algeria	723	2,576	1,906	40
Indonesia	817	1,118	1,061	1,035
Nigeria	1,000	825	1,373	1,349
United Arab Emirates	1,086	726	401	100
Venezula	1,666	2,054	6,830	6,557
Other	2,189	3,099	1,373	1,423
Communist countries	3,394	3,767	7,325	2,609
China	—	—	3,395	181
East Germany	832	642	796	303
Hungary	300	700	260	550
Poland	19	374	849	800
Other[c]	2,243	2,051	2,025	775
International organizations	190	160	275	429
TOTAL	41,775	70,169	82,812	66,197

Source. Morgan Guaranty. *World Financial Markets.* New York: Morgan Guaranty Trust Company, November 1980.
[a]Includes multinational organizations revised.
[b]Includes regional development organizations.
[c]Includes COMECON Institutions.

EXHIBIT 12c NEW INTERNATIONAL BOND ISSUES
(NEW ISSUES IN PERIOD, IN MILLIONS OF DOLLARS)

	1977	1978	1979	1980 (January–November)
By type:				
Eurobonds, total	17,771	14,125	18,726	22,355
By category of borrower				
U.S. companies	1,130	1,122	2,872	3,948
Foreign companies	7,347	4,540	7,183	8,275
State enterprises	4,667	3,291	4,524	5,522
Governments	2,936	3,643	2,433	2,826
International organizations	1,691	1,529	1,714	1,784
By currency of denomination				
U.S. dollar	11,627	7,290	12,565	15,159
Deutsche mark	4,131	5,251	3,626	3,544
Dutch guilder	452	394	531	1,022
Canadian dollar	655	—	425	279
European unit of account	28	165	253	65
Other	878	1,025	1,326	2,286
Foreign bonds outside the United States, total	8,777	14,359	17,749	13,316
By category of borrower				
U.S. companies	40	245	217	278
Foreign companies	1,421	2,110	3,463	2,776
State enterprises	2,427	3,163	3,284	2,616
Governments	2,043	5,771	7,663	4,020
International organizations	2,846	3,070	3,122	3,626
By currency of denomination				
Deutsche mark	2,181	3,789	5,379	4,482
Swiss franc	4,970	5,698	9,777	6,862
Dutch guilder	211	385	75	259
Japanese yen	1,271	3,826	1,833	1,088
Other	144	671	685	625
Foreign bonds In the United States, total	7,428	5,795	4,515	3,195
By category of borrower				
Canadian entities	3,022	3,142	2,193	2,136
International organizations	1,917	459	1,100	550
Other	2,489	2,194	1,222	509
By country of borrower:				
Industrial countries	23,851	24,964	31,886	30,621
Australia	1,074	1,218	593	525
Austria	1,384	1,027	1,218	1,703
Canada	5,277	4,764	4,197	3,635
Denmark	796	1,018	752	1,108
Finland	358	952	699	392
France	1,945	1,286	2,106	2,566
Japan	1,979	3,467	5,775	4,762
Netherlands	682	251	832	1,536
New Zealand	567	744	553	293
Norway	1,889	2,751	1,955	769

EXHIBIT 12c   CONTINUED

	1977	1978	1979	1980 (January–November)
Sweden	1,574	876	1,530	2,815
United Kingdom	1,915	1,365	1,181	1,733
United States	1,353	2,973	6,767	5,399
Developing countries	3,421	4,227	3,093	2,220
Non-OPEC countries	2,676	2,684	2,667	1,677
Brazil	732	843	930	349
Mexico	1,282	568	363	439
Philippines	129	170	175	70
OPEC countries	745	1,543	418	543
Algeria	166	721	208	—
Venezuela	438	588	55	398
Communist countries	248	30	75	65
Hungary	174	—	—	65
International organizations	6,454	5,058	5,936	5,960
TOTAL	33,976	34,279	40,990	38,866

Source. Morgan Guaranty. *World Financial Markets,* New York: Morgan Guaranty Trust Company, November 1980.

The amounts of individual loans vary from under $10 million to over $1 billion, and maturities extend from over 1 year to 15 years. For instance, in 1979 about 24 percent of all loans matured in over 1 to 7 years. The majority of loans, 52 percent, had maturities of over 7 years to 10 years, and 16 percent matured in over 10 to 15 years.

Banks that provide syndicated loans acquire funds for these financings primarily by borrowing in the form of short-term deposits from other banks (i.e., perform maturity transformation). For this reason there are difficulties in financing long-term fixed-interest loans. Therefore, Eurobanks price medium- and long-term syndicated loans on a floating basis, subject to periodic interest adjustments (i.e., on a rollover basis).

Syndicated Eurocurrency loans are rollover credits under which a bank agrees to make funds available for up to 15 years. The price of rollover credits to the borrower has three components: a floating interest rate, a spread, and various fees. The interest rate charged on most syndicated loans is floating, usually computed by adding a spread or margin to the London Interbank Offered Rate. The latter is the rate at which banks lend funds to other banks operating in the Euromarket, adjusted every 3 or 6 months as market rates change. The new base rate is calculated 2 days prior to the rollover date as the average of the offer rates of several reference banks in the syndicate. This procedure enables the lending banks to obtain the funds they need on the market at all times at the prevailing terms and conditions.

The size of the spread depends on the market's assessment of the creditworthiness of the borrower, the maturity of the loan, and market conditions. The spread is negotiated with the borrower and either remains constant over the life of the loan, changes after a number of years, or is floating and is adjusted periodically. The higher the perceived risk associated with a borrower, the wider the spread that would be required.[38]

Evidence shows that the spreads on syndicated loans tend to narrow if the level of interest rates increases, the volatility of rates declines, or the maturities on loans is shortened. Data for 1979 show that 23 percent of all Eurocurrency loans carried a spread of up to 0.5 percent; over 60 percent had spreads ranging from over 0.5 percent to 1.0 percent; about 10 percent had a spread of over 1.0 percent to 1.25 percent; and 5 percent had a spread of 1.251 percent to 1.750 percent. Wider spreads were, however, uncommon.

For the lending bank, LIBOR represents the cost of the funds lent; the spread together with the fees constitute its net revenue, which offsets the cost of funds and intermediation risk. Hence interest on syndicated loans is charged in the same way that the banks have to pay interest to attract the deposits to make these loans, that is, every 3 or 6 months, and there is no interest-rate transformation. The floating-loan pricing method is attractive to both borrowers and lending banks; it avoids being locked into paying more or receiving less than current interest rates when rates change, thereby reducing the risk associated with the interest-rate and maturity transformation.

The cost of arranging a syndicated loan is relatively low. In addition to the interest costs on a Eurocurrency loan, there are also commitment fees, front-end management fees, and occasionally an annual agent's fee. Commitment fees of 0.5 percent are charged against the undrawn amount of the loan and apply on both term loans and revolving credits. Front-end fees include participation fees and management fees and usually range between 0.5 and 1 percent of the value of the loan. Lending banks are paid participation fees depending on the size of their individual participation and managers are paid underwriting fees on the amount of their initial committed participation. All interest payments are paid free of any taxes. Similarly, if reserve requirements are raised or non-interest-bearing deposits are imposed, thereby increasing the cost of funds, the borrower has to pay the higher cost of credit.

The charges on syndicated loans may be summarized as follows:[39]

Annual payments = (LIBOR + spread) × amount of loan drawn
                + Commitment fee × amount of loan undrawn
                + Tax adjustment (if any) + Annual agent's fee (if any)

Front-end charges = Participation fee × face amount of loan
                + Management fee × face amount of loan
                + Initial agent's fee (if any)

Syndicated Eurocredits contain advantages for both lenders and borrowers. They allow banks, both large and small, to share large credits with other banks, participate in many transactions, and diversify their risks.

Loan syndication increases the amount of bank credit available to borrowers without necessarily increasing the risk to individual lenders. It allows for the efficient arrangement of a larger amount of funds than any single lender can feasibly supply relatively quickly and cheaply. The underwriting procedure used in the syndication of Eurocurrency credits may allow the borrower to obtain better terms than those that would otherwise be available. For many sovereign-state borrowers, particularly the less developed countries, the loan market is one of the major international financing options available.

The syndication procedure allows banks to diversify some of the unique risks that arise in international lending. These risks reflect, to some degree, the heavy con-

EXHIBIT 13a   BORROWING IN CAPITAL MARKETS BY BORROWING COUNTRY, PURPOSE OF THE BORROWER AND MATURITY, 1977 TO 1979
(PERCENT OF TOTAL DISTRIBUTION OF AMOUNT BORROWED)

Type of Borrower	Eurocurrency Credits All Categories			Foreign Bonds All Categories			International Bonds All Categories		
	1977	1978	1979	1977	1978	1979	1977	1978	1979
Central government	29.4	28.7	16.9	22.80	34.67	24.13	13.4	22.0	13.1
State or local government	4.4	2.2	2.6	10.70	4.84	5.39	3.6	2.9	2.6
Public nonfinancial enterprise	26.6	29.8	32.6	14.05	8.77	9.52	14.4	10.8	10.4
Private nonfinancial enterprise	14.1	18.6	19.6	13.21	13.94	21.24	28.0	18.5	26.5
Deposit money banks	3.1	2.8	9.8	1.60	3.14	1.69	13.9	15.2	13.6
Central monetary institution	3.3	4.0	3.2	—	—	—	1.1	0.2	—
Other public financial institution	17.7	12.6	12.7	7.28	5.84	7.29	7.1	8.4	9.0
Other private financial institution	0.8	1.1	2.1	1.77	2.07	0.56	6.2	5.0	8.8
International organizations	0.6	0.2	0.4	28.58	26.69	24.39	12.4	17.1	15.9
Others	—	—	—	—	—	—	—	—	—
Unknown	—	—	0.0	—	—	—	—	—	—
All types	100.0	100.0	100.0	100.00	100.00	100.00	100.0	100.0	100.0

Purpose of the Borrower									
Transport	25.0	20.4	27.7	10.6	11.1	9.6	28.3	28.7	31.5
Public utilities	4.5	4.7	5.7	2.9	4.0	4.8	3.8	3.0	3.1
Petroleum and natural gas	10.5	14.2	17.6	10.4	6.7	5.9	5.5	4.3	5.8
Natural resources	8.4	11.4	10.2	4.4	1.8	2.6	12.0	5.3	4.1
Industry	1.0	1.6	3.2	0.2	0.3	—	1.9	—	0.8
Public and community services	16.3	15.9	13.1	9.0	9.9	17.3	19.2	16.4	21.6
International organizations	5.4	1.8	2.2	0.8	—	0.2	0.5	0.5	1.8
General purpose	0.6	0.2	0.4	28.6	26.7	29.4	12.4	17.1	15.9
Unknown	28.4	29.8	19.8	33.1	39.5	30.3	16.5	24.7	15.4
	—	—	0.0	—	—	—	—	—	—
All purposes	100.0	100.0	100.0	100.0	100.0	100.0	100.0	100.0	100.0
Original Maturity (years)									
Over 1 – 3.00	2.7	2.8	4.2	0.3	0.7	0.1	5.2	6.0	5.0
3.01 – 5.00	15.9	5.1	8.5	18.6	21.4	21.7	19.9	21.5	18.1
5.01 – 7.00	65.1	25.2	11.0	16.5	13.2	19.3	27.9	16.3	17.4
7.01 – 10.00	11.7	57.5	51.8	16.3	18.9	19.6	24.2	29.4	34.4
10.01 – 15.00	—	5.7	15.7	21.1	27.1	17.5	19.7	23.4	23.4
15.01 – 20.00	—	—	0.2	9.9	10.5	9.3	2.4	0.8	0.7
20.01 – 25.00	—	—	—	7.1	1.0	2.3	—	—	—
25.01 & over	—	—	—	6.9	4.7	7.5	—	—	—
Unknown	4.6	3.6	8.6	3.3	2.7	2.7	0.6	2.7	1.0
All maturities	100.0	100.0	100.0	100.0	100.0	100.0	100.0	100.0	100.0

Source. World Bank. *Borrowing in International Capital Markets.* Washington, D.C.: World Bank, 1980.

EXHIBIT 13b   EUROCURRENCY CREDITS BY CURRENCY OF DENOMINATION AND TYPE OF CREDIT 1977 TO 1979 (US$ MILLIONS OR EQUIVALENT)

Currency of Denomination	1977	1978	1979
National currencies			
Canadian dollar	—	8.9	—
Deutsche mark	914.3	1,419.1	1,616.3
French franc	10.0	68.7	81.1
Hong Kong dollar	—	125.0	58.2
Italian lira	102.2	56.9	26.5
Japanese yen	136.8	289.3	103.7
Kuwaiti dinar	—	111.5	50.5
Malaysian Ringgit	—	100.0	78.9
Mexican peso	—	—	13.1
Netherlands guilder	8.3	147.7	128.5
Norwegian krone	—	18.4	20.1
Pound sterling	128.7	882.4	656.6
Saudi Arabian riyal	72.8	94.4	251.5
Singapore dollar	—	108.9	90.0
Swedish krona	—	—	33.8
Swiss franc	105.2	21.2	40.8
U.S. dollar	32,707.0	70,271.1	65,641.6
Composite currency units			
All currencies	34,185.3	73,723.5	68,891.2
By type of credit			
Term	30,644.7	65,827.2	61,922.2
Revolving	2,859.2	4,692.0	474.4
Other	473.0	2,115.1	4,057.8
Unknown	208.4	1,089.2	2,436.8

Source. World Bank. *Borrowing in International Capital Markets.* Washington, D.C.: World Bank, 1980.

centration of lending to public-sector borrowers, approximately 70 percent of the total. The legal protection available to a bank is much different if a private borrower defaults compared with the situation when a public borrower defaults. In the former case, creditors can pursue various legal steps. When commercial banks lend to public-sector borrowers, there is much more uncertainty about legal recourse, since some public-sector borrowers are covered by sovereign immunity.

Moreover, syndication allows banks to reduce sovereign risk by giving them the opportunity to diversify their international loans geographically, and it provides more protection against selective defaults. The syndication process tends to increase the penalty associated with selective defaults, that is, if a public-sector borrower chooses not to repay loans from individual banks or a group of banks in a particular country.[40] Banks include a cross-default clause in the loan agreement that states that if one public borrower defaults, the loans of other public borrowers from that country may be called into default as well. In that case, the loans of those borrowers become due and payable.

In summary, a syndicated Eurocurrency loan, compared with a fixed-rate credit arranged by an individual bank, minimizes the various risks that financial institutions participating in the market would otherwise face, through the strategies described below:[41]

Risk	Source of Risk	Risk-Reduction Strategy
Country risk	The ability and willingness of borrowers within a country to meet their obligations	Syndication of the credit and diversification of bank's loan portfolio
Credit risk	The ability of an entity to repay its debts	Syndication of the credit and diversification of bank's loan portfolio
Interest risk	Mismatched maturities coupled with unpredictable movements in interest rates	Matching assets to liabilities by pricing credits on a rollover basis
Regulatory risk	Imposition or reserve requirements or taxes on the banks	A clause in the contract that forces the borrowers to bear this risk

Syndicated Eurocurrency loans are usually unsecured, nonnegotiable, and generally remain on a banks' books until maturity. However, some loan agreements may allow banks to transfer or assign participations to their branches or other banks.

Syndicated loans are arranged by a manager or lead manager, which is usually a commercial bank, or a merchant or investment bank that has a mandate to handle the financing. Most loans are led by one or two major banks that negotiate to obtain a mandate to raise funds from the borrower. Often a potential borrower will set a competitive bidding procedure to determine which lead bank or banks will receive the mandate to organize the loan.

The lead manager of a syndicated loan negotiates its terms and conditions with the prospective borrower and is responsible for arranging the syndicate, preparing loan documentation, and organizing the signing of the loan agreement by the borrower and all participating lenders. After the management group has been formed with other banks that will underwrite part or all of the loan, the lead manager begins syndication by offering banks a chance to participate in amounts usually smaller than the managers' commitments. During syndication, a placement memorandum, which includes a summary of the terms, a description of the borrower's financial conditions, and other relevant information, is prepared and distributed among participants.

The lead bank is normally expected to underwrite a share at least as large as that of any other lender, but in a successful syndication, the managers' own participations may be reduced. Since other banks are willing to participate in smaller credits to frequent borrowers during periods of uncertainty, club loans are often arranged in which the lead bank and managers fund the entire loan and no placement memorandum is necessary.

When the loan is fully syndicated, that is, banks have agreed to provide funds for the entire loan, the loan agreement is signed by the borrower and all the participants. If the loan cannot be underwritten on the initial terms, it must be renegotiated or the lead manager must be willing to take a larger share into its own portfolio than originally planned. After signing the loan, usually the lead bank serves as agent to

EXHIBIT 13c EUROCURRENCY CREDITS WITH VARIABLE INTEREST RATES BY CATEGORY OF BORROWING COUNTRY, BORROWING COUNTRY, AND WEIGHTED SPREAD 1977 TO FOURTH QUARTER, 1979[a]

ALL CATEGORIES

Amount Borrowed
(U.S.$ Millions or Equivalent)

Weighted Spread (percent)	1977[b]	1978[b]	1979[b]	1978 (III)	1978 (IV)	1979 (I)	1979 (II)	1979 (III)	1979 (IV)
Up to 0.500	33.2	7,562.5	13,797.8	704.9	3,839.2	532.0	3,140.3	4,242.4	5,883.1
0.501–0.750	1,270.0	22,088.4	24,847.0	5,337.9	5,435.4	4,583.2	5,007.2	7,972.9	7,283.7
0.751–1.000	9,707.1	15,038.7	12,283.2	4,286.7	4,969.4	3,776.4	3,466.9	3,230.9	1,809.0
1.001–1.250	6,382.9	9,319.9	5,747.6	1,736.4	3,513.8	1,748.5	1,130.1	1,404.4	1,464.6
1.251–1.500	3,883.0	6,779.9	2,196.2	1,525.2	1,738.9	1,137.4	307.4	526.0	225.4
1.501–1.750	6,260.2	2,522.4	828.4	379.2	224.3	148.8	111.5	433.3	134.8
1.751–2.000	2,812.9	1,932.1	327.5	452.4	43.8	28.5	231.0	22.0	46.0
2.001–2.250	569.9	606.2	37.8	92.5	26.5	15.0	22.8	—	—
2.251 & over	493.8	122.7	48.5	—	7.5	34.5	—	14.0	—
Unknown	260.0	1,183.3	440.6	377.3	455.9	22.7	257.0	14.6	146.3
All spreads	31,673.0	67,156.1	60,554.6	14,892.5	20,254.7	12,027.0	13,674.2	17,860.5	16,992.9

DISTRIBUTION OF AMOUNT BORROWED
(percentage of total)[c]

Up to 0.500	0.1	11.3	22.8	4.7	19.0	4.4	23.0	23.8	34.6
0.501–0.750	4.0	32.9	41.0	35.8	26.8	38.1	36.6	44.6	42.9
0.751–1.000	30.6	22.4	20.3	28.8	24.5	31.4	25.4	18.1	10.6
1.001–1.250	20.2	13.9	9.5	11.7	17.3	14.5	8.3	7.9	8.6
1.251–1.500	12.3	10.1	3.6	10.2	8.6	9.5	2.2	2.9	1.3
1.501–1.750	19.8	3.8	1.4	2.5	1.1	1.2	0.8	2.4	0.8
1.751–2.000	8.9	2.9	0.5	3.0	0.2	0.2	1.7	0.1	0.3
2.001–2.250	1.8	0.9	0.1	0.6	0.1	0.1	0.2	—	—
2.251 & over	1.6	0.2	0.1	—	0.0	0.3	—	0.1	—
Unknown	0.8	1.8	0.7	2.5	2.3	0.2	1.9	0.1	0.9
All spreads	100.0	100.0	100.0	100.0	100.0	100.0	100.0	100.0	100.0

Source. World Bank. *Borrowing in International Capital Markets.* Washington, D.C.: World Bank, 1980.

[a]This table only includes loans where the interest rate is variable. Therefore total borrowing for a specific category of borrowing country or borrowing country could be higher than the amount shown.

[b]Includes loans that have not been allocated to a specific month.

[c]Components may not add to the total because of rounding.

EXHIBIT 14a SUMMARY OF BORROWING IN INTERNATIONAL BOND MARKETS 1977 TO 1979
(U.S.$ MILLIONS OR EQUIVALENT)

	Foreign Bonds			International Bonds		
	1977	1978	1979	1977	1978	1979
By type of placement						
Public offering	8,911.8	12,412.5	10,249.4	15,425.2	11,666.2	14,608.3
Private placement	7,698.4	8,964.1	9,131.1	4,058.9	4,273.6	3,118.0
By category of currency of denomination						
U.S. dollar				12,336.4	7,693.4	10,584.5
Deutsche mark				5,215.2	6,531.2	4,654.4
Netherlands guilder				362.7	384.3	308.1
Other European currencies				220.9	390.3	784.0
Composite currency units				33.5	234.9	411.5
Others				1,315.4	705.7	983.8
By type of bond						
Straight	15,689.8	18,769.3	16,696.3	15,715.0	11,086.0	11,098.7
Convertible and warrant	226.2	833.7	1,809.2	1,172.5	1,308.0	1,617.0
'Special' placement	347.1	800.5	486.6	723.9	844.0	844.0
Other	347.1	973.1	373.5	1,840.0	2,603.0	4,166.6
Unknown			14.9	32.7	98.8	
By category of market country						
United States	7,668.2	6,358.6	4,594.0			
Switzerland	4,959.3	7,454.9	8,959.5			
EEC countries	1,892.9	2,602.3	2,453.9			
Other industrialized	1,393.5	4,715.0	3,1844.3			
Developing—oil exporting	685.8	245.8	188.8			
Developing—others	10.5					

Source. World Bank. *Borrowing in International Capital Markets.* Washington, D.C.: World Banks, 1980.

compute the interest-rate charges, to receive service payments, to disburse these to individual participants, and to inform them if there are any difficulties with the loan.

RECYCLING OPEC'S SURPLUSES. The growing financial needs and external burden of the non-oil LDCs, combined with the need to continue recycling OPEC's surpluses, pose serious challenges for the international financial market.

The non-oil LDCs face a large financing gap in the 1980s which, if not met increasingly from official sources, could increase the difficulties of debt servicing and the risk of widespread defaults. Compared with the early 1970s, the LDC debt burden has increased in nominal and real terms, as well as in relation to their exports and their GNP.

A number of developing countries have accumulated large external debts, with maturities that are closely bunched, so that their debt service ratios have risen rapidly. In general, the risks are greater in the 1980s than in the late 1970s although conditions vary greatly from country to country. The sharply increased international bank exposure may reduce the willingness of banks to lend, which may make it more difficult for the recycling mechanism to function properly. In addition, higher risk and narrower profit margins make recycling more difficult.

The adjustment of the LDCs during the first oil crisis was made possible by the decline in the relative price of oil in the late 1970s; the economic recovery in the major industrial countries; austerity programs in many LDCs; and the ability of the international financial markets to finance their debts. The conditions for smooth adjustment by non-oil LDCs in the present environment are worse than in the 1970s because of the sharp increase of real oil prices; the worldwide recession; incomplete adjustment in many LDCs; very high interest rates, and the diminished ability of private banks to intermediate or recycle OPEC's surplus to deficit countries. Recycling in the aftermath of the second oil shock is becoming more difficult since non-oil LDCs' external deficit and debt have risen sharply; banks are reaching or approaching their prudential lending limits vis-à-vis the LDCs; and OPEC's surplus will probably be more lasting than in the mid-1970s.

Financing LDCs external balance-of-payments deficits will be more difficult in the aftermath of the second oil crisis and require innovative institutional initiatives. The commercial banking system will continue to play an important role in the recycling process, but it cannot assume complete responsibility for this task. The ever-rising external debt could destabilize the monetary system.

Some international banks are reportedly trying to reduce their commitments to LDCs, thereby pushing the indebted countries closer to default. If this development becomes widespread (and official financing on a sufficiently large scale is not forthcoming) it could create enormous difficulties for the global banking system. Alternative recycling mechanisms, including direct lending by OPEC or increased intermediation by official institutions, are necessary to alleviate the burden on the international banking system.

THE INTERNATIONAL BOND MARKET

DEFINITIONS.[42] Borrowing in the international bond market takes place either through public (67 percent of total) or private issuing of Eurobonds (also known as international bonds) and foreign bonds. The international bond market has expanded

EXHIBIT 14b   INTEREST RATES ON THE INTERNATIONAL MARKET

| | 1979 | 1980 | | | | | | | | | | |
	December	January	February	March	April	May	June	July	August	September	October	November
EUROCURRENCY MARKET[a]												
3-month deposits												
U.S. dollars in London	14.50	14.41	16.97	19.94	15.00	9.75	9.75	9.81	12.50	13.94	15.25	18.31
Sterling in London	16.88	17.81	18.63	18.69	17.25	17.25	17.13	15.44	16.75	15.81	17.13	14.59
Swiss francs in London	5.81	5.44	5.75	7.13	6.13	5.50	5.75	5.44	6.06	5.94	5.44	6.31
Deutsche marks in London	8.63	8.47	9.19	10.19	9.31	9.13	9.44	8.38	8.63	8.81	9.00	9.69
Guilders	13.90	11.48	12.05	11.46	10.76	11.14	10.70	10.08	10.09	10.50	9.73	9.63
French francs in London	14.25	12.81	14.38	14.25	12.84	12.75	12.50	11.94	12.13	12.63	11.31	11.38
Yen in London	7.75	8.59	10.63	15.56	12.81	12.75	12.31	12.31	11.75	12.00	9.88	10.50
6-month deposits												
1 U.S. dollars in London	14.62	14.41	16.97	19.69	14.12	10.06	10.00	10.00	12.62	13.87	15.00	17.12
12-month deposits												
1 U.S. dollars in London	12.94	13.87	16.50	17.94	13.16	10.06	9.94	10.25	12.62	13.62	14.31	15.68

INTERNATIONAL BOND MARKET[b] (secondary market yields)

DOLLAR-DENOMINATED BONDS												
With remaining maturity of 3 to 7 years												
—issued by private corporations	11.93	12.30	13.67	14.46	14.04	11.88	10.81	10.92	11.73	12.25	12.47	13.33
With remaining maturity of 7 to 15 years												
Issued by international organisations	11.66	12.09	13.33	13.67	13.21	12.02	11.63	11.67	12.10	12.54	12.62	13.10
Issued by the public sector	11.27	11.59	13.29	13.79	12.80	11.50	11.03	11.09	11.79	12.22	12.41	12.97
Issued by private corporations	11.53	11.77	13.20	13.69	13.06	11.87	11.23	11.22	11.89	12.66	13.25	13.54
DM-DENOMINATED BONDS												
With remaining maturity of 3 to 7 years												
Issued by international organisations	7.5	7.7	8.4	9.6	9.4	8.4	8.0	7.9	7.9	8.3	8.8	
Issued by the public sector	7.8	8.0	8.8	10.2	9.9	8.9	8.5	8.3	8.3	8.7	9.2	
Issued by private corporations	8.0	8.2	8.9	10.4	10.2	8.9	8.5	8.4	8.4	8.8	9.3	
With remaining maturity of 7 to 15 years												
Issued by international organisations	7.9	8.1	8.8	9.9	8.6	8.2	8.1	8.1	8.5	8.9	9.1	
Issued by the public sector	7.8	8.0	8.9	10.1	9.6	8.6	8.2	8.2	8.2	8.6	9.1	
Issued by the private corporations	7.7	7.9	8.8	10.1	9.8	8.8	8.3	8.2	8.1	8.6	9.0	
GUILDER-DENOMINATED NOTES												
(with remaining maturity of 3 years and over)	9.39	9.42	9.95	11.41	10.82	9.71	9.53	9.51	9.56	9.70	9.73	10.02
FRENCH FRANC-DENOMINATED BONDS												
(with remaining maturity of 7 to 15 years)	12.55	12.69	12.80	13.94	13.70	13.21	13.07	12.85	12.79	13.02	13.47	13.57

Source. OECD. *Financial Statistics Monthly*, part 1, Paris: OECD, December 1980, p. 30.

[a] Eurocurrency market: end of month rates (for the deposits in guilders; average daily rates).

[b] International bond market: average of rates calculated once a week.

from $4.5 billion in 1970 to $37 billion in 1979, of which $18 billion or 48 percent was Eurobonds and the balance of $19 billion, or 52 percent, was foreign bonds. The market in 1979 accounted for 35 percent of the total medium- and long-term credit raised in the Euromarkets, and provided an important source of credit for borrowers from all over the world, including industrialized countries (67 percent of total in 1979), OPEC (2 percent), non-OPEC less developed countries (9 percent), and international organizations and development institutions (12 percent), public and private sectors. Freedom from regulations has produced innovations and flexibility: Securities are available at fixed as well as floating rates and in various types and exchange denominations.

A summary of foreign and international Eurobond issuing by borrowing country or area, type of borrower, type of placement, market country, type of bond, purpose of borrowing, and currency denomination and maturity is given in Exhibits 12–15.

A Eurobond, or international bond, is a long-term security, underwritten by an international syndicate of banks (commercial, investment, or merchant) and marketed internationally in countries other than the country of the currency in which it is denominated. The issue is not subject to any national restrictions.

A Eurobond is denominated in a currency that is not necessarily that of either the borrower or the investors. Most bonds have been denominated in U.S. dollars (about 60 percent in 1979); however, in contrast to the Eurocurrency market, nondollar issues are of considerable importance (Deutsche Marks, 28 percent). Many investors have a preference for issues in a strong currency, presumably in the belief that the lower interest rate on these issues will be more than compensated for by the appreciation in capital value as the currency appreciates.

Eurobonds are issued in units of, or are equivalent to, $1000 each, and are always available in bearer form, thus preserving anonymity of ownership. Interest is paid free of taxes. In general, bonds tend to have longer maturity than Eurocurrency loans. Bond issues are for over 1 to 15 years life to maturity at fixed and floating rates of interest, whereas Eurocurrency loans are mainly available for shorter maturities, primarily at floating interest rates, which vary every three or six months.

A foreign bond is a long-term security issued by a borrower in the national capital market of another country (as distinct from a Eurobond, which is marketed internationally). Underwritten by a syndicate from one country alone and sold on that country's capital market, the bond is denominated in the currency of the country in which it is sold. Foreign bonds are usually available in bearer form, preserving anonymity of ownership. Normally interest is paid free of withholding tax to bond holders (not resident in the country of issue).

Dollar bonds issued by foreigners in New York are called Yankee bonds. These bonds are underwritten by an international syndicate managed by American banks and placed in the United States. They are subject to U.S. law and have to be registered with the SEC. Most Yankee bonds are sold in the United States, but anyone can acquire them.

THE EMERGENCE OF THE EUROBOND MARKET. Despite numerous international bonds issued during the inter-war period, the market's sharpest expansion occurred in the late 1950s and early 1960s. The development of the bond market since World War II has had three distinct phases: (1) an emerging period, 1958–1963; (2) the period of U.S. capital controls, 1963–1974; and (3) a maturing period, after 1974.[43]

The market expanded significantly after the introduction of the U.S. interest-

EXHIBIT 15   CURRENCY COMPOSITION OF EXTERNAL BOND OFFERINGS (IN PERCENT)

International Bond Offerings	1964–1968	1969–1973	1974–1977	1978–1979
U.S. dollar	82.8	63.6	60.8	54.2
Deutsche Mark	13.4	21.3	23.6	33.6
Canadian dollar	—	0.1	5.5	1.4
Netherland guilder	—	6.2	3.7	2.1
OPEC currencies	—	—	2.4	3.0
International units of account	1.8	2.8	2.;0	1.9
Pound sterling	1.6	1.1	0.5	1.7
French franc	0.4	3.1	0.7	1.4
Japanese yen	—	—	0.2	0.6
Other	—	1.8	0.6	0.1
Total	100.0	100.0	100.0	100.0
Foreign Bond Offerings				
United States	67.9	38.4	51.6	26.0
Switzerland	6.4	21.7	26.8	40.2
Japan	—	10.6	4.0	18.1
Germany	17.0	16.9	6.6	10.5
OPEC	0.5	3.1	7.0	0.7
Netherlands	0.7	0.4	2.0	1.2
Luxembourg	0.0	0.6	0.3	1.1
France	1.3	0.8	0.3	1.0
Belgium	0.6	2.7	0.6	0.7
Italy	2.1	2.2	0.2	—
United Kingdom	2.5	1.4	0.1	—
Other	1.0	1.2	0.5	0.5
Total	100.0	100.0	100.0	100.0

Source. OECD. "The Use of National Currencies for External Bond Issues," *Financial Market Trends,* Vol. XVI (1980), pp. 95–107.

equalization tax, and other balance-of-payments programs after 1963. The U.S. interest-equalization tax had a prohibitive effect on the American capital market, especially for potential bond issuers. The tax was levied on American buyers of all foreign shares, and it increased by maturity. To finance foreign direct investment and expansion abroad, U.S. multinational corporations raised funds offshore by selling bonds to investors holding dollars in Europe. They thus avoided the regulations and tapped a new source of funds. Non-U.S. borrowers also turned to European capital markets for credit.

An adverse U.S. tax and regulatory environment offered foreign banking institutions an opportunity to form underwriting syndicates to service major governments and international companies, which had previously satisfied their capital requirements on the New York market. In this period the Eurobond market developed as an alternative to New York as a source of capital funds.

The interest-equalization tax in the United States was reduced several times to 0 percent in 1974. It seems that a significant impetus for the market's growth was provided by U.S. capital control, but its continued existence does not depend upon it. The gradual abolition of controls allowed the foreign-bond-issue business to re-emerge in New York, but the Eurobond market, which was already well established, continued to expand in the new environment.

EUROBOND-MARKET CHARACTERISTICS.[44]   Borrowing in the Eurobond market in 1979 by category of borrowing country was led by industrialized countries, with $12.5 billion, or 71 percent of the total; international organizations, $2.8 billion, or 16 percent; and developing countries, $2.0 billion, or 11 percent. By country of borrower, the United States headed the list followed by Japan and Canada. Of the total Eurobond issuing, private entities accounted for 60 percent of the total, the public sector for 25 percent, and international organizations for the balance.

The international bond market is sensitive to currency movements, and in recent years it has experienced substantial currency diversification. Although the dollar remains the most significant currency (about 60 percent of the Eurobond market in 1979), the use of other currencies, particularly Deutsche Marks (28 percent), became widespread as investors attempted to diversify their portfolios. Other currencies of significance are the Canadian dollar (2.7 percent), French franc (2.2 percent), Kuwaiti dinar (2.2 percent), Dutch guilder (1.8 percent), and sterling (1.7 percent). Currency composites are also used, and in 1979 the European Unit of Account accounted for 1.7 percent of total Eurobond issues and SDRs accounted for 0.6 percent. Eurobonds are also issued in the form of multiple-currency bonds, parallel issues, and composite units of bonds.

Exhibits 14–15 show the currency composition of international bond issuing. The role of the U.S. dollar declined from 82.8 percent in 1964–1968 to 54.2 percent in 1978–1979. The Deutsche Mark's share increased from 13.4 percent to 33.6 percent during the same period. Other currencies have been used, however, to a limited extent.

Originally the Eurobond market was confined to the issuing of straight bonds, that is, securities without rights of conversion into a borrower's common stock, but since 1968 convertible debentures have also been issued, that is, fixed-interest securities convertible into the borrower's common stock on stipulated conditions. That option can be exercised between two dates fixed in the loan contract, at a fixed price. The difference between the price of ordinary shares at the time of the issue of the bonds and the rate at which they can be converted is the *convertible premium*. The attractiveness of convertible bonds is that there will be a rise in the price of the common stock during the period of the convertible bond's life, or an appreciation in the currency in which the common stock is quoted, or both. Convertible bonds provide a hedge against considerable erosion of their capital due to currency depreciation.

Convertible bonds with detachable warrants allow investors to purchase straight Eurodollar bonds with the option to purchase shares of the issuer's common stock. These options are called warrants. Almost all warrants may be detached from their bonds and traded freely in a secondary market, although they are not listed in Europe. When warrants are exercised, that is, converted into common shares, outside capital is usually used to buy the shares. This is different from a convertible bond; in that case it is the principal amount of the security itself that is used to purchase shares.

In 1979, 63 percent of all Eurobonds issues were straight bonds, 9 percent were convertible and warrant, and other types made up the balance.

By purpose of the borrower, about 32 percent of total Eurobonds in 1979 were issued by banks and financial entities, 22 percent by industry, 6 percent by public utilities, and the balance by transport, petroleum, and other such groups. In the same period, 40 percent of all Eurobonds had maturities of over 1 year to 7 years; 34 percent matured in 7–10 years; 23 percent matured between 10 and 15 years, and only 0.7 percent of all Eurobonds had longer maturities of 15–20 years.

Further growth of Eurobond issues depends on the market's capacity to absorb new issues and on the expansion of the secondary market, both of which give bonds a high liquidity and attract investors. Hence trading Eurobonds on the secondary market after floating an issue is of utmost significance. It satisfies investors' desire for liquidity, which induces demand for bonds.

Eurobonds are listed on a number of stock exchanges, including the Luxembourg Bourse, where there are special fiscal incentives and other concessions to attract foreign issues. A listing of the bonds on the Luxembourg or London stock exchanges is usually applied for since many institutional investors are not allowed by law or internal regulations to invest in unlisted bonds. Inasmuch as dollar bonds are often payable in New York and are deposited there, they are also listed on the New York Stock Exchange.

The secondary market assumes the form of active dealing between financial houses on their own accounts, to or from each other and to or from their clients. Buying and selling is carried out by telephone and telex between banks and brokers, mostly outside stock exchanges. As traders are no longer able to maintain active markets in all outstanding issues, lists are published to indicate those bonds in which they specialize as market makers.

The secondary market is made up of various types of investors, which may be classified into the following categories: (1) central banks, government agencies, and international financial institutions; (2) investment funds, pension funds, and insurance companies; (3) bank trust departments; (4) bank portfolios, and (5) retail investors.[45]

The identity of most Eurobond investors is confidential and unknown since the securities are in bearer form and no records are kept of their ownership. The 20 banks that act as syndicate leaders on the market hold some 25 percent of the Eurobonds that have been issued. More than 50 percent of the outstanding bonds are held by private customers. Institutional investors (e.g., investment trusts, pension funds and multinational corporations, insurance companies and monetary authorities) are holding some 25 percent of the outstanding Eurobonds.[46]

Eurobonds are priced on the basis of both fixed and floating interest rates. Issues with fixed interest rates and fixed maturities, "straight" bonds, represent the most important type. Short-term floating-interest-rate securities, floating-rate notes (FRNs), are also available. Some straight issues carry guarantees by a parent company for its foreign subsidiary if the latter acts as borrower in its own name, or by governments for the issues of public agencies' borrowing.

The FRN's rate of interest is set at 6 months LIBOR, adjusted semiannually, plus a spread, usually between 0.25 percent and over 1.0 percent. These securities are particularly attractive during periods of rising interest rates, when the issues of straight bonds are subject to capital depreciation. Moreover, during periods of tight monetary conditions, this instrument provides an alternative to bank credit.

The maturity of FRNs ranges from 4 to 10 years, but maturities are concentrated in the range of 5–7 years. The notes are typically callable after 2 or 3 years at par.

To protect investors against declining interest rates, an investor in FRNs normally receives a minimum rate below which the interest cannot fall. Floating-rate notes represent an increasing proportion of issuing on the Eurobond market. They are available in a number of currencies, but at a higher cost than straight Eurobonds.

The price at which bonds are sold on issue is normally expressed as a percentage of the bond's face value, which is usually $1000 in the Eurobond market. Par is the equivalent of face value; a sale price of 99½ means that the bond is sold at a discount for $995; quotations above 100 represent a premium over face value. Repayment at maturity is usually at face value, that is, 100 percent of the principal amount. The annual payment of interest is the same each year and it is expressed as a percentage of a bond's principal amount. For instance a $1000 bond with an 8 percent interest will pay an investor $80 per year. The interest payment is represented by a coupon, which must be clipped off each year and presented to an appointed paying agent for payment of interest.

The return, or yield to maturity, on a fixed-interest security is based on coupon price and its average remaining life. An 8 percent bond sold at par yields that return; it yields less than 8 percent if bought above par, and more than 8 percent if bought below par. Current yield is calculated by dividing the interest payment, or coupon, by the security price. For instance the current yield of an 8 percent coupon bond priced at 97½ percent is 8.2 percent (8 percent ÷ 97½ percent). Yield to maturity consists of interest from the coupon and capital gain from the difference between the discount price at the time of purchase and the repayment price at maturity (almost always 100 percent). Using this calculation method at a price of 97½ percent, an 8 percent 7-year bond yields approximately 8.50 percent, taking into account both the coupon and the 2½ percent capital gain that will be realized in seven years and amortized over that same period.[47] Exhibit 14 lists recent yields on the international bond market.

Eurobonds are exempt from taxes and yield a higher return than domestic bonds with the same maturities and currency. The issue cost incurred by the borrower is 2–2½ percent of the issue's principal amount and consists of management fee (⅜–½ percent), underwriting commission (⅜–½ percent), and placement fee or selling concession (1¼–1½ percent).

Eurobonds are placed by a lead bank manager and co-managers, which invite a great number of banks and brokers in a number of countries to participate in the placement of the issue either as underwriters or as members of the selling group. The underwriters undertake to provide a certain portion, ranging from 1.5 percent to 1 percent, of the issue's principal amount, depending whether they are major, submajor, or minor participants. The banks that act as underwriters receive the underwriting commission in addition to the selling concession, whereas the banks belonging to the management group (the lead manager and the co-managers) are also entitled to a management fee.

FOREIGN-BOND-MARKET CHARACTERISTICS.[48] Borrowing in the foreign bond market is concentrated in the industrialized countries ($11.5 billion, or 59 percent of total in 1979), followed by the international organizations ($5.7 billion, or 29 percent), and developing countries ($2 billion, or 10 percent).

By type of borrower, public entities accounted for the bulk of the issuing in 1979; central governments accounted for 32 percent of the market; state or local governments, 9 percent; public nonfinancial enterprises, 32.5 percent; and public financial institutions, 10 percent. Private nonfinancial enterprises issued 32.5 percent of total foreign bonds in 1979, whereas banks and other financial institutions accounted for 3 percent.

The issuing of foreign bonds in a specific market is affected by market conditions, particularly interest and exchange rates. In 1979 the most active market was Switzerland, with 46 percent of the total, followed by the United States, 24 percent.

By type of bond, in 1979 straight bonds accounted for 86 percent of the total, convertible and warrant for 9 percent, and various other types for the balance. By purpose of the borrower, international organizations headed the list with 29 percent of the total, followed by public and community service, 17 percent; industry, 17 percent; and public utilities, 6 percent.

Foreign bonds have long maturities, usually extending to 20 years. In 1979, 22 percent of all foreign bonds matured between 3 and 5 years; 19 percent in 5–7 years; 20 percent in 7–10 years; 18 percent in 10–15 years; 9 percent in 15–20 years, and the balance had longer maturities.

CONTROL OF THE EUROCURRENCY MARKET

The growing international interdependence of financial markets led to increased international cooperation in the area of supervision. International cooperation has been conducted on multilateral and regional levels. However, the division of responsibilities of national supervisory authorities is not too clear and it is a source of disputed interpretation, thereby reducing the effectiveness of existing agreements and allowing some banks to escape supervision.

Since the Euromarket operates with a minimum of regulation, demand for its control has been made on many occasions since its emergence, particularly during periods of international monetary problems. The rapid growth in recent years of the Eurocurrency market and international lending has raised three main issues concerning (1) its effects on global macroeconomic conditions (i.e., inflation, balance of payments, etc.), (2) its effects on domestic monetary independence (i.e., the ability of national authorities to control domestic money supply and credit), and (3) its effects on prudential management of international banking activity, including foreign branches and subsidiaries.[49]

Critics have charged that the Eurocurrency markets (1) created excessive expansion of world liquidity and international reserves, which in turn has caused inflation; (2) induced currency speculation and exchange-market instability by playing a role in the diversification of funds out of dollars into other currencies; (3) reduced the balance-of payments discipline or constraint on economic policies and induced inflation by making Eurocurrency credit available with limited conditionality (relatively easy credits enabled countries to postpone the adoption of necessary adjustment policies, including appropriate anti-inflationary measures, with a consequent spillover of inflation); and (4) diminished the effectiveness of domestic monetary policies and contributed to excessive growth of the world money supply, thus worsening world inflation.

The growing role of the Eurobanks in recycling OPEC surpluses and the consequent increase in Eurocurrency lending to non-oil less developed countries have been a source of major concern. In view of the lack of control over the Eurocurrency market, the relatively higher country risk, and the problems of capital adequacy of the Eurobanks, the problem of bank stability in the event of a large-scale default by borrowers has become acute.

Calls for control of the Eurobanks' operations and regulation of their activities have resulted from the above concerns. Accordingly, proposals aimed at controlling the activities have three objectives: (1) to improve global macroeconomic conditions, (2) to enhance the effectiveness of domestic monetary policies, and (3) to improve the stability of the international financial system. Usually government intervention in, or control of, the financial markets and the domestic banking system is designed to meet three main goals: (1) to control the domestic money and credit supply, (2) to maintain a stable banking system, and (3) to affect the allocation of credit.[50]

The rapid growth of the banks' international business has focused attention on a number of prudential problems, which include (1) the need for exercising effective control over banks' foreign subsidiaries, particularly where parent authorities do not supervise their banks on the basis of consolidated balance sheets and where supervisory arrangements in the countries in which the subsidiaries operate are inadequate; (2) the growth of banks' exposure vis-à-vis foreign countries, especially certain developing countries with substantial external indebtedness; (3) the banks' diminished profitability margins and the increase in the degree of maturity transformation; and (4) the weakened capital base of some banks.[51]

The central banks of the Group of Ten countries and Switzerland Committee on Banking Regulations and Supervisory Practices was established in 1974. The Committee aims to establish broad principles, with which all supervisory systems might conform in establishing their own arrangements. In addition, it was charged to search for a means of improving international early warnings systems of potential troubles in national banking systems, which might have international repercussions.

To maintain the soundness of the international banking and the world monetary systems, the governors of the BIS acted in three related areas: (1) lender-of-last-resort responsibilities; (2) information about market activities; and (3) excessive loan-risk concentration and prudent bank-management practices of international banking activities.

Last-resort-lending responsibilities are vital to prevent a banking panic in the event of a sudden withdrawal of deposits and a severe squeeze on liquidity. Default could have serious consequences if the national monetary authorities were not prepared to render aid and support. The central banks of eight European members of the BIS reached an agreement in July 1974 in Basle on lender of last resort for the Eurocurrency market in case of temporary liquidity problems. By the end of the year the United States, Japan, and some 30 additional countries agreed to subscribe to the Basle accord.

The agreement is based on the broad principle of parental responsibility, according to which banks are responsible for their overseas branches. The central bank of the parent bank also has an indirect responsibility for such overseas operations, and would provide emergency facilities for parent banks in the event of a temporary liquidity crisis. Consortium banks, which have multinational bank participation, would be bailed out on a pro rata basis by member parent banks. The latter would be backed by their own central banks.

The BIS agreement is unclear about who bears responsibility for losses or difficulties experienced by foreign subsidiaries of a bank. A subsidiary is legally an autonomous entity incorporated under the laws of the country in which it is located. The government of the parent company has no authority over foreign subsidiaries, and in the case of banks, these subsidiaries are often exempt from regulations by the host government as well. The issue of whose central bank is ultimately responsible to act as lender of last resort for bank subsidiaries is therefore unclear.

There is also doubt as to the ability and willingness of central banks to provide lender of last resort assistance on a coordinated basis. In fact, they are involved in a dispute over their regulatory responsibilities, due to differing interpretations of the Accord.

The main dispute concerns the question of the primary responsibility for supervision of the foreign branch, subsidiary or agency; is it the host or home country responsibility? Some central banks believe that the primary supervisory responsibility for foreign branches or subsidiaries rests with the host country's authorities, while others maintain that it depends on whether the foreign bank is a branch or subsidiary.

The Group of Ten Committee on Banking Regulations and Supervisory Practices has concluded that responsibility for supervising the liquidity of foreign branches must rest with the host supervisory authority, but a branch's liquidity cannot be judged wholly in isolation from that of its parent bank. This consideration brings its liquidity within the sphere of interest of the supervisory authority of the parent bank also. Although the legal position of foreign subsidiaries and joint ventures is different from that of foreign branches, the parent authorities cannot be indifferent to the moral responsibilities of parent institutions for ensuring that their offshoots do not default on their commitments. The division of supervisory responsibilities in relation to foreign banking establishments and the need for cooperation between host and parent supervisory authorities is further hampered by the prohibition of disclosing confidential information, etc.

In ensuring solvency, it was concluded that there must be some sharing of responsibility for supervision between host and home or parent supervisory authorities, with the emphasis varying according to the type of establishment concerned. For foreign subsidiaries and joint ventures, the primary responsibility must rest with the host authorities. However, parent authorities will need to take account of the exposure of parent banks, derived from their moral commitment to support their foreign offshoots.

The lender-of-last-resort agreement does not relieve the Eurobanks from the obligation to exercise prudence and restraint. Although, the central banks have assumed ultimate responsibility for the Euromarkets, the market participants continue to carry primary responsibility for the functioning of the Euromarkets, obliging them to adhere to prudent banking practices.

Recently the Group of Ten and Switzerland adopted the following measures to improve the supervision of banks' international operations: (1) the use of consolidated balance sheets as the basis for supervising banks to determine prudent portfolio management criteria and excessive loan-risk concentration; (2) the supervision of banks' country-risk-assessment procedures to improve the quality of credit and reduce risk; and (3) the monitoring of the their maturity transformation and capital adequacy.

Banks in these countries are subject to close supervision by the BIS Committee on Banking Regulations and Supervisory Practices regarding the above issues. The Committee helps ensure bank solvency and liquidity by promoting cooperation among the supervisory and regulatory authorities. It established guidelines concerning the division of responsibility between national authorities for the supervision of banks' foreign establishments, with the object of ensuring that no foreign banking establishment escapes supervision.

The Group of Ten and Switzerland have agreed to examine the development of international bank lending semi-annually on the basis of data collected by the BIS and to propose harmonized measures. A group of experts has been given the task of clarifying the technical details involved, with the aim of establishing a comprehensive reporting system on maturity transformation and exposure. This information will enable the central banks to assess the significance of the banks' international operations and will provide a framework for further cooperation. The European Community also provides a vehicle for international cooperation of banking supervision, and is promoting coordination of practices and schemes for the exchange of information.

International lending is increasingly carried out through foreign subsidiaries (because of the various advantages of operating offshore), rather than through the parent company or home office. There is full agreement on the necessity to enforce bank-supervision regulations on the basis of consolidated balance sheets for banks.

Proposed controls consider global management of international lending by banks on a coordinated basis. Accordingly, discussions considered imposition of direct controls in the form of capital deposits and loans ratios. One proposal calls for linking international lending to general ratios related to banks' own funds or capital adequacy on a consolidated basis.

The imposition of formal reserve requirements is another possibility that Eurobanks may have to confront, though it would seem highly unlikely that they will be implemented soon. To be effective they would have to apply in all Eurocenters and to all banks and even to nonbanking financial institutions.

The United States proposed that major market participants impose the same reserve requirements on offshore and onshore banking operations. It is recognized that effective measures can only be introduced jointly with other countries and that such measures must be based on a uniform assessment of these markets. Among the obstacles to the implementation of such a proposal is the fact that a number of countries that do not have minimum-reserve regulations would have to modify their national monetary-policy instruments accordingly.

To assess the validity and feasibility of the various arguments for controlling the Eurocurrency market, the proper framework for analyzing the market's mechanism and factors affecting its growth have to be identified. Aspects of particular relevance are the sources, nature, and effects of various policies on the market's growth.

The assessed impact of the Eurocurrency market on the domestic monetary sector is a controversial subject. The main issue is whether, and to what extent, the market's unregulated expansion of credit undermines national financial policies and generates more expansionary financial pressures than are desired.

The effect of the Eurocurrency market on domestic monetary management can be analyzed according to two different aspects, which depend on the interpretation of the market's process and nature. One interpretation of the market's process and effects regards its credit creation as an addition to domestic money and credit. Those using this approach commonly argue that the market has excessively expanded the total volume of the world's bank credit by creation of private and official international liquidity outside national governments' control. The alternative approach views the markets as a substitute for domestic liquidity.

Although the interpretation using either approach remains controversial and depends on the framework of analysis, it is now widely accepted that there is relatively little credit creation in the market.

Initial international agreement on international banking supervision has been reached, but formal regulations of banking activities have not been agreed upon. The agreement on the lender of last resort provided a significant addition of confidence. Controls will be effective only if they apply to all countries; otherwise they stand little chance of being either adopted or effective. In the absence of worldwide agreement, any governments' attempts to impose direct controls on the currency market would result in Eurobanking business shifting either to a different jurisdiction or to a different group of Eurobanks.

The Eurocurrency market performs a significant and valuable function of intermediation in the international money and capital markets. Attempts to regulate it by imposition of controls could have worldwide ramifications and adversely affect the flow of international credit and capital. Opponents of controls argue that the Eurocurrency market is already subject to sufficient national monetary authorities' influence in several ways: They affect domestic monetary conditions; they regulate and supervise banks headquartered and located in their respective countries; and they often regulate their residents' participation in the market through exchange and monetary controls. Thus additional controls are not necessary.

In conclusion, the most-likely developments in the Eurocurrency market in the near future are some agreement on reserve requirements and capital adequacy, and increased reporting requirements.

SUMMARY AND PROSPECTS

Unsettled international economic conditions—both cyclical and structural—create an unfavorable environment for the international financial market. Following two decades of rapid expansion of the world financial markets, we are now experiencing a consolidation process. The system lacks a sustainable mechanism to recycle OPEC's surpluses, and there is no near-term prospect for establishing one.

Multinational banks carry a heavy burden in recycling OPEC's surpluses. But their continued role is becoming increasingly difficult as international payments diseqilibriums persist and less developed countries' external debts expand. Against this background, the ever-growing non-OPEC less developed countries' demand for credit and debt is a major source of potential disturbances.

There is widespread agreement on the need to preserve the safety and soundness of the Eurobanks, but discussions concerning the imposition of controls on the Euromarkets have been controversial. The disagreement concerns whether there is a need for control and the method of applying it. Regardless whether formal controls are adopted, faced by a rapidly expanded LDCs external debt, banks' supervisory authorities have increased their involvement in the market to keep abreast of market developments and protect their domestic banking systems. Lending to LDCs in the future will be greatly affected by regulatory requirements which could reduce the amount of bank credit flowing to those areas. Presently a greater monitoring of the Eurocurrency markets is already taking place, combined with exchange of information.

Attempts to regulate the Eurocurrency market could have worldwide ramifications and could adversely affect the flow of international capital and credit. Eurobanks' more-cautious lending combined with heavy involvement with the less developed countries would diminish the banks' role in the recycling process. This in turn could increase the risk of widespread defaults unless alternative channels were constructed.

The U.S. dollar is the most significant international currency, but its relative role has declined over the past two decades. Other currencies are gradually assuming a greater role, thereby contributing toward the evolution of a multiple-reserve currency system and currency blocs, along the major currencies and the existing regional economic organizations. In addition, the reemergence of gold as an international reserve is well underway.

Evidence shows that in the major countries the exchange system is becoming more stable and disturbances have diminished. It is now recognized that the role of the foreign-exchange rate in the adjustment mechanism is limited; it has to be supplemented by appropriate economic policies, and it occurs after a considerable time lag.

The trend toward greater supervision and control of financial institutions is designed to achieve a greater degree of monetary and prudential control and to restore a greater degree of competitive equity. American efforts to regain international financial competitiveness and equality could lead to a proliferation of offshore financial centers in the United States and around the world. This, combined with likely controls on the Eurocurrency market, could affect the international flow-of-funds pattern.

"Offshore" banking facilities in the United States could provide an impetus for shifts in the geographic locations of markets, and have significant effects on the international banking system and money and capital markets. They could attract international business of American banks and nonbanks that is now conducted abroad because domestic business is subject to higher tax rates and the Federal Reserve regulations.

Events are now moving toward the reemergence of New York as a leading international and Eurocurrency financial center. IBFs in New York will attract business primarily from Nassau and other financial centers in the Carribean, which are in the same time zone, but to a smaller extent from London. Preliminary estimates suggest that by the end of this decade, the business volume of the New York City banks could equal that of London.

NOTES AND SOURCES

1. Poniachek, H.A. "The Role of Gold in the Global Economy," *The Money Manager,* Vol. IX, No. 10 (1980), pp. 12 and 21.
2. The IMF unified and simplified effective January 1, 1981, the currency basket that determines the value of, and the interest rate on, the SDR. The weights for the revised SDR valuation and interest rate basket are as follows: U.S. dollar, 42 percent; Deutsche Mark, 19 percent; Franch franc, 13 percent; Japanese yen, 13 percent; pound sterling, 13 percent. The weights for the five currencies reflect the relative importance of these currencies in international trade and finance, based on the values of the exports of goods and services of the members issuing these currencies and the amounts of their currency officially held by members of the Fund over the five years 1975–1979.

   Until mid-1974 the SDR was fixed in terms of gold. Since July 1, 1974, the IMF has been using a new method of valuing the SDR in terms of currencies. From mid-1978 to the end of 1980, a 16-currency basket based on 16 countries that had the largest share in the world export of goods and services in the five-year period from 1972 to 1976 had been used for the valuation of the SDR. The currency composition of the basket will be adjusted at five-year intervals.

At noon each business day, the Fund values the currency components of this basket at their U.S. dollar middle rates in the London exchange market; in the case of yen, at the Tokyo rate. The sum of the U.S. dollar equivalents of the currency components yields the rate for the SDR in terms of the U.S. dollar. Exchange rates for the SDR in terms of other currencies, as used in Fund operations and transactions, are ascertained by the IMF from the "representative" market exchange rates of these currencies for the U.S. dollar.

3. IMF. *Annual Report of Exchange Arrangements and Exchange Restrictions.*

4. "Exchange Rates and Exchange Arrangements, March 31, 1980," IMF Survey, April 21, 1980.

5. IMF. *Annual Report of Exchange Arrangements and Exchange Restrictions.*

6. Ibid.

7. Poniachek, op cit.

8. Ibid.

9. An eligible value date must be a business day in the home countries of the currencies transacted. For a spot transaction on Monday, value date would be Wednesday, on Tuesday it would be Thursday, etc. Whenever there are ineligible days, e.g., weekends, the value date moves forward to the next eligible business day. For a spot transaction on Thursday the value date would be Monday, and on Friday it would be Tuesday.

10. Gerakis, A.S. "Resort to Forward Exchange Transactions Arises from Fluctuations in Currency Rates," *IMF Survey,* Vol. VIII, No. 9 (1979), pp. 105–107.

11. Kubarych, R.M. *Foreign Exchange Markets in the United States,* New York: Federal Reserve Bank of New York, 1978.

12. Giddy, I.H. "Measuring the World Foreign Exchange Market," *Columbia Journal of World Business,* Vol. XIV, No. 4 (1979), pp. 36–48.

13. Nakamura, T. "The Test of a Currency Is Who Trades in It," *Euromoney,* Vol. (1980), pp. 168–172.

14. Heller, H.R. "The International Role of the Dollar: An Analysis of Long-Term Trends" Bank of America memo. San Francisco, May 1980.

15. Nakamura, op. cit.

16. Giddy, op. cit. and Group of Thirty. *Foreign Exchange Markets Under Floating Rates.* New York: Group of Thirty, 1980. Alternative estimates by commercial and official banking sources suggested that global foreign-exchange trading in 1977 amounted to $30–50 trillion. Heller suggested a $60–70 trillion trade volume for 1978.

17. Federal Reserve Bank of New York. *Survey No. 1371.* New York: FRBNY, June 23, 1980. The 90 banking institutions surveyed account for virtually all currency transactions in the U.S. interbank market, whereas the 11 brokers account for all brokered foreign-exchange activities in the U.S. market. The 90 banks are composed of large money-center and regional domestic commercial banks and several branches operating separately in foreign-exchange operations, Edge Act corporations, and U.S. branches and agencies of foreign banks.

18. The effective exchange rate is an index that shows the change in any currency against those of its major trading partners. It measures a currency's performance vis-à-vis other currencies and reflects trends in international competitiveness. Effective exchange rates have gained broad acceptance in formulation of official exchange-rate policies.

Effective exchange indexes have been developed by the IMF, U.S. Treasury, Federal Reserve Board, Morgan Guaranty Trust Company, The U.K. Treasury, and others. The various indexes vary in the number of countries and the statistical approach.

A weighted-average index involves the multiplication of index numbers by weights and summation of these components. Indexes of effective exchange rates are based on weights for the various currencies that approximate the relative importance of the partner currencies. The most widely used weighting systems are (1) *multilateral*, in which each currency is weighted in proportion to the partner country's share in world trade or trade among the industrial countries; and (2) *bilateral*, in which the weights are proportional to each partner's bilateral share of the country's trade.

19. Calculations of the effective exchange rates based on the IMF multilateral-exchange-rate model (MERM) are as follows. The implicit weighting structure takes account of the relative importance of a country's trading partners in its bilateral relationships with them, of competitive relationships with "third countries" in particular markets, and of estimated elasticities affecting trade flows. Changes in effective exchange rates derived from the MERM may differ from estimated effective-exchange-rate changes based on changes in trade-weighted exchange-rate indexes for which the relative importance of the exchange-rate changes of particular countries is measured in terms of these countries' shares in bilateral trade of the country in question. An additional index of interest is the real effective-exchange-rate index, which is calculated by adjusting the effective exchange index by the weighted inflation rate (i.e., inflation differentials weighted by the same weights that are used in deriving the effective exchange rates). Real effective-exchange-rate indexes provide an analytical instrument for evaluating the degree to which purchasing-power-parity is reflected in the exchange rate. See Caves, D.W. and E.L. Feige. "Efficient Foreign Exchange Markets and The Monetary Approach to Exchange-Rate Determination," *The American Economic Review,* March (1980), pp. 120–134.

20. Artus, J.R. "Methods of Assessing the Longer-Run Equilibrium Value of an Exchange Rate," *Finance & Development,* Vol. 15, No. 2 (1978), pp. 26–28.

21. Isard, P. *Exchange Rate Determination: A Survey of Popular Views and Recent Models.* Princeton Studies in International Finance, No. 42. Princeton: International Finance Section, Department of Economics, Princeton University, 1978.

22. Dufey, G. and I.H. Giddy. *The International Money Market.* Englewood Cliffs, NJ: Prentice-Hall, 1978.

23. Antus, op. cit.

24. Keran, M.W. "The Value of the Yen," Paper presented at American Enterprise Institute Conference on The International Monetary System Under Stress, Washington, DC, February 28–29, 1980.

25. *Federal Reserve Bulletin, Treasury and Federal Reserve Foreign Exchange Operations,* various issues.

26. The data in this section are based on the Bank for International Settlements annual reports if not otherwise stated.

27. Dufey and Giddy, op. cit. The net size includes, within the reporting European area, foreign-currency liabilities due to (1) nonbanks, both resident and nonresident, and (2) banks. The latter includes (1) deposits by official monetary institutions of the reporting area, (2) funds converted by reporting banks from domestic funds into foreign currencies and deposited in Eurobanks, (3) foreign-currency funds obtained by the reporting banks from nonresident banks or nonbanks, which are treated as end uses or suppliers of funds.

28. See Poniachek, H.P. *Monetary Independence Under Flexible Exchange Rates.* Lexington, MA: Lexington Books, 1979; and "Alternative Definitions of Money in an Open Economy; The Case of West Germany," *Kredit Und Kapital,* Heft I (1980), pp. 1–20.
Money has three functions as a means of payment, store of value, and unit of account. Whereas only currency and demand deposits serve the means-of-payment function, the store-of-value function is performed by a wide range of financial assets (e.g., CDs, saving deposits, etc.).

29. Swoboda, A.K. *Credit Creation in the Euromarket: Alternative Theories and Implication for Control.* New York: Group of Thirty, 1980.

30. Ibid.

31. Ibid, as reported in Niehans, J. and J. Hewson. "The Eurodollar Market and Monetary Theory," *Journal of Money, Credit and Banking,* Vol. VIII (1976), pp. 1–27.

32. Swoboda, op. cit.

33. Niehans and Hewson, op. cit.

34. Swoboda, op. cit.

35. McCarthy, I. "Offshore Banking Centers: Benefits and Costs," *Finance & Development,* Vol. XVI, No. 4 (1979), pp. 45–48.

36. Hodjera, Z. "Asian Currency Market," *IMF Survey,* Vol. VII, No. 14 (1978), pp. 218–221.

37. The data on the various loans and borrowing characteristics are based on World Bank, *Borrowing in International Capital Markets,* unless otherwise indicated.

38. Fleming, A.E. and S.K. Howson. "Conditions in the Syndicated Medium-Term Euro-credit Market," *Bank of England Quarterly Bulletin,* Vol. XX, No. 2 (1980), pp. 311–323.

39. Adopted from Goodman, L.S. "The Price of Syndicated Eurocurrency Credit," *FRBNY Quarterly Review,* Vol. XV, No. 2 (1980), pp. 39–49.

40. Ibid.

41. Adopted from Goodman, ibid.

42. The data for this section were adopted or calculated from World Bank, *Borrowing in International Capital Markets,* op. cit., if not otherwise indicated.

43. Frowen, S.F. ed. *A Framework of International Banking.* London: Guildford Educational Press, 1979.

44. The data for this section are based on World Bank, op. cit, if not otherwise indicated.

45. Fisher, III, F.C. *The Eurodollar Bond Market.* London: Euromoney Publications, 1979.

46. Swiss Bank.

47. Adopted from Fisher, op. cit.

48. The data were adopted and calculated from the World Bank, op. cit.

49. Bank for International Settlements, *Fiftieth Annual Report,* Basle, 1980. Wallich, H.C. "Why the Euromarket Needs Restraint," *The Columbia Journal of World Business,* Vol. XIV, No. 3 (1979), pp. 17–24.

50. Swoboda, op. cit.

51. BIS, op. cit.

INTERNATIONAL COMMERCIAL BANKING

CONTENTS

GLOBAL ASPECTS 3

Role of National Banking Systems 3
What Is International Commercial
Banking? 4

DEVELOPMENT OF U.S.
INTERNATIONAL BANKING 6

Stages of Development 6
  Long view 6
  Short view 7

ORGANIZATIONAL STRUCTURES 8

Organizational Forms 8
Foreign Banking in the United States 12

OPERATIONAL ASPECTS 13

INTERNATIONAL LENDING AND
EUROCREDITS 14

  Amount of Bank Lending 14
  Risk Evaluation 15
  Problems and Issues 17

INTERNATIONAL BANKING AND THE
THIRD WORLD 17

Serving the Needs of Developing
Countries 17
Access to International Capital 18

REGULATORY ASPECTS 18

SOURCES AND SUGGESTED
REFERENCES 19

INTERNATIONAL COMMERCIAL BANKING

Francis A. Lees

The past three decades have witnessed the most extensive and penetrating expansion of international banking in world financial history. Although led by the overseas expansion of American banks, this growth has spread to the banks and banking systems of other countries as well. The development of international banking has contributed to the evolution of national financial markets in developing as well as industrial countries. More important, it has established firm linkages between the financial markets of all nations, and these linkages in turn have evolved into full-fledged international financial market sectors.

Whereas the early development of international banking was related primarily to the need to finance export-import trade and provide short-term credit facilities, subsequent stages of growth have witnessed the introduction of new international money-market instruments—dollar certificates of deposit (CDs) in London and complex syndicated-loan agreements. The ability to arbitrage funds through the international money markets has been enhanced by the growing activities of international banks. Moreover, international banks have become more innovative in finding ways to borrow as well as lend internationally mobile funds.

GLOBAL ASPECTS

ROLE OF NATIONAL BANKING SYSTEMS. A discussion of the growth of international commercial banking inevitably begins with an examination of national banking systems and their banks, which furnish the basic building blocks. Several national banking systems have taken the lead in providing international commercial banking services, whereas other nations have been avid consumers. What makes a country prominent in international banking? Why are some countries more successful exporters of foreign banking representation, whereas others tend to attract foreign banking representation?

Although we do not yet have a definitive theory of international comparative advantage to explain why and how some countries export and others import international banking services, we can point to a number of factors that enter into determining how important any single country will be in providing international banking services. These include the importance of that country as a source of lendable funds, the strength of the country's currency, the size and importance of export-import trade, and the size and managerial efficiency of its banking institutions. In addition, a number of less-tangible factors enter into the picture in influencing international banking leadership. These include the degree and type of cooperation provided by government agencies and the national attitude toward banking (liberal, tolerant, or populist).

Comparative statistics for the 10 leading countries in international banking are contained in Exhibit 1. At the top of the listing are the United States and the United Kingdom. These countries play a leading role in international banking because of their substantial position in world export-import trade, the prestige of their financial institutions, and their lead in foreign investment. New York and London have long enjoyed a special role as leading international financial and banking centers. The remaining eight countries play a somewhat different role in international banking.

West Germany has developed into a leading international banking country by means of its strong currency; rapid expansion in foreign trade; balance-of-payments surpluses, which permit foreign investment and foreign bond issue activity; and an inflow of foreign business investment. By contrast, Japan's status in international banking can be associated with extensive offshore borrowing by Japanese banks to finance rapid expansion in foreign trade. Moreover, Japan's capital market was closed to foreign borrowers until fairly recently. Part of the success of Japan's international banks has been due to the support of government agencies and the central bank and close coordination of overseas activities between the nonbanking business sector and the large banks.

In contrast with Japan, the Canadian banks have built a substantial foreign-exchange and international-banking business based on their open economy (exports are 25 percent of GNP), substantial capital inflows from U.S. business investment and sale of bonds in New York, and development of a substantial organization of overseas branches and agencies. Canadian banks hold a large amount of foreign-currency assets as a reserve against foreign-currency liabilities.

Switzerland's status in international banking reflects a well-developed and efficiently managed financial market mechanism, a conservatively-managed monetary system, and the stable value of the Swiss franc in world currency markets. The Swiss have attracted nonresident funds by their adroit and successful portfolio investments at home and overseas. Overseas representation of Swiss banks is moderate, but is directed along the lines of greatest efficiency.

The remaining four countries represented in Exhibit 1 also play an important role in international banking. This is based upon relatively open economies (column 1), substantial volumes of foreign trade (column 2), significant holdings of official reserves, and prominence of their banks in the Eurocurrency market.

WHAT IS INTERNATIONAL COMMERCIAL BANKING?   International commercial banking has become a complex part of global financial relationships. Two decades ago it would have been possible to consider international commercial banking to include three essential activities: foreign-trade finance, overseas lending, and foreign-exchange trading. This relatively narrow definition is no longer valid. International commercial banking now functions as a separate system, in part operating above and beyond the national banking systems from which major international banks have evolved and grown. Using a Darwinian analogy, international commercial banking

EXHIBIT 1 PRINCIPAL FACTORS RELATING TO INTERNATIONAL BANKING ROLE OF MAJOR COUNTRIES[a]

	Openness to International Trends (exports divided by GNP)	Merchandise Export 1979[b]	Foreign Bond Issue[b]	Eurobonds by Currency	Official Reserves[b]	Eurocurrency Deposits in Banks[b]	Home-Currency Banking Liabilities to Nonresidents[b]	Number of Banks in Top 100 in World
U.S.	10%	182	4.6	12.6	18.0	2.3	128.5	15
U.K.	29	91	—	—	17.6	281.8	19.2	5
Germany	26	172	5.4	3.6	42.0	23.4	54.3	12
Japan	10	102	3.1	—	17.8	46.6	3.8	24
Switzerland	34	27	9.0	—	12.2	30.7	7.4	3
Canada	25	58	—	0.4	3.2	29.6	3.1	5
France	20	101	—	—	23.8	99.6	6.6	8
Italy	24	72	—	—	19.3	35.2	2.9	8
Netherlands	47	64	0.1	0.5	10.1	44.5	10.8	3
Belgium	51	56	—	—	7.6	43.5	6.5	5

Sources. IMF, *International Financial Statistics;* Bank of International Settlements, *Annual Reports;* Bank of England, *Quarterly Bulletin;* Morgan Guaranty Trust Co., *World Financial Markets.*

[a]All data is for 1979, except for column 5, which applies to 1980.
[b]Data in billions of U.S. dollars.

is a new species, with essential chromosome and genetic characteristics not to be found in its ancestors.

What are the unique genetic characteristics of modern-day international commercial banking that are not to be found in the large domestic banks of the older era of banking? Three distinct features characterize modern international commercial banking, as follows:

1. International commercial banking has developed to a point where it now operates within international financial markets, which in turn depend on international banking activities for their sustenance. These include the Eurocurrency, Eurobond, and global foreign-exchange markets.

2. International commercial banking services the multinational corporation. This has required that international banks develop special servicing for the multinational corporation, such as funds positioning and money transfer.

3. International commercial banking has extended itself into investment-banking activities. For American banks this is a notable achievement in light of federal banking laws prohibiting the mix of commercial and investment banking. This separation is not characteristics in other national banking systems.

DEVELOPMENT OF U.S. INTERNATIONAL BANKING

STAGES OF DEVELOPMENT.   Analysis of the stages of development of international banking can focus on the long view or on a shorter time perspective. In the discussion that follows we begin with a long view, and then shift our attention to shorter time periods.

Long View.   A long view of the development of international banking would focus on the hundred years prior to 1914 as a historical phase offering expanding opportunities, followed by a shorter three-decade period (1914–1945) in which international banking suffered retrogression. Following this retrogression period, international banking has enjoyed expanding opportunities for over 3½ decades (1945–1981).

The hundred years prior to 1914 witnessed rapid expansion of world trade, a gradual extension of the role of the international gold standard supported by a stable gold–pound-sterling relationship, and the acceleration of European investment into other parts of the world. As Herbert Feis (1930) has described so well in his study, Europe and particularly Britain had become the world's banker:

> Half a hundred types of financial institutions played a part in the process of investment of British capital. The huge commercial banks, where most checking accounts were kept, which financed commodity movements throughout the world, were the greatest source of credit, yet they played but an indirect part in the security issue business. Alongside of them stood the banks, public and private, of the British Dominions. These, growing to power, kept establishments in London to employ their funds, to share in the profits of trade financing, to handle governmental financial affairs.

> There were few governments in the world to which the English people did not make a loan, few corners in which some enterprise was not financed from London. The spread of English commerce, the almost universal range of the British-owned foreign banks, the huge extension of the colonial domain made it natural that British foreign investment should be widely scattered.

World War I and the currency disturbances that followed as an aftermath of hostilities brought an end to the expansion period of international banking. The pound-sterling–gold link was broken, foreign-investment flows were interrupted, and world-trade relationships were thrown out of balance. The world depression of the 1930s and World War II prevented any serious rebirth of international banking until the late 1940s and after. The third period, after 1945, brought with it a gradual expansion of international banking activity, but this expansion was largely confined to the trade-financing aspect until the 1960s. Beginning around 1960 international commercial banking enjoyed a dynamic expansion.

Short View. International commercial banking has not developed in a vacuum. Its expansion has been nurtured by its surroundings, and in turn by its own growth it has modified its own environment. Insofar as the postwar expansion of international banking is concerned, we can distinguish at least four distinct environmental periods, within which the pattern and pace of international banking expansion has varied according to the environment and conditions in the world economy. These periods may be described as follows:

1. *Dollar shortage, 1946-57.* At the conclusion of the World War II, the United States was the only major country that could supply the rest of the world with virtually unlimited amounts of capital goods and consumer products for export. During the decade after 1945, the world was preoccupied with European reconstruction and reviving world trade. The dollar was much in demand because of the scarcity of merchandise for export outside the United States. Dollar credits were much in demand, since other countries had limited opportunities to earn dollars by exporting. By contrast these countries needed U.S. goods. As a result U.S. banks enjoyed a highly favored position in financing the U.S. export-import trade and in providing short-term dollar credits to overseas customers. There was little effective competition from banks outside the United States, since these institutions did not have ready access to hard currencies for loan and foreign-trade financing activities. A world dollar shortage persisted over much of this time period, which gave American banks a decided advantage in rebuilding and strengthening their international correspondent banking networks, and in competing in a growing market for financing export-import trade.

2. *Convertibility and early expansion, 1958–1963.* In 1958 virtually all of the Western European nations declared their currencies convertible for nonresident account. This signaled a return to normalcy insofar as international currency and foreign-exchange-market conditions were concerned. Normalcy in foreign-exchange markets implied more-stable conditions in the markets for goods and services, and the ability of many Western European countries to achieve reasonable balance-of-payments equilibrium. Foreign-trade financing became more competitive as European banks regained the ability to deal more freely in foreign-exchange markets. However, new opportunities for expansion were made available as the newly formed Common Market attracted massive American business investments requiring U.S.-bank financing and servicing. Head-office lending to European and other borrowers provided additional opportunities for U.S. banks to expand their international-loan portfolios.

3. *U.S. capital controls, 1964–1973.* U.S. balance-of-payments problems in the early 1960s led to a series of controls over capital outflows. These were designed to achieve a strengthening of the U.S. balance of payments. Three types of controls were applied including (1) an Interest Equalization Tax (IET) on purchases of foreign securities by American investors, (2) restrictions on U.S. direct-business-investment outflows, and (3) restrictions on U.S. bank lending abroad. These controls accentuated the demand for funds outside the United States, leading to more-rapid development of the Euromarkets. Moreover, they furnished incentives for American banks to establish offshore branches from which rising foreign loan demand could be fed. European banks responded to the challenge by establishing Eurocurrency operations and expanding their Eurobond-underwriting capacities. The international currency crises of 1971 and 1973 led to devaluation of the dollar and a floating-rate currency regime, basically altering the ground rules of international banking.

4. *Petrodollar and currency instability, 1974–1981.* The quadrupling of oil prices in 1973–1974 by the OPEC countries brought opportunities as well as challenges for international banks. U.S. authorities removed the capital controls to facilitate petrodollar recycling through U.S. financial markets. Sizeable payments surpluses of oil-exporting countries required deposit and investment management facilities, which international bankers were agreeable to provide. Competition for petrodollar deposits has been a watchword of international banking since 1974. At the same time international bankers were pressed to find profitable loan and investment outlets for these funds. As a result, the medium-term Eurocurrency lending market expanded, in large part related to the escalation in lending to nonoil developing countries. Bank regulatory agencies in the United States and other countries have maintained a close surveillance of this lending because of its pivotal position in world financial relationships, as well as its importance to the soundness of national banking systems whose banks are participants in this form of lending. In this period the expansion of American bank branches overseas slowed down. By contrast, this period witnessed a sharp growth in the representation of foreign banks in the United States.

ORGANIZATIONAL STRUCTURES

ORGANIZATIONAL FORMS. International banks developing their overseas activities have a range of organizational structures to choose from including correspondent-bank relationships, representative offices, overseas branches, agencies or subsidiary companies. Most major banks maintain correspondent banking relationships with local banks in the countries in which they are developing business contacts. This reciprocal, or two-way, relationship includes placement of deposits as well as performance of services. A foreign correspondent is expected to accept drafts, honor letters of credit, provide credit information, and render other services for the U.S. bank at the other end of the relationship. The reciprocal nature of the relationship mandates "equivalent abilities and status," which must be broadly interpreted. Neither of the correspondent banks in a relationship maintains its own personnel in the other country. Therefore, direct costs are minimal. Benefits include access to banking services in a country in which the U.S. banks' own customers require good execution of banking and financial services. Correspondent relationships suffer from certain disadvantages, including the inability to control performance of services and transactions with certainty, the lack of status and prestige from direct representation in the country, and the inability to accept deposits in the country where correspondent banking relationships are used.

Often a bank relying heavily on foreign correspondents to render services in a given country will establish a representative office. Essentially, a representative office helps the parent bank to serve clients who conduct business in that country. A representative office is not a banking office as such, and cannot accept deposits, make loans, deal in drafts, or cash checks. Representative offices provide direct contacts in the country that can put parent-bank customers in contact with local government officials or local businessmen. In addition, they can provide credit information and analysis, and information concerning local business and economic trends. A representative office may be the first step toward establishing a full branch, or the only alternative in countries that prohibit general banking offices of nonresident banks.

The overseas branch is an integral part of the parent bank, backed up by the resources and lending power of the total organization. A branch does not have a separate corporate charter, does not issue ownership shares, and does not enjoy a separate legal status. Although it maintains its own accounts and sets of books, its financial policies are basically part of the parent organization. American banks have relied heavily on the branch form of organization in their postwar overseas expansion. This is due to the many advantages it provides, including the full credit backing of the parent, the ability to attract corporate customers by use of the parent name and identity, and direct management control. Branches are usually simpler to organize than subsidiary companies. However, the profits of overseas branches are subject to immediate taxation in the home country.

In the period June 1972 to June 1980 the assets of foreign branches increased from $69.6 billion to $376.7 billion. At the later date 73 percent of these assets were denominated in U.S. dollars. Close to 35 percent of foreign-branch assets were located in branches in the United Kingdom. Foreign-branch assets represent close to 27 percent of the total assets in the U.S. banking system. Basic balance-sheet data for all overseas branches of U.S. banks are presented in Exhibit 2. In 1979 U.S. banks were operating 779 overseas branches (Exhibit 3).

Some local jurisdictions permit the representation of a foreign bank through an agency. The agency resembles a branch, with the exception that deposits cannot be accepted. New York State banking law provides for foreign-bank representation by agencies, and a number of these units carry out extensive trade-financing activities and money-market operations. California also provides for agency representation, and it is possible for these units to accept foreign-source but not domestic-source (U.S.), deposits.

Subsidiary corporations are used extensively in international banking. At least three basic types can be isolated from the point of view of American banks: the Edge Act corporation, the foreign-incorporated bank, and the foreign-incorporated nonbank finance company.

Foreign banking subsidiaries provide direct, grass-roots representation. Often banking subsidiaries incorporated in the host country appear to be local in character, and can attract a base of resident clientele. Local management can give a foreign banking subsidiary greater access to the local business base. A special type of sub-

EXHIBIT 2   AGGREGATE BALANCE SHEET OF FOREIGN BRANCHES OF U.S. BANKS, JUNE 1980 (BILLIONS OF U.S. DOLLARS)

Assets			Liabilities		
Claims on U.S.		29.1	To U.S.		76.3
On parent bank	18.5		Parent bank	30.9	
Claims on foreigners			Other U.S. banks	12.4	
Other branches of parent bank		76.1	Nonbanks	32.9	
Banks		132.6	To foreigners		72.1
Public borrowers		25.6	Other branches of parent banks		127.7
Nonbank foreigners		95.9	Official institutions		34.1
Other assets		17.5	Nonbank foreigners		50.7
			Other liabilities		15.9
Total		376.88	Total		376.88

Source. Board of Governors of the Federal Reserve System.

EXHIBIT 3   GROWTH IN FOREIGN BRANCHES AND INTERNATIONAL BANKING CORPORATIONS 1971–1979

	Number		Total Assets (billions of dollars)	
	Foreign Branches	Section 25 & 25(a) Corporations	Foreign Branches	Section 25 & 25(a) Corporations
1971	577	85	55.1	5.5
1972	627	92	72.1	6.1
1973	699	103	108.8	6.9
1974	732	117	127.3	10.1
1975	762	116	145.3	9.1
1976	731	117	174.5	11.1
1977	738	122	205.0	13.4
1978	761	124	232.0	14.8
1979	779	132	290.0	16.3

Source. Board of Governors of the Federal Reserve System.

sidiary bank, the consortium bank, has been utilized. Organized as a joint venture, generally three or more international banks hold ownership in consortium banks. Consortium banks are generally headquartered in London or Luxembourg and engage primarily in medium-term Eurocurrency lending.

Foreign nonbank subsidiaries are organized for two basic purposes. In countries that restrict or prohibit foreign ownership of banking institutions, nonbank companies permit the conduct of near-banking activities including loan, factoring, leasing, consumer-credit, and money-market operations. Where foreign-owned banking is permitted, it may be desirable to establish nonbank finance companies to take advantage of opportunities that are profit generators or that are better separated from the traditional banking operation.

Edge Act corporations are chartered in the United States by the federal government. They provide American banks with the opportunity to conduct international banking activities in locations other than the states in which the banks are organized to operate. For example, Chicago banks that cannot branch outside of the state of Illinois can operate Edge Act subsidiaries in New York, California, Miami, Houston, and other financial centers. In addition, they can operate as holding companies, owning the equity shares in foreign banks and finance companies that represent part of the global banking network of the parent bank. Parent banks are not able to own shares in foreign finance companies directly, but must acquire such ownership through their Edge Act subsidiaries. Finally, Edge Act corporations engage in specialty financing of offshore projects, taking long-term debt and other financing positions in these projects. Two types of Edge Act corporations have developed: the financing corporation and the banking corporation. Banking corporations are subject to lending limits and reserve requirements. Financing corporations can operate more freely with respect to lending and financing activities. Financial transactions of Edge Act corporations must be incidental to foreign or international business. The minimum capital investment in Edge Act corporations is $2 million. The International Banking Act of 1978 liberalized the reserve-requirement and liabilities limits so that

Edge Act corporations could more competitively finance U.S. export trade. In 1979 American banks were operating 132 such corporations (Exhibit 3).

FOREIGN BANKING IN THE UNITED STATES.   The decade of the 1970s witnessed a rapid expansion in the number of foreign banking offices in the United States—in the volume of banking assets and liabilities in the United States held by foreign banks. At year-end 1972, foreign banks held U.S. assets in excess of $23 billion. By 1978 this had grown to $96 billion. Over 140 foreign banks operate representative offices, agencies, branches, and subsidiaries in the United States. The range of operations of foreign banks has expanded in recent years, and includes lending in the domestic loan markets, money-market activities, retail banking, stock market transactions, securities underwriting, and servicing the needs of multinational corporations. Foreign banks now account for over 20 percent of the commercial and industrial loans made to borrowers in the United States.

Foreign banks have followed the inflow of foreign investment entering the United States. This foreign investment takes three principal forms: direct business investment, portfolio investment, and short-term investment in liquid assets. The growth of foreign banking is closely related to this inflow of foreign investment.

The following represent key aspects of foreign bank operations in the United States:

1.   *Corporate services.*   Foreign companies have accelerated their investment in the United States. Major foreign banks have followed their home-country corporate customers to retain their business. In addition, foreign banks have attempted to develop bank-service relationships with U.S. corporations. As a result, the foreign-bank share of commercial and industrial loans in the U.S. market has increased to over 20 percent.

2.   *Money market.*   New York offices of foreign banks have been important participants in the U.S. money markets. Canadian agencies in New York have been active in the call-loan and dealer-loan market sectors. Nearly all foreign banks operate in federal funds and certificates of deposit.

3.   *Dollar sourcing.*   A major consideration for foreign banks in establishing U.S. banking offices is the desire to have a base to secure dollar funds. Closely related is the fact that a U.S. office provides a clearing and deposit center for parent-bank operations. An office in New York may provide dollar funds to other units of the parent bank within prescribed limits. A dollar-based banking office can operate in the exchange market after European foreign-exchange markets have closed for the day.

4.   *Retail banking.*   A small number of foreign banking units in the United States have extended their operations beyond wholesale banking into retail activities. Often these have been banks with ethnic links such as the Puerto Rican and Israeli banks. In California foreign-owned subsidiary banks are heavily retail oriented.

5.   *Securities-market linkages.*   In the past, foreign banks have been prompted to extend their securities-trading and securities-underwriting activities in the United States. This activity has given foreign banks a competitive advantage, since domestic American banks are prohibited from simultaneously engaging in investment banking and commercial banking by the Glass-Steagall Act.

With passage of the International Banking Act of 1978, foreign banks are prohibited from further developing investment-banking activities in the United States. Existing facilities have been grandfathered.

OPERATIONAL ASPECTS

International commercial banking has developed a diverse and complex set of operational activities. In our discussion five important operational areas are examined. The first four are discussed in this section. The fifth, international lending, is discussed in the following section. The five areas are as follows:

1. Financing exports and imports.
2. Foreign exchange.
3. Money market.
4. Corporate services.
5. Lending and Eurocredits.

Export-import financing is the oldest operational aspect of international commercial banking. Traditionally, export-import finance has been the bread-and-butter business of commercial-bank international departments. In cases where the foreign trade of customers is facilitated by a letter of credit, the bank places its name behind the buyer. Time drafts drawn under letters of credit incorporate the financing of the transaction, and by accepting the draft the bank creates a bank acceptance, which tends to provide lower-cost financing. U.S. banks open import letters of credit in favor of overseas sellers at the request of American buyers. Export letters of credit are advised by American banks on behalf of their foreign correspondent banks. In addition to issuing, confirming, endorsing, and paying against letters of credit, international departments of commercial banks provide loans and credits to support foreign trade. In addition to facilitating letter-of-credit transactions, banks process documents under standardized collection procedures. In such cases no bank obligation to honor drafts is involved.

International departments of major banks carry out a variety of foreign-exchange functions for customers and bank correspondents. These include buying and selling foreign exchange, providing advisory services to customers regarding management of foreign-exchange exposure, facilitating corporate-funds positioning to take advantage of currency and interest-rate relationships, and arranging for speedy money transfer and check collection on a global basis.

Money-market operations of international banks include dealing in different national money markets, international money markets, and facilitating arbitrage of funds across different money-market sectors. Eurocurrency dealing is a central aspect of money-market activities. Funding international loans by means of purchasing short-maturity Eurocurrency deposits is an extremely competitive aspect of money-market operations. Foreign banks with New York offices run a complete money-market operation in the United States dealing in federal funds, CDs, and commercial paper.

Corporate services provided by international banks have brought them closer to the field of investment banking. This is because many of the services they provide are investment-banking oriented. For example, long-term financing in the international capital markets requires an underwriting syndicate. It is interesting to note that many U.S. banks participate in such underwriting activities overseas, although the Glass-Steagall Act prohibits such activities domestically. Another important corporate service is locating and arranging mergers and acquisitions (and arranging divestments). Outside of the investment-banking area, international bankers provide valuable assistance to corporate management of working capital. This includes multicountry and multicurrency cash management, collections on receivables, inventory financing, general working-capital financing, fronting loans, provision of centralized depositories for more-effective regional cash management, and provision of speedy money-transfer and funds-remittance facilities.

INTERNATIONAL LENDING AND EUROCREDITS

AMOUNT OF BANK LENDING.   The international loan portfolios of American banks underwent dramatic increase in the period 1960–1980. This resulted from the interplay of several forces including (1) expansion of overseas activities of U.S. multinational corporations, (2) U.S. government restrictions on capital transactions, (3) the strategic needs of large American banks to achieve growth and diversification, (4) rising petroleum prices and the need of many countries to finance petroleum-payments deficits, (6) opportunities to recycle or intermediate petrodollars, and (7) the increased competitive efficiency of the enlarged Euromarkets compared with many domestic financial markets. The first three factors played a prominent role in the 1960s, whereas the remaining three were important in the 1970s.

We must distinguish between head-office lending by U.S. banks, which is essentially in the form of dollar credits, and foreign-branch lending, which is a combination of Eurocurrency and local currency lending. Data in Exhibit 4 provide insight into the rapid growth of claims on foreigners by U.S. banking offices. The slow growth in 1965–1970 reflects the U.S. capital-control program, which terminated early in 1974. The amounts in Exhibit 4 include various types of claims on foreign banks, corporations, and governments.

Claims on foreigners include direct loans, acceptances created by American banks for the account of foreign banks, claims of U.S. banks on foreign banks that are in

EXHIBIT 4   CLAIMS ON FOREIGNERS REPORTED BY BANKS IN THE UNITED STATES 1955–1980 (BILLIONS OF DOLLARS)

	Short-Term	Long-Term	Total	% Short-Term
1955	1.5	0.7	2.2	70
1960	3.6	1.7	5.3	68
1965	7.7	4.5	12.2	63
1970	10.7	3.1	13.8	78
1975	50.2	9.6	59.8[a]	84
June 1980	115.2	34.2	149.4[b]	87

Source.   Board of Governors of the Federal Reserve System.
[a]Includes $12.1 billion due from banks' own foreign branches.
[b]Includes $56.1 billion due from banks' own foreign branches.

the process of being collected, and other types of claims. Exhibit 5 provides a breakdown of the types of borrowers at the opposite end of the credit relationship at midyear 1980.

Lending from the United States is conducted almost exclusively in dollars. Foreign claims of U.S. banks arise in connection with extension of commercial credits covering foreign trade, stabilization and standby credits, development credits, and medium-term credits to industrial borrowers to finance capital-equipment purchases.

Lending by foreign branches of U.S. banks is more diversified than lending by head offices. This lending varies based on differences in the national and international banking markets in which foreign branches operate. Lending is carried out in local currencies, mainly in cases of loans to local corporate and U.S.-affiliated borrowers. Lending is carried in U.S. dollars in cases where the borrower has a need for dollar-denominated credits. A large part of the lending in primarily European and offshore-island (Nassau and Cayman Islands) branches is in Eurocurrencies. Branch systems, or networks, channel funds to bring together surplus and deficit money and loan markets. Multicurrency lending arrangements have developed in Europe, where credits can be transferred from branch to head office or in reverse, or can be participated among branches and head office in response to the needs of the borrower.

With the rapid escalation of international bank lending commencing in 1974 with the OPEC payments surpluses and need to finance payments deficits of oil-importing nations, the Bank for International Settlements undertook a comprehensive estimate of lending in the international markets. The most-recent data available at this time are reproduced in Exhibit 6, in which four lender bank groups are identified. Banks in European countries include the European branches of American banks. The largest part of this lending is in foreign-currency (Eurocurrency) lending. Branches of U.S. banks in offshore centers include those in the Bahamas, Cayman Islands, Panama, Hong Kong, and Singapore. The data in Exhibit 6 are incomplete in that they exclude the offshore activities of banks in Bahrain and business done by non-U.S. banks in the offshore Caribbean centers and Far East.

RISK EVALUATION.   Although international lending offers significant rewards in the form of profit, the lending banks inevitably must assume a measure of risk over and beyond what is normally encountered in domestic lending. In practice these risks can be considered to include credit risk, country risk, currency risk, and funding risk.

EXHIBIT 5   U.S. BANK CLAIMS ON FOREIGNERS JUNE 1980 (BILLIONS OF DOLLARS)

Total claims on foreigners	$149.4
Foreign public borrowers	15.7
Own foreign offices	56.1
Unaffiliated foreign banks	44.1
Of which deposits	6.5
All other foreigners	33.6

Source.   Board of Governors of the Federal Reserve System.

EXHIBIT 6   ESTIMATED LENDING IN INTERNATIONAL MARKETS: CHANGES IN EXTERNAL CLAIMS OF BANKS IN DOMESTIC AND FOREIGN CURRENCIES (BILLIONS OF DOLLARS)

Lenders	Changes			Amounts Outstanding
	1977	1978	1979	1979
Banks in European reporting countries	+80.6	+145.2	+164.8	776.2
Of which in foreign currency (Euromarket)	+68.5	+117.2	+137.9	639.9
Banks in Canada and Japan	+0.8	+16.2	+15.0	71.0
Banks in the United States	+11.5	+37.8	+17.1	136.0
Branches of U.S. blanks in offshore centers	+16.2	+15.4	+21.2	127.7
Total	+109.1	+214.6	+218.1	1110.9
Minus double counting due to redepositing among reporting banks	34.1	104.6	88.1	445.9
New International bank lending	75.0	110.0	130.0	665.0

Source.   Bank for International Settlements.

In lending to private-sector business firms and multinational corporations, credit risks are always present. To evaluate the degree of credit risk assumed, we must consider the type of lending international bankers ordinarily undertake. International bankers ordinarily lend on a wholesale basis to large business firms in host countries where overseas branches may be located (Morgan Guaranty, Paris, to a large French company), or to multinational companies. In such cases credit risks often are well screened out, and only the more-creditworthy and more substantial borrowers are approved. In addition, there is a considerable amount of interbank funds placement, either as part of the Eurocurrency trading activity or local money-market operation. Again, there is a tendency to deal mainly with good-quality Eurobanks or money-market institutions. As a result, credit risks are perceived to be relatively low, often lower than in the case of domestic loan portfolios.

Country risks relate to the exposure a bank has in its loans in a given country when events (economic or political) in that country could make it difficult or impossible for debtors to continue to make loan-servicing payments in the hard currency in which the loan was denominated. The event could be a business recession, a central-bank blockage of foreign exchange available for servicing commercial loans, or civil strife disrupting exports and foreign-exchange earnings. Excessive concentration of international loans in one country may leave an international bank lender in serious difficulties should economic or political conditions turn unfavorable in that country. A special type of country risk applies in cases where a bank lends to the central government, or an official agency created by the central government. This sovereign risk is an exposure that carries with it special problems for the commercial-bank lender. First, a sovereign entity may not be sued or brought to court for nonpayment in courts subject to its jurisdiction. Second, many countries, including those whose banks are actively engaged in international lending, will not support claims brought against sovereign entities in their own courts unless the sovereign entity was engaged in a commercial activity, or unless the sovereign gives permission to be sued.

Currency risk arises whenever a bank denominates loans in one currency but obtains borrowed funds or deposits in another currency. In general, international bankers try to avoid this type of risk. However, there are occasions where the interest differential between two currencies is highly conducive to currency-arbitrage activities.

Funding risk tends to be ever present, in domestic as well as international banking operations. Since international deposit funds are more competitively wholesale oriented and more responsive to interest-rate volatility than domestic funds, the international funding risk may be of a higher degree. Funding risk is considered to be an important factor whenever short-term deposit funds are utilized to fund medium-term loan portfolios. This is because rising interest rates may expose the bank to higher deposit-interest costs at a period when it is locked into relatively less attractive fixed interest rates on medium-term loans. International bankers have found a way out of this dilemma by use of floating-rate loans. The majority of medium-term Eurocurrency loans are made on a floating-interest-rate basis, where the borrower pays an interst rate equal to the London Interbank Offered Rate (LIBOR) plus a premium over LIBOR. LIBOR is the cost of funds of Eurocurrency-lending banks. This is the cost of short-term-deposit funds in the London wholesale interbank market. Periodically (3-6 months) the LIBOR rate is adjusted in the loan to reflect the changed level of interest costs of the lending banks.

PROBLEMS AND ISSUES. Several problem areas emerged in the late 1970s and early 1980s as a result of the escalation in international lending. These focused on possible excessive loan concentration and excessive country exposure of individual banks, the issue of developing-country debt-service capacity, and the locked-in effect experienced by bank lenders as borrowing nations find it not possible to service outstanding debt. Solutions to these problems are not easy. In the past two decades a number of international loan reschedulings have taken place, either on a multilateral or narrower basis. These reschedulings have involved stretch-out of principal repayments and temporary relief from interest payments. Such reschedulings have provided necessary relief, but do not get at fundamental issues such as the need for a more controlled expansion in international loans.

Another problem issue is the need for control over total international credit creation. Competitive financing of exports, loans to strengthen political alliances, and an overall lack of effective coordination between different credit-creating agencies and institutions represent basic problems to be dealt with. We return to these questions below in the section "Regulatory Aspects."

INTERNATIONAL BANKING AND THE THIRD WORLD

SERVING THE NEEDS OF DEVELOPING COUNTRIES. International commercial banking can contribute to the development efforts of the Third World in the following ways:

1. Assisting in the development of local financial institutions.
2. Supporting foreign trade.
3. Facilitating an inflow of capital and supplementing availability of foreign exchange.
4. Promoting thrift and savings habits.

A number of the developing countries have larger and more-sophisticated banking institutions of their own. In such cases some of the above-mentioned contributions are provided by local or indigenous banks.

ACCESS TO INTERNATIONAL CAPITAL. International commercial banking has assisted in channeling capital to developing nations. In general the developing nations have found it difficult to gain access to the international financial markets. Approximately three dozen (one out of four) developing nations have been able to tap the medium-term Eurocurrency loan market each year, and only a dozen developing nations have been able to issue bonds in the international bond markets. Inasmuch as developing nations have been able to obtain over half the funds made available in the medium-term Eurocurrency market in recent years, we can judge that the contribution here has been important.

Three factors influence the access of developing countries to international capital. These include the policies of industrial countries vis-à-vis the operation of their own capital markets, the stage of development of the borrowing country, and the ability of the borrower to maintain effective financial-management policies.

Financial-management policies followed by developing countries can influence the access they enjoy to international loan funds, as well as the loan terms they will be exposed to. For example, there is a close conformity between financial-management effectiveness of developing countries and LIBOR spreads paid by borrowing countries. Indicators reflecting central-government financial-management effectiveness include budget deficit as percentage of gross domestic product (GDP), increase in cost of living, growth of money supply, growth of real per capita GNP, growth or real gross domestic investment, current-account deficit as percentage of exports, debt-service ratio, official reserves as percentage of imports, and the percentage of compressible imports.

REGULATORY ASPECTS

International commercial banking has grown in relative importance in world financial markets to the point where it can affect credit flows and the safety and stability of national banking systems. The United States has had to make special provision for the ability of American banks to circumvent domestic credit controls, by imposing marginal reserve requirements on the Eurodollar borrowings of head offices from their foreign branches. One of the alleged reasons for support of the regulation of foreign banks in the United States was their ability to undermine domestic (Federal Reserve) credit controls by obtaining advances from their parent banks.

Intrepid central bankers have managed to erect hurdles around national banking markets, but international bankers have responded by taking up pole vaulting. At present the question of regulation of credit control over international banks has shifted to the Euromarkets and the prospects for applying credit controls to the international credit markets. Basic implementation problems relate to applying reserve requirements on Eurodeposits and forcing the market to shift to Far Eastern or Middle Eastern centers where no such reserve requirements apply.

In the United States, critics of the role of American banks in international banking have argued that the soundness and stability of the domestic banking system may be jeopardized by continued large-scale lending to high-risk developing countries. Alternately, critics may argue that country loan concentrations are too high. National bank examiners in the United States have reorganized their efforts to achieve a more effective and more uniform review and classification of international loans made by U.S. banks. Nevertheless, loan loss ratios on international loans remain considerably lower than those on domestic loans.

International banking has grown to the point where the quality and structure of American banking has changed and continues to change. The important question is: has international banking become large enough and important enough to warrant the application of special rules and regulations in light of these changes?

SOURCES AND SUGGESTED REFERENCES

Angelini, A., M. Eng, and F.A. Lees. *International Lending, Risk and the Euromarkets.* London: Macmillan, 1979.

Bank for International Settlements. *Annual Reports.* Basel.

Bitterman, H.J. *The Refunding of International Debt.* Durham, NC: Duke University Press, 1973.

Feis, H. *Europe the World's Banker: 1870–1914,* New Haven: Yale University Press, 1930.

International Monetary Fund. *Annual Reports.* Washington, DC: IMF.

Lees, F.A. *International Banking & Finance.* London: Macmillan, 1974.

Lees, F.A. and M. Eng. *International Financial Markets.* New York: Praeger, 1975.

Lees, F.A. *Foreign Banking and Investment in the U.S.* New York: Halsted, 1976.

Mathis, F.J. ed. *Offshore Lending by U.S. Commercial Banks.* New York: Bankers Association for Foreign Trade, 1975.

Morgan Guaranty Trust Company. *World Financial Markets.* New York: Monthly.

Scheffer, C.F. *The Institutional Organization of Industrial Credit Throughout the World.* Leiden, the Netherlands: A.W. Sijthoff, 1977.

Quinn, B.S. *The New Euromarkets.* New York: Halsted, 1975.

Wellons, P.A. *Borrowing By Developing Countries on the Euro-Currency Market.* Paris: OECD, 1977.

World Bank. *World Development Report.* Washington, DC: World Bank, 1977–80.

World Bank. *Borrowing on the International Capital Markets.* Washington, D.C.: World Bank, 1977–80.

INTERNATIONAL INVESTMENT BANKING

CONTENTS

THE ORGANIZATION OF
INTERNATIONAL INVESTMENT
BANKING   3

Edge Act Subsidiaries   3
Ownership Provisions   3
Branching under the Edge Act   4
Financial versus Banking Subsidiaries   4
Edge Act Management   5
International Investment-Banking
Competition   5
The Activities of Investment Banking   6
The Embellishment of International
Investment Banking   6
Key Characteristics of Activities   7
Information Networks   7

MANAGEMENT OF SECURITIES
ISSUES   8

Reasons for the Growth of the
Eurobond Market   8
Eurodollar Lending   8
The Eurobond Market   9
The Placement of Eurobond Issues   9
The Popularity of the Eurobond Market   9

PROJECT FINANCING   10

Characteristics of Project Financing   10
Key Elements of Project Financing   11
The Critical Startup Period   11
Laying Off of Risks   12
Spreading Political Risk   12

Forecasting and Prenegotiating Political
Risk   12
PARALLEL LOANS   13

Parallel Loans   13
Currency Swaps   13
Credit Swaps   13

MERGERS, ACQUISITIONS, AND
REORGANIZATIONS   14

Mergers and Acquisitions   14
Spinning Off Expertise   14
Spotting Merger Partners   15
Underwriting Skills   15
Factors Affecting Merger   15
International Business Necessarily
Involves Mergers   16
Reorganization, Liquidiation, and
Bankruptcy   17
Extension and Composition   17
Reorganization   17

TRENDS IN INTERNATIONAL
INVESTMENT BANKING   18

Lowered Barriers to Entry   18
The Advantages of Size   18
Operation in a Protected Market   18
Parallel Domestic and International
Competition   19

SOURCES AND SUGGESTED
REFERENCES   19

INTERNATIONAL INVESTMENT BANKING

Edward B. Flowers

THE ORGANIZATION OF INTERNATIONAL INVESTMENT BANKING

EDGE ACT SUBSIDIARIES. Commercial banks in the United States engage in international investment banking through the incorporation of Edge Act subsidiaries. The law governing the establishment of Edge Act corporations (EACs) can be found in Title XXV of the Federal Reserve Act (12 USCS §§ 601–632). Enacted in 1919 and amended as late as 1978, the law authorizing Edge Act Corporations requires a minimum capital contribution of $2 million, which, under the 1978 amendment to the law, may now be paid in installments (see 12 USCS § 618). These EACs are federally chartered corporations not subject to state banking laws, and are regulated by the Federal Reserve Board. Before 1919 and the Edge Act, international investment banking was transacted through the use of "agreement corporations," which were also chartered by the Federal Reserve Board. These agreement corporations, however, were subject to the more-restrictive, day-to-day supervision of the Fed and required specific agreement with the Fed concerning participation in individual projects, and the law stated that only 10 percent of capital and surplus could be invested in any one international banking operation. The requirements of the 1919 Edge Act are much more liberal, and the 1978 amendments were enacted specifically to make the act more liberal, by extending its provisions more uniformly to banks across the United States, and to allow freer competition with foreign investment bankers.

OWNERSHIP PROVISIONS. The law on Edge Act corporations previously required that a majority of the shares be owned by U.S. citizens, but under the 1978 amendment (12 USCS § 619), a majority of the stock of a U.S. Edge Act subsidiary may be held by one or more foreign banks or institutions organized under the laws of foreign countries if the prior approval of the Fed is secured. This provision allows U.S. commercial banks to compete on a more even basis with, for instance, banks recently chartered in the United States using Saudi money, French banking expertise in Euromoney markets, and the U.S. capital markets, through a mixture of, say, six Saudi bank shareholders, one French Euromoney bank shareholder, and a number of U.S. banking shareholders.

BRANCHING UNDER THE EDGE ACT. Edge Act investment banking operations are an exception to the rule that U.S. banks may not branch across state lines. Edge Act subsidiaries are often located outside the states of the parent U.S. banks. The principal Edge Act banking cities are New York, Houston, Miami, Chicago, Los Angeles, and San Francisco. This provision allows a very large bank to extend the source of its international investment-banking activities to the customers and capital markets located in all major cities and sections of the United States.

Under the amended Edge Act provisions, a U.S. commercial bank may engage in the following activities:

1. Accept deposits outside the United States.
2. Accept deposits in the United States if incidental to U.S. trade transactions.
3. Make loans (not more than 20 percent of capital and surplus to one borrower).
4. Make loans and advances to finance foreign trade.
5. Issue or confirm letters of credit.
6. Create bankers acceptances.
7. Receive items for collection.
8. Buy, sell, or hold securities.
9. Issue guarantees.
10. Act as paying agent for securities issued by foreign governments or foreign corporations.
11. Engage in spot and forward exchange transactions.
12. Purchase and sell coin or bullion.
13. Purchase and sell virtually any evidences of indebtedness.
14. Borrow and lend money.
15. Issue debentures, bonds, and promissory notes.
16. Engage in remittance of funds services.

The 1978 amendment to the Act (12 USCS § 615) liberalized the ability to accept deposits, deal in coin and bullion, make loans, and sell securities.

FINANCIAL VERSUS BANKING SUBSIDIARIES. Edge Act banking activities fall into two broad categories: international commercial banking, and international "financing" activities. The financing activities of Edge Act corporations constitute the traditional range of investment-banking activities, and the rules for the Edge Act subsidiaries are different depending on which type of primary activity the subsidiary is engaged in. Since the 1963 Federal Reserve Board revision of Regulation K, the regulation by which the Fed governs Edge Act activity, however, this distinction has been dropped as a practical matter, although the EACs tend to still operate as if the original distinction continued (Baker and Bradford, 1974).

If the Edge Act subsidiary functions primarily as a banking subsidiary, it may hold shares of foreign banking subsidiaries and behave as a bank holding company. Foreign branch banks may not do this. The subsidiary may also act as a holding company for all or part of the parent bank's foreign commercial-banking subsidiaries, or may do this as a part of a joint venture with foreign or domestic banks or with other nonbanking institutions.

If the EAC functions primarily as a "financing" subsidiary, that is, as an investment bank, its activities are prescribed as follows:

1. It may hold portfolios of equity investments in foreign commercial and industrial firms
   a. Directly.
   b. Through an official or semiofficial development bank or corporation.
2. It may make direct investments in a wide variety of local businesses through the use of intermediate-term loans, purchase of shares of stock, or a combination of the above.
3. It may handle referrals of long-term development projects to the EAC by the parent bank (commitments from $100,000 to $1 million).
4. If engaged only in financing, it may invest up to 50 percent of its capital and surplus in a single venture (if engaged in general international commercial banking, the limit is 10 percent).
5. Profit derived from dividends (from equity participations), interest (on loans made), and capital gains (from the sale of equity participations), as well as interest paid on bonds, and various service fees.

EDGE ACT MANAGEMENT. Although a commercial bank's international investment-banking activities are being channeled through an Edge Act subsidiary, and although the subsidiary may have foreign shareholders, the subsidiary is a U.S.-domiciled and U.S.-regulated corporation. This is, of course, a legal fiction to a certain extent, "the corporate veil" allowing the U.S. multinational commercial bank to participate in investment-banking activities everywhere except in the United States, where the Glass-Steagall Act prevents direct competition between banks and investment bankers. There has, however, been a great deal of commercial-bank lobbying in recent years to allow the commercial banks to compete with investment banks in the United States. Commercial banks anticipate that the 1980s will be an era of major refinancing for plant and equipment of U.S. industry, and this, coupled with the historically greater profit margins of the U.S. investment-banking industry, makes this market attractive domestically as well as internationally. Commercial banks, on the other hand, find their profits severely limited by federal controls, which often precipitate bank disintermediation, or the foreclosure of capital access during credit crunches, and, recently, by direct commercial-bank competition with savings banks' NOW accounts and the attempts of large investment houses to offer a "financial department store" of services virtually identical to (and more extensive than) those that commercial banks are legally able to offer. The one exception to this rule preventing commercial-bank competition with U.S. investment banks appears to be the rule that allows commercial banks to handle the underwriting of the debentures of state and local public corporations. Even here there is no direct competition, since investment houses are not allowed to underwrite these issues.

INTERNATIONAL INVESTMENT-BANKING COMPETITION. The liberalized Edge Act allows U.S. commercial banks the option of competing in the lucrative *international* investment-banking market. It may be argued (Giddy, 1980) that the increasing activity of the multinational commercial banks in these markets has increased competition and has substantially changed the nature of the services offered.

It is also likely that the passage of the International Banking Act of 1978 (12 USCS §§ 3101–3108), which governs the activities of *foreign* banks in the U.S., will have some effect on the ability of U.S. banks to branch and compete with domestic investment bankers.

THE ACTIVITIES OF INVESTMENT BANKING. In the case of domestic investment banking, it has been said that this industry does not engage in investment and neither does it involve banking. In the case of international investment banking, this is less true, because both international banks and investment houses participate side by side in their competition for international investment-banking markets. Unlike domestic investment banking, in the international arena, the device of the Edge Act corporation enables the commercial banker to hold and sell securities and to compete directly with the investment banker, pyramiding its international investment-banking activities atop its international commercial-banking activities in an operational, if not a legal, sense.

THE EMBELLISHMENTS OF INTERNATIONAL INVESTMENT BANKING. In domestic investment banking, the primary business of the investment house is the secondary offerings of stocks and bonds and the arrangement of complicated financial packages, which are often used in connection with mergers and corporate takeovers. Since the primary business of domestic investment banking is the management of securities offerings, the "product" is the securities themselves. In international investment banking, the business is even more diverse and complex because the international networks of multinational commercial banks are involved in merchant-banking activities across national boundaries and national and international capital markets in addition to the international and domestic merchant-banking activities of investment houses. Although the primary business of international merchant banking is still probably underwriting, mergers and acquisitions, and the sale of advisory functions, the breadth and scope of international investment-banking operations is so extensive that in order to grasp the protean nature of the potential of this industry, it is well to list the types of activities involved, as follows:

1. Securities issues
    - *a.* Underwriting.
    - *b.* Syndication.
    - *c.* Management of issue.
    - *d.* Private placements.
2. Arrangement of complex financing packages
    - *a.* Syndicated loans.
    - *b.* Mergers and acquisitions.
    - *c.* Parallel lending, etc.
    - *d.* Financial rescue operations.
    - *e.* Project financing.
3. Trust management
    - *a.* General.
    - *b.* In relation to bond offerings.
4. Raising capital.
    - *a.* Loans: Eurodollar primarily.

   b.   Equity issues.
   c.   Eurobond issues.
5.   Financial adviser services
   a.   Sources of capital.
   b.   Assessing international capital markets.
   c.   Selling financial deals: "feasibility."
   d.   Negotiation of financial packages.
   e.   Financial advisement to major projects.
   f.   Advice in corporate reorganization.
   g.   Advice on mergers and acquisitions.
   h.   Energy-related financial advisement.
      (1)   Government
      (2)   Private
   i.   Advice on corporate strategies.
   j.   Advice on direct investments in the United States.
   k.   Advice on any complex, or unusual financial problem needing international expertise, information, capital, or contacts.

KEY CHARACTERISTICS OF ACTIVITIES.   One reason for the extensiveness and complexity of these international investment activities is the involvement of large multinational banks. These banks, in effect, market the expertise derived from their base in international commercial-banking operations. The information, expertise, contacts, market-monitoring networks, and international access to capital of the international commercial-banking operations can also be used to solve the more-unusual and more-complex problems arising in the merchant-banking field. The existence of the worldwide commercial-banking network of the multinational banks for use in the international investment-banking field tends to competitively extend the range and complexity of international investment-banking activities, at least qualitatively, far beyond the range of domestic investment banking. This is most readily noticed in the extensive range of advisory services offered through the financial operations of the Edge Act subsidiaries of the large multinational banks engaged in international investment banking. This range of services tends to extend beyond the traditional domestic investment-banking core activities of underwriting, mergers, and acquisitions.

INFORMATION NETWORKS.   Although the end result of most international investment-banking operations is the provision of financing or capital, the activities of the Edge Act subsidiaries of the large multinational banks in this industry tend to shift the emphasis of the action more toward information access, rather than capital access. Another way of stating this is to say that a major function of international investment banking is now to define the range of the possible in international financing, based on the banks' information and expertise in international financial markets. Once the investment banking adviser has defined the possible, this is sold in the form of a feasibility study, which makes possible the securing of the financial package advised. It is much more likely that international capital-market access will be standardized in the future than will the process of organizing such access in investment banking. Thus based on its international banking and information network, an international investment-banking operation and its contacts act as a salesman who secures and certifies financial feasibility for complicated, novel projects that are generally very large and risky. A negative definition of international investment banking might be to say that aside from mergers, acquisitions, and underwriting, international investment banking involves only those projects that are unusual, or require unusual banking expertise.

MANAGEMENT OF SECURITIES ISSUES

One of the major parts of international investment banking is the underwriting, syndication, management, and private placement of both corporate equities and Eurobond issues. Because of the international nature of the distribution process, the large amounts of capital generally involved, and the fact that the regulations of no one nation determine the management of the issues, these activities vary considerably from the domestic underwriting activities of investment banks. Although the Edge Act subsidiaries of multinational banks and other investment houses often manage the issue of equity stock for large corporations, in the international investment-banking field, the management of equity issues is very much parallel to Eurobond issuing, which has, in terms of volume, tended to dominate the development of international investment banking in the field of securities issues since the late 1960s. For that reason this discussion will concentrate primarily on the methods for engaging in and competing with the investment bankers in the rapidly growing Eurobond market dominated by international investment bankers.

REASONS FOR THE GROWTH OF THE EUROBOND MARKET. In the early 1960s, international money-market experts had expected a gradual integration of international capital markets because of the influence of massive direct foreign investment, which seemed to be tying together the international web of business communications. This integration did not take place, primarily because of national credit controls such as the voluntary and then mandatory controls on U.S. direct foreign investment. There were also other restrictions such as the Interest Equalization Tax, which restricted the foreign use of U.S. capital markets during the period of greatest U.S. capital outflow in the form of direct foreign investment. Such governmental regulation apparently interfered with international capital flows to an extent great enough to encourage the rapidly increasing rate of growth of international offshore funds markets—the Eurodollar and Eurobond markets.

In order to precisely understand international investment banking in the underwriting of equity and Eurobond issues, it is first necessary to be able to distinguish these activities from the more-traditional "international banking" activities of Eurodollar lending.

EURODOLLAR LENDING. The dollar-denominated accounts in Europe that were funded by an excess outflow of U.S. funds during the post-World War II years became a source of funds for international lending that was not regulated by any one national government. The lending consortiums (or syndicates) of multinational banks generally accessed these funds through the medium of one of their overseas branch banks located in a European money-market center, such as London. If the funds were sourced in London, the syndicate's lead bank would take down the funds by means of cable in London at the London Interbank Offered Rate (LIBOR) and lend them (under the proper legal loan documents) to a corporation or government anywhere in the world, by means of cable. The lending bank would then take its pro rata share of the spread of the lending rate over LIBOR and the lead syndicate bank would take its management fee for having arranged and managed the lending syndicate.

Such Eurodollar lending is *intermediated* lending, since the European banking system collects the dollars in the Eurodollar accounts and the banking syndicate arranges for the loaning out of this money. This source of some $350 to $800 billion is under the control of no government or central bank; it is an unregulated fund of international money governed only by market supply and demand.

THE EUROBOND MARKET. Although capital from bonded indebtedness is often a substitute for a large, international, syndicated Eurodollar loan, the Eurobond funds are *nonintermediated* funding. The syndicate of international investment bankers who arrange the Eurobond issue merely facilitates the sale of Eurobonds, bonds denominated in any one of some 14 hard currencies, to the ultimate purchaser. The underwriting syndicate immediately provides the issuing corporation with the agreed amount of capital as the bonds are sold to the underwriting syndicate and then distributed by the managing syndicate to the underwriting syndicate (which is multinational in nature), which then *places* (see Giddy, 1975) the Eurobonds through its system of international bankers, brokers, and dealers in various countries.

Unlike domestic bond issues, most of a Eurobond issue will generally be placed outside of the country whose currency is used to donominate the issue. Thus the Securities and Exchange Commission (SEC) or the Fed or the other security and banking regulatory agencies in whose domicile the lead syndicating banker is located generally do not have a determinative regulatory interest in the issue. One important effect of this vacuum of regulatory authority is that generally Eurobond issues are not subject to withholding taxes generally paid on bond interest payments (see Giddy, 1975).

THE PLACEMENT OF EUROBOND ISSUES. Another unique feature of Eurobond issues is that the bonds are not sold directly to the public as they might be if formally issued through a domestic underwriter and its network of brokers. A Eurobond issue generally works its way through a multilayered international distribution network that results in the bonds' being placed with a large number of buyers who have been presold on this issue before it takes place (see Giddy, 1975). Thus this business once again has the flavor of merchant banking in that it involves international connections between large, well-funded institutions that appear to be important in not only the distribution, but also the sale of Eurobond issues.

First the Eurobonds are bought by the managing syndicate of merchant bankers. This syndicate then distributes the bonds to a multinational group of bankers known as the underwriting syndicate. The syndicate members' organization of bankers, brokers, and dealers then place the bonds with their purchasers.

THE POPULARITY OF THE EUROBOND MARKET. Giddy (1975) has outlined how this system results in a market that is able to provide large amounts of capital for often-complicated financing plans, at low cost, with great flexibility, anonymity, and safety. The placement market for Eurobonds is virtually worldwide, and the creditworthiness of the leading syndicate banks is generally impeccable. All of this works for the safe provision of large amounts of capital funds. Since Eurobond issues generally bypass official authorizations, requirements for financial-disclosure queuing arrangements, and exchange-listing obligations, and are not under the regulation of the agencies of any one government, there is great flexibility in managing the issues. Interest costs have been competitive with other markets, and the management fees on these issues, about 3.5 percent of the face value of the issues, are low. It is often possible to avoid withholding taxes on the interest paid on the bonds, further reducing their cost (and increasing the yield of the issues). Corporations like the fact that they are able to rely on a sound and tightly knit institutional framework of investment bankers and their connections, and purchasers of the bonds like the fact that there is a vigorous market in "secondhand" Eurobonds, increasing the liquidity of their investment.

PROJECT FINANCING

Project financing has all of the earmarks of business in the area of merchant banking. Project financing is generally involved in extremely large, mining, energy, or raw-materials projects in remote locations and in countries of high political risk. Typically the sponsoring company could not, by itself, sustain the additional leverage it would have to incur to finance such a large project. This is especially true in the recent environment of high inflation rates, low depreciation rates, high costs of replacing capital equipment, high interest rates, and volatile prices in product and capital markets. Nonetheless, such projects generally offer great potential profits, both for the host country, sponsoring firm, and financiers. Thus the typical project is large, and requires special sources of capital, unique investment-analysis expertise, sharp negotiating skills, and the sort of financial-feasibility study that investment bankers often do best.

CHARACTERISTICS OF PROJECT FINANCING. The characteristics of project financing as organized by an international investment banker would involve the following:

1. The undertaking would be a separate financial entity from that of the sponsoring company.
2. Heavy leverage would be involved; debt would typically represent 65–75 percent of capital.
3. The recourse of borrowers would not be primarily to the sponsoring company, but would generally rely upon
   a. the assets of the project or
   b. the potential cash flow of the project.
4. Supplier commitments would generally be a significant part of the credit support.
5. The sponsoring firm's guarantees to lenders typically would not cover all the risks involved (called "laying off the risk").
6. The project debt would be differentiated from general debt on the sponsoring firm's balance sheet to avoid intolerable levels of leverage for the sponsoring firm.

This type of organization (see Wynant, 1980) allows the sponsoring firm to direct the operations of a development or mining project so large that the financing would overwhelm the firm itself. In one instance, the financing of a single project was equal to 70 percent of the capital of the sponsoring firm. Project financing also enables the prospective cash flows to be used to secure financing in a way that is not possible when many sponsoring firms act alone.

KEY ELEMENTS OF PROJECT FINANCING. Key elements (these elements were gleaned from Wynant, 1980) in project financing are typically provided by the investment banker as follows:

1. The banker makes an assessment of start-up and operating risks that would lead to startup-cost overruns and quick failure of the venture before break-even is achieved.
2. The banker identifies the major sources and terms for financing.
3. The banker develops a risk-analysis approach and may advocate methods for either avoiding or laying off some risks.
4. The banker may advocate unique ways for reaching leverage targets necessary to make the project viable:
   a. Special sources of financing: governmental or international agency sources.
   b. Support arrangements: governmental guarantees of loan arrangements.
5. The banker designs in flexibility to facilitate the availability of future financing.

THE CRITICAL START-UP PERIOD. The investment banker is expected to anticipate start-up problems that can quickly knock out a project (Wynant, 1980). For example:

1. Problems in the recovery process (in a mining venture).
2. Poor engineering for product quality or product specifications.
3. Problems related to low labor productivity, especially in less developed countries.
4. High and inflated costs of replacement equipment, or supplies, possibly due to
   a. inflation in the host country or
   b. adverse movements in the exchange rate.
5. Effects of inflation, which may be quite significant in underdeveloped countries.
6. Problems involved with volatile prices in product markets upon which the project cash flows rely.

One method of anticipating the effects on the project of these diverse risks is to run a computer simulation of the project's start-up to assess project riskiness, and to judge the project's sensitivity to various operating and financial variables. These studies, combined with the banker's expertise and experience, provide a basis for entering the complex financial negotiations between governments, bankers, sponsoring firms, and other parties to the project.

LAYING OFF OF RISKS.   Various methods can be used to lay off some of the risks of the project. In the case of large mining operations, where the cash flows from the project depend on the export sale price of the ore, it is common to include a number of sponsoring firms from different countries in order to secure long-term contracts for the mine's output. This is one way of insulating the projected cash flows from the project from typically volatile raw-materials prices. The spread of nationalities in long-term contracting parties also tends to spread the risk of default as well as the anticipated project profits. It is in the interest of the contracting parties both to receive profits from the mine and to secure stable, long-term supplies of raw materials for their factories. The long-term contracts also take into account anticipated exchange-rate fluctuations that might have just as damaging an effect on project cash flow as falling raw-materials prices; thus the exchange rates for contract prices are often also agreed on.

SPREADING POLITICAL RISK.   Another benefit of securing participants of many nationalities in the project, both among financing parties and parties sponsoring and/or contracting for the project's output, is to bring the political clout of these large companies and banks into bargaining play during any threatened default or nationalization by a host-country government or a host-government joint-venture partner. An example of the use of such bargaining clout was when, in 1976, Peru sought $300 million in balance-of-payments financing from a group of U.S. money-market banks. The financing was conditioned upon Peru's satisfying the syndicate's demand for compensation to Newmont Mining Corporation for Peru's 1975 expropriation of the Marcona Mining Company, and for settlement of a back-tax dispute with Southern Peru Copper Company, owned by AMAX Inc.

FORECASTING AND PRENEGOTIATING POLITICAL RISK.   Eiteman and Stonehill (1979) recommend a technique of forecasting and negotiating away any excessive political risk before the project investment is made. The international investment banker would typically be a lead negotiator in such bargaining for a project-financed venture, because investment bankers are peculiarly well situated to pull together the interests involved. In fact, if the banker does not do this, the project will probably not receive the banker's approval, which is generally necessary in order to induce other sources of financing to participate.

The industries in which project financing is generally employed are transportation, power, chemicals, and agribusiness. All of these industries have a developmental flavor, and many recent project-financed ventures in these industries have been located in less developed countries. Thus negotiations with these host-country governments have often involved the host-country government or its development corporations or banks in some way in the venture as a partner in order to make the host's point of view more congruent with that of the venture.

Wynant (1980) has pointed out that in 1976, 200 projects of this type were project financed with capitalizations of over $200 million apiece. These projects could not have been made by the corporate sponsors alone because either the projects were too large, or the environmental constraints of high corporate leverage, high interest rates, and high inflation rates would have prevented it. Wynant believes that without the intervention of project financing, the world may experience a financial crisis of the type that was avoided by capital-market growth during the 1970s. If Wynant is right, this will be an important growth area for international investment.

PARALLEL LOANS

Parallel loans, currency swaps, and credit swaps are arranged by international investment bankers either to aid going concerns or to aid in project financing organizations, reorganizations, or other offbeat financial situations.

PARALLEL LOANS.   Parallel loans are a method of avoiding the risk that the exchange rate may change on the foreign currency denominating a loan before the loan matures. If, for instance, the exchange rate on a U.S. dollar loan made by a Belgian subsidiary of a U.S. company rises in favor of the dollar before the loan is repaid, then the Belgian subsidiary will book a loss upon repaying the loan because of the need to repay the loan in dollars that are now more expensive in terms of Belgian francs.

To avoid such a risk, Belgian subsidiary A might seek a parallel loan through the services of its investment banker. To do this, the investment banker would find Belgian subsidiary B, of an American firm, which was willing to loan the Belgian subsidiary A the francs that it needed. To complete the arrangment, the banker must have found a Belgian subsidiary B that had a U.S. parent corporation that *needed* a loan in dollars equal in value to the franc loan that its Belgian subsidiary B was making to Belgian subsidiary A.

It is easy to see why an investment banker is necessary to put together a deal like this. Since the foreign-exchange market is avoided, the banker's services are used to arrange a set of congruent loan needs that are simultaneously both equal and opposite in two countries. This loan arrangement literally takes one back to the days of barter. The advantage of the parallel or "back-to-back" loan is that it avoids, for both the parent companies and their subsidiaries, the need to enter the foreign-exchange market to pay back the loans. The parent of Belgian subsidiary B receives its loan repayment in dollars of local U.S. currency. Belgian subsidiary B receives its loan repayment in local Belgian francs. Thus there is no transaction risk on the repayment of the loans, and, since the loan to the Belgian subsidiary is in the local currency, there is no possibility of foreign-currency-denominated monetary assets getting out of balance with foreign-currency-denominated liabilities so as to cause foreign-exchange exposure on its balance sheet.

The investment banker obviously must demand a fee for arranging this type of transaction, but perhaps the fee is preferable to the foreign-exchange risk. The banker has sold his contacts and his peculiar knowledge of international corporate needs. Nonetheless, the difficulty of arranging such a transaction limits its use mainly to the facilitation of complicated financial deals negotiated by the investment banker.

CURRENCY SWAPS.   A currency swap involves the swap of equivalent amounts of two different currencies for a fixed period of time. These transactions are also arranged by investment bankers, but since these transactions closely resemble forward contracts in the foreign-exchange market (and are treated as such by U.S. accountants), they really do not accomplish much that cannot be accomplished more easily through the foreign-exchange market for a small brokerage fee.

CREDIT SWAPS.   A credit swap is an exchange of foreign currencies between a business firm and a bank under an agreement to repay the currencies at a certain time. In this way, the business (and the bank) gets the use of the foreign exchange for a period of time without entering the foreign-exchange market and subjecting itself to foreign-exchange-transaction risk. Since, however, this device uses the deposit accounts of the foreign bank, it is often arranged through the offices of the branch bank, and is probably not generally considered to be international investment banking unless the transaction was in connection with a more-complicated financing that the Edge Act banking group was negotiating.

MERGERS, ACQUISITIONS, AND REORGANIZATIONS

MERGERS AND ACQUISITIONS.   The Edge Act statutes under which international investment bankers operate is subtly rooted in the idea of mergers, because of the gradual reorientation of interpretation of the Edge Act from being considered a law stimulating short-term trade credit to being considered a law intended to encourage much-needed, long-term development financing. Originally the Edge Act had been sold to Congress as a bill to stimulate the financing of U.S. exports, which were perceived to be threatened. After World War I, however, the United States shifted from being a debtor nation to being a creditor nation, and the perception developed that the Edge Act, which was then in operation, could easily be interpreted as encouraging long-term financing of the kind that war-ravaged nations and less developed nations needed to develop and redevelop their natural resources (Baker, 1974). The provisions for "financing" Edge Act corporations and for equity participation in ventures and their financing especially aided this construction of the law. Thus the EACs began to move into large-scale financing of development projects such as those eventually represented by ADELA and PICA. Projects such as these often had governments as participating partners in the joint ventures, and this encouraged the scouting of many cosponsoring corporations in order to spread the risk of such large undertakings. This tradition in the use of Edge Act corporations has continued in the more-recent popularity of project financing for much the same reasons as those discussed above. Big development projects tend to encourage thoughts of joint venture, which naturally lead to the accumulation of the kind of information and expertise on the part of managing investment bankers that leads them to sell their expertise in financing and arranging mergers. The investment bankers have been in this type of business ever since the reinterpretation of the Edge Act in 1920.

SPINNING OFF EXPERTISE.   It is in the international investment banker's financial interest to develop interest in mergers because mergers are a potential use for the type of expertise developed in other investment-banking ventures. Investment bankers find it natural to operate both offensively and defensively in the merger-acquisition field. The international merchant banker has access to funds outside of the country of the tender-offer issuance, which may provide a surprise defensive punch in the event that his bank is defending against an unfriendly takeover attempt. It is the business of investment bankers to have access to the large amounts of capital necessary for the purchase of a target company's stock in the open market, or in a tender-offer situation in which bidding competition sets off a price spiral in the target stock. Investment bankers, because of their constant need to make financial evaluations, are natural parties to advise about the critical effects on dividends, market price, and the qualitative factors affecting the finances of corporations, both during and after takeover.

SPOTTING MERGER PARTNERS.   The combined information network of multinational banks with Edge Act corporation investment-banking sections is probably unparalleled at screening and marrying merger partners with synergistic "fits." The evidence indicates (Weston, 1979) that none of the usual financial variables is good at predicting the success of merged firms, and this makes it likely that the qualitative factors involved in fitting together two or more firms with different resource strengths are the determinative factors in arranging good mergers. International investment bankers are well situated to aid in this process, firstly, because they are constant participants in the financing of the projects of the very large multinational corporations that tend to be corporate conglomerates that are constantly acquiring and selling subsidiaries. Secondly, the bankers are in on large development-financing projects and on project financings, which both tend to involve mixing corporate resources in a large-scale way. The skills involved in these activities (see Wynant, 1980) give the investment banker a set of experience and negotiating tools that are tailor-made for arranging mergers.

UNDERWRITING SKILLS.   The investment banker's practice in the marketing, placement, and management of large international equity and Eurobond financings provides the skills often needed in the arrangement and defense of mergers and takeovers. Mergers and takeovers often take place simply because they provide the way for growth to take place that, from both a financial and a resource-fit point of view, might not be possible otherwise. The size, diversification, and synergies of large firms make them often-superior competitors both in product markets and in capital markets. Large firms, because they are better diversified and better known, are often able to sell their stock at a lower required rate of return, and thus may be able to finance with cheaper debt and equity than would be available to a smaller firm. Moreover, there are often tax advantages in purchasing one company with the stock of another, since the owner of the target company will not have to pay capital-gains tax on the acceptance of the takeover company's tender offer of stock in the takeover company, rather than cash. This might mean that it would be cheaper for the takeover company to purchase a going concern with stock, rather than to purchase the assets and organize its own company subsidiary. High rates of inflation and the understated book values of many going concerns tend to make them good bargains. International investment bankers are peculiarly able to put together stock-swap packages for successful mergers and takeovers and to shepherd them through the intricacies of international capital markets in an optimal fashion.

FACTORS AFFECTING MERGER.   The banker should make a systematic assessment of the basic factors affecting merger possibilities:

1. Corporate earnings.
2. Rate of growth in earnings.
3. Dividends paid on stock.
4. Market values of stock.
5. Book values of corporations.
6. Net current assets of target corporations.
7. Qualitative factors affecting "fit."
8. Assessment of available legal complications for defense.

The availability of legal complications to impede a merger attempt might include securing legal advice about the following:

1. Federal Trade Commission-approval requirements under the 1976 Hart-Scott-Rodino Act.
2. Relevant legal prohibitions under the Sherman Antitrust Act of 1890.
3. Available remedies under any applicable state law requiring notice before the issuance of a tender offer.
4. Any similar foreign laws applicable under the circumstances.

A survey of the legal environment surrounding any merger attempt suggests that the banker should formulate or aid in the formulation of a merger strategy. Some situations illustrative of the sorts of strategies that are available might be the following:

1. J. Ray McDermott Company outbid United Technologies in its tender-offer bid for control of the Babcock and Wilcox Company in 1977 because the initial tender offer of United Technologies was too low to preempt the stock.
2. In 1977 the stockholders of Kennecott Copper Company accused its managers of "squandering" its cash because it made a $66-per-share tender offer for the stock of the Carborundum Company, which was then selling for $33.25 per share. Kennecott argued that it had sought to defend itself from takeover by investing $1.2 billion from its forced divestment of the Peabody Coal Company in Carborundum at a price that would constitute a successful preemptive bid for controlling interest in Carborundum.
3. The Kern County Land Company was able to successfully defend itself from a $83.50 tender offer for its shares, which were then selling for $60 per share, by saying in print that its underlying assets were worth much more than the $83.50 offer of Occidental Petroleum indicated. Kern solicited higher offers from other, "friendly" tender bidders, and eventually accepted an offer from "friendly" Genneco Corporation, which of course, provided for continued tenure in office for Kern's management.

INTERNATIONAL BUSINESS NECESSARILY INVOLVES MERGERS. The international extension of the already complicated tactical and strategic considerations outlined above is a daunting proposition, but it is one that is inevitably involved in multi-national-business management in today's world, and one that calls for the intervention, advice, intermediation, and negotiations skills of the international investment banker. *Multi*national business, by its nature, demands that corporations be large and have larger-than-average managerial, operational, and financial resources. This underscores merger as an important means of attaining these goals (aside from the previous list of theoretical, economic, and financial advantages). Many multinational corporations must merge in order to be able to successfully compete and survive. Large domestic size of a corporation does not guarantee its adequacy as an international competitor. One reason for this may be the fact that Europe has relatively few legal antitrust traditions. To the contrary, during the late 1960s the French government's program of "indicative planning" forced mergers in order to develop domestic corporations that were perceived to be large enough to thwart *le defi Americain*. International investment bankers will inevitably be involved in wave after wave of financially competitive international mergers. The era of such mergers is upon us, as indicated by studies such as that of Jean Boddewyn (1979) describing the standard patterns of retrenchment used currently as management tools of multinational corporations that may have overextended themselves during the direct-foreign-investment boom of the sixties and early seventies. These corporations appear to rationalize, cut back, and reorganize their worldwide nultinational business. The international investment bankers who originally tagged along to service these multinationals may now be required to help manage their reorganization and merger problems.

REORGANIZATION, LIQUIDATION, AND BANKRUPTCY. International investment bankers are most often involved in reorganization operations rather than either bankruptcy or liquidation proceedings. Bankruptcy is the toiling province of local legal and juridical specialists, and liquidations are generally handled through the auspices of the commercial-banking divisions of international banks. However, the investment banker is, more or less, constantly involved in reorganizations as he participates in project financings and mergers. The management of large-scale, risky international mining and development projects constantly involves negotiations to restructure, or "reorganize," the operations, the management, and/or the finances of these ventures. The spectrum of the reorganization activities ranges from the devising of methods to peacefully let out disenchanted investors to the over-the-weekend tactics for securing rescue capital for a coming insolvency crisis. Investment bankers are the doctors involved in saving the client. When the client dies, he is turned over to other specialists.

EXTENSION AND COMPOSITION. Extension and composition are probably the investment banker's most-common approaches to the most-severe reorganization problems his clients face. These methods avoid the legal technicalities and delays of bankruptcy or state common-law proceedings. Extensions postpone the dates of required payments of past-due obligations. In the case of Eurodollar loans, such permission is often directly within the power of the investment banker, and is commonly called "the management of financial default." In composition, some sort of negotiations must precede an agreement to reduce the creditors' claims on the debtor.

In presiding over, or advising upon, proceedings leading to either an extension or a composition, the banker must satisfy the presence of the prerequisities to a successful reorganization:

1. That the debtor is a good moral risk.
2. That the debtor has the ability to make a recovery.
3. That general business conditions are favorable to a recovery.

Upon the satisfaction of these criteria, there is generally a meeting of the debtors and creditors, the appointment of a committee of creditors, an exhaustive report by the committee, and an eventual meeting to work out the composition agreement.

REORGANIZATION. The term *reorganization* as used in the context of bankruptcy or insolvency implies business failure. Actually, the investment banker is almost constantly involved in the reorganization of corporate financing, and if the reorganizations are well managed, failure is never directly an issue.

A business reorganization that is made to avoid business failure, however, generally involves the following:

1. Scaling down the company's fixed charges.
2. Converting short-term debt into long-term debt.
3. Securing new capital financing:
    a. to provide working capital and
    b. to rehabilitate assets.
4. Discovering the causes for failures:
    a. operational and
    b. managerial.

In order to successfully scale down the claims made upon the failing corporation, the banker must ensure that the reorganization agreement is fair to all parties. Reorganization is, after all, only another form of extension or composition. The feature of reorganization that most characterizes this approach to business failure is the issuance of new securities in return for the retirement of the old securities under whose terms the business appeared to be failing. A crucial issue in this exchange is: What is the market value of the old securities? Once this question is answered to the satisfaction of the parties and any relevant regulatory agencies (i.e., the SEC or the FTC), the exchange can be made. If the reorganization is successful, the corporation will have undergone a successful business analysis and corrected the operational, managerial, or financial problems that led to failure, and will have secured new capital to correct the problems, if necessary. This opens the possibility for the investment banker to profit from the anticipated cash flows of the reorganized business venture either through interest on loans, dividends on shares held, or the receipt of advisement fees.

TRENDS IN INTERNATIONAL INVESTMENT BANKING

LOWERED BARRIERS TO ENTRY.   The modern use of Edge Act corporations has only partially lowered the barriers to entering the international investment-banking industry. Foreign legal barriers still exist, as indicated by the recent study by the U.S. Treasury Department (1979) and by a similar study by the OECD (1978).

THE ADVANTAGES OF SIZE.   Aside from the legal barriers, the operational barriers to entry in the international investment-banking industry are formidable. If international investment banking is an industry composed of EACs selling firm aggregates of high-level banking expertise, the large multinational banks have a decided competitive advantage over traditional domestic investment-banking houses. The competitive advantages of size are evident in other areas as well. Giddy (1980) gives evidence that there are greater profits in the foreign-exchange operations of multinational banks with large branch-bank networks than in those with smaller networks of branch banks.

OPERATION IN A PROTECTED MARKET.   Once the operational and legal barriers to entry have been surmounted, an international investment-banking operation can expect to earn oligopolistic profits in a partially protected market (Giddy, 1980). And if the pattern in the United States extends to international banking, the profits in international *investment* banking will be higher than those in international *commercial* banking. This will encourage international investment bankers to further differentiate their services to sew up their markets. These investment banks' services are partially differentiated to begin with, because of the peculiar mix of international commercial-bank capabilities upon which the international investment-banking operations have been piggybacked. It should be easy enough to further differentiate the services using the appropriate advertising media mixed with word-of-mouth advertising.

PARALLEL DOMESTIC AND INTERNATIONAL COMPETITION. An important question is whether or not the traditional domestic investment-banking houses can continue to compete with the piggybacked Edge Act corporations of large multinational banks. In the domestic (U.S.) investment-banking industry, investment-banking houses are attempting to integrate vertically. Wholesale houses are attempting to develop broad-based sales networks at the same time that retail houses are striving to develop sources of the "product"—original security issues (Hayes, 1979). In international banking the traditional investment-banking houses may feel the need to develop international commercial-banking capabilities in order to develop their own brand of vertical international integration. They may find it difficult to do this unless they can arrange appropriate mergers with other international commercial-banking networks.

SOURCES AND SUGGESTED REFERENCES

Aliber, R.Z. "International Banking: Growth and Regulation." *Columbia Journal of World Business,* Vol. X (1975), pp. 9–15.

Baker, J.C., and M.G. Bradford. *American Banks Abroad, Edge Act Companies and Multinational Banking.* New York: Praeger, 1974.

Battersby, M.E. "Avoiding Risks by 'Parallel Lending.'" *Finance Magazine,* Vol. XXI (1976), pp. 56–57.

Boddewyn, J. "Foreign Divestment: Magnitude and Factors." *Journal of International Business Studies,* Vol. X (1979), pp. 21–27.

Eiteman, D.K., and A.I. Stonehill. "Reacting to Foreign Exchange Risk," "International Capital Markets," and "International Banking," in *Multinational Business Finance,* 2nd ed. Reading, Addison-Wesley, 1979.

Federal Reserve Act (12 USCS §§ 601–632). Section 25(a)1.

Ganoe, C.S. "Foreign Banks: Reciprocity and Equality," *The Bankers Magazine,* Vol. CLVII (1974), pp. 28–30.

Ganoe, C.S. "International Banking Gets Stronger," *The Bankers Magazine,* Vol. CLVIII (1975), pp. 109–111.

Giddy, I.H. "The Blossoming of the Eurobond Market," *Columbia Journal of World Business,* Vol. IV (1975), pp. 66–76.

Giddy, I.H. "Internationalization of Commercial and Merchant Banking: The Competitive Structure of the Industry." Paper presented at the Conference on Internationalization of Financial Markets and National Economic Policy, April 10–11, 1980, at New York University, Graduate School of Business Administration, sponsored by the Salomon Brothers Center for the Study of Financial Institutions.

Hayes, II, S.L. "The Transformation of Investment Banking," *Harvard Business Review,* Vol. LVII (1979), pp. 153–170.

Hutton, H.R. "The Regulation of Foreign Banks—A European Viewpoint," *Columbia Journal of World Business,* Vol. X (1975), pp. 115–119.

Logue, D.E., and J.R. Lindvall, "The Behavior of Investment Bankers: An Econometric Investigation," *Journal of Finance,* Vol. XXIX (1974), pp. 203–215.

Neukomm, H.A. "Risk and Error Minimization in Foreign Exchange Trading," *Columbia Journal of World Business,* Vol. X (1975), pp. 77–86.

Organization for Economic Co-operation and Development. *Regulations Affecting International Banking Operations of Banks and Nonbanks.* Paris: OECD, 1978.

Robinson, Jr, S.W. *Multinational Banking.* Leiden, the Netherlands: A. W. Sitjthoff, 1972.

Rudy, J.P. "Global Planning in Multinational Banking," *Columbia Journal of World Business,* Vol. X (1975), pp. 16–22.

Thoman, G. "International Banking Can Be Profitable for U.S. Regional Banks," *Columbia Journal of World Business,* Vol. X (1975), pp. 23–32.

United States Treasury Department. *Report to Congress on Foreign Government Treatment of U.S. Commercial Banking Organization.* Washington, DC: U.S. Government Printing Office, 1979.

Weston, J.F. and E.F. Brigham. *Essentials of Managerial Finance,* 5th ed. Hinsdale, IL: Dryden Press, 1979.

Wolf, K. "The Impact of Rate Fluctuations on the Profitability of Swap Transactions," *Euromoney,* XXII (1975), pp. 26–29.

Wynant, L. "Essential Elements of Project Financing," *Harvard Business Review,* Vol. LVIII (1980), pp. 165–173.

SECTION **21**

COUNTRY-RISK ASSESSMENT

CONTENTS

ELEMENTS OF COUNTRY-RISK
ASSESSMENT   3

Structural Aspects   5
Monetary Aspects   6
External Economic Aspects   6
Liquidity Aspects   8
Political Aspects   8

DESIGNING A COUNTRY-RISK
INSTRUMENT   10

RISK ASSESSMENT AND
INTERNATIONAL BUSINESS
DECISIONS   17

SOURCES AND SUGGESTED
REFERENCES   19

COUNTRY-RISK ASSESSMENT

Ingo Walter

International business involves a wide variety of inherent risks. Export markets, carefully developed and nurtured, may suddenly collapse because of internal changes in target markets, imposition of exchange controls, or protectionist trade-policy measures. Imports of raw materials, components and parts, or capital equipment may face restricted supplies or major increases in cost due to shifting conditions, economic or political, in principal supplier countries. International lending may face restrictions on repayment of interest and principal, rescheduling, or outright default. Contracts to build turnkey plants abroad may face abrupt cancellations; licensing arrangements may face restrictions on fee remittances; and foreign direct investment may be subject to nationalization, expropriation, confiscation, indigenization, or a variety of domestic measures in host countries that seriously impair profitability.

Such risks are essentially related to economic and political conditions that exist in *countries*—in politically sovereign national states. They can also spill over from one country to another, or affect several countries at once, thereby limiting the ability of firms to diversify away from the risks inherent in country conditions. It is generally agreed that exposure to such risks in international business has risen over the years, requiring banks, manufacturing firms, insurance companies, and others to devote increasing resources to analyzing country-related conditions and ensuring that returns are adequate to compensate them for the risks involved. This is the task of *country-risk assessment,* which has received a great deal of attention by banks, corporations, and others engaged in international business and exposed to shifting country conditions.

ELEMENTS OF COUNTRY-RISK ASSESSMENT

A simple view of the problem focuses on risk that arises out of structural (supply-side) elements, demand-side and monetary elements, and external economic and political developments, as well as the quality of the national economic management team and the domestic political constraints bearing upon decision makers. One might begin with a relationship such as the following:

$$Y + M = A + X$$

representing real flows of goods and services in an economy, where Y is output, M is imports, A is domestic absorption (consumption, investment, and public-sector spending) and X is exports, all in real terms. Clearly, supply-side changes in Y with unchanged demand will require shifts in imports or exports—reduced production capabilities, for example, mean either increased imports or a more limited capacity to export. In a similar way, demand-side shifts affecting A with unchanged supply can be examined—increased government spending will, for example, have to be met from expanded imports or will deflect export production to meet domestic needs. Monetary variables can affect the picture as well—growth in the domestic money supply will, unless relected in exchange rates, tend to raise A relative to Y and, therefore, increase M, decrease X, or both.

In order to bring the money side into the picture explicitly, we can develop an equally simple equation describing international financial flows:

$$VX - VM - DS + FDI + U - K_0 = DR - NBR.$$

Here VX and VM represent the money value of exports and imports, respectively. DS represents debt-service payments to foreigners (usually part of VM in conventional balance-of-payments accounting); FDI is net flows of nonresident foreign direct investments; U represents net flows of private and public-sector grants such as foreign aid, K_0 is net capital flows undertaken by residents, DR is the change in international reserves of the country in question, and NBR is its net borrowing requirement. An overall negative balance on the left-hand side of the equation clearly means that the country will have to increase its foreign borrowing or use up some of its international reserves. At the same time, increases in foreign borrowing will mean increases in DS in future time periods.

Tying the two equations together are typical "country scenarios." For example, a government comes under political pressure to increase spending for domestic social purposes. It does so by running a fiscal deficit, which it finances by issuing government bonds, most of which may end up in the asset portfolio of the central bank, which in turn has paid for them by increasing the money supply (central-bank liabilities). This puts upward pressure on the general price level in the economy, which the government is reluctant to see reflected in a depreciation of its currency—the disequilibrium exchange rate being secured through exchange controls or central-bank intervention on foreign-exchange markets. The whole process is likely to show up as an increase in A offset by an increase in M and/or a decrease in X in the first equation, the financial flows appearing in the second equation as a net reduction in $(VX - VM)$ financed by a reduction in reserve holdings DR (the central bank's external assets) and/or an increase in net borrowing abroad NBR (e.g., the central bank's external liabilities). Many other such scenarios could obviously be sketched out. The problem is to ascertain what each of them may mean for the different variables we have identified as they evolve over time, particularly DS and NBR. This, together with the underlying political scenarios, is the essence of getting a fix on the expected value and variance of an organization's exposure in a particular country. How can this be accomplished?

Effective country-risk assessment ideally requires the employment of a true "Renaissance person"—exceedingly intelligent, a holder of doctorates from respectable institutions in economics, political science, sociology, psychology, and perhaps a few other fields as well, totally objective, with a great deal of common sense. In addition to being rather well traveled, he or she should be up to date on developments in all countries of interest to the bank (and in other countries that might affect them) and personally acquainted with key policy makers. Obviously, there are few such individuals wandering around these days. And so the question is whether international banks or corporations *as institutions* can in some way put together all of these qualities, using relatively "ordinary" individuals and traditional organizational linkages to assemble a superior ability to forecast the future of countries.

STRUCTURAL ASPECTS. The question here is whether developments in the internal workings of a national economy, both on the supply and demand sides, will be such as to seriously threaten markets, profitability, or the ability to service a country's external obligations. We are interested first in the linkages between the supply side's ability to produce export, import-competing, and nontraded goods, and in the qualitative and quantitative dimensions of the labor force, the capital stock, the natural-resource base, technology, and entrepreneurship that combine to determine this capability. At the same time we are interested in the contributions of real-capital inflows to these supply capabilities made possible by foreign borrowing, foreign direct investment, and other types of financial transfers.

Historical measures of supply-side economic performance abound: labor-force growth and participation rates, unemployment rates, migration and labor-force distributional trends, savings and investment trends, productivity trends, natural-resource availability, and the like. The quality, timeliness, and comparability of the relevant data vary widely, but the real problem obviously lies in ascertaining whether the past is likely to be a good guide for the future. Here a great deal of judgment is required in order to identify and project, for example, various types of quantitative or qualitative labor-supply ceilings and possible market disruptions, social and economic infrastructure bottlenecks, capital-adequacy problems, natural-resource constraints, and so on. Of prime importance is the evaluation of government policies that will influence domestic savings and investment, capital flight and foreign direct investment, risk taking and entrepreneurial activity, supply conditions in labor markets, the adequacy of economic and social infrastructure, exploitation, and forward-processing of natural resources—the entire underlying complex of incentives and disincentives built into the nation's fiscal and regulatory system. In many cases such policies are anchored in government planning documents, in which case an assessment of the degree of realism embodied in these plans may be quite important—government attempts to force the supply side of an economy into a mold that does not fit, but to which a political commitment has been made, can lead to severe domestic and international distortions in the real sector, ballooning of external borrowing, and, ultimately, debt-service problems.

On the demand side, we are interested in factors affecting taxes, government expenditures, transfer payments, and the overall fiscal soundness of the public sector, as we are in prospective patterns of demand for goods and services from the private and export sectors. Once again, historical data series covering consumption spending, government taxation and expenditures, gross national product or gross domestic product, and other conventional economic indicators are usually available on a reasonably timely basis to permit an evaluation of the demand picture over a number of years. But forecasts depend in large part on the ability to predict government demand management and income-distribution policies, as well as exogenous demand-side shocks that may emanate from the foreign sector, changing expectations, or other sources.

In attempting to develop a defensible prognosis of the structural aspects of country futures, therefore, the analyst must start from as complete an information base as possible about the historical track record of the domestic economy and its current situation, and then try to project both the demand-side and supply-side dimensions. This may not be a serious problem in the short term, where the exogenous and policy elements are relatively fixed, but the sources of error multiply as the forecasting period is extended, and few or none of the important determinants of economic performance can be considered constant. What will happen to taxes, transfers, government regulation, the pattern of subsidies and other market distortions, consumption and saving patterns, investment incentives, treatment of foreign-owned firms, and similar factors 5 to 10 years into the future? Everything is up for grabs, and forecasting has to rely in large measure on the basic competence of the policymakers, their receptivity to outside advice, and the pattern of social and political constraints under which they operate. Assuming the cast of characters remains the same, past experience in macroeconomic management and reactions to outside shocks may not be a bad guide to the future. But this assumption itself is often open to question.

MONETARY ASPECTS.   A part of the task of projecting future country scenarios —and some would contend the most important part—lies in the monetary sector. Whereas most country analyses contain extensive descriptions of the national financial system, the critical factors obviously relate to prices and exchange rates. Useful indicators are the domestic monetary base, the money supply, net domestic credit, and available price indexes, together with net foreign official assets and net foreign debt. Monetary disturbances may originate domestically or from the foreign sector (e.g., major increases in external reserves that become monetized). Apart from their inflationary and exchange-rate aspects, of course, such disturbances may also have real-sector influences on consumption and savings, capital formation, income distribution, expectations, and the like.

Once again, whereas the mechanisms relating monetary developments to country-risk problems are well understood, and the requisite data usually more readily available than most others, near-term assessments are far easier than formulating a defensible long-range outlook. It is, after all, possible to evaluate the relationship of the existing exchange rate to some hypothetical market-determined rate based on a calculated purchasing-power-parity index, and to project this deviation for the near term based on relative inflation trends. The larger the degree of currency overvaluation, for example, the greater will the need for increased external borrowing tend to be, as well as the likelihood of reserve losses and/or the prospects for a tightening of controls on international trade and payments. Much more difficult is the task of forecasting government responses to problem situations in the monetary sphere—devaluation, liberalization of controls, domestic monetary stringency, and the like—and particularly the timing of such measures. And in the longer term, the problem once again boils down to the competence of the monetary policy makers and the political pressures bearing upon them.

EXTERNAL ECONOMIC ASPECTS.   Because of the importance of foreign-exchange availability in projecting debt service, country assessments usually must pay a great deal of attention to outside factors affecting a country's balance of payments and external finance. On the export side, this requires evaluation of both long-term trends and short-term instabilities. Increasing product and market diversification might be a sign of greater export stability and reduced vulnerability to shifting economic and political conditions, or protectionist trends in a country's major markets. Shifts in the ratio of exports to gross national product may signal changing future balance-of-payments conditions, and an analysis of demand and supply characteristics for major export products may indicate possible sources of future instability in export receipts. Domestic export-supply constraints and export-competing-demand elements link back into the analysis of structural problems, outlined above. Export policies set by the national government and by governments of competing exporters may also be important, along with exchange-rate policies. In general, we are interested here in alignment of a country's exports with its international competitive advantage, in diversification of export risk, and in home and third-country policies that might pose a threat to future export earnings.

On the import side as well, concern must focus on both long-term trends and short-term instabilities. The ratio of imports to gross national product, for example, says little about country risk, but abrupt and sizable shifts in this ratio may be important. The ability to compress imports in times of balance-of-payments trouble may be considered in terms of measures such as the ratio of food and fuel to total imports, or the ratio of food, fuel, intermediate goods, and capital equipment to total imports. Import-price volatility, supplier concentration among trading partners, and trends in import-replacement production are among the other measures that can help identify risk elements orginating on the import side. Here, as in the case of exports, we are also interested in the policy context—the structure of effective tariff and nontariff protection and its impact on domestic resource allocation and efficiency in production.

We have already noted the importance of foreign direct investment for the supply side of a national economy, in terms of its contribution to aggregate and sectoral capital formation, technology transfer, development of human resources, management and enterpreneurial activity, access to markets, and access to supplies—the traditional multinational corporate "bundle" of services. Besides the balance-of-payments gains associated with capital inflows, induced exports, and import-replacement production, outflows may occur through induced imports of goods and services and profit remittances. Each foreign-investment project evidences a more or less unique balance-of-payments profile, in magnitude as well as in timing.

Policies affecting foreign direct investment (e.g., taxation, restrictions on earnings remittances, indigenization pressures, nationalization, and expropriation) may seriously alter this profile and thereby influence country prospects as viewed by international lenders as well. Multinational companies are often extraordinarily sensitive to changes in national-policy environments, and because they can portend change in the overall creditworthiness of countries as a whole, shifts in foreign-direct-investment patterns deserve careful attention. So do capital outflows on the part of domestic residents; these are frequently highly sensitive to the domestic outlook, especially in times of possible discontinuous policy changes.

Finally, it may be important to analyze the magnitude and types of grants and concessional loans that a country receives from abroad, and prospective future developments in these flows. Here domestic developments in the donor countries, donor-recipient relations, and the economic and political attractiveness of the recipient for such transfers may be important. Moreover, is there a "lender of last resort"? Countries of strategic or economic importance are obviously prime candidates for future intergovernmental "rescues" that may to some extent backstop private-bank-lending exposure in severe problem situations and increase the interest of major financial powers in successfully concluding resolution of country problems.

LIQUIDITY ASPECTS.   The aforementioned issues usually involve medium- and long-range forecasts of such aggregates as the balance of trade, the current account, and various other "flow" measures. These will naturally be reflected in a country's future international-reserve position and in its access to international financial markets for future financing needs. Near-term "liquidity" assessments generally focus on such measures as changes in a country's owned reserves and International Monetary Fund (IMF) position and on ratios, such as reserves to monthly imports, intended to indicate in some sense the degree of "cushioning" provided by reserve holdings. Ability to borrow additional sums abroad, or to refinance existing debt, naturally depends on the projected state of financial markets and assessment of country creditworthiness by international banks and official institutions at the time of need. Favorable financial-market and country conditions sometimes lead to "preemptive" borrowing to restructure outstanding debt at market terms and to build up reserves for future use or to improve future creditworthiness.

Analysis of the size and structure of country indebtedness and debt-service payments is equally important in this regard. Ratios such as total debt to exports or to gross national product, and long-term public debt to exports or to gross national product are used in virtually all country analyses, as are the amount and trends in overall external indebtedness, current versus term debt, and total and short-term bank claims. The *debt-service ratio*—debt-service payments to exports or "normal" exports—is perhaps the most common and can be criticized on various grounds. For example, by using only exports in the denominator, it ignores the potentially equivalent contributions of import substitution to debt-service capabilities. And a particular debt-service ratio (say .3) may mean entirely different things for different countries as far as creditworthiness is concerned. Additionally, the ratios of foreign-capital inflows to debt-service payments, exports plus capital inflows and aid receipts to current debt, vital imports plus debt-service payments to exports plus capital inflows and aid receipt (*compressibility ratio*) and the reciprocal of the average maturity of external debt (*rollover ratio*) are commonly used.

All such ratios must be interpreted cautiously and have different meanings for different countries and for the same country at different times and stages of development. There are no valid rules of thumb. The skill lies in the interpretation of any ratios used, particularly changes therein, and in the specific context of particular country situations. Yet even if a good analyst recognizes the limitations of some of the more pedestrian indicators, they may nevertheless figure heavily and perhaps mechanically into how the market views the situation in a debt-rollover context and, therefore, may have to be monitored carefully.

POLITICAL ASPECTS.   Besides domestic structural and monetary factors and external stock and flow variables, country analysis related to term exposure always requires astute political forecasting. Most closely related to the economic variables just reviewed, of course, is the "competence" or "wisdom" of the economic managers, which, insofar as it relates to the cast of characters on the stage, is basically a political matter. Small changes in the actors can cause enormous changes in the quality of the play. There is also the question whether the technocrats have a full political mandate to "do what is necessary" from a debt-service point of view, and ultimately whether the government itself is firmly enough in the saddle and has the political "guts" to carry it out. Recent "horror stories" ranging from Turkey and Zaire to Jamaica, Peru, and Poland illustrate the critical importance of evaluating and forecasting the political "overlay" of national economic policy making—the degree of resolve, the power base, and the tools available for implementing sound policy decisions. Banks and corporations that are leaders in country analysis generally place a great deal of stress on this particular dimension, which requires an entirely different sort of prognostication and information base then some of the more-mechanical aspects of the problem. Beyond this, however, there are more-fundamental political developments that need to be sorted out, monitored, and forecast as well.

Internal political change may range from gradual to abrupt, systemic to nonsystemic, and cataclysmic to trivial in terms of its importance to international firms. For example, political drift to the right or left may mean a great deal in terms of the internal and external workings of the national economy and the quality of economic management, as the recent history of countries like Brazil, Mexico, Chile, and Sri Lanka nicely demonstrates. The symptoms make themselves felt in domestic fiscal and monetary policies, relations with foreign countries, pressures for nationalization or indigenization of foreign direct investments, imposition of exchange controls, and the like. Adverse shifts in this respect may result in soaring imports, reduced capacity to export, drying-up of foreign direct investment, capital flight, aid cutoffs, and problems in accessing international capital markets. The point is that it is necessary to fix on the direction, magnitude, and timing of political drift, if any, before very much that is sensible can be said about future macroeconomic scenarios.

A more dramatic version of the same thing relates to violent internal political conflict, which may ultimately produce the type of political "drift" discussed above, but in the meantime may have serious direct economic consequences as well. Strikes, terrorism, sabotage, and popular insurrection may seriously disrupt the workings of the national economy, with potentially dramatic consequences for the balance of payments. Export industries like tourism are particularly sensitive to such problems. The direct and indirect import requirements of government antiinsurgency efforts can be significant as well. It is obviously necessary to assess the strength of both the insurgency movement and the government in order to forecast the duration and outcome of the conflict, which (if it results in systemic change) may even lead to repudiation of external debt. As the Iranian case shows, such forecasts are as treacherous as they are critical to the whole process of country analysis. The assassination of South Korean President Park Chung Hee illustrates the extreme range of possible outcomes of a descrete event of political violence, from total insignificance to a fundamental political and economic overthrow of the existing order.

External political conflict can likewise take a variety of forms, ranging from invasion (Afghanistan) and foreign-inspired or foreign-supported insurgency (Zaire, Morocco, Tunisia) to border tension and perceived external threats (Peru, Israel, Thailand). Threats from abroad often require far-reaching domestic-resource reallocation in the form of an inflated defense establishment—causing probable adverse trade shifts—and for most countries involve large direct foreign-exchange costs as well. Military hardware, human resources, and infrastructure in an economic sense generally have low or negative productivity in terms of the domestic economy or the balance of payments. Such distortions alone may have a serious bearing on the risk profile of a country as viewed from abroad.

These problems reside in both *potential* and *actual* external conflict. The latter simply makes the various distortions worse—to the extent that the costs are not absorbed by foreign political allies—to which must be added the supply-side possibilities of physical and human-resource destruction and dislocation, obsolescence, and reconstruction costs to the extent that these are not partly offset by reparations or aid receipts. Even if external political conflict is won, there may be derivative internal political upheavals and possibly sizable costs of occupation. If the conflict is lost, continued internal resistance and reparations obligations may have a debilitating effect on the home economy, quite apart from the possibility of debt repudiation by the successor regime. All such assessments have to be undertaken in probabilistic terms, but they are of far more than casual interest in exporting to, investing in, or lending to countries like South Korea, Taiwan, Thailand, Yugoslavia, Pakistan, and even Malaysia and Singapore.

Shifting political alliances, regional political developments, and bilateral relations over such peripheral issues as human rights and nuclear proliferation can provide additional sources of political conflict. All are heavily influenced by global, regional, and national political events. Heavy lending exposure in Eastern Europe and China (insofar as the banks are not backstopped by their home governments) carry with them risks related both to future political developments and to the ability of the borrowers to sever links to Western trade and financial markets at acceptable economic cost to themselves.

Political forecasting is an art that, despite its central role in plotting the creditworthiness future of countries, remains in its infancy. Indexes of political stability developed by political scientists say little that is very reliable about the future or about the ultimate implications for traders, investors, or lenders. The more-sophisticated projections and even on-line information systems detailing possible sources of internal and external political conflict, although useful and necessary, usually leave the critical judgments largely up to the user of the information. There are also problems in the completeness and currency of political information, and the inevitable biases embedded in external and in-house information that consensual approaches such as the "Delphi" technique have only begun to attack. It is not surprising, therefore, that political forecasts by banks and others "missed" on dramatic cases like Iran, Egypt and South Korea, or less-dramatic ones like Zaire and Turkey. It hardly means, however, that significant advances cannot still be made.

DESIGNING A COUNTRY-RISK INSTRUMENT

From a managerial perspective, a key question is how the results of country assessment can be boiled down to "ratings" that can be effectively used in decision making. Clearly, to adequately describe a country's prospects fully would require an extensive and detailed narrative backed up by large quantities of economic data and forecasts. Such extensive and relatively unstructured "country studies" would clearly lack usability in business-decision making. Moreover, they would be relatively noncomparable among countries and highly sensitive to differences in competence among country analysts. Some technique, therefore, may have to be found to organize as much country information as possible and boil it down into usable form. This is the task of *country-risk rating* systems.

Exhibit 1 presents an instrument that might be used to construct a country-risk rating. It involves assigning judgmental values to a series of factors, compiling them

EXHIBIT 1   COUNTRY-ANALYSIS INSTRUMENT

ECONOMIC ELEMENTS

Supply Capability and Resiliency

Describe numerically the prospects during the next 7–10 years the following elements of the supply side of the national economy.

	Favorable			Unfavorable	
	1	2	3	4	5
Labor-force quantity					
Labor-force quality					
Labor-supply bottlenecks					
Labor-supply disruptions					
Savings rate					
Financial intermediation[1]					
Investment levels (domestic)					
Economic infrastructure[2]					
Social infrastructure[3]					
Agricultural development					
Natural resources					
Energy					
Foreign direct investment					
Productivity					
Entrepreneurship					
Character of the people					
Supply-side summary:					
Real-growth potential					
Emergence of bottlenecks					
Ability to withstand adverse shocks					

Demand and Monetary Factors

Describe numerically the prospects during the next 7–10 years for the following elements of the aggregate demand and monetary characteristics of the national economy.

Aggregate-demand factors:	Favorable			Unfavorable	
	1	2	3	4	5
Consumer spending					
Investment spending					
Government spending					
Net foreign demand[4]					
Income-redistribution pressure					
Government deficit					
Monetary factors:	1	2	3	4	5
Money-supply growth					
Demand-side summary:	1	2	3	4	5
Unemployment					
Inflation rate					
Realized GNP growth[5]					

EXHIBIT 1   CONTINUED

Economic policy makers:	1	2	3	4	5

Assessment of competence

External Balance

Describe numerically the prospects during the next 7–10 years for the country's balance of payments.

Trade:	Favorable			Unfavorable	
	1	2	3	4	5

Export growth
Export diversification[6]
Import growth
Import diversification[7]
Import compressibility[8]

Financial flows:	1	2	3	4	5

Investment flows (net)
Foreign-aid receipts
Capital flight
Foreign-borrowing ability

Reserves and debt:	1	2	3	4	5

Size of foreign debt
Debt service "burden"[9]
External reserves
IMF position[10]

Exchange rate:	1	2	3	4	5

Deviation from market rate[11]

External-balance summary:	1	2	3	4	5

Balance of trade
Terms of trade[12]
Balance of payments
External reserves
Foreign debt

POLITICAL ELEMENTS

Leadership Change

Mark the combination that seems to describe best the country's leadership:

	Demo-cratically elected majority party	Demo-cratically elected majority coalition	Non-democratically elected ruling party/ coalition/faction	No real ruling party/ coalition/faction
Leadership in power for past 4–5 years				
Leadership in power for less than 4–5 yrs.				
Leadership facing fragmented opposition				

EXHIBIT 1 CONTINUED

Leadership facing
strong, organized
opposition

	Low				High
	1	2	3	4	5

Describe numerically the level
of violence displayed during
demonstrations, riots, or
strikes by both demonstrators
and police (army?) during the
past 2–3 years

Describe numerically the level
of terrorism (both internally
and abroad, by organizations
belonging to the country)

Goal Change

	YES	NO	DON'T KNOW
Fundamental issues are being debated and the leadership is deeply divided over them			

(If the answer is YES, answer the following:)

	YES	NO
Does the content of these debates touch on matters of economic policy?	☐	☐
Although it does not touch on matters of economic policy, the debates themselves strongly influence the leadership's economic policies	☐	☐

(If the answer is NO, answer the following:)

	YES	NO
Although fundamental issues are not being debated, they do exist and are potentially divisive	☐	☐
Strong pressure groups within the country are likely to bring up requests or demands whose implementation requires a drastic change in officially stated systemic goals	☐	☐

Policy Change

	Yes				No
	1	2	3	4	5

The way laws, regulations, rules, and
orders are implemented has changed over
the last 4–5 years

Administrative procedures are currently
being revised and changed

EXHIBIT 1   CONTINUED

The need for a thorough administrative reform having deep implications on how rules are implemented is felt

Capability

How to you rate the country's . . .

	Favorably			Unfavorably	
	1	2	3	4	5

Efforts to set up and manage an efficient educational system (elementary and high schools, vocational schools, institutes of higher learning)?

Efforts to use its natural resources (land reclamation, extraction of minerals, etc.)?

Efforts to utilize its human capital (providing employment and incentives to specialists, financing research, etc.)?

Efforts to enforce its own laws (prevention and punishment of crime)?

Efforts to avoid and prevent deviance or morally condemnable behavior?

Efforts to cope with environmental problems (pollution, health, etc.)?

Welfare programs?

Other programs for the underprivileged?

Wage and price policy?

Ability to project a good image of the government among its own citizens?

Ability to project a good image abroad?

Ability to convince the public opinion of the worthiness of its own government?

Ability to cope with internal natural emergencies (earthquakes, drought, etc.)?

Ability to cope with social and political emergencies (strikes, terrorism, etc.)?

Ability to respond effectively to explicit military threat from abroad?

Structural Differentiation

Does the political system have specialized structures able to perform the following activities:

	Low specialization			High specialization	
	1	2	3	4	5

   rule making
   rule implementation
   rule adjudication (tribunals)

Does the political system have specialized structures able to convert popular demands and widely felt needs into suitable outputs

EXHIBIT 1 CONTINUED

(a new law, an administrative reform, etc.) through the following activities:	1	2	3	4	5

rule making
rule implementation
rule adjudication

Ideological Polarization

	Low				High
Check the existence of the following:	1	2	3	4	5

Opposing groups characterized by widely differing systems of thought

Historically rooted cleavages among groups

Intolerance among groups and unwillingness to compromise

Use of violence justified and encouraged by the opposing groups

Subsystem Autonomy

Low				High
1	2	3	4	5

Amount of political participation allowed through elections and party/trade-union activism (or whatever group has an official status)

Amount of political participation allowed or tolerated through demonstrations, propaganda, lobbies, professional associations, etc. (informal interest groups)

Level of the activity actually occurring

Internal Political Summary

Favorable			Unfavorable	
1	2	3	4	5

Prospects for domestic political violence

Prospects for "systemic" political change

Prospects for adverse economic effects of emerging political change

Mandate given to economic policy makers

External Political Factors

Favorable			Unfavorable	
1	2	3	4	5

Prospects of border warfare

Geopolitical tension spillovers

Regional political alliances

Economic warfare

EXHIBIT 1   CONTINUED

COUNTRY-REVIEW SUMMARY

	1	2	3	4	5	Weights[a]	Products
Economy: supply side							
Economy: demand side							
Balance of payments, reserves, debt							
Competence of economic policy makers							
Internal political							
External political							
TOTALS						100	

WEIGHTED COUNTRY RATING ⟶

PROJECT-SPECIFIC FACTORS

Aside from the overall country profile you have developed by running through the foregoing analysis, is there anything about the proposed project that might cause you to alter your assessment of risk?

Yes   No

If so, is your assessment of project-specific risk higher or lower than that applying to the country as a whole?

Higher   Lower

By how much (%)?

Why?

_____

_____

_____

_____

_____

_____

Explanatory Notes
[1] Adequacy of existing or prospective financial institutions to channel savings into investment.
[2] For example, rail lines, highways, port facilities, telecommunications, etc.
[3] For example, schools, hospitals.
[4] Exports minus imports.
[5] Outlook for *actual* (as opposed to *potential*) GNP growth.

EXHIBIT 1   CONTINUED

[6] Diversification across export markets and products.

[7] Diversification across import sources of supply (trading partners).

[8] Imports of "necessities" like food and fuel (which cannot be reduced under adversity) as a percentage of total imports.

[9] For example, debt-service payments as a percent of exports.

[10] Net borrowings from the International Monetary Fund.

[11] Is the currency "overvalued" or "undervalued," as projected?

[12] Movement of export prices relative to import prices.

[a] Assign weights to factors A through F in this column according to your assessment of the *relative* importance of each summary factor. Weights must add up to 100. Then multiply the value you have assigned to each factor by its weight, and add all of the products for items A through F. Your total ("weighted country rating") will lie somewhere between 100 (most favorable) and 500 (least favorable).

into aggregates, and then compiling the aggregates into an overall summary "score." This involves the assignment of weights, either explicit or implicit, to the various factors. This process may clearly involve a great deal of subjectivity, and it is not at all certain that the same weights should be assigned to each country—since the relative importance of individual factors differs as potential sources of risk from one country to the next.

What the country-risk-rating approach contributes in usability, it often loses in capturing highly country specific sources of risk. For example, few country-risk-rating systems succeeded in forecasting the 1977 Iranian revolution or its consequences for international business transactions. For this reason, dependence on such "weighted checklist" or "scoring" systems can be quite hazardous. It is recommended that this kind of approach be used only as a preliminary "screen" to identify countries that should be further reviewed in depth with specific reference to the kind of exposure contemplated.

RISK ASSESSMENT AND INTERNATIONAL BUSINESS DECISIONS

Given the nature of the country-evaluation problem within the context of decisions in international lending and investing, and the available techniques, it is useful to discuss briefly the institutional setting within which this process occurs. Exhibit 2 is a simplified schematic of a decision system, one that will vary to some extent among international firms or banks. The solid lines represent reporting relationships, and the dashed lines represent information flows. Information on cross-border exposure can be maintained by a monitoring system at the head office. Care must be taken that exposure is correctly measured in the light of third-country guarantees, insurance, and certain other factors that might be considered to shift the locus of risk. Exposure data should be updated frequently and made available to responsible officers along with any country limits decided upon by management.

The degree of decentralization of decision making differs substantially among international corporations and banks. However, the need to secure competitive advantages through close client contact, quick response times, and adequate decision

EXHIBIT 2   SETTING, MONITORING, AND EVALUATING INTERNATIONAL RISK EXPOSURE

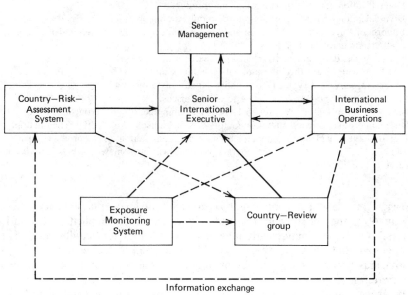

Information exchange

authority often leads to greater decentralization. This puts a premium on the existence of some type of centralized system that assures that objective risk evaluation is in fact undertaken, yet at the same time does not itself unduly restrict the activities of the enterprise in a highly competitive marketplace. In any case, there will normally be a substantial two-way exchange of information between those responsible for the system and line managers insofar as they are not one and the same. In the event that a major project is contemplated, if a shift in existing exposure limits seems justified by profitability trends, or if an alteration in the perceived riskiness of exposure develops, an *ad hoc* country-review group may be formed, consisting of responsible officers, senior executives with regional responsibility, country economists and other country specialists, and possibly other interested individuals under the chairmanship of the firm's senior international corporate officer or his designee. Such a review group may make a recommendation of appropriate action in the case involved. The purpose is to bring together as many different viewpoints as possible, often with conflicting opinions—for example between the country economist emphasizing the risks and executives emphasizing business opportunities, competitive positioning and the associated returns. Ultimate responsibility lies with the senior international corporate officer who reports directly to top management and is charged with monitoring and planning the bank's international loan or investment portfolio within broad policy guidelines.

In the design of a country-analysis function, the emphasis clearly must be on the fact that it is the beginning, not the end, of the task. Approaches that try to be overly precise risk triggering arguments among users over irrelevant points. Those that are too general may fail to concentrate on the true sources of risk in country exposure and on the specific concerns facing a particular bank or corporation. Risk to medium-

and long-term loan or investment exposure requires a far more complex analysis than risk to short-term lending or to exporting. The twin temptations of "quick and dirty" and "overloaded" country assessments often seem to confront international enterprises. The first approach promises mechanical shortcuts and the use of low-priced talent to grind out results at reasonable cost, but often appears to succeed only in producing nonsense—there really is no substitute for high-quality analysis, flexibility, judgment, and familiarity. The second approach may rely on well-qualified internal personnel at high cost, yet encounter a dangerous narrowing of country expertise, possibly cause dissension, and create bottlenecks in the decision-making process.

The conflicting demands of country assessment—ranging from high levels of usability, auditability, and comparability and the need to capture exceedingly complex and country-specific qualitative judgments over extended periods of time, to the need to avoid abuse of the results in decision making—probably mean that there is no such thing as an "ideal" system. "Appropriate" systems will certainly differ for different banks or corporations. The key may reside as much on the *human resources* side as on the *technology* side. To train line bankers or corporate executives in using reasonably unsophisticated yet sensible country assessments properly and in being sensitive to changing country-risk profiles as they go about their business may in the end contribute more to sound decisions than comparable resources devoted to the design and implementation of more-elegant systems. This would appear to follow from the view of multinational corporations' and banks' general competitive advantage as "information factories" to which their global operations and headquarters-affiliate links are ideally suited. The exercise of country assessment should be an integrated managerial process that focuses the network of information and actively involves individuals with different functions and perspectives. The exercise will thus have intangible benefits all its own, quite apart from its more visible output in the form of defensible country-by-country evaluations. Mechanization and decentralization of the country review process will tend to cut down and perhaps eliminate this benefit and may thereby help to stifle an environment conducive to sound international business decisions.

SOURCES AND SUGGESTED REFERENCES

Duff, D., and I. Peacock. "A Cash Flow Approach to Sovereign Risk Analysis," *The Banker,* XXI (1979), pp. 34–39.

Gladwin, T.N., and I. Walter. *Multinationals Under Fire: Lessons in the Management of Conflict.* New York: Wiley-Interscience, 1980.

Goodman, S.H. ed. *Financing and Risk in Developing Countries.* New York: Praeger, 1978.

Goodman, S.H. "How the Big Banks Really Evaluate Sovereign Risks," *Euromoney,* VIII (1977), pp. 41–46.

Haner, F.T. "Rating Investment Risks Abroad," *Business Horizons,* III (1979), pp. 34–42.

Hofer, C.W., and T.P. Haller. "Globescan: A Way to Better International Risk Assessment," *Journal of Business Strategy,* Vol. II (1980), pp. 68–75.

Kobrin, S.J., "Political Risk: A Review and Reconsideration," *Journal of International Business Studies,* Vol. XI (1979), pp. 44–61.

Nagy, P. *Country Risk: How to Assess, Quantify and Monitor It.* London: Euromoney Publications, 1978.

Nagy, P., "Quantifying Country Risk: A System Developed by Economists at the Bank of Montreal," *Columbia Journal of World Business*, XIII (1979), pp. 44–60.

Puz, R. "How to Tell When a Country Shifts from A-1 to E-5," *Euromoney*, Vol. IX (1978), pp. 123–137.

van Agtmael, A. "Evaluating the Risks of Lending to Developing Countries," *Euromoney*, Vol. VII (1976), pp. 88–96.

COMPARATIVE ACCOUNTING SYSTEMS

CONTENTS

TOWARD A TAXONOMY OF NATIONAL ACCOUNTING SYSTEMS 3

Descriptive Comparisons 3
Classification Frameworks and Morphologies for National Accounting Systems 4
  Hatfield's framework 4
  Mueller's framework 4
  The Seidler-Previts framework 4
  AAA's framework and morphology 6
Statistical Classification Schemes 7
  The Da Costa-Bourgeois-Lawson clusters 7
  Frank's clusters 9
  Disclosure and measurement clusters 9

SURVEY OF MAJOR ACCOUNTING SYSTEMS 10

Accounting in Germany 11
  The balance sheet 12
  The income statement 15
Accounting in the Netherlands 17
  Limpberg's replacement value theory 17
  Replacement value accounting practice 18
  Other selected accounting and reporting practices 19
Accounting in Sweden 20

Valuation of fixed assets 21
Inventory reserves 21
Investment reserves 22
Other selected accounting and reporting practices 23
Accounting in Poland 23
  The hierarchical aggregation process 24
  The system of uniform charts of accounts 24
  Uniform valuation principles 25
  Financial reports 26

IMPLICATIONS OF INTERNATIONAL DIFFERENCES 27

HARMONIZATION EFFORTS 29

The International Accounting Standards Committee 29
The International Federation of Accountants 31
The United Nations 31
The Organization for Economic Cooperation and Development 32
The European Economic Community 33
Union Européene des Experts Comptables Economiques et Financiers 34
Other Harmonization Efforts 34

SOURCES AND SUGGESTED REFERENCES 35

COMPARATIVE ACCOUNTING SYSTEMS

Konrad W. Kubin

Financial accounting principles and reporting practices of business enterprises around the world reveal a remarkable blend of diversity and homogeneity. Each nation's set of financial accounting and reporting standards is unique; yet many accounting concepts are universally accepted and have resulted in similar or even identical practices in different countries. This section discusses frameworks for the classification of national accounting systems, surveys the accounting practices in four foreign countries, analyzes the concerns of groups affected by international differences, and describes harmonization efforts.

TOWARD A TAXONOMY OF NATIONAL ACCOUNTING SYSTEMS

Classification frameworks for corporate accounting systems existing in various countries have been developed to accentuate similarities and differences, to help eliminate any unnecessary diversity, and to guide future accounting developments within countries as well as in the international realm. Early classification attempts relied largely on descriptive comparisons. Later, frameworks and morphologies for grouping national accounting systems were developed, and recently statistical investigations have identified clusters of countries exhibiting similar financial reporting practices.

DESCRIPTIVE COMPARISONS. Virtually all early articles in international accounting heralded certain foreign accounting practices unknown at home. Often the relevations were sensationalized and implied that the accounting practices abroad were inferior. The first more comprehensive and objective descriptive studies include Mueller's international business series on accounting practices in various countries (Mueller, various years starting in 1962), *Professional Accounting in 25 Countries* compiled by the American Institute of Certified Public Accountants (AICPA, 1964; see also the 1975 issue entitled *Professional Accounting in 30 Countries*), Zeff's historical analysis, *Forging Accounting Principles in Five Countries* (Zeff, 1972), and series of country studies published by various international CPA firms. For each of the countries included in the AICPA study, for example, information is provided about the accounting profession, auditing and reporting standards, and accounting principles.

In 1973, Price Waterhouse published its first *Survey of Accounting Principles and Reporting Practices*. Now in its third edition (Fitzgerald, Stickler, and Watts, 1979), it is the most comprehensive comparative accounting study analyzing the degree of acceptance of 267 accounting practices in 64 countries. Illustrative concepts and practices for Brazil, Germany, the Netherlands, Sweden, the United Kingdom, and the United States are summarized in Exhibit 1. This exhibit shows unanimity of acceptance by these countries of the first four accounting concepts, but vast differences in the degree of acceptance of the last four. The disclosure of cost of goods sold, for example, ranges from "required" in Brazil to "not permitted" in Germany.

CLASSIFICATION FRAMEWORKS AND MORPHOLOGIES FOR NATIONAL ACCOUNTING SYSTEMS

Hatfield's Framework.   Although Hatfield (1966) did not specifically have in mind to construct a classification framework, his keen observation and analysis of accounting practices as they existed in the United States and several European countries in 1911 can be viewed as an early form of a classification framework. Inductively derived, this framework classifies national accounting systems by the primary initiator of accounting progress. Using this criterion for differentiation, Hatfield identified a Continental European, a British, and an American model. On the Continent, jurists have been the primary initiators of accounting progress. They have codified even detailed bookkeeping requirements, valuation methods, and formats for financial statements. This legalistic approach to the promulgation of accounting principles contrasts sharply with the development of accounting in England, which came largely from chartered accountants, and the United States, where engineers pioneering cost and railroad accounting greatly influenced accounting progress, although public accountants had also made significant contributions. American accountants' inventiveness in designing bookkeeping systems, for example, was so admired on the Continent that any bookkeeping device having peculiar merit was, irrespective of actual origin, usually called "American bookkeeping."

Mueller's Framework.   A more rigorous classification framework was developed by Mueller (1967). His inquiries into international accounting found that it was not as diverse as the more sensational descriptive literature suggested. Rather, he observed that differences in accounting standards and reporting practices among countries could be explained in terms of a limited number of patterns or cores of accounting thought. According to this classification scheme, accounting contains (1) a macroeconomic, (2) a microeconomic, (3) an independent, and (4) a uniform core of accounting thought. Although not a single accounting system has developed exclusively around only one of these cores, Swedish accounting practices typify the macroeconomic pattern of accounting development; the Dutch accounting system can be considered a prototype of the microeconomic orientation; U.S. accounting reflects a strong independent core of accounting thought; and French and German accounting practices are illustrative of the uniform, or legal, pattern. The main concepts of these four models are contrasted in more detail in the "Survey of Major Accounting Systems" presented below.

The Seidler-Previts Framework.   Seidler (1967) traces accounting practices of various countries to the "spheres of influence" of certain "mother countries." His tripartite

EXHIBIT 1   CURRENT ACCEPTANCE OF ILLUSTRATIVE ACCOUNTING CONCEPTS IN SELECTED COUNTRIES

Accounting Concepts	Degrees of Current Acceptance[a]						
	Required	Insisted Upon	Predominant Practice	Minority Practice	Rarely or Not Found	Not Accepted	Not Permitted
Departures from the consistency concept are disclosed	a						
Departures from the historical cost convention are disclosed	a	UK					
Departures from the accrual concept are disclosed	a	S					
Revenues and costs are recorded in the financial statements of the period in which they are earned or incurred, and not as money is received or paid.	a	UK US					
Cost of sales is disclosed	B	US	N	UK	S		G
Leases are accounted for by the lessee as an installment purchase when the substance of the arrangement transfers the usual risks and rewards of ownership from the lessor to the lessee	US		N UK	S	G		B
Consolidated financial statements are prepared when an investor owning less than 50 percent of the voting-share capital has the power to control, by statute or agreement, the financial and operating policies of the management of an investee company	G S N		B		UK		US
Investments in less than 50 percent owned companies, over which the investor can exercise significant influence, are accounted for on the equity basis	UK US		B	N			G S

Source. Special tabulation based on data contained in Fitzgerald, Stickler, and Watts, 1979.

[a]B = Brazil, G = West Germany, N = Netherlands, S = Sweden, UK = United Kingdom, US = United States, a = all of the six countries listed above, except those identified as having a different "degree of current acceptance."

classification scheme consists of a British, an American, and a Continental European model. The British model has influenced accounting in Australia and India as a result of strong colonial, traditional, and political linkages. Following the flow of investment capital, the American model has spread to Mexico and is now expanding into large parts of South America, Japan, and Israel. The Continental, primarily French, accounting model has had an impact on southern Europe, the Mediterranean and those South American countries with commercial codes patterned after the Napoleonic Code.

Elaborating on this classification framework, Previts (1975) associated Canada, New Zealand, South Africa, Nigeria, the British West Indies, Thailand, and Greece with the British model and assigned Germany to the American model.

As Seidler points out, the accounting system of the "mother country" is rarely adopted *in toto,* and in many instances, such as in Canada, spheres of influence overlap. Since accounting practices reflect the dynamic international business environment, classifications of countries according to their accounting practices are bound to change over time, and spheres of influence cannot be viewed as being mutually exclusive.

AAA's Framework and Morphology. A 1975–1976 committee of the American Accounting Association (AAA) adopted a dual approach toward the international comparison of accounting practices ("Report of the American Accounting Association Committee," 1977). Based on historical-cultural-socioeconomic variables that have influenced financial accounting and reporting principles, the committee identified a classification framework consisting of the following five "zones of influence": (1)

EXHIBIT 2   A MORPHOLOGY FOR COMPARATIVE ACCOUNTING SYSTEMS

Parameters	States of Nature				
	1	2	3	4	5
P₁—political system	Traditional oligarchy	Totalitarian oligarchy	Modernizing oligarchy	Tutelary democracy	Political democracy
P₂—economic system	Traditional	Market	Planned market	Plan	
P₃—stages of economic development	Traditional society	Pre-takeoff	Takeoff	Drive to maturity	Mass consumption
P₄—objectives of financial reporting	◀————Micro————		▶ ◀ ————Macro————		▶
	Investment decisions	Management performance	Social measurement	Sector planning and control	National policy objectives
P₅—Source of, or authority for standards	Executive decree	Legislative action	Government administrative unit	Public-private consortium	Private
P₆—education, training, and licensing	◀————Public————		▶ ◀ ————Private————		▶
	Informal	Formal	Informal	Formal	
P₇—enforcement of ethics and standards	Executive	Government administrative unit	Judicial	Private	
P₈—client	Government	Public	◀————Enterprises————	▶	
			Public	Private	

Source. "Report of the American Accounting Association Committee," 1977.

British, (2) Franco-Spanish-Portugese, (3) Germanic/Dutch, (4) U.S., and (5) communistic.

At the same time, the committee developed a morphology that distinguishes financial reporting systems on the basis of eight environmental and endogenous accounting parameters, as shown in Exhibit 2. Within this morphology, the United States would be described in terms of P_1-5, P_2-2, P_3-5, P_4-1, P_5-4, P_6-4, P_7-3, and P_8-4.

In comparison with a strict taxonomy or classification framework, morphologies have the advantage of being more flexible and avoiding the need to force a particular accounting system into one of the basic models, categories, or zones of influence. Morphologies also mitigate the danger of unproductive, emotional discussions attempting to identify "the best" accounting system in the world or rank various national accounting systems without proper perspective for environmental differences.

STATISTICAL CLASSIFICATION SCHEMES. Recent attempts to delineate classification schemes for national accounting systems rely on factor analysis to statistically uncover clusters of countries exhibiting homogeneity in financial accounting and reporting practices.

The Da Costa-Bourgeois-Lawson Clusters. Da Costa, Bourgeois, and Lawson (1978) selected from the 1973 Price Waterhouse study (Price Waterhouse & Co., 1973) 100 accounting principles that were not uniform throughout the world and scaled the survey responses ordinally from one to five as follows:

Survey Responses	Scale
Accounting practice is	
not permitted or found in practice	1
followed by a minority of reporting companies	2
followed by about half of reporting companies	3
followed by a majority of reporting companies	4
required of, or conventionally followed by, all reporting companies	5

In the second step of their analysis, highly correlated practices were grouped into common factors. This procedure resulted in the identification of seven underlying factors labeled as follows:

1. A measure of financial disclosure.
2. Company law as an influence on accounting practices.
3. Stress of reporting practices on income measurement.
4. "Conservatism" as a guiding principle.
5. Tax law as an influence on accounting practices.
6. Inflation as an environmental consideration.
7. Orientation of reported information toward capital market users.

The statistical analysis designed to identify those countries whose accounting practices are similar across all seven factors revealed two distinct groups. As can

**EXHIBIT 3 COUNTRIES GROUPED ON THE BASIS OF THE ASSOCIATION
AMONG THEIR FINANCIAL ACCOUNTING PRACTICES
(1973 survey data)**

	Coefficient with	
Countries	Group 1	Group 2
Group 1 (nc = 26)		
Japan	.95	.28
Philippines	.94	.28
Mexico	.93	.32
Argentina	.93	.32
Germany	.90	.42
Chile	.90	.41
Bolivia	.89	.43
Panama	.89	.45
Italy	.88	.43
Peru	.88	.43
Venezuela	.88	.46
Colombia	.86	.50
Paraguay	.86	.48
United States	.86	.05
Pakistan	.85	.49
Spain	.85	.49
Switzerland	.84	.53
Brazil	.83	.51
France	.83	.53
Uruguay	.82	.52
Sweden	.81	.59
India	.81	.57
Ethiopia	.81	.57
Belgium	.79	.60
Trinidad	.76	.65
Bahamas	.75	.65
Group 2 (nc = 10)		
United Kingdom	.004	.98[a]
Eire	.19	.96
Rhodesia	.48	.87
Singapore	.50	.86
S. Africa	.51	.86
Australia	.51	.85
Jamaica	.54	.84
Kenya	.57	.81
New Zealand	.62	.78
Fiji	.65	.75
Factorially complex countries—unclassifiable		
Netherlands	.66	.74
Canada	.66	.47

Source. Da Costa, Bourgeois, and Lawson, 1978.
[a]The British model: former British Empire members.

be seen in Exhibit 3, accounting practices in Group 2 apparently are patterned after those prevailing in the United Kingdom, since that country exhibits the highest correlation coefficient (.98) in that group. This is also the country most dissociated from Group 1 as indicated by the low (.004) coefficient in column 1. Although the United States does not enjoy a similar clear position, Exhibit 4 shows that the United States ranks first among Group 1 countries in terms of dissociation from the British model.

Frank's Clusters.   Contrary to the findings of Da Costa, Bourgeois, and Lawson, whose analysis did not support the existence of a Continental European group, Frank (1979), also using the 1973 Price Waterhouse survey responses, but different statistical methods, found the following four factor groupings:

Group I	Group II	Group II	Group IV
Australia	Argentina	Belgium	Canada
Bahamas	Bolivia	Colombia	Germany
Ethiopia	Brazil	France	Japan
Eire	Chile	Italy	Mexico
Fiji	India	Spain	Netherlands
Jamaica	Pakistan	Sweden	Panama
Kenya	Paraguay	Switzerland	Philippines
New Zealand	Peru	Venezuela	United States
Rhodesia	Uruguay		
Singapore			
South Africa			
Trinidad and Tobago			
United Kingdom			

The intuitive identification of these four groups with the British, the Latin American, the Continental European, and the United States models was supported by a supplementary multidimensional scaling analysis using various environmental variables, such as the country's language, several economic structure variables, and sets of variables reflecting trade patterns among the countries. According to this analysis, 83 percent of the countries were assigned to the same group under which they were classified on the basis of financial accounting practices.

Disclosure and Measurement Clusters.   Since in several countries financial disclosure standards are promulgated by one rule-making body, whereas valuation or measurement standards are set by a different regulatory body, Nair and Frank (1980) examined whether the classification of countries is the same using accounting measurement standards as it is using financial disclosure practices. Data from the 1973 and 1975 Price Waterhouse surveys relating to these two subsets of financial accounting served as the data base for the statistical inquiry. The groupings that emerged by analyzing measurement standards differed from those based on disclosure practices, as a comparison of Exhibits 5 and 6 reveals. Whereas the analysis of measurement practices is consistent with the classification frameworks proposed by Seidler and Frank with the addition of a fifth group, namely Chile, disclosure practices do not conform to these classification schemes. Contrary to popular belief, there

EXHIBIT 4   GROUP 1 COUNTRIES RANKED ON THE BASIS OF THEIR DISSOCIATION FROM THE BRITISH MODEL OF GROUP 2 (1973 survey data)

Countries	Correlation Coefficient with Group 2
United States	.05[a]
Japan	.28
Philippines	.28
Argentina	.32
Mexico	.32
Chile	.41
Germany	.42
Bolivia	.43
Peru	.43
Italy	.43
Panama	.45
Venezuela	.46
Paraguay	.48
Spain	.49
Pakistan	.49
Colombia	.50
Brazil	.51
Uruguay	.52
France	.53
Switzerland	.53
India	.57
Ethiopia	.57
Sweden	.59
Belgium	.60
Trinidad	.65
Bahamas	.65

Source. Da Costa, Bourgeois, and Lawson, 1978.
[a]The American model: international grouping of countries that dissociate from the British model.

seem to be more international differences in disclosure than in valuation or measurement practices.

However, a word of caution needs to be raised against placing too much reliance on statistical classification schemes. All attempts to delineate clusters of countries exhibiting homogeneity in financial accounting and reporting practices are only as good as the data on which they are based. Nobes (1981) has questioned both the reliability of the data used and their appropriateness for statistical analyses.

SURVEY OF MAJOR ACCOUNTING SYSTEMS

The review of classification schemes for national accounting systems dealt with cross-country similarities and differences in the abstract. To get a more detailed understanding of the international diversity, specific financial accounting and reporting

EXHIBIT 5   COUNTRIES GROUPED ON THE BASIS OF THE ASSOCIATION AMONG THEIR ACCOUNTING-MEASUREMENT PRACTICES (1975 survey data)

Group I	Group II	Group III	Group IV	Group V
Australia	Argentina	Belgium	Bermuda	Chile
Bahamas	Bolivia	Denmark	Canada	
Fiji	Brazil	France	Japan	
Iran	Colombia	Germany	Mexico	
Jamaica	Ethiopia	Norway	Philippines	
Malaysia	Greece	Sweden	United States	
Netherlands	India	Switzerland	Venezuela	
New Zealand	Italy	Zaire		
Nigeria	Pakistan			
Republic of Ireland	Panama			
Rhodesia	Paraguay			
Singapore	Peru			
South Africa	Spain			
Trinidad and Tobago	Uruguay			
United Kingdom				

Source.   Nair and Frank, 1980.

practices in four countries will now be analyzed. For comparison purposes, U.S. accounting practices are used as a point of reference without intending to imply, however, that they are necessarily superior. The objective of this analysis is twofold: to aid in the understanding of foreign financial statements and to explain why accounting principles not acceptable in the United States may make sense within a different environment. The countries included in this comparison have been selected because the legal, economic, social, and political conditions prevailing in them have resulted in relative differences in the objectives of accounting and the practices derived from them.

ACCOUNTING IN GERMANY.   Financial reports of German corporations are largely issued for the benefit of stockholders and creditors. This dual objective can result in inconsistencies among accounting standards. For example, a conservative valuation of assets is frequently esteemed in the interest of protecting creditors. How-

EXHIBIT 6   COUNTRIES GROUPED ON THE BASIS OF THE ASSOCIATION AMONG THEIR FINANCIAL REPORTING PRACTICES (1975 survey data)

Group I	Group II	Group III	Group IV	Group V	Group VI	Group VII
Belgium	Australia	Bahamas	Bermuda	Argentina	Denmark	Italy
Bolivia	Ethiopia	Germany	Canada	India	Norway	Switzerland
Brazil	Fiji	Japan	Jamaica	Iran	Sweden	
Chile	Kenya	Mexico	Netherlands	Pakistan		
Colombia	Malaysia	Panama	Republic of Ireland	Peru		
France	New Zealand	Philippines	Rhodesia			
Greece	Nigeria	United States	United Kingdom			
Paraguay	Singapore	Venezuela				
Spain	South Africa					
Uruguay	Trinidad and Tobago					
Zaire						

Source.   Nair and Frank, 1980.

ever, if conservatism results in the creation of hidden reserves, the objective of providing useful information to stockholders becomes jeopardized.

Germany has attempted to mitigate this dilemma by adopting a unique blend of accounting measurement standards. Strict upper limits for the valuation of assets have been combined with tacit permission to create hidden reserves without, on the other hand, arbitrarily understating net assets.

Since Germany uses accounting more freely than the United States for the protection of creditors, it is understandable that the promulgation of accounting standards rests largely with legislators. Noncodified "principles of proper bookkeeping" exist. However, they do not have the same significance as "generally accepted accounting principles" in the United States, because even detailed valuation principles and financial reporting requirements are prescribed by law.

The primary sources of legal provisions for financial accounting are the Commercial Code, the Corporation Act, the Limited Liability Company Act, and the Publicity Law. In addition, tax regulations have a major, although indirect, impact on financial accounting practices.

The Corporation Act prescribes in detail the format of the balance sheet and income statement to be used by corporations operating in the form of the *Aktiengesellschaft* (AG), explanatory notes to be disclosed, and valuation principles to be applied. Statements of changes in financial position are not required by law and are voluntarily included in only a minority of the annual reports.

Domestic subsidiaries are required to be consolidated, provided their inclusion does not diminish the understandability of the consolidated statements. Although the inclusion of foreign subsidiaries is optional, most large AGs publish consolidated statements on a global basis.

The Balance Sheet. The balance sheet consists of *Aktiva* and *Passiva*. Although these terms are roughly comparable to *assets* and *equities*, there are some distinct classification and valuation differences. As a minimum, an AG must disclose separately the following items on the *Aktiva* side of the balance sheet:

   I.   Subscriptions to capital stock (DM . . . called)
  II.   "Fixed assets" (*Anlagevermögen*)
      A.   Fixed tangible assets and intangibles
         1. Land and leasehold rights together with office, factory, and other buildings thereon
         2. Land and leasehold rights together with dwellings thereon
         3. Land and leasehold rights without buildings
         4. Buildings constructed on land owned by others, not included in 1 or 2
         5. Machinery and mechanized installations
         6. Factory and office fixtures and furniture
         7. Construction in progress and advances on fixed tangible assets
         8. Franchises, trademarks, patents, and similar rights as well as licenses thereto
      B.   Investments
         1. Investments in excess of 25 percent of the voting rights in another entity

      2. Securities held for long-term investments, not belonging to 1

      3. Loans receivable not due within four years (DM . . . secured by mortgages)

III. "Circulating assets" (*Umlaufvermögen*)
- A. Inventories
  1. Raw materials and supplies
  2. Work in process
  3. Finished goods, merchandise
- B. Other circulating assets
  1. Advances not belonging to IIA number 7
  2. Accounts receivable (DM . . . not due within one year)
  3. Notes receivable (DM . . . discountable with the Federal Bank)
  4. Checks
  5. Cash on hand, including deposits with the Federal Bank and in postal checking accounts
  6. Cash in other bank accounts
  7. Securities not belonging to 3, 4, 8 or 9, or IIB
  8. Treasury stock (DM . . . par value)
  9. Participation in a controlling company (including mining enterprises) or in one holding the majority interest (DM . . . par value or, in case of mining shares, number of shares . . .)
  10. Receivables from affiliated companies
  11. Loans and advances regulated by
     a. §89 (receivables from members of the board of management)
     b. §115 (receivables from members of the supervisory board [*Aufsichsrat*])
  12. Other assets

IV. Prepaid expenses and deferred charges

V. "Balance sheet loss" (*Bilanzverlust*)

Under *Passiva,* AGs must disclose at least the following details:

I. Capital stock (*Grundkapital*)
II. "Open reserves" (*offene Rücklagen*)
1. Legal reserves
2. Free reserves
III. "Valuation corrections" (Wertberichtigungen)
IV. "Estimated liabilities" (*Rückstellungen*)
1. Provisions for pensions
2. Other estimated liabilities
V. Liabilities with term of at least four years
1. Bonds payable (DM . . . secured by mortgages)
2. Liabilities toward banks (DM . . . secured by mortgages)
3. Other liabilities (DM . . . secured by mortgages)
(DM . . . of the liabilities included in 1 the rough 3 maturing within four years)

VI.   Other liabilities
    1.   Accounts payable
    2.   Notes payable
    3.   Liabilities toward banks not belonging to V
    4.   Advances from customers
    5.   Liabilities toward affiliated companies
    6.   Other liabilities
VII.   Deferred income
VIII.   "Balance sheet profit" (*Bilanzgewinn*)

In contrast to U.S. balance sheets, which are organized according to liquidity (starting with cash as the most liquid asset), German balance sheets rank assets largely on the basis of materiality, by highlighting fixed assets before disclosing current assets. Acquisitions and disposals of fixed assets as well as depreciation thereof have to be listed separately. Typically this is done in columnar form within the balance sheet itself, starting with the book value at the beginning of the year, adding the cost of acquisitions made during the year, and subtracting the book value of dispositions as well as the depreciation charges for the current year to arrive at the new carrying value at the balance-sheet date. Thus original acquisition costs and related accumulated depreciation are typically not disclosed.

Depreciation charges are usually computed for financial reporting purposes at the maximum rate permissible for tax purposes. The Corporate Act specifically provides that AGs can make writedowns of fixed assets over and above the systematic depreciation charges if a lower book value is acceptable for tax purposes. Similar provisions allowing the creation of hidden reserves apply to the valuation of inventory and accounts receivable, provided again that the lower carrying values are acceptable to the tax authorities.

Organization costs, which in the United States have to be capitalized and amortized over several years, must be expensed by German corporations when incurred. On the other hand, the German Corporation Act permits, at the option of the company, spreading start-up costs over a period of up to 5 years, whereas under U.S. accounting principles such costs have to be expensed immediately.

With respect to goodwill, two cases must be distinguished: goodwill arising from the acquisition of the net assets of a business enterprise, and consolidated goodwill. As in the United States, the amount of goodwill arising from the acquisition of net assets is measured in terms of the excess of acquisition costs over the fair market value of the separately identifiable net assets purchased. Whereas, however, American corporations are required to capitalize and amortize it over the future periods expected to benefit—not to exceed 40 years—German corporations have an option to capitalize such amounts or to write them off against income in the year the net assets were purchased. If the capitalization alternative is selected, goodwill arising from the acquisition of net assets of a business has to be amortized over a period of not more than 5 years.

Consolidated goodwill related to the acquisition of the common stock of another company, on the other hand, is in essence permanently carried forward as a "consolidation adjustment." In contrast with U.S. accounting principles, the amount of the consolidation adjustment is defined as the excess of the acquisition cost of the subsidiary's shares of common stock over the book value, not fair market value, of the subsidiary's net assets. In other words, the asset values contained in the balance sheets of the individual companies belonging to the consolidated group are binding, and German accountants are not permitted to depart from them in preparing consolidated balance sheets.

The strict adherence to acquisition cost as the upper limit for the valuation of assets also does not permit the use of the equity method of accounting for investments.

Accounting for stockholders' equity and especially the provisions for the determination of the "balance sheet profit" manifest vividly the goal of protecting creditors by creating reserves and restricting the amount available for payment of dividends. Any paid-in capital in excess of par, 5 percent of the current year's net income reduced by any loss carried forward, and some other items specified by law have to be credited to "legal reserves" until they equal 10 percent of the par value capital or a larger amount stipulated by the corporation's bylaws. If the stockholders have the right to "legally ascertain" the financial statements as being final, the bylaws can provide that up to one half of the net income after crediting "losses carried forward" and "legal reserves" has to be transferred to "free reserves." This amount can even be larger if the right to vote on the financial statements rests with the board of management and the supervisory board of the corporation. In either case, the residual "balance sheet profit" does not indicate in any way the corporation's real profitability. It merely represents the maximum amount that can be declared as dividends.

The Income Statement.   As a minimum, the income statement must disclose the following items:

1.	Sales revenue (net of sales returns and allowances)	DM _____	
2.	Inventory changes of finished goods and work in process		DM _____
3.	Capitalized costs of self-constructed assets		_____
4.	Total product		DM _____
5.	Expired costs of raw materials, supplies as well as acquired merchandise		_____
6.	Net amount		DM _____
7.	Income from profit-pooling agreements, profit-transfer contracts and partial-profit-transfer contracts	DM _____	
8.	Income from investments in excess of 25 percent of the voting rights in another entity	_____	
9.	Income from other long-term investments	_____	
10.	Other interest and similar income from temporary investments	_____	
11.	Gains from the disposal and appreciation of "fixed assets"	_____	
12.	Gains from the reduction of lump-sum-valuation reserves on receivables	_____	

13. Gains from the reduction or dissolution of "estimated liabilities" (*Rückstellungen*)

14. Other income (including DM of . . . extraordinary income) _____

15. Compensation in connection with loss-absorption agreements _____   DM ____

16. Wages and salaries   DM ____

17. Social security levies   _____

18. Cost of retirement plans and social aid benefits   _____

19. Depreciation and writedowns on property, plant, and equipment as well as intangible assets   _____

20. Writedowns on investments (IIB on *Aktiva* side of balance sheet) except for amounts referring to lump-sum-valuation adjustments on receivables   _____

21. Losses from decline in value or disposal of "circulating assets" except inventories (IIIB on *Aktiva* side of balance sheet) and amounts added to the lump-sum-valuation adjustments on receivables.   _____

22. Losses from disposal of "fixed assets" II on *Aktiva* side of balance sheet)   _____

23. Interest and similar expenses   _____

24. Taxes
    a on income and property (Vermögen)   DM ____
    b other   _____

25. Losses assumed under loss-absorption agreements   _____

26. Other expenses   _____

27. Income transferred pursuant to profit-pooling agreements, profit-transfer contracts, and partial-profit-transfer contracts   _____   _____

28. Net income/loss for the year   DM ____

29. Balance sheet profit/loss carried forward from previous year   _____   DM ____

30. Transfers from "open reserves"
    a from legal reserves   DM ____
    b from free reserves   _____   DM ____

31. Transfers to "open reserves" out of net income for the year
    a to legal reserves   DM ____
    b to free reserves   _____   _____

32. Balance sheet profit/loss   DM ____

Cost of goods sold is not disclosed and cannot be ascertained on the basis of the published financial statements. Given the quite specific provisions of the Corporation Act, voluntary disclosure of cost of goods sold is not considered permissible.

Since the act provides that estimated liabilities for pensions *may* be set up, pension costs are sometimes accounted for on a pay-as-you-go basis, a method not permitted in the United States.

Leases are seldom treated by the lessee as an installment purchase, even if the contractual arrangements transfer the usual risks and rewards of ownership from the lessor to the lessee. Following a strict legal definition of a lease, all payments under such an agreement are typically considered rent expense. Disclosure of commitments under long-term leases is only seldom made.

The legalistic approach to accounting also does not permit the U.S. practice of comprehensive income tax allocation. Thus when accounting and taxable income differ, the income tax expense for financial reporting purposes is based on the tax concept of "taxable income" and not on the accounting notion of "income before taxes." The reason for prohibiting the recording of deferred income taxes payable is typically defended by the fact that deferred taxes neither give rise to a legal claim by the tax authorities against the corporation nor a legal obligation on the part of the company to currently pay such amounts.

The extension of the income statement beyond "net income/loss for the year" picks up the balance sheet profit carried forward and allows for transfer to and from "open reserves" to end up with the "balance sheet profit/loss" disclosed in the balance sheet. The disclosure of earnings per share is not required by law and is rarely found in practice.

ACCOUNTING IN THE NETHERLANDS.   The microeconomic influence on accounting is reflected in the definition promulgated by the Netherlands Institute of Registered Accountants, which perceives accounting as "the systematic recording, processing and supplying of information for the management and operation of an entity and for the reports that have to be submitted thereon" ("Report of the American Accounting Association Committee," 1976). As this definition indicates, "accounting for management" plays a more dominant role in the Netherlands than in the United States, whereas financial reporting to absentee owners does not quite have the preemptive importance that is assigned to accounting in the United States. This slight, but nevertheless discernible difference in the objective of accounting can be explained by the fact that stock ownership is not as broad based as in the United States. In addition, Dutch companies rely more on bond than on stock issues to raise new capital. In 1972, for example, less than 2 percent of the value of all new public issues were in the form of capital stock, compared to more than 98 percent in the form of bonds (Lafferty, 1975).

Limpberg's Replacement Value Theory.   According to business economic thinking as promulgated by Limpberg (for a more detailed discussion of Limpberg's theory see Mey, 1970), management's primary responsibility is to assure the continuing existence of the enterprise. This duty implies that management needs information that indicates whether the wealth, defined in terms of productive capability, of the enterprise has been maintained. Accounting reports based on historical costs do not necessarily provide this information. If, for example, historical costs are used to determine selling prices—which is a widespread practice—the enterprise is essentially making gifts to its customers during periods of inflation. If the company instead increases its selling prices to provide for the higher replacement cost of the goods sold, the profit increase, which traditional income measurement methods would report, entails the danger of raising dividend payments. Again, the effect would be to reduce the enterprise's wealth by the unwarranted transfer of resources to others.

At the same time, artificially overstated profits could also encourage plant expansion. However, such an expansion may not be justified because the investment opportunity is actually not as profitable as the historical-cost income statement indicates.

The use of replacement value accounting, on the other hand, is deemed to be a "sound business practice." It provides information that helps management in assessing whether the productive capability of the enterprise has been preserved. Profit, according to Limpberg's theory, is earned only after the maintenance of the economic substance has been ascertained. It is defined as the difference between sales revenue and the replacement value—at the time of sale and not the time of actual replacement—of the goods sold.

Replacement Value Accounting Practice.   As Exhibit 7 indicates, only 15 percent of all industrial and trading companies quoted on the Amsterdam Stock Exchange presented fixed assets and depreciation in their 1967/68 annual reports on the basis of replacement values, whereas 50.7 percent adhered to historical costs, with the rest using hybrid forms between the two methods. However, the low acceptance rate does not accurately reflect the real significance of replacement value accounting in current practice, since more than 50 percent of the 23 largest companies use replacement value accounting in the pure form and an additional 21.7 percent set up reserves as part of stockholders' equity to assure maintenance of equity capital.

A major reason more smaller corporations do not use replacement values is the insistence of tax authorities on historical costs for the preparation of tax returns. Nevertheless, it is likely that the use of replacement value accounting will increase since the Tripartite Commission—set up in 1971 at the initiative of the Dutch minister of economic affairs and composed of representatives from the employers' association,

EXHIBIT 7   FIXED-ASSET VALUATION AND DEPRECIATION METHODS USED BY INDUSTRIAL AND TRADING COMPANIES QUOTED ON THE AMSTERDAM STOCK EXCHANGE, 1967–1968

Net Fixed Assets of Companies (Fl millions)	Basis for Fixed-Asset Valuation; Income Determination				Total Number of Companies	Percentage of Grand Total
	Historical Cost; Historical Cost Depreciation	Historical Cost; Depreciation above Historical Costs	Historical Cost; Historical-Cost Depreciation Plus Extra Depreciation to Set Up Capital Reserve	Replacement Value; Replacement-Value Depreciation		
0–10	100	27	21	8	156	60.2
10–25	16	10	9	8	43	16.6
25–75	12	7	7	11	37	14.3
Above 75	3	3	5	12	23	8.9
Total	131	47	42	39	259	100.0
Percent	50.6	18.1	16.2	15.1	100.0	

Source. Lafferty, 1975.

the labor unions, and the Netherlands Institute of Registered Accountants—has endorsed this method.

Some of the major companies, such as Philips N.V., revalue their inventories and fixed assets on an annual basis. For practical reasons, Philips uses the average price level pertaining to a homogenous group of assets instead of computing replacement values for each individual asset. Specific price indexes are developed internally to approximate the replacement values of factories, buildings, and self-constructed assets. The purchase department keeps track of trends in the acquisition cost of raw materials and merchandise inventory. Work in progress and finished goods are typically valued at standard costs adjusted to replacement value by means of specific indexes.

For depreciable fixed assets, an increase in the replacement value is recognized by charging the asset account and crediting a corresponding amount to "capital arising from revaluation of assets."

This revaluation capital is not available for distribution in the form of dividends, since capital needs to be retained in real, as opposed to historical, terms. Annual depreciations are based on the new replacement value. Adjustments needed to restate accumulated depreciations for prior years are also made against income for the current year.

To achieve complete maintenance of capital, the effect of changing price levels on the net monetary assets must also be accounted for. If the general purchasing power of money decreases as a result of inflation, companies having a net monetary asset position incur a loss in the real value of these assets. To avoid an erosion of the capital base, these companies charge the "cost of inflation" against income and set up a "capital reserve for the diminishing purchasing power of net monetary assets."

Enterprises whose monetary liabilities exceed monetary assets "gain" during periods of inflation. The principle of conservatism limits the recognition of such inflation gains to the balance of the capital reserve account created in prior years. Thus the "capital reserve for diminishing purchasing power" can never have a debit balance.

Other Selected Accounting and Reporting Practices. The Dutch Commercial Code requires the keeping of books that show the company's financial position and provide information about its business and transactions. The code was supplemented in 1970 by the Act on Annual Financial Statements of Enterprises, which stipulates "that the financial statements should provide such information that a sound judgment can be formed on the financial position and result of the enterprise and, to the extent to which the annual statements permit, on its solvency and liquidity."

Financial statements—consisting of the balance sheet, the income statement and explanatory notes—should reflect fairly and systematically the size and composition of the enterprise's financial position at year-end and the result for the period then ended. The statement of changes in financial position is not specifically mentioned in the act. However, since the financial reports need to provide insight into liquidity and solvency, it can be expected that more and more companies will follow the practice of the larger quoted enterprises to prepare such statements.

Information about subsidiaries must be presented in the annual report of the parent company, either in the form of separate or combined financial statements for the subsidiaries, or in the form of consolidated statements included as part of the notes to the parent's financial statements. The preparation of only consolidated financial statements, which is the predominant practice in the United States, is not permitted. Of the two options open to Dutch companies, most publish consolidated as well as "parent-company-only" financial statements.

Exemptions exist for foreign subsidiaries. Their financial statements, prepared in accordance with applicable foreign statutory requirements, may either be presented as part of the notes to the parent company's statements or be made available for public inspection at the Commercial Register.

Goodwill resulting from the acquisition of subsidiaries is frequently written off against retained earnings in the year of acquisition. Such a bypass of the income statement would not be permissible in the United States.

Income from investments in affiliates in which an enterprise has at least a 25 percent ownership interest must be disclosed separately. The name and domicile of all subsidiaries and affiliates must be disclosed in the annual report, or a statement needs to be filed for public inspection with the Commercial Register, provided the annual report contains an appropriate footnote reference. As in Germany, this Dutch disclosure requirement exceeds U.S. standards applicable to annual reports for stockholders.

Comprehensive tax allocations resulting from timing differences between accounting income and taxable income are as common in the Netherlands as in the United States. Yet in some cases, Dutch accountants are going further than their American colleagues by discounting deferred income taxes.

Although the 1970 act contains other detailed provisions governing financial accounting and reporting by Dutch companies, it does not represent a list of all accounting principles that are acceptable in economic and social life. Other principles, which conform to "sound business practices" and meet the criteria of social accountability, can also be used. "General acceptance" as in the United States is not required.

To further improve financial accounting and comparability of annual reports, the Tripartite Commission mentioned earlier is currently taking inventory of accounting principles used by business enterprises. The commission also tests these principles for relevance in today's economic and social environment and tries to determine whether they provide information needed to form a sound judgment on the enterprise's solvency and liquidity.

The reports, or "opinions," issued so far by the commission do not carry the same weight as FASB statements or APB opinions in the United States. However, the Netherlands Institute of Registered Accountants has proposed a study to ascertain which of the commission's draft opinions should become binding to the business community and the accounting profession.

ACCOUNTING IN SWEDEN.   Financial accounting and reporting practices in Sweden, probably more than in any other country except for Eastern bloc countries, is based extensively on macroeconomic considerations. Granted, the National Bookkeeping Law and the Companies Act stipulate that books must be kept "in accordance with generally accepted accounting principles and sound business practices." However, Swedish tax regulations have significant influence over accounting practices, since certain advantageous income measurement principles can be used for tax purposes only if they are also adhered to in published financial reports. Thus through tax incentives, Sweden has been using accounting as a tool to pursue such macro-economic goals as full employment, avoidance of business cycles, and orderly economic growth.

The macroeconomic impact on financial accounting practices is especially evident in three areas: the valuation of fixed assets, inventory reserves, and investment reserves.

Valuation of Fixed Assets. The valuation of property, plant, and equipment follows largely very liberal tax provisions. Since the depreciation rates allowable for tax purposes are usually higher than rates based on the estimated useful life, fixed assets would be considered undervalued according to U.S. generally accepted accounting principles. Such an undervaluation, however, is not in violation of the Swedish Companies Act. The principle of "prudence," which stipulates that the financial position should not be presented in an overly optimistic manner, and the act's reference to "sound business practices" are deemed sufficient justification for the creation of such reserves.

In general, machinery and equipment can be written off in as short a period as 5 years with an annual depreciation rate of up to 30 percent of the book value of the asset. Thus a company taking full advantage of this liberal depreciation schedule can write off 51 percent of the acquisition cost within the first 2 years. Moreover, in some cases depreciation can already be taken from the date of the purchase contract instead of the date the asset was actually put into service. If fixed assets have an expected life of no more than 3 years, they can be expensed immediately.

Fixed assets can be written up to an "enduring value" significantly above book value if the amount of the revaluation is used either to offset depreciation charges on other fixed assets or to increase capital stock by issuing stock dividends. Real estate cannot be revalued to an amount exceeding the assessed tax value.

If fixed assets have been revalued, this fact, the amount of the writeup, and its treatment need to be disclosed. However, the Companies Act does not require disclosure of the depreciation method used.

Agreement on the balance sheet presentation of property, plant, and equipment does not exist. The Companies Act recommends that accumulated depreciation be shown as a valuation reserve under "equities"; the Swedish Association of Authorized Public Accountants favors treating accumulated depreciation as a contra-asset account; and many companies, in practice, reveal neither the acquisition cost nor the accumulated depreciation, but merely the net carrying value. Irrespective of the disclosure method used, fixed assets of most Swedish corporations contain hidden reserves, so that the companies can survive lean years.

Inventory Reserves. The Companies Act and the income tax law require that inventories are valued at cost or market, whichever is lower. Since the tax law insists that costs are determined using the first-in, first-out method, FIFO is also the predominant practice for financial reporting purposes.

To smooth out business cycles and ensure the survival of business enterprises, Swedish tax regulations permit the creation of "inventory reserves." Obsolete or unsalable inventory items can be written off in full. If individual identification of unmarketable merchandise is not feasible or is too cumbersome, a 5 percent across-the-board deduction is typically allowed. The remaining inventory balance can be further reduced by up to 60 percent. To take advantage of this liberal tax provision, companies make charges against income and corresponding appropriations to inventory reserves. The reserves must be reversed and become taxable income in the next year, but new reserves can be established in essence to defer taxes indefinitely. A voluntary reduction of inventory reserves is made primarily in order to avoid taxable losses that would otherwise occur.

An alternative to this general rule permits a writedown of up to 60 percent of the average inventory (after deductions for obsolescence) of the 2 preceding years. If ending inventories (after 5 percent blanket deductions) for 1979 through 1981 amount to SKr120,000, 100,000, and 60,000, respectively, the company is entitled to a reserve of SKr66,000, that is, 60 percent of (SKr120,000 + SKr100,000) ÷ 2, at the end of 1981. Thus the company would show a "negative inventory" of SKr6000 in the sense that the reserve of SKr66,000 exceeds the inventory carrying amount of SKr60,000.

A second supplementary rule applies to raw materials and staple products. To provide for the risk of a price decline in these inventory items, the company may value them at an amount as low as 70 percent of their lowest market price in effect during the 10 years preceding the balance sheet date.

Investment Reserves.   Tax-free investment reserves are designed as an anticyclical device to fight unemployment and economic recessions. The basic idea is to encourage savings during prosperous years and capital expenditures in periods when the economy threatens to slow down.

According to tax regulations, a company can set aside up to 40 percent of its net income (before taxes and contributions to investment reserves) by a charge against taxable income and a corresponding allocation to "investment reserves." To be able to take advantage of this tax relief, the company has to transfer cash equal to 46 percent of the allocation, that is, about the amount saved in taxes, to a restricted non-interest-bearing account with the National Bank of Sweden. The purpose of this mandatory deposit is to prevent companies from utilizing their tax savings during periods when additional investments would funnel inflation.

The use of the investment fund deposited with the National Bank is regulated by the Labor Market Board. If adverse economic conditions make additional investments desirable, the board can release part or all of the funds for qualifying investment purposes. The release can apply generally, or it can be limited to depressed regions, industries, or specific enterprises.

At the time the investment funds become unblocked, the company also dissolves the corresponding amount of the "investment reserve." This amount, however, does not become part of taxable income; rather it reduces the acquisition cost of the qualifying asset. In addition, companies using investment reserves with government approval are entitled to a 10 percent investment deduction.

If the investment reserve is used without permission by the Labor Market Board, the amount involved plus a 10 percent penalty will be subject to tax. In this case the corresponding deposits with the National Bank will be returned to the company.

After 5 years from the date a tax-free allocation is made to the reserve account, 30 percent can be dissolved and used for qualifying investments without government approval. At the same time, the company can withdraw the corresponding 46 percent deposited with the National Bank. No penalties are levied, but the 10 percent investment deduction does not apply.

To encourage large investment projects that require more capital than could be accumulated in prior years, companies may obtain special authority to use investment reserves expected to be appropriated in future years. The liberal tax regulations also permit the transfer of investment reserves within a group of affiliated companies.

Other Selected Accounting and Reporting Practices.   All companies must issue financial statements consisting of the balance sheet, the income statement, and explanatory notes. Companies that are subject to statutory audits must also prepare a statement of changes in financial position.

Consolidated statements are mandatory in addition to, but not in lieu of, the statements prepared exclusively for the parent company. The Companies Act does not prescribe the method of consolidation, but requires that generally accepted accounting principles be used. Since the Swedish Association of Authorized Public Accountants has endorsed the use of the purchase method to account for business combinations, this method is widely adhered to. Only if the merged companies are comparable in size and the acquisition was accomplished through the issuance of common stock is the pooling-of-interest method acceptable.

Goodwill arising from the purchase of a business can be written off against retained earnings in the year of acquisition—a method not acceptable in the United States—or it can be capitalized and amortized over a period not to exceed 10 years. In practice, most companies adhere to the second alternative.

Since favorable income measurement principles, as a general rule, can only be employed for tax purposes if they are also used in preparing financial statements, deferred income taxes are seldom encountered in practice. If accounting income and taxable income are at variance, the difference is neither recorded nor disclosed in accompanying footnotes. Rather, the amount of income tax expense shown on the income statement is taken directly from the tax return.

Pension costs are sometimes accounted for when pensions are paid. However, most Swedish companies provide for such costs over the term of employment. Past service costs not provided for have to be disclosed in the notes to the financial statements.

Contrary to American practice, long-term lease commitments do not have to be revealed and are rarely shown on a voluntary basis. Only a minority of the companies account for leases as an installment purchase, even if the lessee assumes the normal risks and rewards of ownership.

Similar to German statutory requirements, the Swedish Companies Act stipulates that 10 percent of the annual profit has to be allocated to legal reserves until they reach 20 percent of the par value of common stock or a higher amount specified by the bylaws. However, contemplated proposals to reform the Companies Act and to harmonize it with the anticipated European Company Law call for the abolition of such mandatory reserves.

ACCOUNTING IN POLAND.   In centrally planned economies, such as Poland, the primary functions of accounting are to facilitate the management of state enterprises, to enable central planning and control, and to serve as the basis for preparing national income statistics. To accomplish these functions, information about the financial

---

Informative discussions with Professor Alicja Jaruga, University of Lodz, and Professor Tadeusz Peche, Central School of Planning and Statistics, Warsaw, and constructive comments by Professor Peche about an earlier draft of "Accounting in Poland" are thankfully appreciated.

position, the results of operations, and numerous other aspects of state-owned enterprises are produced for management and various governmental agencies.

Management is primarily interested in accounting information that helps to evaluate the performance of the enterprise. Since its objective is not to maximize profits, but to manufacture the number of products prescribed by the central planners within the budget allocated to the enterprise, accounting for management focuses more on the evaluation of effectiveness than efficiency.

The Hierarchical Aggregation Process. Besides providing enterprise information to the National Bank of Poland, the Workers' Selfgovernment, and the Internal Revenue Office, accounting and reporting to various state agencies can be viewed as a hierarchical aggregation process that on the one hand is linked to the five-year plan and on the other hand culminates in national income statistics. The first level of aggregation normally takes place at the enterprise level. Even enterprises operating more than one plant rarely prepare complete financial reports for each plant, since plants are typically treated as cost, not as profit or investment centers.

The second level of aggregation occurs by industries or industry branches. The financial reports of enterprises belonging to the same industry are aggregated by a process that resembles consolidation without, however, resulting in a complete set of consolidated reports. *Combinats,* which are state enterprises whose fully integrated stages of production cut across two or more industries, are typically excluded from aggregation at this level, since an allocation of their activities to various industries would be too arbitrary.

The third level of aggregation occurs at the industrial-ministry level. Each ministry in charge of a group of industries and *combinats* summarizes certain accounting information of industries and *combinats* under its supervision into a limited number of statistical indexes. This aggregation process has very little in common with the preparation of consolidated financial statements.

The Central Planning Committee, the Ministry of Finance, and the Central Statistics Office, in turn, aggregate indexes for the entire Polish economy. At this final level of aggregation, highly summarized enterprise information is used in the central-planning and review processes, as well as in the preparation of national income statistics. Since some state enterprises have to submit accounting reports directly to the Central Statistics Office, the link between enterprise accounting and national income accounting is, at times, established both directly and indirectly through the aggregated reports of industries and industrial ministries.

This hierarchical aggregation process requires that accounting be highly standardized to assure comparability of data. Standardization has been facilitated through the introduction of uniform charts of accounts, the promulgation of uniform valuation principles, and the insistence on uniform financial reports.

The System of Uniform Charts of Accounts. Structurally the system of uniform charts of accounts parallels the governmental hierarchy. The Uniform Accounting Plan covering the entire economy represents the highest level of aggregation. Issued by the Ministry of Finance, it serves as a framework for developing industrial-branch accounting plans. These branch accounting plans, in turn, serve as the basis for the uniform chart of accounts to be used by a state enterprise.

The Uniform Accounting Plan consists of a chart of accounts, detailed descriptions of the functions of each account, and rules for expanding the chart by adding subsidiary accounts for analytical purposes. To facilitate industrial-branch accounting, the Ministry of Finance also issues uniform charts of accounts for specific industries, such as manufacturing, domestic trade, foreign trade, agriculture, construction, transportation, and budget institutions (i.e., schools, operas, museums, and banks).

The charts are based on the decimal numbering system. They consist of 10 classes of accounts, each of which is divided into 10 subclasses. If necessary, these subclasses in turn are further subdivided to assure that a given account contains only homogenous transactions and events. Thus each account is identified by a three-digit number. These so-called synthetic accounts can be expanded by the enterprise for analytical purposes by adding as many additional digits as desired.

The 10 main classes of accounts for manufacturing enterprises are as follows:

0. Fixed assets and investments.
1. Cash (including bank accounts and bank loans).
2. Receivables and payables.
3. Raw materials, merchandise inventory, and supplies.
4. Costs classified by nature.
5. Costs classified by cost centers.
6. Work in process and finished goods.
7. Income from sales (including sales revenue, cost of sales, selling expenses, turnover taxes, subventions from the budget system, and extraordinary income).
8. Basic (i.e., statutory and reserve) funds and financial results.
9. Budget and special funds (such as funds for development, premiums, investments, risk, and social purposes).

Uniform Valuation Principles.   Uniformity is also accomplished through the issuance of detailed valuation principles. The three primary sources of accounting standards are the regulation of the Ministry of Finance dated November 23, 1972, entitled "General Rules of Accounting of State-Owned Enterprises" (*Monitor Polski*, 1972), the ordinance of the Council of Ministry No. 210 dated August 24, 1973, which deals with the "Duties of Chief Accountants and CPAs, and Methods of Auditing of Financial Reports and Statements of State Enterprises" (*Monitor Polski*, 1973), and numerous, very specific ordinances, regulations, and instructions concerning the financial system of state enterprises. These ordinances, regulations, and instructions are issued, among others, by the Chamber of Deputies, the Council of Ministry, the Ministry of Finance, the Ministry of Internal Trade, and the president of the Central Planning Commission.

Except for land, which does not show up on the books of the enterprise at all, fixed assets are recorded at their historical acquisition costs. Depreciation methods (typically straight-line) and rates to be followed are set by the government. As a result, all enterprises use the same depreciation rate for a given class of fixed assets, unless the proper state authorities adjust the rate to reflect, for example, the more extensive use of an asset than originally estimated.

Annual depreciation is not only treated as a cost; it simultaneously requires payments to the state budget if the asset to which the depreciation relates was originally supplied to the enterprise through state appropriations. The amount of the cash transfer is equal to the depreciation charges for the year.

Salvage values are not considered in computing depreciation. If fixed assets are retired before they are fully depreciated, the book value at the time of retirement is treated as a loss.

Receivables and payables are valued at their nominal amounts. Allowances for doubtful accounts are not necessary, since accounts receivable representing claims against other state enterprises are not at risk. They are also typically settled within a few days.

Inventories of raw materials and merchandise are valued at cost. Since prices are set by the government, enterprises can only make adjustments to costs if the proper authorities issue new price lists or indexes. The necessary adjustments do not affect the performance of the enterprise, since they are treated as increases or decreases of the enterprise's fund balances.

To discourage holding of raw materials that are chronically in short supply, enterprises receive funds from the governmental budget system equal to only a certain percentage, such as 70 percent, of their investment in raw materials. The balance is provided by bank loans on which the enterprise has to pay interest.

Work in process and finished goods are generally valued at full cost. Only some products are measured at actual or budgeted costs, whichever is lower. If the manufacturing costs exceed net realizable value, finished goods are valued at budgeted costs.

Financial Reports. The primary financial reports are the balance sheet, the income statement, the sales-performance report, and the production-cost-performance report. The format of these reports is prescribed by the government. It tends to change over time as new reporting forms are issued by the Central Statistics Office in cooperation with the Ministry of Finance.

The balance sheet consists of *Aktiva* (assets) and *Passiva* (liabilities and funds), each being subdivided as follows:

Aktiva	*Passiva*
A. Investment projects (including investments in fixed assets under construction, cash set aside for future investments in fixed assets, receivables related to future investments in fixed assets)	A. Investment funds (including bank loans for investment projects, and accounts payable related to such projects)
B. Fixed assets	B. Statutory funds for fixed assets and accumulated depreciation.
C. Balance sheet loss and division of financial results (division among special funds and the governmental budget system)	C. Balance sheet profit and profit given to enterprise by the governmental budget system.
D. Inventories and accounts receivable	D. Statutory funds concerning current assets, bank loans for operations, accounts payable for inventories
E. Cash and receivables other than accounts receivable	E. Other payables, reserves, and unearned income

Aktiva	*Passiva*
F. Special assets (including cash of special funds, inventory for special purposes)	F. Special funds

Not only must the sum of *Aktiva* equal total *Passiva,* but ideally the subtotals for each of the *Aktiva* sections A through F should equal the corresponding subtotals on the *Passiva* side. For example, if the investment projects listed under section A on the *Aktiva* side are financed strictly according to financial rules, their total value should be identical to the investment funds disclosed under section A on the *Passiva* side. This heavy influence of fund accounting on corporate financial reporting is understandable, since state enterprises are an integral part of the governmental budget and accounting system.

Information about income has to be supplied on a form that vaguely resembles an expanded multiple-step income statement. Very simplified, income is determined and allocated as follows:

$$
\begin{aligned}
&\text{Revenues} \\
-\,&\text{Expenses} \\
\hline
=\,&\text{Fund accumulations} \\
-\,&\text{Turnover tax} \\
-\,&\text{Budget payments} \\
\hline
=\,&\text{Net income (residual income)} \\
-\,&\text{Transfers to premium fund for executives} \\
-\,&\text{Transfers to enterprise development fund} \\
-\,&\text{Transfer to reserve fund} \\
\hline
=\,&\underline{\underline{0}}
\end{aligned}
$$

Since workers and executives are interested in wage and salary increases, premiums, and transfers to the development fund, attention in performance evaluation focuses on the value added by the enterprise and residual income. As Jaruga (1976) points out: "The size and increase of value added determine the size and increase of wages. On the other hand, the size and growth of residual income (net income) determine the level of the premium fund for executive managers as well as the development fund of the firm."

The performance evaluation relies also on the sales-performance report and the production-cost-performance report. Both facilitate an analysis of factors contributing to the enterprise's residual income by comparing actual results to corresponding planned amounts. Thus accounting in Poland has more in common with U.S. management and fund accounting than with financial reporting.

IMPLICATIONS OF INTERNATIONAL DIFFERENCES

In assessing the implications of international accounting differences, a distinction needs to be made between the concerns of at least six different interest groups. Briefly stated, the concerns about the comparability of various national accounting systems can be summarized as follows:

1. *Multinational enterprises* are faced with having to maintain corporate accounting systems in many different national currencies, different languages, and different sets of accounting principles. Reports to satisfy the diverse informational needs of numerous governments and international agencies must be prepared using various accounting measurement and reporting standards. To meet the informational needs of stockholders and management itself, countless reports from subsidiaries around the world have to be adjusted to reflect the same set of accounting principles, translated into one common language and monetary unit, and consolidated into a single set of financial statements.

    A no-win situation exists in using a single standard for evaluating the performance of responsibility centers in various countries and the managers in charge of them. If a multinational enterprise employs the same standard throughout the world, environmental differences that have a bearing on the performance in various countries are disregarded. If, on the other hand, local standards are used to evaluate a subsidiary vis-à-vis its competitors in a given foreign country, a comparison of responsibility centers within the multinational enterprise is seriously hampered. An international harmonization of accounting principles would significantly simplify financial reporting, management planning and control, as well as decision making within multinational enterprises.

2. *Investors and financial analysts* have to cope with similar problems of comparability. Since they are primarily familiar with financial reporting practices in their own country, they prefer annual reports in their country's language, currency, accounting principles, and auditing standards. Yet corporations issuing multiple financial reports to improve the effectiveness of transnational reporting would confuse those investors who happen to read financial statements intended for two different national audiences. Harmonization of accounting would improve the communication with the worldwide family of stockholders and thus contribute to a more efficient allocation of scarce investment capital on a global basis.

3. *Host countries* are concerned about the multinational companies' ability to "manipulate" accounting data. Excess power ascribed to multinational corporations, which supposedly lifts them above the control of any one country, has resulted in charges of
    a. hiding information behind the veil of consolidation,
    b. evasion of local taxes,
    c. exploitation of local resources and capital,
    d. unfair competition with indigenous companies,
    e. perpetuation of technological dependence,
    f. lack of social responsibility and accountability, and
    g. disruption of the foreign-exchange market.

    Third World countries are concerned about North-South as well as East-West implications of accounting systems. Should an emerging nation pattern its accounting system after those prevailing in highly advanced Western countries, or should it adopt a system tailor-made for Eastern bloc countries? The system that is best for highly industrialized nations of the West may not necessarily be optimal for pursuing the goals of developing countries. On the other hand, the system utilized by centrally planned economies may contribute to a socioeconomic system that stifles private initiative and freedom of choice. Thus the developing countries are interested in international harmonization of accounting that considers their need for improved income measurement, financial disclosure, and social accountability.

4. *Home countries* have almost similar concerns as host countries about the "supranational" power of multinational enterprises. They have started to question the validity of the saying "What is good for General Motors is good for the country." Some of the more frequently voiced concerns are the ability of large multinational corporations to export jobs, worsen the balance of payments, enjoy tax loopholes, and weaken the currency of any country, including that of the country of domicile. Although international harmonization of accounting cannot solve all of these problems, it can at least provide comparable data for establishing and maintaining sound international economic relations among sovereign nations.

5. *The International Labor Office* has voiced concern about the diversity of corporate disclosure standards among countries and the inadequacy of disclosure in general. Organized labor maintains that multinational companies have an unfair advantage by dealing with labor unions on a country-by-country basis. The corporations can readily avoid the bargaining power of a union by shifting production to their subsidiaries abroad without adequately disclosing their overseas involvement. Harmonized and improved disclosure would be a first step toward reestablishing bargaining parity between multinational companies and labor unions.

6. *The accounting profession* itself has been concerned over the years about the discrepancy of accounting practices among countries. If accounting is truly the language of businessmen, international accounting needs to become the language spoken in multinational companies. Only by harmonizing accounting around the world can international accounting improve communication among international business executives.

HARMONIZATION EFFORTS

The six interest groups—identified earlier—concerned about the diversity of accounting systems have become involved to various degrees in attempts to harmonize accounting practices around the world. The dominant forces behind setting international standards are the following organizations.

THE INTERNATIONAL ACCOUNTING STANDARDS COMMITTEE. Established in 1973 by the professional accountancy bodies of Australia, Canada, Germany, Japan, Mexico, the Netherlands, the United Kingdom and Ireland, and the United States, the IASC now has the support of national institutes in 43 countries representing more than 400,000 certified accountants. Each member organization of the IASC has agreed to use its best effort to ensure that (1) financial statements published in its country adhere to international accounting standards promulgated by IASC, (2) auditors satisfy themselves that the financial statements conform with these standards or that the fact of noncompliance is disclosed in the financial statements or the auditor's report, and (3) appropriate action is taken against auditors who disregard international standards.

The operating procedures of the IASC are similar to those followed by the FASB. The board of the IASC identifies the subject areas to be studied and appoints a steering committee for each area to write an exposure draft. After the exposure draft has been approved by a two-thirds vote of the board, the draft is sent to the professional accountancy bodies and others for comment. The steering committee reviews all comments and drafts the final standard, which must be approved by a three-fourth vote of the board to become effective. So far the IASC has issued the following international accounting standards:

IAS	1	Disclosure of Accounting Policies (1975)
IAS	2	Valuation and Presentation of Inventories in the Context of the Historical Cost System (1975)
IAS	3	Consolidated Financial Statements (1976)
IAS	4	Depreciation Accounting (1976)
IAS	5	Information to Be Disclosed in Financial Statements (1976)
IAS	6	Accounting Responses to Changing Prices (1977)
IAS	7	Statement of Changes in Financial Position (1977)
IAS	8	Unusual and Prior Period Items and Changes in Accounting Policies (1978)
IAS	9	Accounting for Research and Development Activities (1978)
IAS	10	Contingencies and Events Occurring after the Balance Sheet Date (1978)
IAS	11	Accounting for Construction Contracts (1979)
IAS	12	Accounting for Taxes on Income (1979)
IAS	13	Presentation of Current Assets and Current Liabilities (1979)
IAS	14	Reporting Financial Information by Segment (1981)

As of summer 1981, the following exposure drafts were outstanding:

Accounting for Foreign Transactions and Translation of Foreign Financial Statements

Accounting for Retirement Benefits in the Financial Statements of Employers

Information Reflecting the Effects of Changing Prices

Accounting for Property, Plant and Equipment in the Context of the Historical Cost System

Accounting for Leases

Revenue Recognition

Various steering committees are also currently working on the following:

Disclosures in financial statements of banks

Business combinations

Accounting for government grants

Accounting for the capitalization of finance costs

Related party transactions

The effectiveness of the IASC in harmonizing accounting practices has been questioned, since several member bodies, including the AICPA, do not have the power to set accounting standards and cannot enforce international standards under their respective codes of professional ethics. However, Nair and Frank (1981) found that considerable progress toward harmonization of accounting practices occurred between 1973 and 1979 with respect to topics on which the IASC had issued pronouncements. Nevertheless, it remains to be seen whether the United States would make substantial changes in its accounting standards in the interest of international harmony if the IASC should issue standards in conflict with U.S. principles.

THE INTERNATIONAL FEDERATION OF ACCOUNTANTS. Established in 1977, IFAC has a membership of 75 professional accountancy bodies from 57 countries. Its objectives are (1) to initiate, coordinate, and guide efforts aimed at (a) harmonizing technical, ethical, and educational aspects of the profession, and (b) granting reciprocal recognition of qualifications for practice, (2) to encourage and promote the development of organizations working toward regional harmonization, and (3) to arrange the holding of international congresses of accountants. Seven standing committees have been appointed to accomplish these objectives. As of spring 1981, IFAC has issued the following international auditing guidelines:

IAG   1   Objective and Scope of the Audit of Financial Statements (1980)
IAG   2   Audit Engagement Letters (1980)
IAG   3   Basic Principles Governing an Audit (1980)
IAG   4   Planning (1981)
IAG   5   Using the Work of an Other Auditor (1981)
IAG   6   Study and Evaluation of the Accounting System and Internal Control in Connection with an Audit (1981)

Exposure drafts have been issued on the following topics:

Control of the Quality of Audit Work
Audit Evidence
Documentation
Using the Work of an Internal Auditor

THE UNITED NATIONS. In 1974, a "group of eminent persons"—appointed by the U.N. secretary-general in response to a resolution of the U.N. Economic and Social Council—issued a report that noted the limited comparability of corporate reports and a serious lack of financial and nonfinancial information useful for assessing the activities of multinational companies. At the recommendation made in this report, a "group of experts in international standards of accounting and reporting" was appointed to consider—under the auspices of the U.N. Commission on Transnational Corporations—the promulgation of international accounting and reporting standards.

In 1977 this group issued a report, "International Standards of Accounting and Reporting for Transnational Corporations," which advocated extensive disclosures in financial and social accounting. In response to criticism, an "*ad hoc* intergovernmental working group of experts on international standards of accounting and reporting" was set up to review the report and issue a new one. The *ad hoc* group is consulting with the IASC, but will not necessarily adopt IASC standards in its own recommendations. So far it has issued an interim report entitled "Comprehensive Information System: International Standards of Accounting and Reporting," which deals with the feasibility of a proposed international code of conduct.

Other U.N. reports and background papers related to harmonization and improved disclosures are the following:

International Standards of Accounting and Reporting: Work of the United Nations (1979)

International Standards of Accounting and Reporting: A Comparative Study (1979)

International Standards of Accounting and Reporting: Regional and International Organizations Promoting Accounting and Reporting Standards (1979)

Ongoing Efforts of Harmonization (1980)

Information Disclosure: Numbers of Employees (1980)

Information on Gross Operating Profit and Depreciation (1980)

Besides striving for more disclosure and comparability, the United Nation's effort is also directed toward establishing a comprehensive financial data bank on multinational enterprises.

THE ORGANIZATION FOR ECONOMIC COOPERATION AND DEVELOPMENT. In 1976, OECD adopted the Declaration of International Investment and Multinational Enterprises. In essence, this declaration is a code of conduct for multinational companies and host governments. The "Guidelines for Multinational Enterprises," which are part of the declaration, call for, among other things, the disclosure of (1) geographic areas where operations are carried out and the principal activities carried on therein, (2) operating results and sales by geographic areas, (3) significant new capital investments by geographic areas, (4) the average number of employees by geographic areas, (5) transfer-pricing policies, and (6) accounting principles, including those on consolidation, observed in preparing financial statements.

The guidelines have been endorsed by the U.S. government and the International Chamber of Commerce. Australia uses them in deciding on applications by foreign companies for investments in Australia, and labor unions in Europe have cited them in disputes with management.

To assess compliance with the guidelines and review international accounting in general, the OECD Committee on International Investment and Multinational Enterprises (CIIME) organized a working group on accounting standards. Specific tasks of the working group are to (1) assist CHME by clarifying the accounting terms contained in the OECD guidelines, (2) encourage exchanges of views between governments and professional accounting organizations, (3) provide technical advice relating to accounting and disclosure standards, and (4) consider ways to constructively further international accounting harmony. The working group's 1980 report "International Investments and Multinational Enterprises—Accounting Practices in OECD Member Countries" found a lack of standards for measuring items to be disclosed under the guidelines. It also identified areas of significant differences that need to be considered in future efforts toward harmonization.

THE EUROPEAN ECONOMIC COMMUNITY. The harmonization efforts of the EEC are carried out under the provisions of Article 3 of the Treaty of Rome. This article states, among other things, that the objectives of the EEC are (1) the abolition of obstacles between member states to freedom of movement for persons, services, and capital, and (2) the institution of a system ensuring that competition in the Common Market is not distorted. To accomplish these objectives, the EEC has embarked on two major efforts contributing to the harmonization of accounting: the creation of a European company, and the issuance of "directives" dealing with accounting principles.

The creation of a European company, to be known by the Latin name Societa Europea (SE), would enable companies operating simultaneously in several European countries to incorporate as supranational legal entities. A draft of a regulation, which would be binding in every respect and have direct force of law in every member country, was passed by the EEC Commission and submitted to the Council of Ministers in 1970. Although the economic and social committee of the EEC reported favorably on the draft, it is currently bogged down by extensive redrafting.

The harmonization in the form of directives has been more successful. Directives are binding on member countries with respect to the results to be achieved, but leave the ways and means of implementation to the discretion of the national authorities. So far the council has issued the following directive to achieve accounting harmony:

First Directive—Corporate Powers and Disclosures (1968)

Second Directive—Incorporation of Public Companies and Transactions in Capital Shares (1976)

Third Directive—Merger of Public Companies (1978)

Fourth Directive—Principles of Accounting and Disclosure (1978)

Directive—Coordinating the Conditions for the Admission of Securities to Official Stock Exchange Listing (1979)

Directive formerly titled the Sixth Draft Directive—Publication Requirements for Listing Securities (1980)

Directive—Protection of Employees in the Event of Insolvency of the Employer (1980)

By far the most important of these directives is the fourth, dealing with the preparation of annual financial statements by corporations operating in the EEC. It also prescribes accounting standards for intercompany investments, goodwill, research and development, and the valuation of fixed assets, inventory, and other current assets. Some of these standards as well as the formats to be used for the preparation of financial statements differ from practices adhered to in the United States and other non-EEC countries.

In addition to these directives, which have received final approval by the Council of Ministers, the European Commission has issued the following proposed directives for council action:

Proposal for a Fifth Directive—Corporate Management Structure and Employee Participation

Proposal for a Directive—Scissions of Public Limited Companies

Amended Proposal for a Seventh Directive—Consolidated Statements

Amended Proposal for an Eighth Directive—Auditor's Qualifications

Proposal for a Directive—Procedures for Informing and Consulting Employees of Companies with Complex Structures, Transnational Firms

Amended Proposal for a Directive—Interim Financial Data to Be Published by Listed Companies

The most important draft proposal is the one covering consolidated statements. If adopted in its present form, it would require enterprises operating within the EEC but domiciled elsewhere to prepare combined financial statements for all subsidiaries incorporated in the EEC and all companies controlled by them.

UNION EUROPÉENE DES EXPERTS COMPTABLES ECONOMIQUES ET FINAN-CIERS. Similar to IFAC's worldwide harmonization efforts in auditing, the main objective of UEC is the mitigation of differences among auditing standards in Europe. Founded in 1951, UEC currently consists of 28 professional accounting organizations from 20 European countries. All member organizations have agreed to support UEC auditing statements by:

1. Informing their members about the content of UEC draft statements.
2. Either informing their members about the content of UEC definitive statements or incorporating these statements into their national auditing standards.
3. Using their best endeavors, in those countries where audit procedures are prescribed by law, to get the law adapted accordingly.
4. Using their best endeavors to ensure that bodies responsible for the maintenance of professional standards are aware of UEC auditing statements.

As of spring 1981, UEC has issued eight auditing statements, four additional exposure drafts on auditing, two statements on professional ethics with an additional three ethics statements in exposure form, and two studies by its technical and research committee that deal, among other things, with generally accepted accounting principles. These statements are not binding unless they have been incorporated into national auditing standards.

OTHER HARMONIZATION EFFORTS. Over the years many other contributions toward harmonization have been made. The international congresses of accountants have highlighted the need for more accounting harmony since the first congress was held in St. Louis in 1904. The congresses in Sydney and Munich in 1972 and 1977, respectively, can take credit for the establishment of the IASC and IFAC. Regional conferences organized by UEC, the Confederation of Asian and Pacific Accountants, and the Inter-American Accounting Association have made indirect, albeit very valuable, contributions to the reduction of international accounting differences.

The international conferences on accounting education held in conjunction with the last four international congresses of accountants have focused attention on international accounting issues. World congresses sponsored by the Academy of Accounting Historians have traced the development toward international harmonization in accounting. University-based centers and institutes for international accounting studies have been established at the Universities of Illinois, Washington, Texas at Dallas, California State at Northridge, Lancaster in England, and other institutions.

The international accounting section of the American Accounting Association has become a major vehicle for research and exchange of ideas related to international accounting issues. Its approximately 600 members not only have been active in teaching international accounting, but they also have researched international problems and have responded to exposure drafts issued by the IASC and other standard-setting organizations.

Although not all contributions to international harmonization can be properly acknowledged, one would go amiss by not mentioning the international public accounting firms. They continue to play an active role in the harmonization process by standardizing their accounting and auditing practices in offices around the world and establishing uniform training programs for their professional staff and clients. Their international exchanges of staff and partners may not directly result in harmonization, but they create a greater awareness for the international dimension of the profession that is conducive to the eternal striving for harmony.

SOURCES AND SUGGESTED REFERENCES

Accountants International Study Group. *International Financial Reporting.* New York: AICPA, 1975.

American Institute of Certified Public Accountants. *Professional Accounting In 30 Countries.* New York: AICPA, 1975.

American Institute of Certified Public Accountants. *Professional Accounting in 25 Countries.* New York: AICPA, 1964.

Arpan, J.S., and Radebaugh, L.H. *International Accounting and Multinational Enterprises.* Boston: Warren, Gorham & Lamont, 1981.

Arthur Young & Company. "Keeping Up-To-Date With International Accounting Developments," *Arthur Young Client Memorandum,* March 31, 1980.

Choi, F.D.S. and Mueller, G.G., *An Introduction to Multinational Accounting.* Englewood Cliffs, NJ: Prentice-Hall, 1978.

Coopers & Lybrand. *International Financial Reporting and Auditing.* New York: Coopers & Lybrand, 1979.

Da Costa, R.C., Bourgeois, J.C., and Lawson, W.M. "A Classification of International Financial Accounting Practices," *International Journal of Accounting,* Vol. XIII, No. 2 (1978), pp. 73–85.

Deloitte Haskins & Sells. *International Accounting Standards and Guidelines.* New York: Deloitte Haskins & Sells, 1981.

"Duties of Chief Accountants and CPAs, and Methods of Auditing of Financial Reports and Statements of State Enterprises," *Monitor Polski,* 1973, No. 37, Item 226.

Ernst & Whinney. *The Fourth Directive.* London: Kluwer, 1979.

Fitzgerald, R.D., Stickler, A.D., and Watts, T.R. *International Survey of Accounting Principles and Reporting Practices.* Scarborough, Ontario: Butterworths for Price Waterhouse International, 1979.

Frank, W.G. "An Empirical Analysis of International Accounting Principles," *Journal of Accounting Research,* Vol. XVII, No. 2 (1979), pp. 593–605.

"General Rules of Accounting of State-Owned Enterprises," *Monitor Polski,* 1972, No. 56, Item 300.

Hatfield, H.R. "Some Variations in Accounting Practice in England, France, Germany and the United States," *Journal of Accounting Research,* Vol. IV, No. 2 (1966), pp. 169–182.

Jaruga, A.A. "Problems of Uniform Accounting Principles in Poland," *International Journal of Accounting,* Vol. VIII, No. 1 (1972), pp. 25–41.

Jaruga, A.A. "Recent Developments in Polish Accounting: An International Transaction Emphasis," *International Journal of Accounting,* Vol. X, No. 1 (1974), pp. 1–18.

Jaruga, A.A. "Recent Developments of the Auditing Profession in Poland," *International Journal of Accounting,* Vol. XII, No. 1 (1976), pp. 101–109.

Kubin, K.W. and Mueller, G.G. *A Bibliography of International Accounting.* Seattle: University of Washington, 1973.

Lafferty, M. *Accounting in Europe.* Cambridge, England: Woodhead-Faulkner, 1975.

Mey, A. *On the Application of Business Economics and Replacement Value Accounting in the Netherlands.* Seattle: University of Washington, 1970.

Miller, E.L. *Accounting Problems of Multinational Enterprises.* Lexington, Mass.: Lexington Books, 1979.

Mueller, G. *Accounting Practices in (Various Countries).* Seattle: University of Washington, various years starting in 1962.

Mueller, G.G. *Accounting Practices in the Netherlands.* Seattle: University of Washington, 1962.

Mueller, G.G. *International Accounting.* New York: Macmillan, 1967.

Nair, R.D. and Frank, W.G. "The Impact of Disclosure and Measurement Practices on International Accounting Classifications," *Accounting Review,* Vol. LV, No. 3 (1980), pp. 426–450.

Nair, R.D. and Frank, W.G. "The Harmonization of International Accounting Standards, 1973–1979." *International Journal of Accounting,* Vol. XVII, No. 1 (1981), pp. 61–77.

Nobes, C.W. "An Empirical Analysis of International Accounting Principles: A Comment," *Journal of Accounting Research,* Vol. XIX, No. 1 (1981), pp. 268–270.

Nobes, C.W., and Parker, R.H., *Comparative International Accounting.* Oxford, England: Irwin, 1981.

Oldham, K.M. *Accounting Systems and Practice in Europe.* Epping, England: Grower Press, 1975.

Previts, G.J. "On the Subject of Methodology and Models for International Accountancy," *International Journal of Accounting,* Vol. X, No. 2 (1975), pp. 1–12.

Price Waterhouse & Co. *Accounting Principles and Reporting Practices: A Survey in 38 Countries.* Toronto, Canada: Price Waterhouse International, 1973.

Price Waterhouse & Co. *Information Guide for Doing Business in Germany.* New York: Price Waterhouse, 1978.

Price Waterhouse & Co. *Information Guide for Doing Business in the Netherlands.* New York: Price Waterhouse, 1980.

Price Waterhouse & Co. *Information Guide for Doing Business in Sweden.* New York: Price Waterhouse, 1980.

"Report of the American Accounting Association Committee on International Accounting, 1974–75," *Accounting Review,* Vol. LI, supplement (1976), pp. 70–196.

"Report of the American Accounting Association Committee on International Accounting Operations and Education, 1975–1976," *Accounting Review,* Vol. LII, supplement (1977), pp. 67–132.

Seidler, L.J. "International Accounting—The Ultimate Theory Course," *Accounting Review,* Vol. XLII, (1967), pp. 775–781.

Watt, G.C., Hammer, R.M., and Burge, M. *Accounting for the Multinational Corporation.* Homewood, IL: Dow Jones-Irwin, 1977.

Zeff, S.A. *Forging Accounting Principles in Five Countries.* Champaign, IL: Stipes, 1972.

SECTION **23**

ACCOUNTING FOR MULTINATIONAL OPERATIONS

CONTENTS

FOREIGN-CURRENCY TRANSLATION	**3**	The International Response	28
Reasons for Translation	3	International Accounting Standards	
Terminology	3	Committee	28
The Problem	3	Other international accounting	
Foreign-Currency Transactions	4	organizations	29
Single-transaction perspective	5	The United Kingdom	29
Two-transaction perspective	6	Argentina	30
Foreign-Currency Financial Statements	**7**	Australia	30
Translation Methods	**8**	Belgium	31
Single-rate method	8	Brazil	31
Multiple-rate methods	9	Canada	31
Financial-statement effects	10	France	31
Accounting for Translation Gains and		Japan	31
Losses	**13**	The Netherlands	31
New Translation Proposal	**14**	New Zealand	32
Foreign-currency transactions	14	South Africa	32
Foreign-currency financial statements	14	West Germany	32
Forward Exchange Contracts	**16**	**OTHER REPORTING ISSUES**	**32**
The Controversy Continues	**18**	Consolidated Financial Statements	**32**
Concept of income	18	Purpose	32
Reporting perspective	18	Requirements for consolidation	33
To smooth or not to smooth	18	Consolidation issues	34
Effective hedges	19	Foreign-Operations Disclosure	**37**
Foreign-currency translation and		Reporting requirements	37
inflation	20	Policy issues	40
		Examples of foreign-operations	
		disclosures	41
ACCOUNTING FOR INFLATION	**20**	Transnational Financial Reporting	**46**
The Problem	20	Reporting requirements	46
Types of Inflation Adjustments	21	Convenience translations	46
General-price-level adjustments	21	Special information	46
Current-cost adjustments	22	Limited restatements	47
The U.S. Response	23	Primary-secondary statements	47
Major provisions	23	**SOURCES AND SUGGESTED**	
Foreign operations	26	**REFERENCES**	**48**
Major issues	27		

ACCOUNTING FOR MULTINATIONAL OPERATIONS

Frederick D. S. Choi

FOREIGN-CURRENCY TRANSLATION

REASONS FOR TRANSLATION. Foreign-currency translation, the restatement of account balances from one national-currency framework to another, is undertaken for several reasons, including the following:

1. Recording foreign-currency transactions in the financial statements of a reporting enterprise.
2. Preparing combined or consolidated financial statements coupled with accounting for foreign investments under the equity method.
3. Reporting the results of independent operations to foreign audiences of interest.

Item 3, convenience translation, is discussed in the section "Transnational Financial Reporting."

TERMINOLOGY. *Translation* is not synonymous with *conversion*. Conversion is the physical exchange of one currency for another. Thus a U.S. citizen vacationing in Japan would convert dollars into yen if he were interested in purchasing Japanese goods. Translation is simply a change in monetary *expression*, as when a balance sheet expressed in British pounds is restated in U.S. dollar equivalents. No physical exchange occurs, no accountable transaction takes place. Exhibit 1 defines other terms used in this section.

THE PROBLEM. The traditional medium for translating foreign currency is the foreign-exchange rate which denotes the price of a unit of foreign currency in terms of the domestic or reporting currency. If foreign-exchange rates were relatively stable, as they were prior to the early 1970s, the translation process would be as easy as translating inches or feet into their metric equivalents. However, exchange rates today are free to fluctuate in response to complex forces of supply and demand,

EXHIBIT 1   GLOSSARY OF FOREIGN-CURRENCY-TRANSLATION TERMS

Attribute   The quantifiable characteristic of an item that is measured for accounting purposes. For example, historical cost and replacement cost are attributes of an asset.

Conversion   The exchange of one currency for another.

Current Rate   The exchange rate in effect at the relevant-financial-statement date.

Discount   When the forward exchange rate is below the current spot rate.

Exposed Net Asset Position   The excess of assets that are measured or denominated in foreign currency and translated at the current rate over liabilities that are measured or denominated in foreign currency and translated at the current rate.

Foreign Currency   A currency other than the currency of the country being referred to; a currency other than the reporting currency of the enterprise being referred to.

Foreign-Currency Financial Statements   Financial statements that employ foreign currency as the unit of measure.

Foreign-Currency Transactions   Transactions (for example, sales or purchases of goods or services or loans payable or receivable) whose terms are stated in currency other than the local currency.

Foreign-Currency Translation   The process of expressing amounts denominated or measured in one currency in terms of another currency by use of the exchange rate between the two currencies.

Foreign Operation   An operation whose financial statements are (1) combined or consolidated with or accounted for on an equity basis in the financial statements of the reporting enterprise and (2) prepared in a currency other than the reporting currency of the reporting enterprise.

Forward Exchange Contract   An agreement to exchange at a specified future date currencies of different countries at a specified rate (forward rate).

Functional Currency   The primary currency in which an entity conducts its operation and generates and expends cash. It is usually the currency of the country in which the entity is located and the currency in which the books of record are maintained.

Historical Rate   The foreign-exchange rate that prevailed when a foreign-currency asset or liability was first acquired or incurred.

Local Currency   Currency of a particular country being referred to; the reporting currency of a domestic or foreign operation being referred to.

Monetary Items   Obligations to pay or rights to receive a fixed number of currency units in the future.

Reporting Currency   The currency in which an enterprise prepares its financial statements.

Settlement Date   The date at which a payable is paid or a receivable is collected.

Spot Rate   The exchange rate for immediate exchange of currencies.

Transaction Date   The date at which a transaction (for example, a sale or purchase of merchandise or services) is recorded in a reporting entity's accounting records.

Unit of Measure   The currency in which assets, liabilities, revenue, and expense are measured.

Source.   Adapted from Statement of Financial Accounting Standard No. 8, 1975.

creating difficulties in multinational companies' foreign-exchange translation and conversion procedures.

FOREIGN-CURRENCY TRANSACTIONS. Foreign-currency transactions occur whenever an enterprise purchases or sells goods for which payment is made in a foreign currency, or when it borrows or lends foreign currency. Translation is necessary to maintain the accounting records in the currency of the reporting enterprise.

In October of 1975, the U.S. Financial Accounting Standards Board (FASB) issued Statement of Financial Accounting Standards No. 8 (F.A.S.B. 8) providing, for the first time, authoritative guidance on accounting for foreign-currency transactions and foreign-currency financial statements. Paragraph 7 of the statement mandates the following:

1.   At the *transaction date* [italics added], each asset, liability, revenue, or expense arising from the transaction shall be translated into (that is, measured in) dollars by use of the exchange rate (rate) in effect at that date, and shall be recorded at that dollar amount.

2.   At each *balance sheet date* [italics added], recorded dollar balances representing cash and amounts owed by or to the enterprise that are denominated in foreign currency shall be adjusted to reflect the current rate.

Similar accounting provisions are specified in Exposure Draft 11 of the International Accounting Standards Committee (IASC), an international organization concerned with developing international accounting standards. Entitled *Accounting for Foreign Transactions and Translation of Foreign Financial Statements,* the exposure draft contains the additional proviso (par. 28) that "the forward rate specified in a foreign exchange contract may be used to record a transaction in a foreign currency if the forward contract is entered into in order to establish the amounts of the reporting currency at the date on which the foreign currency transaction is settled." On this basis, a foreign-exchange adjustment is necessary whenever the exchange rate changes between the transaction and settlement dates of a foreign-currency payable or receivable to reflect the difference between the amount originally recorded and the settlement amount. Should financial statements be prepared prior to settlement, the accounting adjustment equals the difference between the amount originally recorded and the amount presented in the financial statements.

Single-Transaction Perspective.   Under a "single transaction" perspective, an exchange adjustment would be treated as an adjustment to the original transaction accounts on the premise that a transaction and its subsequent settlement are a single event. This is illustrated below.

On December 1 of 19X1, a U.S. manufacturer sells, on account, goods to a French importer for $10,000 when the dollar/franc exchange rate is U.S.$1/FF4. The franc receivable is due in 60 days and the U.S. company operates on a calendar-year basis. Prior to collection of the receivable, the franc begins to depreciate. By year-end, the dollar/franc exchange rate is $1/FF4.5; on February 1, 19X2, it is $1/FF5.0.

U.S. Company's Record

		Foreign Currency (decrease)	U.S. Dollar Equivalent (decrease)
12/1/1	Accounts receivable	FF40,000	$10,000
	Sales		10,000
	(to record credit sale)		

U.S. Company's Record

		Foreign Currency (decrease)	U.S. Dollar Equivalent (decrease)
12/31/1	Sales		(1,111)
	Accounts receivable		(1,111)
	(to adjust existing accounts for initial exchange-rate change; FF40,000/FF4 minus FF40,000/FF4.5)		
2/1/2	Retained earnings		(889)
	Accounts receivable		(889)
	(to adjust accounts for additional rate change; FF40,000/FF4.5 minus FF40,000/FF5.0)		
2/1/2	Cash		8,000
	Accounts receivable	(40,000)	(8,000)
	(to record settlement of outstanding foreign-currency receivable.)		

In this illustration, the initial dollar amount recorded for both Accounts Receivable and Sales is considered an estimate until the account is collected. These accounts are subsequently adjusted for changes in the dollar/franc exchange rate. Further depreciation of the franc between the financial statement date (December 31) and the settlement date (February 1) would entail additional adjustments.

Two-Transaction Perspective. Under a "two transaction" perspective, collection of the franc receivable is considered a separate event from the sale giving rise to it. Using the previous data, the export sale and related receivable would be recorded at the exchange rate in effect at that date. Depreciation of the franc between December 1 and December 31 would give rise to a *translation* loss (i.e., exchange loss on an unsettled transaction) and would leave unaffected the previously recorded revenue figure. Settlement of the foreign-currency receivable on February 1, 19X2, at the even-lower exchange rate would give rise to a *conversion* loss (i.e., exchange loss on a *settled* transaction).

U.S. Company's Record

		Foreign Currency (decrease)	U.S. Dollar Equivalent (decrease)
12/1/1	Accounts receivable	FF40,000	$10,000
	Sales		10,000
	(to record credit sale at 12/1/1 exchange rate)		

U.S. Company's Record

		Foreign Currency (decrease)	U.S. Dollar Equivalent (decrease)
12/31/1	Foreign-exchange loss		1,111
	Accounts receivable		(1,111)
	(to record effect of initial rate change)		
2/1/2	Cash		8,000
	Foreign-Exchange Loss		889
	Accounts receivable	(40,000)	(8,889)
	(to record settlement of foreign-currency receivable)		

To achieve uniformity, F.A.S.B. 8 requires the two-transaction method of accounting for foreign-currency transactions which appears to be consistent with international practice. A Price Waterhouse International survey, cited here and subsequently (Fitzgerald et al., 1979), suggests that this treatment is prescribed or the predominant practice in a majority of the 64 countries examined. Unfortunately, uniform application of this methodology to every situation can distort income between reporting periods. As an example, consider our illustration of the U.S.-French transaction from the French importer's point of view. Assume further that the U.S. goods purchased during 19X1 are, in turn, resold by the French buyer during 19X2, when the related foreign-currency payable is settled. Anticipating a strengthening of the U.S. dollar and a concomitant increase in its foreign-currency liability, the French company raises its selling price. The result, per F.A.S.B. 8, would be an unusual charge to earnings of 19X1 followed by an unusually high gross margin on the sale during 19X2.

Distortions of this nature, if material, merit explanation. To its credit, F.A.S.B. 8 encourages such disclosure to the extent "practicable." Therefore, it behooves managers to comment on the effects of F.A.S.B. 8 when it produces income effects not in accord with the economic effects of exchange-rate changes.

FOREIGN-CURRENCY FINANCIAL STATEMENTS. Financial statements of a multinational company's foreign branches and subsidiaries are translated for purposes of consolidation. Fluctuating exchange rates complicate this translation process by increasing the number of translation rates that may be employed; namely, historical rates, current rates, or averages of either (see Exhibit 1 for exchange-rate definitions). Choice of a translation rate, historical or current, is important, as each produces significantly different financial-statement effects. Historical rates preserve the original cost of a foreign-currency item in the domestic-currency statements. If, for example, a German subsidiary of a U.S. parent company acquired a piece of equipment for DM 90,000 when the exchange rate was DM2/$1, this asset would have a U.S.$45,000 equivalent upon consolidation. Should the mark devalue to DM3/$1 by the next financial statement date, the dollar equivalent of the German asset would remain at $45,000, its historical cost in dollars, as long as it continued to be translated at the *historical* rate of DM2/$1. Thus historical rates shield financial statements from foreign-currency *translation gains or losses,* that is, increases or decreases in the dollar equivalents of foreign-currency balances due to fluctuations in the exchange rate between reporting periods. The use of *current* rates produces translation gains or losses. In our previous example, translating the foreign-currency asset at the new current rate would yield a translation loss of $15,000 (DM90,000 ÷ DM2 − DM90,000 ÷ 3).

Basic issues surrounding the translation of foreign-currency financial statements thus include the following:

1. Which exchange rate should be applied to specific foreign-currency-financial-statement accounts?
2. How should translation gains or losses be accounted for?

TRANSLATION METHODS. Varying exchange rates give rise to four major translation methods: current, current-noncurrent, monetary-nonmonetary, and temporal. Exhibit 2 summarizes the treatment of specific balance sheet items under each of the four methods.

These methods, in turn, are grouped into two categories. The first uses a single translation rate; the second, multiple rates. Each category, premised on different concepts of foreign-operations and translation objectives, is useful.

Single-Rate Method. A single rate to translate foreign-currency financial statements is appropriate when foreign entities are viewed from a *local,* as opposed to a parent-

EXHIBIT 2   EXCHANGE RATES EMPLOYED IN DIFFERENT TRANSLATION METHODS FOR SPECIFIC BALANCE SHEET ITEMS

| | Single-Rate Method | Multiple-Rate Methods | | |
	Current-Rate	Current-Noncurrent	Monetary-Nonmonetary	Temporal
Cash	C[a]	C	C	C
Accounts receivable	C	C	C	C
Inventories				
Cost	C	C	H	H
Market	C	C	H	C
Investments				
Cost	C	H	H	H
Market	C	H	H	C
Fixed assets	C	H	H	H
Other assets	C	H	H	H
Accounts payable	C	C	C	C
Long-term debt	C	H	C	C
Common stock	H[b]	H	H	H
Retained earnings	*[c]	*	*	*

[a] C = Current rate.
[b] H = Historical rate.
[c] * = Residual, balancing figure representing a composite of successive current rates.

company, perspective. This method recognizes a foreign-based operation as a separate unit doing business in a foreign currency, retaining the foreign currency as the appropriate unit of measure, and preserving the initial relationships (e.g., financial ratios) in the foreign-currency statements by translating all foreign-currency items—assets, liabilities, revenues, and expenses—by a constant, namely, the current rate. Only the form, not the nature of the foreign accounts, is changed.

When a local-company perspective is maintained, reflection of any translation adjustments in current income would defeat the purpose of preserving relationships in foreign-currency statements. Adjustments to Owners' Equity is preferable. (Choi and Mueller, 1978).

The current-rate method was first supported by the Institute of Chartered Accountants in England and Wales (ICAEW) in their 1968 Statement N25 (1968). It is one of two methods recommended by the IASC in their Exposure Draft 11, used more frequently in Europe and Japan than in the Americas.

Multiple-Rate Methods. Multiple-rate methods utilize a combination of historical and current rates, premised on a parent-company perspective. Foreign-based operations are viewed as mere extensions of the parent company as opposed to independent entities. Hence the objects of translation are to change the unit of measure for the financial statements of foreign subsidiaries from foreign currency to the parent company's reporting currency and to make foreign statements conform to accounting principles generally accepted in the country of the parent company. Thus if the historical-cost principle is embraced by the parent, translation of a subsidiary's foreign-currency-denominated assets at the historical rate assures that they will also be reflected at cost in the consolidated statements. Translation at the current rate would restate foreign-currency assets to a basis other than cost. Three historical-rate methods are discussed in turn.

Current-Noncurrent Method. Prior to F.A.S.B. 8, this was the most authoritative foreign-currency-translation method in the United States. No longer permitted there, its use is still advocated in the authoritative literature outside the United States. It remains the predominant practice in countries such as West Germany, Iran, New Zealand, Pakistan, and South Africa.

Under the current-noncurrent method (described in Chapter 12 of *Accounting Research Bulletin No. 43* of the AICPA), a foreign subsidiary's current assets and current liabilities are translated into their domestic-currency equivalents at the current rate. Noncurrent assets and liabilities are translated at historical rates.

Income-statement items, with the exception of depreciation and amortization charges, are translated at average rates applicable to each month of operation or on the basis of weighted averages covering the whole period to be reported. Depreciation and amortization charges are translated at rates in effect when the related assets were acquired.

Monetary-Nonmonetary Method. Formally recognized in the United States with the issuance of Accounting Principles Board (APB) Opinion No. 6 (amending Accounting Research Bulletin No. 43), this method, like the current-noncurrent method, uses a balance-sheet-classification scheme to determine appropriate translation rates. *Monetary* assets and liabilities (see Exhibit 1) such as cash, receivables, and payables including long-term debt, are translated at the current rate. *Nonmonetary* items—

fixed assets, long-term investments, and inventories—are translated at the historical rate. Income-statement items are translated under procedures similar to those described under the current-noncurrent framework. Although no longer permitted in the United States, the method is practiced extensively in Central America, the Philippines, Sweden, and Taiwan (PWI Survey).

Temporal Method.   Under this method, foreign-currency assets and liabilities are translated in a manner that retains their original measurement bases. Cash, receivables, and payables are translated at the current rate. Assets carried in foreign financial statements at historical cost are translated at the historical rate. Assets carried at current values such as inventories, under the lower-of-cost-or-market rule, are translated at the current rate. Revenue and expense items are translated at rates prevailing when the underlying transactions take place, although average rates are suggested when revenue or expense transactions are voluminous.

Under a historical-cost-valuation framework, the translation procedures resulting from the temporal principle are virtually identical to those resulting from the monetary-nonmonetary method. Translation procedures differ, however, if other asset-valuation bases, such as replacement cost, market values, or discounted cash flows, are adopted.

The temporal method of translation became a part of U.S. generally accepted accounting principles with the issuance of F.A.S.B. 8. Canada has since adopted the method (currently under revision) and the IASC accepts it as one of the two methods supported in its Exposure Draft 11. Australia is also seriously considering its adoption in light of a recent exposure draft released by the Australian Accounting Research Foundation. A comprehensive tabulation of the rates at which certain common balance sheet accounts are to be translated under F.A.S.B. 8 is contained in Exhibit 3.

Financial-Statement Effects.   Exhibit 4 highlights the financial-statement effects of the various translation methods described. The balance sheet of a hypothetical Swiss subsidiary of a U.S.-based multinational appears in the first two columns of the exhibit. The third column depicts the U.S. dollar equivalent of the Swiss franc (SF) balances when the exchange rate is $1/SF2. Should the franc appreciate by 33⅓ percent in relation to the dollar (now $1/SF1.5), a number of different accounting results are possible. (Bracketed expressions in the exhibit identify those foreign-currency balances affected by exchange-rate changes, giving rise to translation gains or losses.)

Under the current-rate method, exchange-rate changes affect the dollar equivalents of the Swiss subsidiary's *total* foreign-currency assets (TA) and liabilities (TL) in the current period. Since their dollar values are affected by changes in the current rate, they are said to be *exposed,* in an accounting sense, to foreign-exchange risk. Accordingly, under the current-rate method, an exposed net-asset position (TA > TL) would give rise to a translation loss should the Swiss franc depreciate in value and an exchange gain should the franc be revalued. An exposed net-liability position (TA < TL) would produce a translation gain in the event of a Swiss franc devaluation and conversely. In our example, current-rate translation yields a $300 translation gain, since the dollar equivalent of the Swiss subsidiary's net-asset position after the franc appreciation is $1200 ($3600 − $2400), whereas the dollar equivalent *before* the appreciation was $900 ($2700 − $1800).

**EXHIBIT 3   RATES USED TO TRANSLATE ASSETS AND LIABILITIES
UNDER F.A.S.B. 8**

	Translation Rates	
	Current	Historical
Assets		
Cash on hand and demand and time deposits	x	
Marketable equity securities		
Carried at cost		x
Carried at current market price	x	
Accounts and notes receivable and related unearned discount	x	
Allowance for doubtful accounts and notes receivable	x	
Inventories		
Carried at cost		x
Carried at current replacement price or current selling price	x	
Carried at net realizable value	x	
Carried at contract price (produced under fixed-price contracts)	x	
Prepaid insurance, advertising, and rent		x
Refundable deposits	x	
Advances to unconsolidated subsidiaries	x	
Property, plant, and equipment		x
Accumulated depreciation of property, plant, and equipment		x
Cash surrender value of life insurance	x	
Patents, trademarks, licenses, and formulas		x
Goodwill		x
Other intangible assets		x
Liabilities		
Accounts and notes payable and overdrafts	x	
Accrued expenses payable	x	
Accrued losses on firm purchase commitments	x	
Refundable deposits	x	
Deferred income		x
Bonds payable or other long-term debt	x	
Unamortized premium or discount on bonds or notes payable	x	
Convertible bonds payable	x	
Accrued pension obligations	x	
Obligations under warrants	x	

Under the current-noncurrent method, the U.S. company's accounting exposure is measured by its net current asset or liability position, under the monetary-non-monetary method, by its net monetary asset or liability position. Exposure under the temporal principle depends on whether the Swiss subsidiary's inventories or other assets are valued at historical cost or some other valuation basis.

EXHIBIT 4   TRANSLATION GAINS AND LOSSES UNDER DIFFERING METHODOLOGIES ASSUMING AN APPRECIATING FOREIGN CURRENCY[a]

Swiss Subsidiary Balance Sheet in Swiss Francs		U.S. Dollars Before Franc Appreciation ($1/SF2.0)	U.S. Dollar Equivalents After Swiss France Appreciation ($1/SF1.5)			
Amount	Item		Current Rate	Current-Noncurrent	Monetary-Nonmonetary	Temporal
	Assets					
SF 600	Cash	$ 300	$ 400	$ 400	$ 400	$ 400
600	Accounts receivable	300	400	400	400	400
	Inventories:					
	Cost (SF900)					
1200	Market	600	800	800	600[b]	800
3000	Fixed assets, net	1500	2000	1500	1500	1500
SF 5400		$2700	$3600	$3100	$2900	$3100
	Liabilities and *owners' equity*					
SF 1200	ST payables	$ 600	$ 800	$ 800	$ 800	$ 800
2400	LT debt	1200	1600	1200	1600	1600
1800	Owners' equity[c]	900	1200	1100	500	700
SF 5400		$2700	$3600	$3100	$2900	$3100
	Translation gain (loss)		$ 300	$ 200	$ (400)	$ (200)

[a]Note that if the exchange rate remained unchanged over time, the translated statements would be the same under all translation methods.

[b]Under some interpretations, this item would be reclassified as a monetary item and translated at the current rate.

[c]In the translated statements, Owners' Equity is a residual balancing figure.

ACCOUNTING FOR TRANSLATION GAINS AND LOSSES. The last row of Exhibit 4 reveals a wide array of accounting results—ranging from a $400 loss under the monetary-nonmonetary method to a $300 gain under the current-rate method. Yet each method presumably describes the same factual situation! This raises the issue of how these "translation gains or losses" are accounted for.

A distinction between conversion and translation gains or losses should be acknowledged at the outset. In the former case, there is an actual exchange of foreign currencies. Thus if a U.S. company borrows SF300,000 when the exchange rate is $1/SF2 and immediately converts the franc proceeds to dollars, it will receive $150,000. If, at the time of repayment, the franc appreciates to $1/SF1.5, the U.S. borrower will actually have to expend $200,000 to discharge its SF300,000 debt. A $50,000 conversion loss occurs. In accounting parlance, this loss has been *realized,* and accountants would generally agree that such losses (or gains) should be reflected immediately in period income.

In contrast, translation adjustments are "unrealized" gains or losses (i.e., bookkeeping entries) that result from the application of different translation rates to foreign-account balances. Under these circumstances the appropriate accounting disposition is less obvious.

Prior to F.A.S.B. 8, the prevalent accounting treatment for translation adjustments under U.S. historical-translation methods was to net translation gains and losses incurred during the period. Excess translation losses were reflected in current income, excess translation gains were deferred in the balance sheet and used to absorb future translation losses. Outside the United States, immediate recognition of both gains and losses is frequently practiced. Moreover, the accounting disposition of such translation adjustments appears to be independent of the particular translation method utilized. Other accounting treatments, less commonly practiced, range from reflecting all gains and losses directly in Owners' Equity to deferral and amortization over future periods.

F.A.S.B. 8 significantly altered U.S. practice as well as that of foreign companies subscribing to U.S. GAAP. In addition to mandating use of the temporal principle, F.A.S.B. 8 required affected companies to include both translation gains and losses in operating results in the period of the rate change. Designed to assure accounting uniformity, this F.A.S.B. 8 feature proved more controversial than any other. In effect, F.A.S.B. 8 eliminated the use of balance sheet reserves to buffer current earnings from fluctuating exchange rates causing concern among executives of multinational companies that reported earnings of their companies would appear more volatile than those of purely domestic entities, and would depress their stock prices. Despite evidence to the contrary (Dukes, 1978), F.A.S.B. 8 had a significant effect on corporate-management practices. Studies on the economic impact of F.A.S.B. 8 by organizations such as the FASB (in 1978), Conference Board (in 1979), and Financial Executives Research Foundation (in 1980) found management incurring current and/or potential cash costs to minimize noncash (translation) adjustments, including the opportunity costs of management time diverted away from mainstream operating problems.

Dissatisfaction with F.A.S.B. 8 also centered around the unrealistic results often produced by specific translation provisions. In particular, the use of multiple rates as translation coefficients distorts both income-statement and balance sheet relationships (e.g., gross margins as a result of translating sales at current rates and cost of sales at historical rates) in the foreign-currency statements. Similar distortions are produced when exchange gains or losses mask what has actually occurred. Furthermore, forward contracts and other hedging transactions were often not accounted for as such.

NEW TRANSLATION PROPOSAL.   In May 1978, the FASB invited public comment on its first 12 pronouncements. Most respondents urged that F.A.S.B. 8 be reconsidered. Accordingly, in August 1980 the FASB issued an exposure draft (since revised) of a proposed Statement of Financial Accounting Standards, *Foreign Currency Translation,* which would replace F.A.S.B. 8 on or after December 15, 1981 recently postponed to December 15, 1982. (Canada is also reconsidering its pronouncement and the United Kingdom has issued a proposed standard along the lines of the new U.S. exposure draft.) If adopted, the FASB proposal supercedes in addition to F.A.S.B. 8, F.A.S.B. 20, *Accounting for Forward Exchange Contracts,* FAS Interpretation No. 15, Translation of Unamortized Policy Acquisition Costs by a Stock Life Insurance Company; and FAS Interpretation No. 17, *Applying the Lower of Cost or Market Rule in Translated Financial Statements.*

Foreign-Currency Transactions.   The new FASB proposals are similar to those under F.A.S.B. 8 with two major exceptions. Transaction adjustments—translation gains or losses on unsettled transactions as well as conversion gains or losses on settled transactions—are reported in a separate component of Stockholders' Equity in the following cases:

1. When the foreign-currency transaction (including a forward exchange contract, discussed shortly) is intended as a hedge of a foreign operation's exposed net-asset or net-liability position.
2. When the adjustment relates to transactions between a parent company and an affiliate that is combined, consolidated, or accounted for by the equity method in the parent's financial statements.

Transaction adjustments between two or more affiliates of the parent company, however, are reflected in current income.

Foreign-Currency Financial Statements.   The FASB's new proposal also calls for major changes when translating foreign-currency financial statements. Although retaining U.S. accounting principles as basic, the FASB now considers a local-company perspective appropriate for reporting foreign operations. By requiring the current-rate method of translation discussed earlier, the financial results and relationships, as measured and expressed in the primary, or *functional,* currency (see Exhibit 1) in which the foreign entity conducts its business, are preserved. All assets and liabilities would be translated at exchange rates prevailing as of the financial-statement date, whereas revenues and expenses, *including* cost of goods sold and depreciation, would be translated at an average of the exchange rates in effect during the reporting period. If the foreign-currency statements were denominated in a currency other than its functional currency, then restatement to its functional currency (using the temporal method) would have to occur before translation to its parent's currency by means of the current-rate method.

   In line with F.A.S.B. 8, the current rate to be used for translation is the rate prevailing at the financial-statement date. The dividend-remittance rate is preferred where multiple exchange rates exist. Should a foreign affiliate's financial-statement date differ from that of its reporting parent, the rate in effect at the foreign entity's statement date should be used. Nonconsolidation and hence no translation is considered appropriate for subsidiaries located in countries with extremely unstable or controlled currencies.

Another translation objective, ignored by F.A.S.B. 8, is to obtain results generally compatible with the expected effects of a rate change on an enterprise's foreign-exchange exposure. In the FASB's view:

> Compatibility in direction is achieved if the accounting results are favorable when an exchange rate is favorable to an enterprise's exposed position and vice versa. Compatibility in financial statement classification is achieved if adjustments that are reasonably expected to be realized are included as gains or losses in determining net income and adjustments that are only remote and have uncertain implications for realization are excluded from determining income.

Compatibility is accomplished by distinguishing between gains and losses arising from foreign-currency transactions (settled and unsettled) and those arising from the translation of foreign-currency financial statements. The former would be included in current income, whereas the latter would be included as a separate component of Stockholders' Equity. Adjustments to Stockholders' Equity, in turn, would be included in income only when a substantial, partial, or complete liquidation occurs or when a permanent impairment of the net investment in the foreign affiliate has occurred. ("Permanent impairment" is not defined in the exposure draft.)

The following illustration assumes that a Canadian subsidiary of a U.S. parent company borrows 100,000 Dutch guilders (DG), given the facts below:

	Canadian Books	U.S. Books
Foreign currency loan	DG100,000	
Exchange rate at transaction date	C$2.6^a = DG1	$0.85 = C$1
(= financial-statement date 12/31/1)		
Exchange rate at financial-statement date (12/31/2)	C$2.1 = DG1	$1 = C$1
Loan balance at:		
Transaction date (12/31/1)		
(DG100,000 × C$2.6)	C$260,000	
(C$200,000 × $0.85)		$221,000
Financial statement date (12/31/2)		
(DG100,000 × C$2.1)	C$210,000	
(C$210,000 × $1)		210,000
Translation gain		
Reflected in income	C$ 50,000	
Reflected in Stockholders' Equity		$ 11,000

^{a}C$ = Canadian dollar

In this example, the Dutch guilder loan constitutes a foreign-currency transaction on the Canadian subsidiary's books. In the U.S. consolidation, it simply constitutes a foreign-currency liability that needs to be restated to its U.S. dollar equivalent.

EXHIBIT 5 COMPARISON OF F.A.S.B. 8 TO EXPOSURE DRAFT

Criticisms of F.A.S.B. 8	Effect of Exposure Draft
Unnecessary fluctuations are reported in Income	Translation gains or losses on net investments in foreign operations are excluded from income and reported as a separate component of Stockholders' Equity
Accounting exchange gains or losses can be reported where the reverse has occurred from an economic standpoint	All assets and liabilities are translated at the current rate and thus the translation process is directionally sympathetic with the economic effect of the exchange-rate movement
Financial-statement relationships are restated from those reflected in the foreign-currency operations	Changes in financial-statement relationships largely are eliminated by translating all items within each statement at the same exchange rate; i.e., current rate for balance sheet; weighted-average rate for income statement
Effective hedges are ignored	Gains or losses on effective hedges of a net investment in foreign operations are applied as an offset to translation gains or losses reported as a separate component of Stockholders' Equity. Also, the conditions for a hedge of a foreign-currency commitment are modified

Source. Peat, Marwick, Mitchell & Co., 1980.

Differences between the translated balance sheets under F.A.S.B. 8 and the new exposure draft can be seen in Exhibit 4. Whereas the $200 translation loss under the temporal method would be shown in the income statement (per F.A.S.B. 8), the $300 translation gain under the current-rate method would be credited directly to a separate equity account that would not be amortized (per exposure draft). Exhibit 5, in turn, summarizes how the proposed standard attempts to remedy criticized features of F.A.S.B. 8.

FORWARD EXCHANGE CONTRACTS. This section elaborates upon the last comparison in Exhibit 5. Forward exchange contracts, defined in Exhibit 1, may be secured to (1) hedge a foreign-currency payable or receivable (a foreign-currency commitment), (2) hedge an exposed net-asset or net-liability position of a foreign operation, or (3) speculate in foreign currencies. Under F.A.S.B. 8, each of these categories dictated a different accounting treatment for discounts, premiums, gains, or losses on contracted forward exchange. These adjustments might arise in the following manner.

On March 1, 19X1, a U.S. company enters into a contract to exchange one million Swedish krona (SKr) for U.S. dollars on June 1, 19X1. Exchange-rate information and related accounting adjustments appear below.

Amount of Forward Contract	Skr1,000,000
Spot rate on 3/1/1	$0.24 = SKr1
3-month forward contract rate on 3/1/1	$0.23 = SKr1
Discount [($0.24 spot rate − $0.23 forward rate) × SKr1,000,000]	$10,000

Amount of Forward Contract	Skr1,000,000
Spot rate on 6/1/1	$0.21 = SKr
Gain [($0.24 spot rate − $0.21 future spot rate) × SKr1,000,000]	$30,000

The following matrix illustrates how these accounting adjustments would be reported following F.A.S.B 8 dicta:

	Gains/Losses	Discount/Premium
Identifiable foreign-currency commitments	Deferred and included in dollar basis of foreign-currency transaction[a]	Amortized over duration of contract[c]
Exposed net asset or liability position	Recognized in income of period in which they occur	Amortized over duration of contract
Speculation	Recognized in income of period in which they occur[b]	Recognized in current income

[a]The amount deferred is limited to the amount of the related commitment, on an after-tax basis.

[b]Gains/losses in this category are a function of the difference between the forward rate available for the remaining period of the contract and the contracted forward rate (or the forward rate last used to measure a gain or loss on that contract for an earlier period).

[c]The portion that is amortized during the commitment period may be included in the dollar basis of the related foreign-currency transaction.

The foregoing scheme is modified by the new FASB proposal in that gains or losses related to a hedge of an exposed net-asset or net-liability position would be reported in a separate component of Stockholders' Equity rather than in periodic income. Conditions qualifying a forward contract as a hedge of an identifiable foreign-currency commitment under F.A.S.B. 8 and the FASB's new proposals (less stringent) are listed below:

F.A.S.B. 8	New Proposal
Life of the forward contract must match that of the related foreign-currency commitment.	Forward contract must be intended and designated as a hedge of a foreign-currency commitment.
Forward contract must commence at the commitment date.	Forward contract need not commence at the commitment date.
Forward contract must be denominated in the same currency as the foreign-currency commitment.	Forward contract must be denominated in the same currency as the foreign-currency commitment or in a currency that moves in tandem with it.

F.A.S.B. 8	New Proposal
Foreign-currency commitment must be firm and uncancelable.	Foreign-currency commitment must be firm.

THE CONTROVERSY CONTINUES.   While the recent FASB proposals are designed to still many of the criticisms leveled at F.A.S.B. 8, new issues stir new controversies; perhaps inevitable given the complexity of multinational operations and the many purposes of translation. Several basic issues are set forth below.

Concept of Income.   Under the FASB exposure draft, adjustments arising from the translation of foreign-currency financial statements and certain transactions are made directly to Shareholders' Equity, thus bypassing the income statement. The apparent intention was to provide statement readers with more-accurate and less-confusing income numbers, that is, translated results that are "directionally sympathetic" with the economic effect of exchange-rate movements. Some, however, dislike the idea of "burying" translation adjustments, heretofore disclosed. They fear possible reader confusion as to the effects of fluctuating exchange rates on a company's worth. Equity adjustments, moreover, violate the *all-inclusive concept of income* (APB Opinion No. 9, December 1966), which requires that companies disclose (1) operating revenues and expenses, and (2) all unusual, nonoperating, and infrequently occurring items in the computation of income, the latter category being reported separately in the income statement. This provision was designed to provide statement readers with all information bearing on a firm's "profitability." Which income concept is right?

Reporting Perspective.   In adopting the notion of a "functional currency," the FASB accommodates both a local as well as a parent-company reporting perspective in the consolidated financial statements. The first adopts the currency of the foreign operation's domicile as functional; the second, the U.S. dollar. As an example, a Brazilian subsidiary might manufacture a component to be shipped to its U.S. parent for inclusion in a product resold in the United States. In this case, the Brazilian subsidiary is merely an extension of the U.S. operation; its functional currency is the U.S. dollar. Should the Brazilian entity maintain its records in cruzeiros, its financial statements would be translated to U.S. dollars using the temporal method, and any translation adjustments would be included in current income (as per F.A.S.B. 8). However, several questions arise. First, are the translation adjustments just described any different from those resulting from use of a current-rate method (per exposure draft)? If not, is any useful purpose served by disclosing some translation adjustments in income and others in Stockholders' Equity? Are financial-statement readers better served by incorporating two different reporting perspectives and, therefore, two different currency frameworks in a single set of consolidated financial statements? The F.A.S.B. 8 concept of a single consolidated entity and a single unit of measure (the dollar) may prove the lesser of two evils.

To Smooth or Not to Smooth.   F.A.S.B. 8's treatment of exchange gains and losses was designed, among other things, to minimize a smoothing option permitted by the earlier use of balance sheet reserves to account for net translation gains. Ironically, the FASB's new proposals would reintroduce smoothing opportunities. Consider, once again, the notion of functional currencies. When a foreign entity's functional currency is not readily apparent, its determination is left to management. Once determined, the functional currency is expected to be used consistently, unless management ascertains a change in the underlying circumstances. Ernst & Whinney (1980) state that "a change in the functional currency would not be considered a change in accounting principle under APB Opinion No. 20, 'Accounting Changes.' We believe a change in the functional currency of a foreign entity would be viewed as a change to reflect new events or economic circumstances." This means that the cumulative effect of a functional currency change, computed for all prior periods to the beginning of the period in which the change is made, would not have to be disclosed.

As an example of a smoothing opportunity, assume that a U.S. parent company has a manufacturing subsidiary in Germany whose functional currency is the *U.S. dollar*. The U.S. parent wishes to borrow deutsche marks for use in its Frankfurt operations. If the parent were to take out the deutsche mark loan, an appreciation of the deutsche mark by the repayment date would be reflected in consolidated income. However, if the German *subsidiary* borrowed the funds and the deutsche mark were designated as its functional currency, an exchange adjustment, stemming from a rise in the deutsche mark's value, would bypass consolidated income and appear in Stockholders' Equity instead.

Assume now that the U.S. parent desired use of the deutsche mark loan proceeds. Again, borrowing deutsche marks through the German subsidiary would shield consolidated income from the effects of a fluctuating DM/$ exchange rate, regardless of the functional currency of the German subsidiary. Under the FASB's proposal, transactions between an investor and investee (e.g., intercompany receivables or payables) are viewed as increases or decreases in a parent company's foreign investment. Accordingly, foreign-exchange adjustments, whether attributed to settled or unsettled transactions, are treated as adjustments to Stockholders' Equity. Under these circumstances, parent-company borrowing of deutsche marks would be a logical tack when the deutsche mark was expected to depreciate; appreciation of the mark would dictate intercompany borrowing.

Intercompany transactions, however, only apply to transactions between a parent company and its affiliates, not to transactions between two or more affiliates of the same parent. Adjustments from these latter transactions would be recognized immediately in period income. With the exception of transactions that are essentially permanent investments, some people question whether transactions between a parent and its affiliate are any different from those between related affiliates. Opportunities for income manipulation also arise. A parent company, for example, could serve as a clearinghouse for intersubsidiary transactions to avoid having to report related gains or losses in consolidated income.

Effective Hedges. Transactions intended as economic hedges of foreign net investments (exposed net-asset or net-liability positions) get special treatment under the new exposure draft. For example, a U.S. parent company with an Australian exposed net-asset position could arrange to borrow Australian dollars to hedge its net investment in Australia. Translation adjustments relating to the foreign-currency transaction would then appear in Stockholders' Equity rather than periodic income. Unfortunately, the converse situation, that is, maintaining an exposed-asset position as a hedge against a foreign-currency commitment, would not be recognized. Thus a U.S. company with a Chinese yuan bank balance might contract to purchase textiles from a manufacturer in Canton. If the purchase price was payable in yuan, any translation loss on the yuan payable owing to a rise in the dollar/yuan exchange rate would be offset by the exchange gain on the yuan bank deposit. Whether this hedge is different from the Australian hedge described above is for the reader to decide.

Foreign-Currency Translation and Inflation.   An inverse relationship between a country's rate of inflation and its currency's external value has been empirically demonstrated. Consequently, use of the current rate to translate the cost of nonmonetary assets located in inflationary environments will eventually produce domestic-currency equivalents far below their original measurement bases. At the same time, translated earnings will be greater because of correspondingly lower depreciation charges. Such translated results could easily mislead rather than inform. Lower dollar valuations would usually understate the actual earning power of foreign assets supported by local inflation and inflated return on investment ratios of foreign operations could create false expectations regarding future profitability.

In light of these considerations, would some form of inflation adjustment be appropriate prior to translation? The FASB considered this, but faced a number of dilemmas. For example, should inflation adjustments apply to all foreign entities or just those domiciled in "high inflationary" environments? If the latter, when would an inflation rate be considered hyperinflationary? This question is especially troublesome given double-digit inflation rates in the United States. Indeed, would special accounting treatment be appropriate for subsidiary accounts denominated in currencies with significantly lower inflation rates than that in the parent's country?

In a recent meeting (April 1981), the FASB supported an approach that would adjust local currency statements for changes in the local general price level whenever the cumulative rate of local inflation for the preceeding three years exceeds 100 percent. In addition, price level adjustments would be permitted for operations in countries having inflation rates below the level for which inflation adjustments would be mandatory if the inflation rate exceeds that in the parent company's country. While an improvement, this modification to the FASB's original exposure draft raises further issues. Thus, are cumulative rates of inflation of, say, 75 percent any less significant than 100 percent? Are statement readers better served by price level adjusting the results of some foreign operations and not others? Given the nature of current exchange rates, the problem of foreign currency translation may very well be inseparable from the issue of accounting for inflation.

ACCOUNTING FOR INFLATION

THE PROBLEM.   Accepted accounting principles in most countries, including the United States, have traditionally assumed stable prices. With global inflation the major economic malady of the 1980s, the relevance of historical-cost accounting is being increasingly questioned. Thus matching revenues realized during an inflationary period against the historical costs of resources (notably inventories and property) acquired in the past generally result in overstated income, which may lead to the following:

1.   Increases in proportionate taxation.
2.   Demands by shareholders for more dividends.
3.   Demands by labor for higher wages.

4. Unfavorable actions by home and/or host governments.
5. Unoptimal business decisions.

With inflation, there is always the danger that a firm may not preserve sufficient resources internally to replace higher priced assets. Also, failure to adjust corporate accounts for changes in the purchasing power of the monetary unit makes it difficult for statement readers to interpret and compare operating results both within and between countries. Conventional disregard for purchasing-power gains and losses from holding monetary items further distorts business-performance comparisons during inflationary periods.

Many are cognizant of the need to consider price changes when interpreting historical-cost-based statements. Nevertheless, explicit recognition of inflation's effects in financial reports is useful for several reasons (FASB, 1979):

1. The effects of changing prices depend partially on the transactions and circumstances of an enterprise, and users do not have detailed information about those factors.

2. Alleviation of the problems caused by changing prices depends on a widespread understanding of the problems; a widespread understanding is unlikely to develop until business performance is discussed in terms of measures that explicitly allow for the effects of changing prices.

3. Statements by managers about the problems caused by changing prices will have greater credibility when enterprises publish financial information that addresses those problems.

TYPES OF INFLATION ADJUSTMENTS.   Accounting for inflation requires that a distinction be made between general-and specific-price movements. A *general-price-level change* (inflation or deflation) refers to a movement in the prices of all goods and services in an economy on the average, that is, the purchasing power of the monetary unit changes in terms of its ability to command goods and services in general. A *specific-price change* refers to a change in the price of a specific commodity, inventories and equipment, for example. General-and specific-price series seldom move in parallel fashion. Each differs in its financial-statement effects; each is accounted for with different objectives in mind. Henceforth, accounting for the financial-statement effects of general-price-level changes is referred to as the *historical-cost/constant-dollar model*. Accounting for specific-price changes is referred to as the *current-cost model*.

General-Price-Level Adjustments.   From a balance sheet perspective, income represents that portion of a firm's wealth (net asset) position that can be disposed of during an accounting period without decreasing its original net-asset position. To illustrate, assume a U.S. merchandiser starts the calendar year with $100,000 in cash (no debt), which is immediately converted into salable inventory. The entire inventory is sold on the last day of the year for $150,000 cash. Assuming stable prices, enterprise income would equal $50,000, measured as the difference between the ending and beginning net assets, or revenues minus expenses (cost of goods sold). In this case, a dividend distribution of $50,000 would indeed leave the firm with as much money capital at the end as it had at the beginning, namely, $100,000.

During periods of inflation, however, the $50,000 may no longer represent the amount of a firm's disposable wealth. General-price-level adjustments take this into account by measuring enterprise income so that it represents the maximum amount of resources that could be distributed to various income claimants while preserving the firm's ability to command as many goods and services, in general, at the end of the period as it could at the beginning.

Assume now that the general level of prices, as measured by the consumer price index, increases from a level of 100 at the beginning of the period to 120 at the end. (It would take $120 at year-end to purchase what $100 would have purchased at the beginning.) Income, under the historical-cost/constant-dollar model, is thus measured by taking the difference between wealth at the end of the period ($150,000) and wealth at the beginning adjusted to its end-of-period purchasing-power equivalent ($100,000 × 120/100 = $130,000) or $30,000. Alternatively, historical-cost-based expenses in the income statement could be restated to their end-of-period purchasing-power equivalents (constant dollars) and subtracted from period revenues, which are already stated in end-of-period dollars. In our example,

Revenues ($150,000 × 120/120)	$150,000
less Cost of goods sold ($100,000 × 120/100)	120,000
Price-level-adjusted income	$ 30,000

Disbursing no more than $30,000 would help assure that the company could command as many goods and services, in general, at the end of the period as it could at the beginning.

It is possible to convert measurements of historical cost to their beginning-of-period purchasing-power equivalents by multiplying the foregoing figures by the ratio of the general-price-level index at the beginning of the period to the price index prevailing at the end. Either method, if used consistently, is satisfactory.

Current-Cost Adjustments.   The current-cost model views income as the amount of resources that could be distributed during a given period while maintaining a company's productive capacity or earning power. One way is to adjust a firm's original net-asset position using appropriate specific price indexes or direct pricing to reflect changes in an item's current-cost equivalent during the period. In our current example, if during the same period prices of the firm's inventories increased by 40 percent, income under the current-cost model would be measured as ($150,000 − $100,000 × 140/100) or $10,000. Again, the $150,000 figure could represent ending net assets or sales revenues and the $100,000 figure, beginning net assets or cost-of-goods-sold expense. In this case, distributing no more than $10,000 would help ensure that the firm would preserve sufficient resources internally to enable it to replace specific assets whose prices had risen during the period. Thus whereas the objective of general-price-level adjustments is to preserve the general purchasing power of an enterprise's original money capital, the current-cost model attempts to preserve a firm's physical capital or earning power.

National accounting responses to inflation generally reflect the historical-cost/constant-dollar *or* current-cost models. Those favoring the former argue that the latter violates the historical-cost-valuation framework, is too subjective, and is difficult to implement. It also ignores changes in the purchasing power of money and the resulting monetary gains or losses from holding monetary items such as debt. Those favoring current-cost adjustments argue that businesses are not affected by general inflation; they are affected instead by increases in specific operating costs and plant expenditures. Moreover, recording purchasing-power gains from holding debt during inflation could be misleading. Highly levered firms could show large monetary gains while on the brink of bankruptcy (Vancil, 1976).

Methods combining features of both current-cost and adjusted-historical-cost models are also under limited experimentation in the United States. This financial information recognizes both changes in asset values and changes in the monetary-measuring unit.

THE U.S. RESPONSE. In September 1979, the FASB issued Statement of Financial Accounting Standards No. 33 (F.A.S.B. 33), *Financial Reporting and Changing Prices,* the result of intermittent efforts by the U.S. accounting profession to integrate inflation adjustments into U.S. annual reports. Highlights of the lengthy standard follow.

Major Provisions. Applicable for fiscal years ending after December 23, 1979, F.A.S.B. 33 requires disclosure of both price-level-adjusted historical-cost and current-cost information. The FASB concluded that preparers and users of financial reports should have further practical experience with inflation accounting. Hence the required disclosures *supplement* rather than *replace* historical cost as the basic measurement framework for primary financial statements.

The statement presently applies to public U.S. enterprises that have either

1. Inventories and property, plant, and equipment (before deducting accumulated depreciation) of more than $125 million, or
2. Total assets amounting to more than $1 billion (after deducting accumulated depreciation). Assets include those in foreign locations.

It also applies to publicly held non-U.S. companies that prepare their basic financial statements in U.S. dollars and in accordance with U.S. GAAP, such as the Royal Dutch-Shell Group when reporting to their U.S. shareholders.

A comprehensive review of F.A.S.B. 33 by the FASB is contemplated no later than September 1984. In the meantime, the Board intends to assess the usefulness of the inflation disclosures as a basis for possible revision.

Supplementary disclosure requirements of F.A.S.B. 33 are summarized below.

Information for the Current Year
    Historical-Cost/Constant-Dollar Basis
      Income from continuing operations.
      Purchasing-power gain or loss on net monetary items.
    Current-Cost Basis (beginning in 1980)
      Income from continuing operations.
      Current-cost amounts of inventory and property, plant, and equipment at year-end.
      Increases or decreases in the current-cost amounts of inventory and property, plant, and equipment, net of inflation (general-price-level changes).

Information for Each of the Five Most-Recent Years
   Net Sales and Other Operating Revenues
   Historical-Cost/Constant-Dollar Information
      Income from continuing operations.
      Income per common share from continuing operations.
      Net assets at year-end.
   Current-Cost Information
      Income from continuing operations.
      Income per common share from continuing operations.
      Net assets at year-end.
      Increases or decreases in the current cost amounts of inventory and property, plant, and equipment, net of inflation.
   Other Information
      Purchasing-power gain or loss on net monetary items.
      Cash dividends declared per common share.
      Market price per common share at year-end.
      Level of the consumer price index used to measure income from continuing operations.
      Explanations of the information disclosed and discussions of the significance of the information in the circumstances of the reporting enterprise.

Firms are allowed and encouraged to experiment with statement presentations of the required information. Exxon Corporation offers a useful reporting format that exceeds F.A.S.B. 33's disclosure minima. It appears in Exhibit 6.

EXHIBIT 6   EXXON CORPORATION'S INFLATION ACCOUNTING FORMAT

INCOME FROM CONTINUING OPERATIONS AND OTHER CHANGES IN SHAREHOLDERS' EQUITY ADJUSTED FOR CHANGING PRICES FOR THE YEAR ENDED DECEMBER 31, 1979 (MILLIONS OF DOLLARS; ADJUSTED FOR MILLIONS OF AVERAGE 1979 DOLLARS)

		Adjusted for	
	As reported	General Inflation	Specific Costs
Income from continuing operations			
Total revenue	$84,809	$84,809	$84,809
Costs and other deductions			
Crude oil and product purchases	40,831	40,831	40,831
Depreciation and depletion	2,027	3,270	3,932
Other	14,070	14,070	14,070
Interest expense	494	494	494
Income, excise and other taxes	23,092	23,092	23,092
Total costs and other deductions	$80,514	$81,757	$82,419
Income from continuing operations	$ 4,295	$ 3,052	$ 2,390
Gain from decline in the purchasing power of net amounts owed		998	998
Increase in current cost of inventories and property, plant and equipment during 1979			9,333

EXHIBIT 6   CONTINUED

	As reported	Adjusted for	
		General Inflation	Specific Costs
Less effect of increase in general price level during 1979			6,634
Excess of increase in specific prices over increase in the general price level			2,699
Net income	$ 4,295		
Adjusted net income		$ 4,050	
Net change in shareholders' equity from above	$ 4,295	$ 4,050	$ 6,087

SUMMARIZED BALANCE SHEET ADJUSTED FOR CHANGING PRICES AT DECEMBER 31, 1979

	(millions of dollars)	(millions of average 1979 dollars)	
		Adjusted for	
	As reported	General Inflation	Specific Costs
Assets			
Inventories	$ 5,481	$ 7,585	$11,558
Property, plant and equipment	26,293	35,796	45,418
All other assets	17,716	16,892	16,892
Total assets	49,490	60,273	73,868
Total liabilities	26,938	25,599	25,599
Shareholders' equity	$22,552	$34,674	$48,269

SUPPLEMENTARY FINANCIAL DATA (MILLIONS OF DOLLARS EXCEPT PER SHARE AMOUNTS)

	Years ended December 31				
Unadjusted for inflation	1975	1976	1977	1978	1979
Income from continuing operations	$ 2,456	$ 2,615	$ 2,443	$ 2,763	$ 4,295
Per share	5.49	5.84	5.45	6.20	9.74
Return of income from continuing operations on average shareholders' equity, percent	15.4	15.1	13.1	14.0	20.1

Historical Cost Information Adjusted for General Inflation (average 1979 dollars)

Income from continuing operations	1,961	2,355	1,983	2,052	3,052
Per share	4.38	5.26	4.43	4.60	6.92
Gain from decline in purchasing power of net amounts owed	337	277	441	617	998
Adjusted net income	2,298	2,632	2,424	2,669	4,050
Per share	5.14	5.88	5.41	5.99	9.19
Total revenue	65,765	67,059	70,023	72,191	84,809
Dividends, per share	3.37	3.47	3.59	3.67	3.90

EXHIBIT 6 CONTINUED

	Years ended December 31				
	1975	1976	1977	1978	1979
Market price at year-end, per share	58	69⅜	56¼	52⅝	52⅛
Net assets at year-end	30,114	31,146	31,847	32,599	34,674
Return of adjusted net income on average shareholders' equity, percent	7.7	8.6	7.7	8.3	12.0
Historical Cost Information Adjusted for Specific Costs (Average 1979 Dollars)					
Income from continuing operations		1,944	1,336	1,245	2,390
Per share		4.34	2.98	2.79	5.42
Gain from decline in purchasing power of net amounts owed		277	441	617	998
Excess of increase in specific prices over increase due to general inflation		2,999	1,807	(377)	2,699
Net change in shareholders' equity		5,220	3,584	1,485	6,087
Per share		11.66	8.00	3.33	13.81
Net assets at year-end		42,781	44,642	44,211	48,269
Return of net change in shareholders' equity on average shareholders' equity, percent		12.8	8.2	3.3	13.2
Average consumer price index	161.2	170.5	181.5	195.4	217.4

Compliance with *F.A.S.B. No. 33* requires that a firm adjust, at a minimum, inventory, fixed assets, and their related charges to income, using the Consumer Price Index for all Urban Consumers to restate these data to a constant dollar basis. Greater flexibility is permitted when obtaining information on current cost equivalents, including the use of specific price indexes or direct pricing.

F.A.S.B. No. 33 replaces Accounting Series Release No. 190 of the U.S. Securities and Exchange Commission (SEC) (March 1976), which called for footnote disclosures of certain replacement cost data by large U.S. enterprises in their 10-K filings with the Commission. ASR No. 271 removed this requirement for fiscal years ending on or after December 25, 1980, when the FASB's current cost disclosures became mandatory.

Foreign Operations. F.A.S.B. No. 33 also applies to foreign operations included in the consolidated statements of U.S. parent companies. In this regard, should the amounts of foreign subsidiaries and branches be adjusted for foreign inflation and then translated to U.S. dollars (restate-translate method)? Or, should they be translated to dollars and then adjusted for U.S. inflation (translate-restate method)?

Under a historical cost/constant dollar framework, the restate-translate method involves adjusting foreign currency account balances for foreign general-price level changes and then translating the adjusted amounts to U.S. dollars. The translate-restate option would translate the accounts of foreign subsidiaries to U.S. dollars and then adjust these amounts for changes in the U.S. Consumer Price Index.

To illustrate, assume that a U.S. parent company's Brazilian subsidiary starts and ends its calendar year with an inventory balance of $5 million cruzeiros. The dollar/cruzerio exchange rate on January 1 was $0.02 = Cr1. During the year, the U.S. general price level advances from 100 to 110; the Brazilian general price level doubles. At year-end, the foreign-exchange rate stands at $0.015 = Cr1. Employing the temporal method of translation, the dollar equivalent of the cruzerio inventory balance under both foreign-currency/price-level adjustment methods would be derived as follows:

Restate-Translate (Thousands)

	Foreign-Currency Balance	Foreign-Inflation Adjustment	Historical-Cost/Constant Cruzeiros	Translation Rate	U.S. Dollar Equivalent
Inventories	Cr5000 ×	200/100 =	Cr10000 ×	0.015 =	$150

Translate-Restate (Thousands)

	Foreign-Currency Balance	Translation Rate	U.S. Dollar Equivalent	Domestic-Inflation Adjustment	Historical-Cost/Constant Dollars
Inventories	Cr5000 ×	0.02 =	$100 ×	110/100 =	$110

From a U.S. parent-company perspective, the $150,000 in the restate-translate method *overstates* the amount of *U.S. purchasing power* invested in Brazilian inventories. From a local-company perspective, the $110,000 in the translate-restate method *understates* the *foreign-purchasing-power equivalent* of the translated inventories.

The FASB considered the problem of consolidating the accounts of foreign subsidiaries domiciled in inflationary environments. It concluded that the preferred method for achieving constant dollar measurements is first to translate foreign-currency historical amounts into U.S. dollars in accordance with U.S. GAAP and then to restate the translated amounts for U.S. inflation. The translate-restate alternative was preferred because (*F.A.S.B. 33,* par. 192):

> The usefulness of constant dollar measurements is partly to provide information about the erosion of investors' purchasing power and the relevant measure of purchasing power for most investors in U.S. enterprises is the purchasing power of the U.S. dollar.

Major Issues.   The issuance, however, of the FASB's recent exposure draft on foreign-currency translation (see section "Foreign Currency Translation: New Translation Proposal") raises a number of perplexing issues that have yet to be resolved. Although F.A.S.B. 33 suggests a parent-company perspective as a reporting stance for foreign operations, its exposure draft supports a local-company perspective, implying that the restate-translate method may be the appropriate mode to follow when reflecting inflation's effects in consolidated financial statements. Although the

FASB now favors inflation adjustments prior to translation, this is mandated only for operations domiciled in "hyper-inflationary" environments.

Implementation of F.A.S.B. 33 is also complicated by the Board's preference for the current-rate method of translation. If the exposure draft is approved in its present form, companies adhering to the translate-restate option will have to translate foreign accounts at the current rate, then restate the resulting dollar amounts accounting for U.S. inflation. An issue that may be difficult to resolve, quantitatively, is: To what extent do exchange rates between the foreign currency and the U.S. dollar reflect changes in the relative general purchasing powers of the respective currency units involved? To the extent that the current exchange rate reflects purchasing-power parity between currencies, translated foreign-currency amounts may already be expressed in inflation-adjusted dollars. To the extent that they are, further adjustments for U.S. inflation may be redundant.

Even if the foregoing issue were resolved, translation of cost-based foreign-currency assets at the current rate would change the resulting dollar equivalents to a basis other than cost. In the previous inventory example, translation of the Brazilian subsidiary's inventories at the historical rate preserved their cost of $100,000 in the U.S. statements. Translation at the current rate would change this basis to $75,000, a figure that resembles neither historical nor current cost. Similar considerations apply to the restate-translate method in conjunction with restatements for general price level changes prior to translation. Restating a foreign-currency account, measured at cost, for foreign inflation does not change the *valuation base*.

Use of the current-rate method appears most compatible with a current-cost-valuation framework. Multiplying a foreign-currency item valued at current cost by a current market exchange rate provides a current-cost equivalent of that item in U.S. dollars. This viewpoint, is in fact, supported by *F.A.S.B. 33* (par. 59):

> If current cost is measured in a foreign currency, the amount shall be translated into dollars at the current exchange rate, that is, the rate at the date of use, sale, or commitment to a specific contract (in the case of depreciation expense and cost of goods sold) or the rate at the balance sheet date (in the case of inventory and property, plant, and equipment).

THE INTERNATIONAL RESPONSE. The worldwide nature of the problem of disclosing the effects of changing prices has led to active development of inflation-accounting proposals internationally. Some major developments are briefly sketched. Addresses of organizations that will provide further information are appended to each subsection.

International Accounting Standards Committee. Established with the objective of harmonizing accounting standards internationally, the IASC has maintained an accommodating posture in the area of inflation accounting. International Accounting Standard 6, *Accounting Responses to Changing Prices,* (1977) summarizes major inflation-accounting alternatives in a preface. The standard merely states that

> enterprises should present in their financial statements information that describes the procedures adopted to reflect the impact on the financial statements of specific price changes, changes in the general level of prices, or of both. If no such procedures have been adopted that fact should be disclosed.

IAS 6 became operative for financial statements covering periods on or after January 1, 1978.

In August 1980, the IASC also issued Exposure Draft 17 (ED 17) *Information Reflecting the Effects of Changing Prices*. More specific than IAS 6, ED 17 proposes that large publicly traded enterprises disclose the following information using a method that adjusts for the effects of changing prices:

1. The amount of the adjustment to, or the adjusted amount of, depreciation of property, plant, and equipment.
2. The amount of the adjustment to, or the adjusted amount of, cost of sales.
3. A financing adjustment(s), if such adjustment(s) is generally part of the method adopted for reporting information on changing prices.
4. The enterprise results recomputed to reflect the effects of the items described in (1) and (2) and, where appropriate, (3), and any other items separately disclosed that the method adopted requires.

The information, *if provided,* should be disclosed on a supplementary basis unless inflation-adjusted accounts constitute the basic financial statements. (*International Accounting Standards Committee, 3 St. Helen's Place, London EC3 6DN, England*)

Other International Accounting Organizations.   In an effort to harmonize financial disclosures among member countries of the European Economic Community (EEC), the EEC Commission issued its Fourth Directive in 1978. In the area of asset valuation, the directive retains the historical-cost principle as its basic valuation method. However, it allows member states to authorize the use of replacement-value measurements or other methods based on current or market values. Any differences between historical-cost valuations and replacement-cost or current-market valuations must be aggregated and separately disclosed as an item of "revaluation reserve" in Owners' Equity. The summarized revaluation reserves must be disaggregated according to the main asset categories to which they pertain. (U.S. Office, 245 East 47th Street, New York, NY 10017)

The U.N. Group of Experts on International Standards of Accounting and Reporting (GEISAR), whose major aim is harmonizing the disclosure practices of transnational corporations, has not yet concerned itself with accounting measurement rules. In its 1977 report *International Standards of Accounting and Reporting for Transnational Corporations,* the U.N. group simply calls for the disclosure of accounting policies including overall valuation methods such as historical cost, replacement value, general-price-level adjustments, or any other valuation basis. (Center on Transnational Corporations, United Nations, Box 20, Grand Central P.O., New York, NY, 10017)

The Organization for Economic Co-operation and Development (OECD), which serves as a policy forum for its 24 member nations, has thus far adopted a posture similar to that of the U.N. group. (U.S. office, Suite 1207, 1750 Pennsylvania Avenue, N.W., Washington, DC 20006)

The United Kingdom.   In a development pattern paralleling that in the United States, the U.K. Accounting Standards Committee (ASC) issued Statement of Standard Accounting Practice No. 16 (SSAP 16), *Current Cost Accounting,* in March 1980. Effective for financial reporting periods beginning on or after January 1, 1980, the U.K. standard differs from F.A.S.B. 33 in two major respects. First, whereas the U.S. standard requires both constant-dollar and current-cost accounting, SSAP

16 adopts only the current-cost method for reporting. Second, whereas U.S. inflation adjustments have an income-statement focus, the U.K. current-cost statements must include both a current-cost income statement and balance sheet, together with explanatory notes. The U.K. standard may be complied with by

1. presenting current-cost accounts as the basic statements with supplementary historical-cost accounts, or
2. presenting historical-cost accounts as the basic statements with supplementary current-cost accounts, or
3. presenting current-cost accounts as the only accounts accompanied by adequate historical-cost information.

SSAP 16 applies to all listed companies and unlisted companies that satisfy any two of the following criteria: sales of £5 million or more, total assets of £2.5 million or more, and 250 or more employees.

Although concepts of and methods for determining current costs are roughly similar in both F.A.S.B. 33 and SSAP 16, the latter differs in its method of accounting for purchasing-power gains and losses related to certain monetary items. In addition to an adjustment that recognizes the effects of changing prices on a firm's monetary-working-capital position, the U.K. standard includes a "gearing" adjustment. This gearing adjustment reduces the *total* of the adjustments made to reduce historical-cost-based income for the higher current-cost equivalents of depreciation expense and cost of goods sold, including the purchasing-power loss from a monetary-working-capital position. Based on the ratio of total debt to total capitalization, the gearing adjustment acknowledges that it is unnecessary to recognize in the income statement the additional replacement cost of assets to the extent they are financed by debt. (Chartered Accountant's Hall, P.O., Box 433, Moorgate Place, London EC2P 2BJ, England)

Argentina. A 1972 pronouncement of the Argentine Technical Institute of Public Accountants now mandates, in certain provinces, that publicly held corporations with paid-in capital exceeding 5 million pesos present complete restatements of all nonmonetary items using a general price index. The supplemental information may be disclosed in (1) a second column in the basic financial statements, (2) footnotes to the basic statements, or (3) a complementary set of financial statements.

More recently (September 1980), the Argentina Professional Council of Economic Sciences of the Federal District, which regulates the public-accounting profession in Buenos Aires, declared that basic financial statements should, in the future, disclose historical-cost/constant-dollar figures in one column and historical cost in another. (Federacion Argentina de Colegios de Graduados en Ciencias Economicas, Avenida Cordoba 1261, 2 Piso 1055, Buenos Aires, Argentina)

Australia. Inflation-accounting developments in Australia have proceeded in several phases. In phase 1, a provisional accounting standard (October 1976) was issued recommending current-cost accounting as applied to fixed assets and inventories in the basic financial statements. In phase 2, attention turned to the required treatment of purchasing-power gains and losses, culminating in the issuance (August 1979) of an exposure draft, *The Recognition of Gains and Losses on Holding Monetary Items in the Context of Current Cost Accounting*. In the most recent phase, Australian accounting bodies have issued an "omnibus" exposure draft extending current-cost provisions to other financial-statement categories including those denominated in foreign currencies. (Australian Accounting Research Foundation, 49 Exhibition Street, Melbourne, Victoria 3000).

Belgium. An October 1976 *Royal Decree on Financial Statements of Enterprises* permits use of current-cost data with respect to inventories, fixed assets, cost of goods sold, and depreciation in the basic financial statements by means of footnote disclosure. Valuation differences are to be charged or credited to a revaluation account. (Institut des Reviseurs d'Enterprises, Rue Caroly 17, 1040 Brussels, Belgium)

Brazil. Under the new Brazilian corporation law, companies are required to reflect in the basic financial statements the general-purchasing-power equivalents of all "permanent-asset accounts," including fixed assets, investments, and deferred charges, using an official general-price-level index. Inventories are not adjusted. The new requirement applies to all companies for fiscal years beginning after January 1, 1978. (Instituto dos Auditores Independentes do Brazil, Rua Antonia de Godoi, 83-16 Andar, Conjunto 161, São Paulo, Brazil)

Canada. Having aired the relative merits of both the historical-cost/constant-dollar and current-cost models, the Canadian Institute of Chartered Accountants (CICA) produced a draft proposal (February 1980) on current-cost accounting. Applicable to large public companies with inventories and fixed assets of at least C$50 million or total assets of at least C$350 million, the proposal calls for supplementary disclosure of the impact of specific-price changes on operating results. Current-cost restatements would apply to fixed assets, inventories, depreciation, and cost of goods sold. The effect of changing prices on monetary working capital would also be disclosed. (The Canadian Institute of Chartered Accountants, 250 Bloor Street East, Toronto M4W 1G5, Canada)

France. Listed companies in France were required to reflect in their basic financial statements the current replacement costs of fixed assets in 1978. Asset-revaluation adjustments were to be disclosed in Stockholders' Equity. Mandated by the French Finance Acts of 1977 and 1978, the disclosures were restricted to fixed assets and did not take into account the effects of inflation on debt and cost of goods sold. The disclosure requirements were also limited to one year.(La Documentation Française, 31 Quai Voltaire, Paris)

Japan. With the exception of the early 1950s, when land and certain depreciable assets were revalued by legislative initiative, valuation principles in Japan have been based on historical cost. Owing to accelerating rates of inflation, especially in the area of property values, the Japanese Institute of CPAs and the Business Accounting Deliberation Council are actively studying the issue. No formal pronouncement has yet been issued. (The Japanese Institute of Certified Public Accountants, the Kabuki Building, 4-12-15, Ginza, Chuo-Ku, Tokyo, Japan)

The Netherlands. Despite the absence of any formal requirements to do so, a generally accepted accounting principle in the Netherlands is the inclusion of current-replacement-value measurements in annual accounts. Larger Dutch companies especially carry certain inventory and depreciable fixed assets at their current replacement values with corresponding replacement-value-based depreciation and cost-of-sales expenses in income statements, and replacement-valuation "reserves" in the Owners' Equity section of balance sheets. Support for this practice is contained in an accompanying note to an IASC exposure draft, *Accounting for Changing Prices,* issued in January 1976 by the Council of Netherlands Instituut van Registeraccountants. (Netherlands Instituut van Registeraccountants, Mensinge 2, Postbus 7984, Amsterdam 1011, Netherlands)

New Zealand.   Instead of a formal accounting standard, New Zealand issued a guideline to inflation accounting in January 1979, which became operative for financial statements prepared by listed public companies on or after April 1, 1979. They require the preparation of supplementary current-cost-adjusted financial statements. Specifically, all nonmonetary assets are to be revalued in terms of their current-replacement cost or net realizable values. Adjustments for depreciation, cost of goods sold, and gearing are required in computing income from current operations. (New Zealand Society of Accountants, Willbank House, 57 Willis Street, P.O. Box 11342, Wellington, New Zealand)

South Africa.   Like New Zealand, the National Council of Chartered Accountants in South Africa issued, in 1978, a guideline to inflation accounting, recommending the adoption of a supplementary income statement prepared in accordance with the current-cost-accounting concept. (The National Council of Chartered Accountants (S.A.), P.O. Box 964, Johannesburg 2000, South Africa)

West Germany.   As a result of a 1975 accounting standard, public companies in West Germany are encouraged to supplement their basic financial statements with information disclosing the effect on earnings of cost of goods sold and depreciation restated to their replacement-cost equivalents. However, that portion of inventories and fixed assets that is considered to be financed by debt, as opposed to equity, is excluded in determining the effect on net earings. (Institut der Wirschaftsprüfer in Deutschland e.V., 4 Düsseldorf 30, Cecilienallee 36, West Germany)

OTHER REPORTING ISSUES

CONSOLIDATED FINANCIAL STATEMENTS.   Consolidated financial statements (or group accounts) result from the line-by-line combination of the assets, liabilities, revenues, and expenses of a parent company and its principal subsidiaries. Reciprocal accounts stemming from intercompany transactions are typically eliminated.

Purpose.   Statement 3 of the IASC (1976) describes the purpose of consolidated statements thus:

> Certain parties with interests in the parent company of a group, such as present and potential shareholders, employees, customers, and in some circumstances creditors, are concerned with the fortunes of the entire group. Consequently, they need to be informed about the results of operations and the financial position of the group as a whole. This need is served by consolidated financial statements, which present financial information

concerning the group as that of a single enterprise without regard for the legal boundaries of the separate legal entities.

The preparation of consolidated accounts is being required in more and more countries. Practices, however, are not yet uniform. The United States and Canada, for example, present only consolidated results in their annual reports. In many other countries separate parent-company statements are presented together with group accounts. German annual reports often become rather voluminous because they contain not only consolidated financial statements and separate statements for the parent company, but also separate financial statements for two or three major subsidiary companies. In some German reports a dual set of consolidated statements is presented—one that includes only domestic subsidiaries, the other both domestic and foreign.

Requirements for Consolidation. In the United States, professional support for consolidated financial statements is contained in Accounting Research Bulletin (ARB) No. 51 and Chapter 12 of ARB No. 43. Although these pronouncements do not mandate consolidation in all instances, companies and their auditors are compelled to justify nonconsolidation. Governmental provisions are contained in the SEC's Regulation S-X. Rule 4-02 of that regulation states:

> The registrant shall follow in the consolidated financial statements principles of inclusion or exclusion which will clearly exhibit the financial position and results of operations of the registrant and its subsidiaries.

Private-capital-market institutions, the New York Stock Exchange in particular, require as a condition for listing the provision of consolidated accounts. A consolidated balance sheet and income statement is permitted in lieu of financial statements of the corporation as a whole and each majority-owned corporate subsidiary.

International interest in consolidation is also very evident today. In 1976 the International Accounting Standards Committee, whose membership currently spans 61 professional accountancy bodies from 47 countries, issued a formal standard recommending that

> a parent company should issue consolidated financial statements, except that it need not do so when it is a wholly owned subsidiary.. . . Investments in associated companies.. . . and in subsidiaries which are not consolidated.. . . should be included in the consolidated financial statements under the equity method of accounting.

Three developments at the governmental level are especially noteworthy. The first event was the issuance in 1976 of a proposed EEC directive calling for annual publication of consolidated financial statements. Seventh in a series aimed at achieving uniform legal requirements in the EEC, the initiative is likely to have a significant impact on multinational companies with extensive operations in the Community. The scope of this impact is described in the following excerpt from the draft directive (EEC, 1976):

> Multinational companies registered in the EEC will be required to draw up and publish clear and complete information, which will ensure that both their relationships with other members of the group and their activities will be clearly visible. They will have to publish

consolidated accounts covering all their affiliated companies throughout the world and drawn up on the basis of principles and methods of consolidation that are uniformly applicable throughout the EEC. MNC's whose registered offices are outside the EEC will also have to comply with the directive's provisions for the activities of their subsidiaries incorporated in the EEC.

The second event was agreement (also reached in 1976) by the 24 member countries of the OECD on a set of guidelines for the conduct of multinational corporations. The accounting dimensions of these guidelines call for the annual publication of financial statements for each enterprise as a whole. Supplementary disclosures on a consolidated basis are also entailed. Although voluntary, these guidelines will probably be adhered to by large multinational companies in the member countries.

The third event was the issuance of a report by the U.N. Center on Transnational Corporations in October 1977 detailing minimum disclosure items for general-purpose reporting by multinational companies. The recommendations were drafted by a U.N. group of experts to improve the availability and comparability of information made available by multinational corporations to host-government and other user groups. As presently constituted, they call for the disclosure of both financial and nonfinancial information by the consolidated enterprise, including separate reports by the parent company and individual member companies of the group. The recommendations have been approved in principle by the U.N. secretary-general. Governments and national accountancy bodies will be invited to use the proposed reporting standards as guidelines in establishing or reviewing their individual reporting and disclosure requirements vis-à-vis national and transnational companies.

Consolidation Issues. Multinational enterprises encounter a number of problems when consolidating the accounts of both domestic and foreign subsidiaries. Translation and the effects of inflation, were discussed earlier. Additional problems stem from differences between foreign and U.S. accounting methods, intercompany transactions, and questions related to appropriate consolidation criteria.

Consolidation mechanics would be straightforward were it not for differences in measurement bases underlying foreign and domestic accounts. Thus adding fixed-asset and accumulated-depreciation balances of a 100-percent-owned Philippine subsidiary to those of its U.S. parent for consolidation purposes would not be proper if the Philippine accounts were restated for local inflation. Even if asset valuation principles were the same in both countries, the resulting additions could still mislead, as most Philippine companies do not estimate the residual value of an asset when calculating depreciation. Additional differences in fixed-asset measurement internationally include the following:

1. Capitalization of interest expense on funds borrowed to finance construction of fixed assets is permitted in many countries; not so in others.

2. Depreciation of fixed assets is not a generally accepted practice in all countries (e.g., several countries on the African continent).

3. Whereas many countries employ straight-line depreciation for financial reporting purposes and accelerated depreciation for tax purposes, countries such as Japan and Korea use accelerated-depreciation methods for both.

4. Required in most countries, disclosure of the valuation basis of fixed assets

remains the exception in countries such as Austria, Greece, Japan, Italy, and Switzerland.

These accounting differences are not limited to fixed assets but permeate almost all financial-statement accounts. As a result, there is now a serious effort to reduce international accounting diversity. A leading force in the accounting-harmonization movement is the IASC. Established in 1973, the IASC has since issued over a dozen definitive accounting standards with many more in process. (Topics covered by IASC standards issued thus far include disclosure of accounting policies, inventory valuation, consolidated financial statements, depreciation, information disclosure, statement of changes in financial position, unusual and prior-period items and changes in accounting policies, research and development, contingencies and post-balance-sheet events, construction contracts, income taxes, and presentation of current assets and liabilities.) Complementing the IASC's efforts are those of the International Federation of Accountants (an organization aimed at promoting the development of a coordinated worldwide accounting profession), the U.N. GEISAR group, the OECD, and several regional accounting organizations.

Despite this progress, accounting diversity continues to characterize the international accounting scene. Adjustments of foreign accounting principles to a basis consistent with those of the reporting parent is therefore necessary prior to consolidating foreign with domestic accounts.

When consolidated statements are prepared, intercompany receivables, payables, sales, profits, and the like are generally eliminated to avoid double counting. Elimination of intercompany profits can be troublesome, especially where a minority interest exists in the subsidiary. Thus whenever profits arise from a sale by the parent to a partially owned subsidiary ("downstream" sales), a common practice is to eliminate 100 percent of the intercompany profit. Sales from a partially owned subsidiary to a parent ("upstream" sales) may be accounted for either in terms of (1) a 100 percent elimination by a charge against consolidated income or (2) an elimination to the extent of the parent company's ownership interest in the subsidiary. The usual practice here is also 100 percent elimination. A view gaining support in the United States, however, is that 100 percent elimination should only apply when intercompany transactions are not at arm's length. Otherwise intercompany profits should be eliminated in proportion to the parent's ownership interest in the subsidiary where the equity method of accounting is used (Accountants International Study Group, 1972).

Watt, Hammer, and Burge (1977) provide helpful insights on the issue of complete versus partial elimination of intercompany profits. They favor 100 percent elimination of profits on downstream sales as a matter of practicality. The partial elimination method, for example, would require a case-by-case analysis of each transaction to determine timely realization of the profit recognized. In their words,

> This would involve an analysis of the financial position of the investee, an evaluation of the influence of the minority interest and assurance that the parent did not force "sales" to the investee near the period end to develop consolidated income. The application of this procedure, therefore, becomes burdensome to the point of impracticality in companies having a multiplicity of investments and intercompany sales.

Partial recognition, however, is preferred for upstream sales in the case of a subsidiary with a minority interest. Complete elimination in this case will involve a double charge against consolidated income; one for the minority interest's share in the profit of the selling subsidiary, and another in connection with the consolidating entry that eliminates the entire intercompany profit. Although the foregoing practice may not have a significant effect on reported earnings in any one year, the cumulative effect on consolidated results could. According to Watt et al.,

> The cost of the assets in consolidation should include the profit which accrues to the minority interest in a subsidiary on sales to the parent. This is a properly recognized cost element which the parent incurs as a result of the lack of complete ownership of the subsidiary, that is, using the capital of the minority interest. Moreover, an investor company brings into its income only its share of the profit reported by the investee on the intercompany transaction and that amount is all that should be eliminated. Income taxes, or the appropriate portion paid on intercompany sales, should be included in the cost of the asset that remains in the consolidation.

Consolidation criteria are called for when deciding whether or not to include the accounts of an associated company in consolidated results. An accepted consolidation prerequisite in many national jurisdictions is control over investee companies by the investor. Unfortunately, different interpretations exist as to what constitutes "control." In the United States, control is presumed to exist when 50 percent or more of the outstanding voting stock of an investee is owned by the parent (APB Opinion No. 18, par. 3). That this criterion is popular is evidenced by its embracement in International Accounting Standard 3, *Consolidated Financial Statements* (IASC, 1976). IAS 3, however, also acknowledges other interpretations of control, as follows:

> A company in which a group does not have control, but in which a group:
> (a) owns more than half the equity capital, but less than half the voting power, or
> (b) has the power to control, by statute or agreement, the financial and operating policies of the management of the company, with or without more than one half of the equity interest, may be treated as a subsidiary and consolidated in the consolidated financial statements. In such circumstances, the reasons for consolidating the company should be disclosed.

The tenor of these provisions find expression in the EEC's proposed Seventh Directive (issued in 1976). In this document, control is associated with the power to exercise such dominant influence over group members that all related undertakings are managed on a central and unified basis. Hence the *power of control* is emphasized over the actual *exercise of control*. Based on these criteria, a parent corporation with a registered office in the EEC might be required to prepare consolidated statements, including its subsidiaries both within and outside the EEC. And whether the parent company were headquartered within the EEC or not, any of its subsidiaries with a registered office in the EEC and that, in turn, controlled other subsidiaries, might have to prepare subconsolidations. Business International (1979) observes further that the directive may even require consolidated financial statements for groups in which no one enterprise dominates any other. A horizontal group of companies (e.g., groups of companies related by a formal management contract) might be consolidated based on EEC definitions.

Reasons justifying nonconsolidation of subsidiaries include the following:

1. Parent-company control is likely to be temporary.
2. Business activities of the subsidiary are so dissimilar to those of the parent

that combined financial statements would not be meaningful (e.g., when finance companies are subsidiaries of industrial companies).

3. Host-government restrictions impair parent-company control (e.g., currency-exchange restrictions and the like).

4. Foreign accounts are insignificant in terms of amounts involved.

Companies electing not to consolidate the accounts of foreign subsidiaries may account for these investments under one of two methods: cost or equity. Under the *cost* method, an investment in the securities of a foreign investor is recorded at cost. The parent company subsequently recognizes income from such an investment only to the extent that dividends are distributed by the investee (save for international tax considerations). Dividends received, however, may bear little relation to the actual performance of the investee, as dividends may be distributed to suit the income or cash needs of the parent.

To remedy this, more countries are requiring adoption of the *equity* method. Here the carrying value of the investee is adjusted to reflect the investor's proportionate share of the investee's profits or losses. Dividends received from an investee are treated, in turn, as reductions in the carrying value of the parent-company's investment. The decision to consolidate internationally, while governed by numerous considerations, ultimately should be governed by two general factors: (1) the significance of the degree of consolidation to the various users of the financial statements and (2) the meaningfulness of consolidated statements that report in a single currency what in fact occurred in several.

FOREIGN-OPERATIONS DISCLOSURE. The growth and geographic spread of business operations has stimulated public demand for information on a reporting enterprise's foreign operations. Proponents of such disclosures argue that consolidated statements, although desirable for their synergistic insights, do not allow investors and other financial analysts to assess the relative importance of foreign segments which experience patterns of profitability, growth, and risk that often differ from aggregate trends. Some express concern that foreign-operations disclosures may (1) harm a reporting company's competitive position, (2) be too detailed for general-purpose financial statements, or (3) confuse the reader. Others feel they are no more onerous than information currently provided in conventional accounting reports.

Arguments notwithstanding, there is today a push at both national and international levels to require more disclosure of a firm's foreign operations, which are viewed as useful supplements to consolidated information.

Reporting Requirements. Foreign-operations-disclosure requirements are commonly treated in conjunction with reporting for business segments. In the United States, F.A.S.B. 14, *Financial Reporting for Segments of a Business Enterprise* (issued December 1976), is the authoritative pronouncement on such disclosures. In addition to information concerning industry segments, the statement requires separate information disclosure for an enterprise's foreign operations, which can be done in an aggregate fashion, or, if appropriate, by geographic area. This requires, however, that foreign operations contribute 10 percent or more of consolidated revenue, or the assets identifiable with the foreign operations must be 10 percent or more of consolidated assets. Excluding unconsolidated subsidiaries and investees, a foreign operation is defined as a revenue-producing operation located outside the

United States (for U.S. enterprises) that generates revenue either from sales to unaffiliated customers or from intercompany sales or transfers between geographic areas. Information sought by F.A.S.B. 14 for foreign operations includes the following:

1. Revenue, with separate disclosure of (a) sales to unaffiliated customers, (b) sales or transfers between geographic areas, and (c) transfer-pricing bases used.
2. Operating income, net income, or some other measure of profitability in between, as long as a consistent measure is used for all geographic areas.
3. Identifiable assets.

ARS No. 236 was issued by the U.S. Securities and Exchange Commission in 1978 to conform its earlier line of business reporting rules with F.A.S.B. 14. Now all SEC filings must contain revenue, income, and identifiable-assets information for foreign operations as required in F.A.S.B. 14.

Foreign-operations-disclosure provisions, similar to those of F.A.S.B. 14, are also contained in an IASC exposure draft on segmental reporting. Issued in March 1980, its intended purpose is "to enable users of financial statements to assess the effect that operations in different industries and in different geographical areas may have on the enterprise as a whole."

Governmental interest in foreign-operations disclosure stems from their concern over the economic and social effects of multinational corporation operations on the countries concerned, irrespective of the relative importance of such operations for the transnational corporation as a whole. Accordingly, the EEC, OECD, and United Nations have also joined the disclosure bandwagon. The EEC's Fourth Directive requires that sales be disaggregated by categories of activity and geographic markets to the extent that these categories and markets differ substantially from one another. The OECD's *Guidelines for Multinational Enterprises* include the following pertinent disclosure provisions:

1. The geographic areas where operations are carried out and the principal activities carried on therein by the parent company and the main affiliates.
2. The operating results and sales by geographic area and the sales in major lines of business for the enterprise as a whole.
3. Significant new capital investment by geographic area and, as far as practicable, by major lines of business for the enterprise as a whole.
4. The average number of employees in each geographic area.
5. The policies followed in respect of intragroup pricing.
6. The accounting policies, including those on consolidation, observed in compiling the published information.

The most comprehensive disclosure standard yet to be proposed on the international front is that originally recommended by the U.N. Group of Experts on International Standards of Accounting and Reporting. Not yet completed, the proposal contains detailed lists of minimum financial- and nonfinancial-disclosure requirements for enterprises as a whole as well as individual member companies.

EXHIBIT 7   GEISAR'S FOREIGN-OPERATIONS-DISCLOSURE PROPOSALS

SECTION B.   INDIVIDUAL MEMBER COMPANY

List of minimum items for general purpose reporting of an individual member company (including the parent company) of a group of companies comprising a transnational corporation. (Each major category also applies to the enterprise as a whole.)

1. Labour and employment
    (a) Description of labour relations policy
          (i) Trade union recognition[a]
          (ii) Complaints and dispute settlement mechanism and procedure[a]
    (b) Number of employees as at year end and annual average
    (c) Number employed by function (professional, production, etc.)
    (d) Number of women employees by function
    (e) Number of national employees by function
    (f) Average hours worked per week
    (g) Labour turnover, annual rate
    (h) Absenteeism—working hours lost (number and as percentage of total working hours per year)
    (i) Accident rates (describe basis)
    (j) Description of health and safety standards
    (k) Employee costs
          (i) Total wages, salaries and other payments to employees (before tax)
          (ii) Social expenditures paid to institutions and Government for benefit of workers (excluding pension schemes reported in the profit and loss statement)
          (iii) Summary description and cost of training programmes

2. Production
    (a) Description of practices regarding acquisition of raw materials and components (indicate percentage acquired from intercompany foreign sources and percentage from all foreign sources)
    (b) Indicate average annual capacity utilization in accordance with normal industrial practice
    (c) Physical output by principal lines of business in accordance with normal industrial practice
    (d) Description of significant new products and processes

3. Investment programme
    (a) Description of announced new capital expenditure
    (b) Description of main projects, including their cost, estimate additions to capacity, estimated direct effect on employment
    (c) Description of announced mergers and takeovers, including their cost and estimated direct effect on employment

4. Organizational structure
    (a) Names of members of board of directors and, where applicable, the supervisory board and a description of their affiliations with companies outside the group
    (b) Number of owners or shareholders and, where known, the names of the principal owners or shareholders

5. Environmental measures
    Description of types of major or special environmental measures carried out, together with cost data, where available

---

[a]For reporting of these items, reference may be made to the application of national laws, agreements with trade unions or publicly available written company policies.

Required financial disclosures on foreign operations parallel closely those of the FASB, IASC, and OECD. Nonfinancial disclosures (see Exhibit 7) contain items seldom disclosed even in U.S. general-purpose reports. These disclosures could very well signal additional or enlarged general-purpose reports by foreign operations.

Policy Issues. Policy decisions are required in at least three basic areas of foreign-operations reporting. The first concerns identification of the geographic segment(s) to be reported, on the premise that operations in different parts of the world may be subject to different degrees of risk or profit opportunities. Although this operating characteristic provides a conceptual basis for identifying geographic areas, operationalizing the concept is difficult. Thus a U.S. subsidiary located in the Far East (e.g., Taiwan) may generate the bulk of its revenues from exports to the EEC. The appropriate geographic classification, assuming the Taiwanese operation is significant, is unclear. Whereas the foreign operation's revenue source may be in Europe, its political-risk complexion may be colored by its Far East location. Environmental risk, in turn, may change over time, often abruptly. Unfortunately, little help is provided by standard setters in suggesting appropriate geographic categories. F.A.S.B. 14 offers the following guidance:

EXHIBIT 8 GEOGRAPHIC CLASSIFICATIONS USED BY U.S.-BASED MULTINATIONAL CORPORATIONS IN THE PHARMACEUTICAL INDUSTRY

Classifications	Number of Companies Using Classification
Three Classifications	
U.S. / Europe / and Other	4
U.S. / Americas and Far East / Europe and Mideast and Africa	1
U.S. / OECD / Other	1
U.S. / Europe and Mideast / Other	1
U.S. / Canada and Latin America / Europe and Africa and Far East	1
Four Classifications	
U.S. / Europe / W. Hemisphere (– U.S.) / Africa and Asia and Pacific	1
U.S. / Europe and Africa / Canada and Latin America / Other	1
U.S. / Latin America / Europe and Mideast and Africa / Pacific and Far East and Canada	2
U.S. / Pacific / W. Hemisphere (– U.S.) / Europe and Mideast and Africa	1
U.S. / W. Hemisphere (– U.S.) / Europe and Africa / Other	1
Five Classifications	
U.S. / Canada / Latin America / Asia and Pacific / Europe and Mideast and Africa	1
U.S. / Europe / Asia / Africa and Mideast / Canada and Latin America	1
U.S. / North America (– U.S.) / South America / England and Continental Europe / Africa and Asia and Pacific	1
Total	17

Source. Bavishi and Wyman, 1980.

For purposes of this statement, foreign geographic areas are individual countries or groups of countries as may be determined to be appropriate in an enterprise's particular circumstances. . . . Each enterprise shall group its foreign operations on the basis of the differences that are most important in its particular circumstances. Factors to be considered include proximity, economic affinity, similarities in business environments, and the nature, scale, and degree of interrelationship of the enterprise's operations in the various countries.

Guidance offered by international organizations such as the IASC and OECD are similarly phrased.

A recent disclosure survey (Bavishi and Wyman, 1980) suggests that geographic categories currently employed by many U.S. companies are arbitrary and possess limited information content. Categories discerned in the pharmaceutical industry (see Exhibit 8) are used to illustrate this contention. In the absence of more-specific institutional guidance, meaningful geographic categories will ultimately depend on reasoned, if necessarily subjective, interpretations of existing guidelines.

Approximately 225 of the 300 largest U.S.-based multinationals examined in the previously cited survey limited the number of their geographic reporting categories to two or three. This may be attributed, in part, to numerical materiality guidelines prescribed in F.A.S.B. 14. Thus a particular geographic area is considered a separate reporting unit if identifiable assets or area revenues from sales to unaffiliated customers are 10 percent or more of worldwide totals. Under these criteria, a company whose multinational operations made up less than 30 percent of group totals would be limited to two geographic segments, or one if multinational operations were less than 20 percent of consolidated totals. Companies wishing to emphasize the geographic breadth of their operations should, according to Business International (1979), increase the number of their geographic partitions in the fashion of the Clark Equipment Company. In 1977 Clark reported five geographic areas, even though some of the segments did not meet the 10-percent-materiality criterion.

In requiring disclosure of foreign operations' profitability by significant geographic areas, paragraph 10 *d* of F.A.S.B. 14 requires that "operating expenses incurred by an enterprise that are not directly traceable to specific geographic areas should be allocated on a reasonable basis among those reporting segments." To the extent that such expense allocations are arbitrary, disclosed operating results will vary in their objectivity and relevance. Reporting entities must thus decide whether to (1) further improve upon the information being provided, or (2) in the absence of any theoretically correct or cost-efficient solution, alert statement readers to the data's limitations. Until further experience is gained on reporting foreign operations, the latter alternative, perhaps by means of a cautionary note, would appear to be a logical expedient.

Examples of Foreign-Operations Disclosures.   On the basis of recent surveys, Lafferty (Lafferty *et al.,* 1979) concludes that foreign-operations disclosures on the European front are also lacking in clarity and information content. In particular, "information given on local currency amounts fails to indicate the magnitude of the local operations in terms of the total group activities and is of very limited value."

Experience in the United States and Europe suggests that foreign-operations disclosure is still at an early stage of development. Nevertheless, heightened interest in the foreign operations of multinational companies ensures that further reporting innovations are forthcoming. Excerpts from the annual reports of Alcan Aluminum

EXHIBIT 9   EXAMPLES OF FOREIGN-OPERATIONS DISCLOSURES (INFORMATION BY GEOGRAPHIC AREAS IN MILLIONS OF DOLLARS)

ALCAN ALUMINUM COMPANY

	Canada and Caribbean	United States	Latin America	Europe and Africa	Asia and South Pacific	Eliminations	Alcan Consolidated
Year ending December 31, 1979							
Sales and operating revenues							
To subsidiary companies	734	62	—	17	65	(878)	—
To other companies	1,005	1,073	439	1,439	425	—	4,381
Total	1,739	1,135	439	1,456	490	(878)	4,381
Net income	214	48	40	107	46	(28)	427
Capital expenditures	224	34	53	134	49	—	494
December 31, 1979							
Current assets	870	475	165	676	236	(233)	2,189
Fixed assets (net)	984	163	217	371	180	—	1,915
Investments and other assets	119	5	57	157	48	—	386
Identifiable assets	1,973	643	439	1,204	464	(233)	4,490
Current and other liabilities	393	173	101	394	143	(177)	1,027
Capital employed	1,580	470	338	810	321	(56)	3,463
Number of employees (thousands)	22.4	4.8	9.5	17.0	11.7	—	65.4

Year ending December 31, 1978

Sales and operating revenues							
To subsidiary companies	801	52	1	19	48	(921)	—
To other companies	891	980	314	1,148	378	—	3,711
Total	1,692	1,032	315	1,167	426	(921)	3,711
Net income	151	38	41	62	37	(32)	297
Capital expenditures	137	20	57	73	34	—	321
December 31, 1978							
Current assets	749	403	187	628	243	(228)	1,982
Fixed assets (net)	847	141	192	314	144	—	1,638
Investments and other assets	84	7	40	170	46	—	347
Identifiable assets	1,680	551	419	1,112	433	(228)	3,967
Current and other liabilities	338	156	115	409	136	(189)	965
Capital employed	1,342	395	304	703	297	(39)	3,002
Number of employees (thousands)	21.8	4.8	8.4	16.8	11.6	—	63.4

Certain 1978 amounts have been restated to give retroactive effect to the accounting changes described in note 2 to the financial statements.

Sales to subsidiary companies are made at a fair market price recognizing volume, continuity of supply and other factors.

Net income is total revenues less expenses directly related to the geographic area in accordance with generally accepted accounting principles.

Capital employed represents the total book value of the net assets located in each area.

Of the Canada and Caribbean sales and operating revenues to other companies, $167 million in 1979 ($230 in 1978) were export sales from Canada, principally to the United States.

Consolidated Sales of Aluminum by Markets (thousands of tonnes)

	1970	1971	1972	1973	1974	1975	1976	1977	1978	1979
Canada	144	172	177	213	225	195	211	220	220	241
United States	323	351	377	435	410	295	352	374	450	402
Latin America	66	86	101	103	113	110	115	116	121	145
European Economic Community	353	303	346	429	448	348	408	364	382	434
Asia and South Pacific	233	251	220	249	235	262	216	185	335	255
All others	102	105	95	91	77	62	72	59	89	55
	1,221	1,268	1,316	1,520	1,508	1,272	1,374	1,318	1,597	1,532

DUPONT COMPANY

Consolidated Sales and Net Income by Geographic Area

	Sales		Net Income	
	1979	1978	1979	1978
Europe, Middle East, & Africa	$ 2,060	$ 1,580	$234	$111
Canada	672	523	38	22
Latin America	710	534	59	32
Asia/Pacific	540	355	45	65
Total International	3,982	2,992	376	230
United States	8,590	7,592	563	557
Total	$12,572	$10,584	$939	$787

The above breakdown reflects the destination of the sale rather than the location of the corporate unit making the sale. Net income is determined by charging manufacturing costs and other related expenses directly against sales, regardless of the area in which such expenses were incurred, and by allocating other elements of income and expense to geographic areas. A breakdown of results based on the location of the corporate unit making the sale, as required by the Securities and Exchange Commission and the Financial Accounting Standards Board, can be found on page 47.

Sales outside the United States of products manufactured in and exported from the United States totaled $1,764 in 1979 and $1,266 in 1978.

Other Consolidated Geographic Data (capital expenditures, investment, and average employment of DuPont and its consolidated subsidiaries)

	Capital Expenditures		Investment December 31		Average Employment	
	1979	1978	1979	1978	1979	1978
Europe, Middle East, & Africa	$ 81	$ 46	$ 1,757	$ 1,435	12,300	12,100
Canada	21	21	801	740	5,600	5,400
Latin America	11	20	492	452	8,000	8,000
Asia/Pacific	14	3	311	216	2,100	1,400
Total International	127	90	3,361	2,843	28,000	26,900
United States	802	696	12,867	11,871	106,200	104,900
Total	$929	$786	$16,228	$14,714	134,200	131,800

Capital expenditures, investment, and average employment are assigned to geographic areas generally based on physical location. Investment is the sum of all assets, before deduction of accumulated depreciation and obsolescence.

Affiliated Companies (sales, net income, and net assets of nonconsolidated affiliates accounted for by the equity method).

	Sales		Net Income		Net Assets December 31	
	1979	1978	1979	1978	1979	1978
Europe, Middle East, & Africa	$249	$165	$ 42	$(58)	$ 17	$ (26)
Latin America	251	197	25	13	137	116
Asia/Pacific	364	303	8	26	100	105
Total International	864	665	75	(19)	254	195
United States	1	16	(54)	(9)	144	95
Total	$865	$681	$ 21	$(28)	$398	$290
DuPont Equity in:						
Net Income			$ 9	$(10)		
Net Assets					$207	$150
Advances to Affiliates					27	28
Investment in Nonconsolidated Affiliates					$234	$178

23 · 45

(Canada) and DuPont (U.S.) are provided in Exhibit 9 as examples of the current state of the art in this new area of financial reporting.

TRANSNATIONAL FINANCIAL REPORTING. The sale of corporate securities in foreign and international capital markets raises additional reporting problems for multinational companies, who must often report the results of operations and financial position to audiences of interest unfamiliar with the language, currency framework, accounting principles, auditing standards, and general business milieu of the reporting enterprise. Under these circumstances, the challenge is effective communication of intended messages to foreign readers. Failure might mean higher capital costs and other disadvantages.

Reporting Requirements. At present, little formal attention has been accorded the transnational-reporting dimension. As a condition for listing their shares on the major U.S. securities exchanges, foreign companies must conform to the financial-reporting requirements of the SEC. In seeking comparability in financial statements issued to U.S. investors, the Commission permits, with certain exceptions, foreign issuers to prepare their financial statements in accordance with accounting principles generally accepted in their home countries. Any material differences between the foreign and U.S. generally accepted accounting principles must be reconciled by way of footnotes to U.S. GAAP. Although aware of it, the FASB chose to disregard the problem of transnational reporting in F.A.S.B. 8. With the exception of foreign disclosures, international accounting organizations have also been silent on the subject of reporting to foreign audiences of interest.

In the absence of enforceable transnational accounting and reporting norms, one must look to existing practice for guidance. Four distinguishable approaches are described next (Choi and Mueller, 1978).

Convenience Translations. Many reporting entities continue to send copies of their *primary* financial statements to foreign readers, prepared in terms of the language, currency, accounting, and auditing framework of the reporting company's country of domicile. But many large multinationals in the United States and Europe with foreign shareholders regularly publish their annual reports in as many as six foreign languages. Japanese companies go a step further. In addition to language translations, companies such as Fujitsu Ltd. present monetary expressions in parallel columns, for example, Japanese yen and U.S. dollars when reporting to American readers.

Although *convenience* translations lend an international appearance to primary statements and may offer some public-relations benefits, they may also mislead. For example, English language and/or U.S. dollar translations of Japanese financials often give the American reader the impression that the accounting principles underlying the convenience statements have been translated as well. If such is not the case, erroneous conclusions can be drawn. This problem may be minimized by disclosures that specifically identify the national accounting principles and auditing standards underlying convenience statements.

Special Information. A small number of companies, notably those from Sweden, have made an effort to explain to foreign readers the major accounting principles behind their annual reports. Thus a company like Beijerinvest makes available to its U.S. readers an English language edition of its annual report, along with a little pamphlet explaining Swedish accounting principles employed. This practice, unfortunately, presumes that the foreign reader possesses accounting expertise and is able to quantitatively reconcile disclosed accounting differences. This is seldom the case.

Limited Restatements. A partial remedy to the reconciliation problem just described is used by several Netherlands-based multinationals. For instance, in addition to language translations, the Philips Company estimates what earnings adjustments would be required if accounting principles generally accepted in the United States rather than in the Netherlands were followed. A direct result is that Dutch investors see earnings and per-share numbers that are consistent with local accounting practices, while their U.S. counterparts are at least provided with earnings numbers that are readily understood and can be used comparatively. The disadvantage of partial restatements are fairly obvious; that is, rate-of-return comparisons are hardly meaningful when earnings restated to U.S. GAAP are compared with total assets and other financial-statement categories that reflect Dutch accounting norms.

Primary-Secondary Statements. In a 1975 study entitled *International Financial Reporting,* the Accountant's International Study Group (1975), which has since disbanded, recommends that two kinds of financial statements be recognized as part of a country's official set of generally accepted accounting principles. *Primary* financial statements, as previously defined, would be prepared for a reporting company's domestic readers. *Secondary* financial statements would be prepared specifically for foreign readers. These statements would reflect one or more of the following characteristics:

1. The language of the reader's country of domicile.
2. The currency of the foreign country.
3. The accounting principles of the foreign country.
4. The auditing standards of the foreign country.

An alleged advantage of the primary-secondary reporting system is that it accommodates more than a single set of accounting and reporting standards. In doing so, full recognition is afforded different national viewpoints. Tailoring published corporate reports to specific readership groups also eliminates the generalized traditional reporting formats, resulting in information more germane to user decisions.

But aside from considerations of production cost, the issuance of secondary statements can prove to be misleading. If one accepts the proposition that accounting principles are shaped by a particular social, economic, and legal environment, and that national accounting environments differ, translation of financial statements from one set of accounting principles to another could distort the original message. Even if accounting principles between two countries are similar, business and financial mores that govern the interpretation of accounting-based financial statement ratios may vary internationally. This could lead to further message distortion. As an example, high debt ratios, viewed with alarm in the United States, are an accepted part of the business scene in Japan.

Shortcomings of the AISG proposal can be remedied by footnote disclosure of the main differences between accounting principles of the reporting company's and reader's countries of domicile, together with their effect on net income and financial position. Environmental disclosures that assist foreign readers in properly interpreting secondary-statement information (i.e., financial ratios) should also be disclosed. Several Japanese companies have begun to provide such disclosures in their registration filings with the U.S. SEC as a result of past misunderstandings.

SOURCES AND SUGGESTED REFERENCES

Accountants International Study Group. *Consolidated Financial Statements*. New York: AISG, 1972.

Accountants International Study Group. *International Financial Reporting*. New York: AISG, 1975.

Accounting Standards Committee. *Current Cost Accounting*. Statement of Standard Accounting Practice No. 6. London: ASC, 1980.

American Institute of Certified Public Accountants, Committee on Accounting Procedure. "Restatement and Revision of Accounting Research Bulletins," in *Foreign Operations and Foreign Exchange*. Accounting Research Bulletin No. 43, Chapter 12, New York: AICPA, 1953.

American Institute of Certified Public Accountants. *Status of Accounting Research Bulletins*. Accounting Principles Board Opinion No. 6. New York: AICPA, 1965.

Arthur Young. *Financial Reporting and Changing Prices: A Survey of How 300 Companies Complied with FAS 33*. New York: Arthur Young, August 1980.

Bavishi, V., and H. Wyman. "Foreign Operations Disclosures by U.S.-Based Multinational Corporation, Are They Adequate?" *International Journal of Accounting,* Vol. XVI, No. 1 (1980), pp. 153–168.

Business International. *Corporation, International Accounting, Auditing, and Taxation Issues*. New York: BI, 1979.

Choi, F.D.S. "Primary-Secondary Reporting: A Cross Cultural Analysis," *International Journal of Accounting,* Vol. XVI, No. 1 (1980), pp. 83–104.

Choi, F.D.S., and G.G. Mueller. *An Introduction to Multinational Accounting*. Englewood Cliffs, NJ: Prentice-Hall, 1978.

Choi, F.D.S. and G.G. Mueller. *Essentials of Multinational Accounting: An Anthology*. Ann Arbor, MI. University Microfilms International, 1979.

Coopers & Lybrand. *Foreign Currency Translation,* New York: Coopers & Lybrand, 1980.

Deloitte Haskins & Sells. *Foreign Currency Translation*. New York: Deloitte Haskins & Sells, 1980.

Dukes, R. *An Empirical Investigation of the Effects of Statement of Financial Accounting Standards No. 8 on Security Return Behavior*. Stamford, CT: Financial Accounting Standards Board, 1978.

"EEC Proposed Seventh Directive," *EEC Bulletin,* Supplement, September (1976).

Ernst & Whinney. "Foreign Currency Translation: FASB Exposure Draft," in *Financial Reporting Developments*. Cleveland: Ernst & Whinney, 1980.

Financial Accounting Standards Board. "Foreign Currency Translation," in *Exposure Draft,* Stamford, CT: FASB, 1980.

Financial Accounting Standards Board. *Accounting for the Translation of Foreign Currency Transactions and Foreign Currency Financial Statements*. Statement of Financial Accounting Standards No. 8. Stamford, CT: FASB, 1975.

Financial Accounting Standards Board. *Financial Reporting for Segments of a Business Enterprise*. Statement of Financial Accounting Standards No. 14. Stamford, CT: FASB, 1976.

Financial Accounting Standards Board. *Financial Reporting and Changing Prices*. Statement of Financial Accounting Standards No. 33. Stamford, CT: FASB, 1979.

Fitzgerald, R.D., A.D. Stickler, and T.R. Watts. *International Survey of Accounting Principles and Reporting Practices*. New York: Price Waterhouse International, 1979.

Institute of Chartered Accountants in England and Wales. "The Accounting Treatment of Major Changes in the Sterling Parity of Overseas Currencies," in ICAEW. *Member's Handbook, Statement N25*. London: ICAEW, 1968.

International Accounting Standards Committee. *Accounting For Foreign Transactions and Translation of Foreign Financial Statements*. Exposure Draft 11. London: IASC, 1977.

International Accounting Standards Committee. *Reporting Financial Information by Segment*. Exposure Draft 15. London: IASC, 1980.

International Accounting Standards Committee. *Information Reflecting the Effects of Changing Prices*. Exposure Draft 17. London: IASC, 1980.

International Accounting Standards Committee. *Consolidated Financial Statements*. International Accounting Standard 3. London: IASC, 1976.

International Accounting Standards Committee. *Accounting Responses to Changing Prices*. International Accounting Standard 6. London: IASC, 1977.

Lafferty, M., D. Cairns, and J. Carty. *1979 Financial Times Survey of 100 Major European Companies' Reports and Accounts*. London: Financial Times, 1979.

Lees, F.A. *Reporting Transnational business Operations*, Washington, DC: The Conference Board, 1980.

Organization for Economic Cooperation and Development. *International Investment and Multinational Enterprises: Accounting Practices in OECD Member Countries*. Paris: OECD, 1980.

Organization for Economic Cooperation and Development. *International Investment and Multinational Enterprises*, revised ed. Paris: OECD, 1979.

Peat, Marwick, Mitchell & Co. *Foreign Currency Translation*. New York: Peat, Marwick, Mitchell, 1980.

U.N. Commission on Transnational Corporations. *International Standards of Accounting and Reporting for Transnational Corporations*. New York: U.N. Economic and Social Council, 1977.

U.S. Securities and Exchange Commission. "Regulation S-X," in *Form and Content of Financial Statements*. Washington, DC: US SEC, 1972.

Vancil, R. "Inflation Accounting—The Great Controversy," *Harvard Business Review*, Vol. LIV, No. 2 (1976), pp. 58–67.

Watt, G.C., R.M. Hammer and M. Burge. *Accounting for the Multinational Corporation*. New York: Financial Executives Research Foundation, 1977.

INTERNATIONAL TAXATION

CONTENTS

COMPARATIVE TAX SYSTEMS	**3**
Why International Tax Problems Arise	3
Key Elements of All Tax Systems	4
Who is subject to the tax?	4
Taxation of branch income	4
Statutory tax rates	4
Imputation systems	5
Taxation of foreign-source income	6
Inventory valuation	6
Depreciation methods	7
Intercompany dividends	7
Capital gains	7
Net operating losses	8
Consolidated returns	8
Foreign losses	8
Taxation of nonresidents	9
Bilateral Tax Treaties	9
FOREIGN-TAX-CREDIT PROBLEMS	**10**
The Direct Foreign-Tax Credit	**10**
Creditable foreign taxes	10
The foreign-tax-credit election	11
The foreign-tax-credit limitation	11
Source-of-income rules	12
Allocation of deductions	13
Allocation of interest expense	13
Allocation of research and development expense	14
The Indirect Foreign-Tax Credit	**14**
The deemed-paid credit	15
Illustrative example	15
TAX-DEFERRAL PROBLEMS	**17**
Controlled Foreign Corporations	**17**
When is a foreign corporation a CFC?	17
Taxation of U.S. shareholders	17
Subpart F Income	**18**
Foreign-base-company income	18
Foreign-personal-holding-company income	18
Foreign-base-company sales income	19
Foreign-base-company services income	19
Foreign-base-company shipping income	20
Exclusions from foreign-base-company income	20
Insurance of U.S. risks	20
Bribe-and boycott-related income	20
Increase of investments of earnings in U.S. property	20
Other amounts taxed currently	21
Creation, Reorganization, and Disposal of a Foreign Corporation	**21**
Transfers of property from the United States	21
Transfers of property to the United States	22
INTERCOMPANY-TRANSACTION PROBLEMS	**22**
The Transfer-Pricing Problem	**22**
The Section 482 Regulations	**23**
Application of Section 482	23
Interest charges	23
Service fees	24
Lease rentals	24
Sales of tangible property	24
Sale or licensing of intangible property	25
SPECIAL TAX OPPORTUNITIES	**25**
Exporting Through a Domestic International Sales Corporation	**25**
Requirements for qualification of a DISC	25
Intercompany-pricing rules	26
Taxation of DISC income	26
Deemed distributions	27

The Section 936 Tax Credit   28
    Requirements for claiming the credit   28
Borrowing Through an International
Finance Subsidiary   28
International Tax Compliance, Tax

Morality, and Tax Havens   29

SOURCES AND SUGGESTED
REFERENCES   30

INTERNATIONAL TAXATION

Lowell Dworin

COMPARATIVE TAX SYSTEMS

WHY INTERNATIONAL TAX PROBLEMS ARISE. Tax factors are likely to be of greater importance in the case of transnational activity than in a purely domestic context for several reasons:

1. The income generated in one country (the *host* country) may be subject to taxation by both the host country and the country in which the management of the business is located or the business organized (the *home* country). This overlap of taxing jurisdictions may result in the problem of *double taxation*.

2. Conversely, most countries do not tax the earnings of foreign corporations owned by resident individuals or domestic corporations until such earnings are remitted to the resident stockholders (or until the disposal or liquidation of the foreign corporation). By operating through a foreign subsidiary, home-country *tax deferral* may generally be obtained. To the extent that financing, marketing, transportation, and other activities not requiring the existence of a *permanent establishment* in the host country are conducted by a foreign subsidiary located in a *tax haven* (a country that imposes little, if any, taxes on these activities), both home and host-country taxation may be minimized.

3. Thus in contrast to domestic activity, where the income earned is roughly taxed at the same rate irrespective of the location or form of organization (ignoring differences between corporate and individual tax rates), the income earned by related entities engaged in foreign commerce may incur a tax burden ranging from full home-country and host-country taxation to the absence of any current tax burden. Tax provisions such as the *foreign-tax credit* against home-country taxation for all or a portion of the profits taxes paid to the host country will likely mitigate the problem of double taxation. Other tax laws designed to preclude the improper shifting of income between related parties and limit tax-haven activities may reduce the benefits of tax deferral. Income earned abroad is thus likely to be taxed at an effective rate somewhere between the two extremes noted. However, by appropriate choice of business organization, dividend policy, or even method of tax accounting, this effective rate may be substantially reduced.

4. Not only may greater tax savings result from proper tax planning in the case of transnational activity, but because the reorganization of international operations is likely to incur tax costs (*toll charges*) that would not have arisen in a purely domestic reorganization, the penalty for rectifying an inappropriate plan is also greater.

KEY ELEMENTS OF ALL TAX SYSTEMS.   Despite the multitude of taxing jurisdictions and variety of taxes that may be encountered in the conduct of international enterprise, all tax systems may be characterized in terms of certain basic features as follows:

1. The nature of the tax.
2. The scope of the tax.
3. The calculation of the tax base.
4. The treatment of losses.
5. The taxation of nonresidents.

Who Is Subject to the Tax?   Countries that tax the profits of commercial activities generally impose such tax on both resident individuals and resident corporations. The definition of a resident and the statutory rates of taxation differ. The residency of an individual is generally determined by reference to a number of factors, including the location of the individual's principal home and business activities. A number of countries (e.g., the United Kingdom, Japan, West Germany) define a resident corporation as one whose management or principal place of business is located within the country. Although several countries (e.g., Canada, the Netherlands, France, West Germany) presume a corporation organized within the country to be a resident corporation, other countries do not. The United States is nearly unique in subjecting the income of its citizens and corporations organized in the United States to the federal income tax even if they may be regarded by U.S. tax law as residents of other countries. This question is of importance in the determination of the maximum level of activities that may be carried out within the host country without subjecting such activity to host-country taxation, and is generally addressed in all *tax treaties* between home and host countries.

Taxation of Branch Income.   The earnings of a domestic branch of a foreign corporation are generally taxed under the host country's corporate tax laws, although often at rates that differ somewhat from the corporate rates. Most countries require resident corporations to withhold a certain portion of the dividends remitted to nonresident stockholders. Generally no corresponding amounts need be withheld upon the remittance of branch earnings. To offset this comparative advantage given to branch operations, the tax rate on branch income is generally somewhat greater than the corporate rate. The rates are the same, however, in Canada and France, both of which impose a withholding tax on branch remittances (with some exceptions).

Statutory Tax Rates.   Although profits taxes are generally imposed on the taxpayer's total operations within the country, a few countries (e.g., the United States, Norway, the United Kingdom) have enacted special taxes on oil-production income. It is not uncommon, however, for different sources of income (or income generated in different industries) to be subject to tax at different rates (generally manufacturing is taxed preferentially whereas oil production is taxed much less favorably). In many countries the various political subdivisions (provinces, states, prefectures, municipalities, etc.) levy an additional tax on the profits earned within the subdivision. Such jurisdictions generally apply the national corporate-tax laws (except as they relate to the taxation of foreign-source income) at substantially lower rates than the national corporate rates. These additional taxes are typically deductible from the national tax (in Canada a limited credit against the federal tax is given for the provincial tax incurred). When these additional taxes are included, the combined statutory rates of taxation on undistributed corporate profits for many of the major capital-exporting countries are seen to approximate the U.S. statutory combined federal and state tax rate of 46–51 percent, as follows:

Canada	
Normal rates	45–51 percent
Manufacturing and processing	39–45 percent
France	50 percent
The Netherlands	48 percent
United Kingdom	52 percent

The corresponding tax rates on undistributed profits are significantly higher in West Germany (61–64 percent) and Japan (53–54 percent).

Imputation Systems.   The above statutory rates may not be representative of the effective rates of taxation on corporate earnings for several reasons. More-liberal depreciation methods and other differences in the tax laws may result in a taxable income to which the above rates apply which differs significantly from that calculated under U.S. tax laws. Both West Germany and Japan utilize a *split-rate* tax system, whereby the statutory rate of taxation on distributed corporate earnings is lower than that on retained earnings, but both countries also impose a *withholding tax* at the corporate level on dividend remittances to resident stockholders (most countries, including all of those discussed above, impose such withholding tax on distributions to nonresident stockholders). Finally, several of these countries (e.g., West Germany, Canada, France, the United Kingdom) utilize an *imputation system,* whereby resident stockholders are allowed to credit a portion of the tax paid at the corporate level (as well as the tax withheld) against the tax imposed at the stochholder level. In such cases the stockholder must also gross up the dividends received by both the tax withheld and the credit allowed (i.e., add the imputation credit and withholding tax to the actual cash received to determine taxable income). Although the specifics vary, the overall effect is that the combined tax at both the corporate and stockholder level is substantially lower than it would have been if a *classical* system (as in the United States) were in use. Thus for a resident individual stockholder in the base-rate tax bracket (30 percent) in the United Kingdom, the imputation credit just eliminates the tax at the stockholder level, whereas for a resident stockholder in West Germany, the imputation credit just eliminates the impact of the corporate-profits tax. *These imputation credits are not generally allowed to nonresident stockholders,* although a 1970 amendment to the U.S.-France tax treaty allows such benefits to U.S. stockholders with less than 10 percent ownership interest. The recently adopted Third Protocol to the U.S.–U.K. tax treaty is unique in that it allows half of the imputation credit that would be available to a U.K. resident stockholder to be claimed by a U.S. parent corporation of a British subsidiary. The resulting benefit may be seen by comparing the statutory tax rates (including the appropriate withholding tax) if it is assumed that the wholly owned foreign subsidiary distributes all of its earnings (after tax payments to the foreign government) to its U.S. parent:

West Germany	51–55 percent
Japan	46–48 percent
Canada	
Normal rate	53–58 percent
Manufacturing and processing	45–53 percent
France	53 percent
The Netherlands	50 percent
United Kingdom	45 percent

Taxation of Foreign-Source Income.   Many countries (e.g., the United States, the United Kingdom, Japan) utilize a *global* tax system under which the worldwide income of its citizens or residents is subject to tax. Such countries generally allow a foreign-tax credit against home-country taxation for profits taxes paid to the host government. Although differences exist with respect to the ability to credit the underlying corporate taxes paid by the foreign subsidiary (rather than just the parent's foreign-branch tax and the tax withheld on subsidiary or branch remittances), the credit allowed is generally limited to the home-country tax that would have been imposed on the foreign-source income were such income earned in the home country. Thus—ignoring differences in the computation of taxable income, surtax exemptions, and certain other complexities—by comparing the statutory foreign tax rates on earnings remitted to a U.S. parent with the 46 percent U.S. corporate tax rate, it may be seen that dividends from a foreign subsidiary in each of the countries listed, with the exception of the United Kingdom and perhaps Canada, will generate *excess foreign-tax credits* (host-country tax payments that produce no corresponding home-country tax benefit). Some countries (e.g., West Germany, Canada, the Netherlands), although nominally using a global tax system, provide either through their internal tax laws or through bilateral tax treaties an effective exemption of foreign-source income earned in a particular set of host countries. A few countries (e.g., France with respect to the corporate tax, Argentina, Denmark) utilize a *territorial* tax system, under which all income earned outside the country is fully or partially exempt from tax. These countries thereby provide greater tax incentive to their domestic firms to invest abroad in low-tax-rate host countries than do countries such as the United States, which utilize a global tax system. Some of the advantage may be reduced in those countries that utilize an imputation system, since an additional tax (an *equalization* tax) may be imposed when such exempt foreign earnings are ultimately distributed to the parent corporation's stockholders. Moreover, a global system allows foreign losses to offset domestic income, whereas in a territorial system such losses will provide at best only temporary tax benefits.

Inventory Valuation.   Relatively few countries (e.g., the United States, Japan, the Netherlands) allow the use of last-in-first-out (LIFO) inventory valuation for tax purposes. Alternative methods designed to limit the taxation of inventory profits arising from the use of historical rather than current costs may be used (e.g., the stock-relief scheme in the United Kingdom, the inventory inflation adjustment in Canada, the reserve for inventory price increase in France). Both U.K. and Canadian allowances may provide permanent benefits, whereas LIFO and reserve methods in principle provide only tax deferral.

Depreciation Methods.   The rapidity with which the cost of fixed assets may be written off varies greatly. The cost of machinery and equipment (except cars) may be fully expensed in the year of acquisition in the United Kingdom, and if used for manufacturing and processing operations, in the first two years in Canada. If such rapid writeoff is not desirable (perhaps because of current losses), both countries allow the depreciation to be written off more slowly. In other countries (e.g., the United States, France, Japan, Norway) the cost of such assets must be depreciated over a period approximating the service life of the specific assets, although accelerated methods of depreciation may be used. Buildings and structures are not generally allowed to be written off as rapidly as machinery and equipment, but even for such assets as much as 50 percent of the cost may be written off in the year of acquisition in the United Kingdom. A number of countries (e.g., United States, France, West Germany) allow rapid writeoff of assets used for specific purposes (e.g., pollution-control equipment) or located in specific regions of the country. An *investment tax credit* (based on a percentage of the cost of qualifying assets acquired) is also allowed against the tax otherwise due by several countries (e.g., the United States, the Netherlands, West Germany, the United Kingdom). Such investment tax credits are generally not available for assets used outside the country. Expenditures for scientific research are often given preferential treatment, either through an allowance for additional depreciation (e.g., France) or the qualification of such investment for an investment tax credit (e.g., Japan, the Netherlands).

Intercompany Dividends.   Most countries substantially exempt dividends received by a corporation from another *domestic* corporation from taxation either expressly (e.g., the United Kingdom, Japan), through the allowance of a deduction (e.g., the United States, Canada, France), or by application of the imputation-credit system to the corporate stockholder (e.g., West Germany). Although the income out of which such dividends are paid has been subject to taxation at the corporate level, dividends paid out of such income to the recipient corporation's stockholders may either trigger the application of an additional equilization tax (e.g., France, if distributed more than 5 years after receipt) or not qualify for tax benefits otherwise available (e.g., the reduced tax rate in Japan).

Capital Gains.   Several countries (e.g., the United States, Canada, the United Kingdom) tax capital-gains income preferentially, generally by allowing a deduction equal to a fraction of the gains realized on the sale of capital assets held for more than a specific period of time. Other countries (e.g., West Germany, Japan, the Netherlands) generally tax such gains as ordinary income. Long-term corporate capital gains are taxed preferentially when realized in France, but the benefit is lost when the gains are distributed to the stockholders. Tax on the gains realized on the disposal of plant and equipment may often be deferred if replacement property is acquired within a specific period before or after the disposal (e.g., the United States, the Netherlands,

West Germany). Gains realized from the sale of depreciable property, which might otherwise be subject to preferential capital gains treatment, may be taxed as ordinary income to the extent of all or a portion of the depreciation previously claimed with respect to the property (e.g., the United States, France, the United Kingdom).

Net Operating Losses.   Most countries that tax the profits from commercial activities allow losses incurred from one activity to offset the income from the taxpayer's other activity within the country. This general rule is most likely to be altered (if at all) in the case of mineral extraction, where there may be restrictions on the allowance of losses from other activities to offset mineral-extraction income (as in the *ring-fence* provisions of the British corporate tax) or even the allowance of losses from one mine or oilfield to offset income from other mines or oilfields (as in the United Kingdom's petroleum-revenue tax). Those countries that tax capital gains preferentially are also likely to allow *capital losses to offset only capital gains* (e.g., Canada, the United States, the United Kingdom). The tax treatment of a net operating loss from aggregate activities within the country varies. Many countries allow such losses to be carried back to the previous year (e.g., Canada, the United Kingdom if other than from accelerated depreciation, the Netherlands, Japan, and West Germany to a limited extent with respect to corporate tax) and allow the balance to be carried forward for varying periods. The United States provides more-liberal treatment by allowing such losses to be carried back 3 years and/or forward 7 years. In those countries where capital losses may only be offset against capital gains, a limited carryback and carryforward is also allowed (only an unlimited carryforward is provided in the United Kingdom, and a 10-year carryforward in France).

Consolidated Returns.   In some countries (e.g., the United States, the United Kingdom, France, the Netherlands, West Germany), a related group of corporations may be taxed as a single taxpayer. This may allow the deferral of the tax on intercompany profits and the utilization of one member's losses against another member's gains. Generally only domestic corporations controlled by a common parent corporation may be included, although even foreign subsidiaries may be included in France. In addition to minimum ownership requirements, certain other conditions (e.g., local ownership of the parent corporation in France, financial and organizational integration of the member corporations in West Germany) may be imposed on the group electing such treatment.

Foreign Losses.   Foreign losses may be used to offset domestic income in the case of countries that utilize a global tax system. However, such losses may also reduce the allowable foreign-tax credit for taxes paid with respect to other profitable foreign operations if an *overall* foreign-tax-credit limitation (the foreign-tax credit allowed is limited to the home-country tax on total foreign-source income) is used. For a company in an excess-foreign-tax-credit position, the tax benefits of the loss offset will just compensate for the reduced foreign-tax credits, resulting in no net benefit. In those countries (e.g., Canada, the United Kingdom) that utilize a *per-country* foreign-tax-credit limitation (the allowable foreign-tax credit from each country is limited to the home-country tax on the income from that country), the foreign-tax credits from profitable foreign-country operations are preserved. Although Japan uses an overall limitation, losses from foreign projects may be excluded from the calculation of aggregate foreign-source income producing the same effect. The United States requires the *recapture* of an overall foreign loss by reclassifying a portion of the subsequent foreign-source income as U.S.-source income, thereby reducing the allowable foreign-tax-credit limitation.

Taxation of Nonresidents. If a nonresident alien or foreign corporation is considered to be engaged in a trade or business in the host country (and in some countries such as the United Kingdom and Japan if such trade or business is conducted directly or through an agent from some fixed place of business) the income from such activity is generally taxed at regular rates and in the regular manner. If not, the income earned in the host country (which would generally be of a passive nature such as dividend, interest, royalty, or rental income) is generally taxed at a *flat rate based on the gross payment;* this tax is required to be *withheld from the amount distributed.* Because of this diverse treatment, the characterization of a trade or business or the requisite establishment of a fixed place of business is an important issue that unfortunately is often inadequately defined in the internal tax laws of the host country. Even if the taxpayer conducts a business in the host country in a manner that calls for regular taxation, passive income of the type noted above may in some countries (e.g., the United States, West Germany, the Netherlands) be subject to the withholding tax rather than the regular tax unless such income is *effectively connected* to the trade or business (the economic nexus required being defined in the tax laws).

BILATERAL TAX TREATIES. Although commonly thought of as conventions for the avoidance of double taxation, the major purpose of bilateral tax treaties is to limit the taxation *by one contracting state* of certain activities conducted by residents or citizens of *the other contracting state.* Thus, for example, most tax treaties preclude the host country from taxing business profits of a resident of the other contracting state unless such profits are attributable to a *permanent establishment* in the host country (the treaties moreover define the criteria by which such permanent establishment may be identified). Tax treaties also exempt from host-country taxation certain entire classes of income earned in that state by residents of the other state (e.g., shipping and air transportation income, income earned by a commercial traveler present in the host country for only a limited time, capital gains). Moreover, the applicable withholding rates on passive income that is not attributable to a permanent establishment are generally reduced below the nontreaty rates. Although bilateral tax treaties attempt to address many issues that arise from the disparity in the internal tax laws of the contracting states, not all such issues are expressly dealt with, nor is the interpretation of the treaty provisions always clear. For this reason many treaties establish a grievance procedure for residents of the contracting states who feel that the actions of one or both contracting states will result in a tax liability that is not in accordance with the objectives or provisions of the treaty. Such residents may request the *competent authority* of the state of residency to resolve the issue by consultation with the competent authority of the other state. Such authorities may agree on the same attribution of income for the residents' permanent establishments in the other state, the same allocation of income and expense between related entities (see "Inter Company-Transaction Problems"), the same source of income rules, and so forth. Without such uniformity of treatment, the problem of double taxation often cannot satisfactorily be resolved.

FOREIGN-TAX-CREDIT PROBLEMS

THE DIRECT FOREIGN-TAX CREDIT.   The foreign-tax credit (FTC) is the major unilateral mechanism for alleviating the problem of double taxation in countries such as the United States that tax the worldwide income of their citizens and residents. In practice it does not completely eliminate the problem of double taxation for a number of reasons:

1. The foreign jurisdiction may impose taxes other than income taxes, such as wealth taxes and turnover taxes, for which only a deduction, rather than a credit, may be claimed.

2. Many foreign countries levy income taxes at rates in excess of the U.S. tax rates (especially when the withholding tax incurred on the repatriation of the foreign earnings is included), but the United States limits the allowable credit to the U.S. tax on foreign-source income.

3. Many foreign countries have rules for calculating taxable income and for determining the source of such income that are quite different from the U.S. rules. These differences may result in foreign-tax payments for which no U.S. foreign-tax credit (computed according to U.S. laws) may be claimed, without competent-authority adjustments.

Creditable Foreign Taxes.   The United States allows a foreign-tax credit only for income taxes or taxes *in lieu of* income taxes paid or accrued by the taxpayer (the *direct*-tax credit) or deemed paid by the taxpayer (the *indirect*-tax credit). Whether or not a payment to a foreign government is a creditable income tax or a creditable payment in lieu of an income tax is based on U.S. standards. The most troublesome issue of classification has arisen in the context of foreign mineral extraction, where the distinction between an income tax and a payment that represents licensing fees, royalties, or other compensation for the privilege of conducting such operations in the foreign country is least clear. The general requirements for regarding a payment as an income tax are as follows:

1. The profits on which the foreign tax is levied must be realized according to U.S. standards of income recognition.

2. The tax must be on net gain. This does not preclude a tax on gross income, providing it is unlikely that taxpayers subject to the tax will be required to pay it when they have no net gain by U.S. standards.

3. The tax must be imposed on the receipt of income by the taxpayer rather than on specified activity of the taxpayer, such as the extraction and processing of minerals.

The general requirements for regarding a payment as being in lieu of an income tax are as follows:

1. The foreign government must have a general income-tax law in effect.

2. The taxpayer must be subject to the general income tax if the in-lieu-of payments are not made.

3. Both the in-lieu-of payments and the income-tax payments must not be imposed on the same activity in the same year.

In November 1980 the U.S. Treasury Department issued temporary and proposed final regulations that add the requirement that the tax not be compensation for the receipt of an economic benefit. A tax will be presumed to be compensation for an economic benefit if the charge on those receiving the economic benefit (such as the right to drill for oil) is significantly greater than the charge on those who do not receive such benefit.

The Foreign-Tax-Credit Election.   An individual who is a citizen of the United States and a domestic corporation are eligible to elect to utilize the foreign-tax-credit provisions rather than deduct the creditable foreign taxes. Such election is available on an annual basis. However, the option elected for a given year applies to *all* creditable foreign taxes paid or accrued during that year, even if some portion of such creditable taxes may not provide a current tax benefit because of the foreign-tax-credit limitations. Once made, the election may be changed at any time prior to the expiration of the statute of limitations for claiming refunds for that year (generally three years after the return is filed). Although the choice of the foreign-tax credit will generally be more advantageous, there may be cases, such as the occurrence of an overall net operating loss, when the deduction of creditable foreign taxes might be considered.

The Foreign-Tax-Credit Limitation.   The maximum amount of foreign taxes that may be credited in any year is limited to the U.S. tax that would be due on the taxpayer's *total* foreign-source taxable income (the *overall* limitation):

$$\text{maximum credit} = \frac{\text{U.S. tax on worldwide income}}{\text{before credits}} \times \frac{\text{foreign-source taxable income}}{\text{worldwide taxable income}}$$

Several points should be noted in connection with this formula:

1.   Separate application of the formula must be made with respect to non-business-related interest income, dividend income from domestic international sales corporations (DISCs), foreign oil-related income (foreign-extraction income for individuals), and all other income. Thus creditable foreign taxes paid by an oil company with respect to oil production may not be used to reduce the U.S. tax that would otherwise be due on foreign petrochemical operations. However, foreign-source income from transportation, refining, and marketing of crude oil and gas (as well as extraction income) are regarded as oil-related corporate income, as are certain dividend and interest payments from subsidiaries engaged in such activities.

2.   The U.S. tax on worldwide income does not include the accumulated earnings tax, the personal-holding-company tax, or the minimum tax. Foreign-tax credits may, however, be claimed against the alternative minimum tax.

3.   The taxable income appearing in both the numerator and denominator in the limitation formula is calculated according to U.S. tax laws. An individual's personal exemptions, income excluded by various tax laws, and income for which a Section 936 tax credit (see "The Section 936 Tax Credit") is claimed are excluded from the calculation.

4.   Certain reductions in the amounts appearing in both the numerator and denominator must be made to reflect the reduced tax rates on capital gains. Moreover, gains from the sale of personal property sold outside the United

States by a domestic corporation or sold outside the country of residency by an individual may *not* be included in the numerator if the country in which the property was sold taxes the gains at a rate less than 10 percent, subject to certain exceptions.

Creditable foreign taxes that may not be used in the current year because of the limitation formula may be carried back 2 years and forward 5 years. They may be used in these years only to the extent that the foreign taxes for the year to which the credit is carried, together with foreign-tax credits carried over to that same year from prior years, do not exceed the maximum credit allowed in that year. In addition, excess credits may not be carried to a year a deduction for foreign taxes rather than a credit was elected (although the credits remaining to be used in future years are reduced as if such excess credits could be carried to the deduction year).

Source-of-Income Rules.   Since the FTC-limitation formula requires the determination of foreign-source taxable income, the rules by which the source of income is determined are of interest. These rules generally determine the source of *gross* income; *taxable income* is obtained by reducing the gross income by the allocable expenses. The general rules are listed in Exhibit 1. In the case where the income is

EXHIBIT 1   SOURCE-OF-INCOME RULES

Type of Income	Source of Income
Interest income paid by	
Domestic corporation	United States
Foreign corporation	Foreign country
Individual	Residency of debtor
Dividend income from	
Domestic corporation	United States
Foreign corporation	Foreign country
DISC	Foreign country
Compensation for personal services	Where performed
Rents and royalties	Where property located or used
Sale of real property	Where property located
Sale of purchased personal property	Where sold
Sale of personal property manufactured by taxpayer	
In United States and sold in United States	United States
Outside United States and sold outside United States	Foreign Country
In United States and sold outside United States	Part United States, part foreign country
Outside United States and sold in United States	Part United States, part foreign country
Losses on sale of capital assets	Where income would be sourced in absence of sale

shown as "part U.S., part foreign," the specific apportionment depends on whether an *independent factory price* may be established. If the taxpayer regularly sells the product to independent distributors, the income attributable to the country of production can be taken to be that obtained by assuming the product were sold by the manufacturer at the independent factory price. If no independent factory price may be established, the total taxable income generated by the taxpayer's sales of such goods must first be obtained taking into account all relevant expenses. *One half* of the total taxable income is then allocated to the United States *in proportion to U.S. gross sales* of such products, *and the other half* of total taxable income from the sale of such goods is allocated to the United States *in proportion to the value of the taxpayer's property that is U.S. property.* For this purpose, only property held or used to produce the goods is considered, and investment in foreign affiliates and accounts receivable from foreign purchasers are treated as non-U.S. property. In the simplest case, where goods are manufactured in the United States and sold abroad, at least one half of the total taxable income from such sales is treated as foreign-source income (the full gross-sales factor and some of the property factor). For the purpose of determining the source of income, a sale is considered to occur *where title to the property passes to the buyer.* When the seller retains mere legal title, the sale occurs where the risks of ownership pass to the buyer.

Allocation of Deductions. After several years of consideration, the U.S. Treasury Department in 1977 adopted Regulation 1.861-8 dealing with the allocation of expenses for the purpose of determining income from specific sources and activities. The regulation requires that all deductions for the year first be allocated to classes of gross (or *potential* gross) income in accordance with reasonable factual relationships between the deduction and the class of gross income. Deductions that are not directly related to any class of gross income (e.g., the zero-bracket amount) are to be allocated to all classes of gross income in proportion to the gross income in each class. Exempt or excluded income is also to be considered a class of income to which a portion of the deductions must be allocated. The deductions within each income class are then apportioned to the statutory groupings of interest (e.g., foreign-source taxable income) in a manner that reflects the factual relationship between the deductions and the statutory grouping. For many classes of income, apportionment will be automatic.

Allocation of Interest Expense. The allocation of interest expense is predicated on the view that except in very limited circumstances a firm's interest expense is attributable to all activities and assets irrespective of the specific purpose for which debt was issued. The preferred method of allocation of interest is in proportion to the *value of the assets* utilized in generating each class of income. Either the average fair market value or tax basis for the year may be used for this purpose. As in the allocation of total taxable income from goods produced in the United States and sold abroad, foreign-related assets would include investments in foreign subsidiaries, loans to foreign corporations, foreign accounts receivables, and a portion of working capital and plant attributable to the supervision of the foreign subsidiary's activities. An optional *gross-income method* may also be chosen, in which the interest expense is allocated to the relevant classes of gross income in porportion to the gross income in each class. This method may be used unless the amount of interest expense so allocated to any class is less than 50 percent of the expense that would have been allocated to that class under the asset-value method. In such case an *alternative optional gross-income method* may be used, whereby 50 percent of the interest expense as determined under the asset-value method is allocated to that class that did not meet the test under the optional gross-income method (the balance allocated to the remaining classes). The same choice of allocation method must be made by all members of a consolidated-return group.

Allocation of Research and Development Expense.   Research expenses deductible under Internal Revenue Code (IRC) Section 174 are viewed as definitely related to specific classes of gross income based on the two-digit Standard Industrial Classification (SIC) Manual. Basic research not identifiable with any one SIC category is considered to apply to all classes of gross income. Research undertaken to meet legal requirements (such as federally mandated safety standards) imposed by one government that cannot be expected to benefit products marketed outside that government's jurisdiction may be apportioned solely to gross income from that country, but it may be difficult to convince the I.R.S. that no benefits from such research accrue elsewhere.

The preferred method of apportionment of R&D is the *sales method*. Under this method, if more than 50 percent of the costs of R&D are expended in a single geographic area (e.g., the United States) then 30 percent of the R&D expense after deduction of the legally imposed R&D costs may be *exclusively apportioned* to that geographic area (a greater exclusive apportionment may be claimed if there is very limited or long-delayed application outside the geographic area). The balance of the R&D expense is apportioned to the specific classes of gross income under consideration in accordance with the amount of sales in each product classification. Although it is only the taxpayer's R&D expense that is being allocated, the sales of both the taxpayer and the taxpayer's controlled subsidiaries enter into the apportionment calculation. The taxpayer may elect to apportion the R&D expense (after deduction of the legally mandated expense) on the basis of *gross income,* provided the resulting apportionment results in an allocation of 50 percent or more of the expense that would have been allocated to each relevant class of income under the sales method. If such is not the case for a particular class of gross income, an *alternative optional gross-income method* may be used, in which 50 percent of the expense is allocated to that class, with the balance of the expense allocated to the other classes. The same choice of allocation method must be made by all members of a consolidated-return group. It should be noted that if the foreign marketing and distributing function is conducted by a foreign sales subsidiary that does not engage in manufacturing, such sales subsidiary is viewed as a wholesale or retail subsidiary, with the result that none of the R&D definitely related to specific manufacturing categories need be allocated to income from that subsidiary. In addition, the establishment of a cost-sharing arrangement between foreign and domestic entities will preclude the need for allocation of the R&D (other than that called for in the cost-sharing agreement). In 1981 Economic Recovery Act suspends application of these rules for two years, during which time U.S. R&D is allocated entirely to U.S. source income.

THE INDIRECT FOREIGN-TAX CREDIT.   U.S. domestic corporations may claim an indirect (deemed paid) foreign-tax credit upon receipt of a *dividend* from a foreign subsidiary for a portion of the foreign taxes *paid by the subsidiary*. Such indirect credit may also be claimed with respect to a portion of the foreign taxes paid by second- and third-tier foreign subsidiaries when the earnings upon which the foreign taxes are levied are ultimately distributed through the chain of foreign corporations and remitted by the first-tier corporation to the domestic parent. In order to claim these credits, the domestic corporation must own at least 10 percent of the voting power of the first-tier foreign corporation, which in turn must own 10 percent or more of the second-tier corporation, which in turn must own at least 10 percent of the third-tier foreign corporation. In addition, the domestic corporation must have an indirect ownership interest in each of the second and third-tier foreign corporations of at least five percent.

The Deemed-Paid Credit. The indirect-foreign-tax credit is obtained as a fraction of the foreign taxes paid (or deemed paid) by the first-tier foreign corporation as follows:

$$\frac{\text{deemed-paid-}}{\text{foreign-tax credit}} = \frac{\text{foreign taxes paid}}{\text{or accrued}} \times \frac{\text{dividends paid}}{\text{accumulated profits after foreign taxes}}$$

A corresponding formula is used to determine the foreign taxes deemed paid by the second-tier foreign corporation for taxes paid by the third-tier corporation. *Such taxes are included together with the actual foreign taxes* paid by the second-tier corporation in the corresponding formula to obtain the foreign taxes deemed paid by the first-tier corporation (which are added to the actual taxes paid by the first-tier corporation in the above expression). If the dividends remitted from any tier reflect earnings from several years (rather than just the current year) the total deemed-paid credit is obtained by summing the product of the factors on the right-hand side of the expression for the individual years. Dividends paid within the first 60 days of the taxable year are assumed to be distributions of the previous year's earnings.

When dividends are received by the domestic corporation with an associated deemed-paid credit, the taxable (foreign source) dividend income is *grossed up* by the associated deemed-paid credit. If a withholding tax is imposed on the domestic corporation resulting in a reduced amount received, the dividend income is also grossed up by the taxes withheld (for which a direct-foreign-tax credit may be claimed).

Illustrative Example. As an illustration of the indirect-foreign-tax credit and allocation of deduction rules, consider the situation described in Exhibit 2. Corporation X, a U.S. corporation, is the sole owner of Corporation Y, a foreign corporation. Corporations X and Y manufacture similar products, X sells its output in the United States and Y sells its output outside the United States, with the results shown in the exhibit. Note that the deemed-paid-tax credit that may be claimed by Corporation X is $9200, resulting in a grossed-up dividend income of $20,000. Were it not necessary to allocate X's interest and R&D expense to its foreign-source income, the foreign-tax-credit limitation for X would be:

$$\$69,000 \, \frac{\$ \, 32,000}{\$150,000} = \$14,720$$

EXHIBIT 2 ILLUSTRATIVE EXAMPLE

	X	Y
Income		
Sales	$ 600,000	$200,000
Cost of goods sold	(232,000)	(80,000)
Gross income	368,000	120,000
Dividend income[a]	20,000	
Interest income[b]	12,000	
Interest expense	(150,000)	(12,000)
R & D expense[c]	(100,000)	
Taxable income	150,000	108,000
Gross U.S. tax[d]	(69,000)	
Foreign tax paid[d]		(49,680)
Net income	$ 81,000	$ 58,320
Assets		
Current and fixed assets	$3,200,000	
Investment in Y	600,000	
Loan to Y	200,000	
Total assets	$4,000,000	

[a]Cash dividend from Y to X: $10,800
 Deemed-paid credit: $49,680 (10,800/58,320) =   9,200
                                                   $20,000

[b]Paid by Y on loan from X.
[c]All performed in United States; no federally mandated costs.
[d]Both U.S. and foreign tax rate taken as 46 percent of taxable income.

which exceeds the $9,200 deemed-paid credit; the entire deemed-paid credit may thus be utilized. However, the situation is quite different when the Regulation 1.861-8 rules are applied to X as follows:

	U.S. Source	Foreign Source
Gross sales income	$ 368,000	
Dividend income		$ 20,000
Interest income		12,000
Interest expense	(135,000)	(15,000)
R & D expense	(91,250)	(8,750)
Taxable income	$ 141,750	$ 8,250

Foreign-tax-credit limitation = $69,000 (8250/150,000) = $3795, where allocation of the interest and R&D expense was made using the alternative optional-gross-income method as follows:

$$\$15,000 = 0.5[\$150,000(800,000/4,000,000)]$$
$$\$\ 8750 = 0.5[(\$100,000 - \$30,000)\ (200,000/800,000)]$$

It may thus be seen that without a more-judicious organizational structure, less than half of the deemed-paid-foreign-tax credit may be used against X's current gross U.S. tax liability, resulting in a net U.S. tax liability of $65,205.

TAX-DEFERRAL PROBLEMS

CONTROLLED FOREIGN CORPORATIONS. An important modification of the general rule that a stockholder in a foreign corporation does not recognize income earned by the corporation until that corporation remits a dividend was introduced by Congress in 1962 and broadened in 1975. A set of new sections were introduced as *subpart F* (of Part III of subchapter N) of the Internal Revenue Code. Under subpart F, a U.S. stockholder owning directly or indirectly at least a 10 percent interest in a *controlled foreign corporation* (CFC) is liable for taxes on certain undistributed earnings of the CFC. The income so tainted is that which Congress felt may as easily have been earned by a domestic corporation, such as passive investment income or income from the sale by the CFC of goods produced by a related person for use or consumption in a country other than that in which the CFC is organized. Several other countries (e.g., Canada, West Germany, Japan) have also developed tax laws that result in the current taxation of a stockholder on the undistributed earnings of a foreign corporation, but these laws are generally less broad than the U.S. laws. It is important to note that all such laws *do not affect the home-country taxation of the CFC;* they only relate to the taxation of certain stockholders of the CFC.

When Is a Foreign Corporation a CFC? A controlled foreign corporation is defined as a foreign corporation of which more than 50 percent of the total voting power of the stock is owned by *U.S. shareholders.* A U.S. shareholder is any U.S. individual, corporation, or other entity *owning directly or indirectly 10 percent or more of the total voting power.* When several classes of voting stock are outstanding, these tests are made with respect to the stockholder's ability to elect the directors or cast the deciding vote. The substance rather than the formal measure of control is examined. In most cases (e.g., where a U.S. parent corporation is the sole owner of the foreign corporation), the identification of the U.S. shareholders and the characterization of the foreign corporation as a CFC is obvious. In cases where an attempt is made to avoid classification of the foreign corporation as a CFC (e.g., by spreading ownership over a set of related entities such that no one entity has 10 percent of the voting power) the relevant *attribution rules* under which one person's interest in the foreign corporation may be regarded (for the purpose of the ownership tests) as owned by another must be examined. The general thrust of these attribution rules is to preclude non-CFC status unless a significant degree of control over the foreign corporation has actually been given up by its majority U.S. stockholders.

Taxation of U.S. Shareholders. All U.S. shareholders of a foreign corporation that maintains CFC status for 30 days or more during the year are required to recognize their share of certain income of the CFC in proportion to their ownership of the CFC on the last day of the year. This income is viewed as a deemed distribution and increases the basis of the stock of the CFC. A later actual distribution of this previously taxed income will not again be taxed (but the basis of the stock of the CFC will be reduced). Since this deemed distribution is viewed as an actual dividend from the CFC, a deemed-paid-foreign-tax credit may be claimed by a corporate U.S. shareholder. When an actual distribution is made, the ordinary deemed-paid credit is available only to the extent that a credit had not previously been claimed at the time of the deemed distribution. In addition, the foreign-tax-credit limitation is increased in the year of the actual distribution to the extent the deemed distribution increased the limitation in the year it was taxed and such increase was not then absorbed by the corresponding deemed-paid credit. It should be noted that whereas actual distribution must flow from lower-tier foreign corporations to the parent corporation through the chain of intermediate foreign corporations and thus generate a lesser ordinary-deemed-paid-tax credit (because of the undistributed earnings of the intermediate corporations), the subpart F deemed distribution is viewed as flowing directly to the U.S. shareholder from the lower-tier CFC, generating in general a greater deemed-paid credit. It may thus sometimes prove more beneficial to have a lower-tier CFC loan funds to the domestic parent (which may give rise to a deemed distribution) than to remit such funds through a chain of foreign corporations. It is possible for an individual U.S. shareholder to elect to have the deemed distribution taxed as if the individual were a corporation (and thus enjoy the benefits of the deemed-paid credit), but these benefits are only temporary and are recaptured when actual distributions are made.

SUBPART F INCOME.   It is possible for a foreign corporation to be a CFC without having the U.S. shareholders taxed on the undistributed earnings (indeed, this is the more usual situation). The U.S. shareholders will be taxed currently only when the CFC either (1) earns *subpart F* income (or acts in a manner such that previously excluded subpart F income is currently recognized), or (2) increases its investment of earnings (whether subpart F or not) in U.S. property.

Foreign-Base-Company Income.   Subpart F income consists of three types of income—*income from the insurance of U.S. risks, bribe- and boycott-related income,* and *foreign-base-company income,* which is generally the major component. In computing the subpart F income, an allocation of expenses and deductions in accordance with Regulation 1.861-8 must be made. *Foreign-base-company income* is made up of four types of income as follows:

1.   Foreign-personal-holding-company income.
2.   Foreign-base-company sales income.
3.   Foreign-base-company services income.
4.   Foreign-base-company shipping income.

Regardless of the amount of subpart F income earned during the year, the deemed distribution is limited to the *earnings and profits* (an approximation of economic income) for the year.

Foreign-Personal-Holding-Company Income.   Passive investment income, such as dividends, interest, royalties, rents, and gains from the sale of securities may constitute foreign-personal-holding-company income of both a CFC or a foreign personal holding company (FPHC). If the corporation also qualifies as a FPHC, the foreign-personal-holding-company income will be taxed under the FPHC provisions; if not, the income will be foreign-base-company income of a CFC, unless the rents and royalties are received from unrelated parties in the active conduct of a trade or business, or the interest, dividends, and gains from the sale of securities are received from unrelated persons in the active conduct of a banking or insurance business. A *related person* is any person (individual, corporation, partnership, trust, or estate) that controls the CFC, a corporation controlled by the CFC, or a corporation that is controlled by the same person or persons who control the CFC. Control is ownership of more than 50 percent of the voting power. Dividend and interest income from a related corporation will not constitute FPHC income of a CFC if the related corporation is organized in the same country as the CFC and the related corporation's assets are substantially used in that country. This means that a holding company may be interposed between the U.S. shareholder and a foreign operating company provided the holding company is organized in the same country as the operating company. Likewise, rental or royalty income from a related person is not FPHC income if the property is located in the same country as the CFC.

Foreign-Base-Company Sales Income.   As may be seen from the exceptions to FPHC income, the subpart F provisions are more likely to apply to income from transactions with a related person than to income from transactions with an unrelated person. Moreover, subpart F provisions are more apt to apply to income from transactions with a related person who has no business in the country in which the CFC is organized than to income when the related person is organized in or has property in that country. These same *antitax haven* concepts apply in the definition of foreign-base-company sales income. Thus income from the purchase of personal property from (or on behaf of) a *related person* and its sale to any person, or the purchase of personal property from any person on behalf of (or sold to) a *related person* is foreign-base-company sales income if the property is manufactured and sold for use outside the country of organization of the CFC. Thus the income from the sale of goods purchased by a Swiss sales corporation from its U.S. parent to French, West German, and Italian customers will be currently taxable to the U.S. parent as a subpart F deemed distribution. However, income from sale to Swiss customers or income from the sale of goods produced by a Swiss manufacturing subsidiary and sold to customers throughout the world is not foreign-base-company sales income. In order for the CFC to be regarded as producing or manufacturing the product (components of which may be purchased from a related person), the CFC must have substantially transformed the product or incurred conversion costs of 20 percent or more of the total cost of the product. Generally minor assembly and packaging operations will not suffice. To prevent the manufacturing operations of a CFC to shield from subpart F status the income from sales activities in other countries, the subpart F character of the income from such branch operations will be tested as if each branch were a separate corporation if the branch income is taxed by the host country at an effective tax rate that is less than 90 percent of (and at least five percentage points less than) the effective tax rate of the country *in which the CFC is organized.* A corresponding *branch rule* applies in the case of a manufacturing branch of a selling CFC.

Foreign-Base-Company Services Income.   If a CFC performs services for (or on behalf of) a related person, and the services are performed outside the country in which the CFC is organized, the compensation of the CFC will constitute foreign-base-company services income. However, services performed in connection with the sale of personal property manufactured by the CFC are not included. If the related person performs substantial assistance to the CFC, the service performed by the CFC will be regarded as service on behalf of the related party; such would not be the case if the related party merely acted as guarantor for the CFC.

Foreign-Base-Company Shipping Income.   The income from the use or leasing of any aircraft or vessel in *foreign commerce* constitutes foreign-base-company shipping income. In addition, the performance of services related to such activity and the gains from the sale of shipping assets are included, as well as a portion of dividend and interest income from a foreign corporation engaging in such activities. However, to the extent the shipping income is reinvested in qualified shipping assets, the subpart F characterization is deferred until such investment is withdrawn.

Exclusions From Foreign-Base-Company Income.   If less than 10 percent of the CFC's gross income is foreign-base-company income, then none of the CFC's income is considered foreign-base-company income. This implies, for example, that each foreign manufacturing subsidiary may engage in a limited amount of foreign-base-company activity without triggering current taxation of the U.S. parent on such activity. Conversely, however, if more than 70 percent of the CFC's gross income is foreign-base-company income, then all of the CFC's gross income is considered to be foreign-base-company income. If the I.R.S. can be convinced that the creation or organization of the CFC and the effecting of the transaction through the CFC were not undertaken with tax avoidance as a significant factor, the income generated may be excluded from foreign-base-company income.

Insurance of U.S. Risks.   In addition to foreign-base-company income, subpart F income also includes income derived by a CFC from the insurance of U.S. property, life and health insurance of U.S. residents, and liability insurance in connection with U.S. activities. However, if the insurance premiums received by the CFC from the insurance of U.S. risks are less than 5 percent of the CFC's total insurance premium receipts, such income is excluded from subpart F characterization.

Bribe- and Boycott-Related Income.   Bribes, kickbacks, and other illegal payments paid by a CFC to any foreign official or government employee are not deductible, and the corresponding increase in taxable income is considered subpart F income. Income arising from operations in any foreign country requiring participation in an international boycott as a condition of doing business in that country is also considered subpart F income. If it is not possible to trace income to operations within the country, an *international-boycott factor* (essentially the ratio of boycott operations to total foreign operations, as measured by sales, purchases, and payroll) must be used. Such bribe- and boycott-related income also reduces the available foreign-tax credits.

Increase of Investments of Earnings in U.S. Property.   Even if none of the earnings of a CFC are subpart F income, the U.S. shareholder may be taxed currently on that portion of the earnings of the CFC that is invested in U.S. property. The actual calculation is rather complex, but the following points may be noted. First, U.S.

property includes tangible property located in the United States as well as stocks and obligations of a U.S. person (including loans to the CFC's U.S. parent) and, with some exceptions, patents, know-how, and copyrights acquired or developed by the CFC for use in the United States. However, U.S. government obligations, the obligations of any U.S. person to the extent commensurate with the business transactions between the CFC and the U.S. person, the stock of a domestic corporation (other than a U.S. shareholder) provided the U.S. shareholders do not own directly or indirectly 25 percent or more of the voting power of such domestic corporation after the acquisition by the CFC, and certain other property may be excluded.

Second, the U.S. shareholder is not taxed currently on the increase of investment in U.S. property if such increase is out of undistributed earnings which were or are currently taxed to the shareholder as subpart F income (or effectively connected U.S. income).

Other Amounts Taxed Currently.   Foreign-base-company shipping income that was previously excluded because of investment in qualified shipping assets is included in the deemed distribution when such investment is withdrawn (either through depreciation or disposal). Since subpart F income could be excluded prior to 1975 to the extent qualified investments were made in certain less developed countries, the withdrawal of such investment is included in the deemed distribution (even though such deferral is no longer allowed).

CREATION, REORGANIZATION, AND DISPOSAL OF A FOREIGN CORPORATION.
The contribution of property to a domestic corporation in return for the corporation's stock does not generally result in the recognition of taxable income. Likewise, the acquisition, reorganization, and liquidation of a domestic corporation may often be effected without the recognition of taxable income. Because of the potential for avoidance of U.S. taxation of the gains on the sale of appreciated U.S. property or the undistributed earnings of a foreign corporation that might otherwise result, such *tax-free* transactions will generally require some income recognition if one or more of the corporations that are parties to the transaction are foreign corporations.

Transfers of Property from the United States.   The *outbound* transfer of property (other than stock or securities of a foreign corporation that is a party to the organization or reorganization) by a U.S. person in a transaction that would otherwise be tax-free if purely domestic entities were involved requires approval by the I.R.S. for corresponding tax-free treatment. Such approval must be sought within 183 days of the transfer of the property. Generally such approval will not be forthcoming in the case of the transfer of property to a foreign corporation unless such property is used in the active conduct of a trade or business and is needed in that business. Moreover, such permission will generally require that the gain that would have been recognized if the following properties had been sold be recognized by the transferor:

1. Inventory.
2. Copyrights.
3. Unrealized accounts receivable.
4. Stock or securities.

5. Property that the transferor leases or licenses (to parties other than the transferee).

6. Property that will be leased or licensed by the transferee.

7. U.S. patents, know-how, and so forth used in the conduct of a business in (or the manufacture of goods for sale in) the United States.

8. Foreign patents and other intangibles to be used in connection with the sale of goods manufactured in the United States.

Such income (*toll charge*) must also be incurred in connection with the liquidation of a U.S. corporation into a foreign parent corporation or acquisition of a U.S. corporation's assets by a foreign corporation in a qualified reorganization. Moreover, the toll charge required for the conversion of a foreign branch into a foreign subsidiary will include the recapture of any unrecovered foreign losses.

Transfers of Property to the United States.   A ruling request for tax-free treatment for transfers of property to the United States (or transfers that are purely foreign) is not necessary; such transactions are governed by recent temporary Treasury Department regulations. Under these regulations, when a foreign corporation is liquidated into a domestic parent, the parent is required to treat the transaction as if just prior to the liquidation the foreign corporation remitted all of its earnings and profits. The parent will thus pick up dividend income (effectively limited to the gain that would be realized if the foreign subsidiary were sold) and will be allowed to claim a deemed-paid-foreign-tax credit. Similar treatment is also generally required when a domestic corporation disposes of its foreign subsidiary in a tax-free reorganization. Although gain on the sale of a domestic corporation generally receives capital-gain treatment, all or part of the gain on the sale by a U.S. person who owned 10% or more of the stock of a foreign corporation that was a CFC at any time within the 5-year period preceding the sale may be treated as dividend income (and thus carry with it a deemed-paid credit). Such dividend income will be limited to the post-1962 earnings and profits of the corporation for the period during which the corporation was a CFC and the stock was owned by the U.S. person. Undistributed earnings that were already taxed to the U.S. shareholder as subpart F income are excluded from the determination of the dividend income. Additional limitations restrict the amount of such dividend income for both individual and corporate stockholders. Although the general thrust of these provisions is to reduce, at the stockholder level, the preferential taxation of the undistributed (and thus previously untaxed) earnings of the foreign corporation, for corporate stockholders the deemed-paid credit may in fact make dividend income more advantageous than capital gains.

INTERCOMPANY-TRANSACTION PROBLEMS

THE TRANSFER-PRICING PROBLEM.   A substantial portion of international trade occurs between related affiliates of multinational corporations (e.g., 50 percent of U.S. exports in 1970, 30 percent of British exports in 1973, 59 percent of Canadian exports in 1971). Since even a modest change in the prices at which goods are transferred between related entities may result in a significant shift of income from a high-tax-rate to a low-tax-rate country, the appropriateness of such prices has long been of concern to the fiscal authorities of many countries. Relying on the authority granted by Congress in *Section 482* of the Internal Revenue Code, which gives the Commissioner of Internal Revenue the right to allocate income among related tax-payers if such allocation is necessary to clearly reflect income or prevent the avoidance of tax, the I.R.S. has increasingly questioned the appropriateness of transfer prices and charges for other intercompany transactions. In response to a specific request by the House-Senate conference committee considering the 1962 act (which introduced the subpart F provisions), the Treasury Department promulgated a set of *Section 482* regulations that attempt to provide guidance in an area where there may be no "correct" answer that would apply in every case. These regulations have also been generally approved in a 1979 OECD report, "Transfer Pricing and Multinational Enterprises."

THE SECTION 482 REGULATIONS. The basic premise of the regulations (and the OECD report) is that the principal standard for the intercompany pricing of goods and services is the price that would be charged by unrelated parties (an *arm's-length* standard). When such price is readily apparent (e.g., when goods are sold to both unrelated distributors and related sales subsidiaries in comparable quantities and terms), the application of this standard presents no problems. In most cases, however, an arm's-length price cannot be unambiguously determined. For certain charges (interest rates, service fees, lease rentals) the regulations nevertheless provide *safe-haven* rules (generally favorable to the taxpayer), which establish a charge that will be acceptable to the I.R.S. even if such charge may be a poor approximation of the arm's-length standard (and for this reason the OECD report was generally critical of such rules). With respect to transfer prices, the regulations merely provide several methods (as well as a ranking of these methods) that must be used to determine an appropriate price. These methods are not meant to be used in a purely mechanical fashion. An appropriate adjustment reflecting the specific facts and conditions of each particular situation must be made.

Application of Section 482. Section 482 applies to two or more entities that are owned or controlled directly or indirectly by the same interests (a *controlled group*). Control generally means ownership of at least 50 percent of the total voting power (or at least 50 percent of the total value of all classes of stock). When the I.R.S. makes an adverse change in the income of one member of the group, it is required to make a generally favorable *correlative adjustment* to the income of the other member engaged in the transaction in question (thus the total amount of income of the group is left unchanged). In the case of a foreign member, such correlative adjustment may be of no use if the adjustment is not recognized by the host government. In addition, the I.R.S. must allow adverse changes with respect to certain transactions to be *set off* against favorable correlative adjustments with respect to other transactions. In general, if a Section 482 adjustment results in an increase in income of a domestic parent corporation, the parent is allowed to receive a corresponding payment from its foreign subsidiary with no further U.S. tax imposed (either through the mechanism of a dividend-income exclusion or establishment of an account receivable).

Interest Charges. When one member of a controlled group lends money to another member, if the interest rate charged is at least 11 percent but not more than 13 percent simple interest, the interest rate charged will not be questioned. If no interest is charged or the interest rate is outside the allowed range, 12 percent simple interest will be required, except in the following case:

1. The funds were obtained by the lender from a creditor located in the same country in which the borrowing member is organized. In such a case the interest rate charged must reflect the interest charge to the lending member adjusted for the lender's transaction costs.

2. The market rate exceeds the rate charged and the rate charged is greater than 13 percent, or the market rate is lower than the rate charged, and the rate charged is less than 11 percent. In such case *the rate charged* is accepted.

3. The lender is in the business of making loans. In such a case the market rate will be required.

Service Fees. When one member of a controlled group performs services for the benefit of another member and such activities are an integral part of the business activity of either member, an arm's-length charge is required. If such services do not constitute a significant portion of either member's operations, a safe-haven charge for such services is the cost (both direct and indirect) of such services to the performing member.

Lease Rentals. When tangible property owned or leased by one member of a controlled group is leased to another member and either member is engaged in the business of renting such property, an arm's-length rental is required. When neither member is in the rental business, a safe-haven annual rental charge is the sum of the following:

1. The direct and indirect expenses of the owning member.

2. An allowance for depreciation for the period the property was used by the leasing member (using the straight-line depreciation method).

3. A return on capital equal to 3 percent of the *depreciable basis,* prorated for the period the property was used by the leasing member.

Sales of Tangible Property. When one member of a controlled group sells tangible property to another member, the *comparable uncontrolled price* charged in similar transactions between unrelated parties must be used. Adjustment for differences in the quantity and quality of the product sold, the terms of the sale, the level of service provided to the buyer, and the condition and location of the market in which the product is sold must be made. However, if there are no comparable uncontrolled sales or the number of required adjustments would be excessive, the *resale-price method* must be used. The arm's-length price under this method is the price at which the product is resold by the buying member (within a reasonable time before or after purchase) in an uncontrolled sale, *less a markup* based on the uncontrolled activities of the buying member. If the buying member does not engage in corresponding transactions with unrelated parties, the markup may be determined by reference to industry experience, but adjustment for differences in markets, functions, or other relevant factors must be made. For example, if the selling member guarantees the buying member against loss, whereas independent distributors must bear the entire risk of loss, such a difference must be reflected in the markup used. If the buying member adds a substantial amount of value to the product before resale, the *cost-plus method* must be used. Under this method, the arm's-length price is the cost of producing the product, *plus a markup* based on the selling member's similar transactions with unrelated parties. As in the case of the resale-price method, if no comparable uncontrolled sales are made by the selling member, industry experience may be used to determine the appropriate markup, provided adjustment is made for all relevant differences. The taxpayer is entitled to use some other pricing method providing that it can be shown that such method is more appropriate than the suggested methods. Although frequently used in the past (particularly at the agent level), profit-allocation methods (such as a 50/50 split) that cannot be justified in terms of the business activities and risks of each member will not be sustained by the courts.

Sale or Licensing of Intangible Property.   When intangible property rights are transferred from one member of a controlled group to another, an arm's-length standard measured with respect to transfers of comparable rights to unrelated parties must be used. In the absence of comparative transfers, the regulations list a number of factors (but do not provide the weighting) to be used in establishing the appropriate charge. They do allow such a charge to be based on the profits earned by the transferee, which may prove more desirable than a charge based on sales in the initial years of a new foreign manufacturing operation. Cost-sharing arrangements will also be respected, providing they reflect each participant's share of the costs and risks of the development of intangible property.

SPECIAL TAX OPPORTUNITIES

EXPORTING THROUGH A DOMESTIC INTERNATIONAL SALES CORPORATION.
The Revenue Act of 1971 created a new type of domestic corporation for tax purposes—a domestic international sales corporation (DISC). The major advantage of exporting through a DISC (a DISC cannot itself manufacture or produce goods) as originally conceived was the ability to defer from U.S. taxation approximately 25 percent of the total income from the manufacture and sale of the goods exported. In the face of repeated Treasury Department studies that failed to detect an increase in U.S. exports resulting from the DISC provisions, these provisions were modified so as to provide reduced benefits for DISCs that failed to maintain an increased level of export sales.

Requirements for Qualification of a DISC.   Because Congress viewed the DISC provisions as an incentive for increased trade, the requirements for a domestic corporation to qualify as a DISC are quite modest. The major requirement is that 95 percent or more of the DISC's gross income must consist of qualified export receipts (receipts from the sale or lease of goods manufactured or produced in the United States for use or consumption outside the United States, provided not more than 50 percent of the value of such goods is attributable to imports). Crude oil, natural gas, coal, uranium, and certain intangible property such as patents, copyrights, and know-how are not qualified export property. A second requirement is that at least 95 percent of the DISC's assets must be export assets (assets used primarily in an exporting business, such as inventory and accounts receivable). In addition, the DISC must have at least $2500 capital and only one class of stock, must maintain separate books and records, and must elect to be treated as a DISC. However, a DISC need not have any employees, nor (in the case of a commission DISC) have any tangible assets. A DISC may contract with its parent for a sales franchise whereby the parent will continue all export functions (except invoicing, which must be done by a buy-sell DISC) in return for the maximum commission allowable (for a commission DISC) or at transfer prices that provide the DISC the maximum profit allowable (for a buy-sell DISC).

Intercompany-Pricing Rules.   The DISC provisions provide two safe-haven rules for determining the maximum allowable commission or profit. These rules are generally far more advantageous than the Section 482 rules (although the Section 482 rules may be used if desired). The first safe-haven rule allows the DISC an *income* equal to *4 percent of qualified export receipts,* plus 10 percent of the export promotion expenses incurred by the DISC (if any) on such sales. The second rule allows the DISC an income equal to 50 percent of the combined taxable income of the DISC and its related supplier, plus 10 percent of the export promotion expenses. In computing the total combined taxable income, the DISC may use marginal costing (including the export-promotion expenses to the extent that such expenses are used to increase the allowable profit), providing the ratio of the resulting income to the DISC sales does not exceed the *overall profit percentage limitation* according to the following formula:

$$\frac{\begin{array}{l}\text{combined taxable income of DISC}\\\text{and related supplier, plus supplier's}\\\text{income from domestic sales of}\\\text{same product under full costing}\end{array}}{\text{total gross receipts from above sales}} = \text{overall profit percentage limitation}$$

The DISC is given considerable flexibility in applying these rules by grouping transactions according to product lines and applying the method that generates the maximum income to each group (which need not exactly coincide with the grouping used in the overall profit percentage limitation computation). When the combined taxable income with respect to any grouping is positive, neither method may result in a loss to the related supplier. However, if the combined taxable income is negative, the DISC is nevertheless allowed the income calculated under the 4 percent gross receipts method to the extent that the ratio of the DISC income to the DISC sales does not exceed the overall profit percentage limitation for the particular grouping.

Taxation of DISC Income.   A DISC is not subject to the corporate income tax. However, a portion of DISC income is taxed at the stockholder level as a *deemed distribution,* even if no earnings are actually distributed. Such deemed distribution does not qualify for the 85 or 100 percent dividend-received deduction. However, that portion of DISC income that is not deemed distributed is not taxed to the stockholder until such income is actually distributed, the corporation no longer qualifies as a DISC, or the DISC is sold, exchanged, or liquidated (unless the DISC or DISC assets are transferred to a corporation that is itself a DISC in what otherwise would qualify as a tax-free transaction). Actual dividend distributions are not taxable to the stockholders to the extent that they are out of earnings that had previously been taxed to the stockholders as deemed distributions. These rules are similar to the subpart F provisions regarding the taxation of a CFC. Unlike the subpart F provisions, however, a DISC *can* invest its earnings in U.S. property without subjecting to taxation the *accumulated DISC income* (the untaxed protion of the DISC's earnings). A DISC may loan its related supplier (or other U.S. export manufacturer) its accumulated DISC income, provided such *producers' loans* increase the export-related assets of the borrower. A producer's loan is a qualified export asset and the interest from such a loan a qualified export receipt.

Deemed Distributions. The portion of DISC income taxed currently to the stockholders consists of:

1. Interest from producers' loans.
2. Gain on the sale or exchange of nonqualified export assets acquired in a nontaxable exchange.
3. Gain to the extent of depreciation recapture on the sale or exchange of qualified export assets acquired in a nontaxable exchange.
4. Fifty percent of the taxable income attributable to military property.
5. Taxable income attributable to *base-period export gross receipts*.
6. The amount of foreign investment attributable to producers' loans.
7. Fifty percent of DISC income in excess of items 1–5.

Item 5 is the mechanism by which DISC benefits have been tied to increases in export sales. Taxable income attributable to base-period export gross receipts is defined as

$$\begin{array}{l}\text{taxable income attributed} \\ \text{to base-period export} \\ \text{gross receipts}\end{array} = \begin{array}{l}\text{adjusted} \\ \text{taxable} \\ \text{income}\end{array} \times \dfrac{\begin{array}{l}\text{adjusted base-period} \\ \text{export gross receipts}\end{array}}{\begin{array}{l}\text{export gross receipts} \\ \text{for current year}\end{array}}$$

Adjustable taxable income is the DISC income reduced by items 1–4, and adjusted base-period export gross receipts is 67 percent of the *average* of the export gross receipts for the base period (the fourth through seventh preceding taxable years). If the DISC has taxable income of $100,000 or less, this item may be ignored (and may be partly ignored to the extent the DISC income exceeds $100,000 but does not exceed $150,000). Item 6 arises when a DISC lends money to its related supplier to the extent there has been an increase in the foreign assets of the members of the controlled group to which the DISC belongs, and such increase results from foreign investment by the domestic members. In the simplest case, where items 1–6 are zero, the deemed distribution is 50 percent of the DISC income. If the 50 percent of combined taxable income method were used to determine DISC income, the tax on approximately 25 percent of the combined taxable income (50 percent of 50 percent) would be deferred. For a mature DISC, where items 1–6 may represent a fair portion of DISC taxable income, the deferral benefits may be significantly reduced. Moreover, since DISC income is generally foreign-source income that is free of foreign taxation, it may not be advantageous to use a DISC if the parent corporation is in an excess-foreign-tax-credit position.

THE SECTION 936 TAX CREDIT.   Prior to the Tax Reform Act of 1976, a domestic corporation engaged in an active business in Puerto Rico (and certain other U.S. possessions) was permitted, subject to certain requirements, to exclude from U.S. taxation all income earned in Puerto Rico or elsewhere outside the United States. Such a *possession corporation* was generally engaged in activities that qualified its Puerto Rican earnings for exemption from Puerto Rican taxes as well. As long as such a corporation did not remit dividends to its domestic parent (possession-corporation dividends did not generally qualify for the 85 or 100 percent dividend-received deduction), its earnings went untaxed, with the result that substantial accumulated earnings were invested *outside the United States and Puerto Rico.* Since such investments were not felt to provide the benefits to either the United States or Puerto Rico that were envisioned by Congress, the 1976 act made the income earned by the possession corporation taxable, but provided a new tax-sparing credit (the *Section 936 credit*) equal to the U.S. tax on the possessions-corporation income from the active conduct of a business in Puerto Rico and from *qualified possession-source* investment income. The foreign-tax-credit limitation does not apply to the Section 936 credit, and the income upon which the Section 936 credit is based is ignored in computing the limitation with respect to the ordinary foreign-tax credit.

Requirements for Claiming the Credit.   A domestic corporation must elect to claim the credit. Once elected, it remains in force for 10 years, provided the corporation satisfies the following two requirements:

1.   Eighty percent or more of gross income from the 3-year period preceding the close of the taxable year must be derived from sources within a possession of the United States.

2.   At least 50 percent of gross income for the same period must be derived from the active conduct of a trade or business within a possession. A corporation electing the Section 936 credit is not allowed to join in the filing of a consolidated tax return. However, the domestic parent of such corporation is eligible for the 85 or 100 percent dividend-received deduction on dividends received from such a corporation. Because qualified possession-source investment income is limited to income from investments that are made in Puerto Rico (and are not reinvested outside the possession), the general result of the 1976 act is to effectively continue to exclude from U.S. taxation income earned *in Puerto Rico* while encouraging repatriation of funds that had previously been invested outside the United States and Puerto Rico. The imposition of a Puerto Rican withholding tax (*tollgate* tax) on dividend remittances by a possession corporation to its U.S. parent may, however, reduce somewhat the desirability of repatriating the previously accumulated funds.

BORROWING THROUGH AN INTERNATIONAL FINANCE SUBSIDIARY.   If a domestic corporation borrows funds from a foreign creditor who is not otherwise engaged in a U.S. trade or business, the interest payments will be subject to a withholding tax. However, if the domestic corporation were to borrow from a creditor in a country such as the Netherlands Antilles, which has entered into a tax treaty with the United States that exempts from U.S. withholding tax interest payments from U.S. borrowers, payment may be made to the Netherlands Antilles creditor free of U.S. withholding tax. Moreover, if the treaty country itself does not impose any withholding tax on interest payments made to nonresidents, as is the case in the

Netherlands Antilles, the Netherlands Antilles creditor could in turn borrow funds in the Eurobond market without subjecting the interest payments to foreign investors to any withholding tax. Thus by establishing a Netherlands Antilles finance subsidiary and structuring its payments to the finance subsidiary to match the Eurobond payments, a domestic corporation can tap the Eurobond market. Since the finance subsidiary's interest expense offsets its interest income, the finance subsidiary need not pay any taxes to the Netherlands Antilles. Despite the lack of any business activity with unrelated parties and the fact that the domestic parent generally guarantees the Eurobond loan (which often is convertible into stock of the domestic parent), the subsidiary has generally been recognized as a separate corporation for tax purposes, although the I.R.S. has indicated that such determination would have to be made on a case-by-case basis. This use of an intermediate entity located in a country with more-favorable tax-treaty provisions than those in effect directly between the United States and the foreign investor's country of residence is illustrative of the general practice of *treaty shopping*. The establishment of holding companies in the Netherlands, Netherlands Antilles, and British Virgin Islands in order to take advantage of favorable U.S. treaty provisions has also been frequently chosen by nonresidents seeking to invest in the United States. Such practice is expressly disallowed under the U.S. Model Treaty and some recently concluded treaties, but only if the treaty partner taxes holding-company income preferentially (as is the case in the Netherlands and Netherlands Antilles, but not the British Virgin Islands).

INTERNATIONAL TAX COMPLIANCE, TAX MORALITY, AND TAX HAVENS. The use of tax-haven corporations and trusts to maximize the benefits of tax deferral may serve the legitimate purpose of reducing a taxpayer's tax exposure. However, with the introduction of the subpart F provisions, the imposition of a *35 percent excise tax* on the transfer of appreciated property by a U.S. person to a foreign corporation or trust (other than in exchange for corporate stock), and other changes in the U.S. tax laws, the ability to use tax havens to shelter property and business income from U.S. taxation has been significantly reduced. However, because of their bank- and corporate-secrecy laws, many tax havens continue to be used by taxpayers who misrepresent or conceal facts in order to obtain by illegitimate means those benefits that no longer are legitimately available.

In addition to the filing of tax returns and supporting schedules, the Internal Revenue Code and the Bank Secrecy Act of 1970 establish a number of information-reporting requirements with respect to transactions with or relationships to foreign entities as follows:

1. Every U.S. person who owns more than 50 percent of the stock of a foreign corporation for 30 days or more during the year must file a Form 2952, which requires detailed information concerning the corporation, including summaries of certain transactions between the corporation and related persons as well as a listing of all U.S. stockholders owning more than 5 percent of the corporation's outstanding stock.

2. Every U.S. shareholder of a CFC must file Form 3646, which shows the shareholder's pro rata share of foreign-base-company income, increase in earnings invested in U.S. property, and previously excluded subpart F income withdrawn from investment in shipping operations and less developed countries.

3. Every U.S. officer or director of a foreign personal holding company must so indicate by filing an information return on Form 957 for the company's tax year, and must report operating results on Form 958.

4. Every U.S. officer or director of a foreign corporation must file Form 959 with respect to each U.S. person who acquires 5 percent or more of the corporation's stock or an additional 5 percent of such stock.

5. Every U.S. person who physically transports or causes to be transported into or out of the United States any currency or monetary instruments exceeding $5000 at any one time must file Form 4790 with the Customs Service.

6. Every U.S. individual (including trust beneficiaries) who has signature or other authority over a foreign-bank, securities, or other financial account, is required to file information return Form 90-22.1 with the Treasury Department, as well as indicate the existence of a foreign account or trust on Schedule B of tax return Form 1040.

7. Every financial institution covered by the Bank Secrecy Act must indicate each deposit, withdrawal, exchange of currency, or other transfer of currency in excess of $10,000 by or through a financial institution on Form 4789.

8. Every U.S. person who transfers property to a foreign trust that has a U.S. beneficiary must file an information return Form 3520-A and Form 3520 if the trust was created by a gift.

Because of the taxpayer's ability to structure certain transactions in such a way as to avoid the necessity of filing one or more of the information returns (or the outright disregard of the need to file such returns), the general level of tax enforcement with respect to tax-haven activity is rather poor, as evidenced by the results of the I.R.S. Project Haven investigation. In view of the difficulty of negotiating satisfactory agreements for the exchange of information with the tax-haven governments, the most likely method of attack on tax-haven abuse by the I.R.S. is through a more-comprehensive examination of those records of the U.S. banking, accounting, and legal professions that are currently available (e.g., Forms 4789 and 4790) or may be obtained by legislative or judicial action.

SOURCES AND SUGGESTED REFERENCES

Burns, O. "How I.R.S. Applies Intercompany Pricing Rules of Section 482," *Journal of Taxation*, Vol. LII (1980), pp. 308–314.

Commerce Clearing House. *Income Taxes Worldwide*. Chicago: Commerce Clearing House, 1976.

Commerce Clearing House. "OECD Model Double Taxation Convention on Income and Capital and Department of the Treasury Model Income Tax Treaty," in *Tax Treaties*. Chicago: Commerce Clearing House, 1965.

Committee on Fiscal Affairs of the OECD. *Transfer Pricing and Multinational Enterprises*. Paris: Organization for Economic Cooperation and Development, 1979.

Deloitte Haskins and Sells, *International Tax and Business Service*. New York: Deloitte Haskins & Sells, various years.

Diamond, W.H. *Foreign Tax and Trade Briefs*. New York: Matthew Bender, 1980.

Granwell, A., M. Amdur, G. Fritzhand, and A. Weiner. "Prop. Regs. on CFC's U.S. Property Contain New Concepts, Create New Problems," *Journal of Taxation, Vol. LII* (1980), pp. 368–373.

International Bureau of Fiscal Documentation. European Taxation. Amsterdam: International Bureau of Fiscal Documentation, 1961.

Kurtz, J., M.C. Ferguson, and D. Rosenbloom. "Statements on Foreign Tax Havens by I.R.S. Commissioner Jerome Kurtz; M. Carr Ferguson, Assistant Attorney General, Tax Division; and International Tax Counsel David Rosenbloom Before the House Ways and Means Subcommittee on Oversight," *B.N.A. Daily Tax Report,* April 24, 1979. pp. J-1.

Moore, M.L. and R.N. Bagley. *U.S. Tax Aspects of Doing Business Abroad,* Studies in Federal Taxation No. 6. New York: American Institute of Certified Public Accountants, 1978.

Prentice-Hall. *U.S. Taxation of International Operations.* Englewood Cliffs, N.J.: Prentice-Hall, 1973.

Price Waterhouse Information Guide *Corporate Taxes in 80 Countries.* New York: Price Waterhouse, 1980.

Rhoades, R. von T. and M.J. Langer. *Income Taxation of Foreign Related Transactions.* New York: Matthew Bender, 1980.

Tax Management Foreign Income Portfolios. Washington, D.C.: Bureau of National Affairs, Inc.

Watt, G.C., R.M. Hammer, and M. Burge. *Accounting for the Multinational Corporation.* Homewood, IL: Dow Jones-Irwin, 1977.

PART 4

LEGAL ASPECTS OF INTERNATIONAL BUSINESS

LEGAL ASPECTS OF
INTERNATIONAL INVESTMENT

CONTENTS

SCOPE OF SECTION	3	JOINT VENTURES IN THE EEC	12
Ramifications of Expanded Trade and Foreign Investment on the Field of Law	3	Attempt at a Definition	12
		Legal Ramifications	13
Domestic law	3	Research-and-Development Agreements	14
International law	3	Specialization Agreements	16
Supranational law	4	Manufacture and Sale Agreements	20
		Conclusions	22
MODES OF ENTRY INTO BUSINESS IN THE EEC	5		
		INDUSTRIAL PROPERTY RIGHTS AND EEC LAW	23
General	5		
Legal Principles of the Common Market	6	Patent Licensing Agreements	23
EEC Antitrust Concepts	8	Restraints on the Use of Legal Status	27
Extraterritorial Application of EEC Law	11	NOTES	37

LEGAL ASPECTS OF INTERNATIONAL INVESTMENT

Utz P. Toepke

SCOPE OF SECTION

RAMIFICATIONS OF EXPANDED TRADE AND FOREIGN INVESTMENT ON THE FIELD OF LAW. The extent of today's international business operations is a result of the political, economic, and technological interdependence of nations in our world. As they penetrate all parts of the globe, such operations meet with tariff and monetary policies, antitrust and tax regulations, investment controls, and so on. These regulations affect not only the growth of domestic economies but also the volume and channels of foreign trade and investment. Nowadays individuals or corporations engaged in international business activities are introduced to questions and problems previously not experienced in such trade. For instance, the law in its role to encourage and facilitate, as well as to regulate and referee, transnational economic activity has become more complex. It must respond not only to tremendously increased volumes of trade and ensuing problems of diverging marketing practices, distribution schemes, and financing requirements, but also to the demands of steady growth and stability for the economies of all participants in international business.

Domestic Law. As it exists in the infrastructures of national legal systems of trading nations, domestic law has always dealt with certain aspects of international business. Recognized as a field of private activity that was historically regulated by national law, the commercial operations of aliens, be they individuals or corporations, were treated and protected very much like those of domestic residents. Special protection was usually granted to foreign investment, the observance of contracts entered into with aliens, and the safety of foreign persons. The international businessman had thus grown accustomed to the fact that he had to turn to national law whenever and wherever conflicts arose and disputes had to be settled.

International Law. On the other hand, international law, although contributing toward the spirit and mode of the resolution of such disputes on the national level, was until recently not concerned with business operations. The law of nations, as it is also called, imposes duties and confers rights only upon sovereign states, its sole subjects in the classical view of international law. Brierly defines it as "the body of rules and principles of action which are binding upon civilized states in their relations with one another.''[1] Although there is no certain way to ascertain which rules and principles make up all or part of the international law, Article 38 of the Statute of the International Court of Justice has been used to describe what is comprised by this type of law.[2] It follows that the business executive could hardly resort to international law as a source for help in cases of conflict during the pursuit of business goals across borders. Even after it had to be recognized by international law as an existing entity, the corporation engaged in international business was still regarded by the International Court of Justice "as an institution created by states in a domain essentially within their domestic jurisdiction.''[3] This in turn required that whenever legal issues arose concerning the rights of states with regard to the treatment of foreign companies and shareholders, international law had to refer to the relevant rules of domestic law. In short, any aggrieved private party seeking redress in the arena of international business could not hope for relief from the rules of international law.

Recently this has changed. A new category of instruments organizing relations among sovereign states has emerged since World War II. These are regional treaties of economic and/or political cooperation and integration between independent nations of a certain geographic area. In at least one case, to wit, the Treaty of Rome establishing the European Economic Community (EEC), this has led to the establishment of a new, supranational type of law providing individuals as well as corporations engaged in international business with *locus standi* in the framework of a supranational judicial system.

Supranational Law. As created by this type of international agreement, supranational law not only confers rights upon the businessperson, it also imposes duties beyond those of the national legal system in which he or she operates. To be sure, treaties among nations have for quite some time—long before these regional cooperation treaties appeared—imposed a certain order upon the international community that often had a direct and specific impact upon private parties engaged in business. Sometimes called by some other name than *treaty,* such international agreements have determined the conditions under which the nationals of one country may export to, or do business within, the other country's territory. The difference, though, lies in the fact that these treaties of old days, usually bilateral in nature, did not create any supranational law separate from the legal system of the signatories. In effect, the law created by such treaties remained national in character, with recourse for any aggrieved private party favored under the treaty to the national courts only.

The novelty to be dealt with by anyone engaged in transnational business today is a truly international framework with an ensuing *two-tier system of laws and regulations* that may be of regional character (e.g., the EEC) or of worldwide dimension (e.g., the General Agreement on Tariffs and Trade, known as GATT). The question no longer is whether national or international law applies. Today both national and international (supranational) law may apply to transnational business activities of private parties. International business has called for, and resulted in, a new kind of international law quite different from the traditional law of nations. This type of law is not concerned with "the demarcation of land and sea boundaries . . . the formalities and courtesies of diplomatic relations . . . (or) responsibilities of a state for injuries to aliens . . .'' and so forth.[4] Supranational law addressed here goes to the very heart of international business. In the case of the EEC, it often forms the basis for the validity of certain business relations.

The other important new aspect to be reckoned with by the international businessman today is the emergence of a very large number of *international organizations.* These are usually created by the international treaties and tend to have permanent staffs who monitor and enforce the supranational laws that the treaties established. Sometimes these organizations have the power to develop further norms and enact additional regulations, and this results in a machinery creating a life of its own, as is the case with the EEC. In fact, such a legislative function, coupled with the judicial system mentioned before, represents the very essence of the supranational character of the international framework created by those treaties of economic and/or political cooperation and integration.

Although most of the existing treaties of this kind declare the attainment of supranational goals of one kind or another as an objective, many of them have yet to produce practical results. It is only the *Treaty of Rome,* which was enacted more than two decades ago and established the *European Economic Community* that has led to a truly supranational cooperation of states that have relinquished some of their sovereign powers to international organs or agencies, most notably the European Court of Justice. It is for this reason that the following remarks are focused entirely on the EEC. The importance of this grouping of states for the international business community is highlighted not only by the competence of EEC bodies to issue regulations that are binding upon business and that can be judicially enforced but also by the impressive trade statistics of the European Common Market.[5] Moreover, the Treaty of Rome is unique in the sense that it has no time limitation (Article 240) and it does not sanction withdrawal by any member state. Most importantly, however, the Treaty of Rome, through its famous four freedoms allowing for *free movement of goods, persons, services, and capital,*[6] has created a zone of free trade and investment unprecedented in the history of international business.[7] It has also provided for the most sophisticated judicial system of international nature enacted to date anywhere in the world.[8]

Before turning to a detailed discussion of a selected number of legal aspects of international investment in the Common Market, it appears necessary to review, in the context of EEC law, the choices facing the businessman who wants to do business abroad. However, the reader is spared a detailed description of both the economic alternatives of EEC investment and the EEC legal system, because this would take this section far beyond its proposed scope.

MODES OF ENTRY INTO BUSINESS IN THE EEC

GENERAL. A business operation that has decided to sell its goods abroad has a *variety of organizational structures* to choose from. First a decision has to be made about the principal way of doing business in another country, that is, whether to restrict the activity to the traditional form of pure trade—an export operation—or whether to go one step further and undertake a direct foreign investment by setting up a subsidiary company. Apart from other considerations, this decision will depend upon the attractiveness of an establishment within the desired trading area in light of existing tariff and nontariff barriers. Between these legal extremes of running a transnational business operation, that is, on a *merely contractual basis* (export sales contracts with foreign agents/distributors) *as opposed to a proprietary basis* (controlled foreign subsidiary or branch), there are also *intermediary forms* for organizing an international business enterprise. These are franchising, patent or trademark licensing, and joint ventures with a foreign partner.

In the EEC, all of these approaches are at the international businessman's disposal. EEC legislation will have a more or less serious effect on the individual operation, depending on the organizational choice in each case. Dealing with the aspects of international investment, this section will not focus on the many questions and risks facing a businessman who enters into trade arrangements in the Common Market. It must be pointed out, however, that agency agreements, franchising arrangements, and, most importantly, all dealership contracts or networks of authorized distributors, can run serious risks of violating the antitrust provisions of the Treaty of Rome. No trade contract extending to the territory of the EEC ought to be signed by a private businessman in a nonmember state country without prior consultation with a legal adviser expert in the laws and regulations of the Common Market. The *financial risk of* attracting a fine for intentional or negligent *violation of EEC law* has become greater over the years, to the extent that today no responsible businessman can afford such violation, either from an ethical or a financial point of view.[9]

Instead of providing a broad description of all legal aspects of business investment (as opposed to capital investment) in the EEC, ranging from environmental requirements, regional planning considerations, transport regulations, and customs regulations to aspects of competition policy, the following discussion will concentrate on those questions and problems that have occurred in cases previously decided in the EEC in relation to the modes of entry into business that involve investments. More specifically, it will deal with those *areas of international investment in the EEC that,* by way of decisions of the European Court of Justice and the EEC Commission, *have proven to be stumbling grounds* for businessmen from anywhere: the *utilization of industrial property rights* such as patents, trademarks, or copyrights in the Common Market, and the establishment of an economic base in the EEC through a *joint-venture operation.* Both areas have shown a *high degree of legal vulnerability* under the provisions of the Treaty of Rome. The more-traditional forms of international investment such as the creation of a foreign subsidiary or a merger with, or takeover of, an existing company in the EEC will result only in incidental effects of Community law. For the purpose of this section, the legal aspects of such investments can be disregarded. However, one important proviso must be made: If a *merger* were to *result in the abuse of a dominant position* of a particular company in the EEC, the consequences would be severe and could certainly not be neglected by any businessman, as the EEC Commission might insist on a divestiture of all assets taken over by a company in such a merger. This will be discussed later.

Prior to entering into a detailed discussion of substantive issues of EEC law in relation to joint ventures and the use of industrial property rights, it is necessary for the reader to understand some of the basic principles of this law as well as the concept of EEC competition rules. The remaining comments in this section are therefore devoted to these subjects.

LEGAL PRINCIPLES OF THE COMMON MARKET. The European Economic Community presents itself to the international businessman as one large single market of approximately 265 million consumers in which goods and services *can* move freely despite the remaining borders among the ten member-state countries. To the international lawyer the Community appears as one coherent legal system in which goods and services *must* move freely. This, in short, symbolizes the legal significance of the historic attempt, in 1957, undertaken by six politically independent countries of rather diverse economic structures and cultural traditions, to forge a common market among themselves. Whether or not the attempt has been successful is periodically questioned, and the answer will probably depend on the questioner's personal attitude toward the desirability of the total integration of the member-state economies. Notwithstanding personal opinions, it is an indisputable fact of today's political and economic environment in Western Europe that the legal aspects of the *approximation of previously separate economies* are present, visible and, in the integration sense, successful. Nobody involved in business operations in any of the EEC member states can ignore the existence of Community law as created by the Treaty of Rome and secondary legislation by the Council or the Commission. One of the most striking examples of Community law is the abolishment of all customs duties on trade among member states and the establishment of a common tariff on all imports into the Community from third countries. The idea of a *customs union* is, in fact, at the very heart of the Treaty of Rome, as evidenced by its famous Article 3, which describes the activities of the Community.[10]

The variety of EEC laws and regulations affecting business in Europe is such that they cannot be explained meaningfully here. It must suffice to impress upon the reader that the overriding goal and central objective of the EEC is *economic integration*. Consequently any attempt by a businessman to hamper the free flow of trade through adoption of measures that are counterproductive to the idea of a single market can be expected to run afoul of the Community legal system. Balkanization of the Common Market is perhaps the clearest form of business practice that would lead to troubles with the EEC institutions commissioned with the enforcement of Community law. It is the *partitioning of markets* through reerection of borders in the EEC by private action that creates obstacles to trade of any kind, for instance through contractual export prohibitions in dealership agreements or pricing schemes that provide for disincentives to sell abroad. Such action would violate the spirit underlying the EEC; it would turn back the clocks of Europe. No international business operation can expect to be permitted to do this with impunity. A new form of legal-political consciousness has emanated from the existence of the Community that makes this kind of business behavior the nearest equivalent in Europe to what is known in the United States as a *per se* violation of the law. That it will be severely punished can be seen from a long and consistent line of decisions of both the EEC Commission and the Court of Justice.[11]

Another general aspect of the new reality created by the Common Market that has to be reckoned with by the international business community is the existence of *Community institutions*. The Treaty of Rome established a complex constitutional framework of legislative, executive/administrative, and judicial powers that is distinct from the parallel system remaining in the member states. Very often the international businessman and his counsel will have to deal with Common Market officials rather than national representatives, although their business activity might be primarily in one EEC country. The center of attention is almost always Brussels, the seat of the EEC Commission. Although there are established procedures for dealing with the Commission in certain fields and for certain purposes,[12] the importance and effectiveness of inofficial contacts with the right people in the EEC establishment in Brussels should not be underestimated.[13]

EEC ANTITRUST CONCEPTS. Rules of competition are usually the centerpiece of any legal system with respect to its effects on the business world. The EEC is no exception. In its *Article 3,* already referred to, the *Treaty of Rome* calls for the *institution of a system ensuring that competition* in the Common Market *is not distorted.* This demand is the necessary corollary to the creation by the treaty of a customs union and the resulting single market. *Articles 85–89* implement this demand in that, as stated by the Court of Justice, they "put into operation the provisions of Article 3".[14] Accordingly, business conduct and the EEC provisions most directly concerned with it, namely Articles 85 and 86, must be viewed in light of the general principles of the Treaty of Rome. The principles are expressed in the treaty's preamble relating to "the removal of existing obstacles" and the guarantee of "fair competition," both of which are necessary for the realization of a single market.[15] This wider interpretation, through application of the competition rules by the Commission or the Court of Justice, will lead to severe consequences in all cases of attempted reerection of obstacles to intra-Community trade.

Articles 85 and 86, Treaty of Rome, form the backbone of these competition rules. They have been compared with Sections 1 and 2, Sherman Act, in the United States, and, despite obvious disparities in implementation, there is a surprising degree of similarity of substantive areas covered by both sets of rules.[16]

Article 85 relates to conduct of at least two independent enterprises. It outlaws all agreements or concerted practices the object or effect of which is to prevent, restrict, or distort competition within the Common Market. An added jurisdictional prerequisite is the requirement that the agreement or concerted practice "may affect trade between Member States." Whether or not such an effect on interstate commerce is sizable will not provide a defense as long as one of the enterprises involved is of "sufficient importance for its behavior to be, in principle, *capable* of affecting trade."[17] On the other hand, an agreement between two companies of two separate member states will not be caught by Article 85 regardless of its content, even if absolute territorial protection is stipulated by the parties, if the effects of the agreement on competition are insignificant owing to the weak position of the parties on the relevant market.[18] No relevance can be attached to the fact that a *horizontal agreement* might be involved in one case and a *vertical agreement* in another. The Court of Justice held in *Italy* v. *EEC Council*[19] that Article 85 does not distinguish between one kind of agreement or the other. The prohibition in Article 85 can catch any restriction of competition resulting from an agreement, whether it be concluded at the same economic level (horizontal) or at different levels (vertical; i.e., between manufacturer and distributor).

Article 86, in contrast, regulates the conduct of a single company in the Community, for all practical purposes. The situation of shared dominance among various companies, which is also covered by Article 86, will not be discussed here. For Article 86 to apply, dominance of the accused firm must first be established, and a relevant market must be defined. Both terms embrace complex legal concepts that have been at the heart of protracted litigation in the EEC. For purposes of this discussion it must suffice to caution the reader to devote specific attention to these two criteria when the application of Article 86 is in question.

Generally speaking, the presence of a *dominant position* in a given case derives from a combination of several factors that, taken separately, are not necessarily determinative. The market share of the company involved can be taken as sufficient proof of dominance only when it reaches 65 percent or more; below this margin other additional indicia of control over the market are required, such as relative strength and number of competitors, technological superiority, integrated marketing and service organizations, and research and development power.[20] Dominance, therefore, is a concept of relativity, its threshold being considerably lower than that of monopoly power in U.S. antitrust law. It might be added that profitability is not a decisive factor. In *United Brands* v. *Commission* the Court held that "an undertaking's economic strength is not measured by its profitability."[21] Even a loss for a certain time is not incompatible with a dominant position, according to the Court's language. It was added, as a consolation perhaps, that the reverse is also true, namely that "large profits may be compatible with a situation where there is effective competition,"[22] that is, no dominant position exists. In summary, then, it may be said that a company's overall economic strength and its ability for independent action on the market, both with respect to its actual and potential competitors, are determinative in the evaluation of whether or not the company possesses a dominant position.

Defining the *relevant market* has proven to be much less of a problem for the EEC Commission pressing its cases before the Court in Luxembourg. Usually the justices have agreed to a very narrow definition, both from the standpoint of the products involved and from a geographic viewpoint. In *General Motors* v. *EEC Commission,* the approval procedure with respect to legally required road-safety inspections for motor cars imported into Belgium, which was delegated by the state to the manufacturer for each make of car, was held to be the relevant market.[23] The result was that GM Belgium possessed a dominant position with regard to the inspections carried out by them on GM cars, notwithstanding that this was a legal monopoly entrusted upon them by Belgian law. In another case, *Hugin* v. *EEC Commission,* a manufacturer of cash registers was held to possess a dominant position on the market for his own spare parts, produced by no one but himself. The supply of spare parts for Hugin machines was seen as constituting a specific relevant market in light of the existence of independent enterprises specializing in the maintenance and repair of cash registers.[24] Conversely, the definition of the relevant market has to be broadened to include products with a sufficient degree of substitutability with the product under consideration.[25] Also, potential competition has to be taken into account when ease of entry of other manufacturers into the market is a distinct possibility, for instance by way of making simple adjustments to their manufacturing processes.[26]

Another prerequisite for the application of Article 86 is the requirement that the conduct complained of *may affect trade between member states*. It is the same jurisdictional requirement already addressed in the context of Article 85, and the same wide-ranging interpretation of the meaning of this phrase applies here. Transferred into the realm of single-company conduct, instead of joint action between two or more companies, this interpretation leads to the conclusion that the requirement is satisfied "when an undertaking in a dominant position within the Common Market abusively exploits its position in such a way that a competitor in the Common Market is likely to be eliminated";[27] then it does not matter, said the Court of Justice, "whether the conduct relates to the latter's exports or its trade within the Common Market, once it has been established that this elimination will have repercussions on the competitive structure within the Common Market."[28]

Finally, for Article 86 to apply, it is necessary to prove that there has been an *abuse* of the dominant position previously established. As a first observation it must be stated that the law itself does not provide any definition of the term *abuse,* as is also the case with the other requirements for Article 86 application discussed above.

The treaty provision does, however, provide by way of example four cases in which an abuse can be found to exist. Two of them deal with pricing methods (unfair pricing and price discrimination) and the other two with specified business practices prejudicing consumers (tying and marketing restrictions). This catalog of examples is not exhaustive. It resembles the illustrations given in Article 85 for illegal agreements distorting competition. This leads to the second observation, namely that *Articles 85 and 86 are interchangeable* when the situation would allow application of either provision. In other words, if the tests of both articles are satisfied, proceedings may be initiated against a company based on Article 85, Article 86, or both.[29] The observation is important not so much because it might be easier for the Commission to adduce the necessary evidence in one case as opposed to the other, but because of the possibility to apply for an exemption from the prohibition of Article 85 but not Article 86.

It was established in the *Continental Can* case[30] that the word *abuse* in Article 86 refers not only to actions of enterprises that have a direct effect on the market as being detrimental to production or distribution, to purchasers or consumers such as those described in Article 86, but also applies to changes in the structure of a particular enterprise that result in a serious alteration of competition in a substantial part of the Common Market. This holding opened the *application of Article 86 to mergers* between two competing enterprises. In view of the fact that the Commission proposal for a merger-control directive in the EEC is still in the negotiating phase with the member countries, the Court's language in *Continental Can* carries special weight.

Recently, in its decision of the *Hoffmann-LaRoche* case,[31] the Court has expanded on this thought of structural effects and has widened the *concept of abuse*. Drawing on earlier precedents describing Article 86, as well as Article 85, as an implementation of the general principles of the treaty laid down in Articles 2 and 3, Article 3(f) in particular, the Court declared that Article 86 "covers not only abuse which may directly prejudice consumers but also abuse which indirectly prejudices them by impairing the effective competitive structure as envisaged by Article 3(f) of the Treaty."[32] Therefore, abuse presents itself as an *objective concept.*[33] Abuse does not require intent, although this consideration will become decisive with respect to the imposition of fines (Article 15(2), Regulation 17/62). As an objective concept, abuse can manifest itself in business conduct that simply influences the structure of a market "where, as a result of the very presence of the undertaking in question, the degree of competition is weakened and which . . . has the effect of hindering the maintenance of the degree of competition still existing in the market or the growth of that competition."[34] This is an extremely broad concept. Indeed, it appears capable of embracing nearly all conceivable business conduct once two conditions are met: first, the existence of a dominant position, and second, as held in the *Hoffman-LaRoche* Case, the influence on the market by way of "*any* further weakening of the structure of competition."[35]

Thus it is no surprise that the Court rejected the suggestion that an abuse implies that the use of the economic power bestowed by a dominant position is the means whereby the abuse must have been committed.[36] In other words, *no requirement of causality between the dominant position and the abuse* can be construed. The suggestion would have hardly suited the concept of objectivity now read into the term *abuse.* Puzzling, however, is the relationship of this new interpretation with the Court's own statements of exactly one year earlier in the *United Brands* case. Here the Court had expressly acknowledged a dominant company's right to protect its own commercial interest and to fight back if attacked.[37] The Court seemed to have drawn the line in this earlier judgment based on the *principle of proportionality,* that is, the counterattack of the dominant firm was not objectionable as long as that attack was proportionate to the threat emanating from the original onslaught by the smaller company, considering the economic strength of both companies. The *Hoffman-LaRoche* decision casts doubt on the continuing validity of this principle. If it is just the influence on the structure of the market in terms of "the effect of hindering the maintenance of the degree of competition still existing in the market or the growth of that competition" that decides whether a specific business conduct is abusive, then the safe margin for action by a dominant firm might well be reduced to zero, or close to it, notwithstanding the principle of proportionality. This seems hard to believe, but only future case law in the EEC will tell. In any event, dominant firms are now on notice that they cannot simply rely on previous decisions taken by the Commission or the Court. In *Hoffman-LaRoche,* a Commission decision was cited by the company in defense of one of its contract clauses that had been attacked by the Commission as abusive. The Court, pointing to the lack of dominance of the companies involved in the earlier case, rejected the argument and held that "an undertaking in a dominant position cannot reasonably believe that a negative clearance issued in such circumstances would serve as a precedent for justifying its own behaviour in the context of Article 86."[38] Case distinguished on dominance, one might say, and add, as a summary, that almost anything could constitute an abuse, no matter what previous case law says.

EXTRATERRITORIAL APPLICATION OF EEC LAW.   The extraterritorial application of EEC law was one of the major subjects of earlier decisions where U.S. or other foreign-based corporations were the defendants.[39] This is no longer the case. In the *United Brands* case the dispute regarding the administrative authority of the Commission or the jurisdiction of the Court with respect to enterprises domiciled outside the Community such as the defendant in this case did not even come up. Only a few years earlier, most notably in *Continental Can* v. *Commission,* this dispute had aroused elaborate argument by counsel involving the general principles of international law, which supposedly prevented the Commission from investigating an American company directly, and which were said to deny the Court of Justice jurisdiction to impose sanctions on such a company. This is all over now. In the *Continental Can* case the Court expressed unequivocally that the fact that a company "does not have its seat in the territory of one of the Member States is not sufficient to remove this enterprise from the application of Community law."[40]

In all cases, the non-EEC companies had acted within the Common Market through a *subsidiary established in one of the member states.* The Court rejected the argument commonly advanced by the foreign corporation that the separate legal personality of the subsidiary should shield the parent company from EEC action. The Court's reasoning applied the facts of real life in that it turned on the possibility that the subsidiary's conduct can usually be imputed to the parent company. This, the Court said, "applies particularly where the subsidiary does not determine its market conduct autonomously but in the main follows the instructions of the parent company."[41] In the *Commercial Solvents* case, this appraisal of parent-subsidiary relationships was carried one step further. The Court of Justice abandoned the American-born "effects theory,"[42] which by some analyses was underlying the

Court's thinking in previous holdings of extraterritorial application of EEC law, and which might or might not have been expressed in the Court's language in the *Continental Can* case, quoted above. The Court substituted its own analysis of international corporate affiliations for the American effects theory. In the *Commercial Solvents* case, the Court held alien parent companies of EEC subsidiaries that exercise control by virtue of a majority of stock to form a *single economic unit* with their subsidiary. Consequently, there is only one company in the economic sense to deal with for purposes of antitrust enforcement, be it a case of Article 85 application as in *ICI* and *Geigy*,[43] or the enforcement of Article 86 as in *Continental Can* and *Commercial Solvents*.[44] Therefore, the Commission can choose in a situation of this kind whether to bring a case against the EEC-based subsidiary or the foreign parent company, or against both. They are both responsible, and consequently all necessary *service of formal documents* during an investigation against either of them can be effected by service upon the other.[45]

JOINT VENTURES IN THE EEC

ATTEMPT AT A DEFINITION.   For the non-EEC-based company with international business activities, one of the possible *modes of entry* into the Common Market is to seek the cooperation of a company already established there. For EEC-based companies, the coordination of interests with another company of a member state where they are not yet represented can also constitute a viable alternative to other ways of establishing an economic base in new markets. This cooperation, or pooling of interests, commonly referred to as joint venture, can take various legal forms. The reality of business life shows considerably more inventiveness than can be described within the scope of a section such as this. Therefore, it is easier to start off by first excluding those modes of entry that will usually not be considered as constituting joint ventures, such as direct foreign investment through creation of a new company without a partner, acquisition of an existing company through takeover or merger, and any kind of dealership arrangement.

In its purest form, a *joint venture* presents itself as the *creation of a jointly owned subsidiary* by two or more legally and economically independent enterprises, where the subsidiary itself constitutes a genuine economic entity. The joint venture can be a national or an international one, the latter being present if the participants come from different countries. This is the type with which EEC law concerns itself.[46] In this form, a joint venture has both the appearance and effect of a partial loss of identity of the participating companies; it is a *quasi-merger*. The benefits to be derived from this kind of cooperation between formerly independent companies from a business viewpoint are obvious. The combined capital, assets, and know-how of two companies may facilitate entry into new markets and thereby enhance competition; it may create efficiencies or new productive capacity not achievable by the participants separately. The perils resulting from joint ventures from the viewpoint of competition policy are equally obvious. Any kind of cooperation or joint action among formerly independent companies active in the same product markets is inherently dangerous to competition as it eliminates actual or potential contest between the companies involved.

Joint venture arrangements with a lesser degree of fusion exist where the parties involved do not depend on the creation and control of a separate company for the pursuit of their joint interest but simply execute *agreements* between themselves. These agreements can range in complexity from the simple pooling of certain functions such as buying or selling, to extremely sophisticated constructions of mutual responsibilities of the participants, such as in the case of research-and-development agreements.

LEGAL RAMIFICATIONS.   The legal ramifications of joint ventures under EEC antitrust law correspond to the character of cooperation between the joint venturers and vacillate in the gravitational field of rules pertaining to mergers on the one hand and restrictive agreements on the other. Article 86, Treaty of Rome, would apply in the first case and Article 85 in the second. In complex cases, though, *both Article 85 and 86 may be applicable.* There is no distinction of substance between a situation in which the two companies forming a joint venture hold shares in a separately incorporated economic entity and the case in which they provide for the unified, joint, and equal control of all their activities relating to the joint venture in a distinct agreement, including planning, financing, research, development, construction or manufacturing, and sale. As a rule of thumb, however, it may be permissible to delineate the application of Articles 85 and 86 to joint ventures as follows: Where the parent companies of a pure joint-venture subsidiary transfer all their assets to the joint venture and become themselves no more than holding companies, without continuing as competitors to each other or the joint venture, albeit maintaining some other remaining business activity, the situation will be *treated as a merger,* and only *Article 86* ought to be considered.[47]

The consequences are known since the Court's judgment in the *Continental Can* case. Article 86, correctly interpreted in light of Article 3(f), Treaty of Rome, relates to practices harmful to consumers, including those that affect the structure of actual competition. Thus the strengthening of the position held by one enterprise that is already in a dominant position can be an abuse regardless of the methods or means used to attain it. A merger, consequently, is subject to the prohibition of Article 86 when the degree of dominance achieved through it substantially hampers competition. This is the case when virtually all competition is eliminated, and also when competition is affected to the extent that any remaining competitors can no longer provide a sufficient counterbalance so that the *consumers' freedom of action* on the dominated market is *seriously jeopardized.*[48]

A joint-venture case where this situation would have occurred had the parties been allowed to go through with the joint venture is described in the Commission decision of October 1978 regarding the Wasag/ICI cooperation with respect to black-powder in the *WANO* case.[49] However, the Commission reviewed the case under Article 85 as well, based on the specific factual circumstances in the situation. The joint-venture subsidiary, WANO Schwarzpulver GmbH, already existed before the reallocation of its stock was arranged by agreement between its parent company, Wasag A.G., and ICI Ltd. This agreement and others related to it prompted the Commission to examine the case mainly under the rules pertaining to restrictive agreements.

Article 85(1) will apply and prevent a joint venture, unless an exemption can be granted under Article 85(3), where the formation of a joint venture creates an independent company, but the *parent companies,* which are the partners in the joint venture, *continue to be competitors* on the relevant markets. This was the case in *De Laval/Stork.*[50] Article 85(1) will apply, as well, in all other cases where the joint venture takes the form of an agreement, no matter of what type. In summary, it can be said that the application of EEC antitrust law to joint ventures does not turn on the legal formalities chosen by the companies involved so much as on the economic realities of the particular business situation.[51] It may be added that the common concern in the legal sense regarding all joint ventures is the question whether the cooperation between the participants is likely to restrict or lessen competition. If it does, the question then becomes whether there are counterbalancing advantages attached to it that allow *exemption* of the agreement from the prohibition of Article 85(1) under paragraph 3 of this article.

The following comments will describe three actual cases of joint ventures, based on recent Commission decisions. Each one of these cases is representative for a specific category of joint venture. However, to obtain a complete picture of EEC treatment of joint ventures, the reader would have to resort to the full body of case law now existing in the Community.

RESEARCH-AND-DEVELOPMENT AGREEMENTS.   On occasion, companies engaged in specialized research may face situations where the continuation of a particular project, or the original embarkation on a totally new field of research, is not economically feasible. Lack of special skills, high risks of success and financial burdens may be the reasons why a company cannot afford to undertake some *specified research* on its own. Nevertheless, it would be desirable, or even necessary, for the economic success of the company as well as the benefit of its customers to go through with the research. EEC law provides for a vehicle to allow for a joint effort where the company finds another one that is willing and capable to complement the research activity by joining in its tasks and sharing in its costs. Article 85(3) permits exemption of agreements between companies otherwise prohibited by paragraph 1 of the same article that are related to "promoting technical or economic progress, while allowing consumers a fair share of the resulting benefit."[52] The EEC Commission has sole authority to grant such exemptions (Article 9(1), Regulation 17/62).

A recent example of representative importance for situations of the type described here is the *Beecham/Parke, Davis* decision of 1979,[53] involving a joint research-and-development agreement. Two multinational companies of considerable size, both engaged in the research, production, and marketing of a wide range of pharmaceutical products, entered into an agreement with the aim of *creating a new type of product* intended for the prophylactic treatment of heart disease caused by problems of blood circulation. Neither Beecham Group Ltd. of England nor Parke, Davis and Company (a subsidiary of Warner Lambert) of Michigan, had a product with therapeutic effects such as these available. Prior to their agreement, both parties had independently made preliminary investigations in the field of research pertaining to the development and manufacture of the desired drug. However, this individual research had yielded few positive results, and considering the risk factors involved, they both terminated their work in this field. It was not until 1973, when they agreed on a framework of cooperation that met the financial and technological criteria that made the risk factors acceptable, that both firms restarted their work. They now divided the necessary research in such a way that each company had its own range of compounds for evaluation in separately conducted laboratory tests, based on joint planning and with exchange of results. This avoided unnecessary overlap and duplication of cost.

Following this stage, referred to in the joint-venture agreement as the Project, the parties were to enter a second stage, called the Development Programme. The aim of the Project was to identify promising candidate substances for the new drug and to complete the required tests. By 1978 the parties had completed this *research stage* and moved on to the Development Programme. This stage involves extensive pharmacological and clinical tests and is expected to last a further 5–10 years. It will be superseded by the *marketing stage,* envisaged by the agreement with a view to commercial exploitation of the joint effort. The agreement includes a royalty-free *cross-licensing* arrangement, with power to sublicense, for patents and know-how resulting from the research and test activities. Once in the marketing stage, the parties are also obliged, for a period of 10 years from the date of first marketing of the drug by either party, to *exchange information of improvements* related to the product.

The parties notified their agreement to the Commission in January 1974, shortly after inception of the initial stage of the cooperation, as the United Kingdom had at that time joined the EEC. Five years later, the Commission granted an exemption for 10 years from the date of the decision to the joint research-and-development agreement of both parties. It was first determined that the *agreement* is *caught by Article 85(1)* as Beecham and Parke, Davis are competitors[54] and because the close collaboration between them at every stage of the agreement results in the fact that neither party can obtain a competitive advantage over the other at any point in the innovative cycle or during the phase of joint commercial exploitation. Hence, competition is restricted.[55] The new drug will be manufactured by the same process and under the same patents, assuming a successful outcome to the common research, and will then be marketed throughout the EEC by the parties or their subsidiaries or licensees. It will therefore by the subject of trade between member states. Consequently, the restrictions imposed upon the parties by the agreement during all phases will affect trade between member states.[56]

Nevertheless, the Commission saw *justification* under Article 85(3), *to exempt* the parties' joint-venture agreement, "since its aim is to create a novel therapeutic effect in a pharmaceutical sector recognized as one in which the required tests are especially complex. The time and cost involved in this research are such that consumers have much greater chance of obtaining an effective product if the research is done jointly by Beecham and Parke, Davis."[57] In other words, the conclusive element seems to have been the fact that the jointly researched and developed *drug will be different from currently known medicines,* coupled with the fact that the required investigations and tests are unusually long and costly.[58] From a purely legal viewpoint, the justification for the Commission's positive decision in this case is to be seen in the fact that the new drug, if found and successfully produced, will contribute to *promoting technical progress* (Article 85(3) Rome Treaty). The drug "would lead to the effective prevention or treatment of the impairment of blood circulation in certain sufferers for whom there is presently no known marketed compound having such effects."[59] *Consumers will see quicker and better results* in the form of such a new product, as the reasonable likelihood of success is much greater in case of this joint endeavor of Beecham and Parke, Davis than in the case of independent research. The exemption was granted for a period of 10 years to allow the Commission a review of the situation within a reasonable term.

The *decision* thus clearly *distinguishes* the *Beecham/Parke, Davis* agreement from those types of agreements relating to joint implementation of research work that are addressed in the *Commission Notice of 1968.*[60] Those agreements covering the joint research up to the stage of industrial application were held not to affect competition.

In the case at hand, there is to be close collaboration between the parties during all stages, restricting competition. The approval that was nevertheless given to the agreement will serve as a valuable example in guiding future applicants who desire to conclude a joint research-and-development contract.

The decision has some added value, too. In its original form, the agreement between Beecham and Parke, Davis contained some *overly restrictive clauses* that were not indispensable to the attainment of its objectives. The parties were to pay each other *royalties* for all cross-licenses. The Commission felt that in this case these provisions would have extended the scope of the cooperation from the desirable joint research and development into the area of marketing of the products independently manufactured by each partner. This was unacceptable, as the royalty payments appeared to be intended not as equal contribution to joint research expenditure but rather to ensure *profit sharing* among the parties. Such an arrangement is likely to create a considerable disincentive for the parties to compete with one another, particularly in areas of difficult marketing, that is, where no production facilities or sales forces are available. Profit sharing through royalty payments would present a convenient alternative to competition in such situations. The Commission took the position that royalty payments would seem reasonable only "if the results of the common research can, particularly for technical reasons, only, or mainly, be used by one of the parties."[61] Then, the Commission said, the other party could participate in the benefits obtained from marketing the jointly developed product by way of royalty payments.

A final consideration not to be overlooked in the analysis of any research-and-development agreement is the partners' *freedom of action* at the conclusion of the development stage. The Commission, in the *Beecham/Parke, Davis* case, allowed the obligatory exchange of information on improvements to the product for 10 years. But it attached great importance to the fact "that both parties remain completely free to manufacture and market the product wherever, in whatever quantities and under whatever conditions, trademarks and prices they individually consider appropriate."[62] The Commission emphasized strongly that *joint research can only be approved where the results can be used freely by the parties* without any territorial or other restrictions on production or marketing within the EEC. This warning is clearly intended to counsel future candidates for joint ventures in this field.

SPECIALIZATION AGREEMENTS.   For a long time, it has been the policy of the EEC Commission to encourage and support cooperation of small and medium-sized companies where such cooperation leads to benefits for the companies involved, the consumers, and the economies in the Common Market at large. Recognizing the inherent advantages of agreements for the specialization of production, as an example, the EEC authorities have accepted that companies can, in general, operate on a more rational basis and offer their products at more-favorable prices when they specialize in the manufacture of certain products. The improvements to be gained from specialization agreements, both in the production and distribution of goods, have led the EEC Council to authorize the Commission to adopt a regulation exempting certain categories of agreements of this kind from the prohibition of Article 85(1).[63] The result was Regulation 2779/72,[64] which determined what restrictions on competition may be included in a specialization agreement. In general, the regulation allows companies to *limit* their *production contractually* and enter into mutual exclusivity with the other contract party with respect to the products in question. In addition, *mutual supply arrangements* on an exclusive basis are allowed, and Article

2, Regulation 2779/72, permits a company to grant *exclusive distribution rights* to its partner in a specialization agreement for the products that are the subject of specialization.

Resolved to ensure that competition is not eliminated in respect to a substantial part of the goods in question—a Treaty of Rome requirement laid down by Article 85(3)—the Commission established certain *limits in size for companies privileged* under this regulation. Article 3, Regulation 2779/72, excludes agreements that have as their object products that represent more than 15 percent of the market for all such products in a substantial part of the Common Market.[65] Also, where the aggregate annual revenue of the participating parties to the specialization agreement exceeds 300 million units of account,[66] the exemption provided by Article 1, Regulation 2779/72, does not apply. However, this does not mean that *large companies* are totally deprived of the benefits of specialization under EEC antitrust law. They do have the opportunity to apply for an *individual exemption* pursuant to Article 85(3), and the Commission may well decide positively if the circumstances of the situation warrant this.

A case in point is the decision of December 1975 relating to the *Bayer/Gist-Brocades* agreement with respect to a long-term specialization in the area of penicillin production.[67] Two large European drug manufacturers, Bayer A.G. of Germany and Gist-Brocades N.V. of the Netherlands, concluded a series of agreements between May 1969 and May 1971. During the late 1960s, Bayer and Gist-Brocades were confronted with an expansion of the penicillin business. Both companies at that time were producing raw penicillin and an intermediate product called 6-aminopenicillanic acid (6-APA) in their own plants. They were faced with the choice of either increasing production or entering into long-term supply contracts with outside sources. In particular Bayer had to decide whether to cover its increased requirements for raw penicillin by a heavy investment in new production facilities or by finding a reliable source of supply. In 1969 the two companies concluded two *contracts for mutual supply* of raw penicillin and 6-APA, respectively. Bayer declared not to expand its raw penicillin plant but to purchase its increased requirements from Gist-Brocades, who in turn agreed to enlarge their raw-penicillin capacity, partially with the financial help of Bayer, who were to provide Gist-Brocades with long-term loans totaling DM25.6 million. Gist-Brocades, on the other hand, agreed to abstain from expanding their 6-APA production facilities and to obtain any additional volumes required from Bayer, who would increase their capacity accordingly and would receive financial assistance from Gist-Brocades for doing so, totaling DM14.9 million.

The agreements contained a number of detailed obligations for both parties related to the purchase and supply of the products in question, including sections on quality control and the pricing of raw penicillin or 6-APA to be delivered to the other partner. Through a *licensing agreement* concluded at the same time, Gist-Brocades granted Bayer a nonexclusive, nontransferable license for its chemical process to manufacture 6-APA. Up to that time, Bayer had been using a biological process. The license was royalty-free as long as Bayer continued to supply Gist-Brocades with 6-APA. Both firms undertook to inform each other of any improvements in the manufacturing process for raw penicillin or 6-APA, respectively, and to grant each other licenses in respect of such improvements. They also agreed that neither would contest the validity of existing or future industrial property rights of the other party.

In 1971 these supply contracts and licensing agreements were supplemented by another agreement, called the basic agreement. This accord led both firms into a pure joint venture in the sense described above.[68] The 1971 agreement not only spelled out the details of mutual financing of new production plants or extensions to existing ones for raw penicillin in the case of Gist-Brocades and for 6-APA in the case of Bayer, but it also provided for the transfer of these plants to two *jointly owned subsidiaries*. The creation of a joint cooperation committee for the coordination of all related activities, including the exchange of information and research results, was also part of the agreement. Each company was to take a 50 percent share in the two subsidiaries and to appoint an equal number of directors. However, both companies retained complete autonomy regarding the conduct of their research-and-development programs, with the proviso that Gist-Brocades was to concentrate on raw penicillin and Bayer on 6-APA and results would be exchanged.

When the EEC Commission started to investigate this case on its own initiative in December 1974, pursuant to Article 3, Regulation 17/62,[69] the results of the various agreements between the two companies had started to affect the penicillin market. Gist-Brocades, through its plant extensions, had become one of the world's largest, if not the largest manufacturer of raw penicillin, with 16 percent of total world production. Bayer, too, had become one of the leading manufacturers in the world for 6-APA, its portion of the specialization agreement with Gist-Brocades. Its 6-APA production at that time accounted for an estimated 15 percent of world production. Moreover, the Commission found that the highest concentration of production for both raw penicillin and 6-APA was located in the Common Market, with approximately 60 percent of worldwide output manufactured there. Under these circumstances, and based on the terms of the agreements outlined above, the Commission had no difficulty finding that the *specialization agreed upon* by the two chemical giants *violated Article 85(1)*, Treaty of Rome. In each giving up part of its business in favor of the other, Bayer and Gist-Brocades were operating a specialization arrangement (supported by long-term supply contracts and joint-investment agreements) that was based, in effect, on an *agreement not to compete*. Both companies were sufficiently large and experienced, in the Commission's view, to be able independently to expand their production plants or set up new plants in order to meet rising demand. There was also no doubt that the agreements for reciprocal long-term supply between the two firms were capable of affecting trade between EEC member states, as the two parties were from different Common Market countries, and the products covered by the agreements are in fact dealt with in EEC trade.

However, in May 1975, after the Commission had opened its investigation, the companies filed a formal notification of their agreements with the Commission in accordance with Article 4, Regulation 17/62, asking for an exemption under Article 85(3), Treaty of Rome.[70] *After certain changes* in their relationship *were made* and amendments to the agreements implemented, Bayer and Gist-Brocades were granted an *exemption* by the EEC Commission. The most important of these changes involves the joint venture between the parties. The *Commission opposed the creation of the* two production *subsidiaries* for raw penicillin and 6-APA, as it would have deprived the parties of the opportunity of separate action on the market. The formation of these joint subsidiaries would have led to bringing the production of a major portion of the total world output of raw penicillin and 6-APA under joint control. Since each partner was to be equally represented in the management of the two subsidiaries, they both would have had the chance to veto any operational or investment decision with regard to either subsidiary. "The result would inevitably have been that output would have been determined by joined agreement," said the Commission.[71] Neither company could have increased, without the other's approval, the quantities of raw penicillin or 6-APA available for resale to third parties and hence to increase competition on the market for these products.

After the Commission had objected to the formation of these joint subsidiaries as a means of *joint control of production and investment* (Article 85(1) (b), Treaty of Rome), Bayer and Gist-Brocades agreed to terminate the basic agreement relating to the joint venture. This cleared the way for the Commission's examination of the applicability of Article 85(3) and eventually secured the exemption granted to the remaining arrangement of specialization between the parties. Both companies are now free to make their own decision about the utilization or expansion of that part of their production capacity in the field covered by the agreements that is not required to meet their supply commitments. There were *other changes,* as well, that had to be made to the agreements before the Commission was able to grant an exemption. For one thing, the agreements relating to the reciprocal supply with raw penicillin or 6-APA had to be written in a way to make it clear that there are *no exclusive-supply conditions* among the parties' obligations. If additional supplies are required over and above the contract quantities, each party remains free to obtain its needs on the open market. Another change insisted upon by the Commission was the *removal of the no-challenge clause* in the licensing agreement. This clause was held to be unnecessarily restrictive and not indispensable to the attainment of the stated objectives of the specialization arrangement.

The *justification for the exemption* in this case was seen in the fact that the specialization agreement between the parties, after excluding the joint subsidiaries from the collaboration, contributes to the *improvement of production* (Article 85(3), Rome Treaty).[72] The Commission pointed out that the question of a contribution to economic progress can only arise in exceptional cases, where the free play of competition is unable to produce the best result economically speaking. In the circumstances at hand, the Commission added, it could not be assumed, without further facts, that the companies involved could not have undertaken the necessary expansion of their respective capacities independently to achieve the required rationalization of production. However, account had to be taken of Bayer's limited abilities to expand its raw penicillin plants economically to meet its increased requirements, according to the Commission. Bayer's raw penicillin production was apparently not up to the latest technical standards; its quality and yield were very low. Bayer, therefore, had to obtain the assistance of a firm experienced in raw-penicillin fermentation techniques. Gist-Brocades was in a position to provide that assistance. For technical reasons, though, it was not as economical to improve and expand Bayer's existing manufacturing facilities as to finance jointly an expansion of Gist-Brocades' raw-penicillin capacity. This arrangement, of course, made it also possible for Bayer to change from the production of raw penicillin to the production of 6-APA in larger quantities and under modernized conditions.

In summary, both partners to the specialization agreement achieved better economies of scale under improved manufacturing conditions. The results were already visible when the Commission investigated the case. The average prices for raw penicillin and 6-APA were falling, as a comparison of 1974 prices with those of 1970 showed. Another positive outcome of the agreements was the fact that Gist-Brocades, whose sales to other firms of raw penicillin and of 6-APA had nearly tripled during the years 1971–1974, was supplying a much larger number of firms with penicillin-base products than before the specialization went into effect. Consequently, those other firms were able to produce larger quantities of penicillin specialities in competition with Bayer and, to some extent, Gist-Brocades. This, in turn, resulted in *benefits to consumers*. Article 85(3) mandates that consumers must be allowed their fair share of the resulting benefits of an agreement scrutinized for exemption. The Commission stated that this was the case here as documented in the greater number of end products available on the penicillin market and the general trend to lower prices.

To enable the Commission to observe the practical effects of the *Bayer/Gist-Brocades* specialization agreement, particularly with respect to its impact on third parties, each company was required to provide the Commission periodically with information on the actual implementation of the agreements, that is, investments, production quantities, prices charged, supplies to the other party, and to third companies. The exemption was granted for a period of eight years to give the Commission a chance to review the situation within a reasonable time.

MANUFACTURE AND SALE AGREEMENTS. A very special form of specialization was intended by a British and a German company at around the time the Commission approved the accord between Bayer and Gist-Brocades. In late 1975, *Imperial Chemical Industries Ltd.* of England and *WASAG A.G.* of Germany, part of the Bohlen Group, concluded a series of agreements for the equal ownership and control of companies already existing in West Germany. The objective was to create a joint venture for the manufacture and sale of black powder. The *WASAG/ICI* arrangement provided for the two multinational groups of companies to pool their mutual interests in the market for black powder, henceforth to *make and sell the product jointly*. The means by which to achieve this goal was for ICI to purchase 50 percent of the shares and to make certain other capital contributions so as to achieve *joint and equal control of* a WASAG *subsidiary*, WANO Schwarzpulver GmbH. *WANO,* as then constituted, supplied all of WASAG'S black-powder requirements and, since 1974, had started to supply ICI. By October 1976, WANO met all or substantially all of ICI's black-powder requirements as well. ICI, according to the plan, had phased out its own production of black-powder and shut down its plant.

The agreements between WASAG and ICI were notified to the EEC Commission persuant to Article 4, Regulation 17/62, asking for an exemption from Article 85(1), Treaty of Rome, or for a negative clearance under Article 2, Regulation 17/62,[73] in the alternative. Later this notification was withdrawn, and the companies informed the Commission that it had been decided not to implement the notified agreements. Prior to this, however, the Commission had already informed the parties of its objections to the agreements. The Commission, on its own initiative, pursued the matter and in October 1978 issued a *negative decision* in this case.[74] The official reason provided for this unusual procedure, that is, an official decision in a case rendered moot by the parties' withdrawal of the notification, was the importance of the case as a precedent. The Commission wanted to establish clearly, for the benefit of other producers and customers of black- powder, "that the agreements in question infringed Article 85(1) and could not be exempted under Article 85(3)."[75] The parties were also informed "that implementation on their part of the joint agreements could in this case have additionally amounted to an abuse of ICI's dominant position in the UK black-powder market,"[76] that is, Article 86 would have been applicable next to Article 85 in the case of this joint venture. Most importantly, however, the parties had already acted as if the joint venture were fully implemented, albeit a provision in the agreements that they would not come into operation until approved by the Commission.[77]

It is important to understand some more details of the *factual situation* than described so far to be able to follow the Commission's appraisal of the agreements as being designed solely to *eliminate competition.* The agreements between WASAG and ICI not only ensured equal control by the parties of WANO as well as equal sharing of WANO's profits and losses, but accompanying correspondence established that both partners in the joint venture would buy their total requirements of black-powder from the joint venture. WANO was to operate under the management of general managers appointed in equal numbers by each party, resulting in the fact that no question regarding the production or sale of black-powder could in future be resolved by unilateral action of either company. Prior to the agreements of 1975, WASAG and ICI were competitors in the black-powder market. ICI was the only producer of black-powder in the United Kingdom, with a near-100 percent market share. WASAG manufactured more than two thirds of the black-powder produced in Germany. The joint venture would have controlled approximately 58 percent of the total EEC output of black-powder. In addition, ICI and WASAG both control extensive storage and transport facilities for explosives within their respective countries, an indispensable condition for the success of any black-powder business operation.

Another important aspect was the use of black-powder in the production of safety fuse, a follow-on product. Although the joint venture did not extend to include the related market for safety fuse, it proved to be a determinative fact in the Commission's consideration that ICI was by far the leading producer of safety fuse in the EEC. WASAG was the only manufacturer of safety fuse in Germany. According to the Commission, the *existence of the joint venture* for the base product, that is, black-powder, *would have afforded* the two companies *opportunities and inducements to restrain* their *competition in a related market,* that is, the market for safety fuse. The combined safety-fuse production of ICI and WASAG amounted to more than double the aggregate production of all other safety-fuse producers in the EEC. It was not conceivable in these circumstances, held the Commission, that the parties would have resisted the temptations provided through the joint operation of the black-powder business to align their prices and to share markets for safety fuse.[78]

The most important fact of all, however, in the Commission's view was the situation created by the joint venture for the U.K. black-powder market. ICI's participation in the joint venture would have had the effect that ICI would make all or substantially all of its future black-powder purchases from the production of WANO, rather than leave itself free also to obtain black-powder from other sources available in the Common Market. In view of ICI's overwhelming position as a distributor on the U.K. market for black-powder, this would have resulted in commiting more or less the entire future black-powder requirements of Britain to the joint venture. It cannot surprise anyone that the Commission mentioned this fact as the overriding reason why it was *not possible to grant an exemption* under Article 85(3) in this case.[79] In purely legal terms, this situation, had it been allowed to come about, would have afforded the participants in the joint venture "the possibility of eliminating competition in respect of a substantial part of the products in question" (Article 85(3) (b), Treaty of Rome). The *joint venture would have insulated the United Kingdom,* for all practical purposes, from existing or potential competition. Entry by black-powder producers other than WANO into the U.K. market would have been precluded. Consequently, questions of contribution to the improvement of the production or distribution of the goods covered by the agreement, or to the promotion of technical or economic progress did not have to be considered in this case,[80] pursuant to the law (Article 85(3) (b), Rome Treaty).

In withdrawing their application for an exemption, the companies have signaled their concurrence with the Commission's analysis of their agreements. In a way, the *WASAG/ICI* decision therefore constitutes a rare occasion of all-around acclaim of the legal interpretation given a specific joint-venture agreement. The case will therefore serve as a valuable precedent, indeed, for future considerations in this field.

CONCLUSIONS.   Commission decisions in joint-venture cases can be categorized along some general lines of comment. The specific decision related to individual terms and conditions of a joint-venture agreement, though, always results from a legal analysis of a particular situation that appears in almost as many different forms as the joint-venture agreements themselves. Therefore, it should first be stated that every single joint venture will have to be examined on its own merits. The EEC Commission uses a *case-by-case approach,* carefully examining in each situation whether the benefits of the joint venture outweigh, or at least balance, the disadvantages produced by the restrictions of competition inherent in almost every joint-venture agreement.

Decisions in this field so far allow the general comment that the *EEC Commission looks favorably upon research-and-development agreements* between companies, no matter whether or not they are direct competitors, where the type of research required to lead to a successful product or design is such that it would entail financial and technical resources to an extent that neither of the partners in the joint venture could reasonably provide alone. Usually this happens in advanced-technology areas or the field of medical/biological research, because highly specialized skills will be necessary, and the costs involved normally exceed the level that can be expected in any type of general research. In addition, the probability of success is often so low that the overall financial risk of undertaking the research project separately would be so high as to make it imprudent for a businessman not to seek a joint venture with a suitable partner, that is, a company that can provide complementary expertise and additional financing.

Joint ventures of this kind result in appreciable economic advantages and usually allow the consumers in the EEC their fair share of the benefits of the cooperation as required by Article 85(3), Treaty of Rome. The Commission has therefore found enough justification in cases falling into this category to grant an exemption from the prohibition laid down in Article 85(1), Treaty of Rome. In all cases, however, the *period of exemption* was *limited* to afford the Commission an opportunity to review the situation within a reasonable lapse of time. This appears necessary to ensure that the approved joint venture does not last longer than can be economically justified and thus legally defended. A prime example for a joint venture belonging into this category is the *Beecham/Parke, Davis* agreement, discussed above.[81]

Another category of joint-venture agreements can be identified from Commission decisions that granted exemption to arrangements between two competitors where the thrust of cooperation shifts from research-and-development work to the manufacture and subsequent marketing of the products covered by the agreement. Here it is usually not a new type of product that is the subject of the joint venture. The parties normally try to achieve a rationalization of their manufacturing processes, a better utilization of their production capacities, a penetration of new geographic markets, or an extension of their product range. They may attempt to achieve a combination of all these factors and look for a joint venture to overcome technical difficulties and financial risks. The EEC Commission is *reluctant to exempt manufacture and sale agreements* (which these types of joint ventures represent), but it has done so, for limited periods of time, where the arrangement resulted in an immediate improvement of the production or distribution of the products in question, as well as direct consumer benefits, either through lower prices or a wider range of products available on the market, or both. Usually obligations were attached for the companies that allowed the Commission to monitor the progress of the agreements, for example, annual reporting by the parties on production, sales, and financing of the joint venture. An example of this is the specialization agreement of the type examined in the *Bayer/Gist-Brocades* case.[82]

The Commission has insisted in all these cases that the cooperation between the two companies did not result in unnecessary limitations of the parties' freedom to decide their own production and marketing policies independently. In addition, the justification for an exemption under Article 85(3), Treaty of Rome, was held to exist only if independent production of the joint venturers was economically impractical. Finally, the Commission reviewed in each case whether the agreement afforded the parties opportunities or inducements to align their activities in other areas than the one covered by the joint venture. Lastly, Article 85(3) itself requires the Commission to check whether or not the joint venture would lead to market dominance by providing the parties a chance to eliminate competition for a substantial part of the products in question. For all these reasons, an exemption in the *WASAG/ICI* case was not possible and the *WANO* joint venture had to be prohibited, as described above.

It may be *concluded,* then, that joint ventures in the Common Market will be allowed if they offer companies a unique opportunity of overcoming more or less urgent problems in the operation of their business; if they result in direct benefits for EEC consumers in the medium term; and if competition in the Community will increase in the long run. Judging from the cases decided to date, the creation of joint subsidiaries will be allowed only on an exceptional basis.

INDUSTRIAL PROPERTY RIGHTS AND EEC LAW

PATENT LICENSING AGREEMENTS. In no other area of international business is the structure of the particular legal environment more important and the need for help from the law more necessary than in the field of worldwide exploitation of technical inventions. In the majority of cases, the individual inventor lacks the resources to exploit his invention himself in all the geographic or technical areas where such exploitation may be desirable. Modern legislation, in almost all countries, has therefore provided the necessary system for an inventor to achieve full commercial exploitation of his invention. The only form of protection for a new idea prior to the advent of patent laws was secrecy. By recognizing the invention as a form of property, the law has granted the necessary protection for an inventor who wants to involve others in the exploitation of his ideas and thus has to give up his secrets. Today, through the legal protection of the patent system in the world, an inventor enjoys the possibility of entering into *vertical agreements* to use his patented process with third parties simultaneously in many countries. He may, thereby, benefit from his intellectual property through the payment of royalties, without himself engaging in any particular commercial activity in the area in question. The individual right to use the patented process (typically to manufacture a product) is called a license, and the agreements bestowing such rights by the patent holder to third parties are referred to as patent licensing agreements.

These agreements, as in other parts of the world, play an important role in the distribution of products throughout the EEC. It is recognized that patent licensing agreements, in general, contribute to technical progress and improve the distribution of goods. They usually increase the number of production facilities in the Common Market, and thereby the quantity of goods produced in the Community, as they enable companies other than the patent owner to manufacture products using the latest and presumably most-efficient techniques. On the other hand, *patent licensing agreements normally contain clauses that go beyond the simple right to exploit the patented process for the payment of royalties.* For this reason, such agreements are usually of a restrictive character as far as competition is concerned, and therefore come under *Article 85,* Treaty of Rome. From the beginning, EEC law had thus to wrestle with the issue of patent licensing agreements. However, the problem was not the legal monopoly created for the patentee by the national laws (which by definition restricts competition); the problem was the *exercise of the industrial property right through an agreement* with third parties that had *to be reconciled with the requirements of a single market* represented by the various member states. In *Parke, Davis and Co.* v. *Centrafarm,*[83] the Court of Justice, after first having declared that the use of a patent granted under the law of a member state does not in itself violate the treaty rules of competition, stated the problem this way: "On the other hand, the provisions of Article 85 could be applicable if the utilization of one or more patents by enterprises acting in concert were to result in creating a situation likely to fall within the concepts of agreements between enterprises . . . within the meaning of Article 85, paragraph 1."[84]

One of the most typical and frequent *clauses* in patent licensing agreements *suspected of violating Article 85(1)* is the one relating to territorial exclusivity, that is, the patentee agrees not to manufacture or sell the goods in question in the licensee's territory and vice versa. Apart from exclusivity for one or both contract parties, which always involves export bans, such agreements typically contain the following other clauses that may subject them to Article 85(1): field-of-use restrictions, non-competition clauses, quantitative output limitations, no-challenge clauses, and restrictions on duration of the agreement.

As is the case with marketing agreements that contain restrictive clauses in contradiction to Article 85(1), patent licensing agreements may also be notified to the Commission pursuant to Article 4, Regulation 17/62, in order to obtain an *individual exemption* from the prohibition of Article 85(1) for the agreement in question. Such an exemption would be based on the special authorization contained in subparagraph 3 of Article 85, which makes this situation identical to the ones described above dealing with agreements such as specialization contracts or research-and-development agreements. However, in one particular area, namely, the field of exclusive dealing, EEC law has provided a special vehicle in form of a block exemption to settle the majority of cases occurring in this connection. The Commission enacted, upon authority provided by the EEC Council, Regulation 67/67 and thereby solved for itself a pressing administrative problem resulting from thousands of applications for individual exemptions.

The situation in the area of patent licensing today is what it used to be in the area of exclusive dealing prior to the adoption of Regulation 67/67. At year-end 1979, approximately two thirds of all notifications and applications pending before the Commission related to patent licenses; the Commission calls it a "problem of sheer bulk."[85] Not surprisingly, the Commission has therefore sought to equip itself with an equally effective instrument as in the area of exclusive distribution agreements to master the flood of applications for individual exemption of patent licensing agreements. Regulation 19/65 of the EEC Council, which provided the legal basis to enact Regulation 67/67, also contains sufficient authority for the Commission to adopt a similar regulation granting a block exemption to certain bilateral agreements "which include restrictions imposed in relation to the acquisition or use of industrial property rights, in particular of patents, utility models, designs or trademarks" (Article 1(1)(b), Regulation 19/65). The Commission has worked on such a *block-exemption regulation* for patent licensing agreements for many years. After several futile attempts a *draft* of such a regulation was finally *published* in 1979.[86]

This draft document indicates that the Commission intends to issue a regulation for the block exemption of patent licensing agreements that, in its structure, will closely resemble Regulation 67/67. The *main provisions of the 1979 draft regulation* are as follows: Article 1 contains obligations that may be imposed upon a party to a patent licensing agreement without concern about Article 85(1); included here is the exclusive right for the licensee to manufacture or use the patented product or process in the licensed territory. Article 2 lists a number of obligations that do not prevent exemption; examples are the obligations not to divulge business secrets, to respect certain quality standards, and to comply with field-of-use restrictions. Article 3 mentions clauses whose presence in an agreement precludes the benefit of the block exemption; however, clauses mentioned here (such as a no-challenge clause or a noncompetition clause) may still be exempted individually, pursuant to Article 85(3). Although Article 1(2) exempts exclusive selling rights and accompanying export bans for small-to-medium-sized firms, the *Commission is holding onto its general policy of rejecting export bans* in patent licensing agreements. The rationale, according to the Commission, is "that export bans within the Common Market are contrary to the very idea of a single market and are as a matter of principle caught by Article 85(1)."[87] The exception with respect to small and medium-sized companies is justified because they lack the resources necessary to exploit their inventions and consequently have to issue licenses; equivalent protection is justified for these types of firms when they receive patent licenses and have to make corresponding investments.

It is already clear that the Commission, based on the comments and criticism it has received after publication of the draft regulation, will publish an *amended draft sometime in the future.*[88] This new draft will have to go through another round of consultations, which are required by Regulation 19/65 (the legal basis for the future block-exemption regulation). It is therefore premature to make any further comments on the draft as it stands today, and there is certainly no way of predicting when the proposed regulation will finally be adopted. The international businessmen planning to enter into a patent licensing agreement that covers all or part of the EEC will therefore have to *continue to apply to the Commission for a single-case exemption* in all cases where the agreement is subject to the prohibition of Article 85(1). Whether such is the case will, until further notice, continue to depend, in part, on the *Com-*

mission Notice on Patent Licensing Agreements of December 1962.[89] To a larger extent, this determination will depend on the individual decisions that the Commission has taken in this field and on the applicable judgments of the Court. The latter will be explored in greater detail in this section, but it will serve no lasting purpose to explain the dozen or so Commission decisions over the last 10 years in detail when it can reasonably be expected that the draft regulation (which, after all, contains all the legal wisdom of these decisions) will be enacted in the foreseeable future. Therefore, it will suffice to mention only some of the highlights of these Commission decisions.

The *kind of patent licensing agreement that would qualify, today, for exemption* from the prohibition in Article 85(1) is, of course, similar to the one described in *Article 1* of the *draft regulation*, and represents a combination of elements that have passed muster on previous occasions.[90] It is easier to list those *elements of a contract that would not be exempted* by the Commission. Foremost of these is the *noncompetition clause*. In the *Campari* case,[91] the Commission had indicated that such a clause in a licensing agreement concerning industrial property rights would constitute a barrier to technical and economic progress by preventing the licensee from taking an interest in other techniques and products. Just over a year later, the Commission confirmed this position in the *Vaessen/Moris* case,[92] a decision that dealt with a license agreement regarding a patented process in manufacturing meat sausages. At the same time, this decision makes it clear that a *no-challenge clause* in a patent licensing agreement violates Article 85(1), in that it deprives the licensee of the possibility available to everyone else, namely to remove, through the challenge of the patent, an obstacle to his freedom of commercial action. The Commission added, with respect to the licensee's obligation not to use competitive sausage casings in the patented manufacturing process of meat sausages (but only those casings supplied by the patentee) that this was also a violation of Article 85. Neither of these clauses qualified for exemption, because they did not contribute to improving the production or distribution of the goods in question, nor did they promote technical or economic progress. "On the contrary," said the Commission, "these clauses are impediments to such progress, the first [i.e., the no-challenge clause] because it prevents [the licensees] from being free to carry on activities within the limits of the patent claims, and the second by preventing them from obtaining casings from another supplier at a more favourable price."[93]

In the *AOIP/Beyrard* case,[94] the Commission had to address the question whether an *obligation* imposed upon the licensee in a patent licensing agreement *to continue to pay royalties after the expiration of the patent* could be tolerated. The means by which this result was to be achieved in the *Beyrard* case were simple. The license agreement provided that the duration of agreement would be extended automatically with each improvement patent to the ones subject to the original contract. When the Commission, in 1975, looked at this license agreement, which dated from 1953, the life of the contract had already been extended to 1989. But the licensee was obliged to pay the full royalty, even after all the patents in force at the time of original signature had expired, and even if he was not making use of the patents after that date.[95] The Commission decided that this clause constituted an infringement of Article 85(1) and ordered the parties to terminate the infringement. As this decision also deals with a number of other restrictions typically contained in a license agreement, it provides good guidance for the interested businessmen until the Commission's block-exemption regulation finally becomes law.

Recently, the Commission has confirmed its position taken in *Beyrard* with respect to the *payment of royalties after the expiration of the patent*. In a situation involving a Belgian company, an inventor had asssigned his patents for making a new kind of precast cement girder and other equipment against the promise of a percentage of the company's sales "for so long as the agreement was being applied" (*Preflex/ Lipski*).[96] The Commission intervened upon the complaint of Preflex and pointed out that a licensee's obligation to pay royalty after the patent has expired is in *violation of Article 85(1)*. This is true, *even if the previously patented process is still used after expiration of the patent*, because the continued payment of royalties would place the licensee at a disadvantage in relation to others who are now free to use the same process without having to pay. As the parties terminated the agreement on this point, the Commission did not have to take a formal decision.

Basically, the same rationale as with respect to royalty payments applies in cases of *attempted territorial protection after expiration of the patent*. A case in point is that of *Fondasol*, a French company, reported in May 1980.[97] Again, no Commission decision was taken, as the firms voluntarily complied after the Commission had intervened. Three EEC companies were the makers and users of a patented device to measure certain soil properties. When the original patent expired in Belgium, Fondasol decided that it was now free to supply its services in that country using the measuring technique, which also used to be covered by the expired patent. One of the three firms mentioned before, however, had previously been granted the exclusive right to use the process in Belgium. All three firms went to court in Belgium against Fondasol, based on this exclusive right. The Commission advised the parties that *contract clauses ensuring territorial protection can be permitted only if a patent is in force in the protected territory,* and then only under certain circumstances. The three firms withdrew their court action.

These cases allow the conclusion that the *Commission will oppose any attempts by a patent holder to extend the life of his patent through any contractual means beyond* the effective date of *expiration*. Other than that, it appears to be the best advice for the businessman entering into a patent licensing agreement in the EEC today to study carefully the draft regulation of 1979, described above. Unfortunately, this area of EEC law is currently in a state of change that does not yet allow certainty of opinion, usually resulting from the existence of a statute, nor does it necessarily permit reliance on older precedents that may or may not be obsolete.

RESTRAINTS ON THE USE OF LEGAL STATUS.   No EEC-wide system has been adopted to date for the uniform protection of industrial and commercial property rights.[98] Instead, the Treaty of Rome recognizes, in Article 222, the various systems of property ownership that exist in the member states. Patents, trademarks, and copyrights are protected as property rights in all EEC countries by national legislation granting the exclusive right to sell and/or manufacture the protected product on the territory of the member state in question. Therefore, *protection of industrial property rights in the Common Market* today is still a *national affair,* based on the well-established *principle of territoriality,* which has been acknowledged throughout the world ever since legislation for the protection of industrial property occurred.

In contrast, the European Economic Community was created to overcome all kinds of barriers to trade existing between the member states at the time of its inception in 1958. Article 3(a), Treaty of Rome, therefore demands "the elimination, as between member states, of customs duties and of quantitative restrictions on the import and export of goods, and of all other measures having equivalent effect.'' Accordingly, the *integration of the separate national markets into one single market* has been called the *essential goal of the EEC Treaty*.[99] To achieve this aim of integration, the treaty provides, in Article 9 and following, for a system of *free movement of goods,* and it also relies, as a second pillar of the "European edifice," on its *rules of competition*. As was explained before,[100] these rules are part of a system called for in Article 3(f), Treaty of Rome, which demands "that competition in the Common Market is not distorted." Regarding the free movement of goods, Article 30 specifically prohibits "quantitative restrictions on imports and all measures having equivalent effect . . . between the member states." Although it is not difficult to understand what creates a "quantitative restriction" on imports (classic example: tariff quotas), it was subject to disputes how far the other part of this prohibition in Article 30, Treaty of Rome, would reach. The Court of Justice finally gave an authoritative interpretation in 1974 when it decided the case of *Public Prosecutor* v. *Dassonville*.[101] The Court held: "All trading rules enacted by Member States which are capable of hindering, directly or indirectly, actually or potentially, intra-Community trade are to be considered as measures having an effect equivalent to quantitative restrictions."

With these *two systems of law coexisting in the Community* after 1958, a *basic conflict* thus existed *with respect to the treatment of products protected by a patent, a trademark, or a copyright*. The respective claims of the two systems can be staked out by the *national* protection of industrial property rights with territorial nature on the one hand and the *supranational* rules relating to the free movement of goods as well as those regarding competition on the other. The Court of Justice itself recognized and admitted this conflict in two judgments, for patents and trademarks, separately. Noticing that the national rules relating to the protection of industrial and commercial property have not yet been rendered uniform within the Community framework, the Court acknowledged first with respect to patents in its 1968 judgment of *Parke, Davis and Co.* v. *Centrafarm*[102] that "in the absence of such a unification, the national scope of industrial property protection and the differences between the laws in this matter are likely to create obstacles both to the free movement of patented products and to competition within the Common Market." It also used the same thought with respect to the free movement of trademarked goods throughout the Community when it decided the *Sirena*[103] case in 1971.

On the other hand, the Court had decided the underlying conflict between EEC and national law many years earlier in favor of Community law. Drawing upon the rule contained in Article 5, Treaty of Rome, which establishes a general obligation for the member states to abstain from any measure that could jeopardize the attainment of the objectives of the treaty, the Court of Justice declared in *Costa* v. *Enel*[104] in 1964 the *supremacy of EEC law over national laws*. Therefore, when the Court was faced with the conflict of laws in the area of industrial property rights, it was only a question of implementing this general principle of law without compromising the essential contents of the national rights, guaranteed under Article 222, Treaty of Rome (see above). A balance had to be struck between both systems, allowing for the continuation of the national protection of property-right holders as well as enforcing the treaty objectives of uninhibited trade throughout the Community. This delicate task fell onto the EEC Court of Justice. In a long line of judgments, stretching over a period of 12 years, *the Court reconciled EEC law and national laws regarding the protection and the utilization of industrial property rights* in the Common Market by extrapolating from Article 36, Treaty of Rome, an interface delineating the existence and the exercise of a particular right such as a patent or a trademark. *Article 36* provides an exception to the fundamental principle of free movement of goods in the EEC in that it permits, for the purpose of safeguarding some general goals of public interest (among them "the protection of industrial and commercial property"), certain prohibitions or restrictions on trade between the member states. At the same time, however, Article 36 refers to these permissible prohibitions and restrictions, specifically demanding that they shall not be used as "a means of arbitrary discrimination or a disguised restriction on trade between Member States."[105]

The first time that the issue of an industrial property right colliding with EEC law principles came before the Court of Justice was in the landmark case of *Grundig, Consten*[106] in 1966. Here the Court had to decide the *relationship between trademark rights* under German and French law *and EEC antitrust law*. The facts of the case, in this respect, were as follows. Based on an agreement between Grundig, the German manufacturer of home-electronic equipment, and its sole French distributor, Consten, the trademark *GINT* (for *Grundig-International*) had been registered in France in the name of Consten. However, Consten had agreed that at the termination of the exclusive distributorship agreement with Grundig, the trademark would be assigned to Grundig or would be allowed to expire. The GINT trademark, which was affixed to all Grundig products, was introduced by Grundig after it had lost a court decision in the Netherlands against a parallel importer. In this former case Grundig had attempted to ensure for its Dutch distributor exclusivity and territorial protection through the Grundig trademark registered in Grundig's name. After this had failed, Grundig established the second mark and had it registered in the name of its various exclusive dealers in the EEC countries other than Germany, with the explicit understanding of reassignment at the termination of the dealership contract mentioned before. When parallel imports of Grundig products occurred in France, Consten sued the parallel importer based on infringement of "its" GINT trademark.

The Commission, which became involved upon the complaint of the parallel importer, took issue with this exercise of the trademark right, as well as the underlying contract between Grundig and Consten. It issued a *cease-and-desist order* pursuant to Article 3, Regulation 17/62, *to refrain from using the national-trademark right to prevent imports* and addressed this decision both to Grundig and Consten. When the two companies appealed this decision to the Court of Justice, they alleged, among other things, "that the Commission violated Articles 36, 222, and 234 of the EEC Treaty and also exceeded its authority in declaring that the agreement on the registration of the GINT trademark in France serves to ensure absolute territorial protection for Consten and in thereby prohibiting . . . Consten from invoking rights stemming from national trademark law to prevent parallel imports."[107]

The Court dismissed this argument entirely. It recognized that the purpose of Consten's right to be the only one in France to use the GINT trademark was nothing else but the attempt to make it possible for Consten to control and prevent imports. "For this reason," said the Court, "the agreement whereby Grundig, as holder of that trademark by virtue of an international registration, authorized Consten to register it in France in its own name is designed to restrict competition."[108] Such an agreement, the Court added, is illegal under Article 85(1), Treaty of Rome. Articles 36, 222, and 234 do not change this assessment as they "do not prevent Community law from having an influence on the *exercise* of industrial property rights under domestic law."[109] The *Commission's order* to refrain from using the trademark rights to prevent parallel imports "leaves these rights untouched," said the Court, in that it *limited* their *exercise only,* and only to the extent necessary to enforce the prohibition of Article 85(1).

This, then, was the beginning of the now-famous *existence/exercise doctrine in EEC law* that distinguishes between the existence of an industrial property right, not to be tampered with, and its exercise, which is controlled by Community law. In its later attempts to define more clearly the interface between national and Community law regarding the trade in products protected by a patent, trademark, or copyright, the Court of Justice has heavily relied on this distinction. In fact, the existence/exercise doctrine has been at the heart of every single judgment decided in the area of industrial property rights since the *Grundig, Consten* case. Although the foundation of this doctrine on Article 36 may still have been somewhat opaque in the 1966 judgment (because of the obiter-kind hint, cited above, that Articles 36, 222, and 234 do not prevent Community law from having an influence on the exercise of industrial property rights), the Court made it clear five years later in the *Sirena* case that the *relationship between EEC antitrust law and national laws relating to industrial property rights* is indeed *governed by Article 36.* "Article 36, while it is included in the chapter on quantitative restrictions on trade between Member States, is based on a principle that can also find application to competition law in the sense that while the *existence* of industrial and commercial property rights granted under the law of a Member State is not affected by Articles 85 and 86 of the Treaty, the *exercise* of such rights may come within the prohibitions contained in these provisions."[110] With this judgment of 1971, the Court formalized the doctrine that has become the ground rule for all courts in the Community faced with the problem of interpreting the interface between national legislation granting exclusive rights on patents, trademarks, and copyrights and the principle of unity of the Common Market.

The judgment in the *Grundig, Consten* case allows the conclusion that the EEC system of competition rules does not permit a trademark owner to use his rights resulting from the trademark law of different member states for purposes that are contrary to Community antitrust law. Accordingly, a cease-and-desist order by the Commission to refrain from using a national trademark right to prevent parallel imports is compatible with the Treaty of Rome rules on competition as well as those relating to the free movement of goods. It is particularly compatible with Article 36, as it leaves the trademark right itself untouched but limits only its exercise insofar as necessary to enforce the prohibition of Article 85(1).

Grundig, Consten was a trademark case that also involved an agreement between the two parties that squarely violated the provisions of Article 85 by attempting to partition the Common Market. During the following 12 years, *12 more cases* came before the Court of Justice *in which companies attempted to exercise their industrial property rights in order to prevent imports, reimports, or parallel imports of the protected products into their territories.* All of these cases reached the Court by way of the procedure provided for in Article 177, Treaty of Rome, that allows national courts (and in some cases forces them) to ask the European Court of Justice for a preliminary ruling on questions of EEC law in cases that are pending before them. In all cases the company owning the property right had sued the importer in a national court for infringement of its rights under national law, and the national court was thus faced with the obvious discrepancy between national and EEC law (principle of territoriality versus free movement of goods), described above. The vehicle of an Article 177 referral has helped these courts out of this dilemma in each instance, and the resulting decisions of the Court of Justice, which cover the whole spectrum of industrial property rights from copyright to trademark to patent, have created an *invaluable body of case law.*

The majority of cases decided by the Court in this area have ended in defeat for the companies that attempted to partition the Common Market through the use of their legal status as owner of an industrial property right. In other words, most judgments held that national laws had to yield to Community provisions where the conflict between the two legal systems occurred. These judgments can be divided into two categories in the sense that two of them, the *Grundig, Constent* and *Sirena* cases, were based on the treaty rules of competition, in particular Article 85, whereas the majority were decided through *direct application of Articles 30 and 36 to the conduct of private enterprises,* although these treaty articles, according to their text, are addressed to member states only. The latter group of judgments represent the core of *EEC jurisprudence that outlaws the partitioning of national markets through the use of industrial property rights.* They are, in time sequence, the judgments in *Deutsche Grammophon*[111] for copyrights (1971); *Van Zuylen Frères* v. *Hag A.G.* (Cafe Hag)[112] for trademarks (1974); and *Centrafarm B.V.v. Sterling Drug Inc.*[113] for patents (1974).

In the *Deutsche Grammophon* case, the Court said with respect to an exclusive right under German law to sell a product, which is akin to a *copyright,* that the legality of exercising this right (in order to prevent the sale on the domestic territory of products normally sold in other EEC countries) depends on a special determination whenever such exercise escapes the elements of contract or concert addressed in Article 85. This determination makes it necessary to consider "whether the exercise of the right . . . is compatible with other provisions of the treaty, particularly those relating to the free movement of goods."[114] As the Court explained, this means that the extent to which the exercise of a national right to protection, akin to a copyright, might prevent the sale of products coming from another member state must be determined in light of Article 36 in particular. In the *Deutsche Grammophon* case, this led to the conclusion that the *exercise of the copyright* in order to prohibit the sale in that member state (Germany) of products that were distributed in another member state (France) by the producer, or with his consent, solely for the reason that such distribution did not take place in the territory of the first state (Germany) is *contrary to the rules providing for the free movement of goods* within the Common Market.

In the *Cafe Hag* case, the Court faced a situation in which two companies, economically and legally independent of each other, were rightful owners of the same *trademark* for an identical product, namely *Cafe Hag* for decaffeinated coffee. The Germany company Hag A.G., which is the original owner of the mark, had assigned this trademark regarding Belgium to its subsidiary established in that country before World War II. In late 1944, Cafe Hag S.A. Belgium, the subsidiary, came under sequestration as enemy property. Later the shares in the company were sold off by the Belgian sequestration office to a private Belgian entrepreneur. In 1971 he assigned the trademark to the plaintiff in this case, Van Zuylen Frères, for Belgium and Luxembourg. When Hag A.G. in 1972 started to sell its coffee bearing the trademark *Cafe Hag* in Luxembourg, Van Zuylen brought a trademark infringement action in a national court. This court referred the case to the European Court of Justice.

The EEC Court pointed out at the outset that under the circumstances, Article 85 was not applicable because no agreement for the specific purpose of partitioning the market existed between the parties, or one of them and a third party. The original assignment of the trademark from Hag A.G., Germany, to Cafe Hag S.A., Belgium, was between parent company and subsidiary, and the Court had decided in earlier judgments that Article 85 does not apply in cases of parent/subsidiary agreements.[115] Thus, the Court held, "the question must be examined by reference only to the rules relating to the free movement of goods."[116] The Court, in the *Cafe Hag* case, recognized the basic conflict between these rules and a national trademark and expressly deplored that the *exercise of a trademark right tends to contribute to the partitioning of markets* and thus to impair the free movement of goods between EEC countries. *Accordingly,* the Court concluded, "the *holder of a trademark cannot be permitted to rely on the exclusiveness of a trademark* right . . . with a view to prohibiting the marketing in a Member State of goods legally produced in another Member State under an identical trademark having the same origin. Such a prohibition, which would legitimize the isolation of national markets, would conflict with one of the essential aims of the Treaty, which is to unite national markets in a single market."[117]

In *Centrafarm* v. *Sterling Drug,* the Court had to deal with a manufacturer (Sterling Drug) that owned *parallel patents* in several member states. After the product had been put into circulation by the manufacturer (or his consignee) in one member state, these patents were *invoked to prevent imports of the protected product from that member state, where they were cheaper, into another.* The Court referred to its own distinction between the existence and the exercise of an industrial property right and defined the *specific subject matter of a patent right,* which falls under the "existence" guarantee and is not affected by the treaty provisions, as the "exclusive right to use an invention with a view to manufacturing industrial products and putting them into circulation for the first time." The Court concluded that an *obstacle to the free movement of goods may be justified* on the ground of protection of industrial property *where* such *protection is invoked against a product coming from a member state where it is not patentable,* or in cases where separate patents exist that belong to legally and economically independent companies. However, "a derogation from the principle of the free movement of goods is not . . . justified where the product has been put onto the market in a legal manner, by the patentee himself or with his consent, in the Member State from which it has been imported, in particular in the case of a proprietor of parallel patents."[118] The Court did not try to avoid the basic issue of the case, namely the underlying conflict between the national legislation concerning industrial and commercial property and the treaty rules on the free movement of goods within the Common Market. It specifically said that any provisions in national laws "under which a patentee's right is not exhausted when the patented product is marketed in another Member State, with the result that the patentee retains the right to prevent importation of the product into his own State" is an obstacle to the free movement of goods.[119] This statement marked the beginning of the now-famous *"exhaustion of rights"* doctrine, which has been applied to trademarks as well in the judgment of the parallel case of *Centrafarm B.V.* v. *Winthrop B.V.*[120] In both cases, the application of this doctrine led to the *preclusion of the industrial-property-right holder* (patentee or trademark owner) *from exercising his rights to prevent parallel imports:* "The exercise, by a patentee [or the owner of a trademark] of the right he enjoys under the laws of a Member State to prohibit the sale, in that State, of a patented product [trademarked product] that has been marketed in another Member State by the patentee [trademark owner] or with his consent is incompatible with the rules of the EEC Treaty concerning the free movement of goods within the Common Market."[121]

Some *general conclusions from this case law* are possible. First, since the Treaty of Rome has come into force the *privileges provided* to holders of industrial property rights *under national legislation* have been *severely curtailed*. The built-in limitations on free trade in the Community, resulting from the territorial character of the national laws, today are counteracted by the treaty rules on competition as well as those relating to the free movement of goods. Second, however, it remains necessary to balance the conflicting interests of the two legal systems coexisting in Europe today regarding the existence and the exercise of industrial property rights. While the total partitioning of national markets in the EEC by means of industrial property is no longer possible, *the law continues to respect the basic rights of patent, trademark, and copyright owners*. The key to the understanding of this difference between the existence of rights and their exercise by their owners is the specific subject matter of the right in question. The Court has defined what constitutes the specific subject matter of a patent right and a trademark right.[122] If a restriction, applied by the owner of the right, is not necessary to guarantee the exclusive rights that constitute this specific subject matter (i.e., not necessary to guarantee the existence of the right), then if this restriction is to survive, it must be compatible with the rules relating to competition or the free movement of goods.

Third, so long as only national laws exist to protect industrial and commercial property, the unity of the Common Market is only incompletely attained. This has the practical side effect that, on occasion, a holder of a patent, trademark, or copyright may prevail against a parallel importer who threatens the territorial exclusiveness of the right by importing protected products from other member states. In the present state of Community law, it remains possible to invoke an industrial property right, legally acquired in a member state, to prevent, under certain circumstances, the import of products into the protected territory under the *exception from the principle of free movement of goods* that is *allowed by Article 36, first sentence*. This will be the case whenever the facts of the particular situation are such that the objective of industrial and commercial property protection (i.e., reward to the inventor/investor) would be undermined, if the Community law principles were to prevail over the protection given by the respective national laws. Obviously, such situations will be rare inasmuch as they represent exceptions from the general rule of supremacy of EEC law. Only special circumstances can justify these exceptions, and insofar every single case creates a precedent of its own. To date, *four* such *cases* exist in which the Court has decided to *uphold the industrial-property-right owner's position over that of the parallel importer*. One case involves a patent, and the other three are trademark protection cases. The remaining comments are devoted to these cases.

The first was the *Parke, Davis*[123] judgment of 1968. Here the patent holder, Parke, Davis, was successful in its efforts to prevent the importation of its drugs from Italy through an independent Dutch importer, Centrafarm. The decisive criterion in the Court's deliberation of the case appears to have been the conclusion that "the exercise of the rights flowing from a patent granted under the laws of a Member State does not in itself violate the rules of competition set forth in the Treaty."[124] However, it must be pointed out that Italy, at that time, *did not allow patent protection for pharmaceutical products* under its legislation, and the situation in *Parke, Davis* was thus not one of parallel patents in two member states, but rather unique in the sense that products protected by a patent in Holland were free and without protection against third companies in Italy. The Italian prices for the identical drugs were considerably lower than the Dutch prices. It was presumably this *unusual set of circumstances* that prompted the Court to allow Parke, Davis to invoke its patent rights in Holland against imports from Italy, where no exclusive rights to manufacture and sell the drugs were available. In passing, the Court mentioned with respect to the allegation of abusive exploitation of Parke, Davis' patent rights that "the fact that the price of the patented product is higher than that of the non-patented product does not necessarily constitute an abuse."

The second case occurred in 1976, namely *Terrapin* v. *Terranova*.[125] This case involved a trademark dispute between a German and a British manufacturer of construction materials. Again the case was built on the *unusual circumstances whereby the two trademarks,* which were used by the companies as their commercial names at the same time (*Terrapin* for the British company and *Terranova* for the German), *were said to be confusingly similar.* Consequently, the German company opposed the British competitor's attempt to have its mark registered in Germany. After many years of litigation, the case reached the German Supreme Court, which found itself bound by Article 177(3), Treaty of Rome, to refer the matter to the European Court of Justice, as issues regarding the compatibility of Terranova's action with the treaty rules on the free movement of goods had been raised during the process by the British company. The *question referred to the Court of Justice* can be paraphrased as follows: Provided there are no commercial relationships or common ownership between the two companies, is it compatible with the provisions of Articles 30 and 36, Treaty of Rome, that a German company, using its commercial name and trademark rights that exist in Germany, should be allowed to prevent the importation into Germany of similar goods made by an English company, if these goods have been lawfully given a distinguishing name that may be confused with the commercial name and trademark of the German company?

The Court answered in the affirmative, holding that in the present state of Community law, an *industrial or commercial property right may be used to prevent,* under Article 36, first sentence, *the importation of goods marketed under a name giving rise to confusion,* provided the rights in question have been acquired by different and independent proprietors under different national laws. The Court based its judgment on its *definition of the subject matter of the trademark right* as one "of guaranteeing to consumers that the product has the same origin." It was this concern for the protection of the consumer's interest to be able to conclude from the trademark whether a product has the same origin that led the Court to uphold the German company's claim against the British company for risk of confusion between the two trademarks. Based on Article 36, second sentence, however, the Court did not fail to admonish that it is the duty of the national court, "after considering the similarity of the products and the risk of confusion, to inquire further in the context of [Article 36, second sentence] whether the exercise in a particular case of industrial and commercial property rights may or may not constitute a means of arbitrary discrimination or a disguised restriction on trade between Member States."[126] And the Court added that it is *of particular importance* in this respect for the national court to ascertain *whether the trademark owner is exercising his rights with the same strictness regardless of the national origin of any possible infringer.*

After the *Terrapin* case, two more cases ended with victory for the company suing a parallel importer for infringement of its national trademark rights in a national court. While the *Court upheld,* under Article 36, first sentence, the *claims* of both plaintiffs *against improper use of* their *trademarks by a third party,* it *nevertheless* gave broad authority, under Article 36, second sentence, to the national courts to allow, in certain specified circumstances, a kind of *self-help* on the part *of parallel importers against trademark owners where the trademark is abused* to impede the free movement of goods in the Common Market, artificially. The two judgments are *Hoffman-LaRoche* v. *Centrafarm*[127] and *Centrafarm* v. *American Home Products,*[128] both of 1978.

In the first case, Hoffman-LaRoche was able to prevent Centrafarm from buying its Valium drugs in Britain (where they are offered in larger-size packets and are considerably cheaper than elsewhere in the Community) and reselling them in Germany. The reason was that *Centrafarm had repackaged the drugs* for the German market into larger packets *and had affixed the "Valium-Roche" trademark to the new packets* without authorization from Hoffmann-LaRoche. Having regard to the essential function of the trademark, "which is to guarantee the identity of the origin of the trademarked product to the consumer or ultimate user," the Court did not hesitate, in these circumstances, to declare that the exercise of the trademark right appeared justified under Article 36, first sentence. At the same time, however, the Court said that a "disguised restriction on trade between Member States" could arise where the proprietor of a trademark adopts a *marketing system of "putting onto the market in various states an identical product in various packages"* while availing himself of the rights inherent in the trademark to prevent repackaging by a third person, even if it were done in such a way that the identity of origin of the trademarked product and its original condition could not be affected."[129]

The Court gave two examples in which the latter situation would be present. First, the proprietor of the trademark has marketed the product in a double packaging and the repackaging affects the external packaging, only. Second, the repackaging process is inspected by a public authority for the purpose of ensuring that the product is not adversely affected. In these cases, the *exercise of the trademark rights* to fetter the free movement of goods among EEC countries *would constitute a disguised restriction prohibited by Article 36, second sentence,* if it is established that this exercise contributes to the artificial partitioning of the Common Market. The Court admitted that this "amounts to giving the trader who sells the imported product with the trademark affixed to the new packaging without the authorization of the proprietor a certain license."[130] But it added that this *license to self-help for the parallel importer* "is unavoidable in the interests of freedom of trade."

In the other case, *Centrafarm* v. *American Home Products,* the results were virtually the same, but the facts of this dispute were sufficiently different to make this later case a valuable precedent of its own. American Home Products (AHP) was the proprietor in various member states of *various trademarks for the same pharmaceutical product.* For instance, in the Benelux countries the trademark *Seresta* was registered in AHP's name for the product in question, a tranquilizer. In Britain, the mark for the same type of product with identical therapeutic effects was *Serenid D. Centrafarm* imported the product from Britain, *removed the British trademark, and affixed* to the product *the Dutch trademark* for purposes of marketing the tranquilizer in Holland. Centrafarm's reasons for this action were twofold. First, considerable price differences between Britain and Holland existed for pharmaceuticals in general and for this AHP product in particular. The parallel import of the tranquilizer from the United Kingdom was therefore economically enticing for Centrafarm. Secondly, affixing the Seresta trademark in Holland was essential, according to Centrafarm, to overcome an otherwise-strong impediment to competition with AHP's local trademark in that country. Launching a new trademark on the Dutch market such as *Serenid D* in light of another, already well established mark for an identical product in this market (namely *Seresta*) would have led to considerable expenses for Centrafarm, so they said, and this would have neutralized all benefits of importing the cheaper product from the United Kingdom.

Under these circumstances, the Court reached the conclusion that *only the proprietor of a trademark may confer an identity upon the product by affixing the trademark.* The guarantee of origin to the consumer, which is the specific subject matter of the trademark, would otherwise be jeopardized, if it were permissible for third parties to affix the trademark to products without authorization, "even to an original product."[131] Nevertheless, the Court continued, although it may be lawful for a manufacturer to use varying trademarks in different EEC countries, the *proprietor of a trademark could follow* such a *practice of different trademarks for identical products* "as part of a system of marketing intended *to partition the markets artificially.*" If such a marketing practice would be established (and it is for the national court to find out about the facts), the *Court would not hesitate* to preclude the trademark owner from exercising his right and *to grant a license to self-help to the parallel importer*: "In such a case, the prohibition by the proprietor of the unauthorized affixing of the mark by a third party constitutes a disguised restriction on intra-Community trade for the purposes of [Article 36, second sentence]."[132]

These judgments show that a trademark owner in a particular EEC country may keep out products from another EEC country if this is necessary to preserve the very essence of his trademark (the specific subject matter of the right), namely the guarantee to the consumer that the trademarked goods are in fact produced by him and have not been altered by third parties. This is all the more true if the *products are imported from countries outside the EEC,* as has been made clear in three parallel judgments of 1976 deciding the *EMI* v. *CBS* cases.[133] The Court confirmed that Community law principles do not prevent the owner of the same trademark in all member states from exercising his rights, in order to keep out products bearing the same trademark that is owned by a third party in a non-EEC country. However, this exercise of trademark rights is lawful only if it does not result from an agreement with the third party or a concerted practice which has the object or effect of partitioning the Common Market. The Court expressly confirmed that a requirement that the proprietor of the trademark in a non-EEC country must, prior to exporting the goods to the Community, obliterate his mark on the goods and perhaps apply a different mark "forms part of the permissible consequences flowing from the protection of the mark." These *CBS* judgments are hardly surprising, because the basic conflict between national laws and EEC law usually creating the difficulty in a particular case did not occur in this instance. Rather, in all three cases the conflict was between the British, Danish, and German trademark rights of EMI, respectively, and the U.S. rights of CBS Corporation. This was not considered by the Court to be "trade between Member States," as the CBS products were not in free circulation in any of the member states but came in from outside the Community.

In summary, then, it can be said that industrial property rights of the traditional type, that is, with territorial character, which the international businessman is used to are still alive in the EEC and may provide protection against third parties in certain cases. However, the restraints on the use of the legal status of a patent, trademark, or copyright owner resulting from the Treaty of Rome rules on competition and those on the free movement of goods are normally stronger and override national laws that seem to grant shelter from competition of parallel importers. For the international businessman looking for advice, the only safe conduct for purposes of trading in patented, trademarked, or copyrighted goods in the Community appears to be to assume that a particular case will always be decided by the Commission or the Court of Justice in favor of Community interests over national law, a principle that might be called *in dubio pro communitate*.

NOTES

1. J. L. Brierly, *The Law of Nations,* 6th ed., H. Waldock, ed. New York: Oxford University Press, 1963, p.1.

2. Article 38 reads as follows:
    "1. The Court whose function is to decide in accordance with international law such disputes as are submitted to it, shall apply:
        a.   international conventions, whether general or particular, establishing rules expressly recognized by the contesting states;
        b.   international custom, as evidence of a general practice accepted as law;
        c.   the general principles of law recognized by civilized nations;
        d.   subject to the provisions of Article 59, judicial decisions and the teachings of the most highly qualified publicists of the various nations, as subsidiary means for the determination of rules of law.
    "2. This provision shall not prejudice the power of the Court to decide a case *ex aequo et bono,* if the parties agree thereto." The subject matter treated is thus "directly relevant to the function which international law served; bringing minimum order to relations between states by imposing certain restraints upon them and allocating certain competences among them," as stated by Steiner and Vagts, 1976, *Transnational Legal Problems,* 2nd ed. The Foundation Press, Inc., N.Y. p. 329.

3. International Court of Justice, 1970, I.C.J. Rep 4, *Belgium* v. *Spain,* paragraph 38. Case reported in Steiner and Vagts, 1976, p. 222.

4. Cf. Steiner and Vagts, 1976, p. 329.

5. So called because Article 2, Treaty of Rome, calls for the establishment of a common market among the member states. The latest available figures indicate that the Community of Nine is the single largest trading partner in the world, by far. The exports reported for 1979 for the EEC, the United States and Japan, respectively, were as follows: $577.5 billion, $181.8 billion, and $102.3 billion (all f.o.b.). The corresponding import figures were $604.5 billion for the EEC, $218.9 billion for the United States and $109.8 billion for Japan (all c.i.f.). Source: *International Monetary Fund, Direction of Trade Yearbook,* 1980.

6. Cf. Articles 9, 48, 52, 58, and 59. These freedoms apply to foreign companies, too, as long as they establish a subsidiary in one of the member states and then deal through this subsidiary in the EEC, Article 58.

7. This is in contrast to the situation created by the notorious Decision 24 adopted by the Ancom Commission on December 31, 1970, for the Andean Pact countries. Decision 24 all but prevented future foreign investments in the Andean Pact countries by requiring prior government approval and prohibiting new foreign investments in most key commercial areas.

8. For instance, Article 173 allows full judicial review of all acts of the EEC Council and Commission other than mere recommendations or opinions. In cases of conflict, EEC law enjoys supremacy over national law. The statement in the text does not imply, however, that the system could not be improved; it is only a comparison with other international systems.

9. Most recently, Pioneer, a Japanese manufacturer of home electronics, was fined approximately $10 million by the EEC Commission; decision of December 14, 1979, *Official Journal of the European Communities* (referred to as OJ in the following footnotes) No. L 60 of March 5, 1980, p. 21; reported in *Common Market Reporter,* Commerce Clearing House, Inc. (referred to as CCH in the following footnotes), §10.185. The firm had attempted, through trade agreements, to prevent parallel imports of its equipment into France from Germany and the United Kingdom, thereby trying to maintain high price differences between these countries.

10. Article 3, Treaty of Rome, reads as follows:
    "For the purposes set out in Article 2, the activities of the Community shall include, as provided in this Treaty and in accordance with the timetable set out therein

    a. the elimination, as between Member States, of customs duties and of quantitative restrictions on the import and export of goods, and of all other measures having equivalent effect;
    b. the establishment of a common customs tariff and of a common commercial policy towards third countries;
    c. the abolition, as between Member States, of obstacles to freedom of movement for persons, services and capital;
    d. the adoption of a common policy in the sphere of agriculture;
    e. the adoption of a common policy in the sphere of transport;
    f. the institution of a system ensuring that competition in the common market is not distorted;
    g. the application of procedures by which the economic policies of Member States can be coordinated and disequilibria in their balances of payments remedied;
    h. the approximation of the laws of Member States to the extent required for the proper functioning of the Common Market."

11. See the Commission's answer to written question No. 542/74 reported in CCH §9711. See also judgments of the Court in the *Sugar* cases (Nos. 40–48, 50, 54–56, 111, 113—114/ 73) of December 16, 1975, CCH §8334, as well as in case 85/76, *Hoffman-LaRoche* v. *Commission* of February 13, 1979, CCH §8527.

12. E.g., Regulations 17/62 and 99/63 in the area of antitrust.

13. J. Drew, *Doing Business in the European Community,* London: Butterworths, 1979. Gives an excellent account of such opportunities and provides a useful insight into the workings of the Common Market.

14. *Italy* v. *EEC Council and EEC Commission,* judgment of July 13, 1966, case 32/65, CCH §8048, p. 7717. The Court has repeatedly referred to this general thought expressed in this 1966 judgment in later decisions and declared both Articles 85 and 86 to be detailed expressions of the principle laid down by Article 3(f) of the Treaty of Rome.

15. Cf. *Italy* v. *EEC Council* (note 14), p. 7718.

16. *Article 85,* Treaty of Rome, has the following text:
    "1. The following shall be prohibited as incompatible with the Common Market: all agreements between undertakings, decisions by associations of undertakings and concerted practices which may affect trade between Member States and which have as their object or effect the prevention, restriction or distortion of competition within the Common Market, and in particular those which:

    a. directly or indirectly fix purchase or selling prices or any other trading conditions;
    b. limit or control production, markets, technical development, or investment;
    c. share markets or sources of supply;
    d. apply dissimilar conditions to equivalent transactions with other trading parties, thereby placing them at a competitive disadvantage;
    e. make the conclusion of contracts subject to acceptance by the other parties of

supplementary obligations which by their nature or according to commercial usage, have no connection with the subject of such contracts.

"2. Any agreements or decisions prohibited pursuant to this Article shall be automatically void.

"3. The provisions of paragraph 1 may, however, be declared inapplicable in the case of:

any agreement or category of agreements between undertakings;

any decision or category of decisions by associations of undertakings;

any concerted practice or category of concerted practices, which contributes to improving the production or distribution of goods or to promoting technical or economic progress, while allowing consumers a fair share of the resulting benefit, and which does not:

a.   impose on the undertakings concerned restrictions which are not indispensable to the attainment of these objectives;

b.   afford such undertakings the possibility of eliminating competition in respect of a substantial part of the products in question."

Article 86, Treaty of Rome, reads as follows:

"Any abuse by one or more undertakings of a dominant position within the Common Market or in a substantial part of it shall be prohibited as incompatible with the Common Market in so far as it may affect trade between Member States.

"Such abuse may, in particular, consist in:

a.   Directly or indirectly imposing unfair purchase or selling prices or other unfair trading conditions;

b.   limiting production, markets or technical development to the prejudice of consumers;

c.   applying dissimilar conditions to equivalent transactions with other trading parties, thereby placing them at a competitive disadvantage;

d.   making the conclusion of contracts subject to acceptance by the other parties of supplementary obligations which, by their nature or according to commercial usage, have no connection with the subject of such contracts."

17.   *Miller International Schallplatten* v. *Commission,* Court of Justice, judgment of February 1, 1978, case 19/77, CCH §8439, p. 7925 (Emphasis added.) In this case approximately 6 percent in terms of volume of sales in the relevant market (sound recordings in West Germany) was held to be sufficient to produce such effect. In an earlier judgment the Court had stated that the agreement must "be such as to give rise to a reasonable expectation that it might directly or indirectly, actually or potentially, influence the flow of trade between Member States that is likely to hamper the realization of a single market between those States." Case 56/65, *Societe Technique Miniere* v. *Maschinenbau Ulm GmbH (LTM* v. *MBU),* judgment of June 30, 1966, CCH §8047, p. 7697.

18.   Cf. *Völck* v. *Vervaecke,* case 5/69, judgment of July 9, 1969, CCH §8074. The market share of the German company involved in this case for the product covered by the agreement in question had declined from 0.2 percent in 1963 to 0.05 percent in 1966. The Court held that an agreement escapes the prohibition of Article 85 when it only affects the market insignificantly, account being taken of the parties' weak market position. The old Roman rule of *de minimis non curat praetor* is therefore applicable in EEC law.

19.   See note 14.

20.   Cf. judgments of the Court in cases 27/76, *United Brands* v. *Commission,* judgment of February 14, 1978, CCH§8429, and 85/76, *Hoffmann-LaRoche* (see note 11). See in particular judgment in case 26/76 of October 25, 1977, *Metro SB Grossmärkte* v. *Commission,* CCH §8435, p. 7849, where a stereotype approach considering just the percentage of the market held by the enterprise in question was expressly rejected as a means of determining whether a dominant position exists.

21.   Paragraph 126 of the judgment, CCH § 8429, p. 7711.

22. Ibid.

23. Judgment of November 13, 1975, case 26/75, CCH §8320, p. 7734 (paragraphs 7–9 of the original judgment).

24. Judgment of May 31, 1979, case 22/78, CCH §8524, p. 7458 (paragraphs 7 and 8 of the original judgment).

25. Cf. *Kali und Salz A.G.* v. *Commission,* judgment of May 14, 1975, cases 19/74 and 20/74 CCH §8284, p. 7249. See also *United Brands,* (note 20), p. 7705 (paragraph 12 of the original judgment).

26. Cf. *Continental Can* v. *Commission,* Case 6/72, judgment of February 21, 1973, CCH § 8171, page 8301.

27. *Commercial Solvents* v. *Commission.* judgment of March 6, 1974, cases 6 and 7/73, CCH § 8209, p. 8821 (paragraph 33 of the original judgment). See also *United Brands,* (note 20), p. 7715 (paragraph 201 of the original judgment).

28. *Commercial Solvents,* ibid.

29. Cf. the Commission's statements in this regard in *Report on Competition Policy* (in the following footnotes referred to as Comp. Rep.), for 1977 (seventh), published April 1978, point 13. In agreement also H. Smit and P. E. Herzog, *The Law of the European Economic Community,* New York: Matthew Bender, 1976, Vol. 2, point 86.06.

30. Note 26, p. 8299.

31. Note 11.

32. Ibid., p. 7559 (paragraph 125 of the original judgment).

33. So stated expressly by the Court of Justice in *Hoffmann-LaRoche* (note 11), p. 7553 (paragraph 91 of the original judgment).

34. Ibid.

35. Note 11, p. 7559 (paragraph 123 of orignal judgment).

36. *Hoffmann-LaRoche* (note 11), p. 7553. See also the judgment in *Continental Can* (note 26), p. 8300.

37. Note 20, p. 7714 (paragraph 189 of the original judgment).

38. *Hoffmann-LaRoche* (note 11), p. 7561 (paragraph 136 of the original judgment).

39. Cf. the dyestuffs cases: *Imperial Chemical Industries Ltd.* v. *Commission,* judgment of July 14, 1972; case 48/69; CCH § 8161 and *Geigy A.G.* v. *Commission,* judgment of same date, case 52/69, CCH § 8164. See also *Continental Can Co.* v. *Commission* (note 26) and *Commercial Solvents Corp.* v. *Commission* (note 27). The reason for the dispute might be seen in the fact that EEC law, unlike German or U.S. law, contains no explicit provision regarding the application of antitrust law to actions committed outside its jurisdiction.

40. Note 26, p. 8298.

41. *Continental Can,* ibid.

42. A doctrine of U.S. antitrust law, in respect of its application to foreign commerce. It was used, for example, in *U.S.* v. *Alcoa,* 148 F. 2d 416 (2d Cir. 1945).

43. If the subsidiary does not in fact have autonomy in determining its course of conduct on the market, said the Court in both judgments, then the prohibition of Article 85, paragraph 1, is inapplicable to the relationship between it and the parent company with which it forms an economic unit; see note 39, p. 8031 re *ICI* v. *Commission,* and p. 8143 re *Geigy* v. *Commission.* This means that the parent is directly responsible for the actions of the subsidiary, as the separate legal personality of both companies does not prevent the two from being considered one single enterprise in their relationship with the outside world.

44. The relevant passage in *Commercial Solvents* reads as follows: " . . . the conduct of CSC and ISTITUTO has thus been characterized by an obviously united action which,

taking account of the power of control of CSC over ISTITUTO, confirms . . . that as regards their relations with ZOJA the two companies must be deemed an economic unit and that they are jointly and severally responsible for the conduct complained of,'' CCH § 8209, p. 8822 (paragraph 41 of the original judgment).

45. In the dyestuffs case the commission had effected service on the German subsidiary of 1C1 instead of attempting service in London, seat of the company's headquarters. The United Kingdom, at that time, was not a member of the Common Market. The Court confirmed the validity of this service; see CCH § 8161, p. 8026.

46. Strictly national joint ventures are of interest to the Commission only in the event that they might affect trade between member states.

47. Cf. Comp. Rep 1976 (sixth), point 55. A case in point is *SHV/Chevron,* Commission Decision of December 20, 1974; OJ No. L 38/14 of February 12, 1975, CCH § 9709. However, the Commission did review the case under both Articles 85 and 86, which may be explained by the fact that this was the Commission's first decision ever involving the formation of joint subsidiaries in a joint-venture situation. Four years later, in *Kaiser/ Estel,* the Commission remained consistent and applied a clean Article 86 rationale in the case of this 1979 joint venture, which had to be regarded as a partial merger. Cf. Comp. Rep. 1979 (ninth), point 131. This shows that the legal approach to joint ventures had to be developed on a case-by-case basis; see the Commission's own explanation, cf. point 53, sixth Comp. Rep.

48. *Continental Can* (note 26), pp. 8300 and 8301.

49. This decision will be discussed below.

50. Commission decision of July 25, 1977 OJ No. L 215/11 of August 23, 1977 CCH § 9972. Cf. the Commission's comments in Comp. Rep. 1976 (sixth), point 176 and in Comp. Rep. 1977 (seventh), point 151. See also decision of the Commission in the *General Electric/Weir* case of November 23, 1977, OJ No. L 327/26 of December 20, 1977, CCH § 10,000 relating to sodium circulators for the production of nuclear reactors.

51. This was expressly confirmed by the Commission in its comments related to the *Henkel/ Colgate* case; cf. Comp. Rep. 1978 (eighth), point 89.

52. More-limited forms of joint implementation of research-and-development projects may be deemed not to restrict competition and may not fall under Article 85(1), consequently. Cf. Commission Notice on Agreements, Decisions, and Concerted Practices Concerning Cooperation Between Enterprises of July 29, 1968, OJ No. C 75, corrected by OJ No. C 84 of August 28, 1968, CCH § 2699.

53. Commission decision of January 17, 1979, *Bulletin of the European Communities* (hereafter referred to as Bulletin EC) 1979/1, point 2.1.32, CCH § 10,121.

54. Cf. Commission decision (note 53) paragraph 26.

55. Ibid., paragraph 32.

56. Ibid., paragraph 34.

57. Commission press release No. IP (79) 42 of March 7, 1979 CCH § 10,121.

58. Cf. Commission decision (note 53), paragraph 37.

59. Ibid., paragraph 36.

60. See note 52.

61. Commission decision (note 53), paragraph 43 (c).

62. Ibid., paragraph 42.

63. Council Regulation No. 2821/71 of December 20, 1971 OJ No. L 285/46, December 29, 1971 CCH § 2729.

64. Issued on December 21, 1972, OJ No. L 292/23, December 29, 1972, with an amendment extending the validity of this regulation through December 1982, Regulation 2903/77 of December 23, 1977, CCH § 2731.

65. Each of the member states, with the exception of Luxembourg and possibly Ireland, can be taken to represent "a substantial part of the Common Market."

66. A unit of account is the EEC internal measurement base used for budgetary and other financial purposes. On December 31, 1980, one unit of account equalled $1.31, see Bulletin EC 1980/10, p. 125.

67. Commission decision of December 15, 1975, OJ No. L 30/13 of February 5, 1976, CCH § 9814.

68. Cf. beginning of this section.

69. Where the Commission suspects an infringement of EEC competition rules, it can open a formal investigation, activating all the special powers that it is given under Council Regulation 17/62.

70. It is not until such a notification is filed that the Commission can start to consider the applicability of Article 85 (3), Treaty of Rome, in a given case.

71. Decision of December 15, 1975 (note 67), paragraph III 3 (b).

72. Ibid., paragraph III 1.

73. The Commission can certify, under the provisions of this article, that "there are no grounds under Article 85(1) or Article 86 of the Treaty for action on its part in respect of an agreement, decision or practice."

74. Commission decision of October 20, 1978, OJ No. L 322/26 of November 16, 1978, CCH § 10,089. It is said to be the Commission's first decision under Article 85 prohibiting agreements to set up a joint venture (cf. Bulletin EC 1978/10, p. 32). This is only partially true, considering the *Bayer/Gist-Brocades* agreement, where the joint-venture subsidiary intended by the parties was also disallowed by the Commission. The end result, of course, was different in that Bayer and Gist-Brocades obtained an exemption, and WASAG and ICI did not.

75. Comp. Rep. 1978 (eighth), point 136.

76. Ibid.

77. Cf. part IV of the decision.

78. Cf. part II, paragraph 2(d) of the decision.

79. Comp. Rep. 1978 (eighth), point 135.

80. The Commission did it anyway, but discarded the companies' arguments in this respect; cf. part III, paragraphs 2–4 of the decision.

81. Other examples are the *Vacuum Interrupters* case, Commission decision of January 20, 1977, OJ No. L 48 of February 19, 1977, CCH § 9926, also the *General Electric/Weir* agreement (note 50).

82. Other examples are the decision in *De Laval/Stork* (note 50), and *SHV/Chevron* (note 47); see also Commission decision of December 21, 1977, OJ No. L 70 of March 13, 1978, CCH § 10,014, *Sopelem/Vickers*, relating to the joint distribution of microscopes, and the *ICI/Montedison* agreement, reported in Comp. Rep. 1977 (seventh), points 156–159 (this agreement was not implemented, though, as the two companies abandoned the joint venture).

83. Court of Justice, judgment of February 29, 1968, case 24/67, CCH § 8054.

84. Ibid., p. 7825. Preceding this statement the Court had declared, in the same context, that "a patent of invention, viewed by itself and apart from any agreement of which it might be the subject, does not belong in any of these categories [of agreement] but results from a legal status granted by a state for products meeting certain criteria, and thus avoids the elements of contract or concert required by Article 85, paragraph 1."

85. Comp. Rep. 1979 (ninth), point 7.

86. "Proposal for a Commission Regulation on the Application of Article 85(3) of the Treaty to Certain Categories of Patent Licensing Agreements," OJ No. C 58 of March 3, 1979, p. 12, CCH § 10,118.

87. Comp. Rep. 1979 (ninth), point 11.

88. Ibid.

89. Notice of December 24, 1962 ("Christmas Message"), OJ No. 139, p. 2922.

90. One of these decisions was discussed in this paper, namely *Bayer/Gist-Brocades* (note 67); some others were the Dutch Drainage case—*Bronbemaling Heidemaatschappij,* decision of July 25, 1975, OJ No. L 249 of September 25, 1975, p. 27, CCH § 9776, and the *Maize Seed* case, decision of September 21, 1978, OJ No. L 286 of October 12, 1978, p. 23, CCH § 10,083.

91. Commission decision of December 23, 1977, OJ No. L 70 of March 13, 1978, p. 69, CCH § 10,035; cf. paragraph III A (2) of the decision, p. 10,204.

92. Commission decision of January 10, 1979, OJ No. L 19 of January 26, 1979, p. 32, CCH § 10,107.

93. Ibid., paragraph 23 of the decision, p. 10,370.

94. Commission decision of December 2, 1975, OJ No. L 6 of January 13, 1976, p. 8, CCH § 9801.

95. Ibid., p. 9793–7.

96. Cf. Commission press release of April 23, 1980, CCH § 10,224.

97. Cf. CCH § 10,217.

98. In the area of patents, a step into the future has been taken with the *Convention for a European Patent,* signed in Luxembourg on December 15, 1975. This convention creates a Community patent, valid in all the countries forming the Common Market, within the framework of the *European Patent Organization,* which was established approximately two years earlier and comprises other European countries not belonging to the EEC. However, the basic conflict between Community law and its concern for undistorted, uninhibited trade among the member states on the one hand and national laws granting territorial protection to patent holders on the other hand has not been resolved with the Community patent. The reason is a special section in the Convention that allows territorially limited licenses and grants the right to the patent holder to institute infringement actions against licensees who are in breach of this territorial restriction (i.e., make use of the patent license outside their allotted territory, for example, by selling the patented product in another EEC country). This is the famous *Article 43(2) of the Convention.* The Commission has taken the view "that the existence of the patent in no case gives the holder the right to shield one licensee against competition from another," and it was therefore "not able to give its approval to Article 43(2)." See Comp. Rep. 1975 (fifth), point 11. The conflict between the supranational EEC system and the national legal systems has thus been perpetuated by the European Patent Convention. The Commission characterized this by stating that "it will be for the Court of Justice of the European Communities to resolve this difficulty in the final instance" (Ibid.).

99. Court of Justice, in *Deutsche Grammophon* v. *Metro SB Grossmärkte,* case 78/70, judgment of June 8, 1971, CCH § 8106, p. 7192.

100. Cf. chapter on business in the EEC, under "EEC Antitrust Concepts."

101. Court of Justice, judgment of July 11, 1974, case 8/74, CCH § 8276, p. 7129.

102. Note 83, p. 7825.

103. *Sirena Srl.* v. *Eda GmbH,* case 40/70, judgment of February 18, 1971, CCH § 8101, p. 7111.

104. Court of Justice, judgment of July 15, 1964, case 6/64, CCH § 8023.

105. *Article 36,* Treaty of Rome, has the following text: "The provisions of Articles 30 and 34 shall not preclude prohibitions or restrictions on imports, exports or goods in transit justified on grounds of public morality, public policy or public security; the protection of health and life of humans, animals or plants; the protection of national treasures possessing artistic, historic or archaeological value; or the protection of industrial and

commercial property. Such prohibitions or restrictions shall not, however, constitute a means of arbitrary discrimination or a disguised restriction on trade between Member States.''

106. Court of Justice, judgment of July 13, 1966, cases 56 and 58/64, CCH § 8046.

107. Ibid., p. 7654.

108. Ibid.

109. Ibid. (emphasis added).

110. Note 103, p. 7111 (emphasis added). The Court has consistently held that the exception permitted by Article 36, first sentence, has to be applied as narrowly as possible because of the built-in restriction evident from Article 36, second sentence. See the text of the law (note 105).

111. Note 99.

112. Court of Justice, judgment of July 3, 1974, case 192/73, CCH § 8230.

113. Court of Justice, judgment of October 31, 1974, case 15/74, CCH § 8246.

114. Note 99, p. 7192.

115. Cf. note 43.

116. Note 112, p. 9124.

117. Ibid., p. 9125 (emphasis added).

118. Note 113, pp. 9151–56 (paragraph 11 of the original judgment).

119. Ibid., (paragraph 10 of the original judgment).

120. Court of Justice, judgment of October 31, 1974, case 16/74, CCH § 8247.

121. Ibid., p. 9151–67 regarding trademarks (paragraph 12 of the original judgment), and note 113, p. 9151–56 regarding patents (paragraph 15 of the original judgment).

122. Cf. *Sterling Drug* (above) with respect to patents and *Terrapin* (below) with respect to trademarks. The Commission has expressed its opinion with respect to copyrights in connection with a recent case involving an *attempt to partition the Common Market by means of copyright licenses*. It is ''the Commission's general view . . . that once a copy of a book has been sold by or with the consent of the copyright owner in one Member State, that copy must be free to move throughout the EEC in the same way as patented or trademarked goods.'' Bulletin EC 1979/10, point 2.1.27 (page 27). The specific subject matter of the copyright is therefore to be seen in the right to put into circulation a copy of the protected product for the first time, for purposes of commercial exploitation. It can be expected that the Commission will apply its view to all copyrighted products, not just books.

123. Note 83.

124. Ibid., p. 7825.

125. Court of Justice, judgment of June 22, 1976, case 119/75, CCH § 8362.

126. Ibid., p. 7605.

127. Court of Justice, judgment of May 23, 1978, case 102/77, CCH § 8466.

128. Court of Justice, judgment of October 10, 1978, case 3/78, CCH § 8475.

129. Note 127, pp. 8400–8401 (emphasis added).

130. Ibid., p. 8401.

131. Note 128, p. 8592.

132. Ibid.

133. Court of Justice, judgments of June 15, 1976, cases 51/75 (CCH § 8350), 86/75 (CCH § 8351), and 96/75 (CCH § 8352).

LEGAL ASPECTS OF INTERNATIONAL TRADE

CONTENTS

HISTORICAL OVERVIEW	3	Subsidies Resulting in Countervailing Duties	19
TARIFFS	6	Dumping	24
Valuation of Goods for Customs Purposes	8	Section 337 Relief from Unfair Trade Practices	25
Generalized System of Tariff Preferences for Developing Countries	9	Standards as a Barrier to Trade	26
		GOVERNMENT PROCUREMENT	28
IMPORT-RESTRAINT ACTIONS	12	Nondiscrimination	29
''Escape Clause'' Action	12	Code Rules and Transparency	29
Section 22 Restraints on Agricultural Imports	16	Dispute Settlement	32
Section 204 of the Agricultural Act of 1956	16	Government-to-government consultations	33
National Security Provision	16	Multilateral settlement	33
		General Limitations on Code Coverage	33
UNFAIR COMPETITIVE PRACTICES IN INTERNATIONAL TRADE	17	Country limitations on coverage	34
		Other Code Provisions	35
Enforcement of U.S. Rights—Section 301	18	U.S. Implementation of the Code	35
		SOURCES AND SUGGESTED REFERENCES	36

LEGAL ASPECTS OF INTERNATIONAL TRADE

Morton Pomeranz

HISTORICAL OVERVIEW

An elaboration of the elements of U.S. law that affect our international trade will be more understandable if one is aware of their development over the 200 years of our history. Our trade law reflects the history of our growth from a small trading country to a world economic power in an era of increasing international interdependence.

Congress, under the Constitution (Article I, Section 8), has the authority to impose and collect taxes and duties and also to regulate commerce with foreign nations. James Madison, the first Speaker of the House of Representatives, the congressional body in which all revenue measures must originate, introduced our first tariff act in 1789, largely to generate the revenues needed to fund the new government. Fundamentally, tariffs are nothing more than taxes applied to imported goods. Until the passage of the income tax in 1913, the primary function of the U.S. tariff system was to provide the government with income adequate to finance its operations. Until the latter year, tariffs collected at customs offices accounted for between 50 and 90 percent of government revenues.

From the beginning, the enactment of tariff acts by Congress, notwithstanding their principal revenue aspect, has been attended by attempts to prevent or restrict the importation of certain goods from abroad. Some sector of the economy would always be lobbying to raise the duty level on one or more categories of imported goods on the thesis that such higher tariffs were needed to "protect" one or more domestic industries or producers from foreign competition and to preserve domestic employment levels. But it was not until after the Civil War and the flowering of the industrial revolution in the United States that protectionism became an increasing factor in congressional tariff making.

At various times throughout U.S. history, Congress has delegated to the President its powers concerning the regulation and promotion of international trade and commerce. During the first century of U.S. history such delegations were few. Throughout most of that period, Congress itself established the levels of import duties. By 1890 Congress began to recognize its limitations in ascertaining precise duty rates on anything approaching a scientific basis. Moreover, due to a history of regional and industrial pressures, there grew a consensus to remove specific tariff making from politics as much as possible. Constituent interest was such that no tariff bill could be passed without warping compromises, bargains, and special concessions. Although recognizing this problem, Congress addressed it initially only reluctantly and in a piecemeal fashion.

A first small step was taken in the "McKinley" Tariff Act of 1890 (26 Statutes at Large 567, 612). In that act, Congress provided that the President, by proclamation, could enter into and carry out agreements with other countries that would allow for duty-free importation of sugars, molasses, coffee, tea, and hides from that country if he determined that U.S. exports enjoyed reciprocal advantages in that country. In the short span of 4 years before repeal of the McKinley Tariff, the President proclaimed agreements with 10 countries under this authority. The concept was reactivated in the "Dingley" Tariff Act of 1897 (30 Statutes at Large 151, 203). The Dingley Tariff also allowed reciprocal agreements on the basis of a limited list of agricultural products. In the next 10 years, nine agreements based on this authority were entered into with European countries. It is particularly interesting to note that another section of the Dingley Tariff authorized the President to negotiate agreements for wide reductions in tariffs with other countries, but only through conclusion of a treaty, which, of course, requires Senate ratification.

In spite of these modest steps to "depoliticize" the tariff-making process by delegation to the President, a number of unfortunate chapters would have to be written before the Congress was prepared to delegate the extensive kind of tariff-reduction authority to the President that began in 1934 and has continued virtually uninterrupted to this day. The infamous "Smoot-Hawley" Tariff Act of 1930, the most protectionist in our history, probably represented the final stage in Congress' becoming aware of its limitations in reaching any kind of scientific result in its own tariff-making efforts.

The Reciprocal Trade Agreements Act of 1934 represented a bipartisan commitment of the Congress to a program of reducing the "beggar-thy-neighbor" tariff levels that had sprung up internationally at the beginning of the Great Depression. This was to be done by lowering U.S. tariffs in return for reciprocal concessions from other countries. It totally altered the process of changing U.S. tariffs by turning the power to reduce rates by as much as 50 percent over to the Executive Branch for an initial 3-year period. The act eliminated the practice of periodic wholesale rewriting of the U.S. tariff law and rates. Except for a 7-year period prior to 1974, that original delegation of tariff authority has been consistently extended to the present day. Since 1934, in response to domestic pressures and international trade developments, those delegations have become broader in scope and much more complex in their administration.

The rationale for congressional delegation of its authority to the President found its expression in the Senate Finance Committee report on the Trade Agreements Act of 1934:

Time is of the essence in international negotiations of a commercial nature under the emergency conditions of today. Practically all of the important commercial nations of the world can take prompt action with regard to tariff adjustments. Under our form of government general tariff policies can be and should be formulated by the legislative branch; broad principles governing our long-term relations with foreign countries are properly established by statutes or treaties. On the other hand, plain limitations upon the scope permitted for Executive discretion, such as are embodied in the Trade Agreements Act, are essential in regard to domestic matters and frequently are desirable in regard to our foreign relations. To attempt more may often thwart important general policies and principles; to attempt to require in every instance senatorial disposition of the manifold and constantly changing details involved in the carrying out of such policies and principles would frequently be to render the legislative branch incapable of effective exercise of its functions. S. Rept. 111, 75th Cong., 1st. Sess., 1G.3

The courts have upheld congressional delegations of its trade authority to the President so long as Congress had laid down, by legislative act, intelligible policy and plans for the President to follow. The courts have recognized that in this process Congress may provide that the enforcement of the law may depend on future events or the ascertainment of facts, leaving to the President the determination of the happening of the events or the existence of the facts.

Beginning with the 1890s, aspects of trade law other than tariffs also began to be the focus of congressional action and consequent additional delegations to the Executive Branch. To a large extent this additional focus was the result of domestic pressures to respond to international practices that were deemed to be unfair to U.S. trade and to the U.S. economy generally. Illustrative of these early beginnings for the much more complex body of legislation that applies today are the following:

1. *Antisubsidy.*   The pioneering Dingley Tariff Act of 1897 provided that the Secretary of the Treasury should impose an additional duty on imports equal to the amount of the bounty or grant paid or bestowed by a foreign government for the benefit of the exported goods.

2. *Antidumping.*   The Antidumping Act of 1921 (42 Statutes at Large 11) authorized the Secretary of the Treasury to add a dumping (additional) duty to equalize prices of goods being imported and sold in the United States at "less than fair value."

3. *Unfair import practices.*   Section 337 of the Tariff Act of 1930 (building on earlier legislation of 1922) provided for the prohibition of imports that are found to have been brought in or sold by unfair methods and thus to have caused substantial injury to an efficient domestic industry.

A further historical insight into the development of U.S. trade law can be gained from comparing the 1897 one-paragraph simple antisubsidy delegation to the Secretary of the Treasury to the dozen pages in the Trade Agreements Act of 1979, containing much more detailed provisions insuring complex investigative, regulatory, and enforcement procedures. This phenomenon has also occurred with regard to many other elements of U.S. trade law.

No historical overview would be complete without reference to the General Agreement on Tariffs and Trade (GATT). In the grand design of post-World War II planning that was to result in the United Nations, the International Monetary Fund (IMF), and the World Bank, it was envisaged that an International Trade Organization (ITO) would also be established, to provide international rules not only in the trade area but in such other areas as foreign investment, commodity agreements, and monopoly practices as well. The planners were determined that the restrictionist trade policies enacted during the 1930s had to be dismantled and ways found to prevent a repetition of the destructive "beggar-thy-neighbor" trade and economic policies that accompanied the Depression and contributed to bringing on the war.

GATT was negotiated in 1947. The United States and the 22 other countries who were the original signatories were then in the process of drawing up the charter for the ITO. The GATT, an instrument drawing upon selected parts of the ITO charter, was looked upon as a way of getting trade liberalization under way quickly and was provided with only minimum institutional arrangements, because it was expected that the function would soon be assumed by the ITO. Cold War tensions and other disenchantments of the late 1940s doomed the ITO, leaving the GATT as the only international instrument laying down rules to govern trade among the nations responsible for most of the world's trade.

The United States, as the leading planner for the postwar world, in order to avoid the need for congressional approval of the GATT, did not want to enter into an agreement that was not consistent with the then-current U.S. trade legislation. Consequently, the original GATT could not provide a complete framework for the general regulation of world trade. The more limited undertaking that it represents carries forward two main thrusts of the reciprocal-trade-agreements program that the United States embarked upon in 1934—the need to lower tariff levels throughout the world and the need to extend the benefits of those tariff reductions to all countries on a most-favored-nation nondiscriminatory basis. Equally important, the GATT established a series of normative rules covering subjects such as dumping, subsidies, taxation on goods, state trading, and import quotas, as they may impact on the reduced tariff levels that member countries would agree to negotiate and to maintain as one of their principal commitments under the GATT. In the years since 1947, the ever-increasing membership of the GATT participated in seven so-called rounds of tariff negotiations. It was evident, even before the 1973 beginning of the last round (the "Tokyo Round," which concluded in 1979) that tariff reductions had proceeded to a point where tariffs no longer represented as great an obstacle to international trade as the nontariff barriers to that trade. As one might therefore expect, the last round of negotiations was largely devoted to making substantial improvements on earlier efforts to expand GATT rules in the nontariff areas. The resultant GATT codes on such subjects as subsidies, dumping, technical standards, valuation for customs purposes, and government procurement represent a substantial enlargement of GATT rules and the machinery for enforcing rights under the GATT. At appropriate points later in this section, more-detailed references to the GATT codes and rules will be provided as they interplay with U.S. domestic legislation.

The remainder of this section is broken down into four major parts covering the most important aspects of our international trade law. The first part, "Tariffs," is devoted to (1) the basic tariff authority, (2) valuation of goods for customs purposes, and (3) the generalized system of tariff preferences for developing countries. "Import Restraint Actions" treats (1) the "escape clause" action, (2) Section 22 restraints on agricultural imports, (3) Section 204 of the Agricultural Act of 1952, and (4) the national-security provision. The third part, "Unfair Competitive Practices in International Trade," covers (1) enforcement of U.S. trade rights, (2) subsidies resulting in countervailing duties, (3) dumping, (4) Section 337 relief from unfair trade practices, and (5) technical standards as a barrier to trade. The final part is devoted entirely to government procurement.

TARIFFS

The most recent grant of tariff authority to the President was contained in the Trade Act of 1974 (19 U.S.C. 2101). It is a far more complex delegation by Congress than the act of 1934 and one that reflects the development of such delegations over the years. Principally it provided for a 5-year extension, which expired January 3, 1980, of the authority to negotiate, enter into, and implement multilateral and bilateral trade agreements, modifying, continuing, or increasing import duties and excise taxes. Under this delegation, the President could not reduce duties to a level below 40 percent of existing duties, although duties already at a level of five percent or less could be negotiated down to zero. Further, the Act provided that large duty reductions (exceeding 10 percent) had to be phased in over a period of years (not more than three percentage points or one tenth of the total reduction annually). Congress, in passing the 1974 Act, anticipated that this basic authority would be used by the President to negotiate and carry out U.S. commitments that were expected to result from the round of multilateral trade negotiations then in progress. These negotiations had been initiated in 1973 in Tokyo by the more than 80 countries who participate in the GATT. This Tokyo Round of negotiations, concluded in 1979, resulted in an agreement by the United States to a more than 30 percent average reduction in the then-existing U.S. tariff levels on industrial products on a reciprocal basis. Specific tariff rates and the means of implementation of the reductions agreed to in the Tokyo Round are contained in *Tariff Schedules of the United States Annotated* (1980, Publication No. 1011) published by the U.S. International Trade Commission (ITC).

Although the President's basic tariff authority lapsed on January 3, 1980, the 1974 Act also provided that for an additional two-year period (ending January 3, 1982), the President could enter into further trade agreements reducing duties on articles that account for no more than two percent of the value of imports for the most recent 12-month base period for which statistics are available. This so-called residual authority is further limited in that the total duty changes on any tariff item, using both the basic and residual tariff authority, may not exceed the 40 percent "floor" that was possible under the basic negotiating authority. Thus if a 10 percent duty had been reduced to 5 percent as a result of the Tokyo Round of negotiations, it could only be reduced to 4 percent under this residual authority.

The 1974 Act is also noteworthy in that it set up two other new presidential authorities affecting tariffs. The first of these is called the "balance of payments" authority. When, in the early 1970s, for the first time in our history we experienced balance of payments problems, questions were raised about the President's authority to respond to such a situation. Consequently Congress authorized the President to proclaim, for a period up to 150 days, an import surcharge (an additional import duty of up to 15 percent *ad valorem*) or import quotas, or a combination of the two, as may be necessary to deal with large and serious balance of payments deficits, to prevent an imminent and significant depreciation of the dollar, or to cooperate with other countries in correcting international balance-of-payments disequilibriums. Import restrictions are to be applied on a nondiscriminatory basis unless the President determines that circumstances warrant restrictions on imports from individual countries. Conversely, if the President determines that the United States has experienced large persistent trade surpluses that require an offsetting increase in U.S. imports, he is authorized to proclaim for a period of up to 150 days: (1) a temporary reduction in the rate of duty, or not more than five percent of the value of any article, (2) a relaxation of import quotas, or (3) a temporary suspension of other import restrictions.

The second new presidential tariff authority provided by the 1974 Act is labeled the "compensation" authority. In essence, it provides for the ability to provide offsetting lower duties to countries that suffer a loss of trade because the United States has determined, in response to unexpected import competition, that it is necessary to raise duties on particular tariff items, when the rate of duty was earlier guaranteed to those countries. A fuller discussion of this authority is provided in the "escape clause" section in the second part of this chapter.

The 1974 act set up very elaborate procedures that the President must follow before utilizing any of his delegated authorities. They include advising the ITC of the articles on which he intends to negotiate, obtaining from the ITC its advice about the potential consequences of tariff reductions on the articles so listed, holding public hearings concerning the intended negotiations, and obtaining advice about such proposed tariff action from executive departments and from private sector and congressional advisory groups set up for the purpose.

VALUATION OF GOODS FOR CUSTOMS PURPOSES.   There are two basic kinds of import duties: *specific* and *ad valorem*. Specific duties are assessed and applied in terms of units of money for a specified quantity of goods imported (e.g., 10 cents per pound or 5 cents per yard). *Ad valorem* duties are assessed and applied in terms of a percentage of the value of the imported good. Throughout the world over the last 50 years, there has been a full-scale movement toward the phasing out of specific duties in favor of *ad valorem* duties. This has required development of precise rules for determining the value of goods to which the duty is applied when moving through customs.

Article VII of the GATT represents the 1947 attempt to establish an international rule for determination of value. It set out the basic rule that "The value for customs purposes . . . should be based on the actual value of the imported merchandise on which duty is assessed, or of like merchandise, and should not be based on the value of merchandise of national origin or on arbitrary or fictitious values." This general rule was then elaborated as follows:

1. "Actual value" should be the price at which at a time and place determined by the legislation of the country of importation, such or like merchandise is sold or offered for sale in the ordinary course of trade under fully competitive conditions.

2. When actual value is not determinable under number 1 above, "the value for customs purposes should be based on the nearest ascertainable equivalent of such value."

3. The value for customs purposes should not include the amount of any internal tax, applicable within the country of origin or export, from which the imported product has been exempted or has been or will be relieved by means of refund.

Notwithstanding the establishment of this GATT rule, customs valuation continued to constitute an important form of trade restriction, and arbitrary valuation methods continued to appear in virtually all of the major trading countries. Thus it was one of the major issues to be confronted in the Tokyo Round of trade negotiations. The result was the so-called Customs valuation agreement (more formally termed the Agreement on the Implementation of Article VII of the General Agreement). The rather substantial changes in U.S. valuation rules resulting from U.S. signature of the agreement were implemented by Congress through the 1979 Trade Act (Title II as amended by P.L. 96-490).

The Valuation Agreement eliminates to a large degree the potential for arbitrary valuation by providing for a primary method that must be used whenever possible

and a series of alternative methods that traders and Customs officials must attempt
to apply in a prescribed sequence as follows:

1. *Transaction value.* The primary method of valuation is the transaction value
   of the imported merchandise, that is, the price actually paid or payable for
   the goods with a limited number of adjustments. Upward adjustments in value
   shall be made for such as the following if not already included in the price:
   a. Packing costs and selling commissions incurred by the buyer.
   b. Items or services, when supplied by the buyer free of charge or at reduced
      cost, for use in connection with the production or sale for export to the
      United States of the imported merchandise, such as materials incorpo-
      rated in, and tools, dies, and so forth, used in the production of the goods,
      as well as engineering, development, and design work necessary for the
      production of the imported merchandise and undertaken elsewhere than
      in the United States. (In the technical parlance of Customs these are
      called "assists".)
   c. Royalties and license fees the buyer is required to pay as a condition of
      the sale of the merchandise to him.
   d. Proceeds of a subsequent resale, disposal, or use of the imported mer-
      chandise accruing to the seller.

If any of these additions cannot be determined for lack of sufficient information,
then the transaction value cannot be determined, and another method of valuation
must be used.

The following items are illustrative of those not to be included in transaction
value (they must be identified separately): reasonable charges incurred for the
construction, erection, assembly or maintenance of, or technical assistance provided with respect to, the merchandise after its importation; transportation of the
merchandise after its importation; and certain duties and taxes payable on the
merchandise by reason of its importation.

Sales between related parties where the relationship may affect price are subject
to special rules to determine whether the transaction value can be used or not.

2. *Transaction value of identical merchandise and similar merchandise.* If
   transaction value of the merchandise, the primary test, is not acceptable to
   the Customs Service, the first alternative valuation method to be applied is
   that of the previously accepted transaction value, adjusted for commercial
   and quantity levels as appropriate, of identical merchandise sold for export
   to the United States and exported at or about the same time as the goods
   being valued.*

3. *Deductive value.* In simplistic terms, deductive value is determined by taking
   the price of the first sale after importation of either the imported good or
   identical or similar goods and deducting therefrom certain costs and charges
   incurred after importation. Normally this method would be used when the

*If these two methods of valuation, based on transaction, cannot be accepted for customs
purposes, the value under the new code will be determined on the basis of the *deductive* value
or *computed* value, in that order, unless the importer opts to reverse their application. Should
it prove impossible to determine an acceptable computed value after the importer requests this
option, the deductive method will be applied.

imported product is not further manufactured after importation, but the importer may request its use for goods later processed if due allowance is made for the value added by the processing.

4. *Computed value.* The computed value of imported merchandise is the sum of:

   a. Material and manufacturing costs.

   b. Profit and general expenses, normal in sales of merchandise like or similar to that imported, by producers in the country of exportation when producing for the United States.

   c. Any "assists" not included in the above.

   d. Packing costs.

5. *If valuation cannot be arrived at under prior methods.* The final method of appraisement, to be used only when a value cannot be accepted under any of the previous valuation methods, is the "value that is derived from the methods set forth [above], with such methods being reasonably adjusted to the extent necessary to arrive at a value." The reader should recognize this rule for what it is—not a very good rule, but one sufficient to force use of the prior methods of valuation or risk, under this alternative, what amounts to "anything goes." However, the Customs Valuation Code (implemented in the United States by the 1979 Trade Act), does put a good measure of constraint on this method by prohibiting the use of certain valuation methods that had earlier been used both in the United States and elsewhere. Most notable of such prohibited valuation methods is the American Selling Price method, under which goods were valued solely on the basis of the price at which the comparable American good was sold or offered for sale in the United States. Another method now prohibited is that of appraisement of merchandise at the higher of two alternatives.

In the event of a dispute under the Customs Valuation agreement a committee on Customs Valuation, made up of signatories to the customs agreement, is established to effect implementation of the agreement and to resolve disputes arising under it. The code also establishes a Technical Committee, drawing on the talents of the Brussels-based Customs Cooperation Council, to provide expertise to the Committee on Customs Valuation when technical aspects of the agreement require such assistance.

Initially, the concerned parties should seek to resolve the dispute between themselves. Failing such resolution, either party may request the matter to be taken up by the Committee on Customs Valuation. To assist the work of that committee, the Technical Committee can be brought in to provide its expertise and either party can request the establishment of a panel of independent experts to review facts and the applicable law in the case.

GENERALIZED SYSTEM OF TARIFF PREFERENCES FOR DEVELOPING COUNTRIES. "Trade, not aid" became a catch phrase of some consequence among developing countries as early as the 1950s. The underlying argument noted that export earnings represented not only the source of funds needed for economic development but also the wherewithal for financing food imports and other commodities necessary for improving the standard of living of the populations of the developing countries. Those countries argued strenuously that developed countries could lessen their aid burdens by extending tariff preferences to goods originating in the developing countries. This would help developing countries increase exports, diversify their economies, and make them less dependent on foreign aid. Of course it was also argued that such preferences could be extended without undue harm to the international trade of the developed countries.

The idea of preferences for the developing countries was formally introduced at the first United Nations Conference on Trade and Development (UNCTAD) in Geneva in 1964. At that meeting the developing countries argued that their inability to compete on an equal basis with developed countries in the international trading system was one of the major impediments to accelerated economic growth.

Pressures on the developed countries continued to build, and, at the second UNCTAD conference in New Delhi in 1968, the United States joined other nations in supporting a resolution to establish a mutually acceptable system of preferences. Any such system of preferences would, of course, have to be squared with Article I of the GATT, which provides that trade be conducted on a nondiscriminatory most-favored-nation basis. Consequently in June 1971, the United States and other developed countries requested and received a 10-year waiver from Article I. The European Community implemented its preference system shortly thereafter, and most other major powers had their system in place before the U.S. program became effective in January 1976. During the Tokyo Round, the GATT member countries took an action that for all practical purposes extends the GATT Article I waiver indefinitely. The generalized system of preferences (GSP) systems of the various countries are generally similar in coverage and eligible recipients. They all include machinery to protect domestic industry from undue import competition.

Under the terms of Title V of the Trade Act of 1974, the U.S. GSP system will remain in effect until January 3, 1985. The essential features of the U.S. program are as follows:

1. In designating the products that will be subject to preferential rates, the President must exclude (1) textile and apparel items whose importation is being otherwise limited through other international agreement, (2) watches, (3) "import-sensitive" (e.g., products deemed to be suffering considerable import competition) electronic articles, (4) import-sensitive steel articles, (5) certain specified footwear articles, (6) import-sensitive semimanufactured glass products, and (7) any other articles that the President determines to be import sensitive for this purpose or that are subject to any of the import-restraint actions described below.

2. The President designates beneficiary developing countries. In essence, the Trade Act of 1974 provides that he may not designate most communist countries or those that have taken specified unfair actions against the United States, its trade, or the property of its citizens.

3. Eligible articles must be imported directly from the developing country. The value of the good added in that country must be at least 35 percent of the value of the article. Under the 1974 Act, in those cases where the country was a member of a free trade association, the local content from two or more associated countries would have had to be 50 percent of the value of the article. This was changed to 35 percent under the 1979 Act.

4. An article imported from any one country will no longer enjoy the preferential rate if the imports of that article from that country in any year exceed $25 million (adjusted to reflect growth in U.S. gross national product; the adjusted figure for 1979 was $41.9 million) or 50 percent of total U.S. imports of that article, with certain limited exceptions (e.g., the 50 percent rule will not apply if article imports do not exceed $1 million, with that figure also subject to adjustment).

The U.S. program now covers about 40 percent of the approximately 7000 classifications in the Tariff Schedules of the United States (TSUS). Information about specific tariff items affected in these preferences can be obtained by reference to the ITC publication cited earlier in this chapter.

IMPORT-RESTRAINT ACTIONS

By the nature of the U.S. political process, it was not unreasonable to expect that as Congress increased the delegations of trade-liberalizing authority to the President, it would also provide for a number of devices by which the consequences of such actions could be counterbalanced. This part of the chapter is devoted to such provisions of U.S. trade law.

"ESCAPE CLAUSE" ACTION. When the trade agreements program was first proposed in 1934, the major element in the arguments of its opponents was that the reductions in U.S. tariff duties that would be made could result in serious injury to domestic industries. Advocates of the program contended that by careful selection of the classifications of imports on which negotiated tariff reductions would be made and by careful consideration of the extent of the reductions of these tariffs, serious injury to domestic industries could and would be avoided. As the program developed, it became evident that it was not possible to forecast accurately developments in trade and industry that might affect the impact of trade-agreement concessions on individual domestic industries. In order to meet this problem, the Roosevelt administration adopted the practice (subsequently ratified by statute) of including in trade agreements negotiated after 1941 a provision that is referred to as the "escape clause." Under this clause, tariff concessions on particular goods may be withdrawn or modified if increased imports of such goods cause or threaten serious injury to domestic industries producing like or directly competitive goods. When the GATT was negotiated in 1947, marking the beginning of the U.S. move to multilateral rather than the earlier bilateral approach to trade, an escape clause, closely patterned after U.S. law, was inserted therein as Article XIX of the Agreement.

Under the 1974 Trade Act, an escape clause action can be initiated by a petition to the ITC "by an entity, including a trade association, firm, certified or recognized union, or group of workers, which is representative of an industry." ITC action can also be initiated by a request of the President, the U.S. Trade Representative or by either of the two congressional committees with jurisdiction over trade matters (Senate Finance Committee and House Ways and Means Committee).

In an escape-clause action, the ITC investigates "to determine whether an article is being imported into the U.S. in such increased quantities as to be a substantial cause of serious injury, or the threat thereof, to the domestic industry producing an article like or directly competitive with the imported article." In the long history of the escape-clause investigation, there has been heated debate over the elements of this statutory rule. What is *serious injury, substantial cause,* and *like article?* At this point in U.S. history, "substantial cause" is defined as a cause that is important but not less than any other cause. In providing further guidance, Congress has stipulated that the ITC in its investigations must take into account all economic factors that it considers relevant, including the following:

1. For purposes of *serious injury,* the significant idling of productive facilities in the industry, the inability of a significant number of firms to operate at a reasonable level of profit, and significant unemployment or underemployment within the industry.

2. For purposes of the *threat of serious injury,* a decline in sales, a higher and growing inventory, and a downward trend in production profits, wages, or employment (or increasing underemployment) in the domestic industry concerned.

3. For purposes of *substantial cause,* an increase in imports (either actual or relative to domestic production) and a decline in the proportion of the domestic market supplied by domestic producers.

In the course of an escape-clause investigation the ITC must, after reasonable notice, hold public hearings and afford interested parties an opportunity to be present, to present evidence, and to be heard at such hearings.

Within 6 months of the initiation of the escape-clause action, the ITC must report its findings to the President. In addition to providing the basis for its findings, the ITC must include in its report any dissenting or separate views of the Commissioners. If the Commission does find serious injury or the threat thereof it is required (1) to find the amount of the increases in, or imposition of, any duty or import restriction (e.g., import quotas) on such article as would be necessary to prevent or remedy such injury, or (2) if it determines that adjustment assistance to affected workers, firms, or communities can effectively remedy such injury, provide its recommendations for such assistance.

The concept of adjustment assistance may be more meaningful if one is aware of its antecedents. In its 1954 *Report to the President and the Congress,* the Randall Presidential Commission summarized its view as follows:

> In a free economy, some displacement of workers and some injury to institutions is unavoidable. It may come about through technological change, alterations in consumer preferences, exhaustion of a mineral resource, new inventions, new taxes, or many other causes. Since it has never been seriously proposed that the burden of all such injury arising in a free economy should be assumed by the Government, the Commission felt that it was not appropriate to propose such a plan in the tariff area only.

David McDonald, then president of the steelworkers' union, was alone among the Commission members in proposing a plan to provide such assistance. Senator John F. Kennedy unsuccessfully sought to have a proposal similar to the McDonald plan embraced in trade legislation being considered by Congress in 1954. As one of his first major legislative programs, President Kennedy, in January 1962, sent to Congress his bill for the Trade Expansion Act of 1962. Title III of the bill stated that:

In order to facilitate adjustment of United States firms and workers to conditions that may result from action taken by the President in carrying out trade agreements, the President is authorized, after receiving the advice of the Tariff Commission, to determine that adjustment assistance may be furnished in the form of trade readjustment allowances, training and relocation allowances for workers; technical assistance, financial assistance, and tax relief for firms; and, *as extraordinary relief,* increased duties or other import restrictions for industries, all as provided in this title. Such forms of assistance may be granted singly or in combination. (italics added)

Congress, in enacting the Trade Expansion Act, did not go along with the President's concept that tariff or other import relief would be "extraordinary," that is, a lesser recourse than relief through adjustment assistance. It is the author's belief, however, that Congress did agree to the alternative of adjustment assistance for two reasons: (1) it was responsive to labor demands, and (2) as long as the GATT required compensation for import-relief actions that impaired tariff concessons agreed to under the GATT tariff negotiations, it was anticipated that an escape-clause action involving some major import items such as textiles, steel, or automobiles, would require compensatory tariff reductions that the United States would find difficult to effect (for matter of GATT compensation relating to escape clause actions, see below). Despite its controversial beginning, the periodic Congressional discontent with its implementation, and the unusually large budget costs now being experienced through unemployment in the auto and steel industries, adjustment assistance was expanded to include affected communities under the 1974 Act and continues in that form to date.

After the ITC forwards its decision to the President, he has 60 days in which to act, unless he requests further information from the ITC, in which case the time period is extended an additional 30 days. The President, unless he determines that providing import relief is not in the national interest, has several alternative courses he may take after he has received an affirmative finding by the ITC. He may:

1. increase the duty (up to 50 percent), or impose a duty not exceeding 50 percent if the item is then entering duty-free
2. proclaim a tariff-rate quota (e.g., an arrangement whereby quantity X may enter at rate Y, whereas values above quantity X enter at a rate of duty higher than Y) on such article
3. proclaim a modification of, or imposition of any quantitative restriction (quota) on the import into the United States of such article
4. negotiate "orderly marketing agreements" with foreign countries limiting their exports to the United States (as implied, an agreement under which the foreign country controls its exports to the United States)
5. take any combination of such actions.

Whether or not the ITC has recommended the grant of adjustment assistance and regardless of whether he chooses to proclaim import relief, the President may direct the Secretary of Labor and the Secretary of Commerce to expedite petitions for adjustment assistance by affected firms, workers, and/or communities. On the day that the President determines that providing import relief is not in the national economic interest, he must transmit to Congress a document setting forth that decision and the reasons why he chose not to and also what other steps he is taking to help the industry to overcome serious injury and the workers to find productive employment. Congress then has a period of 90 days to decide, through a concurrent resolution of both houses, to override the President's decision and thereby have the ITC recommendation for import relief implemented. Congress has not yet overridden the President in an escape-clause case, although it came within one vote of doing so in the 1980 case on leather apparel.

Import relief may not be granted for a period greater than five years, but a single extension for a period of 3 years is available if the President, after advice from the ITC, determines that such an extension is in the national interest. To the extent feasible, import relief granted for a period of more than 3 years shall be phased down beginning no later than the end of the third year.

GATT Article XIX provides that a member country that invokes the escape-clause action "shall afford [to other member countries] having a substantial interest as exporters of the product concerned an opportunity to consult with it in respect to the proposed action." Under this GATT rule, a country taking import-restrictive actions under the escape clause must either compensate countries adversely affected by such action or be subject to retaliatory import restrictions by them. Until the congressional grant to the President, in the 1974 Trade Act, of the special compensatory tariff reduction authority, the United States did not have the option of choosing what compensatory action it might offer and thereby ran an undesirably high risk of compensatory withdrawal by others in cases where the United States took escape clause action.

In addition to the conventional-escape-clause action, Congress also provided for a special escape clause that applies to communist countries. In the U.S. tariff schedule, a second column of rates, considerably higher than conventional rates, applies to most communist countries. Under the 1974 Trade Act, the President is authorized under strictly defined circumstances to extend most-favored-nation (nondiscriminatory) treatment to those communist countries whose products did not then receive such treatment. As one of a number of conditions for such agreements, however, Congress has provided for application of a special escape clause whose criteria involve the concept of *market disruption*. Thus a firm, trade association, or union may petition the President to initiate the bilateral consultation procedures (which for this and other purposes must be a part of such agreements) upon a showing of likelihood of market disruption as a result of imports entering under the more-favorable tariff rates resulting from the agreement. An ITC finding of market disruption is based upon a showing that an article produced by a communist country is competitive with a U.S. product and that such imports from that communist country are increasing rapidly so as to be a significant cause of material injury or threat thereof to a domestic industry. This obviously is an easier test to satisfy for import relief than that provided in the conventional-escape-clause action. It is therefore understandable why domestic interests have tried, during recent trade bill revisions, to have the market disruption test applied in the conventional escape clause procedure.

For market disruption cases, ITC has 3 months within which it must complete its report rather than the basic 6 months provided for conventional escape clause cases. Additionally, the President is authorized to take immediate action whenever he determines that a condition exists requiring emergency treatment. This "fast track" authority permits the President to take any of the remedial actions he may take under the conventional escape clause provisions (e.g., increased tariffs, quotas, orderly marketing agreement), but in this procedure he may impose import restrictions only for products from the communist countries that are causing the market disruption.

SECTION 22 RESTRAINTS ON AGRICULTURAL IMPORTS. Section 22 of the Agricultural Adjustment Act of 1933 (as amended) directs the Secretary of Agriculture to advise the President whenever the Secretary has reason to believe that any article or articles are being imported under circumstances that would negate or interfere with any price-support or other agricultural-commodity program undertaken by the Department of Agriculture, or to reduce substantially the U.S. processing of any agricultural article under such a program. The President may direct the ITC to conduct an investigation including a public hearing and to return a report to him of its findings and recommendations. On the basis of such findings, the President is authorized to proclaim such fees, duties, or import quotas, in addition to the basic tariff duty, as he may determine to be necessary. Existing fees and/or duties may not be increased by more than 50 percent. Quota limitations to be imposed may not be less than 50 percent of the quantity imported during a previous representative period of time, as determined by the President. The President may take action before the report by the ITC if he is advised by the Secretary of Agriculture that an emergency situation exists. In that case, presidential action continues in effect pending the report and recommendations of the ITC and action thereon by the President. In recent years, there has been decreasing use of this provision as a result of the declining use of agricultural support programs. At present writing only peanuts, cotton, sugar, and certain dairy products are affected by Section 22.

SECTION 204 OF THE AGRICULTURAL ACT OF 1956. Closely akin to the Section 22 import restraints are those provided in Section 204. This provision authorizes the President, when appropriate, to negotiate agreements with foreign governments limiting the export from such countries and the importation into the United States of any agricultural commodity or product manufactured therefrom or any textile or textile product. He is authorized to issue regulations to implement import procedures under such agreements. In addition, if a multilateral agreement exists among countries accounting for a significant part of world trade in the articles concerned, he may also issue regulations controlling imports from countries that are not parties to the international agreement. Section 204 provides the statutory basis on which the United States participates in the Multifiber Arrangement Regarding International Trade and Textiles. Under this international agreement, the United States and other countries that account for a significant part of world trade in textiles and apparel control the volume of textile and apparel imports that enter their countries. This control is effected under either bilateral agreements or unilaterally.

No procedures have been provided by Congress for petitioning action under this section or under Section 22, leaving such initiation to political action.

NATIONAL SECURITY PROVISION. Under the national-security provision (Section 232 of the Trade Act of 1974, as amended) the President is directed to reserve from trade-agreement negotiations any article on which a reduction in duty or change in some other import restriction would threaten to impair the national security. More importantly, in the context of import relief, he is directed to control entries (e.g., by quotas or an increase of duties) of any article being imported in such quantities or under such circumstances as to threaten to impair the national security.

The Secretary of Commerce is required, upon the request of the head of any department or agency, upon the application of an interested party, or on his own motion, to conduct an investigation to determine the effects on the national security of imports of any article. The Secretary must send his decision to the President within a year of the initiation of his investigation.

If the Secretary, after advice from other affected agencies, is satisfied that the subject article is being imported in such quantities or under such circumstances as to threaten to impair the national security, he is to so advise the President. If the President agrees with the Secretary, he is to take such action as he considers necessary to "adjust" imports of such article so that they do not threaten to impair the national security. Such authority is not limited (unlike the escape clause, according to which he may not increase by more than 50 percent).

The Act instructs the Secretary and the President, in determining the impact on national security, to consider, *inter alia:*

> . . . domestic production needed for projected national defense requirements, the capacity of domestic industries to meet such requirements, existing and anticipated availabilities of the human resources, products, raw materials, and other supplies and services essential to the national defense, the requirements of growth of such industries and such supplies and services including the investment, exploration and development necessary to assure such growth, and the importation of goods in terms of their quantities, availabilities, characters and the capacity of the United States to meet national security requirements. [They] shall further recognize the close relation of the economic welfare of the Nation to our national security, and shall take into consideration the impact of foreign competition on the economic welfare of individual domestic industries; and any substantial unemployment, decrease in revenues of government, loss of skills or investment, or other serious effects resulting from the displacement of any domestic products by excessive imports. . . .

Considering this language, the reader will easily understand why the early history of this section was marked by numerous petitions from import-impacted industries more interested in protecting themselves than the national security in any strategic or military sense. Notwithstanding the number of petitions under Section 232, in only one case was there a determination that imports were adversely affecting national security. That case involved petroleum imports, and the existing regime for such imports is a result of that determination.

The GATT, in Article XXI, also recognizes that trade actions may be taken for national-security reasons.

UNFAIR COMPETITIVE PRACTICES IN INTERNATIONAL TRADE

This section is devoted to those provisions of U.S. trade law designed to prevent or suppress unfair trade practices in international trade. Although some of this legislation traces its roots back half a century, this group of statutes has achieved a high degree of usage and importance only in the last two decades. As duty rates have dropped as a result of multilateral tariff negotiations, thereby increasing the visibility of non-tariff barriers to trade, and as governmental interventions in international trade have become more sophisticated, Congress has manifested heightened concerns for what it perceives to be enlargement of foreign unfair practices against U.S. trade.

These conditions have led Congress to reexamine and enlarge the arsenal of U.S. trade-law elements directed against unfair competitive practices in our international trade. Over the last two decades, Congress has added new tools for the President to use to cope with such unfair practices. Where Congress has deemed the Administration to be remiss in fully utilizing those tools, additional strictures have been put on the delegations to the President for the purpose of insuring closer adherence to the expressed will of Congress. In the process Congress has also spelled out in more detail and more carefully the rules for enforcing the rights of U.S. traders under U.S. and international law.

Recent Administrations and Congress have also recognized the need to establish international rules to be applied in cases of unfair competitive practices. Consequently, much of the effort in the recently concluded Tokyo Round of GATT negotiations was devoted to negotiating international codes to govern national actions, principally in the areas of subsidies, dumping, technical standards, and valuation of goods for customs purposes. U.S. concerns about unfair trade practices gave impetus to the negotiations, and the content of the resultant codes reflects those concerns. As might therefore be expected, the legislative changes involving unfair practices effected by the 1979 Trade Act fully reflect the obligations undertaken by the United States under the codes.

ENFORCEMENT OF U.S. RIGHTS—SECTION 301.   The GATT, the codes recently negotiated under the aegis of the GATT, and other international agreements to which the United States is a party, are government-to-government agreements that create no rights for individual U.S. citizens and companies to participate directly in the enforcement of those agreements. Only the U.S. government has the right to pursue the rights created under these agreements.

Recognizing this, Congress created in Section 301 of the Trade Act of 1974 (building on an earlier provision in the 1962 Trade Act and since amended by the 1979 Act) a mechanism whereby U.S. citizens and companies could bring their trade complaints to the attention of the U.S. government for action to remedy foreign violations of the agreements. Under that section the President is authorized to act (1) to enforce the rights of the United States under any trade agreement; or (2) to respond to any act, policy or practice of a foreign country that is inconsistent with the provisions of, or otherwise denies benefits to the United States under, any trade agreement, or is unjustifiable, unreasonable, or discriminatory and burdens or restricts United States commerce.

In its reports on this legislation, Congress has recorded that *unjustifiable* refers to restrictions that are inconsistent with trade agreements, whereas *unreasonable* refers to restrictions that are not necessarily inconsistent with trade agreements, but that nullify or impair benefits accruing to the United States under trade agreements or otherwise restrict or burden U.S. commerce. This somewhat-circular definition of *unreasonable* has given concern to foreign interests who consider the language broad enough for the United States to act under Section 301, even though the complaint is not based on a situation that the international community would consider to be a violation of the GATT or other international commitments.

Where any of the Section 301 conditions exist, the President must take all appropriate and feasible actions within his inherent and statutory authority to enforce such rights and obtain the elimination of the complained-of act, policy, or practice. For such purposes he may suspend, withdraw, prevent the application of, or refrain from proclaiming, benefits of trade-agreement concessions to carry out a trade agreement with the offending country. He may also impose duties or other import restrictions on the products of, and fees and restrictions on the services of, the offending country for such time as he deems appropriate.

Citizens and companies initiate action under Section 301 by filing a complaint with the U.S. Trade Representative (USTR). To assist petitioners in this regard, the Act provides that upon written request the USTR will provide nonconfidential information on the nature and extent of specific foreign-trade practices, U.S. rights under any trade agreement and remedies available under that agreement and under U.S. law, and current and earlier actions regarding a foreign policy or practice. If the government does not have the requested information, the USTR must either request the information from the foreign government or inform the requesting party why it declines to do so.

Within 45 days of receipt of the petition, the USTR is required to review the allegations and determine whether to initiate an investigation. A decision to initiate a Section 301 investigation must be published in the Federal Register. For a negative decision, he must publish his reasons. When the decision is affirmative, the Federal Register notice will contain the text of the complaint. The USTR must begin consultations with the offending government on the date that he decides to initiate the investigation. The petitioner may, as a matter of right, request that a public hearing be held within 30 days of the initiation of the investigation. As a part of the investigation, the USTR must also seek information and advice from the petitioner and other private-sector representatives. If the case involves a trade agreement, and a mutually acceptable resolution is not reached during the consultation period, if any, specified in the trade agreement, the USTR must promptly request proceedings on the matter under the formal-dispute procedures provided in that agreement.

Perhaps the most important change in Section 301 effected by the 1979 Trade Act was the establishment of time limits (in a new Section 304) for USTR and presidential action. Thus from the date of initiation of an investigation, the USTR would be required to make a recommendation to the President (1) within 7 months if the complaint involves an export subsidy under the new GATT subsidies code; (2) within 8 months if the complaint concerns a matter under the subsidies code involving more than an export subsidy; (3) within 30 days after the dispute-settlement procedure is concluded if the petition concerns some other trade agreement; or (4) within 12 months for all other situations.

Within 21 days after the receipt of a recommendation from the USTR, the President must determine what action he will take on the matter. Publication is required, in the Federal Register, of all presidential determinations to take or not take action, including the reasons for the determination and for the action.

The President may take action without providing opportunity for a public hearing and presentation of views when he determines that the national interest requires expeditious action. In that event, however, he must provide an opportunity for the presentation of views and, when requested, public hearings, after any action is taken.

SUBSIDIES RESULTING IN COUNTERVAILING DUTIES. Subsidies are bounties or grants bestowed on the production or export of goods, usually with the effect of providing thereby some competitive advantage over other-country producers. Countervailing duties are special duties imposed by the importing country to offset the amount of the foreign subsidy.

GATT rules (Article VI) provide that countervailing duties shall not be imposed unless subsidization of the imported product causes or threatens to cause material injury to a domestic industry, or materially retards establishment of a domestic industry. Because the U.S. countervailing-duty law predated the adoption of the GATT in 1947, and because of a grandfather clause represented by the GATT Protocol of Provisional Application, the United States was not obligated to change its historical practice of not requiring an injury test. However, when the United States amended its law in 1975 to apply countervailing duties to duty-free imports for the first time, the United States did require that the injury test be applied with respect to those duty-free imports of products from GATT member countries.

For many years the United States has sought greater discipline over the use of subsidies by its trading partners. The substantive rules and dispute settlement procedures provided in the GATT have not been sufficient to cope with the increasingly sophisticated range of domestic and export subsidies granted by these countries. On the other hand, the United States has long been urged by other countries to adopt the injury test that is the GATT precondition for application of countervailing duties.

These were the principal motivating forces that led to the successful negotiation of the Subsidies Code (technically named The Agreement on Interpretation and Application of Articles VI, XVI, and XXIII of the General Agreement on Tariffs and Trade) as a part of the Tokyo Round of trade negotiations. In the remainder of this section, the rights and obligations of the code signatories, as implemented in the United States by the Trade Act of 1979, are delineated.

Essential to an understanding of the GATT Subsidies Code and U.S. implementation of the code is the distinction drawn between *export* subsidies and *domestic* subsidies and the sub-distinction between export subsidies on primary products and export subsidies on non-primary products. As indicated above, subsidies are usually thought of in terms of export subsidies, where a government makes some sort of payment to a producer or forgives some obligation due from him, the net effect of which is to lower the cost of the product so that the producer can be more competitive in international trade. But the increasing problem in the modern world is the impact on foreign trade of domestic actions taken by governments in implementation of social or economic programs (domestic subsidies). All governments, for example, grant economic assistance to foster the elimination of regional economic disparities—in the United States this may take the form of incentives to firms to locate in the depressed areas of Appalachia; in Germany the government aids firms in West Berlin. As governments increasingly take over ownership of elements of their economy, such as a depressed steel industry, the question arises as to when the degree of aid to such industries represents a domestic subsidy that adversely affects international trade. The pioneering effort of the subsidies Code to address this problem of domestic subsidies is perhaps the most important one for the future.

For the purposes of the Subsidies Code, a primary product is any product of farm, forest, or fishery in its natural form or one that has undergone such processing as is customarily required to prepare it for marketing in substantial volume in international trade.

But for certain specified exceptions for a limited time for signatory developing nations, the code prohibits the use of export subsidies on primary mineral products and all non-primary (industrial) products. The Annex to the code provides an illustrative list of export subsidies. This list represents an enlargement and refinement of an earlier GATT list. Export subsidies on primary products are not limited by the code so long as they do not displace the exports of other countries in world markets. Thus the subsidy cannot result in the exporting country gaining "more than an equitable share of world export trade" in the primary product. *Equitable share* is interpreted to mean that a country shall not grant export subsidies that have the effect of displacing the exports of another Code signatory. Finally, the code prohibits a subsidy on a primary product that results in prices materially lower than those of other suppliers to the same market.

By the very nature of domestic subsidies, it could not be expected that they would also be outlawed by the code. Rather, the code provides ground rules for use of domestic subsidies so that they do not have adverse effects on the international trade interests of other signatory governments. The most important element is that governments agree to be confronted and examined by other signatories as to whether the domestic advantages of the subsidy are outweighed by the undesirable consequences to international trade.

Thus it is clear that Code rules are largely normative ones, and it is only with regard to export subsidies that they come anywhere close to being objective ones. Consequently, the review-and-dispute-settlement procedures provided under the code take on unusual importance. The code establishes a *Committee of Signatories* made up of representatives of each adhering government. The committee is to meet at least twice each year and reach decisions on a one-country-one-vote basis. Disputant countries are enjoined to seek a bilateral solution initially, with the aim that such a bilateral solution should be reached within 30 days in the case of an export subsidy or within 60 days in the case of any other subsidy. If the disputants fail to resolve the problem between themselves, either party is free to refer the matter to the committee of Signatories for conciliation. Failing resolution through such a "good offices" effort, either party may request that the committee establish, within 30 days, an impartial panel of experts to investigate the matter and report back to the committee within 60 days. So that the parties will have another chance to resolve the problem bilaterally, the factual part of the panel report and at least an outline of conclusions will be provided to the disputants before the report goes to the committee. Within 30 days of receipt of the panel report, the committee may make recommendations for a solution. When the committee is agreed that a subsidy is being granted in violation of the code and the offending country does not follow the recommendations of the committee, the latter may authorize the complainant to take countermeasures (what those may be are not stated in the code) against the guilty country.

Under the 1979 Trade Act, which conforms U.S. law to the new code, domestic rules in subsidy cases will depend on whether the subsidizing government is or is not a signatory to the code. For the United States, adherence to the code is on a conditional most-favored-nation basis, that is, the United States will extend its benefits solely to those nations who have accepted the code's obligations. Consequently, in deciding whether to apply a countervailing duty, the U.S. procedures will not involve an injury determination if the subsidy in question (other than on a duty-free import) is granted by a country that has not adhered to the code.

A countervailing duty investigation can be initiated by petition to the Secretary of Commerce in behalf of an "interested party." The latter is defined as (1) a manufacturer, producer, or wholesaler in the United States of a like product (defined as a product that if not identical is most similar in characteristics and uses with the imported article that is the subject of the subsidy action); (2) a certified or recognized union or group of workers that is representative of an industry engaged in the manufacture, production, or wholesale in the United States of a like product; or (3) a trade or business association, a majority of whose members manufacture, produce, or wholesale a like product in the United States. The Secretary may, without such a petition, initiate an investigation if he determines that his own information warrants it. A copy of the petition must simultaneously be submitted to the ITC if an injury determination will be necessary. Another copy must also be provided to the Washington embassy of the country whose subsidy is the subject of the petition. This is to provide the earliest opportunity for that country to clarify its position and to enter into consultations that might remove the problem.

A countervailing duty will be applied only after it has been determined that (1) a product imported into the United States benefits from a subsidy, and (2) a domestic industry in the United States has been injured by reason of the subsidized imports. Consequently, the petition must contain sufficient detail about both the alleged subsidy and the consequent injury as to make a prima facie case (for further details about what the petition must contain see 19 Code of Federal Regulations 207.11, 207.26, and 335.26).

The Commerce Department (with informal-injury advice from the ITC) must determine within 20 days of receipt of the petition whether that petition provides a basis on which a countervailing duty may be required. If the petition is deemed to be sufficient, a notice to that effect is published in the Federal Register with a copy furnished to the ITC. A negative determination, also published in the Federal Register, terminates all action on the case at both the Commerce Department and the ITC.

Normally within 85 days of submission of the petition, the Commerce Department must reach a preliminary determination that a subsidy is being provided. Within the first 45 days of that period, the ITC must make a preliminary determination as to whether there is reasonable evidence of injury from the subsidy in question. If that determination is negative, the ITC will give public notice thereof, and further action at the Commerce Department and the ITC will not be necessary. If the determination is positive, Federal Register notice of that fact will issue, the interested parties will be informed, and the Commerce Department will proceed with its work in arriving at a preliminary determination.

A positive preliminary determination by the Commerce Department triggers important consequences. All customs entries of the subsidized product after notice of the determination will not be liquidated. For each entry thereafter, a cash deposit, bond, or other security equal to the estimated amount of the net subsidy applicable to the affected goods will be required by the appropriate District Director of Customs. It will also trigger the formal beginning of the ITC's final injury investigation.

From this point, the Commerce Department has an additional 75 days to arrive at its final determination as to the existence of the subsidy. A negative final determination terminates the matter at both the Commerce Department and the ITC. A positive final determination, as with a preliminary one, requires notice to the affected parties and to the general public through the Federal Register. That notice must include the Commerce Department's judgment of the amount of the net subsidy and whether the subsidy involved is an export or domestic subsidy. For this purpose, a *net subsidy* is defined as the gross subsidy reduced by (1) any payments made to qualify for a subsidy, (2) any loss in value of the subsidy through the fact that its payment is mandatorily deferred, and/or (3) the amount of export taxes levied specifically to offset the subsidy involved. If the Commerce Department had reached a negative preliminary determination, with the consequence that posting of security and suspension of liquidation of entries had not earlier been decreed, those actions would be triggered by the Commerce Department's final determination. On the other hand, a negative final determination will lift the earlier suspension of liquidation, and deposits of cash or security will be refunded. If an injury determination is required, the ITC has 45 days after the Commerce Department's final determination within which to produce that determination. This time period is increased to 75 days if the Commerce Department's preliminary determination was not in the affirmative.

For the ITC, the standard *material injury* means that there must be harm to an industry that is not inconsequential, immaterial, or unimportant. Both the Subsidy Code and U.S. law require the ITC to take the following factors into account in making the injury determination:

1. whether there has been a significant increase in the volume of subsidized imports, either absolutely or relatively.
2. what the price effect of subsidized imports on the like U.S. product is; whether or not there has been undercutting, suppression, or depression of prices.
3. the effects of the subsidized imports on the domestic industry's output, sales, market share, cash flow, profits, prices, inventory, work force, and so forth.
4. with regard to agricultural products, whether there has been an increase in the burden to the government of firm income or price-support programs.

For purposes of the ITC injury finding, an *industry* is generally considered to mean the domestic producers, as a whole, of the like product. However, domestic producers in a geographic region in the United States will be considered to be an industry if they sell most, if not all, of the like product in that regional market and the demand for the like product in that market is not substantially supplied by producers of the product located elsewhere in the United States. There must be a concentration of the subsidized imports in that regional market for the countervailing duty to be levied.

The Commerce Department must publish a countervailing duty order within seven days of receipt of an affirmative injury determination by the ITC. That order will direct the Customs Service to assess the duty only on the merchandise found to be benefiting from the subsidy and in an amount equal to the net subsidy determined to exist. In "critical circumstances" countervailing duties are imposed retroactively from the date of a final finding of injury to the date 90 days before the date on which liquidation of entries was suspended. Critical circumstances exist when the ITC determines that there is injury that would be difficult to repair, caused by what the Commerce Department has determined to be massive imports, over a relatively short period, benefiting from export subsidies. Countervailing duties will continue in effect as long as the subsidy is present, but the finding and the amount of the net subsidy will be reviewed by the Commerce Department at least once a year.

At any time prior to a final determination, the Commerce Department may suspend or terminate its investigation upon receipt of an "undertaking" by either the offending government or the exporter of the affected product that the subsidy will cease or that the subsidized exports to the U.S. will be halted. In the rare case in which the suspension of the investigation will be more beneficial to the domestic industry than its continuation and the investigation is complex, the Commerce Department can accept an agreement that will completely eliminate the injurious effect of the sub-sidized product. The Commerce Department may not accept any undertaking that it cannot effectively monitor for compliance. The Commerce Department must give the petitioner and other interested parties 30 days notice of the proposed agreement and provide an opportunity for them to comment thereon on the record. Interested parties may seek review of the Commerce and ITC decisions in subsidy cases through the U.S. Court of International Trade.

We have so far seen that interested parties in the United States can attack foreign-subsidy practices in two ways—by petition to the Commerce Department under the countervailing-duty statute or by alleging an unfair trade practice to the U.S. Trade Representative under Section 301. In the light of the Subsidy Code and the history of U.S. subsidy legislation, some simplistic conclusions can be drawn about which of the alternative routes will be used. In virtually all cases involving an export subsidy and in those involving a domestic subsidy that has an impact in the United States, the likelihood is that the petitioner will go the Commerce Department route, since within a statutorily prescribed timetable, he can look forward to a remedy that his own government will apply without prior concurrence of other governments. Con-versely, the Section 301 route will likely be used only in cases in which a foreign government provides a domestic subsidy with that subsidy having an effect in a third country rather than in the United States. Such latter cases obviously can bring satisfaction to a domestic petitioner only after the U.S. government has, through the Subsidy Code Committee of Signatories, convinced others that the complained-of subsidy action is in fact actionable, and the United States is thereby authorized to take retaliatory action if the offending subsidy is not removed.

DUMPING.   The Trade Agreements Act of 1979 amended U.S. law to make it conform to the Antidumping Code that resulted from the Tokyo Round of trade negotiations. Unlike the conditional most-favored-nation situation in subsidy cases, U.S. antidumping duties will be applied, on the usual GATT most-favored-nation basis to dumped merchandise from all sources, whether or not the government of the country in which the dumped merchandise originates is a party to the code.

An antidumping duty will be levied on a class or kind of foreign merchandise that is being, or is likely to be, sold in the United States at less than its fair value if an industry in the United States is materially injured or threatened with material injury, or if the establishment of an industry in the United States is retarded, by reason of imports of that merchandise. The term *fair value* is not defined by the law, but Congress has recorded that it "intends the concept to be applied essentially as an estimate of what foreign market value will be so as to provide [the Department of Commerce] with greater flexibility during its investigation." The terms *industry* and *material injury* are defined in the same way as in subsidy situations.

Antidumping investigations may be initiated by the Secretary of Commerce on his own initiative or by petition presented by an interested party (as earlier defined for subsidy purposes). The Commerce Department must determine within 20 days of the filing of the petition whether it alleges the elements and information necessary for relief. An affirmative decision will trigger the Commerce Department investigation as to whether dumping exists, whereas a negative decision would end all proceedings. ITC has 45 days after the filing of the dumping petition to determine whether there is a reasonable indication of injury to a domestic industry by reason of dumped imports. In this instance too, a negative decision will terminate all action on the case.

The Department of Commerce, within 160 days of the petition, must make a preliminary determination, on the best evidence available to it at that time, whether there is a reasonable basis to believe or suspect that dumping exists. The time period is extended to 210 days if the case is extraordinarily complicated. A positive preliminary determination will trigger the immediate requirement of bonds or cash deposits to be posted on allegedly dumped imports in an amount equal to the estimated margin of dumping and suspension of the liquidation of entries of the affected goods, and the ITC will initiate an investigation as to whether injury exists. Even with a negative preliminary determination, the Commerce Department would continue its investigation leading to a final determination. That final determination is due within 75 days thereafter (135 days upon request of exporters or petitioners). With a negative final determination, proceedings would, of course, end. The ITC's final determination as to injury is due within 120 days of the Commerce Department's affirmative preliminary determination or within 75 days of the Commerce Department's final affirmative determination following a negative preliminary finding that dumping did not exist. An ITC affirmative final determination must result in the imposition by the Commerce Department of antidumping duties within 7 days.

In "critical circumstances," antidumping duties are imposed retroactively from the final finding of injury to the date 90 days before that on which liquidation was suspended. Critical circumstances exist when Commerce determines that (1) there is a history of such dumping of the class or kind of merchandise under investigation, or the importer knew or should have known that dumping was occurring; and (2) there have been massive imports of the merchandise in a relatively short period, and the ITC determines that the material injury results from the massive imports to the extent that it is necessary to retroactively impose an antidumping duty in order to prevent such injury from recurring.

At any point before a final determination, the Department of Commerce may suspend the process if (1) exporters accounting for substantially all of the importers under investigation agree to eliminate dumping or to cease exporting the offending goods within 6 months of the suspension, or (2) extraordinary circumstances exist and the exporters described in (1) agree to revise prices so that the injurious effects of the imports are completely eliminated. Such latter agreement for suspension will not be effected if, on petition, ITC finds that the injurious effect will not be completely eliminated. Should the Commerce Department determine that a suspension agreement was being violated, the investigation would then be resumed and unliquidated imports covered by the agreement would be subjected to antidumping duties retroactively if entered on or after the later of (1) 90 days before the date of the affirmative preliminary determination, or (2) the date of the violation.

Dumping duties are reviewable by the U.S. Court of International Trade under the same terms as described above for countervailing duties.

SECTION 337 RELIEF FROM UNFAIR TRADE PRACTICES. Section 337 of the Tariff Act of 1930, as amended (19 United States Code 1337) provides that "Unfair methods of competition and unfair acts in the importation of articles into the United States, or in their sale . . . , the effect or tendency of which is to destroy an industry, efficiently and economically operated, in the United States, are declared unlawful . . . ." Congress has charged the ITC to investigate alleged violations of Section 337 upon complaint under oath. If a violation is found, the Commission may order that the articles involved be excluded from entry into the United States, or it may issue a cease and desist order regarding the unfair practice. These remedies can be applied temporarily by the ITC while a determination is pending if the Commission has reason to believe that Section 337 is being violated and it finds immediate and substantial harm to the industry or trade and commerce. When temporary orders are in effect the articles in question may, however, be entered under a bond that will insure compliance with the ultimate disposition of the case.

Because of the lack of definition of *unfair* and the general broad sweep of Section 337, the history of the provision has been marked by a long period of disuse alternating with flurries of cases seeking new applications of it. Congressional concern regarding its use has resulted in a recent amendment that requires the ITC to terminate an investigation, or not begin an investigation, when it has reason to believe that the complained-of facts and effects are within the purview of the dumping or countervailing-duty law. Such a situation must be notified to the Secretary of Commerce. Where the case involves additional elements, the ITC may proceed with its investigation, but will be bound by the final decisions of the Department of Commerce with regard to the dumping and subsidy aspects of the case.

A review of Section 337 cases pending in 1979 confirmed that the section had largely been used in patent infringement cases. Of the 21 cases pending in that year, all but four involved the unlicensed importation of goods falling within the claims of a U.S. patent. Two cases involved alleged trade-secret misappropriations and antitrust involvement; one presented a violation of common law trademarks as well as deceptive advertising and marketing; whereas the fourth alleged trademark violations, unlawful copying of trade dress and packaging, and false country of origin markings.

The courts have determined that the ITC, for purposes of this section, must consider any patents involved in the case to be valid unless and until a court of competent jurisdiction has held otherwise.

In investigations under this section, the ITC is required to consult with the Departments of Justice, Health and Human Services, the Federal Trade Commission, and other appropriate government agencies. In making its determination for action, the commission is required to consider also the effect that such action would have on the general health and welfare, on competitive conditions in the economy, on the production of like or competitive merchandise in the United States, and on consumers. These considerations may be overriding. The ITC must complete Section 337 investigations within one year (18 months in complicated cases). All legal and equitable defenses may be presented in Section 337 cases. In cases involving patents, remedies may not be applied to imports by the U.S. government. Such actions against the government would be brought in the Court of Claims. Final ITC determinations may be appealed to the U.S. Court of Customs and Patent Appeals.

The President has 60 days following the issuance of exclusion or cease-and-desist orders by the ITC to override the Commission's decision if he determines it to be necessary for public or foreign-policy reasons.

STANDARDS AS A BARRIER TO TRADE.   The preparation, adoption, and application of product standards, product certification systems, and procedures for determining conformity of products with standards have often been used to distort international trade. Numerous ways exist to manipulate product standards to exclude imports. Certification systems, which provide assurances that products conform to standards, may limit access to imports or deny the right of a certification mark to imported products. Testing can be done arbitrarily or in a manner that increases expenses needlessly so that importers are further disadvantaged. To discourage discriminatory manipulation of product standards, product testing, and product-certification systems, the countries of the GATT who participated in the Tokyo Round of trade negotiations produced an Agreement on Technical Barriers to Trade (popularly known as the Standards Code). The Standards Code, implemented in the United States by Title IV of the Trade Agreements Act of 1979, contains specific obligations to ensure that mandatory and voluntary standards are not prepared, adopted, or applied by signatory countries with a view to creating, or have the effect of creating, unnecessary obstacles to international trade. The code does not restrict a signatory's right to adopt standards necessary to protect human, animal, or plant life or health, the environment, to ensure the quality of its exports, or to prevent deceptive practices.

The code is applicable to both agricultural and industrial spheres. Its provisions are not applicable to standards involving services, technical specifications related to government procurement contracts (although this issue is addressed in the new International Procurement Code, see below), or to standards established by private companies for their own use. Even though the code applies only to new and revised standards, a signatory country that believes that an existing measure conflicts with the underlying concepts of the code can ask that the measure be considered by the signatories under the dispute mechanism of the code.

Standards are to be specified, to the extent possible, in terms of performance rather than design or descriptive characteristics. Where appropriate in the preparation of new standards or the revisions of old standards, signatories should base their actions on existing international standards.

Although only central government standards and certification systems are bound by the code, those of state and local governments and those of private sector organizations are indirectly subject to its provisions. The code requires that signatories shall "take such reasonable measures as may be available to them" to ensure compliance by state and local governments and private organizations—a so-called second level of obligation. The nature of such reasonable measures is for each signatory to determine within the frame of its own domestic political and legal systems. However, if these second level entities act, in standards matters, so as to create unnecessary obstacles to international trade, their central government could be subjected to a complaint procedure under the code.

Where certification systems are in effect, they must permit foreign or nonmember suppliers to have their goods certified under the rules of the system on the same basis as domestic or member suppliers. Signatories are encouraged to accept test results, certificates, or marks of conformity issued in the country of export when they are satisfied that such testing and certification is performed by a technically competent body using appropriate methods. Open procedures are to be used whenever a new or revised domestic standard or technical regulation is being drafted or a new certification system introduced. These procedures include publishing of proposed measures, affording interested parties an opportunity to make comments and taking such comments into account.

To ensure transparency, the code requires the following:

1. all standards and details of certification systems must be published.
2. each signatory must establish an inquiry point where all interested parties

may obtain answers concerning specific domestic standards and certification systems.

3. each signatory undertakes to forward to the GATT Secretariat, for distribution to other signatories, central-government notices or technical rules of certification systems under preparation.

The code provides for a dispute-settlement mechanism similar to that described above for other Tokyo Round codes. In the first instance there is an obligation to engage in bilateral consultations at the request of any other signatory. Failing resolution bilaterally, the matter can be put to the code's Committee on Technical Barriers to Trade, which can draw on technical expert groups and panels for assistance in its determinations. It is expected that disputes will be resolved expeditiously, particularly in the case of perishable products. Retaliatory action in the form of withdrawal of code benefits may be authorized if a signatory's standard, testing method, or certification system is found by the Committee on Technical Barriers to Trade to be creating an unnecessary obstacle to international trade. The vehicle for a U.S. individual or company to utilize for a request that the U.S. government pursue its rights under the Code is the Section 301 procedure described earlier.

U.S. implementing legislation directs the U.S. Trade Representative to coordinate trade policies related to standards, and he is given responsibility for coordinating discussions and negotiations on standards with other countries. Technical offices are established in the Department of Commerce for nonagricultural products and in the Department of Agriculture for agricultural products to perform a variety of functions, including steps necessary to enable U.S. exporters to take advantage of opportunities opened by the code. The Secretaries of Commerce and Agriculture are to keep informed of international standards-related activities, identifying those that may substantially affect U.S. commerce, and to encourage private interests to participate in particular international standards-related activities. The Commerce Department will maintain a Standards Information Center (in the National Bureau of Standards) to disseminate information to U.S. interests about foreign standards-related activities and to serve as the *inquiry point* that the United States is obligated to maintain under the code for fielding standards questions from other signatories. The USTR and the Departments of Commerce and Agriculture are authorized to make grants, provide technical assistance, and enter into contracts with other federal agencies, state or local governments, or private individuals for the purposes of implementing and complying with the code. The structure of the trade agreements private sector advisory committee is to be used by the USTR and Departments of Commerce and Agriculture to obtain technical and policy advice on standards.

GOVERNMENT PROCUREMENT

When the GATT was negotiated in 1947, Article III was written to exclude government purchases from the national treatment provision (e.g., treating foreign suppliers on the same basis as domestic ones), notwithstanding a U.S. effort for the opposite result. Consequently, over the years since, nations have continued to discriminate in favor of domestic suppliers in government procurements, in some cases to the total exclusion of foreign suppliers.

By the 1960s it was becoming obvious that government procurement was assuming larger importance because governments were taking increasingly greater ownership shares of their national economies, thereby insulating tremendous amounts of purchases from the otherwise-applicable international trade rules. During that time it was internationally recognized that the United States was not alone in favoring domestic suppliers in the procurement process. The major difference between the United States and other countries was that the United States prescribed clearly visible percentage preferences (e.g., 6 or 12 percent of the bid price) for domestic suppliers, whereas most other countries used highly invisible administrative procurement practices and procedures to achieve the "buy national" result. In simplistic terms what the United States was doing had the effect of an additional import duty on foreign-supplied goods, whereas other countries were, in effect, applying import quotas of a size usually approaching zero imports.

In the light of these circumstances, it was understandable that during the late 1960s the idea was evolving that the most productive course for addressing the procurement issue would be a movement toward an international agreement to open procurement markets to foreign suppliers on a reciprocal basis. This idea reached fruition in the Tokyo Round of trade negotiations. The resultant procurement code went into effect on January 1, 1981.

No international code could possibly provide a full set of rules to substitute for domestic procurement processes. The code contains, for the most part, only those rules that past experience indicated were essential to a viable international agreement. They are largely addressed to areas where in the past it was found that without such rules—and the visible use of those rules—it was possible to shut out foreign suppliers to a greater or lesser degree.

NONDISCRIMINATION.   The most important element of the code is the elimination of discrimination against foreign suppliers when governments purchase articles for their own use. Under the code the visible forms of such discrimination, the percentage price preferences accorded by such countries as Canada and the United States to domestic bidders over foreign bids, cannot be continued, since foreign suppliers must be treated no less favorably than domestic bidders ("national treatment"). The more difficult task addressed by the code is the elimination of discrimination brought about by the absence of procurement rules on the invisible use of existing discriminatory practices and procedures. Consequently, the largest part of the code is devoted to establishing appropriate rules and the means for ensuring that they will be applied openly so that all will be entirely aware that the procurement process is carried out in a fair and equitable manner.

CODE RULES AND TRANSPARENCY.   The code establishes a number of rules and the means for insuring transparency (full disclosure) in the use of those rules, as follows:

1. Countries must publish their procurement laws and regulations, and they must not conflict with code rules.
2. Purchasing entities must publish all bid opportunities in the following detail in a publication specifically listed for that purpose by each country in a code annex:

    a. Kind and quality of products to be supplied.

    b. Whether the bidding procedure is open or selective.

    c. Delivery dates.

    d. Address and final date for submitting an application (as well as the language in which it must be submitted)
        (1) to be invited to bid,
        (2) for qualifying for the bidders list, or
        (3) for receiving bids.

    e. Address of the agency awarding the contract.

    f. Any information necessary for obtaining specifications or other documents.

    g. Any information required of bidders, including economic and technical requirements and financial guarantees.

    h. What the cost and payment terms are for obtaining the bidding documentation.

3. A synopsis of the bid opportunity, in one of the official languages of the GATT (English, French, or Spanish), must also be published.

4. To further ensure transparency and that all bidders will start off equally, the code prescribes the minimum information that must be contained in the bidding documentation. Two of these requirements that are particularly important are as follows:

    a. A complete description of the required products; any requirements to be fulfilled by the products, including technical specifications or conformity certification; necessary plans, drawings, and instruction materials.

    b. The criteria for awarding the contract, including any factors other than price used to evaluate bids.

5. The code prohibits the use of technical specifications that would create or might have the effect of creating obstacles to international trade. Technical specifications must be based on international standards or recognized national standards. If the only way to describe the product in question is by reference to a brand or patent name, the bid invitation must also contain the words "or equivalent."

6. Procurement officers have discretion in their choice of the following purchasing procedures, so long as they observe the requirement of providing the maximum degree of competition possible:

    a. *"Open" procedure.* All interested suppliers may bid.

    b. *"Selective" procedure.* The government may invite bids from selected suppliers, due account being taken of all those on lists of qualified suppliers that the procuring agency maintains. Suppliers not yet on bidders' lists are able to participate provided they have qualified within the time frame of the procurement. The number of such not-yet-listed suppliers that are allowed to participate may be limited to that number that would permit "the efficient operation of the procurement system." The code requires annual publication of those bidders' lists that agencies maintain as well as publication of procedures for getting on those lists. Governments undertake that applicants will be considered for such lists within a reasonably short time. The underlying principle is that "the process of, and the time required for, qualifying suppliers shall not be used . . . to keep foreign suppliers off suppliers' lists or from being considered for a particular proposed purchase." The code recognizes that in selective procedures there are frequently too many qualified bidders on the list to permit all of them to be invited to tender on any one contract. Consequently, "any selection shall allow for equitable opportunities for suppliers on the lists." The underlying thought is that over a series of invitations, all qualified bidders will have a chance to compete for one or another of the contracts.

 c. *"Single tendering."*   The code recognizes that no procurement system can operate efficiently without the ability to go to a single supplier when circumstances require it. One of the most difficult aspects of the negotiation was to arrive at strictly defined criteria for single tendering so as not to subvert the competitive procedures set up by the code. Five criteria are provided for single tendering as follows:

  (1)   When there have been no responses to a bid invitation or when the responses are either non-responsive or collusive.

  (2)   When there is an extreme time emergency that could not have been foreseen by the procurement entity and the product could not be obtained in time by competitive procedures.

  (3)   When the goods needed are protected by an industrial property right and only the owner thereof can supply the good for which no reasonable alternative exists.

  (4)   To get additional deliveries of replacement parts from the original supplier in cases where without such parts it would be impossible to meet the requirements of interchangeability with already-existing equipment.

  (5)   When an entity purchases a prototype or prototypes that are developed at its request as part of a research or development contract (all purchases after the prototype must be by competitive bidding).

7.   In procurements across national borders, time limits within which bids must be submitted become increasingly important. The code addresses this issue in considerable detail. Generally at least 30 days must elapse between initiation and receipt of bids.

8.   Additional rules are provided to cover various contingencies such as when bid invitations are amended or reissued, bids are submitted by telecopy, telex, or telegram to meet bid deadlines, errors in bids have been made, or all bids received are considered unacceptable.

9.   "The entity shall make the award to the tenderer who has been determined to be fully capable of undertaking the contract and whose tender, whether for domestic or foreign products, is either the lowest tender, or the tender which *in terms of the specific evaluation criteria set forth in the notices of tender documentation* is determined to be the most advantageous" (italic supplied).

10.   Information about awards

 a.   *Open procedures.*   Bids resulting from open procedures are to be opened in the presence of bidders or their representatives, or alternatively, in the presence of an "appropriate and impartial witness not connected with the procurement process." A written report of such openings shall be drawn up and maintained in the purchasing office for such use as may be necessary in the dispute settlement process. Governments have the right to obtain information concerning such awards.

b. *General rules.* The United States argued throughout the negotiations that one of the most essential elements for ensuring openness (transparency) in the procurement process is the guarantee that the name of the winning bidder and the amount of the award will be published for each procurement contract. The European Community and others maintained that such publication is unnecessary and would also lead to collusive bidding in future procurements of the same item. A solution was found in the following set of rules:

(1)   Not later than seven working days from the date of an award, unsuccessful bidders must be informed in writing or by publication that the contract was awarded.

(2)   Upon request, the purchasing entity must promptly provide to the unsuccessful bidder "pertinent information concerning the reason why the tender was not selected, including information on the characteristics and the relative advantages of the tender selected, as well as the name of the winning tender."

(3)   An unsuccessful bidder's government can obtain the contract price and, in most cases, discreetly make that price known to the bidder. However, "in cases where release of this information would prejudice competition in future tenders, this information shall not be disclosed except after consultation with and agreement of the party which gave the information to the government of the unsuccessful tenderer."

DISPUTE SETTLEMENT.   The thrust of the code is that it will be largely self-policing. Code rules are structured to provide maximum opportunity for resolving problems between the potential supplier and the procurement agency at any stage of the procurement process.

1.   *For qualifying suppliers.*   "Any supplier having requested to become a qualified supplier shall be advised by the entities concerned of the decision in this regard."

2.   *During the tendering procedure.*   "Entities shall reply promptly to any reasonable request for relevant information submitted by a supplier participating in the tendering procedure."

3.   *Overall rule.*   The above rules are capped by the following: "Entities shall establish a contact point to provide additional information to any unsuccessful tenderer dissatisfied with the explanation for rejection of his tender or who may have further questions about the award of the contract. There shall also be procedures for the hearing and reviewing of complaints arising in connection with any phase of the procurement process so as to ensure that, to the greatest extent possible, disputes under this Agreement will be equitably and expeditiously resolved between the suppliers and the entities concerned."

Given the business premium of resolving disputes during the process of procurement, the drafters of the code contemplated that only a few cases would fail to be resolved in this manner.

Government-to-Government Consultations. For cases not resolved between the potential supplier and the procuring agency, the code provides for bilateral consultations between the procuring government and the government of the aggrieved supplier. In such consultations, governments are obligated to provide the information needed for that purpose and are directed "to conclude such consultations within a reasonably short period of time."

Multilateral Settlement. Failing such bilateral resolution of the problem, the code provides for a multilateral settlement mechanism. It establishes a Committee on Government Procurement composed of representatives of each of the signatory governments to handle disputes (as well as other matters relating to the code). When requested, the committee will meet within 30 days to consider the dispute and provide a "good offices" effort for solution. If the committee examination does not bring about a resolution within 3 months, either government may request establishment of an impartial panel to make findings of fact, reach conclusions, and make recommendations to the committee, normally within 4 months from the date the panel was established. The panel shall be of three or five members drawn from the committee chairman's list of experts "in the field of trade relations"; experts may be drawn from either the government or private sector; and panel members may not be citizens of countries involved in the dispute.

Committee action on the panel report should normally be taken within 30 days of the receipt of the report. The only code guideline for committee action is that it "shall aim at the positive resolution of the matter on the basis of the operative provisions of this agreement and its objectives set out in the Preamble." If the country addressed by the committee's recommendations is unable to implement them, it must provide its reasons promptly to the committee in writing. The final step is that if the recommendations are not accepted and if the committee determines "that the circumstances are serious enough to justify such action," it may authorize the aggrieved country or countries to suspend code obligations toward the offending country.

GENERAL LIMITATIONS ON CODE COVERAGE. The code applies *solely* to the procurement of goods. Services are included only where they are "incidental" to the procurement of goods (i.e., services making up less than 50 percent of the value of the contract). The code applies only to procurement contracts of a value of 150,000 Special Drawing Rights (SDRs)—approximately $190,000—or more. Contract splitting to avoid this threshold is prohibited. Aid programs of some of the signatory developed governments for developing countries do sometimes require that aid-financed procurements must originate in the grantor country. The code notes that this practice is being phased out and, consequently, provides that so long as aid remains tied in this fashion, the underlying procurements will not be subject to the code. The code also does not cover procurement of arms, ammunition, or war materials nor procurements indispensible for national security or national-defense purposes. The code does not apply to measures necessary to protect public morals, order, or safety, human, animal, and plant life, industrial and commercial property, or relating to the products of handicapped persons, philanthropic institutions or prison labor.

Country Limitations on Coverage.   One aim of the negotiations was that all agencies or entities under the direct or substantial control of participating governments would be subject to the code. When it became clear that some governments were not prepared to go that far, it was agreed that the code would apply initially only to those entities listed by each country in an Annex to the code. The U.S. list is, in part, a response to the less-than-complete offers from other countries and their general unwillingness to include entities in the fields of transportation, power generation, and telecommunications. U.S. exclusions from code coverage are

1. Department of Energy.
2. Department of Transportation.
3. Tennessee Valley Authority.
4. Corps of Engineers of the Department of Defense.
5. Bureau of Reclamation of the Department of the Interior.
6. Two parts of the General Services Administration National Tool Center and Federal Supply Regional Office No. 9).

Other qualifications on U.S. coverage as follows are: (1) COMSAT, AMTRAK, CONRAIL, and the U.S. Postal Service are not covered by the code since they are deemed not to be under the direct or substantial control of the U.S. government; (2) the code will not apply to Department of Agriculture purchases made for agricultural support programs or human feeding programs such as the school lunch program; (3) Department of Defense coverage is qualified so that the code will not affect that agency's existing obligation to buy textiles, clothing, shoes, food, stainless steel flatware, certain specialty metals, buses, ships and components thereof solely from domestic sources; (4) transportation is not included in services "incidental" to the purchase of goods; (5) state and local governments are not listed entities, and consequently their purchases, whether or not based on federal grant funds, are not subject to the code; and finally (6) the U.S. coverage does not apply to contracts reserved ("set-asides") for small and minority businesses.

The above description of U.S. coverage is indicative of the coverage of other countries. An unusual difference is to be found in the coverage of Switzerland and the Nordic countries. They have reserved to themselves a right to favor domestic bidders where "important national policy objectives" are involved. They have assured other countries that such instances will be extremely rare and that action will be based only on a Cabinet decision.

The code countries have given a clear signal that they anticipate building on what is already in the agreement by agreeing that "Not later than the end of the third year from the entry into force of this Agreement and periodically thereafter, the Parties thereto will undertake further negotiations, with a view to broadening and improving the Agreement on the basis of mutual reciprocity. . . . In this connection, the Committee [of Signatories] shall, at an early stage, explore the possibilities of expanding the coverage of this Agreement to include service contracts."

OTHER CODE PROVISIONS. The code entered into force on January 1, 1981, for those governments that adhered to it by that date. For governments adhering later, it will enter into force on the thirtieth day following the date of accession. There is no obligation whatsoever to extend the treatment mandated by the code to countries that have not adhered to it. The code will not apply between any pair of countries if either government does not consent to it. In this vein, a number of countries have informed India that its initially tabled coverage offers were inadequate and will have to be expanded if India is to get the benefits of the code. Any country can withdraw from the agreement 60 days after written notice.

U.S. IMPLEMENTATION OF THE CODE. Title III of the Trade Agreements Act of 1979 implements the code in the United States by eliminating those U.S. legislative barriers that are inconsistent with the code. It does this by providing that the President may waive the Buy American Act (and an important part of the "set-aside program" for labor-surplus areas) for other code signatories. However, in accordance with the terms of the code, the Buy American Act will not be waived for contracts below the code threshold (150,000 SDRs) nor with regard to government agencies that are not on the list of U.S. entities covered by the code.

Congress has provided that presidential waivers be applied to countries on one of four bases, depending on the stage of industrial development of each country as follows:

1. Major industrial countries (defined as Canada, the European Economic Community and its member countries, Japan, and any other country so designated by the President) can only qualify if they sign the code and provide reciprocity to the United States.

2. Any other country willing to provide reciprocity and apply the agreement de facto with respect to U.S. products (e.g., a country willing to enter into a bilateral agreement based on the code, although not prepared to join the multilateral agreement) can qualify.

3. A country willing to provide appropriate reciprocal procurement opportunities for U.S. products without assuming the procedural obligations of the code (e.g., a developing country that could not undertake so radical a change in its primitive procurement system) can qualify. Congress has recorded that this kind of waiver "will be granted only after thorough, careful deliberations."

4. The 29 "least developed" countries (so defined in a United Nations list) can enjoy a waiver without offering reciprocity.

For major countries, the consequence of failing to obtain a waiver would be complete disbarment from participating in procurement covered by the code. After January 1, 1981, the date for the first waivers under the code, countries that are not major countries or least developed countries and that fail to obtain a waiver can participate in U.S. procurements for a period of two years after January 1, 1981, but only under the terms of the system that existed in the United States prior to the operation of the code (e.g., including application of Buy American preferences).

As might be expected, Congress provided that U.S. citizens and companies can bring their procurement-code problems to the attention of the government through use of the Section 301 procedures described earlier in this chapter.

SOURCES AND SUGGESTED REFERENCES

Agreements Reached in the Tokyo Round of the Multilateral Trade Negotiations, H.R. Doc. No. 153, 96th Cong., 1st sess., pt. 1, 1979.

Agricultural Act of 1956, 70 Stat. 188.

Agricultural Adjustment Act, 48 Stat. 31.

Anti-Dumping Act of 1921, 42 Stat. 11.

Commission on Foreign Policy, *Report to the President and the Congress,* 1954, so called "Randall" Commission.

General Agreement on Tariffs and Trade, text published in *Basic Instruments and Selected Documents,* Vol. IV, GATT, Geneva, 1969.

A Guide to the U.S. Generalized System of Preferences (GSP), Office of the USTR, Exec. Off. of the President, Washington, D.C., November 1980.

Havana Charter for an International Trade Organization, published in Dept. of State Publication 3206, Commercial Policy Series 114, September 1948.

Pomeranz, *Toward a New International Order in Government Procurement,* 11 Law and Policy in International Business 1263, 1979.

S. Rept. 111, 75th Congress, 1st sess., p. 3, Senate Finance Committee Report on the Trade Agreements Act of 1934.

Tariff Act of 1890, 26 Stat. 567 (1890) (McKinley Tariff).

Tariff Act of 1897, 30 Stat. 151 (1897) (Dingley Tariff).

Tariff Act of 1930, 46 Stat. 590 (1930) (Smoot-Hawley Tariff).

Tariff Schedules of the United States Annotated, Publication No. 1011, US ITC, 1980.

Trade Act of 1974, P.L. 93–618, 19 U.S.C. 2101.

Trade Agreements Act of 1934, 48 Stat. 943.

Trade Agreements Act of 1979, P.L. 96–39.

Trade Expansion Act of 1962, 76 Stat. 872.

LEGAL ASPECTS OF INTERNATIONAL LENDING

CONTENTS

BASIC CONCEPTS OF A LOAN AGREEMENT   3

Conditions of Lending   3
  Need for closing conditions   3
  Government approvals; exchange control   3
  Legal opinions   4
  Conditions for each disbursement   5
Representations and Warranties   5
  Purposes of representations   5
  Typical representations   6
  Absence of material adverse change   6
Covenants of the Borrower   7
  Functions of covenants   7
  Negative covenants   7
Events of Default   8
  Typical events of default   8
  Grace periods and notice requirements   8
  Remedies   9

EURODOLLAR LOANS   9

Nature of Eurocurrency   9
Funding   10
London Interbank Offered Rate   11
Yield Protection   11
Funding Interruption   12
Place of Payment   12

Foreign-Currency and Multicurrency Loans   12

LOANS TO SOVEREIGN BORROWERS   13

General Considerations   13
Immunity from Suit, Attachment, and Execution   13
  Immunity   13
  Service of process   15
  Representation   15

SYNDICATION AND PARTICIPATION   15

Syndicated Loans   15
Participations   16
Liability of Manager and Lead Bank   17

GOVERNING LAW   17

Need for Governing-Law Clauses   17
Scope of Governing-Law Clauses   18
Reasonable-Relationship Requirement   18

STIPULATION OF JURISDICTION   19

Submission to Personal Jurisdiction   19
Subject-Matter Jurisdiction   20
Forum Non Conveniens   20
Ouster of Jurisdiction   20
Arbitration   21

SOURCES AND SUGGESTED REFERENCES   21

LEGAL ASPECTS OF INTERNATIONAL LENDING

Michael Gruson

BASIC CONCEPTS OF A LOAN AGREEMENT

CONDITIONS OF LENDING

Need for Closing Conditions. A loan agreement between a bank and a borrower (the following assumes a loan agreement drafted in accordance with U.S. practice and governed by New York law) is usually signed by the parties well in advance of the actual making of the loan (the disbursement of funds). The loan agreement represents a legally binding obligation of the bank to make the loan, and if the bank refuses to advance funds after having signed the loan agreement, it may be liable to the borrower for damages. The bank can protect itself by specifying in the loan agreement conditions, so-called closing conditions, that must be satisfied before it is obligated to disburse funds. If one of the conditions is not met, the bank may have the legal right to refuse to make the loan. If all conditions are satisfied, the bank is normally legally obligated to make the requested advance even though there have been significant changes in the borrower's circumstances. Thus these conditions assure the bank that the factors that constitute the basis for the bank's credit decisions are true and that the legal aspects of the loan are in order not only at the time of signing the loan agreement, but also remain unchanged at the time of disbursement of funds.

Customarily, most of these documentary closing conditions must be met only when the bank makes the first advance under the loan agreement and not also at the time of subsequent advances. At a minimum, banks generally require evidence that the loan was and still is *duly authorized* by the appropriate governing body of the borrower (usually banks require resolutions of the borrower's board of directors authorizing the loan transaction and authorizing certain officers to execute and deliver the loan documents) and that the loan agreement was duly executed and delivered by an authorized officer.

Governmental Approvals; Exchange Control. It is customary to require the borrower to deliver copies of any necessary governmental approvals. Although the bank will require the borrower's representation and an opinion of borrower's counsel that all necessary governmental approvals have been obtained, it is advisable to receive copies of such approvals so that the bank and its counsel are able to verify for themselves that the transactions contemplated by the loan agreement have been approved. If it is known at the time of drafting the loan agreement which governmental approvals will be required, they should be specifically referred to in the loan agreement. This procedure helps counsel to focus early on the legal requirements.

A bank lending U.S. dollars or Eurodollars expects to be repaid in U.S. dollars; however, exchange-control laws of the country of the borrower may restrict availability, convertibility, or transferability of U.S. dollars. Accordingly, the bank should obtain the agreement or other assurance from the appropriate authorities that (1) U.S. dollars will be available to the borrower when needed to pay interest and principal and other amounts under the loan agreement, and (2) the convertibility of the borrower's currency into U.S. dollars and the transferability of U.S. dollars for purposes of the loan will not be restricted.

The International Monetary Fund (IMF) Articles of Agreement prohibit enforcement in any member country of an *exchange contract* involving the currency of any other member country that is in violation of the exchange-control laws of such other member country (assuming such laws are consistent with the IMF agreement). Though a loan agreement itself may not be an exchange contract for purposes of the IMF agreement, an exchange-control license or other approval would be such an exchange contract. Furthermore, the refusal by a foreign government to honor agreements by its currency-exchange agency to provide U.S. dollars for local currency is an *act of state* the validity of which is not reviewable by a U.S. court [*French v. Banco Nacional de Cuba,* 23 N.Y. 2d 46, 295 N.Y.S. 2d 433 (1968)].

Legal Opinions.   Most major loan agreements contain a closing condition that the bank obtain a favorable opinion of counsel. The purpose of this requirement is to obtain counsel's judgment that the legal assumptions upon which the credit decision has been made are correct. In addition, negotiating the scope of the opinion may bring into the open legal problems and uncertainties before the loan agreement is signed or the loan proceeds are disbursed. In some cases these problems can be solved, whereas in other cases the bank must decide whether it will accept these problems and uncertainties as a credit matter. The opinion of counsel has the additional function of helping to establish the bank's prudence and good faith in making the loan.

Traditionally, banks require an opinion from borrower's counsel. This opinion usually covers the same subject matters as the representations made by the borrower in the loan agreement relating to legal matters, but does not cover representations by the borrower relating to financial matters. The borrower's counsel is usually more familiar than the bank's counsel with the subject matters covered by the opinion, and his opinion reinforces his client's representations. In many loan transactions the bank is satisfied with a legal opinion by the borrower's inside counsel. In more-difficult transactions where the opinion requires more-specialized expertise, or in unusually important transactions where the bank desires the safeguard of perhaps more-independent judgment, the bank may insist on a legal opinion from borrower's outside counsel. In addition, some banks do regularly require an opinion of their *own* outside counsel about the validity and enforceability of the loan agreement or other matters.

In the case of loans to foreign borrowers, the bank, because of its unfamiliarity with the foreign law, usually insists on an opinion by a foreign counsel of its own selection, which may cover substantially the same subject matters as the opinion of borrower's counsel. But even where the bank retains local counsel in a foreign country, the bank usually expects its U.S. counsel to make a diligent effort to uncover problems that might arise under the relevant foreign law and to ascertain that these problems have been addressed and solved. In addition, U.S. counsel should ascertain that foreign counsel is familiar with the purpose and meaning of the proposed opinion. This requires close interaction between the bank's U.S. counsel and foreign counsel.

In the case of syndicated loans, the loan agreements usually provide for an opinion of special counsel selected by the lead manager who represents all members of the syndicate or the agent bank or both. This opinion is much more limited than the opinion of borrower's counsel and frequently is simply to the effect that the loan agreement and notes are legal, valid, binding, and enforceable against the borrower. Sometimes this opinion is to the effect that the legal documentation is "in substantially acceptable legal form" and that the closing documents are "substantially responsive to the requirements of the loan agreement."

Foreign borrowers, in particular foreign sovereign borrowers, have sometimes expressed annoyance at the requirement of an opinion of counsel. They do not understand why the opinion of a private attorney should determine whether or not the borrower obtains the loan. The answer is simply that a prudent bank will make a loan only if the loan agreement is legal, valid, and enforceable, and the legal opinion is a method of ascertaining whether the loan agreement meets these requirements.

Conditions for Each Disbursement. If the loan is not disbursed in a lump sum but in a series of disbursements or advances, the loan agreement usually contains conditions designed to permit the bank to refuse to make advances if changes have occurred in the legal or financial assumptions underlying the credit decision. Normally the loan agreement will require as a condition of each advance that the representations and warranties remain true and accurate as of the date of the advance and that no event of default, or event that may become an event of default upon giving of notice or lapse of time, has occurred and is continuing at the time of the advance. If the loan agreement contains a representation that no material adverse change has occurred in the borrower's financial condition or operations since the date of the financial statements upon which the credit decision was based, this representation is repeated as of the date of each advance, and the bank could refuse to make an advance if there were a material adverse change. The requirement that no default has occurred picks up, through the provision making a breach of a covenant an event of default, all the covenants of the borrower, and again would permit the bank to refuse to make advances if the borrower were not in compliance with a covenant.

REPRESENTATIONS AND WARRANTIES

Purposes of Representations. The representations and warranties set forth in the loan agreement state the legal and, to some extent, the financial assumptions upon which the bank's credit decision is based. They serve several functions. If the loan agreement provides that it is a condition of the bank's obligation to make advances that the representations be correct on the date of each advance, the bank could refuse to make an advance if a representation were not correct on that date. If a material misrepresentation were to occur—either on the date of the loan agreement or on the date of an advance—it would constitute an event of default and would permit the bank to accelerate the loan. These rights are not conditioned upon a misrepresentation being the fault of the borrower. Rather, the representations operate to allocate the risk to the borrower for the matters covered by them. Borrowers unwilling to give a representation sometimes argue that they themselves are not certain whether the representation is correct; this argument is misdirected. The proper question is who should bear the risk if certain factual assumptions upon which the credit decision is based are not correct.

In addition, the representations serve as a disclosure device during the negotiations by requiring the borrower to disclose information inconsistent with the requested representations. Finally, the representations may assist the bank in establishing that it acted in good faith in the transaction.

Typical Representations. Representations relating to legal assumptions typically cover (1) the proper incorporation and good standing of the borrower in the jurisdiction of its incorporation; (2) the corporate power of the borrower to enter into the loan transaction; (3) the proper authorization of the loan transaction; (4) the absence of the need for obtaining authorizations or approvals from governmental entities for the loan or, if such authorizations or approvals are required, their validity and effectiveness; (5) the absence of violations of law or any contract binding on or affecting the borrower resulting from the loan (e.g., the loan may violate other financing agreements of the borrower that limit the amount of indebtedness that the borrower is permitted to incur, and such violation could permit the other creditors either to declare defaults under their agreements or to bring suits against the bank for causing or inducing a breach of contract); and (6) the fact that the loan agreement is a legal, valid, and binding obligation of the borrower, enforceable against the borrower.

In each loan, the bank must consider whether its credit decision is based on any particular assumptions that should be covered by representations. If, for example, the business of the borrower depends upon a particular contract or permit, it may be useful to have a representation of the borrower concerning it. If the credit decision is made on the basis of certain nonpublic information supplied by the borrower (for example, projections or cash-flow statements), the loan agreement may contain representations as to the accuracy of such information.

A loan agreement normally contains a representation as to the accuracy of the financial statements upon which the bank based its original decision to extend the credit. This representation usually refers to the latest audited financial statements as well as any more-recent interim financial statements.

The representations relating to financial assumptions reflect only the minimum assumptions as to financial matters; usually the borrower provides much more financial information to the bank than is set forth in the representations.

Absence of Material Adverse Change. A common representation is that there has been no material adverse change in the financial condition or operations of the borrower since the date of the latest financial statements. Such change may or may not be reflected in the balance sheet or income statement of the borrower. This provision enables the bank to refuse to lend to a borrower whose financial situation has materially deteriorated. It does not permit the bank to declare outstanding loans due and payable unless the representation was materially false when made (at the time of signing or of any advance).

The *material adverse change* standard is designed to cover circumstances in which the borrower's ability to perform its obligations under the loan agreement has become doubtful. The standard lacks precision and the bank's refusal to make further advances to the borrower because of a material adverse change is likely to cause disagreement. The bank's position obviously would be more certain if it were able to point to a violation of a financial covenant or some other provision of the loan agreement. However, because of the difficulty in defining clearly all possible material adverse changes, having the ability to invoke this standard, however imprecise, remains very important. Even in cases where the bank and the borrower disagree on whether a material adverse change has occurred, the existence of the clause alone may improve the bank's negotiating position.

COVENANTS OF THE BORROWER

Functions of Covenants. The affirmative and negative covenants bind the borrower in the conduct of its business during the period of the commitment and for the duration of the loan. Covenants permit the bank to influence the future conduct of the borrower in a manner that will reduce the risk that the loan will not be repaid. Violations of covenants serve as warning signals of difficulties. Covenants accomplish this in several ways: by requiring the borrower to comply with applicable legal requirements, by restricting excessive leveraging (restrictions on debt and leases), by preventing the borrower from preferring other creditors (the negative pledge), by maintaining assets in the borrower (restrictions on dividends and the net-worth covenant), or by requiring the borrower to retain liquidity (working-capital covenant). Also typically included in the covenants is an agreement by the borrower to supply financial and other information so that the bank can monitor the condition of the borrower and take corrective action if the situation warrants such action. If the borrower has subsidiaries, the bank must decide whether to apply the covenants to the borrower alone, the borrower and its subsidiaries generally, or the borrower and a group of specified subsidiaries (frequently referred to as restricted subsidiaries).

A violation of these agreed-upon minimum standards for the borrower's future conduct should give the bank the right to refuse to make additional advances because such violation (in some cases upon notice and passage of an applicable grace period) creates an event of default, which should prevent the conditions of lending from being met and which should permit the bank to accelerate the loan and cancel its commitment.

Negative Covenants. The negative covenants may be more significant than the affirmative covenants, because they provide clear restrictions upon managerial decisions. These restrictions normally cover such areas as creation of liens, incurrence of indebtedness and lease obligations, payment of dividends, mergers, sale of assets, and investments.

The negative-pledge covenant usually prohibits the borrower from granting any security interest, lien, or mortgage on its property or its income to secure the payment of obligations to other lenders. The problem created by any such security interests, liens, or mortgages in favor of other creditors is that they subordinate the bank's loan to the borrower's obligations to other creditors in case of financial difficulty of the borrower. The purpose of a negative pledge is to provide a pool of assets that will be available for payment of the claims of unsecured creditors equally without any preference of one over the other; it does not create a security interest in favor of the bank. The negative-pledge covenant should apply to the borrower's right to receive income as well as its properties to prevent the use of devices that dedicate income streams to the payment of certain debts.

There are a variety of possible covenants. Which covenants the bank wishes to include in a loan agreement depends on the nature of the borrower's business, its financial condition, and the term of the loan. The covenants may be tied directly to detailed financial projections provided by the borrower if the credit risk is high, or may be limited to a few general financial benchmarks if the credit risk is low. In devising financial covenants for foreign borrowers, the bank should take into account the foreign accounting principles applicable to the borrower.

EVENTS OF DEFAULT.   Events of default are circumstances in which the bank has the right to declare the loan immediately payable and to terminate the bank's commitment to extend credit under the loan agreement.

Typical Events of Default.   Most loan agreements contain at least the following events of default: nonpayment of principal or interest, inaccuracy in the representations and warranties, violations of covenants, cross-default to other debt of the borrower, bankruptcy events, expropriation, and failure to pay a final judgment in excess of a certain amount.

A cross-default provision is important in circumstances in which the borrower has defaulted under another credit agreement, thus enabling other creditors to demand payment or negotiate improvements in their positions. The cross-default provision gives the bank the right to accelerate its loan in such event. The cross-default can be broadened to include events that have not yet become events of default under other credit agreements because notice requirements or cure (grace) periods are still applicable. This latter type of cross-default gives the bank the same opportunity to negotiate with the borrower as the other creditors prior to the occurrence of a formal event of default under their credit agreements.

In addition to the events of default mentioned above, the bank must consider whether, in the context of the particular loan transaction, there are other circumstances in which the bank should have the right to call the loan. However, many of these circumstances could more appropriately be located in other parts of the loan agreement. For example, if the purpose of the credit is to finance the construction of a hotel, the loan agreement could provide for mandatory prepayment rather than an event of default if the hotel is destroyed. If it is important for the bank that the borrower continues to be owned by its parent corporation, then instead of simply making the transfer of the borrower's stock an event of default, it might be preferable to have the parent corporation covenant to continue to hold the stock of the borrower, and then make the violation of this covenant an event of default. The advantage of covering these circumstances in parts of the loan agreement other than the events of default is that because of the requirement for notice and grace periods or because of the wording of the cross-default clauses in other credit agreements, such circumstances may not immediately trigger a cross-default in other credit agreements, and under proper circumstances, may enable the bank to obtain a court order enjoining the borrower or its parent corporation from violating a covenant.

Grace Periods and Notice Requirements.   Certain events of default may contain grace periods or notice provisions, whereas others are considered so significant that the mere occurrence of the event gives the bank the immediate right to accelerate. Grace periods are granted very infrequently in the case of a default for failure to make principal payments. Since the representations and warranties reflect the fundamental assumptions upon which the credit is extended, any material inaccuracy is considered serious and usually treated as an automatic event of default. A cure period is usually not provided because misrepresentations often are not susceptible to being remedied. Violations of covenants become events of default frequently after notice is given by the bank to the borrower and a grace period lapses without the borrower correcting the default. However, a loan agreement may create an automatic event of default upon violation of certain covenants, especially financial covenants, because they are fundamental to the basic credit decision or because the opportunity for correction is limited.

Automatic events of default may be disadvantageous to the bank because they may trigger cross-default provisions in credit agreements between the borrower and other creditors and may thereby introduce an element of instability in the borrower's financial affairs. This consideration would not be relevant, however, if another credit agreement contained a cross-default provision that was violated irrespective of notices and cure periods in the loan agreement or waivers by the bank.

Remedies.   Upon the occurrence and during the continuance of an event of default, the bank has the right to accelerate the loan and terminate its commitment. An event of default sometimes accelerates the loan automatically, especially upon the occurrence of bankruptcy or similar events, but automatic accelerations are unusual. This right to accelerate is not intended to be the only remedy available to the bank. In addition, the bank has the right to set off deposits of the borrower against the borrower's obligation to repay the loan either by virtue of a specific provision contained in the loan agreement, or by statute or by common law. If the borrower is not in bankruptcy, the bank is normally able to obtain a judgment against the borrower for the amount of the debt due and then has available the remedies under the legal system for the enforcement of judgments. Furthermore, the bank may be able to resort to legal proceedings to enforce certain provisions of the loan agreement. For example, the bank may be able to obtain a court order requiring the borrower to comply with a covenant or enjoining the borrower and third parties from violating a covenant.

In practice, banks rarely exercise the right to accelerate the loan, because an acceleration is likely to trigger acceleration by other creditors of the borrower and thus cause a bankruptcy. The most frequent result of an event of default is a renegotiation by the bank and the borrower of the loan agreement together with a renegotiation of the borrower's other credit relationships. Even though rarely used, the right to accelerate is an essential remedy, because having this right substantially strengthens the bank's negotiating position with the borrower and other creditors. It also serves as a powerful incentive for the borrower to remain in compliance. However, if bankruptcy appears inevitable, or if other creditors accelerate, or if there exists fraud or some other situation with which the bank cannot live, the bank may be forced to accelerate and set off deposits.

EURODOLLAR LOANS

NATURE OF EUROCURRENCY.   Eurodollars are deposits of U.S. dollars with foreign banks or foreign branches of U.S. banks located outside the United States. Euro-Deutsche Marks are deposits of Deutsche Marks with banks located outside the Federal Republic of Germany. Thus a Eurocurrency is a bank deposit liability (or a claim against a bank) denominated in a currency other than the monetary unit of the country in which the bank is located. Eurodollars are created when a U.S. or foreign owner of a deposit with a bank in the United States transfers a U.S. dollar credit balance to a foreign bank (or to a foreign branch of a U.S. bank) located outside the United States. The foreign bank assumes a deposit liability to the transferor owner payable in U.S. dollars, and itself has a corresponding claim in U.S. dollars against the bank in the United States (owns a deposit or credit balance with that bank). The foreign bank may transfer its U.S. dollar deposits to a second foreign bank, the second foreign bank may transfer the deposit to a third foreign bank, and so forth. In each case the transferee foreign bank becomes owner of the dollar deposit in the United States and assumes a deposit liability payable in U.S. dollars to the transferor foreign bank. The dollars never leave the U.S. bank or the United States, so the total of bank deposits in the United States remains unchanged, but additional dollar deposits have been created abroad. When a bank, supported by such a U.S. dollar claim against a U.S. bank, transfers to a borrower a claim *against itself* for an equivalent amount of U.S. dollars, it makes a Eurodollar loan.

FUNDING.   The theory of a Eurodollar loan is that the lending bank acquires short-term Eurodollar deposits and lends the funds so borrowed by it to the borrower on a long-term basis. The interest rate on a Eurodollar loan is equal to the funding cost of the bank plus an agreed-upon *margin* or *spread*. The funding cost is expressed by reference to a specified Eurodollar interbank market (for instance, London) in which, theoretically, the bank expects to obtain the Eurodollars to lend. The loan agreements, however, do not restrict the bank to one market, and it may obtain the Eurodollars in any market it chooses. Because the bank passes the funding cost on to the borrower, the interest rate payable by the borrower fluctuates with the change of the funding cost.

The periods used for setting the interest rate payable by the borrower on the loan (interest periods) correspond, in theory, to the maturities of the U.S. dollar deposits acquired by the bank to fund the particular Eurodollar loan. At the end of any given term for a funding deposit the bank would, in theory, cause the maturity of such deposit to be extended, or would acquire another U.S. dollar deposit, for a term that similarly "matches" the next interest period (either selected by the borrower or set by the terms of the loan agreement). In practice, many large banks do not match deposits to interest periods of particular loans, but rather acquire an inventory of Eurodollar funds without consideration to any particular loan. In that case, the Eurodollar rate determined in accordance with the interest-period concept is a convenient and relatively verifiable way to establish a certain rate. Generally speaking, longer interest periods will result in higher current rates but may be preferred by the borrower if he believes interest rates are rising.

Because in theory the term of each funding deposit matches the term of an interest period for the loan, the bank might suffer a loss if the borrower repaid or prepaid the loan or a portion thereof in the middle of an interest period. The bank would have to continue to pay interest on its funding deposit until the maturity of such deposit, but the borrower would not have to pay the corresponding interest on the "matching" loan. In addition, the bank may be unable to reinvest the funds at the interest rate previously paid by the borrower. To avoid this possibility, Eurodollar loan agreements provide that the interest periods (at least for an amount equal to the principal due) will end on each principal-repayment date, and that the borrower cannot prepay any portion of the loan except at the end of an interest period for such loan. If prepayment is allowed at some other time, the borrower should agree to reimburse the bank for any loss resulting from such prepayment.

LONDON INTERBANK OFFERED RATE (LIBOR).   Eurodollar loan agreements generally define the Eurodollar rate as the rate of interest at which U.S. dollar deposits (Eurodollars) are offered by the principal office of the bank to other banks in the specified interbank Eurodollar market (e.g., London) at a certain hour a certain number of days (usually two business days) before the first day of the applicable interest period for a period equal to such interest period and in an amount equal to the loan or advance to be made available during such interest period. Most agreements refer to the rate for U.S. dollar deposits *offered by* the bank for sale to prime banks, the Eurodollar rate *posted* by the bank. In a syndicated loan the Eurodollar rate is determined by reference to an average (arithmetic mean) of the Eurodollar rates offered by specified reference banks. This averaging of rates takes into account both the relatively lower rates of the large dealer banks and the relatively higher rates of the non-dealer banks (which are more likely to "match" funding deposits to interest periods).

Eurodollar loan agreements in which dealer banks do not participate sometimes provide for a Eurodollar rate based on the rate *offered to* the bank or the reference banks in order to take the higher rate into account that such banks have to pay for U.S. dollar deposits.

YIELD PROTECTION.   The Eurodollar interest rate consists of funding cost plus fixed spread, and customarily Eurodollar loan agreements guarantee this spread by providing that the borrower must indemnify the bank for *increased costs*. Increased costs could be incurred if because of a change in law (in the case of a loan through a London branch of a U.S. bank, U.S. law, or English law) reserve or other monetary requirements were imposed on the bank or its branch. It is possible that U.S. or overseas monetary authorities will become concerned enough about the present lack of regulation in the Eurodollar markets that they will impose, or request "voluntary" compliance with, requirements intended to restrict, and make more costly, Eurodollar lending. Banks lending Eurodollars generally expect that the borrowers will assume the risk of such requirements and therefore will agree to pay the increased funding costs resulting from such requirements. If these additional costs unduly burden the borrower, Eurodollar loan agreements customarily permit the borrower to prepay the loan, at which time the bank's commitment terminates.

As additional yield protection, banks generally require that all payments by the borrower must be made free and clear of withholding and all other foreign *taxes*. In addition, the loan agreement may provide that the borrower must indemnify the bank against income taxes imposed on the bank by its own country for imputed income attributable to withholding taxes paid on its behalf by the borrower (so-called gross-up provision). For example, under present U.S. tax law, if the interest due and paid by the borrower is $100 and the withholding tax rate is 25 percent, the bank is generally taxed in the United States on an income of $133 (*i.e.*, 75 percent of $133 ≈ $100) rather than $100. The borrower frequently argues that a gross-up provision is unjustified if the bank is entitled under its tax laws to a foreign-tax credit for the withholding taxes even if paid by the borrower.

FUNDING INTERRUPTION. The determination of the Eurodollar rate is based on the assumption that the Eurodollar market will continue to exist substantially in its present form and Eurodollars will remain available, and Eurodollar loan agreements frequently provide that if this assumption (which may be expressed in different ways) is no longer true (e.g., because of a major dislocation of the specified Eurodollar market), the interest rate will be redetermined to reflect the cost to the bank of funding the loan. The procedure usually requires the bank and the borrower to negotiate with a view to agreeing on an alternative basis for the loan or for determining the rate. If no such agreement results after a specified period of time, then, many loan agreements provide, the bank is required to notify the borrower of the alternative rate at which the bank is prepared to lend. At that point the borrower has two choices: either to pay the alternative rate as determined by the bank or to prepay the loan. The borrower bears the risk that the Eurodollar market will not continue in its present form.

Frequently Eurodollar loan agreements cover the risk that it may become *unlawful* for the bank to continue to fund or to make its Eurodollar loans. This risk includes the possibility that the United States or the country of the lending office of the bank might prohibit, or permit on untenable conditions, transfers or purchases of U.S. dollar claims overseas or might regulate the volume or type of Eurodollar lending by banks. Loan agreements frequently (1) require that in such an event the borrower prepay the loan and (2) provide that the bank's commitment terminates.

PLACE OF PAYMENT. Most Eurodollar loan agreements require the borrower to repay the loan at a bank located in the United States for account of the lender or, if the loan is made by a foreign branch of the U.S. bank, for account of such lending office. This requirement is important. First, the bank passes the *exchange control* risk to the borrower, for it is the borrower, not the bank, who is responsible for returning the U.S. dollar claims to the United States, where the claim becomes a currency in available funds. U.S. dollar credits overseas may not be worth as much as U.S. dollars in the United States if the uses to which such credits can be put are restricted or if exchange-control laws restrict their transfer. Second, the bank minimizes the risk of something happening to the payment resulting from expropriation or other *adverse action* of the government of the foreign branch that acted as lending office or other overseas government. Third, the place of repayment under a loan agreement is, under New York law and the law of many other states, the most important contact for determining the governing law; thus specifying New York City as the place of repayment greatly reinforces the New York governing-law clause. Fourth, a requirement for repayment in New York may be necessary to create subject-matter jurisdiction in a suit by a foreign bank against a foreign borrower to recover damages for breach of a loan agreement.

FOREIGN-CURRENCY AND MULTICURRENCY LOANS. A bank that makes a loan in a foreign currency may avoid the foreign-exchange risk by funding the loan in the same currency. However, U.S. banks often base Eurocurrency loans on U.S. dollars: The lending commitment is in U.S. dollars or the Eurocurrency equivalent of a stated U.S. dollar amount. If the borrower requests an advance in Euro-Deutsche Marks, the bank would theoretically acquire Eurodollars in the relevant interbank market and use these Eurodollars to buy (convert into) Euro-Deutsche Marks. In order to have sufficient Eurodollars at the end of the interest period to repay the Eurodollar-funding loan, the bank may cover itself by selling forward the Euro-Deutsche Marks for the necessary amount of Eurodollars. At the end of the interest period, the bank would use U.S. dollars to buy Euro-Deutsche Marks to perform the forward transaction. Any exchange loss or gain arising from this last transaction is usually for the account of the borrower. If the borrower wishes to convert the outstanding Euro-Deutsche Mark advance at the end of an interest period into a Eurofrancs advance, the bank would theoretically convert the Euro-Deutsche Marks back into U.S. dollars and then convert the U.S. dollars into Eurofrancs. The change of value of the borrowed foreign currency against the U.S. dollar affects the commitment of the bank: The borrower may only borrow an amount of Eurocurrency that if converted to U.S. dollars does not exceed the U.S. dollar commitment. Some loan agreements provide for a prepayment of outstanding Eurocurrency advances to the extent that, because of fluctuating exchange rates, their dollar equivalent exceeds the U.S. dollar commitment.

LOANS TO SOVEREIGN BORROWERS

GENERAL CONSIDERATIONS.   Most major banks require even in the case of a government borrower a loan agreement that establishes a basis for effective enforcement proceedings. Such banks anticipate that a defaulting government may not always be motivated by a desire for continued access to the capital markets or may have access to alternative markets, that the banks would be in a weak negotiating position if the loan agreement provided for no legal action except that controlled by the government borrower, and that the bank's government may, for political reasons, be reluctant to intervene on behalf of the bank. Finally, the absence of provisions for effective legal action in one government-loan agreement creates a precedent for loan agreements with other government borrowers.

The legal protection of a bank should include a waiver of sovereign immunities by the government borrower, submission by the government to a neutral and commercially experienced forum, and the choice of a developed commercial law as governing law. A bank would not want its loan to a sovereign borrower to be governed by the law of the jurisdiction of the borrower. Such law is susceptible to being changed by and for the benefit of the sovereign borrower, and history has shown that a sovereign, when in trouble, tends to change its law to alleviate its troubles. If the law of the sovereign was specified as the governing law, courts may (and New York courts probably will) give effect to such changes in the specified law.

IMMUNITY FROM SUIT, ATTACHMENT, AND EXECUTION

Immunity.   Submission by the borrower to the jurisdiction of a court does not give much protection to a bank if the government borrower and its property are immune from suit, execution, and attachment. Under the U.S. Foreign Sovereign Immunities Act of 1976 (28 U.S.C. §§ 1330, 1332, 1391, 1441, and 1602 et seq.), (1) a *foreign state* is immune from suit in federal and state courts in the United States, and (2) assets in the United States of a foreign state are immune from attachment, arrest, and execution, except in each case as otherwise specifically permitted by the immunities act. *Foreign state*, with minor exceptions, is defined to include a political subdivision of a foreign state and an agency or instrumentality of a foreign state; and *agency or instrumentality* is defined to include a separate legal person that is an organ of a foreign state or political subdivision thereof and a corporation organized under the laws of, and the majority of whose shares are owned by, a foreign state or political subdivision thereof. The exceptions from immunity from the jurisdiction of the federal or state courts in the United States are as follows:

1. A foreign state can explicitly or implicitly *waive* its *immunity from suit* in a federal or state court. Obviously, an explicit waiver is preferable over a waiver merely by implication.

2. A foreign state is *not immune from suit* in any case in which the action is based upon an activity of the foreign state that is *commercial* by its nature and that is carried on in the United States, or upon an act performed within, or having a direct effect within, the United States in connection with such foreign state's commercial activity elsewhere.

3. A foreign state can explicitly or implicitly *waive* its *immunity from attachment in aid of execution*, and its immunity from execution, upon a judgment entered by a federal or state court. Whereas a foreign state (that is not an agency or instrumentality) can waive immunity from attachment in aid of execution and from execution only for property used for a commercial activity in the United States, an agency or instrumentality of a foreign state engaged in commercial activity in the United States can waive these immunities for any property (whether commercially used or not) in the United States.

4. The property of a foreign state is *not immune from attachment in aid of execution* or from execution upon a judgment entered by a federal or state court if the commercially used property is or was used for the *commercial activity* upon which the claim was based, or if the property (whether commercially used or not) belongs to an agency or instrumentality of a foreign state engaged in commercial activity in the United States and the judgment relates to a claim based upon a commercial activity carried on in the United States or upon an act performed within, or having a direct effect within, the United States in connection with such agency's or instrumentality's commercial activity elsewhere (regardless of whether the property is or was used for the activity upon which the claim is based).

5. Commercially used property of a foreign state in the United States is *not immune from attachment prior to judgment* in any action brought in a federal or state court if the foreign state has explicitly waived its immunity from attachment prior to judgment *and* the purpose of the attachment is to secure satisfaction of a judgment that may ultimately be entered against the foreign state (and not to obtain jurisdiction).

6. Notwithstanding the above exceptions to immunity from attachment and execution, the property in the United States of a *foreign central bank* or monetary authority "held for its own account" is immune from any attachment and execution whatsoever, unless such bank or authority, or its parent foreign government, has explicitly waived its immunity from attachment in aid of execution or from execution. But property of a foreign state of a *military character* or controlled by a foreign military authority and funds payable by certain *international organizations* to or on the order of a foreign state are absolutely immune from attachment or execution.

Each waiver of immunity is effective irrespective of any subsequent attempt to revoke it, unless the waiver is interpreted to be revocable.

The legislative history of the immunities act indicates that a foreign state's borrowing of money from U.S. commercial banks would be of a "commercial" nature and that a foreign state's incurring of indebtedness in the United States (if the loan agreement is negotiated and executed in the United States) would be a commercial activity carried on in the United States (House of Representatives, 94th Cong., 2d Sess. H. Rep. 1487 (1976) pp. 10 and 16.). The courts, however, have a great deal of latitude in determining what is *commercial* and whether a particular commercial activity has been performed in the United States, and it is advisable to include in all loan agreements with foreign states an explicit waiver of all three immunities, that is, immunity from suit; immunity from attachment in aid of execution, and from execution, upon a judgment; and immunity from attachment prior to judgment.

Service of Process.   The immunities act specifies various ways for making service of process on a foreign state. However, if the potential plaintiff and the foreign state agree upon any special arrangement for delivery of summons and complaint, service must be made in accordance with such method. The immunities act intends to encourage potential plaintiffs and foreign states to agree on a procedure for service. A usual procedure is for the foreign state to appoint a process agent in the jurisdiction to which the foreign state submits. Such agent should accept the appointment, agree to forward all process to the foreign state and agree not to resign such appointment during the term of the loan. The consul of a foreign state in the United States may be appointed process agent, but may have its own diplomatic immunity from process; such immunity should be waived either by the consul itself or by the foreign state on behalf of the consul.

Representation.   A loan agreement with a governmental borrower often contains a representation to the effect that the borrower is not subject to sovereign immunity and that the execution, delivery, and performance of the loan agreement constitutes a commercial act. Such a representation may help to establish the commercial nature of the transaction.

SYNDICATION AND PARTICIPATION

SYNDICATED LOANS.   When a borrower's need for funds exceeds the amount that any single bank is able, willing, or legally permitted to lend, several banks may join together in a syndicate to provide the required funds. A multibank syndicated loan represents an aggregate of commitments by the syndicate members, who agree to make the loan and to receive payments pro rata in accordance with the commitment of each. Each syndicate member is a party to the loan agreement and receives a separate note evidencing the portion of the loan made by it. The obligations of the syndicate members are separate, and one lender is not responsible for the commitment of another lender. In syndicated loans, one bank usually serves as *agent* for the syndicate in order to centralize the administration of the loan. An agreement between the agent bank and the syndicate members (which may, but need not, be part of the loan agreement) should clearly spell out the responsibilities and liabilities of the agent bank. Although loan agreements frequently state that the agent bank's function is limited to ministerial duties expressly set forth in the agreement, the agent stands in a fiduciary relationship to the syndicate members. This relationship may, for instance, obligate the agent bank to disclose to the syndicate members inside information relating to the borrower and possibly even to keep itself informed about the borrower. An agent bank might find itself confronted with conflicting interests and duties due to other contractual and trust relationships with the borrower and its affiliates.

Frequently a syndicate is organized by a *manager* or a limited number of co-managers under the leadership of a *lead* manager (frequently the agent bank or one of its affiliates). Acting as manager involves responsibilities with the correspondent risk of liability. The lead manager has several roles that may conflict: The lead manager commits to the borrower to syndicate the credit; the borrower looks to the manager for informed advice; the syndicate participants rely on the manager to negotiate and structure the terms of the loan to their advantage; and in addition, in most cases the manager commits a substantial portion of the loan.

One of the most important provisions in a syndicated-loan agreement is the sharing-of-payments provision: To what extent must a bank that sets off a deposit maintained by the borrower with it against its portion of the loan share with the other banks? Sometimes a syndicated-loan agreement provides for a sharing among the banks of amounts set off and of other payments received with respect to the borrower's obligation to pay principal and interest. Such a provision prevents the borrower from favoring one bank in the syndicate when it is unable to satisfy all banks in full, and prevents any bank from receiving an advantage over the other banks because the borrower happens to maintain deposit accounts with that bank.

PARTICIPATIONS.   A participant "purchases" from the lending or lead bank an undivided percentage interest in the lead bank's loan to the borrower (*i.e.*, the lead bank's existing right to receive payment in respect of the debt owed by the borrower) upon payment to the lead bank of a commensurate percentage of the principal amount of the participated loan. A lead bank may "sell" participations in a loan when the loan exceeds its lending limit, when it desires to reduce its risk or to increase its liquidity or to raise the funds for the loan, or in order to promote its correspondent-bank relationships. In many cases the loan agreement makes no reference to a sale of participations.

The relation between the lead bank and the participant is governed by a participation agreement or a participation certificate or both. The participant is not a co-lender to the borrower and does not enter into any debtor–creditor relationship with the borrower. Thus the participant cannot under common law set off against the borrower's funds on deposit with it [*In re Yale Express System, Inc.*, 245 F. Supp. 790 (S.D.N.Y. 1965)]. Participation agreements typically provide that recourse against the lead bank is limited: The participant's right to repayment arises only upon the receipt by the lead bank of payment from the borrower, and in case of a default by the borrower the participant shares in the losses pro rata with the lead bank. Of course the participation agreement may provide for a different relationship between the lead bank and the participant. For example, the participation agreement may provide that the participant will have full recourse against the lead bank irrespective of a default by the borrower. The loan agreement between the lead bank and the borrower may give the participant certain rights against the borrower, for instance, protection against withholding taxes, the benefit of indemnities, and possibly the right of setoff.

LIABILITY OF MANAGER AND LEAD BANK.   It is an open and much-debated question whether (1) a loan participation agreement or a participation certificate and (2) a note issued by a borrower to the bank, or even a noteless loan agreement, constitute *securities* in the meaning of the U.S. securities laws. [Compare *Provident National Bank* v. *Frankford Trust Company,* 468 F. Supp. 448 (E.D. Pa. 1979) (loan participation is not a security) with *Commercial Discount Corporation* v. *Lincoln First Commercial Corporation,* 445 F. Supp. 1263 (S.D.N.Y. 1978) (loan participation is a security).]

If a syndication of a loan involves a security, the manager may be liable to the syndicate members under the disclosure requirements of the antifraud provisions of the U.S. securities laws (especially Section 10(b) of the Securities Exchange Act of 1934). The manager would be liable if his written or oral communications to the prospective syndicate members (especially an information memorandum delivered by the manager) included any untrue statement of a material fact or omitted to state a material fact necessary in order to make the statements not misleading, and if the manager knew, or in the exercise of due diligence could have known, of such misstatements or omissions. The manager would be under an affirmative duty to disclose material "inside information" (information in the possession of the manager and known not to be available to the prospective syndicate members). Ryan (1980) summarizes, "It is still unsettled, however, whether or to what extent a manager would have to satisfy the requirement for a due diligence investigation of the borrower and other aspects of the syndicated credit. A manager's duty of due diligence could reasonably vary from one transaction to another in proportion to its role in the syndication." It is doubtful whether and to what extent a manager can avoid liability by disclaiming responsibility for, and by each syndicate member confirming that it has not relied on the manager for, the accuracy of statements made in connection with the loan agreement or the creditworthiness of the borrower.

If a participation involves a security, the same considerations would apply to the liability of the lead bank as to the participant.

GOVERNING LAW

NEED FOR GOVERNING-LAW CLAUSES.   Nearly every international loan agreement contains a *governing-law* or *choice-of-law* clause that sets forth the law that the parties intend to govern the agreement. It is important that the parties stipulate the applicable law because otherwise, under the principles set forth in the well-known case *Auten* v. *Auten* [308 N.Y. 155, 124 N.E. 2d 99 (1954)], the courts in the United States apply the law of the jurisdiction "which has the most significant contacts with the matter in dispute." Under the similar *governmental interest* approach, the courts apply the law of the jurisdiction having the most interest in the disputed issue. Under these approaches it is usually quite unpredictable which law the courts will apply to an agreement.

A bank usually insists on the law of the country or state in which it is located, because it prefers a familiar to an unfamiliar legal system, or on the law of a major commercial country or state, such as New York, on the theory that such jurisdiction has a well-developed commercial law that results in a relatively predictable interpretation and enforcement. In recent years, foreign borrowers, especially sovereign borrowers, have sometimes requested (or for internal or legal reasons insisted) that the law of their jurisdiction should govern the loan agreement. In the view of most banks this request is unjustified. After the bank has disbursed the loan, it is in a weak position, because it has performed its part of the bargain and has rights only under the agreement, primarily the right to receive payment of principal and interest. The borrower has only obligations, primary of which is the obligation of payment of the principal and interest. The bank alone bears a risk of loss. It would be unjustified to render the exercise of the bank's rights more difficult by asking it to enforce them under a law unknown to it. The borrower does not need the protection of a legal system familiar to it, because the obligation to pay principal and interest is very clear.

SCOPE OF GOVERNING-LAW CLAUSES. In the United States, questions of validity and scope of a choice-of-law clause in a loan agreement are governed by state law. The court in which suit is brought to enforce a loan agreement analyzes under its own law (the law of the forum) the validity and scope of the governing-law clause, even if the clause stipulates the law of another jurisdiction as governing the agreement. If it finds the clause valid, it will apply the stipulated law. Therefore, it may be desirable for the bank to obtain legal opinions as to the validity of the governing-law clause from all jurisdictions in which it might seek to sue the borrower on the loan agreement.

If action to enforce a loan agreement is brought in the court of a country or state other than the country or state whose law is stipulated, the application of the validly stipulated law is limited in one respect: The stipulated law will not be applied by the court to the extent that it violates an *important public policy* of the law of the forum or, according to some authorities, even to the extent that it violates a public policy of another jurisdiction that has a materially greater interest in the determination of the disputed issue than the country or state whose law was selected.

As a general rule, a stipulation of the law of a country or state is a stipulation of the substantive rules of law of that country or state and not of the whole law, including the conflict-of-laws rules of that country or state. If the parties agree on New York law, they wish the substantive New York law to apply and not the law of that state that a New York court would apply under the New York conflict-of-laws rules absent a governing-law clause. However, even though a loan agreement stipulates the law of a particular jurisdiction as governing, questions of the corporate power of the borrower to enter the loan agreement, questions of authorization of the loan agreement by all appropriate corporate actions of the borrower, and questions of due execution and delivery of the loan agreement by appropriate officers of the borrower will most probably be determined by the law of the country or state of the borrower.

REASONABLE-RELATIONSHIP REQUIREMENT. Most courts in the United States (including New York courts) follow the rule that the parties to an agreement may choose any governing law so long as there is a reasonable relationship between the transaction and the country or state whose law was chosen. This concept is also expressed in Section 1-105(1) of the Uniform Commercial Code, which does not directly apply to loan agreements but, as one of the very few statutory expressions of a general principle of conflict of laws, carries great weight. This reasonable-relationship requirement should not create any problem if a loan agreement is governed by the law of the country or state where the bank's lending office or the head office of the borrower is located.

If the bank and the borrower wish to agree on the law of a third country because neither of them is located in a country with a developed body of commercial law or because this solution offers itself as a compromise, the reasonable-relationship test becomes important. A reasonable relationship between a transaction and a country or state is probably given, for instance, if the agreement is made or will be performed in that jurisdiction. It is helpful if substantial negotiation of the transaction took place in that jurisdiction. A U.S. dollar or Eurodollar loan agreement will probably be performed in the location in the United States where the loan must be repaid.

STIPULATION OF JURISDICTION

SUBMISSION TO PERSONAL JURISDICTION.   Most international loan agreements contain a provision in which the borrower agrees to submit to the jurisdiction of the courts of one or more states or countries, frequently specifying the city in which suit may be brought. This facilitates enforcement by the bank of its rights under the loan agreement in case of a default by the borrower. Although there is no conceptual connection between this clause and the governing-law clause, it is usually preferable to litigate a dispute in the courts of the country or state the law of which governs the agreement, because proof of that law in the courts of another country or state can be difficult. At any rate, the selected forum should have a judiciary that has integrity and is experienced in commercial litigation. Another important consideration is whether a judgment by the selected courts would be enforced by the country in which the borrower has assets, that is, frequently the home country of the borrower.

Submission to the jurisdiction of a particular court by the borrower gives that court personal jurisdiction over the borrower (power of the court to render judgment binding on the defendant personally). The threshold question is whether the selected court accepts such advance contractual submission by a party that without such submission would not be subject to its jurisdiction. For instance, both New York State courts and federal courts in New York sitting in diversity actions accept a submission to their jurisdiction. A New York court recognized consent jurisdiction in *National Equipment Rental, Ltd.* v. *Graphic Art Designers, Inc.* [36 Misc. 2d 442, 234 N.Y.S. 2d 61 (Sup. Ct. 1962)] and the U.S. Supreme Court recognized consent jurisdiction in *National Equipment Rental, Ltd.* v. *Szukhent,* [375 U.S. 311 (1964)].

Valid submission by the borrower to the jurisdiction of a court does not dispense with the requirement of proper service of process on the borrower in accordance with the law of the country or state of such court. In many loan agreements, the borrower expressly appoints an agent located in the jurisdiction of the selected court on whom process may be served. It may be sufficient under applicable law if the borrower agrees to another manner of service of process, for example, being served by being sent by registered mail a copy of the process. [See *Fidan* v. *Austral American Trading Corp., 8 Misc. 2d 598, 168 N.Y.S. 2d 27 (Sup. Ct. 1957).]* If an agent for service of process has been appointed by the borrower, it is advisable to obtain the agent's formal acceptance of the appointment and his agreement to transmit to the borrower all process served upon him.

In the absence of the borrower's express consent to personal jurisdiction, personal jurisdiction of the forum over the borrower would have to be obtained under the forum's "long-arm" statutes, which require some contact between the defendant and the forum.

SUBJECT-MATTER JURISDICTION. A court must have not only jurisdiction over the person of the defendant, which can be created by a submission to its jurisdiction, but in addition subject-matter jurisdiction (power of the court to take cases of the kind in question), which cannot be conferred upon the court by the parties.

U.S. *federal courts* have subject-matter jurisdiction in actions involving loan agreements usually only if there is "diversity of citizenship" between the plaintiff and defendant (28 U.S.C. § 1332). Diversity of citizenship requires that one party to the litigation is a citizen of a state of the United States whereas the other party is a citizen of another state or of a foreign country. Thus diversity jurisdiction is not available where both parties are citizens of foreign countries, for example, in a suit by a foreign bank against a foreign borrower. In that case submission to jurisdiction is of no avail. Because federal jurisdiction based on diversity of citizenship is derived from the U.S. Constitution, a statute cannot broaden the concept, and the argument that the Foreign Sovereign Immunities Act of 1976 permits a diversity action even if two non-U.S. parties are involved in the suit is incorrect.

State courts, which are not subject to the above requirements, may be subject to other limitations relating to subject-matter jurisdiction. For example, Section 1314(b) of the N.Y. Business Corporation Law permits actions by one foreign (*i.e.*, non-New York) corporation against another foreign corporation before New York state courts only in certain enumerated cases, the most important being actions brought to recover damages for the breach of a contract "made or to be performed" in New York. The New York Banking Law contains the same provision for actions involving foreign banks. Thus a New York court has subject-matter jurisdiction over an action for damages for breach of a loan agreement between a foreign bank and a foreign borrower only if the agreement was executed and delivered in New York or if disbursement and repayment of the loan is made through a New York bank account of the lender. The requirements of Section 1314(b) apply also to a federal court in New York sitting in a diversity action.

FORUM NON CONVENIENS. Even if a federal or state court has the power to hear a case, it may in its discretion still decline to hear the case on the ground of the doctrine of *forum non conveniens*. Under this doctrine a court may dismiss an action over which it has jurisdiction if it is a seriously inconvenient forum for the trial, provided that a more appropriate forum is available to the plaintiff. A valid submission-to-jurisdiction clause precludes the borrower from asserting its own inconvenience but does not necessarily prevent the court from ordering a dismissal or transfer of the case because of third-party or public interests.

OUSTER OF JURISDICTION. If a loan agreement selects the courts of one jurisdiction, for example, England, as the exclusive forum for the litigation of disputes arising under the agreement, and an action is brought in that jurisdiction, the court will look at the forum-selection clause as a submission to its jurisdiction. However, if an action is brought in another jurisdiction, for example, New York, the courts of that jurisdiction will look at the forum-selection clause as an ousting of its jurisdiction. An exclusive-forum selection clause is both a submission to jurisdiction of a particular court and an ouster of all other jurisdictions. The U.S. Supreme Court in *The Bremen* v. *Zapata Off-Shore Co.* [407 U.S. 1 (1972)] upheld a forum-selection clause (the clause in that case selected English courts and thereby excluded U.S. courts) if the choice of forum was made in an arm's-length negotiation by experienced and sophisticated businessmen. The courts of several states, including New York, have adopted the same rule. [See, e.g., *Gaskin* v. *Stumm Handel GmbH,* 390 F. Supp. 361 (S.D.N.Y. 1975).]

ARBITRATION. Most banks are skeptical of arbitration. Arbitrators are apt to render a compromise award, and banks feel that the repayment of a defaulted loan is not susceptible to compromise or equitable considerations. The award, once given, is not subject to judicial review except on grounds of fraud or other extreme conduct on the part of the arbitrators. Further, if arbitration fees are based on the amount in dispute, costs of arbitration could be substantially higher than costs of a court proceeding.

SOURCES AND SUGGESTED REFERENCES

Effros, R.C. "The Whys and Wherefores of Eurodollars," *The Business Lawyer,* Vol. XXIII (1968), pp. 629–644.

Gruson, M. "American Lawyers and Legal Opinions of Foreign Counsel," in Sweeney, J.C. ed., *1975 Annual Proceedings of the Fordham Corporate Law Institute*, New York: International Project Finance, 1976, pp. 296–305.

Gruson, M. "Governing Law Clauses in Commercial Agreements—New York's Approach," *Columbia Journal of Transnational Law,* Vol. XVIII (1979), pp. 323–379.

Logan, F.D. "Term Loan Agreements," in R.S. Rendell, ed., *International Financial Law,* London: Euromoney Publications, 1980.

Rendell, R.S. ed., *International Financial Law: Lending, Capital Transfers and Institutions.* London: Euromoney Publications, 1980. (herein cited as "Rendell, *International Financial Law*).

Ryan, R.H. "International Bank Loan Syndications and Participations," in Rendell, *International Financial Law*, pp. 25–38.

Special Committee on Legal Opinions in Commercial Transactions. "Legal Opinions to Third Parties: An Easier Path," *The Business Lawyer,* Vol. XXXIV (1979), pp. 1891-1926.

Stevenson, J.R. and J.F. Browne "United States Law of Sovereign Immunity Relating to International Financial Transactions," in Rendell, *International Financial Law*, pp. 85–103.

CODES OF CONDUCT FACING TRANSNATIONAL CORPORATIONS

CONTENTS

THE NEED FOR INTERNATIONAL
CODES 4

ELEMENTS OF THE CODES OF
CONDUCT 4

SCOPE, NATURE, AND
CHARACTERISTICS OF THE CODES 6

PROSPECTS AND EFFECTS 7

HISTORICAL PERSPECTIVE 8

Transnationals on the World
Stage 9

THE U.N. CODE OF CONDUCT
ON TRANSNATIONAL
CORPORATIONS 12
Structure of the Code 13
Negotiating Procedures 13

THE CODES IN UNCTAD 15
Restrictive Business Practices 16
Transfer of Technology 17

THE ILO TRIPARTITE DECLARATION 19

THE OECD GUIDELINES 20

NOTES 22

CODES OF CONDUCT FACING TRANSNATIONAL CORPORATIONS

Sotirios G. Mousouris

At the threshold of the 1980s, the international community seems to be absorbed in drafting and implementing codes of conduct related to transnational corporations (TNCs). Two instruments, the International Labor Organization (ILO) Tripartite Declaration and the Organization for Economic Cooperation and Development (OECD) Guidelines, are already in effect. Another, a set of principles and rules regarding restrictive business practices, negotiated in UNCTAD, has just been adopted by the U.N. General Assembly. Two more codes of conduct—those on transfer of technology and on transnational corporations—are reaching decisive points in negotiations.

These developments, startling as they appear, must be seen against the world's rising awareness during the 1970s of the phenomenon of transnational corporations and the concerns expressed in various quarters regarding their activities and effects.

A decade ago, a new and forceful actor advanced gradually to the proscenium, and the international community turned the spotlight upon it. Transnational corporations became a challenge to national sovereignty and to intergovernmental relations. They offered both perils and opportunities. Governments individually and collectively voiced their concerns and expressed their determination to tame this new force and harness its powers and capabilities to the purposes of their developmental objectives. Vigorous debates and close examinations followed. The conclusion quickly reached by governments was that an international phenomenon such as the emergence of transnational corporations had to be dealt with by international action.

Thus the issue of attempting to introduce certain "rules of the game," regarding transnational corporations, acceptable by a number of governments came to the forefront. However such "rules of the game," guidelines, standards or norms of behavior, or conduct cannot be considered at this stage as constituting a legally binding international regulatory framework. Since there is no global authority to enforce these rules and the interests of countries are so diverse, for various reasons which will be discussed below, the international community is in most cases settling for something less than an international regulation. Usually the codes containing guidelines are issued as resolutions or declarations of governments rather than as international treaties. They carry moral rather than legal force.

This section first deals with some of the reasons and origins that gave impetus to the elaboration of codes and examines briefly the history of these efforts. Second, it outlines the scope, nature, and objectives of these codes. Finally, it describes the background, the negotiation process, and the contents of the codes prepared at the United Nations, the ILO, and the OECD.

THE NEED FOR INTERNATIONAL CODES

The transnational character of these corporations' activities is such that national action alone is insufficient to handle their implications.

A transnational corporation is a commercial enterprise composed of a number of entities operating in various countries. (These entities may or may not be incorporated in the host countries and can be subsidiaries, affiliates, branches, or offices of a corporation). The enterprise usually works under a system of decision making which permits one or more decision-making centers (headquarters) to exercise influence over the other entities. Such influence can be exercised by way of ownership or other links between the entities, entails the sharing of information, resources, and responsibilities among the entities and often reflects a global strategy.

It is evident then, that no single national jurisdiction can cover the enterprise as a whole, since each entity has to observe the laws of the individual country in which it operates. What for instance would happen if the home government of a transnational corporation, say the United States, prohibited by law its corporations from exporting to country X? Does that prohibition cover affiliates of the transnational corporation established in another country which is interested in having trade relations with country X? What happens when a transnational corporation faces conflicting demands in two countries in which it operates? What happens if a host country feels that the affiliate of a transnational corporation serves the global interests of the enterprise as a whole rather than the interests of the host country? There are these types of considerations that highlight the need for international cooperation in this field.

Furthermore, it has been realized that while the world has developed international norms covering major aspects of international economic activities, such as trade and monetary relations, it has left, despite several efforts, a gap in the case of foreign investment. For instance, there is nothing analogous to the International Monetary Fund (IMF) or to the General Agreement on Tariff and Trade (GATT) when we come to direct foreign investment. Finally, incidents of political interference by transnational corporations in the early 1970s made the need for international action more acute. In some cases such incidents became the proximate cause of international action involving codes of conduct and other international arrangements.

ELEMENTS OF THE CODES OF CONDUCT

The codes of conduct are conceived as instruments designed to enhance the positive and reduce the negative effects of transnational corporations; to ensure that their activities are in accordance with the development objectives of countries in which they operate; to improve the investment climate; to protect the economies of host countries and the interests of workers and consumers; to encourage contributions that transnational corporations can make towards redressing the imbalance between developed and developing countries; and to solve conflicts among governments arising from the operations of transnational corporations.

These are some of the objectives of the codes that appear more or less in most of the relevant documents, albeit with varying degrees of emphasis. The guidelines issued in 1972 by the International Chamber of Commerce, for example, place emphasis on a favorable investment climate, while the OECD Guidelines for Multinational Enterprises, adopted in 1976, attempt to strike a balance by referring to the improvement of the foreign investment climate, the encouragement of positive contributions, and the minimization and resolution of difficulties. The ILO Tripartite Declaration concerning Multinational Enterprises and Social Policy, adopted in November 1977, addresses such issues as employment, vocational training, conditions of work and life, and industrial relations. It aims at encouraging positive contributions and minimizing and resolving difficulties in the light of the goals of the New International Economic Order (NIEO).

The United Nations Conference on Trade and Development (UNCTAD) has been the forum of two parallel negotiations: one on a set of principles and equitable rules for the prevention, elimination, and control of restrictive business practices, and another on a code of conduct for the transfer of technology. The first, adopted by a Conference in April 1980, and by the General Assembly later the same year, has provisions on restrictive business agreements and acts, concentration of economic power and prices, and conditions of sale. The code of technology transfer, which is still under negotiation, includes a long list of objectives, among them international regulatory action, the encouragement of the *unpackaged* transfer of technology, improvement of access to technology at fair and reasonable prices and costs, effective transfer arrangements, and development of the technological capabilities of recipients.

At the United Nations, under the auspices of the Commission on Transnational Corporations, a comprehensive code of conduct is under formulation. Although there is not yet agreement on the language of the preamble to the code, the Commission's general objective is to secure effective international arrangements for the operations of transnational corporations, designed to promote their contribution to national developmental goals and world economic growth while controlling and eliminating their negative effects.

This apparent proliferation of codes of conduct should not give the impression of confused duplication or overkill. The existing codes and those under negotiation differ substantially in their comprehensiveness, content, and application. Some are universal, while others are limited in geographic scope, covering the activities of transnational corporations only in certain countries. Some are comprehensive, while others are limited in substantive scope, covering only some aspects of transnational corporation activities. However, for the time being all have one common characteristic: adherence to these codes is voluntary. Various groups of countries are still too far apart in their interests and motivations to establish the binding rules implicit in multilateral treaties. Thus, the effectiveness of these codes of conduct relies much on their general acceptability, the comprehensiveness and specificity of their rules, as well as on their means of implementation. Notwithstanding their nonbinding character, the effects of these codes and their implications for transnational corporations may be far-reaching.

SCOPE, NATURE, AND CHARACTERISTICS OF THE CODES

The various codes mentioned above have both similarities and differences among them as regards to their aims, coverage, content, negotiating procedures, and follow-up mechanisms.

The United Nations code on transnational corporations, currently in its final stages of negotiation, is the most universally comprehensive to date. The code purports to incorporate, or refer to, codes on specific issues, such as restrictive business practices and transfer of technology, as well as employment and labor. It may even refer appropriately to relevant parts of the Treaty on Illicit Payments when the latter is adopted. Thus it should be seen as a general "umbrella" code dealing with all issues related to transnational corporations.

Its aims are on the whole similar to those underlying the exercises in UNCTAD and to some degree the ILO Declaration. Its means of implementation, not yet agreed upon, may be similar to that envisaged in the two instruments of UNCTAD, and if the developing countries have their way, will be at least as strong as the OECD Guidelines. The fact that the Commission on Transnational Corporations works on the basis of consensus rather than majority voting may facilitate negotiations on the issue of the follow-up machinery and its particular functions.

The negotiating procedures followed in the formulation of these different codes differ substantially. In UNCTAD the negotiations were based on three texts prepared by developed Western countries (Group B), the developing countries (Group of 77) and the socialist countries of Eastern Europe (Group D) and aimed at preparing a fourth agreed text. The Working Group under the Commission on Transnational Corporations of the United Nations on the other hand initially adopted the use of a series of single texts prepared by a neutral source, namely the Chairman of the Group or the U.N. Center on Transnational Corporations (which is the secretariat of the Commission). Later the Chairman's tentative formulations served as the basis for drafting by the governments themselves. Again, a single text was used. In cases of disagreement, brackets around words or sentences were used. The negotiating procedures in the ILO and OECD were less time-consuming and the drafting was carried out by a smaller number, in the former, by a tripartite group (business, labor and government), and in the latter, by representatives of governments only. The involvement of business and labor representatives, which was direct in the case of the ILO, was more indirect in the OECD and the U.N. Commission on Transnational Corporations, and almost absent in the case of UNCTAD.

The specificity of provisions in the various texts ranges from the detailed standards of some chapters in the code of conduct on transfer of technology to the general and relatively brief contents of the OECD Guidelines.

The common characteristic of all these instruments is that they address transnational corporations and to a lesser degree governments themselves. They all rely on cooperation among governments and, as it appears likely at this stage, on voluntary observance by the transnational corporations.

The interrelationship of these codes is apparent. Similar notions and even phrases are found sometimes in two or more texts. However, discernible differences exist in some cases in the treatment of similar subjects. The provisions of the U.N. Code of Conduct on Transnational Corporations are, as one might expect, much more restrictive and more comprehensive than those included in the OECD Guidelines.

Although each code has its own logic and bias and each will require the separate attention of the actors to which it is addressed, a basic premise transcends them all: transnational corporations should contribute to the economic and social progress of the countries in which they operate and should show sensitivity to the needs of the poor and to the rights of workers and consumers. Governments, on the other hand, should provide a fair framework for the operations of Transnational Corporations, keeping in mind the implications of interdependence and self-reliance.

PROSPECTS AND EFFECTS

A question that often arises is the practical effect that the codes of conduct will have on the parties concerned. It should be remembered that no code of conduct has yet been adopted as a treaty. The codes discussed here appear to be concealed in declarations and resolutions, and therefore are not legally binding. A treaty that is ratified usually becomes part of the national legislation of the signatory parties and its provisions become legally binding on the addressees. A nonbinding code, on the other hand, rests upon the voluntary observance of its provisions by the parties to which it is addressed. The force of a nonbinding code rests on the strength of moral suasion and the fact that a large number of countries have negotiated and accepted its provisions. Undoubtedly such an instrument would have some effect on the behavior of its addressees, although not as strong an effect as a treaty, with legal obligations, would have. Regardless of whether resolutions adopted by consensus at the United Nations can become customary law, the mere adoption of an agreement that has been negotiated over a number of years undoubtedly has political impact.[1]

In addition, codes may serve as models for national legislation. Governments, especially of developing countries, may be inspired to introduce or revise legislation amplifying and elaborating the provisions of a code. Furthermore, governments might require transnational corporations operating in their territory to state that they will adhere to the principles and specific provisions included in the code. Indeed, such a statement could become a standard clause in contracts and agreements involving the entry of transnational corporations into a country.

Furthermore, there might be some specific provisions of the code of conduct which could not be easily ignored; for instance, those requiring transnational corporations to disclose information to the public or trade unions. The act of disclosure is an objective act that can be easily established. Lists of noncomplying transnational corporations compiled by trade unions or other bodies lead easily to embarrassments. Governments that would be expected to report on the observance of the code by transnational corporations would tend to do their part to ensure a cooperative attitude from their transnational corporations in this regard.

The final question relates to the practical effects that a code of conduct might have on transnational corporations. What action will they be expected to take and what gains should they envisage? They will probably be required to study the agreement carefully and to disseminate its contents to their various management centers. Entities of transnational corporations might be asked to inform headquarters of their experience regarding the observance of the code or to send information that would be used by the headquarters for their reporting requirements. The headquarters, on the other hand, might implement the code by issuing specific instructions to their affiliates and company policy might be influenced by the code's provisions. One impact of the decision making at various levels would be the spirit, if not the letter, of the code (the letter of the code might be in some cases too vague to have operational value).

A benefit that business could expect to have from codes of conduct is the reduction of uncertainty or a larger degree of stability in relations with governments. The code might help transnational corporations to extricate themselves from conflicting requirements imposed on them by two or more countries. In a few words, the code would entail a set of acceptable standards of behavior by transnational corporations and governments. Major deviations from this set or yardstick would expect to meet with general disapproval.

HISTORICAL PERSPECTIVE

The efforts of the international community to implement rules regarding direct foreign investment and the conduct of the agents of such investment date back to the proposed Charter for an International Trade Organization prepared in Havana in 1948. This charter dealt with foreign investment and restrictive business practices (Articles 12 and 46-54; U.N. Conference on Trade and Employment, UN Sales No. 1948.II.D.4). The provisions called upon capital-importing countries to provide reasonable security to investors and to avoid "unreasonable and unjustifiable actions" against them; but they also upheld the right of these countries to screen foreign investments, place restrictions on ownership, and take other reasonable actions. However, this charter was never adopted.

Following this, other initiatives were undertaken in different quarters, both intergovernmental and private. At the United Nations, resolutions on permanent sovereignty over natural resources have been adopted since 1952; a draft convention on restrictive business practices was discussed in 1953, and 1954; and the International Development Strategy for the First and Second Development Decade (1960s and 1970s) touched upon issues related to foreign direct investment (UNCTC, E/C.10/9 and Add.1).

Outside the United Nations, the developed countries dealt with the issue in the forum of the OECD. A draft convention on the Protection of Foreign Property prepared in OECD, but not put into effect, has been the basis for a number of standards (OECD, Draft Convention on the Protection of Foreign Property and Resolution of the Council of the OECD on the Draft Conventions, publication No. 23081).

Developing countries, particularly the nonaligned countries (those developing countries which do not maintain formal alliance with major powers), raised the issue of foreign private investment at some of their early meetings and conferences. In 1971, the Second Ministerial Meeting of the Group of 77 (developing nations in the United Nations) stated that "private foreign investment, subject to national decisions and priorities, must facilitate the mobilization of internal resources, generate inflows and avoid outflows of foreign reserves, incorporate adequate technology, and enhance savings and national investment" (UNCTAD, *The Declaration and Principles of the Action Programme of Lima,* TD/143). In 1972, the Conference of Foreign Ministers of Non-Aligned Countries called in their Georgetown Declaration for a study of criteria, techniques, and procedures for making private foreign investment "subserve national development objectives" in order to facilitate the adoption of a common approach to private foreign investment (The Georgetown Declaration, Action Programme, Economic Co-operation of Foreign Ministers of Non-Aligned Countries, August 1972).

Paralleling these governmental attempts and intentions have been proposals by a number of private groups. A draft convention, for instance, providing for protection of foreign investment was prepared in 1958 by a group chaired by Lord Shawcross (A.A. Fatouros, "An International Code to Protect Private Investment; Proposals and Perspectives," *University of Toronto Law Journal*, Vol. XIV, No. 1, 1961, pp. 77–102). Similar drafts were presented by a British parliamentary group for world government, by the German Society to Advance the Protection of Foreign Investments, and by other groups, conferences, and institutions. In 1972, the International Chamber of Commerce issued Guidelines for International Investment which were addressed to investors, and to the governments of home and host countries (Guidelines for International Investment, International Chamber of Commerce, Paris, 1972).

Obviously these efforts reflect the objectives of their initiators. While initiatives by private groups and developed countries aimed at protecting foreign investment and ensuring a favorable investment climate, those stemming from developing and nonaligned countries were intended to protect the interests of host countries and affirm their right to regulate foreign investment. Taken as a whole, these efforts show a deep appreciation of the role of foreign investment and a desire to attract it in order to serve the development efforts of nonindustrial countries.

As the years went by and the scarcity of capital together with the urgent need for industrialization became less acute, a shift was registered in the focus and emphasis of these initiatives. Developing countries began to stress the need for regulation and supervision. The late 1960s and the beginnings of the 1970s were also years during which the developing countries began to form a front of solidarity to present their demands in a decisive manner. The process started at that time culminated in the Program of Action for the Establishment of a New International Economic Order.

TRANSNATIONALS ON THE WORLD STAGE.   One of the first references to transnational corporations, in general still called multinationals, appeared in the context of the United Nations in its 1971 *World Economic Survey*. It read "while these corporations are frequently agents for the transfer of technology as well as capital to developing countries, their role is sometimes viewed with awe, since their size and power surpass the host country's entire economy. The international community has yet to formulate a positive policy and establish effective machinery for dealing with the issues raised by the activities of these corporations." A few months later, the International Confederation of Free Trade Unions called for a code of conduct for "multinational companies" (The ICFTU Executive Board, "Resolution on Freedom of Association and Multinational Companies," December 1970 in ICFTU, *The Multinational Challenge,* 63, ICFTU World Economic Conference Reports No. 2, 1971). This initiative reflects the strong interest that trade unions have shown in this matter and the fact that they have been in the forefront in the call for regulating transnational corporations.[2]

In 1972, Salvador Allende, then recently elected President of Chile, denounced ITT for its involvement in the internal affairs of that country. President Allende himself, in an impressive speech before the United Nations General Assembly, spoke of the need for regulating transnational corporations and for prohibiting their interference in the political affairs of nation-states.

In the same year, the Third Conference of UNCTAD, held in Santiago, adopted one resolution on the transfer of technology, and another on restrictive business practices, which led eventually to the convening of conferences to adopt codes of conduct.

Finally, in July 1972, the representative of Chile at the United Nations Economic and Social Council (ECOSOC) proposed a comprehensive study of the effects of multinational corporations. Thus the first comprehensive global effort was launched. ECOSOC adopted by consensus a resolution which, after noting the work in ILO and UNCTAD, requested the Secretary-General to appoint a group of eminent persons to study the impact of multinational corporations on world development and international relations, and to formulate conclusions "which may possibly be used by governments in making their sovereign decisions regarding national policy in this respect, and to submit recommendations for appropriate action" (ECOSOC resolution 1721 (LIII), 28 July 1972).

The Secretary-General appointed 20 individuals who were prominent in the field of international economic relations to form what became known as the Group of Eminent Persons.[3] The Group of Eminent Persons conducted a number of hearings with about 50 representatives from governments, transnational corporations, labor unions, consumer groups, and universities (*Summary of the Hearings before the Group of Eminent Persons to Study the Impact of Multinational Corporations on Development and on International Relations*, UN publication, Sales No. E.74.II.A.9). On the basis of these hearings and a study prepared by the Secretariat in 1973, entitled "Multinational Corporations in World Development,"[4] the group issued a report in the spring of 1974.

The report made a number of recommendations on issues such as ownership and control, balance of payments, transfer of technology, competition, transfer pricing, and consumer protection and proposed the establishment of a commission on multinational corporations and an information and research center at the secretariat level. It also called for the formulation of a code of conduct, which was seen as a voluntary step toward the eventual conclusion of an international agreement.

The Secretary-General submitted the report with his approval to the Economic and Social Council, which in the autumn of 1974 decided by consensus to establish a Commission on Transnational Corporations. The Commission was designed as an intergovernmental body subsidiary to ECOSOC, consisting of high-level experts from 48 governments, to act as a forum for the comprehensive consideration of issues relating to transnational corporations. It was to be assisted in a private consultative capacity—and this is a unique feature for a United Nations body—by a number of persons on the basis of their practical experience, from trade unions, business, public interest groups, and universities from both the developed and developing countries.[5] This decision acknowledged the need to establish a focal point for the deliberations already being conducted by the international community on transnational corporations. In addition, it recognized the importance of involving individuals from the quarters directly concerned and immediately affected by these deliberations.

The U.N. Center on Transnational Corporations was also set up by this resolution, as part of the United Nations Secretariat. The center was given a mandate to assist in the formulation of international arrangements, agreements, and a code of conduct; to research the political, legal, economic, and social aspects relating to transnational corporations; to develop a comprehensive information system on their activities; and to organize programs of technical cooperation aimed at strengthening the capacity of host, particularly developing, countries.

Thus the stage was set for the continuing involvement of the United Nations in the issue of transnational corporations and the work on a code of conduct. The adoption by the General Assembly of the resolution on a New International Economic Order (May 1974) was to give a strong impetus to the whole endeavor. The subject of transnational corporations was henceforth firmly inscribed in the agenda of the United Nations and became part of the North-South dialogue.

The activities of the Commission on Transnational Corporations and of the ECO-SOC are taken to represent an all-encompassing global approach by the international community to the issue of transnational corporations, but they have not been alone. Other U.N. bodies and specialized agencies started work on the subject within their respective areas of competence at the same time. Both the International Labor Organization (ILO) and UNCTAD began to deal with aspects of the operations and effects of transnational corporations during the 1970s.

As early as 1972, ILO convened a tripartite meeting of experts to pursue a resolution adopted at the fifty-sixth session of the International Labor Conference, and to consider the relationship between multinational enterprises and social policy. Experts representing the workers' interests insisted on the need to prepare a "code of good behavior" to respect trade union rights and collective bargaining. Following a number of studies conducted by the ILO, the Tripartite Declaration Concerning Multinational Enterprises and Social Policy was adopted by the governing body of ILO in 1977. In this instance, governments, business, and labor joined in the first international declaration dealing with social policy and labor aspects of the operations of transnational corporations.

The work of UNCTAD on restrictive business practices was started in 1974 by a committee of experts acting in their individual capacity, whose report was rejected at first by the Trade and Development Board of UNCTAD on the basis that it was not thorough enough. However, following an effort by a second group, the Fourth UNCTAD Conference, held in Nairobi, in its resolution 96(IV) gave a mandate to a third *ad hoc* group of governmental experts to prepare proposals and recommendations, *inter alia,* on the negotiation of a set of multilaterally agreed equitable principles and rules for the control of restrictive business practices, including those of transnational corporations, adversely affecting international trade, particularly that of developing countries and their economic development. This group completed its work in 1978.

Also in Nairobi in 1976 UNCTAD initiated work on formulating an international code of conduct on the transfer of technology. In July 1978, an intergovernmental group of experts completed the drafting of a code, though several issues were left unresolved. The work continued at a U.N. conference.

While the United Nations was occupied with the drafting of codes, other intergovernmental institutions were carrying out similar endeavors, sometimes reaching more prompt results. The OECD Guidelines for Multinational Enterprises represent the most important accomplishment in this regard. It is significant because it is the first instrument adopted on transnational corporations that covers major aspects of their activities and also because its adoption must be attributed to the efforts of the industrial countries, most of them homes of transnational corporations. In addition, the follow-up to the guidelines represents an interesting example of the effect of a voluntary instrument on transnational corporations as well as the effectiveness of intergovernmental cooperation.

There was a feeling in some quarters that the OECD exercise was an attempt to consolidate and harmonize western positions in view of the forthcoming negotiations in the United Nations. If this was the primary motivation of some of the parties, it would seem that the exercise has exceeded the initial expectations: the follow-up machinery in OECD has proved to be quite effective, and the guidelines have their own impact and their own evolution. The value of the work in the OECD goes beyond the scope and objectives of the instrument. It has become a forerunner to the United Nations code of conduct. The OECD exercise has alerted the parties concerned and has had a significant educational effect. Governments have consolidated national positions; business, labor and other groups have consulted with their constituencies and have articulated positions. The level of awareness has risen among businessmen regarding existing and impending guidelines that attempt to set standards for their behavior. Last but not least, the follow-up procedures provide models for imitation and improvement.

The sections that follow provide a brief description of the instruments dealing with transnational corporations which are either in effect or still in negotiation.

THE U.N. CODE OF CONDUCT ON TRANSNATIONAL CORPORATIONS

The code of conduct on transnational corporations that is being negotiated by the U.N. Commission on Transnational Corporations is a comprehensive general instrument dealing with the behavior of transnational corporations and their treatment by governments.

The formulation of a code of conduct was one of the main tasks entrusted by the ECOSOC to the Commission on Transnational Corporations in the autumn of 1974.

The Commission on Transnational Corporations is an intergovernmental body, composed of 48 governments and assisted by 16 expert advisers. The members of the Commission are elected for 3-year terms by ECOSOC. The 16 advisers who participate in their individual capacities from business, labor, university, and other interest group backgrounds, are selected by the Commission from a list prepared by the Secretary-General. The Center on Transnational Corporations, on the other hand, is an autonomous part of the Secretariat of the United Nations that became operational in November 1975 as the central unit at the secretariat level of the United Nations system to deal with all aspects related to transnational corporations. The Center receives its work program primarily from the Commission to which it submits reports and provides all services needed to achieve the objectives set by the Commission.

The explanation above should help the reader understand the background and the procedures involved in the formulation of the code. First to expound the usefulness of a code of conduct was the U.N. Secretariat in its study *Multinational Corporations in World Development* (U.N. Sales No. 73.II.A.11). The idea was subsequently endorsed by the Group of Eminent Persons and was later retained by ECOSOC as one of the functions of the Commission.

The Commission itself at its second session held in Lima in 1976, unanimously decided that the formulation of a code of conduct had highest priority in its work program and proceeded in establishing an Intergovernmental Working Group for this purpose. The Group, composed of the same 48 governments participating in the Commission, began its work in 1977 under the chairmanship of Sten Niklasson,

Undersecretary of Industry of Sweden. Since then, the Group has held 11 sessions, the last in October 1980. According to a decision by the Commission at its June 1980 session in Mexico, the Working Group should complete its task by the spring of 1981. To date the Group has concluded the drafting of more than half the provisions; they cover, with few exceptions, all the provisions which relate to the activities of transnational corporations. The language of half of these concluded provisions has been agreed upon while for the other half, a number of disagreements persist; they are indicated by brackets around words or sentences which are not yet accepted by consensus. The sections of the code not yet drafted—and which relate mostly to the treatment of transnational corporations by governments—contain some of the most controversial issues, such as the questions of nationalization and compensation, jurisdiction, definitions, and implementation.

STRUCTURE OF THE CODE. The code consists of the following sections: I. Preamble and Objectives; II. Definitions; III. Major Principles and/or Issues Relating to the Activities of Transnational Corporations; IV. Principles and/or Issues Relating to the Treatment of Transnational Corporations; V. Legal Nature and Scope; VI. Implementation.

Section III contains the following subsections: A. Respect for national sovereignty and observance of domestic laws, regulations, and administrative practices; adherence to economic goals and development objectives; adherence to sociocultural objectives and values; respect for human rights and fundamental freedoms (including noncollaboration by transnational corporations with racist minority régimes in southern Africa); noninterference in internal political affairs; noninterference in intergovernmental relations; abstention from corrupt practices; B. Ownership and control; balance of payments and financing; taxation; competition and restrictive business practices; transfer of technology; employment and labor; consumer protection; environmental protection; C. Disclosure of information. Section IV contains: A. General treatment of transnational corporations by the countries in which they operate; B. Nationalization and compensation; C. Jurisdiction.

NEGOTIATING PROCEDURES. The negotiating technique that the Group adopted has been quite innovative and deserves mention. When the Working Group first met in 1977, it was faced with two documents prepared by its secretariat, the Center on Transnational Corporations, analyzing the views of governments and nongovernmental interests as well as long lists of "areas of concern" submitted by developing, developed, and socialist countries. These documents revealed some diametrically opposed views concerning both the possible content of the code and its eventual legal form. Most developed countries, strongly endorsing a voluntary code, placed emphasis on "balanced" content, which in effect meant the inclusion of obligations of governments, while developing and socialist countries, opting for a binding code, sought to regulate transnational corporations and ensure that their activities were in line with development objectives expressed in the new international economic order.

A way out of an impasse was found when, responding to the Group's request for a draft outline, the Center presented a list of items which covered all the areas of concern. Thus the headings of the sections and the subsections of the code were born at the first session of the Group. In subsequent sessions, at the Group's request, the Chairman and the Center presented texts which, beginning from simple annotations, eventually became full-fledged formulations. In other words, each section of the code was built up with each round of discussions of the Group, from annotations to key elements to common elements; from tentative formulations, to chairman's formulations. The objective was to elaborate the language covering the concerns of governments and to reach, as much as possible, a consensus. This method of drafting was a step-by-step approach based on a single text prepared by neutral sources. This approach prevented early polarization and inflexibility in the positions of participating governments.

In the last few sessions the Group began drafting on the basis of the Chairman's formulations and proposals by the developing countries. This effort led to concluded provisions—still a single text—some of which contained brackets signifying current lack of agreement.

The role of the Group's secretariat, namely the Center on Transnational Corporations, in facilitating the formulations of the code is worth noting. Conceptual issues, such as the implications of the legal nature of the code or the options regarding means of implementation, were elucidated by a number of background papers prepared by the Center over the last few years.[6] The Center has also actively assisted the Chairman and the Working Group in most phases of their work.

In drafting the code, the Group has faced several difficulties. On the issue of national sovereignty, the developing countries wish to see transnational corporations subjected to the sovereignty, jurisdiction, and laws and regulations of the countries in which they operate; the developed countries stress the importance of international law and obligations in this regard, as well as the use of arbitration in case of difficulties. While the developing countries would have transnational corporations adhere to the development objectives and policies of host countries, the developed countries insist that such policies should be clearly defined and that transnational corporations should not be expected to carry out requirements beyond their resources and capabilities, bearing in mind their commercial character. Developed countries would like to see provisions calling on governments to extend fair, equitable, and nondiscriminatory treatment to transnational corporations, and the right of transnational corporations to call on their home governments to represent their interests in case local means do not resolve difficulties in a satisfactory manner. The perennial differences between developed and developing countries on the issues of nationalization and compensation are well-known and remain one of the most formidable stumbling blocks in the process to form guidelines. Other matters to be resolved include the scope of implementing the code at the international level and, in particular, whether the Commission, which will be the body responsible for the follow-up, will have the right to clarify the provisions of the code at the request of governments. The role of trade unions in these follow-up procedures may also create some problems. Finally, the difficulty regarding the definition of a transnational corporation centers on the question of whether state-owned enterprises should be included. The socialist countries strongly oppose the inclusion of these enterprises in the definition. The question of the legal nature of the code, on the other hand, seems to be moving toward resolution by silence. Most governments assume that the code will not be legally binding at this stage, which stresses the importance attached to the provisions for its implementation.

In other words, the North wishes to avoid all-encompassing requirements on transnational corporations, which want their commercial character to be acknowledged, to maintain their international viability and to be allowed to be good corporate citizens. These corporations also want to have the option of calling on their home countries when relations with the host give rise to serious problems. Not surprisingly, these efforts are strongly opposed by the developing countries, and in some specific cases by some developed host countries as well, which expect transnational corporations to identify as much as possible with the interests of the countries in which they operate, to refrain from interfering in internal affairs, and to contribute fully, beyond the requirements arising from their global strategy, to the economic and social progress of host countries.

In essence, the problem seems to turn upon the fine tuning between the autonomy of the entities and the demands of the global strategy of the transnational corporation as charted at its headquarters. Ultimately the issue is the redressing of the economic imbalance between North and South.

In spite of these unresolved problems, the prospects of concluding the code in the next few months are not bleak. A consensus resolution adopted in Mexico on July 4, 1980, at the sixth session of the Commission contains certain formulations which would prove helpful in removing some brackets from the present text of the concluded provisions and in settling some outstanding issues.

The meeting of the Commission in Mexico has indeed given political impetus to the work on the code of conduct. It appeared that all sides were determined to make every effort to complete the task within a year. The recent declaration of the ministers of the OECD countries in favor of a prompt conclusion of the work reaffirms that the developed countries are anxious to contribute to achieving an open North-South dialogue. A code of conduct might reduce present instability in economic relations; it might also permit the conclusion of the treaty on illicit payments, a treaty worked out at the United Nations, chiefly at the initiative of the United States, and at present in a state of abeyance. The developing countries are also anxious to finalize the work, though not at all cost, which occupies an important place in the Program of Action for the New International Economic Order.

In case the Group fails to complete the draft code by May 1981, the Commission might have to decide whether to prolong the life of the Group or to call for a conference in 1982. The first approach would have the advantage of continuity by giving the opportunity to the Group, which is familiar with the subtleties and complications involved, to complete the drafting of all the parts of the code and remove some of the existing brackets before it presents it to the international community for adoption. The second approach, the convening of a conference, possibly preceded by preparatory meetings, would have the advantage of involving all U.N. member states. Whatever the final outcome might be, it appears that barring unforeseen circumstances, the code will be adopted by the U.N. membership sometime in 1983.

THE CODES IN UNCTAD

The casual observer might find it bewildering that the United Nations should be proceeding with the establishment of three parallel codes: one at the Commission on Transnational Corporations, and two in UNCTAD. A closer examination, however, shows that the United Nations will produce only one comprehensive code on transnational corporations: that negotiated by the Working Group of the Commission on Transnational Corporations discussed above. The codes on the transfer of technology, and the set of principles and rules on restrictive business practices, will be specialized instruments on these subjects whose coverage is not limited to transnational corporations and will be appropriately incorporated—under the headings of "transfer of technology" and "restrictive business practices" presently appearing without text—in the general code of conduct on transnational corporations (United Nations Center on Transnational Corporations, *Transnational Corporations: Aspects of Possible Relationships Between the Work on a Code of Conduct and Related Work in UNCTAD and ILO*, E/C.10/AC.205, 18 July 1976).

RESTRICTIVE BUSINESS PRACTICES.   Of the two exercises undertaken in UNCTAD, one has already been completed. On 21 April 1980, the Conference on Restrictive Business Practices approved the set of "Multilaterally Agreed Equitable Principles and Rules for the Control of Restrictive Business Practices," and transmitted them to the General Assembly. The Conference recommended that the set of principles should be adopted by a resolution of the General Assembly and that it should be reviewed under the auspices of UNCTAD five years after its adoption by the General Assembly.

This successful outcome represented more than a decade of work by UNCTAD in this field. As mentioned above, following initial work by groups of experts, the Fourth Conference of UNCTAD in Nairobi established the third *Ad Hoc* Group of Experts. It was given a mandate to work toward: (1) the identification of restrictive business practices likely to injure international trade, particularly the trade and development of developing countries; (2) the formulation of principles and rules to deal with such practices; (3) the development of systems for information exchange and collection; and (4) the formulation of a model antitrust law for developing countries.

The *Ad Hoc* Group accomplished its mandate in the course of six sessions held between November 1976 and April 1979. In addition to an agreed system for providing information to the UNCTAD secretariat on antitrust legislation and its enforcement, and on a draft model antitrust law and a list of restrictive business practices likely to be injurious to trade and development, the Group completed the drafting of the set of principles mentioned above, although some of the provisions were contained in brackets. In the autumn of 1979, a United Nations Conference on Restrictive Business Practices was convened. It concluded its work at a second session held in April 1980 in Geneva ("Report of the Third *Ad Hoc* Group of Experts on Restrictive Business Practices on its sixth session" TD/250).

The text of the set of principles represents one of the most ambitious efforts of the international community to draw up specific international rules on a subject which has raised controversy even at the national level. The accomplishment is even more impressive if one contemplates the different objectives that brought countries together for this purpose and the ideological connotations of the exercise. In developed countries, antitrust doctrines aimed at free competition and free trade have gained over-all acceptance, though there is a discernible variation among the doctrines in approach, scope, and firmness. The developing countries' interests on the other hand, were in protecting their economies from abusive practices of transnational and other enterprises.

The text of the Set of Principles on Restrictive Business Practices adopted by the Conference contains about 50 provisions and includes the following sections: (a) Objectives; (b) Definitions and scope of application; (c) General principles; (d) Principles and rules for enterprises including transnational corporations; (e) Principles and rules for states at national, regional and subregional levels; (f) International measures; and (g) International institutional machinery.

The aims of the principles and rules are to ensure that restrictive business practices do not impair or negate the realization of benefits from trade liberalization measures; to attain greater efficiency in international trade and development; to protect and promote social welfare in general; to eliminate the disadvantages to trade and development which may result from restrictive business practices of transnational corporations or other enterprises; and finally, through adoption of the principles and rules at the international level, to facilitate the adoption and strengthening of laws and policies at national and regional levels.

"Restrictive business practices" are defined as acts or behavior of enterprises which, through an abuse of a dominant position of market power, limit access to markets or otherwise unduly restrain competition, and have, or are likely to have, adverse effects on international trade, particularly of developing countries and on the economic development of those countries. "Dominant position of market power" is defined as a situation where an enterprise, alone or with a few others, is in a position to control the relevant market. "Enterprises" are defined as including all forms of partnerships or corporations, whether created or controlled by states or not, which are engaged in commercial activities, and any branches, subsidiaries, or affiliates directly or indirectly controlled by them.

The general principles call for action at the regional, national, and international levels to eliminate restrictive business practices, and call on countries to collaborate, exchange information, and hold consultations. Some preferential treatment is provided for developing countries in connection with the need to establish domestic industries and to cooperate at a regional or global level.

These principles and rules call upon enterprises to conform to the restrictive business practices laws of the countries in which they operate, and contain a list of cartel practices which enterprises are not supposed to engage in, as well as a number of other practices considered as an abuse of a dominant position of market power. With regard to principles and rules for states, the text calls on them to introduce and effectively enforce appropriate legislation, to ensure fair and equitable treatment of enterprises, to obtain information from enterprises (while protecting its confidentiality), to take measures to prevent the use of restrictive business practices when the trade and development of the developing countries are affected, and to exchange information and experiences with other states.

Action at the international level is envisaged as embracing the following: the achievement of common approaches to the control of restrictive business practices; notification of exceptions or exemptions granted by states; consultations; the dissemination of information on restrictive business practices; technical assistance, advisory and training programs; and future institutional arrangements at the international level to facilitate efforts for the control of restrictive business practices.

Finally, the text provides for an international mechanism, consisting of an Intergovernmental Group of Experts on Restrictive Business Practices operating within the framework of a UNCTAD Committee, which will be the forum for the exchange of views, consultations, collection and dissemination of information, and for making recommendations to states on matters within its competence.

TRANSFER OF TECHNOLOGY. The Intergovernmental Group of Experts on an International Code of Conduct on the Transfer of Technology, established by the Fourth UNCTAD Conference in 1976, completed the drafting of an international code of conduct in July 1978. This draft code was submitted to the United Nations

Conference on an International Code of Conduct on the Transfer of Technology, which met first in Geneva from October 16 to November 11, 1978, under the auspices of UNCTAD. It has met again twice, the last time during the spring of 1980. Thus far the Conference has been unable to complete its work. It may meet again in early 1981, to try to iron out differences in the sections of the text dealing with restrictive business practices, the applicable law, and guarantees.

The negotiating procedures in UNCTAD involved drafting on the basis of three texts, prepared respectively by the Group B countries (developed market economies), the Group of 77 (developing countries) and Group D (socialist countries of Eastern Europe). At the conclusion of the last session of the Conference, the spokesmen for these three groups made several points. The spokesman for the Group of 77 identified three groups of problems, the most important concerned the *chapeau* to the chapter on restrictive business practices, i.e. the nature of the practices to be covered by the chapter and the extent of the application of the code to the parent/subsidiary relationship. The Group of 77, according to the spokesman, believes that the provisions of the code should apply to transactions between all parties, including those covered by the parent–subsidiary relationship. Another group of problems centers on the more general exceptions sought by Group B to the application of a number of restrictive practices—exceptions which the Group of 77 does not accept. The third concerns practices which the Group of 77 considers restrictive but which Group B does not. As regards the chapter on guarantees, the Group of 77 had offered an important compromise which, however, had not been accepted by the developed countries.

The spokesman for the Group B countries said that, although some careful and measured steps had been taken, agreement had not been reached at the Conference, particularly in the matter of restrictive business practices, although it was quite close as regards the chapter on guarantees. Nevertheless, an optimistic note was struck by both these spokesmen, as well as by the spokesman for Group D and the Chairman of the Conference.

The difficulties the Conference is facing undoubtedly reflect the complexity of the problem of restricting business practices, the strong interests involved, the rather inflexible negotiating techniques adopted, and the ambitious scope of the code.

The role of technology in development cannot be overestimated. While protection of industrial property rights has been covered by the Paris Convention and several other multilateral agreements, no rules exist on agreements for the transfer of technology and the licensing of industrial property rights, either nationally or internationally. The developed countries are emphatically not interested in permitting these agreements to undermine the present system of protecting industrial property. They are willing to purge anticompetitive practices which hamper the transfer of technology and to call on the parties to observe fair and honest practices, while allowing such parties to choose freely the law applicable to their particular transactions. For the developing countries, the purpose of the code is to assist them in strengthening their own technological capacity and to alleviate some of the burden that they feel they are carrying under the present terms and conditions of transfer of technology ("Arusha Programme for Collective Self-Reliance and Framework for Negotiations," 1979, TD/236). The socialist countries are interested in avoiding discrimination in the technology they obtain from the West.

The present draft of the code of conduct on the transfer of technology contains the following chapters: (1) Preamble, (2) Definitions and Scope of Application, (3)

Objectives and Principles, (4) National regulation of transfer of technology transactions, [The regulation of practices and arrangements involving the transfer of
technology] [Restrictive business practices] [Exclusion of political discrimination
and restrictive business practices], (5) Guarantees/Responsibilities/Obligations, (6)
Special Treatment for Developing Countries, (7) International Collaboration, (8) International Institutional Machinery, (9) Applicable Law and Settlement of Disputes,
(for the present state of the text see UNCTAD, "Draft International Code of Conduct
on the Transfer of Technology, as of 6 May, 1980," TD/CODE TOT/25).

The text is considerably detailed and includes at this stage several bracketed
clauses and alternative formulations proposed by each of the three groups.

The issue of the legal nature of the code has been a central point of disagreement.
The developing countries are strongly in favor of a legally binding code, while developed countries squarely oppose any obligatory agreement. It is probable that the
code will be adopted in nonbinding form and the issue will be discussed again 5 years
after its adoption. Another problem is whether the code would apply to affiliates of
transnational corporations transferring technology to local enterprises, where the
transfer does not cross national borders. The question of whether the code would
apply to intrafirm transactions still remains unresolved. The issues of the relevance
of international law regarding the applicable law, the forum for the settlement of
disputes, and the circumstances in which restrictive business practices, otherwise
prohibited, may be allowed, constitute some of the remaining stumbling blocks (for
a detailed discussion of the negotiations on the code, see Gabriel M. Wilner, "Transfer of Technology: The UNCTAD Code of Conduct" in N. Horn, ed., *Legal Problems*).

Regardless of the timing of the outcome, the code on transfer of technology will
be a positive step toward intergovernmental cooperation in this field and will provide
inspiration for the regulation of the transfer of technology and the introduction of
antitrust legislation by developing countries. It will also contribute to the redressing
of certain abuses by transnational corporations in developing countries.

THE ILO TRIPARTITE DECLARATION

The Tripartite Declaration of Principles Concerning Multinational Enterprises and
Social Policy, adopted by the Governing Body of the ILO on November 16, 1977,
contains principles commended to the governments, and the employers' and workers'
organizations of home and host countries, and to the multinational enterprises. The
Declaration consists of 58 paragraphs and in addition to a section on general policies,
contains chapters on employment, training, conditions of work and life, and industrial
relations.

A working group consisting of four governments, four employer, and four worker
group members prepared a draft between January and April 1977. Following some
revisions at a Tripartite Advisory Meeting, the draft was submitted for adoption to
the Governing Body. After its adoption, the Director-General of the ILO transmitted
it to the Secretary-General of the United Nations with the suggestion that it should
be incorporated as a whole in the United Nations code of conduct. At the tenth
session of the Working Group on a Code of Conduct, it was decided that a reference
should be made in the section of the code on employment and labor to the ILO
Declaration. This facilitates the task of the Working Group, which has been spared

from having to draft its own provisions on the matter, and maintains coherence between these rules within the U.N. system. Some problems may arise, however, with regard to implementation. Certainly, the Commission on Transnational Corporations would not wish to deny itself the possibility of offering access to trade unions in matters related to the code. If, however, the matters raised by labor before the Commission fall within the competence of the follow-up machinery of the ILO, it is likely that the Commission would normally transmit them.

The ILO Declaration has some notable features. Having been drafted by governments, employers, and workers, it is addressed to all three parties. It applies to multinational enterprises whether they are of public, mixed, or private ownership. It is a universal, voluntary instrument which aims at recommending good practice for both multinational enterprises and national enterprises, wherever relevant, and at times assigns to multinational enterprises a model or pioneering role. It encourages consultation between the parties concerned, although it falls short of providing for global consultations between representatives of workers with the management of all affiliates of a transnational corporation. The Declaration calls on transnational corporation to provide such information to workers' representatives as is required for meaningful negotiations. It makes specific reference to the goals of the New International Economic Order, calling on governments to pursue an active policy designed to promote full, productive, and freely chosen employment (*Tripartite Declaration of Principles Concerning Multinational Enterprises and Social Policy,* ILO, Geneva, 1977).

At its session in February–March 1978, the ILO Governing Body decided to request governments to report periodically on the effect given to the Declaration, after full consultations with employers' and workers' organizations, and to prepare a first report 2 years after the adoption of the Declaration. Such reports would be considered by a Tripartite Governing Body committee composed of 15 members. The committee would survey the observance of the Declaration, consider difficulties or inadequacies that might appear in the survey and suggest ways of dealing with them, and advise on further follow-up procedures (Hans Günter, "The Tripartite Declaration of Principles (ILO): Standards and Follow Up," in N. Horn, ed., *Legal Problems of Codes of Conduct*).

To implement these decisions, the Governing Body has sent a questionnaire to governments, which have been requested to complete it after consulting with employers' and workers' organizations. Multinational enterprises can participate in the follow-up procedure through their employers' organizations.

The last World Employment Conference (June 1979) strongly backed these follow-up procedures, and requested the Director-General of ILO to follow closely the work in the United Nations on the adoption of a code of conduct.

It is still too early to evaluate the follow-up procedures of the Declaration. It is quite probable that some workers' groups or governments which were unsatisfied by the nonbinding nature of the Declaration will press for stronger follow-up agreements. Developments in the OECD and the United Nations may have certain repercussions in this regard.

THE OECD GUIDELINES

The Guidelines for Multinational Enterprises adopted by the governments of the OECD form part of a package called "Declaration on International Investment and

Multinational Enterprises and Decisions of the OECD Council," containing together with the guidelines, (which consist of a series of recommendations to multinational enterprises), decisions of the Council on National Treatment, on International Investment Incentives and Disincentives, and on Consultative Procedures (OECD, *International Investment and Multinational Enterprises,* OECD, Paris, 1976). Thus the guidelines for multinational enterprises are voluntary, while the three related decisions are binding for the participating members. (Turkey did not participate in the Declaration and abstained from the decisions.)

The work on the guidelines was initiated in 1974. Following the submission of the Rey Report on Trade and International Economic Relations, and during the year which the U.N. General Assembly was negotiating the declaration on the New International Economic Order, the Executive Committee of the Council proposed, among other things, the preparation of guidelines for business practices. A Committee on International Investment and Multinational Enterprises (CIME), established for this purpose, met several times between March 1975 and May 1976 under the chairmanship of Helga Steeg (Federal Republic of Germany). Assisted by a drafting group chaired by Professor Theo Vogelaar, special consultant to the Secretary-General of OECD, the Committee, in consultation with the Business and Industry Advisory Committee and the Trade Union Advisory Committee, completed the drafting of the Guidelines and presented them to the Ministers of the OECD countries. On June 21, 1976, the Declaration was issued, along with the decisions of the Council.

Transnational corporations are increasingly recognized as legitimate agents of development, provided they act in accordance with the development objectives of the countries in which they operate and show greater sensitivity to the needs and concerns of these countries. The international community is declaring that it is ready to assume the task of watching to see that this role is played properly, according to the new rules of the game.

The Declaration recognizes the important role that multinational enterprises play in the investment climate, encourages the positive contribution that multinational enterprises can make to economic and social progress, and attempts to minimize and resolve difficulties which may arise from their various operations. The importance of intergovernmental cooperation and consultation regarding the guidelines and decisions is stressed. It was further declared that the governments could review these matters within 3 years, to improve the effectiveness of cooperation among member countries on issues relating to international investment and multinational enterprises. (Such a review took place in 1979.)

The Guidelines contain an introductory part which enunciates the philosophy embedded in the text, its scope and its nature, and a description, rather than a definition, of a multinational enterprise. It is noted that "observance of the guidelines is voluntary and not legally enforceable" and that "every state has the right to prescribe the conditions under which multinational enterprises operate within its national jurisdiction, subject to international law and to the international agreements to which it has subscribed. The entities of a multinational enterprises located in various countries are subject to the laws of these countries." The same section establishes the Nondiscriminatory Treatment Council to CIME. The latter prepared a review which was submitted to the ministerial meeting of OECD in June 1979. The report of CIME contains comments on 12 general issues, reflecting in an indirect way the specific cases, complaints, and requests submitted to it. On the suggestion of the CIME, the Council has given the Committee clear responsibilities for the clarification of the OECD Guidelines. In addition, the Business and Industry Advisory Committee and the Trade Union Advisory Committee can initiate exchanges of views with CIME and individual enterprises that are subject to complaints and will be able to present their views to CIME either directly, or through the Business and Industry Advisory Committee or a government. During the recent review it was decided that a further review of the Guidelines would be held in 1984, and a mid-report to be prepared in 1982. Thus the Guidelines have remained on the whole unchanged, while the follow-up procedures have been strengthened.

The attention that the OECD Guidelines command has been strong. This is un-derstandable since they represent the first international instrument in the field of transnational corporations and involve all the developed-market economy countries which are both home and host countries to transnational corporations. The reaction of transnational corporations to an instrument agreed upon by their own governments is being closely watched. Moreover, the effectiveness of a voluntary instrument is a question of primary concern to developing countries, trade unions, and other interests, which are gradually realizing that the time for generally accepted binding obligations for transnational corporations may not have come. If the Guidelines prove to be effective, the demands for legally binding codes may subside.

Governments might become more intent on obtaining greater effectiveness of codes through achieving practical solutions aimed at dealing with future problems rather than formulas based on old doctrines reflecting historical grievances and spe-cific, rather than, general language of provisions and follow-up procedures (which ensures that the codes remain operational and evolutionary) might be the answer to successful codes at this stage. Finally, the wide acceptance and involvement of all the actors affected by the provisions of the codes appears to be a critical element in breathing life through these instruments.

The codes of conduct may indeed signal the passage to a new era. It appears that governments are trying to agree on the proper role of transnational corporations. Transnational corporations are increasingly recognized as legitimate agents of de-velopment, provided they act in accordance with the development objectives of the countries in which they operate and show greater sensitivity to the needs and con-cerns of these countries. The international community is declaring that it is ready to assume the task of watching to see that this role is played properly, according to the new rules of the game.

NOTES

1.   Niklasson, S. "The OECD Guidelines for MNEs and the UN Draft Code of Conduct: Some Political Considerations," in N. Horn, ed., *Legal Problems of Codes of Conduct for Mul-tinational Enterprises,* The Hague: Kluwer/Deventer, 1980. Vernon, R. *Storm Over the Multinationals: The Real Issues* Cambridge, Mass.: Harvard University Press, 1977. Barret, R.J. and R. Muller, *Global Reach: The Power of Multinational Corporations* New York: Simon and Schuster, 1974.

2.   Baade, H.W. "The Legal Effects of Codes of Conduct for MNEs," and Fatouros, A.A. "The UN Code of Conduct on Transnational Corporations" in Horn, *Legal Problems of Codes of Conduct for Multinational Enterprises.*

3.   The ICFTU also issued in the mid-1970s a "Charter of Trade Union Demands for the Legislative Control of Multinational Companies" (ICFTU document 11/GA.9).

4.   The Group of Eminent Persons was composed of the following members: Emerik Blum (Yugoslavia), Tore Browaldh (Sweden), John J. Deutsch (Canada), Mohamed Diawara

(Ivory Coast), John Dunning (United Kingdom), Antonia Estrany y Gendre (Argentina), Ahmed Ghozali (Algeria), I.D. Ivanov (USSR), Jacob Javits (United States), L.K. Jha (India), C. George Kahama (United Republic of Tanzania), Ryutaro Komiya (Japan), Sicco Mansholt (Netherlands), Hans Matthoefer (Federal Republid of Germany), J. Irwin Miller (United States), Mohammad Sadli (Indonesia), Hans Schaffner (Switzerland), Juan Somavia (Chile), Mario Trindade (Brazil) Pierre Uri (France). The Secretary-General was represented by Philippe de Seynes, Under-Secretary-General on Economic and Social Affairs who directed the work of the United Nations in this field until his retirement. Secretaries of the Group were Gustave Feissel and Sotirios Mousouris.

5.   United Nations publication, Sales No. E.73.II.A.11. In its final chapter the study proposed that a general agreement on multinational corporations could be the ultimate objective of the work of the United Nations but, in case this was too ambitious, it went on to add that "some general agreement on a code of conduct for multinational corporations is not beyond reach."

6.   See for instance *Transnational Corporations: Issues Relevant to the Formulation of the Code of Conduct* (United Nations publication, Sales No. E.77.II.A.5); "Transnational Corporations: Material Relevant to the Formulation of a Code of Conduct" (E/C-10/18) and "Transnational Corporations: Certain Modalities for Implementation of a Code of Conduct in Relation to its Possible Legal Nature" (E/C.10/AC.2/9).

PART 5

INTERNATIONAL MARKETING

SECTION **29**

INFORMATION FOR INTERNATIONAL MARKETING DECISIONS

CONTENTS

COLLECTING INFORMATION FOR
STRATEGIC INTERNATIONAL
MARKETING DECISIONS   4

Data Relating to the National
Investment Climate and Market
Environment   4
   Information sources   4
   Data accuracy, equivalence, and
   interpretation   7
   Risk factors   8
   Indicators of market potential   9
   Costs of market operation   10
   Applications of aggregate
   macroindicators   12
Data Relating to the Product Market
and to Company Performance   **15**
   Market size and structure   15
   Company sales and product-market
   performance   15
   Sales and demand projections   17

USING INTERNATIONAL MARKETING
INFORMATION   **22**

Market Entry and Mode of Entry
Decisions   **23**
   Evaluating market entry   24
   Determining the mode of entry   27
Reallocation Decisions   **28**
   Monitoring environmental change   28
   Reallocating resources and
   management time and effort across
   different regions, countries, and
   product markets   29

CONCLUSIONS   **31**

SOURCES AND SUGGESTED
REFERENCES   **31**

INFORMATION FOR INTERNATIONAL MARKETING DECISIONS

Susan P. Douglas
C. Samuel Craig

As competition for world market share intensifies in many industries, such as those purchasing automobiles, steel, watches, apparel, and electronics, attention to international marketing strategy becomes even more crucial. Lack of familiarity with foreign environments coupled with the greater degree of uncertainty in operation across national boundaries imply, however, a high level of risk. Collection of relevant information can aid in reducing the level of risk and thus lead to more effective international business decisions.

Information is required for two types of decision-making situations: when a company is considering initial entry into international markets, and when a company has existing operations in foreign markets. In the first case, information is required to determine (1) which countries, product markets, and target segments to enter, and (2) what mode of entry (i.e., export, direct sales, joint venture) to use in each country and product market. In the second case, information is needed (1) to monitor business changes in the environment of the different national markets where the company has operations, and (2) to determine the appropriate allocation or reallocation of resources across different countries, products, and target segments.

The type of information needed in these two decision-making situations is somewhat different. For the first set of decisions, heavy reliance is placed on the use of secondary data, in particular, macrocountry indicators such as GNP, population, measures of country political stability, and financial risk. These enable assessment of the investment climate in a country, as well as marketing threats and opportunities. In addition, data concerning specific product markets and competition should be obtained, where available.

The plethora of information relating to international markets suggests, however, the importance of selectivity in collecting such information. Not only are high costs associated with collecting and processing information in relation to a multiplicity of international markets, but in addition the human mind has a limited capacity to handle, organize, and interpret information on this scale. The collection of information for international business decisions should thus be guided by the specific requirements of each type of decision. Such an explicit focus avoids both decision making based on inadequate or inaccurate data and the collection of an overabundance of unnecessary or little-used information.

The second set of decisions not only requires, or rather assumes, the availability of such secondary market data, but also requires internal company data relating to sales and performance within each national market. In addition, projections of sales and performance data are needed in order to assess future market potential in each country and product market. The specific types of information which can aid in making both sets of decisions are next discussed in more detail.

First, the different types of information required for making international marketing decisions are identified. Alternative sources of these data and their relative merits and limitations are then discussed. Finally, the various uses of this information both in relation to initial market entry and in reallocating resources across countries and product markets are examined.

COLLECTING INFORMATION FOR STRATEGIC INTERNATIONAL MARKETING DECISIONS

In making strategic international marketing decisions, three types of information are required:

1. Secondary data relating to the national business and market environment.
2. Internal company data relating to past sales and performance.
3. Estimates of projected sales and market potential.

The specific data and relevant sources for each of these categories are next examined in more detail.

DATA RELATING TO THE NATIONAL INVESTMENT CLIMATE AND MARKET ENVIRONMENT

Information Sources. An important type of data that is needed in making international business decisions and that is unique to international, as opposed to domestic, business relates to the national business-investment climate and environment. These data can be obtained from a variety of secondary sources, including statistics published by Business International, Euromonitor, the United Nations, and Predicasts.

Those published by Business International are among the best and most widely known. They are revised every six months and are computerized. As indicated in Exhibit 1, they include numerous variables covering key indicators of economic structure, historical population and labor force statistics, wages, prices, foreign trade, and consumption patterns. These are available for 131 countries. Special analyses of these data can be conducted using in-house or standardized programs, and the data can be mixed with company data to make relevant analyses. Forecast reports covering key market variables for 35 major world markets for 2-year periods can also be purchased.

The main advantages of these data are their up-to-dateness and the fact that they are computerized. Analyses tailored to specific company or market situations can be made, and the data can be related to internal company sales and performance

EXHIBIT 1   INTERNATIONAL BUSINESS DATA

Demographic data
National income
Gross domestic product (GDP)
Private consumption expenditure
Capital formation
GDP by types of activity
Components of manufacturing
Currency and balance of payments
Labor force
Production and productivity indexes
Hourly wages, manufacturing
Price trends
Foreign trade
Selected production and consumption data
  Passenger cars in use
  Trucks and buses in use
  Telephones in use
  Radios in use
  Television sets in use
  Steel consumption
  Cement production
  Energy consumption
  Electricity production
  Consumption of newsprint
  Residential construction

data. The range of variables included is, however, not as extensive as that provided by other sources.

A broad range of indicators is to be found in the Euromonitor statistics. These are contained in two volumes, one relating to European markets, the other to all other countries. The indicators available in relation to international markets are shown in Exhibit 2. The information and data available for European markets is considerably more detailed than that for other markets. The major limitations of the data are that they are not computerized nor updated as frequently as those published by Business International.

The U.N. and UNESCO yearbooks provide extremely detailed statistics for an extensive number of countries, focusing predominantly on economic and demographic data such as income, population, literacy, educational levels, and birth, death, and marriage rates. The major limitation of these data, although extremely detailed and carefully collected, is that they do not always focus on information of the most relevance for marketing decisions. Emphasis is placed on analysis of past trends, rather than the projection of future trends, which is required for international business decisions.

The World Bank also publishes a number of statistics for 125 countries throughout the world (World Bank 1980). These include basic indicators such as population, G.N.P. per capita, inflation, literacy, food production, as well as statistics relating to the economy, i.e., growth of production by sector, growth of consumption, trade

EXHIBIT 2   EUROMONITOR INTERNATIONAL MARKETING DATA

Population
  Total population
  Area, population distribution and
    density
  Population growth and forecasts
  Vital statistics
  Household population
  Demographic breakdowns by age and
    sex

Employment
  Labor force by age
  Unemployment
  Average working week
  Industrial disputes
  Accidents at work
  Female working population
  Economically active population
  Employment by activity

Production
  Land use and irrigation
  Indices of agricultural and food
    production
  Livestock
  Meat production
  Animal and fishery products
  Fruit and vegetables
  Cereals
  Forestry products
  Other crops
  Manufactured foods
  Beverages and tobacco
  Natural resources
  Refined metals
  Building materials
  Energy resources and production
  Electrical energy
  Chemical products
  Automotives
  Consumer durables
  Clothing and textiles

Trade
  Balance of trade
  Direction of trade (imports and
    exports)
  Imports of selected manufactured
    goods

Economy
  Economic indicators
  Gross national product
  Productivity
  State budget
  Gross domestic product (origin and
    distribution)
  Money reserves and supply
  Exchange rates

Standard of Living
  Comparative wages and earnings
  Consumer prices
  Comparative costs
  Radios and televisions in use
  Car ownership
  Ownership levels for consumer
    durables
  Household expenditure
  Retail trade

Consumption
  Industrial products
  Energy
  Agricultural requisites
  Food
  Beverages
  Tobacco
  Sales of durables

Housing, Health, Education
  Dwelling stock
  Size of dwellings
  Facilities in dwellings
  Hospital establishment
  Health personnel
  Primary education
  Secondary education
  Higher education
  Expenditure on education
  Illiteracy level

Communications
  Cultural indicators
  Libraries, museums
  Communication services
  Telephones, telegrams
  Transport statistics
  Roads, railways, air traffic, shipping
  Tourist statistics

movements, capital movements, and various demographic and social statistics. These are carefully compiled, in some cases using U.S. or UNESCO data, and are highly reliable. On the other hand, they suffer from the same limitations as the U.N. data, namely, their general economic focus and lack of up-to-dateness.

The Worldcasts division of Predicasts also contains information on national income, population, the labor force, industrial production, trade and service, and government. Their main focus has, however, been on commodity and product-market data for industries such as chemicals, metals, instruments, transportation equipment, and fabricated products, that is, the export-oriented industries. These are also projected by country for selected product markets, notably that for industrial goods. In general, one-, two-, three-, and four-year projections are developed.

Data Accuracy, Equivalence, and Interpretation.   There is, nonetheless, considerable variation in data from one source to another, as is evident from the range of values reported for a given statistic such as GNP per capita, number of television sets in use, vehicle registration, or number of retail institutions. In addition, accuracy of data varies from country to country. Data from the United States and the highly industrialized nations is likely to have a higher level of accuracy than that from developing countries. This is largely due to the mechanisms for collecting data. In the United States and other industrialized nations, relatively reliable and sophisticated procedures for collecting population or industry census data, national accounting, or other macrodata are utilized. In developing countries, however, such data may be based on estimates, or rudimentary procedures incorporating a high component of measurement error may be used.

Measurement units are also not necessarily equivalent from country to country. In the case of income, for example, annual-income figures in France and Belgium are likely to include the thirteenth month—a bonus automatically received by all salaried workers—hence providing a measurement construct different from that in other countries. Similarly in some countries, such as the United Kingdom, use of a company car is provided to many employees as a fringe benefit. Consequently, registration of personal-vehicle ownership does not necessarily provide an accurate reflection of "actual" levels of personal-vehicle consumption.

Interpretation of apparently equivalent measures also poses a number of problems. Comparisons of GNP per capita, may, for example, be misleading. Differences in personal taxation structures and in relative prices imply, however, that purchasing-power parity is not necessarily equivalent. Recent studies (Kravis *et al.,* 1978) adjusting national income statistics for purchasing-power parity have, for example, tended to result in significant readjustment of apparent relative wealth, especially for developing economies.

An important limitation to all of these data in assessing market potential is that they relate to the general business environment. In addition, individual companies will require, wherever feasible, data relating to specific product markets, and a linking of the macroindicators to these markets.

A valuable source of product-market data is the U.S. Department of Commerce. The department publishes (1) global market surveys, in-depth reports covering 20 to 30 of the best foreign markets for a single U.S. industry such as micrographics, biomedical equipment, metalworking and finishing, building products and construction equipment; (2) producer and consumer-goods research, in-depth reports covering the best foreign-sales opportunities for a single U.S. producer or consumer-goods industry; and (3) country-market sectoral surveys, in-depth reports covering the most promising U.S. export opportunities in a single foreign country. The focus is, however, on specific industries, particularly those with export potential.

In collecting information to assess market entry, a company should, therefore, collect information relating to both the macrocountry environment, and the specific product market.

In essence, four major categories of information relevant to market-entry decisions may be identified, as follows:

1. Indicators of *risk* associated with operation in an overseas market.
2. Indicators of market *potential* and control.
3. Indicators of *costs* of exploiting market potential, which also vary with different modes of operation.
4. *Product*-specific market data.

Risk Factors.   Three major types of risk may affect the success or profitability of operations in a foreign environment. These are as follows:

1. *Political risk.*   These include risks of expropriation or imposition of restrictions on foreign corporations by host governments, as well as internal political instability and insurrections. The former can be assessed on the basis of historical data, that is, the number of expropriations that have taken place in a particular country (Bradley, 1977). It should, however, be noted that such indicators are not always the most accurate, because of changes in government. Consequently, different approaches, using expert opinion, Delphi techniques, and impressions, as well as quantified approaches may be desirable (Rummel and Heenan, 1978). Syndicated services for evaluating risk are also available, such as Business Environment Risk Index, the Business International Index or Faust and Sullivan's World Political Risk Forecasts.

2. *Financial and foreign-exchange risks.*   These include factors such as the rate of inflation, currency depreciation, or restrictions on capital flows and repatriation of earnings. Again, a variety of commercial services are available. These include services for predicting foreign-exchange rates in the long run, such as those provided by the major international banks (i.e., Chemical Bank, Citibank, Chase Manhattan), or specialized econometric forecasters such as Chase Econometrics, Data Resources, Inc., or the Wharton Econometric Forecasting Associates. A number of smaller organizations specialized in assessing foreign-exchange rates have also developed, such as Predex, Mureenbeld, Conti Currency, and the European-American Bank. The accuracy and reliability of these services has been extensively investigated, and shows variation depending on the currency and time horizon (Levich, 1980). Also provided by other sources are summary indicators such as the rating of 93 countries' creditworthiness by 90 international bankers, recently published in the *Institutional Investor* (1979).

3. *Legal and regulatory factors.*   These include factors such as import-export restrictions on various forms of ownership, modes of operation, tariff barriers, product regulation, and legislation. Information on these has generally to be analyzed on a country-by-country basis for a specific product category, and

is to be found in sources such as the *Price Waterhouse Information Guides*, or Dun and Bradstreet's *Exporters' Encyclopaedia*, which contain information on foreign commerce, language, weights and measures, price controls, distributor agreements, marking and labeling, and commercial practices.

Some illustrative examples of variables that might be included under each of these categories are shown in Exhibit 3. It should, however, be noted that these are illustrative only, and in each case the variables specifically relevant for a particular company or product will need to be determined.

Indicators of Market Potential.   The second set of variables are surrogate indicators for market growth and development. These include the following:

1. *Demographic characteristics.*   Here factors such as population size, rate of population growth, degree of urbanization, and age structure and composition can be obtained from U.N. data, demographic and other statistical yearbooks, or from the other information sources previously cited.

2. *Economic characteristics.*   These are essentially factors such as GDP or GNP per capita, rates of growth, income distribution, and so forth. Again, information on such factors can be obtained in most international data banks.

3. *Geographic characteristics.*   Here factors such as the physical size of the country, climatic, and topographical conditions need to be considered. These are most likely to be found in geographic atlases. Information on climate can also be obtained from tourist guidebooks.

4. *Technological characteristics.*   In this category are included factors such as the level of technological education, and sophistication of consumer education, and existing production or consumption technology. These are available in various sources such as Berry's *Atlas of Economic Development* (1961), for example, which contains information relating to factors such as percentage of land area cultivated, wheat yields, and rice yields. Information relating to consumer education and literacy rates can be found in the U.N. and UNESCO

EXHIBIT 3   RISK FACTORS

Political Factors
    Internal political stability
    Communist influence
    Expropriation risks
    Host-government attitudes to foreign investment

Legal Factors
    Import-export restrictions
    Legal systems
    Restrictions on ownership

Financial factors
    Rate of inflation
    Capital-flow restrictions
    Foreign-exchange risk

---

handbooks. The level of consumption technology can be evaluated from the level of household-appliance ownership, the number of libraries and museums, consumption of newsprint, or expenditure on higher education. Technological development can be evaluated from the existence of more sophisticated industries such as electronics or microprocessing, and from the level of energy consumption, and productivity indexes, which are found in most data sources.

5. *Sociocultural characteristics.* These include factors such as dominant cultural values and life-style patterns, linguistic fragmentation, and cultural or ethnic homogeneity. Here considerably greater difficulty is likely to be encountered in obtaining relevant data and developing quantitative indicators. Information on aspects such as linguistic fragmentation or the number of ethnic or subcultural groups can be obtained from U.N. demographic and statistical handbooks. However, the extent to which this provides evidence of market potential is not always clear. More detailed studies of cultural values and life-style patterns have been conducted in relation to a number of countries, typically the more industrialized countries (Segnit and Broadbent, 1973, McCann-Erickson, 1978). Interpretation of the implications for product potential and marketing strategy is, however, not always clear (Douglas and Macquin, 1977).

Some illustrative examples of relevant factors to be included from these categories are shown in Exhibit 4. Again, however, it should be emphasized that these are only illustrative, and the specific indicators will depend on the product market and the individual company.

Costs of Market Operation. The third set of variables includes factors relating to the infrastructures that affect the costs of operating in a specific country environment. These are of two kinds: (1) *integrative networks,* which affect the feasibility or desirability of utilizing specific types of marketing programs and strategies, and (2) *basic resource requirements,* which affect the feasibility or costs associated with different modes of operation within a given national market.

Integrative Networks. A variety of factors might be included here, as for example, the availability of television advertising, commercial radio networks, and supermarkets or other self-service outlets, the development of the transportation network and the communication system, and the existence of banking, financial, and credit services, advertising agencies, or market-research organizations. Information on these factors can be obtained from a variety of sources. Information relating to the number of television sets or radios owned, mail flow per capita, newspaper circulation, transportation statistics (such as kilometers of railroads, roads, ton kilometer of freight per kilometer of road or railroad), number of commercial and consumer motor vehicles, and number of wholesalers and retailers are available in most international data sources. Information relating to the existence of service industries is, however, likely to have to be obtained from the international association relevant for the industry, as for example the International Advertising Association (IAA), or the International Association of Department Stores, or other trade sources.

**EXHIBIT 4   BUSINESS AND MARKET
ENVIRONMENT INDICATORS**

Demographic characteristics
  Size of population
  Rate of population growth
  Degree of urbanization
  Population density
  Age structure and composition of population

Geographic characteristics
  Physical size of country
  Topographical characteristics
  Climate conditions

Economic factors
  GNP per capita
  Income distribution
  Rate of growth of GNP
  Ratio of investment to GNP

Technological factors
  Level of technological skill
  Existing production technology
  Existing consumption technology
  Education levels

Sociocultural factors
  Dominant values
  Life-style patterns
  Ethnic groups
  Linguistic fragmentation

Resource Requirements.   Essentially cover three basic categories as follows:

1. *Physical resources,* such as electricity, energy, or water. Again information on the availability of these, for example, electricity production or energy consumption, can be obtained from most international data sources. More detailed information relating to specific regional and site availability is, however, likely to require more detailed investigation.

2. *Human resources,* such as the availability of labor, work skills, management training, and attitudes. Once again, aggregate information on the size of the labor force, levels of productivity, or hourly wages, is contained in sources such as Business International data, but specific regional or industry availability will require more explicit investigation.

3. *Capital resources,* such as financial and capital resources and technology availability and sophistication. As in the preceding two cases, aggregate information on, for example, capital formation and financial markets is available in sources such as *International Financial Statistics.* Technology can be assessed in terms of the existence of high-technology industries. Again, however, the relevancy of these to specific industries and companies will require further examination.

Examples of both types of variables are noted in Exhibit 5. But again, as in the case of the two preceding variable sets, the examples are illustrative only, and the specific indicators selected are contingent on the specific product and company and the mode of operation or market entry that is envisaged.

Applications of Aggregate Macroindicators.   These aggregate macroindicators have been used in two ways: to develop classification schemata for countries with similar business environments, and to develop indexes of market potential in different countries.

Classification Schema of Countries.   Macroindicators have been used in a number of studies to classify countries according to their business environment and hence investment potential. The classic study of this type was that conducted by the Marketing Science Institute (Liander *et al.*, 1967). In addition to a regional-typological approach, two approaches were adopted. One was based on two dimensions—a country's degree of demographic and economic mobility, and its domestic stability and cohesion. Position on the economic-demographic dimension was measured by 21 variables relating to development and industrialization, marketing orientation, communications, transportation, organization of population, education, and health. The second dimension, internal stability and cohesion, was measured by three indicators: deaths from group violence, cultural homogeneity and fragmentation, and duration of national identity. In the second approach, countries were first classified into Berry's five levels of technological development: most highly developed, developed, semideveloped, underdeveloped, very underdeveloped. Similarity among countries within each level was then examined based on 12 environmental and societal characteristics such as population growth, urban population, and religious and racial homogeneity.

EXHIBIT 5   INFRASTRUCTURE REQUIREMENTS

Integrative networks
  Transportation infrastructure
  Distribution network
  Availability of mass media, TV, radio, magazines
  Availability of communication networks, mail services
  Existence of other marketing or functional organizations

Basic resources
  Physical
    Electricity
    Energy
    Water
  Human
    Availability of labor
    Work skills of labor
    Management training and attitudes
  Capital
    Financial resources
    Technological capabilities
    Housing for expatriate labor

Litvak and Banting (1968) have proposed that investment climates be evaluated in terms of major categories of variables, relating to political stability, cultural homogeneity, geocultural distance, legal and physiographic barriers, market opportunity, and economic development. Sheth and Lutz (1973) have developed an operational means of applying this framework using 15 indicators to classify the investment climates of 80 countries on a hot—cold continuum.

Another schema is that developed by Sethi (1971), which uses 29 variables relating to political, socioeconomic, trade, transportation, communications, biological, and personal consumption data to classify 91 countries. In a later study, (Sethi and Curry, 1973) more sociocultural variables were added, reaching a total of 56, and 93 countries were classified. A more recent study (Johansson and Moinpour, 1977) classifies countries within the Pacific Rim and Atlantic Ocean regions, based on 29 economic, social, and political variables.

Similarly, Doyle and Gigendil (1976) used 26 indicators drawn from several U.N. yearbooks, the UNESCO *Statistical Yearbook,* and Business International data to identify countries with similar characteristics and hence market potential. The matching of countries based on their profiles was then investigated as a basis for grouping countries for market entry or strategy development.

Piper (1971) in an early investigation of factors used by U.S. firms to evaluate investment opportunities, also found similar types of information were used in investment studies. These are shown in Exhibit 6. In addition to the macroeconomic indicators, as might be anticipated in an investment study, a number of financial variables were also included.

The major limitation of such classification schemata is, however, that they are based solely on macro, economic, social, and political indicators. Consequently, they assume that the same indicators are relevant for all product markets and companies. Whereas this may be true for certain indicators such as GNP or population size, it is not for others. Political factors are, for example, likely to be more important for companies in strategic industries such as the extraction industries or telecommunications than for those in consumer-goods industries such as soft drinks or high-technology industries such as electronic components. Furthermore, such schemata do not contain any information concerning product markets. This, nonetheless, is likely to be crucial in assessing market potential in a given country.

Multiple-Factor Indexes.   Multiple-factor indexes are also published by various commercial services. Business International, for example, publishes each year information on three indexes: (1) market growth, (2) market intensity, and (3) market size for countries in Western and Eastern Europe, the Middle East, Latin America, Asia, Africa, and Australia. The specific variables included in each of these indexes vary somewhat from region to region, reflecting different market characteristics. The market-growth index is based on the average of 10 indicators of percentage growth over the past 5 years. In Europe, these are population, steel consumption, cement and electricity production, passenger cars, GDP., national income, private consumption, telephones, and television sets. In Latin America, the last five are omitted, and energy consumption and trucks and buses in use, are added.

Market intensity is an index that measures the "richness" of a market, or degree of concentrated purchasing power. The region is taken as the base, and a score for each country is calculated based on certain indicators. In Europe these are the same 10 indicators, with double weighting of private-consumption expenditure and own-

EXHIBIT 6   DECISION VARIABLES IDENTIFIED IN 16 INVESTMENT STUDIES

Financial considerations
1. Capital acquisition plan
2. Length of payback period
3. Projected cash inflows (years one, two, and so forth)
4. Projected cash outflows (years one, two, and so forth)
5. Return on investment
6. Monetary-exchange considerations

Technical and engineering feasibility considerations
7. Raw-materials availability (construction/support/supplies)
8. Raw-materials availability (products)
9. Geography/climate
10. Site locations and access
11. Availability of local labor
12. Availability of local management
13. Economic infrastructure (roads, water, electricity, and so forth)
14. Facilities planning (preliminary or detailed)

Marketing considerations
15. Market size
16. Market potential
17. Distribution costs

18. Competition
19. Time necessary to establish distribution/sales channels
20. Promotion costs
21. Social/cultural factors affecting products

Economic and legal considerations
22. Legal systems
23. Host-government attitudes toward foreign investment
24. Host attitude toward this particular investment
25. Restrictions on ownership
26. Tax laws
27. Import/export restrictions
28. Capital-flow restrictions
29. Land-title acquisitions
30. Inflation

Political and social considerations
31. Internal political stability
32. Relations with neighboring countries
33. Political/social traditions
34. Communist influence
35. Religious/racial/language homogeneity
36. Labor organizations and attitudes
37. Skill/technical level of the labor force
38. Socioeconomic infrastructure to support American families

Source. Piper, 1971.

ership of passenger cars. In Latin America only per capita energy and steel consumption, telephones, and television sets are used, and in addition to private-consumption expenditure and ownership of passenger cars, proportion of the urban population also receives double weighting.

The market-size index measures the relative size of each national market as a percentage of the total market. Again, in Latin America this ranking is based on population (double weighted), urban population, private-consumption expenditure, energy and steel consumption, cement production, and telephones, cars, and televisions in use.

Other similar indexes have been constructed as, for example, the J.W. Thompson index. This uses similar factors including population, value of imports, private-consumption expenditure, number of cars, radios and telephones to rank Western European countries according to their buying potential.

The principal limitation of these indexes is that they focus on macrocountry indicators, which are then used as surrogate indicators or proxy variables for evaluating the general business climate. As such they are useful as a first step in identifying countries that are likely to be attractive candidates for initiation or expansion of international operations. Individual companies will, however, need more detailed analyses, tailored to corporate objectives and the specific product markets in which they are involved. Consequently, their use is somewhat limited, particularly for companies already involved in, or seriously committed to, international operations.

DATA RELATING TO THE PRODUCT MARKET AND TO COMPANY PERFORMANCE

Market Size and Structure.   In addition, wherever feasible, data relating to the specific product market should be collected. These should include information with regard to product usage, usage of complementary and substitute products, and competitive market structure. The relevant types of variables are essentially the same as those that would be used to assess potential-market size and structure in relation to the domestic market.

Product-Usage Data.   Here information relating to levels of product ownership for durable products, or sales-purchase and repeat-purchase rates for nondurables, is desirable. Availability of such data is likely to depend on the development of the product market and the specific country. Nielsen data can, for example, be obtained for most major industrialized countries. The Economist Intelligence Unit also pub- '
lishes studies relating to different products such as shoes, confectionery, and radios in various European countries. In developing countries such as the African countries or the Asian markets, greater difficulty is likely to be encountered in obtaining such data.

Usage of Complementary or Substitute Products.   Data relating to usage of complementary or substitute products, as for example, automobiles for tires, cameras for film, or the construction industry for float glass are also desirable. Similarly, data on bourbon consumption might be collected by companies marketing Scotch whiskey. Difficulties are likely to be encountered in collecting such data as in relation to product usage. Data for some industries, for example, the construction industry or major industrial markets, are readily available. In relation to consumer goods, such as soft drinks or electronic toys, much may depend on the state of market development.

Competitive Market Structure.   Data relating to the competitive market structure should also be collected. This might include, for example, the number and size of competitors in the marketplace, their sales volume and rates of growth, relative market share, and so forth. Again, the feasibility of obtaining such data is likely to vary significantly with the specific product. In industrial markets, some data may be obtained from company reports or trade sources. In developing countries these may, however, be scanty. In consumer-goods industries in general, greater difficulty is likely to be encountered, as firms often have diverse product lines and do not break down aggregate figures on this basis.

Some illustrative indicators are shown in Exhibit 7. Specific operational definitions will, however, need to be established for each product market.

Company Sales and Product-Market Performance.   Internal company data are also an important component of the information system. The same types of information

EXHIBIT 7 PRODUCT-SPECIFIC
INDICATORS

Product usage
    Sales volume of product
    Ownership of product

Usage of complementary or substitute products
    Sales volume of complementary products
    Existence of user industries
    Sales of substitute products

Competition
    Number of firms
    Sales analysis
    Growth rate of competing firms

needed to evaluate domestic marketing decisions are required. The exact information required is, however, likely to vary considerably from company to company depending on the nature of existing operations. Regardless of interfirm variation in information requirements, however, they should include aggregate measures of market performance, as for example, return on investment, market share as a percentage of total industry sales, market share relative to the top, or leading three, competitors, trends in market share, marketing expenditure relative to sales ratios, or growth in sales by product line.

Depending on the size of the market, these may be broken down to reflect territorial or regional measures of performance, for example, market-share estimates and trends by specific geographic regions, sales and sales trends by region, expenditure relative to sales ratios by region and so forth. Measures of performance relative to specific marketing variables or tasks such as sales force advertising, sales promotion, pricing, and distribution efficiency should also be included.

These data will, however, only be available in relation to the specific national or product markets in which the company is already involved and are essentially needed for decisions relating to the reallocation of resources and effort across different country and product markets.

Collection of data for international operations and incorporation of these data into the information system initially appears relatively straightforward. Data comparability from one country to another presents, however, a major obstacle. It is important to realize that a value or number supplied by a subsidiary in one country is not necessarily identical to the supposedly comparable figure supplied by a subsidiary in another country. Consequently, values or figures need to be adjusted into equivalent units so they can serve as a meaningful input for marketing decisions.

Sales-volume measures, for example, may be expressed in real or monetary units. Real units, although accurately reflecting the number sold, may be misleading in that the nature of the product can vary from country to country corresponding to different market requirements. Automobiles and pharmaceutical products, for example, frequently require modification to conform to specific national product regulations, thus entailing different costs.

Monetary units may thus be doubly misleading. The price of the product may not only reflect design differences, but in addition, differences in pricing policy, transfer-pricing practices, and local taxation rules, as, for example, a value-added tax. In addition, monetary units require conversion by an appropriate exchange rate. This gives rise to further difficulties to the extent that exchange rates are floating and may sometimes artificially reflect shifts in capital funds or temporary balance of payments. Procedures or mechanisms that adjust for such factors are thus required.

These difficulties are further compounded by variations in accounting procedures and standards in different countries. Costs may not be estimated in the same way or may include different expense items. Countries have different rates of social security payment and methods for allocating and billing these. Some adjustment has therefore to be made to make calculation of sales force costs as a percentage of total sales comparable.

Even seemingly unambiguous measures of performance such as market share may be misleading. The definition of the relevant product market may vary from country to country as, for example, in the case of soft drinks or pharmaceuticals, thus understating or overstating a firm's share of the market. In examining sales response to various marketing-mix elements, differences in distribution channels and their efficiency, media availability and effectiveness, and market structure and pricing have to be taken into consideration. Distribution channels, such as supermarkets, used in one country may not exist in another, and hence distribution costs will be higher. Advertising sales ratios may be affected by the availability of various media and their reach. In some countries, television advertising may not be available. Consequently, print or radio media may be more widely used. Media mixes thus vary considerably, rendering strict comparison of advertising and sales ratios of limited value.

Sales and Demand Projections.   In addition to estimating current market potential, estimates of future market potential and growth are also required to evaluate future rates of return. This is important when considering initial market entry because of the high costs and uncertainty associated with entering new markets. Such estimates are also necessary in countries where a company has existing market operations to assess whether resources and effort should be shifted from one product market and country to another.

If the company has been involved in the product market a sufficient time for historical data to be available, procedures similar to those followed in the domestic market can be used. For example, time-series trend analysis, or double-exponential smoothing analyses can be conducted. Since the application is identical to that in the domestic-market situation, these are not discussed here.

If, however, management is considering entry into new markets or is in the initial stages of market development, other procedures will be required. Often many of these markets, particularly in developing countries are likely to be small and fragmented, and few data are available (Moyer, 1968). The small size of the markets, as well as the difficulty and high costs of undertaking research under such conditions, suggests that techniques commonly used in domestic markets, such as surveys of buying intentions or market tests are likely to be prohibitively expensive. In some cases, they may in fact be infeasible. Consequently, low-cost rudimentary procedures are likely to be required.

Data-extrapolation techniques offer considerable potential in this regard, since they make use of experience and data collected in one or more countries to develop estimates or forecasts of potential in other countries. Such extrapolations may either be made using time-series or cross-sectional data.

It is, however, important to note that use of extrapolation techniques requires a number of assumptions concerning the relevance in one country of data collected in another country. It requires, first, that countries be equivalent units or comparable in certain relevant respects. Thus, for example, extrapolation between countries that have similar market structures or demand characteristics is likely to be the most successful. Secondly, it assumes that the measurement units are comparable or equivalent in all countries. Thus, for example, if monetary units are used, their currency equivalents have to be established. Even if real units are utilized, equivalence has to be established, since these may not be defined similarly in different countries. Thirdly, it assumes that the relationship between demand determinants and sales is the same in all countries, that is, if GNP is related to cement consumption in one country, it will be related to cement consumption in another country. Finally, it requires that product classes are comparable and equivalent in all countries. For example, comparability of different shampoo variants or soft drinks in all countries has to be established. Furthermore, if projections over time are to be made, it requires that the rate of change in all markets be approximately equivalent.

Lead-Lag Analysis.   The first and most simplistic method of data extrapolation is lead-lag analysis. This is based on the use of time-series data from one country to project sales in other countries. It assumes that determinants of demand in the two countries are identical and the only factor that separates them is time. Thus, for example, sales trends in France can be predicted on the basis of sales trends in the United States, with a lag of x years. Exhibits 8 and 9 show this for television sets in the United States, the United Kingdom, and West Germany. This method is, however, generally not widely used, because of the difficulty of identifying the relevant time lag. Furthermore, the accuracy of the estimate is open to some question. It is likely to be most effective in the case of innovations, which have the same penetration rate in different countries.

Barometric Analysis.   A second technique, which relies on the use of cross-sectional data, is analogous to the use of barometric procedures in domestic sales forecasting. This assumes that if there is a relationship between the product category and a gross indicator in one country, the same relationship will hold in other countries. Exhibit 10 shows the relationship between glass consumption and GNP in different countries. Various models can be applied to these data, including linear regression, logarithms, or exponential or more-complex models, to develop relevant model parameters, as

EXHIBIT 8   PERCENTAGE OF HOUSEHOLDS OWNING TELEVISION SETS

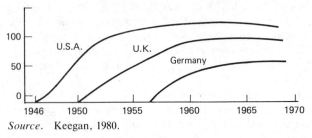

Source.   Keegan, 1980.

EXHIBIT 9   YEARLY PERCENTAGE INCREASE IN HOUSEHOLD OWNERSHIP OF TELEVISION SETS

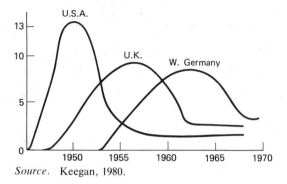

Source.   Keegan, 1980.

in Exhibit 11. These can then be used to predict sales based on level of GNP in other countries.

An analogous procedure, which has been effectively used in relation to consumer markets, is the development of multiple-factor indexes. Thus rather than using one factor such as GNP to predict sales, a number of different variables are included in the model. Dickensheets (1963) has, for example, developed a multiple-factor index

EXHIBIT 10   GLASS CONSUMPTION AND GNP

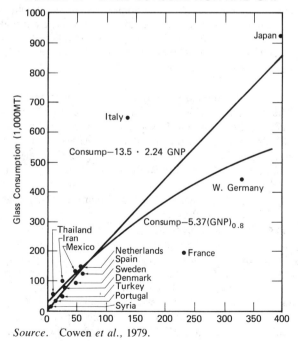

Source.   Cowen et al., 1979.

EXHIBIT 11   REGRESSION MODELS FOR PREDICTING GLASS CONSUMPTION BASED ON GNP

Country	Glass Consumption (metric tons)	GNP ($ Billion)
Syria	15	3
Portugal	36	13
Thailand	46	11
Turkey	50	23
Denmark	74	26
Iran	95	28
Sweden	99	48
Mexico	128	50
Netherlands	138	58
Spain	132	59
France	197	230
West Germany	454	330
Italy	686	135
Japan	1,230	393

$$\text{Model I} \quad C = A + B(GNP) = 13.5 + 2.24GNP$$
$$\text{Model II} \quad C = A(GNP)^B = 5.37(GNP)^{.8}$$

for refrigerators with larger storage capacity, consisting of 11 indicators including food-shopping habits, number of supermarkets and self-service food stores, auto ownership, consumption of frozen foods, per capita private-consumption expenditure, employment of women, availability of domestic help, availability of consumer credit, cost of electricity for residential use, dwelling construction and size of new dwellings, and refrigerator saturation in high-income families. Where weights for each factor are developed, these indexes can be used to rank countries in terms of their attractiveness or market potential.

Segment Extrapolation.   A modified version of the barometric procedure is segment extrapolation. The barometric procedure assumes that certain gross indicators are related to aggregate market potential. In some cases, there may be different market segments, in which different factors underlie demand. Alternatively, different market segments may have different levels or rates of market penetration.

In the first case, different indicators will have to be developed for each market segment. In the case of diesel engines for small boats, for example, there may be two potential markets, that for pleasure boats and that for fishing boats. In the first case, the relevant indicators might include, for example, per capita disposable income, whereas in the second case, the length of the coastline or estimates of fish haul would be more appropriate. Similarly, in the case of hotels, there may be two potential market segments, one for tourist, and one for business travel. The first may be estimated on the basis of the number of tourists traveling to different countries, and the second on the basis of growth in GNP.

In the second case, where different market segments have different rates of consumption or market penetration, extrapolation by segment, rather than for the total market, is desirable. This is particularly likely to occur in relation to up-scale luxury goods such as premium wine or wristwatches. If, for example, market penetration of expensive wristwatches is related to income, the number of units sold to different income groups can be identified in one country, for example, the United States. The number of household units in each of these income groups is then identified in the second country and multiplied by the relevant group penetration rate to obtain potential-market size by subgroup. This is shown in Exhibit 12.

Similarly, in relation to industrial markets, different user industries can be identified, and rates of penetration in each of these industries determined for one country. The number of companies in each of these industries in another country can then be assessed and multiplied by the relevant penetration rate in order to determine potential-market size. In the case of minicomputers, for example, the key user industries might be financial institutions or commercial data-processing and market-research companies.

This technique can be further refined by breaking down companies within each of these industries by size, sales volume, or other factors indicative of sales potential. Penetration rates in each of these within-industry segments can then be estimated in the base country. The number of companies in each of these segments in the second country is determined and multiplied by the relevant segment-penetration rates. Thus, for example, in estimating market potential for microwave ovens in the industrial sector, three major groups of potential users might be identified—hotels, fast-food chains, and restaurant chains. For hotels, the number of units likely to be purchased might vary with the number of rooms. Sales potential can be estimated by size class in the base country. The number of hotels in each size class can then be estimated in the second country from tourist-board data or tourist guides. This can be multiplied by the relevant-size-class sales-potential figure to obtain market-potential estimates. This is shown in Exhibit 13. Similarly in the case of fast-food chains, if the number of units purchased varies with sales volume, penetration rates can be estimated by these segments in the base country. Again, these rates can be multiplied by the number of chains in each segment in the second country to obtain market-potential estimates.

Econometric Forecasting Models.   More complex forecasting models can also be developed using econometric procedures. These typically require both cross-sec-

EXHIBIT 12   PREDICTING SALES OF WRISTWATCHES

| | Country 1 | | Country 2 | | |
| | Number Sold Annually | × | Number Household Units (thousands) | = | Potential Sales Volume (units) |
Household Income					
$35,000 and over	0.51		240	=	122
$30,000–34,999	0.47		300	=	141
$25,000–29,999	0.39		310	=	121
$20,000–24,999	0.38		600	=	228
$15,000–19,999	0.35		580	=	203
$10,000–14,999	0.21		610	=	128
$ 5,000– 9,999	0.20		1920	=	384
$ Under 4,999	0.19		2040	=	388
					1715

EXHIBIT 13 ESTIMATING MARKET POTENTIAL OF MICROWAVE OVENS BY USER SEGMENT (MARKET SEGMENT—HOTELS)

Number of Rooms	Number of Units Purchased	×	Hotels	Potential Market
50–100	5		200	1000
30– 49	2		100	200
<30	0		0	0
				1200

tional and time-series data. The cross-sectional data might, for example, relate variation in sales to macroindicators such as population, income, literacy, and proportion of the population in agriculture (Armstrong, 1970). Data on these indicators and sales can then be collected over time for selected countries. Regression analysis can be used to identify causal relationships and develop model parameters. The model can then be used to predict sales in other countries or to project sales over time in the same country where predictions for the macroindicators can be obtained.

Such models do, however, require the availability of historical sales data. Furthermore, they assume that extrapolation of these data is relevant in predicting future trends. This is likely to be the case only in relation to a relatively limited number of products that are in the mature phase of the product life cycle. In addition, trends, and hence underlying relationships between sales and indicators, often change very rapidly in foreign markets. Consequently, such techniques are likely to be often subject to substantial error. The models are complex to develop, and frequent updating of relevant model parameters is required.

The Macrosurvey. A technique likely to be particularly effective in developing countries, where there is low market potential, predominantly in scattered rural areas, is the macrosurvey (Carr, 1978). A differentiation scale first has to be developed, consisting of different indicators, or relevant combinations, each of which corresponds to a level of market potential. For example, in Exhibit 14, the presence of a church in a village might indicate that a sales call would be worthwhile, but the community might need to have several telephones before it was considered worthwhile to establish a distribution facility.

Data has then to be collected on the presence or absence of these various items. This may be accomplished by aerial photography, or in some cases, the equivalent of the *Yellow Pages* can be useful. The most comprehensive approach would include a community visit in order to complete and update the index. An example of a scale developed to assess the potential for U.S. products in rural Thailand is shown in Exhibit 15.

USING INTERNATIONAL MARKETING INFORMATION

The four types of information about the international business environment can be used in two distinct decision-making situations—where management is contemplating market entry, and where the company already has operations in overseas markets. For a company considering international market expansion, information is needed

EXHIBIT 14   GUTTMAN SCALE OF DIFFERENTIATION FOR 24 MEXICAN
VILLAGES

Step Number	Item Content	Proportion Discriminated
1	Named and autonomous locality group	1.00
2	One or more governmentally designated officials; more than one street	.92
3	One or more organizations in village	.88
4	A church	.84
5	A school building; a government organization; Mass said in the village more than annually	.80
6	A functional school	.76
7	Has access to a railroad or informant voluntarily includes railroad in list of village needs	.63
8	Access to electric power; informant estimates that a majority have electricity; six or more streets	.46
9	Railroad station; four or more bus or train trips daily	.41
10	School has four or more grades	.37
11	Village has a public square; village market patronized by people in other villages	.29
12	Doctor; priest resides in village; 10 or more streets; school has six or more grades; six or more stores; two or more television sets in village; public monument	.20
13	Has one or more telephones	.16
14	Forty percent or more have radios; settlement area one square mile or more	.12
15	Secondary school; 20 or more stores	.08
	(Coefficient of scalability is .92)[a]	

Source.   Carr, 1978.
[a]The coefficient of scalability is a measure that "varies from 0 to 1, and should be above .6 if the scale is truly unidimensional and cumulative."

to determine *which* countries or markets to enter, and *how* to enter, that is, what mode of operation to use in entering these markets. For the company already in international markets, information is required to monitor business environment change and to assess how to re-allocate resources and effort across different national boundaries and product markets. In the latter case, data relating to the product market and to company performance is also required. These information requirements are next discussed in more detail.

MARKET ENTRY AND MODE OF ENTRY DECISIONS.   For companies entering international markets for the first time, a dual decision has to be made concerning the appropriate combination of countries and modes of entry to be used. This requires the collection of information to assess the investment climate and market potential in all countries to be considered.

EXHIBIT 15 DIFFERENTIATION SCALE OF RURAL THAILAND AND ASSOCIATED MARKETS

Step Number	Item Content	Estimated Population	Markets
1	Market square	1,000–3,000	Piece-good cloth and light agricultural implements (e.g., shovels)
2	Fairground; agricultural support shops (e.g., hand forges, wheel wrights); food shops	3,000–8,000	Manufactured clothes (e.g., work clothes, sandals); canned/dried foods (e.g., evaporated milk, dried shrimp and squid); radios, bicycles, and mopeds
3	Raimie *fiber* mill and pond; Buddhist temple; elementary school; urban support shops (e.g., auto-repair shop)	5,000–10,000	Service for mopeds; hardware, (e.g., hammers, saws, roofing material); school supplies; one-man motorized agricultural equipment (e.g., front-end tiller)
4	Government administration building; ambulatory health care; secondary school; police services	7,000–10,000	Window/door-screen material, glass; social dresses; primitive plumbing equipment (e.g., lavatories, shower heads, etc., with support piping)
5	Raimie *sack* mill and water reservoir; high school and/or technical college; sewer-and water-purification systems	22,000–30,000	Light-industrial machinery (welding, pipe-threading equipment); air conditioning; cement; construction services; office supplies and equipment

Source. Carr, 1978.

Evaluating Market Entry. A major problem in the initial stages of international market entry is the bewildering array of countries and markets which could be entered. Since it is clearly prohibitive to examine all possible countries and markets, an initial screening procedure to determine which countries to investigate in depth is required. Secondary data can provide the basis for this evaluation, in conjunction with a screening or scanning routine developed to evaluate countries on relevant variables (Douglas et al., 1972). This screening procedure is modeled after the management decision-making process, selecting relevant variables and weighting them according to their perceived importance to management to rank countries in terms of priority for further investigation.

A modified version of the conceptual framework used to develop this procedure integrating international information needs is outlined in Exhibit 16. Three stages in the procedure may be identified. First, a number of preliminary screening criteria for eliminating countries are identified. Next, criteria for evaluating countries and the weights to be assigned to them under different modes of operation or entry are determined. Finally, countries are evaluated, based on these criteria, utilizing information relating to the general business and investment climate and, where avail-

**EXHIBIT 16   A CONCEPTUAL FRAMEWORK FOR COUNTRY/MODE-OF-ENTRY
SELECTION**

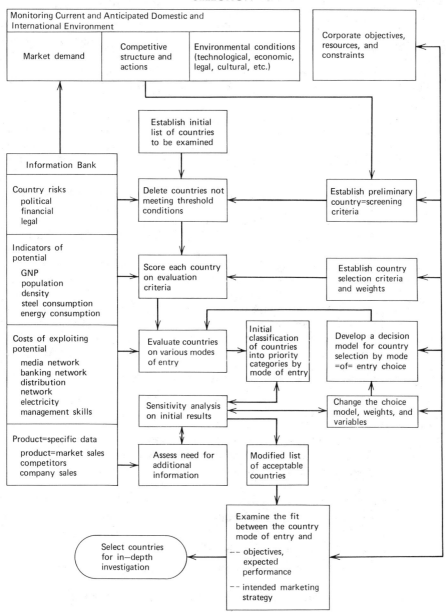

Source.   Adapted from Douglas *et al.*, 1972.

able, to the specific-product market. A sensitivity analysis is then conducted to assess the robustness of the classifications.

Step 1: Preliminary-Screening Criteria.   The first step in the macroevaluation phase is to establish the preliminary-screening requirements. These consist of go–no-go criteria applied by management to establish the feasible list of countries for the evaluation process. This assumes that countries may be excluded from further consideration on the basis of certain attributes.

Two types of attributes may be relevant as follows:

1. *Prohibitions* or restrictions on the sale of specific products or services by foreign companies, as for example, firearms or narcotics, or restrictions by home governments on marketing to certain countries, as for example, to the Soviet Union.

2. *A priori* rules of thumb established by management for eliminating countries. The latter may reflect ideological or political influences, for example, a U.S. company might eliminate South Africa, or a company selling pork products might eliminate Moslem countries. They might also reflect the need for a minimum level of demand or market size. For example, a manufacturer of fur coats might eliminate countries with tropical climates, or a cigarette manufacturer, countries below a certain level of GNP per capita or population size. The specific criteria will depend on the nature of the product market and corporate objectives. Companies marketing similar products will not necessarily use similar sets of criteria. For example, interest and willingness to trade with communist countries or to assume risk may vary with the individual company. In any given situation, therefore, the onus is on management to identify the set of relevant criteria.

Step 2: Selecting Variables and Determining Weights for Evaluating Countries.

Identifying Relevant Variables.   The second step is to determine which country characteristics are to be used in evaluating marketing opportunities and how these should be weighted. Following the four information components identified earlier, four types of variables need to be taken into consideration in evaluating international markets:

1. The *risks* associated with operating in a given national or product market.
2. The market *potential* and growth of the country and the specific product market.
3. The *costs* of operating in that environment.
4. The strength of potential *competition*.

The variables listed earlier (in Exhibits 3,4,5, and 7) provide some illustrative characteristics that might be used in evaluating international marketing opportunities. Information relating to each of these can be obtained from the sources indicated previously. In each specific case, however, the specific variables to be included need to be carefully selected by management based on the nature of the product market and corporate objectives.

Establishing the Relative Importance of Each Variable.   Once the relevant variables to be included have been selected, the weights to be assigned to each of these have to be determined. These are likely to vary from company to company. For example, one company may be willing to accept a higher degree of political risk and less economic stability than another company. Similarly, a company emphasizing a mass-media approach may attach importance to a well-developed communication structure or the existence of television advertising. This implies that the weights should be provided by the judgments of relevant decision makers within the firm. Such judges should be selected on the basis of their involvement and importance in decisions to enter international markets.

Various data-collection and analytical procedures may be utilized to generate these weights. If, for example, decisions to enter an overseas market are typically made on the basis of group judgments, a Delphi technique may be appropriate. Weights initially attributed by individual judges are modified by group discussions. If, on the other hand, a hierarchical decision-making procedure is used, independent judgments may be collected from all relevant decision makers and weighted according to their relative importance in the decision-making process.

Such judgments may be collected using different scaling techniques, ranging from a simple rank order to the more-rigorous interval scales. For example, each decision maker may be presented with a set of variables. He then assigns a value of 0 to the variable rated lowest and 100 to that rated most important. Values ranging from 0 to 100 are then assigned to the remaining variables corresponding to their relative importance. Aggregating across decision makers, an interval scale for the weights is obtained. More-complex procedures such as conjoint or trade-off analysis may also be developed.

Determining the Mode of Entry.   Country-selection decisions are also affected by, and interact with, the mode-of-entry, or operation, decision. The importance of tariff barriers is, for example, critical when exporting, and may encourage local production. Similarly, factors such as the level of local technological, mechanical, or managerial skills are substantially more important if local production is being envisaged as opposed to licensing or exporting.

The variables included in the evaluation procedure and the importance attached to them therefore need to be adjusted according to the mode of entry. Judges or decision makers can be asked to select and weight variables under different modes of operation and entry as, for example, exporting, licensing, contract manufacturing, joint venture, or local production. Where significantly different variables or weights are assigned for different modes of entry, these can then be incorporated into the evaluation model.

Step 3: Country Evaluation and Sensitivity Analysis.   Countries can then be evaluated based on these variables using information from the international information bank and ranked according to their score. If more than one set of weights is used, evaluations can be made sequentially based on the different sets. The highest ranking obtained for the country on any one of these sets is then retained as its score. The rank orderings of countries and the implied financial investment is then reviewed and the initial list of countries for in-depth evaluation selected.

The robustness of this procedure and overall congruence with initial management objectives is then examined. A sensitivity analysis is conducted to evaluate the explicit and implicit decision rules used by management and their implications. At the same time, the need for more-accurate information on countries where minor changes either in the value of variables or their weights would affect acceptance or rejection may be assessed. This sensitivity analysis thus consists of two subphases: analysis of the weights used for each mode of entry or operation, and analysis of the effect of variation in the value of a variable for the country rating. In both cases, simulation procedures are used to assess the impact of alternative weights and values for variables on country scores. Particular attention is focused on cases that would shift the country dramatically from a high-priority to a medium- or low-priority zone.

The possibility of collecting additional information or redefining information needs may then be considered. This may entail either collecting more accurate or more detailed information with regard to a particular variable for a given country or set of countries or redefining and reassessing a particular variable or unit of measurement in the information bank. A reevaluation of countries may then be introduced, leading to the development of a modified list of acceptable countries.

Finally, the congruence of the procedure with initial management objectives is assessed. The rank ordering of countries with top priority for in-depth investigation is then examined. Each country ranking implies a specific mode of entry or operation, for example, exporting to Venezuela, local production in the Philippines. The compatibility of this country/mode-of-entry alternative with initial management expansion and financial objectives can be assessed. If the country rankings do not appear to be consistent with these objectives, reassessment of the procedure is required. More explicit incorporation of financial or other investment criteria may, for example, be desirable.

Other procedures can be developed for evaluating target countries based on secondary data. They may vary in the degree of complexity and sophistication, depending on company size and resources available for international market evaluation. Simple country-rating schemata may, for example, be used or more intricate models developed incorporating political and financial-risk analysis (Stobaugh, 1969). In either case, however, careful selection of country indicators relevant to the specific company or product market and the availability of an appropriate information bank is crucial to effective country-market assessment.

REALLOCATION DECISIONS. For companies already involved in international markets, decisions with regard to the reallocation of resources and effort across different countries and product markets also need to be made. These require (1) the monitoring of environmental change in different countries, and (2) assessing relative profitability in different countries and product markets.

Monitoring Environmental Change. Monitoring environmental change requires surveillance of a number of key indicators. These should be carefully selected and tailored to the specific product or range of products with which management is concerned. Two types of indicators are required. The first monitors the general health and growth of a country and its economy and society; the second, those aspects of the specific product market. Again, information with regard to these indicators can be obtained from the sources previously cited.

The first type of indicator might include factors such as the growth of GNP, population growth, percentage of GDP in agriculture, level of steel or cement consumption, imports of gasoline, or employment in service industries. In this context, it is helpful to include not only indicators that relate to the general economic and business trends and market growth, but also financial data, such as the rate of inflation or balance-of-payments figures and foreign-exchange rates, which provide indicators of the health of the financial climate. These are likely to be particularly critical when a company is involved in exporting or in sourcing across international boundaries.

The second type of indicator might include data relating to product sales in units and in dollar volume, market-share data, prices of leading competitors, number and growth of user industries, and so forth. If such data is not available or the product market is not well developed, surrogate indicators of potential demand may be developed, such as those discussed earlier. In the case of marine engines for small boats, for example, the length of the coastline in miles might provide an appropriate indicator, whereas for corn pickers, the acreage or annual volume of corn production might be suitable. Similarly, minicomputer industries might be concerned with the growth of the service sector of the economy. In each case, however, the particular indicators to be included should be tailored to the specific objectives and strategy of the company and the nature of the product market. Companies reluctant to assume financial risk might, for example, place greater emphasis on financial indicators and rates of inflation.

Reallocating Resources and Management Time and Effort across Different Regions, Countries, and Product Markets. Companies already involved in international markets also need to reassess periodically the allocation of resources and management time and effort across different regions, countries, and product markets. This may be desirable either because of changes in market conditions in a given country, for example, in inflation rates, or in economic growth, which affect profitability. Alternatively, management decisions to diversify or to enter new product markets or new countries may stimulate such a reevaluation.

Profitability in existing markets and countries thus has to be assessed relative to that anticipated from entering new product markets or expanding the current company product line in new countries. In addition to short-term profitability, a critical input to the resource-allocation decision is sales trends in each country or product market. These provide an indication of how resources and marketing effort should be shifted over time to anticipate changing conditions and to help ensure the long-term viability of the firm's international operations. As indicated earlier, in areas where the firm has a history of operations, sales-forecasting techniques similar to those employed domestically can be used. When new countries are being considered, methods of sales forecasting outlined earlier can be utilized.

Current profitability levels coupled with the sales forecast may suggest the desirability of reallocating resources from the product markets and countries in which the company is currently operating to other product markets and countries.

The international-product-portfolio model provides an appropriate conceptual framework for examining this decision and for determining the appropriate mix of countries, product markets, and operational modes for the firm. Various alternative formulations of this model have been developed, ranging from the simpler Boston Consulting Group portfolio model (Larreche, 1978) to the more-complex, risk-return model (Wind, 1976). None of these have, however, yet been clearly developed nor operationalized.

Following the Boston Consulting Group portfolio model, product markets can be characterized on the basis of market share and market growth (Day, 1977), both of which are assumed to be linked to profitability. Applying this model to international markets, the growth rate for a given product market in each country and the company's market share can be examined. Assuming that world market share is a major objective, resources and effort should be shifted from countries with low rates of market growth to countries with high rates of market growth to enable the company to maintain or increase long-run global market share (Larreche, 1978). This does, however, necessitate availability or development of information relating to product-market growth. This could be developed from historical data.

This approach does not, however, take into consideration the possibility of cost economies for multiproduct companies nor of counterbalancing growth rates in different product markets. Companies may also prefer to concentrate efforts in countries with similar market characteristics, so that standardized strategies can be used in different countries throughout the world, thus reducing costs associated with strategy adaptation and development. This may also be true if there are significant costs of country-market entry or when products have shared marketing costs, for example, when they share a common sales force or distribution network or have a common brand identification (Doyle and Gigengil, 1976). Assessment of such economies does, however, require information, providing a breakdown of current and projected production and marketing costs for each product at different levels of output in each country considered.

A more complex approach is to follow a risk-return portfolio model (Wind and Douglas, 1981). This assumes that the allocation of effort to different product markets is based on the expected rate of return from each product market and the risks associated with operating in a given market. Risk can be limited by the mode of operation within a country. Licensing, for example, reduces the level of risk, though with a communsurate limitation on rate of return. The optimal combination of countries, target segments, and product markets, and modes of operation to maximize profitability relative to a given level of risk has thus to be evaluated in relation to all product markets, and countries under consideration.

This approach requires information related to the rates of return and risks associated with each of the components of the portfolio. A number of measures can be used to evaluate returns, such as net present value, ROI, net cash flow, or any other measure of performance for each product line in all countries to be considered. Attention needs to be paid to obtaining data that is comparable from one country to the next, particularly where the product line or segment differs and hence the basis for allocating overhead costs differs. Equally, accounting procedures or fiscal-authority requirements may vary, generating data that is not strictly comparable from one country to another.

Risk can be evaluated based on a number of indicators as discussed in relation to financial, political, and legal risks. Then the best set of alternative portfolios, can be selected, given some assumptions concerning the nature of risk management is willing to accept. In countries or product markets in which the company is not currently operating, management judgements with regard to the potential attractiveness and risks associated with these markets, can be obtained, applying an hierarchical approach (Saaty 1980). This enables extension of the range of portfolios to be considered beyond the product markets and countries where the company has current operations. Expansion into new product markets, segments and countries can thus be evaluated as well as divestment in other products or countries.

The impact of alternative international scenarios, for example, expected rates of inflation or sharp or moderate rises in oil prices, on expected rates of return has also to be taken into consideration. Since a variety of different scenarios may be feasible, estimation of the most likely scenarios and the probability of their occurrence may be desirable. Delphi techniques might be used. Once these scenarios have been identified, their impact on specific product markets and also on individual countries has to be determined. Again use of expert opinion or Delphi techniques may be effective.

The complexity of this approach, and in particular its information requirements, suggests that at this point in its development it is most likely to be appropriate only for multinational corporations with a highly diversified product line. In this case, the range of alternatives is sufficiently large, and hence potential impact on profitability of reallocating resources substantial enough, to warrant the cost and complexity of the data collection and assessment required. Other companies may prefer to use the less complex procedures, which have less stringent information and estimation requirements.

CONCLUSIONS

Collection of information is a key element in developing and implementing effective international business strategies. In particular, it is important to gather information relating to macroeconomic indicators in order to monitor the business-investment climate and marketing environment in different countries throughout tbe world.

Companies committed to international markets and global market expansion should develop an international information bank. This should link relevant macroeconomic, social, political, and technological indicators and information to internal company sales and market-performance data. Analyses of these data provide important input into decisions relating to market entry and the reallocation of resources on a global scale.

In domestic markets, an effective information system is essential to success. Because of the rapidly changing nature of international markets, the development of an efficient information system is even more important if the company is to remain a viable force in world markets. Yet even companies whose main focus is on domestic markets cannot afford to ignore international developments. The plight of the U.S. textile, television, automobile, and watch industries serves to underscore the importance of monitoring international development. Adoption of a global perspective in business is thus increasingly essential as the pace accelerates toward the emergence of a world economy and globally integrated markets.

SOURCES AND SUGGESTED REFERENCES

Armstrong, J.S. "An Application of Econometric Models to International Marketing," *Journal of Marketing Research*, Vol. VII, No. 2 (1970), pp. 190–198.

Berry, B.J.L. "Basic Patterns of Economic Development," in N. Ginsberg, ed. *Atlas of Economic Development*. Chicago: University of Chicago Press, 1961.

Bradley, D.G. "Managing Against Expropriation," *Harvard Business Review*, Vol. LV, (1977), pp. 75–83.

Business International. *B.I. Data*. New York: Business International, 1980.

Business Week, June 30, 1980.

Carr, R.P. "Identifying Trade Areas for Consumer Goods in Foreign Markets," *Journal of Marketing*, Vol. XII, (1978), pp. 76–80.

Cowen, J., R.R. Galan, F. Gallione, B. Gardner, C. Sullivan, and J-C. Tshishimbi. *International Expansion of PPG, Float Glass Technology*. Unpublished working paper, 1979.

Day, G.S. "Diagnosing the Product Portfolio," *Journal of Marketing*, Vol. XLII (1977), pp. 29–38.

Dickensheets, R.J. "Basic and Economical Approaches to International Marketing Research," in *Proceedings American Marketing Association*. Chicago: American Marketing Association, 1963.

Douglas, S.P., P. LeMaire, and Y. Wind. "Selection of Global Target Markets: A Decision-Theoretic Approach," in *Proceedings of the XXIII ESOMAR Congress*, September 1972.

———, and A. Macquin. *L'Utilisation du Style de Vie dans le Media Planning*. Paris: Jours de France, 1977.

Doyle, P., and Z. Gidengil. "A Strategic Approach to International Market Selection," in *Proceedings, European Academy for Advanced Research in Marketing*. Copenhagen: 1976.

Dun and Bradstreet. *Exporters' Encyclopaedia*. New York: Dun and Bradstreet, annual edition.

The Economist Intelligence Unit. *Marketing in Europe*. Special Reports, 1981.

———. *Quarterly Economic Reviews*. London: The Economist Intelligence Unit, 1981.

Euromonitor Publications Ltd. *European Marketing Data and Statistics*, London: Euromonitor Publications Ltd., 1981.

———. *International Marketing Data and Statistics*, 1977/1978.

International Financial Statistics, Washington, D.C.: International Monetary Fund.

Institutional Investor, September, 1979.

Johansson, J.K., and R. Moinpour. "Objective and Perceived Similarity of Pacific Rim Countries," *Columbia Journal of World Business* Vol. XII (1977), pp. 65–76.

Keegan, W.J. *Multinational Marketing Management*, 2nd ed. Englewood Cliffs, NJ: Prentice-Hall, 1980.

Kravis, I.B., A. Heston, and R. Summers. *International Comparisons of Real Product and Purchasing Power*, United Nations International Comparison Project: Phase II. Baltimore and London: Johns Hopkins University Press, 1978.

Larreche, J.C. "The International Product Market Portfolio," in S. Jain, ed. *Research Frontiers in Marketing: Dialogues and Directions*, Proceedings of the American Marketing Educators' Conference. Chicago: American Marketing Association 1978.

Levich, R.M. "Analyzing the Accuracy of Foreign Exchange Advisory Services: Theory and Evidence," in R.M. Levich and C.G. Wihlborg, eds. *Exchange Risk and Exposure*. Lexington, MA: D.C. Heath, 1980.

Liander, B. ed. *Comparative Analysis for International Marketing*. Boston: Allyn & Bacon, 1967.

Litvak, I.A., and P.M. Banting. "A Conceptual Framework for International Business Arrangement," in R.L. King, ed. *Marketing and the New Science of Planning*. Chicago: American Marketing Association, 1968.

McCann-Erickson. *Youth in Europe*. London: McCann-Erickson, 1978.

Moyer, R. "International Market Analysis," *Journal of Marketing Research*, Vol. V, (1968) pp. 353–360.

Piper, J.R. "How U.S. Firms Evaluate Foreign Investment Opportunities," *M.S.U. Business Topics*, Vol. XIX (1971), pp. 11–20.

Predicasts. *Worldcasts*. Cleveland: Predicasts. Annual.

The Price Waterhouse Information Guides, *Doing Business in . . . Value Added Tax*, etc.

"Rating Country Risk," *The Institutional Investor*, September 1979.

"The Reindustrialization of America," *Business Week*, special issue, June 30, 1980.

Rummel, R., and D. Heenan. "How Multinationals Analyze Political Risk," *Harvard Business Review*, Vol. LVI (1978), pp. 67–76.

Segnit, S. and S. Broadbent. "Lifestyle Research," *European Research*, Vol. I, No. 1 (1973), pp. 6–19; Vol I., No. 2 (1973), pp. 62–68.

Sethi, S.P. "Comparative Cluster Analysis for World Markets," *Journal of Marketing Research*, Vol. VIII (1971), pp. 348–354.

—— and David Curry. "Variable and Object Clustering of Cross-Cultural Data: Some Implications for Comparative Research and Policy Formulation," in S.P. Sethi and J.N. Sheth, eds. *Multinational Business Operations*. Pacific Palisades, CA: Goodyear Publishing, 1973.

Sheth, J., and R. Lutz. "A Multivariate Model of Multinational Business Expansion," in S.P. Sethi and J.N. Sheth, eds. *Multinational Business Operations*. Pacific Palisades, CA: Goodyear Publishing, 1973.

Saaty, T. *The Analytic Hierarchy Process*, New York: McGraw-Hill, 1980.

Stobaugh, R. "How to Analyze Foreign Investment Climates," *Harvard Business Review*, Vol. XLVI, (1969), pp. 100–108.

United Nations, *The Demographic Yearbook*, New York: United Nations, annual edition.

——. *Yearbook of Industrial Statistics*, New York: United Nations, annual edition.

Wind, Y. and S. Douglas. "International Portfolio Analysis and Strategy: The Challenge of the '80s," *Journal of International Business Studies*, special issue, Fall 1981.

World Bank, *World Tables*, 2nd ed. Baltimore: Johns Hopkins University Press, 1980.

MARKETING RESEARCH IN THE INTERNATIONAL ENVIRONMENT

CONTENTS

ISSUES IN CONDUCTING
INTERNATIONAL MARKETING
RESEARCH   4

Types of International Marketing
Research   4
Managerial Issues in International
Marketing Research   5
  Demand estimation   5
  International segmentation decisions   5
  Marketing-strategy development   5
  Strategic marketing planning   6
Issues in Designing International
Marketing Research   6
Organizational Issues in International
Marketing Research   7
  Centralization vs. decentralization   7
  In-house vs. external research
  services   8

TYPES OF DATA FOR
INTERNATIONAL MARKETING
RESEARCH   10

Secondary Data   11
Primary Data   11
  Selecting the sampling frame   12
  Sampling procedures   14
  Sampling techniques   16
  Sample size   17
  Comparability of sample composition   18
  Comparability in sampling procedures   18

INSTRUMENT DESIGN   19

Issues in Instrument Design   19
  Functional equivalence   20
  Conceptual equivalence   20
  Category equivalence   21
Potential Sources of Response Bias   21
  Social acquiescence or courtesy bias   22
  Topic bias   22
  Response style   22
  Respondent characteristics   22
Instrument Development and Question
Formulation   23
  Use of nonverbal stimuli   23
  Instrument translation   24
Response Format   26
  Scoring device   26
  Scoring procedures   28

DATA-COLLECTION PROCEDURES   29

Survey-Administration Techniques   29
  Mail surveys   30
  Telephone interviewing   30
  Personal interviewing   31
Data Quality   32
  Nonsampling error   32
  Sampling error   32

CONCLUSION   34

SOURCES AND SUGGESTED
REFERENCES   35

MARKETING RESEARCH IN THE INTERNATIONAL ENVIRONMENT

Susan P. Douglas
C. Samuel Craig

Prowess in domestic markets does not necessarily transfer to international markets. There are countless examples of blunders made by otherwise knowledgeable and successful companies entering international markets for the first time. Philip Morris, for example, tried unsuccessfully to convert Canadian smokers to one of its popular U.S. cigarette brands. Traditionally, Canadians have favored so-called Virginia-type tobacco blends, and despite a substantial advertising and promotional campaign, they retained their preference. General Mills encountered a similar misfortune with its Betty Crocker cake mixes in the U.K. market. The English housewife simply could not believe that a mix would be able to produce the exotic devil's food cake pictured on the package (Ricks *et al.*, 1974). In both cases, adequate prior market research would have revealed such potential problems.

Why do companies not engage in adequate market research? The answer lies in part in a lack of sensitivity to the differences in consumer tastes, preferences, and response patterns in foreign markets. The high costs associated with research in overseas markets and sometimes the lack of adequate research competence constitute further barriers to international market research. In addition, the conceptual, methodological, and organizational problems associated with such research in many cases lead companies to doubt its value.

Such attitudes are, however, largely unwarranted. Although it is true that research in international markets is often more expensive, of lower quality, and less reliable than comparable data in the U.S. market, it is nonetheless, essential to collect such data. Only with the aid of such information can effective international marketing strategies be developed and the costly mistakes of Philip Morris, General Mills, and numerous other shortsighted companies be avoided.

Secondary information sources useful in relation to market entry and resource allocation decisions are discussed in the following section. The present chapter aims to provide some guidelines for the collection of primary data in international markets, focusing in particular on multicountry research. Issues arising in relation to single-country research in foreign markets are not examined here, since they are similar to those in domestic market research, and are covered adequately elsewhere (Cochran, 1977; Green, 1978; Green and Tull, 1978; Lehmann, 1979; Sudman, 1976).

In this chapter, the major issues in designing multicountry research are examined first. Next the types of data and the associated sampling issues are discussed. Instrument design and alternative data-collection procedures are then covered. Finally, the main conclusions are highlighted.

ISSUES IN CONDUCTING INTERNATIONAL MARKETING RESEARCH

Two views are commonly held with regard to the design of international market research. The first holds that international market research is essentially the same as domestic market research. The second, on the contrary, conceives of international market research as a very different type of operation from single-country research, requiring a fund of experience and a combination of skills very different from that required for research in one country. The answer probably lies between these two extremes, as the same basic principles and procedures apply. However, a number of problems may arise that although present to some degree in domestic market research are magnified in conducting international research. To indicate more specifically what difficulties may be encountered, the various types of international market research are first examined, and the issues arising both from a managerial and a research standpoint are outlined.

TYPES OF INTERNATIONAL MARKETING RESEARCH.   The significance of problems arising in international marketing research depends on the specific type of international market research being conducted. In general, four types of international market research may be identified: (1) single-country research, (2) independent multicountry research, (3) sequential multicountry research, and (4) simultaneous multicountry research (Barnard, 1976). Single-country research is that undertaken in one country by a foreign company. Independent multicountry research is that undertaken by subsidiaries of multinational organizations in different countries and not coordinated across countries. In both of these cases, as noticed previously, the issues encountered are similar to those in domestic market research, and hence are not discussed further in this context.

In sequential multicountry research, research is conducted first in one country and then in other countries. This is attractive insofar as lessons learned in one country can be applied in another. This procedure may increase the efficiency of research, as the key findings of earlier studies influence the focus of later ones. In addition, costs are spread over a longer period.

Simultaneous multicountry research is research conducted at the same time in different countries, coordinated across countries. This is the most difficult to undertake and is particularly difficult to organize and coordinate. It tends to entail high costs and be relatively time-consuming. Consequently, although a growing number of such studies are beginning to be undertaken they are still relatively rare.

A number of conceptual and methodological issues also hamper the execution of such research. In the first place, the relevant unit of analysis, that is, country, group of countries, and target segments has to be selected. Then appropriate sampling and data-collection procedures have to be determined, in particular, whether the same procedures will be used in each country or location. Designing a research instrument that provides comparable results and is of equivalent reliability is a further consideration, particularly in view of the need for linguistic and stimulus translation from one context to another. Despite such difficulties, multicountry research is essential to the development of effective international marketing strategy and in making many tactical decisions with regard to foreign markets. These are next discussed in more detail.

MANAGERIAL ISSUES IN INTERNATIONAL MARKETING RESEARCH.   Research is an important input into a number of international marketing decisions. In the first place, research may be undertaken to estimate demand in foreign markets. Second, it may be designed to determine appropriate bases of international market segmentation. Research may also be required to determine whether various marketing-mix elements such as advertising and pricing should be standardized across countries or adapted to the idiosyncrasies of specific national or product markets. Finally, it is an important element in developing long-run strategy with regard to international markets.

Demand Estimation.   Here two types of research may be required. First, research may be required to estimate the income elasticity of demand. This measures the relationship between the amount demanded of various goods and economic progress, or, more specifically, how demand for goods changes with changes in levels of income (Moyer, 1968). This may aid in indicating how demand for a product will increase or decrease as income levels rise in different countries. Second, research may be required to estimate current demand, examining current market penetration, that is, the number of customers currently owning or purchasing the product, and repurchase rates. Similarly, surveys of purchase intentions and expected purchase rates may be undertaken to estimate future potential.

International Segmentation Decisions.   An important decision in developing international marketing strategy is how to segment international markets. Here a key decision is whether to segment markets on a country-by-country basis and then identify relevant segments within countries as in domestic markets (Wind and Douglas, 1972). Alternatively, transnational segments cutting across national boundaries may be appropriate. This requires investigation of whether the response patterns of similar segments or customer groupings, such as businessmen, teenagers, or upper-socioeconomic-status consumers in different countries are more similar to each other than to other segments within the same countries.

Research to determine the appropriate base for market segmentation may also be required. Here it is important to assess whether similar bases of segmentation can be used in different countries. Although in some countries certain benefit or life-style segments may be viable, these may not exist or be reached easily in other countries.

Marketing-Strategy Development.   In developing international marketing strategy, a fundamental decision is whether a global as opposed to a country-specific positioning strategy is selected. Products and concepts developed in relation to a specific national market need to be evaluated in other national markets to see whether they can be launched in these markets. In particular, evaluation of whether modification, either in the physical characteristics of the product or of its positioning relative to competing products and selected target segments, is required. Equally, research to determine whether and how concepts and products, for example, automobiles, can be developed specifically for multicountry markets may be desirable.

Appropriate operationalization of such positioning strategies in terms of marketing-mix tactics must also be examined. This requires testing the effectiveness of using the same advertising theme and copy or similar sales-promotion tools in each country. Research to assess whether price elasticities are similar in different countries, and hence similar pricing strategies can be used, may also be desirable. In relation to media and distribution decisions, the infrastructures are likely to differ from country to country and hence limit the feasibility of utilizing similar strategies.

Strategic Marketing Planning.   Research can also provide much valuable information in developing long-run marketing strategy. Here two major strategic issues need to be considered. The first concerns the selection of appropriate countries, product markets, target segments, and modes of operation in each of these markets for long-run market growth. This requires identification of opportunities in different countries and product markets (as well as assessment of the ease of effective market penetration and exploitation). The second concerns the extent to which similar product positioning strategies can be used and hence marketing strategies standardized across different countries, and economies of scale achieved relative to world markets. This requires assessment of the efficacy of standardized relative to country-specific production lines and communication appeals in different country markets.

Research can thus aid in making more effective strategic and tactical decisions relative to international markets. Observational and qualitative data can be useful in the exploratory stages of research and market entry. Survey research is, however, likely to constitute the primary mode of investigation in overseas markets, providing relevant quantitative information on which to base decisions. Consequently, the primary focus of this chapter is on the issues and problems arising in the design of survey research.

ISSUES IN DESIGNING INTERNATIONAL MARKETING RESEARCH.   Conducting research in multicountry markets is considerably more complex than conducting research in a domestic market. Traditional marketing-research concepts, designs, and measures are often ill suited and inadequate to cope with the problems encountered in a multicountry environment. In particular, the need to establish the conceptual and linguistic equivalence of measurement instruments and their interpretation gives rise to problems.

Many of the concepts, measurement instruments, and procedures to administer these have been developed and tested in the United States. Their relevance and applicability in other countries is, however, far from clear. Explicit administrative and analytic procedures for modifying and testing the relevance of concepts and measures developed in one country should thus be incorporated into the research design. In addition, procedures should enable the identification of concepts and measures unique to a specific country or culture. More specifically, it is suggested that a hybrid approach should be adopted (Wind and Douglas, 1980). Concepts and measures developed and tested in one national or cultural context, for example lifestyle statements, are then translated and adapted for use in other countries and contexts. Constructs and measures unique to a specific country or culture should also be identified. This suggests a need to conduct exploratory research to identify country-specific constructs and to test the applicability of those used in other national contexts. The relevance of both sets of measures, using either internal- or external-validation criteria, are then examined to determine what should be incorporated in the design. Potential biases associated with the use of various instrument administration and analysis procedures need also to be taken into consideration. Data-collection techniques such as personal interviewing, telephone, or mail surveys differ from country to country in terms of their reliability and sources of bias (Webster, 1966).

Elimination of cultural bias from data interpretation is also an important issue. Individual researchers are likely to interpret data in terms of their own cultural self-referent (Lee, 1966). Consequently it is desirable to develop research procedures allowing for participation of researchers from all cultures or countries investigated in both the development of research instruments and the stage of the data analysis and interpretation.

Although such procedures add considerably to research costs and time required to conduct the research, they are nonetheless important in developing more reliable and better-quality data for international marketing decisions. This is a necessary consideration insofar as much of the data available for making international marketing decisions tends to be scantier, of poorer quality, and less reliable than that available for domestic marketing decisions.

ORGANIZATIONAL ISSUES IN INTERNATIONAL MARKETING RESEARCH. In organizing and coordinating international marketing research, two main issues can be identified. The first concerns the extent to which research is centralized or decentralized within a corporation and is managed and organized by local subsidiaries or, alternatively, central headquarters. The second is whether in-house resources of a research department located either at central headquarters or locally are utilized, or external research services purchased from a large international research organization or from local suppliers.

Centralization vs. Decentralization.   The desired degree of centralization depends to a large extent on whether standardized or locally modified strategies are adopted. Centralization is likely to prove optimal in coordination of research across countries, but there is a danger of misinterpretation of local nuances and downplaying of environmental factors. If, on the other hand, a decentralized approach is adopted, emphasis is likely to be placed on local idiosyncratic factors at the expense of comparability across countries and cultures.

If a centralized approach is adopted, the central coordinating unit develops guidelines and establishes research specifications in the initial phases of the project. These are then communicated to local research units, or are centrally administered with little delegation to local research organizations (Berent, 1975; Adler, 1975; Barnard, 1976). Such an approach maximizes the coordination of research across countries, as well as facilitating control.

On the other hand, there is the danger of a cultural bias. A central coordinating unit is likely to favor a standard uniform research design with minimal adaptation to differences in local conditions (Adler, 1975). This considerably facilitates control of research. Problems of communication and coordination can, however, arise between the central organizing unit and the local units. Local research units are likely to complain that there is lack of attention to specific local factors and environmental conditions. Administrative costs may also be entailed in the development of coordination and control procedures.

Alternatively, a decentralized approach can be adopted. The major responsibility for development of the research design and its implementation is placed on local research units in each country, and coordination is provided through international committees and meetings (Adler, 1975). Whereas such an approach provides optimal adaptation to local conditions, problems with regard to comparability in research design are likely to arise, and an inclination to adopt a country-specific perspective is more likely to occur. Scheduling of fieldwork and reports also needs to be carefully planned, and frequently gives rise to some difficulties due to operation across geographic distances and international boundaries. Consequently, delays can occur in mailing or receipt of data and reports.

Standardized procedures for coding and categorization of data, as well as for data analysis and report preparation in order to ensure comparability are required (Franzen and Light, 1976). Development of standardized procedures is likely to be critical to ensure effective communication and coordination of local activities undertaken by researchers of different cultural backgrounds and different research traditions.

Problems arising in this context suggest that in various cases the fieldwork can most effectively be carried out from a central location. This is particularly desirable if sophisticated quantitative data-collection procedures are to be utilized. Questionnaires can thus be centrally developed and telexed to local branch units, and results telexed back for central analysis. If, however, emphasis is to be placed on adaptation of research instruments to the local environment, or if qualitative research is to be undertaken, more decentralization and allowance for local input and analysis will be required.

The organization of international research should thus strike a delicate balance between centralization and direction of research from central headquarters, and decentralization or local autonomy in research design and implementation. The former may result in lack of attention to specific local idiosyncracies and problems of implementation. The latter is likely to lead to research and data that is not comparable across countries. In particular, mechanisms to ensure effective communication and control between local operating units and central administrative units are essential.

In-House vs. External Research Services.   A second issue concerns the use of internal research capabilities versus the purchase of external research services. Here it is unlikely that many companies will have the in-house expertise to design and implement research for all international markets. The need for familiarity with the local research environment and multiple linguistic competence is typically critical for effective field research. Consequently, unless a study entails predominantly desk research, purchase of outside services is likely to be required.

The four largest, specialized organizations and the four largest full-service organizations are shown in Exhibit 1. The four largest are specialized services such as Nielsen, which provides retail-store audit data, and SAMI, which offers as its main service a warehouse-withdrawal monitoring service. The four largest full-service organizations offer worldwide research services including consumer, industrial, agricultural, and feasibility studies, and various data-collection and data-processing services. Sometimes these are carried out by local branch offices (Research International has, for example, offices in 30 countries) and sometimes by traveling multilingual executives using quality local suppliers.

Some organizations specialize in particular product markets. IMS International,

EXHIBIT 1a   THE FOUR LARGEST RESEARCH SUPPLIERS IN THE WORLD

	Worldwide Research Sales (1979 estimate) (millions of U.S. $)	Number of Countries with Office	Head Office
Nielsen	301.9	23	U.S.A.
IMS	88.8	51	U.S.A.
SAMI	55.5	1	U.S.A.
Arbitron	44.4	1	U.S.A.

EXHIBIT 1b   THE LARGEST FULL-SERVICE RESEARCH COMPANIES

	Worldwide Research Sales (1979 estimate) (millions of U.S. $)	Number of Countries with Office (Including Majority Holdings)	Head Office
Research International	42.2	30	U.K.
Infratest	33.3	3	Germany
GFK	28.9	6	Germany
AGB	28.9	5	U.K.

Source.   Barnard, 1980.

the second-largest research organization in volume of sales, is the dominant researcher in the pharmaceutical area, and offers audits and doctor panels worldwide. Other organizations specialize in qualitative market research, including discussion groups and projective techniques.

Most research tends to be *ad hoc,* that is, focusing predominately on product development and testing, attitude and image studies, and qualitative studies, as shown by the profile of the "typical" research market in Exhibit 2. In more industrialized countries, however, a higher proportion is spent on continuous, that is, audit or monitoring research, since understanding of the market, the primary purposes of *ad hoc* research, has already been gained. There is, of course variation from country to country in the type of research. In Australia, Malaysia, Denmark, and Finland there is substantial use of omnibuses. Equally, there are changes over time. In India, for example, there is less product testing than previously, as market monitoring and understanding of consumer tastes has grown.

Choice of organizations or type of service depends to a large extent on the type of research required, and in particular, the degree of methodological sophistication required. In the case of exploratory market research, use of traveling research executives and qualitative research may be appropriate. If more extensive *ad hoc* market surveys are required, use of one of the large international full-service organizations with offices in the countries to be investigated may be desirable. Similarly, if highly specialized research is required as, for example, in pharmaceuticals, use of organizations specialized in the product market is likely to be preferable.

In purchasing outside services, an important consideration is whether to purchase all services from the same supplier, or whether to "patch together" services from different suppliers. Use of a single supplier helps in building a working relationship

EXHIBIT 2   PROFILE OF "TYPICAL" RESEARCH MARKET
(BY VALUE IN %)

Continuous research	35
Ad hoc research	
Habit/attitude/image studies	15
Product development and testing (quantitative)	15
Qualitative	10
Industrial/agricultural/pharmaceutical/other nonconsumer	10
Others	5
Media research	5
Omnibuses	5

EUROPEAN MARKET RESEARCH MARKET STRUCTURE
(BY VALUE IN %)

Country	*Ad Hoc*	Continuous
Austria	62	38
Belgium	52	48
Denmark	75	25
Finland	60	40
France	69	31
West Germany	65	35
Greece	75	25
Ireland	67	33
Italy	50	50
Netherlands	65	35
Norway	55	45
Portugal	59	41
Spain	47	53
Sweden	48	52
Switzerland	59	41
United Kingdom	65	35

Source.   Barnard, 1978.

and minimizes the administrative effort required, but can, on the other hand, lead to a monopoly situation. As Exhibit 2 indicates, only a limited number of companies provide a range of services and are likely to cover all countries desired. Consequently, either such organizations are used or services are purchased from multiple suppliers, that is, medium and small *ad hoc* agencies. This will, however, entail substantial costs, inconvenience, and difficulties for management. Use of different suppliers for different projects and types of research (i.e., qualitative vs. survey research) may, however, be desirable.

TYPES OF DATA FOR INTERNATIONAL MARKETING RESEARCH

In collecting data for international marketing decisions, two types of data may be considered—secondary and primary. Secondary data are data already available and collected for other purposes, such as GNP or income data, or the Reader's Digest European Survey. Primary data are those expressly collected as input to a specific decision. In an international context these data are highly complementary in nature. Secondary data are frequently used in the early stages of research to identify countries and target segments and product markets to be examined. Primary data are collected in subsequent phases of research to determine appropriate marketing strategies and tactics to reach these segments and product markets.

SECONDARY DATA. The various sources of secondary data are covered in a later section of this handbook, and hence will not be reexamined here. The principal advantages of these data are their ready availability and low cost. They may eliminate the need to undertake primary data collection and provide some initial indication of the attractiveness of various markets.

The disadvantage of such data is that they are typically collected on a region, country, or region-within-country basis, and hence may not be comparable. This is the case even in relation to such vital data as population and GNP. In addition, these data are frequently somewhat out of date, which is often a critical limitation given the rapid pace of change in many international markets. They also tend to be macroindicators relating to factors such as income, population, the economy, or social trends, rather than the more specific market data required for marketing decisions.

The major problem is, however, that the data are aggregated across regions, countries, or regions within countries and thus tend to give the illusion of homogeneity. This masks the existence of wide diversity within many regions and countries. In Europe, for example, the wealthiest of the 119 regions of the Common Market, Hamburg, had an income in 1970 seven times as great as that of the poorest region, Irish West Country (Morello, 1977). Similarly, data relating to aggregate values or living patterns, as for example, the Yankelovich data (de Vulpian, 1974) or the Reader's Digest European Survey hide significant differences with regard to values or living standards among different sectors of the population.

In general, therefore, it is important to realize that although the country has traditionally been used as the relevant unit for defining the target population, this may not necessarily be appropriate. Countries are often highly heterogeneous with regard to a variety of factors such as language diversity, socioeconomic and technological development, social cohesion, and wealth. Consequently, the relevant target population might be subgroupings within countries such as cities, regions, communities, or cultural and minority subgroups such as teenagers, businessmen, blue-collar workers, or career women.

Since these groups face similar problems and decision situations from country to country, they may be expected to have similar behavior and response patterns (Douglas, 1976). In some cases these may be closer to those of a comparable segment in another country than to other groups within the same country (Thorelli *et al.,* 1975). Consequently, the relevant target population may consist of such segments considered transnationally or on a global basis.

For some purposes, clusterings of countries may exhibit similar patterns of behavior, and hence the country cluster is the relevant target population. In the automobile industry, for example, regional groupings of countries often define the relevant target market, because of the existence of economies of scale and the need for integration of small markets. The same also applies to the pharmaceutical industry.

PRIMARY DATA. Once secondary-data sources have been examined and have provided some initial indication about the nature of different markets, the next step is to collect primary data, tailored to meet information needs relating to specific management decisions. In particular, primary data are likely to be required in order to make tactical decisions for example, market segmentation or marketing-mix decisions relative to the extent to which strategies can be standardized across countries, or need to be adapted to specific national market conditions. Such data are also desirable in making long-term strategic target market selection decisions.

A first step in the collection of such data is the development of an appropriate sampling plan. Here two main issues are important: (1) the *representativeness* and (2) the *comparability* of the samples relative to the target population. In the multinational context, choice of appropriate sampling procedures is particularly complex, since it often involves sampling at multiple levels as well as determining the sequencing of sampling at each of these levels. Furthermore, cost considerations are often an important issue, and may dominate decisions relating to the choice of sampling procedures.

In designing a sampling plan, the first step is to find a sample frame appropriate for the target population. Then the appropriate respondents have to be selected. Next, techniques for sampling have to be selected, the sample size determined and procedures for dealing with sampling nonresponse established. Each of these steps is next discussed in more detail.

Selecting the Sampling Frame.   Once the target population to be sampled has been established, the sampling frame, or list of population elements from which the sample is to be drawn, has to be determined. In an international context, this frequently presents difficulties because of limited availability and inherent limitations of sampling frames such as electoral or municipal lists, directories, telephone books, or mailing lists available in domestic market research. When available, they frequently do not provide adequate coverage, particularly in less developed countries, and hence give rise to frame error.

The most aggregate level at which a sampling frame can be constructed is the world; the next level consists of geographic regions such as Europe or Latin America. Following this is the country, and the geographic units or other subgroups within countries, for example, regions, cities, precincts, neighborhoods, or local associations and community groups.

The level at which the sampling frame is developed will depend in part on the specific product market and research objectives and the availability of lists at each level. The sequencing of research and whether, for example, one region or country is investigated first and then another will also determine the appropriate level for constructing a sampling frame. The advantages and limitations of each of these levels as sampling frames are next discussed in more detail.

World.   The first level at which a sampling frame may be developed is the world. This is likely to be appropriate in industrial markets, such as injection molders, surgical equipment, machine tools, and mainframe computers. In industrial markets, worldwide or regional lists of manufacturers can be obtained from sources such as Bottin International, which registers names and addresses of over 300,000 firms in 110 countries under 1000 product classifications, by trade and by country, and *Kelly's Manufacturers and Merchants Directory,* which lists firms in the United States and other major trading countries in the world. In some cases, trade associations are able to provide such information. These are listed in the *World Guide to Trade Associations.*

Use of a world sampling frame is likely to be relatively rare in the case of consumer research. It might, however, occur if the target population is a relatively small transnational market segment. For example, subscribers to the *National Geographic* or American Express card holders might be appropriate sampling frames for testing a new foreign-travel publication. Similarly, subscribers to *European Research* might be an appropriate sampling frame for testing new market-research services. The major restriction on the use of sampling frames that transcend national boundaries is thus likely to be the availability of appropriate sampling lists of the target population.

Country Groupings.   The next level for developing a sampling frame is that of country groupings. These are most likely to be regional. As in the case of global sampling frames, regional sampling frames are most likely to exist in industrial markets. Regional listings of manufacturing companies, banks, and other organizations, such as the *Directory of European Associations* (1976) may, for example, be found, particularly in the more-developed countries.

In some cases, however, regional sampling frames suitable for consumer markets may also be available. *Paris Match,* for example, has an extensive number of subscribers throughout Europe, and the *Economist,* among English-speaking businessmen throughout the world. But it is important to note that these will generate a relatively particular sample, and hence relevance to the desired target population needs to be assessed.

Country.   The country is the most commonly used level for developing a sampling frame in multicountry research. Here frames such as electoral lists, population censuses, and telephone books can be utilized. It should, however, be recognized that such sampling frames are not always available, particularly in developing countries, and in addition coverage will vary.

Sampling frames commonly used in U.S. market research, such as electoral or municipal lists, census tract and block data, or telephone listings, are often not available or are not current in other countries. For many years, for example, neither Cairo nor Teheran, with populations of 8 and 5 million respectively, have had a telephone book. Some countries, notably in Southeast Asia and Africa, lack any type of population lists, and hence sampling frames have to be constructed from scratch. In many cities in South America and Asia, even street maps are not available, and in extreme cases (for example, Saudi Arabia) streets have no names and houses are not numbered.

Different biases may also be inherent in different sampling frames. In most countries outside the United States, for example, use of telephone lists (except in the case of industrial research) will provide a relatively skewed sample. Similarly, use of block data will not necessarily ensure a random sample, and may result in underrepresentation of lower socioeconomic respondents living in caves, hovels, or riverboats.

Subcountry Groupings.   The next level of sampling frames is subgroups within countries. These might be geographic units such as cities or neighborhoods, or ethnic, racial, cultural, age, or demographic subgroupings such as Catholics, Protestants, blacks, Indians, foreigners of different origins, children, cat owners, members of the

PTA, or senior citizens. Similarly, in an organizational context, specific industries or organizations within certain regions might constitute the relevant population.

The availability of an appropriate sampling frame is likely to vary with the specific subgrouping. For geographic units, this is likely to pose the least problem, if maps or local electoral lists can be obtained. In some countries, however, even such frames may not be available. Information on demographic groupings will generally be available from census data, and religious groups from church membership or organizations. Greater difficulties may be encountered getting information on other ethnic groups unless there are local ethnic organizations.

The Choice of Respondent. Once the sampling frame has been determined, the specific respondents to be sampled have to be determined. Here, as in domestic market research, an important consideration is whether a single respondent is used or whether multiple respondents will be required, for example, husbands, wives, and children in the family, or buyers, users, prescriptors, and gatekeepers in organizations.

This decision depends to a large extent on the degree of involvement of different participants in purchase decisions. In organizations, for example, the purchasing agent may merely act as the agent in making purchases, whereas actual decisions about what to purchase are made by a buying committee or are influenced by the user. Similarly, in the household the housewife may act as the agent in purchasing food and groceries, but choice decisions may be heavily influenced by other family members and explicit purchase requests or feedback on choices may be important. Consequently, multiple respondents may be desirable.

Identification of the relevant respondent(s) in each country is also an important consideration, since these may vary from country to country. In some countries, for example, there may be a tendency among organizations toward highly centralized decision making. Hence the industrial buyer may be merely an agent. In Anglo-Saxon cultures, on the other hand, there is a greater tendency to delegate authority. Consequently, the buyer may play an important role.

Similarly, among upper socioeconomic families in Latin American countries and among white non-Afrikaaner South African families, the maid is frequently responsible for purchasing food and groceries. Therefore, relevant participation in purchase decisions is difficult to ascertain. This is in marked contrast to the family decision making common in relation to grocery purchasing in the United States, or the housewife-dominated decision making more prevalent in Europe. Prior examination of such factors is therefore necessary to determine appropriate choice of respondent(s).

Sampling Procedures. The next step is to determine appropriate sampling procedures. Here a first consideration is whether research is to be undertaken in all countries and contexts, or whether results and findings are generalizable from one country or context to another.

Ideally, research should be conducted in all countries and contexts in relation to planned marketing operations. In some cases, given the high costs of multicountry research, management may consider it desirable to use findings in one country as a proxy for another. For example, market response patterns in Scandinavian countries may be sufficiently similar to sample only one of these countries. Similarly, response patterns in the Netherlands may be sufficiently close to those in Germany to generalize from a survey of the Dutch to the German market. It is, however, important to realize that such a procedure is fraught with danger. Even though previous experience suggests that response patterns are the same in both countries, this may change, or not be relevant in relation to the specific case examined.

Furthermore, there is a trade-off between the number of countries in which research is undertaken and the depth or quality of the research. Either a limited number of countries can be investigated in depth or a larger number can be studied, but less extensively. This often becomes an important issue when the sampling lists have to be developed or extensive interviewer training is required. Consequently, substantial costs may be entailed in generating reliable, good-quality data, and it may be more desirable to investigate a single or limited number of countries rather than several countries with less reliable methods.

Differences in the cost-effectiveness of research organizations from one country to another is often an important consideration in this regard. Costs do not always parallel wage rates in each country but also depend on the efficiency and experience of market-research organizations. As Exhibit 3 indicates, research costs are, for example, substantially lower in the United Kingdom than in the rest of Europe, largely because the market-research infrastructure is better developed in the United Kingdom. Consequently, it may be desirable to select a country where research organizations are more cost-effective or to use these as the preferred location from which to conduct international market research.

The importance attached to representativeness as opposed to comparability is a consideration. Data can be collected that are representative of the countries or contexts studied, drawing, for example, probability or quota samples. Such samples are, however, unlikely to be equivalent with regard to variables such as income, education, age, or size, or organization, structure, and industry, because the underlying distribution of these variables varies from country to country. If, on the other hand, the samples are comparable and matched on key background characteristics, national representativeness will be lost.

The selection of sampling procedures is related to decisions with regard to how the data will be collected. Use of mail questionnaires requires, for example, the existence of a mailing list, whereas personal interviews facilitate the use of cluster sampling. In establishing sampling procedures, a decision has to be made about whether random or purposive sampling should be used. The sample size has to be determined, as well as procedures for dealing with nonresponse.

EXHIBIT 3   INDEX OF FIELDWORK OUT OF POCKET (INCLUDING SOCIAL) COSTS, 1980[a]

Austria	1.8	Italy	2.0
Belgium	1.7	Netherlands	1.7
Denmark	2.6	Norway	2.3
Finland	1.6	Spain	1.6
France	2.2	Sweden	3.4
Germany	2.4	Switzerland	2.6
Greece	0.9		

Source. Marketing Research Society Newsletter, June 1980.
[a]United Kingdom = 1.0.

Sampling Techniques.   The distinction between probabilistic sampling and purposive sampling is an important one. In probabilistic sampling, each respondent in the target population has an equal chance of being in the sample. In purposive, or judgmental, sampling some criteria are established on the basis of which respondents are selected. Although in domestic market research, random, or probabilistic, sampling is generally considered to be the most desirable, this is not always the case in international market research. Difficulties of obtaining reliable sampling frames and costs associated with their development suggest that other methods such as judgment or convenience sampling may be more cost-effective. Alternatively, samples matched across countries with regard to key background characteristics may be desired, suggesting the use of quota sampling.

Random Sampling.   A major problem with the use of random sampling in international market research is that it requires the existence of a frame or list. Respondents are then picked at random from this list, selecting, for example, every *n*th name or person successively, until the desired sample size is obtained. These respondents constitute the sample population and are then questioned by personal interview, mail, or telephone. This technique is, however, difficult to apply in many developing countries because of the limited availability of appropriate sampling frames.

In cases where no adequate sampling frame is available, an alternative procedure is to use the *random walk* method. The interviewer then also becomes the sampler. The interviewer is provided with a walk route and instructed to select every *n*th house to interview (Frey, 1970). This actually sounds easier than it is, since the interviewer may have difficulty following the route or determining exactly what constitutes a "dwelling unit" in urban slums or villages, or where buildings include multiple dwelling units. Such difficulties suggest why random sampling, although from a statistical standpoint the only valid procedure, has frequently been replaced by the use of purposive or judgmental sampling.

Judgmental Sampling.   Another procedure is to select respondents based on judgment. This may be particularly appropriate in certain industrial markets, where "experts" can provide valuable information, as for example in the aerospace industry or where specific individuals are known to have key influence. The sales force is often a valuable source of information, since they know customer needs and interests, though care should be taken in using them, for example, to obtain quantitative estimates of sales potential. Importers or export agents may also be used as "key informants," though some bias may be introduced reflecting their own self-interests.

This procedure may also be used in consumer markets, notably in developing countries. Here questioning of village elders, priests, or other local authority figures may provide a reliable method of obtaining information about the number of inhabitants, current purchase behavior, and problems. This may be particularly desirable in countries with high levels of illiteracy, where the purpose of the research is to estimate sales potential rather than response to alternative marketing strategies.

Quota Sampling.   A procedure commonly used in both industrialized and developing countries is quota sampling. The number of respondents required within a given category (e.g., in consumer research, in different age or income groups, working vs. nonworking wives, or in industrial markets, industry or firm size) is specified. Again, this procedure is particularly likely to be appropriate for industrial markets, where, depending on the product, customers are likely to be found in specific industries. Although this procedure ensures that the sample will be representative on the selected quota characteristics, there is clearly a danger that these characteristics are systematically associated with other factors, which will introduce confounding effects (Campbell and Stanley, 1963).

In a comparison of consumer innovators in France and the United States, for example (Green and Langeard, 1975), the French population was stratified along the variables of age, income, education, and employment status to ensure equivalence to the U.S. population on these characteristics. This stratification, rather than any fundamental differences in innovative behavior, may account for their lower levels of communication about grocery products and less television viewing compared with the U.S. sample, since they come from the more-sophisticated, better-educated elite of the French population.

Convenience Sampling.   Another alternative is to use convenience sampling. This implies selecting any respondent who is readily available. In developing countries, for example, convenience sampling in the marketplace provides a low-cost procedure for generating a sample (Mayer, 1978). Given the difficulties and costs of developing reliable sampling frames in such countries, this is often appropriate for developing a sample that although not strictly representative, may nonetheless be free of any systematic bias.

Sometimes in cross-national research, sample designs involve a mix of different approaches. In industrial market research, for example, specific industries may be selected for investigation and then quota sampled within each industry. Similarly, different regional units or areas, for example, certain major cities in industrialized countries, or villages in developing countries, may be selected. Then random-walk or block sampling within the city, or judgmental sampling of village elders can be applied.

Sample Size.   Another important decision concerns the appropriate sample size. Here, assuming a fixed budget, there is a trade-off between the number of countries or contexts sampled, the sample size within each country, and the extensiveness of the data collected from each respondent. As in many domestic market-research projects, a choice has to be made between small samples and high-quality in-depth research or larger samples and less extensive data.

Use of statistical procedures to determine appropriate sample size poses some difficulties, since to apply these procedures, some estimation of population variance is required (Cochran, 1977). In many cases these may not be available or where available may differ from one country to another. Hence appropriate sample sizes can only be determined on a country-by-country, rather than transnational, basis. Sample sizes may thus in many cases be determined arbitrarily, on an *ad hoc* basis. Management may, for example, decide that samples of 200–300, or 20 focus groups in each country, are required.

Diversity with regard to other factors within country units also needs to be taken into consideration. Differences with regard to the distribution of key determinants and related variables or sampling characteristics such as income, age, and education are likely to arise. This suggests that larger-than-normal sample sizes are likely to be required to test for the impact of differences in these variables on cross-national findings. This does, however, entail high sampling costs and hence may pose difficulties from a budgetary standpoint. Use of large sample sizes such as those in the *Reader's Digest European Survey* or the Leo Burnett/International lifestyle survey, are, therefore, rare.

Small sample sizes may, however, be defensible, particularly in the exploratory stages of research, where there is likely to be less concern with representativity. Use of large samples, although increasing statistical reliability and reducing random error, may increase error from nonsampling sources (Lipstein, 1975; Frey, 1970). Additional interviewers will be required, as well as additional coders, thus increasing the possibility of errors from interviewing and data processing. Consequently, additional quality controls will be required, necessitating expenditures to train competent interviewers and to supervise editing and coding. This is likely to pose problems in international market research, particularly in developing countries, where the quality of fieldwork may be frequently poor, and availability of trained interviewers or qualified research organizations limited.

Comparability of Sample Composition.   A key issue in developing a sampling design is the importance attached to the representativity as opposed to the comparability of the samples. If samples are drawn that are representative of the target population, they are unlikely to be comparable with regard to certain key characteristics such as income, age, and education. This can create a problem if, as is frequently the case, such variables affect the behavior or response pattern studied. For example, in comparing interest in tropical fruit in different countries, income or education might be important factors affecting response. Mistaken inferences about national differences or similarities in interest in tropical fruits might, therefore, be made, when these reflect differences between samples in income distribution, rather than "true" national differences. One might, for example, conclude there was lack of adequate market potential, when in fact a small high-income segment constituted a potential spearhead for market entry. Equally, a myriad of other factors, such as life-style patterns or subcultural influences, may vary across countries. These introduce a confounding effect that may make it extremely difficult to isolate the impact on the behavior studied.

Statistical procedures can be used to evaluate the impact of different sample compositions on results. Either univariate or multivariate analysis of covariance can be conducted, with the different countries or target populations being entered as experimental units and the sampling characteristics as covariates. Tests of the significance of the covariates indicate whether findings are attributable to differences in the composition of national samples. Covariance analysis can also be used to adjust national means for differences in sampling characteristics, so that the impact of such variables is removed from the analysis, as well as identifying the strength of the association for specific variables. Initial applications of this procedure (Douglas, 1980) suggest, however, that substantial differences in composition will be required before there is a significant effect on results.

Comparability in Sampling Procedures.   A further issue is whether the same sampling procedures are used. Sampling procedures vary in reliability from one country to another. Thus rather than using identical sampling procedures and methods in each country, it may be preferable to use different methods or procedures that have equivalent levels of accuracy or reliability (Webster, 1966). If, for example, in one country random sampling is of known validity and in another country quota sampling is known to be of equivalent validity, the results will be more comparable in terms of response rate and quality of response if two different procedures are used than if the same sampling procedure were used. Similarly, it is not safe to assume that if the same sampling procedures are used in each country with known biases, the results will automatically be comparable (Holt and Turner, 1970). A sampling procedure underestimating commercial travelers might have a different effect in various countries because of a different incidence of commercial travelers. Thus the results would not be comparable.

Similarly, costs of sampling procedures may differ from country to country. Cost savings achieved by using the same method in many countries and centralizing analysis, coding and so forth, may be outweighed by use of the most efficient sampling method in each country. For example, in one country random sampling may necessitate the purchase of a special list at a high price, whereas in another country quota sampling produces acceptable results at half the cost. Consequently it may be more appropriate to use the quota method in the latter country while using random sampling in the first.

Differences in sampling methods can also be utilized to provide a check on the reliability of results and potential bias in different methods. In one industrial survey, different sampling procedures with different sources of potential bias were used in five different countries (Webster, 1966). A constant pattern was found on one of the main variables studied, namely, the percentage of firms in each size category owning the test product. If the same sampling procedure had been utilized in each country, this might not have been detected.

In brief, therefore, use of similar sampling procedures will not necessarily ensure comparability of results, since each procedure is subject to different types of bias, and these vary from country to country. Deliberate variation of procedures, on the other hand, if intelligently used, can provide a means for checking the validity of results and detecting biases inherent in different types of procedures.

INSTRUMENT DESIGN

Once sampling procedures have been set up to obtain the desired data, the next step is the design of the research instrument. Here, as in other aspects of international market research, a key issue is to establish the comparability of the research instrument in different countries and cultural contexts. In so doing, it is important to ensure that the research instrument is adapted to the specific national and cultural environment and is not biased in terms of any one country or culture. Such bias may enter in both the design and development of the instrument, as well as in its application and scoring.

Bearing such factors in mind, the issues arising in instrument design for multicountry research are first examined. The main focus is on survey research and questionnaire design, since these are the methods predominantly used in multicountry research. The various sources of response bias associated with survey instruments are discussed. Issues with regard to instrument translation and use of verbal and nonverbal stimuli are then covered. Finally, different methods of instrument calibration and scoring procedures are discussed.

ISSUES IN INSTRUMENT DESIGN.   In designing a research instrument for survey research, the key aspects concern: (1) the method of approach to the respondent, that is, how the sponsorship and/or purpose of research is presented and the degree of confidentiality promised, (2) how questions are formulated and in what sequence or order they are asked, and (3) what response format is used, and (4) whether these are precoded or unstructured (Oppenheim, 1966). In multicountry research, instrument design becomes even more complex because of the multilinguistic and sociocultural contexts.

Equivalence of comparability of the content, that is, behavior and topics studied, has to be established. Different response biases may also tend to be more or less prevalent, or be a source for concern in different countries and cultures. Operation in multilingual and cultural contexts also implies that instruments, whether verbal or nonverbal, will need to be translated so that they have equivalent meaning in each context. High levels of illiteracy imply that use of nonverbal stimuli instead of, or in conjunction with, verbal stimuli may be desirable. Finally, differences in perception and ability to grasp both verbal and nonverbal stimuli imply that response scales and formats will need to be designed to eliminate or reduce bias arising from such sources. It may also be desirable to include a test that alerts the researcher to the presence of such biases.

Functional Equivalence. In examining the equivalence of the research context, a first issue to be considered in conducting international marketing research is that the behaviors studied may not necessarily be *functionally* equivalent and have the same role or function in all countries and contexts studied (Berry, 1969). Thus, for example, although bicycles are predominantly used for recreation in the United States, in the Netherlands, as in various developing countries, they provide a basic mode of transportation. This implies that in designing the research instrument, the relevant competing product set will need to be defined differently in the two contexts. In the United States it will include other recreational products, whereas in the Netherlands it will include alternative modes of transportation.

Similarly, in examining different components of life-style in different countries or cultures, apparently similar activities may have different functions. In some countries such as the United States, for example, adult education may be regarded a leisure activity, whereas in other contexts, for example, Japan, it is designed to improve work performance. In the same way, whereas shopping is predominantly a work activity in the United States, in other cultures and countries, it is an important aspect of social life.

Conceptual Equivalence. Another and related issue is that of the *conceptual* equivalence of different attitudes and behavior in different countries and contexts. A personality trait such as aggressiveness may not be relevant in all countries and cultures, or may be expressed in different types of behavior, hence requiring different measures. Some attitudes or behavior may be unique to a specific country or culture. The concept of *philotimo,* or conformity to norms and values of the in-group, and the importance attached to making sacrifices to family, friends, and others is, for example, unique to the Greek culture (Triandis and Vassilou, 1972).

Examination of this issue is particularly necessary in relation to attitudinal, psychographic, and life-style variables, which cannot be objectively measured. Even where the same construct is identified, it may best be tapped by different types of statements in different cultural settings. Innovativeness, for example, may be a relevant construct in both the United States and France. In the United States it is commonly measured by self-designated measures and statements such as ''I frequently talk about new products with friends and neighbors," or "I am generally the first among my friends to buy a new product." In France, however, to be innovative is not socially valued, and in addition, new food products or brands are not a common topic of discussion (Green and Langeard, 1975). Consequently, use of behavioral rather than attitudinal measures will be preferable.

Similarly, social interaction is measured in the United States by statements such as "We frequently dine with friends." This is not appropriate to measure social interaction in other cultural contexts, such as developing countries, where dining with friends is not a common practice, and meals are taken almost exclusively with the family. Social interaction may take other forms such as participation in communal dancing or other festivities.

Such problems can also arise in relation to behavioral variables. For example, the question "Are you engaged?" has a different meaning in different cultures (Berent, 1965). In the United Kingdom it implies a formal commitment to be married, whereas in Italy and Spain it merely means having a boyfriend or girlfriend.

Category Equivalence.   Equivalence with regard to different categories also has to be established. Product class definitions may, for example, differ from one country to another. In the soft-drink and alcoholic-beverage market, for example, forms of soft drinks such as carbonated sodas, fruit juices, and powdered and liquid concentrates vary significantly from one culture to another. In Mediterranean cultures, for example, beer is considered to be a soft drink (Berent, 1975). Similarly, in the dessert market, items that are included will vary substantially, ranging from apple pie, jellies, and ice cream to baklava, rice pudding, and zabaglione. In some societies, cakes or cookies are included as desserts, whereas in China sweet items do not form part of the meal. This implies that what is included in the relevant competing product set will vary. Careful attention to such factors is thus an important consideration when designing concept or product tests, or alternatively, developing product-related measures.

Equivalence has also to be considered in relation to demographic characteristics. In the case of marital status, for example, in various African countries it is not uncommon for a man to have several wives, and in some cases women may have several husbands. Occupational categories also do not always have strict equivalence in all countries. The counterpart of the U.S. lawyer or the Japanese subway packer may be difficult to find. Occupations may also have different status categories in different countries and societies. Priests and ministers, for example, often occupy higher prestige categories in the less-developed than in the more literate industrialized nations. Similarly, the social prestige attached to government administrative positions or to being a lawyer varies from society to society.

POTENTIAL SOURCES OF RESPONSE BIAS.   Once the equivalence or comparability of the content of the research has been established, the next step is to design the research instrument. First, it is important to establish a method of approach and questionnaire administration that avoids generating a response bias. Here four major types of bias can be identified: that (1) arising from a respondent's desire to be socially acquiescent, (2) arising from the topic being considered, (3) arising from specific response styles such as yea-saying, and (4) associated with specific categories or types of respondents.

Social Acquiescence or Courtesy Bias. The desire to provide the socially desirable response, and in cases where an interviewer is present to give the response wanted by the interviewer, is particularly prevalent in certain countries and contexts. This type of bias appears to be particularly common in Asia, everywhere from Japan to Turkey (Mitchell, 1965). Some of the effects of this bias can be reduced by concealing sponsorship of the study, more effective training of interviewers, and more careful wording of questions to avoid use of "moral" or judgmental wording. In particular, it is important to maximize the ease of providing a socially unacceptable response by prefacing questions with phrases such as, "Some people feel this way, some people feel that way—how do you feel?"

Topic Bias. Differences also arise with regard to topics that are socially sensitive in different national and cultural contexts. Willingness to respond to questions about income or discuss topics such as sex or alcoholism vary from one country or culture to another. In the Scandinavian countries, for example, respondents are considerably more willing to admit to overdrinking than in Latin countries (Lovell, 1973). In India, sex tends to be a taboo topic.

  This suggests the need to identify what topics are socially sensitive in each country and cultural context. Measures to reduce bias from this source, as, for example, by collecting observational data or using an influential sponsor or improved interviewer probing techniques, can thus be introduced.

Response Style. Differences in response-style bias from country to country also occur. Studies have, for example, found variation in the existence of yea-saying and nay-saying (Chun *et al.*, 1974) and also in tendencies to use extreme points in verbal ratings (Douglas and LeMaire, 1974). Another study, applying multiple-scaling devices, suggested, however, that such tendencies were "true" responses, rather than an artifact of the scaling device (Crosby, 1969).

  This suggests the need to use multiple-scaling instruments such as unipolar and bipolar scales as well as Likert or other types of scales to check for the existence of such biases. In addition, where scales equivalent to the Crowne-Marlowe measure (Crowne and Marlowe, 1964) or other similar scales measuring social acquiescence, and adapted to specific cultural environments are available, these should also be included.

Respondent Characteristics. Differences in response bias have also been found to be related to certain respondent characteristics. These appear in general to be the same in different countries and cultures. Yea-saying and nay-saying biases, have, for example, been found, in other countries as in the United States, to be stronger among women, the less-educated, and respondents of lower socioeconomic status (Landsberger and Saavedra, 1967). Item nonresponse has also been found to be related to similar factors, namely, sex, age, and education (Douglas and Shoemaker, 1979) in nine European countries.

  This suggests that the distribution of different national samples on variables such as income and education will need to be examined, to identify the extent to which such factors are likely to affect the comparability of results. In general, however, preliminary research indicates that substantial differences in such distributions will be required, before there is any significant effect (Douglas and Shoemaker 1979).

INSTRUMENT DEVELOPMENT AND QUESTION FORMULATION. Once the mode of approach to avoid response bias has been determined, the next step is to develop an instrument and decide how questions should be posed. In this context, high levels of illiteracy in many developing countries suggest that use of nonverbal stimuli may be desirable. In addition, administration of the instrument in multilinguistic and cultural contexts will require translation to ensure instrument comparability.

Use of Nonverbal Stimuli.   Where research is conducted in countries or cultures with high levels of illiteracy, as for example, Africa and the Far East, (Exhibit 4) it is often desirable to use nonverbal stimuli such as show cards. Questionnaires can

EXHIBIT 4   ILLITERACY IN DEVELOPING COUNTRIES[a]

Country	Year	Percentage of Illiteracy	Year	Percentage of Illiteracy
Ethiopia	1965	94.0	—	—
Senegal	1961	94.4	—	—
Liberia	1962	91.1	—	—
Afghanistan	—	—	1975	87.8
Nigeria	1963	84.6	—	—
Morocco	1960	86.2	1971	78.6
Pakistan	1961	84.6	—	—
United Arab Republic	1960	80.5	—	—
Libya	1964	78.3	—	—
Iran	1966	77.0	1971	63.1
India	1961	72.2	1971	66.6
Syria	1960	70.5	1970	60.0
Jordan	1961	67.6	—	—
Honduras	1961	64.8	1974	43.1
Guatemala	1964	62.1	1973	53.9
Turkey	1960	61.9	1975	39.7
Zambia	1963	58.6	1969	52.7
Nicaragua	1963	50.4	1971	42.5
Malaysia	—	—	1970	41.5
Peru	1961	39.4	1972	27.5
Brazil	1960	39.3	1970	33.8
Portugal	1960	38.1	1980	29.0
Dominican Republic	1960	35.5	1970	32.8
Mexico	1960	34.6	1970	25.8
Venezuela	1961	34.2	1971	23.5
Thailand	1960	32.3	1970	21.4
Ecuador	1962	32.2	1974	25.8
Colombia	1964	27.1	1973	19.2
Panama	1960	26.7	1970	21.7
Paraguay	1962	25.2	1972	19.9
Sri Lanka	1963	24.9	1971	22.4

Source.   U.S. Department of Commerce, 1969.
[a]Improvement during 1960s indicated in selected countries.

be administered orally by an interviewer, but respondent comprehension will be facilitated if pictures of products or concepts or test packs are provided.

Show cards such as those shown in Exhibit 5 and 6 can, for example, be used in concept testing or to assist in answering product-usage questions. Product samples can also be shown to respondents. A drawback of this approach is that respondents tend to become irritated if the samples are removed for the next interview. Consequently, it is wise to be able to leave a free sample or alternative reward (Corder, 1978).

Even where literacy levels are high, it may be desirable to use nonverbal stimuli as a complement to verbal stimuli to provide a check on instrument equivalence and potential biases from instrument translation and adaptation to different linguistic and cultural contexts.

Instrument Translation.   Both verbal and nonverbal stimuli require translation for use in different linguistic and cultural contexts. Where a verbal instrument is used, a procedure widely advocated in the social sciences is that of *back-translation* (Brislin, 1970, Werner and Campbell, 1970). A questionnaire is translated from the initial or base language by a native speaker of the language of translation and then retranslated back into the original language by a native speaker of that language.

EXHIBIT 5   SHOW CARDS

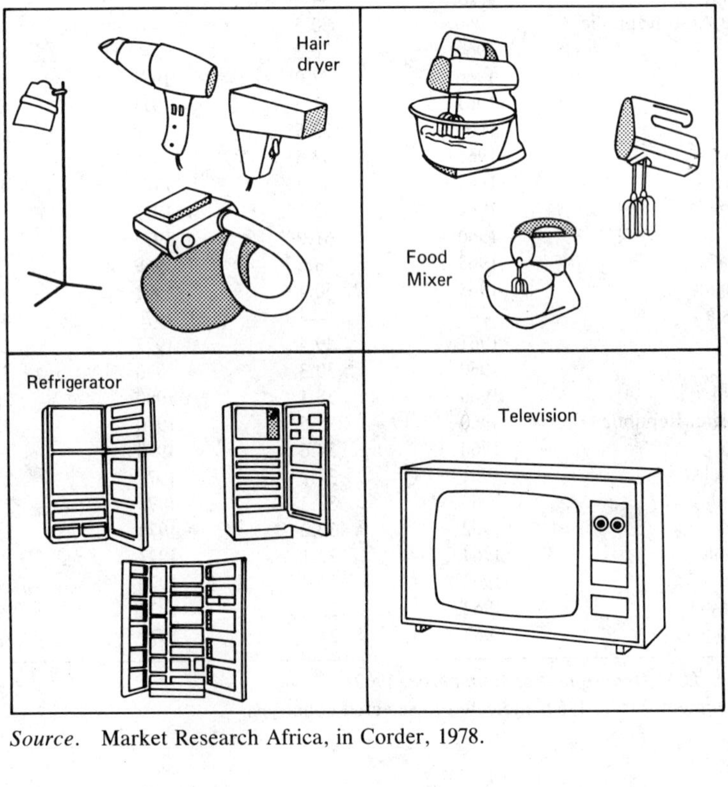

Source.   Market Research Africa, in Corder, 1978.

Although useful in identifying translation errors, back-translation is not always totally effective (Brislin, 1970). Bilinguals often develop a particular language structure and usage and hence may not translate into the idiom commonly used by the mass of the population. Furthermore, back-translation assumes the existence of equivalent terms and concepts in all languages and that a "totally loyal" translation is required. This may not always be the case. The terms *fair play* and *lonesomeness* are, for example, difficult to render in German (Brislin *et al.*, 1973). Also, in some cases it may be more desirable to translate into equivalent colloquial phrases, rather than attempting to make a "totally" faithful and accurate translation.

Such considerations suggest that use of *parallel* translation may be desirable (Frey, 1970). A committee of translators conversant with at least two of the languages employed can then go through successive iterations of translation and retranslation. In international market research, members of different local research organizations

EXHIBIT 6   INTERVIEW SHOW CARD USED IN CONSUMER SURVEY IN SOUTH AFRICA[a]. (ASSIST TO ANSWER QUESTION "WHAT IS YOUR SEWING MACHINE USED FOR?")

Source.   Singer Sewing Machine Company, New York.
[a]This freehand style of drawing proved to have good appeal in interviews conducted in developing countries.

could be used. This could result in *decentering* of the original questionnaire (Werner and Campbell, 1970), so that the terminology is equally comprehensible in all language contexts, and the dominance of one language structure and cognitive context is eliminated.

In addition, in countries such as Belgium, India, Canada, and South Africa that have multilanguage subgroups, separate versions of the questionnaire or research instrument will need to be developed. Even if the linguistic subgroup can understand another language, as is, for example, often the case in more-developed countries such as Belgium or Canada, translation into the local idiom will enhance willingness to respond and to provide complete and accurate answers.

Even if nonverbal stimuli such as pictures, show cards, or graphics, are used, the equivalence of their meaning in each context has to be evaluated. Although it might appear that pictorial stimuli are universal, this is not always the case. The Bantu of South Africa, for example, do not distinguish between blue and green. Consequently, use of these colors to distinguish between two objects or symbols would be of no avail. Similarly, African blacks do not always interpret Western three-dimensional perceptual cues correctly, which may give rise to some difficulties in the use of pictures and scenes. Interpretation of meaning attached to colors, shapes, or objects varies from country to country and culture to culture, and hence may affect perception of pictures, scenes, and other visual stimuli. The symbolism evoked by color, for example, varies widely from country to country. In Japan white is a color of mourning, whereas in Malaysia green symbolizes danger. Consequently, product, package, or picture stimuli may be inappropriately interpreted, or different associations may be evoked.

Studies of word associations with basic objects such as table, dark, man, mountain, house, deep, and soft among West European subjects (Rosenzweig, 1961) have generally found these to be highly similar. It is, however, questionable whether the same similarities would be found if a more diverse set of countries were studied. Similarly, at lower levels in the hierarchy of associations, for example, specific products such as dining tables or low-sudsing detergents, or in relation to brands, it is likely that much greater diversity will be found.

RESPONSE FORMAT. Although it is generally recognized that instruments need to be designed to eliminate bias due to content and mode of presentation to the respondent, there is generally less appreciation of biases that may arise from response format and recording procedures. These are next examined further.

Scoring Device. In designing response format, an important consideration is whether different or similar response formats should be used. It has, for example been argued that different response scales, adapted to specific cultural and educational traditions will be required. Thus, for example, in France a 20-point scale is commonly used in rating performance in primary and secondary schools. Such scales are, however, somewhat cumbersome, and existing studies suggest that little bias will be introduced by use of 5- or 7-point rating scales common in U.S. research (Douglas and LeMaire, 1974).

In countries with low literacy levels, where responses are to be scaled, some ingenuity will be required in the development of appropriate response-recording devices. Although interviewers can pose questions and record categorical responses concerning behavior and background characteristics, some difficulties can arise in obtaining response to attitudinal questions, where indication of position on a scale by the respondent is required.

One such scale is the *Funny Faces* scale, which has been used to good effect among blacks in South Africa (Corder, 1978). This is shown in Exhibit 7. Respondents are shown a concept, or given an attitudinal statement, and asked to indicate their degree of agreement or interest by indicating their position on this scale. Another device is the use of a wooden notched scale. The ends of the scales are explained to the respondent. These may, for example, represent positive or negative positions with regard to certain attitudinal statements. Respondents are then asked to indicate their positions by placing a stick in one of the notches on the scale.

Steps of a ladder can also be used to indicate the various response alternatives open to respondents (Cantril, 1965). Respondents are shown a sketch of a ladder and asked to indicate their position with respect to steps on the ladder. In countries or cultures where ladders are not known, other items can be substituted. For example, for Zulus a picture of a mountain with successive terraces was substituted. This represented the different stages or steps in climbing the mountain and was a much more familiar set of alternatives.

Techniques in which respondents define their positions relative to the cultural self-norm or to a self-defined response continuum may also be appropriate. In developing life-style measures, for example, adaptation of methods developed in other social sciences such as Cantril's self-anchoring scale (Cantril and Free, 1962) may

EXHIBIT 7 THE FUNNY FACES SCALE

Very happy

Happy

Not happy but also not unhappy

Unhappy

Very unhappy

Source. Corder, 1978.

be desirable. Here the individual indicates his own anchor point and its position or distance from a culture-specific stimulus set. In the research conducted by Cantril (1965), concerns of different kinds were studied. Yet although this eliminates cultural differences, it also eliminates differences in adaptation relative to the cultural norm.

Use of scaling instruments that have been tested in different countries and cultures and are believed to be culture free, such as Osgood's semantic differential (Osgood *et al.*, 1975), may also be desirable. These are, however, somewhat rare, particularly in relation to scales commonly used in marketing research. One exception is the adaptation of the Myers and Warner Colloquial and Formal Rating Scales for use in France (Angelmar and Pras, 1978). Similar adaptation and testing of verbal rating scales should be undertaken before they are used in other countries or linguistic contexts.

Scoring Procedures. Procedures to avoid bias in the recording and scoring of the response are also required (Meade and Brislin, 1973; Straus, 1969). These can arise as a result of random errors, such as incorrect recording by the interviewer or respondent, or because of some systematic source of error. Although the former can only be reduced by improved design of the research instrument, clearer, more graphic scales or greater attention to interviewer training and procedures to eliminate systematic bias can be incorporated into the research design.

An important source of systematic error that is a potential danger in international marketing research arises from the cultural self-referent bias (Lee, 1966). Thus a researcher of a specific nationality or culture may tend to interpret data in terms of his own cultural self-referent or cultural values. This is best resolved by the use of multiple judges, each with different self-referents, to interpret the data, and in the case of open-ended or qualitative data, to develop appropriate coding or categorization schema. For example, in a two-country/culture study, one monolingual judge from each country or culture should be used, and two bilingual judges, each a native speaker from a different country. An iterative, back-checking process, similar to that used in linguistic translation, can then be applied to ensure decentering of interpretation and elimination of the cultural self-referent bias (Werner and Campbell, 1970).

Furthermore, given the existence of differences in response set and respondent bias in different countries and cultures, use of different standards of scoring and interpretation may be desirable (Straus, 1969; Cunningham *et al.*, 1977). Measures can thus be culturally *ipsatized*, that is, the identical measure is used, but standards for scoring and interpretation differ across countries and cultures. For example, if results are being compared between an Irish and a British sample, where the Irish may be expected to respond to items in a more emotional manner, the data can be ipsatized by national group.

An alternative procedure is normalization. Thus rather than using raw scores for individuals in the analysis, differences from the country mean are utilized. For each variable, country averages are computed. An individual's score on each variable is then deducted from the country average and used as input in the comparative analysis. This procedure will, however, clearly only be necessary if responses are not elicited relative to a cultural self-norm.

Once the instrument has been designed to ensure comparability or equivalence across all countries and contexts studied and to minimize response bias from administration in different national and cultural contexts, the next step is to determine appropriate procedures for its administration in these different contexts.

DATA-COLLECTION PROCEDURES

In determining how to implement the research design, decisions have to be made with regard to appropriate data-collection techniques, for example, survey, experimentation, depth interviewing, observation, and so forth, and also their execution. This depends to a large extent on the purpose of the research. This may be either exploratory, that is, designed to identify relevant constructs to be examined in subsequent phases of research, or concerned with more-precise estimation as, for example, predicting new-product response, or testing advertising effectiveness. As noted previously, research in developed countries tends to be predominantly *ad hoc* or audit research and there is less need to conduct exploratory research. In developing countries, however, where little is known about market trends, it is often important to conduct exploratory or qualitative research.

Where exploratory research is to be undertaken to identify relevant concepts or product classes, or attitudes and behavior relative to these, unstructured data-collection techniques such as protocols, depth interviews, and focus groups can be particularly useful. Such techniques avoid the imposition of a cultural bias, since no prespecified conceptual model is imposed *a priori* by the researcher. Rather the respondent(s) is left to respond freely in selecting criteria or attitudinal statements most relevant to him. The specific terminology used by respondents when thinking about products, sources, or purchase situations, may be identified (Douglas *et al.*, 1981). On the other hand, the burden of interpretation is placed on the researcher to identify concepts, attitudes, or behaviors that are considered relevant. Consequently, in order to eliminate any potential cultural bias, it is generally desirable, as in the case of instrument design, to make use of multiple judges from different cultural and linguistic backgrounds when interpreting the data. Although collection of these data is relatively simple, care in supervision of data-collection procedures in order to minimize potential reactivity is required. Experience in data interpretation is also important and will require skilled and well-trained researchers.

If more precise quantitative estimation is required, survey research is likely to be more appropriate. As noted previously, the survey has traditionally been the instrument most frequently used in international marketing research. It does, however, require the availability of trained interviewers and a field-research organization. Such services are generally available in most countries in the world, either from local research organizations or the major international market research organizations, though the way in which they are organized may vary.

In determining appropriate data-collection procedures, decisions have to be made about how the survey should be administered. As in domestic research three major alternatives can be identified: mail, personal interview, and telephone. In making this choice, care needs to be taken to ensure that reliable good-quality data are generated. Here a number of factors have to be taken into consideration. These are next examined in more detail.

SURVEY-ADMINISTRATION TECHNIQUES. In domestic market research, relative cost, length of survey, and time constraints largely determine the choice of questionnaire-administration procedures. In international markets, however, other aspects such as availability of mailing lists and trained interviewers, the quality of the postal service, levels of literacy, or private telephone ownership also affect the decision. Of particular importance, especially in consumer research in developing countries are low levels of literacy (see Exhibit 4). These, coupled with lower wage levels, often dictate frequent use of personal interviewing. The advantages and disadvantages of each method in international markets are next discussed in more detail.

Mail Surveys. Mail surveys can typically be used effectively in industrial market research. Mailing lists such as those of Bottin International or directories for specific industries are generally available. The key problems are to identify the relevant respondent within a company and to personalize the address to increase the likelihood of response. Appropriate sponsorship or prior telephone verification can also aid in increasing response rates.

In consumer research, and particularly in developing countries, use of mail surveys may give rise to some problems. As in the case of sampling frames, mailing lists may not exist or sources such as telephone directories may not provide adequate coverage. Available lists such as magazine subscription lists or membership-association lists may be skewed to better educated segments of the population. In addition, in some countries, the effectiveness of mail surveys is limited by low levels of literacy, reluctance of respondents to respond to mail surveys, and extremely inefficient mail services. In countries with high levels of illiteracy, the proportion of the population likely to be reached by mail survey is limited. Even in countries where levels of literacy make use of mail surveys feasible, reluctance to respond and a tendency to regard surveys as an invasion of privacy may limit their effectiveness. Inefficiency of mail services constitutes a further hazard in using mail surveys in other countries. In Brazil, for example, 30 percent of the domestic mail is never delivered, whereas in Nicaragua all mail has to be delivered to the post office.

Thus although mail surveys may be effectively used in industrial market research, in consumer research they may be appropriate only in industrialized countries. Here levels of literacy are high, and mailing lists are readily available. In other countries they may only be appropriate if it is desired to reach a relatively up-scale and well-educated segment of the population. Thus although costs of administering mail surveys appear low on a per-questionnaire mailed-out basis, low response rates or poor quality data in developing countries may render such surveys less cost effective than other methods of data collection.

Telephone Interviewing. Telephone interviewing is a method of questionnaire administration that has developed substantially in the United States in recent years. The availability of WATS lines and special volume rates have changed the economics of telephone interviewing as opposed to other methods of administration. Furthermore, use of telephone interviewing from a centralized location facilitates control over the interviewers. This has been found increasingly to be a problem in personal-interview surveys.

In industrial market research, use of telephone surveys may be quite effective. The majority of businesses, other than some small or itinerant retailers or craftsmen, are likely to have telephones. It is important, as in the case of mail surveys, to be able to identify the relevant respondent(s). This is, however, facilitated in telephone surveys by the ability to conduct initial probing or ask preliminary screening questions. Willingness to respond may, however, depend on relative time pressures at work and the desired target population. Where the target population is upper management, some resistance is likely to be encountered unless substantial interest in the survey can be aroused. Use of personal contacts, or obtaining sponsorship from some appropriate organization or association may also be desirable.

In consumer research, the feasibility of using telephone surveys varies from country to country. In countries such as Sri Lanka, only 4 percent of the population have telephones, whereas even in relatively affluent societies such as France and Italy, there are only 29 and 27 public and private telephones per 100 inhabitants and in Portugal only 11. Volume rates and grouped lines such as those in the United States are rarely available.

Telephone linkages vary substantially in quality and are often inadequate for efficient interviewing. As in the case of mail surveys, respondents may be reluctant to respond to strangers or to questions posed by an anonymous interviewer, and may be unaccustomed to lengthy conversations. Consequently, telephone surveys may only be appropriate where the research is designed to reach relatively up-scale consumer segments, people who are accustomed to business transactions by telephone, as for example, doctors and lawyers. In addition, the questionnaire needs to be short, simple, and easily administered by telephone.

Personal Interviewing.   The third method of administering questionnaires is by personal interview. In industrial marketing research, personal interviewing is likely to be the dominant mode. Response to mail surveys may tend to be low and adaptation cannot be made to specific company situations. In telephone interviews only limited information can be obtained from certain respondents and in relation to specific nonconfidential topics. Furthermore, probing is carried out less effectively. In consumer research, for the reasons noted previously, that is, lack of mailing lists, inadequate mail services, and high levels of illiteracy, personal interviewing will often be required.

In personal interviewing, a key problem is the interaction between the interviewer and the respondent. In international market research this is affected by a number of factors. These vary from country to country and can affect the quality of data obtained. As noted previously, attitudes toward questioning by strangers, feelings that interviewing constitutes an invasion of privacy, and suspiciousness about the interviewer's motivations vary from country to country or culture to culture. This affects the willingness of respondents in both industrial and consumer surveys to participate or cooperate in surveys, as does the extent to which respondents will deliberately conceal information or give false answers.

In industrial marketing research, willingness to participate and provide information may depend to a large extent on the competitiveness of the market environment. In certain countries or with certain product markets such as pharmaceuticals or electronics, management may be considerably more reluctant to provide information than in product markets such as crafts, etc. In the former case, suspicion may be aroused that information may leak to competition, or be used to the company's detriment. In consumer surveys in Latin countries, and in the Middle East, interviewers are regarded with considerable suspicion. In Latin countries, where tax evasion is a national pastime, interviewers are often suspected of being tax inspectors. In the Middle East, where interviewers are invariably male, interviews with housewives often have to be conducted in the evenings when husbands are at home.

An important factor in deciding whether or not to use personal interviewing is the availability of trained interviewers. In certain developing countries, the availability of field staff is open to some question. There may be a lack of competent trained professional interviewers. This is often the case in cultures such as the Middle East where it is not acceptable for women to hold such posts. This implies that interviewers will have to be recruited and trained expressly for a specific piece of research.

Political and social surveys conducted in developing countries have typically found recruitment of socioeconomically up-scale individuals in leadership positions to be desirable. Thus, for example, village headmen, teachers, and country prefects have been found to be good interviewers (Frey, 1970). In such situations extensive training programs have to be developed prior to the survey, and standard procedures for interviewing developed.

Yet even in more-developed countries, attention to interviewer training and briefing and debriefing is desirable to ensure the maximum response rate and to avoid bias arising from interviewer–respondent interaction. This is particularly desirable when the interview involves open-ended or complex questions and tasks such as, for example, projective techniques or multidimensional scaling.

The personal interview is typically the most expensive method of questionnaire administration. It is, however, the method most commonly used outside the United States. Lack of sampling frames, higher rates of response, and low wage rates in developing countries often offset the higher costs. Furthermore, in countries with low levels of literacy, personal interviewing is mandatory. The improved quality of the data is also a major consideration.

DATA QUALITY. An important consideration in collecting data in multicountry research is the quality of the data obtained. The sampling plan can be set up to ensure comparability of the samples from country to country. The instrument may be well designed to avoid cultural bias. Effective survey administration procedures may be established. Yet there may still be a number of underlying problems that need to be carefully evaluated.

Little is known concerning factors that affect rates of nonresponse or the quality of data provided by respondents in other countries. With a few rare exceptions, the reliability of data obtained in cross-national research has been little investigated, using either test-retest, or interjudge-reliability procedures. It is, nonetheless, critical that checks of this type be included as standard procedure in multicountry research. As in domestic research, two major sources of error in survey research can be identified—sampling and nonsampling error. Problems arising from sampling error can generally be readily identified and hence pose somewhat less of a threat to the quality of data than the problems arising from the somewhat invidious nature of nonsampling error.

Nonsampling Error. Nonsampling error can arise as a result of the individual respondent's unwillingness to respond accurately and completely, his personality and response set, purposeful misreporting of data, faulty recall, respondent fatigue, interviewer error, the interaction between the interviewer and the respondent, or other extraneous factors. Since these sources of bias have been discussed in relation to questionnaire administration, they are not discussed further here.

Sampling Error

Survey Nonresponse. Differential rates of nonresponse to surveys can affect the quality of the data. Again, some evidence exists to indicate differences in the rates of nonresponse to surveys in different nations (Almond and Verba, 1963) and also among different categories of respondents. In the classic Almond and Verba study, the percentages of the samples actually interviewed were United Kingdom, 59 percent; Mexico, 60 percent; Italy, 74 percent; Germany, 74 percent; and the United States, 83 percent. This, however, is a more significant problem in mail and telephone interviewing, and can be more effectively controlled in personal interviewing except in countries where there are high rates of refusal. This problem is compounded by the inadequacies of many sampling frames discussed earlier.

Available evidence tends to suggest that background characteristics of nonrespondents are likely to be the same. Samples will thus be underrepresented with regard to the same segments, for example, low-income or less-educated consumers. It is, therefore, important to make adjustments for such factors to ensure comparability of samples and that national representativeness is not lost. This can be corrected by double-sampling on high nonresponse segments. If, however, other factors such as suspiciousness of interviewers or hostility surveys underlie nonresponse, the relevant determinants and their impact will need to be investigated in each specific case.

Little research also appears to have been conducted into ways to increase rates of nonresponse in other countries or in multicountry surveys. One study of elites found that use of large incentives increased response and improved the probability of providing complete responses (Godwin, 1979). Other standard procedures, such as personalization, sponsorship, and follow-ups are also used in other countries, although little has been published with regard to their relative effectiveness.

The efficacy of several return-increasing techniques in South America and Africa has also been examined (Eisinger et al., 1974). In Kenya and the Ivory Coast, the effects of registration and personalization in a mail survey were examined. In neither case did personalization significantly increase returns, though registration increased returns by eight percent in Kenya. Registration was also found to increase returns in Venezuela and Argentina. In all cases, follow-up mailings increased return rates. This is comparable to similar findings in the United States.

Reliability of the Data.   Another issue is the reliability of data obtained in cross-national surveys. Here the prime concern is whether the same result is obtained when a measure is repeated in a different context, fashion, or time. Despite all efforts to design an instrument that is adapted to all countries and cultures, it may not be equally reliable in all these contexts. Similarly, different forms, for example, of attitudinal or life-style measures, may vary in their level of reliability. The stability of data over time is yet another consideration.

Despite its significance, the reliability of the data in cross-national research has received little attention. Available evidence suggests, however, that the reliability of data varies from country to country. Studies of public opinion data, have, for example, investigated the reliability of data on age and education in the United Kingdom and the United States over time (Schreiber, 1975/76). For age, 91 percent of the U.S. sample, and 98 percent of the British sample gave consistent reports in both waves of measurement. However, for education the figure was only 74 percent in the U.S. sample. Another study based on self-administered questionnaires to couples in five countries from two linguistic groupings, the United States, the United Kingdom, France, Belgium, and Canada, found generally somewhat higher levels of reliability for 10 background characteristics ranging from a low of 84 to 100 percent. Reliability did, however, vary from country to country, though no systematic or consistent patterns emerged (Davis et al., 1980).

Reliability has also been found to vary with the type of data. The same five-country study found reliability to be greater for background data than behavioral data, and this in turn more reliable than attitudinal data. In the first two instances, comparison of husband-wife reports were used as measures of reliability, whereas in the third instance, attitudinal variables, a measure of internal consistency was applied to multiple-item attitudinal constructs. As in the case of background characteristics, the level of reliability was found to vary from country to country, though again there was no systematic tendency for any particular national sample or language group to exhibit high or low reliability across different variables of the same type.

Such findings suggest that in addition to efforts to design instruments so as to control and minimize nonequivalence from one country or context to another, attention should also be directed toward monitoring the reliability of these instruments. This requires that reliability be investigated routinely in cross-national surveys, just as interview verification and examination of sampling errors are an accepted part of research practice. Adjustments for unreliability can also be made, but entail complex statistical procedures (Bagozzi, 1980; Griliches 1974).

CONCLUSION

International research provides an essential input into the design of effective strategies for international marketing operations. Further, it aids in decisions concerning appropriate tactics to be used in different country markets. In particular, research is required to evaluate long-run market potential relative to different countries, product markets, and target segments. Research can also aid in determining appropriate modes of market segmentation, that is, by country or across countries, as well as relevant bases for market segmentation. Decisions with regard to the adaptation of marketing-mix tactics to specific national environments should also be research based. Finally, research provides a valuable input for long-run strategic planning and selection of countries, product markets, target segments, and modes of operation for long-run market growth.

The heart of the research design is the sampling plan and the research instrument. The sampling plan has to be developed to ensure that accurate and reliable data are collected in the most cost-effective manner. An appropriate balance between comparability of samples and representativeness of the target population has to be maintained. Instruments should be designed to ensure as far as possible comparability across countries and cultural contexts. In particular, elimination of cultural bias in the instrument itself and in its analysis is an important consideration.

In analyzing data from multicountry research, a number of problems arise because of multiple levels of measurement units, that is, countries, industries, companies, respondents within companies, and households, particularly when these vary in their underlying composition (i.e., different buying centers, household composition, etc.). The hierarchical character of the research design (i.e., across countries and target segments, and different levels of product markets and product lines) adds further to the difficulties of analysis. This implies that use of a multistage hierarchical approach will frequently be required. Data are first analyzed *separately* for each unit examined, and then *across* all the units studied (Frey, 1970). Although tedious and time consuming, this has the advantage of tailoring the analysis to, and gaining understanding of, the specific problems or situations in each country or context before integrating findings across countries. However, more efficient analysis awaits development of adequate multivariate statistical techniques that can effectively deal with the complex hierarchical nature of multinational data.

International marketing operations clearly emerge as one of the major trends of the 1980s. Yet existing research procedures and organization appear ill-suited to aid management in meeting new developments in the internationalization of business operations. Although the high costs and conceptual and methodological difficulties associated with international marketing research appear to constitute a barrier, the expected payoff is high. Collection of better and more reliable information is an important step in improving international marketing decisions. Thus increased attention to the design and execution of international market research constitutes an important priority in the agenda of the international marketer.

SOURCES AND SUGGESTED REFERENCES

Adamopoulos, J. "The Dimensions of the Greek Concept of Philotimo," *Journal of Social Psychology,* Vol. X (1977), pp. 313–314.

Adler, L. "Managing Marketing Research in the Diversified Multinational Corporation," in E.M. Mazze, ed. *Marketing in Turbulent Times and Marketing: The Challenges and the Opportunities—Combined Proceedings.* Chicago: American Marketing Association, 1975.

———, and C.S. Mayer. "Meeting the Challenge of Multinational Marketing Research," in W. Keegan and C. Mayer, eds. *Multinational Product Management.* Cambridge, MA.: Marketing Science Institute, 1976.

Almond, G., and S. Verba. *The Civic Culture: Political Attitudes and Democracy in the Nations.* Princeton: Princeton University Press, 1963.

Anderson, B.R. "On the Comparability of Meaningful Stimuli in Cross-Cultural Research," *Sociometry,* Vol. XXX, No. 2 (1967), pp. 127–136.

Angelmar, R., and B. Pras. "Verbal Rating Scales for Multinational Research," *European Research,* Vol. VI (1978), pp. 62–67.

Bagozzi, R.P. *Causal Models in Marketing.* New York: Wiley, 1980.

Barnard, P. "The Role and Implementation of International Marketing Research," in *International Marketing Research Seminar.* Brussels: ESOMAR, 1976.

———. "Market Research in the World Economy," *Marketing Research Society Newsletter,* No. 150 (1978), pp. 9–14.

———. "The World of Research," *Marketing Research Society Newsletter,* No. 171 (1980), pp. 31ff.

Berent, P.H. "International Research is Different," in E.M. Mazze, ed. *Marketing in Turbulent Times and Marketing: The Challenges and the Opportunities—Combined Proceedings.* Chicago: American Marketing Association, 1975.

Berry, J.W. "On Cross-Cultural Comparability," *International Journal of Psychology,* Vol. IV (1969), pp. 119–128.

Bottin International, U.S.A. 5714 West Pico Boulevard, Los Angeles, CA 90019.

Boyd, H.W., R.E. Frank, W.F. Massy, and M. Zoheir. "On the Use of Marketing Research in the Emerging Economies," *Journal of Marketing Research,* Vol. I (1964), pp. 20–25.

Brislin, R. "Back-Translation for Cross-Cultural Research," *Journal of Cross-Cultural Psychology,* Vol. I (1970), pp. 185–216.

——— W.J. Lonner, and R.M. Thorndike. *Cross-Cultural Research Methods,* New York: Wiley, 1973.

Campbell, D.T., and J. Stanley. *Experimental and Quasi-Experimental Design and Research.* Chicago: Rand McNally, 1973.

Cantril, H. *The Pattern of Human Concerns.* New Brunswick, NJ: Rutgers University Press, 1965.

———, and L.A. Tree. "Hopes and Fears for Self and Country," *American Behavioral Scientist,* Vol. VI supplement (1962), p. 8.

Chun, K.T., J.B. Campbell, and J. Hao. "Extreme Response Style in Cross-cultural Research: a Reminder," *Journal of Cross-Cultural Psychology,* Vol. V (1974), pp. 464–480.

Cochran, W.G. *Sampling Techniques.* New York: Wiley, 1977.

Corder, C.K. "Problems and Pitfalls in Conducting Marketing Research in Africa," in B. Gelb, ed. *Marketing Expansion in a Shrinking World,* Proceedings of American Marketing Association Business Conference. Chicago: American Marketing Association, 1978.

Crosby, R.W. "Attitude Measurement in a Bilingual Culture," *Journal of Marketing Research,* Vol. VI (1969), pp. 421–426.

Crowne, D.P., and D. Marlowe. *The Approval Motive: Studies in Evaluative Dependence.* New York: Wiley, 1964.

Cunningham, W.H., I. Cunningham, and R.T. Green. "The Ipsative Process to Reduce Response Set Bias," *Public Opinion Quarterly,* Vol. XLI, No. 3 (1977), pp. 379–394.

Davis, H.L., S.P. Douglas, and A.J. Silk. "Reliability: The Underlying Danger in Cross-national Surveys," *Journal of Marketing,* Spring 1981.

Douglas, S.P., and P. LeMaire. "Improving the Quality and Efficiency of Life-style Research," XXV ESOMAR Congress, Budapest.

———. "Cross-National Comparisons and Consumer Stereotypes: A Case Study of Working and Non-Working Wives in the U.S. and France," *Journal of Consumer Research,* Vol. III (1976), pp. 12–20.

———, and R. Shoemaker. *Item Non-Response in Cross-National Surveys.* European Research, October 1981.

———. "Adjusting for Sample Characteristics in Multi-Country Survey Research," in *Proceedings, 9th Annual Meeting of the European Academy for Advanced Research in Marketing.* Edinburgh, 1980.

———, C., S. Craig, and J.P. Faivre. "Protocols in Consumer Research: Problems, Methods and Uses," in J. Sheth, ed. *Research in Marketing,* Vol. V., Greenwich, Conn.: JAI Press, 1981.

Eisinger, R.A., W.P. Janicki, R.L. Stevenson, and W.L. Thompson. "Increasing Returns in Mail Surveys," *Public Opinion Quarterly,* Vol. XXXVII (1974), pp. 124–130.

Encyclopaedia of Associations, Detroit: Gale Research Company, Book Tower, 1980.

Franzen, M.P., and L. Light. "Standardize Process Not Programs," in *International Marketing Research* seminar. Brussels: ESOMAR, 1976.

Frey, F. "Cross-Cultural Survey Research in Political Science," in *The Methodology of Comparative Research,* R.E. Holt and J.E. Turner, eds. New York: The Free Press, 1970.

Godwin, R.K. "The Consequences of Large Monetary Incentives in Mail Surveys of Elites," *Public Opinion Quarterly,* Vol. XLII (1979), pp. 378–387.

Goodyear, J. "The World of Research," *Marketing Research Society Newsletter,* No. 171 (1980), pp 81ff.

Green, P.E. *Mathematical Tools for Applied Multivariate Analysis.* New York: Academic Press, 1978.

———, and D.S. Tull. *Research for Marketing Decisions.* Englewood Cliffs, NJ: Prentice-Hall, 1978.

Green, R., and E. Langeard. "A Cross-National Comparison of Consumer Habits and Innovator Characteristics," *Journal of Marketing,* Vol. XLIX (1975), pp. 34–41.

Griliches, Z. "Errors in Variables and Other Inobservables," *Econometrika,* Vol. XLII (1974), p. 971–998.

Holt, R.T. and J.E. Turner (eds.) *The Methodology of Corporative Research,* New York: Free Press, 1970.

Kelly's Manufacturers and Merchants Directory. NY: Kelly's Directories, annual edition.

Landsberger, H.A., and A. Saavedra. "Response Set in Developing Countries," *Public Opinion Quarterly,* Vol. XXXI, No. 2 (1967), pp. 214–229.

Lee, J.A. "Cultural Analysis in Overseas Operations," *Harvard Business Review,* Vol. XLIV (1966), pp. 106–114.

Lehmann, D.R. *Market Research and Analysis.* Homewood, IL: Richard D. Irwin, 1979.

Linton, A., and S. Broadbent. "International Life-Style Comparisons," *European Research,* Vol. III, No. 2 (1975), pp. 51–56, 84.

Lipstein, B. "In Defense of Small Samples," *Journal of Advertising Research,* Vol. XV (1975), pp. 33–42.

Lovell, M.R. "Examining the Multinational Consumer," in *Developments in Consumer Psychology,* Maidenhead: ESOMAR, 1973.

Mayer, C.S. "Multinational Marketing Research: The Magnifying Glass of Methodological Problems," *European Research,* Vol. 6 (1978), pp. 77–84.

Meade, R.D., and R.W. Brislin. "Controls in Cross-Cultural Experimentation," *International Journal of Psychology,* Vol. VIII, No. 4 (1973), pp. 231–238.

Mitchell, R.E. "Survey Materials Collected in Developing Countries: Sampling Measurement and Interviewing: Obstacles to Intra- and Inter-National Comparisons," *International Social Science Journal,* Vol. XVII, No. 4 (1965), pp. 186ff.

Morello, G. "Understanding the European Market." Paper presented at the 60th American Marketing Association conference, Cleveland, May 1977.

Moyer, R. "International Market Analysis," *Journal of Marketing Research,* Vol. IV (1968), pp. 353–60.

Oppenheim, A.N. *Questionnaire Design and Attitude Measurement.* London: Heineman, 1966.

Osgood, C.E., W.H. May, and M.S. Miron. *Cross-Cultural Universals of Affective Meaning.* Urbana, IL: University of Illinois Press, 1975.

Pike, K. *Language in Relation to a Unified Theory of the Structure of Human Behavior.* The Hague: Mouton, 1966.

Poortinga, Y.M. "Some Implications of Three Different Approaches to Intercultural Comparison," in *Applied Cross-Cultural Psychology,* J.W. Berry and W.J. Lonner, eds. Amsterdam: Swetts and Zeitlinger, 1975.

Reader's Digest. *A Survey of Europe Today—the peoples and markets of sixteen European countries.* London: Readers Digest, 1970.

Ricks, D.M., Y.C. Fu, and J.S. Arpan. *International Business Blunders.* Columbus, OH: Grid, 1974.

Rosenzweig, M.R. "Comparisons of Word Association Responses in English, French, German and Italian," *American Journal of Psychology,* Vol. LXXIV (1961), pp. 347–360.

Rusby, P. "Europe, One Market for Market Research," *European Research,* Vol. II (1974), pp. 22–28.

Schreiber, E.M. "Dirty Data in Britain and the U.S.A., the Reliability of 'Invariant' Characteristics Reported in Surveys," *Public Opinion Quarterly,* Vol. XXXIX, No. 2 (1975/76), pp. 493–506.

Straus, M.A. "Phenomenal Identity and Conceptual Equivalence of Measurement—A Cross-Cultural Comparative Research," *Journal of Marriage and the Family,* Vol. XXXI, No. 2 (1969), pp. 233–239.

Sudman, S. *Applied Sampling.* New York: Academic Press, 1976.

Thorelli, H., H. Becker, and J. Engledow. *The Information Seekers: An International Study of Consumer Information and Advertising Image.* Cambridge, MA: Ballinger, 1976.

Triandis, H.C. *The Analysis of Subjective Culture.* New York: Wiley, 1972.

———, and Vassilou "A Comparative Analysis of Subjective Culture," in H.C. Triandis, *The Analysis of Subjective Culture.* New York: Wiley, 1972.

U.S. Department of Commerce, Bureau of the Census. *Statistical Abstract of the United States,* 100th ed. Washington, D.C.: U.S. Government Printing Office, 1969.

De Vulpian, A. "Les Courants Socio-culturels en France," in *Les Styles de Vie* Journées de L'IREP. Paris: IREP, 1974.

Webster, L. "Comparability in Multi-Country Surveys," *Journal of Advertising Research,* Vol. VI (1966), pp. 14–18.

Werner, O. and D.T. Campbell. "Translating Working Through Interpreters and the Problems of Decentering," in *A Handbook of Method in Cultural Anthropology,* R. Naroll and R. Cohen, eds. New York: Columbia University Press, 1970.

Wind, Y. and S.P. Douglas. "International Market Segmentation," *European Journal of Marketing,* Vol. IX (1972), pp. 17–25.

———. "Comparative Consumer Research: The Next Frontier," *European Journal of Marketing,* 1981 (special issue on comparative marketing).

"World of Research," *Marketing Research Society Newsletter,* June 1980.

World Guide to Trade Associations, Vols. 1 and 2, New York and London, 1973.

ENTERING INTERNATIONAL MARKETS

CONTENTS

THE ELEMENTS OF FOREIGN-MARKET-ENTRY STRATEGY   **3**

The Need to Plan   3
Constituent Product/Market Plans   4
Foreign-Market-Entry Modes   4

ENTERING FOREIGN MARKETS THROUGH EXPORTS   **5**

Exporting as a Learning Experience   5
Getting Started: Indirect Exporting   6
  Indirect and direct export channels   6
  Export management companies   7
Direct Exporting   8
  Deciding on the direct export channel   8
  Choosing a foreign agent or distributor   9
Export Operations   10
  Export documents   10
  Export price quotations   10
  Payments arrangements   11
  Export organization   11

ENTERING FOREIGN MARKETS THROUGH LICENSING AND OTHER CONTRACTUAL ARRANGEMENTS   **12**

International Licensing   12
  Advantages and disadvantages of licensing as a primary entry mode   12
  Profitability analysis of a proposed licensing venture   14
  Negotiating and managing licensing agreements   14
Other Contractual Entry Modes   14

International franchising   14
Contract manufacturing   15
Management contracts   15
Turnkey construction contracts   15
Coproduction agreements   15

ENTERING FOREIGN MARKETS THROUGH INVESTMENT IN LOCAL PRODUCTION   **16**

Advantages and Disadvantages of Investment Entry   **16**
The Decision to Invest in a Target Country   **16**
Investment Entry Through Acquisition   **17**
  Advantages and disadvantages of acquisition entry   18
  Acquisition strategy   18
Investment Entry Through Joint Ventures   **19**
  Advantages of joint ventures   19
  Disadvantages of joint ventures   19
  Choosing the right partner   20

DECIDING ON THE RIGHT ENTRY MODE   **20**

Three Decision Rules   **20**
An Application of the Strategy Rule   **21**

MONITORING FOREIGN-MARKET-ENTRY STRATEGIES   **21**

NOTES   **21**

SOURCES AND SUGGESTED REFERENCES   **22**

ENTERING INTERNATIONAL MARKETS

Franklin R. Root

Today companies need to plan for growth and survival in a world of global competition. Many companies will choose to remain at home to confront international competitors in once-familiar domestic markets. But other companies will choose to meet their competitors in foreign markets (as well as in domestic markets) by going international in one or more ways. To do so, they will need to design and carry out entry strategies that can sustain a continuing presence in foreign markets.

THE ELEMENTS OF FOREIGN-MARKET-ENTRY STRATEGY

THE NEED TO PLAN.   A foreign-market-entry strategy is a comprehensive plan that lays down the objectives, resources, and policies that will guide a company's international business over a period of time long enough to achieve a sustainable growth in world markets. The time horizon for an entry strategy should be distant enough to compel company managers to raise and answer fundamental questions about the direction and scope of their international business. For most companies the entry-strategy time horizon will be 3 to 5 years.

Managers in small and medium-sized companies tend to view strategic planning for foreign-market entry as something only large companies can afford to do because they think it calls for elaborate techniques applied by expert planners to mountains of data acquired by costly research. But this is a misconception. Planning foreign-market entry is actually a process of deciding on the direction of a company's international business by combining reason with empirical knowledge. It forces managers to examine critically all assumptions about foreign markets and competition. Once a company accepts the *idea* of strategic planning, it can surely find a way to plan foreign-market entry—however limited its resources may be. Indeed, no company can afford *not* to think systematically about where its international business should be three to five years from now, because it will be competing against strategy-minded Japanese, European, and other firms. Without an entry strategy, a company is confined to short-run, *ad hoc* responses to changing markets and competition. Such a "sales" approach to foreign markets is no longer a viable form of international business.

CONSTITUENT PRODUCT/MARKET PLANS. A company's overall foreign-market-entry strategy is an aggregation of several individual product/market strategies. Managers need to design an entry strategy for *each* product and *each* foreign market. Differences among foreign markets make highly risky the assumption that a particular entry strategy would draw the same response across different products or different country markets. This statement does not gainsay the desirability of identifying clusters of *similar* country markets that can be entered with the same strategy. Indeed, market clustering is a natural outcome of the reconciliation by managers of the constituent product/market plans to form a company's overall foreign-market-entry strategy.

The constituent plans call for decisions on the following issues:

1. The target product and target foreign market.
2. The company's objectives and goals in the target market.
3. The entry mode to penetrate the target foreign country.
4. The marketing plan to penetrate the target market in the target country.
5. The control system to monitor performance in the target country/market.

These entry decisions are interdependent, making the planning process iterative, with several feedback loops. For instance, the evaluation of alternative entry modes may bring about a revision of market objectives or even start a search for a new target country. Or the design of the marketing plan may call into question an earlier preference for a particular entry mode. Once operations begin in a foreign target market, variances in performance may lead managers to revise any or all of the other entry decisions. Thus managers should regard planning for foreign-market entry as a continuing, open-ended process.

This section addresses primarily the third and fifth entry issues: the choice of an entry mode and the revision of foreign-market-entry strategies to sustain market performance. Section 32 examines the other entry issues, particularly the formulation of a marketing plan to gain penetration of a foreign target market.

FOREIGN-MARKET-ENTRY MODES. A foreign-market-entry mode is an institutional arrangement that enables a company to transfer its products, technology, management, and other resources to a foreign *country*. The need to penetrate a country as well as a market is unique to international business because in domestic business a company is already located inside the country that contains its market. Since an entry mode that is successful for one country may not be successful for another, managers need to decide on the most appropriate entry mode for each target country.

Foreign-market-entry modes may be classified as follows:

1. Export entry modes:
   a. Indirect.
   b. Direct agent/distributor.
   c. Direct branch/subsidiary.
   d. Other.
2. Contractual entry modes:
   a. Licensing.
   b. Franchising.
   c. Technical agreements.

     d. Service contracts.
     e. Management contracts.
     f. Construction/turnkey contracts.
     g. Contract manufacture.
     h. Coproduction agreements.
     i. Other.
3. Investment entry modes:
     a. Sole venture: new establishment.
     b. Sole venture: acquisition.
     c. Joint venture: majority.
     d. Joint venture: 50–50.
     e. Joint venture: minority.

In deciding on the most appropriate entry mode for a particular product and target foreign country, managers need to consider several, often conflicting, external forces in the target country as well as several factors internal to the company.

Target-country factors include *market factors* (such as sales potential, competition, and distribution channels), *production factors* (such as the quality, quantity, availability, and cost of inputs for local production) and *political, economic, and sociocultural factors* (such as government policies toward international trade and investment, geographic distance, attributes of the economy, and the cultural "distance" between the home and target-country societies).

How managers respond to external country factors in choosing an entry mode depends on factors internal to the company. They include *product factors* (such as degree of differentiation, pre- and post-purchase services, technological intensity, and the need for adaptation), and *resource/commitment factors* (such as resources in management, capital, technology, and functional skills, and the willingness to commit them to foreign markets).

The diversity of forces and the need to assess their strengths and future directions combine to make the entry-mode decision a complex process with many trade-offs among alternative entry modes. To deal with this complexity, managers can benefit from an analytical model that facilitates systematic comparisons of entry modes with respect to a particular product and target country. This model is offered later, after the reader has become acquainted with the general advantages and disadvantages of the different entry modes.

ENTERING FOREIGN MARKETS THROUGH EXPORTS

EXPORTING AS A LEARNING EXPERIENCE. Most manufacturers enter international business for the first time as exporters. By using an indirect channel, a manufacturer can begin exporting with low start-up costs, modest risks, and the prospect of early profits on sales. He can then step up his effort over time by penetrating new country markets, adding new export products, and eventually moving on to direct export channels. Exporting allows a manufacturer, therefore, to test the acceptance of his products in foreign markets in an exploratory, experimental fashion. And so, exporting becomes an international learning experience that carries a company into a growing commitment to international business.

Licensing and investment entry modes can seldom offer manufacturers the advantages of exporting as a first learning experience. Although they may have low start-up costs, licensing arrangements are not good learning experiences because the foreign-licensee firms have full control over the marketing of licensed products. Thus the licensee stands as a buffer between the licensor (manufacturer) and the foreign market. Furthermore, licensing may create a future competitor in world markets, a contingency that is likely to be overlooked by the neophyte international company. In contrast, equity investment in local production can provide an intense learning experience, but only at a high risk. Investment entry calls for a much-higher commitment of resources than exporting and is much-more exposed to political risks. Moreover, the information and experience needed by managers to make good investment decisions are simply unavailable to the neophyte international company.

As managers gain knowledge and experience from export operations, they also learn to assess the true risks of international business as distinguished from its imagined risks. They are inclined to move, therefore, toward entry modes that offer greater control over the marketing effort in target countries. They may also discover that some excellent foreign-market opportunities can be exploited only through licensing, investment, or other nonexport entry modes. The story of a small building-products manufacturer (call him Alpha) reveals this process of growing international involvement.

Alpha entered foreign markets for the first time in 1965 by exporting to Europe and Australia, and it now has distributors in all the major industrial countries. In the late 1960s, Alpha negotiated licensing agreements in Europe, Japan, and South Africa. The Japanese licensee later became a joint-venture partner. As sales reached substantial volumes in certain countries, Alpha began to establish local production facilities. It opened its first plant in Europe in 1970 and its second plant in Australia the following year. By the early 1970s, Alpha was getting about 80 percent of its income from foreign operations, which included exporting, licensing, joint ventures, and wholly owned subsidiaries in countries on all continents.

Although few manufacturers become as dependent on international business, Alpha's story is representative of how many companies have developed their international business. It may help managers in neophyte international firms to know that even the giant multinational manufacturers got their start in international business as exporters.

GETTING STARTED: INDIRECT EXPORTING

Indirect and Direct Export Channels. In exporting to a target country, a company may use any of several export channels. Exhibit 1 illustrates the principal channels.

The primary distinction among the alternative export channels is the presence or absence of export middlemen in the home country. Channels that utilize domestic intermediaries are called *indirect* because the manufacturer does not export on his own but instead relies on an export middleman. Channels that utilize foreign agents or distributors, the manufacturer's own foreign sales facilities, or any other channels that circumvent domestic export middlemen are called *direct*. With direct channels, the manufacturer carries on his own export operations.

There are several kinds of domestic export middlemen: export merchants who deal mainly in staple goods, resident foreign buyers and commission houses who source products for export, exporting manufacturers who take on complementary lines, and export management companies. In the United States, the most important middleman is the export management company.

EXHIBIT 1

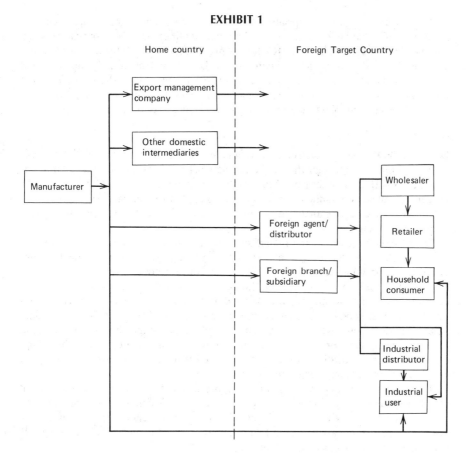

A U.S. Department of Commerce study of 5000 manufacturing companies in 1978 disclosed five major obstacles to exporting: (1) lack of knowledge of how to find foreign agents and distributors, (2) lack of knowledge about foreign markets, (3) lack of interest in foreign markets, (4) fears of not getting paid, and (5) lack of adequate personnel (U.S. Dept. of Commerce, 1978). Manufacturers who want to export but experience one or more of the other obstacles should consider using an export management company to handle their export business.

Export Management Companies.   An export management company (EMC) is a specialist in international marketing that acts as the export department for several manufacturers in noncompetitive lines. In the United States there are some 800–1000 EMCs who represent some 10,000 manufacturers and account for about 10 percent of U.S. manufactured exports.

EMCs vary greatly in size, product/market specialization, services, and experience. The representative EMC is small (one or two individuals in management and sales), relies on foreign agents or distributors rather than on its own foreign sales offices, takes title to its clients' products, specializes in certain geographic areas (such as Europe or Latin America), handles lines in three or more industries, and is willing to accept exclusive rights for a single country (Brasch, 1978).

The selection of an appropriate EMC is a key decision. Manufacturers need to identify EMCs that have experience in their product lines and target foreign markets, and then screen the candidate EMCs for the most suitable one. Information on EMCs may be obtained from trade publications, the U.S. Department of Commerce, and EMC associations.[1] After signing a contract, the manufacturer should support the EMC by helping to draw up a foreign-marketing plan, by supplying sales aids (such as literature and samples), and by promptly servicing export orders.

DIRECT EXPORTING.   Indirect exporting gives the manufacturer immediate access to foreign markets through the marketing networks of EMCs and other export intermediaries. But the other side of the coin is the manufacturer's lack of control over his foreign sales. A manufacturer who wants to exploit foreign markets aggressively will move on to direct exporting after gaining his initial international exposure through indirect exporting.

Direct exporting offers the manufacturer the following specific advantages: (1) greater control over the foreign-marketing plan (pricing, advertising, personal selling, distribution, product services, etc.), (2) greater concentration of marketing effort on the manufacturer's own product line, (3) quicker information feedbacks on markets, competition, and performance, and (4) better protection of the manufacturer's trademarks, patents, goodwill, and other intangible property. These advantages become actual, however, only when a manufacturer organizes for exporting and commits the resources necessary for an active penetration of foreign markets. The higher start-up costs and risks of direct exporting compared to indirect exporting can only be justified by greater marketing effectiveness.

The most-common channels in direct exporting are those using foreign agents or distributors and foreign branches or subsidiaries. A less common channel is direct contact with final foreign buyers through company representatives working out of the home country, an arrangement that is generally suitable only for industrial products (including services) with high unit values.

Deciding on the Direct Export Channel.   In deciding on a direct export channel, managers need to make decisions on three levels: (1) *performance specifications* —what should the channel do? (2) *channel type*—which alternative channel most closely matches the performance specifications? (3) *channel member*—which intermediary (particular agent, distributor, or branch/subsidiary manager) in the most appropriate channel type is best qualified to carry out the foreign-marketing plan?

Channel-performance specifications indicate what the export manager wants in geographic market coverage in the target country, the intensity of that coverage, sales and promotional efforts, inventory and delivery systems, customer credit, product services (such as installation, maintenance, and repairs), and other channel performance. These specifications will depend on the company's product line, its objectives, its resources, and its foreign-marketing plan.

Performance specifications provide guidelines for the choice of the right channel type. For most manufacturers, the first step in this selection process is a comparison of the branch/subsidiary channel against the agency/distributor channel. The former requires the manufacturer to establish his own sales operations in the target country.[2] The major advantage of this channel type is greater control over the foreign-marketing plan; its major disadvantage is higher fixed costs. The choice between these two channel types, therefore, rests on a comparative assessment of their respective sales and costs over the entry-planning period. Manufacturers tend to use an agent/distributor channel for early export entry because of its lower start-up costs. If so, the second screening step compares foreign agents against foreign distributors in the target country.

A foreign agent is an independent middleman who represents the manufacturer in the target market. As an agent, this middleman does not take title to the manufacturer's product but rather sells that product on a commission basis. Furthermore, an agent seldom holds inventory (beyond samples) or extends credit to customers. Usually the manufacturer receives orders from his agent and then ships directly to the foreign buyer. A foreign agent, therefore, is essentially a salesman.

In contrast, a foreign distributor is a merchant who buys the manufacturer's product for resale to other middlemen or to final buyers. The distributor performs more functions than the agent (such as maintaining inventories, extending credit, servicing orders, and providing after-sales services), and he also assumes the ownership risks. His compensation is his profit margin on resale of the manufacturer's product.

In choosing between an agent and a distributor, export managers need to determine their profit contributions over the entry-planning period by estimating their respective sales and costs. In addition to the expected profit contribution of the channel, managers should also consider control, risk, and other nonprofit channel specifications.

The most attractive export channel today may become obsolete tomorrow as changes occur in markets, competition, channel systems, and public policy, as well as in a manufacturer's own products, resources, and entry strategy. For this reason manufacturers should avoid getting locked in to a particular channel, and they need to monitor channel performance continually to know when new channel arrangements become desirable.

Choosing a Foreign Agent or Distributor.   Finding good agents or distributors is a recurring problem for export managers. It is recommended that they begin the recruitment process by drawing up an agent (distributor) profile that lists all the desirable features of an agent (distributor) in a particular foreign target market. Exhibit 2 suggests the nature of such a profile.

Manufacturers are well advised to make the final selection of a foreign agent or distributor only after personal interviews with the best prospects. Interviews are the most reliable way for manufacturers to gain a feel for a particular agent (distributor) and his organization. But interviews should come only after desk research has identified the best candidates. The time and expense needed for a careful selection of an agent or distributor is justified by the critical importance of this decision. An old saying in exporting goes: "Your line is only as good as your foreign representative."

A final point on export entry. The manufacturer's agreement with his foreign representative should be a written contract that clearly sets forth the rights and obligations of both parties. Provisions relating to sole and exclusive rights, competitive lines, the resolution of disputes, and contract termination are of particular importance. A written agreement is most needed when things go wrong. It cannot, of course, insure that things will go right. Much of an export manager's job is the "care and feeding" of his foreign representatives—a never-ending task of building and sustaining an export-channel team that works together in a common endeavor.

EXHIBIT 2   ELEMENTS OF A MANUFACTURER'S PROFILE FOR EVALUATING PROSPECTIVE FOREIGN DISTRIBUTORS

Lines handled
Experience with manufacturer's or similar product line
Trading areas covered
Size of firm
Sales organization
Physical facilities
Willingness to carry inventories
After-sales service
Knowledge and use of promotion
Reputation with suppliers, customers, and banks
Record of sales performance
Cost of operations
Financial strength and credit rating
Relations with local government
Knowledge of English and other relevant languages
Knowledge of business methods in manufacturer's country
Overall experience
Willingness to cooperate with manufacturer

EXPORT OPERATIONS.   It is beyond the scope of this section to describe export operations, but certain features deserve some comment: documentary requirements, price quotations, payments arrangements, and organization.*

Export Documents.   The variety of export documents appears as a formidable obstacle to the newcomer in international business. Fortunately, manufacturers can call on international-freight forwarders to prepare most documents (as well as arranging shipment) and on banks for assistance in handling documents relating to international payments. Export documents must be prepared meticulously in the correct number of copies and at the right time. With the assistance of forwarders and banks, new export managers can learn quickly all they need to know about documentation.

Probably the single most important document is the ocean (or airway) *bill of lading* issued by an international carrier. Apart from serving as a receipt for goods delivered to the carrier and a contract for its services, the bill of lading controls possession of the shipment. When made out to the exporter's own order, it becomes a document of title necessary to obtain the goods at the foreign point of destination.

Export Price Quotations.   Standard price quotations are widely used in exporting. The two most important codifications are *International Commercial Terms* (Incoterms) adopted by the International Chamber of Commerce and *Revised American Foreign Trade Definitions* adopted by the Chamber of Commerce of the United States. Manufacturers should specify one of these codes in making export price quotations and negotiating export sales contracts.

---

*Useful publications on export operations include *Exporters' Encyclopaedia*; Small Business Administration, 1979; Dowd, 1977; and the *Foreign Trade Handbook*.

The most-common price quotations are *ex named point of origin* (Ex factory, Ex mill, Ex warehouse, etc.), f.a.s. (free along side), and c.i.f. (cost, insurance, freight). Under an Ex quotation, the exporter quotes a price that applies only at the named point of origin with the importer assuming all the responsibility and cost to transfer the merchandise to the ultimate foreign destination. A close variant of this quotation is f.o.b. (free on board) named inland carrier at named inland point, under which the exporter prices his goods as loaded on a specified carrier. An f.a.s. quotation includes delivery of the manufacturer's goods alongside a designated vessel (that is, within reach of its loading tackle) with the importer responsible for all subsequent movement of the goods. Under a c.i.f. quotation, the manufacturer's price covers the cost of the goods, the marine insurance, and all transportation charges to the foreign port of entry.

The quotation easiest for the manufacturer to prepare is ex point of origin, but importers generally prefer a c.i.f. quotation. F.a.s. is a good compromise because it is not difficult for the manufacturer to prepare and for the importer to use in calculating his landed cost. Manufacturers should be flexible in price quotations; it is inexcusable to lose a sale because of unwillingness to quote f.a.s. or c.i.f.

Payments Arrangements. The exporter assumes two nonpayment risks: (1) default by the importer, and (2) inconvertibility resulting from exchange restrictions imposed by the host government. Hence exporters need to check out not only the importer but also the convertibility of the importer's currency. A third risk is the foreign-exchange risk from variations in the rate of exchange. The exporter can avoid this risk by quoting the price in his own currency, a practice that is usually open to U.S. manufacturers given the international role of the dollar. When the exporter does quote his price in a foreign currency, he can hedge against the foreign-exchange risk by using the forward exchange market. In most circumstances, the exporter should hedge rather than speculate on foreign-exchange rates.

Ranked by a rising risk of nonpayment, the alternative forms of international payment are (1) cash in advance, (2) irrevocable, confirmed letter of credit, (3) documentary draft, (4) open account, and (5) consignment. An *irrevocable, confirmed letter of credit* enables the exporter to draw his draft (bill of exchange) against a domestic bank without recourse, an arrangement amounting to payment at the time of shipment.[3] With the *documentary draft* form of payment, the exporter draws his draft against the importer and sends it along with the negotiable bill of lading and other documents through his bank for collection. The importer can obtain the bill of lading (and therefore the goods) only after paying the draft or accepting it for later payment when the exporter extends credit. Because of the high risk, open-account and consignment-payment terms should be restricted to the exporter's own foreign affiliates or to old customers in convertible-currency countries.

In today's competitive markets, manufacturers need to be flexible in their payments arrangements, balancing risk against opportunity. Dogmatic insistence on letter-of-credit terms will lose sales to competitors who are offering credit under documentary drafts. U.S. manufacturers can obtain export credit insurance against both commercial and political risks from the Foreign Credit Insurance Association (FCIA).

Export Organization. A company just starting out in direct exporting is most likely to establish an export department staffed by an export manager and a few assistants.

This "built-in" department depends on other departments for order filling, accounting, credit approval, and other support activities. Although a good way to gain export experience with low start-up costs, the built-in export department should be viewed as a transitional device to be replaced later with a full-function export department or division.

Another aspect of export organization is the authority granted to the export manager. Too commonly that authority is limited by constraints (particularly in pricing and promotion) that weaken the export manager's ability to exploit foreign-market opportunities. Manufacturers who want an aggressive export strategy need aggressive export managers with the authority and resources to plan and execute that strategy.

ENTERING FOREIGN MARKETS THROUGH LICENSING AND OTHER CONTRACTUAL ARRANGEMENTS

Companies may enter foreign markets under a wide variety of contractual arrangements: licensing, franchising, technical agreements, service contracts, construction/turnkey contracts, contract manufacture, coproduction agreements, and others. Licensing is by far the most common contractual arrangement.

INTERNATIONAL LICENSING.   The essence of an international licensing agreement is the transfer of industrial property rights (patents, trademarks, and/or proprietary know-how) from a licensor in one country to a licensee in a second country. Industrial property rights are seldom assigned or sold outright to a foreign company. The usual practice is for the licensor to allow the licensee to use the rights for a specified period of time in return for a royalty compensation.

Manufacturers may license foreign companies for reasons that have little or nothing to do with foreign-market entry. Licensing may be viewed as simply a way of obtaining incremental income on "shelf" technology that has already been written off against domestic sales. Or a manufacturer may agree to exchange technology with a foreign counterpart, a practice known as cross-licensing. Again, manufacturers may license abroad to get legal protection for their patents and trademarks in countries where they must be "worked" to remain valid or to guard against infringement. Multinational companies commonly license their own foreign subsidiaries to establish legal ownership of industrial property, to facilitate repatriation of income, or to satisfy home and host governments. These uses of licensing do not concern us here; we are interested in licensing as a way of entering foreign markets.

Advantages and Disadvantages of Licensing as a Primary Entry Mode.   Licensing offers the manufacturer both advantages and disadvantages as a primary entry mode. Compared to export entry, the most evident advantage of licensing is the circumvention of import restrictions and transportation costs in penetrating foreign markets. Instead of transferring physical products to a target country, the manufacturer transfers intangible property rights and technology. In contrast to investment entry, the outstanding advantages of licensing are low entry costs and low direct risks. Although licensing incurs transfer costs, it requires no fixed investment by the manufacturer. For the same reason, licensing arrangements are exposed to far fewer political risks than foreign investments.

The most critical disadvantage of licensing as an entry mode is the licensor's lack of control over the licensee's marketing program. Although the licensor ordinarily maintains quality control over the licensed product, he does not control the licensee's volume of production or marketing strategy. The market performance of the licensed product, therefore, depends on the motivation and ability of the licensee. A second disadvantage is the lower absolute size of returns from licensing compared to returns from export or investment. In the representative agreement, licensing revenues take the form of running royalties over the life of the agreement. Today royalty rates seldom exceed five percent of the licensee's net sales, and agreements seldom run beyond 5–10 years.

Another disadvantage of licensing is its exclusivity. Ordinarily, a licensing agreement grants to the licensee exclusive rights to use the technology or trademark in the manufacture and sale of specified products in the licensee's country. For the duration of the agreement, therefore, the licensor is prevented from marketing those products in the licensee's country by using another entry mode, such as export or investment. This *opportunity cost* is particularly irksome when the licensee fails to exploit market opportunity. For example, in 1956 a U.S. manufacturer of construction materials granted to a Japanese firm an exclusive license for 20 years to manufacture and sell one of its specialty products that was highly successful in the United States. It so happened, however, that the Japanese firm failed to promote the product, paying it only marginal attention. Since the licensing agreement did not provide for a minimum royalty, the licensor received very little income. Nonetheless, the U.S. manufacturer was precluded from entering the Japanese market until the expiration of the agreement in 1976 (Ricks et al., 1974, p. 40).

The opportunity cost of foresaken income may be substantial even when the licensee does a very good job. For instance, a U.S. manufacturer of technical products granted a British firm not only an exclusive license to manufacture and sell its products in the United Kingdom but also an exclusive right to sublicense its know-how in all other foreign countries. At the time, the manufacturer had no plans to go abroad, and the licensing arrangement promised a continuing royalty income without the need for any foreign investment. Within a few years, the British licensee had sublicensed firms in several countries who, in turn, exploited very attractive market opportunities. Restricted to modest licensing royalties, the U.S. manufacturer could only watch his products creating much more income for the British licensee and the sublicensees (Mace, 1966, p. 76).

Licensing can also generate another kind of opportunity cost—the creation of a competitor in third markets or even in the manufacturer's home market at a later time.

Manufacturers can somewhat alleviate opportunity costs in licensing through contractual provisions that require minimum royalties or make possible the termination of the agreement because of poor performance. They can also participate more in their licensees' success by receiving some compensation in the form of equity or by an option to buy equity in licensee firms. In this way licensing entry may be transformed into investment entry. But the best safeguard is for managers to make licensing decisions only in the context of a comprehensive foreign-market-entry strategy.

For manufacturers who want an aggressive exploitation of foreign markets, licensing is generally a third-best entry strategy. Only when export or investment entry are not feasible or appropriate because of external or internal factors does licensing become attractive to such firms. This is most likely to be the case for developing and communist countries where exports may be kept out by import restrictions and, at the same time, investment entry may be barred by government policy, or the market may be too small or political risks too high to justify it. Small manufacturers are more attracted to licensing than large manufacturers because it is a low-commitment entry mode.

International licensing is most commonly combined with other entry modes. Indeed, the majority of licensing agreements by U.S. manufacturers are with their own foreign subsidiaries. Licensing is also frequently associated with joint ventures in which the licensor has an equity position. Licensing/equity mixes are popular because they allow the manufacturer to benefit from the growth of the licensee firm to a much higher degree than with a pure licensing agreement. Licensing may also be used by the manufacturer to source products for sale on world markets. Despite its limitations as a *primary* entry mode, therefore, licensing has become a flexible *secondary* entry mode that can be combined with other entry modes to form a mixed entry mode superior to its individual constituents.

Profitability Analysis of a Proposed Licensing Venture.   Many manufacturers view international licensing as a marginal activity that does not warrant a careful evaluation of its benefits and costs. This attitude fosters bad licensing decisions. Managers should decide on licensing as a primary entry mode for a target foreign country only after comparing licensing with alternative entry modes with respect to profitability, risk, and strategy objectives. Not to do so is to treat licensing as an *ad hoc,* tactical decision when it is truly a strategic decision that will determine a company's long-run participation in a target market and possibly in third markets as well. We offer an approach to profitability analysis of alternative entry modes later on in this section.

Negotiating and Managing Licensing Agreements.   Apart from helping managers to decide on the desirability of licensing entry for a particular target country, profitability analysis can also help managers negotiate better licensing agreements. It can provide an understanding of the licensor's objectives, the value of the technology package to the licensee, and the many trade-offs among the elements of a licensing agreement.

The signing of the licensing contract ends formal negotiations, but it is only the start of the licensing venture. In most ventures, the licensee will require continuing technical support from the licensor who, in turn, will have a continuing interest in helping the licensee achieve market success. Manufacturers, therefore, should view their international licensing arrangements as *nonequity* joint ventures that join together the strengths of the two partners in pursuit of a common goal—the creation of a sustainable role in the target market.

OTHER CONTRACTUAL ENTRY MODES.   In addition to licensing, several other contractual entry modes have become prominent in recent years, particularly in doing business with developing and communist countries. We can offer here only some brief comments on these arrangements.

International Franchising.   Unlike conventional licensing, the franchisor licenses a *business system* to an independent franchisee in a target foreign country. The franchisee carries on a business under the franchisor's trade name and in accordance with policies and practices laid down by the franchise agreement. In the decade

1965–1975, over 200 U.S. companies established 11,000 franchise outlets in foreign markets (Business International, 1977, p. 52). Through franchising, Holiday Inn, McDonald's, Kentucky Fried Chicken, Avis, and many other U.S. firms have become household names in scores of countries. The classic international franchisor, of course, is Coca Cola. International franchising has become, therefore, a powerful entry mode for companies that have products and services that can be reproduced by independent franchisees.

Contract Manufacturing.   In contract manufacturing, an international firm negotiates a long-term arrangement with a company in the foreign target country to manufacture a product for subsequent sale by the international firm. To get the product manufactured to its own specifications, the international firm usually transfers technology to the contract manufacturer.

Contract manufacturing can offer several advantages to the U.S. manufacturer as a mode of foreign-market entry. It requires only a modest commitment of capital and management resources compared to investment entry, avoids the political problems of local ownership, and allows the manufacturer to exercise full control over the foreign-marketing program. On the other hand, the manufacturer may find it difficult or impossible to locate a good contract manufacturer (especially in developing countries), he must often provide substantial technical assistance to bring the contract manufacturer up to desired quality levels, and—as in licensing—he may be creating a future competitor.

Management Contracts.   Under an international management contract, a company undertakes the day-to-day management of an independent enterprise in a foreign target country. In return for its management services, the company ordinarily receives fees over the fixed life of the contract.

Manufacturers usually enter management contracts only in conjunction with other arrangements, such as joint ventures or turnkey projects, because they seldom see themselves as primary suppliers of management services. Apart from fees, management contracts can provide manufacturers with a way of controlling foreign ventures in which their ownership is zero or minimal.

Turnkey Construction Contracts.   Under a turnkey project, a company provides not only engineering and construction services but also the additional services needed to bring the project up to the point of operation before it is turned over to the owner. At times a company may also operate the project for a transition period, an arrangement called *turnkey plus*. In short, a turnkey contract calls for the international transfer of a package of services—engineering, construction (often including financing), training, and (possibly) management.

Coproduction Agreements.   Coproduction is a kind of nonequity joint venture that is prominent in East-West business. Under a long-term contract, the Western company provides technology, components, and other inputs to a communist state enterprise in return for a share of the resulting production, which it then markets in the West. A U.S. manufacturer may gain several advantages from a coproduction agreement, including the sale of equipment and other products to the communist enterprise, a low-cost source of products for sale in the West, licensing royalties, and presence in a communist country that can generate future business. But these advantages must be weighed against certain possible disadvantages—the failure of the communist partner to maintain quality standards or meet delivery schedules, difficulties in protecting technology from disclosure, and the creation of a future competitor in third markets. Coproduction arrangements are very attractive to communist countries because payments to the Western companies come out of production rather than out of scarce foreign exchange.

ENTERING FOREIGN MARKETS THROUGH INVESTMENT IN LOCAL PRODUCTION

ADVANTAGES AND DISADVANTAGES OF INVESTMENT ENTRY. Companies invest abroad in production for three fundamental reasons—to acquire minerals and other raw materials through exploitation of natural resources, to source manufactured products at a low cost for use or sale at home and in third countries, and to build a logistical base for the penetration of a local market in the target country. Our interest here is with the third group of investors who use investment as a mode of foreign-market entry.

Through investment entry, a company can establish a full-function enterprise in the target country and thereby exploit its competitive advantages to a higher degree than is ordinarily possible through export or contractual entry modes. Investment entry allows a company to control the foreign-marketing program and to gain logistical advantages that may arise from the circumvention of import barriers, savings in transportation costs, or lower production costs. Because of its manifold advantages, investment entry has become the hallmark of the multinational corporation.

Investment entry also poses certain disadvantages. Compared to other entry modes, it requires a far greater commitment of capital, management, and other company resources. This higher commitment, in turn, means a higher exposure to business and political risks. Substantial start-up costs, long payback periods, and the cost of disinvestment in the event of failure must also be considered disadvantages of investment entry. Again, managers need more information to make good investment decisions than is true of export and licensing decisions. In particular, investment becomes a high-risk entry mode when the investor has no prior experience in the target country. Understandably, therefore, manufacturers are inclined to invest in a country only after gaining knowledge and experience through export or contractual entry modes.

THE DECISION TO INVEST IN A TARGET COUNTRY. The investment-entry decision is the outcome of a lengthy process that ordinarily involves several managers from different functions and at different levels of the company organization. We can structure this process as a sequence of checkpoints that must be passed before the final approval of a foreign-investment proposal: (1) Should we investigate the foreign-investment proposal? (2) Is the present investment climate in the target country acceptable? (3) Will the investment climate remain acceptable over our strategic planning period? (4) Will the investment project meet return on investment and other objectives after taking account of business and political risks? If not, can we redesign the project to make it acceptable? (5) Have our entry negotiations with the host government reached a satisfactory outcome?

Probably the most critical checkpoint is the first one—the decision to investigate.

The usual form of a positive decision to investigate is the creation of a management team drawn from marketing, finance, engineering, and other relevant functions. Not only is investigation costly in management time and money, it also tends to generate a commitment to invest. That is to say, the management team is quite likely to become a champion of the investment project. Before making a decision to investigate a proposal in depth, therefore, managers should review the alternative entry modes available to the company, including alternative investment modes (*de novo* versus acquisition and sole venture versus joint venture). Such a review helps prevent a premature decision to investigate by safeguarding against tunnel vision that considers only the investment proposal in question.

Following the decision to investigate, the next two checkpoints call for a thorough evaluation of both the present and future investment climates of the target country. The investment climate includes all the political, social, economic, and other environmental factors that can have a significant effect on the profitability and safety of the project over its planning horizon. Managers need to identify the critical or "killing" variables in the investment climate, and then assess their present and likely future behavior. Because so many critical variables relate to the political system and government of the host country, an assessment of the future investment climate is mainly an assessment of *political risk*: Will the current rules of the game (e.g., ownership rights, the right to import raw materials and parts used in production, and the right to repatriate profits) remain acceptable over the project's time horizon? To answer this question, managers should make explicit judgments on the stability of government policies and the political system in general.

If the investment climate checkpoints are passed, managers can turn to a full investigation of the project's economic feasibility—the market, production and supply, labor, capital sourcing, tax, and other factors. The recommended approach to measure the expected return on investment is a discounted cash-flow analysis with adjustments for political and other risks.

The last checkpoint is negotiations with the host government. Increasingly, governments are establishing screening systems to insure that foreign investment projects contribute net economic and social benefits to the host country. It has become vital, therefore, for managers to know the investment-screening criteria used by the government of a target country. Then it is often possible to design an investment project so as to enhance its acceptability by the host government and, at the same time, maintain its profitability.

The checkpoints identify the key elements of the investment-entry decision. But, in practice, that decision is seldom the outcome of a successive consideration of checkpoints. It is more likely to be a process with many twists, turns, and iterations. In most instances, managers will run through checkpoints several times before deciding on negotiations with the host government. And those negotiations can sometimes lead back to a general reassessment of the investment climate and project before the decision process comes to an end.

INVESTMENT ENTRY THROUGH ACQUISITION. A foreign-investment proposal may be a proposal to acquire a firm in the target country rather than start a venture from scratch. The checkpoints apply to all forms of investment entry, but acquisition entry has its own special features. Our interest here is with horizontal acquisition (the product line is similar to the investor's) the dominant purpose of which is entry into a foreign target market.

Advantages and Disadvantages of Acquisition Entry.   Acquisition entry offers a company several *potential* advantages compared to new-venture entry. They are only potential advantages because they depend critically on the choice of the acquired firm. A poor choice can transform a potential advantage into an actual disadvantage.

The most evident advantage of acquisition entry is a faster start in the target country. The investor gains control over a going concern with a product line, manufacturing facilities, managers, workers, and customers. To achieve the same market penetration through a new venture could take several years. For the same reason, acquisition entry promises a quicker return on investment. But this advantage presumes that the acquired firm is viable or can be made viable through a "quick fix" by the investor. Moreover, even when the acquisition is a good one, the time needed to fit it to the policies and operations of the investor company can easily take a year or more. In the event of a poor acquisition, the start-up period may exceed that of a new venture. One mistake is the acquisition of a firm with a product line radically different from the investor's. As an entry mode, the basic purpose of a foreign acquisition should be market diversification—not product diversification.

Through acquisition entry, an international company may also obtain a scarce resource that would be more costly to mobilize in a venture started from scratch. This resource can be any one or several of the acquired firm's assets—a product line, a manufacturing facility, goodwill, a dealer network, a work force, managers, technology, and so on. But once again, a poor acquisition can turn this advantage into a disadvantage. For example, a U.S. housewares company, frustrated by its inability to get distribution for its exports to West Germany, acquired a local housewares manufacturer. Unfortunately, this strategy backfired because the manufacturer also suffered from a weak distribution system. As a consequence, the U.S. company not only failed to solve its export distribution problem but also created a new problem—what to do with the products of its new German subsidiary.[4] To conclude on this point, if an international company is seeking a specific resource through an acquisition, it needs to make certain that an acquisition candidate actually possesses that resource and that it will become available to the investor after the acquisition is made. Other potential advantages of acquisition entry include a lower overall cost than building from scratch, synergistic effects on the investor's other operations, and the elimination of a competitor.

Acquisition entry may run into obstacles that are absent or weaker for new ventures. Acquisitions by foreign investors are opposed by many host governments because they eliminate locally owned enterprises. This negative policy is most prominent in developing countries, but it is also encountered in certain industrial countries, notably Australia, Canada, France, and Japan. For example, the French government is inclined to reject acquisitions involving "sensitive" industries (such as computers) or industry leaders.[5] Foreign acquisitions can also be blocked by U.S. antitrust policy, as shown by the recent attempt of Rockwell International to take over Serck Ltd., a British manufacturer of industrial valves.[6]

Finding a good acquisition candidate can take a great deal of time and money. In some countries, good candidates are simply not available. Further, the assessment of candidates is often arduous because of peculiar accounting systems, false or deceptive financial records, and the concealment of problems by local owners and managers.

Acquisition Strategy.   A study of 407 acquisitions in Europe by U.S. and European firms over the period 1965–1970 concluded that the payoff from acquisitions was lower than the payoff from investments in new manufacturing plants and the risk of failure was high. Only half of the acquisitions were rated successful by managers. It is prudent, therefore, for an international company to evaluate acquisition entry from the perspective of an overall foreign-market-entry strategy. If acquisition is judged the best way to enter a target country, then managers should articulate an acquisition strategy that specifies and ranks objectives; identifies the desired features in a candidate firm; and provides guidelines for pricing, financing, and assimilating the acquired firm. The proper execution of a good acquisition strategy can bring an international company an ongoing enterprise that has immediate access to a target market and can form a base for future market development.

INVESTMENT ENTRY THROUGH JOINT VENTURES.   Joint-venture entry occurs when an international company invests in a business enterprise in a target country together with a local partner firm. The foreign investor may hold a majority, a minority, or half of the joint venture's equity. Joint ventures are usually started from scratch, but they may also result from the purchase of equity in an existing local firm.

Advantages of Joint Ventures.   In developing and communist countries, joint ventures may be the only investment-entry mode available to international companies because host governments prohibit sole ventures. Many governments also prohibit majority joint ventures. Since the most common reason for joint-venture entry is host government policy, it follows that in many instances joint ventures are viewed by international managers as second-best to sole ventures. Nonetheless, joint ventures can offer foreign investors certain advantages apart from host-government acceptance.

By contributing capital to the joint venture, the local partner reduces the foreign partner's investment outlay and risk exposure. But the local partner's most valuable contribution is his knowledge of the local business environment and his ongoing contacts with local customers, suppliers, banks, and government officials. That is why joint ventures can be attractive to companies with little experience in foreign operations. It is also why many U.S. manufacturers have entered joint ventures in Japan even when sole-venture entry was open to them. In some cases, a joint venture may be the only way for an international company to gain an acceptance of its products by local middlemen and customers. The story of a U.S. manufacturer of poultry feed who invested in a sole venture in Spain illustrates this point. After production got underway, the manufacturer discovered he could not sell his feed because local poultry growers and feed producers were linked by generations-old business ties, resembling a closely knit family. In effect, the chicken-feed market was barred to newcomers. To circumvent this problem, the manufacturer bought several chicken farms in Spain only to learn that no one would buy his chickens. At last report, the manufacturer was thinking about buying restaurants in Spain! Clearly, the manufacturer could have avoided this sad experience by entering a joint venture with a Spanish feed company (Ricks, et al., 1974, pp. 24–25). Summing up, the local partner's resources combined with those of the foreign partner can sometimes exploit a target market more effectively than a sole venture.

Disadvantages of Joint Ventures.   International managers commonly complain that joint ventures dilute their control over foreign operations. Even with majority joint ventures, international managers must accommodate the interests of local partners.

The importance of control ultimately depends on a company's international strategy. One study of joint ventures concluded that companies attempting to penetrate multiple-country markets with a narrow product line found joint ventures an obstacle to the creation of global marketing and production systems. In contrast, companies that were continually introducing new products into foreign markets over several product lines showed a high tolerance for joint ventures (Franko, 1971).

Management control need not be synonymous with the degree of ownership. International companies may achieve a dominant control even over minority joint ventures in several ways. If, for example, a joint venture is continually dependent on the foreign partner for a critical input (say, technology), then that partner can exert a decisive control regardless of the ownership split. A minority foreign partner can also gain significant control through formal arrangements, such as the issuance of voting and nonvoting equity shares, bylaws that give him the right to select key executives or veto key decisions, or a management contract.

Choosing the Right Partner.   After managers have decided on a joint venture as the most appropriate entry mode for a target country, the most critical decision is the choice of a local partner. Joint ventures are often compared to marriages, and like marriages they frequently founder on the rocks of divorce.

Managers should first determine what they want the joint venture to accomplish in the target country over a strategic planning period, and how the joint venture fits into their overall international business strategy. Next they need to find out the objectives and policies of the prospective local partner, as well as the resources he would bring to the joint venture. Only after agreement on the purpose of the joint venture should managers go on to negotiate specific issues—ownership shares, the allocation of management responsibilities, profit reporting, dividend policy, the settlement of disputes, and others. If all the issues are not resolved during negotiations, they are certain to return at a later time. But even a comprehensive joint-venture agreement marks only the end of the venture's beginning. The venture will prosper only if the partners trust each other and continually support their common endeavor.

DECIDING ON THE RIGHT ENTRY MODE

THREE DECISION RULES.   We have now reviewed several foreign-market-entry modes. As we have seen, each mode has its general advantages and disadvantages. But managers must move from the general to the specific: They must decide on an entry mode for a particular product and for a particular foreign country/market. To do so, they may follow one of three different decision rules.

The *naive rule* is for managers to use the *same* entry mode, such as agent/distributor exporting, for all target countries. Because country markets and entry conditions are heterogeneous, this rule leads managers to forsake promising markets that cannot be penetrated with their single entry mode or to end up in markets with an inappropriate mode.

The *pragmatic rule* is for managers to find an entry mode that "works." In most instances, managers start by assessing export entry, and only if such entry is infeasible do they go on to assess another mode. This rule avoids the two pitfalls of the naive rule, and it also saves management time and effort. But it fails to lead managers to the most appropriate mode. A workable mode is not necessarily the right mode.

The *strategy rule* is for managers to decide on the right entry mode as a key element in a company's foreign-market-entry strategy. It is the most difficult rule to follow because managers must make systematic comparisons of alternative entry modes. But the payoff is better entry decisions.

AN APPLICATION OF THE STRATEGY RULE. It should be evident from our discussion of the different entry modes that the choice of a particular mode for a target country is influenced by many, often conflicting, forces. It is, therefore, a complex strategic decision that demands management judgment.

Our approach to the entry decision is an interpretation of the strategy rule: Choose the entry mode that maximizes profit contribution over the strategic planning period within the constraints of company resources, risk, and nonprofit objectives. Managers initiate this approach by screening all entry modes for *feasibility*: Is it possible for my company to enter the target country with this mode? Next managers make three comparisons of the workable modes that survive this screening—profit contribution, risk, and nonprofit objectives. Then these comparisons are brought together to form an overall comparative assessment. This final ranking of alternative entry modes requires managers to decide on trade-offs among profits, risks, and objectives. The principal advantage of this approach is that it compels managers to compare alternative modes and thereby directs them toward the right mode.

MONITORING FOREIGN-MARKET-ENTRY STRATEGIES

In this section we have focused our attention on one element of a foreign-market-entry strategy—the choice of an entry mode. We now close with a brief reference to another element—a control system that monitors the performance of the overall strategy.

International managers should establish performance standards for the current budgetary period that reflect their strategic objectives in target country/markets. Deviations between planned and actual performance become warning signals that trigger an investigation of causes. Only after that is done can managers take proper remedial action. More generally, strategic planning for foreign-market entry is a continuous process involving the assessment of past performance as well as changes in the international business environment. The right strategy for today may not be the right strategy for tomorrow. The evolution of a company's international business should describe a sequence of entry strategies designed by managers to create and sustain a presence in markets throughout the world.

NOTES

1. The National Federation of Export Management Companies, located in New York City, is the association of the regional trade associations. The U.S. Department of Commerce has published a *Directory of U.S. Export Management Companies.*

2. The distinction between a sales branch and a sales subsidiary is purely legal: A branch has the same legal identity as the parent company, whereas a subsidiary has its own legal identity. Whether a company chooses to use a branch or a subsidiary is a legal and tax question—not a marketing question.

3. The details of letter of credit and other international payments arrangements may be ob-

tained from banks. The major banks have publications in this field, such as *Financing of U.S. Exports* by the First National Bank of Chicago.

4. *Princess Housewares GmbH (A)* (Boston: Intercollegiate Case Clearing House, 1968).
5. "French Acquisition Climate Remains Highly Charged," *Business International*, April 13, 1979, pp. 113–114.
6. "Rockwell International: Reaching for the Automotive Market Abroad," *Business Week*, May 5, 1980, p. 87.

SOURCES AND SUGGESTED REFERENCES

Aharoni, Y. *The Foreign Investment Decision Process*. Boston: Graduate School of Business Administration, Harvard University, 1966.

Brasch, J.J. "Export Management Companies," *Journal of International Business Studies*, Spring–Summer 1978.

Business International. *International Licensing*. New York: BI, 1977.

Dowd, L.P. *Introduction to Export Management*. Burlingame, CA: Eljay Press, 1977.

Exporters' Encyclopaedia. New York: Dun and Bradstreet International, annual.

Foreign Trade Handbook. Chicago: Dartnell Corporartion, latest edition.

Franko, L.G. "Joint Venture Divorce in the Multinational Company," *Columbia Journal of World Business*, May–June 1971.

Mace, M.L. "The President and International Operations," *Harvard Business Review*, November–December 1966.

Newbould, G.D., P.J. Buckley, and J.C. Thurwell. *Going International: The Experience of Smaller Companies Overseas*. New York: Wiley, 1978.

Ricks, D., M. Fu, and J. Arpan. *International Businesss Blunders*. Columbus, OH: Grid, Inc., 1974.

Robinson, R.D. *National Control of Foreign Business Entry*. New York: Praeger, 1976.

Small Business Administration. *Export Marketing for Smaller Firms*, 4th ed. Washington, D.C.: U.S. Government Printing Office, 1979.

U.S. Dept. of Commerce. *Export Promotion Strategy and Programs*, study prepared by the Industry and Trade Organization. Washington, D.C.: Dept. of Commerce, 1978.

World Intellectual Property Organization. *Licensing Guide for Developing Countries*. Geneva: WIPO, 1977.

INTERNATIONAL MARKETING MIX

CONTENTS

MARKETING MIX AND MARKETING
STRATEGY   3

The Marketing Mix   3
Product Decisions   4
    Strategy one: product-promotional
    extension   4
    Strategy two: product
    extension—promotional adaptation   5
    Strategy three: product
    adaptation—promotional extension   5
    Strategy four: dual adaptation   5
    Strategy five: product invention   5
Pricing Decisions   6
Advertising   7
    Advertising strategy   8
    Stages of development   9
Coordinating International Advertising   9
Channel-of-Distribution Decisions   11
    Middlemen   11

INDUSTRIAL VERSUS CONSUMER
MARKETING   12

Buying Motives and Behavior in the
Consumer Market   13
    Buyer characteristics   13
    Product characteristics   14
    Seller characteristics   14
    Situational characteristics   14

Buying Motives and Behavior in the
Industrial Market   15
    Environmental factors   15
    Organizational factors   16
    Interpersonal factors   16
    Individual factors   16

UNCONTROLLED VARIABLES AND
MARKETING-MIX DECISIONS   16

Cultural and Social Factors   17
    Innovation and change   17
Legal Environment   18
    U.S. laws and international marketing   18
    Foreign laws and international
    marketing   19
Political Environment   20

Economic Environment   21

PLANNING THE INTERNATIONAL
MARKETING MIX   22

Developing a Marketing Mix   22
    Demographic variables   25
    Psychographic variables   25
    Geographic variables   25
    Product-usage variables   25

SOURCES AND SUGGESTED
REFERENCES   25

INTERNATIONAL MARKETING MIX

Samuel Rabino

MARKETING MIX AND MARKETING STRATEGY

Effective management of international marketing-mix strategy is a key ingredient of a successful enterprise. The caliber of a firm's product-market strategy and its execution separates the high performers from the low performers. Differences in market share, in technological accomplishments, in customer loyalty, in product innovation, in quality of the product manufactured, in sales growth, in after-tax profit, in return on investment, and in reputation and image all tend to derive to a large extent from a well-developed strategy and execution of marketing-variables decisions.

Luck and Ferrell (1979) suggest that strategic planning, the determination of strategies, should take place in three phases:

1. Marketing objectives—the creation of a viable, sustainable customer base and market for the firm's products/services.
2. Policies—the rules that guide the selection of strategies as well as the subsequent actions that implement them.
3. Strategies—the fundamental means of reaching the objectives.

The discussion will concentrate on the third stage—identifying and selecting marketing strategies—but a prerequisite to that stage is the sound and explicit determination of objectives and policies.

THE MARKETING MIX. Marketing consists of an integrated strategy that is aimed at providing customer satisfaction. To do this, a company has certain demand-influencing variables that together constitute the *marketing mix*. The mix includes the product or service offered by the firm, the distribution channels used (e.g., wholesalers, distributors, retailers) to make the product available to customers, the price charged for the product, advertising and sales promotion, and personal selling effort. The four marketing-mix variables—product, distribution, promotion, and price—are traditionally viewed as controllable, that is, variables that are under the control of the firm and can influence the level of consumer response.

In the following sections each of the marketing-mix variables will be discussed separately. Subsequently, implications for marketing planning will be derived.

PRODUCT DECISIONS.   Two issues are particularly relevant for the development of international product plans. The first involves a decision between a product-differentiation or a market-segmentation approach and the second deals with product-life-cycle analysis.

Product differentiation provides one basis upon which a supplier can appeal to selective buying motives. Products may be perceived to be different by buyers; these differences can be either real or imaginary. Simply stated, products are different if the consumer believes that they are different. When a company designs a single marketing mix and directs it at an entire market for a particular product, it is using a market, or undifferentiated, approach. For example, Levi, Wrangler, and Lee use essentially the same appeals and the same products in all of Western Europe ("Blue Jeans," 1975). Frequently a company will attempt to use promotional efforts to differentiate its products from competitors' products. It hopes to establish in customers' minds the superiority and preferability of its product compared to competing brands. Thus Levi in an effort to differentiate its products, markets them in Europe with the theme "The Original Jeans."

The product-life-cycle refers to a sales pattern that most successful products undergo. The sales pattern is frequently described in terms of four basic states: introduction, growth, maturity, and decline. In the introduction stage, the product is new in the marketplace. Sales begin to build as initial buyers become aware of the product, try it, and ultimately decide to adopt it. As interest in the product expands, the product moves into its growth stage, characterized by a rapid increase in sales. Other firms, attracted by a potential market opportunity, introduce similar products, which expand both the availability of the product and marketing efforts aimed at building sales. As sales continue to expand, the product moves into the maturity stage. Competition is typically keen as the market reaches a saturation, or leveling-off, point. Severe price competition often prevails, thus reducing profits. After reaching a maturity stage, the sales of some products actually decline from their peak-sales level and the product may enter a period of decline.

The product-life-cycle concept is important for two reasons. First, it applies in an international as well as a domestic marketing situation. Products are introduced in export markets, create a market or capture market share, attract competitors, and finally may be squeezed out of a market. Second, and perhaps more important, many firms attempt to expand sales and prolong the growth and maturity phases of the life cycle by seeking new markets in other countries. The general approach is to find a product strategy that meets the needs of foreign customers at a reasonable cost to the firm. According to Keegan (1980), five policy alternatives can be used to expand international markets.

Strategy One: Product-Promotional Extension.   This is the easiest marketing strategy to implement and probably the most profitable one. The strategy entails selling in every country in which the company operates exactly the same product with the same advertising and promotional themes and appeals that it uses in the United States. Pepsi Cola, for example, has been successful in selling the same product with standard promotional themes in a variety of markets. Pepsi has estimated that the cost of preparing ads would be raised substantially by tailoring promotions to each foreign market. Although this strategy has worked for soft drinks, other American firms have run into problems trying to export prepared foods that do not fit local preferences. A case in point is the unsuccessful effort by a U.S. company to capture the British cake-mix market. It offered U.S.-style cake mix with fancy frosting only to discover that English consumers prefer their cake at teatime, and that the cake they prefer is dry, spongy, and suitable for being picked up with the left hand while the right hand manages a cup of tea.

The advantages of this strategy lie not only in the substantial economies associated with standardization of marketing communication, but also in cost saving resulting from manufacturing economies of scale and the elimination of product R&D costs.

Strategy Two: Product Extension—Promotional Adaptation.   This strategy involves selling the same product in foreign markets but adapting it to local conditions. American firms marketing analgesics in Japan sell essentially the same product under a somewhat different theme. The copy theme for Bufferin, for example, is "gentle for your stomach," whereas in the United States it is positioned primarily as a headache reliever ("Marketing in Japan," 1978).

As with the product-promotion strategy, the principal appeal of this strategy is its relative low cost, because R&D and manufacturing costs remain the same. The only costs incurred are those associated with the development of different promotional strategies.

Another example is Colgate's introduction of a soap bar to Mexico. Colgate has put its Irish Spring formula to use here in a new "double protection" bar soap called Nordiko. The choice of the name Nordiko (as opposed to Irish Spring) was based on the assumption that it projected a fresh and cool image to the Mexican consumers ("Colgate's Nordiko," 1976).

Strategy Three: Product Adaptation—Promotional Extension.   This approach to international product planning extends without change the basic communications strategy developed for the United States, and adapts the American product to local use conditions. Exxon (then Esso), for example, adapted its gasoline to meet different climate conditions in foreign markets, but used its famous "Put a tiger in your tank" promotion in all areas.

Strategy Four: Dual Adaptation.   When the sociocultural and economic conditions are such that using the same product and/or promotion is rendered impossible, a strategy of adaptation of both the product and the communications efforts is suggested. Brazil, for example, had been one of the world's leading importers of Scotch whisky until about 5 years ago, when the military government began to tax heavily all imports it considered "superfluous." Brazilian and other manufacturers came up with a score of new brands, all bottled and some even distilled in Brazil. The products are sweeter than the traditional Scotch whisky and are promoted as thirst-quenching, cooling drinks ("Scotch: On the Rocks," 1978).

Strategy Five: Product Invention.   Perhaps the most risky market expansion strategy is to try to invent something to meet the special needs of overseas customers. Colgate, for example, saw potential in the estimated 600 million people in the world who wash clothes by hand. To tap this market they developed an inexpensive (less than $10), plastic, hand-powered washer that has the tumbling action of a modern automatic machine. This product has sold well in Mexico and could help expand the demand for Colgate's laundry detergent.

Although there is no specific criterion for selecting one strategy over another so that a company's profits will be maximized over the long run, marketing research of multinational markets should result in a set of decision rules aiding a company in the selection of the optimal strategy. The first step in formulating an international product policy is the identification and definition of the potential market for the product. Prospective buyers have to be identified. Their ability to buy through income, credit, or other means has to be ensured as well as their willingness to buy. Often marketing-opportunity analysis must delve into many attitudinal, experiential, and life-style aspects of individuals in order to determine how best to sort out those who do not want to buy from those who do. In Italy, for example, purple is considered a negative color and labels bearing female religious figures are considered poor taste ("Adapting Export Packaging," 1979). Obviously the final strategy decision should be consistent with corporate objectives (e.g., geographic expansion), research and development capacities, and financial constraints.

PRICING DECISIONS. Efficient pricing of goods and services is often a critical factor in the successful operation of a firm. Although the basic pricing ingredients—costs, competition, demand, and profit—are the same for all firms, the optimum mix of these factors varies according to the nature of products, markets, legal and ethical constraints, and corporate objectives.

Price is of unique strategic importance to marketing planners for a number of reasons. It is an important consideration in matching firm resources and supplies to buyer demand. "Unlike product, promotion, and distribution, price can be adjusted quickly and frequently to match supply or demand fluctuation," (Luck and Ferrell, 1979).

Pricing strategies are influenced by a variety of factors that affect ultimate price decisions. These factors may be more involved than traditional microeconomic determinants such as supply, demand, and competitive considerations, and can include such considerations as internal corporate policies and the stage in the product life cycle.

Pricing strategies of U.S. manufacturers affect the competitive posture of the United States in export markets as well as the level of export involvement. It has been observed that more than 90 percent of U.S. manufacturers have never developed export markets (Lang, 1968). Part of the reason for the limited export performance by U.S. firms lies in pricing policies. The export-pricing policy most frequently used by U.S. companies is a cost-plus method (Keegan, 1980). To use this method, a fixed dollar amount is added to the cost of an item to yield a selling price. This amount is the markup designed to cover overhead expenses and produce a profit for a firm. This approach clearly does not take into account competitive conditions in export markets.

Two important disadvantages are associated with the cost-plus approach, according to Keegan. First, it ignores demand elasticity, which changes seasonally along a business cycle. Theoretically, we can be in a situation of rising costs and an upswing of the economy while the economies of other exporting countries are depressed or lagging behind the United States and the costs of factors of production are cheaper. Second, and perhaps an even more serious problem with markup pricing, is the tendency to apply the same average markup percentage to broad classes of goods with little or no regard for possible differences in price sensitivity. In both situations the exporter might miss an opportunity in an export market where a relatively low price would have resulted in large orders.

Cateora and Hess (1979), observe that pricing, from the standpoint of the international marketer, is probably the most complicated decision variable among the four marketing-mix variables. Its sensitivity to variations in the competitive conditions, taxation procedures, legislation, intracompany competition, and monopolistic purchasers makes the issue of who sets a price for a product more and more important. It appears that there are three alternative positions a company can take toward worldwide pricing (Keegan, 1980), as follows:

1. *The ethnocentric pricing policy.* This policy states that the price of a product will be the same whether it is sold domestically or in export markets. Obviously this approach does not take into account demand sensitivity in the various product markets.

2. *The polycentric pricing policy.* This policy is used in a situation in which a subsidiary or affiliate is entitled to pursue pricing policies that are independent of the parent company. The flexibility of this approach allows for more maneuverability in responding to local market conditions. One disadvantage that is associated with this approach is that local managers do not benefit from corporate experience and more-sophisticated types of analyses that the parent company could have provided.

3. *The geocentric pricing policy.* This is an approach that is less flexible than the polycentric approach and yet not as rigid as the ethnocentric pricing policy. The assumption here is that there are some local market factors that should be recognized, but the local decision making is accompanied by headquarters' guidance. A case in point is TRW's pricing strategy. TRW's Automotive Worldwide Group puts pricing to final consumers in the hands of its operating subsidiaries. Local prices are determined by the local marketplace. Similarly, at American Can International, pricing to customers is left to the local affiliates. Headquarters is available for assistance on pricing matters, and affiliates may call on it if they so wish (*Managing Global Marketing,* 1976).

In the final analysis, companies have tried to keep a fairly tight rein on local decision making. A relatively unified pricing structure, one that operates if not worldwide, then at least regionally, aids in discouraging source switching by customers (if free access to various sources is permitted by the company) and minimizes counterproductive competition among various subsidiaries for third-market business.

ADVERTISING. Marketing communications are attempts by a firm to influence the behavior of the markets for its products and services. According to Kotler (1980), advertising consists of nonpersonal forms of communications to target buyers and publics conducted through paid media under clear sponsorship.

Kleppner (1980) states that advertising may be geared toward the following:

1. Increasing the frequency of use of a product.
2. Increasing the variety of uses of a product.
3. Adding a new product to a well-known line.
4. Reinforcing credibility of important claims.
5. Launching a special promotional campaign.

   6. Turning a disadvantage into an advantage.

   7. Dispelling a misconception.

   8. Enhancing the image of a company (corporate advertising).

One of the most-basic marketing objectives is the creation of repeat-purchase behavior or branch loyalty. Brand loyalty implies a repeat purchase on the basis of preference rather than habit. Once a brand loyalty has been established with an identifiable consumer group, the next objective is to increase the rate of consumption. The advertising of most consumer packaged goods (e.g., detergents) includes just such a theme. Experience has shown that it is easier to interest old customers in buying more of a product than to find new ones. Clorox, for example, long known as a bleach, is now promoted as an efficient disinfectant to encourage sales to its existing customers.

Promotion can be used when adding a line in order to benefit from the reputation the firm has generated for its brands. Similarly, advertising efforts are used to enhance or fine tune implementation of other marketing objectives and programs.

The last application area, corporate advertising, is deemed by this writer to be especially important in the context of international marketing. Given the suspicions and controversy surrounding the operations of multinationals, especially in developing countries, it appears that corporate advertising, that is, advertising aimed at creating a favorable corporate image rather than selling a particular product, could be particularly useful. Exxon's corporate advertising, for example, emphasizes its educational and training programs around the world.

Advertising Strategy.   Ultimately, advertising strategy entails two broad groups of decisions. The first is the writing of a copy platform. It sets forth the actual themes and claims to be used and usually includes the mood of an ad and expressions of product features. The second decision set, media planning, involves media-mix decisions, that is, the selection of a combination of television and radio programs, magazines, newspapers, and other media vehicles that will maximize profits, given a budget constraint.

Quantitative models have been developed to help structure and evaluate media and audience data. Obviously the development of media models is predicated on an understanding of the appropriateness of media vehicles and a knowledge of how media are matched with markets. In general, advertisers prefer media whose audience characteristics are closest to the profile of market characteristics of their consumers (Sissors, 1971). Characteristics by which the target population may be identified include demographic, psychographic, and purchase-behavior variables. The goal for international advertisers is to direct market-research efforts toward data about the available media in a desired export market and the demographics or psychographic profiles of local target markets. Media availability and target-market characteristics will dictate the selection of a media mix with an optimal combination of cost and exposure value.

A central component in the development of an advertising plan is the creation of the appeal or the message to be communicated to the target audience. Since the appeal is usually expressed in a combination of words and a picture, language and cultural barriers complicate the task of the international advertiser. The problem involves not only different languages but also different connotations of expressions that are meaningful in one setting but not in another. Thus "Body by Fisher" became "Corpse by Fisher" in some translated versions, and Pepsi's "Come Alive" came out instead "Come out of the Grave" (Dunn, 1976).

Stages of Development. Another important variable to be considered in international-advertising planning is the target export market's stage of economic development. There is a clear association between advertising volume as a percentage of GNP and the general level or stage of economic development of a country—the higher the general level in a country, the higher is the proportion of income spent on advertising (Keegan, 1980). One general implication for the exporting firm or a multinational is that the per capita spending on advertising can be used as a rough indicator of the relative importance of advertising vis-à-vis other elements of the marketing mix.

Regional differences exist also in terms of media availability. Literacy, for example, influences the relative effectiveness of print medium vis-à-vis other media (e.g., radio). Radio and television services either may not be offered or may be offered so minimally that they cannot really be considered viable media options. Promotion in India is a case in point. Half of the total advertising spending is aimed at the literate middle-class urban citizen. However, when aiming ads at the illiterate rural segment of the population, advertisers screen commercials at movie houses. Radio is only a secondary medium, since most government-controlled radio stations are not permitted to carry commercials. Although television stations are allowed to carry commercials, advertisers consider television to be too expensive a medium ("India Offers," 1978).

In general, the proportion of advertising spent on print is relatively low in Latin America and high in the Middle East and Africa. Television expenditures, as a percentage of all advertising, are notably above average in Asia and very low in the Middle East and Africa. Radio receives a higher-than-average proportion of expenditures in the Middle East, Africa, Latin America, and Australia/New Zealand in comparison with the United States, Canada, and Europe (Keegan, 1980.) These spending patterns can be used as one guideline when planning and developing a media mix in any given region.

COORDINATING INTERNATIONAL ADVERTISING. Peebles *et al.* (1978) suggest six steps to govern the conduct of the international-advertising effort. These steps or decision rules are aimed at circumventing the "standardized versus localized" debate (a worldwide standardized advertising campaign vs. a custom-tailored, country-specific campaign).

As shown in Exhibit 1 the steps are as follows:

1. *Marketing and advertising strategy and objectives.* At this stage, the home office and its subsidiaries jointly clarify their understanding of the firm's marketing objectives. In many cases, subsidiary management will be able to offer valid and useful insights when establishing objectives. Recurrent themes may alert the home office to market problems and opportunities of which they were previously unaware.

2. *Individual market input.* Based upon the home office's reaction to their strategies and objectives, each separate market builds a tentative advertising campaign. A sufficient amount of visual material and copy must be prepared

EXHIBIT 1 FRAME WORK FOR PROGRAMMED MANAGEMENT APPROACH

1. Strategy and Objectives

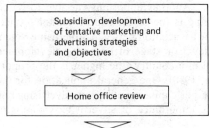

2. Individual Market Input

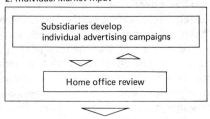

3. Testing

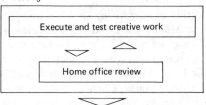

4. Campaign Review

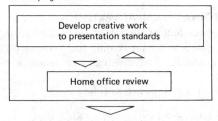

5. Budget Approval

6. Campaign Implementation

Source. Peebles, 1978.

to indicate the primary creative thrust of the campaign. The home office will review all the campaigns and offer suggestions.

3. *Testing.*   Each campaign is market tested in its particular country. The home office will review the test results and offer comments and suggestions.

4. *Campaign review.*   Based upon market test results and the home office critique of those results, subsidiaries develop their campaigns to presentation standards. Each subsidiary's campaign is then submitted to the home office for review and approval or modification.

5. *Budget approval.*   Final budget approval for each subsidiary is delayed until the home office evaluates the campaign.

6. *Implementation.*   Upon reviewing budget approval, the subsidiaries may start a full-scale campaign implementation. Media commitments may be made and final production work begins.

Thus an overall campaign resulting from this approach may be highly standardized, or it may be a campaign consisting of several elements aimed at unique market conditions.

CHANNEL-OF-DISTRIBUTION DECISIONS.   Distribution is concerned with organizing systems of transportation, storage, and communication so that goods and services will be readily available to customers (Dalrymple and Parsons, 1980). The objective is to minimize the costs of storing and shipping merchandise while maintaining or improving sales to the ultimate user. Perhaps more than any other marketing-mix variable, distribution decisions are the least controllable by an exporting firm or a parent company's headquarters. Furthermore, the search for a reliable distributor is considered to be one of the most important barriers to exporting for small companies. Ultimately, channel decisions determine how the firm will reach its target markets, and thus the choice and performance of the channel are major determinants of the firm's financial performance. It is important, therefore, to review some of the complex issues surrounding the selection and evaluation of middlemen.

Middlemen.   The selection of middlemen for use in distribution channels should be based on sales and profit considerations. There are four key determinants of channel strategy: market targets, the marketing program, product or service characteristics, and corporate skills and resources.

According to Cravens *et al.* (1980), direct distribution, whereby a manufacturer performs all channel functions by making contact with consumers and/or industrial and institutional end users through a sales force or by mail, is favored when consistent with the following type of setting: Target markets include a few large customers or customers concentrated geographically, a major component of the marketing program is personal selling, the product is complex (e.g., computers) and requires the manufacturer's personnel in selling and maintenance, and the manufacturer possesses sufficient skills and financial resources to accommodate direct distribution.

When attempting to reach a more-diffuse customer base with products that are frequently purchased in small amounts by a variety of users (e.g., food items), where promotion through advertising is more effective than personal selling, or when corporate capabilities are limited, the use of intermediaries becomes a more realistic option.

One of the most effective and economical ways of locating foreign representation, especially for the smaller firm, is by utilizing the services of the Department of Commerce ("Locating Foreign," 1979). Computer files containing information on more than 150,000 importing firms, trade lists, trade missions, and other services are all available to the prospective buyer and should aid him or her in getting exposure in export markets through intermediaries. Consider the lucrative Middle Eastern market. Black & Decker, Beecham, Union Carbide, Unilever, Nestlé, Kraft, General Electric, and Gillette all have one thing in common: They rely on independent distributors to sell their products ("Developing Middle East," 1977). Union Carbide, for example, works with seven trading companies in the Arabian Gulf area to market the full range of consumer products. Its industrial products currently are sold direct by product specialists, working out of regional headquarters in Athens, because of their high level of specialization.

In general, a strategy of using a single distributor is recommended to the new exporter who is still ambivalent about involvement in foreign markets and when product acceptability is uncertain. After a product "takes off" in the export market there might be a justification for opening a local selling branch or agency or employing more distributors. This pattern of evolution in distribution approaches typifies, for example, the market behavior of U.S. firms operating in the United Kingdom ("Surveying," 1979). Firms new to the market find it more convenient to appoint one distributor to cover the whole country. Later, in order to achieve greater market penetration, other distributors may be appointed. A number of larger U.S. firms maintain their own sales organizations in the United Kingdom as familiarity with the British market increases. Others appoint sales agents who are manufacturers of similar or contemporary products and take on additional items on a commission basis.

It is clear that channel decisions are particularly difficult to implement and supervise from the home country just because, as a general rule, the longer the channel, the more middlemen there are and the less the control in the export market is. Different cultural and economic systems further aggravate this problem. Legal constraints, such as the laws governing termination of foreign distributors' services, sometimes limit the use of such distributors and might lead to a costly establishment of a selling branch by the exporting firm.

In conclusion, it should be recognized that a proper distribution strategy offers a firm the best means of reaching its export market. Although some companies may find that going directly to consumers is more appropriate than using intermediaries, many are compelled either to form new channels or to become members of existing channels. When selecting a foreign distributor it becomes cirtically important to refer to data sources provided by organizations such as the United Nations or the U.S. Department of Commerce. They can help provide information on issues such as reputation and quality of service provided by a foreign distributor as well as the legal/economic environments.

INDUSTRIAL VERSUS CONSUMER MARKETING

Defining and analyzing markets is an early activity in developing a marketing strategy. "To the marketer, a market is the set of all individuals and organizations who are actual or potential buyers of a product or service" (Kotler, 1980). This section focuses on the opportunities originating from the fact that consumers differ.

Segmentation is the strategy of developing different marketing programs directed to different market subgroups or segments. These market subgroups are the market targets. A market target is any group of potential customers toward whom a company decides to direct its marketing efforts. A company may choose to view all potential customers within a product market as sufficiently similar to treat it as a single market, for example, developing one marketing strategy for all the Arab countries in the Middle East.

Other market-target options involve separating potential customers within product markets into different groups based on some demand-related characteristic. For example, somewhat different marketing campaigns could be developed for France than for England. In such a situation different marketing mixes would be designed for different target markets. Thus the essence of marketing strategy becomes the fine tuning of the market mix according to the target market to which it is applied.

The objective of the marketer is to know and understand the market or submarket. In this context two general types of markets will be discussed: the consumer market and the industrial market. These markets are essentially distinguished on the basis of the buyers' role and motives rather than the characteristics of the purchased product. Consumers are individuals and households buying for personal use. Industrial buyers purchase for the purpose of producing.

In the following section, the motives and reasons for buying decisions in consumer- and industrial-market settings will be discussed. Gaining insight into the dynamics of the decision process will result in a better fit between the desired target market (e.g., individual consumers, organizations) and the marketing mix of the exporting firm. Applications of buying-behavior information generally have one or both of two objectives. The first is to make demand predictions. The other objective is demand diagnosis, which is concerned with describing what markets are like and explaining why management should expect certain kinds of market behavior to take place.

BUYING MOTIVES AND BEHAVIOR IN THE CONSUMER MARKET.   The consumer market buys products and services to satisfy a variety of needs—physiological, psychological, social, and spiritual. Literature of consumer behavior is very extensive and relies on clinical and social psychology , economics, and sociology. Only factors that can clearly be related to marketing-mix variables will be discussed here. According to Kotler (1980), the major factors influencing consumer buying behavior are in turn as follows:

1.   Buyer characteristics.
2.   Product characteristics.
3.   Seller characteristics.
4.   Situational characteristics.

The objective of the international marketer is to collect information about each of these factors.

Buyer Characteristics.   Cultural, social, personal, and psychological factors are relevant to buyer characteristics. Thus, for example, mood is very extensively used as a theme in Japanese advertising and reflects the cultural characteristic of avoiding confrontation. "Interestingly, one spot might look very much like another mood spot, yet Japanese viewers seem to clearly note the difference." *Advertising Age* ("Marketing in Japan," 1978.) Social factors include the influence of other people in the consumer's life, particularly the reference groups, family, roles, and status. Reference groups, for example, are all those groups that influence an individual's attitudes, opinions, and value system. A reference group's opinions of a product or service could be important in influencing a buyer's decision. Continuing the Japanese example, one observes that a large part of the advertising efforts is directed toward a group rather than toward the individual, since the Japanese, particularly the men, feel themselves to be part of a group. Hence "we" and "us" are popular pronouns in ad copy.

Another way of analyzing group influence on individual buying behavior is to examine the social stratification or social classes in a given country. Separation of classes can lead to important differences in behavior within the same culture. Many American companies that aim their marketing programs at the middle class can appeal to the same target market in other cultures. In Latin America, for example, the emerging middle class is expected to be more receptive to work-saving appliances, convenience foods, and disposable items—product concepts that up until recently were not particularly meaningful in societies consisting primarily of two classes: the very poor, who had no purchasing power, and the very rich, who preferred luxury items ("Is the Well," 1977).

Personal factors include the consumer's age, sex, occupation, economic circumstances, life-style, and personality. The worsening economic conditions in the United Kingdom, for example, resulted in the introduction of Economy Fish Fingers by the market leader, Birds Eye. An economy pack, the product was modified by a gradual reduction of the amount of cod in it ("Today's European Consumer," 1977). An earlier attempt to use cheaper cuts of fish failed because the consumers were not ready for such a radical downgrading.

Finally, psychological characteristics include consumers' motivations, perceptions, attitudes, and beliefs.

Product Characteristics. Various characteristics of the product influence buying decisions—color, styling, quality, price, and taste. For food items, backup services might also influence consumer decisions. The marketer has control over these product attributes and can design or rearrange them so that the appeal of the product to the target market of interest will be maximized.

Seller Characteristics. Characteristics of the seller will also influence the buying-decision outcome. The seller in this context could be the manufacturer. The reputation associated with his name, with the retail outlet, or with the combination of the two is critical. The image of the manufacturer's reliability and the retailer's knowledgeability, friendliness, and service are considerations important to buying decisions.

Situational Characteristics. Various situational factors influence the buying decision. Climate, seasonability, weather, economic outlook, current fads, and other variables that the manufacturer does not control but has to contend with, all have an impact.

BUYING MOTIVES AND BEHAVIOR IN THE INDUSTRIAL MARKET. The differences between industrial and consumer buying stem largely from the fact that the industrial buyer is responsible to an organization. The characteristics of the organization become important influences on buying decisions. Size will dictate quantity needs, for instance. Furthermore, there are typically fewer buyers in industrial markets than in consumer markets, which makes it possible to offer more-personalized services (Cravens *et al.*, 1980).

Several individuals may be involved in the industrial buying process, including product users, top management, purchasing agents, financial specialists, and research-and-development specialists. This complicates the decision process. Industrial buyers are likely to have greater training and technical knowledge about the product in question. Thus the American firm exporting industrial products must offer a marketing mix that is more technical than that of consumer marketing.

As in consumer marketing, many theories have been advanced to explain how industrial buyers make their purchase decisions. A widely accepted model of industrial buying behavior is that of Webster and Wind (1972). According to this model the variables influencing industrial buying decisions can be classified as belonging to one of the two following categories: task and nontask. Each set contains four classes of variables as illustrated in Exhibit 2.

The task category includes variables that are directly related to the buying problem. The emphasis here is on maximizing the economic objectives of the buyer, such as favoring a supplier with the lowest total cost or most reliable after-sale maintenance. The nontask category includes variables that extend beyond the buying problem. Personal motives such as ego enhancement or risk aversion are more important here.

One implication of this model for the American seller is the need to evaluate the foreign buyer from the perspectives of both economic incentive and the human and social aspects.

Equally important is the evaluation of the four classes of variables that appear in both categories: environmental, organizational, social, and individual.

Environmental Factors.   These factors are external to the organization, where buying decisions are influenced by the level of primary demand, economic outlook, the cost of borrowing, the rate of technological change, political and regulatory development,

EXHIBIT 2   CLASSIFICATION AND EXAMPLES OF VARIABLES INFLUENCING ORGANIZATIONAL BUYING DECISIONS

Type of Influence	Task	Nontask
Individual	Desire to obtain lowest price	Personal values and needs
Social	Meetings to set specifications	Informal, off-the-job interactions
Organizational	Policy regarding local suppliers preference	Methods of personal evaluation
Environmental	Anticipated changes in prices	Political climate in an election year

Source. Webster and Wind, 1972.

and competitive developments. These environmental influences are normally beyond the control of both buyer and seller and have to be considered as given.

Organizational Factors.   Each company spells out objectives, policies, procedures, structures, and systems to guide the buying process. Buying decisions are affected by the company's systems of reward, authority, status, and communication.

Interpersonal Factors.   These factors involve the interaction of several persons of different status, authority, empathy, and persuasiveness in the company. It would be very difficult for the American seller to know in advance how interpersonal factors work in a particular company.

Individual Factors.   Individual factors are all those factors that influence individuals' preferences and choice rules, such as demographic characteristics and general attitudes toward risk taking (Kotler, 1980).

The model described above could be used as a framework for developing marketing and selling strategies aimed at industrial buyers. The marketing practitioner should be aware of the four buying determinants—environmental, organizational, interpersonal, and individual—and conduct an in-depth analysis of how these factors affect the specific target market for his product.

In the international market setting, environmental influences on buying behavior, including economic, technological, physical, political, legal, and cultural factors, could be the most-important determinants of values and norms of the client organization, and an understanding of them is essential. American suppliers should also be aware of the personal risks involved in industrial buying. The decision maker runs the risk that the product that is purchased will not perform satisfactorily. He also incurs the psychosocial risk of how other members of the organization will view the decision (Moriarty and Galper, 1978). Since perceived risk plays a dominant role in the individual's decision-making process, the industrial marketer must evaluate all aspects of the marketing mix in terms of their impacts on perceived risk.

UNCONTROLLABLE VARIABLES AND MARKETING-MIX DECISIONS

Marketing strategy consists of target-market selection and the offering of a marekting mix. Marketing-mix variables are viewed as controllable variables, or variables that are influenced and manipulated by internal managerial decisions. Thus, for example, management has to a large degree control over the characteristics of the product it manufactures, the price it sets, the media it selects, and the distributor it uses. The degree to which an optimal mix of marketing variables could be developed by a firm is limited, however, by uncontrollable variables—factors that the firm has to contend with without really being able to influence them, at least in the short run.

These variables are as follows:

1. Cultural and social factors.
2. Political and legal factors.
3. Economic factors (conditions).

CULTURAL AND SOCIAL FACTORS. Cultural and social considerations are probably the most-constraining uncontrollable variables when marketing in a foreign setting. There are various definitions of *culture*, but there are three aspects of culture on which there is widespread agreement: "It is not innate, but learned; the various facets of culture are interrelated—you touch a culture in one place and everything else is affected; it is shared and, in effect, defines the boundaries of different groups" (Hall, 1977). Culture has a profound effect on the political-economic system in any given country.

In general, the firm's long-run survival depends upon how it relates to conditions in its environment. Each of these conditions is capable of presenting a firm with constraints and opportunities that are relevant to its operations. Maintaining effectiveness depends on the adjustment of strategy and structure to constraints imposed by the environment. Although this holds true both domestically and internationally, the task of matching firm to environment is more difficult in an international setting.

The cultural setting of any given foreign market includes diverse areas such as language, religion, local values and attitudes, education, social order or classes, politics, law, and technology and material culture, that is, the role of technology in the cultural and economic development process. Each of these factors, by itself or by interacting with other factors, can significantly influence the effective application of a marketing mix in any foreign setting. International-business literature has been evaluating the interaction of business, especially the multinational firm, and the cultural environment for many years. In our context it is germane to suggest to the firm contemplating introduction of products in a foreign setting some guidelines by which it can evaluate the receptivity of a foreign culture to its marketing offerings.

One approach describing the process by which a product that is new to a given foreign market is accepted locally was developed by Sheth and Sethi (1977). They link acceptability to the degree of resistance to change of any given culture. The less resistant to change a culture is, the easier is the application of the relevant marketing mix.

Although societies and cultures differ externally, unique identifying features exist that position various cultures on a continuum of social change—from traditional to developed societies. The criterion for placing a society at a point on the continuum is the amount of resistance to change—the lower the degree of resistance to change, the higher a society will place on the continuum (Sheth, and Sethi, 1977). Sheth and Sethi suggest that an understanding of the process by which different cultures move on the continuum can help in understanding and predicting the circumstances under which a given product or idea tends to be accepted in a society. A propensity to change is contingent upon the nature of the product and how it fits with traditional and social values of a given society.

Innovation and Change. International marketing efforts can be viewed as engaging a process of innovation and change. Products are introduced to a foreign target market in combination with a marketing-mix strategy. This marketing effort involves a communication about the innovation with identifiable source, channel, and message components. Communication about the product influences the country's propensity to change, as well as generating an evaluation of the product. The product is evaluated according to its ability to satisfy a set of relevant criteria for the product class. However, the influence of communication on either the propensity to change or the evaluation of the product is limited by two major constraints. The first constraint relates to the selectivity with which potential customers process information. Unless the culture is ready for a change, customers will be insensitive to communication on the new product and will pay little attention to it. Similarly, unless the product is favorably perceived by a culture, the acceptability of a communication will be minimal.

The second constraint relates to the compensatory manner in which a country's change agents and opinion leadership exert influence on propensity to change and product evaluation. If the adoption tendency is strong, the innovation will be tried. Satisfaction resulting from a trial may lead to the creation of product loyalty.

In general, the long-run adoption of an innovation will influence both the propensity to change and product evaluation. If there is satisfaction with the product over the long run, the propensity to change will be affected. Satisfaction will lead to greater receptivity to change and more-favorable predisposition toward the exporting firm or the manufacturer that introduced the innovation.

LEGAL ENVIRONMENT.   The laws of a society are one dimension of its culture. They present a more concrete manifestation of its attitudes and cultural norms and usually reflect its religious tradition. Because laws reflect the culture that gave birth to them, one finds great diversity among the laws of different nations (Terpstra, 1978).

One framework to evaluate the legal environment of international marketing has been developed by Terpstra. Pertinent dimensions are: (1) United States laws, and (2) domestic laws of each of the firm's foreign markets.

U.S. Laws and International Marketing.   The international-marketing considerations most affected by U.S. laws are exporting, antitrust, and organization and ownership arrangements.

Exporting.   The United States has a variety of controls on export trade. Since many of these controls reflect the ever-changing international and domestic climate, we shall allude here only to the kinds of control imposed.

One type of control relates to the country involved. Generally there are restrictions on trading with communist countries. Another control relates not to the prospective export market but to the nature of the product. For certain types of products considered strategic or sensitive there are tighter controls and even prohibition. Products such as nuclear weapons, armaments, and components used for surveillance of communications fall into this category. Another set of restrictions applies to pricing. Specifically, the Internal Revenue Service can examine and have a voice in the price set for exports to foreign subsidiaries.

Antitrust.   The United States antitrust laws affect the foreign business activities of American companies. The opinion and practice of the United States Justice Department is that even if an act is committed abroad, it falls within the jurisdiction of U.S. courts if the act produces consequences within the United States. One exception is the Export Trade Act. The act specifically excludes from antitrust prosecution the cooperation of competitive firms in the development of foreign markets. This antitrust exemption is subject to two qualifications. The first is that collaboration in export markets will not affect competition with the United States. The second is that in their business practices abroad, American firms must follow the same standard of behavior that is required in the United States.

In addition to some exemptions from the antitrust legislation, the government offers exporters some tax incentives. One such incentive is the Domestic International Sales Corporation (DISC). A DISC is a domestically based subsidiary for export sales. When a DISC is set up, it enjoys tax benefits on a portion of the income derived from export sales.

Foreign Laws and International Marketing. The legal system of a foreign-market country affects all marketing-mix variables. The object here is not to list all possible constraints, but to highlight some important considerations that should be included in any analysis prior to a target-market selection.

Product. Many regulations affect product and product-related issues such as packaging, in order to ensure local consumers of the products' purity, safety, or performance. The issue of product liability is becoming more and more important. Despite significant variations in rules from one country to another, the evolution everywhere is in the direction of more constraints, and the rate of change toward higher standards of liability is accelerating. In fact, the Common Market countries are now considering international agreement on rules for product liability that are significantly tougher than most existing national laws (Siegmund 1978).

Price. In some countries the concept of monopolistic competition is not as threatening as it is in the United States. As a result, one may find price agreements between businesses. Price controls also constrain pricing strategies of international marketers. For example, in the mid 1960s, France had an economywide price freeze.

Distribution. According to Commerce Department experts, the most problematic distribution issue concerns the local laws governing the relationship between the exporting firm and its foreign distributors. When disagreement between an exporter and a distributor occurs, these laws typically override the provisions in the contract and can make the severing of an undesirable relationship with a foreign agent or distributor very painful for the exporting firm because of the indemnification it is obliged to make. Occasionally a termination, even if carried out according to the requirements of the local law, may result in protracted litigation or unwarranted settlement when the foreign agent utilizes the nuisance possibilities in the often-ambiguous legislation ("Lessening Terminal Rules," 1978). It is, therefore, crucial to gain information on the agency-termination laws of various countries as well as to include specific features protecting the exporting firm in any representational agreement. The foreign-business-practices division of the Office of International Finance and Investment of the Department of Commerce provides such information and sample guides for the preparation of agreements.

Promotion. Most nations have some kind of laws regulating advertising, and advertising regulation takes several forms. Moreover, Boddewyn (1980) suggests that there is a global spread of advertising regulation, so that not only do U.S. regulatory developments quickly spread abroad (e.g., the issues of imposing corrective ads and of restricting children in ads), but other countries' discomforts with advertising are having an effect here. Boddewyn identifies seven key factors that influence the global multiplication of advertising regulation. These factors and major regulatory developments are listed in Exhibit 3. The implications of this phenomenon for corporate decision makers are a need for more self-regulation, collaborating with consumer organizations, lobbying and public advocacy, and revision of some marketing and promotion policies.

POLITICAL ENVIRONMENT. Corporate involvement in international business ranges from minor exporting operations to investment in factories and total control of the marketing infrastructure in an overseas market. The more a firm commits resources in the form of direct investment in manufacturing abroad, the more it should be attuned to the political environment. In this context, the firm should be aware of the potential confrontation it might face with a host government. Kobrin (1978) takes the position that the root of this conflict lies in the fact that the scope and objectives of the firm and state differ. The firm's interest lies in allocating and utilizing resources so as to maximize profits on a global basis. The state's interest lies in achieving objectives such as growth, employment, stability, and so forth for itself. Four potential conflict areas can be identified as follows:

Control. By accepting a subsidiary of a foreign parent, the host country gives up some degree of control over its industrial and economic affairs.

Protection from Outside Threats. If multinationals are viewed as exploiting elements of the local population, hostility against the outside threat can be aroused.

Cultural-change Agents. Foreign firms can be viewed by both individuals and society at large as a threat to the established culture.

EXHIBIT 3   REGULATORY TRENDS IN INTERNATIONAL ADVERTISING

Key Regulatory Factors	Major Regulatory Developments
Consumer protection (e.g., against untruthful, unfair, misleading ads)	Prior substantiation of advertising claims is becoming the norm
Protecting competitors (e.g., against the misuse of comparison and cooperative advertising)	Growing product restrictions affect their advertising
	More informative ads are in order
Environmentalism (e.g., against outdoor advertising)	Advertising language is being restricted
Civil rights (e.g., against sexist ads)	"Vulnerable" groups, such as children, are becoming the particular target of advertising regulations
Religion (e.g., against the advertising of contraceptives)	
Standards of taste and decency (e.g., against sexy ads)	More groups and people can now sue advertisers
Nationalism (e.g., against the use of foreign languages, themes, and illustrations)	Penalties are getting stiffer

Source. Boddewyn, 1980.

Planning and Budgeting.   The main aspect of promotional planning that can be stand-ardized is the *method* of setting the total amount to be spent. The firm can decide to use *competitive parity, percentage of sales, task-objective,* or some other method, and can apply that method to each national operation. Of course there should be flexibility to adapt to special circumstances, as when the percentage of sales method is being used and competitors in a given country are substantially increasing their expenditures on promotion.

The Promotional Mix.   This term refers to the relative emphasis to be placed on advertising, sales promotion, public relations, publicity, and personal selling. A sim-ple answer is to follow the trade custom and do whatever is normal for a given product in a given country. A more useful (but more complex) answer is to try to assess the costs and benefits of money spent on each type of promotion. This is especially difficult in the case of public relations, which may not directly produce any sales, but which may ultimately make the difference between staying in a country and having to leave it.

ORGANIZATION, PLANNING, AND CONTROL

ORGANIZATION FOR INTERNATIONAL MARKETING.   The concept of organizing for international marketing can be thought of in two ways—the place of international operations in the organization, and the way in which the international operation is structured internally.

The Place of International Operations.   If a firm is not committed to international operations, but is only exporting as opportunities arise, it can simply expand the roles of its domestic sales, shipping, credit, and other divisions to include foreign markets. This is inexpensive, but is also risky because domestic operating personnel may not understand or care about foreign markets, and there may be conflict because of a lack of leadership and coordination.

At a higher level of commitment, the firm can organize a separate international department. It may have only administrative and sales personnel at first, but these can be followed by experts in international shipping and credit. Later, personnel can be added as required to take care of international market research, licensing, finance, personnel, and other functions.

A firm that becomes fully committed to serving international markets can create a specialized subsidiary such as the IBM World Trade Corporation. This kind of subsidiary is a nearly self-contained business entity in charge of international op-erations, and relates with the parent company almost at arm's length except at the highest levels.

There is one more stage in the placement of international operations—to become a world company. A world headquarters is established to supervise the various divisions, including the former home office. This world headquarters may be with or near the former home office, or it may be in a different country that offers simple organizational procedures and low corporate income taxes.

Internal Structure of International Operations.   There are four basic ways of struc-turing a firm's international operations—by function, geographically, by type of product, and by type of customer. Most firms use a combination of two or more of these systems. In a functional form of organization, the head of international marketing might supervise international sales, international credit, and so forth. He might also be in charge of any sales offices in other countries. His responsibility would include all products sold abroad and all foreign markets.

In a *geographic* form of organization, international operations are simply divided by market areas, for example, Eastern Europe, Western Europe, the Middle East, and the Andean Group countries. Each area can contain from 1 to about 50 countries, which do not necessarily have to be contiguous. For example, an area of responsibility might be "developed countries in Africa and Asia" or "all Spanish-speaking countries in Latin America and the Caribbean."

In organization by *type of product,* an office products firm might set up international paper products, desk accessory, and photocopier divisions. Each of these would perform the various functions required to market its assigned products throughout the world.

Organization by *type of customer* is important when similar customers have similar needs and are scattered in several countries. A producer of pneumatic tires, for example, might have its international marketing organization divided to cater to (1) automobile and truck manufacturers, (2) producers of construction equipment, (3) manufacturers of bicycles and small trailers, and (3) the aftermarket.

In practice, firms that do large volumes of international business compound these various structures. That is, a firm might have its international operations structured first by function; then the major functions, such as international sales, could be broken down geographically. Finally, each of these geographic groups could be subdivided by type of product or customer.

INTERNATIONAL MARKETING PLANNING.   Successful international marketing normally requires detailed, long-range, worldwide profit planning. Haphazard international selling with the objective of maximizing profits each year in every market does not produce optimum benefits to the firm.

Detailed Profit Planning.   A firm's sales, profit, market share, or other objectives usually follow its organizational structure. That is, if a firm's international operations include an export sales department that is divided geographically and then by product, its specific export sales objectives will be divided by geographic area and then by product.

Types of Objectives.   *Sales and profit* targets can be set globally, then broken down by region and country (if the firm is organized on a geographic basis). Planners at the world level set the overall goal and then meet with regional managers to allocate it to the regions. Then each regional goal is divided among the countries or areas that make up that region. On the contrary, the managers of the smallest marketing units can be asked to make their projections first. Then these can be combined into regional and finally world totals. In practice, planning discussions usually move simultaneously both up and down the corporate structure until world, regional, and national goals are set.

Market share objectives are more likely to be set at the local level, where planners can take full account of forecasts and opinions of future market conditions. There are some firms, like Bic, that talk in terms of shares of the *world* market, but this approach is useful only for firms that are major competitors in a large number of countries.

A firm can set as its goal a minimum *return on investment* from each market area or type of product. In doing so, however, it should keep in mind the concept of long-term, worldwide planning, which will be discussed later in this section.

It is common to combine two or more objectives. For example, an automobile manufacturer in Argentina might plan on a 20 percent market share in year X with a return on investment of at least 18 percent. The use of multiple objectives can help prevent a local manager from taking actions that make him look good in the short run, but which will hurt the company's future profitability.

Strategies and Tactics.   If a firm is to meet its international marketing objectives, its managers must develop product, price, distribution, and promotion *strategies* for specific products and markets. Detailed tactics are thus planned to implement the strategies.

For example, a firm that intends to capture 15 percent of a foreign market for greeting cards might develop the following strategies:

Product.   Use single fold only, make some cards with no text and others with very brief messages (written, not just translated, locally); sell only single cards, and wrap each one in cellophane; use standard local sizes.

Price.   Maintain price to consumer about two thirds of the way up the range of prices in the market. Give retailers a discount that is slightly larger than average; give wholesalers a normal discount.

Distribution.   Distribute through normal channels, but try for more market penetration by placing cards in medium-price general-merchandise stores.

Promotion.   Give dealers display racks. Concentrate on radio, year-round, peaking before major holidays.

Detailed tactics to carry out these strategies would include, for example, the *media plan* giving radio stations to be used, the advertising schedule and budget, and major themes.

Long-Range Profit Planning.   Many new ventures operate at a loss in their first year. This is even more true with international operations because it takes considerable investment in time and money to acquire a full understanding of laws that affect marketing and *the extent to which* they are enforced in each country, to hire the required sales, service, and other personnel, train them adequately, and move in any necessary expatriate staff members, to establish distribution, whether company-owned or through independent representatives, including warehousing and service facilities, to build up a supply of products and parts, to gain familiarity with a new and distant market that may have very different characteristics from the home market, and to persuade industrial customers that the firm is there for the long haul; it won't pull out suddenly and leave them with unserviceable products. It may also take time to ride out a period of political uncertainty, as during recent years in Chile and Lebanon.

A classic book on this subject is *Strategic Planning for Export Marketing*, by Franklin W. Root (1964). It stresses the need for *5-year* profit plans, which may include planned losses during the initial years in new foreign markets.

Worldwide Profit Planning. Domestic firms sometimes continue to market an unprofitable product because it is a vital part of a lucrative line, or continue to sell in an unprofitable area if it is important to the company's overall strategy. The case with international marketing is similar. A firm may want to stay with an unprofitable product or market country to make it harder for competition to gain a foothold, to be in the market and ready when economic or political conditions improve, to not leave any gaps in a market area, for example, the European Community, or to pick up or test ideas that may be useful in other areas. This international gathering and application of ideas has been called *synergism*—the whole is greater than the sum of its parts.

CONTROL OF INTERNATIONAL MARKETING. Control in international marketing is the complement of planning. It requires systematic collection and feedback of information so the firm will know whether it is meeting its objectives, and if not, where and by how much it is failing. If any objectives are not being met, the situation should be analyzed, and corrective action taken at the earliest possible moment.

SOURCES AND SUGGESTED REFERENCES

Arab Business. London, International Communications, 1975- (monthly).

Bill Communications, Inc. "Exhibits Schedule," in *Successful Meetings* magazine annual.

Bottin Europe. Paris, Didot-Bottin, 1978.

Bottin International. Paris, Didot-Bottin, 1979. 2v.

Brandon's Shipper & Forwarder. N.Y., New York Foreign Freight Forwarders and Brokers Association, 1929- (weekly).

Bureau of National Affairs, Inc. *International Trade Reporter; Export Shipping Manual.* Wash., D.C., 1947- 3v.

Croner's Reference Book for World Traders. Queens Village, N.Y., 1949-.

Day, A.J. *Exporting for Profit.* London: Graham & Trotman (International Publications Service), 1976.

Dun & Bradstreet Exporters' Encyclopedia; World Marketing Guide. N.Y., Dun and Bradstreet International. Annual.

Dun & Bradstreet, Inc. *Principal International Businesses.* N.Y., 1974- Annual.

Food and Agriculture Organization of the United Nations. *Trade Yearbook.* Rome, 1958-.

International Bank for Reconstruction and Development. *World Development Report 1979.* New York: Oxford University Press, 1979.

International Marketing Institute. *Export Marketing for Smaller Firms,* 4th ed. Washington, D.C.: Small Business Administration, 1979.

Jeune Afrique. Paris, Groupe J.A., 1960- (weekly).

Kahler, R. *International Marketing,* 4th ed. Pelham Manor, NY: South-Western, 1977.

Keegan, *Multinational Marketing Management.* Englewood Cliffs, NJ: Prentice-Hall, 1974.

Kotler, P. *Principles of Marketing.* Englewood Cliffs, NJ: Prentice-Hall, 1980.

Majaro, S. *International Marketing: A Strategic Approach to World Markets.* New York: Wiley, 1977.

Organization for Economic Cooperation and Development. *Import/Export Microtables.* Paris, 1975-.

Robinson, R.G. *International Business Management.* Hinsdale, IL: Dryden Press, 1978.

Root, F.R. *Strategic Planning for Export Marketing.* Scranton, PA: International Textbook, 1966.

Standard Trade Index of Japan. Tokyo, Japan Chamber of Commerce and Industry, 1979.

Successful Export Strategy. Proceedings of a conference sponsored by the London Chamber of Commerce and Industry and The Institute of Export. London: Graham & Trotman, 1977.

Terpstra, V. *International Marketing,* 2nd ed. Hinsdale, IL: Dryden Press, 1978.

Trade Channel. Amsterdam, Trade Channel Organization, 1946- (monthly).

United Nations. Statistical Office. *Statistical Papers:* Series M. (Commodity Trade Statistics). NY, 1949-. Irregular.

United Nations. Statistical Office. *Yearbook of International Trade Statistics.* NY, 1951-. Annual.

U.S. Dept. of Commerce. Domestic and International Business Administration. *Overseas Business Reports.* Wash., D.C., GPO.

U.S. Department of Commerce. *Foreign Business Practices.* Washington, DC: U.S. Government Printing Office, 1975.

Vision. Grand-Saconnex, Switzerland, m.d.- (11/yr.).

World Aviation Directory. Wash., American Aviation Pubs., 1940-. v.l-. Biennial.

World Trade Annual. Prepared by the Statistical Office of the United Nations. N.Y., Walker & Co. 5v.

Worldwide Projects. Westport, Conn., Intercontinental Pubs., 1967- (6/yr.).

PART 6

MANAGEMENT OF
INTERNATIONAL OPERATIONS

SECTION **34**

INTERNATIONAL FINANCIAL MANAGEMENT

CONTENTS

THE EXPOSURE PROBLEM	3	International Capital Budgeting	**10**
		The Decision to Invest Overseas	**11**
How Much Hedging?	4	**CONCLUSION**	**12**
Hedging Strategies	5		
Taxation	6	**SOURCES AND SUGGESTED**	
Country Risk	8	**REFERENCES**	**12**

INTERNATIONAL FINANCIAL MANAGEMENT

James L. Burtle

Many of the requirements for operating a business overseas are not essentially different from the requirements for operating at home. Both foreign and domestic businesses are unlikely to succeed without strong overall management, an effective marketing strategy, and adequate cost controls. There are, however, special problems in an international business that are not usually found in a domestic business. The most important of these are (1) the risk of losses from exchange-rate changes, (2) the risk of losses as a result of tax management policies in either the home country or in the country of foreign investment, and (3) political risks including confiscation, wars, civil disturbances, restrictions on convertibility, debt repudiation, and types of discriminatory action in which a foreign business is treated less advantageously than a domestic business.

To put it another way, financial officers of international businesses, in addition to having the financial worries of any business, are typically concerned about the company's losing from exchange-rate changes, from paying taxes unnecessarily, and because of political actions of foreign governments. Each of these risks will be considered separately, and against this background, capital budgeting and the choice of investments abroad will be discussed for a multinational company.

With the advent of widespread floating of exchange rates in early 1973, a new and often formidable dimension was added to international business planning. Most companies became aware that success in production and marketing abroad does not necessarily guarantee profits for the parent company if earnings abroad are eroded because of exchange-rate changes. But although there is agreement that currency fluctuations have created a "problem," there have been wide variations in the policies that companies have followed to protect themselves. Company strategies differ with respect to (1) what is considered at risk under conditions of fluctuating exchange rates, (2) the extent that risks should be hedged, and (3) the appropriate hedging strategy.

THE EXPOSURE PROBLEM

The problem of what is at risk under conditions of variable exchange rates is known as the exposure problem. A great many definitions of exposure have been proposed. From an analytical point of view, exposure can be broken down into three categories:

transaction, translation, and operational exposure. *Transaction exposure* arises when one currency will be converted into another currency at a specific date in the future. For example, a U.S. importer may have ordered a shipment of glassware from Italy and agrees to pay in *lire* when the goods arrive. He thus runs a risk that the *lira* might rise in value in relation to the dollar. On the other hand, a U.S. exporter runs the risk that a foreign currency will depreciate before payment is received. In these and other cases of transaction exposure, there is an actual conversion of one currency into another.

In *translation exposure,* there is no currency conversion. Instead, assets and liabilities held abroad are adjusted in value for the changed exchange rate. In a simple case, a bank account in British pounds is worth less in dollars if the pound is depreciated. Thus the holder of the bank account suffers a translation loss. On the other hand, if the U.S. citizen owes British pounds, his debt is reduced by depreciation of sterling, and he shows a translation gain. In practice, the calculation of translation exposure is more complicated than indicated in the above examples because in the balance sheet of a company operating abroad, there is a wide range of different assets and liabilities, and accounting practices differ as to which of these items should be considered exposed, that is, adjusted for exchange-rate changes. In their financial statements, American companies are currently required to follow Financial Accounting Standards Board Bulletin 8 (F.A.S.B. 8), which specifies that cash, accounts receivable, accounts payable, and long-term debt are exposed. On the other hand, most inventories and fixed assets are not exposed. Rules governing translation exposure are subject, however, to widespread controversy. In actual management policies, many companies follow a variety of translation rules, although reported results are required to conform to F.A.S.B. 8. More recently, the FASB has asked for comments on a proposed new set of accounting rules that would consider all assets and liabilities exposed.

Operational exposure arises from the risk to company profits from the indirect effects of exchange-rate changes. For example, if a subsidiary of a U.S. company is exporting from England, there is an operational risk that a rise in the exchange rate of the pound will discourage export volume and thus lower profits. Likewise a company importing into the United Kingdom may be adversely affected if sterling depreciates and the price of imports rises.

Overall exposure encompassing transaction, translation, and operational exposure is known as *economic exposure.* In principle, economic exposure is defined as the difference between discounted cash flows of future earnings of a company with and without exchange-rate changes. In actual practice, however, most companies do not have the resources to calculate their overall economic exposure. Instead, there is a monitoring of the elements of translation, transaction, and operational exposure that appear to be of greatest significance to profits of the particular company. A firm engaged mainly in exporting and importing might emphasize transaction exposure. A company with an affiliate operating abroad might be concerned mainly with translation exposure. Operational and economic exposures are likely to be of special interest to a company that can afford a long-term planning apparatus.

HOW MUCH HEDGING?   Some companies, having defined exposure, attempt to avoid it entirely. In other words, they attempt to equalize exposed assets (sometimes known as long positions) and exposed liabilities (sometimes known as short positions) so that their P/L statement is unaffected by changes in exchange rates. Other companies are willing to leave exposed positions open if it is believed that the exchange rate is unlikely to move in an unfavorable direction or that the cost of protection (often known as *cover*) from foreign-exchange losses is excessive. Some observers would regard the latter viewpoint as speculative; a contrary view is that a company is speculating only when it takes foreign-exchange positions not related to the ordinary business of the company. Under this definition it would not be speculation if a company did not cover a Japanese *yen* exposure, but it would be speculation if a company took a position in *yen* even though it had no business connection with Japan. One simple rule, sometimes applied by companies that are willing to permit open positions, is that a company should not cover exposed positions unless the expected loss from an uncovered position is greater than the cost of cover.

HEDGING STRATEGIES.   Companies that adopt a policy of not covering all exposed positions should organize a group that will monitor (1) changes in exchange rates, (2) changes in the costs of covering exposed positions, and (3) changes in the exposed position of the company. In an effective foreign-exchange-management group, each of these three elements is forecast, and on the basis of the forecasts, it is decided whether or not to hedge an exposed position. A decision on whether or not to hedge the exposed position may depend on the cost of the hedge compared with the expected loss from not hedging.

If a company decides that it should cover an exposed position, a number of alternative hedging strategies are often available. The most frequently used strategies are (1) the forward market, (2) the money market and (3) restructuring the company balance sheet. In the forward market, foreign-exchange contracts are traded with the requirement that foreign exchange be bought or sold at a specific time in the future. For example, if a foreign currency is sold forward, there is an agreement with someone to buy it at a specific rate at some period ahead. Usually foreign-exchange contracts can be negotiated for 1, 2, 3, 6, 9, and 12 months ahead. A currency may be at either a discount or a premium. At a discount, a currency sells forward for less than the spot rate. At a premium, the currency sells forward for more than the spot rate.

If a currency is expected to depreciate, a company in a long position can protect itself from losses from depreciation by selling the currency forward. However, this protection against foreign-exchange loss from depreciation will usually involve the cost of paying the discount on the forward contract. Likewise, a company in a net liability position in a particular currency can protect itself from exchange losses from appreciation by buying that currency forward, though again such protective action will usually involve paying the cost of a premium on the forward contract.

An alternative hedging strategy for protection against foreign-exchange losses is to use the money market. Money-market strategies involve borrowing a currency that is expected to depreciate or placing a currency that is expected to appreciate. If a currency has been borrowed and converted into dollars and there is a depreciation of the currency, repaying the loan in depreciated currency will offset most of the foreign-exchange loss on a net asset position. On the other hand, if funds are placed in a potentially appreciating currency—in the form of bank deposits or short-term government securities—a foreign-exchange loss on a net liability position can be offset by the gain from appreciation of the funds placed in the appreciating currency. As in the case of the foreign-exchange market, however, there is usually a cost connected with using the money market as protection against foreign-exchange losses. When a currency is expected to depreciate, interest rates are usually higher in the potentially devaluing currency compared with the home currency. Thus cover by borrowing means paying higher interest rates. On the other hand, for a currency likely to appreciate, interest rates are usually lower than in the home currency. Thus cover by placing money means earning less interest income. There is a tendency known as *interest arbitrage* for the costs of using the money market as a hedge against currency changes to be approximately the same as the costs of foreign-exchange contracts. Because of market imperfections, however, interest arbitrage does not always work out exactly, and it is worthwhile for the foreign-exchange manager to investigate carefully which method of coverage of exchange risks is likely to involve maximum protection at the least expense.

In many cases a company can avoid either a forward contract or a money-market hedge by eliminating the exposed position on the company balance sheet. A net asset position may be reduced by remitting dividends, or by collecting receivables and placing the collected funds in nonexposed assets, or by allowing payables to rise. If inventories are not considered exposed, financial assets may be shifted into inventories. However, there may be costs connected with restructuring balance sheets. Profit remittances may be subject to withholding taxes. A company may lose customers if it sharply reduces accounts receivable. Lines of credit may be lost if accounts payable are allowed to become excessive.

TAXATION. It is convenient to begin the taxation section of this section with an oversimplified example of the calculation of foreign and U.S. taxes for both the foreign affiliate of a U.S. company and for the parent company. (U.S. firms operating in less developed countries calculate the tax somewhat differently, but the general methods are similar.)

Suppose that a subsidiary of a hypothetical U.S. company is operating abroad with pretax earnings of $1 million. These earnings are assumed to be subject to a foreign income tax of 25 percent and a foreign withholding tax on dividend remittances of 10 percent. The U.S. corporate income tax is taken at 48 percent. It is assumed that 50 percent of earnings abroad are remitted as dividends to the U.S. parent. Calculations of the foreign and U.S. taxes are shown in Exhibit 1.

From this exhibit it should be understood that a withholding tax is a misnomer; it is simply a tax paid on dividends that is not returned.

One principle of U.S. taxation is that double taxation should be avoided, that is, if a U.S. company has already paid taxes abroad, it should pay only enough taxes in the United States to bring the overall rate up to the U.S. rate. Thus foreign taxes already paid are subtracted from the U.S. tax as indicated in lines 7, 8, 9, and 14. However, the tax credit does not include all taxes paid abroad. It includes all of the withholding taxes but only a fraction of the total income tax abroad. The latter is known as the *deemed tax* and is calculated by multiplying the tax paid abroad by the proportion of aftertax income that is remitted as dividends. In the above example, the income tax abroad was $250,000, but since only half of the aftertax earnings were remitted as dividends, the deemed tax was ½ × $250,000 = $125,000. If a third of the aftertax earnings were remitted as dividends, the deemed tax would be equal to ⅓ × $250,000 = $83,333. (There is no tax credit for property taxes, excise taxes, value added taxes, and other nonincome taxes paid abroad.)

In a process known as the *gross-up* the deemed tax (line 11) is added to the gross dividend (line 10) to obtain the U.S. taxable income (line 12). The U.S. tax rate is

EXHIBIT 1 CALCULATION OF FOREIGN AND U.S. TAXES ON A U.S. SUBSIDIARY ABROAD ($ THOUSANDS)

(1)	Pretax foreign earnings	1,000
(2)	Foreign income tax @ 25 %	250
(3)	Foreign aftertax earnings	750
(4)	Earnings remitted as dividends @ 50%	375
(5)	Withholding tax @ 10%	38
(6)	Net dividend received	337
	Foreign-Tax Credit	
(7)	Withholding tax	38
(8)	Deemed tax @ ½ × 250	125
(9)	Total tax credits	163
	U.S. Taxable Income	
(10)	Gross dividend (line 4)	375
(11)	Deemed tax (line 8)	125
(12)	Total	500
(13)	U.S. Tax @ 48%	240
(14)	Tax credit (line 9)	163
(15)	Net U.S. tax	77

applied to this sum (line 13), and tax credits for the deemed tax and the withholding tax are subtracted (line 14) to obtain the net U.S. tax (line 15). Note that in addition to the principle of *no double taxation,* the above calculation also involves the principle of *deferral of taxation* on earnings of foreign affiliates: no tax is levied on the parent company until dividends are actually remitted. The rule is different, however, if the foreign operation of a U.S. company is a *branch* of the parent company rather than a separate foreign *affiliate.* Then the earnings of the branch are consolidated with the earnings of the parent company and taxed on an annual basis.

When foreign affiliates' income taxes are lower than those in the parent country, there is a strong incentive for the parent company to attempt to shift profits to areas of lower taxes. This can be done in a number of ways including (1) charging overhead costs to the parent corporation, (2) selling to the affiliate below cost—sometimes called transfer pricing—and (3) setting up a separate company in areas of no income taxes and funneling profits to the so-called tax haven. To prevent each of these practices, special I.R.S. rules and statutes have been adopted as follows:

1. Section 1.861-8 of the *U.S. Treasury Regulations* requires an allocation of overhead costs of the parent to the affiliate. This has the effect of reducing the company's earnings abroad on which the tax credit is calculated.

2. Section 482 of the *U.S. Internal Revenue Code* requires that prices on transactions between the parent and an affiliate should be at the same price that would be charged a third party. Thus transfer pricing is, in effect, prohibited.

3. Subpart F of the tax code provides that when a foreign affiliate is set up in a tax-haven country as a "sham" to siphon income from a higher-tax area, that income in the tax-haven country should be considered "tainted" income. Tainted income may be treated as *deemed dividend* and is subject to U.S.

taxes whether or not it is remitted to the United States. The proceeds from liquidating a tax-haven company may also be subject to deemed-dividend treatment and therefore subject to tax. This is sometimes called the "doomsday tax" (*Internal Revenue Code* 1248).

In earlier periods a company could reduce its taxes by switching from branch to affiliate status. Before the relevant legislation was adopted, a company might at a time of heavy start-up costs operate as a branch. Since branch losses are consolidated with the parent company earnings, the effect was to reduce overall taxes. When start-up costs were completed, however, and the foreign operation was earning profits, it would change to affiliate status. This practice is now limited because of a *recapture provision* in the Tax Reform Act of 1976 that provides that such tax savings may be claimed by the I.R.S.

Most tax legislation would appear to reduce the benefits of tax deferral to U.S. international companies. There is, however, an exception. This is the domestic international sales corporation (DISC) law of 1971. This legislation provides that a U.S. company can set up part of its export operation in a special DISC corporation that is permitted to defer payment of taxes on 50 percent of its income. Thus the DISC corporation, even though it operates in the United States, is treated somewhat like a foreign affiliate of a U.S. company. Under current legislation, a company may incorporate under DISC rules 67 percent of its incremental export sales over a past 4-year period. There are also special regulations concerning transactions between a parent company and its DISC. As in the case of foreign affiliates, these rules are designed to prevent siphoning earnings from the parent company to the DISC.

Although this section has attempted to give a bird's eye view of taxation of earnings abroad, the treatment is highly oversimplified. Solutions of actual tax problems should not be attempted without consultation with international tax attorneys.

COUNTRY RISK.   Country risk covers a very broad area including political as well as economic risks. The essential element in country risk is, however, some form of government action preventing the fulfillment of an implicit or explicit contract or agreement. It would not be a country-risk problem if because of poor management, a foreign business failed and it could not pay for imports. It would be a case of country risk, however, if the company was prohibited from payings its bills by government exchange controls. The most frequently cited examples of country risk are expropriation, debt repudiation, and delays in payments for imports. However, there are many less-evident variants of these practices. Companies may not be confiscated but can be reduced to impotence by punitive taxation, lack of police protection, discriminatory labor regulations, and restrictions on remitting earnings. Debts that are not repudiated may be restructured with heavy losses to the lenders. Imports may be "paid for," but only after long delays and in depreciating local currencies.

Thus there is serious ambiguity in the definition of an unfavorable outcome of a country-risk gamble. Not only is there extreme difficulty in assessing and forecasting country risk; there is also difficulty in identifying when it turns unfavorable. Thus the country-risk problem can be compared to the uncertainties of rolling loaded dice in darkness. Nevertheless, the great importance of the subject led to a maximum effort, especially by banks, to analyze the problem in an effort to reduce potential losses to the greatest extent possible.

Earlier efforts at country-risk analysis were somewhat simplistic. Company officials would visit the country in question, or experts in the country would give subjective opinions. Sometimes these opinions were tested for internal consistency by probability-tree methods: The expert would be required to place probabilities on each step in a sequence of events leading to a favorable or unfavorable outcome. For example a joint probability might be formulated for the conditions of (1) a radical change in government, (2) confiscation, and (3) no compensation (see Stobaugh, 1969).

In a more advanced approach to country risk proposed by Haendel, West, and Meadow (1975), specific variables affecting country risk are identified and favorable or unfavorable points are assigned to each variable. Points for different variables are added. Typically a greater number of points means less country risk. Rated variables include GNP per capita, number of riots and demonstrations, number of government crises, size of internal security forces, and legislative effectiveness. There are, however, two basic difficulties with this method. First, because the models affecting country risk are complex, many of the variables may be Janus-faced, sometimes raising country risk and sometimes lowering it. As Knudsen (1974) has pointed out, rising GNP may lower country risk if it creates a level of welfare greater than the aspirations of the population. On the other hand, rising GNP may create an even greater rise in aspirations. Thus by widening the gap between aspirations and achievements, GNP may become negative for country risk. The second difficulty with a point-scoring method is that no system has been developed for testing whether or not a particular point system actually measures country risk. This is at a much lower stage of development than other forecasting models used in international finance. For example, no one would propose a model for forecasting exchange rates without first testing it out against past experience. In country-risk analysis, however, even past experience is foggy with respect to what events could be clearly identified as "succeeding" or "failing" as indicators of country risk. More recently, however, variables relating to country risk have begun to be tested. In these tests of the significance of variables affecting country risk, three definitions of success or failure have been developed.

1. Success is identified with repayment of loans on schedule, whereas failure is identified with restructuring loans.
2. Success is identified with a rise in U.S. direct investment in a country, whereas failure is identified with a decline.
3. Success is identified with the payment of lower interest rates (usually in margins over the London Interbank Offered Rate), whereas failure is identified with higher interest rates.

The search for indicators that can give early warnings of debt rescheduling has usually applied variants of a statistical method known as discriminant analysis. This technique classifies the dependent variable categorically with respect to independent variables. Thus in a useful model, the independent variables will indicate whether the debt will be rescheduled or not rescheduled. In a successful test, "predicted" reschedulings will match actual reschedulings. On the other hand, there will be Type 1 error if reschedulings occur but are not predicted. Moreover, there will be Type 2 error if reschedulings are predicted but do not occur. Empirical attempts to "explain" debt rescheduling and other international debt problems are discussed by Walter (1980).

Another approach to testing for the impact of country risk involves direct investment as a dependent variable. To a considerable extent, U.S. foreign direct investment has been explained by regression analysis. One "simple" explanation relates foreign direct investment to a lagged value of investment itself and to changes in real GNP (see State Department, 1974). In another study, by Kobrin (1978), foreign direct investment was related to size of markets, market growth, previous export involvement, tariffs, and dummy variables for areas. Residuals from the regression may give indications of country risk, that is, indications of when investors, because of their risk outlook, put more or less into particular countries. Kobrin divided these residuals into low and high categories and, using a variant of the chi-square test, related the classified residuals to high and low cases of political variables that he calls turmoil, internal war, and conspiracy. No significant relationship was found between turmoil or internal war and the direct-investment residual. But a significant relationship was found between the residual and conspiracy, especially in cases of higher levels of economic development and governmental efficiency. The Kobrin analysis is important in its rejection of some political variables that on a common-sense basis might appear to affect perceived political risk.

A third attempt to quantify country risk relates country-risk indicators to interest rates on international loans. The hypothesis is that when a country pays a higher interest rate, it is being charged a risk premium. Walter (1980) found that there is an 0.81 Spearman rank correlation between interest-rate differentials and the risk rating of 93 countries provided in an *Institutional Investor* survey. Similar results appeared in a regression analysis by Angeloni and Short (1980).

One difficulty with relating residuals from explained investment and interest-rate differentials to risk variables is that the independent variables explain not actual risk but risk as perceived or believed by investors and bankers. But these perceptions may turn out to be wrong, as seems evident from investment in Iran and interest differentials on loans to Iran. Looking further back, the radicalization of Cuba was by no means widely expected. There is, however, the basic difficulty that the "sample" of truly revolutionary developments has been too small to be explained by any quantitatively rigorous methods. Thus situations, such as debt restructuring that are setbacks rather than disasters are used as dependent variables. This method is on methodologically stronger ground than purely subjective evaluations, but it may ignore the really key questions.

INTERNATIONAL CAPITAL BUDGETING.   Against the background of unsteady exchange rates, internationally differing tax systems, and political risks, capital budgeting for an international firm becomes a complex process, though the basic procedures are not different in principle from capital budgeting for a purely domestic business.

Usually an international capital budget begins with a determination of the internal rate of return on the investment abroad, all in the local currency of the host country. The second step is to calculate the internal rate of return on the investment in the currency of the parent company, assuming that funds from the subsidiary are remitted to the parent. As discussed by Eiteman and Stonehill (1979), this involves considerations of exchange rates, taxes, exchange controls, and possible impacts of the foreign operation on the domestic business, as, for example, the impact of exports to the subsidiary from the parent company.

In calculating the internal rate of return on an investment abroad, there are two approaches for dealing with country risk. In the first approach, the cash flow is adjusted downward to reflect risk. In the second approach, the cost of capital, that is, the required rate of return on the project, is raised to account for country risk. The first approach has the advantage of greater flexibility, because projected cash flow can be allowed to vary over the life of the project if it is expected that risk will be concentrated in particular periods. The second approach is probably easier to manage if it is desired to take into account differences in risk between areas. Then it is easier to compare risk premiums rather than cash-flow streams.

One advantage of a capital budget in local currency for an investment abroad is that it gives an indication whether or not a direct investment in a country is reasonable. If the rate of return on an investment abroad is less than the return on government securities of the country, then the extra management effort of the project would be wasted. It would be simpler for the parent company to buy the government bonds of the host country. Likewise if the planned direct investment earns no more than publicly traded stocks, then it would be simpler to buy a security portfolio in the host country rather than to go ahead with the direct investment.

If funds can be transferred to the United States, a rate of return on the project can be calculated from the point of view of the parent company. This calculation becomes complicated when funds to be transferred are partially or fully blocked. Blocked funds are assumed to be reinvested in the host country. Thus losses from exchange-rate depreciation and inflation may be minimized. This procedure may, however, tend to understate the loss to the parent company, since there may be unfavorable psychological effects on financial markets from "bad news" abroad. The company in the United States may suffer from an overall higher cost of borrowed funds and a low price/earnings ratio for its securities as a result of perhaps-distorted information relating to adversity in its foreign operations.

THE DECISION TO INVEST OVERSEAS.   The previous section sketched out a very much oversimplified picture of international capital budgeting. Once there is agreement on capital budgeting methods, the decision to invest abroad may appear simple: Choose the area (including investment possibilities in the country of the parent company) where the internal rate of return is highest. One problem in applying such a rule—and this problem also arises in choosing investments on the domestic scene—is that opportunities do not all appear at the same time. If the firm expands by acquisition, a particular acquisition offer may expire in a few days and may have no realistic alternatives readily available. Thus it must be compared with projects that may turn up. But many executives with large cash positions or borrowing capabilities find this waiting process painful. Money is truly likely to burn holes in their pockets.

Aside from the problem that alternatives for investment may not be presented simultaneously, there are a number of special considerations that may lead a company to invest overseas even though the internal rate of return may be no higher abroad than in the home country. As has been fully developed in the so-called product-cycle literature (Vernon, 1976), an exporting company may face tariffs on its products. The only way to avoid serious losses may be to jump the tariff wall and manufacture abroad. (Analytically this may be forced into a capital budgeting mold with the choice between losing on an export business and holding the line, with an investment abroad.)

In other cases a company operating abroad may want to spread out its investments among several countries in order to spread country risk instead of facing the possibility of losing everything if all investments are in one country. (Again this choice might be manageable with capital-budgeting methods by raising the adjustment for risk—either in the projected cash flow or the discount rate, as discussed—in countries with a heavy concentration of the company's investment.)

Another special reason for overseas investment is the possibility of achieving economies of scale. In some cases, where it is important to spread fixed costs, an optimal scale in the country of the parent company may be impossible because of the small size of the country or, especially in the United States, because antitrust laws may limit the growth of the parent company.

As has been stressed by Knickerbocker (1973), a firm in a worldwide oligopolistic industry may establish itself abroad, even though the rate of return is lower, in order to prevent the growth of a competitor. This strategy might be handled by capital-budgeting methods, but in some cases the marketing strategy of an oligopolist has a horizon that extends far beyond the horizon of its financial strategy.

Finally, in literature stemming from Cyert and March (1963), the firm may not have a consistent overall maximization goal. Instead, the divisions of the company will attempt to apply some maximization rule to their own activity with no or very little concern for the rest of the company. Against this background, the foreign investment decision will arise out of the process of resolving intracompany conflicts. Certainly, in many such cases, conflict resolution will go a long way from the kind of rational decision implied by capital-budgeting methods. Instead, as has been suggested by Allison (1971), the conflict may be resolved by a compromise, perhaps involving logrolling agreements among company divisions. Another type of conflict resolution is the adoption of a rule or reference to precedent for determining the allocation of investment. By a type of pseudo-legal reasoning, past decisions are carried forward regardless of their validity for the overall operating results of the firm. For example, a rigid rule of one third of funds available for investment may be pushed (or pulled) overseas.

CONCLUSION

This chapter considered three major problems faced by companies operating abroad: foreign-exchange risk, tax-management risk, and the risk of political upheavals.

Many other problems of management abroad are basically the same as management problems in a domestic company. Nevertheless, exchange-rate changes, taxes, and political risks do complicate capital budgeting for an international company. It turns out, however, that business decisions to invest abroad are complex and cannot be fully explained by capital-budgeting considerations.

SOURCES AND SUGGESTED REFERENCES

Aliber, R.Z. *Exchange Risk and Corporate International Finance*. New York: Wiley, 1979.

Allison, G. *The Essence of Decision*. Boston: Little Brown, 1971.

Angeloni, I. and B.K. Short. "The Impact of Country Risk Assessment on Eurocurrency Interest Rate Spreads." International Monetary Fund, 1980, (unpublished).

Antl, B., ed. *Foreign Exchange Risk and the Multinational Corporation*. London: Euromoney Publications, 1981.

Cyert, R. and J.G. March. *The Behavior Theory of the Firm*. Englewood Cliffs, NJ: Prentice-Hall, 1963.

Eiteman, D.K. and A.I. Stonehill. *Multinational Business Finance,* 2nd ed. Reding, MA: Addison-Wesley, 1979.

Esnor, R. and B. Antel, ed. *The Management of Foreign Exchange Risk*. London: Euromoney Publications, 1978.

George, A. *Foreign Exchange Management of the International Corporation*. New York: Praeger, 1978.

Haendel, D., G.T. West, and R.G. Meadow. *Overseas Investment and Political Risk*. Philadelphia: Foreign Policy Research Institute, 1975.

Jacque, L.L. *Management of Foreign Exchange Risk*. Lexington, MA: Lexington Books, 1978.

Knickerbocker, F.T. *Oligopolistic Reaction and Multinational Enterprise*. Boston: Harvard Business School, 1973.

Kundsen, H. "Explaining the National Propensity to Expropriate: An Ecological Approach," *Journal of International Business Studies,* Vol. VII, No. 1, (1974), pp. 51–71.

Kobrin, S.J. "When Does Political Instability Result in Increased Investment Risk," *Columbia Journal of World Business,* Vol. XIII, No. 3 (1978), pp. 113–122.

Kobrin, S.J. "Political Risk, A Review and Reconsideration," *Journal of International Business Studies,* Vol. X, No. 1 (1979), pp. 67–80.

Lessard, D.R., ed. *International Financial Management*. New York: Warren, Gorham and Lamont, 1979.

Levich, R.M. and C.G. Wihlborg, ed., *Exchange Risk and Exposure*. Lexington, MA: Lexington Books, 1980.

Nagy, P. *Country Risk*. London: Euromoney Publications, 1979.

Rodriguez, R.M. and E.E. Carter. *International Financial Management,* 2nd ed. Englewood Cliffs, NJ: Prentice-Hall, 1979.

Sargen, N. "Economic Indicators and Country Risk Appraisal," Federal Reserve Bank of San Francisco *Economic Review,* Fall, (1977), pp. 19–35.

State Department Bureau of Public Affairs. *Factors Influencing Private Foreign Investment Among LDC's*. Washington, D.C.: State Department Bureau Intelligence Research, January 1974.

Stobaugh, Jr., R. "How to Analyze Foreign Investment Climates," *Harvard Business Review,* Vol. XLVII, No. 5 (1969), pp. 100–108.

Vernon, R. *Manager and the International Economy*. Englewood Cliffs, NJ: Prentice-Hall, 1976.

Walter, I. "International Capital Allocation," in R.G. Hawkins, R.M. Levich and C. Wihlborg, eds. *Internationalization of Capital Markets,* Greenwich, CT: JAI Press, 1982.

SECTION **35**

INTERNATIONAL LABOR RELATIONS

CONTENTS

The Importance of Industrial Relations 3
The Importance of International
Industrial Relations 3

**COMPARATIVE INDUSTRIAL-
RELATIONS SYSTEMS** 4

What Is an Industrial-Relations System? 4
Selected Industrial-Relations Systems 5
  United States 5
  West Germany 6
  United Kingdom 8
  Japan 9
Comparing the Systems 11

INTERNATIONAL LABOR ACTIVITIES 11

Identifying the Spectrum 11
Intergovernmental Organizations 12
International Associations Involving
Unions 13
  Global internationals 13
  Regional and specialized
  internationals 14
  Industrial internationals 14

International Activities of U.S. Unions
and the AFL-CIO 16
  A special case—Canada 16
  Coordinated bargaining attempts 16
  Attempts to limit foreign sourcing 16
  AFL-CIO activities 17

**INTERNATIONAL MANAGEMENT OF
INDUSTRIAL RELATIONS** 17

Locus of Decision Making 17
The Headquarters-Staff Role 19
  The advising function 19
  The interpretive function 20
  The stewardship function 20

**INTERNATIONAL BUSINESS
STRATEGY AND INTERNATIONAL
AND COMPARATIVE INDUSTRIAL
RELATIONS** 21

The Foreign-Direct-Investment Decision 21
The Production-Allocation Decision 22
The Disinvestment Decision 23

**SOURCES AND SUGGESTED
REFERENCES** 24

INTERNATIONAL LABOR RELATIONS

Duane Kujawa

THE IMPORTANCE OF INDUSTRIAL RELATIONS. No manager would deny the importance of industrial relations to the success formula of the company. Collective employee-employer relationships implemented within a union-management understanding determine costs (wages, fringe benefits, etc.) per unit of labor input, management's rights (or lack of unilateral discretion) in deciding the work flow, defining the job, assigning personnel, altering production methods, and fixing work schedules and quality standards, and the procedure for resolving questions of rights granted to the parties by the labor contract. In addition, most union agreements confirm a production commitment through no-strike/no-lockout provisions. Successful industrial-relations management involves the maintenance of competitive labor costs and production continuity and the protection of management's right to initiate changes in work force organization and to innovate in production technology and work methods.

Industrial relations is no less important to the multinational firm. It is, however, much more complex.

THE IMPORTANCE OF INTERNATIONAL INDUSTRIAL RELATIONS. Managers located at the operating subsidiary level are invariably responsible for the conduct of industrial relations. Nonetheless, parent-company, or headquarters, management is vitally concerned with the subsidiary's industrial relations. Part of this concern is based upon the stewardship function of the headquarters group and the need to assess and evaluate local management's performance. The parent is concerned too since subsidiary-level production costs, flexibility in staffing and work assignments, prospects regarding industrial peace, and so forth are all key ingredients in planning processes and important strategic decisions at the multinational enterprise (MNE) level. Relevant topics here include production location and reallocation decisions, intraenterprise production-integration networks, plant closings, and major equipment purchases. Additionally, the control function at the MNE level utilizes production, financial, and other data generated by subsidiary operations. Significant variances between budgeted, anticipated events and actual events can result because of industrial-relations problems at a subsidiary. Such problems must be appraised in terms of their cost and schedule impacts on anticipated performance. Operations elsewhere within the MNE system may well be affected.

These and other management-related issues will be discussed later in this chapter. But first some of the institutional foundations affecting international labor-relations management will be identified and clarified. These include the various, usually country-bound, industrial-relations systems within which subsidiaries operate, as well as the international structures and activities of unions (and governments) that are distinctive and unique to industrial relations at an MNE level.

COMPARATIVE INDUSTRIAL-RELATIONS SYSTEMS

WHAT IS AN INDUSTRIAL-RELATIONS SYSTEM? Labor-relations issues and practices can vary considerably among countries, and even within countries across industries or geographic regions. Diversity among systems can be immense. Unions may or may not exist. Management or government may dictate terms and conditions of employment. Labor agreements may or may not be contractual obligations. Management may conclude agreements with unions that have little or no membership in the plant, or with nonunion groups that wield more bargaining power than the established unions. Some principles and issues are relevant in some contexts but not in others (e.g., seniority in layoff decisions, or even the concept of the layoff).

Such diversity in experiences provides fertile ground for analysis, especially regarding causes and effects, and for speculating on the potential impact of (proposed) changes. (For example, in France, this happened. But why? Could it happen here?) However, such diversity also makes understanding systems and comparing across systems more difficult. Yet understanding industrial-relations systems is fundamental to successful management practice. Fortunately, the conceptual framework used in the analysis of industrial-relations systems is straightforward and simple, yet universal and insightful.

Dunlop (1958) characterizes an industrial-relations system as one comprising actors and contexts, a body of rules and an ideology (unifying or destabilizing). The actors encompass supervisors and management hierarchies, workers and their representatives, and (relevant) government agencies. Any single actor, or set of actors, may dominate decision making, may be irrelevant, or may accommodate others in the decision-making process. Different actors, across or within these three key groups, may conflict or collaborate with one another. One actor may participate in several ways, depending on the times and the issues. Government, for example, may legislate (or dictate) terms and conditions of employment, abstain from influencing labor-management relations, and/or structure union-company processes such as union recognition and collective bargaining either by law or administrative behavior.

The contexts are the givens of the environment of the system. Dunlop (1958) notes that they are determined exogenously by the larger society and consist of the following:

1. Technological characteristics—as they affect product configuration, workforce size and deployment, management organization, supervisory problems, skill-level and skill-mix requirements of the workers, potential for public regulation, profit potential, safety requirements, and so forth.

2. Market, or budget, constraints—as they include the extent or lack of competition, the ability of a firm to afford higher wages and/or to administer prices

to pass along wage increases, ease of entry among suppliers of labor, and so forth.

3. The locus and distribution of power (in the larger society)—as it reflects and determines power relationships among the actors and circumscribes or influences the control of each over rule setting.

The body of rules is the output of the system and is universal to all systems. It includes procedures for setting up the rules, the substantive rules themselves, and procedures for the administering of rules. For example, the body of rules might include union recognition, the duty to bargain in "good faith," the job-classification scheme, wages, overtime and shift premiums, fringe benefits, seniority rights in promotions and layoffs, the grievance procedure, and so forth. The determining of these processes and rules is the core of the industrial-relations system (Dunlop, 1958). Certain actors may dominate in setting certain rules. Specific rules may reflect technical or market constraints (such as safety rules in bituminous-coal mining and seniority as a preference determinant in work assignments among airline pilots). Rules, in a sense, are the dependent variables that are explainable in light of the other factors.

Ideology is what holds the system together by defining acceptable roles of behavior by the actors, including the common recognition of the limits of the system and the acceptable use of power. For example, the concept of private property militates against the occupation of a plant by workers as a bargaining tactic.

As a final note, industrial-relations systems are *systemic* in nature, not *systematic*, or preplanned. Industrial-relations systems are interactive processes in which individuals or groups seek to optimize a position at a point in time, and do so in light of constraints and power relationships. The behavior rationale is time- and place-bound, and perhaps opportunistic. It is pragmatic in stable systems, revolutionary in unstable systems.

SELECTED INDUSTRIAL-RELATIONS SYSTEMS. To illustrate variations among systems and the usefulness of Dunlop's systems model to facilitate inquiry, brief commentaries on different country-level systems follow. The United States is included as a familiar base point, West Germany and the United Kingdom since they have been significant donors and recipients of MNEs' direct investments, and Japan since it provides rich contrasts to the others and is, to some observers, superior to the other systems in terms of productivity and harmony.

United States. Government's role in industrial relations in the United States has traditionally been concerned with supporting free, decentralized collective bargaining, and at the same time defining certain practices as contrary to the national interest. Such illegal practices include recognition strikes, the closed shop (where workers must belong to the union before being hired), and secondary boycotts. Other employment-related practices are legally mandated, such as those in the areas of equal employment opportunity, safety and health, social security (retirement and disability insurance), and unemployment compensation. U.S. law acknowledges the labor agreement as a contractual obligation of the parties, with performance deliberately contrary to the contract enjoinable in U.S. courts and with employees surrendering individual employment rights (generally) in favor of those set forth in the contract.

The government is a direct party to the union-management relationship in several ways: for example, in determining the appropriate bargaining unit, conducting and certifying union-recognition elections, and requiring "good faith" bargaining limited to terms and conditions of employment. Federal and state governments have also established legally prescribed minimum wages, maximum hours to be worked per day and per week at regular pay, amounts of overtime and holiday premium pay, and so forth.

A core concept in U.S. industrial relations is *exclusive jurisdiction:* Only one union represents and bargains collectively on behalf of the workers in the bargaining unit. This is legally required and is certainly compatible with the *business unionism* (as contrasted with *political unionism*) culture in the United States. The in-plant administration of the labor contract, involving company management and union members and officers exclusively, displays similar roots. Notwithstanding what the law requires of the parties, the body of rules is substantially determined, or altered through time, through collective bargaining between management and union. Power, implemented mainly through the strike and lockout weapons, is essential to collective bargaining, and a balance in power between the parties promotes mutual respect and a need for mutual accommodation. U.S. labor law supports this balance of power as being in the national interest.

Typically, collective bargaining is conducted at company-specific, local, and national levels with industrial or trade-oriented unions. Some industrywide bargaining also occurs, most notably in the steel industry on a national basis, and in the building trades and trucking on a regional basis. In the auto industry, binational (Canada and the United States) collective bargaining is conducted on a company basis. Usually only a single union participates in company-specific negotiations. An exception arises, however, in conglomerated or multidivisional firms with bargaining units represented by different unions, and where "coordinated bargaining" occurs.

Labor contracts in the United States are for fixed periods of time. Contents invariably cover union recognition and security, management rights, job classifications and wages, wage premiums, standard work periods, holidays, vacations, medical and retirement insurance, seniority rights, grievance handling (frequently culminating in binding arbitration), and no-strike/no-lockout commitments.

In the U.S. system, the right to strike is limited legally to issues germane to terms and conditions of employment, and is usually prohibited during the contract period. Strikes then invariably relate to disputes over interests of the parties as proposed contractual relationships are under consideration (as contrasted with disputes over rights of the parties granted through an existing contract or agreement). "Wildcat," or spontaneous, strikes do occur but are more frequently over local (adverse) conditions, are brief (half-day or so) and are not union initiated or sanctioned. If an impasse in collective bargaining is reached and a strike appears imminent, the parties may agree to call in outsiders to mediate the dispute. Such outsiders may be private individuals or representatives from either federal or state mediation and conciliation agencies. With the notable and recent exception in steel, interest arbitration is not evident.

West Germany.   Similar to the situation in the United States, labor law in West Germany is quite influential and extensive. Gunter and Leminsky (1978) observe that the state originally conceived of itself as a guarantor of security and order and an intervenor, "in a compensatory way, to prevent economic and social disruptions."

Lately, however, the state has become more active, especially regarding social security, full employment maintenance, and worker participation in management.

Fundamental legislation includes two types of laws: those relating to collective bargaining between unions and employers, and those relating to workers' rights and interests at plant and company levels. The Collective Agreements Act of 1949 guarantees the independence of employers and unions, circumscribes the use of strikes and lockouts, and acknowledges the validity of collective agreements. The Works Constitution Act of 1952 mandates employee-elected works councils in larger firms to conclude enterprise-level agreements covering local practices, such as the typical secondary conditions of employment (e.g., start and quit times, vacation schedules, etc.), and periodically to receive information on the firm's economic/commercial situation (present and anticipated). In addition, laws passed in 1972 and in 1976 responded to workers' interests to be on companies' boards of supervision and share in decision making at the very top with the shareholders' representatives. Together, works-council and supervisory-board participation constitute the German experience characterized as *codetermination*.

Collective agreements are fixed-period, legally binding contracts spelling out the mutual obligations of the parties. The works council is responsible for handling employee grievances, but, since the collective agreement is seen as an addendum to an individual's employment contract, a worker also has access to the Labor Court regarding a grievance. Usually collective bargaining occurs at the industry and state levels between the union for that industry and the relevant employer's association. The agreement applies to all employers who are members of the contracting association, and to all employees of such employers whether they are union members or not. Nonfederated firms may apply the terms and conditions of (relevant—i.e., by industry and state) association agreements to their employees if they wish. In some situations, the Ministry of Labor may extend obligations under collective agreements to all firms in the industry (Seyarth, *et al.,* 1969).

Typically, several agreements (which are not necessarily coterminous) together define terms and conditions of employment. For example, in metalworking, Kujawa (1971) has noted four contracts:

1. The wage- and salary-structure agreement—covering wage and salary grades, percentage compensation differential between grades, remuneration systems, and special allowances.
2. The wage (tariff) agreement—covering minimum-wage and salary rates.
3. The general-employment-conditions agreement—covering working time, dismissals and personal leave, short-time work, vacation and overtime pay, and vacation periods.
4. The agreement protecting employees against the effects of rationalization—covering special compensation, redundancy payments (for dismissals), and retraining allowances for employees displaced by technological change.

Other, specialty types of agreements occur from time to time and have, for example, related to conciliation and arbitration, and the recognition and rights of "union men of confidence," shop stewards appointed at the firm level and functioning parallel to the works council (Gunter and Laminsky, 1978). In metalworking, the four agreements noted above were negotiated on behalf of both hourly and salaried workers by the industry union Industriegewerkschaft Metall (IG-Metall) and the salaried-employees union Deutsche Angestellten Gewerkschaft (DAG).

Association-level wage agreements set minimum rates, reflecting perhaps a history of employer cooperation within industries not unlike that typified in cartel-type models. Actual wages, that is, incorporating increments above the minimum required, are set at the company or plant level in response to labor-market, union and/or works-council pressures. Holidays are designated by law (at the state level) and are not usually supplemented by additional holidays defined in collective agreements. Unemployment compensation for laid-off workers is publicly provided, as are disability insurance and pension benefits.

Use of the strike and lockout weapons is constrained by German law, which imposes a peace obligation on both management and labor. Strikes and lockouts may only occur over an issue related to collective bargaining and only when the issue is not covered by an agreement currently in effect. Since various agreements with varying termination dates are usually evident, these limitations on strikes and lockouts greatly diminish the potential for confusion over important issues. Wildcat strikes, once rare in the German system, have been occurring more frequently recently—especially as inflation has offset wage increases called for in fixed-term contracts (Gunter and Laminsky, 1978). As in the U.S. case, strikes are overwhelmingly interest related (not rights related). Interest arbitration is absent, but mediation and conciliation may be required by collective agreement or may be voluntarily utilized.

United Kingdom.   In contrast to the situation in the United States and West Germany, British industrial relations is characterized by the relative absence of legal constraints and structuring. Trade unions are voluntary associations and not legal persons; collective agreements are understandings and not contracts. Neither has legal status. Thomson and Hunter (1978) have noted, however, that the state is becoming increasingly involved in industrial relations and is searching for ways to control or substantially influence the system. For example, the Employment Protection Act of 1975 accords unions rights to certain information and to consult with management over redundancies (i.e., work-force reductions or layoffs). It established arbitration, mediation, and conciliation agencies to implement and secure individuals' and unions' rights granted by the act. It also allows unions to claim, as a right, comparable levels of pay for their constituents in line with industry or district norms. Experience to date on this aspect of the law has been quite limited, however (Thomson and Hunter, 1978). Government involvement has also been seen in its income policies, which have been various schemes and attempts, since the early 1960s, to limit pay increases outright or link them to productivity gains and to restructure, in some cases, the employment patterns in manufacturing and service industries.

Collective bargaining is conducted at both industry levels between groups of employers and unions, and at company or plant levels with a union or group of unions identified at a district (regional) level. Fixed-term agreements are becoming more evident, but the stable sections refer to procedural matters. Negotiations on substantive issues, such as wages, are frequently reopened. The concept of the agreement is that it reflects the understanding between the parties, given present underlying conditions. If these conditions change, a new understanding is required. Agreements typically cover wages (or minimum piece rates), the job classification, pay for overtime and shift work, the standard workweek, starting times, work breaks, and procedures for settling disputes and changing the agreement. In some industries, agreements also cover job or machine-manning levels and schedules, job demarcations, work-sharing and redundancy rules and apprenticeship programs (Thomson and Hunter, 1978).

Industrial relations in the United Kingdom, however, cannot be so handily characterized in terms of union-management relations and collective bargaining. There is a dual system of industrial relations. As Sturmthal (1972) noted:

> Britain [has] . . . not one but two industrial relations systems . . . often in conflict . . . [one] based on . . . collective agreements; the [other] . . . derived from understandings on the factory floor between management and individual work-place groups . . . This conflict expresses itself in a gap between contract and effective wages, in choatic forms of grievance handling, and in a disturbing number of "unofficial strikes."

The shop steward is as much evident in rule making and in administering rules as is the union, if not more so. He is especially concerned with the application of the labor agreement, its interpretation on the shop floor, the changing needs and interests of the workers as times change, and the reestablishment of acceptable compensation, working conditions, and so forth. The situation can be delicate in several ways. The steward, elected by the workers, channels company or plant-specific issues and problems to management for attention and resolution. He must be acknowledged. Yet there is no organic link between stewards and union negotiating committees, which conduct (more formal) collective bargaining (Roberts and Rothwell, 1974). *Ad hoc* arrangements to accommodate stewards during company-level (union) bargaining have been attempted, but one must still admit the potential for steward-union rivalries and conflict remains high. (For an example involving the Ford Motor Company, see Kujawa, 1971.)

Voluntarism, a social philosophy characterized by undisputed self-pursuit of self-interests, is a hallmark of industrial relations in the United Kingdom. Thus there are few, if any, limitations on the right to strike (or the use of the lockout, for that matter). Frequently, strikes are thus also unanticipated (when compared to the expectation of a strike that occurs during a collective-bargaining impasse at the termination date of a labor contract, as in the United States or West Germany). They are more disruptive, therefore, to supplier relationships and are generally viewed as having a more destructive, adverse industrial impact than those in the United States (for instance). In the early 1970s, workdays in the United Kingdom lost per 1000 employed averaged two to three times the French experience, but total workdays lost per year were considerably less than in West Germany.

Japan.   Government involvement in industrial relations in Japan works toward three objectives: delivering tangible, financial-welfare benefits to workers, establishing minimum standards for wages, hours, overtime, and so forth, and securing workers' rights to engage in collective bargaining. Social security legislation is fairly extensive and mandates employer/employee-supported funds for health, welfare, accident, pension, and employment insurance. Company-provided welfare benefits are generally regarded as more extensive than those covered by social security and include housing, medical and health care, daily-living support (e.g., company-provided meals, barber shops, laundries, commuting tickets, day nurseries, etc.), mutual-aid credit facilities, and cultural, recreational, and sports activities and facilities.

The 1947 Labor Standards Law and subsequent amendments prescribe minimums for wages, hours, overtime, rest periods, vacations, sick leave, sanitary and safety conditions, and discharge notice; these are as high as those of other advanced, industrial societies (Shirai and Shimada, 1978). Unions in Japan have special committees for shop-floor inspection to identify, document, and report violations of legally required labor standards.

Regarding unions, Article 28 of Japan's constitution stiuplates workers have a "right to organize, to bargain and to act collectively," and that (as noted in Article 12) this right is "eternal and inviolable" (Hanami, 1979). In addition, the Trade Union Law also spells out workers' rights to organize, to bargain collectively, and to engage in strike action. Patterned after the U.S. labor legislation, the Japanese law identifies (employer) unfair labor practices and, to protect unions, establishes tripartite (i.e., with labor, management, and public representatives) labor-relations commissions to examine and prohibit unfair labor practices and to provide mediation, conciliation, and arbitration services upon request (Shirai and Shimada, 1978).

There is little, if any, direct government participation in collective bargaining. The policy is one of "noninterference," even in the event of a strike. Nonetheless, a labor-relations commission can require collective bargaining in good faith if an employer refuses to bargain with a union. The union-management agreement is an enforceable contract and it supersedes individual labor contracts that do not meet its standards.

The predominant form of union organization in Japan is the enterprise union, which usually includes both hourly and salaried employees (except managerial). Over 90 percent of union members belong to enterprise unions, about 5 percent to industrial unions, and the remainder to craft unions and others (Hanami, 1979). The enterprise unions are company-, branch-, or plant-specific and, as may be expected, are fairly numerous—over 70,000 were in existence in the latter 1970s (Hanami, 1979). If a union is recognized, all workers are included in the bargaining unit.

Collective bargaining in Japan can be conducted at both enterprise and industry levels. With the former, joint labor-management negotiations (company-specific) cover contract revisions concerning wages, bonuses, working conditions, grievances, personnel affairs, and welfare issues. The latter level involves *shunto,* or the annual spring offensive, and is more evidenced in oligopolistic industries where firms have the capability of passing on industrywide wage increases to their customers. Enterprise unions affiliate with industry federations, which in turn negotiate with employer associations. Wages are the subject matter of *shunto.* Unions not affiliated with those involved in the spring offensive often conduct simultaneous, but independent, wage negotiations with their employers.

The extent of strike activity in Japan is relatively low compared to Western experiences. Moreover, about half the strikes are less than 4 hours long. About half are coordinated with and supportive of *shunto.* About two thirds of all labor disputes are usually over economic issues. As mentioned before, a labor-relations commission can, upon request, participate in resolving strike issues, and typically does so in about 10 percent of the cases.

Several key characteristics of Japanese industrial relations have developed fairly independently of union pressure, but should be mentioned. One is the permanent employment commitment to certain classes of employees at the larger firms. Another is the *ringi* system of consensus-building in decision making, which rises from the bottom up. There is also the group identification of the workers and the absence of

Affronting National Pride. Corporate skills and technical know-how and resources may be painfully obvious and resented by local nationals.

Kobrin suggests that the political risk that the firm must be concerned with involves home, host, and third-country relationships and their mutual and often complex interactions.

Operations may be disrupted by internal conflict; restrictions on repatriations may limit profits or even result in expropriations. It is suggested, therefore, that some risk estimates be introduced into the analysis of any investment decision overseas. The result of such analysis would affect not only the type of international involvement (e.g., exporting vs. direct investment) but marketing-mix strategies (e.g., owning a distribution channel vs. using an agent, developing a somewhat-modified product in the home country vs. developing a product manufactured specifically for host-country target markets).

ECONOMIC ENVIRONMENT. There are a number of criteria by which one can assess the impact of the economic environment on marketing-mix decisions. The stage of economic development appears to be particularly appropriate, since it suggests the kind of options that the international marketer has when assembling marketing-mix variables. Economic conditions are related to the existence of mass media as well as the level of education, literacy, and consumption patterns. Rostow (1971) identifies five stages or five sequential categories of economic development as follows:

Stage 1.   *The traditional society.*   Countries in this stage lack the capability of significantly increasing the level of productivity. Another characteristic is a low degree of literacy.

Stage 2.   *The preconditions for takeoff.*   During this stage the advances of modern science are beginning to be applied in agriculture and production. The development of transportation, communications, power, education, health, and other public undertakings are begun in a small but important way.

Stage 3.   *The takeoff.*   Human resources and social overhead have been developed to sustain steady development. Agricultural and industrial modernization lead to rapid expansion in these areas.

Stage 4.   *The drive to maturity.*   Modern technology is extended to all fronts of economic activity.

Stage 5.   *The age of mass consumption.*   This stage leads to a shift in the leading economic sectors toward durable consumer goods and services. Real income per capita rises to the point where a large number of people have significant amounts of discretionary income.

Economies of most developing countries fall into one of the first three categories. The industrialized countries fall into the last two categories. In general, the less developed the country, the smaller the size of potential markets, defined geographically or based on per capita income. The distribution networks in less developed countries are minimal. The more advanced the economy, the more flexibility the international marketer has in terms of segmenting target markets by offering different price points, a number of product lines, various media mixes, and shopping outlets at alternative distribution networks.

PLANNING THE INTERNATIONAL MARKETING MIX

DEVELOPING A MARKETING MIX.   Initial market scanning probing should indicate to an exporting firm or a multinational whether or not some potential exists for penetration in a new foreign market. External documentary sources such as the information offered by U.S. Department of Commerce field offices, company executives based abroad in company subsidiaries, affiliates, branches, distributors, suppliers, and government officials can all aid in one form or another in providing initial information about a market.

Keegan (1980) suggests a general framework for the collection of data in international markets. This framework includes 25 information categories, which are listed in Exhibit 4. The framework is comprehensive and particularly suits the needs of a multinational interested in the creation of an ongoing global data base. For our purpose, the most-relevant research needs are listed in section I of the exhibit and

EXHIBIT 4   TWENTY-FIVE CATEGORIES FOR A GLOBAL BUSINESS INTELLIGENCE SYSTEM

Category	Coverage
I. MARKET INFORMATION	
1. Market potential	Information indicating potential demand for products, including the status and prospects of existing company products in existing markets
2. Consumer/customer attitudes and behavior	Information about attitudes, behavior, and needs of consumers and customers of existing and potential company products. Also included in this category are attitudes of investors toward a company's investment merit
3. Channels of distribution	Availability, effectiveness, attitudes, and preferences of channel agents in company's system or a competitor's system, or of independent distributors; wholesalers, retailers, and so on
4. Communications media	Media availability, effectiveness, and cost
5. Market sources	Availability, quality, and cost
6. New products	Nontechnical information concerning new products for a company (this includes products that are already marketed by other countries), ideas, and market potential
7. Competitive sales	Sales performance of competitve products
8. Competitive marketing programs and plans	Marketing programs and plans (sales promotions, advertising, area coverage, etc.) for existing and new products
9. Competitive products	Prices and features for existing and proposed products
10. Competitive operations	Information relating to a competitor's operating capability. Employee morale, transfers, production efficiency, and so on.
11. Competitive investments	Information concerning competitive investments, expansion plans, or moves. New capacity, investment proposals, indications of manufacturing resource commitments

EXHIBIT 4   *CONTINUED*

Category	Coverage
II. PRESCRIPTIVE INFORMATION	
12. Foreign exchanges	Information concerning changes or expected changes in foreign-exchange rates by exchange-control authorities and immediate influences upon these authorities
13. Foreign taxes	Information concerning decisions, intentions, and attitudes of foreign authorities regarding taxes upon earnings, dividends, and interest
14. Other foreign prescriptions	All information concerning local, regional, or international-authority guidelines, rulings, laws, decrees other than foreign-exchange and tax matters affecting the operations, assets, or investments of a company
15. U.S. government prescriptions	U.S. government incentives, controls, regulations, restraints, etc., affecting a company
III. RESOURCE INFORMATION	
16. Manpower	Availability of individuals and groups. Employment candidates, sources, strikes, etc
17. Money	Availability and cost of money for company uses
18. Raw material	Availability and cost
19. Acquisitions and mergers	Leads or other informationn concerning potential acquisitions, mergers, or joint ventures
IV. GENERAL CONDITIONS	
20. Economic factors	Macroeconomic information dealing with broad factors, such as capital movements, rate of growth, economic structure, and economic geography
21. Social factors	Social structure of society, customs, attitudes, and preferences
22. Political factors	"Investment climate," meaning of elections, political change
23. Scientific technological factors	Major developments with broad but relatively untested implications
24. Management and administrative practices	Management and administrative practices and procedures concerning such matters as employee compensation, report procedure
25. Other information	Information not assignable to another category

Source.   Keegan, 1980.

include information on market potential, consumer and customer attitudes and behavior, channels of distribution, communication and market services, new products, and every other aspect of competitive sales and operations.

We will take this analysis one step further under the assumption that a *geographic* target market has been identified as a potential area of interest for the firm. Such a designation should result from the interaction of two factors: corporate objectives (e.g., penetration into the lucrative Middle East market) and preliminary research (e.g., exploratory contacts with local distributors, information about activity and competing firms). Once a target market has been identified, more-comprehensive research, such as that proposed by Keegan (1980), should be undertaken to develop a segmentation strategy and to examine whether or not the needs of segment(s) could be satisfied by developing appropriate marketing mix(es) while simultaneously meeting corporate objectives. To this end, a framework for international marketing planning has been developed as shown in Exhibit 5.

This framework meets two needs of the firm contemplating foreign-market penetration: market description and market diagnosis. Given rules by which the firm will decide whether or not it is worth its while to exert marketing efforts in the target market of interest, it can now focus on identifying and developing a segmentation

EXHIBIT 5   INTERNATIONAL MARKETING-MIX PLANNING

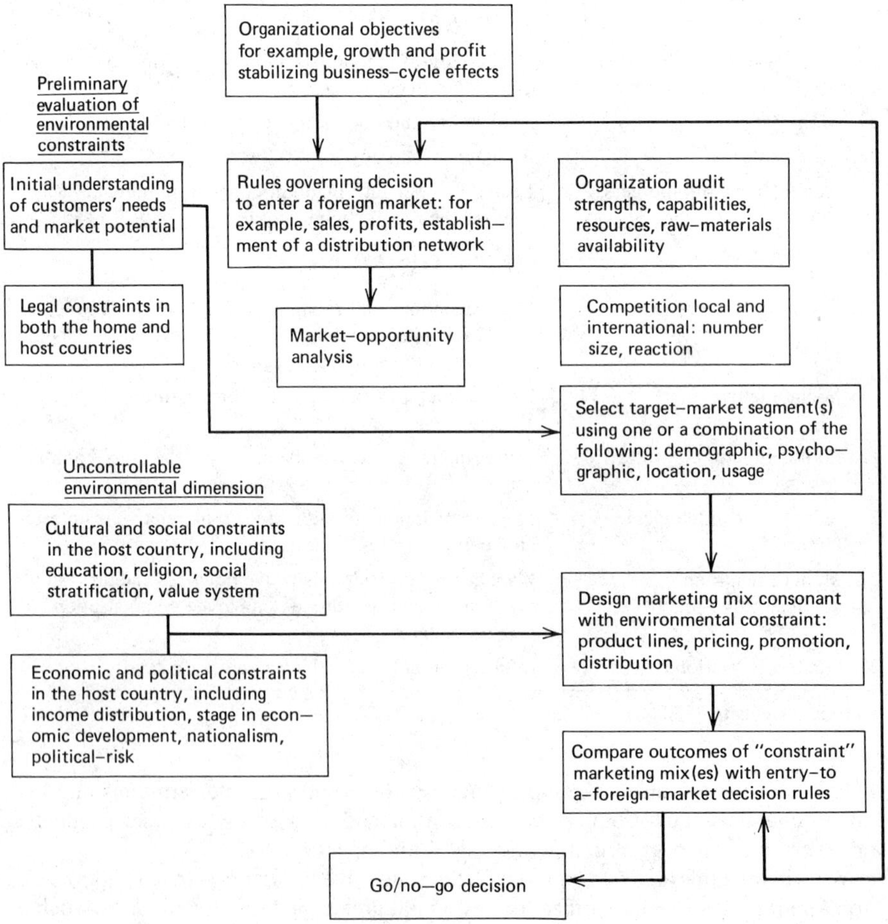

scheme. Typically, the variables used to segment and describe a market are demography, location, site, and usage. Each of the variables will be discussed briefly.

Demographic Variables.   Markets can be segmented or described according to age, sex, income, family size, religion, social class, and other variables. Existence of many young people, for example, could influence a decision of sporting-goods manufacturers to enter a market.

Psychographic Variables.   These variables can be used as supplements to demographic variables. The focus here is on general buyer habits, life-styles, and attitudes as they might be related to a specific product class or consumption in general. People's attitudes toward leisure time might influence a decision to introduce "time saving" products or establish a fast-food chain.

Geographic Variables.   A decision to enter a market can be based on geography and population density. For example, entering a market in a developing country may depend on proximity to a transportation center, or a marketer may concentrate only on urban areas where the more educated and affluent middle class is likely to be found.

Product-Usage Variables.   A market can be divided on the basis of product usage. Thus a market may be divided into users and nonusers. Users may be classified further as heavy, moderate, or light. A separate campaign could be developed for each of these segments or subsegments.

Once a market description or a segmentation scheme is developed, a marketing mix should be developed taking into account company resources, external uncontrollable constraints, and the segment's descriptors (demographic, psychographic, etc.) and requirements. Obviously the net result would be a mix that is not optimal. The more restricted the international-market planner is by the uncontrollable variables, the fewer options he has in terms of assembling the most effective mix. The firm should therefore compare what it can do, given the various environmental constraints and the cost of market penetration, to the decision rules it established beforehand with regard to satisfactory marketing and profit outcomes. After evaluating what can and cannot be done, the firm might very well conclude that the options it has in terms of marketing mix are very limited, and it cannot develop an effective marketing mix. Such a diagnosis should lead to a no-go decision.

Often, though, appropriate market research will lead to the identification of untapped markets that will increase the likelihood of a market penetration.

SOURCES AND SUGGESTED REFERENCES

"Adopting Export Packaging to Cultural Differences," *Business America* (1979), pp. 1–7.

Zahn, P., "Blue Jeans Marketers Battle for Share in Europe," *Advertising Age*, Vol. XLVI, No. 34 (1975), p. 63.

Boddewyn, "The Global Spread of Advertising Regulations," paper presented at the regional meeting of the Academy of International Business in New York, January 1980.

Cateora, R. and M. Hess, *International Marketing,* Homewood, IL: Richard D. Irwin, 1979.

"Colgate's Nordiko Aims at P&G in Mexico," *Advertising Age,* Vol. XLVII, No. 45 (1976), p. 27.

Cravens, W., E. Hills, and B. Woodruff, *Marketing Decision Making,* Homewood, IL: Richard D. Irwin, 1980.

Darlymple, J. and J. Parsons, *Marketing Management,* New York: Wiley, 1980.

Shilling, A., "Developing Middle East Is All It Claims to Be, A New Frontier," *Advertising Age,* Vol. XLVIII, No. 28 (1977), pp. 64–110.

Dunn, S. W., "Effect of National Identity on Multinational Promotional Strategy in Europe," *Journal of Marketing,* Vol. XL (1976), pp. 50–57.

Hall, T., *Beyond Culture,* Garden City: Anchor, 1977.

"India Offers a Diverse, Complex Advertising Market," *Advertising Age,* Vol. XLIX, No. 28 (1978), p. 96.

Criswell, B., "Is the Well Going Dry? Try Getting off the Main Drag," *Advertising Age,* Vol. XLVIII, No. 23 (1977), p. 56.

Keegan, J., *Multinational Marketing Management,* 2nd ed., Englewood Cliffs, NJ: Prentice-Hall, 1980.

Kleppner, O., *Advertising Procedure,* 7th ed., Englewood Cliffs, NJ: Prentice-Hall, 1980.

Kobrin, J., "The Political Environment," In V. Terpstra, ed. *The Cultural Environment of International Business,* Cincinnati: South-Western, 1978.

Kotler, P., *Marketing Management,* 4th ed., Englewood Cliffs, NJ: Prentice-Hall, 1980.

Giberga, M., "Lessening Terminal Risks With Overseas Agents," *Commerce America* (September 1978), pp. 30–33.

"Locating Terminal Rules with Overseas Agents," *Commerce America* (April 1979), pp. 6–8.

Luck, J. and O. C. Ferrel, *Marketing Strategy and Plans,* Englewood Cliffs, NJ: Prentice-Hall, 1979.

Managing Global Marketing, New York: Business International Publications, 1976.

"Marketing in Japan," *Advertising Age,* Vol. XLIX, No. 3 (1978), pp. 43–90.

Moriarty, T. and M. Galper, *Organizational Buying Behavior: A State-of-the-Art Review and Conceptualization,* Cambridge: Marketing Science Institute, 1978.

Peebles, M., K. Ryans, Jr., and I. R. Vernon, "Coordinating International Advertising," *Journal of Marketing,* Vol. XLII, No. 1 (1978), pp. 28–34.

Rostow, W., *The Stages of Economic Growth,* 2nd ed., Cambridge: Cambridge University Press, 1971.

"Scotch: On the Rocks," *Advertising Age,* Vol. XLIX, No. 28 (1978), p. 96.

Sheth, N. and S. Sethi, "A Theory of Cross Cultural Behavior," in G. Woodside, N. Sheth, and P. Bennet, eds., *Consumer and Industrial Buying Behavior,* New York: North-Holland, 1977.

Siegmund, J., *Current Development in Product Liability Affecting International Commerce,* Staff Study, Washington, D.C.: Department of Commerce, 1978.

Sissors, J., "Matching Media with Markets," *Journal of Advertising Research,"* Vol. XI (1971), pp. 39–43.

"Surveying the United Kingdom's Distribution and Sales Channels," *Business America* (1979), pp. 12–14.

Terpstra, V., *The Cultural Environment of International Business,* Cincinnati: South-Western, 1978.

Webster, E. and Y. Wind, "A General Model for Understanding Organizational Buying Behavior," *Journal of Marketing,* Vol. XXXVI (1972), pp. 12–19.

"Today's European Consumer: Skeptical and Uncertain Target," *Advertising Age,* Vol. XLVIII, No. 12 (1977), p. 24.

MANAGEMENT OF THE INTERNATIONAL MARKETING FUNCTION

CONTENTS

TARGET MARKET SELECTION	**3**	Standards and specifications	12
		Patent protection	13
Selecting Target Countries	**3**	Brand and Trademark	**13**
Which countries import	3	Selection of names and trademarks	13
Market indicators	3	Protection of names and trademarks	14
Marketing considerations	4	Package and Label	**14**
International Market Segmentation	**5**	Handling conditions	14
Segmenting the world	5	Shopping habits	14
Segmenting foreign markets	5	Laws	14
International market segments	6	Extent of self-service	14
Targeting specific customers	6	Consumer preferences	14
		Economic conditions	14
INTERNATIONAL PRICING	**7**	Creating the label and package	15
		Instructions, Warranties, and Service	**15**
Global Pricing Strategy	**7**	Instructions	15
One world price	7	Warranties	15
Different price in each market	8	Service	15
Intermediate pricing policies	8	International Product Strategy	**16**
The Price Position or Level	**9**	Product cycles	16
High price position	9	The product line	16
Medium price position	9	Product development	16
Low price position	9		
Barter	9	**INTERNATIONAL DISTRIBUTION**	**16**
Transfer pricing	9		
Working Back to First Cost	**10**	Distribution Functions	**16**
Foreign retail price	10	Information functions	17
Standard multipliers	10	Physical functions	17
Other Considerations	**10**	Types of Distribution Channels	**17**
Price changes	10	Channels in the source country	17
Currency of quotation	11	Channels in the market country	17
Terms of payment	11	Selecting a distribution channel	19
The confirming house	11	Selecting Foreign Representatives	**19**
International tenders	11	Identifying potential representatives	19
		Criteria for selection	19
PRODUCT CONSIDERATIONS	**12**	Contracting with foreign	
		representatives	20
Product Design and Quality	**12**	Working with Foreign Representatives	**20**
Design considerations	12	Training	21
Quality considerations	12		

Objectives   21
Consultation   21
Assistance   21
International Physical Distribution   21
Order processing   21
Packing and marking   21
Documentation   21
Shipping   22
Insurance   22
Warehousing   22
Multimodal distribution   22

INTERNATIONAL PROMOTION   22

Advertising   22
Print media   22
Broadcast media   23
Other advertising media   23
Advertising agencies   24
Sales Promotion   24
Trade fairs and exhibitions   24
Contests and premiums   24
Public Relations and Publicity   25
Public relations   25
Publicity   25

Personal Selling   25
Export sales personnel   26
Foreign sales personnel   26
Other Aspects of Promotion   26
Standardization or adaptation   26
Planning and budgeting   27
The promotional mix   27

**ORGANIZATION, PLANNING, AND
CONTROL**   27

Organization for International
Marketing   27
The place of international operations   27
Internal structure of international
operations   27
International Marketing Planning   28
Detailed profit planning   28
Types of objectives   28
Strategies and tactics   29
Long-range profit planning   29
Worldwide profit planning   30
Control of International Marketing   30

**SOURCES AND SUGGESTED
REFERENCES**   30

MANAGEMENT OF THE INTERNATIONAL MARKETING FUNCTION

Kenneth D. Weiss

TARGET MARKET SELECTION

SELECTING TARGET COUNTRIES. The international marketer who aims at the world in general, like pointing a shotgun at a flock of birds, is unlikely to score a hit. He will do much better if he shoots at specific targets.

Which Countries Import. A simple approach to market selection is to suppose that the highest-potential target markets for a product are countries that import substantial quantities of it. Import statistics are found in several publications, including the following:

1. U.S. Department of Commerce *Market Share Reports*, commodity series, which give for a single commodity the level of imports, main suppliers, and U.S. share of the market of each major importing country.
2. United Nations publications, including *Commodity Trade Statistics*, the *International Trade Yearbook*, the *World Trade Annual*, and the U.N. Food and Agriculture Organization's *FAO Trade Yearbook*.
3. Organization for Economic Co-operation and Development (OECD) "Microtables," on microfilm, which give current, detailed import and export statistics of the 24 OECD member countries.

It is usually possible through desk research to identify the nations that import a product, with quantities, values, supplying countries and major trends. Some drawbacks are that very specific products may be buried in larger product groups, international trade statistics are never entirely accurate, and target-market decisions cannot be based on statistics alone.

Market Indicators. A second approach to target-market selection is the use of market indicators; for example, an indicator of the size of a national market for nurses' caps is the number of nurses in a country. A source of many market indicators is the annual International Bank for Reconstruction and Development's *World Development Report*. This report reveals, for example, that the mid-1977 population of Nigeria was 79 million, increasing by 2.6 percent per year, and there was one nurse for every 3210 persons. If each nurse will purchase, on the average, 3 caps a year, the 1981 market potential is about 86,000 caps.

This approach can be very useful as a starting point, although it doesn't consider local production, import competition, or economic, social, political, or legal factors that may affect sales of a product.

Marketing Considerations.   After selecting *possible* target markets from statistics or indicators, a number of marketing considerations must be examined. These can be summarized as follows:

1. *Suitability of product,* including brand name, label, package, instructions, and warranty. Some pertinent questions are, "Will my product have to be adapted to a different type of electrical current?" "Will my brand name sound appealing in another language?" "Will my label and instructions have to be translated?" and "Will the terms of my warranty have to be changed?"
2. *Ability to meet the price,* considering the costs of production, transportation, and market access.
   a. Most manufacturers know how their *cost structures* compare with those in other producing countries, and many can make comparisons of the approximate *per unit* costs of raw materials, labor, capital, administration, and taxes.
   b. *Transportation costs* depends on several factors, including quantities shipped, traffic on the route, competition among shipping companies, and distance. There seems to be a trend toward the breakdown of the conference-line system and the negotiability of ocean shipping rates.
   c. *Market access* includes import duties, quotas, licenses, and other restrictions. An exporter can ascertain his access to a specific market by contacting the consulate of that country or the U.S. Department of Commerce country specialist in Washington, D.C.
3. *Ability to promote and distribute* the product in the foreign market. Several publications, such as the U.S. Department of Commerce *Overseas Business Report* series, contain information on distribution and promotion in each country. Some distribution systems, for example, those in Japan, are hard for a foreign firm to get a product into. Also, some countries, for example, those in Eastern Europe, lack the advertising agencies and media that are necessary for mass marketing a consumer-convenience good.
4. *Potential for achieving a substantial market share.* This potential depends on many factors, including local and import competition and the image of a firm's products in the target market. The U.S. image is a strong competitive advantage for some products, for example, blue jeans, but is less beneficial for other products, such as consumer electronics.
5. *The economic situation,* specifically, whether or not a country can pay for its imports, and whether or not it allows foreign investors to take out earnings in hard currency. Most international banks have systems of rating countries on their ability to meet foreign-exchange obligations. More specifically, the Chase World Information Service gives statistics on the payment terms used for each country by American exporters and on the delays experienced in receiving payment under letters of credit and drafts.

6. *The political situation,* as an indication of a country's future stability. The country-rating systems of international banks consider the possibility of internal upheavals or external aggression, which could lay waste to the most carefully planned marketing campaign. Less dramatically, political conditions can result in product-safety laws, price controls, or restrictions on advertising that may seriously hamper marketing activities. A case in point is the Kenyan manufacturer who was left with a warehouse full of miniskirts when his market country, Uganda, unexpectedly outlawed this form of dress.

INTERNATIONAL MARKET SEGMENTATION. The term *market segmentation* is used in two ways in international marketing—to segment the world and to segment a particular country. In addition, there is the concept of the *international market segment.*

Segmenting the World. For marketing purposes, countries can be grouped according to many different criteria. For example, grouping by *language* would put French-speaking countries in one segment, Spanish-speaking countries in another segment, and so forth. This would be useful to firms selling language-dependent products such as books and greeting cards.

Some other segmentation criteria that can be used are the following:

1. Religion.
2. Political/economic system.
3. Level of development.
4. Climate.
5. Geographical location (the most common).

Segmenting the world may lead to grouping countries that are in different geographic areas, and even to splitting countries. For example, segmentation based on level of development would place the whites of South Africa with advanced countries and the nonwhites with the emerging nations. This in turn can affect the way a firm is organized for international marketing.

Segmenting Foreign Markets. Any national market can be segmented according to a number of variables, which are summarized as follows by Kotler (1980):

1. *Geographic,* including region, city size, and climate.
2. *Demographic,* including age, sex, income, and so forth.
3. *Psychographic,* including social class, life-style, and personality.
4. *Behavioristic,* including product benefits sought, rate of usage, and sensitivity to changes in price, advertising, or other elements of the marketing mix.

Of course these categories often overlap. For example, a segmentation of Cyprus based on ethnic background would produce a geographic division of the Turkish population and the Greek population.

Geographic segmentation is useful wherever people in different parts of a country have very different purchasing behavior, for example, the sophisticated customers of Bogotá compared with the Colombian *campesinos.*

Demographic segmentation has many uses overseas, such as suggesting small package sizes for small German families and visual advertisements for poorly educated Haitians. In fact, the "illiterate" segment would include 90 percent of the adult population in about 15 countries.

Psychographic segmentation can consider attitudes toward foreign goods and the "westernization" or modernization that such goods often bring or accelerate. In traditional societies such as Japan or Saudi Arabia, most customers for many types of products are in the westernized market segment.

Behavioristic segmentation is vital internationally. A bicycle used for delivering groceries will be very different from one used for racing, although the two might operate on the same street. A refrigerator in many countries must be decorative, because it will be placed where visitors to the house can see it. The consumers who are least loyal to national, or traditionally imported, brands may be the logical targets of market-introduction publicity campaigns.

The information needed to segment foreign markets is becoming increasingly available from international, national, state, and local government organizations, local and international market-research firms, and foreign companies and trade associations.

The danger in market segmentation is the temptation to overdo it by formulating unique marketing plans for segments too small to warrant them. Adaptations in product, pricing, promotion, and distribution should be thought of as investments, each with a payback potential or net present value.

International Market Segments. The concept of international market segments is transnational. It recognizes that consumers located in various countries but having similar purchasing characteristics can be reached by similar marketing procedures.

This concept is especially relevant to marketers of *industrial products*. For example, a supplier of small gasoline engines might single out the following worldwide market segments:

Builders of small boats.

Producers of motorcycles, snowmobiles, and related products.

Manufacturers of lawn mowers, grass trimmers, and other outdoor tools.

This firm would then organize internationally by *market segment*.

The concept is relevant also to some consumer markets. There are people in all countries who like to have the best Scotch whiskey, the most prestigious perfume, the finest wristwatches, and weekly news in English. These international market segments respond worldwide to similar products, prices, promotion, and distribution.

Targeting Specific Customers. International customers can be categorized as either industrial users that import for their own account, including military and other government organizations, or other industrial users and private consumers, reached through various types of intermediaries (including state trading corporations in socialist countries).

Prospective customers in the first category can be identified from directories, and their purchasing behavior can be ascertained by field research. Two very useful directories are *Bottin Europe* and *Bottin International*, which list for each country federal government ministries, industry federations having foreign-trade departments, domestic and foreign chambers of commerce, principal manufacturing and importing companies, state trading corporations, and a great deal of other useful information. Also, Dun and Bradstreet's *Principal International Businesses* covers the entire free world. There are several other useful general directories.

More-specific information is available for individual countries and industries. A country example is the *Standard Trade Index of Japan,* published by the Japan Chamber of Commerce and Industry. An industry example is the *World Aviation Directory,* by the Ziff Davis Publishing Company in New York; it describes civil air carriers, aviation/aerospace and components manufacturers, overhaul facilities, and relevant publications and government organizations (including air forces) in all countries.

Industrial users of a product can often be identified from publications of national trade associations, membership lists of chambers of commerce and/or industry (in some countries chamber membership is obligatory), or lists maintained by government ministries. These sources usually give only the companies' names, addresses, telephone numbers, and perhaps main products and activities. Any additional information, such as years in business or approximate size, must usually be obtained by field research. Importers, import agents, brokers, wholesalers, and retailers that channel merchandise to individual consumers can be identified from publications such as the *Directory of British Importers,* or the U.S. Department of Commerce *Foreign Traders Index* and *Trade Lists.* These publications, however, do not tell a marketer which organizations can handle his product effectively or which *will be willing* to handle it. This kind of information is obtained through field data collection.

INTERNATIONAL PRICING

GLOBAL PRICING STRATEGY.   An important question in international pricing strategy is whether to maintain one price worldwide, a different price in each market, or some intermediate system. The answer depends largely on the number of producing facilities a company operates and the number of markets it sells in.

One World Price.   Many firms that produce in only one country and sell to many establish a uniform export price, f.o.b. factory or port of lading. Warren Keegan (1980) calls this "ethnocentric pricing."

The uniform export price is often, but not always, below the normal domestic selling price. This can be justified by the following arguments:

Competition is more severe in foreign markets.

The country-of-origin price must be low in order to compensate for the high cost of moving goods overseas.

Foreign customers should not be charged for purely domestic expenses, such as advertising and delivery in the home country.

Export sales are really extra, or incremental, sales, so only incremental costs plus profit must be covered (export pricing based on incremental costs may violate antidumping laws, which now exist in most countries).

There are several advantages to a uniform export price:

It is the simplest. Price quotations can be given quickly and easily.

An export price list can be published and distributed to foreign representatives and customers.

The firm can pay more attention to nonprice elements of the marketing mix.

There is of course a major disadvantage to one world price—inflexibility. It will undoubtedly be too low for some markets and too high for others, thus depriving the firm of larger margins in the first case and larger sales volumes in the second.

Some firms that have sources of supply in several countries also try to establish uniform prices, f.o.b. Country of origin, although this implies a different profit margin at each plant because of differences in costs of production. With this system, producing firms prefer to allocate production to the lowest-cost plant, whereas customers prefer to buy from the location from which transportation cost and import duties are the least expensive.

It is rare for a firm to try to maintain a uniform worldwide price, c.i.f. port of unlading or closer to the consumer. This is difficult even within common-market areas because of different frieght rates, disparate local price levels, and fluctuations in the exchange rates of currencies. One product for which the final price to the consumer can be adapted immediately to exchange-rate fluctuations is the weekly news magazine, which can change its prices every week in any country by simply printing the new price on the cover.

Different Price in Each Market.   To set and maintain a different price for each market requires a degree of market knowledge and control that few firms possess. The companies best equipped to do this are multinationals, such as the Coca Cola Comapny, that produce in nearly every country in which they sell. This system of *market differentiated pricing* is described by Richard Robinson (1978). Its main advantage is that price can be adjusted according to purchasing power and competitive conditions in each country.

Separate pricing for each market almost has to be done at the local level, as it is hard for a world, or even a regional, headquarters staff to know enough about conditions in each country to set the most profitable price. Also it is very hard for a headquarters organization to control price once the products leave the company-owned portion of the distribution channel.

Some potential difficulties with market-differentiated prices are jealousies and unauthorized reselling. A foreign representative may be jealous of his counterparts in other countries who pay lower prices than he does, and a representative who pays low prices may make unauthorized sales through alternate distribution channels in countries where prices are higher.

Intermediate Pricing Policies.   At least three alternatives are available:

A Different F.O.B. Factory (or F.O.B. Port of Lading) Price From Each Producing Unit.   This is a cost-based pricing policy that favors lower-cost producing units, although higher-cost factories can still sell because of cheaper transportation, quicker delivery, or other advantages.

Delivery From Free Zones.   Goods can be shipped from different producing units to free-trade zones, such as the one in Panama, and all buyers can be quoted the same price, F.O.B. free zone. It is even possible to use a free zone as a *basing point* for c.&f. or c.i.f. prices. For example, a customer in Buenos Aires could be given a c.&f. price for delivery from Panama, even though the goods were actually shipped from a factory elsewhere.

Same Final Sale Price Throughout a Region.   This system can be used, for example, with heavy industrial equipment throughout the Andrean Common Market. Buyers within the market area are likely to compare price quotations with each other, and the goods, once installed, cannot easily be reshipped to another region in which prices may be higher.

THE PRICE POSITION OR LEVEL.   A firm that is using market-differentiated prices should determine its products' *price positions* in the market country. This is where a product's price fits in the range of prices of all competing products.

High Price Position.   High price levels can be used if a firm's image and the quality of its products are equal or superior to those of the best of the competition. A firm must be able to sell enough at the high price position to meet its profit objectives. This is facilitated if the product has new or unique characteristics that allow it to be *differentiated* from the competition. As in domestic markets, a new product may be sold initially at a high price in order to *skim* the market.

Medium Price Position.   Medium prices for consumer goods can be used in countries where the middle class is substantial (it is still small in many less developed countries). Marketing competition in the middle of the price range is often active and diversified, with special price offers, new product developments, and promotional campaigns, all based on market research. Firms selling industrial goods abroad often select the middle price levels and compete by means of personal selling, product information, and service.

Low Price Position.   An international marketer can choose a low price position if he is able to sell profitably at the bottom of the price range, and if he can capture a large enough share of the market to meet his profit objectives. Often firms choose *penetration* prices because they are the simplest competitive weapon to use, but they are also the easiest for competitors to duplicate. This can result in competitive pressure to lower prices still further.

Barter.   When merchandise is not sold for cash, but is bartered for other goods, the question of price level is still important. A barter deal usually involves fixing a monetary value per unit for all merchandise to be included in the transaction. Then the exchange is, for example, $500,000 worth of tractors for $500,000 worth of grain.

Transfer Pricing.   Special difficulties with pricing arise in intracompany sales from one country to another. The exporting country would like a high transfer price to maximize taxable profits within its borders. On the other hand, the importing country would prefer a low transfer price to maximize taxable profits there (although the customs department in the importing country would frown on unjustifiably low prices). The company, for its part, would like to show the most profit in the country with the lowest tax rates.

There seems to be a trend toward the general acceptance of *arm's length* transfer prices, which means that goods moving intracompany from one country to another are priced as if the transaction were between unrelated business entities.

WORKING BACK TO FIRST COST.   A firm that selects a *price position* in the target market must work back to determine its f.o.b. factory price and then decide whether it can profitably sell at that price level. The process for an exporter using a normal consumer goods distribution channel is explained in the following section.

Foreign Retail Price.

Less retail markup and freight-in equals *foreign wholesale price;*

Less wholesale markup and freight-in equals *importer's price;*

Less importer's markup equals *landed cost;*

Less customs clearance and duty equals *c.i.f. port of unlading;*

Less international shipping and insurance equals *f.o.b. vessel, port of lading;*

Less freight forwarding and documents charges equals *f.a.s. vessel, port of lading;*

Less delivery to pier equals *f.o.b. shipping point,* packed for export.

There may also be charges for port warehousing and/or special handling.

In deciding whether it can meet a calculated price f.o.b. shipping point, a firm should consider the cost of financing as well as any export incentives such as Domestic International Sales Corporation (DISC) tax deferments.

Standard Multipliers.   Firms that frequently do business with the same countries may develop standard multipliers for estimating prices. For example, an exporter of frozen beef from Kansas City to Japan might determine that the Tokyo retail price multiplied by 0.2 will give a close approximation of the f.o.b. packing house price.

The multiplier system can be used also to estimate prices forward. For example, a Dallas manufacturer of machine tools might determine that its normal export prices times three give the approximate final sales price to a customer in Bogotá.

OTHER CONSIDERATIONS.   Some other factors to consider in international pricing are price changes, currency of quotation, terms of payment, confirming houses, and bidding on international tenders.

Price Changes.   Price *increases* in foreign markets are often made necessary by increases in manufacturing, transportation, or other costs, or by inflation in market countries. Occasionally price *decreases* are made possible by reductions in import duties, or are made necessary by increased competition.

Care must be taken to advise all foreign representatives before a price change is to take place and to honor former prices for all sales made before the effective date of an increase.

In countries with high rates of inflation, prices can be averaged over time to make increases less frequent. That is, in a country where the rate of inflation is 10 percent per month, prices can be increased by 20 percent every 2 months. They will be too high right after an increase, and then too low, but there will be fewer disruptive changes.

Price control in several countries restricts price increases, and violations of price-control regulations can have serious consequences for a foreign-owned firm.

Currency of Quotation.   For exporters, the safest currency of quotation is the one that is least likely to be devalued before payment is received. This implies quoting in the currencies of countries with low inflation rates, such as Switzerland.

It is possible to quote in a currency at a fixed exchange rate. For example, an American exporter to Brazil can agree to quote in cruzeiros at the rate of exchange on the day the contract was signed. Then the importer will be able to pay in cruzeiros, but if a devaluation takes place before payment is made he will have to pay enough cruzeiros to give the exporter the number of dollars he requires.

Finally, when receiving foreign currencies in payment for merchandise, an exporter can *hedge* to protect himself against devaluation. For example, an exporter who is to receive 1 million yen in 90 days, can sell the yen for dollars, at a discount, for delivery in 90 days. Of course the discount will be large if the banking community thinks the yen is likely to be devalued against the dollar.

Terms of Payment.   International terms of payment are extremely important, to the point that credit is often more important than price itself. The following general comments can be made with respect to exporting:

Open account sales save time and money, and can be used when both the customer *and his country* are known to be able and willing to pay.

Time drafts give the exporter, as assurance of payment, the customer's signature on a bank document. To dishonor a draft is quite shameful in some countries, but unfortunately not in all.

Sight drafts are safe in theory, but there are hazards. An importer may choose to claim his merchandise late, or not at all, and a country's banking system may be very slow in making payment.

Letters of credit can be secure payment instruments; however, they are costly, and they bind the exporter to rigid terms. A letter of credit issued by a reliable foreign bank can be factored, or the exporter can borrow against it.

Cash in advance is sometimes obtained for small or special orders, or from unknown customers, or in periods when merchandise is in short supply. Many foreign importers maintain bank accounts in the United States to facilitate making cash payments.

The Confirming House.   For sales to customers or countries that have poor credit ratings an exporter can seek to arrange payment through a confirming house. European confirming houses are well acquainted with African markets, for example, and can evaluate credit risks much more effectively than less experienced American exporters.

International Tenders.   Major international tenders from foreign government organizations usually specify the currency of quotation and the payment terms. The main task in preparing a quotation is to evaluate the competing firms and their probable price offerings. The practice of bidding high to cover large payments to agents in foreign markets is now restricted by the Foreign Corrupt Practices Act, and by laws in several countries.

PRODUCT CONSIDERATIONS

PRODUCT DESIGN AND QUALITY. A prominent question in marketing literature is whether to standardize a product for the world or adapt it to each market area. The usual answer is that a firm should standardize as much as possible to reduce expenses, while adapting where it must to increase sales. The ideal procedure would be to compare the projected costs and benefits of each adaptation in product design, quality, packaging, and service.

Design Considerations. The design of a product for international markets is influenced by many factors including the following: the way in which it will be used, the conditions of use, consumer preferences, and legal and economic conditions.

The use of a product varies from place to place. For example, bicycles are for transportation, recreation, racing, or product deliveries. The design varies according to the *type of use*.

Conditions of use also affect product design. Very rough roads require strong suspension systems on motor vehicles; high altitudes necessitate low-pressure tennis balls, and so forth.

Consumer preferences vary enormously from country to country; for example:

The *size* of chairs is larger in Sweden than in Indonesia.

The *scent* of detergent is milder in the Middle East than in most parts of Europe.

Color preferences are many and surprising, including *green* crosses on medical supplies in South Korea and *black* false teeth in Thailand.

The *taste* of soft drinks is sweeter in many countries than in the United States.

Laws such as product-safety regulations can influence the design of toys and other products, and *economic conditions* can require designs that lend themselves to low-cost production techniques.

Quality Considerations. The important point about quality is that it should be *appropriate* for the market and the price position at which a firm is aiming. A firm can price itself out of a market by keeping its product quality unnecessarily high, or it can damage its reputation by selling goods of very low quality.

Often *industrial goods* must be of high quality even in countries in which private consumers buy mainly on price. This is because buyers of industrial goods everywhere are somewhat more sophisticated than the average household consumer. They are better able to judge quality and to understand the dangers of installing shoddy machines and equipment.

Standards and Specifications. Most countries now have industrial standards institutes that publish nationally accepted standards for each product. These are often patterned after those of a leading industrial nation.

An important service for international marketers of manufactured products is *Technical Help to Exporters,* from the National Technical Information Service in Springfield, Virginia. This service provides manufacturers and exporters with information about the standards, certification requirements, and regulatory agencies that will affect sales of their products in foreign countries.

Some of the more-common product adaptations for foreign markets pertain to electrical characteristics (voltage and cycles) and sizes (metric).

Patent Protection. Patent laws around the world are varied and often complicated. In general, an international marketer should have his product patented in every country in which he plans to sell as soon as a decision is made to go ahead. According to *Foreign Business Practices* (1975), the United States is a party to the Paris Union International Convention for the Protection of Industrial Property, the Inter-American Convention of 1910 on Inventions, Patents, Designs and Models, and a number of bilateral agreements. These conventions serve basically to place a foreign firm in the same position as a domestic firm with regard to patents in a signatory country.

There are also agreements in Western Europe that make it possible to obtain patent coverage in several countries by filing only one application. Even so, a firm must be alert to keep its patent protection in force in each market country for as long as the law allows. This is true in both civil-law and code-law countries.

The complexity of international patent laws makes it advisable to use a competent international patent attorney to obtain and maintain protection.

BRAND AND TRADEMARK. A great deal of attention is given to the *selection* and *protection* of brand names and trademarks in international marketing.

Selection of Names and Trademarks. An alternative chosen by many companies is the uniform *worldwide* company and/or product identification. Such identification helps build the image of firms such as *Kodak,* whose products are often purchased by international travelers, and *Exxon,* which has just five letters including two high-visibility *X*'s. The main criteria for a worldwide name are that it be short and that it not have an offensive or derogatory meaning in any major language.

Many other firms *translate or adapt* their brand names to make them more acceptable in various target markets. Terpstra (1978) gives seven variations of the name of an ethical drug product of the Eli Lilly Company. This is an intermediate policy between the worldwide brand and complete adaptation.

Complete adaptation means using in each country or region a brand name and a trademark that seem ideal for that market area. This policy deprives a product of the image of strength associated with multinational firms, but gives it the appearance of local ownership. It may be the best policy in countries in which nationalistic feelings are high and the image of multinational firms is unfavorable.

The use of *private or store brand* merchandise is growing in most developed countries, and may be a means of market entry for a manufacturing firm that does not want to go to the expense of promoting its own brand.

Although some unbranded products are for sale the world over, the use of *generic* products is mainly a U.S. phenomenon. Both brand consciousness and brand loyalty are higher in most foreign countries than in the United States.

Protection of Names and Trademarks.   The United States is a party to the Paris Union International Convention for the Protection of Industrial Property, the Madrid Agreement Concerning the International Registration of Trademarks, and other multinational conventions. Their basic purpose is to allow an individual or firm to register a trademark under the same conditions as a citizen of the country in which registration is being made. The agreements also contain a *right of priority* clause, which gives the first owner of a trademark in any participating country six months in which to file for registration in other participating countries.

Even though brands and trademarks can be protected indefinitely if they continue to be used, *imitation* and *counterfeiting* are both common. There are many examples of imitation brands, with just one or two letters different from the well-known originals, and outright counterfeiting of products such as *Levis*. A firm's representatives around the world must remain alert for imitation and counterfeit merchandise and should be ready to initiate or recommend the most effective corrective action.

PACKAGE AND LABEL.   Usually at least some adaptations are made in the packages and labels of products to be sold in foreign markets. Several factors affect this process, as described in the following sections.

Handling Conditions.   The way in which a product will be handled affects the amount of *protection* a package must provide. Products to be sold in rural stores in developing countries are often subject to rough and frequent handling and thus need stronger packaging.

Shopping Habits.   In countries where people are in the habit of shopping every day, *package sizes* are smaller than in the United States. Also, customers in this type of country usually like to *see* the merchandise they are buying. This leads to greater use of transparent packaging.

Laws.   Most countries have at least some laws that affect labeling and packaging. Some examples are legal requirements that a product's contents be shown on the label, or that an opaque container be filled to at least a specified percentage of its capacity. When an exported product reaches a foreign country and does not meet all legal requirements, the exporter and the importer usually blame each other for their mutual oversight.

Extent of Self-Service.   In countries where self-service has not yet become the accepted way of retailing, packages and labels do not need to have the promotional impact that is required in other countries.

Consumer Preferences.   People's tastes with regard to design and color vary widely from place to place. A company marketing laundry detergent in Somalia tested the package with many different illustrations, showing Somali women at different socioeconomic levels, wearing different clothes, and engaged in different activities. The outcome was an illustration of a decidedly middle class woman wearing a brightly colored striped dress and hanging very white clothes on a clothesline.

Economic Conditions.   Poor economic conditions dictate the use of small package sizes, relatively inexpensive packaging, and, if possible, reusable containers.

Creating the Label and Package. In a majority of countries there are no qualified package-design consultants. International marketers often have packages and labels designed in world or regional headquarters and then tested locally by market-research firms.

For some types of products such as French perfume, Japanese cameras, and Italian wines, the country image as a producer of that product is so strong that very little adaptation must be made in the package or label. For products for which a country is not noted, such as Russian wine and American *sake,* the *appearance* of the product in the retail store is exceptionally important.

INSTRUCTIONS, WARRANTIES, AND SERVICE. These three aspects of the product may have little effect on *initial* sales, but they are paramount for repeat sales of both consumer and industrial goods.

Instructions. Several countries, such as Venezuela, require that product instructions be provided in the local language. A product like a transistor radio, which can be sold worldwide with little or no adaptation, may be packaged with an instruction sheet printed in six or eight different languages. Instructions to be read in foreign countries should be exceptionally simple, clear, and complete.

Warranties. A product warranty can be uniform throughout the world, or it can vary from country to country. Some factors that favor nonuniform warranties are the following:

Location of Manufacture. One factory may not be able to achieve the same product quality as others.

Condition of Use. Marine engines may break down more in salt water than in fresh water, more in industrial applications than if used by individual consumers.

Competition and Promotion. A firm may *have* to offer an attractive warranty because the competition is doing so, or it may *choose* to offer an attractive warranty as a promotional tool.

A company using nonuniform warranties must limit service under warranty to a specified market area, that is, the country of purchase. Thus an African customer who buys a television set in Europe might not be able to have it serviced under warranty in his home country.

Service. It is shortsighted, and in some countries illegal, to sell a product without maintaining adequate service facilities and parts inventories. Service facilities usually have to be maintained in each country because it is time-consuming, risky, and expensive to ship products across national boundaries for servicing. There are some exceptions, such as when photocopiers used in Mexico are sent to the United States for repair.

Whether servicing is done in company-owned service centers or by independent distributors, two very difficult problems are *training* and *control*. Training of servicemen is done through manuals, visits to the service centers by central-service personnel, and training courses at national, regional, or world headquarters. Control is carried out through inspections, reporting systems, and sometimes follow-up with customers who have had products repaired.

Some multinational suppliers of industrial goods such as elevators emphasize *preventive maintenance* more abroad than in their home countries. This is done to minimize the frequency of breakdowns, repairs, and costly rush shipments of replacement parts.

INTERNATIONAL PRODUCT STRATEGY.   Some of the important aspects of international product strategy are product cycles, the product line, and product development.

Product Cycles.   There are two theories relating to international product cycles. One is the familiar theory that every product goes through several phases from introduction to extinction, and a product's natural life can be extended by marketing techniques. The international application is that a product's life can also be extended by taking it to countries in which it will still be appreciated. Chamber pots, washboards, and kerosene stoves are still in demand in some parts of the world.

The other product-cycle theory holds that a new product is first manufactured and sold in its country of origin. Then it is exported. Then it is manufactured and sold both domestically and abroad. Finally it is manufactured abroad and imported to its country of origin, which by that time should be starting the cycle all over again with another new product.

The Product Line.   Multinational firms usually do not try to market all their products and models in every country. This holds true for exporters, but to a lesser degree.

Firms usually try to sell in each country the products that best fit the market and meet competition. Local subsidiaries are often given autonomy, subject to approval by or consultation with a central office, to choose the products and models that they will actively market.

Product Development.   International operations promote product development by providing many new sources of product ideas. Often a distributor in Asia will come up with a product variation that will meet a need in Latin America, Europe, or perhaps worldwide.

The work of new-product research and development is usually done at the regional or world level, especially if technically sophisticated processes are involved. There is however a gradual trend toward decentralization of R&D, partly in response to pressure from countries that would like to increase their technological capabilities. *Product testing* is usually done at the regional or local levels. This helps prevent the introduction of new products or product developments into countries for which they are not suitable.

INTERNATIONAL DISTRIBUTION

DISTRIBUTION FUNCTIONS.   A channel of distribution must serve both information functions and physical functions. Furthermore, movement through the channel must be efficient in both directions—outward to the customer and inward to the international marketer.

Information Functions. The kinds of information that move *out* through a channel of distribution include product data, prices, promotion and special offers, and changes in products, prices, and warranties. Information that moves *in* from the customer includes market data, inquiries, credit verifications, orders, and suggestions of product changes.

A channel that does not facilitate the passage of information becomes a closed door that separates the international marketer from his customers.

Physical Functions. Physical flows out through a channel of distribution include products, parts, service, documents, and financing. The physical flow inward is payment.

The channel selected must be able to perform the functions required to market a particular product. That is, if sales of a product require large local inventories, the channel must be able to maintain them. If service is important, the channel must provide adequate service facilities.

TYPES OF DISTRIBUTION CHANNELS. Firms engaged in exporting can use either direct or indirect channels of distribution. The tendency is for firms to begin with indirect channels and progress to more-direct ones. Firms that are truly committed to international marketing usually want the market knowledge and control that are easier to have with direct distribution.

Channels in the Source Country. If a firm sells directly from its source country to a customer in a foreign market, it is said to be involved in *direct* exporting. There are, however, many kinds of *indirect* channels. Sales can be made to the *buying office of a multinational firm* in the source country. They can be made to the *buying office* of a foreign government or to the *buying agent* of a foreign retail organization. They can be made to an *export merchant* or *trading company,* which buys for its own account and resells abroad. They can be made through *export agents or brokers.* A firm's products can be exported by another firm that carries complementary goods. The U.S. Department of Commerce gave this a name—the "piggyback" system. A company can join with producers of similar products in a Webb-Pomerene Association, which permits joint exporting that would otherwise be in violation of antitrust laws. There are now about 30 active Webb-Pomerene Associations handling such products as woodchips, dried fruit, and motion pictures. Finally, a company can form its own DISC. This is a registered subsidiary that can export American products worldwide. Corporate income-tax payments on half of the DISCs profits can be deferred indefinitely, although possible changes in DISC benefits are often discussed in Washington, D.C.

Channels in the Market Country. Distribution channels vary greatly, even in neighboring countries, as shown by Terpstra in Exhibit 1. The activities of multinational firms are tending to reduce these differences. Some noticeable trends are toward a smaller role for middlemen who do not take title; toward larger wholesale and retail organizations; and toward shorter (more direct) marketing channels. These trends do not appear in all countries, or with regard to all products.

Large volumes of business and large individual sales in foreign markets are often made directly to government organizations, major industrial users, and large retailing

EXHIBIT 1 VARIATIONS IN EUROPEAN DISTRIBUTION CHANNELS BY PRODUCT AND COUNTRY[a]

	Furniture		Domestic Appliances		Books and Stationery		Textiles		Footwear		Clothing	
	France	U.K.	Germany	Netherlands	Belgium	Netherlands	Belgium	U.K.	Germany	U.K.	France	U.K.
Department and variety stores	8.3	13.2	15.6	11.1	25.1	5.3	6.2	10.2	23.8	14.5	17.4	20.6
Multiple chain stores	4.8	26.9	16.8	22.6	9.1	33.4	7.2	16.0	16.0	48.5	4.1	50.7
Mail order	3.1	12.8	24.9	1.5	6.3	3.9	2.5	12.0	0.7	14.0	3.2	10.3
Cooperatives	2.2	7.8	2.3	0.3	0.1	0.3	0.8	3.6	0.2	3.6	1.2	2.8
Independents and street trade	81.6	39.2	40.3	64.5	59.4	57.1	83.3	58.2	59.1	19.4	74.1	15.6

[a]Percentage of sales in each channel.
Source. Terpstra (1978), p. 363. Adopted from *Vision* magazine, June 1975, p. 38.

organizations. Such transactions may be arranged by seller's *agents* or by company-owned sales offices in the market country. Smaller volumes of business are usually handled through agents or brokers to wholesalers and industrial distributors, or through importer-distributors to industrial users and retailers. There are numerous variations of these basic channels.

Finally, there are some instances of *direct* export sales *by mail order*. This method seems to be used mostly for selling articles of clothing to countries having well-developed postal systems, especially where textile products imported in quantity face quotas or high import duties.

Selecting a Distribution Channel.   The selection of a distribution channel is very important because of the difficulty of changing a channel once it is established. A more complete discussion of channels selection can be found in Majaro (1977).

Some of the factors to consider in selecting an international distribution channel are the following:

The Functions It Has To Perform.   If product sales must be financed, the channel should be strong financially, and so forth.

The Firm's Objectives and Financial Ability.   A firm that plans to compete actively in a foreign market for several years and is financially strong should consider setting up a company-owned distribution system.

Channels Used in the Market.   At times it is nearly impossible to enter a market except through the traditional distribution system. At other times the traditional system is effectively closed to a new foreign competitor, and an alternate distribution scheme must be employed.

In general, distribution channels are more direct for industrial products, large sales orders, large selling and/or buying organizations, and goods that are expensive, sophisticated, perishable, custommade, or in frequent need of service.

SELECTING FOREIGN REPRESENTATIVES.   If the distribution channel is to include independent distributors or agents in market countries, they must be selected with great care because (1) the firm will be known in the market country by the quality of its representatives, (2) the firm's success in the market will depend largely on the work of its representatives, and (3) once named, an agent or distributor may be very hard to replace, because of personal, business, and legal considerations.

Identifying Potential Representatives.   Potential foreign representatives can be identified from U.S. Department of Commerce *Trade Lists,* national, international, and industry directories, and personal contacts and market research. Their credentials can be checked through U.S. Department of Commerce *World Trade Directory Reports,* credit-reporting agencies such as Dun & Bradstreet International, or personal visits.

Criteria for Selection.   The following are some important factors to consider in the selection of foreign representatives:

Availability and interest in the firm's products. This can be a difficult criterion because qualified agents and distributors in important market countries have their desks piled high with letters of inquiry from suppliers throughout the world.

Market knowledge that can help the supplier to properly adapt its products and marketing techniques.

The ability to represent a firm adequately, by virtue of management capabilities, areas covered, customers served, product lines carried, sales organization, auxiliary services, and financial strength.

The right "chemistry" with executives of the supplying firm to facilitate understanding and cooperation toward the achievement of mutually beneficial objectives.

Contracting with Foreign Representatives.   An international representation agreement is normally set forth in a written contract—usually enforceable under the laws of the country in which it is to be executed. Some of the usual provisions of such contracts are the following:

Legal nature of the contract—commercial representation.

Parties to the contract—names, addresses, and whether contracting parties are signing as individuals or for their business firms.

Authentic text—if in more than one language, which one is official.

Dates of entering into force and of termination.

Products covered.

Territory included.

Whether the foreign representative will have exclusive sales rights to the covered products.

Kinds of customers included; kinds exempted.

Rights and obligations of the supplying firm to accept or reject orders, provide information, establish factories in the contractual territory, protect the rights of the representative, prevent competition from unauthorized imports and counterfeit brands, assist with sales promotion and advertising, and pay travel or other expenses of the representative.

Rights and obligations of the representative to protect his supplier's interests, to take or not take legal actions in the supplier's name, to observe the supplier's standard conditions of sale, to refrain from handling competing products (unless expressly permitted), to maintain merchandise inventories, to provide after-sale service and spare parts, to provide market and credit information, to advertise and sell, to protect the supplier's industrial property rights, and to assist with collections (if working as an agent).

Commission arrangement (for an agency agreement) or mark-up/discount (for a distributorship agreement).

Provision for termination of the agreement.

Legal jurisdiction.

Absence of conflicting agreements.

Arbitration of disputes.

WORKING WITH FOREIGN REPRESENTATIVES.   The following are some of the considerations involved in working with foreign representatives:

Training. Both agents and distributors need in-depth understanding of the company's products and how to sell them. Adequate training not only helps the representatives do a better job, but gives them assurance that the supplying firm is concerned about their performance.

Objectives. Yearly sales objectives, by product and area or type of customer, should be worked out during face-to-face meetings with each representative. This can be difficult because in many countries the concepts of detailed planning, objective reporting, and early corrective action are not widely accepted.

Consultation. There should be planned, regular two-way communications between the supplying firm and its foreign representatives. Although improvements in international telephone and telex communications have led to dramatic increases in their use, periodic written reports and personal visits are still vital.

Assistance. Serious international marketers strive to assist their foreign representatives by accepting special product orders, sending technicians to help at trade fairs and with special problems, sending missionary salesmen to help call on important customers, giving top priority to urgent shipments, providing catalogs, ad mats, and cooperative advertising, extending credit whenever possible, and trying to eliminate mistakes in production, shipping, and documentation.

INTERNATIONAL PHYSICAL DISTRIBUTION. International physical distribution is a complex, multimodal world of logistics, shipping, insurance, warehousing, and documentation. The following sections describe some of the important considerations.

Order Processing. Processing and filling an order involves various departments of a company—sales, shipping, credit, and perhaps manufacturing. The work of these departments must be coordinated to reduce intracompany conflict and costly mistakes. It is common in small firms for the international-sales department to have to rely on credit and shipping departments that are oriented toward the domestic market and lack both interest and expertise in the international area.

Packing and Marking. International shipments by sea require special packing in order to reduce damage from pilferage, breakage, and water. The marking of crates and containers follows generally accepted practices, but many countries have peculiar marking requirements. Export-packing, freight-forwarding, shipping, and insurance companies have valuable expertise in this field.

Documentation. In spite of frequent efforts to simplify the paperwork involved in international shipments, correct documentation is an exacting and time-consuming process. All documents produced by the supplying firm should be double-checked for accuracy, and all documents produced by the freight forwarder should be examined as soon as they are received. This is especially important when shipping under letters of credit.

Also, the supplying firm should carefully check the import documentation requirements of each country to which it is shipping. Useful information can be obtained from customers abroad, consulates of the market country, freight forwarders,

Croner's *Reference Book for World Traders,* the Bureau of National Affairs *Export Shipping Manual,* the Dun and Bradstreet *Exporter's Encyclopedia,* and Brandon's *Shipper and Forwarder.*

Shipping.   The use of *air* freight, both to and within international markets, has been increasing dramatically. The high cost of air freight may be offset by its speed, relative safety from breakage and pilferage, simpler packing and documentation requirements, and lower insurance costs. In many foreign countries air freight reaches customers who are practically inaccessible by surface transportation.

In *marine* shipping it appears that the conference system is gradually breaking apart, thus increasing the opportunities for negotiation of rates, routes, and schedules.

International *surface* transportation is now dependable throughout Western Europe, but still faces serious difficulties in many parts of the developing world.

Insurance.   A number of countries now require that import shipments be insured by local firms. Thus, c.i.f. shipping terms are giving way to c.&f. The exporter should normally insist on *proof* that the importer has purchased adequate insurance coverage. If the exporter feels that he might bear liability for loss or damage even though insurance coverage was not his responsibility, he can purchase *contingent insurance* to be sure there is adequate, effective coverage.

Warehousing.   International firms often make use of bonded warehouses, or warehouses in free zones. Product inventories have to be especially well controlled, and special packing may be needed for storage in very cold, hot, or humid climates. Many ports do not have adequate cold-storage facilities. Also many warehouses in developing countries are short of materials-handling equipment. This requires smaller and lighter shipping units and stronger packing.

Multimodal Distribution.   There is a clear worldwide trade toward the use of large containers, land bridges, roll-on roll-off, barge-aboard-ship, trailer-on-flat-car, and related equipment that can reduce the costs of export packing, insurance, shipping, and warehousing.

INTERNATIONAL PROMOTION

ADVERTISING.   International advertising is done at all levels—world, region, country, and locality. Variations in media and message from one place to another make this an especially challenging function of international business management. Total expenditures on advertising vary from well over $100 per person per year in the United States to almost zero in some of the least-developed countries. The *media mix* also varies enormously according to the availability of media, legal restrictions, the rate of literacy, and consumers' habits.

Print Media.   International advertising is done at the *world* level through publications such as *Trade Channel* and *Worldwide Projects.* These publications reach selected audiences in wide geographic areas and are used for advertising products that are distributed worldwide.

Some examples of *regional* publications are *Visión* for Latin America, *Arab Busi-*

ness for the Middle East, and *Jeune Afrique* for French-speaking African countries. Most advertising in these publications is directed at industrial users or sophisticated household consumers.

Most developed countries have a variety of *national* newspapers or magazines, and most developing countries have one or more of them. The advertising content of these varies with the country and publication.

Throughout the world most print media advertising is done in local newspapers and, where available, specialized magazines. One aspect that varies a great deal from country to country is the use of color in local newspapers and magazines. Some publications do not offer it. Others do, but lack the color separation and printing techniques and equipment for accurate reproduction. In general, foreign countries are not yet making extensive use of in-ad couponing or newspaper inserts.

Broadcast Media.   *Radio,* including AM, FM, and shortwave, is perhaps the most universal advertising medium. There are in Western Europe several *regional* stations that reach most of the European Common Market and carry advertising by multinational firms. There is also a great deal of transborder radio coverage, for example, Laredo stations reach the English-speaking audience in northern Mexico, and French stations broadcast to the French-speaking portion of Switzerland.

Advertisers and advertising agencies around the world seem to reach their highest levels of creativity when working with radio. An unlimited mixture of music, voices, tempos, volumes, and approaches appeals to target audiences.

Some difficulties with this advertising medium in many countries are fragmentation of the market by a large number of competing stations and the lack of adequate information on listenership. This often results in "overkill," by advertising on more stations than should be necessary to reach a given sales objective.

Television has now reached nearly all countries, and color broadcasting is available in most developed and many developing nations. There is a large amount of transborder television reception, such as programs from Jordan reaching over to Arabic-speaking residents of Israel.

A difficulty with television advertising in many countries is the poor quality of local production. Multinational firms that do local advertising often have the storyboard made up locally, then have the ad produced in a country that has high-quality facilities, and then have it reviewed and/or tested at the local level before being broadcast. Another important difficulty is legal restriction of television advertising. In several countries television stations are noncommercial; advertising is not allowed at all, except perhaps "public service" announcements by official organizations. In other countries advertising is allowed, but severely restricted. Examples of such restrictions are no ads for liquor or tobacco products, none directed to children, and none during peak viewing hours.

Other Advertising Media.   Newspaper, magazine, radio and television ads are supplemented in most countries by billboards, fliers, loudspeaker announcements, transportation placements, movie theater advertising, direct mail, point-of-purchase advertising, and ads positioned in football stadiums and other public places. The motoring public is attracted by billboard ads wherever they are legal, and most market-economy countries now have firms that own and rent billboard space.

Movie theater advertising is useful in many countries in which a routine form of diversion is to see a movie about once a week. The same messages can be used both in movie theaters and on television if the viewers' characteristics are not markedly different. The development of point-of-purchase advertising follows closely the introduction of self-service. Window signs, "shelf-talkers," and other forms of point-of-purchase advertising are used to reinforce messages placed in the mass media.

Advertising Agencies.   There are now qualified local advertising agencies in nearly all countries, and many international agencies offer virtually worldwide coverage. There is a trend by multinational firms to give more of their advertising to the large agencies, most of which are headquartered in the United States, Japan, and Great Britain.

Advertising that is standardized at the world or regional level (except perhaps for language translation) is usually developed by international agencies. Many local agencies have prospered, however, because of in-depth knowledge of local thought patterns, nuances of language, media coverages, and rate structures. It is common to have ads *produced* by international agencies but *placed* by local firms.

SALES PROMOTION.   International sales promotion takes three principal forms—trade fairs and exhibitions, trade missions, and contests and premiums.

Trade Fairs and Exhibitions.   A great deal of international sales promotion is done through trade fairs and exhibitions held throughout the world. They are especially important in countries with centrally planned economies, where other methods of generating sales may be severely restricted.

National fairs open to the general public (often similar to state and county fairs in the United States) are useful for showing new consumer products or increasing brand awareness. Much more important, however, are specialized industry fairs, usually held annually in industrialized countries and closed to the general public. There are several reasons for attending and exhibiting in these fairs—to introduce new products, to see what the competition is doing, to carry out informal market research, to generate inquiries and sales, and to support local agents/distributors. Information on important fairs can be found in the Bill Communication, Inc. *Exhibits Schedule,* published annually. Also important are foreign-trade exhibitions sponsored by the U.S. Department of Commerce, state government agencies, associations of exporters, chambers of commerce, and individual firms. These are held in U.S. trade centers, hotel rooms, and other facilities in major market cities.

The key words for success in all trade exhibitions are *preparation, execution,* and *follow-up.* Successful exhibitors take care to identify their target customers and invite them specifically to their stands or booths, and to select products that will be of interest to those customers. With technical products it is important to have the exhibit manned at all times by both *technical* and *sales* personnel who can speak the languages of their target customers. Interpretors can be hired to work at exhibitions, but direct communication is highly preferable. Finally, successful exhibitors keep records of their conversations with all promising visitors and follow up as soon as possible.

Contests and Premiums.   The promise of something for nothing has universal appeal, especially in countries in which economic conditions are difficult and public lotteries are common. The variety is endless, from small bills (currency) packed randomly in cereal boxes to a free battery with a new transistor radio. In several countries the governments have determined that contests and premiums are *too* effective, economically wasteful, and unfair. They have responded with laws that restrict the maximum value of prizes and other conditions of this kind of sales promotion. It is important to check the legality of a special promotion in each country before putting it into effect.

PUBLIC RELATIONS AND PUBLICITY.   National pride, and prejudice, make public relations an important function in foreign-owned firms worldwide. Publicity is often combined with public relations or with advertising. A highly oversimplified definition of these two terms is that *public relations* means doing nice things for people, and *publicity* means telling them about it.

Public Relations.   A firm has many "publics" in each country in which it operates—suppliers, customers, the government, the military, religious organizations, students, and the population in general. A very bad image with any of these groups can diminish sales and even jeopardize the firm's future in a particular country. In addition, global communications have helped social concerns to become contagious. A campaign against a product in one country can quickly spread to others. In particular, a campaign against infant formula led to a United Nations resolution.

World, regional, and national public relations personnel should continually monitor the attitudes of a firm's various publics about (1) foreign business in general and (2) the firm in particular. This can be done by watching news media and talking with leaders of the various publics and with foreign diplomats and company employees who have contact with the media.

Public relations, then, is both *preventive* and *corrective*. *Preventive* activities include minimizing environmental pollution from company operations, educating consumers to minimize hazardous misuse of the firm's products, giving expatriate employees training in the local language, and buying uniforms for a local baseball team. *Corrective* activities include quickly changing commercials that have been found to be offensive to any segment of the population, taking some products off the market if local competitors are being driven out of business, and counteracting calls of exploitation by showing how much the firm is contributing to the local economy by its purchases, wages, and taxes.

Publicity.   A very effective way for a firm to improve its image or its sales at the retail level is through stories and articles in the news media. Personal and written contact with media executives can result in published or broadcast information that has high impact. Many companies issue regular press releases about product improvements, key local employees, new distributors, and other favorable aspects of their operations.

In many countries there is a direct and open link between advertising and publicity, as when a magazine editor promises an article on a new product in return for so many inches of paid advertising. The manager of promotion in each country should understand this system and how it works.

PERSONAL SELLING.   Personal selling has two dimensions in international marketing—export and missionery salespersons sent by the home office, and local salespersons in the market country.

Export Sales Personnel. A person in charge of selling a nontechnical product in a region of the world may have to be on the road as much as 90 percent of the time. His task is to sell directly to major buyers, and/or to support and train local agents and distributors.

This person should have complete knowledge of the company and its products, because on foreign travels he will not have backup support readily at hand. He should know also the language and culture of the countries to which he is traveling. One simple blunder, like pointing the sole of his shoe at a buyer in South Korea or complimenting a buyer's wife in Spain, could cost him a sale. Finally, the international salesperson should know the buying history of each of his customers and each country's production, consumption, imports, exports, customs duties, and regulations concerning his product.

The export salesperson should continually gather market information, both in his office and on the road. In the field he will also have to motivate foreign representatives, settle disputes involving the company, its representatives, and its customers, and resolve any technical problems that may have arisen.

The carrying of *commercial samples* from country to country has been simplified by the *carnet,* which is available from the New York office of the International Chamber of Commerce.

Foreign Sales Personnel. Products that rely on *supply push* (as opposed to *demand pull*) marketing strategies need personal selling. Unfortunately the sales profession suffers in many countries from a lack of prestige. Adequate training, compensation, and foreign travel have improved the image somewhat, but in many countries young people from "good" families are still reluctant to go into sales.

Except in very unusual circumstances, foreign salespersons are company employees, and are thus subject to minimum-wage, severance-pay, and other laws in each country. The best ways of motivating them vary greatly from one culture to another. In Japan, for example, company-wide recognition of good performance can have as much effect as a substantial commission.

The supervision of field sales personnel presents special difficulties in countries where loose supervision is taken as a sign of disinterest, and tight supervision as a signal of distrust. Sales managers must be selected with great care, especially where personal selling is to be emphasized and the salespersons are from different ethnic groups.

OTHER ASPECTS OF PROMOTION. Some other aspects of promotion that should be considered are standardization or adaptation, planning and budgeting, and the promotional mix.

Standardization or Adaptation. Advertising *media plans* cannot be standardized at the world level; however, *messages* can be if they appeal to *universal buying motives.* The standard message can be adapted in each country as required. Worldwide standardization saves a great deal of expense, but does not lead to maximum sales.

The details of successful sales-promotion, public-relations, and publicity activities can be communicated to each country for information and possible adoption. Personal-selling knowledge and techniques are similar around the world. Whether sales training is done at the country level or above depends largely on the product's complexity.

narrowly defined job classifications. Last, but not least, is the quality circle, which embraces the worker's commitment to error-free performance and his willingness to participate in defining and improving products and production processes. Quality circles, as with many things in Japan, are adaptations of practices imported from the West, especially the United States.

COMPARING THE SYSTEMS.   Although the preceding country-level descriptions of industrial-relations systems were hardly detailed, they do illustrate how the roles of the actors vary (among unions, workers, stewards, governments—legislators and administrators—and management). Think of how the extremes might be characterized if a country governed by a totalitarian regime were included. Cultural influences are evident too—note the orderly, almost regimented logic of the German system and the classic liberalism in the United Kingdom. Contrast these to the paternalism evident in Japan, and the influence of the U.S. occupation of Japan following World War II. Note too how each country's economy is broadly market based and how this supports decentralization in industrial-relations decision making. For contrast within market-based systems, compare the grouping of industrial-relations experiences by industry in Germany, where historically cartels have been a hallmark of industrial organization, to the company-oriented business unionism predominant in America's more competitive, free-enterprise industrial society. These are all rational—that is, intrinsically logical—observations.

It would appear almost obvious that the different systems exhibit certain features that are of critical importance to management. Such features would include the nature and frequency of strikes and the nature and incidence of other modes of worker resistance (ranging from "work-to-rule," as may likely be experienced in Great Britain, to worker occupation of the factory, which would appear more likely in more-communist or socialist-oriented societies, such as France or Italy). They would also include the ability of industrial relations to accommodate technological change. When a production process is improved in the United Kingdom, management may indeed be confronted immediately with a "gain-sharing" demand by the workers (who operate within a representative and legal structure that allows for such). Contrast this to the Japanese environment, where it's not the production improvement, per se, that enhances workers' incomes, but the demonstrated success of the improvement in terms of profit impact and experience that (later) enhances workers' periodic bonus and wage levels.

Obviously the questions and concerns become quite real and detailed. The more-crucial concerns certainly require on-site investigation and analysis beyond the country level to industry, regional, and company (or plant) levels. The more detailed the analysis required, the more relevant and useful is Dunlop's systems approach, which allows for cause-effect relationships to be identified and the rationale of each system (at the different levels) to be understood. This should be the starting point for further management inquiry and analysis.

INTERNATIONAL LABOR ACTIVITIES

IDENTIFYING THE SPECTRUM.   International labor activities can perhaps be best categorized in terms of the identity of the predominant actor or influence—which, in turn, fairly well determines the constituency of issues and interests confronted by the actor or organization at that level. Broadly speaking, three such groupings come to mind.

Some international organizations that involve national governments as members are concerned with workers' and unions' interests. Examples include the International Labor Office (ILO) and the Organization for Economic Cooperation and Development (OECD). These organizations are not directly involved in collective bargaining (with one notable case experience—to be discussed later), but are more likely concerned (more or less) with public-policy formulation (usually within their member countries) related to workers and unions, the evaluation of national policies affecting workers and unions, and the construction and publication of relevant data bases.

Several kinds of union associations function at the international level. They range from those involving national union confederations concerned with the more broad, political issues (either among or within countries or among union/worker movements and philosophies) to those involving workers and unions at different national locations of a single multinational enterprise. Perhaps the most influential of these types of organizations have been the different industry-based international trade secretariats, especially relative to MNE activities, and the regionally identified groups of unions, especially those active in Western Europe, seeking to influence public policy and industrial relations in important industrial sectors.

The third category is identified with activities of U.S. unions and the AFL-CIO, which are international in scope and involve collective bargaining directly, the international extension of a free-trade-union philosophy, or practices aimed at constraining the international activities of U.S. MNEs or offsetting the allegedly onerous domestic-employment and industrial-relations effects of MNEs' activities.

INTERGOVERNMENTAL ORGANIZATIONS. The ILO is undoubtedly the most important intergovernmental organization concerned with worker and union-related issues. Its origins trace back to the League of Nations period, and its membership consists of governments, trade-union organizations, and employer associations. One major focus of the ILO has been directed toward establishing and promulgating fair labor standards covering working conditions (including safety and health standards) and workers' rights (including freedom of association). Another relates to its gathering and publishing of data bases (covering, for example, wages and working conditions by country and industry) and the presentation and analysis of empirical data and other firsthand information useful in modeling future trends (for example, such as employment and income concerns and effects associated with the oncoming shakeout in the world semiconductor industry).

The ILO has completed three major projects of special relevance to MNEs. The first was a broad inquiry in the early 1970s involving testimony and the presentation of evidence, positions, and so forth, from the parties directly concerned (mainly MNE and trade-union representatives), seeking to ascertain the social-policy implications of multinational enterprise. This was followed in the latter 1970s by a series of empirical studies on MNEs' activities in Western Europe, covering, for example, social and labor policies and practices of both U.S.- and non-U.S.-owned MNEs in selected industrial sectors, wages, and working conditions in MNEs, and so forth. In 1980—1981, the ILO published a series of country studies on the employment effects of MNEs. Specific attempts were made to quantify these effects both in terms of job numbers and job quality in some of these studies.

The International Institute for Labor Studies was established by the ILO in 1960 to promote a better understanding of labor problems in all countries through education, discussion, and research. Like the ILO itself, the institute covers a broad spectrum of issues and interests, including those related to MNEs.

The U.N. Centre on Transnational Corporations, its Committee for Trade and Development, and so forth certainly touch on labor- and MNE-related issues, but these are not their main concerns. They defer, in many instances, to their U.N. affiliate, the ILO, for inquiry and expertise on these issues.

The member countries of the OECD agreed in 1976 on a set of "guidelines for multinational enterprises." The guidelines are voluntary, but are felt to be morally binding and sanctioned by public opinion and government action (Blainpain, 1977). They espouse the principle of national treatment by member countries to all MNEs in their territories and an MNE obligation to respect laws, regulations, and administrative practices in member countries. Trade unions and business and industry associations were very active in the preparation of the guidelines and there is no doubt that the direction of the guidelines is toward employment and worker-related social-policy issues, as well as toward tax treatment, financial subsidies, and other policies affecting MNEs' investment decisions.

A landmark case involving the application of the guidelines to an MNE and an interpretation of "national treatment" occurred in 1976. At issue was the inability of the Belgian subsidiary of the Badger Company, Inc., which is in turn owned by the (U.S.) Raytheon Corporation, to compensate discharged Belgian workers at the legally required indemnification limit as it was closing down. The Belgian operation had been marginally profitable and had a positive net worth when abandoned. The Belgian unions pressed the point with the Belgian government and the other OECD members that the parent company intentionally bled the Belgian operation of its finances, that it was the parent's responsibility to cover the shortfall in indemnification funds, and that a national firm would not behave in such fashion. The Badger Company denied the allegation, but settled nolo contendere when several OECD governments pledged not to award engineering contracts to Badger until the indemnification issue was settled (Blainpain, 1977).

The fundamental question in this case is important. Do subsidiaries enjoy the limited liability granted them when they are incorporated, or is there a contingency liability on the parent's part? (Notwithstanding fraudulent or other criminal behavior, the liability of an individual person as a stockholder is certainly limited.) In Badger's case, the market vulnerability of the company to the government's actions tipped the balance of power in favor of the unions' interests. The basic issue, however, of "national behavior/national treatment" as a counterpoint to limited liability remains unanswered.

INTERNATIONAL ASSOCIATIONS INVOLVING UNIONS.   Windmuller (1967) identifies four categories of international trade unionism with reasonably distinctive jurisdictions and functions: global internationals, regional internationals, specialized internationals, and industrial internationals.

Global Internationals.   The global internationals comprise the International Confederation of Free Trade Unions (ICFTU), the World Federation of Trade Unions (WFTU) and the International Federation of Christian Trade Unions (CISC). Windmuller notes they are global internationals because they claim constituencies in nearly every country, and their vertical structures include industrial, regional, and specialized internationals. The global internationals tend to emphasize representation (i.e., present union views to international organizations such as the U.N., ILO, etc., and pressure governments on union rights violations) and missionary activities (Windmuller, 1969).

From an MNE viewpoint, the ICFTU is the most important global international. It claims nearly exclusive jurisdiction in North America and Western Europe, heavy representation in Latin America and the Caribbean, and affiliates in Africa and Asia. The spread of its constituency and its locus of power generally (geographically) parallel that of the MNE (exclusive of Japan). The WFTU monopolizes representation from communist countries and communist unions in noncommunist countries. The CISC is the smallest of the three, is European oriented, and relates to Christian trade unionism (centered mainly in France, Belgium and the Netherlands).

Regional and Specialized Internationals. Most of the regional internationals are geographically defined subdivisions of the ICFTU and CISC. Those of the ICFTU operate in Europe (ERO), the Americas (ORIT), Africa (AFRO), and Asia (ARO); the CISC has a Latin American subdivision (CLASC). Regional internationals that are not affiliated with global internationals include the African Trade Union Confederation (ATUC) and the All-African Trade Union Federation (AATUF). The activities of these organizations parallel those of the global internationals with ERO and ORIT, with their greater financial and organizational resources, operating comparatively more independently of ICFTU direction than their sister organization (Windmuller, 1967).

Specialized internationals focus on intergovernmental agencies to function as a component of such agencies or to lobby them. The Worker Group in the ILO, the Trade Union Advisory Committee in the OECD, and the European Trade Unions Congress, which provides worker representation in the European Economic Community (EEC), are examples of specialized internationals. These organizations are important to MNEs in that the larger bodies (e.g., ILO, OECD, and EEC) to which they relate are very involved in public-policy issues impinging on MNEs' interests. They are not, however, directly involved in multinational collective-bargaining attempts.

Industrial Internationals. The membership of the industrial internationals consists of national trade unions that share a common industrial identification. The industrial internationals themselves are affiliates of the global internationals, that is, the International Trade Union Secretariats (ITSs) in the ICFTU, the Trade Union Internationals (TUIs) in the WFTU, and the Trade Internationals (TIs) in the CISC. From an MNE perspective, the most important are the ITSs, which are fairly independent of ICFTU influence on industrial issues (but acknowledge ICFTU leadership on major political and economic issues—Windmuller, 1967).

Northrup and Rowan (1979) report 17 ITSs active as of 1979. These include those especially concerned with MNEs, for example, the International Metalworkers' Federation (IMF) and the International Federation of Chemical, Energy and General Workers' Unions (ICF).

To illustrate how an ITS responds structurally to implement its interests, the IMF, for example, consists of departments, such as the automotive department, and worldwide company councils, such as the Ford Motor Council, the General Motors Council, and so forth. The identification of these councils relative to MNEs' concerns appears intuitively obvious. The membership of the councils consists of representatives of unions that relate to an MNE in its different national subsidiaries or at the parent company. The activities of the councils can be categorized conceptually into four rather distinctive types: information, intervention, involvement, and intimidation (Kujawa, 1978).

The "information" function represents union interests in providing adequate data and knowledge of MNE management structures to member (country-bound) unions in support of existing collective-bargaining relationships. It has been implemented rather successfully within the world company-council concept. Data are exchanged among council members that cover contract surveys as well as legally required benefits (by country) and on-line experiences (e.g., safety practices). Unions use this information offensively, to push for concessions in collective bargaining to equal conditions elsewhere in the global MNE structure, and defensively, to attempt to balance the power equation in (national) collective bargaining by providing the union (concerned) with specific information on company operations, profits, and decision-making structures.

The "intervention" function has also been implemented rather successfully. It involves direct contact between union representatives and parent-company management to identify and resolve specific labor-relations problems or eliminate onerous management practices at the subsidiary level. Union claims to success in interventions are often difficult to substantiate, but in many cases parent companies have responded responsively to unions' complaints on behalf of other unions in other countries. These complaints ranged from the lack of advance notice by a General Motors subsidiary in Switzerland regarding a plant closing to the discharge of workers at Chrysler Corporation's Spanish subsidiary (Kujawa, 1971). Parent-company management has acknowledged, off the record, that information such as that provided by unions through their intervention activities can often be quite welcome.

The "involvement" function means multinationally coordinated and conducted collective bargaining involving unions in different countries and a single MNE. Notwithstanding some ITSs' claims to the contrary, substantial transnational collective bargaining has yet to be experienced, except in very few instances (Northrup and Rowan, 1979, and Kujawa, 1978). The reasons for this are several, and include legal, structural, cultural, and economic barriers (Kujawa, 1975).

The "intimidation" function relates to the manipulation of the press by certain ITSs (most notably the ICF) to create an image of transnational union activity eminently more successful than the facts imply. The message here, of course, is to get at the facts of each reported instance of union success.

Aside from the ITSs, industrial regional internationals exist, such as the European Metalworkers' Federation, which support the work of regional internationals, such as the ETUC vis-á-vis the EEC, as well as seeking to coordinate transnational collective bargaining at international and regional levels, for example in the case of Philips (Dronkers, 1975).

The bottom line for management regarding transnational collective-bargaining attempts by ITSs (or others) is that much of the content and process of collective bargaining is place-bound and not really open to transnational influence. Moreover, organized labor has little power to bring to bear on such bargaining.

INTERNATIONAL ACTIVITIES OF U.S. UNIONS AND THE AFL-CIO

A Special Case—Canada.   Aside from their participation in ITSs' activities, U.S. unions are directly involved with MNEs in several other ways. Many U.S. unions (e.g., the United Auto Workers and United Steel Workers) are distinctly binational regarding the United States and Canada—the latter is often one of several geographic regions comprising the "international union." The binational unionism on the labor side, combined with many technical, market, and cultural similarities within industries that span the two countries (indeed, including many firms that operate in both countries), has resulted in binational collective bargaining, coordination in collective bargaining between firms and subsidiaries and union representatives from the United States and Canada, and assistance from union and management personnel from one country involving issues, at impasse, perhaps, in the other country.

Following the implementation of the 1965 free-trade agreement in automobiles and automotive parts and accessories, Chrysler, Ford, and General Motors (separately) negotiated wage-parity agreements with the UAW to equalize wage structures and levels and other employment practices between their U.S. and Canadian operations (Kujawa, 1971). Other examples and evidence on the extensiveness of U.S.–Canada binationalism in industrial relations can be found in a special report on the topic by The Conference Board (Hershfield, 1975). Both U.S. and Canadian companies have also experienced situations in which a contract settlement in one country set a pattern for subsequent negotiations in the other country, and, albeit on a much less frequent basis, union and company representatives from a Canadian parent (for example) sometimes seek to mediate a dispute at a U.S. subsidiary.

Coordinated Bargaining Attempts.   In their U.S. collective bargaining, American unions have attempted to confront MNE-related issues through coordinated bargaining and contract control over information disclosure on international operations and allocation of production to foreign subsidiaries. Neither approach has been particularly successful from a union perspective. The lead experience in coordinated bargaining developed by a U.S. union and involving a U.S. MNE is the General (GE) Electric case with the International Union of Electrical Workers (IUE). In conjunction with the 1969 and 1973 meetings of the GE world council (an ITS activity), representatives of unions at GE's foreign plants were invited to attend and observe subsequent contract negotiations between GE and the IUE. Notwithstanding those in attendance, there has never been any collective bargaining during U.S. negotiations on conditions or interests of workers at foreign plants. Northrup and Rowan contend, moreover, that IUE pressure to do so would be contrary to the (U.S.) court order allowing the IUE to select attendees to U.S. bargaining sessions so long as only matters pertaining to the IUE bargaining unit are bargained over, and thus likely considered a "refusal to bargain in good faith" (Northrup and Rowan, 1979).

Attempts to Limit Foreign Sourcing.   Two cases involving attempts by U.S. unions to bargain collectively over MNEs' foreign-sourcing decisions have been reported (Kujawa, 1972). One involved a UAW challenge to the decision by Ford Motor to produce engines and gear boxes at England and German subsidiaries for car assembly operations in the United States and Canada. The union contended that this practice transferred work traditionally done by U.S. UAW members to foreign plants and could lead to U.S. employment losses, production interruptions, and so forth. The company denied these contentions, and the UAW pressed no further (Kujawa, 1972). The other case involved GE and the IUE. During the negotiations on the 1969–1972 contract, the union proposed a clause forbidding GE to transfer work from U.S. to foreign operations or to establish an overseas plant to perform work customarily done by U.S. (unit) employees. In support of this proposal, the IUE requested a substantial amount of information from GE on its foreign operations. The company refused this request, and the union filed an unfair-labor-practice charge. The general counsel of the National Labor Relations Board denied the charge, noting that the detailed information was not needed to bargain over a broad prohibition covering foreign-production transfers, and that the union had not substantiated its claim that such transfers were even occurring (Kujawa, 1972).

AFL-CIO Activities. The AFL-CIO is involved in MNE issues mainly in its attempts to influence U.S. public policies affecting MNE activities. Kujawa (1981) notes that the AFL-CIO, with its social-movement orientation and concern, contends that society's interests supercede those of MNEs and that MNEs are therefore subject to social control. In promoting this perspective, the AFL-CIO has conducted and supported positions and research concluding that U.S. MNEs export employment, sell high-technology expertise (developed often with U.S. government funding support) to overseas affiliates and other customers, contribute to balance-of-payments problems and foreign-exchange crises, and so forth. Moreover, it contends the U.S. government grants MNEs substantial tax benefits supportive of multinational expansion at the expense of (U.S.) domestic growth, and that the deterioration of key U.S. industries occasioned by MNEs' activities contributes to the demise of urban areas and U.S. defense capabilities (Jager, 1975). This is certainly a substantial set of allegations and should be understood by MNE management personnel.

Beginning with its support of the proposed Foreign Trade and Investment Act of 1972 (the Burke-Hartke bill), which called for import quotas, government approval of licensing technology abroad, and so forth, the AFL-CIO has been noticeably active in promoting its public-policy objectives. With few exceptions, it has not been as successful as it would like, however.

Regarding multinational collective bargaining, the industrial union department of the AFL-CIO has been especially supportive. The action, nonetheless, has involved mostly certain key unions and firms, as already discussed in the GE/IUE situation.

Internationally, especially in Latin America, the AFL-CIO cosponsors organizations to promote the development of free trade unionism, such as the American Institute for Free Labor Development. In these instances, some MNEs have joined with the AFL-CIO through direct support.

INTERNATIONAL MANAGEMENT OF INDUSTRIAL RELATIONS

LOCUS OF DECISION MAKING. Labor relations is a very place-bound activity. Issues, actors, structure and method may change considerably from one industry and country to the next. With but few exceptions, industrial relations decision-making is taken at the local, subsidiary level. For example, Robert Copp the overseas liaison manager, labor relations staff, at Ford Motor Company's world headquarters, notes (Copp, 1977):

Every Ford subsidiary has . . . an appropriate staff . . . to develop and administer an industrial relations program appropriate to the national setting. Indeed, this staff, along with the managing director and the board of the subsidiary, is the principal management decision maker in industrial relations matters.

Supportive of Copp's view, Frank Angle director of industrial relations in General Motors' overseas operations division, states (Angle, 1975):

Management in General Motors has always been based on the line-and-staff principle. Line executives, whether based in the United States, Canada, or overseas, have full operating responsibility and authority . . . to ensure the flexibility necessary to adapt individual operations to local conditions.

Similarly, Jack Belford, Massey-Ferguson's vice-president of personnel and industrial relations, states (Belford, 1977):

. . . it would be a brash corporate management that would substitute its judgement of an industrial relations situation for the judgement of the local management. If they do, they are asking for trouble. There is no substitute for local judgement. In this regard I feel strongly about the importance of senior industrial relations managers in every location being national and indigenous.

Exxon's George McCullough, the manager of employee relations, reports that industrial-relations management is highly decentralized (McCullough, 1977):

My company operates in 13 / countries. The variations in our labor relations processes, the manner in which we go about collective bargaining, and the differences in items included in collective agreements are staggering. Even in two countries like Holland and Belgium, where the proximity between Rotterdam and Antwerp has caused us to consolidate some management functions, the labor relations processes are totally independent of each other and the contracts bear little resemblance.

More broadly based studies (involving groups of multinationals) confirm these management statements (Walker, 1972, and Roberts and May, 1974).

Behavioral dimensions of collective bargaining also support the concept of decentralized decision making. Tradeoffs among objectives are made during negotiations, and these reflect specific local priorities. Complete agreements, incorporating the outcome of this process, are either accepted or rejected by local worker constituencies. Management that participate in this process had better be well aware of what will "work" in these give-and-take exchanges.

A few limited exceptions involving parent-company management in subsidiary-level labor relations have been noted, however (Kujawa, 1972). These include the example of a parent's participation in setting an overall industrial-relations strategy at the subsidiary to restructure labor relations away from plant-level agreements and piece rates to a multiplant agreement pattern and time-measured day rates accompanied by a substantial infusion of funds by the parent to modernize production processes. Another situation more commonly evidenced involves a parent's participation in negotiations over pensions when the parent's staff includes actuarial expertise not available locally (to management) and where the pension commitment itself is viewed as a potential liability of the parent company.

THE HEADQUARTERS-STAFF ROLE.   Since labor relations is so localized, there is no line responsibility or function for it at the headquarters level. There is frequently a staff function, however, and it is concerned with effectiveness in industrial relations at the subsidiaries and in operations at the multinational level, and in implementing the stewardship role of the MNE management.

The Advising Function.   An MNE's labor-relations staff usually embraces considerable industrial-relations expertise, especially in terms of the firm's technology and its work-force-management requirements and the corporate philosophy regarding the role and handling of workers, unions, and other aspects of employee relations. This capability at the MNE staff level is not used to intimidate local industrial-relations managers or to impose a unified approach to labor-management relations. Rather, it is made available to local management (frequently only at the request of local management) to respond to ideas and/or to suggest alternatives. The frequency of this parent-company supportive participation increases when an impasse and strike occurs at the subsidiary level, but even then, decisions on both contract substance and management tactics are invariably locally taken. (Of course, if a strike occurs during industrywide negotiations, as may be evidenced, for example, in either Germany or France, any kind of participation by MNE staff is far removed from what may or may not be effective in securing an agreement.)

In most MNEs, the parent-company labor-relations staff monitors subsidiaries' labor relations to ensure that agreements do not compromise the integrity of the local labor market and determines what is required to secure a local agreement. This is done to prevent the establishment of a global company-specific pattern in local collective agreements. The role of the MNE staff in this regard is not one of dictating to subsidiary managers, but rather one of information gathering on local conditions and situations and the sharing of this information with all the subsidiaries. The monitoring function is useful in developing data, not in imposing conditions and bargaining positions. It is becoming increasingly important as unions in different countries are themselves becoming increasingly knowledgeable about contract settlements and employment conditions in other subsidiaries (of the same MNE) and identify and/or press for similar treatment or concessions during local bargaining.

As a side note, what may first appear as exceptions to this MNE objective of localizing wages, benefits, and other employment conditions are the labor agreements in the auto industry to include U.S. and Canadian UAW members in a single wage- and job-classification system. This was accomplished in the inital contracts by bringing Canadian workers' wages up to parity ($1 Canadian = $1 U.S.) with those of U.S. workers. Exchange rates (over time) reflect productivity differentials and money-supply changes between countries. As these have changed between the United States and Canada since wage parity in the auto industry was established, the real purchasing power and the U.S. dollar cost of the wages paid Canadian workers have declined substantially. Nonetheless, the U.S.-dollar–Canadian-dollar parity in the auto industry remains. The foreign-exchange market has effectively matched local labor-market and other economic conditions between the United States and Canada and factored the contractually determined parity condition by whatever differentials found. The integrity of local markets, as they relate to wage payments, remains intact!

The Interpretive Function. Being aware of labor issues and conditions at the subsidiary level, the MNE labor-relations staff performs a very important interpretive role to staff with other functions at the parent-company levels. It provides others with data and other information necessary to their planning activities and to their understanding and assessments of local situations. Production, of course, is affected by strikes at the subsidiaries, and, depending on the extent of intersubsidiary production integration, contingency plans to maintain production elsewhere and to supply market needs must be developed. Or, in the event of multiple production capabilities among subsidiaries, production elsewhere may need to be expanded. The MNE staff's interpretation of the local strike situation as it affects production continuity is essential to these contingency plans.

Budgeting at the headquarters level is also related to the MNE labor-relations staff's functions. What may be required to secure a labor agreement at a subsidiary will likely affect overall production costs and necessitate new cost forecasts. These in turn may affect product prices and sales and revenues forecasts. It is quite common for the MNE's labor-relations staff to be called upon to give estimates (developed with local input) of anticipated labor-cost changes to both the corporate finance and marketing functions.

A third interpretive activity follows from the need of the senior line management that deals with subsidiary management at the parent-company level to be knowledgeable about local labor conditions and problems. This allows them to respond intelligently, responsibly, and responsively to the line-management decisions.

The Stewardship Function. Stewardship is often equated to control. Regarding subsidiary-level labor relations and the role of the MNE staff, stewardship is implemented through indirect control, that is, through input on the selection of industrial-relations executives at the local level, the professional development of these executives, and, in some cases, the influencing of the compensation paid local executives and the staff capabilities evidenced at the subsidiary level. In nearly every case, the line management controls the appointment of management personnel to key positions. This means the managing director at the subsidiary selects the (local) senior labor-relations officer and that person selects his subordinates. The management level above that identified with the selection decision most frequently concurs with the decision, or, sometimes, takes exception to it (invariably prior to the announcement of a final decision). The MNE staff usually advises the MNE line management (invariably on a continuous basis) on the advancement potential of labor-relations executives at the different subsidiaries and offers specific inputs when specific personnel are nominated by subsidiary management for the (local) senior industrial-relations position. It must be emphasized, however, that both initiative and ultimate control are at the subsidiary level. The MNE-level line management and staff would rarely, if ever, impose the appointment of a certain manager on the subsidiary management. Likewise, the appointment of (subsidiary) managers below the level of the senior industrial-relations executive is commonly totally contained at the local level—including the nomination, selection, and approval decisions.

In larger firms, professional development and career-tracking of executives at subsidiary levels are frequently evidenced at the parent level. Training (aside from that locally provided) is often accomplished through intersubsidiary meetings of industrial-relations personnel (on either a regional or global basis) at which information and experiences are shared and ideas tested. Sometimes parent-company personnel may perform (usually informal) functional audits of local industrial-relations management and offer ideas for improvement. Quite commonly, the parent-company labor-relations staff follows the development of local industrial-relations personnel and assesses their promotion potential. This may or may not lead to specific promotional opportunities, and the procedure and interest is not unlike that accorded subsidiary executives in other functional areas.

Occasionally (definitely not frequently), the MNE staff advises line management on compensation levels for subsidiary industrial-relations executives and on the general functions and capabilities necessary to support the conduct of labor relations locally. This is more often than not done on an exceptions basis and then (most likely) only to promote minimum performance levels. The MNE staff is most likely performing an advocacy role to convince local management to upgrade salaries or local competencies.

INTERNATIONAL BUSINESS STRATEGY AND INTERNATIONAL AND COMPARATIVE INDUSTRIAL RELATIONS

Most MNEs confront a variety of strategic decisions on a fairly routine basis. These decisions might encompass product design, product-market identification. long-term financing, research and development support, political involvement, and so forth. Regarding industrial-relations considerations, and limiting our inquiry to include only MNEs in manufacturing or processing, three such decisions appear particularly relevant: the foreign-direct-investment decision, decisions on the allocation of production among parent and subsidiaries, and the disinvestment decision. Care should be taken in making these decisions, both to weigh industrial-relations effects as elements in the decision process and, once the decision is made, as expectations of what may ensue as labor-management opportunities or problems.

THE FOREIGN-DIRECT-INVESTMENT DECISION. Most direct investments by MNEs are defensive in nature; that is, to protect or maintain what had been export sales to foreign markets, usually in advanced, industrialized economies, or to protect or enhance domestic (U.S.) market shares by production cost cutting derived from the location of production facilities in low-labor-cost, developing countries. In other words, foreign direct investments are made to serve foreign markets with local (foreign) production, or domestic (home) or third-country markets with foreign ("offshore") production.

In the former case, the MNE had most likely been serving foreign markets with U.S. exports, but as foreign-based firms have cut into these markets, the premium return on the product's sales has declined, and distant and (local) less-market-responsive operations are no longer economically optimum (or justified). What's required is an actual production presence in the foreign market that is sensitive to and likely adjusted to specific market needs and the actions of competitors. Success in this type of venture also requires a competitive edge in terms of product or process uniqueness, or financial or marketing strength enjoyed by the MNE. In most cases, product, process, or managerial technological superiority is the key. The foreign industrial-relations environment where the prospective direct investment is sited, must be accommodative to the implementation of these competitive strengths. This implies that a production environment characterized by shop-floor militancy and social-class cleavages would be less desirable to the MNE than o.·· in which in-plant labor-management relations were more harmonious and less strike prone. Likewise, an environment in which management is able to capture the economic benefits of improved technologies, at least for the first few years, is preferred to one in which nearly immediate "gain-sharing" with the workers is required. Both considerations point to West Germany or perhaps Spain as preferred plant location sites compared with the United Kingdom, for example. Production continuity, either because of transnational production integration or the inability to stockpile finished product may also be a key factor. A plant site prone to wildcat strikes (including strikes at key local suppliers) would not be satisfactory. Unit labor costs are also important, as are the distance from the production location to the consumers, tariff barriers, and so forth. Analysis of the entire situation lends itself to probabilistic modeling with alternative outcomes and expected costs (e.g., foregone sales, reduced profits, etc.) delineated.

In the offshore production situation, the direct-investment motivation is essentially production cost cutting. The product is likely to be a mature product and the profit margin likely to be thin. Import competition (including that generated by other U.S.-based firms) is heavy. The economics of the situation compels the export of labor-intensive production to low-wage foreign production sites. The quality of the offshore work force, as well as the potential for demand changes in the (U.S.) product market, may well necessitate segmentation in the production process—for example, with garments, where design and cutting are done in the U.S. plant and sewing in the offshore facility. Labor quality, labor cost, and production continuity are likely the key industrial-relations considerations in deciding on a location for offshore production. Most low-wage countries that can respond to this type of direct-invest-ment opportunity (e.g., because of proximity to the United States) have commercial- and economic-development agencies and production "free zones" that will gladly work with a U.S. firm in establishing an offshore facility.

If the firm bargains with a U.S. union whose unit members will be affected by the location of production to the offshore facility, the company is clearly obliged by U.S. labor law to consult with the U.S. union over the effects of that decision on unit members. Enlightened management would also consult with the union before a final decision was made to see if the economic rationale favoring the offshore location could be reversed, for example, by changing U.S. work practices, foregoing wage and benefit increases, and so forth (Kujawa, 1972).

THE PRODUCTION-ALLOCATION DECISION   If production allocation affects U.S. employment of bargaining unit members and is essentially a reallocation situation, the economics of the decision should be addressed within the legal context and union-consultation suggestion discussed above. If production involves new products, then the pertinent industrial-relations considerations are likely to be similar to those dis-cussed already in the foreign direct investment to serve the foreign market situation.

As multinationals themselves have matured, they have expanded product lines in foreign markets and have continued to rationalize production of more mature lines through interplant (including transnational) production integration. The MNE is thus diversifying regarding product-market risk, but becoming less diversified regarding labor-resource risk. This is occurring while product profit margins are becoming increasingly thin because of growing worldwide resource competition and producer cartelization (especialy in financial and energy markets) and increasing (especially international) product-market competition. This means that the production-allocation decision is more important than ever (no product-market staying power) and that it may well turn on narrow differentials in comparative unit labor costs, or on the firm's ability to negotiate with governments over location incentives (e.g., financial subsidies, tax holidays, etc.) that might reverse the direction of these differentials. Firms should be careful to investigate alternatives in detail and to base decisions on present value expectations that factor comparative trends in the growth of unit labor costs and the potential for future successful negotiations with governments in their cash-flow analyses. (Unit labor costs, incidentally, include costs of production stoppages, legally required fringes, etc., and changes in unit labor costs would include workweek and holiday/vacation trends, etc. Anticipated foreign-exchange-rate changes would also be relevant to trend analyses in comparative unit labor costs. Changes in productivity in the specific industry the MNE operates in must be evaluated with expected overall country-level productivity changes that in turn affect exchange rates and the comparative competitiveness of the firm's production in foreign markets, especially in the shorter time periods. In the long run, exchange rates move with productivity changes, and unit money costs of production are not as important to the comparative analysis required.)

THE DISINVESTMENT DECISION.   Disinvestment is not an unusual event for an MNE. Indeed, Vernon (1977) has observed that

> . . . between 1968 and 1974, 180 U.S. based multinational enterprises sold or liquidated 717 manufacturing subsidiaries located in foreign countries . . . out of a total population of about 6,500 such subsidiaries, . . . suggesting the existence of an entropic process in the multinational enterprise.

As noted earlier, many products and industries have matured with little prospect for substantially altering product or process technology. In these cases, profit margins are likely not sufficient to cover the extra costs associated with internationally distributed management. Disinvestment, or even abandonment of a market, is the result, and in many cases should even be anticipated.

Anticipation may be the key to handling disinvestment successfully regarding industrial relations. Selling off an operation while it is still profitable may entail some foregone benefits, but these should be measured against the potential of not selling the operation once it is unprofitable, or of having the facility occupied (and perhaps run) by irate workers who do not want to lose their jobs. Plant closings in Western European countries (England excepted) usually involve an indemnification payment to the discharged workers—which (as discussed earlier in the Badger Company case in Belgium) can amount to several thousand dollars per employee (Blainpain, 1977). The amount of this payment should be the first ingredient used by an MNE in determining the discount applied to the selling price of the subsidiary!

Planning for disinvestment is also important. In countries where employee works councils are legally franchised to receive economic and financial data and forecasts, a surprise disinvestment decision could hardly be expected. Planning the disinvestment beforehand, allowing workers time to adjust to the pending closure (maybe by finding alternative employment early on), and offering workers employment elsewhere (within the MNE system) are all sensible activities.

Country policies on required indemnification payments have raised some interesting problems (for countries) and opportunities (for MNEs). Some companies (with dual production capabilities) have been known to cut back employment more in the country with the less-costly indemnification requirement. This saves the firm money (all else being equal). The problem is then that the country with the less-onerous requirement receives a disproportionate share of the unemployment. The countries of the EEC are presently investigating the need for harmonizing social policy on this issue. Finally, there is the case of the U.S. MNE that traded a "no-layoff" commitment in local collective bargaining for some union concessions. The company's action were based upon detailed analysis of the severance payments due the work force in the event of layoffs factored by the probability of such layoffs occurring during the 3-year life of the contract, and then balancing of this expected cost against the expected gains resulting from the concessions.

SOURCES AND SUGGESTED REFERENCES

Sources

Angle, F. "The Conduct of Labor Relations in General Motors Overseas Operations," in D. Kujawa, ed. *International Labor and the Multinational Enterprise*. New York: Praeger, 1975.

Belford, J. "Comment," in R.F. Banks and J. Stieber, eds. *Multinationals, Unions and Labor Relations in Industrialized Countries*. Ithaca: New York State School of Industrial and Labor Relations, Cornell University, 1977.

Blainpain, R.G. *The Badger Case and the OECD Guidelines for Multinational Enterprises*. Deventer, The Netherlands: Kluwer, 1977.

Copp, R. "Locus of Industrial Relations Decision Making in Multinationals," in R.F. Banks and J. Stieber, eds. *Multinationals, Unions and Labor Relations in Industrialized Countries*. Ithaca: New York State School of Industrial and Labor Relations, Cornell University, 1977.

Dronkers, P.L. "A Multinational Organization and Industrial Relations: The Philips' Case," in D. Kujawa, ed. *International Labor and the Multinational Enterprise*. New York: Praeger, 1975.

Dunlop, J.T. *Industrial Relations Systems*. New York: Henry Holt, 1958.

Gunter, H., and Laminsky, G. "The Federal Republic of Germany," in J.T. Dunlop and W. Galenson, eds. *Labor in the Twentieth Century*. New York: Academic Press, 1978.

Hanami, T. *Labor Relations in Japan Today*. Tokyo: Kodansha International, 1979.

Hershfield, D. *The Multinational Union Challenges the Multinational Company*. New York: The Conference Board, 1975.

Jager, E. "U.S. Labor and Multinationals," in D. Kujawa, ed. *International Labor and the Multinational Enterprise*. New York: Praeger, 1975.

Kujawa, D. "Foreign Sourcing Decisions and the Duty to Bargain Under the NLRA," *Law and Policy in International Business,* Vol. IV, No. 3 (1972), pp. 41–66.

Kujawa, D. *International Labor Relations Management in the Automotive Industry: A Comparative Study of Chrysler, Ford and General Motors*. New York: Praeger, 1971.

Kujawa, D. "Transnational Industrial Relations and the Multinational Enterprise," *Journal of Business Administration,* Vol. VII, No. 1, (1975), pp. 23–37.

Kujawa, D. "U.S. Labor, Multinational Enterprise and the National Interest," *Law and Policy in International Business,* Vol. X, No. 3 (1978), pp. 192–206.

Kujawa, D. "U.S. Manufacturing Investment in the Developing Countries: American Labour's

Concerns and the Enterprise Environment in the Decade Ahead," *British Journal of Industrial Relations,* Vol. XIX, No. 1 (1981), pp. 74–91.

McCullough, G.B. "Comment," in R.F. Banks and J. Stieber, eds. *Multinationals, Unions and Labor Relations in Industrialized Countries.* Ithaca: New York State School of Industrial and Labor Relations, Cornell University, 1977.

Northrup, H.R. and Rowan, R.L. *Multinational Collective Bargaining Attempts.* Philadelphia: Industrial Research Unit, The Wharton School, University of Pennsylvania, 1979.

Roberts, B.C. and May, J. "The Responses of Multinational Enterprises to International Trade Union Pressures," *British Journal of Industrial Relations,* Vol. XII, No. 3 (1974), 34–70.

Roberts, B.C. and Rothwell, S. "Recent Trends in Collective Bargaining in the United Kingdom," in *Collective Bargaining in Industrialized Market Economies.* Geneva: International Labour Office, 1974.

Seyfarth, Shaw, Fairweather, and Geraldson. *Labor Relations and the Law in West Germany and the United States.* Ann Arbor: Bureau of Business Research, Graduate School of Business Administration, University of Michigan, 1969.

Shirai, T., and Shimada, H. "Japan," in J.T. Dunlop and W. Galenson, eds. *Labor in the Twentieth Century.* New York: Academic Press, 1978.

Sturmthal, A. *Comparative Labor Movements: Ideological Roots and Institutional Development.* Belmont, CA.: Wadsworth Publishing, 1972.

Thomson, A.W.J. and Hunter, L.C. "Great Britain," in J.T. Dunlop and W. Galenson, eds. *Labor in the Twentieth Century.* New York: Academic Press, 1978.

Vernon, R. *Storm over the Multinationals: The Real Issues.* Cambridge, MA: Harvard University Press, 1977.

Walker, Kenneth F. *Labor Problems in Multinational Firms.* Report on a Meeting of Management Experts, Paris, June 21–23, 1972. Paris: Organization for Economic Cooperation and Development, 1972.

Windmuller, J. "International Trade Union Organizations: Structure, Function, Limitations," in S. Barkin, *et al,* eds. *International Labor.* New York: Harper and Row, 1967.

Additional Suggested References

Bomers, G.B.J. *Multinational Corporations and Industrial Relations: A Comparative Study of West Germany and the Netherlands.* Assen/Amsterdam: Van Gorcum, 1977.

Dore, R. *British Factory/Japanese Factory: The Origins of National Diversity in Industrial Relations.* Berkeley/Los Angeles: University of California Press, 1973.

Gennard, J. *Multinational Corporations and British Labour: A Review of Attitudes and Responses.* London: British–North American Committee, 1972.

Jacobs, E., et al. *The Approach to Industrial Change in Britain and West Germany.* London: Anglo-German Foundation for the Study of Industrial Society, 1978.

Kennedy, T. *European Labor Relations.* Lexington, MA: D.C. Heath, 1980.

Kujawa, D, ed. *American Labor and the Multinational Corporation.* New York: Praeger, 1973.

Kujawa, D. *Employment Effects of Multinational Enterprises: A United States Case Study.* Working Paper No. 12. Geneva: International Labour Office, 1980.

Kujawa, D *The Labour Relations of United States Multinationals Abroad: Comparative and Prospective Views.* Research Series, No. 60. Geneva: International Institute for Labour Studies, 1980.

Martin, B. and Kassalow, E.M., eds. *Labor Relations in Advanced Industrial Societies.* Washington, D.C.: Carnegie Endowment for International Peace, 1980.

Multinational Enterprises and Social Policy. Geneva: International Labour Office, 1973.

Spalding, H.A. *Organized Labor in Latin America.* New York: New York University Press, 1977.

RESEARCH, DEVELOPMENT, AND TECHNOLOGY TRANSFER

CONTENTS

INTRODUCTION 3

Importance of Technology for Business 3

TECHNOLOGY STRATEGY,
PLANNING, AND MANAGEMENT 4

Technology Strategy 4
Technology Planning 4
Organization 4
Manufacturing 5
Marketing of Technology 5
Technology Management 6
Marketing and Innovation Strategy 7
Technology from Developing Countries 8
TCDC as an Opportunity 9

TECHNOLOGY-TRANSFER
AGREEMENTS AND
IMPLEMENTATION 10

Instruments of Technology Transfer 10
Industrial-Cooperation Agreements 11
Technology-Transfer Agreements 11
Managing Transfer of Technology:
After the Agreement 12

NATIONAL APPROACHES TO
TECHNOLOGY 13

Developed-Country Concerns over
Technology Transfer 14
Developing-Country Concerns over
Technology Transfer 14
Western and Japanese Technology in
Developing Countries 15
Costs of Technology Transfer 16

RESEARCH-AND-DEVELOPMENT
MANAGEMENT 17

Types of Studies on R&D Management 17
Risks, Costs, and Time in Technological
Innovation 17
Time and Cost Overruns 17
Guidelines for R&D Management 18
Overseas R&D by Transnational
Corporations 20
Increasing R&D Overseas 21
R&D in Developing Countries 21
Relocation of Development and
Engineering Activity 22

SOURCES AND SUGGESTED
REFERENCES 23

RESEARCH, DEVELOPMENT, AND TECHNOLOGY TRANSFER

A. J. Prasad

INTRODUCTION

IMPORTANCE OF TECHNOLOGY FOR BUSINESS. Technology has been a subject of considerable interest to business, government, and academia. Each of these groups has a characteristic axis with which it views research, development, and technology transfer. There are others, who are less involved, whose views on technology can be termed relatively philosophical and thus do not have immediate relevance to business decision makers. This section has been organized to reflect the different perspectives of, and insights drawn by, the three major groups.

The impact of technology has always been a matter of concern for thoughtful people. Their arguments have acquired increasing significance in view of the accumulating consequences of unrestricted technological exploitation on nature and on the mental and physical state of mankind. Technology has prevailed, however, probaby more because of the contribution it makes to the capacity to destroy; it has to be acquired for its contribution, direct or otherwise, to "defense." International executives collectively may have a long-term responsibility in this context by virtue of their capacity to influence events, although competitive forces determine short- and medium-term actions.

The contents of this section have been chosen in the context of two important phenomena that emerged in the last two decades and are likely to acquire further momentum in the next two decades.

First, the need for technology (both technical and organizational skill) is growing as a consequence of the drive for economic development over large parts of the globe and for improving the quality of life in the developed countries.

Second, the potential transferees are becoming more aware of the cost and impact of unregulated transfers, as occurred until recently. They are resisting the classic modes of transfer. Both these phenomena suggest that international managers should know more about technology creation and transfer and the global environment in which business strategy has to be evolved.

TECHNOLOGY STRATEGY, PLANNING, AND MANAGEMENT

TECHNOLOGY STRATEGY. Technology strategy is an essential and identifiable component of a firm's overall strategy, and "demands explicit attention to technical, economic, social, political and behavioral considerations simultaneously, as it embraces factors within the firm and external to it" (Kantrow, 1980). Every firm need not be a technological leader to succeed, and in fact, technological leadership does not by itself ensure success. Several distinctly different approaches may be noticed in practice. Firms with marketing and/or financial strengths may opt to buy technology through licensing and/or acquisition of smaller technology-intensive firms.

TECHNOLOGY PLANNING. Technology planning includes evaluation of existing technology in the context of anticipated quantity and quality of output and technological alternatives that may be available or need development. Alternatives may involve quality improvements, resource- or cost-saving developments, and new products. Changes may therefore be required in the operating plans of each functional area of the firm and in the strategic plan that integrates the functional plans. A global view, monitoring technological developments of all competitors, is needed.

ORGANIZATION. International expansion of business has occurred on the basis of one or more strengths—technology, control over raw materials, or marketing. Few companies can claim simultaneous superiority in all three. Research has pointed out that the organization structure, at the headquarters level, of a transnational corporation that exploits its technological superiority through introduction of diverse new products abroad is likely to evolve toward global product divisions. Transnational corporations exploiting marketing strengths, or whose products are becoming mature, adopt global area divisions. But "despite the strong association between area divisions and mature products, area divisions can go with new products as long as the product line is narrow" (Stopford and Wells, 1972). Exhibit 1 illustrates the concept:

EXHIBIT 1   ORGANIZATION OF WORLD HEADQUARTERS. FOREIGN SALES AS PERCENTAGE OF TOTAL GLOBAL SALES

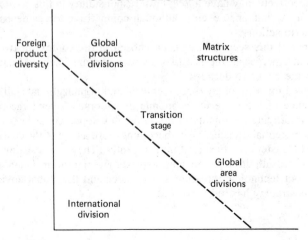

MANUFACTURING.   Technology has, as it has become a central part of business and development literature, acquired a broader meaning. The term now includes management, particularly the planning and production systems and sometimes marketing systems as well. Manufacturing strategy has been, after more than a decade of comparative neglect, again recognized as important. Competition for world markets has increased in many products, leading to a need for lower prices and consistent quality at higher levels of production. It has been hypothesized that "just as the product and market pass through a series of major stages, so does the production process used in the manufacture of that product" (Hayes and Wheelwright, 1979). Thus a product-process matrix can help anticipate the tradeoffs between flexibility and efficiency of the process.

It is also now recognized that process changes, especially learning-curve economies, influence changes in the product, and that a product line and its associated production process should be considered together for purposes of analysis (Utterback, 1978). "Managers can no longer afford to view [manufacturing] as a neutral apparatus for turning out goods. Manufacturing has significant data to contribute to . . . strategic planning" (Kantrow, 1980).

MARKETING OF TECHNOLOGY.   International firms having recognized technology as a marketable asset, it is not immediately clear why many large corporations, particularly the widely diversified firms, do not enter the global market for technology more aggressively. A few companies have taken first steps. General Electric of the United States has a small division, the Technology Marketing Operation, to sell its licenses and provide other technological services.

In principle, transnational corporations could identify independent potential buyers and offer technology "packages" that were tailored to their needs. At present, firms respond to queries from buyers. However, many potential buyers are simply unaware of possible sources of supply. A new dimension could be added to the scope of the international marketing function of a transnational corporation by including technology, braodly defined, as a product.

By doing this, all the benefits of a marketing approach could be realized, both by the buyers and by the sellers. Marketers could, at little expense, forecast and plan their offers and gain an inside track, rather than compete on equal terms after a bid is out. However, transnational corporations appear to be currently pursuing a selling approach characterized by: (1) waiting for buyers to make contact, or (2) offering most of them a similar initial package, often based on direct foreign investment.

Significant industrialization in the developing world has been concentrated in a relatively small number of countries, around 20 by many estimates. The larger and more successful among these have embarked on a determined effort to produce indigenously basic products such as petrochemicals, steel, transport equipment, and numerous light-engineering goods. Import-substitution strategies rely on imports of intermediates, components, or other inputs, and have amplified the need to increase exports of manufactured goods. This in turn has led to an increased demand for licensing agreements to obtain the necessary technology.

Competition from other technology suppliers often makes it imperative for transnational corporations to sell technology as such, without control. Such sale provides resources for investment in new technologies provided that the firm has the ability to manage this task. In consequence, developing countries have become an important and expanding market for technology in many industries, and through the technology-transfer agreement, for products, equipment, and services.

Eastern Europe is another market for technology outside the scope of direct foreign investment. Although direct foreign investment will continue to be important, technology has its own, larger markets.

In technology marketing "the whole planning process must be converted from a resource rationing process into an opportunity seeking process" (Quinn, 1979).

TECHNOLOGY MANAGEMENT.   Technology has an important influence in determining the range of strategic possibilities open to a firm, and may be viewed as an asset to be acquired, managed, and increased, analogous to capital, trademarks, market shares, and human resources. *Ceteris paribus,* technology-intensive firms generally demonstrate higher growth rates, and even firms with established market positions may gradually find themselves outflanked by competitors with superior product or process technology. This may happen in spite of the fact that the new technology may create new markets and threaten traditional technology only progressively—through one submarket at a time. In a market open to unrestricted competition, technological innovations can pose serious threats to a traditional business. Late or inadequate responses designed to permit participation in the new technology may lead to a loss of market position from which recovery may be difficult, and on occasion, impossible.

Management's approach to technology can be shown in a framework with the response mode and activity level on two axes (Exhibit 2).

In technical industries there will continue to be invention and innovation, and for companies in such industries, decisions on technology will have an impact on survival and growth that may be felt only many years later. Management's response to this reality will lead to several "primary technological decisions" to maintain the long-term viability of the firm. Together, these constitute *technology management.* The major purpose is simply to act early enough to ensure that the firm has technology as needed—whether through external acquisition or through internal development. Among these "primary technological decisions" will be the following:

1. Establishment of a mechanism to assess technology required to maintain competitive strength and to monitor developments globally.

EXHIBIT 2   A FRAMEWORK FOR TECHNOLOGY MANAGEMENT

Activity Level (increasing difficulty)	Response Mode	
	Passive: Managerial orientation; wide scope; lower risk and gain	Active: Entrepreneurial orientation; limited scope; higher risk and gain
Monitoring technological change	Learn how to use new technologies as a customer	Purchase technology to become an efficient manufacturer
Managing technological change	Steer organisation through impact of change; assimilate and absorb new technology	Adapt and develop new technology
Exploiting technological change	Launch new products and services based on new technologies	Sell technology domestically and abroad

2. Strategic evaluations of the type of technology needed, covering the following:
   a. Scale of production.
   b. Production process (capital-labor ratio).
   c. Raw materials.
   d. Technical personnel.
   e. Output/product-mix.
3. Decisions on how to obtain the technology, whether from outside the firm or through R&D.

All the major functional areas of the firm have an important role in technology management. Technology decisions often involve considerable risk, and strategic allocation of corporate resources. Therefore, although functional support is necessary, top management has to be thoroughly familiar with the issues.

R&D management is only one of the subsequent tasks of ensuring efficient exploitation of resources allocated for technology management. R&D management thus can have two distinct facets. One is the development of new or modified processes and/or products. The second is assisting operations, through advice on (1) technological developments in the industry, (2) choice of channels by which to acquire technology, (3) fabrication and supply of equipment, and (4) quality control over raw material, processes, and products.

MARKETING AND INNOVATION STRATEGY.   Although top-management involvement in R&D is important, its involvement in understanding the marketing dimension is critical for success. All the research evidence to date suggests that marketing assessments must be injected into the decision process as early as possible to reduce the commercial risks of innovation.

Although this is unquestionable in principle, practical problems arise. Both technologists and marketing managers are often found to be optimists when it comes to the assessment of the initial prospects for new products. "The marketing manager . . . will usually carry out some rudimentary market research . . . most respondents will . . . react favourably; this is little indication of their response later when presented with an order form" (Twiss, 1975).

It may be desirable to attempt an innovation of significance, rather than a marginal improvement. A significant innovation can command a higher price, which will be necessary because costs will be high until, eventually, sales volume increases, leading to lower costs through learning and scale economies. Because a smaller sales volume for an innovation is easier to achieve quickly, a significant innovation is less likely to be unprofitable, because the break-even volume can be reached quickly. Minor innovations may involve less risk, but need higher break-even volumes, which may be more difficult to achieve.

Significant technical progress involves higher technical risk prior to accomplishment; the project is also likely to be more demanding on funds and manpower. In such cases, it has been found that "to compensate for the higher technical risks involved . . . firms apparently screen these projects carefully to make sure that the commercial risks involved are relatively low. . . . Indeed, the probability of commerical success (given technical completion) is . . . greater for projects attempting large or medium advances in the state of the art . . . than for a project attempting a small advance" (Mansfield, 1971).

Marketing analysis includes anticipating the product life cycle and its implications.

Initially, sales will grow slowly, and overinvestment must be avoided. Once growth begins, supplies must be maintained. At the peak, development of new markets and competition must be anticipated and an appropriate strategy (withdrawal?) adopted. Ansoff and Stewart (1967) have presented a now-classic framework that lists the major options open to a firm.

"By way of summary, let us consider the impact of these characteristics on a strategic issue: the timing of the technologically intensive firm's entry into an emerging industry. The alternatives may usefully be grouped into four major marketing strategies, recognizing that most companies will—or should—adopt a blend of these according to the requirements of their different markets or product lines:

- First to market—based on a strong R&D program, technical leadership and risk taking.
- Follow the leader—based on strong development resources and an ability to react quickly as the market starts its growth phase.
- Application engineering—based on product modifications to fit the needs of particular customers in a mature market.
- "Me-too"—based on superior manufacturing efficiency and cost control.

Each of these strategies has different strengths and weaknesses in particular competitive situations. Intelligent selection and execution of the appropriate strategy normally will strengthen the company's competitive posture" (Ansoff, and Stewart, 1967).

TECHNOLOGY FROM DEVELOPING COUNTRIES.   Technical cooperation among developing countries (TCDC) is basically a post-1960 phenomenon and constitutes a source of technology that is complementary to technology from developed countries. A basic question is the type of technologies in which developing countries will be prominent on grounds of market acceptance and technoeconomic characteristics.

"It has been widely presumed that, in technology, [TCDC] serves only in intermediate–traditional, indigenous–technology. Yet not so: the adaptive, modular and more mobile re-designing by India of [Western] nuclear irradiation technology (for medical supplies, agriculture and industrial processes) has been disseminated through TCDC to other Third World countries" (Childers, 1979).

TCDC is not limited to intragovernment projects alone. Technology transfer is occurring frequently enough among private firms in developing countries to merit notice by those interested in international technology transfer. Technology exports by indigenous enterprises in response to market forces take the following major forms (Lall, 1979):

1. Turnkey projects involving exports of complete industrial plants, based in India, Argentina, Brazil, and Mexico. Initially involved in simple industries (textiles, sugar, cement), Indian firms have during the 1970s moved to more-sophisticated industries (large-scale power plants, pharmaceuticals, fertilizers, steel, machine tools, etc.).
2. Engineering consultancy (chemicals, power generation, railway technology, metals, etc.).

3.   Managerial services and training programs.
4.   Direct investment, involving varying degrees of equity participation.

There is little information on the sale or licensing of patents and trademarks among developing countries. "The basis of comparative advantage in technology exports by developing countries is threefold: the low cost of highly skilled manpower; the suitability of the technology to conditions in developing countries (particularly smaller scale production) and the 'unpackaged' nature of technology sales" (Lall, 1979).

India is prominent among technology exporters from developing countries, the probable cause being "the protection and promotion given to the process of learning at different levels by the government . . . in particular to the protection and promotion of learning within locally controlled enterprises vis à vis the import of technology through direct investment by TNCs" (Lall, 1979).

Childers (1979) has summarized the historical context, which currently circumscribes the opportunities for TCDC. Although "Europe's debt to Asian science was total before 1500 AD," the colonial era led to a "mind set" in which much existing wisdom and technology in developing countries was simply scorned. The mind set affected "not only the governors but also the governed." For example, a particularly disastrous mistake made by developing countries, even after political independence, was to adopt the Western model of medicine as the only model, neglecting all indigenous systems without scientific examination of their potentials.

Some thoughtful people have been and are aware of such dangers in using Western technology exclusively, but are still unable to influence events significantly. It was only in the 1970s that the Western model "had come under profound and steadily widening questioning, by environmentalists, fiscal specialists, students of the sociology and economics of dying inner cities, and economists" (Childers, 1979). This questioning has contributed to a new confidence among political leaders of developing countries, greater support for indigenous science, and TCDC.

TCDC AS AN OPPORTUNITY.   The implications of TCDC for international business follow from the convergence of several factors. Recognition of the inadequacy and inappropriateness of total reliance on Western models of production does not by any means pose a threat to the market for Western technology. On the contrary, TCDC is bedeviled by several serious problems: concerns that the technology may be second best just because it is not from the West, absence of capital investment from the transferor to endorse or guarantee the technology, and the nearly universal familiarity of Western trademarks and brand names. Little can be done about these formidable barriers in the near future.

In fact, international executives should find in TCDC an opportunity. TCDC is complementary and therefore expands the global market for technology by increasing supply. Many transfers that are not feasible because of the high costs of Western manpower may become feasible when undertaken in cooperation with firms from technology-exporting developing countries. Although these firms may by themselves be unable—because of lack of capital, brand names, or other reasons—to handle a project, they can participate with transnational corporations.

Oil-exporting countries have become enormous markets for technology. Business International of New York pointed out in 1974 that American firms may not be able to compete on cost for many projects in these countries without the participation of Indian firms, to lower engineering costs.

Apart from this business opportunity, TCDC also demonstrates that there is an effective demand for technology adaptation.

It should be noted that TCDC so far has occurred in spite of a major handicap that has led to serious underutilization of the limited resources devoted to R&D in developing countries. Most R&D in less developed countries is funded by government and conducted in government establishments, where the potential users are typically not involved. The resulting inefficiency is being recognized, however slowly. In the future, increases in R&D effort, especially that directed through business enterprises, may be expected to yield encouraging results. Indeed, there appears to be no other feasible solution than TCDC for the technology needs of most developing countries, because many projects are too small to be of interest to transnational corporations, and/or adaptation is too expensive for transnational corporations to do themselves.

TECHNOLOGY-TRANSFER AGREEMENTS AND IMPLEMENTATION

INSTRUMENTS OF TECHNOLOGY TRANSFER.   Several categorizations may be made of the various instruments of technology transfer. Four instruments are normally recognized:

1. Capital-goods sales.
2. Technical services and consultancy, including turnkey contracts.
3. Licensing of patents, know-how, and trademarks.
4. Direct foreign investment.

One or more may be used in any case of technology transfer.

A useful categorization of possible combinations of these instruments has been suggested by UNIDO (1979, p 27).

1. "Simple direct" sales of technological assets and services to unrelated buyers in mature industries. Exports of equipment, consultancy, and turnkey projects may be appropriate channels.
2. "Process packaged" sales, which include preinvestment studies; design, supply, and commissioning of equipment; and training of personnel. Licensing may often accompany such transfers and is appropriate when the industry is neither mature nor very dynamic.
3. "Project packaged" sales where management, finance, and marketing of output may be undertaken by the transferor. Such sales normally involve managerial control, implying some sort of direct foreign investment. Justification for this may be strong when the technology is dynamic and the transferee can thus retain access to ongoing developments, or when the transferee does not have the competence for independent management of the project.

Technology transfer from Eastern European countries to developing countries occurs through intergovernmental agreements and export of equipment. Intergovernmental agreements provide for exchange of technical documentation, supply of engineering designs, exchange of scientific delegations, and so forth. The Soviet Union has more than 40 such agreements; Bulgaria, 25; Czechoslovakia, 33; German Democratic Republic, 19; Hungary, 42; and Poland, 22. "When the technology supplied by governmental organizations comes without parallel sales of machinery and equipment, the technological services transfers occur through organizations set up specifically for this purpose" (UNIDO, 1979). Eastern European countries have many licensees in the OECD countries.

INDUSTRIAL-COOPERATION AGREEMENTS. In technology transfer agreements from the OECD countries to Eastern Europe, "industrial cooperation agreements" involving buyback arrangements are common. This ensures that the technology transferred is fairly recent and also helps to pay for the technology. Yugoslavia and Poland have signed many joint-venture agreements in which the rights of Western firms—management, marketing, and income—are accommodated by separate agreements between the parties concerned.

TECHNOLOGY-TRANSFER AGREEMENTS. Technical assistance, licensing, and direct foreign investment involve some type of negotiation and resulting agreements prior to commencement of technology transfer.

"For a contract to be considered a 'licence,' there must be some right over which the licensor has legal claim and which he can consequently confer on the licensee by licence. Such rights arise in the area of patents, and by legal convention, (intellectual property rights) extend to know-how" (UNIDO, 1980).

The distinction between know-how and patents, and technical assistance is important. Know-how and patents confer rights on the licensor and obligations on the licensee; technical assistance involves knowledge in the public domain and thus imposes no obligations. Know-how and patents are generally priced taking the licensee's earning power into account, the concept being income sharing; technical assistance is based on market prices for such services. "The nature, content and specificity of knowhow is established or secured only in the licence agreement. Traditionally, the licensor declares he is in possession of novel, valuable and useful technical information, at least some of which he has held in secrecy. The licensee examines this claim (to the extent possible) and contractually accepts it. Through such a declaration and acceptance, the licensor seeks to use established laws, particularly contract and trade secret laws, to create property (or proprietary) right and title in knowhow" (UNIDO, 1980.

Licensors have traditionally maintained that a know-how license is a leased right to use information (intellectual property) and not sale. However, although this may be reasonable in cases where the licensee is involved as a subcontractor, it is not so reasonable when investments have been made by the licensee. Most governments now do not permit automatic renewal of know-how agreements indefinitely, on the ground that know-how has been purchased by the licensee.

A patent is a legal right, enforced by the state from which the patentee has obtained the grant of the patent. Patents have limited lives. "The make, use and sell rights are separate rights, and the patentee has discretion over the extent of the rights he confers on his licensees. Under use and sale rights, a patent system can operate to prevent the importation of a patented product or in some countries prevent importation of a product made by a patented process" (UNIDO, 1980).

International conventions on patents date from 1883 and are being modified to improve the system's efficiency for registering patents. At the same time, both developing and developed countries are contemplating reform of the system.

Even when technical assistance, patents, and know-how are provided by the same transferor, separate agreements are recommended to minimize subsequent contractual disputes. The nature of rights, obligations, payments, and guarantees is different in each case. When a third party is involved as an engineering contractor, another agreement is necessary. Similarly when trademarks are involved, another agreement is used. Most governments accept the permanent right of a trademark holder, although they may not always agree to pay for the privilege of its continued use.

The term *license agreement* has, in common usage, become synonymous with an agreement for transfer of technology. "The general form and structure of the licence agreement is about the same whether executed between industrialised countries or between a developed and developing country. It is a universal and prime document in the transfer of technology, with characteristic clauses" (UNIDO, 1980).

Experts on taxation should be consulted by both licensor and licensee, because the tax implications may be altered by appropriate drafting of the terms of the agreement. In addition, legal experts should also be consulted. Several agencies have published guides that assist the inexperienced negotiator in obtaining insights into the various issues involved, and also serve as checklists. Two such guides are particularly recommended: (1) *Guidelines for Evaluation of Transfer of Technology Agreements* (UNIDO, 1980) and (2) *Licensing Guide for Developing Countries* (World Intellectual Property Organisation, 1977).

MANAGING TRANSFER OF TECHNOLOGY: AFTER THE AGREEMENT. The business aspects of technology transfer are negotiated and covered by a set of agreements. Those charged with subsequently managing the transfer have to be concerned with the components of technology and the most appropriate mechanism for transfer of each component of technology. For this purpose, components must be identified in greater detail than as technical services, know-how, patents, and trademarks. Depending on the scope of the transfer, such components may include the following:

Project-feasibility studies that establish the broad parameters of the project, such as capacity, capital, and quantity and sources of other inputs required.

Product-mix choice and product design.

Plant design and erection.

Initial operation (start-up).

Production and quality-control systems.

Other management support, which may include marketing.

A nucleus for further product and process development.

The manager charged with effecting the transfer has several mechanisms available, including the following:

Equipment, or specifications on the equipment to be purchased, can be supplied to the transferee.

Specifications on raw materials and other inputs can be supplied.

Designs and drawings can be supplied.

Manufacturing and quality-control specifications (manuals that describe procedures in required detail) can be supplied.

On-the-job training at the licensor's plant or at the licensee's plant can be provided.

Seminars/conferences/workshops, before, during and after the transfer, can be held. Some arrangement to answer questions rapidly may also be provided for.

Supply of equipment, manuals, and training are thus the three basic mechanisms. The choice of the mechanism depends upon the component to be transferred, the ability of the transferee to absorb the information, the experience of the transferor in transfer, and the agreement that defines the boundaries, including time and cost, for the transfer.

In practice, one other, less-obvious, factor influences transfer—reluctance on the part of key individuals. Behrman and Wallender (1976) found that "the practice of not communicating all knowledge exists even among affiliates of the same company." Several reasons, rational and human, appear to be the cause. Rivalry may be present with respect to production efficiency and can be expected to be strong when research proposals themselves are the subject of transfer. There may be reluctance at the transferee's end also, to accept ideas originating elsewhere, or to make changes in established practice. Personal visits are perhaps necessary to minimize the barrier of reluctance. In such situations it is not surprising that "only with the closest of business associations (a wholly owned relationship) can an affiliate expect to tap fully the technology of the parent company" (Behrman and Wallender, 1976). In such an association there are no limitations—except those imposed by company policy. Thus policy makers in host countries have realized that even having wholly owned affiliates is no guarantee of significant technology transfer.

NATIONAL APPROACHES TO TECHNOLOGY

Nations view technology as intrinsically desirable and therefore worth paying for. In providing access to their markets to foreign firms, through licensing or direct investment, all countries try to examine the extent of technology transfer that may result. As European and Japanese investment in the United States increased significantly during the 1970s, several such studies were conducted in the United States also (National Academy of Engineering, 1977).

When governments examine foreign investment proposals or licensing agreements, manufacturing on host-country territory, by itself, is increasingly being viewed as inadequate grounds for claiming that technology transfer has occurred. Although manufacturing provides limited control over supply, there may be no control over technology. "Control over supply is usually the direct objective of industrialization; control over technology, on the other hand, is an objective of development" (UNIDO, 1980). "Width of control" can be obtained through provisions of the licensing and know-how agreements; "depth of control" is fully achieved only at the end of a three-stage process, including access, absorption, and freedom to use the technology. Restrictions on use are now unlikely to be allowed in most countries, and international agencies (U.N. Conference on Trade and Development, Organization for Economic Cooperation and Development, the U.N. Commission on Transnational Corporations) are currently engaged in developing codes of conduct on the transfer of technology.

DEVELOPED-COUNTRY CONCERNS OVER TECHNOLOGY TRANSFER.   Technology transfer is not neutral in its impact, and this is true even within a technology-exporting country. Although such a country as a whole may benefit from its transfer, the varying impact on different economic groups and on noneconomic national objectives may lead to conflict and thus create pressures for export controls. National objectives related to international transfer of technology may be grouped as follows:

Primarily economic objectives—economic growth, employment, prices, income distribution, structural adjustment.

Social objectives—environment, consumer protection, promotion of humanitarian behavior.

Strategic objectives—national security.

No policy posture can satisfy all groups in a society, particularly because of impacts on income distribution. The impact on workers whose jobs may be displaced compared with the revenue to the exporting company is a common example. Policy formulation is made more complex because there may be conflicts among the classes of objectives listed above, in addition to conflicts within the same class of objectives.

Finally, the effectiveness of any policy depends very largely on whether alternative sources of technology are available to the potential buyers. If restrictions are applied when alternatives are available, the policy may often be counterproductive.

One concern of technology-exporting firms is that technology may leak out to firms other than subsidiaries or licensees. Some recent evidence suggests that this is more likely in process technologies than in product technologies. In half the cases studied, there was no impact, but in one fourth of the cases it was held that transfer hastened access of other firms to the technology by 3 years (Mansfield and Romeo, 1979).

There is no evidence that the technological lead of an exporting country in any industry has been lost as a result of the technology-transfer activities of its firms. On the contrary, there is some evidence that technology transfer provided additional revenues, and otherwise stimulated R&D. Mansfield and Romeo (1979) noted the "age" of technology transferred—the number of years between transfer overseas and its initial introduction in the United States. Average age (over 27 cases) for transfer to controlled subsidiaries in developed countries was 5.8 years. Average age (over 12 cases) for transfer to controlled subsidiaries in developing countries was 9.8 years. Average age (over 26 cases) for transfer to licensees or joint ventures was 13.1 years.

DEVELOPING-COUNTRY CONCERNS OVER TECHNOLOGY TRANSFER.   "While technology is critical to industrialisation, the specific part it has come to play is that of an instrument of power in the industrial system. Technology is in no sense a neutral entity. . . . On the contrary, it embodies the objectives of one or the other economic entity, and its use has the potential to exclude or curtail the interests of others. Transnational corporations as the major global diffusors (if not the creators) of technology have centralised power to apportion global technology stocks over geopolitical spaces and to direct the flows of future global technological innovation" (UNIDO, 1979).

However, by virtue of their own limitations, in managerial bias and in organizational imperatives that necessitate metropolitan structures, transnational corporations are widely seen as unsuitable agents for bringing about global welfare. In fact, transnational corporations are often seen as accentuating inequalities between countries, and even within a host country, by empowering favored economic groups with the power of technology.

From the perspective of developing countries, technology transfer from transnational corporations has three basic problems:

1. The market for technology is imperfect, thus favouring transnational corporations in negotiations. Three sources of imperfection in technology markets are commonly identified:

   a. Legal protection for patents and trademarks, which has been too often extended beyond justification because of the inability of developing countries to protect their own interests.

   b. Lack of information on alternative sources among developing-country buyers.

   c. Incompetence among developing-country decision makers in making proper choices and negotiating thereafter. Restrictive and unfavorable conditions on the transfer were too often accepted.

2. The products and processes of transnational corporations are often socially inappropriate for developing countries, although they may benefit both elite consumers and producers in these societies. Purchase of inappropriate technology may be due to the absence of appropriate technology anywhere in the world or the buyer's lack of knowledge of the source of appropriate technology.

3. The cost of technology can be very high for a developing country, both directly and indirectly. Developing-country markets are often small and cannot amortize the initial costs of technology, as a large market can. This is of little concern to the seller. Further, the seller's superior bargaining position leads to very expensive terms and conditions. Direct foreign investment, in particular, can prove very expensive because it imposes a continuing drain and provides scope for rigging transfer prices.

   U.N. agencies now attempt to fill the knowledge gap on sources of technology and to train developing-country decision markers. Discussions toward international codes of conduct for transnational corporations, and on technology transfer, have made little practical progress over the last decade. Opposition from transnational corporations, the vast diversity in the status (and therefore viewpoint) among developing countries, and the fact that "there is no institutional machinery for implementing whatever type of code might be adopted" have even led to serious doubts on the value of a code. However, "the strongest argument which is in favour of this activity is precisely that it has educated developing country officials. . . . This educational impact may manifest itself in the creation of national laws and institutions concerned with technology acquisition" (UNIDO, 1979).

WESTERN AND JAPANESE TECHNOLOGY IN DEVELOPING COUNTRIES. Technology transfer from the United States and Europe has traditionally been determined by consideration of the market in the host country. When the market was unattractively small, little transfer occurred. In many cases, although the market by itself could not economically support the scale or capital intensiveness of the technology, protection from imports was generally available in developing countries; resulting higher costs—due to underutilization of plant—were borne by consumers in the local market. Only when the market was large did modification of the technology occur, either in product or process design. Profits were earned either on the strength of technological monopolies or marketing/capital barriers to entry. This has led to growing criticism from perceptive observers of Western technology transfers.

Technology transfer from Japan has often been noticeably different. It has been argued that Japanese direct foreign investment is characterized by "large spillover effects in the host country and [this] makes the new industries competitive in the international market. In short, the most suitable manufacturing industry for developing countries is traditional industry which is labor intensive, well-standardised and price competitive. This is the kind of industry which Japanese direct investment has transplanted" (Kojima, 1977).

Although the same global market conditions are faced by Western and Japanese firms, the strategies, and therefore responses, are different. First, Japanese firms are more oriented to exporting and the global market. As superexporters, they can produce more than the limited demand of the local market and export the surplus. Second, Japanese firms are very efficient at product design and manufacturing technology and have used these as competitive weapons. This fact has been widely recognized in the West only recently; earlier views attributed low Japanese export prices to low wages and government support. Although these factors are relevant, production management gets more attention in Japan than in probably any other country. For example, it has been noted that in a Japanese subsidiary, the production manager is often the last Japanese expatriate. By contrast, Western firms tend to make the finance manager the last expatriate. Third, Japanese overseas investment is characterized by a large percentage of small firms. Small firms from the West do not invest or license technology as frequently. In particular, the smaller Japanese firms have projects, products, processes, and technologies that are more in line with a developing-country environment. Small firms in the West are frequently either too modern in their products or insufficiently oriented to the global market. Fourth, Japan's national policy has been to relocate (export) its labor-intensive industry and use overseas sources of labor to meet global market needs. These factors give Japanese technology transfers a different profile of being more appropriate and successful, although the Japanese may not have made any conscious effort to modify or adapt their technology for the project.

However such projects in traditional industries are only part of the requirements of developing countries. Any technology transfer occurring from "Japanese" manufacturing activity is probably complementary to that which may occur from characteristically "Western" projects.

COSTS OF TECHNOLOGY TRANSFER. The cost of technology transfer depends upon the method used, the competence of both the parties involved, and experience with respect to the specific technology being transferred. David Teece (1977) found that transfer costs ranged from 2.25 percent to 59 percent of total project costs, with a mean of 19.16 percent. These costs must be shared in some fashion by transferor and transferee.

Clearly the more the transferee knows, and the greater the effort and risk of satisfactory performance that the transferee is willing to undertake, the less is the likely payment demanded by the transferor. At the extreme, large transnational corporations simply swap patent rights or know-how without monetary transactions. Transferees in developing countries should be careful in choosing a position between the two ends of a spectrum of possibilities:

Total reliance on the transferor, including engineering and involving developed-country wage rates and overhead, for tasks that may be cheaper (and possibly more appropriate) when done locally.

versus

The costs due to delays and initial problems arising out of "self reliance." In large projects, a delay of even one or two years can mean a substantial permanent drop in the expected rate of return on investment, calculated on a discounted cash-flow basis. This may eventually cost more than the payments to the transferor if this involvement saves time.

RESEARCH-AND-DEVELOPMENT MANAGEMENT

TYPES OF STUDIES ON R&D MANAGEMENT.   Studies on research and development during the last two decades can be broadly divided into three groups. One group focused on the economic analysis of innovation and diffusion of technology (including industrywide studies) attempting to find guidelines for public-policy and corporate-risk management. Another group focused on application of operations-research (management science) techniques for project selection. The inherent uncertainty of information about R&D severely limits the use of such models, however, and this approach has been losing momentum. The third group adopted a microapproach to study individual cases of technological innovation and transfer. The attempt has been to identify causes of success and failure and thus arrive at guidelines for management.

RISKS, COSTS, AND TIME IN TECHNOLOGICAL INNOVATION.   The basic risks are the following:

1. Technical difficulties may become insuperable, or very expensive to overcome.
2. Production costs may be higher than estimated, making market-demand estimates irrelevant.
3. Market analysis, or time of entry, may be inappropriate.
4. Competition may preempt the firm by faster and/or superior entry.

Risk, cost, and time are interrelated. If costs of development and production are higher than original estimates, the price of the product may be too high for the market to bear. The time of introduction of a new product or process has marketing implications in competitive situations. Attempts to cut time of development may lead to disproportionately high increases in the cost of development.

TIME AND COST OVERRUNS.   Apart from the additional demand on company finances, time and cost overruns have an even more dangerous consequence. Markets are defined at given prices—if the end price is much higher than the originally anticipated price, the market may become severely restricted. As a rule of thumb, based on averages of research findings, actual costs and time tend to be around twice the original estimates (Mansfield, 1971). The more ambitious the project, the greater the overrun. Several reasons for these "unanticipated" overruns have been noted by observers:

1. Some degree of optimism is a necessary condition for the motivation to sponsor an R&D project. Like the typical entrepreneur, the technologist may be temperamentally biased in the direction of hope. Consequently, more of the unexpected developments tend to be "bad" rather than "good."
2. Management may not appreciate other costs involved in the innovation. Several studies have found that the research element costs only around 10 to 15 percent of the total cost of bringing a product to market. Engineering, tooling, start-up, and launch costs account for the balance. The people who can estimate these costs should therefore be closely involved before the project is well under way.
3. There may be deliberate underestimation to increase the chances of the project's being approved by management.
4. General management also sometimes causes bias. Technologists may be told that their estimates are "too high." Contingency allowances and desirable features may initially be trimmed; these will later become essential.

Two methods are often suggested to tackle the cost-escalation problem:

1. Management asks: How high could the total cost conceivably become? What then are the implications for the firm and the project? What is the risk of throwing good money after bad, once the project is under way?
2. Management adjusts the estimate of the sponsor to arrive at a more-accurate measure of real costs for purposes of decision making.

GUIDELINES FOR R&D MANAGEMENT.   A persistent theme in the literature on R&D management has been the recognition that although it is a difficult and uncertain area, R&D management cannot be delegated to technical specialists. The time spans required for significant innovations are very long, requiring decision making far too early, in the absence of as many facts as managers would like. In addition, there are inherent risks in R&D. Many managers reportedly feel "uncomfortable" in dealing with technology for these reasons, and naturally tend to avoid facing such a difficult and unprogrammed task. Surveys have indicated that some managers seem to rely on the hope that current technology leadership will be automatically maintained and think that guidance through budgetary control is adequate involvement.

Useful guidelines for R&D management have emerged from extensive research over the last two decades. This research began with concern over the "technology gap" of other OECD countries behind the United States and has subsequently been propelled by the realization that technology is playing a critical role in the prosperity of firms and countries. Some of these guidelines are summarized as follows:

1. Efficient R&D is not a stop-go operation, and this should be borne in mind both when expending R&D budgets and when considering cutbacks. There is also a minimum critical size for a project team.

2. Technical success does not guarantee the success of the project. In fact, it has repeatedly been noted that "a great deal of the risk stems from potential difficulties faced by a new product or process in the marketplace, not from purely technical uncertainties" (Mansfield, 1971). Successful innovations thus require close coordination between marketing and R&D from early stages in the project until introduction in the market.

3. At the basic conceptual level, it has been established that it is useful to see innovation as being bounded by the current states of technical knowledge on one side, and societal and environmental conditions on the other. Simultaneous recognition of both technical feasibility and market need is the key to profits.

4. Top management must understand enough about technology to relate technical, marketing, and entrepreneurial dimensions and thereby develop and implement a conscious technological strategy. Performance characteristics of products, the inputs demanded, limitations of processes, cost, and efficiency implications are also essential parts of the knowledge required. The long-term competitive strength of the process may in certain cases be increased by being flexible and in other cases by being highly specialized (dedicated).

5. Key technological decisions involve considerable risk and involve judgments that should balance long-term and short-term gains; it is thus necessary for top management to make these decisions on a continuing basis during the planning and implementation stages of a project, rather than wait for crises to develop before intervening.

6. Management must be alert to resistance to technological changes within the organization and must support those involved in managing change.

7. Entrepreneurial and managerial skills must both be recognized and encouraged. Taking risks should not prove fatal to the careers of competent people, and separate career ladders should be designed for technical expertise and managerial skill. Some companies have been found not to take the trouble of even a quick examination of all ideas originating in their own research laboratories.

8. Perhaps the most important factor to be recognized is the need for communication. Specialized communication with the external scientific community is obviously important. What is noteworthy is that attention to ensuring adequate communication among the firm's own R&D group has been found to be important. In fact, internal communication flows have been studied over a long period to facilitate such flow, and to detect important contributors—"technological gatekeepers"—defined as those who are most frequently consulted by their peers (Allen, 1977). It has been noted that firms with a high degree of success had even designed the floor space in their laboratories to encourage internal communication, because "the distance people will walk to talk to a colleague is very small."

9. It is of interest to note the factors that did not appear to be significant in explaining success or failure of research projects. Among these were organization structure of R&D teams, techniques of project evaluation, incentives, use of management by objectives, representation of technical personnel on corporate boards, or tight controls on projects (Freeman, 1974).

10. Although tight controls were not a significant factor, it has been noted that management attention is necessary, particularly at the beginning and end of a project. Key decisions must be made at early stages. Toward the end of a project, management involvement seems to be useful in avoiding unnecessary delays in implementation. Left to themselves, project teams may recommend continuing development work that should be done outside the scope of the R&D project.

11. Related to the above findings is the often-noticed existence of a project champion—an executive with adequate authority and commitment to the project to see it through to completion. R&D management in a large corporation must establish priorities among the many opportunities that are available to a multiproduct multimarket firm. At the same time, available financial, technical, and managerial resources must be allocated between short-term improvements and long-term developments.

12. James Quinn (1979) has compared the circumstances under which individuals have innovated and those under which corporate R&D has to work. The table below is based on Quinn's observations and those of others.

For every successful individual innovation that achieves publicity, there are an uncounted number of failures; it is thus not possible to compare success rates of the two environments. However, the comparison does indicate the direction in which an R&D culture should be structured. R&D cannot be managed by a hands-off approach or by a budgetary-control approach, but needs a unique managerial type.

OVERSEAS R&D BY TRANSNATIONAL CORPORATIONS.   The traditional motive for overseas R&D by transnational corporations has probably been that adaptation is frequently necessary to earn the maximum return from a foreign market. To the extent that local manufacturing creates both the need and opportunity for such adaptation, it is reasonable to expect overseas R&D to be related more closely to the sales from foreign subsidiaries than to the exports of a transnational corporation. Empirical support for this view has been discovered (Mansfield, Teece, and Romeo,

Individual Innovation Environment	Corporate Innovation Environment
Fanaticism/commitment	Cannot normally employ fanatics
Chaos acceptance	Demand for others
Low early costs	High overhead
No detailed controls	Financial controls may be stringent
Incentives/risks	Risk of failure high to career-minded personnel
Long time horizons accepted	Pressure for quicker returns
Absence of "not invented here" complex	Interpersonal organizational problems
Varied sources of finance	Absence of venture-capital attitude

1979). The following table shows some trends, although the data have minor gaps in each period.

During the 1960s, overseas R&D, as a percentage of total R&D of U.S. transnational corporations, was around 4.4 percent. During the 1970s this rose to about 7.2 percent. However, 82.5 percent of this overseas R&D in 1975 was concentrated in six EEC countries (Germany, 29.9 percent; United Kingdom, 18.8 percent) and Canada (13.1 percent). If Brazil (2.9) percent is separated, all the other developing countries accounted for only 3 to 4 percent (UNIDO, 1979).

INCREASING R&D OVERSEAS.   It has been noted that R&D done by U.S. manufacturing firms overseas, as a percentage of their total R&D budget, may be increasing. Richard Robinson (1978) points out that several factors may push firms in this direction. Among these are the following:

1. Cost advantage of doing R&D outside the United States.
2. U.S. government regulations that pose difficulties for introducing new products (e.g., pharmaceuticals).
3. Host-government pressure and incentives for local R&D.
4. Reluctance of less-developed-country governments to allow subsidiaries to pay the parent for technology.
5. Tax advantages in owning patents through a subsidiary in a low-tax country, because taxes on income from the patent can then be deferred.

R&D IN DEVELOPING COUNTRIES.   Developing countries are recognizing that continuing technological dependency can be reduced only by acquiring capability for technology development. This has led to many policies; of these, two are relevant to transnational corporations. First, licensees are encouraged to establish R&D programs to make maximum use of the license agreement. Second, transnational corporations are asked to set up R&D laboratories. It may be noted that the Soviet Union reportedly insists on establishment of R&D facilities with every license it buys.

Transnational-corporation controlled R&D centers can pose problems for less developed countries. One fear is that these centers may absorb local talent and then not utilize it, the loss being that such talent has been diverted from, possibly, more-productive tasks. However, given the record of inefficiency of even the more-industrialized less developed countries on R&D management, this fear may not be of key importance.

Percentage of Company-Financed R&D Carried Out Overseas

	1960	1965	1970	1972	1974	1980
35-firm subsample						
Weighted mean	2	6	6	8	10	10
20-firm subsample						
Weighted mean	—	—	4	—	9	14

However, "the local establishment of R&D activities may not be very satisfactory if it is used as an antenna with which to monitor promising research being conducted by local enterprises, or if TNCs try to internalise all of the benefits of R&D rather than diffusing them through the local productive system. As always, the main consideration is the degree to which locally conducted TNC technological innovation is successful in creating stronger and more useful linkages with the domestic system" (UNIDO, 1979).

"The attraction of TNC R&D is relevant only to a few developing countries . . . which have relatively large internal markets, advanced industrial structures, good education systems . . . and some local technological capability. For these countries [such] R&D may offer benefits as long as it can be ensured that the results of innovation are . . . relevant to local needs and . . . wherever the product and process innovations are aimed at the international requirements of the TNC, the skills developed should nevertheless be usable (locally)" (UNIDO, 1979).

RELOCATION OF DEVELOPMENT AND ENGINEERING ACTIVITY. "Relocation" of D&E should be examined by transnational corporation management in the same framework in which decisions on location of R&D are made. It is now widely held that D&E activity should be located as close to the target market as possible. This is an essential feature of successful innovation and has been considered as one of the major reasons for the United States' lead in technology—being the world's largest market, U.S. firms have a natural advantage in innovation, even if the invention occurred elsewhere.

Although proximity to the market may be the dominant consideration for successful commercialization (innovation), other factors can be expected to be important when generation of technology is itself the product. In an age increasingly dominated by concerns over generation and transfer of technology, it is perhaps useful to examine afresh the economics of such activity.

Technology generation and development are activities characterized by two features:

1. They are skilled-labor intensive. One estimate is that 60 percent of R&D expenditure is on salaries of researchers and support personnel (*International Management*, 1979).
2. They are communications intensive. Communications among researchers, and between researchers and management (especially marketing), are critical for success.

Global communication has made enormous progress in the preceding two decades and may have relaxed the constraint of physical proximity required earlier for scientific communication. Yet all communication required for effective R&D is not reducible to data or voice communication, and inspiration may be influenced by interpersonal contact and ambience.

An important distinction may now be made between research, development, and engineering. Research output may be characterized by original concepts. Development is the task of investigating alternatives to implement the concepts to meet (or create) market needs. Engineering is the subsequent task of choosing and erecting a structure for production, which takes into consideration local relative factor costs, scale of production, and so forth. Engineering is more closely related to choice of technique than to research or development.

It is known that development and engineering account for a very large fraction of the total cost of an innovation, especially in the business context; fundamental research is usually funded by governments, even in developed countries. As an example, in the pharmaceutical industry, testing of a new drug is often the most expensive component of development.

It would appear that it is economical to locate such expensive development and engineering activity where the costs are the lowest, provided, as always, the necessary skills and infrastructure exist. The infrastructure for research itself may not be available in the same location and is not essential. Analogous to the search for offshore sources of supply for labor-intensive goods, searching for overseas locations for D&E may be necessary. And just as some transnational corporations saw the opportunity for offshore production before others, some transnational corporations have been "relocating" in the D&E area. The experiences of Corning, Union Carbide (in India), IBM, CPC International, and Otis have been studied by Robert Ronstadt (1977).

SOURCES AND SUGGESTED REFERENCES

Sources

Allen, T. *Managing the Flow of Technology*. Cambridge, MA: MIT Press, 1977.

Ansoff, I. and J. Stewart. "Strategies for a Technology Based Business," *Harvard Business Review*, Vols. XLV, No. 6 (1967), pp. 71–83.

Behrman, J. and H. Wallender. *Transfers of Manufacturing Technology Within Multinational Enterprises*. Cambridge, MA: Ballinger, 1976.

Childers, E. "Technical Cooperation Among Developing Countries," *Journal of International Affairs*, (1979), pp. 8–19.

Freeman, C. *The Economics of Innovation*. London: Penguin, 1974.

Hayes, R. and S. Wheelwright. "Link Manufacturing and Product Life Cycles," *Harvard Business Review*, Vol. LVII, No. 1, pp. 133–140.

International Management, Vol. XXXIV, No. 2, pp. 17–20.

Kantrow, A. "The Strategy—Technology Connection," Harvard Business Review, Vol. LVII, No. 4 (1980), pp. 6–21.

Kojima, K. *Direct Foreign Investment*. London: Croom Helm, 1978.

Lall, S. "Third World Technology Transfer and Third World Transnational Companies," in *International Flows of Technology*. Vienna, UNIDO IOD. 326, 1979.

Mansfield, E. *Research and Innovation in the Modern Corporation*. New York: Norton, 1971.

Mansfield, E. and A. Romeo. "Technology Transfer to Overseas Subsidiaries of US Firms," Research Paper, University of Pennsylvania, Philadelphia, 1979.

Mansfield, E., D. Teece, and A. Romeo. "Overseas R&D by US Based Firms," *Economica* Vol. XLVI, No. 182 (1979), pp. 187–196.

National Academy of Engineering. *Technology Transfer from Foreign Direct Investment in the United States*. Washington, DC: National Academy of Engineering, 1977.

Quinn, J. "Technological Innovation, Entrepreneurship and Strategy," *Sloan Management Review* Vol. XX, No. 3 (1979), pp. 19–30.

Robinson, R. *International Business Management*, 2nd ed. Hinsdale, IL: Dryden Press, 1978.

Ronstadt, R. Research and Development by U.S. Multinationals. New York: Praeger, 1977.

Stopford, J. and L. Wells. *Managing The Multinational Enterprise*. Boston: Basic Books, 1972.

Teece, D. *The Multinational Corporation and the Resource Cost of Technology Transfer.* Cambridge, MA: Ballinger, 1977.

Twiss, B. "A Practical General Management Approach to the Evaluation of New Technologies," *Journal of Management* Vol. II, No. 4 (1975), pp. 61–65.

Utterback, J. "Management of Technology," in A. C. Hax, ed. *Studies in Operations Management.* Amsterdam: North-Holland, 1978.

UNIDO. *International Flows of Technology.* Vienna, IOD. 326, 1979.

UNIDO. *Guidelines for Evaluation of Transfer of Technology Agreements.* Vienna, ID/233, 1980.

World Intellectual Property Organisation. *Licensing Guide for Developing Countries.* Geneva: WIPO, 1977.

Suggested References

Bright, J. and M. Schoeman. *A Guide to Practical Technological Forecasting.* Englewood Cliffs, NJ: Prentice-Hall, 1973.

Dean, B. *Evaluating, Selecting and Controlling R&D Projects.* American Management Association Research Study 89. New York, 1968.

Hawkins, R. and A. Prasad, ed. *Technology Transfer and Economic Development.* Greenwich, CT: JAI Press, 1982.

Hughes Aircraft Company. *R&D Productivity,* 2nd ed. Culver City, CA: Hughes Aircraft, 1978.

OECD Development Centre. *Transfer of Technology by Multinational Corporations,* two vol. Paris: OECD, 1977.

TRANSFER OF PROPRIETARY TECHNOLOGY TO DEVELOPING COUNTRIES

CONTENTS

TECHNOLOGY AND ECONOMIC GROWTH 3

PRODUCTION AND CONCENTRATION OF TECHNOLOGY 3

MECHANISMS OF TRANSFER 5

COST OF ACQUISITION 8

APPROPRIATENESS OF TECHNOLOGY 9

POLICIES OF DEVELOPING COUNTRIES 11

INTERNATIONAL INTERVENTION 13

CONCLUSION 15

NOTES 15

SOURCES AND SUGGESTED REFERENCES 16

TRANSFER OF PROPRIETARY TECHNOLOGY TO DEVELOPING COUNTRIES

Walter A. Chudson

The title of this section fixes two boundaries to the discussion: It will be limited to that part of knowledge which is conveyed through commercial transactions, and to that part of such knowledge which is acquired by developing (relatively poor) countries. To focus on proprietary technology does not serve completely to define technology, but at least narrows the discussion to matters of direct concern to business enterprises (including state enterprises) as producers, sellers and buyers of technology, excluding governmental, educational, scientific, and charitable institutions that may transfer technology for a fee but not for a profit. Further, limiting the scope to developing countries implies that the relationship between such countries and the suppliers of technology has some features that call for special consideration.

No precise definition of technology is needed for present purposes. It may be useful, nevertheless, to think of two elements: production or engineering technology (*hardware*), and management, marketing, and financial skills (*software*).

TECHNOLOGY AND ECONOMIC GROWTH

The connection between technology and economic growth is both unquestioned and empirically demonstrable. Whether due to technology embodied in capital goods or consumer goods of higher value or disembodied in intellectual capability (human capital), a large part of the increase in the real output of nations can be attributed to innovation rather than to the growth of capital and labor as such.

Despite differing individual and national goals and life-styles, there is no difference of view over the disparity in technological endowment between the industrialized and the developing countries and the need to reduce this gap as a necessary, if not sufficient, condition for economic development.

PRODUCTION AND CONCENTRATION OF TECHNOLOGY

By definition, the production and stock of proprietary technology is concentrated in the industrialized world; conversely, the developing countries lack know-how and must narrow the gap either by importing technology or by indigenous technological development, or by a combination of both. Ensuing issues then become (1) production and supply of technology, (2) mechanisms of transfer, (3) cost of acquisition, (4) appropriateness of technology to the acquirer's requirements (by private or social criteria), (5) policies of developing countries for the acquisition and production of technology, and (6) international intervention in the process of international technology transfer.

The theory and practice of the production and supply of proprietary technology is indifferent between its national or international transfer. In either case, commercialization can take place only when an economic agent, say a transnational corporation, possesses technology with a degree of monopoly power. The bulk of this exclusivism and the corresponding market power result from private innovation (typically scientific activity and/or research and development) leading to unpatented know-how; but a substantial part results additionally from a legally conferred monopoly bestowed by national patent and trademark regimes.

The regime of patent protection in developing countries has come under criticism in recent years. Part of this criticism has been directed toward treaty obligations assumed by these countries under the International Convention for the Protection of Industrial Property, the so-called Paris Union of 1888, as amended.

It is contented that whatever the merits of the patent system as an incentive to invention, this is irrelevant to the concerns of developing countries, which are mainly to acquire—at the lowest possible cost—technology, not to generate it, which is largely beyond their reach.

It is, of course, open to any developing country (or any other country, for that matter: Italy, for example) not to adhere to a patent regime, fully or to a limited extent. Few if any reciprocal rights would be lost. However, what most developing countries seek is not abolition of the system but a more or less radical reform of its monopolistic attributes; in other words, they seek a reduction of the economic rents they must pay to licensors under the existing system.

One complaint is that the bulk of patents granted by developing countries is held by nonresidents, and most are not worked but are used under the existing rules of the game to block imports by firms competing with the patentee firm. The system automatically restricts exports to other countries where a corresponding patent applies, and cross-licensing of patents carves out protected markets, inhibiting exports. When commercial production does prove feasible, the remedy of compulsory working of a patent is slow and inefficient, supporting the argument that patents have tended to discourage, rather than encourage, foreign investment, though lack of evidence leaves that point moot.

These points refer to the patent system as such, the awarding of a legal monopoly. Of greater contention is the terms on which industrial property—patented or unpatented—is licensed. Discussion of this issue is reserved for a later section on the cost of acquiring technology. Here it is relevant to note certain developments in the patent field proper.

One recent development is reform of the international patent system itself. For example, the duration of patents in developing countries has gradually dropped to 11 years while remaining 17 years in most developed countries. In lieu of the traditional long-term patent, a so called *utility model* (under which patents are easier to obtain but have a duration of only 3–6 years) has been introduced in some countries, including industrial ones. Certain products considered of high social value, particularly pharmaceuticals and processed foods, have been excluded from patentability, though the effect of such a policy on innovation if adopted universally is not clear since it appears that in the pharmaceutical industry patentability appears to promote innovation.

For one thing, the bulk of technology desired by developing countries is unpatented know-how (including some expired patents) or, if patented, cannot be effectively transferred without detailed unpatented information on processes and techniques as well as managerial software. Further, even in the absence of patents, other sources of market power over technology limit its potential importation.

Legal recognition of trademarks is another device by which a government confers market power on an enterprise. The cost/benefit balance of a trademark regime concerns many developing countries. Its benefits may be a guarantee of quality and a stimulus to investment, mainly in the production of consumer goods. The negative side concerns the economic rents extracted (with the support of heavy advertising) and the discouragement of potential local competition. Developing countries appear reluctant to abolish the trademark system if for no other reason that the recognition of its usefulness for indigenous firms. However, some limited movement toward the use of generic names for pharmaceuticals has occurred. There has also been a limited requirement for the use of joint trademarks designed to facilitate an ultimate shift to local marks, it is hoped without loss of marketability.

Basic to the pricing of technology (discussed below) is the question: What is the real cost of producing technology? Welfare economists have observed for some time that the production of knowledge differs in important respects from, say, the production of shoes. As stated by Harry G. Johnson (1970):

> . . . the creation or development of new productive knowledge requires an investment
> of resources which must be compensated if there is to be an incentive for private investment
> in knowledge creation, but . . . once new knowledge has been created it has the character
> of a public good, in the sense that the use of such knowledge by one person does not
> preclude its use by another, so that optimality requires that it be made available to all
> potential users without charge.

The fact that much of the technology sought by developing countries has been developed for use in other markets—mainly in developed countries—reinforces this distinction between the average and marginal cost of production. It is not denied by welfare theorists that marginal costs are incurred in the *delivery* of technology. At issue is the balance between stimulating an optimum production and delivery of proprietary technology and the appropriation of the economic rents accruing from the possession of know-how.

MECHANISMS OF TRANSFER

The predominant mechanism for the international transfer of proprietary technology continues to be the transnational corporation. Over 80 percent of royalties and similar fees received by the United States in recent years has consisted of payments by majority-owned affiliates of U.S. corporations.[1]

In addition to wholly owned direct investments, the mechanisms of transfer include the following:

Joint ventures
    Majority foreign equity.
    Minority foreign equity.
    Equal foreign and local equity.
Contractual agreements
    Licenses.
    Franchises.
    Management contracts.
    Technical-assistance contracts (sometimes combined with production-sharing contracts).
    Subcontracting contracts.
    Engineering and consulting contracts.
    Construction and start-up of "turnkey" plants.[2]

The supplier of technology through contractual means—ranging from fractional-equity participation to pure arm's length arrangements—may or may not be a transnational corporation, and combinations of mechanisms may be used, particularly licensing and/or management contracts in joint ventures. The list excludes certain contractual arrangements that have become more common in natural-resource projects, primarily for the purpose of allocating profits and control (and for political reasons) rather than as alternatives for the transfer of technology. It should not be overlooked, however, that arrangements aimed at control may also influence the transfer of technology and vice versa.

Analysis of the alternative delivery mechanisms for technology can best be viewed as part of the issue of the emerging relationship between transnational corporations (and other foreign business participants) and host countries. Broadly, the object of host countries (not exclusively developing countries) has been (1) to regulate the entry (or exit!) and operation of foreign participants so as to promote the perceived national economic, social, and political objectives, and (2) to extract the maximum economic rents consistent with the first objective. It is generally appreciated that there may be a trade-off between these objectives. (See United Nations, *Transnational Corporation,* 1978.)

A key word in this process, with special implications for the transfer of technology, is *unpackaging* (or sometimes *unbundling*). This is identified with the belief that the acquisition separately of the constituent elements of the transnational corporations full package of capital, technology, management, global marketing, and other facilities—and particularly the technology component, sometimes labeled the transnational corporation's trump card—will loosen the transnational corporation's grip, promote various development goals, and strengthen the bargaining position of the host country. (Stopford and Wells, 1972.)

Much attention has been given to the benefits and costs to host countries (and also to transnational corporations) of the various forms of unpackaging and to the attitude and behavior of transnational corporations, when faced with these various options—or in some instances, demands. The analysis starts with the proposition that transnational corporations prefer to internalize as much of their activity as possible in order to extract the maximum return from the market power conferred by their technology (both hardware and software). Not all of the technology, particularly the managerial software, can be transferred by licensing or other contractual arrangements; hence transnational corporations tend to prefer direct foreign investment.[3] For their own reasons, host countries increasingly prefer some degree of unpackaging. The outcome of this incompatibility can be expected to be reflected in the price, quality, and quantity of technology transferred, and also in the externalities experienced by the host country.

One thread in the ongoing debate over unpackaging is the Japanese experience, with its discouragement, indeed blocking, of direct investment until recently, and its heavy reliance on arm's length licensing of technology. The disparity between Japan's absorptive capacity and infrastructure and that of even the more-advanced developing countries has not gone unnoticed. Furthermore, the size of the Japanese market appears to support an Adam Smithian paraphrase that the capacity to absorb and attract technology through contractual or noncontractual means depends on the size of the market. Still another facet is the greater emphasis of Japanese negotiators on the duration rather than on the rate of royalty, suggesting a high priority on catching up.

Another thread of the unpackaging question emanates from is the so-called product-life-cycle hypothesis, which offers an explanation of the international diffusion of technology and an accompanying shift from direct investment to licensing. With due regard to its complexities and revisions, the central element of the life-cycle theory is that production of a new product passes through several stages, as a consequence of which the transnational corporation's choice shifts from exporting to production by a foreign subsidiary and finally to licensing of indigenous firms, which may then complete the cycle by exporting to the originating country. In the last two stages, locational factors in the host country preponderate; appropriation of technology rents by the transnational corporation is eroded by standardization and diffusion of knowledge, and the process may end with imports into the innovating country. Several qualifications to this model have been proposed, based essentially on the more-protracted retention of monopoly power by the transnational corporation than originally implied by the "leapfrogging" effect of vertically integrated international production, subcontracting, and so forth, under a global policy of transnational corporation and the reinforcing industrial policies of developing host countries. At any rate, the life-cycle hypothesis remains of interest in understanding the forces allowing feasible unpackaging.

Still another thread is the increased competition resulting from the growing number of sources of technology, including even some newly industrialized countries. This is the technological parallel of the so-called follow the leader syndrome in direct investment; threatened erosion of appropriability of economic rents serves to *encourager les autres* to accept unpackaged arrangements. This is reinforced by diffusion of information and more sophistication in acquisition of technology by would-be licensees.

Despite these considerations, the data do not show a radical shift toward unpackaged arrangements in recent years, except perhaps through joint ventures. Over the past 15 years, licensing receipts of U.S. firms from nonaffiliated licensees have grown more slowly than licensing receipts and dividends from majority-owned affiliates. In 1978 royalties and fees from unaffiliated licensees abroad were $1.1 billion compared with $4.4 billion from affiliates.[4]

Qualitatively "there have been significant changes in recent years in the form and content of contractual arrangements between host governments and transnational corporations, notably in the natural resources sector. (United Nations, *Transnational Corporation,* 1978.) Among the technological aspects associated with such changes have been an increased degree of local processing, improved design of products for export, creation of backward linkages in the host country, and increased local research and development.

In evaluating this experience, however, caution is indicated in attributing the changes to the mechanism. Earlier tendencies to regard joint ventures as a panacea have given way to more hardheaded appraisals. Joint ventures with passive local partners are open to exploitation and control by the foreign partner and may not provide much of a training ground for "infant entrepreneurs." They appear to be most successful for the host country when they offer specialized marketing and managerial skills specially suited to local conditions.

With imported technology, as with the entire foreign investment package, the "frontier of optimality" at which local inputs (management, technology, capital) can be efficiently substituted for foreign inputs is dynamic. The object of host-country policies, discussed in the remainder of this chapter, is, or should be, to foster a continuing process of substitution of imported by domestic technology, or even parts of domestic technology, along with the other inputs. As with the application of an infant-industry policy in general, the pace of the process can be overdone, or the reverse; host governments face a process of trial and error in the task of building up a domestic infrastructure to develop and, perhaps more important, to diffuse internally available technology. The particular constellation of foreign and domestic inputs and the mutually acceptable contractual form will vary from industry to industry and probably from firm to firm.

COST OF ACQUISITION

To analyze the cost of acquiring technology, it is necessary to distinguish between intrafirm and "arm's length" acquisition. In the former case we are dealing with the price of internalized transactions that are determined by managerial decisions, in the latter with more or less arm's length transactions between more or less unrelated parties.[5]

The terms and conditions for acquiring technology consist of two parts: (1) the financial payment (royalty, lump sum, or possible payment in kind under coproduction or similar relationship) and (2) explicit stipulations regarding its use. The most-important nonfinancial stipulations are various restrictive business practices imposed on the licensee, tied purchases of equipment and other inputs, restrictions on exports with respect to territory, quantity and price, exclusive dealing, exclusive sales or representation agreements, restriction on research and adaptation, preventing licensee from using competitive technology or from manufacturing or selling competitive products based on different technology, requiring the licensee to participate in a patent pool or cross-licensing or other collusive arrangements. Representatives of developing countries often point out that most such practices are illegal prima facie under the antimonopoly legislation of many industrial countries.

Here we focus on the financial aspects of contractual arrangements; the nonfinancial costs represented by restrictive business practices are discussed below in connection with host-country policies and a proposed international code of conduct. This separation should not, however, obscure the interconnection and possible trade-off between the two.

Regardless of whether the transfer is internalized or not, the price of technology over the long run is bound to reflect the special conditions of the production of knowledge previously referred to. The marginal cost of production is zero, and the cost of delivery is variable but generally small in relation to its contribution to production. But the initial cost of production (average cost) must be met fully under private-market conditions. In the absence of a subsidy, the cost must be met by payments to the producers (or owners) of know-how; and the producers must anticipate, at a minimum, sufficient proprietary control to enable them to appropriate the profits required to stimulate innovation. This reasoning applies to both patented and unpatented knowledge.

The establishment of the degree of monopoly thus sets the stage for determining the price of technology through a "bargaining model," with due allowance for internal and external transfers.

Charges by parent firms to their wholly owned or partly owned affiliates are internalized "transfer prices" and constitute one part of the return on the whole package of inputs supplied by the parent firm. The private costs of production and delivery of technology must be met, but the actual price charged to the affiliate for know-how can be fixed for a variety of reasons designed to shift profits out of (or possibly into) the host country, as long as the total return on the inputs and risk is attractive to the supplier.

For this reason and because of the notion that technology is practically costless to the supplier (i.e., has already been paid for by other users), a number of developing countries, particularly in Latin America, have adopted responsive fiscal policies. These consist of imposing a withholding tax on intrafirm royalty payments, sometimes at a rate approaching the rate on corporate profits. Alternatively, some countries have adopted a harsher policy of entirely disallowing royalty payments as a cost of production, thus treating royalties like profits.

For interfirm transactions, however, a bargaining model applies.[6] The licensor and licensee each have ceiling and floor prices. The licensor's flow price reflects his estimate of the marginal cost of transfer and possibly an imputed part of these sunk costs or ongoing R&D outlays, which have to be met if he is going to maintain a certain level of technological activity. The licensor's ceiling price is his calculation of the optimum monopoly price based on a judgment of the perceived value of the technology to the licensee.

The licensee's ceiling price is based on his estimate of the net profit he will earn from acquiring the know-how, qualified by the possibility of obtaining it cheaper elsewhere—partly a function of information—or of replicating it himself, which is usually an academic question, except if the alternative exists of unbundling the technology package itself by producing some part of the technology indigenously.

The licensee's floor price is based on an estimate of the marginal cost of delivery incurred by the licensor, with perhaps a perception of the rents that might be earned by the licensor at various prices above that level. Although the final price is indeterminate, an important factor is the estimate by each party of the opportunity cost or benefit of alternative sources of supply (licensee) or uses of the technology (licensor).

APPROPRIATENESS OF TECHNOLOGY

Of all the aspects of technology transfer, the appropriateness of technology to the conditions and needs of developing countries has perhaps received the most attention, at least until recently. Much, but not all, of this concern has been focused on the alleged failure of foreign private suppliers of technology, notably transnational corporations, to produce and supply the "right" technology, including both processes and products, and the reasons therefor.

There has also been concern over the inadequacies of the developing countries' scientific and technological establishments in innovating appropriate technology and assisting local governments in exercising discrimination in fostering the importation of appropriate technology. Yet another tendency is to supplement private enterprise by international action to foster the development and choice of appropriate technology (data banks, the "intermediate technology" movements, etc.).

There are two basic aspects to the subject to appropriateness: (1) the microeconomic analysis of the choice of technology in the light of indigenous factor proportions (labor intensity and employment creation), and (2) the performance of foreign technology suppliers, in particular, transnational corporations, judged by the development criteria of host countries. These aspects overlap, but attention here is directed mainly to the latter.[7]

For present purposes, an appropriate technology can be defined as a relatively labor-intensive process that optimizes the use of the relatively abundant labor supply that is a feature of developing countries. The definition can be extended to include *products* that embody a high labor content compared with the "product mix" of the industrialized countries. These simple definitions conceal certain complexities: There are relatively capital-intensive production functions whose private *and* social efficiencies are absolutely superior to labor-intensive production functions at any socially valued ("shadow") price of labor. But the concern of developing countries is with the socially efficient utilization of relatively abundant labor in general.[8]

There are three broad issues of fact concerning the role of transnational corporations in regard to appropriate technology: (1) Are their technologies adaptable to labor-abundant conditions? (2) Is there in fact adaptation by transnational corporations to local conditions? (3) Do transnational corporations adapt more or less than indigenous firms?[9] Underlying these questions is the question: What factors in the host country or in the transnational corporation obstruct a socially optimal adaptation?

The evidence indicates that no radical adaptations in technology have occurred in transferring transnational corporations' operations to developing countries, although some labor-intensive procedures have been adopted, mainly in peripheral activities such as materials handling.[10] Also, the redesigning of plants to accommodate smaller markets has resulted in some increase in labor intensity. A final factor, which can hardly be considered technological, is the working of more shifts with a consequent higher ratio of labor to capital per unit of output.

On the comparative utilization of labor by local versus foreign firms, the evidence is unclear. There has been little comparison of matched pairs of firms in research, since in many developing countries there are few comparable manufacturing enterprises.

The reasons for suboptimal substitution of capital by labor, by foreign and local firms alike, are the subject of an extensive literature. Unless competitive pressures (for example, from imports) stimulate cost minimization, both domestic and transnational firms choose a more-capital-intensive technology than would be indicated by a private cost-minimization approach. (See Chudson and Wells, 1974.) Among the possible reasons are the following:

1. In developing countries, interest rates are subsidized and wage rates are maintained above the opportunity (social) cost of labor through government policies.

2. Overvalued exchange rates effectively subsidize imports of capital goods; excessive protection subsidizes local production of capital-intensive consumer goods.

3. The smallness of local markets and the lack of competition offer little additional profit from adaptation to labor-intensive processes.

4. Human capital in the form of skilled labor is relatively scarce, and mechanized processes are introduced to economize on this type of labor and to reduce supervisory and managerial costs. Management may be willing to forego profit maximization using labor-intensive processes in order to avoid problems associated with managing large numbers of unskilled workers.

5. A capital-intensive plant may allow the firm to respond more flexibly and quickly to unexpected fluctuations in demand, particularly when it is necessary dismiss workers.

The issue of the "product mix" tends to be identified with that of capital-labor substitution because the "consumerism" in many developing countries contains a bias toward products of relatively high technology that are produced by capital-intensive methods. This situation is largely the outcome of inequality in income distribution in developing countries. It is, of course, also affected by advertising and the emulation of consumption patterns of the "affluent society" of the industrialized countries.

The approach of developing countries to appropriate technology has reflected their concern with massive unemployment or underemployment. How much of a contribution to this problem can be made by adopting labor-intensive processes in manufacturing remains an open question. It is hardly to be expected that the growth of the industrial sector will absorb most of the increase in the labor force or the existing unemployed or underemployed, regardless of the technology employed. Perhaps this is less true of technological adaptations in the agricultural sector. There seems to be a diminishing interest in recent years by governments of developing countries and by analysts in the subject of appropriate technology.

POLICIES OF DEVELOPING COUNTRIES

The movement toward control by developing countries of the entry and operation of transnational corporations and other forms of foreign business participation is largely an outgrowth of two phenomena of the post-World War II period: first, the widespread penetration of the transnational corporation and the transformation of its industrial character, and second, the preoccupation of governments with economic development. The obvious political precondition was decolonization and attendant nationalism.

Already in the 1950s certain restrictive tendencies in host-government policies toward foreign investment were discerned. (See Chudson, 1954.) Action was focused on limiting foreign equity participation (particularly in certain sectors), exclusion from certain sectors, exchange control, technical aspects of taxation, and expropriation. Since then the main emphasis has been the integration of direct investment with development, limitation on foreign control, and a more-favorable sharing of economic rents. This has meant emphasis by host governments on "performance conditions" designed to attain specific objectives of economic and social development, and experimentation with new contractual forms of foreign participation.

Since the main channel of transmission of technology remains the wholly owned subsidiary or minority-owned joint venture of a transnational corporation, it is difficult to isolate a host-country's regulation of incoming technology from its policy toward direct investment as such. In a number of developing countries, the relevant policies are administered by the same or a closely linked agency. However, with the growth of industrialization, the regulation of incoming technology has become a matter of specific policy and administration.

In essence, this policy (with due allowance for varying rigidity and degrees of enforcement) can be said to contain a negative and a positive element.

The negative element consists largely of barring restrictive business practices that have been identified with the licensing of technology and trademarks. Inheriting their definition largely from antimonopoly concepts of industrialized countries, restrictive business practices in the international context have been defined in a recently adopted U.N. agreement as follows:

> Restrictive business practices means acts or behaviour of enterprises which, through the abuse or acquisition of a dominant position of market power, limit access to markets or otherwise unduly restrain competition, having or being likely to have adverse effects on international trade, particularly that of developing countries, and on the economic development of these countries, or which through formal, informal, written or unwritten agreements or arrangements among enterprises have the same impact.[11]

As discussed in the next section, a draft international code of conduct on the transfer of technology, prepared under the aegis of the United Nations Conference on Trade and Development (UNCTAD) and not yet adopted, contains a similar definition of restrictive business practices, but in that case supplemented by practices characteristic of licensing agreements.

The list of putative restrictive business practices identified with licensing is extensive: export restrictions, various tying arrangements, price fixing, exclusive dealing, restriction on the adaptation of technology by the licensee, restrictions on research, exclusive sales agreements, compulsory grant-back of technology developed by the licensee, payments after the expiration of industrial property rights, restrictions after the expiry of the license, and more.[12]

Such restrictions have been included in many technology contracts. What is unclear is how harmful they have been. Restrictions on exports carry little weight unless the country is in a position to export competitively. On the other hand, opposition by business groups to "blacklisting" such practices may likewise have a more ideological than practical implication. Furthermore, in the UNCTAD code on restrictive practices, at least, the internal arrangements between parent firm and affiliate are practically excluded from the list. All in all, it may be that the extraction from a licensor of positive commitments to perform certain functions with regard to training, local research and development, exports, and import substitution of required inputs (so-called backward linkages) may be more significant for development objectives.

In the last decade or so, an increasing number of developing countries have adopted formal "screening" procedures to regulate the terms and conditions of technology transfer, as well as of direct investment. As mentioned, this has been partly inspired by the model of the Japanese Ministry of Industry and Trade (MITI), with due allowance for the differing levels of economic and administrative development.

Broadly speaking the object of such machinery is (1) to reduce the cost of technology, both financial and nonfinancial, including the duration of licenses, (2) to enhance the appropriateness in its several aspects, and (3) to attract suitable technology, while promoting domestic substitution of imported technology. An important aspect of such machinery is the acquisition of information in order to bolster the bargaining capability of the screening agency and encourage competition among potential suppliers.

According to a recent survey, the following countries have introduced official control over technology transfer during the past decade or so (Janiszewski, 1981):

Latin and Central America. Argentina, Brazil, Peru, Colombia, Ecuador, Bolivia.

Africa. Algeria, Egypt, Libya, Tanzania.

Europe. Spain, Portugal, Turkey, Yugoslavia, Romania

Asia. Iraq, Pakistan, India, Malaysia, Philippines, Sri Lanka, People's Republic of China, Israel, Republic of Korea, Socialist Republic of Vietnam.

In other countries a certain amount of regulation is done in conjunction with the administration of foreign-investment laws.

Unfortunately, very little information is available by which to evaluate the performance of these regulatory agencies. In the case of two of the oldest, those in Colombia and Mexico, a large number of restrictive clauses were eliminated from many contracts. It is also reported that the royalty payments were reduced in a number of cases (Vaitsos, 1971). However, it should be acknowledged that such regulation does not affect, by and large, intrafirm technology transfers. Furthermore, the quality of regulation can be only as good as the information, selection criteria, and technical capability of the officials concerned.

It is important to recall that much of the technology required for industrial development in the majority of countries is available "off the shelf" in the open market. A considerable amount of it in fact often exists in one or more enterprises within the host country. Improving the institutional framework for the *internal* diffusion of technology is therefore a task just as urgent as regulating the transfer of technology.

INTERNATIONAL INTERVENTION[13]

All of the issues and policies discussed in this chapter, and more, have been debated in the United Nations and some of its agencies (UNCTAD, UNIDO and ILO) and, regarding the interests of developed countries, in the forum of the OECD.[14]

Under the aegis of UNCTAD, two international codes of conduct relevant to the transfer of technology have been in preparation since 1974. One, entitled *The Set of Multilaterally Agreed Equitable Principles and Rules for the Control of Restrictive Business Practices,* was approved by the U.N. General Assembly toward the end of 1980 (UNCTAD, *Conference on Restrictive Business Practices,* 1980). The other, entitled *Draft International Code of Conduct on the Transfer of Technology,* remains an unagreed-upon document, as the title implies, still peppered with proposed conflicting formulations, some of major importance (UNCTAD, *Conference on an International Code,* 1980).

What follows is an attempt to distill from hundreds of pages and seemingly endless hours of discussion the essence of the U.N. negotiations on the transfer of technology, their objects, their outcome, and their potential implications for the way in which technology is transferred to developing countries.

Bearing in mind the objectives of national regulation, it comes as no surprise that the objectives of the code are essentially the same: to reduce imperfection in the international market for technology and to strengthen the bargaining power of the developing countries.

What may be called the negative part of the proposed code is concerned with listing and defining restrictive business practices that may be associated with licensing, from which parties to technology-transfer transactions (shall) (should) refrain. The code on restrictive business practices per se is concerned with all forms of such practices, whereas the technology code deals only with practices peculiar to the licensing relationship.

Apart from the negative provisions for policing restrictive business practices, the thrust of the technology code is toward helping the developing countries to equalize their bargaining position and to legitimize—for what it is worth—the aspirations of developing countries to establish national policies of the type described in the preceding part of this Section. Formalized in the draft are provisions for international collaboration, including international machinery for consultation and review (the U.N. code word is *implementation*). Included are numerous statements, more or less explicit, committing the industrialized countries to collaboration and assistance (vaguely defined) in fostering technological development.

A major issue, at least in debate—as with all proposed U.N. codes of conduct—is the issue whether compliance with the code should be "binding" or voluntary. The developed countries have unqualifiedly resisted a binding code, even to the point of rejecting a review of the question at a specified future date. The legal and practical reasoning behind this position is outside the scope of the present discussion, but it would appear to be based on the interpretation that the existing structure, based on private contracts and national law, might be displaced by a form of higher international authority. Some legal theorists regard the issue between binding and nonbinding as less sharp than might be implied, given acceptance of the substantive principles. In any case the cutting edge of national regulation would be unaffected. Perhaps the underlying point is that a binding code would encourage and strengthen national regimes to do what they can do already in principle.

Another big issue, on which the code on restrictive business practices almost foundered, is whether relationships between parents and affiliates should be subject to the provisions outlawing restrictive business practices. The industrial countries reject the view that the parent and affiliate should or can be treated as independent entites on the grounds that they are subject to separate legal regimes. Their proposed formulation is as follows:

> Recognizing that restrictions for the purpose of rationalization and reasonable allocation of functions between parent and subsidiary or among enterprises belonging to the same concern will normally be considered not contrary to this chapter unless amounting to an abuse of a dominant position of market power within the relevant market, for example

unreasonable restraint of the trade of a competing enterprise (UNCTAD, *Draft International,* 1980).

Having obtained agreement to a similar formula in the code on restrictive business practices, the industrial countries want a parallel provision in the code on technology.

Another section of the code contains what amounts to a model contract for the transfer of technology. The potential sellers of technology resist such specification on the ground that it will restrict their freedom of negotiation and may, in fact, obstruct transfers that are in the interest of the purchasing country.

An important issue in this, as in other codes, is the machinery for implementation. Since information, analysis, and publication are major sanctions for this type of international accord, much depends on the procedures to be followed and on the quality of the data and analysis of both the secretariat and the governments.

CONCLUSION

In the economics of development, as in macroeconomics generally, everything depends on everything else. What has changed over the past several decades is the priority accorded to particular aspects of the development process. The early emphasis on capital shortage gave way to emphasis on import substitution, then terms of trade, regional integration, export expansion, structural distortions in resource allocation, the role of the transnational corporation and recently the acquisition and development of technology. The ventilation of the technology aspect during the last decade has served to define the issues, accumulate some facts, and clarify the policy options. It remains to be seen what effect it will have on the production and transfer of technology.

NOTES

[1]The data are equivocal in the sense that the charge for an internalized transfer of know-how is an internally determined "transfer price," whereas the rest constitutes arm's length transactions between unrelated parties. It is unlikely, however, that this misrepresents significantly the relative importance of intrafirm technology transfers.

[2]Frequently two or even more of these arrangements are combined in a single project.

[3]Root states: "Few industrial firms create technology to sell as technology. Rather technology is viewed as a source of new products that the firm itself will sell in the market." Root, 1981.

[4]Kroner, 1980. Reference kindly supplied by Prof. F.J. Contractor, Rutgers University from his forthcoming article, "International Technology Transfer," *Journal of International Business Studies* (1981) in collaboration with T. Sagafi-Nejad.

[5]"More or less" connotes a gradation of external control from the wholly owned subsidiary through the joint venture to the completely uncontrolled arm's length transaction between unrelated parties.

[6]For a general statement see Streeten, 1971, and Root, 1981. Of course such models cannot explain all the variations in contractual practice.

[7]On the microeconomic aspects, see the references attached to this chapter.

[8]Side effects of using excessively capital-intensive technology may include income equalities

(although the causality more likely runs the other way) and imitation of inappropriate technology by indigenous firms.

[9]This follows the analysis of Lall, 1978.

[10]This and the following paragraph are based largely on Lall, 1978.

[11]U.N. Conference on Restrictive Business Practices, *Principles and Rules,* 1980; subsequently approved by the U.N. General Assembly in 1980.

[12]There is no lack of evidence of the incorporation of such provisions in license agreements affecting developing countries (and no doubt others). See, for example, UNCTAD, 1975. The leading practices identified in a number of countries were tied imports; restrictions on exports, territorial and other; limitation on competing supplies; and discouragement of local research and development. It is, of course, not possible to measure the real cost of such restrictions from this information. Undoubtedly some of the restrictions govern potential actions, for example, exports, that the licensee would be incapable of taking for purely economic reasons.

[13]For a general survey of international codes of conduct see Section 28.

[14]Discussion of problems of technology transfer dates back to the earliest days of UNCTAD in 1964, and the first U.N. approach to an international code of conduct on the transfer of technology can be traced to the so-called Pugwash (Nova Scotia) conference of 1974, informally supported by UNCTAD.

SOURCES AND SUGGESTED REFERENCES

General

Baranson, J. *Technology for Underdeveloped Areas: An Annotated Bibliography.* New York: Pergamon Press, 1967.

Chudson, W.A. and L.T. Wells, Jr. *The Acquisition of Technology from Multinational Corporations by Developing Countries.* New York: United Nations Sales No. E.74.II.A.7, 1974.

Lall, S. *Private Foreign Manufacturing Investment and Multinational Corporations: An Annotated Bibliography.* New York: Praeger, 1975.

Sagafi-Nejad, T., and Belfield, R. eds. *Transnational Corporations, Technology Transfer and Development: A Bibliographic Sourcebook.* New York: Pergamon Press, 1980.

Sagafi-Nejad, T., R.W. Moxon, and H. Perlmutter, eds. *Controlling International Technology Transfer: Issues, Perspectives and Implications.* New York: Pergamon Press, 1981.

United Nations. *Transnational Corporations in World Development: A Reexamination.* New York: United Nations Sales No. E.78.II.A.3., 1978.

Vaitsos, C. *The Commercialization of Technology in the Andean Pact.* Washington, D. C.: Organization of American States, 1971.

Economic Growth

Denison, E. *The Sources of Economic Growth in the U.S. and the Alternatives Before Us.* Washington, DC: Brookings Institution, 1962.

Eckaus, R.S. "Technological Change in the Less Developed Areas," in *Development of the Emerging Countries: An Agenda for Research.* Washington, DC: Brookings Institution, 1962.

Sen, A.K. *Employment, Technology and Development.* Oxford: Clarendon Press, 1975.

Production of Technology

Chudson, W.A. *Foreign Capital in Latin America*. New York: United Nations Sales No. 1954, II G. 4., 1954.

Janiszewski, H. "Technology Importing–National Perspectives," in Sagafi-Nejad, T. et al., eds. *Technology Transfer*. New York: Plenum, in press.

Johnson, H.G. "The Efficiency and Welfare Implications of the International Corporation," in C. Kindleberger, ed. *International Corporations*. Cambridge, MA: MIT Press, 1970.

Machlup, F. *The Production and Distribution of Knowledge in the U.S.* Princeton: Princeton University Press, 1962.

Wells, Jr., L.T. ed. *The Product Life Cycle and International Trade*. Cambridge, MA: Harvard University Press, 1972.

Mechanisms of Transfer

Baranson, J. *Technology and the Multinationals*. Lexington, MA: Lexington Books, 1978.

Behrman, J. and H. Wallender. *Transfer of Manufacturing Technology within Multinational Enterprises*. Cambridge, MA: Ballinger, 1978.

Davies, H. "Technology Transfer Through Commercial Transactions," *Journal of Industrial Economics,* Vol XXXI (1977), pp. 34–62.

Dunning, J.H. "Alternative Channels and Modes of International Resource Transmission," in T. Sagafi-Nejad, R.W. Moxon, and H. Perlmutter, eds. *Controlling International Technology Transfer*. New York: Pergamon Press, in press.

Franko, L. *Joint Venture Survival in Multinational Corporations*. New York: Praeger, 1971.

Fund For Multinational Management Education. *Public Policy and Technology Transfer: Viewpoints of U.S. Business*, four vols. New York: FMME, 1978.

Lall, S. "The Patent System and the Transfer of Technology to Less-Developed Countries," *Journal of World Trade Law,* Vol. XXI (1976), pp. 19-26.

Patel, S. "Trademarks and the Third World," *World Development,* Vol. XIV (1979), pp. 324–360.

United Nations Conference on Trade and Development, *Major Issues Arising from the Transfer of Technology to Developing Countries*. Geneva: UNCTAD document TD/B/AC/ 1975.

Vaitsos, C.V. "Patents Revisited: Their Function in Developing Countries," *Journal of Development Studies,* No. 1 (1972).

Appropriateness of Technology

Agarwal, J.P. "Factor Proportions in Foreign and Domestic Firms in Indian Manufacturing," *Economic Journal,* Vol. XXI (1976), pp. 589–94.

Bhalla, A.S., ed. *Technology and Employment in Industry*. Geneva: ILO, 1975.

Goulet, D. *The Uncertain Promise: Value Conflicts in Technology Transfer*. New York: IDOC-North America, 1977.

Lall, S. "Transnationals, Domestic Enterprises and Industrial Structure in Host LDCs: A Survey," *Oxford Economic Papers,* Vol. XXX (1978), pp. 217–248.

Mason, H. "Some Observations on the Choice of Technology by Multinational Firms in Developing Countries," *Review of Economics and Statistics,* Vol. XX (1978), pp. 221–260.

Stewart, F. *Technology and Underdevelopment*. Boulder: Westview Press, 1977.

Cost of Acquisition

Aguilar, E. *Restrictive Business Practices*. Vienna: UNIDO, 1975.

Contractor, F. *International Technology Licensing: Compensation, Costs and Negotiations*. Lexington, MA: Lexington Books, in press.

Kroner, N. "U.S. International Transactions in Royalties and Fees," *Survey of Current Business*, January 1980.

Lall, S. "Transfer Pricing and Developing Countries: Some Problems of Investigation," *World Development*, Vol. XIV (1979), pp. 42–66.

Magee, S.P. "Information and the Multinational Corporation: An Appropriability Theory of Direct Foreign Investment," in J. Bhagwati, ed. *The New International Economic Order*. Cambridge, MA: MIT Press, 1977.

Root, F. "The Pricing of International Technology Transfers via Non-Affiliate Licensing Arrangements," in T. Sagafi-Nejad, R.W. Moxon, and H. Perlmutter, eds. *Controlling International Technology Transfer*. New York: Pergamon Press, 1981.

Timberg, S. "The Role of the International Patent Systems in the International Transfer and Control of Technology," in T. Sagafi-Nejad, R.W. Moxon, and H. Perlmutter, eds. *Controlling International Technology Transfer*. New York: Pergamon Press, 1981.

Policies of Host Countries

Balasubramanyan, V. *International Transfer of Technology to India*. New York: Praeger, 1973.

Beranek, W. *Science, Technology and Economic Development*. New York: Praeger, 1978.

Helleiner, G.F. "International Technology Issues: Southern Needs and Northern Responses," in *Mobilizing Technology for World Development*. Washington, DC: Overseas Development Council, 1979.

Mytelka, L. "Technological Dependence in the Andean Group," *World Development*, (1978), pp. 221–260.

Morawetz, D. "Employment Implications of Industrialization in Developing Countries," *Economic Journal*, Vol. XXX (1974), pp. 491–542.

Sauvant, K.P. ed. *The New International Economic Order*, Westview Press, 1977.

Streeten, P. "The Theory of Development Policy," in Dunning, J. ed. *Economic Analysis and the Multinational Enterprise*. London: Allen & Unwin, 1971.

UNIDO. *Guidelines for Evaluation of Transfer of Technology Agreements*. Vienna: UNIDO, 1979.

UNIDO. *National Approaches to the Acquisition of Technology*. Development and Transfer of Technology Series No. 1. Vienna: UNIDO, 1977.

Codes of Conduct

Fatouros, A.A. "International Controls of Technology Transfer," in T. Sagafi-Nejad, R.W. Moxon, and H. Perlmutter, eds. *Controlling International Technology Transfer*. New York: Pergamon Press, 1981.

Moxon, R. and T. Sagafi-Nejad. "Technology Transfer and the Transnational Enterprise: The Outlook for Regulation," *Journal of Contemporary Business*, (1977), pp. 46–70.

OECD. *Guidelines for the Multinational Enterprises*, revised version. Paris: OECD, 1979.

Sagafi-Nejad, T. and H. Perlmutter. *International Technology Transfer: Codes, Guidelines and a Muffled Quadrilogue*. New York: Pergamon Press, in press.

Stopford, J.M. and L.T. Wells, Jr. *Managing the Multinational Corporation*. New York: Basic Books, 1972.

United Nations Conference on Trade and Development. *Draft International Code of Conduct on the Transfer of Technology.* UNCTAD document TD/CODE/TOT/29, 2 June 1980.

United Nations Conference on Trade and Development. *The Set of Multilaterally Agreed Equitable Principles and Rules for the Control of Restrictive Business Practices.* UNCTAD document TD/RBP/CONF/10, 2 May 1980.

United Nations Conference on Trade and Development. *Conference on International Code of Conduct on the Transfer of Technology.* Geneva: UNCTAD document TD/CODE/TCT/25, 1980.

United Nations Conference on Trade and Development. *Conference on Restrictive Business Practices,* Geneva: UNCTAD document TD/RBF. CONF/10, 1980.

United Nations *Transnational Corporations: Code of Conduct: Formulations by the Chairman.* U.N. document E/C.10/AC.2/8, 13 December 1978.

OFFSHORE SOURCING, SUBCONTRACTING, AND MANUFACTURING

CONTENTS

SELECTING THE FORM OF OFFSHORE SOURCING   3

Alternatives   3
  Offshore purchasing   3
  Offshore subcontracting   4
  Joint-venture offshore manufacturing   4
  Controlled offshore manufacturing   4
Selection Criteria   4
  Company capabilities and resources   5
  Availability and capabilities of suppliers or partners   5
  Projected sourcing volume and variability   6
  Degree of integration of offshore and domestic operations   6
  Summary   6

EVALUATING PRODUCTS FOR OFFSHORE SOURCING   6

Main Cost Tradeoffs   6
  Labor   7
  Materials and components   7
  Factory overhead   7
  Corporate overhead   7
  Shipping and duties   7
Products Suitable for Offshore Sourcing   7
  Labor-intensive products   7
  Standardized products   8
  Products with a predictable sales pattern   8
  Products that are easy to ship and face low import duties   8
Trends in Product Selection for Offshore Sourcing   8

EVALUATING SOURCES AND PARTNERS   9

General Characteristics   9
Evaluating Independent Sources   9
Evaluating Partners   9
Negotiating with Prospective Sources and Partners   10

EVALUATING PRODUCTION SITES   10

Important Criteria   10
Labor Factors   11
  Labor costs   11
  Labor availability   11
  Labor productivity   11
  Labor reliability and unions   12
Infrastructure Factors   13
  Industrial sites   13
  Transportation and communication   13
  Local suppliers of goods and services   13
Government Policy Factors   13
  General attitudes   14
  Government regulations   14
  Government incentives   14
Stability Factors   15
  Economic instability   15
  Political instability   15
Sources of Information on Production Sites   16

U.S. CUSTOMS REGULATIONS   16

Normal Treatment of Imported Goods   16
Generalized System of Preferences   17
Quotas   17
Items 806.30 and 807.00   18

**LEGAL AND FINANCIAL
CONSIDERATIONS**   **18**

**ORGANIZATION AND
COORDINATION OF OFFSHORE
SOURCING**   **19**

Communications Problems and
Solutions   **19**

Causes of problems   19
Solutions to communication problems   19
Organization Links   **20**

**SOURCES AND SUGGESTED
REFERENCES**   **21**

OFFSHORE SOURCING, SUBCONTRACTING, AND MANUFACTURING

Richard W. Moxon

One of the fastest-growing international activities of U.S. companies in recent years has been the importation of products formerly manufactured in the United States. Although imports have always been important in some sectors, companies in more and more industries find offshore sources of components and finished products a means of increasing their profitability. As offshore sourcing has spread across industries, it has also spread to countries in Asia, South America, and other developing areas that were not traditionally viewed as exporters of manufactured products. Offshore sourcing is today an important part of business for retailers, wholesalers, and manufacturers in industries as different as apparel and electronics.

The motivations for offshore sourcing are usually to obtain lower-cost products. The degree of overseas involvement by the U.S. buyer varies widely. Some do no more than order products from a catalog, whereas others invest time and money in the establishment of their own offshore manufacturing subsidiaries. The main focus in this section is on sourcing in which the U.S. buyer has some substantial involvement abroad, either in subcontracting or in manufacturing. Furthermore, since developing countries have emerged as important sites for offshore sourcing and provide the most challenges for U.S. buyers, much of the discussion will focus on those countries. Finally, the discussion pertains only to manufactured products, not raw materials or agricultural goods.

SELECTING THE FORM OF OFFSHORE SOURCING

ALTERNATIVES. Although the specific forms of offshore sourcing arrangements vary widely, the basic distinction is the degree of control exercised by the U.S. buyer over the foreign source. Exhibit 1 diagrams the four major buyer–seller relationships.

Offshore Purchasing. This is a relationship between independent buyers and sellers in which goods are exchanged for money. The arrangement may vary in many ways, including whether the transactions are directly between the buyer and seller or through one or more agents in the U.S. or overseas, whether the buyer and seller

EXHIBIT 1   ALTERNATIVE OFFSHORE SOURCING RELATIONSHIPS

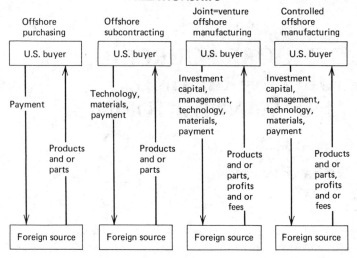

deal on a transaction-by-transaction basis or have some longer-term contract, and whether purchasing in undertaken by an individual enterprise or by a buying group. Choices among these variations are essentially not very different than they are for domestic transactions.

Offshore Subcontracting.   This term covers many different relationships between independent companies in which the buyer is more involved with the source than in a simple buyer–seller relationship. The buyer may provide detailed product specifications, technical assistance, raw materials, or needed components, or even some financing to the foreign manufacturer. Again, such relationships vary as to their duration, the degree of involvement by the U.S. buyer, and whether intermediaries such as agents are involved.

Joint-Venture Offshore Manufacturing.   This relationship involves the joint ownership by a U.S. and a foreign company of an offshore manufacturing enterprise. These arrangements vary by the extent of ownership of each partner, the extent of control exercised by each, what resources each partner contributes, and the specific type of legal entity involved.

Controlled Offshore Manufacturing.   This relationship is that of a parent and a wholly owned foreign operation, generally a subsidiary corporation, that supplies the parent's needs for a product. Such foreign plants vary in how closely they are tied to the rest of the parent's world operations, whether they also serve outside customers, and the legal and financial arrangements.

SELECTION CRITERIA.   A company's decision regarding the form of offshore sourcing it chooses is strongly influenced by what forms other companies in its industry have selected. The needs of different industries vary, and so do their offshore sourcing patterns. In the apparel industry, offshore sourcing is done mainly through purchasing or subcontracting, whereas in electronics there is much more controlled manufacturing. But the needs of all companies in an industry are not the same, and it is important for a firm to look closely at what it is trying to achieve with offshore sourcing, and which form is most appropriate for that objective. Four important considerations are (1) company capabilities and resources, (2) availability and capabilities of suppliers or partners, (3) projected sourcing volumes and variability, and (4) degree of integration of offshore sourcing with other operations.

Company Capabilities and Resources.   Different forms of offshore sourcing demand different abilities on the part of enterprises and vastly different commitments of resources. Simple offshore purchasing requires little experience or investment, whereas controlled offshore manufacturing requires a considerable commitment of investment capital and management time.

Investment capital requirements increase as a company chooses to have more control over its foreign sourcing. Even with minimal control as in subcontracting, there may be a need to help finance working capital for the supplier; controlled offshore manufacturing requires investment in fixed assets as well. In many developing countries, there are methods for reducing these capital requirements, whether through leased, instead of purchased, plants, low-cost development loans, or even outright capital grants from the government. Nevertheless, some investment capital will be required, and the investment will often be in a country regarded as politically and economically less stable than the United States. Companies with limited financial resources or hesitant about "risky" foreign investments will find purchasing or subcontracting more attractive than alternatives involving more control.

Often as crucial as capital requirements is the necessary investment of management time. Again, the establishment of an offshore manufacturing facility normally will require more attention from management than the other alternatives. The actual time investment needed, however, will depend on the type of operation and on the company's previous experience. Time is invested both in establishing an operation and then in operating it. Setting up a simple purchasing agreement normally will require little time, whereas establishing a wholly owned offshore manufacturing plant will require considerable management attention. The time needed to maintain a relationship will depend mainly on the complexity of the interactions between the two parties. If the U.S. company is transferring a lot of technology to the foreign source, or if it owns all or part of the foreign source, the time devoted to managing the relationship is greater. The amount of management time needed to establish and maintain offshore ventures depends also on the company's previous experience with sourcing in general, with the particular form of sourcing, and with the region and particular country with which it is dealing. An inexperienced company needs to budget considerable time for solving unexpected problems especially when setting up its own offshore plants.

Availability and Capabilities of Suppliers or Partners.   An important determinant of how a company sets up offshore sourcing is whether or not acceptable partners or suppliers exist in the countries in which the U.S. company wants to locate a source. Suppliers with the needed production experience, technology, and management capabilities can be hard to find, as can partners with investment capital and other important inputs. Whether acceptable suppliers and/or partners are available depends, of course, on the country, on the complexity of the production requirements, and on the size of the proposed operation. Small operations for relatively simple products may have a wide choice of suppliers or partners, whereas larger investments for more complex products will be more limited in this respect. This partly explains why more controlled offshore manufacturing exists in electronics than in the apparel industry.

Projected Sourcing Volume and Variability. The size and variability of a company's offshore sourcing requirements will be a major determinant of which form of offshore sourcing the company chooses. Companies needing large volumes of foreign products can often justify a large fixed investment, as the fixed costs can be spread over the high volume of output. For companies with smaller needs, an independent supplier will be more attractive. The variability of a company's requirements is also important. If the company establishes its own manufacturing plant, it will want to keep it running steadily to cover its fixed costs. If the business is variable, the company will be more likely to choose the purchasing or subcontracting alternatives. These alternatives are often chosen for fashion-type products, where sales are difficult to project.

Degree of Integration of Offshore and Domestic Operations. If a company wishes to integrate its offshore sources tightly within the company's operations, it will need considerable control over all sources. This will require controlled offshore manufacturing unless a very tight relationship with a foreign company can be established. A closely controlled offshore operation will facilitate coordinated production scheduling, ease transfer of technology, and provide flexibility in financial decisions regarding transfer pricing of components and finished products, dividend payments, and capital investments. Many companies that perform one stage (such as assembly) offshore in a multistage manufacturing process find that they must establish their own manufacturing facility in order to achieve sufficient coordination. But when a company can tolerate a somewhat-looser relationship with its sources, or when requirements are so predictable that control is less important, foreign purchasing or subcontracting is often preferable to controlled offshore manufacturing.

Summary. The factors listed above are important for any company to consider when deciding how to do its offshore sourcing. No one method is obviously best for all companies; a careful balancing of the advantages and disadvantages of the various alternatives is necessary.

EVALUATING PRODUCTS FOR OFFSHORE SOURCING

MAIN COST TRADEOFFS. Some products are sourced offshore because they are not available domestically. In these cases there is no alternative to offshore sourcing. But such cases are rare. In most cases offshore sourcing is chosen because it is cheaper than domestic sourcing. Whether offshore sourcing is cheaper depends on a product's manufacturing cost structure, that is, the mix of labor, material, and other inputs needed in its fabrication. The relative costs of different inputs vary greatly among countries; the differences are greatest between industrialized countries like the United States and the developing countries of Asia, Latin America, and Africa. Some costs are likely to be lower for offshore sources, but others are higher.

The best products for offshore sourcing are those that use intensively the inputs that are cheaper abroad.

Labor.   Direct labor costs are often much lower outside the United States and provide the basic attraction of offshore sourcing. Some examples of relative labor costs are given in a later section. The differences are generally greater for lower-skilled production labor than for skilled workers, technicians, and managers, but significant differences exist in all categories.

Materials and Components.   Local and imported material inputs are often an important part of production costs. Whether they are cheaper or more expensive for an offshore source than for domestic production depends on the country; this varies widely among countries and products. In a few cases, cheap sources of materials may be an important attraction of offshore sourcing.

Factory Overhead.   Some indirect production costs will typically be lower overseas, especially those related to indirect labor or the provision of certain labor-intensive services. Other cost inputs, such as utilities or the amortized costs of construction may be higher or lower than in the United States. In the developing countries, net factory overheads are generally lower than in the United States.

Corporate Overhead.   Corporate overhead associated with offshore sourcing includes the cost of headquarters or domestic managers involved in supervising or coordinating offshore sourcing, and travel and communication costs between the offshore source and domestic operations. These can generally be expected to be higher for offshore sourcing. Distances are greater, so travel and communication costs increase. And offshore sources often need more attention in order to assure adequate performance. Communication difficulties occasioned by language and cultural differences may also increase costs.

Shipping and Duties.   Two major cost disadvantages of offshore production are shipping costs and import duties. Sometimes offshore sourcing involves sending materials and components abroad for assembly and shipment back to the United States. Such transport costs can be high, as can the costs of having capital invested in goods in transit. U.S. import duties can also be significant cost items for some products.

PRODUCTS SUITABLE FOR OFFSHORE SOURCING.   Products suitable for offshore sourcing generally are those for which savings in production costs are sufficient to offset higher costs of transportation, duties, and corporate overhead. Although each product must be evaluated individually, certain products are generally more suitable for offshore sourcing. Products that are labor intensive and standardized in product specifications and manufacturing technology, that have a predictable pattern of sales and a high ratio of value to weight, and that are not subject to high duties are the best candidates. These characteristics are discussed below.

Labor-Intensive Products.   Most products or components suitable for offshore sourcing have a significant labor input. Especially attractive are articles requiring large amounts of low-skilled labor, which is relatively expensive in the United States.

Finding sufficient numbers of U.S. workers for such tedious jobs as sewing garments or assembling semiconductors has become increasingly difficult. Workers overseas can often be trained to perform such jobs well at costs dramatically lower than in the United States. Often a product can be produced in a series of steps, only some of which are labor intensive. In these cases it may be possible to perform only the labor-intensive operations—for example, assembly—overseas. For example, semiconductor chips are manufactured in the United States in a capital-intensive and technology-intensive process, shipped abroad for assembly, into finished products, and then reimported into the United States. There are many reasons why it is undesirable to locate the capital-intensive parts of the process in developing countries. Maintenance of capital equipment is costly, exposure to political risk is increased, and it may not be consistent with the employment goals of the foreign government.

Standardized Products. Products whose design, specifications, and production technology do not rapidly change are likely to require less supervision by the U.S. buyer. Changes in product design or technology must be communicated to the source, and such communications are often difficult and expensive. With standard products, once the production technology is transferred, the foreign source can operate with little outside help. It is also likely that the manufacturing process can be routinized to the point where few skilled workers are required and where the number of supervisory personnel is minimized.

Products With a Predictable Sales Pattern. This topic is closely related to product standardization. Products with steady sales, or at least predictable sales, are more suitable for manufacturing than are products that face abrupt shifts in demand. Offshore sources can be given long production runs that can be programmed well in advance of required delivery dates. Little communication is needed between the U.S. buyer and the overseas source, whether they are independent companies or parts of the same enterprise. Likewise, disruptions in supply due to strikes or transportation problems can normally be overcome in time to meet delivery dates. Products subject to rapid changes in sales levels require sources that can rapidly vary production levels and delivery schedules. This is difficult for offshore sources, and disruptions in supply have very serious consequences. For these reasons, fashion products are less suitable for offshore sourcing than more-stable product lines.

Products That Are Easy To Ship and Face Low Import Duties. Products with high value relative to weight (and volume) will have low transportation costs relative to their total manufacturing costs and sales prices. They also may be shipped by air freight, allowing quicker responsiveness to the market. The import duties faced by different products and components vary greatly. Also, some goods are eligible for special duty treatment, whereas others are not. These duty considerations are discussed in detail in the section on U.S. customs considerations.

TRENDS IN PRODUCT SELECTION FOR OFFSHORE SOURCING. Over the last few years of dramatic growth in offshore sourcing from developing countries, both U.S. companies and their offshore sources have increased their capabilities for managing this activity. Offshore sources have improved their technology, and have gained valuable manufacturing experience. Likewise, U.S. manufacturers and buyers have learned more about working with offshore sources. The result is that more-complex products are being sourced offshore. Increasingly it is not just the most-labor-intensive products that are made abroad, and smaller runs of less-standardized products have become feasible. Such upgrading to more-sophisticated technologies and to products with higher values is in the interest of the developing countries and the more-experienced U.S. and foreign companies.

EVALUATING SOURCES AND PARTNERS

GENERAL CHARACTERISTICS. Most criteria for selecting foreign companies as sources or as joint-venture partners are similar to those used for domestic business. A prospective supplier or partner must be reliable. It may be more difficult to evaluate foreign partners because of lack of information or cultural differences, but identifying partners with desired qualities is essential to successful offshore sourcing. Before selecting a source or a joint-venture partner, it is important to decide what capabilities are required of the foreign company and what kind of relationship is optimal. Many relationships have failed because these requirements were not clarified or because the objectives of the two parties were too divergent. Since many U.S. companies have little experience with subcontracting or joint-venture relationships before moving offshore, and since the opportunity for misunderstanding is greater when the parties are from different countries, it is especially important to clarify objectives before entering into such relationships.

EVALUATING INDEPENDENT SOURCES. For a supplier or subcontractor, the most important selection criteria relate to the source's capabilities for manufacturing and deliverying acceptable products on time at acceptable costs. It is important for the U.S. buyer to define explicitly for itself and the source its expectations in terms of quality, delivery schedules, and expected production volumes and their variability. Next it is necessary to evaluate the source's ability to meet these expectations. Here the company's record in serving other clients is important. A difficulty is that many of the best potential sources in developing countries are relatively young and inexperienced. They have capabilities that are growing and being refined with each job they do, but they may not have a long-established track record.

Sources should also be evaluated in terms of their willingness to be good long-term suppliers. Some firms with the best capabilities may not wish to tie themselves very tightly to a U.S. buyer, wishing instead to diversify customers or to eventually move out of subcontracting into producing and marketing their own products. They may consequently give little attention to the U.S. buyer's needs. It is important, therefore, to raise questions about a source's interest in an enduring relationship.

EVALUATING PARTNERS. A joint-venture partner should be selected with considerable care, as the relationship is likely to be long term, and requires relatively complex interactions between the partners. First, it is important to clarify what a partner is expected to contribute and its capability to actually make such contributions. A partner is generally expected to bring to the venture considerable expertise in addition to its capital investment. Experience in managing operations in the local business environment is most important. Managing large groups of workers in a developing country demands management skills that local partners may already have developed, and which can be a very important contribution.

Important too may be the government and business connections that a foreign partner brings to a venture. Government relations is often a much more important part of management's job in developing countries than in the United States, and the right partner can provide valuable experience and contacts for smoothing such relations. Nevertheless, a local partner does not guarantee good government relations, and it is important to know how the partner views this function. Clearly it is desirable to obtain as much information as possible from objective sources on the prospective partner's connections and abilities in this regard.

Finally, it is crucial to understand whether the goals and expectations of the U.S. company and foreign partner are congruent. A joint-venture relationship implies joint decisions on matters such as capacity expansion, profit-payout policies, transfer prices, and product diversification, which can be quite controversial if the partners have different objectives. Joint ventures contain both mutuality of interest and conflicts of interest, and these must be recognized and dealt with if the partnership is to be successful. Discussing such problems during the formation phase can reduce problems later.

NEGOTIATING WITH PROSPECTIVE SOURCES AND PARTNERS.   Negotiating purchasing, subcontracting, and joint-venture agreements with foreign enterprises requires all the same negotiating skills that a domestic venture requires. In addition, however, cultural differences and differences in the role of the host-country government are important to recognize. Bargaining styles differ greatly across countries, and the best U.S. negotiator may make a mess of a foreign negotiation. The hard versus soft sell, the role of haggling over prices, the use of entertainment and social occasions in negotiating, and the value of personal relationships may differ from practices in the United States. Many errors can be avoided by getting advice from people with experience and by reading available material on cultural differences that cause problems in doing business abroad.

The foreign country's government is often part of any negotiation, especially for joint ventures. It may have to give its approval to any agreement that is negotiated, and often will have definite opinions on how the venture should be set up and run. It may also have views on the relative desirability of different local partners. Even if the government is not actively involved, it is important for the U.S. company to understand its views, as government incentives and controls may be crucial to the success of the venture.

EVALUATING PRODUCTION SITES

IMPORTANT CRITERIA.   One of the most important decisions related to offshore sourcing is the choice of the country from which to source, especially if a firm contemplates the establishment of its own manufacturing facility. Many factors must be considered in evaluating the desirability of a site; they can be grouped into four categories as follows:

1. Labor factors.
2. Infrastructure factors.
3. Government policy factors.
4. Stability factors.

LABOR FACTORS.   Since labor-cost savings provide the major motivation for off-shore sourcing, choosing a country with low labor costs is obviously important. But low labor costs are of little help unless sufficient productive and reliable labor is available. In fact, since wage rates are so uniformly low throughout the developing world, other factors assume a larger importance.

Labor Costs.   Wages vary greatly throughout the world. Exhibit 2 presents some estimates of wage rates in different countries. Although the data are somewhat out of date, the basic relationships still hold. It must be remembered when making such estimates that the level of fringe benefits is often much higher abroad than in the United States, sometimes approaching the base wage itself. Also savings are often available in other job categories. Many companies find that technicians, engineers, accountants, and other professionals can be hired for relatively low wage rates in developing countries, and that their training is often very good.

Labor Availability.   Although unemployment rates are high in many developing countries, labor of the right kind is often scarce. People with skills may be in short supply, and turnover rates for such people may be high. A company locating in such an area must plan an extensive training program. In countries that have recently experienced rapid economic development skilled workers may be abundant, but it may be difficult to find workers willing to do tedious assembly work. Successful economic development increases worker-skill levels; companies needing unskilled assembly workers may have to move to new locations.

Labor Productivity.   Labor costs are determined not only by wage rates but also by worker productivity. Low productivity has a number of undesirable side effects besides its direct effect of increasing unit labor costs. If productivity is low, more workers are required, thereby generating extra overhead and other problems associated with managing a larger work force. Low productivity also implies an increase in required investment in working capital as work-in-process inventory increases.

Labor productivity depends on the experience of the workers, the technology available to them, and the management of the enterprise. The value of experience

**EXHIBIT 2   AVERAGE HOURLY WAGES IN
MANUFACTURING IN SELECTED COUNTRIES (1976)**

Country	Hourly Earnings in Dollars
Hong Kong	0.69
Republic of Korea	0.56
Malaysia	0.47
Philippines	0.25
Singapore	0.65
Taiwan	0.61
Mexico	1.47
Japan	3.27
United States	5.22

Source. For United States, *Monthly Labor Review,* December 1980. For other countries, Business International, Inc., *Investing Trading and Licensing Conditions Abroad,* 1979.

depends on the type of job. Some jobs can be learned quickly, whereas others require months or years of training. But it is clear that technology and management are crucial. Workers with the right tools and equipment, organized and managed effectively, are much more productive than those who are poorly equipped and managed. Effective plant scheduling, worker training and supervision, and other aspects of good management are important determinants of productivity.

It has generally been found in the overseas operations of U.S. firms, as well as by economists in comparative studies, that foreign workers can be just as productive as U.S. workers if they are given the same technology and management. A U.S. Tariff Commission study (1970) found that workers in offshore manufacturing plants can be trained rapidly for most jobs and they approach or exceed U.S. productivity levels. The importance of management is shown by Japanese experience. Japanese workers are said to be very productive, but part of this productivity is undoubtedly due to Japanese management. When Japanese companies come to the U.S., they are often able to manage U.S. workers to achieve comparable productivity levels.

Productivity is not just a function of management, however. Cultural and historical factors also play a role. The industrial experience of the country influences the extent to which workers have been exposed to modern technology and determines the number of technically oriented people available. Educational levels also influence productivity, especially for some types of jobs. Even nutrition may be an important influence in some of the poorest countries. And culture certainly influences attitudes toward work. The Protestant work ethic may be dying in the West, but many companies have found something comparable in countries of the Far East.

Labor Reliability and Unions.   In many offshore sourcing operations it is important to maintain a steady flow of production, as this output feeds into other parts of the company's operations. Disruptions due to strikes can be very serious. Rapid turnover or high rates of absenteeism are also of concern. Turnover in many offshore plants is high because a high proportion of workers are young women who are only temporarily in the labor force.

Strikes and other disruptions abroad have not been a major concern for most companies engaged in offshore sourcing, although U.S. dock strikes occasionally cause problems. In many countries where offshore plants are located, government policies and regulations sharply circumscribe the rights of labor to organize and/or strike, and in some cases these laws are even stricter for export operations than for companies serving the domestic market. Governments realize that export-oriented enterprises will move elsewhere if disruptions become common.

> As reported in one study (Kassalow, 1978): Among the inducements to foreign investors in Singapore and Malaysia were certain legal provisions limiting the benefits payable to employees in new multinational plants for a specified period. In addition, labour laws recently adopted in those countries have made it difficult if not impossible for unions to bargain over employers' decisions to dismiss, transfer or lay off employees.

But as economic development proceeds, governments may loosen such laws in response to democratic pressures, and labor relations may become more similar to those in the United States.

Whether or not unions are tightly controlled by the government, it is important to become familiar with the role and organization of unions in a prospective offshore manufacturing site. Often the role of unions is quite different than in the United States. In some countries unions are organized on a company basis, as opposed to a craft or industry basis. In others unions are extensions of political parties, and a country may have communist, socialist, and other politically affiliated unions. In such cases, labor disputes often have more to do with the national political scene than with wages and working conditions.

INFRASTRUCTURE FACTORS. Infrastructure includes a wide variety of facilities and services required by any offshore operation, ranging from utilities and plant sites to schools, shopping, and services for expatriate families. Among the factors to consider for offshore location decisions are the availability of industrial sites, communications, transportation services, and suppliers of needed goods and services.

Industrial Sites. A determining factor in some location decisions is how fast a facility can be established and begin operations; construction delays can be extremely long. Some countries have industrial sites available to foreign investors on attractive terms and without legal complications involving the determination of title. Others may have standard industrial buildings available to buy or lease, which if appropriate to a company's needs, can save both time and investment capital. In virtually all developing countries, industrial parks of some type have been established, but these vary widely in terms of the types and reliability of services provided and kinds of facilities available.

Transportation and Communication. Offshore sourcing is a relatively complex logistical operation, often involving imports, exports, and considerable international communication to coordinate plans and schedules. Efficient and reliable transportation and communication is therefore essential. Although these services are constantly improving everywhere in the world, they still differ considerably among countries. International telephone and mail service, which are often taken for granted in the United States, are difficult in some places. Countries also vary in terms of the frequency of air and sea shipping connections to the United States and other countries.

Local Suppliers of Goods and Services. An important ancillary advantage of some offshore sites is the availability of inexpensive supplies of component parts, raw materials, and needed services. If materials and components must be imported, costs are often higher, and problems such as bureaucratic delays or corruption may be encountered. If services are not available, the company will be forced to provide them itself. The negative side of this is that governments sometimes force companies to use local suppliers even if they provide goods or services of substandard quality, all in the name of local economic development. It is important, therefore, to investigate the capabilities of local suppliers as well as government policies regarding their use.

GOVERNMENT POLICY FACTORS. In most developing countries where offshore sources are located, governments play a very active role in shaping economic development. It is important, therefore, to understand the current policies regarding foreign investment and offshore sourcing, as well as to develop a feeling for the government's general attitudes in these areas, so as to be able to anticipate possible changes. Governments can be both a help and a hindrance to foreign investors, and their general attitudes range from hostility to active support.

General Attitudes.   Most governments have had considerable experience with foreign investors, and this has conditioned current attitudes. Much of this experience may be considered by them negative, having colonial or neocolonial overtones of exploitation. In some countries there is a strong Marxist movement, either in power or exerting political and intellectual influence, which sees foreign investment as imperialistic. These critics often see offshore sourcing as having a very negative impact on their countries, interpreting it as exploitation of workers with little lasting benefit for the country. If such attitudes are prevalent, foreign-investment legislation may be, or may become, quite restrictive.

On the other hand, some countries see foreign investment in general, and export-oriented foreign investment in particular, as playing an important role in economic development. Such governments have a more positive view of foreign enterprise and see special benefits such as providing jobs, training, and foreign-exchange earnings. In such countries, the government may be quite supportive of offshore sourcing operations.

Government Regulations.   In most developing countries new foreign investments need formal government approval, and the process differs widely among countries. And government rules and regulations often require constant management attention after operations are set up. Most governments have tried to simplify procedures for offshore sourcing in an effort to attract more of these export-oriented operations. Thus exporters are sometimes exempted from certain regulations, or the government sometimes sets up a free-trade zone or export-processing zone in which many of the normal rules don't apply. A good source of information on export processing zones is Currie (1979). Especially attractive are situations in which authority rests in the hands of an independent zone management, thereby reducing the need to deal with a large number of government offices. In most cases, however, a company needs to learn how to deal with the government and how to expedite needed government services or approvals.

Government Incentives.   Various incentives are offered by many developing countries to companies establishing offshore manufacturing plants. These include favorable tax treatment, subsidized services, and freedom of movement of goods, people, and money in and out of the country. Many countries provide tax holidays or other favorable treatment such as rapid depreciation. The value of such treatment will vary among investors, however, based on their tax situations in their home countries. For example, a tax holiday abroad sometimes simply means that a U.S. investor pays more taxes in the United States, but in other cases U.S. taxes can be deferred. Government subsidies come in the form of low-cost sites, cheap loans for construction or importation of equipment, or provision of low-cost services. And of course tax regulations are often used to subsidize exports.

It is important for offshore sourcing that goods, people, and money be permitted to flow freely in and out of the foreign country. Although the degree of freedom differs, most countries have moved toward satisfying this need. On the imports of materials or components to be incorporated in exports generally duties are not paid (or duties paid are rebated upon export). Likewise, the paperwork and licenses required for imports are generally reduced for export operations. Finally, there are generally looser regulations for exporters than for other companies on employment of expatriates, remission of profits, and requirements for partial local ownership.

STABILITY FACTORS.   Economic or political instability can cause unexpected problems for offshore sourcing operations. Inflation, currency fluctuations, civil disruptions, or changes in government all may have unfortunate consequences. Economic stability is closely related to political stability. High inflation, for example, may lead to social disruption and political change. Likewise, political changes often lead to changes in economic policies.

Economic Instability.   The general economic health of a country is important to any investor, but since offshore sourcing plants serve export markets rather than the local market, inflation and currency changes are more relevant than other economic indicators such as growth rates. Inflation and currency depreciation often occur simultaneously. Inflation affects all local costs and could make some products non-competitive with those of other countries. But if the local currency is depreciating along with inflation, the cost in dollars of the goods will not change. The net effect on a company during a given time period will depend on the relative rates of inflation and currency depreciation, especially compared with competitive countries. Some exporting countries systematically devalue their currencies in line with inflation, in order to remain competitive, whereas in others there is sometimes a time lag between inflation and devaluation. The net effect also depends on the extent to which the company uses imported components and materials, which will increase in price as the currency depreciates.

Political Instability.   A major concern of foreign investors is political risk. With regard to offshore sourcing, investors should consider the potential risks posed by external threats (these have been of particular concern in several popular investment sites in the Far East), internal political disturbances that have the potential for disrupting normal operations, and drastic changes in government policies that could affect the success of a company's operations. Predicting political instability and analyzing political risk is a complex art and is covered in section 22 of this handbook. Approaches range from simple numerical rating schemes to in-depth analysis of the political dynamics of a given country. Several such approaches are analyzed in an article in *Fortune* magazine (1980), which concludes that political risk analysis requires

> anticipating the currents of change abroad, then plotting how to move with them. To do this demands going beyond economic forecasting to gauge other forces, from religious movements to nationalistic passions. It also requires U.S. executives, who have learned the hard way, to refrain from plunging into foreign ventures merely on the strength of Washington's judgments.

Various techniques can be used to reduce the political risks of offshore sourcing. The insurance programs available from government or private sources are covered in Section 10. The best protection, however, is a backup source of supply. Many companies have either multiple offshore sources or a backup production facility available in the United States.

SOURCES OF INFORMATION ON PRODUCTION SITES. Most countries that are potential sites for offshore sourcing have offices, often in the United States, to provide information and assistance to companies interested in investing in the country or finding partners or suppliers. These offices can be very valuable for obtaining basic information, sources of other information, and some feeling for government attitudes.

Another important source is the reports that describe various aspects of the political, economic, and regulatory climates in different countries. Some of the most useful ones are the following:

1. *Overseas Business Reports*, published by the U.S. Department of Commerce.
2. *Investing, Licensing and Trading Conditions Abroad*, published by Business International Corporation.
3. *Quarterly Economic Reviews*, published for most countries by the Economist Intelligence Unit.
4. Reports published by a number of banks and public accounting firms.

Many of these are available in good public or university libraries.

Finally, it is important to talk to other companies with experience in a given country. Valuable information on how the published information translates into reality can be obtained in such interviews. However, companies may have biases, either pro or con, on a given country based on their own experiences, so the opinions of several companies should be solicited.

U.S. CUSTOMS REGULATIONS

U.S. customs regulations on imports should be understood by companies engaged in offshore sourcing. Many products that are selected for offshore sourcing are subject to special treatment under U.S. laws. Some are eligible for favorable treatment because of their origin in developing countries, whereas others come under special restrictions because of the poor health of the competing U.S. industry. Still others make use of special features of the tariff laws that favor certain types of transactions. The purpose of this section is not to cover U.S. import regulations in any detail, but instead to outline some basic considerations that can be studied in more detail in other sections of this handbook and in publications of the U.S. Customs Service. The best source of basic information, itself having extensive references to other sources, is *Exporting to the United States*, published by the U.S. Customs Service. The subjects covered here are (1) normal treatment of imported goods, (2) generalized system of preferences (GSP), covering some imports from developing countries, (3) special quotas on particular goods, and (4) tariff items 806.30 and 807.00, covering imports of products that are produced abroad using U.S. components or materials.

NORMAL TREATMENT OF IMPORTED GOODS. Most products imported to the United States pay duties based on the product's definition, its value, and its national origin.

Products are defined for customs valuation and assessment using the *Tariff Schedules of the United States*, published by the U.S. International Trade Commission.

This document classifies each product into a special category based on one or more product characteristics. Often it is unclear from the tariff schedules exactly how an item should be classified, and seemingly minor product differences may result in a different classification and a widely different rate of duty. It is wise to verify the duty on an imported product by consulting with U.S. Customs Service officials; sometimes it will be necessary to request an official ruling on a controversial duty assessment.

Once the product is identified, the method of calculating the duty is specified in the tariff schedules, as is the applicable duty rate. For most products, duties are calculated on an *ad valorem* basis, that is, as a percentage of the value of the product. There are some products, however, whose duty is based on weight, and some that pay a given duty per unit. For products whose duty is based on value, the normal value used is the so-called export value, which corresponds to the free on board (f.o.b.) price, that is, the price received by the exporter including the costs of transporting the goods to the port of exportation and loading the goods onto the export vessel.

The classification of the product and its country of origin determine the rate of duty that must be paid. In the *Tariff Schedules of the United States,* two applicable duty rates are found, one for most favored nations and the other for countries not having this designation. Currently only a few communist countries do not enjoy most-favored-nation status, and imports from these countries are generally assessed a much higher duty.

GENERALIZED SYSTEM OF PREFERENCES. A wide range of products qualify for duty-free entry into the United States if imported from a developing country. The products that qualify for GSP duty-free treatment and the eligible developing countries are identified in the *Tariff Schedules of the United States.* The GSP applies to roughly 150 developing countries in Latin America, Africa, and Asia. It covers some 2800 products, mostly manufactured industrial goods, *excluding* textiles and apparel, footwear, and selected glass items, steel articles, electronics, watches, and miscellaneous other items. In addition, a "competitive-need criteria" denies GSP treatment for particular products when imported from especially competitive developing countries (these countries and products are identified in the *tariff schedules.* Finally, imports under the GSP must conform to a number of rules regarding origin of component parts and documentation to verify that the products are substantially transformed in an eligible developing country. A good source of information on the GSP is the President's *Report to Congress on Operation of the U.S. Generalized System of Preferences (GSP) (1980).*

QUOTAS. A number of products sourced offshore are subject to absolute quotas as well as duties. Quotas essentially limit the volume of imports into the United States and are normally administered on a product and country-of-origin basis. Such quotas have generally been imposed in response to U.S. industries that are threatened by excessive imports. Hence some of the imports that have enjoyed the most success in the U.S. market are subject to quotas. Some quotas are administered by the U.S. Customs Service itself, and others by foreign authorities under a so-called orderly marketing agreement. In the latter case, a quota level for particular products is negotiated with individual exporting nations, which in turn allocate the quota to individual exporters. Without the exporting government's stamp of approval, the product may not be imported into the United States. Needless to say, access to a country's quota may be very valuable, and the availability of a quota allocation may significantly affect a company's decision on where to source its imports.

Products subject to quota as of 1980 include most textile and apparel products, footwear from Korea and Taiwan, and color television sets from Japan, Korea, and Taiwan. Quotas are no longer in force on footwear from Korea and Taiwan or on color television sets from Japan.

ITEMS 806.30 AND 807.00.   Many products sourced abroad by U.S. companies enter the United State under the provision of items 806.30 and 807.00 of the *Tariff Schedules of the United States.* Item 806.30 provides that articles made of metal produced in the United States will upon importation into the United States be assessed duty only on the value of the processing done outside the United States. Item 807.00 provides that articles assembled abroad, in whole or in part, of components made in the United States will upon importation into the United States be assessed duty on the full value of the imported product less the value of the U.S. fabricated components contained therein. These provisions are subject to many conditions, including elaborate accounting for the U.S. components incorporated in imports. Many companies have had problems in following U.S. customs regulations. Nevertheless, imports under these provisions have increased spectacularly in recent years. Good sources of information on the use of Items 806.30 and 807.00 are the following

1. U.S. House of Representatives, Committee on Ways and Means, Subcommittee on Trade, *Special Duty Treatment or Repeal of Articles Assembled or Fabricated Abroad,* hearings before the 94th Congress, second session, March 24-25, 1976, Washington, D.C., 1976.

2. U.S. International Trade Commission, *Import Trends in TSUS Items 806.30 and 807.00,* USITC Publication 1029, Washington, D.C., 1980.

3. U.S. Tariff Commission, *Economic Factors Affecting the Use of Items 807.00 and 806.30 of the Tariff Schedules of the United States,* TC Publication 339, Washington, D.C., 1970.

LEGAL AND FINANCIAL CONSIDERATIONS

Offshore sourcing involves a number of legal and financial considerations that are covered in other sections of this handbook. The important factors will depend on which form the offshore sourcing takes. If it is simple purchasing or subcontracting, the concerns will relate to contractual considerations and trade financing. Information on these topics is available in publications of banks and public accounting firms. If offshore sourcing takes the form of a joint venture or a wholly owned manufacturing plant, the considerations will relate more to the relative advantages of different legal forms of establishment and the contracts necessary between joint-venture partners. Joint ventures and other such agreements with potential competitors may also lead to issues of U.S. antitrust law.

Of course some factors may be more important in offshore sourcing than in other forms of international business. Special tax incentives and sources of financing may be available from host-country governments. Foreign-exchange management assumes important proportions because of the extensive transfers of products across borders. And large amounts of intracorporate sales between a company's U.S. plants and its foreign subsidiaries mean that special attention must be given to the setting of transfer prices. But in the main, offshore sourcing involves similar financial and legal considerations as other forms of international trade and investment.

ORGANIZATION AND COORDINATION OF OFFSHORE SOURCING

COMMUNICATIONS PROBLEMS AND SOLUTIONS. Communications with off-shore sources, whether they are independent companies or a U.S. firm's own subsidiary, often run into problems common to most international business operations. Because they occur so often, and have such devastating effects, they are summarized briefly here, along with some possible approaches for resolving them.

Causes of Problems.   Time and distance are the most obvious causes of communication problems. The U.S. office and the foreign plant are typically in different time zones. Direct telephone contact is therefore limited to the small "window" in which the working day overlaps, or to situations in which one or the other party is making contact outside normal working hours. This can limit the quality of communication and encourages reliance on less-satisfactory forms of written communication, with attendant delays and mistakes. Communications over long distances, with no face-to-face contact and with time pressures due to the high costs involved, often lead to irritation, misunderstandings, and creation of distrust.

Language is another obvious problem area. Although the source managers may speak English, their language capabilities may be limited, which can be quite problematic in long-distance communications.

Problems of time and distance are exacerbated by the differences in cultural environment in which the two enterprises operate. The U.S. firm may not be able to understand why the local manager of a subsidiary finds it necessary to handle a problem in a certain way, whereas the local manager may feel that such a solution is only normal in the local business environment. The areas of labor relations and government relations are fertile fields for such misunderstandings.

These problems are made worse if the managers at either end of the communication channel have little international experience. This is an inevitable, but unfortunate, fact for many companies. Many firms have little experience overseas before beginning offshore sourcing, and do not have a reserve of experienced international managers to handle these communications. Most problems can be overcome quite easily, but a company should be aware of the opportunities for misunderstanding.

Solutions to Communication Problems.   Many of these communication problems can be solved by having the right people involved, by frequent visits between the U.S. offices and overseas sources, and by organizing communication channels properly. The right people can make a big difference. The ideal qualifications would include language capability, experience in the other party's operations, understanding and emphathy for the other culture, plus the expected technical competence. Such people are hard to find, but fortunately, many people can effectively communicate internationally if they are patient and sympathetic to the position of those on the other side.

Frequent visits by U.S. managers to the foreign source, and by the foreign managers to the United States, are also important. Gaining a firsthand feeling for the foreign operation and its current situation helps put later communications in the proper context, and can reduce misunderstandings. Direct exposure to the U.S. market can also help a source understand the importance of its role in producing quality products. Face-to-face communications also can build trust and personal relationships that can help overcome subsequent problems.

Organizational relationships can also be structured to reduce communication difficulties. On the U.S. side it is often useful to have one person designated as liaison with the foreign source. This person can be responsible for insuring timely and effective communications and for clarifying and reducing misunderstandings. Independent foreign agents, appointed by a U.S. company to handle all dealings with foreign sources, can also perform such a function.

ORGANIZATION LINKS.   For many smaller companies the question of how to link a foreign subsidiary or independent source to the rest of the organization is not important. The link is through the sales, purchasing, production, or other functional department. But for larger organizations, a variety of possibilities present themselves.

Consider a multiproduct, multidivison U.S. company with a variety of foreign sources (assume they are controlled manufacturing plants), some of which serve more than one of the U.S. divisions. A simplified representation of such a situation, with the corresponding product flows, is given in Exhibit 3. Here it is assumed that the product divisions are responsible for U.S. production and sales, and the international division manages international operations. How should the foreign sources be linked to the U.S. operations? Two major alternatives in this situation are to link sources organizationally to the product divisions that they serve, or link sources to the international division which manages other international operations. Neither alternative is without problems. Making source 2 a profit or cost center within product division B would not present problems, since all of its products go to the division. But for source 1, no such simple link is possible. Linking organizationally with either division may distort its relationship with the other.

EXHIBIT 3   COMPLEX MULTISOURCE–MULTIDIVISION
SOURCING SITUATION

Linking all sources to the international division would be consistent with the rest of the company's operations, and the international division is likely to have the experienced international managers for good communications. But these subsidiaries, whose primary mission is serving the U.S. divisions, are quite different from the normal subsidiaries that serve foreign customers. An immediate concern would be who was responsible for the success of these subsidiaries: the international division to which they report, or the product divisions that provide their entire market. This raises the question of the appropriate transfer price between divisions, a messy problem in any circumstances. Problems escalate if the example is extended to a greater number of divisions and sources.

The best advice is to choose the organization that seems most natural, probably the one where the bulk of the communication and coordination efforts will be, and then build in mechanisms to overcome difficulties in coordinating with the rest of the organization. In any case, the foreign source should have a clearly defined mission, whether it be a cost center or profit center, and should have the resources and authority necessary to accomplish this mission. The best performance of a foreign source will result when responsibilities and expectations are clearly defined.

SOURCES AND SUGGESTED REFERENCES

Business International Corporation. *Investing, Licensing and Trading Conditions Abroad.* New York: Business International Corporation. A continually updated looseleaf service covering most major countries.

Currie, J. *Investment: The Growing Role of Export Processing Zones.* Economist Intelligence Unit Special Report No. 64. London, 1979.

Economist Intelligence Unit. *Quarterly Economic Reports.* A series of reports covering most countries.

Kassalow, E. "Aspects of Labor Relations in Multinational Companies: An Overview of Three Asian Countries," *International Labor Review,* Vol. XI (May–June 1978), pp. 273–287.

Kraar, L., "The Multinationals Get Smarter About Political Risks," *Fortune,* Vol. XXXI (March 24, 1980), pp. 86–100.

Report to Congress on the First Five Years' Operation of the U.S. Generalized System of Preferences (GSP), Washington, DC: U.S. Government Printing Office, 1980.

U.S. Customs Service, Department of the Treasury. *Exporting to the United States.* Washington, D.C.: U.S. Government Printing Office, 1979.

U.S. Department of Commerce. *Overseas Business Reports.* A series of reports on different countries.

U.S. House of Representatives, Committee on Ways and Means, Subcommittee on Trade. *Special Duty Treatment or Repeal of Articles Assembled or Fabricated Abroad.* Hearings before the 94th Congress, second session, March 24–25, 1976. Washington, DC, 1976.

U.S. International Trade Commission. *Import Trends in TSUS Items 806.30 and 807.00.* USITC Publication 1029. Washington, DC, 1980.

U.S. International Trade Commission. *Tariff Schedules of the United States.*

U.S. Tariff Commission. *Economic Factors Affecting the Use of Items 807.00 and 806.30 of the Tariff Schedules of the United States.* T.C. Publication 339. Washington, DC, 1970.

ORGANIZATION DESIGN

CONTENTS

THE INTERNATIONAL DIVISION 3

PRODUCT VERSUS GEOGRAPHY 6

ELIMINATING THE INTERNATIONAL
DIVISION 7
  IBM 9
  Pfizer 10
  Eaton 11

THE FUNCTIONAL DIMENSION IN
GLOBAL TERMS 12

ORGANIZING AROUND MARKETS,
NOT GEOGRAPHY 14

GLOBAL MATRIX ORGANIZATION 16

CONCLUSION 18

SOURCES AND SUGGESTED
REFERENCES 20

ORGANIZATION DESIGN

Stanley M. Davis

Methods of organizing and managing multinational industrial corporations have matured considerably in the last 15 years, and the basic rules are now rather well understood. Changes in the external environment, however, together with new complexities that arise from corporate responses to these changes, continually reduce the effectiveness of these basic structures and practices. The result is that new methods and forms are evolving in response to the new exigencies. My purpose in this chapter is to chart and explain these recent trends in the evolving patterns of global organization among U.S.-based corporations.

We will examine the problems arising from the well-recognized patterns, and the refinements that are being made to cope with them. Basic design involves three different ways of organizing units: by *functions*, by *product*, and by *geography*. Neat distinctions between the three, however, have been found inadequate because they only optimize along one of these dimensions. Here are some of the trends:

Worldwide functional structures show definite instabilities.

Corporations organized by country are exploring how and where to place product management more adequately in their frameworks.

Firms with worldwide product groups require better coordination within countries and regions than their structures provide.

Corporate planning and development activities have led some companies to organize around markets, not geography.

Some companies experiment with global matrix management and structure.

These developments all point to a trend of learning to integrate and manage diversity in ways that were not possible with the early generations of multinational organization design. This chapter is intended as a guide to those who are seeking innovative adjustments to organizing the complexities of global corporations.

THE INTERNATIONAL DIVISION

Whereas domestic organization emphasize functional and product bases of structure, international growth introduces the area element for dividing the structure. The transition from a domestic organization to a worldwide organization involves a number of phases in which foreign activities begin as a minor and peripheral part of the firm and end up being so central as to change the geographic basis for organization to global parameters. The strategic changes that led to the development of new organizational forms are understandable in terms of the product-life-cycle concept as it applies to international trade. According to this concept, there are four phases in the life history of any product: introduction, growth, maturity, and decline.[1]

During the early phase of the product's manufacture and sale there is a low price elasticity for aggregate demand and for the individual firm. The nature of demand is not yet well understood. Only a small number of firms are involved, and they rely heavily on R&D, skilled labor, and short production runs. All manufacture is domestic, and exports are limited to developed countries with high GNPs. This phase, historically, was characteristic of the early twentieth century, when U.S. firms found that their strategic shift to product diversification stimulated the growth of exports, and this frequently became an important source of revenue for the domestic companies. Organizationally, however, this seldom meant more than the creation of an export office.

In the growth phase, as the technology and the development of the new products come to be understood, methods of mass production are introduced, firms' price elasticity increases, and price competition begins. There are a large number of firms manufacturing the same product line and production starts in other high-GNP countries. The early investment in direct foreign manufacture generally has been in defensive response to this threat to export markets by local manufacture. The foreign subsidiaries created in the early phases of domestic firm's move abroad are generally quite independent from the managerial and administrative control of the parent. This initial period of subsidiary autonomy, however, is rather short-lived. Sixty percent of the 170 companies studied in the Harvard Multinational Enterprise Project historically grouped their subsidiaries under an international division after the acquisition of only their fourth foreign unit.[2]

There are many variations in organizational design of an international business, but the general tendency is quite clear (see Exhibit 1). Whereas the structure of the domestic company is laid out along product and/or functional lines, the international division is organized around geographic interests. The head of the international division is on a hierarchical par with the heads of the domestic product groups, and all report directly to the president. General managers of each foreign unit report to the boss of the international division, and the units themselves reflect the same functional organization as exists in the domestic product divisions. With an increase in the number of foreign manufacturing units in any one geographic area, an intermediary level of regional direction (e.g., Vice-President Europe) is usually created between the subsidiaries or affiliates and the head of the international division. During the early period of its existence, the international division has little staff of its own, and what staff does exist frequently is more closely tied to its functional department at the corporate level than to the international area division.

The initial impetus for the creation of an international division is to congregate the activities whose specialized character is that they occur outside the borders of the home country. For the parent corporation, the locus of foreign expertise comes to be here, and the coordination of functions and products is still largely in the international division. Coordination between the domestic and foreign sides of the enterprise is very loose and is not paid much attention except at the top of the corporate hierarchy. From the corporate perspective, the formation of an interna-

EXHIBIT 1 ORGANIZATION STRUCTURED BY DOMESTIC PRODUCT DIVISIONS AND INTERNATIONAL (AREA) DIVISION[a]

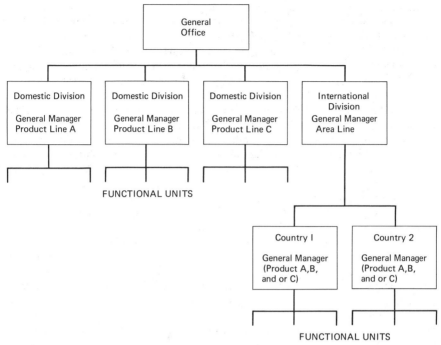

[a]Shows line positions only, not staff.

tional unit gives legitimacy to a policy of multinational expansion not formally recognized and explicitly stated before, and it provides an organizational base from which to develop. In its infancy, the division most generally turns its attention inward and develops under an umbrella of the benign neglect of the domestic company. Although the initiative for foreign expansion begins with the international division, which is strategically distinct from plans for domestic growth, the management of the foreign subsidiaries is now linked more closely with the parent. Thus the symbiotic reality becomes more apparent. For the foreign subsidiaries and affiliates, the international division provides guidance and support, but its creation also increases the control of the center over the periphery and reduces some of their previously enjoyed autonomy.

The creation of an international unit enables the firm to balance the self-interests of individual subsidiaries for the benefit of the company's total international performance. This can only be done by standardizing information and controlling some aspects of the subsidiaries' activities. Once this is done, taxes, for example, are minimized through the transfer price established for goods and services that move between sister subsidiaries in different countries. Central coordination of international activities also enables the company to make more-secure and more-economic decisions about where to purchase raw materials, where to locate new manufacturing facilities, and from where to supply world customers with products. Also, when the financial functions of the international division are coordinated, investment decisions can be made on a global basis and overseas development can turn to international capital markets, instead of just local ones, for funds.

The benefits of coordinating some activities on an international basis, rather than country by country, lead to centralized control at the division level and above. But other activities, such as marketing, often must remain local. The international division begins to reflect the same dual needs as the domestic company: to maintain the specialized inputs at their appropriate levels and locations and, at the same time, to coordinate them to maximize the total utilization of common resources. The two pressures are experienced, however, with a different order of priorities. The typical domestic side of an enterprise is specialized according to a functional division of labor; it coordinates primarily by product groupings and secondarily through centralized staff functions. Area considerations are low priority. The international side of the organization, in contrast, marks its particular expertise by its ability to differentiate geographic areas. It is then faced with the problem of coordinating both products and functions across areas.

The success of the international division provides rationalization for the organization of a company's activities abroad, but it also creates a dual structure that ultimately works against the benefit of the corporation as a whole. "Even with superb coordination at the corporate level, global planning for individual product lines is carried out at best awkwardly by two 'semi-autonomous' organizations—the domestic company and the international division. To add a series of country (or area) management makes the problem more difficult."[3] By creating an international division, the joint problems of specialization and coordination are raised to the top of the corporate hierarchy, but, as is found in the functional design, coordination also has to occur at lower levels in the organization and cannot all be bottlenecked in the president's office. Although the general tendency is to view structure as a static phenomenon, we see its dynamic in the dialectical effect that the success of an international division has on its own potential for survival. Once the international division has grown large enough to rival the largest domestic product division in size, the pressures for reorganization on an integrated worldwide basis become irresistible.[4] The next question becomes: What should be that basis? The two dominant choices involve maximizing either the product or the geographic element.

PRODUCT VERSUS GEOGRAPHY

In the global product structure, the international division is carved up, and its products are fed back into other parts of the organization, whereas domestic units become worldwide product groups. Products that require different technologies and that have dissimilar end-users are logically grouped into separate categories, and the transfer of products into various world markets is best managed within each distinctive product classification. Product diversification may be in related or unrelated lines. A strategy of global product diversification requires heavy investment in R&D, and the global product structure facilitates the transfer and control of technology and new products between domestic and foreign divisions.

To create a global structure based on geography, the domestic business is labeled the North American area and the regional pieces in the international division are elevated to similar status. In contrast to the product-structured firms, with their diversity and renewing growth phases, companies that elect an area mold tend to have a mature product line that serves common end-user markets. They generally place great reliance on lowering manufacturing costs by concentrating and specializing production through long runs in large plants, using stable technology. They also emphasize marketing techniques as the competitive basis for price and product differentiation. Industries with these characteristics that favor the area structure include food, beverage, container, automotive, farm-equipment, pharmaceuticals, and cosmetics industries.

The worldwide area structure is highly suited to mature businesses with narrow product lines because their growth potential is greater abroad than in the domestic market, where the products and brands are in later phases of their life cycles. Since they derive a high proportion of their total sales from abroad,[5] intimate knowledge of local conditions, constraints, and preferences is essential. Many of these firms rely heavily on advertising and benefit from standardizing their marketing as well as production techniques worldwide. But standardization and area differences are sometimes incompatible. In one classical gaffe, for example, advertisement for a major U.S.-based banking firm used a picture of a squirrel hoarding nuts. The idea was to convey an image of thrift, preparedness, and security. When the same advertisement appeared in Caracas, however, it brought a derisive reaction, since Venezuela has neither winters nor squirrels as we know them. Instead, the image evoked a thieving and destructive rat. The major advantage of a worldwide area structure, then, is its ability to differentiate regional and local markets and determine variations in each appropriate market mix. Its disadvantage is its inability to coordinate different product lines and their logistics of flow from source to markets across areas.

Alternative global organizations include a mixture of product and area structures, and in some cases the use of function as the defining element in the macrodesign. All designs, however, represent tradeoffs. The one that is ultimately selected appears to have the greatest advantages. But what about the advantages that are lost by not having chosen the other designs? In the following sections we will see how global corporations are attempting to answer this question and achieve the advantages of several designs simultaneously. We will look at how various industrial corporations have juggled the functional, product, and geographic dimensions in their attempts to get the best global organization design. The first step generally involves elimination of the international division.

ELIMINATING THE INTERNATIONAL DIVISION

Through time, the disjunction between a corporation's product structure in its domestic divisions and geographic structure in its overseas activities creates difficulty. Ironically, the more successful the international division, the more rapidly these difficulties occur. Strategically, the posture shifts from that of a domestic firm with international activities to that of a global corporation. Structurally, the pressures build to reflect this new unity. Although the emergent design is rather predictable in rational economic terms, the speed, clarity, and success with which it is accomplished depends mainly on history, power, and personalities in the firm. As Stopford has pointed out,[6] the major players are bound to have different structural priorities as follows:

Domestic Priorities	International Priorities
Products	Areas
Functions	Products
Areas	Functions

Central staff may compound the conflict by their predominantly functional orientation. While managers are looking for ways to maximize the advantages of all three dimensions simultaneously, resolution is delayed by this need to defend their interests and perspectives. In the process, the existing organization lags behind the evolving strategy, usually catching up in a large quantum jump known as a shake-up, only to begin lagging behind again.

The detailed study by Beer and Davis,[7] gives an example of the conflict and cost experienced during the phase when the international division is dismantled. The process generally takes years, and even then the international division may survive for political and quasi-rational reasons.

Clark Equipment is a company that has been in the process of shifting to a global organization and reducing the scope of its international division for several years. Clark is a highly integrated manufacturer and distributor of industrial end-user products that are sold through a global network of independent dealers. It has sales of over $1 billion, and international sales represent about a third of this amount. In 1970 the company operated with seven domestic product divisions and an international division. At that time there were many discussions about U.S. versus European sourcing and facilities expansion, and about the need for continent-wide product planning. Clark needed a global perspective for its various product lines, but lacked information systems and a formal structure with which to realize this goal. As part of a rationalization program to realize these needs, they separated marketing and operations as independent "profit" centers functioning worldwide. They rationalized manufacturing facilities to eliminate multiproduct plants and to develop product-centered operating subsidiaries. Next the domestic divisions assumed worldwide profit responsibility, and the European headquarters lost its profit-and-loss responsibility.

Still, in 1976 the international division has survived. Wtihin Clark it is seen as a group of "area-based, entrepreneurial generalists." Their job is to enter new markets and to develop global dealer networks; they are not expected to have functional or product expertise. They play a staff role with regard to established operations, yet they maintain operating and profit responsibility for Clark's Latin American and Asian activities. Two continuing questions for the firm are the following:

Organizationally, when is the right time to shift responsibility to the worldwide product divisions?

Strategically, is there sufficient reason to maintain the international division rather than fold it into corporate planning?

In the world of organization theory, the pure answer to the second question is probably no, but historical and political conditions are compelling.

Many international divisions such as the one at Clark and the ones examined by Beer and Davis continue to exist, some as useful anomalies and some as mere anachronisms. The general model assumes that the international division will be replaced by regional or product divisions, whereas in practice international divisions die hard and often linger on in residual roles, sometimes continuing to play important, though reduced, roles. In all cases, the transformation is a struggle to piece together the dimensions of a new global structure. Even firms as sophisticated as IBM have been very slow to break up their international divisions. Although there are no quantitative data to prove it conclusively, it appears that firms that diversify their products before they diversify the countries they operate in attempt to disband their international divisions sooner but may have more difficulty doing so. Corporations that expand globally without or before becoming multiproduct, on the other hand, seem to retain the international divisions longer but are able to make the transition more smoothly, as the IBM and Pfizer examples in the next section will show.

The moral of the tale is that firms assuming a global strategy would do well to adopt a global structure. When they don't, it is likely to be because of the firm's history, politics, and personalities. Companies that want to avoid domestic-international splits in management should avoid the same in structure.

Given: **Geographic Organization**

Needed: **Global Product Management**

The international division and the extension of the geographic basis to a worldwide area structure improve the coordination of all product lines within each zone, but at the expense of reduced coordination between areas for any one product line. The unwillingness to make this tradeoff leads corporations with a geographic structure to introduce global-product-line management into their organization design. Narrow product line companies that embark on a diversification strategy, for example, have drifted away from earlier typical methods of integrating the new lines into the existing geographic setup. These new lines, generally small when considered as a proportion of the whole, tend to drift upward in the geographic hierarchy, gathering product/management identity and independence as they become more centralized. IBM's office-products division and Pfizer's international-diversification efforts are examples of this phenomenon.

IBM. IBM was one of the last holdouts for the international-division (IBM World Trade Corporation) structure long after its international sales suggested that a dichotomous structure of "here and abroad" was inadequate. Shortly after it broke up its international division and created a worldwide area structure, it began to differentiate the global structure for its office-products (OP) business. The OP operations are substantially different from the very large data-processing (DP) operations, and the head of the OP division wanted it to be one profit center, independent of the geographic profit centers for data processing. In less than 3 years, between 1972 and 1975, the locus of OP in the IBM hierarchy moved upward from a position subordinate to DP in each country unit to that of a product division with worldwide responsibility.

Until 1972 there was a single composite sales-and-profit objective at the country level for both DP and OP. Since as much as 90 percent of a country's business was DP, OP would usually be slighted in any tradeoff. Also, staff at World Trade Headquarters were shared, and on critical decisions like pricing, OP did not get the support it needed. Steps were taken to correct this problem in 1972, when the country manager was no longer allowed to make OP-DP tradeoff decisions; they were to be made at the group (Europe, Americas/Far East) level. For a brief while the OP country managers reported to the OP group managers, but then the reporting line was further centralized and they reported directly to World Trade Headquarters. Under that arrangement OP became a separate profit center within the international side of IBM, and the reporting lines effectively bypassed the area and country levels of the old structure. In what must have been read as a moderate challenge to the hegemony of the country managers, who were generally DP types, the OP country manager then had to rely on him only for nonmarketing staff support on a dotted-line basis.

The third structural change in three years took place in mid-1975, when OP was centralized once again. It was taken out of the two geographic groups (United States and Americas/Far East) and set up with the new minicomputers and software as part of a worldwide General Business Group. The General Business Group, an almost $4 billion unit, then set up its own international division based on country management units.

Pfizer.   Pfizer, one of the world's leading pharmaceutical companies, has followed a similar path. With about half of its sales and more of its earnings coming from abroad, it has still held onto its international division rather than shift to a global area design. Beginning in the early 1960s it embarked on a diversification program to counter the decline in new drugs due to the harsh regulatory climate and severe technological obstacles. Its program was both ambitious and haphazard. The company made about 60 acquisitions in 12 years and strayed far afield of its basic business: drugs and health-care products in a science-based company. Organizationally, most of these new product lines were fit into the existing geographic structure of country management. During the period from acquisition through adjustment and often to divestiture, these units would be moved up and down the geographic hierarchy looking for the appropriate way of pitting diversified product lines into a geographically differentiated structure. Many, of course, were dumped along the way, including pesticides, plastics, protein fish meal, door-to-door cosmetics, and baby foods. Those fitting into the more traditional Pfizer product groups finally survived within the international division. Significantly, the more distinct businesses were ultimately organized as separate worldwide product divisions, bypassing the international-domestic split and reporting directly to corporate headquarters. These included Quigley refractories, Howmedia orthopedic supplies, and Coty consumer products.

The reasons and conditions for pulling a product line out of its geographic moorings are similar to the reasons for creating a global structure based on product lines in general. Among the most important are the following:

Sharp differences in marketing or production and supply.

Little or no interdependence between the main line and the new one.

Currently small, but potentially large, growth of the separated product.

Avoidance of rivalry and hostility among managers in different product groups. The lessons of IBM and Pfizer are repeated in other firms that move outside their original, narrow product base. These lessons are as follows:

Pure geographic structures do not permit sufficient integration of any one different product line.

The more differentiated a new product line is from the main business, the more centrally (globally) it should be managed.

The need to introduce product differentiation into a geographically specialized hierarchy increases the managerial and the structural complexity by geometric proportions.

Given: **Global Product Management**

Needed: **Geographic Coordination**

Global corporations that are organized along product lines have the opposite problem: how to coordinate their diverse business activities within any one geographic area. When they have made the strategic choices to carry a diversity of products to new areas, their structures reflect the need to maximize technological linkages among the farflung plants in each business unit. This has been done, however, at the cost of duplicating management and organization in each area. To cope with problems of coordinating and simplifying these parallel managements, firms must reach through their existing product structure and weave an additional dimension across the organizational pattern. In the language of this metaphor, those who do it successfully will have a blend rather than a plaid fabric as the result. Eaton Corporation offers one example of a global firm that has successfully woven a few threads across the straight grain.

Eaton.   Eaton is a highly diversified company in the capital goods and automotive industries. It has sales of over $1.5 billion, employs over 50,000 people, and operates over 140 facilities in more than 20 countries. In 1974 each of its four worldwide product groups had a managing director for European operations. Each of the firm's 29 manufacturing facilities and 6 associate companies in Europe reported to one of these four people. In addition, 18 service operations, a finance operation, and an R&D center in Europe reported to their functional counterparts in the parent company. Senior management was concerned about how well it was coordinating these activities in Europe.

It was important for Eaton to be able to evaluate and respond to significant trends and developments in European countries, such as tariffs, tax matters, duties, government legislation, currency fluctuations, environmental controls and energy conservation, codetermination and industrial democracy, labor matters, nationalization, and government participation in ownership. Its current organization structure did not provide a regular and convenient means of communication among its European units, either for exchanging information, for building a positive corporate identity, or for assessing corporate needs and coordinating programs and procedures to meet them.

Rejecting the notion of country managers and/or one vice-president for Europe, they instituted a European Coordinating Committee (ECC) together with coordinating committees in each country where they had a major involvement. The four European managing directors were permanent members of the ECC and each served as a coordinator for one or more of the country committees; Europeans representing various functions were appointed to one-year terms; and the firm's executive vice-presidents and group vice-presidents were all made *ex officio* members, with one present at each ECC meeting on a rotating basis. Meetings are now held monthly, midway between the monthly meetings of the corporate operating committee, and minutes were sent to world headquarters within five working days. Attendance is required, the chair rotated periodically, and the location rotated among the major facilities. The president and the four group vice-presidents fly to Europe to formally launch the new coordinating committees, and the corporate newsletter devotes an entire issue to the new developments.

Six months after launching the coordinating committees, Eaton formed a Latin American Coordinating Committee, and about a year after that they created a U.S. and Canadian Division Manager's Council using the same model. The same attention was paid to details of the committee's operations and to their implementation. The European committee, then, served as a model for realizing better coordination across business lines in each of the firm's major geographic areas, and it is probable that the capstone in the future will be a council of councils that will take the form of annual or semiannual worldwide coordinating meetings.

This example illustrates a moderate step, in structural terms, toward complementing the warp of a traditional product-line organization with the woof of geographic coordinates. The fabric of the organization is not significantly altered, rather it is reinforced. Little is done to increase the complexity of the global design or management practices. Success depends on thorough implementing of a plan that least disturbs the existing managerial style and corporate culture. The change is supplementary, rather than radical, and it has the desired effect of managing *both* product and country diversity.

Firms that are organized along global product lines will probably experience similar needs to coordinate their activities within a foreign country when they have at least two significant but organizationally independent business units there; there are economies to be gained from pooled information; there are benefits derivable from a more unified corporate identity; or there is a descernible need for assessing and coordinating corporate programs and their implementation.

THE FUNCTIONAL DIMENSION IN GLOBAL TERMS

The product and area structures, and any combinations, all treat the functional dimension in tertiary fashion, locating it in the various parts of the structure after the deck has already been cut twice. The extractive raw-materials ventures are an exception to this rule.

Functional activities play a critical role in, for example, the petroleum industry because of the scale required for economy, the technological complexity involved, and the importance of captive markets for the sale of crude. All major petroleum companies carry out exploration, crude production, tanker and piepline transportation, manufacturing (refining), and marketing, in addition to the logistics of worldwide supply and distribution at each step in these process and product flows. These flows may be managed directly through centralized functional departments acting with worldwide line responsibility and supplemented by corporate staff who coordinate the functions within areas; or, conversely, through area management, with staff coordination for the functions. In any one petroleum company, the structure is either a mixture of the two or else it shifts back and forth. Conoco, for example, dropped its area division and returned to a functional structure. It reasoned that environmental changes, such as the oil import program and the Arab oil embargo, no longer made it feasible to think of domestic and foreign markets separately.

Most oil companies have a petrochemical products division reporting directly to the president, and since they have diversified into other energy sources, they also have a unit for that at the top of the hierarchy. The result is usually a three-dimensional mixture of parallel hierarchies: Some functions, some regions, and some products all report directly to the chief executive. Each of the hierarchies then has its own particular structural sequence: for example, a functional division will be subdivided by regions, whereas a region division reporting directly to the top would subdivide by functions; a product division might subdivide by functions or by regions. The result is a complex array of different hierarchies (Exhibit 2).

Whichever dimension is chosen as the organizing principle for a corporate division, that unit will confront problems integrating the other dimension(s) in its lower levels. Also, the corporation as a whole faces the problems of integrating each dimension as it is variously located in different countries, different hierarchical levels, and different divisions. By varying the primary building blocks, rather than using only one as the basis, the coordinating dilemmas are compounded rather than resolved, no matter how intelligent the choice of mix is. It is an open question whether management is ultimately backing into structural diseconomies; each structural choice is rational, but the totality nevertheless creates complexities that often negate the gained advantages. The structural choice at these macrolevels of design is also motivated by whether they are politically more or less vulnerable to dissection by the government in the event of moves to break up the big oil companies.

The aluminum industry is another example of an industry in which functional activities continue to play a primary role in fixing the structure. Alcan, for example, organized its activities in 1970 around the three major steps in the making and selling of their single-product line. Reporting directly to the president were three executive vice-presidents for raw materials, smelting, and fabricating sales. Within each of these functional divisions, foreign subsidiaries then grouped around area managers. Where a national subsidiary is itself vertically integrated, as in Brazil and India, it reports up the fabricating line. A worldwide functional structure, however, is not very stable, and in 1973 Alcan subsumed its ore activities under the executive vice-president smelting. Its concern was with the vulnerability of its sources of supply.

EXHIBIT 2   STRUCTURAL SEQUENCE OF VARIOUS HIERARCHIES

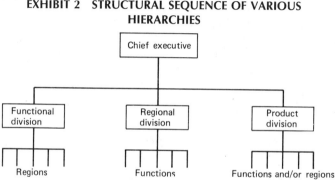

This left the company with a global dichotomy between production and sales in line operations, which continue to drift to an area format with problems of integration for supply and distribution on a global basis.

The lesson is, do not organize global structures around business functions unless you are in extractive raw-materials industries, and even then you will find that these structures are unstable and will have to share primacy with geographic factors and, in some instances, with product differences. For global industrial corporations, basic functions such as manufacturing and marketing are and should be subsumed under product or geographic units. Even European-based companies, which have tended to emphasize functional structures in their domestic activities far more than U.S.-based ones, give this dimension less importance in their multinational design.[8]

ORGANIZING AROUND MARKETS, NOT GEOGRAPHY

Although the basic organizing dimensions for multinational corporations are functions, products, and geographic areas, some firms have begun to think in terms of market differences as a more important basis for determining their global structures. A market is conceived of as an identifiable and homogenous group that has similar patterns of need, purchasing behavior, and product use. Taking this definition and applying it to the nations of the world, companies are less likely to divide the globe on the basis of physical proximity than on the basis of needs and abilities to satisfy them. The traditional categories of Latin America, the Far East, Europe, and the like lose their power, and the new categorization is derived from development economies. Here the oversimplified dichotomy between developed and less developed has yielded to the current preference for dividing the globe into five "worlds." The first world includes the familiar capitalist economies of the industrialized world, and the second world includes the 1.3 billion people in the centrally planned communist economies. The third world comprises developing countries that have a modern infrastructure and/or have exceptional wealth in natural resources. Able to attract foreign investment and borrow on commercial terms, they need time and technology more than foreign aid. They include OPEC members, Brazil, Mexico, South Korea, Taiwan, and Turkey. The fourth-world countries have similar characteristics but in much less generous amounts and therefore need injections of both trade and aid. The fifth-world countries are the complete have-nots, without resources or the likelihood of ever improving their lot.

Business planners and marketers have taken these distinctions and, together with their own companies' historical records, have redrawn their organizational lines. One firm began with Stanford Research Institute's economic projections for 1975–1990 and planned a growth-market group around 10 countries that are expected to have annual growth rates averaging 6 percent or more: Brazil, Iran, Taiwan, Korea, Indonesia, Mexico, Venezuela, Japan, Turkey, and Spain.

Before divesting Merrill Labs, Richardson-Merrill, another multinational, maintained its Latin America/Far East unit, but reorganized the country groupings within it to reflect the same market differentiation as follows:

Group 1.   Andean Group, Southeast Asia, Philippines, and the Caribbean represent small, noncomplex, and underdeveloped markets for their products in places they have chosen to operate.

Group 2. India, Indonesia, and Iran represent large, noncomplex, and high-potential growth markets.

Group 3. Mexico, Brazil, and Australia represent large, complex markets to them, with proven records for their company as well as satellite markets in neighboring countries.

Group 4. Japan stands by itself as another large, complex, and mature market that requires specialized attention.

Ingersoll Rand distinguishes between offensive and defensive strategies when establishing manufacturing plants abroad: "Offensive" plants are to be used for exports as well as for sales in that country, whereas "defensive" location decisions are mainly made to protect against erosion of market share in that country. Other firms are finding it useful to define area managements in terms of a composite scale of key factors: examples include labor–capital intensity of the technology employed, the level of anticipated competition, the character of government (e.g., a socialist-bloc group), the cost of energy, and the availability of skilled personnel.

Market-centered thinking is making deeper inroads into planning and development than into operations, but the evolutionary trend is clear nonetheless. General Electric carries the idea into its planning around "strategic business units," which easily translate into families of businesses laid out on a product/geography grid. Again, the older and already tested structure acts as a supportive framework while new strategies evolve some kinds of metastructures as overlays. As the new language developed in central staffs gets absorbed, and as the future orientation becomes operating reality, it is not unlikely that we will witness a new generation of structural form in global corporations.

The basic principle in this approach is that geography is an obfuscation for conceptualizing global growth strategy and for organizing and managing the multinational corporations' responses. Market segmentation for domestic activities is far from new. A common differentiation in a domestic structure, for example, is between a government sector, an industrial sector, and a consumer sector. Organizing around markets, rather than geography, is recent, however, as applied to worldwide corporate structuring. The country, or nation-state, is kept as the basic unit of analysis, but the grouping together of countries is done on the basis of a different set of questions and assumptions: not on the assumption that understanding management in Mexico helps to start a business next door in Guatemala, but that demographic, income, natural-resource data, and the like are more relevant criteria, and are also ones that lend themselves to country-cluster analysis and hence to market-determined organization design.

The patterns and problems discussed above for the global industrial corporations are also reflected in the multinational spread of service corporations. Here market segmentation around clients and services is analogous to the product dimension in a manufacturing firm, and management searches for ways to integrate this dimension with the familiar geographic design.

The market-center concept is useful to all firms, though few thus far have actually structured their worldwide activities around it. Companies might want to do so when operations in neighboring countries are totally independent of each other; communication networks are good, and the technology for processing information rapidly and accurately is present or is not important; a marketing orientation already exists within the parent company; a set of markets can be identified that have more managerial validity than do sets of countries with geographic regions; the concept is already familiar to managers through the planning process; management is not locked into defense of territories.

GLOBAL MATRIX ORGANIZATION

The trends in organization that we have discussed all start with a primary structural dimension—either functions, products, or geography—and then try to compensate for the benefits lost by not choosing another of these dimensions as the major organizing theme. All of them involve tradeoffs. When a company shifts from organization form A to form B, many benefits of the old form linger on, because they have been deeply ingrained. At some imaginary fleeting moment, there is a balance of benefits, but over time the advantages of the abandoned form are bound to atrophy. This imbalance frequently worsens until there is a sense that the tradeoff has gone too far. Companies then either swing back to the earlier form, as in the familiar centralization/decentralization/recentralization cycles, or else they introduce subordinate coordination schemes such as the ones described in the sections above.

In other words, when companies face multiple goals, they often deal with them in sequence rather than simultaneously. Or else different parts of the company organize around the different subgoals. Translated into structural terms, there is an implicit assumption that the entire organization cannot specialize by two or three dimensions simultaneously. It is this assumption that some firms are rejecting. In doing so, they must reject a pattern of organization based on a hierarchy of power and a unity of command, and they must replace it with a dual or plural model that involves a balance of interest and power. One structural design is not overlaid with elements of another; rather, the two are blended and given coequal weight. The general manager of a French subsidiary, for example, will report to a vice-president for Europe. This is the essence of global matrix organization (Exhibit 3).

Dow Chemical Company is perhaps one of the first industrial corporations to use the matrix form in its global macrostructure. Although Dow does not publish organization charts for internal or external consumption, its 1968 annual report nevertheless did publish a matrix diagram of sorts in the form of a photo cube. Along each dimension of the cube were photos of the key managers for the various functions, product groups, and geographic areas in the Dow organization. At that time the Dow organizational philosophy was that they managed with a three-dimensional matrix. Shortly after that, in fact, one of Dow's senior managers, William Goggin, became

EXHIBIT 3   GLOBAL MATRIX ORGANIZATION

president of Dow Corning and introduced there what he called a four-dimensional matrix, by adding "time" into the sense of structure.

Although these ambitious notions of multidimensional structuring grappled with managing global complexities simultaneously, they proved exceedingly difficult to keep in balance. By 1970 it was apparent that Dow Chemical's matrix was effectively two-dimensional, a worldwide grid of product and geography with functions variously located at different levels in the grid hierarchies. In 1972 the matrix became further imbalanced when the product dimension lost line authority and was kicked upstairs in the form of three business group managers who reported to the corporate product development division. They were to be separate channels of communication for their product groups across the areas, and their clout came from their control over capital expenditures. Life sciences was the only product division that maintained worldwide reporting control.

Around 1974 Dow Chemical held a meeting of its senior managers worldwide. During an anonymous question-and-answer period with the chairman, Carl Gerstaker, the question was asked: "Which dimension of the matrix do you consider to be most important?" The very fact that the question was asked demonstrates that the matrix had deteriorated significantly. Gerstaker's answer was to the point: The most important dimension in a matrix organization is the weakest and/or the most threatened. Despite the chairman's understanding of multidimensional structures, however, the matrix continued to decompose. In 1975 the life sciences division lost its worldwide reporting line and was subsumed under each of the geographic "operating units." Whereas each product used to have an identifiable team linking its business through the area, the basic locus of these teams now exists within each area. Today Dow Chemical would be described more appropriately as using a geographically based structure. In retrospect, it should be noted that, with the exception of the life sciences division, only the areas ever had their own letterhead stationery. Although the ideology of global matrix management still exists in some corners of Dow, the ethos and spirit of it is not to be found.

The example of Dow is not to be read as a failure. As Peter Drucker says, the matrix structure "will never be a preferred form of organization; it is fiendishly difficult."[9] He concludes, nevertheless, that ". . . any manager in a multi-national business will have to learn to understand it if he wants to function effectively himself."[10] Dow's global matrix was a valiant and creative effort, a radical approach to structuring a multinational corporation. Some European firms, such as Phillips, have operated with a matrix organization for years, and some U.S.-based nonindustrial corporations have also relied on the matrix form. Global construction and engineering firms, such as Bechtel Corporation, and one bank, Citibank, are examples that have been more successful than Dow Chemical.

Dow Corning, a twentieth the size of Dow Chemical, had been more successful in maintaining its global matrix. A relatively smaller size may be one reason, but far more important is that Dow Corning pays great attention to the behavioral requirements of matrix management in addition to the structural ones. The chairman is an overt enthusiast of the matrix, amiably stressing to his managers that they will be domocratic and share power. The balance of power and shared decision making are translated into nonconcrete form, for example, by the elimination of walls and corridors in favor of office landscaping around family groupings. Since Dow is purposefully built around a paradox of competing claims, stability rests in managers' behavior more than in structural form. Matrix is a verb.

Corporations need not organize their domestic activities around a matrix in order for the form to be used in their global frameworks. But if they are going to attempt to implement a matrix design, they should only do so when there is diversification of both products and markets requiring balanced and simultaneous attention; the opportunities lost and difficulties experienced by favoring either a product or geographic unity of command cannot be ignored; environmental pressure to secure international economies of scale require the shared use of scarce human resources; there is a need for enriched information-processing capacity because of uncertain, complex, and interdependent tasks; information, planning, and control systems operate along the different dimensions of the structure simultaneously; as much attention is paid to managerial behavior as to the structure.

The corporate culture and ethos must actively support and believe in negotiated management. They have to think matrix.

The increasingly common response during the past five years is to turn to some form of matrix design. As author of a recent book on the subject,[11] I have watched the growth of matrix usage closely. A strange and paradoxical, though understandable, phenomenon is occuring. There is parallel increase in the *usage* of and *dissatisfaction* with the matrix. By now, the structural requirements are rather clear; it is the behavioral changes that are resisted and resented. Little wonder! In common usage, the form is only a few decades old. After centuries of a one-boss model, based around principles of the unity of command, the shift to a two-boss model, based on a balance of power, will take many more years before it is legitimated and accepted.

For the purpose of brevity, two examples of major world corporations will suffice. Only 5 years ago only a few of General Electric's strategic business units were organized around some form of matrix. By 1977, 25 percent reported using a matrix, and only 1 year later as many as 40 percent of the strategic business units were employing it in one way or another. Whereas the matrix is found at middle levels in GE, it has been used as an organizing principle for the entire institution at Citibank, the second-largest bank in the world. The results are mixed, and senior management is searching for a way to get "beyond the matrix" without returning to the either/or world of the already existing models.

The two examples are instructive for another reason. The principal organization models are ones that have been developed by industrial firms in an industrial economy. The United States, however, has a postindustrial or service economy. This has received scant attention for the most part, and few observers or practitioners have understood the implications of this major historical shift for both the strategy and organization of world corporations. IBM, for example, is much less than 20 percent manufacturing-based with the rest service-based, yet the firm is considered an industrial corporation. Corporations in the service sector of the economy have used organization models developed in and for the industrial sector. It is my hunch and prediction that the major breakthroughs in organization design will occur in the now-dominant service sector. It is only a logical extension that if and when there is a major advance in the organization of multinational corporations, it will come from multinational *service* corporations.

CONCLUSION

In summary, the basic patterns of organization for global corporations are rather standard by this time. While the posture of a firm is domestic with only some foreign activities, the latter are generally grouped into an international division. Once a global orientation is assumed by the firm, either a worldwide product structure or worldwide geographic divisions are the most-common alternatives. Functional specialization is seldom used as the organizing basis for a global structure; natural-resource industries are sometimes the exception to this rule.

When organizations experience significant diversification in both their products/ services and markets, the singular structure based on *either* global product divisions *or* geographic area divisions becomes inadequate. Diversification has led to experiments in global organization design that simultaneously structures a corporation by product/service *and* by geography. This occurs through a variety of forms, although the principles of design are the same in each.

In the simpler form of this new design, corporations develop an overlay of the second organizing dimension across the basic dimension used in the global structuring. Examples include using area-coordinating committees in a product-structured firm; shifting the level of product-line reporting, according to the unique requirements of each, between country, region, zone, and worldwide, in a geographical-structured firm; and using the corporate planning function to negotiate product–market interdependencies.

In the more complex form of the new design, corporations are using global matrix management and matrix structures. These involve some manner of dual reporting lines between the product/service and market dimensions; dual accounting and planning; and a sense of shared responsibilities in which tradeoffs have to be negotiated at the point of interface, rather than sent up to a common boss for resolution. Global matrices are structurally unstable, as are their domestic counterparts. Conflict is inherent in the design, and is managed as an acceptable cost of having the best of both forms of organization.

The general trend is clear. Traditional structures, with their simple choice of functional, product, *or* geographical design, are relied on less and less by global industrial corporations because they optimize along only one dimension. Changes in the external environment and the strategic responses to these changes, however, led global corporations to develop and manage more-complex organization designs than were possible only a decade ago. The new designs attempt to integrate and manage competing needs simultaneously. As the new patterns are understood more clearly, it becomes evident that their success does not lie in having made the most rational choice of structure in any given case. Instead, success with the new patterns depends more on managerial ability to live with a paradox.

NOTES

1. For the application of the product-life-cycle concept to international trade, see Wells of *Business Administration, Harvard University*, (1972).

2. The Harvard Multinational Enterprise Project is a large-scale study that has been going on since 1965, under the direction of Raymond Vernon. The 60 percent figure comes from one of the study's volumes. (Stopford and Wells, 1972, p. 21).

3. Clee and Sachtjen (1964, p. 60).

4. Of the 170 firms examined by Stopford and Wells (1972, p. 51), 90 had an international division in 1968, but the international division was the largest in only 4 of the 90.

5. Stopford and Wells (1972, p. 64) report that when foreign sales reach 40 percent of the total, most firms turn to some form of direct area coordination.

6. Stopford and Wells (1972, p. 77).
7. Davis (1976, pp. 35–47).
8. Franko, (1977).
9. Drucker, (1978, p. 598).
10. Drucker (1978).
11. Davis and Lawrence (1977).

SOURCES AND SUGGESTED REFERENCES

Clee, G.H. and W.M. Sachtjen. "Organizing a Worldwide Business," *Harvard Business Review,* Vol. XIV, No. 6 (1964), pp. 60–78.

Davis, S.M. "Creating a Global Organization," *Columbia Journal of World Business,* Vol. VII, No. 2 (1976), pp. 35–47.

Davis, S.M. and P.B. Lawrence, *Matrix,* Reading, MA: Addison-Wesley, 1977.

Drucker, P. *Management: Tasks, Responsibilities, Practices,* New York: Harper and Row, 1978.

Franko, L.G. "The Move Toward a Multidimensional Structure in European Organizations," *Administrative Science Quarterly,* Vol. XVIII, No. 4 (1977), pp. 493–506.

Stopford, M.J. and L.T. Wells, Jr. *Managing the Multinational Enterprise,* New York: Basic Books, 1972.

Wells, L.T., Jr. ed. *The Product Life Cycle and International Trade,* Boston: Division of Research, Graduate School of Business Administration, Harvard University, 1972.

INTERNATIONAL CORPORATE PLANNING

CONTENTS

THE PURPOSES   3

A Bridge Between the Company and Its Environment   3
A Tool for All Seasons   4
   Contingency planning   4
   Centralization and decentralization   4
   The international dimension   5

THE CONTENT—STRATEGY FORMULATION   6

Diversification   6
   Geography   6
   Product diversification   7
The Route   7
   Sale of knowledge   8
   The sale of goods and services   9
   Investment   9

THE STAGES—FROM FORMULATION TO IMPLEMENTATION   10

Long-Term Planning   10
   Decision preparation   10
   The tools of long-range planning   10
   The advantages   11
Planning for the Medium Term   11
   Translation   11
   The tools of translation planning   13
   The advantages   13
Short-Term Planning   13
   Implementation   13

   The techniques   14
   The advantages   14

THE ROLE   14

The Provision of Criteria   14
The Objective View   15
The Linking   16
The Balancing   16

THE INFORMATION   16

The Flow, the Spasm, and the Signal   16
   The cost of information   17
   Indications of change   17
The Questions To Be Answered   17
Sources of Information   18

THE PLANNING DEPARTMENT   19

Function   19
Organization   20
   Integrated   21
   Group   22
Selection of Organization Type   22
Recruitment and Training   22
The Control of the Planning Function   22

THE FUTURE   23

New Emphases   23
International Planning at the Service of the Company   24

SOURCES AND SUGGESTED REFERENCES   25

INTERNATIONAL CORPORATE PLANNING

Michael Z. Brooke

THE PURPOSES

A BRIDGE BETWEEN THE COMPANY AND ITS ENVIRONMENT. Corporate planning provides a company with a sense of direction and a means of coping with opportunities and problems. The activity is one in which every executive engages in some form: The dream as a result of which the company was founded was itself a pioneer corporate plan. Statements to the contrary, like "this company started planning in 1974," are commonly heard at executive seminars, but reflect a limited view of the subject. Such sayings refer to the introduction of a *formal* system of corporate planning, whereas the exercise has its informal side as well. In the formal sense, as it happens, many companies stopped planning in 1974, at least temporarily. They became disillusioned with an expensive activity that, in many instances, failed to make provision for a steep rise in fuel prices. Normally a company that operates across frontiers does come to see the sense in moving toward some formal planning even if the price seems high. Issues that are straightforward at home develop unexpected complications abroad, and the first reason for developing formal procedures is to provide a bridge between the company and its environment. A few examples will illustrate the point.

The *mining company*'s decision about where to locate a mine is mainly determined on geological grounds in its own country. Naturally there is local opposition to contend with, possibly also central government policy, and certainly the fluctuations in the commodity markets during the long period that elapses between the decision to go ahead and the production of salable material. That period is much longer when the exercise is outside the home country, and political, legal, economic, and other considerations external to the company become critical.

The *machinery manufacturer* may well have a protected market at home. Where there are tariff barriers, local specifications, established relations with customers, or other impediments to trade, the full impact of competition is not met until the company starts to sell abroad. Then the environment becomes very competitive indeed; the strategies of the opposition have to be understood along with local laws and customs.

The *food-processing company* is not, at first sight, an obvious candidate for international operations. The technology is not among the most advanced, the materials are relatively simple, and the market is local. But a second impression conveys that a large part of this industry is in fact international. Staple foods—bread, cereals, fruit juices, preserves, butter, margarine—are manufactured or packed by a limited number of companies with plants in numerous countries. The production of cattle fodder is even more concentrated. The wide range (spread) of multinational food manufacturers argues for a subtle international strategy, including the necessity of understanding the local environment at its most mysterious—eating habits and farming methods—and determining where standardization is possible and where variety is required.

Service industries, like banks, advertising agencies, and insurance companies, go international in order to retain existing customers and to relate to the customers' international strategies. Once abroad, such industries usually seek local customers as well and develop their own foreign policies.

Each industry has its own route and its own planning requirements. Difficulties occur if the environment is not understood, and opportunities arise if it is. The lure into international business comes from higher profits to be made abroad, wider sales from the same expenditure on product development, and the opportunity of transferring to other markets the knowledge acquired at home. The task of international corporate planning is to ensure that the potential is realized and the traps avoided.

A TOOL FOR ALL SEASONS. International corporate planning steers the company through a host of pressures and attractions. It is not intended to be a straightjacket restricting the ability to maneuver. One of the problems in 1973–1974 was that overrigid planning systems had been adopted. Not only was the first oil crisis not foreseen by many—it *was* by some—but the plans were not flexible enough to make the necessary adaptations. Companies have now learned what some were practicing in the 1960s, that corporate planning exists to provide a choice of routes that will enable rapid adjustment to opportunities and problems as they arise. The word *contingency* summarizes the planning outlook that underlies these pages.

Contingency Planning. Broad objectives are set, and the piloting of the company toward those objectives is carried out, by a series of criteria and guidelines for responding to changes and difficulties as they arise. This is contingency planning, and it provides a business with the flexibility to switch from one route to another as conditions change instead of being stymied when the chosen path is closed. The intention is that the destination becomes more important than the means of getting there.

The building of a factory in Nigeria, for instance, will absorb much of the resources of a small company; but even so, provision is required for achieving the proportion of income expected from the plant if there is another revolution in that country and foreign property is expropriated. The planning will ensure that such major disasters, as well as smaller inconveniences, will not prevent the income and growth targets from being reached and may indeed assist in reaching that end. Alongside this approach goes the more difficult issue of central and local participation in the planning.

Centralization and Decentralization. The international planner is often accused of assuming a kind of imperialist role by disposing of the world from his ivory tower in the corporate headquarters. The alternative is then seen as the drafting of plans in the local units, with the headquarters approving or amending. The phrases *top down* and *bottom up* are used of these approaches. The former can be insensitive to the local situation, whereas the bottom-up approach can easily sacrifice the advantages of being international. The benefit of the part does not necessarily aid the well-being of the whole. In the example mentioned in the last paragraph, the Nigerian subsidiary might wish to plan for the reinvestment of all its income in its own operation. The parent company, on the other hand, would certainly want to draw as much revenue out of the Nigerian affiliate as possible once an optimum size had been reached. The money could be used to boost dividends while it was still available, but at least some part would be used to finance a project elsewhere to provide a hedge against any setbacks in Nigeria. For this reason the central planning department would see a different purpose for the Nigerian revenue and recognize that the subsidiary needed a skilled finance manager able to gain government agreement to remitting the surplus funds abroad. This is a typical case of a clash of interest between the local operation and the center.

Most companies need a strong central sense of direction, but this has to exist with the consent and cooperation of the local units. Insensitivity at the center is best overcome by fixing formal procedures for local participation—and this participation should not just consist of meetings of professional planners. One company has regular meetings of national chief executives in each region in which it operates as a part of the planning process. Such procedures highlight the third aspect of the purpose: the special nature of *international* planning.

The International Dimension.   A domestic company does not have to concern itself with transferring money across frontiers, and this consideration symbolizes the special requirements of international planning. A chief executive officer recently declared that "it is totally wrong to distinguish between planning for our domestic business and for that abroad." It is unlikely that a company adopting his view will make the most effective use of its foreign operations, but naturally only large companies can afford specialized and full-time international planners. At a rough estimate, annual sales of $40 million are required to support a full-time planning executive, so the specialization will usually have to be carried part time.

Similar techniques as were used before the company thought in such terms may well be employed to design global plans, but much more complex data will be incorporated into the equations, and the resultant strategies will have the geographic as a prominent dimension. Both the resemblances and the differences between countries have to be noted, but the differences are harder to identify. Many a well-ordered plan has been wrecked because insufficient account was taken of the legal system of a country, the accounting conventions, the local prejudices against a particular marketing ploy, or any of the other factors such as customs and immigration procedures that scarcely have to be considered in domestic planning.

The impact of the planning on both the company and the country is another vital consideration. As a company grows abroad, its management system is going to change. There will come a stage—20 percent of the business outside the home country has been suggested—when the organization will have been altered completely and many of the staff with it. The figure of 20 percent is arbitrary, but the process is inevitable. So international planning is concerned with the response at home as well as the development abroad. Part of that development, again, will have a great impact on national economies. One of the reasons for the growing political opposition to the international firm is precisely that planners in one country are effectively, if unconsciously, vitiating the carefully considered plans of another. The word *sensitivity* must be placed alongside the word *flexibility* as a hallmark of international planning.

In sum, the company can expect of the international planner that he will provide an understanding of the conditions that favor and constrain the international business, and that he will mark out a path to make the most profitable use of any favorable circumstances and to overcome the risks. With this understanding of the aims and objects as a background, it is possible to summarize the contents of the global strategy.

THE CONTENT—STRATEGY FORMULATION

DIVERSIFICATION. There are a number of options for corporate development, including making more profitable use of existing resources, but if *expansion* is the selected strategy, it will not be long before *diversification* is considered in addition to the steady growth of existing business. There are two ways to diversify:

1. *By geography.* This is the international route. The planner prepares the evidence for and against the move abroad and works out the implications after the decision has been made.

2. *By product.* The move into new businesses may be an alternative to going abroad or may by itself lead into foreign markets. Frequently a company that was domestic only finds itself purchasing another that already has foreign operations. Tarmac, a British road-surfacing company, bought one of its competitors, which already had contracts in three continents.

Geography. In the discussion on diversification, there are many arguments for an international strategy. Moving into other countries, for instance, brings the company under the influence of different national economies. Since these are unlikely to go through the cycles of boom and slump at the same time, the company achieves some leveling out of its business, which is one of the objectives of diversification. The more even flow of orders and income that results is especially important for concerns that are much affected by the ups and downs of national economies. On the other hand, naturally, an international strategy has its problems, and there are numerous traps to guard against. Compiling a list of these traps is another task of the planner. For instance, a small manufacturer of fancy goods in the United States developed a substantial market in Germany. The growth of sales there encouraged the manufacturer to appoint a local agent. The appointment was made without adequate planning or investigation of the snags. When the United States company gave the agent notice, it was discovered that considerable compensation was owed. There was no mention of this in the contract, but German law includes a clause protecting local firms that act as agents to foreign companies. This is a typical trap because no such law exists in the United States, whereas it does exist in several European countries.

The international planner, then, has to signal the traps. In addition to the need to operate under different legal systems, a selection of common pitfalls includes the following:

1. *Different accounting systems.*   One company was nearly bankrupted because the controller's department at head office failed to see the signs of trouble soon enough as a result of a misreading of the accounts.

2. *Appointing insensitive managers to sensitive parts of the world.*   One company lost much business after putting a racially prejudiced manager in charge of a subsidiary in a newly independent African country. The promotion of the wrong local manager can be equally disastrous in some countries.

3. *Less-obvious traps.*   Some of the traps, such as the failure to adapt to local conditions, are obvious; others, like the offense that can be caused by overadaptation, are less so. More than one writer has commented on the ability to alienate customers abroad shown by companies with a reputation for being market conscious at home.

International diversification may, then, produce difficulties; but a high proportion of companies also express reservation about product diversification.

Product Diversification.   An apparent advantage of emphasizing diversification by product is that existing skills are employed. The routes available can, indeed, be classified by the skills employed—the *marketing* route, whereby different businesses that require similar marketing abilities are acquired, and the *technical* route, in which industry sectors that employ similar technologies are entered.

Another means of diversification is *financial,* the conglomerate, where acquisitions are made for their financial logic. The companies acquired fit specifications the planner has identified, such as return on investment and asset growth potential. Yet another route is *vertical integration,* when a supplier or customer is purchased.

All the methods can have international implications and are to be considered, along with further international developments, as part of the strategic decision-making process. Vertical integration, for instance, is a common route abroad as a company sets out to ensure its supply network as well as its outlets. Every method of diversification has been described as a spread of risk that carries its own risk, and the planner is interested in reducing the uncertainties. For this a set of criteria are required, and these include some simple and arbitrary, but very common, guidelines like: "This company will place half of its new investment each year outside the home country." A more subtle guideline arises from listing the strengths of the company and determining in which parts of the world they are most likely to be profitably employed. The initial decision to move abroad comes from answers to questions about the strengths and resources already possessed by the company; the answers to other questions determine the route to be followed.

THE ROUTE.   A distinctively international decision is about the method of entering the foreign market. There are three main routes: the sale of knowledge (technical, marketing, or general management); the sale of goods; foreign investment (which may include the other two). Each, of course, has many subdivisions.

A prevailing view is that the most profitable route is through foreign investment, and that the sale of knowledge is only for risky markets or companies that cannot afford any other means. This view, repeated in many textbooks, underestimates the opportunities available to the international planner. His object is to make money abroad, and in a form in which it can be brought home. This may mean adopting different strategies from those suggested by a straightforward pursuit of profit. A company does not need one general strategy for the thrust abroad; it requires separate routes for each product and each market. The different approaches need to fit together, and the way they match is obviously an important consideration. Each main strategy will be identified in the following sections.

Sale of Knowledge.   This route to foreign markets includes a wide variety of activities, beginning with licensing and franchising. In their simplest form, these involve planning in one specialist function only—the technical for licensing and the marketing for franchising. But strategic decisions are never that simple. The licensing department is selling the company's skills, but is itself a branch of marketing, with which it has to be integrated. If this does not occur, a spread of manufacture by licensing, with each case considered purely on its merits, will restrict a company's strategies for years ahead. Then again, the licensing contract cannot always be regarded just as a means for making more money out of research and development without any implications for other functions. The licensee, for example, may have inadequate marketing or financial skills, and so a more complicated arrangement will be required to compensate for the deficiencies of the foreign operator. The same applies to franchising, a sale of marketing knowledge that becomes a total corporate strategy.

There is a spectrum of agreements that gradually grow more complex, with the pure licensing agreement at one end and the management contract at the other. Along the line other functions become involved. The management contract includes, on principle, the management of a company in its entirety but without ownership. Originally developed as a means of using surplus management capacity among transport concerns (a management structure required to operate 10 ships, aircraft, or buses can also operate 100) and expropriated firms in tropical agriculture, this method is now being used in a widening selection of businesses. The various forms of knowledge agreement are shown in Exhibit 1, which demonstrates the range available to the strategist and some of the considerations that apply.

It is characteristic of all knowledge arrangements that

1.   Little capital is required for the foreign operation, but expenditure is required at home to ensure that the company remains at the front in research; otherwise the knowledge may soon become unsalable.

2.   The risks of loss are minimized in the short term, but safeguards are needed for the longer term to prevent the foreign partner from becoming a competitor. The only real safeguard against this and other problems that arise is in the

EXHIBIT 1   KNOWLEDGE AGREEMENTS AND THEIR STRATEGIC RELATIONSHIPS

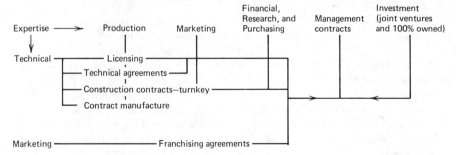

business relationship, which is, therefore, the planner's main concern. The legal contract is usually irrelevant except when the relationship breaks down.

3. The knowledge arrangement is determined as a result of a conscious decision that this is the company's most salable asset.

4. From most countries it is easier to bring money home as payment for know-how (royalties) or for management assistance (fees). The tax position is also more favorable. Until the mid-1970s, both these statements were normally true. More recently, however, suspicions of overcharging for technology have produced changes in some tax systems as well as stricter control of money transfers. The assumption that there are universally applicable tax and remittance rules must now be added to the list of traps for which the planner has to be on the watch.

The amount of money transferred through knowledge agreements is still small, less than 15 percent of world trade, but some forms (like management contracts) have been expanding more rapidly than others.

The Sale of Goods and Services.   Export is the traditional means of making money abroad, and the traditions themselves frequently increase the expenses. Methods that were appropriate when labor was cheap and technology primitive have survived in the transport, dock-handling, revenue service, and other sectors. The total costs of distribution—packing, transport, insurance, clearance across frontiers, and documentation—can add over 100 percent to the cost of a product that is bulky and inexpensive. On the other hand, export is favored by governments concerned with balance-of-payments problems, so assistance to offset the expenses may be available.

The planner is naturally interested in examining the special opportunities for the company's goods and the adaptations, if any, required for the foreign market. He is also concerned that export shall be seen as a strategic option that can be adapted in numerous ways to capture the greatest-possible commercial advantage. For instance, part assembly may ensure orders in some markets, even where it is not legally required, and the advantages that could have been gained by part assembly will eventually be lost if a policy of promoting finished goods is rigidly maintained. The part assembly may be carried out under contract or through a local subsidiary. The assembler sometimes provides after-sales servicing and the stocking of spare parts; both these will improve the sales pitch against competitors. It is, indeed, the competitive pressures that are changing the approach to export planning and ensuring that this is seen as part of a selection of strategies.

Investment.   Most studies of international business in the last 20 years have stressed the growth of foreign investment. In fact, all the routes have been increasingly used in spite of floating currencies, import restrictions, and numerous measures that were once said to be disruptive of trade. Foreign investment has had the most public discussion, because it is the most visible and controversial route, with its political and social implications. There have also been spectacular successes along this route, but these have been accompanied by notable, even if less publicized, failures. The number of withdrawals has been increasing, and one challenge to the planner is to make sure that withdrawal is also an orderly process when it becomes necessary.

This review has been concerned with the planning of two major international strategies—diversification and the route. A profitable, and therefore compatible, package is required when reviewing the plans. Attention is now turned to the part the planner plays in the decision-making process.

THE STAGES—FROM FORMULATION TO IMPLEMENTATION

Planning starts from a question. It may be a general query: "Where is this company going?" In practice it is likely to take a more specific form: "Would it not be a good idea to move into product X?" Or perhaps: "What would be the implications of opening up a business in country Y?" Whatever the starting point, a number of stages occur between the first statement of an idea and its profitable operation. Some of these stages are for the planner, some for the decision maker. In the small company the two will be the same person; where professional planners are employed, their work will be a useless expense unless they cooperate closely with the appropriate decision maker at each stage.

LONG-TERM PLANNING.   The planner picks up a question, or the germ of an idea, and works out some ways in which it can be answered. This stage is usually called decision preparation.

Decision Preparation.   The planning process begins when the planner develops a number of options in the light of the question or statement that forms his brief, and with the corporate objectives in mind. His aim is to provide a reasoned view of where the company could hope to be within 5–10 years, and then to support the findings with some glimpses into the longer term. The exact time horizon will depend upon the industry sector and the type of decision. For a fashion-conscious industry like clothing, 5 years will be long term for product decisions but not for diversification planning. For an industry like mining, 5 years is very short term indeed—perhaps only the time taken to get permission to sink a mine.

The Tools of Long-Range Planning.   The methods used are mainly nonquantitative, although supported by some attempts at forecasting. Increasingly used is scenario-writing. This is a technique for describing some likely situations in which the company may find itself in relation to various changes in the environment. Different companies adapt the technique to their own circumstances, but a typical engineering or chemical concern is likely to start with a look at the prospects for technical change over the next 10–15 years. For this, the planners are very dependent on the research-and-development department. Changes in the market are also considered in the countries in which the company already operates, together with the prospects in other countries. The report includes long-term possibilities for new manufacturing or selling facilities, and the rationalization of the old. Desirable lifetimes for the company's assets are considered. Each scenario, although drafted in general terms, contains a general statement of funding requirements and expected income. Even at this stage the income may be stated in terms of the expected, the best-possible, and the worst-conceivable, requirements and results. The scenarios are constructed from information much of which is external to the company—changes in technical, commercial, economic, social, political, and other factors that are likely to affect the business. Each scenario is then considered in the light of the company's strengths and weaknesses and those of the principal competitors. The story of business in the last 30 years has been full of incidents in which a number of manufacturers have seen a coming gap in the market that they have all moved in to fill. Industry sectors such as basic chemicals and steel have suffered from heavy overcapacity and the resultant losses for individual companies. Hence the planner asks himself how the competitors are likely to react, and who is best placed to win if a commercial war breaks out. Among the techniques for company and competition analysis internationally is the use of a matrix diagram that relates the strengths and weaknesses of the company being analyzed to the opportunities and threats in the environment. Exhibit 2 gives a simplified example of how such a diagram can be designed. In this case a small selection of issues is included for illustrative purposes, and pluses and minuses show the advantages and disadvantages. In actual use, the selection and ordering of the factors would be more systematic, and a number of symbols would be used to identify the most- and the least-advantageous situations and the range in between. From this exercise a list of eligible strategies can be brought together concerning *what* the company is most likely to achieve, to be followed by other strategies suggesting *how* these can be carried out. The resultant report with its recommendations is summarized and handed to the corporate decision-making body. Once this body has decided among the proposals, the next stage of the planning can follow.

The Advantages.   The long-term planning exercise is expected to provide the following:

1. A stimulus to a more detached view about the company's future, since wishful thinking can be a poor adviser.
2. A guide to routine decisions, since the unguided acceptance of opportunities can mean disaster later.
3. An indication of the timing for further decisions and preparations, since delay can destroy a chosen policy.
4. The ability, even for the smallest company, to ensure that corporate resources are used to the greatest possible advantage.
5. A framework for assessing the information constantly becoming available both from inside and outside the company.

PLANNING FOR THE MEDIUM TERM.   Basic decisions have now been made about the strategy, and the transition to tactics is being undertaken. This is a phase of translation.

Translation.   General schemes for the future of the company have to be turned into programs for operating departments, and a decision to enter a particular market must be translated into requirements for facilities and finance. Firm recommendations are made that will determine priorities for a long time to come. The route to a market may be through export, licensing, or investment. Each of the three routes has many subroutes and numerous related decisions. The decisions themselves have different time scales. For instance, investment through starting a new subsidiary from scratch has one set of planning implications. Such an exercise begins with the choice of a site; whereas, if an existing company is to be purchased, a lengthy and painstaking search for a suitable candidate may be involved. If the financing requirements of a project mean a new equity issue, to take a different kind of example, another long

EXHIBIT 2   STRATEGY-FORMULATION MATRIX[a]

Opportunities and Threats in the Environment	Company Strengths and Weaknesses					
	Successful Contracts in Middle East	Limited Sources of Funds	Strong Research and Development	Weak Presence in Europe	Much-Improved Distribution System	Spare Management Resources
Middle East market increasing	+ +					
Steep increase in funding requirements anticipated		– –				
Technological change becoming less important			– +			
Competitors' products unsuccessful in Europe				+ –		
Fast deliveries required					+ +	
Diversification opportunities						+ +

[a]A similar chart, elaborated to any degree required, can be drafted for the company itself and for its competitors.

wait may be necessary before the money market is ready for the placement on suitable terms. In the process of working out the tactics, all the implications of the decision are considered and systematically turned into medium-term plans for each of the departments concerned.

The Tools of Translation Planning.   The methods used are a mixture of the quantitative and nonquantitative; there is a special emphasis on capital requirements supported by income forecasts, market-share proposals, and timing. In some companies the timing is specified in a policy statement containing preferred timings for each major activity from two to five years ahead. Every year the plans are moved further ahead while the current year, or whatever period of time is determined, moves into the sphere of operational planning and budgeting. A number of techniques are available to the medium-term planner, and these will be more quantitative than those used by his long-term colleague, but the figures will be accompanied by general appraisals of the situations under discussion. The techniques include simulation and decision models, in which computer programs are used to show the financial outcomes of the various options. Contingency models are employed in conjunction with the simulations to keep in view the various factors that can affect the outcomes, and criteria are drafted to ensure that the decisions taken are in line with the objectives.

The Advantages.   The company derives a number of benefits from medium-term planning, including the following:

1. A systematic list of deadlines for the progress of a project for both general and departmental decisions and actions.
2. A set of guidelines for appraising opportunities as they arise.
3. Further guidelines for coping with problems that might otherwise deflect the company from its objects.
4. Tactics to meet reactions on the part of competitors.
5. A means of undertaking complicated international logistic exercises with manufacturing units that purchase their supplies from a number of countries and then dispatch their products to numerous other countries. Some of the suppliers and some of the customers may be within the same company, and all the countries may have restrictions on the free movement of goods across their frontiers.
6. Formulas for bringing together the resources of the company into a common decision system.

In general the translation is more complex and specialized than the earlier or the later stages, and it is here that the advantage of employing professional corporate planners is first likely to become obvious.

SHORT-TERM PLANNING.   The final stage is to turn tactical decisions into plans that can be carried out in each operational unit of the firm. This stage is that of implementation.

Implementation.   Precise lead times are now required for the ordering and the delivery of equipment or components and the completion of buildings, renovations, market research, and selling plans, as well as numerous other related activities. The deadlines are carried as far forward in time as such accuracy is possible, but the first year's plans are turned into budgets according to a regular annual procedure. The proposals for the route abroad, determined by the medium-term planners, are turned into courses of action for the selection and appointment of agents or licensors, or for the formation of subsidiaries. Naturally not all the intentions are carried out within the time scales of short-term planning, and some are labeled "search," with contingency plans ready if some decision has to be postponed for lack of a suitable collaborator in the chosen market.

The Techniques.   The short-term planner has a battery of techniques at his disposal, most of them quantitative. Included are short-term forecasting methods that enable him to identify supply and financing opportunities in detail. Similar techniques enable the operations to be geared to seasonal changes and to those of the trade cycle. Market research, which is also used in the earlier stages for more-general purposes, is used at this stage for final decisions about the presentation of the product. One of several forms of network analysis (diagrams designed to show accurately how different activities interrelate) and other scheduling techniques are used to determine precise deadlines for deliveries, funding, establishing facilities, preparing the market, and the launch of the product.

The Advantages.   At this stage of the planning, unlike the two earlier stages, few doubt that the advantages are self-evident. Money can be saved by ensuring that purchases are not made too soon and loans are not acquired with the interest attached before they are needed; there is the equal necessity of avoiding expensive delays when some part of the program is late. Any argument at this stage is about the techniques rather than about the purposes of the planning. The small company should take advice, as the wrong technique or a misinterpretation of facts can be expensive. The larger company is likely to possess its own experts on these subjects.

The advantages of individual elements in the planning process have been suggested, the next section of this section looks at the benefits the company can expect from the planning process as a whole.

THE ROLE

THE PROVISION OF CRITERIA.   The arrival of opportunities cannot be planned, but it can be foreseen, and a reception prepared. A set of guidelines can be formulated to assist in making a judgment about whether a particular opportunity is to be welcomed or whether it is to be regarded as a trap—a short-term advantage that would hinder longer-term developments. The guidelines should be as detailed as possible. Even so, no proposal can be expected to fit all the criteria, but a decision can be taken according to the importance of those that are not met.

Principal factors on the list are the following:

1. *Income.*   If accepted, the income (discounted over the life of the project) has to fit the profit objectives of the company.
2. *Growth.*   Similarly, some statement of anticipated growth is required.

3. *Synergy.* The proposal needs to fit with the company's existing business. The word *synergy* is often used by planners to indicate the degree of mutual adavantage to be found between the suggested operation and the existing activities of the company. In developing the detailed criteria, the synergy heading should be subdivided into the relationship between the project under consideration and each subsidiary, division, and specialist department. Although prospective income is seldom ignored, a proposal that is marginally adequate by return-on-investment forecasts may be worthwhile if it contributes substantially to the profits of an existing part of the business. A high-technology company may set up a subsidiary in a country where relevant expertise exists without the hope of making much impact in that country; the intention is to derive benefits that will be put to profitable use in other markets.

4. *Market.*   A calculation has to be made about market share, sector, and segment to ensure that the new product matches existing capabilities and at least the basic requirements.

5. *Industry Sector.*   Another group of criteria limits the industry sectors and types of technology.

6. *Time scales.*   Preferred time scales are stipulated to ensure that a mixture of long- and short-term projects are made available as required.

7. *Size.*   The size of the project is fixed to some extent. This is determined in the light of a decision about whether it is more opportune, in the current state of a company's development, to spread the corporate risk among a number of small undertakings or to concentrate on a few larger ones.

8. *Resources.*   Another group of criteria ensure that existing resources, including the staff, will be used to their best advantage.

9. *Nature.*   The detailed nature of the project is specified. If, for instance, there is a proposal to buy a company, then another set of criteria is required specifying the minimum requirements for a company that is to be purchased.

Numerous other factors will be listed among the criteria; their systematic consideration before a proposal is accepted is essential and the planning department is well-placed to carry this out. The next element in the role provides a reason why it is so well placed.

THE OBJECTIVE VIEW.   Presenting a detached view of a firm's prospects is a function of the planner. Already mentioned in connection with long-term planning, this is required at the other stages as well. Naturally the detachment is more easily achieved when the planner is full time. If he is also a member of line management, he will find it harder to step out of the biases and the vested interests that are part of his life to take an objective view of his company's prospects. Even the full-time planner often finds himself immersed in corporate politics, or in considerations of personal advancement, that make detachment difficult. Nevertheless, there are obvious advantages to the company in possessing an ability to look at the situation as a whole, as if from the outside, and the use of techniques that resist manipulation will aid such a look. This is one reason for the search for greater quantification in forecasting, but the doubtfulness of the figures and the weakness of some of the gimmicks employed make them liable to manipulation when long-term considerations are at stake. In the end, and when all the aids have been recognized and adopted, objectivity depends on the professional conscience of the planner.

THE LINKING. The planner is able to take an overview of the company's business and point out the weaknesses in the structure. Managers all the way up the hierarchy hold appointments that limit them to certain aspects of the business. The appointments may concern a corporate function, like marketing, or the management of a specific product, or operations in a particular part of the world. The managers are intended to champion their own departments, and are judged according to their successes. This is the time-honored means of managing any organization, and the allocation of responsibilities entailed is usually regarded as essential. But such an allocation does contain divisive pressures. Strong leadership in one unit may advance the interests of that unit against the well-being of the whole company. This is a special difficulty in an international firm, where the contribution that the many parts make to the whole may be obscure, as well as dependent on a number of assumptions about longer-term advantages. The planning department can be expected to provide an overview of all operations so that more-rational decisions can be taken about where the company will place its resources.

THE BALANCING. The twin activity to linking is balancing. The international firm has a variety of facilities and markets, and therefore has numerous logistic questions to answer. There is always scope for improving the supply-and-distribution systems. The balancing of other systems, already mentioned under "Implementation," is of special importance but many other operations have to be balanced as well. Already mentioned under implementation, this is important at all the stages of planning, but balancing includes other issues as well. For instance, rationalization across frontiers is frequently a profitable option but one that is hard to carry out. A concentration of manufacture for a particular product in one country can be desirable on economic grounds but difficult to implement when the closure of a plant in another produces a politically explosive situation. The planner can first determine the measure of rationalization that is desirable, to ensure that the opposition is worth provoking. After that, steps can be worked out to minimize and meet any problems that may arise.

In order to provide balancing, linking, objectivity, and criteria. The planner requires a considerable amount of information. One aspect of his job is that of determining how to collect and process the necessary data.

THE INFORMATION

THE FLOW, THE SPASM, AND THE SIGNAL. The tools of corporate planning require facts, sometimes in large quantities. A principal objective is to reduce the mass of information to a limited number of indicators that can be used as guides to decision making. The world *flow* is used to suggest that a continuous supply of information is being poured into the planner. In practice this is not the way things happen. The data arrive in *spasms,* snowstorms they have been called, since the searches are spasmodic, not continuous. It is not usually possible to maintain a general system of monitoring the environment. Such a system is frequently proposed, but is found to be too expensive; most companies have sufficient difficulty coping with the information required for a particular decision. The planner converts this limited information into signals for action.

The most efficient exercise would be that which could detect the signals in the first place without collecting the information. This may occur sometimes, but usually data have to be collected and sifted to produce a convincing case.

The Cost of Information.   The first requirement in determining the information collected for corporate planning purposes is a policy about the cost. The common arrangement whereby this fluctuates according to the prosperity of the company is wasteful when all is well and unreliable at other times. A satisfactory arrangement is one that ensures a minimum supply of information related to the size of the firm, with a full-time specialist appointed as soon as growth warrants. The person appointed should be briefed to observe signs rather than to assess data. Whatever the size of the information budget, this should be increased to match the needs of specific projects. There is a formula for determining the viable cost of information in relation to a particular project. The calculations are made in the light of the amounts at stake. If the risks are low (say a maximum loss of $1 million if the project fails) but the rewards are high (an income of $10 million in the first 3 years of operation), then an estimate of 1–2 percent of the project budget for information costs would be reasonable. If the rewards are less and the risks greater, then a smaller information cost would be all that could be justified. If, on the other hand, the rewards are higher (say $100 million income over three years) and to fail would carry the risk of bankruptcy, then 5–6 percent of the project budget would be allocated to information collection. These figures are, of course, only broad indications. The actual figures used in a particular company must depend upon its size. The possibility of overwhelming success or disaster is the factor for determining the viable cost of information, not the desirability of knowledge. The purpose is to reduce the gambling element; the information available can never ensure certainty.

Indications of Change.   For the international planner, the cheapest and most reliable information is that which signals change: one market beginning to improve, another to decline; one product at last showing greater potential, and other such general indications. More specifically, the armaments manufacturer watches the national budget while the producer of educational equipment looks out for changes in the birth rate or the law on the school-leaving age. Such indicators often produce little response because they do not signal urgently enough. Attention may be concentrated on current crises while important trends are overlooked. By the time the signs are noticed, they are also obvious to competitors, and any response has become more difficult and less profitable. The search for the early warning is a vital and frequently inexpensive element in the data-collection system.

THE QUESTIONS TO BE ANSWERED.   The purpose of the information is to answer questions, and these will be of a number of kinds:

1.   What evidence is coming to light that offers fresh opportunities or threatens disaster? The difficulty, as has just been suggested, is to receive this information—especially when it comes from abroad and may therefore seem less urgent than it is. Guidelines can be issued and duties allocated, but perhaps the most-effective means of overcoming the difficulty is to ensure that there

is always time at meetings, always space on agendas, and always some listening time available. A few minutes wasted is better than ignoring important messages.

2. What evidence is available for a particular long-term project? How reliable, or how available, is the evidence? Can it be employed in connection with the techniques being used? The answers to these questions enable some calculations of costs related to the issues at stake to be made.

3. What information is required for the tactical and operational planning of the project? This question can be broken down into general and departmental issues. The markets and the competition will have been identified and will now require a closer look. The general view of the prospects will have to be broken down into the following:

    a. *Financial statements,* detailed presentations of the way the new product or national market can be expected to contribute. The financial planning will include the measures to be taken to ensure, as far as possible, that the expected amount of money can be remitted home at minimum cost in delays or tax deductions. If a new subsidiary is to be founded, decisions about its financial structure will depend on knowledge about the local money market, the banking system, relevant legislation and the possibility as well as the desirability of moving funds within the company.

    b. *Marketing requirements* in addition to those that have already been assessed, like the size of the market and the state of the competition. A more detailed market study will be required to demonstrate the changes, if any, that are needed in the presentation of the product and its promotion. Knowledge about the distribution system in the country and how the customer is usually serviced will also be sought.

    c. *Technical information* will be needed if local manufacture is anticipated, and the extent to which the subsidiary will fit into local industry has to be assessed. The equipment available locally and its sophistication will also be studied. The production manager will require information on the availability of staff at all levels and the state of labor relations.

SOURCES OF INFORMATION.   There are two sources of information available to a company, the *internal* and the *external,* and both can be provided *orally* or by *documentation.* Studies have shown that most corporate decision making is based on facts generated internally, and that for external information, oral sources are preferred. Keegan (1974) states: "Businessmen clearly rely very much on information that is not contained in the literature and must have, to be effective, a network of human . . . sources." The construction of such a network by the international corporate planner enables questions to be answered by phone, and can reduce considerably the time taken in documentary searches—even if some additional information from documents is required. The personal sources can be tested, their reliability gauged, and replacements made if necessary. They can also be cross-questioned. Nevertheless, biases and prejudices influence the advice given, particularly when the nuances of foreign markets or the characteristics of local labor are being discussed.

The internal documentary sources, which can also be cross-questioned, since they originate from foreign employees of the firm, are derived mainly from the control system. The planner, as well as the accountant, helps to decide the items on which reports are required. To the financial data are added items of market information, especially on sales and market share. Figures for production—including machine utilization and delays, labor quality and turnover rates, training requirements, and other relevant facts—can also be demanded.

Some problems of using the control information as the basis of the planning information do have to be recognized. One is that data from this source relate to the past and may be misleading in considering the future. At the least a trend, such as the increasing success of a particular product, should be carefully examined before resources are committed. Another problem is the influence on the subsidiary of pressure to collect information not required for its own business. This can imperil its efficiency.

External documentary information is another source, and is provided in a variety of ways—customers, banks, suppliers, and general contacts perhaps operating on a reciprocal basis. The criteria are the ability to meet the requirements suggested earlier in this chapter to provide adequate signals for action at a viable cost, ability to provide an objective check against the information received through the internal and oral routes, and accuracy and costs within fixed limits.

Some of the most useful literature comes either free or at a trivial expense from sources like banks, embassies, trade associations, and the International Monetary Fund. In the next rank come a few indispensable reference books like the *United Nations Yearbook* (beware the dating of the information) and the publications of the Organization for Economic Cooperation and Development. Finally, there are the commercial reference books—the *Europa Handbook* are among the most reliable—and the news services, of which the various publications of Business International are the most useful for the professional corporate planner. An indexing system is required to make the best use of the information and to record where it can be found when required again. Advice on appropriate systems, which should be stored on a computer, is easily obtainable, but the arrangements finally made should be personal to the company. Increasingly, the information can be bought in machine-readable form, and the costs are often far less than the labor costs of library searches.

THE PLANNING DEPARTMENT

FUNCTION. "Planning may be as old as thinking man, but as a recognized part of the equipment of the business firm and with its own organization it is relatively new" (Brooke and van Beusekom 1979, p. 211). A number of approaches to the role have already been discussed. The place of the planning department itself may be understood in relation to its *level* in, and its *degree* of involvement with, the management system of the company. *Level* refers to the position at which the planning department is slotted into the organization. This may be near the top, as an advisory service to the chief executive; at the divisional level; at the subsidiary level; or at any combination of the three. Once the planning function develops, departments emerge at many levels with or without a common organization. The degree of involvement, or the amount of detachment, is likely to be related to the level. The advisory service to top management is mainly objective: The planners are not expected to be concerned with implementation. The lower-level service, which is usually introduced first, is concerned with implementation—ensuring that the implications of longer-term commercial decisions are carried out systematically—and with conducting a search for acquisitions. This last, often a specific duty given to the planning department, is a wasteful confusion of role in an international context. The planner is best employed performing the other activities already outlined—providing the objective standpoint, the linking, and the balancing—while the search for acquisitions is carried out by line management within the framework of whatever international organization the company possesses. The planner provides guidelines and lead times to assist the line manager, and he determines the criteria for purchase, not the companies to be bought. Some aspects of the work of the international planner emerge in a simple example. Assume that an agreed-upon strategy includes developing two products extensively in Latin America, on the grounds that the income objectives for those two products are most likely to be achieved on that continent. Assume also that the company already has extensive business in six of the Latin American countries, this business is in other products as well as the two selected, and it is being conducted at present through a large number of licensees, agents, sales offices, and other outlets. Assume finally that tactical guidelines are developed that include a rationalization of the varous outlets and the purchase of an existing company that can manufacture the products in the area and undertake a major thrust into its own national market, to be extended to other countries later. As soon as word of this policy gets around, the company is going to be inundated by agents, licensees, and others proposing that they become the subsidiary and with plans for the rationalization. In the end, the company may appoint consultants to advise on a suitable firm, after first determining which is the preferred country, or may use an internal team for the purpose. This is a task that is not suitable for the corporate planning department. If it does become involved, there will be no unit that is not subject to the immediate pressures, for and against a particular acquisition or agency, and that is able to ensure that objectives and tactics are fulfilled. The decisions will be made in any case; but the profit contribution from Latin America is likely to be watered down if the planning department does not retain its ability to judge objectively, to balance, and to link. The department plans the implementation and provides the criteria for the final decisions, but leaves the actual selection of units for sale or development to others.

The second element in the department's function is complementary to the first; it is to involve the implementer in the global planning. The planning process internationally consists of much travel and many meetings, so that the benefit of the local unit and its specialized knowledge is fully considered and makes the greatest possible contribution to the well-being of the whole concern.

Other activities vary with the stage of the planning process. In the early stages, the long-range planner stands by the central decision maker with his overarching view of the corporation, while the implementation planner provides a service to the operating managers. At every stage some equilibrium has to be achieved between a planning system that destroys local initiative and that which fails to realize the international potential. If this task is found to be easy, then it is probably not being fulfilled.

ORGANIZATION. There are a number of ways of integrating the planning department with the rest of the organization. Essential is that the department be treated as an independent unit answerable to general management at the relevant level.

The most-useful services of international planning will not be provided if the planners report to marketing executives. Among companies with separate planning functions, there are two main forms of organization. In Exhibit 3 these are called *integrated* and *group*. The relationships of planning with the other departments are shown in the diagrams, and the main characteristics of each type are discussed in the following sections.

Integrated.   This is an arrangement whereby the planning department is organized as a whole throughout the company, with a section attached to the head office and one to each of the divisions and subsidiaries. The department is integrated in that the manager in charge at the head office is also in charge for the whole of the company; there will be considerable division of labor between the units; each will play a different part in the stages of planning and may have special product and geographic interests as well. The actual relationship to the subsidiary management will vary from company to company, but usually the local chief executive will be in charge with a strong link to the center, as is shown in Exhibit 3.

EXHIBIT 3   THE PLACE OF THE PLANNING DEPARTMENT IN THE CORPORATE SYSTEM: (a) INTEGRATED (ONLY P₁ IS INVOLVED IN LONG-TERM PLANNING; P₂ IS MAINLY IMPLEMENTATION.) (b) GROUP (P₁ AND P₂ ARE BOTH INVOLVED IN ALL TYPES OF PLANNING AS RELEVANT TO THEIR UNIT. THE CONTACT BETWEEN THEM IS INFORMAL.)

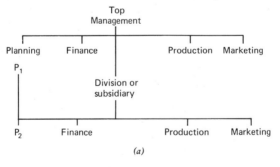

(a)

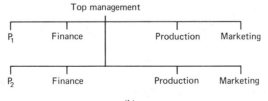

(b)

Group. The other method is for each unit to have its own planning organization, which is unspecialized and performs any functions the local management may require. Links with the center are weak.

SELECTION OF ORGANIZATION TYPE. The type of organization chosen by a particular company depends on many factors unrelated to planning—industry sector, background, management style, and so on. From the point of view of the professional planner, the integrated form has many advantages. There are also dangers. One is that the planning can become overcentralized. Just as the resources of an international group are wasted if there is no strong center taking a global view of resources, so the opportunities will be frittered away if the dialogue with the subsidiaries is weak. The danger then is that planning will develop along esoteric lines remote from the needs of the business. The form of organization needs to avoid this danger, to keep the planners closely in touch with day-to-day management but without damaging their objectivity. Their recruitment and training will be required to serve the same objectives.

RECRUITMENT AND TRAINING. The professional planner has to earn the right to be heard, demonstrate his skills in a convincing manner, and achieve both the detachment and the involvement demanded of him. As soon as the size of the department justifies it, corporate planning can be divided into two groups—the longer term (strategic and tactical) and the short term (operational). Recruits for the former group will need some business experience and to have demonstrated their ability at making judgments and choosing between options under conditions of uncertainty, with evidence that seldom seems adequate. The job also requires imagination. The recruit may well come from line management and perhaps may expect to return there. He may even be on temporary secondment.

The short-term planner, on the other hand, is likely to have a mathematical background and to intend a career in planning. He will be involved in simple day-to-day practicalities and at the same time with complex corporate models. An ability to handle sustained routine activities is required. For the operational planner, qualifications are more important and personal characteristics less so than for his longer-term colleague.

Part of the training program needs to make the planner more familiar with the other aspects of the business, and a joint program to bring together planners and other representatives of both staff and line management is useful. Other aspects of a planning course include the nature of planning, its uses and phases, forecasting, scheduling and other means of fixing deadlines, planning in functional departments, organization, demand analysis, inventory control, the role of the planner and the skills required, the production of planning cycles, and the collection and use of information.

THE CONTROL OF THE PLANNING FUNCTION. There is no known productivity measurement for the planning department, and planners have no difficulty in resisting attempts to find one. Nevertheless, thorough checks are required in an activity that influences so much of a company's most sensitive activity and brings together action and knowledge throughout the most far-flung operations. Significant objectives of appraisal of planning are the following:

1. To determine the size of the department and what resources can be allocated with a reasonable hope of a satisfactory return. A rough and ready calculation of what a company could *afford*, a full-time planner for $40 million dollars' worth of sales, has already been suggested. The object here is to decide what a company *needs*. For the purposes of determining the optimum size, the department must be considered both as an advisory service and as an insurance. Contingency planning provides some hedges against disaster that would be more expensive if paid for in any other way. The cost of the planning department can be compared with the cost of providing the services by other means.

2. To determine whether appropriate techniques are being used and used effectively. To do this, a checklist of available techniques is drafted, as well as an inventory of those used in the company. Then members of staff are asked to answer two questions:

   a. Why are certain techniques being used and others not?

   b. Why does a particular mixture of techniques exist in the company itself?

   These questions check the planner's knowledge of new developments outside the firm and of what is going on inside. The point of the questions is to make such a check, not to question the planner's professional expertise.

3. To examine the detailed results, this is mainly applicable to the short-term planner in whose case some attempt can be made to ensure that the scheduling techniques have given the correct signals to line management and their suppliers. For the longer-term planner, such an attempt is undesirable; it may affect his objectivity by concentrating his attention too much on the obvious and the predictable. Some list of probable reactions to corporate proposals from different parts of the world can be expected of the tactical planner.

4. To ensure that the role of the department is in accordance with corporate policies and management styles—to ensure, for instance, that the planners are not exercising a centralizing influence when the company is attempting to decentralize.

None of these control objectives provide simple quantitative checks, but together they come as near as is possible to an appraisal of the work being undertaken without damaging the objectivity and detachment of the department. Naturally individual planners will also be subject to any personal evaluation schemes employed by the company. The purpose of appraising the planning function as such is to make judgments on its relevance and expertise. The checks will be carried out on the basis of reasonable assumptions about the contribution the planner can make. The department does not exist to provide some magical insight into the future; it exists to provide a sense of direction for steering through the global opportunities for success and failure.

THE FUTURE

NEW EMPHASES. The last decade has seen an increase in the funds committed to international trade; the increase proves steep even after allowing for inflation. This growth has occurred in spite of obstacles that were previously considered fatal. Floating exchange rates alone were once confidently said to be enough to destroy a large sector of commerce; but their effect has hardly been noticed even though accompanied by growing national restrictions and escalating fuel prices. The response of business to national economic problems and growing competition has been to seek every available advantage by selling in more markets, seeking supplies from more sources, and funding from as many centers as possible.

Such developments have increased the need for international corporate planning in spite of the damage to its reputation caused by the first energy crisis. The changing emphasis already noted is likely to continue with more stress on targets and on keeping options open—with carefully calculated deadlines at which particular options have to be jettisoned—and less on detailed routes. This trend will be accelerated by increasing costs. Even with the mechanization of data storage and of the techniques for employing the data, corporate planning will remain labor intensive and will be used with discretion. There is likely to be more effort devoted to reducing uncertainties and less to global scanning. Indeed this latter activity, much recommended in the past, is likely to go out of fashion except where some easily recognizable indicator is being sought in order to forecast changes in a particular market.

One activity that is likely to increase is the use of scenarios, and since this requires specialist skills, some degree of professionalism will be needed. The skills are most appropriately developed inside the company, even on a part-time basis, by an executive trained for the purpose but retaining other duties. If no suitable insider can be seconded, outside assistance may be required. In either case an intimate knowledge of the company is essential. The scenarios will identify the pitfalls likely to be encountered and will enable a number of options to be considered at whatever depth is desired or can be afforded. They will also be as comprehensive as possible in including all the issues that can affect the future of the business, from changing technologies through consumer fashions to government intervention.

Many commentators are preoccupied with discontinuities in the environment —both over time, where new technology has wiped out well-established industries, and over space, where many markets remain bound into established cultural patterns. This preoccupation is likely to grow, and international planners will need to devise new tools to identify where discontinuities are likely to arise for particular products. The competitive advantage will rest with adaptability rather than dramatic innovation, and the ability to adapt will be the subject of increasing pressure.

INTERNATIONAL PLANNING AT THE SERVICE OF THE COMPANY.   The changing emphasis will clearly lead to changing demands on planning services. Questions couched in the form "What will happen if . . ." are likely to be the stock in trade, but the planner will often have to frame the question as well as the answer. He will also provide sets of criteria in the light of which the questions can be answered by others. The place of formal planning in the management system will be partly determined by the size of the company. At any size, companies are increasingly likely to be conducting business across frontiers, but naturally the small (under $100 million a year sales) and the very small (under $10 million sales) will not be able to hire specialized planners for the international operations. Such companies will need to second one executive part time to learn how to devise systems that can greatly simplify the activities abroad and make them more profitable. As the company grows toward the $100 million sales, more resources can be allocated for providing a stimulus and a warning to those units that operate abroad. The ability to set up guidelines for the avoidance of common errors can be a profitable skill. Even before a company is large enough to hire a full-time planner for the international operations, a period in this field may be regarded as a necessary part of the training program for a senior manager. Thus it is possible to appoint a full-time planner for a limited period. During that time the person appointed will devise the guidelines for international management, and the experience gained will still be available to the company when he moves on to a more senior post. Middle-sized companies (sales under $1,000 million) will also be concerned with adequate indicators of the problems and opportunities to be met abroad, but will be able to go further in using linking and balancing activities. The planners will spend more time than is usual at present watching the different markets and assessing the effectiveness of the agents, the licensees, and the other foreign collaborators. In the larger companies, much of the international planning will be delegated to the divisions, but training, recruitment, and the development of new methods will be retained at the center.

The tenor of these concluding remarks is that international planning is both necessary and profitable if used correctly. The proper use is not as a supplement to general management, to perform jobs like seeking acquisitions, which no one else wants. Rather the planner should be encouraged to retain his neutral status and provide, if only part time, an advisory service on how the company can fulfill its objects and where it can avoid the pitfalls. In helping to steer the firm, the planner can often be more effective than the outside consultant.

A final word concerns a strategy for the planning itself. The phased introduction of the more-formal services begins by improving the implementation and moves gradually backward to the tactics and the strategy formation. There are, as already suggested, a number of ways of building international planning into the management system. The executive on secondment in the small company, or operating full time in the large one, constructs a network of contacts for the rapid collection of facts when national markets are being assessed or reappraised. He will then ensure that there is some system of assembling and sifting the data; after this, targets for market entry, expansion, or change can be determined. When the whole process has been organized, the balancing and linking functions can be inserted. This chapter has listed the main provisions. With them a company can accumulate the benefits of international corporate planning without undue disruption or expense.

SOURCES AND SUGGESTED REFERENCES

The following is a list of some of the more readable works published since 1976 that are relevant to the international corporate planner.

Brooke, M.Z. and H.L. Remmers. *International Management and Business Policy.* Boston: Houghton-Mifflin, 1978a.

Brooke, M.Z. and H.L. Remmers. *The Strategy of Multinational Enterprise,* 2nd ed. London: Pitman, 1978b.

Brooke, M.Z. and M. van Beusekom. *International Corporate Planning,* London: Pitman, 1979.

Buckley, P.J. and M. Casson. *The Future of the Multinational* Company. London: Macmillan, 1976.

Channon, D.F. and M. Jalland. *Multinational Strategic Planning*. American Management Association, 1979.

Eitemann, D.K. and A.I. Stonehill. *Multinational Business Finance,* 2nd ed. Reading, MA: Addison-Wesley, 1979.

Keegan, W.J. "Multinational Scanning: A study of the Information Sources Utilized by Headquarters Executives in Multinational Companies," *Administrative Science Quarterly,* Vol. XIX, No. 4 (1974), pp. 411–421.

Leroy, G. *Multinational Product Strategies*. New York: Praeger, 1976.

Naylor, T.H. and D.R. Gattis, "Corporate Planning Models," *California Management Review,* Vol. XVII, No. 4, (1976), pp. 69–78.

Steiner, G.A. *Strategic Planning: What Every Manager Must Know*. New York: The Free Press, 1979.

Vancil, R.F. "Strategy Formulation in Complex Organizations," *Sloan Management Review,* Vol. XVII, No. 2, (1976), pp. 1–18.

Vernon, R. and L.T. Wells. *Manager in the International Economy,* 3rd ed. Englewood Cliffs, NJ: Prentice-Hall, 1976.

SECTION **41**

CONFLICT MANAGEMENT IN INTERNATIONAL BUSINESS

CONTENTS

THE CHALLENGE OF CONFLICT MANAGEMENT   3

Conflict and the Multinational Corporation   3

THE NATURE OF MULTINATIONAL CORPORATE CONFLICT   4

Conflict Issues   4
Conflict Locus   4
Conflict Opponents   5
Conflict Tactics   8
Conflict Consequences   8

THE MANAGEMENT OF MULTINATIONAL CORPORATE CONFLICT   9

Strategies for Dealing with Conflict   9
Deciding on a Conflict Management Strategy   11
  The role of stakes   11
  The role of power   13
  The role of interests   14
  The role of relations   15
  Putting it all together   16

Selecting the Appropriate Strategy   17
  Single-mode strategies   17
  Simultaneous-mode strategies   19
  Sequential-mode strategies   20
  Collaborative paths   21
  Accommodative paths   22
  Competitive paths   23
  Avoidance paths   23
  Compromise paths   23

THE IMPLEMENTATION OF CONFLICT MANAGEMENT   25

Incentive Systems   25
Task Systems   26

CONFLICT MANAGEMENT IN THE YEARS AHEAD   27

A Future of Contradictions   27
Managing the Contradictions   27

SOURCES AND SUGGESTED REFERENCES   28

CONFLICT MANAGEMENT IN INTERNATIONAL BUSINESS

Thomas N. Gladwin

THE CHALLENGE OF CONFLICT MANAGEMENT

CONFLICT AND THE MULTINATIONAL CORPORATION. *The Economist* (1978) has captured "it" well:

> It fiddles its accounts. It avoids or evades its taxes. It rigs its intracompany transfer prices. It is run by foreigners, from decision centers thousands of miles away. It imports foreign labor practices. It overpays. It underpays. It competes unfairly with local firms. It is in cahoots with local firms. It exports jobs from rich countries. It is an instrument of rich countries' imperialism. The technologies it brings to the third world are old fashioned. No, they are too modern. It meddles. It bribes. Nobody can control it. It wrecks balance of payments. It overturns economic policies. It plays off governments against each other to get the biggest investment incentives. Won't it please come and invest? Let it bloody well go home.

"It," of course, is the multinational corporation (MNC)—which from a multiplicity of quarters has found itself under heavy fire. No other institution in history has ever been so pervasively unloved and misunderstood throughout the world. The fact of conflict—of somehow being involved with opposing forces—has surely come to be a dominant connotation attached to the very phrase *multinational corporation*. The causes, course, and consequences of conflict involving the MNC have been persistent and major themes in the international business literature, as reflected in works, for example, by Barnet and Muller (1974); Bergsten, Horst, and Moran (1978); Gilpin (1975); Sauvant and Lavipour (1976); and Vernon (1977).

Gladwin and Walter, in *Multinationals Under Fire* (1980), have summarized the challenge of conflict confronting multinationals as follows. They see multinational corporate conflict as *inevitable,* given that MNCs operate in an environment of multiple interest groups that place conflicting demands on them. Such conflict is *different,* both in kind and degree, from that which is purely domestic because of unique features both of the MNC itself and of the interdependent global system in which conflicts occur. As a result, the disputes are often far more *complex.* And given that the world is moving deeper into an era of growing demands and diminishing resources, it's quite likely that the frequency and intensity of conflicts involving MNCs will be *increasing*. The challenge of conflict is truly *diverse* and *pervasive* with respect to the kinds of issues, opponents, tactics, and areas involved. The structure or focus of conflict, in addition, is growing increasingly *transnational* through time. Finally, the conflicts can be *consequential*, in both destructive and constructive ways, and have often been *mismanaged*. Let's explore this "arena of conflict" in a bit more detail before turning our attention to a new contingency-based approach to conflict management appropriate for use within it.

THE NATURE OF MULTINATIONAL CORPORATE CONFLICT

CONFLICT ISSUES.   Myriad issues give rise to multinational corporate conflict. Exhibit 1 organizes them into nine subject areas: terrorism, human rights, politics, questionable payments, marketing, labor relations, environment, technology, and economics/finance. Case examples from all of these areas are highlighted below. But following from Gladwin and Walter (1980), the diverse and pervasive nature of conflict confronting multinational corporations can be quickly appreciated by considering a typical issue or question associated with each area, as follows:

Terrorism.   Should MNCs be allowed to pay ransom and publish revolutionary manifestos of terrorist groups in order to gain the release of kidnapped employees?

Human Rights.   Should MNCs be allowed to expand present investments or make new investments in nations where human civil and political rights are violated?

Politics.   Should MNCs be allowed to decline doing any business in Israel in order to avoid being blacklisted by Arab League nations?

Questionable Payments.   Should MNCs be allowed to offer or give a bribe in order to obtain or retain business in nations where bribery and corruption are the way of life?

Marketing.   Should MNCs be allowed to advertise and promote in developing nations the sale of infant-formula products that substitute for breast milk?

Labor Relations.   Should MNCs be allowed to threaten to transfer the whole or part of an operating unit from a country in order to influence the results of collective bargaining?

Environment.   Should MNCs be allowed to circumvent restrictive environmental or occupational health laws at home by shifting "dirty" facilities to poor developing nations?

Technology.   Should MNCs be allowed to concentrate most of their R&D activities at home rather than dispersing them widely around the globe?

Economics/Finance.   Should MNCs be allowed to use transfer pricing between subsidiaries that does not conform to an arm's length standard for purposes of reducing taxes in nations with high tax rates?

CONFLICT LOCUS.   Multinational corporate conflict is of course nothing new, as business historians such as Wilkins have extensively documented (Wilkins, 1970 and 1974). The composition of issues at stake in the conflicts has naturally varied over time, reflecting the influence of social and political movements, fads, contagion, and domino effects. Most MNCs' disputes over ecology and bribery, for example, emerged only after 1975.

Conflicts involving multinationals undoubtedly occur in every society in which they operate, but they vary widely in terms of content, frequency, intensity, forms of expression, and duration. This variation is perhaps largely attributable to the diverse economic, social, political, and institutional contexts in which MNC operations take place. Disputes over ownership and kidnapping, for example, have emerged most frequently in developing nations, whereas issues involving labor relations and consumerism have largely occurred in the developed economies.

A valuable locational perspective emerges when MNC conflicts are classified according to "issue locus," that is, whether the conflict emerges in a home nation over a purely domestic matter, in the home nation over a foreign matter, in a host nation over a domestic matter, or in a host or third nation over a foreign matter. Conflicts can be deemed to be over "foreign matters" when the overseas behavior of the multinational corporation is at issue or when foreign transactions, opponents, or reactions are significantly involved. Church-group protests in the United States regarding labor practices of U.S. firms in South Africa, for example, represent home-nation disputes over foreign matters.

Gladwin and Walter (1980) have found that the content of the issues in MNC conflict has been growing increasingly international or transnational over time. This is probably the result of growing economic interdependence, improved global communications, intergovernmental coordination, and a greatly increased propensity on the part of citizen lobbies, politicians, and regulators to concern themselves with events and conditions in foreign lands. The veil that used to insulate MNCs from attacks in one nation for their behavior in others has thus progressively been lifted. The challenges posed by such interdependence and transnationalism have been surveyed by Keohane and Nye (1977); Nye (1974); and Vogel (1978).

CONFLICT OPPONENTS.   Who seeks to hinder, compel, or injure the activities of multinationals? The answer, it seems, is just about everybody. Some of the opponents are small and others very large; some are novices and others old pros at waging conflict; some are poor and others rich; some are *ad hoc* and unorganized, whereas others are long established and highly structured; some are obsessed with a single issue, whereas others dally in multiple issues; some have entire armies at their disposal, whereas others only have typewriters; some are out for a little fun and excitement, whereas others are willing to die for their causes.

The opponents of MNCs can be classified into four general categories: citizen lobby, regulatory, political, and commercial. *Citizen lobbies* (e.g., environmental, religious, human rights, social action, consumer, community, university) tend to have deep-seated and ideological convictions, thus often producing greater rigidity in their conflict behavior and transforming conflicts with MNCs into eternal struggles over fundamental "truths." *Regulatory agencies* (e.g., antitrust, finance, welfare, environment, natural resources, commerce) are generally empowered to carry out mandates entrusted to them from either legislative or executive branches of government. *Politicians* (e.g., heads of state, political parties, legislative bodies, international bodies, nationalist/separatist groups, terrorist groups), wherever they are, are constantly striving to remain in, or get into, power. Politicians in power are often motivated to extract additional benefits from MNCs, whereas those out of power

EXHIBIT 1 ISSUES IN MULTINATIONAL CORPORATE CONFLICT

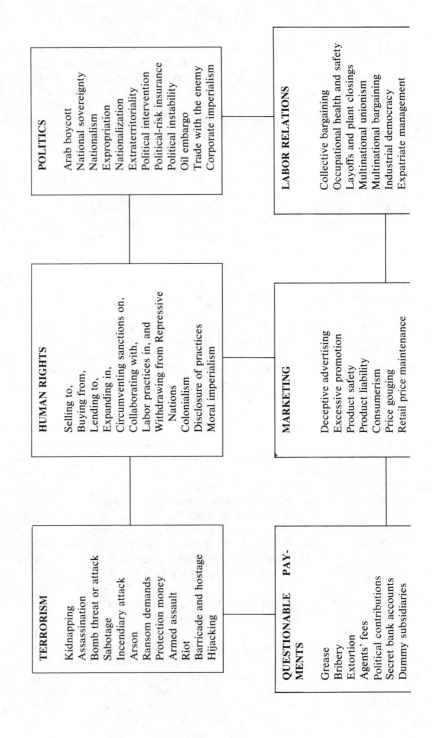

TERRORISM

Kidnapping
Assassination
Bomb threat or attack
Sabotage
Incendiary attack
Arson
Ransom demands
Protection money
Armed assault
Riot
Barricade and hostage
Hijacking

**QUESTIONABLE PAY-
MENTS**

Grease
Bribery
Extortion
Agents' fees
Political contributions
Secret bank accounts
Dummy subsidiaries

HUMAN RIGHTS

Selling to,
Buying from,
Lending to,
Expanding in,
Circumventing sanctions on,
Collaborating with,
Labor practices in, and
Withdrawing from Repressive
   Nations
Colonialism
Disclosure of practices
Moral imperialism

MARKETING

Deceptive advertising
Excessive promotion
Product safety
Product liability
Consumerism
Price gouging
Retail price maintenance

POLITICS

Arab boycott
National sovereignty
Nationalism
Expropriation
Nationalization
Extraterritoriality
Political intervention
Political-risk insurance
Political instability
Oil embargo
Trade with the enemy
Corporate imperialism

LABOR RELATIONS

Collective bargaining
Occupational health and safety
Layoffs and plant closings
Multinational unionism
Multinational bargaining
Industrial democracy
Expatriate management

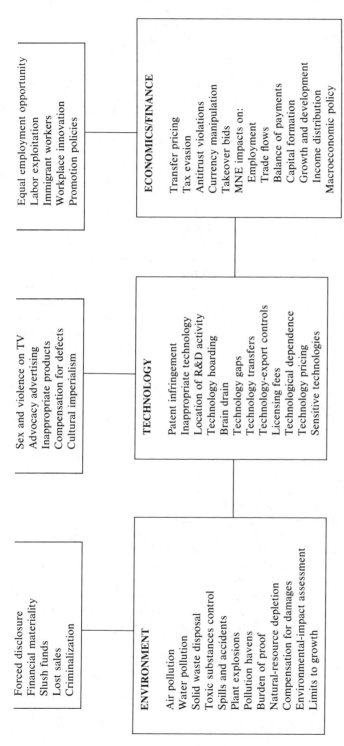

Equal employment opportunity
Labor exploitation
Immigrant workers
Workplace innovation
Promotion policies

ECONOMICS/FINANCE

Transfer pricing
Tax evasion
Antitrust violations
Currency manipulation
Takeover bids
MNE impacts on:
  Employment
  Trade flows
  Balance of payments
  Capital formation
  Growth and development
  Income distribution
  Macroeconomic policy

Sex and violence on TV
Advocacy advertising
Inappropriate products
Compensation for defects
Cultural imperialism

TECHNOLOGY

Patent infringement
Inappropriate technology
Location of R&D activity
Technology hoarding
Brain drain
Technology gaps
Technology transfers
Technology-export controls
Licensing fees
Technological dependence
Technology pricing
Sensitive technologies

Forced disclosure
Financial materiality
Slush funds
Lost sales
Criminalization

ENVIRONMENT

Air pollution
Water pollution
Solid waste disposal
Toxic substances control
Spills and accidents
Plant explosions
Pollution havens
Burden of proof
Natural-resource depletion
Compensation for damages
Environmental-impact assessment
Limits to growth

Source. Gladwin and Walter, *Multinationals Under Fire* (1980).

often tend to fix blame on MNCs for undesirable states of affairs. Finally, *commercial bodies* (e.g., corporations, labor organizations, press), tend to come into conflict with MNCs almost exclusively when matters of direct economic self-interest are at stake.

We should note that many MNC conflicts are multiparty affairs, which means that MNCs often have to contend with radically different opponent-incentive systems in regard to the same general issue. It's also important to note that audiences and/or third parties are also involved in a good portion of the conflicts involving multinationals. Third parties enter into conflicts in several broad role categories: as possessors of superior powers to impose a settlement (e.g., judges, arbitrators), as reconcilers of disparate interests (e.g., fact finders, mediators), and as expert assistants to one or the other contending parties (e.g., attorneys, consultants).

CONFLICT TACTICS. The tactics used against multinationals are as varied as the groups using them and the issues addressed. Opponent arsenals include means that range from violent to nonviolent, direct to indirect, legitimate to illegitimate, persuasive to coercive, simple to complex, and inexpensive to quite costly.

Gladwin and Walter (1980), after examining hundreds of MNC conflicts, have classified the tactics employed against multinationals into eight categories: legal, legislative, administrative, financial, economic, communicative, symbolic, and violent. Although administrative and legal tactics dominate the overall battleground, the kinds of tactics utilized vary widely from issue to issue. Terrorism, by definition, exclusively entails violence. Human-rights controversies are marked by communicative, financial (proxy resolutions and stock divestitures), and symbolic tactics. Administrative interventions mark most political and marketing disputes, whereas economic tactics (e.g., strikes) dominate the labor scene. Conflicts over questionable payments, environmental protection, technology, and economics/finance all have strong legal-administrative flavors. We should note, however, that a wide a variety of tactics are brought to bear on most issues.

CONFLICT CONSEQUENCES. The most critical question about MNC conflict is, of course, so what? Just what is the bottom line? At the extreme, that line for multinationals is nothing less than survival. Conflict has the potential of disrupting or reducing a MNC's vital flow of essential resources and support from relevant interest groups in a variety of ways. Examples would include investments lost due to government takeovers, production lost as a result of strikes, markets lost after bans are imposed on production, and property and executive lives lost from terrorist attacks. The acquisition of future resources can also be seriously impaired by conflict that translates into delays and obstruction.

Conflicts can be costly in still other ways. They can result in badly tarnished public images, consume disproportionate amounts of top-management time and attention, entail skyrocketing legal fees, sink employee morale, and induce role stress within executives. But all is not negative. Conflict can also be legitimate, productive, and desirable for both individuals and organizations. It can serve to foster internal cohesiveness, prevent stagnation, help clarify objectives, direct managerial attention to needed changes, and stimulate adjustment to new conditions. Conflict in MNC operations can thus be functional, dysfunctional, or both at the same time.

The appropriate objective of conflict management should therefore not be that of avoiding or resolving all external conflicts. Since some types of conflict can be detrimental and others beneficial, the goal must rather be one of optimal balance. This can be achieved by constructive management actions that serve to minimize the negative effects and enhance the positive effects of any given dispute. The key is not to misread the "true" nature of a conflict situation, for example, underestimating or overestimating the amount of power at the MNC's disposal, misconceiving the real stakes riding on the conflict outcome, falsely defining occasions that might permit mutual gain as situations of pure "zero-sum" conflict, misinterpreting the quality of the firm's relationship with an opposing party, thereby missing useful communication opportunities, and so forth. The multinational must also strive to avoid a wide variety of other destructive processes: narrowing of vision, heavy-handed power tactics, overreactions, biased perceptions, excessive loyalties, oversensitivity to differences, stereotypic thinking, impoverished communications, failures to adapt to changing circumstances, and so on.

There are of course no simple cookbook approaches to dealing with conflict in MNC operations—no panaceas, no foolproof strategies, no one best answer. There are a wide variety of strategies and tactics potentially available for use in constructively managing conflicts, and the appropriateness of any given strategy or tactic will naturally depend upon the particular circumstances found in a specific conflict situation. Let's turn now to a general model for managing conflicts in international business that embodies this "contingency" perspective.

THE MANAGEMENT OF MULTINATIONAL CORPORATE CONFLICT

STRATEGIES FOR DEALING WITH CONFLICT.   In dealing with any given external conflict, MNC management must primarily concentrate on obtaining a satisfactory outcome rather than resolving the conflict itself, although the latter is, of course, often preferable if feasible. In addition, management must also be concerned with its relationship with the parties who constitute its opposition. Depending on the emphasis placed on these two factors of assertiveness and cooperativeness, one of five styles of conflict management may be chosen as noted by Thomas (1976) and as indicated in Exhibit 2. Management may choose to *compete* tooth and nail (assertive/uncooperative) in an attempt to overcome the opposition. It may opt to *avoid* (unassertive/uncooperative) conflict and withdraw from the fray or to *accommodate* (unassertive/cooperative) the opposition. It may actively *collaborate* (assertive/cooperative), hoping to satisfy both sides of the issue, and, finally, there is always the option of *compromise,* which "splits the difference' in a bargaining context and represents an intermediate position in terms of both assertiveness and cooperativeness. For an in-depth examination of the nature of each of these modes or styles see Gladwin and Walter (1980).

The differences between these conflict strategies are well illustrated by the reactions of the Sperry Rand Corporation, and Dresser Industries to the export controls instituted by the Carter administration during the summer of 1978 to express displeasure with the Soviet trials of political dissidents and American journalists. Sperry was denied an export license to ship a $6.8 million computer system to Tass, the official Soviet press agency. Dresser, a diversified energy-industry supplier, was affected when all American exports of oil-field technology to the Soviets were placed under governmental control. J. Paul Lyet, Sperry's chairman, reportedly greeted the

EXHIBIT 2   MODES OF CONFLICT MANAGEMENT

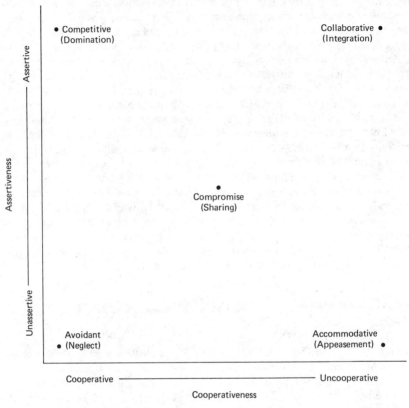

Source. Thomas, 1976.

license denial with, "Bah, humbug," but added that the company had always complied with the wishes of the U.S. government on "where and with whom" the company traded and would "continue to follow that policy." Dresser's reaction was almost the opposite of Sperry's relatively unassertive and cooperative stance of accommodation. Carter's oil decision was labeled "sheer idiocy," and John V. James, Dresser's chairman, speedily and bluntly attacked efforts by the President's senior advisers and a special review panel convened at Defense Secretary Harold Brown's request to stop the firm's $150 million contract to build a drill-bit plant in the Soviet Union. The highly competitive approach helped produce a go-ahead for the Dresser sale. The Carter administration flip-flopped 2 years later and revoked Dresser's license. By this time, however, the bulk of all equipment and technology for the plant had already been shipped. The White House also eventually reversed its decision on the Sperry sale, but unfortunately for the company, the Russians in the meantime had found a new supplier, CII-Honeywell-Bull of France.

There are, of course, many possible combinations of cooperativeness and assertiveness, but most are combinations or variations of the five "polar" positions depicted in Exhibit 2. It should be emphasized that these options are ways of *coping* with conflict and not necessarily ways of *resolving* conflict, that is, only collaboration and compromise involve conflict resolution in the sense that both opposing parties obtain satisfaction. Thus crushing an attempt by unions in Europe to bargain on a multinational basis, terminating business in payoff-prone regions such as the Middle East, or temporarily halting bank loans to the South African government may enable the firm to suppress or bypass the open expression of conflict, but do not really resolve the underlying issues.

DECIDING ON A CONFLICT-MANAGEMENT STRATEGY. Suppose there are demands to get out of South Africa, stop the marketing of infant formula in Haiti, or cut the price of tranquilizers in Great Britain. How should MNC management go about deciding how assertive to be in such situations? That is, what factors ought to determine the levels and kinds of resources that should be invested in an attempt to obtain a favorable conflict outcome? In general, the answer depends on the *stakes* management places on that outcome along with the relative *power* or leverage of the enterprise in the conflict situation.

The Role of Stakes. Stakes can typically be assessed subjectively, but are difficult to pin down rigorously. A great deal naturally depends on management's own perceptions. It was relatively painless, for example, for Procter & Gamble (Folger coffee) and General Foods (Maxwell House) to end their U.S. importation of Ugandan coffee in 1978 in response to pressure from human-rights groups and U.S. congressmen to end America's business connection with Idi Amin's regime, as Ugandan supplies amounted to only 6 percent of U.S. coffee imports. The story certainly would have been different had the supplier in question been Brazil. Tough competition rather than accommodation surely would have been the result.

The most important factor in determining a multinational's stakes in a particular conflict is usually management's own global strategy. Thus conflict outcomes that weaken the heart of that strategy—damaging the firm's distinctive competences, degree of control, or unique capabilities—are likely to be those that management wants most to avoid. And although multinationals often pursue multiple strategies in different product or geographic divisions, it is possible to distinguish between different kinds of strategies, as has been done by Fayerweather (1978), and show how the stakes in any particular conflict depend on them. For example, firms such as IBM that concentrate on exploiting technological leads in a few product areas normally consider it essential to maintain an exceptionally strong R&D program, high product-quality standards, tight control of technological skills, and close supervision of marketing strategy. The need for tight reins on production and marketing, however, is not as critical to those multinationals that are comparatively efficient in the development of innovative leads in a wider range of product lines and markets. Thus companies like Honeywell, Westinghouse, ITT, and L.M. Ericsson have been relatively calm when faced with pressures for local ownership participation in countries like France or Brazil, whereas IBM has fought the same pressures every step of the way.

In contrast, multinationals in the oil, copper, aluminum, and chemicals industries as explored by Vernon in *Storm Over the Multinationals* (1977) tend to pursue strategies resting on the advantages of large scale, and view barriers to entry, coordination of decisions at various stages of production, security of raw materials supply, and stability in product demand as their particular "jugular veins." A serious threat to any of these factors would probably evoke strong reactions. On the other hand, multinationals in the food and pharmaceutical industries rely on strategies based on advanced managerial and marketing skills, proprietary knowhow, strong trade names, or massive promotional expenditures. Tight control of marketing programs is usually viewed as absolutely essential, and conflicts that affect such programs are usually assigned high stakes. There are still other strategies that rest on the multinational's global scanning capability and well-integrated, efficient logistical system. In the automobile and electronics industries, for example, where returns depend on low-cost-production locations and effective global marketing, tight internal control is needed to tie together the multinational network, and threats to that network involve high stakes.

Besides such strategic factors, stakes are affected by the firm's financial condition. If the enterprise is very well off, it may be prepared to offer greater concessions to its opponents than if it is close to collapse. During the winter of 1975–1976, for example, Chrysler, as noted by Young and Hood in *Chrysler U.K.* (1977), was able to translate its financial weakness into what some observers labeled a "triumph of negotiations" in the United Kingdom. Specifically, Chrysler's threats to liquidate its failing British subsidiary enabled management to squeeze an aid package of $360 million out of the Labour government—five times the amount the government first proposed.

Other determinants of stakes include sunk costs, precedents, and accountability to third parties such as joint-venture partners, industry associations, suppliers, customers, and government regulators. At the same time, perceived stakes may be reduced in various ways. One is insurance, such as that provided to U.S. companies by the Overseas Private Investment Corporation against seizure of overseas property by foreign governments, inability to repatriate profits, or acts of war. Another is the existence of options such as the availability of alternate markets or sources of supply. A third is the joint ownership of capital-intensive facilities, such as aluminum smelters, copper mines, oil fields, natural-gas pipelines, and petrochemical complexes, which tend to create a common cost structure and common exposure to risk for the firms involved. Thus if a consortium facility is impaired or expropriated, competitive relationships may remain more or less intact, and losing a conflict does not necessarily set one firm back relative to its rivals. Such stakes-reducing and risk-management techniques are examined in works by the Congressional Research Service (1973); Franko (1971); Haendel and West (1975); Lloyd (1976); Moran (1973); and Robinson (1978).

In trying to ascertain its stakes in a conflict outcome, management also has to consider carefully the time element. For example, as time pressures increase, the perceived need to obtain the most desirable outcome may fade. Urgency tends to increase "decision costs," prompting management to soften its demands, reduce its aspirations, or increase its concessions. Such was the case in Standard Oil Company of Ohio's (52 percent owned by British Petroleum) ill-fated attempt to construct a tanker terminal in Long Beach, California, and pump Alaskan crude oil to Texas refineries. The urgency of servicing the company's huge debt associated with the Trans-Alaska Pipeline and finding a way of getting petroleum products to its Midwest markets cheaply caused Sohio to become an "environmental Santa Claus." The company even agreed to spend $78 million to reduce pollution at a Southern California Edison generating plant as part of a pollution offset arrangement in the hope of gaining a quick green light for the project. Five years of delay, however, eroded the $1 billion project's once-attractive economics, and it was abandoned in 1979.

Whether the stakes are attributable to strategic requirements, financial condition, precedent, available options, or urgency, management should usually try to be assertive in conflict situations in which those stakes are perceived to be high. Among other things this means that considerable time and energy should be spent to either steamroller the opposition or pursue avenues of collaboration. In contrast, when the stakes are low, major outlays of corporate financial and human resources usually do not make sense.

The Role of Power. Although stakes succeed in defining much of management's motivation in social conflict, they don't go very far toward suggesting appropriate levels of assertiveness without reference to the firm's relative influence or power position. This depends on both the multinational's own characteristics and the situation in which it finds itself, and can differ enormously from one conflict situation to another. For our purposes, power can be defined as suggested by Raven and Kruglanski (1970); Swingle (1976); and Wrong (1979) in terms of the range of conflict outcomes through which one party can push another in a conflict situation, with greater power corresponding to a greater range of outcomes. It should be noted that relative power positions can change rapidly, as demonstrated by the rapid and dramatic decline in the leverage of most multinationals operating in Iran following the overthrow of the Shah.

What are the sources of a multinational's power? Generally, the ingredients of power include a firm's size, financial base, human resources, expertise, leadership quality, prestige, communication and persuasion skills, access to the media, cohesiveness, prior experience in dealing with conflicts, intensity of commitment, degree of trust and legitimacy, and risk-taking ability. For example, management may be able to convince the other party that it has superior knowledge or abilities, and may hold out the promise of benefits such as new investment or job creation, whereby it is clear that the reward depends on a conflict outcome that is favorable to the enterprise. Alternatively, management may be able to convince the opposition that the firm is justified in making a particular demand on grounds of precedent, reciprocity, or fair play.

Another important ingredient of relative power in multinational corporate conflict is the formation of coalitions with protagonists having complementary objectives. One example of such a coalition was the joining together of 63 major U.S. multinationals and banks in the early 1970s to form the Emergency Committee for American Trade in order to aggressively lobby against the highly protectionist AFL-CIO-backed Hartke-Burke bill. Similarly, more than 100 U.S. firms agreed to endorse the principles of the Rev. Leon Sullivan aimed at eroding apartheid and promoting fair employment practices in South Africa; 170 U.S. firms represented on the Business Roundtable joined together to bargain with American Jewish groups on the Arab boycott issue; and 9 major companies and 30 industry associations jointly went to court in West Germany during 1977 in an attempt to get that country's codetermination law overturned on constitutional grounds.

The site of a conflict may also affect relative power. Multinationals play most of their conflicts "away" rather than "at home," and usually have to contend with opponents on their own territories, where those parties are more familiar with the local environments and often enjoy the ability to control or influence them. Moreover, the multinational enterprise, as a guest, may be constrained in its assertiveness by a need for caution in an unfamiliar setting—although it can occasionally obtain assistance from its home government. The lack of options is also a power-limiting factor. A classic case that illustrates this point occurred in the early 1970s, when some of the richest oil fields in the North Sea were discovered in the Shetland basin by multinational oil firms including Shell, British Petroleum, Conoco, Burmah, Exxon, and Total. As reported by Baldwin and Baldwin (1975), it became evident to the residents of the Shetland Islands, which lie about 100 miles due west of the field, that the companies would be seeking permission to pipe the oil ashore at Shetland, the nearest possible landing point. But very few of the islands' 19,000 inhabitants wanted oil development encroaching on their way of life. Seizing the initiative, in 1974 the Shetland Island Council pushed an unprecedented piece of private legislation through the British Parliament that gave the council extensive rights to control and participate in oil-related development. With the Shetland landfall and tanker terminal vital to the economic exploitation of the fields, the oil companies were in no position to argue, and yielded at almost every turn to the council's demands on siting, facility design, and inflation-hedged royalties.

The existence of options, on the other hand, naturally enhances the multinational's power. One example is dispersion of production. Enterprises that rely on well-diversified supply sources are less vulnerable to embargoes and nationalizations, and are perhaps more resilient in conflicts in general than firms that rely on more-concentrated sources. They gain in leverage from limitations in the ability of governments or other opponents to reach out for alternative sources of technology or capital. In manufacturing industries, power can derive from breaking down the production process so finely that threats to the firm become meaningless—a government's expropriation of a screwdriver-type electronics-components-assembly operation that puts together imported inputs for export would yield little. Finally, multinationals attain power through a degree of indispensibility, that is, by possessing something unique to offer or withhold when a conflict arises. For discussions of these and other power factors in relation to a firm's vulnerability to expropriation see Jodice (1980); Kobrin (1980); and Truitt (1974).

Although the ingredients of power may be complex, they are also usually the primary determinants of the feasibility of different types of conflict behavior. Thus a clearly superior power position is likely to favor relatively assertive behavior in conflict situations. This can take the form of either a straightforward competitive stance or one of active collaboration, where the firm's problem-solving resources imply a position of strength and low risk. By contrast, an inferior power position normally inhibits management's ability to compel the other side to negotiate or make concessions, and unassertive behavior (avoidance or accommodation) may be most appropriate.

The Role of Interests.   Besides deciding how assertive it should be, management must also decide how cooperative to be. This decision will depend on the interdependence of *interests* between the multinational and its opponent and the ability to translate the need to cooperate into action given the quality of *relations* between the two parties.

The convergence or divergence of interests in conflict situations can arise from interdependence of both "goals" and "means," as noted theoretically by Deutsch (1973), and Rubin and Brown (1975). For example, a cooperative goal situation is one in which the various parties sink or swim together, whereas in a purely competitive situation, if one swims, the other must sink. Means interdependence, in contrast, exists when the methods that one party needs to reach its goal affect those available to the other. Thus management often finds that even though both itself and the opposition are in general agreement on a common goal, there is basic disagreement on how it should be accomplished. Mining companies like AMAX, Rio-Tinto Zinc, and International Nickel, for instance, have often found that even though they are in general agreement with governmental agencies and citizen groups on the desirability of exploiting a particular mineral resource, they still have serious differences on how to go about it—fast or slow, small or large scale, one extractive method or another, and so on.

Goal and means incompatibility often arise because multinationals inevitably affect a wide range of politically sensitive areas in the countries where they operate. As noted in works by Hawkins (1979); Hood and Young (1979); and Walter (1975), these range from economic growth, employment, prices, technical change, income distribution, and taxation to human rights, pollution control, balance of payments, and even national security. Consequently, any actions that they take that are perceived to threaten these interests are likely to represent points of incompatibility with host governments or various local interest groups. This is especially likely when matters of national identity or autonomy are involved. Thus in 1976, Dow Chemical found itself the target of severe criticism from Italian Communist Party economist Eugenio Peggio for "dismantling" the research and sales operations of its 70-percent-owned Italian pharmaceutical subsidiary, Gruppo Leptit S.A., and placing them under the Dow umbrella. The result, according to Peggio, was that "if Dow decides to leave, what is Italy left with?" In his view, those multinationals that "devoured and dismembered Italian companies for their own benefit" had to be opposed.

One of the most fundamental sources of diverging interests, according to observers such as Barnet and Muller (1974); Behrman (1970); Bergsten, Horst, and Moran (1978); and Vernon (1971), is incompatibility between the *global* views of management and the essentially *national* perspective of most of the institutions with which it comes into conflict. Macroeconomic policy at the national level has traditionally been viewed as setting the conditions within which the microeconomic functions of the firm are carried out. With multinationals, however, we have the global microeconomics of the firm often influencing the parameters of macroeconomic policy at the national level. And although the multinational has interests that extend beyond the border of any single country, its managers worry about the problems that arise from overlapping national jurisdictions, particularly with regard to their affiliates being used as political tools, conduits, and hostages by competing sovereign states.

In general, management is likely to be best able and most highly motivated to behave in a collaborative or accommodative manner in situations where both goals and means are positively interdependent. Some multinationals, for example, have chosen to meet the Third World call for "appropriate technologies" by engaging in product innovation designed specifically for the special conditions and needs of developing nations, as Ford Motor did with the "developing nations tractor" and GM with its "basic transportation vehicle." Value conflicts in the transfer of technology have been explored by Goulet (1977).

The Role of Relations.   Conflicts, however, may still occur even when there is no perceived or actual divergence in goals or means among the parties. When this happens, it usually results from poor prior relations and attitudes. A positive relationship will generally serve to foster mutual trust, recognition of the legitimacy of the other party's interests, open communications, and an increased willingness to respond helpfully to the other party's needs. Hostility, on the other hand, tends to feed upon itself and is triggered by factors like isolation, stereotypes, failure or disillusionment in prior conflicts, mutual ignorance, racial differences, distorted perceptions, and institutional barriers. In some instances, local ideologies and values may even reject the multinational enterprise as an institution. For example, in those countries with socialism as a basic commitment, the Marxist concepts of capitalist exploitation, imperialism, and class struggle will naturally place a burden on constructive conflict resolution. Similar problems are caused by anti-American, anti-German, or anti-Japanese paranoia, as well as by questionable behavior on the part of a handful of multinationals, such as ITT in Chile.

The primary sources of negative relations between multinationals and local institutions, however, are probably ethnocentricism and nationalism, which have been studied by Fayerweather (1975); Johnson (1965); and LaPalombara and Blank (1976). Ethnocentrism reflects an inability to appreciate the viewpoint of others whose cultures have, for example, a different morality, religion, or language, and leads to an unwillingness to see the common problems that lie beneath differences in social and cultural traditions. Nationalism, as an extension of ethnocentrism, adds a strong chauvinistic and emotional component to many conflicts involving multinationals. For instance, surges of nationalist sentiment have, from time to time, spurred Canadian governments to impose protectionist measures aimed at reducing the flow of U.S. influence into that economy. One industry particularly affected has been publishing, with classic battles erupting over the government's attempts to drive *Time* and *Reader's Digest* out of the country.

The annals of multinational corporate conflict contain plenty of examples of hostility—Nestlé and the Third World Action Group over infant-formula promotion in developing nations; Firestone and the Young Americans for Freedom over plans for a synthetic-rubber plant in Rumania; Mobil and the Center for Social Action of the United Church of Christ over alleged petroleum supplies to Rhodesia; and ITT and the Senate Foreign Relations Subcommittee on Multinational Corporations over its Chilean activities are just a few of these. Case histories of these "classic" battles can be found in Gladwin and Walter, *Multinationals Under Fire* (1980). Positive relationships, however, are possible, and the factors that can lead to them include experience of successful prior interactions, perceived similarity in beliefs, common values and attitudes, good communications, and the concern of the parties about their ability to work together in the future. In general, management is most likely to exhibit a high degree of cooperativeness (collaboration or accommodation) when relations are open, friendly, and trusting.

Putting It All Together. Our framework suggests that in any given conflict situation, the appropriate combination of assertiveness and cooperativeness ought to be a product of the interaction of four situational variables—*outcome stakes, relative power, interest interdependence,* and *relationship quality* (see Exhibit 3). Multinationals regularly encounter conflict situations of a relatively pure form in which the variables combine to unambiguously suggest a corporate conflict-management position. These four factors are seldom of equal importance, however. Instead, in most situations, the "motivational structure" of conflict (stakes and interest interdependence) is probably a more-important determinant of conflict behavior than the "capability structure" (power and relationship quality). This is because capabilities are more readily changeable than underlying motives. Also there are often linkages

EXHIBIT 3   DETERMINANTS OF APPROPRIATE CONFLICT BEHAVIOR

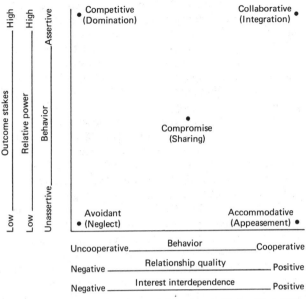

Source.   Gladwin and Walter, *Multinationals Under Fire*, 1980.

among the situational factors themselves—parties who dislike one another, for example, are apt to emphasize or develop incompatible goals. Thus, it's not hard to understand why most multinationals have been unwilling to engage in a dialogue with representatives of the World Council of Churches: the WCC declared its vehement opposition to multinationals in 1977 on the grounds that they are accomplices of "repressive states, predatory local elites, and racism" and thus pillars of a system that "oppresses, excludes, and exploits" (*The Economist,* 1977). And as the stakes in a conflict outcome increase, so does the incentive to utilize every source of power that may be available to each side.

SELECTING THE APPROPRIATE STRATEGY.   External conflicts in multinational corporate operations emerge in many shapes, sizes, intensities, and complexions. Selecting an appropriate conflict management thus critically depends on an accurate diagnosis of the motivational and capability structures at hand. In some conflict situations, a strategy of using one conflict-handling mode alone will suffice, whereas other situations may recommend the use of two or more modes simultaneously. And dynamic situations will naturally necessitate the utilization of different modes at different stages of the conflict. Let's examine these single-, simultaneous-, and sequential-mode strategies in more detail.

Single-Mode Strategies.   A *competitive* (assertive, uncooperative) response to conflict is appropriate when a multinational's stakes and power are relatively high, and when interest interdependence and relations are relatively negative. The objective is domination. Such is the case in the uranium-cartel dispute involving two Pittsburgh neighbors—Westinghouse Electric and Gulf Oil—along with 28 other uranium producers, with Westinghouse charging Gulf and the others with creating an international cartel that forced the price of uranium from $8 a pound to more than $40 a pound over a two-year period. This thorny legal imbroglio—dubbed the "lawyers full-employment case" by a federal judge—began trial in late 1980. The direct dispute between Westinghouse and Gulf was settled in 1981 when Gulf agreed to pay Westinghouse $25 million and to supply six of Westinghouse's utility customers with uranium valued at about $350 million.

An *avoidant* (unassertive, uncooperative) approach to handling conflict is useful when the firm's stakes and power are relatively low, and when interest interdependence and relations are relatively negative. The objective is to throw in the towel or move on to greener pastures at lowest possible costs. A clear example would be the quiet withdrawal of the U.S. executives of GM, Exxon, Ford, Coca-Cola, and other firms from Argentina in 1973–1974 when the executive-kidnap rate in that country reached 10 per month. Other cases of responding to terrorism in this manner are reported in Clutterbuck (1978). Avoidance can be useful in many kinds of situations, such as when alternate projects or markets are readily available, when the issues in conflict are trivial and represent only minor annoyances, or when potential disruption and negative publicity seem to outweigh the benefits of conflict resolution.

A *collaborative* (assertive, cooperative) approach to handling conflict is likely to be best when the multinational's stakes and power are relatively high, and when interest interdependence and relations with the opposition are relatively positive. The widely publicized experiment in workplace innovation in the Volvo assembly plant at Kalmar, Sweden, represents a case in point. The goals of that experiment, not yet fully achieved, are to upgrade workers' tasks into ones that are more creative and satisfying for the individual, thereby leading to a higher level of worker motivation, greater productivity, reduced absenteeism, and reduced strike activity. Collaboration is especially effective when both sides want to achieve the same objective, but differ over the means.

An *accommodative* (unassertive, cooperative) response to conflict is suitable when stakes and power are relatively low, and when interest interdependence and relations are relatively positive. The objective is appeasement, and this makes sense when issues are more important to others than to the firm itself, when the firm finds that it has been wrong on matters of substance, and when organizational energy is needed for other conflicts where the stakes are higher. How else can one explain the unprecedented "orgy of self-flagellation" noted by Gladwin and Walter (1977) during which some 400 American-based multinationals voluntarily disclosed to the Securities and Exchange Commission that they had made a total of almost $1 billion in questionable payments abroad?

Finally, a *compromise* (moderately assertive and cooperative) mode tends to be useful when the firm's stakes are moderate and power advantage or disadvantage is slight, and when interest interdependence and relations are mixes of positive and negative elements. The objective is to "split the difference," especially when conflicts involve differences in goals, attitudes, and values, and when many issues are involved that are given different priorities by the various parties in conflict. During 1976–1977, for instance, the American Jewish Congress (AJC) negotiated agreements with a number of major U.S.-based multinationals regarding the Arab boycott of Israel, a subject investigated by Chill (1976) and Turck (1977). Gulf Oil, Bethlehem

Steel, Goodyear Tire & Rubber, Standard Oil of California, and Tenneco were among those who agreed to provide requested information about boycott practices and/or to revise corporate policies in return for the AJC's withdrawing its shareholder resolutions on the matter. Compromise makes sense when goals are important but not worth the effort or potential delays associated with more-assertive kinds of behavior. It can produce expedient solutions under time pressure as well as temporary settlements to complex issues. And it can be a primary backup strategy when collaboration or competition are unsuccessful.

Simultaneous-Mode Strategies. Let's turn to more-complex conflict situations. One of the reasons multinational corporate disputes often become so protracted is that the bones of contention become fused into a monolithic whole that is not easily broken apart. Each side comes to view the issues as so interconnected and the resulting complex so overwhelming that the give-and-take process of compromise and concession appears impossible. The likelihood of reaching a satisfactory solution to a conflict can often be increased, according to Fisher (1964), by separating or "fractionating" the large issues involved into smaller and more-workable ones. The issues can often be manipulated—sized up or down, hooked together, broken apart, or stated in different language. They can be differentiated in terms of importance and relatedness, and different conflict-management techniques applied to each at the same time. Some questions can be avoided, others compromised, and still others subjected to intensely assertive behavior on the part of management. Fractionation of issues in conflict can help alleviate the stultifying effects of excessive commitment often associated with attempts to deal with large and complicated conflicts.

Opponents can also be divided, a procedure that is especially useful when the opponents themselves have divergent interests. For instance, Enka Glanzstoff, the fiber subsidiary of the Dutch chemical firm AKZO, announced plans in 1975 to close fiber operations in three countries and eliminate 6000 jobs by 1977 in an effort to regain profitability. AKZO's two major Dutch and German unions, inspired by the International Federation of Chemical, Energy, and General Workers Unions, called for discussions with the company to be held only an international basis, hoping to set a precedent in multinational labor cooperation against multinationals. Dutch Prime Minister Joop den Uyl publicly supported the union demands. But AKZO steadfastly refused to talk on a multinational basis and successfully shattered the front orchestrated by Charles Levinson of the international federation by appealing to the desires of small Dutch unions that did not want an all-out confrontation during a recession. AKZO was thus able to negotiate the plant closings with its labor unions in each country separately. For studies of multinational unionism and bargaining see Hershfield (1975); Kujawa (1979); and Northrup and Rowen (1974).

Certainly unique to conflicts facing multinational companies are issues involving parties in different nations, and the multinational can easily become the "monkey in the middle." Because of its "double identity" and questions of overlapping and conflicting jurisdiction, management often finds itself wedged between the hauling and pulling of parties in several countries whose interests point in fundamentally different directions. Consider Fruehauf's majority-owned subsidiary in France, sandwiched between conflicting U.S. and French government positions in 1965 regarding shipment of truck trailers to China; or Volkswagen angering the Brazilian government during the 1975 recession when the company reassigned an export production order from its Brazilian subsidiary back to Germany to appease workers at home; or Gulf

Oil confronting incompatible demands with respect to disbursement of royalty payments from its Angolan operations in 1975 exerted by the Ford administration and the three factions vying for control during the Angolan revolution; or British Petroleum losing its assets in Nigeria to nationalization in 1979 when it got caught in the middle of a dispute over the African policies of the government of Prime Minister Margaret Thatcher.

Even in single-country conflicts, management may find it advantageous to use different conflict-handling strategies simultaneously to block the formation of powerful opposing alliances, encourage counter-coalitions, or promote division or contention among weaker parties. Boeing, for example, found it useful to collaborate with the State Department while competing with the SEC on disclosure of the names of its agents and consultants abroad who had received more than $70 million in questionable payments. The company refused to comply with the SEC demands, claiming that the disclosure of "proprietary and confidential information" could cause "substantial, irreparable harm." This position was supported by the State Department, which on Boeing's behalf told the U.S. Appeals Court that disclosure "could reasonably be expected to cause damage to the foreign relations of the United States."

Sequential-Mode Strategies.   Conflicts, in addition to often being complex, are generally also dynamic. They usually do not appear suddenly, but rather pass through a series of progressive stages during which the degree of conflict may either escalate or abate as described and modeled in works by Gulliver (1979), Lockhart (1979), Schelling (1960), and Zartman (1977). Moreover, conditions related to stakes, power, interest interdependence, and relations with opponents often shift significantly from one time period to the next. Consequently, a firm's conflict-management strategy should be adapted accordingly. The saga of IBM in India, which followed a path of collaboration→competition→compromise→avoidance illustrates this point quite well. The company responded positively to an invitation of Jawaharlal Nehru to establish an accounting-machine plant in Bombay in 1951 (*collaboration*). IBM went on to dominate the Indian computer industry, and eventually the Indian government pressed the firm both to reduce its 100 percent owership to 40 percent and to extend its computer design and manufacturing operations in India for the domestic as well as export markets. IBM was initially highly reluctant to consider any deviation from its traditional global policy of keeping all of its foreign affiliates under 100 percent IBM ownership (*competition*). However, an equally rigid position on the part of the Indian government forced IBM to propose a range of concessions in the hope of *compromise*. These concessions were not enough for the Indians, though, and IBM's proposals were rejected. Finally, IBM concluded that the equity dilution demanded by the Indian government "would seriously impair [IBM's] ability to manage an international high technology company requiring sharing of resources and know-how across national borders," and it subsequently announced its withdrawal from the nation on November 15, 1977 (*avoidance*).

It is not sufficient for a conflict strategy to be adaptive, however. It should also be proactive at times, for the various elements that determine the nature and intensity of conflict management can be consciously altered as time goes by. Values, beliefs, and perceptions of the opponents, for example, can be changed through communication and persuasion. In short, the quality of relations can be improved, as noted by Behrman, Boddewyn, and Kapoor (1975); Blake (1977); and Dunn, Cahill, and

Boddewyn (1979) through skillful public affairs. Likewise, the power balance may be shifted by working on the firm's leverage points or the effectiveness with which they are used. Coalitions, for instance, can be formed to offset an initial power disadvantage. The perceptions of the stakes involved in a conflict can also be changed dramatically by restricting or expanding the options available to oneself or one's opponents. Similarly, perceptions of interest interdependence can be altered by substitute goals, third-party intervention, reformulating the issues involved, or introducing "superordinate" goals or threats that outweigh the existing hostility and divergent objectives.

There may also be changes in conflict circumstances beyond the control of the parties concerned. This is perhaps best illustrated by the inevitable cycles that appear in the bargaining strength of multinationals and governments of developing countries in the natural-resource industries, where the initial contractual arrangements between these firms and governments tend to obsolesce over time. Such agreements are normally reached in order to facilitate development of the country's natural resources. However, once the capital has been sunk and the initial risks have been taken, attitudes often change. In these circumstances, management almost always perceives the project as offering even more promise than before. But the government—with the project now "captured"—often comes to view at least some of the original terms of the agreement as unreasonable. And knowing that the terms needed to retain the essential benefits or the project are much less now than those needed to attract it in the first place, it typically presses for renegotiation. The ingredients of conflict management for both sides have thus changed. Examples of this "obsolescing bargain" phenomenon are legend and have been explored in efforts by Mikdashi (1976); Mikesell (1975); Moran (1974); and Smith and Wells, Jr. (1975). The government of Papua New Guinea, for example, demanded a renegotiation of the terms of the Bougainville copper-mining agreement with Bougainville Copper Ltd. (Rio-Tinto-Zinc) just one year after the world's fourth-largest copper mine had been in operation—partly a consequence of extraordinarily large profits earned during the first year.

As follows from above, Exhibit 4 illustrates 16 potential paths of change in a multinational's conflict behavior. Several of these paths may be used during the course of one particular conflict. Even in such circumstances, however, the "opening moves" in the form of offers, gestures, and actions are often critical in the creation of the psychological setting that may prevail throughout, since it is at this early stage that rules and norms are first implanted, the issues such as trust and toughness are considered for the first time, and each party's preferences, intentions, and perceptions are first exposed.

Collaborative Paths. In general, initial use of the *collaboration* mode is recommended whenever possible. This is because outcomes of such behavior are likely to come close to outcomes that are viewed as substantively "fair" or in the "public interest." The assumption here is that, over the long term, the interests of the enterprises will best be safeguarded if they coincide with perceptions of public interest in home and host nations. But joint problem-solving efforts are fragile and may break down. And so the collaborate→compromise shift (*path 1*) may be needed to resolve remaining issues. Moreover, if the breakdown is severe enough, and if management finds itself in a weak bargaining position, then the collaborate→accommodate route (*path 2*) may be necessary to maintain a positive working relationship with the

EXHIBIT 4   SEQUENTIAL PATTERNS OF MODE UTILIZATION

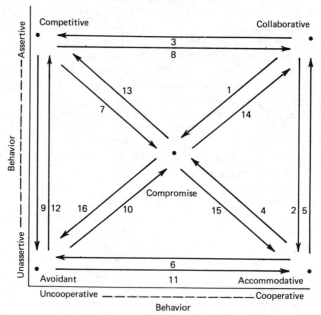

Source. Gladwin and Walter, *Multinationals Under Fire*, 1980.

opposition. However, if the multinational's power base is sufficiently strong and the relationship is viewed as expendable, then the collaborate→compete path (*path 3*) may be a viable last resort should irreconcilable differences emerge.

Accommodative Paths.   When a multinational confronts an issue that generates intense and aggressive feelings, however, *accommodation* may be more useful than collaboration as a starting point. In particular, if management can fully understand and empathize with the other side, the accommodative approach may establish a relationship that can eventually employ either compromise (*path 4*) or possibly even collaboration (*path 5*). Accommodation may also facilitate influence by gradations—the "foot in the door" technique—or even induce guilt or obligation in the other party, making that party less likely to resist the more assertive and/or uncooperative behavior that follows. Nevertheless, a shift from accommodation to avoidance (*path 6*) may be necessary if the enterprise is pushed too far or if things just don't work out. Polaroid's experience in South Africa, chronicled by O'Connell (1973), is an example of the latter situation. In this case, demonstrations, sit-ins, and an attempted product boycott in the United States in 1971 led management to acquiesce to some of the demands of the Polaroid Workers Revolutionary Movement. In particular, the company, as part of a widely publicized "experiment," required its independent distributor in South Africa to improve the wages and job opportunities for blacks and banned sales of its products to the South African government. Unfortunately, Polaroid was forced to pull out of the country altogether in 1977 when it confirmed reports from exiled black activists that its local distributor had sold film to the South African government in violation of the earlier understanding.

Competitive Paths.   Initial collaboration or accommodation should be avoided whenever such early cooperation could lead to a superficial or unstable agreement before the underlying issues in the situation were really worked through. In such circumstances, competition, even with its threat of losses to both sides, may be necessary in order to motivate the parties to approach the negotiation process in a mature fashion. By starting out tough, management can systematically soften its position by making positive concessions, either as part of a compromise (*path 7*) or as an attempt for full collaboration (*path 8*). One illustration of this approach was observed in the head-on clash between Hoffmann-LaRoche and the U.K. Monopolies Commission and Department of Health and Social Services over the pricing of librium and valium. Roche chose to get involved in a battle of "epic proportions" in order to prevent the spread of price-cutting demands in a dozen other nations. But the stakes declined as Roche's patents in these tranquilizers expired, and the Swiss firm compromised not long afterward. And, as with all other modes, the enterprise always has the option to throw in the towel (avoidance) should the going get too rough or too costly (*path 9*). Three examples of this sequence are Coca-Cola's withdrawal from India in the face of that government's demands that it disclose its secret formula; Firestone's termination of a Rumanian rubber-plant deal as a result of the protest orchestrated by the Young Americans for Freedom; and the Shell Oil Company's departure from the state of Delaware after a bitter "To Hell With Shell" campaign by environmentalists fighting the firm's local refinery-construction plans.

Avoidance Paths.   When the firm's stakes or power are low, where a zero-sum game is involved, or where there is a great deal of hostility, avoidance-oriented behavior often makes sense for openers. Management can let it be known that it won't touch the issue with the proverbial "10-foot pole." Yet if it backs off and lets the situation cool down, it is possible that a basis may later emerge for meaningful dialogue and negotiation (*path 10*). For example, in 1976 it became known that Coca-Cola's independent bottler in Guatemala had engaged in repressive actions against employees exercising their right to union representation. Faced with church groups demands that it terminate the franchise agreement, Coca-Cola argued that it was not the owner of the plant and had no control over its labor practices, and thus tried to disassociate itself from the conflict. The pressure of a shareholder resolution eventually led the company to agree to investigate the charges in exchange for a withdrawal of the church action. Church sponsors even visited Guatemala in 1978 and witnessed the signing of an agreement between the bottler and the workers. But murders, the use of riot squads, and abductions reportedly continued, and this led church groups to again press Coca-Cola into adopting a "code of minimum labor standards" that would be required of its franchisees around the globe. The company then returned to an uncooperative stance, restating that allegations involving independent bottlers were none of its business. In other circumstances, a transition from avoidance to accommodation may be appropriate (*path 11*), should the relationship improve or interests converge. Or if the stakes go up or the power balance reverses, a switch to competition (*path 12*) may become the logical course of action.

Compromise Paths.   As noted earlier, *compromise* is an appropriate initial course of action when stakes are relatively moderate, power is about equally distributed, and when interests and relations are mixed in character. However, it occasionally makes sense to move away from the compromise model. Thus when negotiations are moving slowly or when additional leverage is needed, the enterprise may find it expedient to introduce some threats into the picture (*path 13*). Goodrich in 1976, for instance, was attempting to reorganize the profitless non-tire section of Rubberfabriek Vredestein N.V. of Holland, which it had acquired in a bitter takeover battle with Goodyear in 1971. The unions protested the proposed reorganization, which would have meant layoffs of 762 of 4700 employees. This brought the Dutch government into the dispute. Negotiations ambled along until Goodrich, fed up with the slow pace, delivered an ultimatum—it offered to sell Vredestein to the government in June 1976 and announced it would sell off or close down if no agreement could be reached. The pace then quickened with negotiating teams flying back and forth between Akron and The Hague, and a fade-out agreement was reached in October 1976.

In other cases, the very experience of "good faith" bargaining and the development of mutual trust between the multinational and another party may allow compromise to evolve into collaboration (*path 14*). For example, when faced with intensifying nationalistic pressures in Guyana in the 1960s, Booker Sugar Estates, a subsidiary of Britain's Booker McConnell Ltd., embarked upon a comprehensive program, as reported by Litvak and Maule (1975) to win Guyanese acceptance by drastically increasing its contribution to the local economy. Working closely with government departments, the company promoted the formation of new business ventures, encouraged the expansion of independent cane farming, helped develop a local economic infrastructure, sought local equity participation in its own operations, progressively "Guyanized" its management, and generally attempted to reduce the industry's traditional paternalism. In sum, Booker's efforts to embody Guyanese goals in its corporate strategy allowed the company to operate unscathed until 1976, when a government takeover was negotiated. Other multinationals, such as Alcan, which had not engaged in such efforts in Guyana, were nationalized a number of years earlier.

In other circumstances, especially when the firm faces a decline in power or has a strong desire to maintain a particular relationship, a movement toward accommodation (*path 15*) may be called for. Perhaps the most classic case of this approach involves the relationship between the oil majors and OPEC examined in Vernon, *The Oil Crisis* (1976). In that instance, the entry of lean and hungry independent oil companies into the Middle East caused the leading "Seven Sisters" to lose their ability to set the terms of doing business. As a result, decisions that were the product of compromise in the 1950s and 1960s became products of accommodation in the 1970s and 1980s.

Finally, if bargaining fails to produce an acceptable agreement and competition or accommodation are inappropriate, management always has the option of pulling out (*path 16*). In early 1979, for example, the Swiss banking subsidiaries of Citicorp and Dow Chemical withdrew at the last minute from a syndicate that was floating a $33 million loan to Algeria. The eleventh-hour exit was prompted by a complaint made public by a manager of Banque Rothschild of Paris that his bank had been excluded from the syndicate because of its Jewish connections. Withdrawal was the only way in which the two American firms could comply with U.S. antiboycott laws that outlaw discrimination in the underwriting of loans.

In sum, since conflicts are not static, conflict management cannot be either. The 16 two-point incremental sequences above show some of the possibilities for change.

Even more extreme changes in behavior, say from competition directly to accommodation (bypassing compromise), or collaboration to avoidance, and vice versa, may be appropriate when stakes, power, interests, or relations change abruptly and radically. The point is that multipoint sequences are compelled by the dynamics of conflict, and in many cases the pattern of emergent behavior must "track" all over the grid that has been presented.

THE IMPLEMENTATION OF CONFLICT MANAGEMENT

INCENTIVE SYSTEMS.   Accepting the logic and value of the above contingency approach to constructive conflict management is one thing; executing such an approach effectively and efficiently on the part of MNC management is another. How can implementation of the approach best be encouraged or facilitated? The answer, according to Gladwin and Walter (*Multinationals Under Fire,* 1980) lies in creating a conducive management environment *within* the MNC. This, in turn, depends vitally on two systems—the *incentive system* under which MNC managers operate, and the

EXHIBIT 5   INCENTIVES AND TASK SYSTEMS FOR CONSTRUCTIVE CONFLICT MANAGEMENT

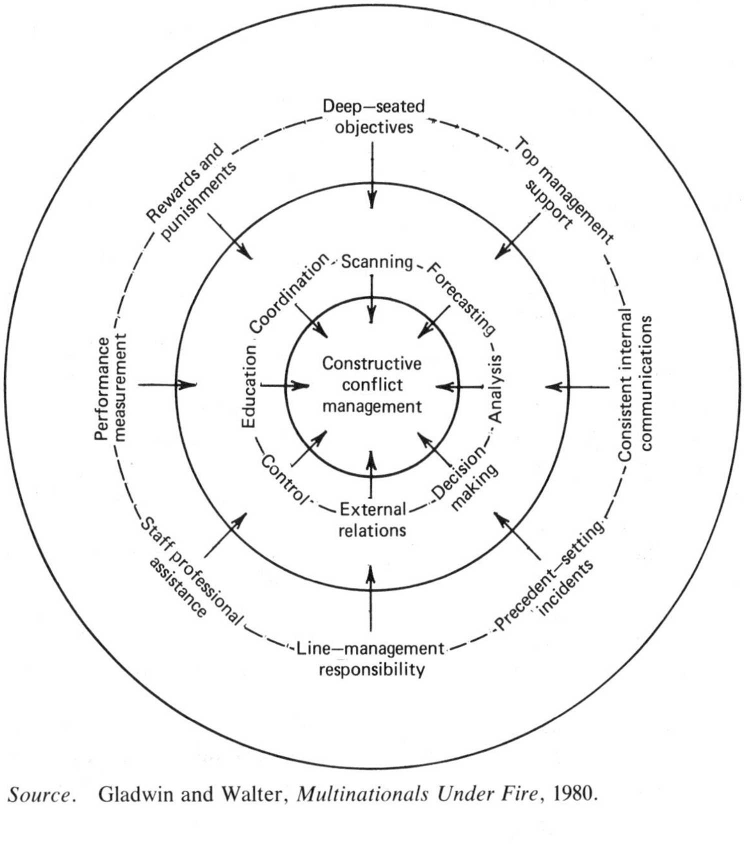

Source.   Gladwin and Walter, *Multinationals Under Fire,* 1980.

task system necessary for carrying out conflict management itself. Some of the more important "points of leverage" bearing upon the organizational climate for constructive conflict management are shown in Exhibit 5.

The outer ring of Exhibit 5 shows various elements of the corporatewide incentive system that can be shaped by senior management. Constructive conflict management must be a deeply ingrained facet of the MNC's corporate personality—shared in, believed in, and acted upon at every level. To become an integral part of the normal planning and decision-making process, conflict management must gain strong and consistent support at the highest levels of management. Senior managers need to communicate clearly and forcefully how much constructive conflict management means to the firm—one effective way of doing this is to creatively use a conspicuous incident (e.g., an investment project that has been blocked because of obviously poor conflict management) as a corporate learning experience in order to send a strong message to the middle managers who are most directly involved in managing such conflict.

Conflict management should be primarily a "line" function; a sure route to disaster is to leave conflict-management strategies and tactics totally in the hands of staff specialists and then issue them to line managers as directives. Staff professionals can, of course, play a useful support role to the line organization, but responsibility and authority should clearly rest in line-management hands. This is because conflict management will only be effective if it is a continuous and major element in the line manager's decision system. As such, the function of conflict management should be tested by periodic measures of performance and organizational "carrots and sticks" used to reinforce desired managerial behavior.

TASK SYSTEMS. Attention can now shift to the inner ring of Exhibit 5, which identifies the primary tasks essential to effective *implementation* of conflict management by MNC management. The MNC's ability to constructively manage external conflict will importantly depend on its expertise in *scanning*, selecting, transmitting, and interpreting information related to the potential emergence and actual character of conflict. Much of the scanning activity can be performed by staff "boundary-spanning" personnel. *Forecasting* is also important, since astute conflict management depends on predictions of the potency and demands of various interests groups and assessments of how the demands may constrain the MNC's actions. Proper scanning and forecasting will make the creative task of *analysis* easier, since formulating specific conflict-management alternatives as well as evaluating differences among them largely depends on the availability of cognitive resources.

The essence of MNC conflict management according to the contingency scheme, of course, is expertise in *decision making* among the various types of conflict-handling behavior. Such decision making cannot be rigid, but must rather be fast and flexible; timing will often be of the essence in conflict management. Implementing the decisions that are made will typically involve *external relations;* the MNC thus needs expertise in representing itself, communicating with and exerting influence over relevant external groups and organizations.

A control system represents an important adjunct to the decision-making system in conflict management. *Control* is essential mainly because external demands change over time—as noted above, stakes, power, relations, and interests are dynamic variables—the effectiveness of conflict behaviors thus must be continuously monitored and corrective actions taken when necessary. *Education* of MNC managers in the "art" of conflict management is also an essential task, and management-development programs can be designed to bridge gaps in required knowledge, attitudes, and skills. The final and most critical task is that of *coordination;* "unity of effort" must be brought about in the performance of all of the tasks described above.

CONFLICT MANAGEMENT IN THE YEARS AHEAD

A FUTURE OF CONTRADICTIONS.   What general trends seem to be shaping the challenge of conflict management as it will confront multinationals in the years ahead? Gladwin and Walter, in *Multinationals Under Fire* (1980), have forecast a "future of contradictions"—a global environment facing MNCs that will be characterized by often-incompatible factors bearing upon corporate objectives and policies. They see many trends that may work in almost dramatically opposed directions.

Some examples include the following. The importance of nationalism may continue to grow, but so will world economic and political interdependence. The power balance between MNCs and host nations may continue to shift in favor of host nations, but at the same time, home countries may increasingly assert their powers in the form of political controls over outward technology transfer, investment, and trade. And most developing nations appear steadfast in their desire for a "new international economic order," but their demands for a more "equitable" share of global prosperity are coming at a time when they need the MNC as much as ever and when developed nations are in no mood to make concessions as a result of unemployment, inflation, and energy problems.

The contradictions continue. The push of technology in telecommunications, computers, and travel will continue to shrink time and space, and will produce increasingly universal standards of behavior, but cultural homogenization appears to be increasingly resisted by groups seeking ethnic, religious, and cultural identity. The new importance given to maintaining local values may translate into more-frequent charges of "cultural imperialism" against MNCs in host nations—yet pressure groups at home seem intent on forcing MNCs to carry homegrown values abroad, particularly regarding ethical and moral dimensions of corporate policy. And employees will continue to demand a greater say in how their companies are run, but at the same time, myriad outside interest groups are bound to continue their struggle to have a say in corporate governance.

MANAGING THE CONTRADICTIONS.   We could go on, but the fact that MNCs will in part create, collide with, and be victimized by contradictions in the 1980s and beyond should be clear. The central task of conflict management on the part of multinationals will be to cope with such contradictions. The opposing trends imply that tensions surrounding the MNC will remain and perhaps intensify. We may increasingly find MNCs being used as political tools, hostages, and bargaining chips by competing sovereignties; the risks of being caught between conflicting parties may thus grow more serious.

Many of the trends also imply that MNCs may experience a loss of autonomy and discretion—the mixture of emerging law, regulation, government intervention, trade-union/employee power, and citizen-lobby pressure can only translate into increased external control. The trends also signal increasing turbulence, with the key factor here being interdependence. Shifts in the external environment are increasingly going to come from anywhere without notice, to produce consequences unanticipated by those initiating the changes and those experiencing the results. In sum, multinationals will have to show far more political-social savvy in the years ahead in order to ensure survival and success. Under fire, the multinational must approach conflict management in a more proactive, contingency-based, and strategic manner.

SOURCES AND SUGGESTED REFERENCES

Baldwin, P.L. and M.F. Baldwin. *Onshore Planning For Offshore Oil: Lessons from Scotland.* Washington, DC: The Conservation Foundation, 1975.

Barnet, R.J. and R.E. Muller. *Global Reach: The Power of the Multinational Corporations.* New York: Simon and Schuster, 1974.

Behrman, J.N. *National Interests and the Multinational Enterprise: Tensions Among the North Atlantic Countries.* Englewood Cliffs, NJ: Prentice-Hall, 1970.

Behrman, J.N., J. Boddewyn, and A. Kapoor. *International Business—Government Communications.* Lexington, MA: D.C. Heath, 1975.

Bergsten, C.F., T. Horst, and T.H. Moran. *American Multinationals and American Interests.* Washington, DC: Brookings Institution, 1978.

Blake, D.H. *Managing the External Relations of Multinational Corporations.* New York: Fund for Multinational Management Education, 1977.

Chill, D.S. *The Arab Boycott of Israel.* New York: Praeger, 1976.

Clutterbuck, R. *Kidnap and Ransom: The Response.* London: Faber and Faber, 1978.

Congressional Research Service. *The Overseas Private Investment Corporation: A Critical Analysis.* Prepared for the House Committee on Foreign Affairs. Washington, DC: U.S. Government Printing Office, 1973.

"Controlling the Multinationals," *The Economist* (January 1978), pp. 68–69.

Deutsch, M. *The Resolution of Conflict: Constructive and Destructive Processes.* New Haven: Yale University Press, 1973.

Dunn, S., M.F. Cahill, and J.J. Boddewyn. *How Fifteen Transnational Corporations Manage Public Affairs.* Chicago: Crain Communications, 1979.

Fayerweather, J. "A Conceptual Scheme of the Interaction of the Multinational Firm and Nationalism," *Journal of Business Administration,* Vol. VII (1975), pp. 67–89.

Fayerweather, J. *International Business Strategy and Administration.* Cambridge, MA: Ballinger, 1978.

Fisher, F. "Fractionating Conflict," *Daedalus,* Vol XCII (1964), pp. 920–941.

Franko, L.G. *Joint Venture Survival in Multinational Corporations.* New York: Praeger, 1971.

Gilpin, R. *U.S. Power and the Multinational Corporation: The Political Economy of Foreign Direct Investment.* New York: Basic Books, 1975.

Gladwin, T.N. *Environment, Planning and the Multinational Corporation.* Greenwich, CT: JAI Press, 1977.

Gladwin, T.N. "Environmental Policy Trends Facing Multinationals," *California Management Review,* Vol. XX (1977), pp. 81–93.

Gladwin, T.N. and I. Walter. "How Multinationals Can Manage Social and Political Forces," *The Journal of Business Strategy,* Vol. I (1980), pp. 54–68.

Gladwin, T.N. and I. Walter. "Multinational Enterprise, Social Responsiveness, and Pollution Control," *Journal of International Business Studies,* Vol. VII (1976), pp. 57–74.

Gladwin, T.N. and I. Walter. *Multinationals Under Fire: Lessons in the Management of Conflict.* New York: Wiley, 1980.

Gladwin, T.N. and I. Walter. "The Shadowy Underside of International Trade," *Saturday Review,* Vol. IV (1977), pp. 16–59.

Goulet, D. *The Uncertain Promise: Value Conflicts in Technology Transfer.* New York: IDOC/North America, 1977.

Gulliver, P.H. *Disputes and Negotiations: A Cross Cultural Perspective.* New York: Academic Press, 1979.

Haendel, D. and G.T. West. *Overseas Investment and Political Risk.* Philadelphia: Foreign Policy Research Institute, 1975.

Hawkins, R.G., ed. *The Economic Effects of Multinational Corporations.* Greenwich, CT: JAI Press, 1979.

Hershfield, D.C. *The Multinational Union Faces the Multinational Company.* New York: The Conference Board, 1975.

Hood, N. and S. Young. *The Economics of Multinational Enterprise.* London: Longman, 1979.

"In hoc Signo," *The Economist* (August 13, 1977), p. 13.

Jodice, D.A. "Sources of Change in Third World Regimes For Foreign Direct Investment, 1968–19776," *International Organization,* Vol. XXXIV (1980), pp. 177–206.

Johnson, H.G. "A Theoretical Model of Nationalism in New and Developing States," *Political Science Quarterly,* Vol. LXXX (1965), pp. 169–185.

Keohane, R.O. and Nye, J.S. *Power and Interdependence: World Politics in Transition.* Boston: Little, Brown, 1977).

Kobrin, S.J. "Foreign Enterprise and Forced Divestment in the LDCs," *International Organization,* Vol. XXXIV (1980), pp. 65–88.

Kujawa, D. "Collective Bargaining and Labor Relations in Multinational Enterprises: A U.S. Public Policy Perspective," in R.G. Hawkins, ed. *The Economics of Multinational Corporations.* Greenwich, CT: JAI Press, 1979.

LaPalombara, J. and S. Blank. *Multinational Corporations and National Elites: A Study in Tensions.* New York: The Conference Board, 1976.

Litvak, I.A. and C.J. Maule. "Foreign Corporate Social Responsibility in Less Developed Economies," *Journal of World Trade Law,* Vol. IX (1975), pp. 121–135.

Lloyd, B. *Political Risk Management.* London: Keith Shipton Developments, 1976.

Lockhart, C. *Bargaining in International Conflicts.* New York: Columbia University Press, 1979.

Moran, T.H. *Multinational Corporations and the Politics of Dependence.* Princeton: Princeton University Press, 1974.

Moran, T.H. "Transnational Strategies of Protection and Defense by Multinational Corporations: Spreading the Risk and Raising the Cost for Nationalization in Natural Resources," *International Organization,* Vol. XXVII (1973), pp. 273–287.

Mikdashi, Z. *The International Politics of Natural Resources.* Ithaca: Cornell University Press, 1976.

Mikesell, R.F. *Foreign Investment in Copper Mining: Case Studies in Peru and Papua New Guinea.* Baltimore: Johns Hopkins University Press for Resources for the Future, 1975.

Northrup, H.R. and R. Rowen. "Multinational Collective Bargaining Activity: The Factual Record in Chemical, Glass and Rubber Tires," *Columbia Journal of World Business,* Vol. IX (1974), pp. 49–63.

Nye, J.S. "Multinational Corporations in World Politics," *Foreign Affairs,* Vol. LIII (1974), pp. 153–175.

O'Connell, J.J. "Polaroid Corporation Case," in C.E. Summer and J.J. O'Connell, eds. *The Managerial Mind,* 3rd ed. Homewood, IL.: Richard D. Irwin, 1973.

Raven, B.H. and A.W. Kruglanski. "Conflict and Power," in Paul G. Swingle, ed. *The Structure of Conflict*. New York: Academic Press, 1970.

Robinson, R.D. *International Business Management: A Guide to Decision Making,* 2nd ed. Hinsdale, IL: Dryden Press, 1978.

Rubin, J.Z. and B.R. Brown. *The Social Psychology of Bargaining and Negotiation*. New York: Academic Press, 1975.

Sauvant, K.P. and F.G. Lavipour. *Controlling Multinational Enterprises*. Boulder: Westview Press, 1976.

Schelling, T.C. *The Strategy of Conflict*. New York: Oxford University Press, 1960.

Smith, D.N. and L.T. Wells, Jr. *Negotiating Third World Mineral Agreements*. Cambridge, MA: Ballinger, 1975.

Swingle, P.G. *The Management of Power*. Hillsdale, NJ: Lawrence Erlbaum Associates, 1976.

Thomas, K.W. "Conflict and Conflict Management," in M.D. Dunnette, ed. *Handbook of Industrial and Organizational Psychology*. Chicago: Rand-McNally, 1976.

Truitt, J.F. *Expropriation of Private Foreign Investment*. Bloomington: Division of Research, Graduate School of Business, Indiana University, 1974.

Turck, N. "The Arab Boycott of Israel," *Foreign Affairs,* Vol. LVV (1977), pp. 472–439.

Vernon, R. *Sovereignty at Bay*. New York: Basic Books, 1971.

Vernon R. *Storm Over the Multinationals: The Real Issues*. Cambridge, MA: Harvard University Press, 1977.

Vernon, R. ed. *The Oil Crisis*. New York: W.W. Norton, 1976.

Vogel, D. *Lobbying the Corporation: Citizen Challenges to Business Authority*. New York: Basic Books, 1978.

Walter, I. "A Guide to Social Responsibility of the Multinational Enterprise," in J. Backman, ed. *Social Responsibility and Accountability*. New York: New York University Press, 1975.

Wilkins, M. *The Emergence of Multinational Enterprise*. Cambridge, MA: Harvard University Press, 1970.

Wilkins, M. *The Maturing of Multinational Enterprise: American Business Abroad from 1914 to 1970*. Cambridge, MA: Harvard University Press, 1974.

Wrong, D.H. *Power: Its Forms, Bases and Uses*. New York: Harper and Row, 1979.

Young, S. and N. Hood. *Chrysler U.K.: A Corporation in Transition*. New York: Praeger, 1977.

Zartman, I.W. *The 50% Solution*. Garden City, NY: Anchor Books, 1977.

INTERNATIONAL PUBLIC AFFAIRS

CONTENTS

WHY PUBLIC AFFAIRS?   3

WHY INTERNATIONAL PUBLIC
AFFAIRS?   4

KEY IPA FACTORS   4

Type of Industry   4
Size, Growth, and Evolution   6
Corporate Culture and Individual
Attitudes   7

IPA INTELLIGENCE AND PLANNING   7

Institutionalizing the Planning Function   7
Establishing Priorities and Targets   8
Sources of Information   10
  Internal sources   11
  External sources   11
  Coordination   11
  The chief executive officer's special
  problems   11
Inventorying Resources   12
Setting Goals, Timetables, and Budgets   12

STRUCTURING THE IPA FUNCTION   13

Beginning Steps: The Minimal Pattern   13
On the Way: The Intermediate Pattern   15
All the Way: The Advanced Pattern   15
  National line executives   16
  National public-affairs staff   17
  Local community level   18
  Regional level   18
  The world corporate global level   18
Special Patterns   19
Concluding Remark   19

IPA STAFFING   20

Rank and Status   20
Background, Nationality, and Rotation   20
Formal and Informal PA Roles   21
  The monitor/analyst/thinker   21

The contact man/door opener/
  introducer   22
The adviser/consultant/trusted
  confidant   22
The negotiator   23
The communications specialist   23
The program man   23
Concluding remark   23
Outsiders   23
Collective Action   25

IPA ACTION   26

Modes of Response   26
Profiling the Multinational Corporation   26
Philosophy   28
  Public affairs is important and
  inevitable   28
  Public affairs is a proper and
  legitimate function   28
  Public affairs is an earning function   29
  Public affairs must be managed   30
  Public affairs works best as a two-
  way process   30
  Public affairs is an inside job too   30

IPA REPORTING AND CONTROLLING   31

Channels   31
Interaction Among Levels   31
Format, Timing, and Contingency
  Planning   33
Locus of Control   34
Criteria of Effectiveness   34
Reward and Penalties   35
Socioeconomic Reporting   36

CONCLUSION   36

SOURCES AND SUGGESTED
REFERENCES   36

INTERNATIONAL PUBLIC AFFAIRS

Jean J. Boddewyn

WHY PUBLIC AFFAIRS?

There are three basic ways of making money in business. One is through *operational efficiency,* by minimizing inputs and maximizing outputs in any given activity and for the whole firm. Such savings and higher productivity translate into greater profits.

The second profit-generating way rests on *market effectiveness* in buying and selling. The old principle of "buy cheap, sell dear" applies here, although nowadays it takes rather sophisticated forms in developing sourcing, marketing, and corporate strategies.

This leaves us with *public affairs*—the third way of making money. A firm may be efficient and well positioned in the market, but what if it is boycotted because of its union-busting and environment-polluting activities? In such a case, the profits resulting from efficiency and market effectiveness will be jeopardized. Conversely, a company can secure favorable legislation, obtain a relaxation of onerous regulations, and gain the goodwill of actual and potential consumers, and thereby achieve greater profits.

To put it more generally, public affairs is about obtaining and retaining *legitimacy* from the firm's "publics." A "legitimate" business is one that not only acts legally but also fairly and in tune with current expectations of good behavior vis-à-vis its own members, the communities in which it operates, and the society it serves. Such legitimacy protects the profits made by the company's producers and marketers. It also opens new avenues for gain through the creation of a better operating environment and the reaping of more immediate benefits such as tax concessions and greater patronage.

This is the domain of public affairs—also called external affairs, social affairs, public relations, and other names.

Public Affairs (PA) is concerned with enlisting the support and negating the opposition of significant nonmarket units (public institutions and private organizations, looser collectivities, and individuals) in the firm's environment. Its targets (constituencies, publics, stakeholders) consist of (1) government in its multiple roles of legitimizer, regulator, and promoter; (2) business, trade, labor, and professional associations as well as other firms in their pressure-group, private-regulator and legitimizing roles; (3) the intellectual, moral, and scientific communities as legitimizers and opinion makers; (4) public opinion at large as voter and general legitimizer; and (5) the firm's stockholders and employees as legitimizers. These targets constitute the "nonmarket environment" of the firm as distinguished from the "markets" for its commercial inputs and outputs.

Some people scoff at such profit protecting and making through public-affairs activities. They feel that business has no business meddling in politics and government, and in manipulating public opinion. This view, however, denies business the right to speak up, to petition, and to avail itself of political and economic benefits open to all private and corporate citizens. Exhibit 1 presents an overall description of the public-affairs function and emphasizes "good conduct" as the basis of all PA activities. It also stresses the continuous feedback that should inform them.

WHY INTERNATIONAL PUBLIC AFFAIRS?

The legitimacy issue looms even larger in international business, because a foreign firm is generally perceived as a "foreign body" whose contributions and loyalty are questionable.

For one thing, headquarters personnel and managers sent abroad are relatively ignorant of host-country policies, laws, legal traditions, local notions of what is considered "fair" business behavior, attitudes, customs, and so on. To make matters even worse, many expatriate managers prove impatient or ethnocentrically intolerant in the face of such differences: "Why are they not like us?"

Some home-based and expatriate managers go even further and flatly refuse to accept local traditions and expectations. This may be caused by sheer intolerance of foreign ways, or it may simply relect the human desire to simplify life and continue operating as at home. It may also be the product of corporate policy and of its bias toward standardized operating procedures, since multinational corporations need some global vision and uniform approach in order to maximize their advantages over local firms that will always know their milieus better.

Consequently, the legitimacy of foreign-owned and controlled companies is frequently challenged by host nations, which then translate their fears and suspicions into special entry, operating, and exit requirements, often stricter than those applying to local firms (see previous sections The Political Environment of International Business, Codes of Conduct Facing Transnational Corporations, and Conflict Management in International Business). The home country also presents PA challenges, since the multinational character of a firm may be perceived as detrimental to that country's welfare by exporting jobs, capital, and technology, among other things.

KEY IPA FACTORS

Identifying targets as well as developing, implementing, and evaluating the appropriate programs to reach and influence them constitute the tasks of international public affairs (IPA). Before analyzing these classical elements of planning, organizing, staffing, directing, and controlling, it is well to focus on some of the key factors that affect the conduct of the IPA functions.

TYPE OF INDUSTRY. Clearly, some industries have more IPA problems than others. Mining and extracting, for example, raise a host of sensitive issues because many countries view their natural resources as a sacred patrimony that is out of bound for

EXHIBIT 1 THE PUBLIC-AFFAIRS FUNCTION

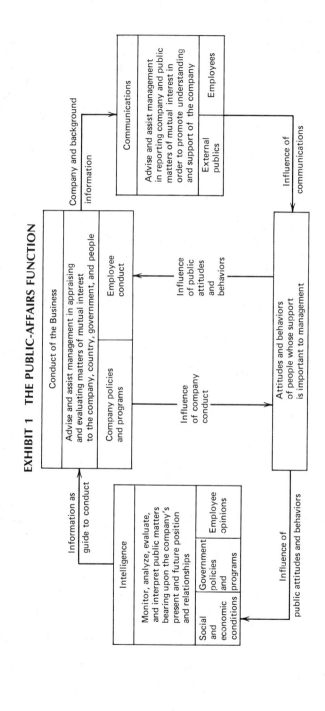

foreigners, who should not own or exploit the "soil"—the national territory—that embodies the concept of sovereignty.

Other industries are vulnerable because they are polluters (e.g., refining and chemicals), or because of some priority assigned to them as a source of export earnings (many commodities, for example), as the basis for economic development (e.g., steel and banks), as necessary for national defense (e.g., transportation, armaments, communications), as the guarantor of low national-health costs (e.g., pharmaceuticals), as the basis for modernization (e.g., machine tools, computers, biochemistry), or simply because they are prestigious and have caught the fancy of some key political leader. Consequently one finds that firms like Exxon (petroleum), Pfizer (pharmaceuticals), IBM (electronics), Citicorp (banking), and Ford (automobiles) have a well-developed IPA function.

On the other hand, some industries are practically invisible and stir very little concern. Eaton, which makes a large number of intermediary products that find their way into better-known ones, could advertise at one time that: "We probably are the largest multinational company you have never heard of!" A particular company, of course, may have many different product lines and thus face varying public-affairs situations. Westinghouse sells both air conditioners and nuclear reactors, but the former line generates far fewer problems than the latter.

Conversely, some economic activities suffer from "benign neglect" and do not generate enough public support because they are taken for granted or considered to be of minor importance. Pure marketing organizations such as department stores and supermarkets often have to clamor for government attention and incentives because economic-development authorities often assume that distribution will take care of itself, or because they consider it to be a parasitic activity.

SIZE, GROWTH, AND EVOLUTION. Large size—absolute or relative to local firms—usually makes for visibility, greater impact on the local economy and society, and vulnerability to the criticisms addressed to monopolistic and oligopolistic companies. This calls for more public affairs to justify the firm's bigness in terms of economies of scale and as part of a multinational organization that can draw on the resources and experiences of its many parts.

The company that grows internally or through acquisitions also creates problems as local firms feel crowded out, and as the specter of foreign domination raises its ugly head. J.J. Servan-Schreiber made *The American Challenge* a common fear in Europe, but Latin Americans resent *dependencia,* and Africans and Asians reject new forms of imperialism and colonialism.

Other changes can be equally bothersome. The multinational that closes a plant in one country and opens another elsewhere is frequently branded as irresponsible and profit thirsty. Expanding here rather than there also rankles the feelings of the neglected governments—especially if several nations competed vigorously for the new plant or expansion.

The *entry* stage poses different problems from those of later stages. There are typically active and multiple contacts with the authorities and various experts to ascertain the overall investment climate, to get the necessary permits and guarantees, and to obtain investment incentives (tax holidays, training allowances, cheap loans, free grants, etc.) if available. At this point, relations with government and the public are often smooth and cordial when the foreign investor has been invited or welcomed by the host country, although some local interests may object.

After the honeymoon period is over and the *ongoing-operations stage* sets in, public affairs may settle into a placid routine, although constant vigilance is necessary in order to avoid being ignored and even harmed as later investors now get new benefits. Besides, governments policies and priorities do change over time; and the cost/benefit ratio tends to look less favorable to government which now sees foreign companies paying fees and royalties to their parent and repatriating profits while the subsidiary's contributions in terms of jobs, exports, taxes, and so forth tend to be taken for granted.

At *exit*—forced or voluntary—time, new public-affairs problems emerge as both the government and public opinion oppose layoffs and the loss of productive capacity unless local ownership and management can take over. Even when forced out, the multinational must negotiate for compensation and try to maintain good relations with its constituencies in order to protect its other investments in the host country and elsewhere, and to prepare for its possible return at a later date.

CORPORATE CULTURE AND INDIVIDUAL ATTITUDES.   Some companies have no significant PA experience at home and are thus unaware of such problems abroad and unprepared to cope with them on an international scale. For example, IBM's European subsidiaries were at one point more sophisticated in public affairs than their parent company because they had first faced in the United Kingdom, France, and Germany public policies designed to favor local computer companies through government purchases and subsidies. Hence there was little that the corporate head-quarters could provide in the way of PA assistance. Conversely, a multinational such as Caterpillar, which has a well-developed corporate public-affairs philosophy at home, is more likely to implement it in host countries.

The implementation of company policy depends on people, but some managers are not temperamentally or professionally suited to be active in public affairs. They may resent the publicity, abuse, and even injuries (kidnapping, kneecap shooting, assassination) associated with visibility and outspokenness. Others object to the required politicking and public-relationing because of their engineering, production, or marketing background, which has oriented them to other forms of profit making.

Executives experienced in legal and financial matters, on the other hand, are more inclined to recognize opportunities in this area and to minimize the concomitant risks, since their regular work requires much contact with government anyway. As the financial director of a multinational in Belgium put it: "The more interesting part of my job is not financial statements and cash flows—I have able assistants to do that—but interacting with numerous bureaucracies to obtain permission to increase prices, to get favorable customs valuations, to repatriate dividends, and so on."

Over time, even managers with little inclination toward public affairs do learn from experience; and strong admonitions from higher corporate levels ("We don't want problems with host governments!") help move reluctant converts in that direction.

IPA INTELLIGENCE AND PLANNING

INSTITUTIONALIZING THE PLANNING FUNCTION.   Setting goals and action plans for tomorrow requires good intelligence today. A major problem here is that public-affairs issues vary so much from country to country, from product to product, and from function to function. One obvious solution is to fully decentralize public affairs among the multinational company's units regions, countries, divisions, and departments.

This approach, however, leaves unattended the central headquarters' tasks of (1) identifying common issues around the world, (2) collecting and sharing worthwhile knowledge and experiences, (3) centralizing those monitoring activities that are best done once and for all, and (4) appraising the units' planning performances so that the latter may be ultimately upgraded. How do multinationals cope with this classical problem?

Ultimately all solutions require the appointment of one or more people at headquarters—the question is who and where? A relatively simple answer consists of expanding the role of the *market-research and/or corporate-planning staff* beyond their traditional economic analyses of the world environment to include IPA matters. Since these staffs' resources are limited in terms of time and expertise, this solution ultimately requires the addition of one or more IPA specialists—often someone with a liberal-arts and/or social-science background, although engineers and scientists are also included when technical problems loom large (e.g., environmental protection).

Alternatively, the chief executive officer may appoint a *special assistant* operating outside of the corporate planning staff in order to emphasize the chief executive officer's concern with these matters, and as the possible nucleus for a full-fledged IPA department. A few multinationals (e.g., Exxon) assign a member of the *board of directors* to the surveillance of IPA matters.

A more elaborate solution consists of placing such intelligence gathering and planning *within the corporate public-affairs department,* whose role is thus extended to encompass international developments. This is a more advanced approach because it signifies that the multinational corporation has seen it fit to create a separate public-affairs function that provides inputs and generates favorable outcomes just like the other major units of the firm (marketing, production, finance, product divisions, geographic areas, etc.).

ESTABLISHING PRIORITIES AND TARGETS. A perusal of any list of topics on the agendas of the U.S. government, foreign governments, and the United Nations reveals scores of long-term issues and immediate problems with which a multinational can concern itself. (See also Gladwin and Walter, 1980). Exhibit 2 illustrates the major topics with which they have to cope to one degree or another.

Can such public-affairs issues be tracked down so that management may take adequate initiatives in time? Several think-tank and consulting organizations are in the process of developing the technology that a small but growing number of multinational corporations are beginning to use and improve. (Molitor, 1977; La-Palombara and Blank, 1977; Kobrin, 1979; Terry, 1977; Haendel, 1979; Kraar, 1980). The techniques and their validity remain crude, but multinationals are undoubtedly expanding and refining their monitoring of the relevant environments (Kobrin et al., 1980).

In any case, some sorting out is essential in terms of *specificity* to the firm, urgency, and danger/opportunity significance. Besides, both *short-term and long-term implications* must be considered—for example, immediate compliance with a new ill-designed regulation on consumer protection *and* prevention of its spreading to other countries through more-effective monitoring and lobbying. (For an excellent treatment of the monitoring function, see Brown, 1979).

EXHIBIT 2   PUBLIC-AFFAIRS ISSUES

Main Issues	Subissues
Multinationalism (pressures on multinational companies)	Protectionism (tariff and nontariff barriers); foreign ownership; indigenization of personnel; exporting jobs; local research and sourcing; import substitution; expropriation and nationalization; choice of appropriate technology; patent/trademark/licensing restrictions; codes of conduct (UN, OECD, EEC, UNCTAD, ICC, ILO, national, industry, etc.); disclosure; bribery and other corrupt practices; Arab boycott; South Africa; human rights; transborder data flows; multinational unions; foreign divestment; disclosure of information to governments, unions, employees, and stockholders; accounting standards.
Employee participation	General industrial relations climate; theory and practice of participation through works councils, trade unions, staff associations, etc.; codetermination; cooperatives; attitudes of employers and employees; layoffs; plant closures; unemployment; motivation; automation; international comparisons and differentials; legislation and regulations.
Environmental pollution	Air, land, water; noise; resource conservation; resource allocation; recycling; new technologies; legislation and regulations (local, national, EEC, UN, etc.).
Individual and organization	Alienation; pressure groups; power groups; role of trade unions; civil rights; women; immigrants; participation in planning; consumer protection; legislation and regulations.
Consumer affairs	Pressure groups; fair trading; customer service; product liability; subsidies; shortages; substitutes; legislation and regulations.
Business and society	Ownership; profit; disclosure; big vs. small business; entrepreneurship; licensure; marketing concept; government intervention; capitalism vs. socialism; mergers, monopolies; social responsibility; social audit; centralized control; move to service economy; inflation; prices and incomes; investment and jobs; company legislation and regulations.
Government	State of politics; political parties; democracy; nationalization; devolution; sovereignty; internationalization; defense; direct intervention; civil-service practices; legislature vs. executive and judiciary.
Technological change	New technologies; technological impact; mass communications; rate of change; investment in research; responsibilities of technologists and scientists; technology transfer; scientific entrepreneurs; social impact/technology assessment; appropriate technology; education for a world of change.

EXHIBIT 2   CONTINUED

Changing values/social trends	Materialism vs. quality of life; growth vs. no growth vs. balanced growth; desire for participation; leisure; crime, security; health (physical, mental); drugs; sex; alienation; elitism; invasion of privacy; morals, ethics, religion; attitudes toward business, government; role of youth; home, family; education; demand for information; racism; sexism; minorities.
Urban affairs	Inner-city slums; infrastructure; decision making, participation; transportation; education; housing; social services; local government finance; minorities.
The third world	North vs. South; power blocs; East vs. West; role of private enterprise; role of EEC, UN, OECD, etc.; foreign aid; population; natural disasters; education; training; pollution; technology; use of power by resource-rich less developed countries (oil, tin, cobalt, etc.).
Resources	Energy; raw materials; basic foodstuffs; fresh water; conservation; recycling; new sources; oceans; manmade substitutes; legislation and regulations (national, regional, international).
International affairs	EEC; East-West relations; Europe-U.S. relations; Far East; Middle East; trends in nation states; GATT, trade bodies; OECD; United Nations and its agencies; Commonwealth; monetary situation; global inflation; expropriation; war; security.

Source.   InterMatrix, Greenwich, CT.

Ultimately, issues translate into specific *targets* that embody problems and opportunities:

1. Who are the people, institutions, and organizations who can cause us trouble or assist us?
2. How do they operate, and what are they likely to do?
3. What do we want them to do or not to do?

These targets are not all external to the firm but include shareholders and employees (see below). Customers and suppliers are also important elements in public affairs, because they represent potential or actual allies and enemies. Without such a target list, no definite action plans can be effectively developed.

SOURCES OF INFORMATION.   The intelligence gathered should be related to the company's main problems around the world. Otherwise, too much unnecessary information clutters the whole process and ultimately dooms the project to failure, since it is not perceived as being sufficiently action oriented. Still, more-sophisticated multinationals allow for the monitoring of "horizon" issues still dimly understood in terms of their corporate implications (Molitor, 1977).

Internal Sources. The plans and reports produced by subsidiaries are being progressively expanded to include public-affairs issues and actions. However, this takes time, pressure, and education because the natural inclination of operations managers is to focus on more-traditional quantitative issues (market trends, operating costs, etc.).

Much information is also gathered through visits to and from foreign subsidiaries, meeting of public-affairs officers from various countries, the debriefing of returnees, and regular intracorporate communications through letters, telephone calls, telex messages, and so on.

External Sources. There is an increasing number of good information sources, ranging from the regular reading of *The New York Times,* the *Wall Street Journal,* the *Economist,* and the *Financial Times,* to subscribing to more-specialized country and issues reports generated by such outfits as the Economist Intelligence Unit, the Conference Board, the InterMatrix Group, Rundt, Business International, and International Business-Government Counsellors. Additionally, conferences provide settings where experiences and current knowledge can be more interactively shared (e.g., the meetings of the Public Affairs Council and the International Public Relations Association).

A major principle here is that multiple sources of information and interpretation should be used, because no single person or department has the necessary expertise, and because several heads are better than one when it comes to analyzing complex issues. This suggests the elaboration of alternative scenarios rather than simple black-and-white diagnoses and prognoses.

Besides, one gets information mostly by sharing one's own, since some topics are too delicate to be put in writing. This requires identifying the people (including experts, government officials, and critics) and associations that have the necessary information and cultivating them regularly through visits and by attending conferences in which they participate.

Coordination. Although some centralized information keeping is necessary, most data remain with the subsidiaries and divisions. This suggests developing a system comparable to British Oxygen Company's "ring and main" approach. The units are conceived of as in a circle, and the corporate planning "center" is only one of the groups on the circle. Each unit has access through requests to information in any other unit, but this requires that the units be made cognizant of each other's store of knowledge through the circulation of master lists (Who keeps track of what?) and periodic meetings of information officers.

The Chief Executive Officer's Special Problems. The chief executive officer's information problems are unique, because much of it comes to him filtered, and because subsidiaries are reluctant to communicate bad news or draw attention to new problems on which they will be queried and prodded. Consequently, he must complement the organization's monitoring system by his own sources: peers in other firms, government officials at home and abroad, membership in key associations (e.g., the Business Roundtable), board members (including foreigners) especially appointed for that purpose, advisory boards, contacts with experts and critics, the commissioning of special studies, and so on.

INVENTORYING RESOURCES.   This step is crucial for deciding what changes are needed in organization structure, staff, activities, and controls after identifying what the firm can already do by itself with its present resources. Additionally, external potential sources of assistance must be identified and evaluated.

Questions include:

1. How much *information* already exists in the firm: Who knows what?
2. Who knows whom, in terms of the necessary *contacts* with the main targets?
3. How good is the *communication system* for collecting, interpreting, storing, retrieving, and sharing public-affairs information?
4. What *budgets* are available and how are they spent?
5. What *outsiders* (consultants, associations, information services) are good at what and at what cost to complement the firm's own resources?

SETTING GOALS, TIMETABLES, AND BUDGETS.   Public-affairs goals cannot simply be *general philosophy statements* of the type: "We will behave as good citizens of the countries where we operate." They have to be translated into specific tasks linked to desired outcomes, and with a timetable—for example, to hire a former U.S. government official of subcabinet rank to head the firm's Washington office within 6 months; or to postpone for at least two years the enactment of regulations barring the use of certain food ingredients in France; or to increase the proportion of Brazilian people who think favorably of the company from 15 to 25 percent within one year.

Headquarters must also issue *policies and guidelines* within which the subsidiaries' public-affairs plans will be developed. Some brook no exceptions (such as the proscription of bribing officials) whereas others simply set broad parameters—for example, representation on the board of major business associations is highly desirable, but the choice of associations and the timetable for obtaining representation is left flexible.

Whenever possible, *financial budgets* must be related to the achievement of particular goals—for example, how much it will cost to conduct a public-relation campaign designed to convey certain messages to a specific target audience within a defined time period. On the other hand, slush funds must be avoided, because they falsify the budgetary process and complicate the assessment of results—not to mention possible legal and legitimacy problems.

Time budgets are also important, since it is estimated that anywhere from 5 to 70 percent of the top managers' time is spent on public-affairs matters. Should new goals require more time, these executives must receive special assistance or delegate some of their other tasks.

As in all other forms of planning, flexibility is essential, because situations and conditions change. Hence it is essential to maintain a constant monitoring of the environment, to develop alternative contingency plans ("If this happens, we do that instead") and to have versatile resources that can be shifted from old to new problems.

STRUCTURING THE IPA FUNCTION

Proper organizing of the IPA function is not easy, because of the multiple factors bearing on it (e.g., type of industry, size of the multinational and its foreign subsidiaries, corporate tradition, personal attitudes, etc). Besides multinational corporate experience in this area is still relatively meager, so that one finds a variety of patterns further complicated by the numerous organizational changes undergone by many multinationals in recent years.

Indeed, the public-affairs function must largely adapt itself to whatever global organizational form (international division, geographic, product, matrix) has been adopted by a multinational. In particular, the move toward a worldwide product-division basis has created problems to the extent that this organizational form complicates the conduct of public affairs at all levels, because product divisions operating in a single country are not typically organized to coordinate their PA activities on a national or regional basis.

A key principle here is that *PA policies and implementing decisions that have major implications for the entire company have to be made at higher levels.* The higher levels are also involved if only they possess the credibility and weight to make corporate policies believable by others—for example, to increase R&D expenditures abroad as a sign of the multinational's commitment to its host nations.

Yet it is desirable to involve those lower levels that have relevant information and/or will have to live with the new policies. Besides, a company spokesman should not be inadvertently caught lying because he did not know that the firm had a particular policy or was engaging in certain practices (e.g., bribery).

It is not unusual to find that the different levels in the firm—global (corporate), regional (e.g., Europe), national, and local (community)—are unevenly developed, and similar variations are found among product divisions and geographic areas. When the field is more active in public affairs than the center, headquarters has problems assisting and supervising the subsidiaries.

The facts that public affairs itself is made up of many parts (public relations, government relations, consumer relations, employee relations, etc.) and that some of them are lodged in other departments (personnel, marketing, finance, legal, etc.) also complicate the design of an effective IPA structure.

Exhibit 3 presents the respective ideal roles of the corporate, regional, and national levels. Such a division of labor is only approximated in a few multinationals such as Caterpillar Tractor Company, which has a definitely centralized headquarters-oriented approach to international public affairs. Other companies are learning, and several other patterns are evident besides such an "advanced" one.

BEGINNING STEPS: THE MINIMAL PATTERN. One finds here firms with no significant public-affairs problems, those with no awareness of, or interest in, such problems, those not quite knowing what to do about them, and those that have taken a few preliminary, tentative, partial steps to develop a PA function within their organizations.

At the national level, the minimal response consists of assigning to some manager or staffer whatever PA tasks have become necessary, besides what the chief executive himself shoulders in this area. Typically, it will be a second- or third-level manager whose function already involves relations with government and other nonmarket

EXHIBIT 3   THE IDEAL ROLES OF THE CORPORATE, REGIONAL, AND NATIONAL LEVELS IN INTERNATIONAL PUBLIC AFFAIRS

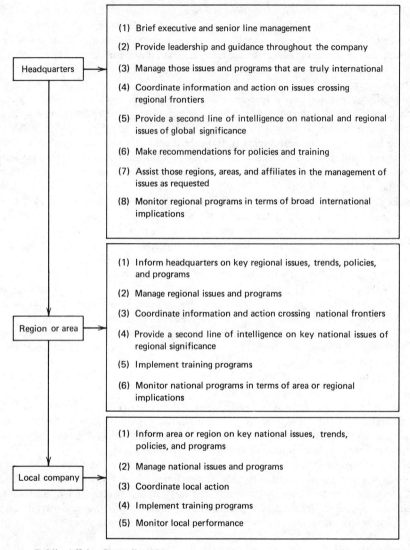

Headquarters

(1) Brief executive and senior line management

(2) Provide leadership and guidance throughout the company

(3) Manage those issues and programs that are truly international

(4) Coordinate information and action on issues crossing regional frontiers

(5) Provide a second line of intelligence on national and regional issues of global significance

(6) Make recommendations for policies and training

(7) Assist those regions, areas, and affiliates in the management of issues as requested

(8) Monitor regional programs in terms of broad international implications

Region or area

(1) Inform headquarters on key regional issues, trends, policies, and programs

(2) Manage regional issues and programs

(3) Coordinate information and action crossing national frontiers

(4) Provide a second line of intelligence on key national issues of regional significance

(5) Implement training programs

(6) Monitor national programs in terms of area or regional implications

Local company

(1) Inform area or region on key national issues, trends, policies, and programs

(2) Manage national issues and programs

(3) Coordinate local action

(4) Implement training programs

(5) Monitor local performance

Source.   Public Affairs Council, 1980.

groups. The personnel manager is therefore frequently assigned the nascent PA activities, but the chief financial officer or the legal counsel are also common choices, since they already deal with labor ministries, tax authorities, foreign-exchange matters, price-controls, and so forth. Besides, lower-level professionals such as engineers and accountants are brought in whenever their expertise is needed to study issues, prepare reports, and make presentations.

This pattern, by the way, is the one generally found at the *plant or community level,* even when the national subsidiary has a more fully developed public-affairs function: The plant manager or his personnel officer carry out on a part-time basis whatever community relations are necessary—sometimes with the assistance of a public-relations man.

A further step consists of appointing a special assistant to the chief executive officer to provide coordination in these matters and prepare the transition to a more elaborate setup.

At this early stage, outsiders such as bankers and lawyers are frequently used to supplement the firm's meager resources, and some firms use the service of the American Chamber of Commerce (and similar bicountry associations) and of their embassy (see below).

The simplicity of such light arrangements should not obscure the real problems connected with the lack of in-depth expertise and full-time attention, and with the difficulty of coordinating all sorts of piecemeal and diffuse efforts. Such problems can be remedied up to a point through training programs and exchanges of information among affiliates. Sooner or later, however, this set-up proves too awkward and ineffective.

ON THE WAY: THE INTERMEDIATE PATTERN. Most multinational firms are at the intermediate stage-—aware of the growing public-affairs problems facing their type of company, curious to find out what others are doing, discussing the problems at various levels within the organization, and building some of the major components of a full-fledged PA function. Major factors prompting greater involvement and the development of a more elaborate structure are the successful examples of other firms active in this area, some crisis (e.g., a negotiation poorly handled or a major attack on multinationals), pressure from higher hierarchical levels, and/or the interest and initiatives of the general manager or of some staffer—for example, the legal counsel or the public-relations officer.

The major characteristic of this intermediate stage is the existence of some *formal* external-affairs position *somewhere* in the international organization—frequently at the regional (e.g., European) level as far as U.S. firms are concerned—but going beyond whatever public-relations activities the firm may already be engaging in. It may be nothing more than the general manager getting a special assistant to deal with public affairs, or some functional manager having his position formally extended and upgraded to include government relations and other PA matters as a way of learning more about what should be done and how.

ALL THE WAY: THE ADVANCED PATTERN. At the advanced stage, all four levels—local, national, regional, and corporate/world—have well-developed public-affairs objectives, structures, and personnel (including the involvement of top executives), although some locations, countries, and regions typically are less grown and sophisticated than others.

These are companies in industries where government relations are crucial, as in petroleum, pharmaceuticals, computers, chemicals, and automobile manufacturing. They are large, or at least affect the country's economy significantly; and they are continuously in the process of expanding, contracting, and rationalizing their production, marketing, and financial operations in a number of countries—with the concomitant changing impacts on home and host countries.

They are usually organized on a geographic basis, but those with worldwide product divisions or of a conglomerate nature (such as ITT) have regional and/or national coordinating and assisting units. Exhibit 4 presents a simplified organizational chart for such arrangements.

National Line Executives.   These executives concentrate on four major tasks:

1.   Identifying problem areas, indoctrinating their managers and employees about them, and assigning accountability for them to various subordinates and staff while remaining ultimately responsible for the PA function.

2.   Assisting in the gathering of information about nonmarket developments through meetings with various elites in economy and society—on a personal basis and in the context of associations, conferences, and select gatherings of executives.

3.   Obtaining support for the firm's actions from decision makers (mainly legislators and government officials), opinion makers (the press, academics, fi-

EXHIBIT 4   ADVANCED PATTERN IN INTERNATIONAL PUBLIC AFFAIRS

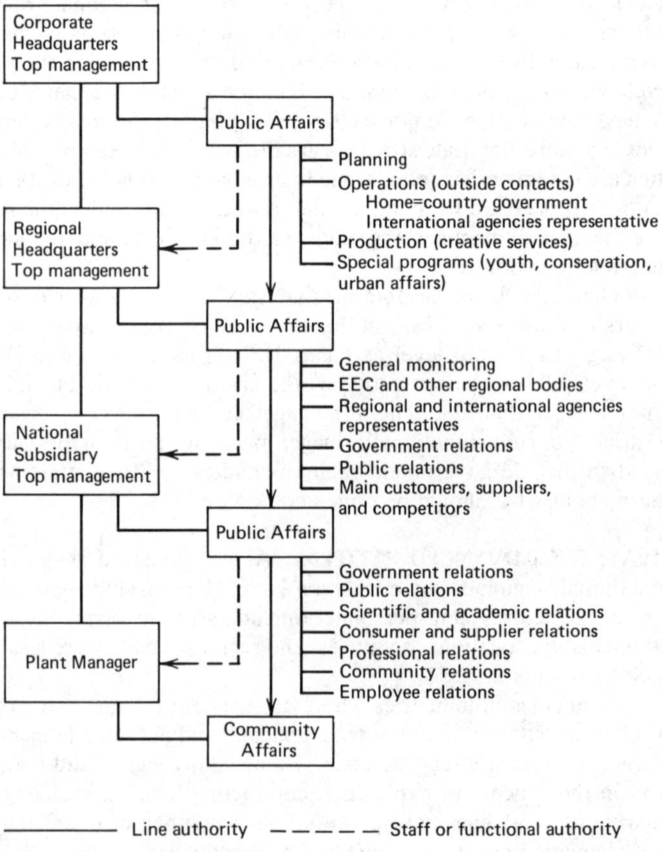

Corporate Headquarters Top management

Public Affairs
— Planning
— Operations (outside contacts)
    Home=country government
    International agencies representative
— Production (creative services)
— Special programs (youth, conservation, urban affairs)

Regional Headquarters Top management

Public Affairs
— General monitoring
— EEC and other regional bodies
— Regional and international agencies representatives
— Government relations
— Public relations
— Main customers, suppliers, and competitors

National Subsidiary Top management

Public Affairs
— Government relations
— Public relations
— Scientific and academic relations
— Consumer and supplier relations
— Professional relations
— Community relations
— Employee relations

Plant Manager

Community Affairs

———— Line authority   — — — — Staff or functional authority

Source.   Business International, 1975.

nancial analysts, etc.), and other significant influencers and public-opinion segments.

4. Negotiating with other decision makers when power and protocol considerations make national line executives the only valid spokesmen for the company.

Lower-level line managers are of course also active in relations with government and the public when their counterparts are of commensurate rank and when these managers' technical expertise is crucial in supporting roles. Here top executives and officials often initiate contacts and negotiations and then leave them to their subordinates to pursue until they have to be formally concluded or some impasse has been reached.

National Public-Affairs Staff. The public-relations function is typically very developed at this advanced stage and includes personnel specializing in such activities as receptions and visits, the production of various publications, press relations, and academic/scientific relations. This staff advises top executives as well as other departments.

However, sophisticated companies do not stop at these more-traditional PR activities (often assisted by the regional and world levels, which have relevant expertise to communicate) designed to project a company's image. They also conduct such activities as consumer-complaint handling, charitable contributions, beautification and safety programs, developing community facilities such as swimming pools, and making free computer time available to worthy causes. Hence PR titles are often upgraded to "public affairs" or "external affairs," and a separate government-relations officer may be appointed.

A few companies include advertising and sales promotion in public affairs, but this is exceptional—as is the full inclusion of the legal department. Similarly, some PA staffs handle employee relations (elsewhere handled by the personnel department), customer relations (elsewhere handled by the marketing department), and/or trade/technical/professional relations (elsewhere handled by the manufacturing department). Thus the U.K. subsidiary of IBM has combined under "communications" the following activities:

Civic affairs (general involvement as a corporate citizen).

Academic and scientific relations.

Press relations.

Employee relations.

Technical and professional relations.

Customer relations.

Community relations.

Government relations.

Some companies organized on a product basis have found it desirable to form national councils for the various product subsidiaries in the same country so as to develop and share information on common environmental concerns, and in order to provide a single voice for the firm. Otherwise, host governments ask: "Who speaks for the company in this country?"

Local Community Level.   Although some public-affairs matters are conducted from the center, distance and the need for close and sustained relationships usually bring about the appointment of at least one local PR-type officer. However, this responsibility may simply be given to the local plant manager or personnel manager.

Regional Level.   This level represents a half-way point between (1) the national level, where needs and resources may be too limited to warrant the formal appointment of a public-affairs man; and (2) the world level, where the task is largely unmanageable on a global scale (see below).

As a fairly typical example of this development, one U.S. firm has a public-affairs director at the European level whose task it is to (1) oversee the creation and up-grading of this function in national subsidiaries; (2) coordinate the sharing of national experiences with other subsidiaries in the region; (3) monitor and influence developments in public and international organizations (EEC, OECD, UN, International Chamber of Commerce) through secondary sources and personal contacts; (4) relay information from and to the world level; and (5) advise the top regional managing director as well as national managers and PA staffs.

The latter task reveals that the regional PA executive has no direct supervisory role over the national subsidiaries but can only exercise influence through his own boss—with the affiliates remaining responsible for PA activities in their countries, as should be the case. Since a number of these regional executives have had national experience during some prior assignment, their advice is typically well accepted—particularly since they are themselves aware of the fact that they can only "sell" but not "tell."

This role is more complex when the company is organized on a product basis—especially when product headquarters are located in different countries (e.g., the European chemical division is based in London, and the textiles division in Rotterdam). One company handles this problem by having a more "philosophically oriented" PA man loosely capping the "day-to-day" staffers attached to the product divisions.

The World Corporate Global Level.   Few international companies have a distinct staff for public affairs at this level. Instead, most do it on a part-time basis or in association with something else—with existing staffs such as legal and corporate planning brought in whenever necessary to plan new investments, to review the performance of subsidiaries in public affairs, and to provide occasional assistance to foreign subsidiaries. For example, General Electric has an international planning staff that evaluates foreign investment proposals in the light of economic and noneconomic variables and assists top management in developing policies in such matters as tariffs, nontariff barriers, and foreign-investment regulations.

One witnesses also the appointment of international specialists such as an international governmental affairs and/or international public relations director—usually under the corporate vice-president for public affairs.

Internal communication is important in terms of diffusing relevant experiences within the multinational company among all countries and regions. It is also essential for foreign-subsidiary executives and staffers to know those corporate-headquarters people that handle public affairs so that communications may be based on more personal relations. This leads to frequent visits in both directions as well as to the regular convening of PA staffers from all over the world so that the company philosophy may be better understood, problems may be aired, new policies and plans may be discussed, fellow practitioners may get to know each other better, and the attitudes and practices of the more-effective subsidiaries and levels may rub off on the others.

A few companies practice a fair amount of "industrial diplomacy" through their top corporate officers. The better-known practitioners have been David Rockefeller (of Chase Manhattan) and Henry Ford II, who traveled widely and met visibly (and sometimes loudly) with foreign elites of various kinds. Other firms choose to do it less flamboyantly, if only because the company name and that of their chief executive are not well known. Such visits provide these travelers with prime sources of key information about investment climates and government policies, but this information appears to be poorly diffused within the organization for lack of good debriefing processes. The major benefit of such visits is symbolic, as they manifest the international commitment of the firm. The visits also open up channels of communication for lower-level executives and staffers who engage in the actual negotiations and routine contacts.

SPECIAL PATTERNS.   When one part of a company has more experience and influence than another on account of size, age, type of industry, and so forth, it is not uncommon to have it assume responsibility for conducting all or most of the public affairs of the others. A classical example here is the oil company assisting its petrochemical affiliate within the same country and/or region.

A parallel arrangement exists when one product division is more experienced and carries out the PA function for the others. Thus the computer division of one U.S. firm in Italy services the office-equipment, industrial-equipment, and consumer-products parts of the subsidiary. This special pattern, however, requires close physical proximity of the related parts.

Similarly, the head of the major Belgian subsidiary of a highly diversified firm has been appointed "senior officer" and is charged with the government relations of the other subsidiaries—largely because the electronics-equipment firm he heads has a long experience in this area, and because he is considered to be most effective. This approach is particularly indicated when the various parts of the conglomerate firm cannot be brought under a single national holding company because of the desire to make some of the affiliates look national rather than American, when the latter image could hurt sales and other external relations.

CONCLUDING REMARK.   About one third of international firms may be said to have a fairly well developed public-affairs function or to be moving in that direction, with some building blocks already in place. Even for them, however, the stage of development is uneven from country to country, particularly at the world level.

Yet there is often more here than meets the eye. In many firms, one looks in vain for a vice-president for international public affairs and/or for a supporting staff in these areas. At the same time, however, one is struck by the fact that all sorts of people have part of the necessary information, the indispensable contacts, the appropriate awareness, and the essential determination to cope with problems in the nonmarket environment of the firm. Indeed, a growing number of these people have been stationed abroad, travel frequently to visit subsidiaries, attend regional and worldwide company seminars and working committees, and communicate regularly and even incessantly with other company executives and staffers at home and abroad by mail, telephone, and telex.

One may well prefer to find something neater and more clearly understandable; one is aware of gaps and weak links; and one wishes that even more attention and resources would be devoted to this area of great and increasing importance. But for most of these companies, such informal arrangements *do work* until a major crisis makes it evident that something more formal and explicit as well as better endowed is necessary.

IPA STAFFING

International public affairs requires a variety of skills and therefore persons—both insiders and outsiders.

RANK AND STATUS.   The more-sophisticated multinationals recognize that their chief executives have to be involved in public affairs for symbolic power and protocol reasons. In the first place, the chief executive officer is the only valid *spokesman* of his organization when it comes to dealing with the nonmarket environment of the firm (including government) over important matters. Symbolically, only the man who is perceived as able to *represent* and *commit* his entire organization is believable and trustworthy in formal contacts and negotiations. It is also a matter of *protocol* to the extent that outside of the United States, people tend to delegate much less authority to their subordinates, so that only the top man is thought to have the necessary knowledge and power.

Of course, the notion of "chief operating executive" is sometimes amorphous, because several executives can share top power in a collegial manner (there are German and Dutch arrangements to that effect in large corporations), and U.S. titles are sufficiently confusing to foreigners so that it is not always clear who the main man is among the chairman, the president, the general manager, the executive vice-president and other "chiefs."

Lower-level executives and specialists (treasurer, accountant, personnel manager, legal counsel, etc.) are regularly involved in more-routine and in more-technical contacts and negotiations, but their symbolic role is small or nil unless their partic-ipation has been preceded by formal introductions and by a meeting of the principals involved, who then retire until the detailed negotiations are over and the official agreement is ready to be ratified and the ribbons cut.

BACKGROUND, NATIONALITY, AND ROTATION.   Public-relations experience—particularly in press relations and speech writing—is commonly found in public-affairs staffers, although people with a technical background are increasingly brought in to provide the expertise needed for dealing with technological and environmental problems. Besides, it is felt by some companies that they also need "thinkers" as PA staffers as well as executive trainees in the process of rounding their exposure to the firm's functions. The pure print-oriented PR man seems to be declining in importance, however.

Government-relations people are seldom hired directly. Instead, they are started in other parts of the company in order to familiarize them with its operations. They are then progressively given more government-relations responsibilities until their task becomes a full-time one.

There is a presumption in favor of the local national, based on his greater familiarity with the local environment, his knowledge of the native language, his greater loyalty toward the host nation (his country), and the notion that his appointment proves the foreign corporation's ability to train and promote its native employees. These are very valid arguments, but they should not be exaggerated, because local nationals are often unaware of and insensitive to major factors and trends in their own countries. After all, how many U.S. managers paid much attention to the nascent civil rights, ecology, women's liberation, and consumerism movements?

Knowledge of the local language is of course a major advantage for the native manager, although less so in multilingual countries (e.g., Switzerland, Belgium, and the Philippines), where English is often the preferred second language. A major handicap for Americans lies in the fact that trade associations conduct their business meetings in the native language(s) without simultaneous translation, thereby discouraging U.S. managers from participating in important discussions and acquiring influence within such groups. Some U.S. managers send a lower-ranking native to represent them, but this move can be misinterpreted, because foreigners do not believe that a number-two or number-three man knows as much as his boss, and because of the symbolic and protocol importance of having the number-one man present.

Language aside, the fact of being a foreigner is not necessarily a handicap for the general manager, because local officials believe that a foreigner is more likely than a native to be heard and heeded at the corporate level. Besides, expatriates are often seen as carriers of such desirable values as efficiency, technology, and entrepreneurship, and thus derive much legitimacy from this perception. In any case, governments usually accept that Americans and other expatriates predominate at the regional and world levels as a recognition of where the ownership and control of the company really lie.

A reverse problem exists as far as relations with home-country embassies are concerned, to the extent that the ambassador and foreign-service officers are more at ease with their compatriots than with native managers in terms of language, the common background that facilitates discussions, and trust in the loyalty and discretion of the managers when sensitive information is being communicated. This problem promises to loom larger as more local nationals become managing directors.

The reassignment of foreign executives certainly poses a problem in terms of developing and maintaining effective rapports with government officials and industrial elites. Frequent rotation, for one thing, prevents the development of language fluency unless the executive is transferred to a country with the same language or to the regional headquarters. Reassignments also discourage government officials faced with the endless task of getting to know the foreign executive and "educating" him about the government's policies and concerns.

FORMAL AND INFORMAL PA ROLES. At least six types of PA men are evident in sophisticated multinationals.

The Monitor/Analyst/Thinker. This kind of specialist is used to "scan the environment," to keep track of relevant developments such as regulatory proposals, public-opinion changes, and initiatives by important interest groups. He interprets them for line managers and other departments, and prepares recommendations for action—frequently in consultation with other knowledgeable people inside and outside the firm. To him is also assigned the task of preparing position papers as well as reports to higher levels within the multinational.

Typically, this kind of PA man has a liberal-arts or social-science background, although a growing number of firms are appointing engineers and line managers as a way of broadening their training in anticipation of higher-level assignments, or in order to draw on their expert knowledge (e.g., of pollution controls if environmental protection is a key issue).

Few subsidiaries have such a monitor/analyst/thinker but rely instead on an economist within the firm, their legal counsel, or some outside firm specializing in monitoring and reporting environmental developments.

The Contact Man/Door Opener/Introducer.   When there is frequent rotation of foreigners at the head of the subsidiary so that they never have the chance to develop personal relationships with key outsiders, intermediaries are used on a permanent or occasional basis. Some of them wear another hat within the organization as in the case of the personnel manager who has an artistocratic background and is well introduced in political and economic circles.

Others sit on the board of directors on account of their political, economic, and social connections. Men of this caliber not only provide introductions, but they also help legitimize the foreign subsidiary for whose "seriousness" they vouch. The problems with such appointments are that some big names lose their usefulness once away from power or do little to stir themselves, and it is very difficult to get rid of them on account of their important symbolic roles. Changes in political regimes can also make them useless if not embarrassing.

There are, however, plenty of less well known contact men who are useful on account of their social (nobility, upper bourgeoisie), educational (elite schools), and professional (former high-level government bureaucrats) background, or because of family and personal connections.

When the subsidiary is a joint venture with a local firm of some standing, this intermediary role frequently devolves to the partner. Practically always, these "introducers" are local nationals, because they require extensive familiarity with national elites, which only a native can acquire.

The Adviser/Consultant/Trusted Confidant.   This group is typically made up of outsiders, but some of them have a more permanent relation with the subsidiary, and have the title of assistant to the president or sit on the board of directors. This category often overlaps with the contact-man category, since the knowledge these people possess is based on the significant relations that they have with various elites. Thus a former prime minister advised a U.S. manufacturer about the timing and manner of its announcement to the host government of a major acquisition to which the latter was bound to object.

Local bankers and well-known lawyers often serve in this advisory capacity on the board of directors or simply as consultants, on account of their knowledge and contacts. Here again, local nationals predominate, although a variety of nationalities are used when it comes to dealing with supranational authorities such as the European

Community (but even here, the tendency is to use an Italian to advise about approaching Italian Eurocrats).

The Negotiator.   This kind of PA person is rarer because the crucial role of the line executive in high-level bargaining and because lower-level managers and staffers conduct most of it at their respective levels. Besides, the chief executive and other managers may have been appointed precisely because of the excellence of their negotiating skills if the subsidiary is involved in some critical dealings with government. However, outsiders such as lawyers are used here when the identity of the foreign investor must remain hidden at an early exploratory stage and when negotiating skills are missing within the firm.

The Communications Specialist.   This category is clearly linked to public relations and its emphasis on mass communication. Typically, such persons write speeches, testimonies, and presentations to officials, commissions, and legislators, and they prepare various brochures about the company. Thus a couple of U.S. electronics firms in the United Kingdom have special newsletters designed to acquaint parliamentarians with the development of the computer industry so that they will be better informed when dealing with protectionist U.K. policy in this regard.

The Program Man.   He frequently overlaps with the public-relations expert, but his expertise lies more in running special programs—for example, charitable contributions, aids to universities, community-action endeavors, and projects (e.g., plant openings).

Concluding Remark.   These six roles overlap to some extent, although the same person is rarely effective in more than a couple of them. Besides, roles can be combined with other assignments within the organization, as when the personnel manager has excellent social connections and can serve as a door opener for others. Furthermore, the higher regional and world levels can assist or replace lower-level ones.

In all cases, the line managers cannot abdicate their responsibilities to the PA staff or part-time participants because the latter two types are only specialists in detecting and appraising external conditions, in suggesting certain responses, and in carrying some of them out. They are "early-warning and bag men," but it is management's responsibility to determine the need for some response, to give the go-ahead signal, and to carry out key negotiations.

OUTSIDERS.   Not even the largest firm can handle all of its public affairs by itself, and this is particularly true in international matters. *First,* many foreign laws and regulations as well as customs simply require that such outsiders as lawyers and notaries be used to incorporate, organize, and run a subsidiary, to apply and report to government agencies, to negotiate taxes, and so on. *Second,* the sheer number of regulatory and policy developments in a large number of countries and the great variety of PA roles usually preclude a company (even a large one) from having the full capacity to follow up and influence these developments at all geographic levels (local, national, regional, world). This forces them to rely on external and shared resources. *Third,* some expert assistance may be only sporadically needed and not warrant the full employment of a qualified person. *Fourth,* some PA expertise is scarce (e.g., about crucial public policies or the likely reaction of a host government to a major investment); and the few experts available have to be shared by several firms, which employ them as consultants, agents, or board members. *Fifth,* it is usually indicated to validate and/or double-check internally generated information through outsiders—either to improve the accuracy of the company's decisions or to appraise the effectiveness of lower hierarchical levels in performing various aspects of the PA function. *Sixth,* some government relations require anonymity, as when a multinational wants to test the host country's reaction to some of its initiatives but without being identified as the inquirer: Here intermediaries are indispensable. *Seventh,* some intermediaries are able to obtain more-accurate and faster information than a single company can because of special relationships (some consultants and lawyers are very well introduced) or because they can legitimately insist on receiving it (for example, the U.S. embassy can easily inquire about the discriminatory treatment of U.S. subsidiaries in violation of a bilateral treaty of establishment).

Exhibit 5 outlines the major forms of outside PA assistance used and received by multinationals.

EXHIBIT 5   TYPES OF OUTSIDE ASSISTANCE

	Influential Elites	International Law Offices and Local Lawyers	International and Local Financial Institutions	International and Local Public-Relations Firms
General information, interpretation and advice about the country		X	X	X
Specific information and advice about an investment	X	X	X	X
Introductions to government people	X	X	X	X
Presentation of company and industry views and demands to government	X	X		
Negotiation	X	X	X	
Compliance with local laws and regulations		X	X	
Mass communication				X
Public-affairs programs (plant openings, philanthropy, etc.)				X

a Denotes a particularly significant role on the part of that type of outsider.

COLLECTIVE ACTION. Working with and through American chambers of commerce, business and trade associations, as well as partners offers the classical advantages of economies of scale and a bigger and more effective voice.

However, collective action is costly in money and executive resources, since many benefits can be obtained only through active participation in associations—possibly in a large number of them. Besides, some associations abroad remain indifferent or hostile to foreign firms considered upstarts, lacking industrial statemanship, and dangerous rivals for leadership. The antitrust problems connected with collective action are real even though often exaggerated.

Still, the principles guiding the choice between single and collective action are fairly clear. As the experienced managing director of a diversified firm put it: "We approach government alone when it is the only way to do it—for example, to apply for some permission, when we have been singled out by some bureaucratic action, when we need an exemption from some general rule, and when one of our subsidiaries is clearly the leader in its industry—when we are the industry in fact! On the other hand, working through a trade association makes a lot of sense when it makes you more credible that way, when it gives you more clout, and when delicate issues have to be explored or novel situations clarified without revealing who is asking and who stands exactly for what!"

SOUGHT AND OF TYPES OF HELP AVAILABLE[a]

International and Local Media	Home-Country Embassy	American (and Similar) Chambers of Commerce	International and National Business and Industry Associations	Host-Government Bureaus and Departments	Local Partners (Joint Ventures)
X	X	X	X	X	X
				X	X
	X		X	X	X
	X		X		X
			X		X
			X		
		X	X		

IPA ACTION

Previous sections have already dealt with the multiple interactions between multinationals and their environments, and with the various tasks required to achieve effectiveness in international public affairs (information gathering, negotiation, etc.). It remains to comment on the response mode, style, and philosophy connected with such actions.

MODES OF RESPONSE.   Multinational firms differ in their responses to nonmarket environmental challenges. Some still exhibit sheer *inactivism* or avoidance (see comments about the low profile below). Most common is *reaction,* that is, adaptation or accomodation on a *post-factum* basis. A few englightened firms are moving toward *proaction* through monitoring, anticipation, and manipulation in order to deflect or kill emerging issues before they harden and can only be reacted to. *Interaction* remains largely an ideal, and would consist of a fairly simultaneous combination of environmental and organizational change designed to narrow the gap between social expectations and corporate performance. (See Post, 1978; and Sethi, 1975).

More concretely, the major operational problem in public affairs remains that of making the *entire organization responsive and committed to its nonmarket environment*. This would roughly correspond to Phase 4 in Exhibit 6.

PROFILING THE MULTINATIONAL CORPORATION.   Different MNCs obtain or choose various profiles or images about (1) their contributions to home and host countries and (2) the clout they carry with government and other target groups.

A particular profile may be inevitable because the firm is too small to be noticed or too important to be ignored by government. Clearly, IBM has a *high profile* in most foreign countries because of its size, dominance of the industry, technological significance, multinational character, U.S. ownership and control, and connection with such hot issues as privacy and transborder data flows.

On the other hand, some MNCs try to achieve a *low profile* because it apparently presents fewer risks, requires less justification, and is usually advised by those intermediaries whose forte consists precisely in quiet face-to-face negotiations (e.g., lawyers). Besides, many executives fear public exposure and the wear and tear of the hostile confrontations that are more readily encountered in high-profile situations.

Ultimately, the *right profile* must be chosen in terms of its effectiveness in helping achieve PA goals. This may require a mixture of high and low profiles. For that matter, a firm is—by definition—always visible to its PA targets, so that a low profile really means: "By whom do we want *not* to be seen as doing certain things?" This perspective raises interesting questions about the preference for such invisibility, since it suggests illegal or unethical practices (Boddewyn and Marton, 1978).

Exhibit 7 outlines the major situations and strategies connected with the various stages in the international firm's investment life cycle. Thus whereas the profile is typically high at entry, a low profile may be needed if the country is going through an antiforeign phase. Besides, the height of the profile varies with the target involved—for example, high with government, but low with the general public; whereas the respective roles of the national and higher levels depend on who has more credibility *and* bargaining strength.

EXHIBIT 6 THE FOUR PHASES OF PUBLIC-AFFAIRS INVOLVEMENT

	Phase 1 Emerging and Diffuse Concern	Phase 2 Early Leadership	Phase 3 Public-Affairs Institutionalization	Phase 4 Public-Affairs Commitment
Policy issue	Are there significant PA problems?	Should the firm concern itself with them?	What responses are appropriate	How is the response to be managed and disseminated throughout the organization?
Requirements	Individual interest	Individual commitment Information	Corporate policy Information and analysis	Corporate policy Information and analysis Organizational concern and commitment
Organizational involvement, structure, and staffing	Minimal, diffuse, sporadic	Chief executive or some other executive Heavy reliance on part-timers and outsiders	Chief executive PA specialists Part-timers and outsiders	Chief executive PA specialists Operating managers Part-timers and outsiders Collective action
Reporting system	None	Reporting conspicuous incidents	Fuller reporting but without action implications	Systematic and action-oriented reporting
Performance evaluation and reward system	None	None	Criticism for specific and blatant errors	Appraisal and approval based on a systematic review against plans

Source. Adapted from Ackerman (1974).

EXHIBIT 7   THE INVESTMENT LIFE CYCLE AND APPROPRIATE PROFILES

Stage	Bargaining Strength	Publicity (Profile)	Role of Geographic Levels
Entry	Higher	High (about terms)	World, regional
Expansion		High (about terms)	National, regional
Implementation		High	National, regional, world
Ongoing operations		Low or medium	National
Acquisitions		High (about terms)	National, regional
Stagnation, decline		Low	National
Disinvestment		Low (preferably)	World, regional, national
Expropriation, renegotiation		High (about terms)	World, regional, national
Reentry after withdrawal	Lower	Medium (about terms)	World, regional

PHILOSOPHY.   The effective performance of international public affairs requires certain attitudes (whether or not translated into official company policy) to inform and dynamize this function.

Public Affairs Is Important and Inevitable.   Unfortunately, too many executives are still ill at ease handling the increasing involvement with government and other constituencies required in today's economic world—either for lack of experience or on account of prejudices and misinformation. Others fear the cost (in terms of time and money) and the obligations entailed by closer involvement with target groups, since such relationships normally involve quid pro quos.

Journalistic exposés of firms like ITT as well as business associations, lobbyists, and "superlawyers" make it appear that large firms are very proficient at government relations and are routinely "walking the corridors of power" and manipulating public opinion. Reality, however, presents a much less flattering or threatening portrait. The first order of business for many multinationals thus remains one of greater awareness about the importance and magnitude of this function.

Public Affairs Is a Proper and Legitimate Function.   What must be extirpated is the false notion that government relations is "not nice," irrational, and unbusiness like, or that it can be "tolerated" only when the company needs to be protected or rescued by government, or must defend itself against some unconscionable action on the part of the authorities. This view is akin to considering the government a "partner of last resort" and viewing government affairs as a "necessary-evil" type of practice best left to some remote Washington representative, some mysterious special assistant to the President, or some hidden "department of dirty tricks"—a deplorable way of tainting this function from the start.

Actually, the notion of "corporate citizenship" that is so highly recommended nowadays includes by definition both the *duty* to serve society (the part usually stressed) and the *right* to be heard (and preferably heeded). This right of petition is guaranteed by the First Amendment to the U.S. Constitution, whereas in Europe, many planning and concertation schemes make such relations with government a matter of routine if not of obligation (e.g., in the context of the mandatory "consultative bodies" of countries like Belgium). Hence it is perfectly proper for multinational firms to contact and try to influence governments at home and abroad.

Obviously there are socially acceptable and unacceptable ways of monitoring and influencing governments and other elites, but occasional improprieties do not invalidate the legitimacy of this function any more than shady advertising claims or "yellow" labor contracts obliterate the fundamental need for marketing and industrial relations or the societal contributions that these functions make. Of course public affairs is more likely to be accepted as legitimate if it is seen as being related to the broad concerns of society, which governments everywhere make explicit and attempt to satisfy, rather than being only concerned with manipulating the state and society for purely selfish personal and corporate interests.

Public Affairs Is an Earning Function. Politics has a negative connotation for many business executives, as is evident in the contrasting of "political *risks*" with "market *opportunities*" in studies of foreign countries. Because of this negative view of politics, there is a tendency to view government relations in a defensive manner and as a protective device against the machinations of political demagogues and power-hungry bureaucrats. The latter certainly exist, and guarding one's firm against unfavorable developments is certainly a critical component of the public-affairs function even if it costs time and money to engage in such purely defensive moves.

Beyond this elementary observation lies the more profitable realization that modern governments control all sorts of scarce and valuable goods in their capacities as creditors through state financial institutions, as regulators, as suppliers and/or partners through state enterprises, as customers through their purchases, as grantors of partial or complete monopolies through their selective distributions of permissions to invest, as subsidizers of research and training programs, as providers of public utilities and "law and order," and so on. There are real political *opportunities* here—not just risks.

Public affairs is thus much more than a "spending" function on the order of a night watchman who protects a firm's real sources of profits. It has, instead, real "*earning*" potential; and it deserves as much executive attention as the other two pillars of profitability, namely, efficient management within the company and business effectiveness in the marketplace.

This emphasis on earnings, of course, should not obscure the fact that the effectiveness of public affairs can seldom be immediately measured in terms of its impact on sales, profits, or return on investment, since so many things contribute to corporate performance, and on account of the special difficulties connected with measuring results in this area (see below). Besides, government relations is no panacea and by itself is usually insufficient to insure a firm's prosperity or survival even though the Lockheed, Penn-Central, and Chrysler cases illustrate the life-saving contribution of this function.

Still, many PA initiatives have delayed and/or indirect effects. In the United States, for example, pressures from business against excessive environmental-protection requirements were not as effective as the energy crisis in getting them reviewed, but they certainly prepared the groundwork for such a review.

Public Affairs Must Be Managed. The test of good management is explicit goals, clear assignments of responsibility, good forecasting, timely action, and relevant reporting. Moreover, effective management of the PA function requires that the chief executive be actively involved in its planning, conduct, and supervision, because representing the firm to the outside world is an intrinsic and fundamental part of top management's job, which cannot be delegated downward even a variety of subordinates can assist. On the other hand, top management should not be overexposed nor its "shock value" spent over minor matters.

A key principle in this respect is that informed commitment is more important than any particular organizational structure or technique. Moreover, simply imitating some competitor's move, coping with problems on an *ad hoc* and crisis basis, or succumbing to the entreaties of a consultant are poor ways of getting started in or conducting public affairs. PA should rest instead on an understanding of the function's importance and an appraisal of risks and opportunities in this area. This awareness and commitment must then pervade the entire organization instead of being relegated to some specialized niche and personnel.

The Watergate scandal has certainly made more executives aware of the fact that financial contributions to political parties is no substitute (in fact, often a bad one) for a professionally developed approach to government affairs.

Public Affairs Works Best as a Two-Way Process. The relation between business firms and governments in the mixed economies of today is increasingly one of symbiosis: They have to rely on each other in order to achieve their respective objectives. The correct perspective is thus not one of a "zero-sum game," where public power grows only at the expense of private enterprise, but rather a frequent "positive-sum game," where both benefit from the relationship. On the other hand, a very uneven relationship where one party can dictate to the other is seldom fruitful in the longer run because it leads to ill feelings, recriminations, renegotiations, nationalizations, stagnation of investment, and/or divestment.

Instead, the best gains are those that leave the other party satisfied too—now and for the foreseeable future. Hence it is essential for firms to consider the problems and goals of governments and to couch their own approaches in terms of what they will contribute to the satisfaction and achievement of public objectives. As one executive put it: "We must talk of 'participating in economic development' rather than of 'coping with the environment'; and we must talk of 'sharing in change' rather than of 'dealing with change.'" Conversely, opposition to government policies must stress how they may be self-defeating or inferior in terms of what a country needs and wants.

Many firms find it hard to adopt such a posture because of the nearly irresistible attractiveness of high profits and of getting something for nothing or cheaply, and because companies prefer to compensate for high overseas risks through quick and handsome returns. Still, getting all one can get with no thought for the morrow and the other party is inviting trouble overseas just like at home. We can expect an increased emphasis on the criteria of fairness and equity in the division of burdens and benefits among countries and companies; firms should therefore try to understand this increasingly important requirement for mutually beneficial solutions.

Public Affairs Is an Inside Job Too. Few companies effectively apply the principle that "external affairs begins at home." There may be various house organs and other publications dealing with the firm's foreign affiliations, international involvement, and contributions to host economies and societies. However, they suffer from the well-known shortcomings of such endeavors—particularly, their low credibility.

For that matter, many firms do not even make the effort to report on pending legislation detrimental to the company, public-opinion attitudes unfavorable to foreign direct investment, or the firm's contributions to its home and host countries. This is in contrast to national and international unions, which are increasingly propagandizing their members, the public, and international organizations about the dangers and problems associated with multinational companies. In Europe the growing importance of works councils and of other forms of worker representation and participation is of course forcing firms to reveal much more about their operations to labor representatives. However, much of this communication is still marked by distrust and undercandidness.

Still, a few companies are improving their efforts in this area, being particularly careful to tailor their communications to the various audiences they address, since a worker's interests are different from those of a stockholder and even of a union leader. Thus British Oxygen publishes a monthly tabloid widely distributed at the workplace. It has gained considerable credibility among its readers by refusing to gild the lily and by reporting company shortcomings. A second quarterly magazine is written for middle and top management, with think pieces on various environmental and internal (e.g., reorganization) topics.

Obviously, multinational firms will have to do much more and much better in this area. As one executive put it: "Having 10,000 employees say good things about the company amounts to both a low profile and a lot of speaking out, and is well worth the effort!"

IPA REPORTING AND CONTROLLING

Performance must be measured in public affairs as in any other business function, but there are special problems connected with the transfer of information and the reporting of activities in this area.

CHANNELS.   National PA staffs formally report to the line management of the subsidiary rather than to the corresponding PA staff at the regional and/or world levels. This adds time and a filter to the reporting of information and action; but in many firms this official/formal channel is supplemented by frequent communications (mail, telephone, telex), by visits by line executives and PA staffers, by regional and worldwide meetings (for example, ITT-Europe meetings in Brussels and the regular convening of public-affairs managers from all over the world by Pfizer), and by board-of-directors meetings in Europe and other operating areas (Caterpillar, IBM, Dow).

Locational factors factors also affect the allocation of PA reporting responsibility, as when the Belgian subsidiary is charged with following up EEC developments, since the EEC Commission is located in that country. Places like London and New York are very important listening posts regarding financial controls everywhere, because major international banks are located there and keep abreast of relevant regulations and financial conditions all over the world.

INTERACTION AMONG LEVELS.   The general principle that decision should be made where the facts are available and understood militates against much reporting to higher levels when the latter do not possess such information. However, international companies qualify this principle in a number of ways.

First, *higher levels have to be kept informed of locally made decisions even if they did not participate in them* in order to (1) appraise the effectiveness of public affairs at lower levels ("We are particularly interested in finding out what subsidiaries were surprised by political and regulatory changes that might have been anticipated"), (2) evaluate the adequacy of the budgets requested and obtained for that function, and (3) form an impression about trends in policies and regulations in the regions or in the world at large—something for which national subsidiaries usually lack perspective.

Second, *reporting systems vary according to the types of external events covered and the types of required company responses.* Some governmental policies are beyond the control of higher levels and are only *ultimately reported* to them for information's sake and/or in order to justify certain actions and performances of the affiliates (e.g., to explain why the subsidiary could not avoid a price freeze in a foreign country). Promptness in reporting such a new regulation is not crucial, because the appropriate response can usually be decided by the local management.

Other local policy developments, however, have more serious implications for the rest of the international company, and therefore require *immediate reporting*. An example would be stricter controls on capital movements in and out of a foreign country. When the financial function is centralized, the regional and world levels want to know of such a regulation or of its imminence right away, because they have to shift funds around, alter financial plans, and make other decisions. It is also a kind of development in which international treaties and special agreements between the parent company and the host government may be relevant and therefore invite representation by the firm or the U.S. government if some violation or discrimination is involved.

Some regulatory or public-opinion developments may be of purely local import, whereas others may interest *other affiliates.* Thus the EEC directive allowing manufactured goods from underdeveloped nations to enter member countries duty free (up to a certain volume) made it possible for the Brazilian subsidiary of a U.S. international company to export more parts to EEC countries at a lower cost.

This example involves a tactical response, but the parent company may also need to know of regulatory developments for *strategic* purposes. For example, the banning of phosphates in detergents is a type of policy change quickly reported because it may require dropping an entire line of products and stepping up research efforts to come up with substitutes. It is also a regulation likely to be adopted by other countries, since concern with protecting the environment is widespread. Consequently, a firm may want to stop using such an ingredient in other countries even before it is obliged to do so.

The distinction made above is between (1) what is urgent and must be immediately reported, (2) what must be ultimately known and, (3) what is of marginal or no interest to higher levels and should be left out of intelligence channels that may already be overburdened. This sorting out process is not always obvious but must be inculcated and implemented through company directives, conferences, reviews, and other means.

Strangely enough, it appears that good news often does not travel as readily as bad news, because overseas subsidiaries are not eager to be asked to do something more or to change procedures because some regulation has been removed or modified. Bad news, on the other hand, provides a handy excuse for not meeting some assigned goals. In addition, perceiving new opportunities requires thinking changes through, but few subsidiaries have been staffed with that kind of managerial and staff talent.

Still, *crisis developments* tend to move very quickly up the organizational hierarchy. This is a reflection of the fundamental principle that higher levels concern themselves with "exceptional" problems—especially when the amounts involved and the possible implications for other parts of the international company are significant and assume policy dimensions. Furthermore, difficult transactions with foreign governments bring about escalation to higher levels in order to impress foreign governments with the fact that the international company has alternatives in other countries and must reconcile its national obligations and opportunities with foreign and international ones. Finally, higher levels are usually brought in to remove the pressure from the national manager—especially if the affiliate is small and its manager a native of the country, because local managers are much more vulnerable to governmental pressures (including physical ones), whereas foreigners at least are somewhat protected by their embassies and bilateral treaties of establishment.

Third, *the assessment of intelligence varies according to the prevalent authority structure.* Multinationals with loosely connected foreign affiliates are much more likely to let them process their own intelligence, decide accordingly, and simply keep the parent company informed, than centralized firms bent on controlling their subsidiaries rather tightly.

Fourth, *the respective competences of field and headquarters affect the reporting system.* National subsidiaries, through their closer association with operations, are more attuned to local developments and better aware of obstacles and unpredictable developments. However, they are also susceptible to that complacency of those who feel that they are doing the right thing simply because they are the local experts. Headquarters, on the other hand, is often better at detecting the uncommon, which may be more clearly perceived from a distance, but it may be deficient at understanding the proper importance of such exceptional developments. Therefore, there are normal disagreements between national and regional subsidiaries and the corporate headquarters about the meaning and magnitude of overseas environmental developments. For example, Italy is always a difficult country to evaluate from a distance because it seems so unstable and messed up, although, on the spot, the same events may look "normal" and manageable. Such a divergence obviously requires a lot of mutual "education" so that reports and plans may be more intelligible and acceptable to all levels concerned.

FORMAT, TIMING, AND CONTINGENCY PLANNING.   National-level reports about government and public affairs have to be condensed and integrated with other subjects in the short summaries prepared for higher levels. What may have started as a 20-page analysis written by the PA director in Germany ends up a 1–2 page component in the more general report of the German general manager to the European headquarters, which itself condenses Germany to a paragraph or two in the European report going to New York, where the worldwide analysis finally reduces it to a couple of lines! *It is then extremely difficult for anyone at that level to interpret and act meaningfully on such scanty information.*

Besides, *the timing of intelligence is frequently faulty.* Most overseas subsidiaries do not catch problems at the incipient stage. Later on, they remain optimistic that things will work out, because they have in the past. Therefore, they usually fail to communicate detailed information and forecasts about such developments. When events finally become unmanageable, they provide handy excuses for no longer performing satisfactorily. However, the matter of urgency should not be overstated, because in fact major policy developments are few and slow in coming, and there is usually time to obtain the necessary information.

Poor timing is compounded by the fact that *there is little contingency planning embodied in most PA reports*. That is, affiliates very seldom report developments in a form outlining what is likely to happen (with various probabilities) and what alternative courses of action are open regarding each possible outcome. Instead, their reports typically present some overall appraisal of the state of the environment and aim at reassuring the parent company that the situation is being carefully followed up. Still, a small but increasing number of international companies are insisting that their foreign affiliates develop flexible responses and build a system for government relations so that channels may be available and in working order when crises develop.

LOCUS OF CONTROL. Public-affairs action gets harder to appraise as one moves away from the locus of their performance. Still, the increasing number of executives and staffers at the regional and world levels who have served in foreign countries is helping to improve the review process, since they can ask better questions and even double-check with former business and government contacts in those countries. A few companies also ask international public-relations firms and consultants to audit the subsidiaries' resources and performance in this area.

In general, higher-level PA staffs monitor the performance of lower-level ones in the process of advising their own superiors about the supervision of the regional and national subsidiaries. A few large companies with complex organizational structures have appointed a number of the corporate executive committee or of the board of directors to act as the contact man for international public affairs.

CRITERIA OF EFFECTIVENESS. "The collection, interpretation, and diffusion of information as well as those relations with the authorities and public opinion conducted for the corporate purposes of acquiring legitimacy, of influencing the contents of public policy, and of obtaining and retaining favorable treatment." This definition of public affairs makes it obvious that most of it is of an *intangible nature and difficult to measure for control purposes.*

Control is undoubtedly easier when careful PA planning has resulted in *specific goals matched with specific budgetary allocations.* More companies now specify in their PA plans such concrete tasks as getting to know certain politicians and officials, improving by five percentage points the proportion of people who think favorably of the company, getting the subsidiary's general manager elected an officer of a key trade association, and so on. These are valuable and even necessary targets, but there is a danger that their use may degenerate into pointless nose counting of favorable press clippings, bureaucrats visited, industry citations received, and so forth.

More important still, *such measurements (preferably of the before-and-after kind) are only loosely and vaguely linked to the achievement of overall corporate objectives of the "hard" kind*: return on investment, share of the market, rate of growth, and so on. It is well to stress such hard goals at this point, because many executives still believe that they are the only ones worth considering. Even those firms that take "social responsibilities" into explicit consideration have the disconcerting habit of becoming hard-nosed about "soft" goals and the corresponding budgetary allocations when profits decline or growth slows down. Hence a solid rationale for public affairs as well as concrete goals (and their commensurate achievement) are most important. This is certainly the way the more reflective PA officers feel, because they have seen axes fall in their areas and in other such soft areas as training and research.

In any case, *some result-measurement problems cannot be eliminated.* The fundamental reason for this situation is that a good part of public affairs is of a defensive or "reserve power" nature, designed to prevent undesirable outcomes (e.g., unfavorable legislation and poor image). The public-affairs function here resembles that of the armed forces in a peace-loving nation, that is, to *prevent* attacks and other destructive actions. However, if the country is never attacked on account of this effective military posture, outsiders have a tendency to ask: "Why do we need an army? They never do anything!" In the same vein, a government-relations officer remarked: "It takes a lot of effort to build good connections in government, but you may never need to use them, and you may never have to pick up that phone for something very important. You need it 'just in case,' but that 'case' may never materialize. However, other people only see those fancy luncheons you had with government people, and they think you wasted a lot of good money and company time in the process!"

Besides, *it is hard to isolate the credit owed PA efforts for some favorable outcome* because other companies, trade associations, foreign embassies, and so forth may have worked at it too. Consequently, reviews and evaluations must also encompass processes and causes:

1. Were the goals well set in the first place?
2. How were they achieved, and how effective was each of the means used?
3. Why were they effective or not?

As one astute observer put it: "Was this a battle we really could have won if our people had been wise enough to talk to the press at the right moment? Or were we really beaten before we started, and did the public-affairs people do the best they could? Did they give away too much in the compromise, or did they do a pretty hard nosed job of negotiating? Did their predictions as to who would do what hold up pretty well, or did they misanalyze the picture from the start? Were there some relationships they should have built earlier?" (Fenn, 1979).

Similarly, the quality of the reports must be appraised in terms of the following questions:

1. How timely were they?
2. How understandable were they in terms of why certain things happened or not?
3. Were they action-oriented in clearly identifying revised goals and contingency actions?

REWARD AND PENALTIES.   Individual performance review must be geared to better results next time. This will depend to a considerable extent on whether people were properly rewarded and/or punished for what they did in managing the public affairs under their control.

International public affairs is an endless task, never completed and never performed perfectly, so expectations should not be higher than in the case of other functions. After all, 9 out of 10 new products fail in the marketplace, and all financial schemes are not profitable. Still, the stakes are high and deserve the best management that the state of the art allows.

SOCIOECONOMIC REPORTING.   The emphasis on this section has been reporting for *managerial* purposes. Multinationals, however, are being increasingly asked to report to such *external constituencies* as governments, international organizations, national and international pressure groups, and public-interest monitors about their contributions to a variety of physical (e.g., environmental protection, safety), economic (e.g., development), social (e.g., training and education), political (e.g., emancipation of minority or downtrodden groups), and cultural (e.g., respect of local traditions and support of local arts) goals.

These demands take various forms, ranging from the mandatory *bilan social* (social balance sheet) in France to requests for information from concerned groups (e.g., about MNC action vis-à-vis the apartheid situation in South Africa). The reports themselves vary in size, scope, and sophistication from brief references in annual reports to jobs created and exports generated, to such lengthy analyses as the 228-page *Nestlé in the Developing Countries* 1975 compendium.

This is a complex topic in itself, which cannot be investigated here. For a recent discussion of the disclosure issue and of various concrete responses to it by multinationals see the handbook written by the Public Affairs Council and the InterMatrix Group (1980).

CONCLUSION

The multinationals have been challenged, and the contest can no longer be avoided. The task of international public affairs consists precisely of presenting a true picture of these firms' contributions and fitting them into the economic, political, and social mechanisms of the societies in which they operate. This is why the IPA function is so much needed now that multinationals have definitely been recognized as significant actors on the world economic sense and have seriously been challenged by some governments and other segments in their home and host societies.

However, there are profit opportunities too in being perceived as legitimate partners in the development of home and host countries. This positive perspective should dominate the further growth, elaboration, and perfecting of this relatively new function.

SOURCES AND SUGGESTED REFERENCES

Ackerman, R.W. "Putting Social Concern into Practice," *European Business,* Vol. VIII (1974), pp. 33–44.

Ackerman, R.W. *The Social Challenge To Business.* Cambridge, MA: Harvard University Press, 1975.

Behrman, J.N., J.J. Boddewyn, and A. Kapoor. *International Business-Government Communications: U.S. Structures, Actors and Issues.* Lexington, MA: D.C. Heath, 1975.

Blake, D.H., and V. Toros. "The Global Image Makers," *Public Relations Journal*, Vol. V (June 1976), pp. 10–12.

Blake, D.H. *International Public Affairs: Programs for the 1980s*. Washington, D.C.: Foundation for Public Affairs/Public Affairs Council, 1978.

Blake, D.H. *Managing the External Relations of Multinational Corporations*. New York: Fund for Multinational Management Education, 1977.

Boddewyn, J.J. and K. Marton. "Corporate Profiles: Low, High and Right," *IPRA (International Public Relations Association) Review*, Vol. VII (September 1978), pp. 9–12.

Boddewyn, J.J. "The External Affairs of Transnational Firms: A Research Note," *Management International Review*, Vol. XIX (1976/3) pp. 47–57.

Boddewyn, J.J. "Western European Policies Toward U.S. Investors." New York University, Graduate School of Business Administration, Institute of Finance, *The Bulletin*, No. 93–95 (1974), pp. 1–95.

Brown, J.K. *This Business of Issues: Coping with the Company's Environments*. New York: Conference Board, 1979.

Business International. *Corporate External Affairs*. New York and Geneva: B.I. 1975. (J.J. Boddewyn, main reporter.)

Carson, J.J., and G.A. Steiner. *Measuring Business Social Performance: The Corporate Social Audit*. New York: Committee for Economic Development, 1974.

Channon, D.F. and M. Jalland. *Multinational Strategic Planning*. New York: American Management Association, 1978.

Dunn, S.W., M.F. Cahill, and J.J. Boddewyn. *How Fifteen Transnational Corporations Manage Public Affairs*. Chicago: Crain Books, 1979.

Fayerweather, J., ed. *International Business-Government Affairs: Toward an Era of Accommodation*. Cambridge, MA: Ballinger, 1973.

Fenn, D.H. "Finding Where the Power Lies in Government," *Harvard Business Review*, Vol. XXII (September–October 1979), pp. 144–153.

Gladwin, T.N. and I. Walter. *Multinationals Under Fire: Lessons in the Management of Conflict*. New York: Wiley, 1980.

Haendel, D. *Foreign Investments and the Management of Political Risk*. Boulder, CO: Westview Press, 1979.

Hargreaves, J. and J. Dauman. *Business Survival and Social Change*. New York: Wiley, 1975.

International Advertising Association. *Multinationals in Confrontation*. New York: I.A.A., 1975.

International Business-Government Counsellors. *Multinational Government Relations*. Washington, DC: I.E.G.C. 1977. (J.J. Boddewyn, main reporter).

Jackson, R.A., ed. *The Multinational Corporation and Social Policy; With Special Reference to General Motors in South Africa*. New York: Praeger, 1974.

Josephs, R. "A Global Approach to Public Relations," *Columbia Journal of World Business*, Vol. VII (Fall 1973), pp. 93–98.

Kobrin, S.J. "Political Risk: A Review and Reconsideration," *Journal of International Business Studies*, Vol. X (Spring–Summer 1979), pp. 67–80.

Kobrin, S.J. et al. "The Assessment and Evaluation of Noneconomic Environments by American Firms: A Preliminary Report," *Journal of International Business Studies*, Vol. XI (Spring/Summer 1980), pp. 32–47.

Kraar, L. "The Multinationals Get Smarter About Political Risks," *Fortune*, Vol. XXIV (24 March 1980), pp. 86–93.

LaPalombara, J. and S. Blank. *Multinational Corporations and National Elites: A Study in Tensions*. New York: Conference Board, 1976.

LaPalombara, J. and S. Blank. *Multinational Corporations in Comparative Perspective*. New York: Conference Board, 1977.

McGrath, Ph.S. *Managing Corporate External Relations*. New York: Conference Board, 1976.

Molitor, G.T.T. "The Hatching of Public Opinion." *Planning Review*, Vol. V (July 1977), pp. 3–7.

Negandhi, A.R. and B.R. Baliga. *Quest for Survival and Growth: A Comparative Study of American, European and Japanese Multinationals*. New York: Praeger, 1979.

Post, J.E. *Corporate Behavior and Social Change*. Reston, VA: Reston Publishing, 1978.

Public Affairs Council and the InterMatrix Group. *Handbook on Socioeconomic Activity and Performance Reporting on Overseas Operations*. Washington, D.C.: Intermatrix, 1980.

Public Affairs Council. *Managing International Public Affairs Perspectives* (newsletter), (1979), p. 2.

Sethi, S.P. "Dimensions of Corporate Social Performance: An Analytical Framework," *California Management Review*, Vol. XVII (Spring 1975), pp. 58–64.

Terry, P.T. "Mechanisms for Environmental Scanning," *Long Range Planning*, (June 1977), pp. 2–9.

Traverse-Healy, T. "Public Affairs Activity by Multinationals in Europe," *IPRA (International Public Relations Association) Review*, Vol. IV (September 1977), pp. 28–35.

U.S. Department of Commerce. *Corporate Social Reporting in the United States and Western Europe*, Report of the Task Force on Corporate Social Performance. Washington D.C.: U.S. Government Printing Office, 1979.

Wells, L.T. "Social Cost/Benefit Analysis," *Harvard Business Review*, Vol. XXII (March–April 1974), pp. 40–56.

APPENDIX **A**

A BIBLIOGRAPHY OF
INTERNATIONAL BUSINESS

CONTENTS

ECONOMIC ENVIRONMENT OF
INTERNATIONAL BUSINESS   3

FINANCIAL ENVIRONMENT OF
INTERNATIONAL BUSINESS   3

SOCIOCULTURAL ENVIRONMENT
OF INTERNATIONAL BUSINESS   4

POLITICAL-LEGAL ENVIRONMENT
OF INTERNATIONAL BUSINESS   5

FORMS OF INVOLVEMENT IN
INTERNATIONAL BUSINESS   5

GLOBAL-STRATEGY FORMULATION   6

MULTINATIONAL CORPORATE
PLANNING   7

MULTINATIONAL ORGANIZATIONAL
DESIGN   7

ACCOUNTING MANAGEMENT FOR
MULTINATIONALS   8

PUBLIC-AFFAIRS MANAGEMENT FOR
MULTINATIONALS   9

HUMAN-RESOURCE MANAGEMENT
FOR MULTINATIONALS   9

MARKETING MANAGEMENT FOR
MULTINATIONALS   10

FINANCIAL MANAGEMENT FOR
MULTINATIONALS   11

POLITICAL-RISK MANAGEMENT FOR
MULTINATIONALS   11

CONFLICT MANAGEMENT FOR
MULTINATIONALS   12

SELECTED INTERNATIONAL BUSINESS
PERIODICALS   13

General International Business   13
Economic/Financial Environment   13
Political/Cultural Environment   13
International Management   14
International Marketing and Public
Affairs   14
International Accounting and Finance   14
Area News and Studies   15

SELECTED SOURCES OF PUBLISHED
INTERNATIONAL-BUSINESS DATA   15

A BIBLIOGRAPHY OF INTERNATIONAL BUSINESS

Thomas N. Gladwin

Economic Environment of International Business

Brunner, K., and A. Meltzer, eds. *Institutions, Policies and Economic Performance*. New York: North-Holland, 1976.

Business International Corporation. *Operating in Latin America's Integrating Markets: AN-COM, CACM, CARICOM, LAFTA*. New York: Business International, 1977.

Dunning, J., ed. *Economic Analysis and Multinational Enterprise*. London: Allen and Unwin, 1974.

Goldman, M. *Detente and Dollars*. New York: Basic Books, 1975.

Gruchy, A.G. *Comparative Economic Systems*, 2nd ed. Boston: Houghton Mifflin, 1977.

Kindleberger, C.P., and B. Herrick. *Economic Development*. New York: McGraw Hill, 1977.

Kumar, K., and M.G. McLeod, eds. *Multinationals from Developing Countries*. Lexington, MA.: Lexington Books, 1981.

Lamont, D.F. *Foreign State Enterprises: A Threat to American Business*. New York: Basic Books, 1979.

Moran, T.H. *Oil Prices and the Future of OPEC*. Washington, D.C.: Resources for the Future, 1978.

Richardson, J.D. *Understanding International Economics*. Boston: Little, Brown, 1980.

Sauvant, K.P., and H. Hasenpflug. *The New International Economic Order: Confrontation or Cooperation Between North and South?* Boulder: Westview Press, 1977.

Todaro, M.P. *Economic Development in the Third World: An Introduction to Problems and Policies in a Global Perspective*. New York: Longman, 1977.

Vernon, R., and L.T. Wells, Jr. *Manager in the International Economy*, 4th ed. Englewood Cliffs, NJ: Prentice-Hall, 1981.

Walter, I., and Areskoug, K. *International Economics*, 3rd ed. New York: Wiley, 1981.

Wilczynski, J. *The Multinationals and East-West Relations*. Boulder, CO: Westview Press, 1976.

Financial Environment of International Business

Aliber, R.Z. *Exchange Risk and Corporate International Finance*. London: Macmillan, 1978.

Aliber, R.Z. *The International Money Game*. New York: Basic Books, 1977.

Baldwin, R.E., and J.D. Richardson. *International Trade and Finance: Readings.* Boston: Little, Brown, 1974.

Bell, G. *The Eurodollar Market and the International Financial System.* New York: Wiley, 1973.

Black, S.W. *Floating Exchange Rates and National Economic Policy.* New Haven: Yale University Press, 1977.

Cohen, B.J. *Organizing the World's Money.* New York: Basic Books, 1977.

Dufey, G. "International Capital Markets: Structure and Response in an Era of Instability," *Sloan Management Review,* (Spring 1981).

Dufey, G., and I.H. Giddy. *The International Money Market.* Englewood Cliffs, NJ: Prentice-Hall, 1978.

Isard, P. "Exchange Rate Determination: A Survey of Popular Views and Recent Models," *Princeton Studies in International Finance,* No. 42 (May 1978).

Lederer, W. "How the U.S. Balance of Payments Affects the Dollar," *Euromoney,* (March 1978), pp. 85–93.

McKinnon, R.I. *Money in International Exchange.* London: Oxford University Press, 1979.

McKinnon, R.I. "The Eurocurrency Market," *Princeton Essays in International Finance,* No. 125 (December 1977).

Solomon, R. *The International Monetary System, 1945–1976.* New York: Harper & Row, 1978.

Wihlborg, C.G. "Currency Risks in International Financial Markets," *Princeton Studies in International Finance,* No. 44 (December 1978).

Willett, T.D. *Floating Exchange Rates and International Monetary Reform.* Washington, D.C.: American Enterprise Institute, 1977.

Sociocultural Environment of International Business

Apter, D.E., and L.W. Goodman, eds. *The Multinational Corporation and Social Change.* New York: Praeger, 1976.

Casse, P. *Training for the Cross-Cultural Mind.* Washington, D.C.: The Society for Intercultural Education, Training and Research, 1980.

Condon, J., and F. Yousef. *Introduction to Intercultural Communication.* New York: Bobbs-Merrill, 1975.

Davis, S.M. *Comparative Management: Organizational and Cultural Perspectives.* Englewood Cliffs, NJ: Prentice-Hall, 1971.

Douglas, S., and B. Dubois, "Looking at the Cultural Environment for International Marketing Opportunities," *Columbia Journal of World Business,* (Winter 1977), pp. 102–109.

England, G.W. *The Manager and His Values: An International Perspective From The United States, Japan, Korea, India and Australia.* Cambridge, MA: Ballinger, 1975.

Hall, E.T. *The Silent Language.* Garden City, NY: Anchor, 1973.

Hall, E.T. *The Hidden Dimension.* Garden City, NY: Anchor, 1969.

Harris, P., and R. Moran. *Managing Cultural Differences.* Houston: Gulf Publishing, 1979.

Hofstede, G. *Culture's Consequences: International Differences in Work Related Values.* Beverly Hills: SAGE, 1980.

Kluckhohn, F.R., and F.L. Strodtbeck. *Variations in Value Orientations.* Westport, CT: Greenwood Press, 1961.

Kobrin, S.J. *Foreign Direct Investment, Industrialization and Social Change.* Greenwich, CT: JAI Press, 1977.

Ricks, D., M. Y.C. Fu, and J.S. Arpan. *International Business Blunders.* Colombus: Grid, 1974.

Terpstra, V., ed. *The Cultural Environment of International Business*. Cincinnati: South-Western, 1978.

Webber, R.A. *Culture and Management*. Homewood, IL: Richard D. Irwin, 1969.

Political-Legal Environment of International Business

Boarman, P.M., and H. Schollhammer, eds. *Multinational Corporations and Governments: Business-Government Relations in an International Context*. New York: Praeger, 1975.

Fayerweather, J. "A Conceptual Scheme of the Interaction of the Multinational Firm and Nationalism," *Journal of Business Administration,* No. 1 (1975), pp. 67–89.

Hahlo, H.R., J. Smith, and R.W. Wright. *Nationalism and the Multinational Enterprise*. Dobbs Ferry, NY: Oceana Publications, 1973.

Jones, R.T. "Executive's Guide to Antitrust in Europe and the U.S.," *Harvard Business Review,* (May–June, 1976).

Keohane, R.O., and V.D. Ooms. "The Multinational Firm and International Regulation," in C.F. Bergsten and L. Krause, eds. *World Politics and International Economics*. Washington, D.C.: The Brookings Institution, 1975.

Keohane, R.O., and J.S. Nye. *Power and Interdependence: World Politics in Transition*. Boston: Little, Brown, 1977.

Kobrin, S.J. "Foreign Enterprise and Forced Divestment in the LDCs," *International Organization,* (Winter 1980), pp. 65–88.

Moran, T.H. *Multinational Corporations and the Politics of Dependence*. Princeton: Princeton University Press, 1974.

Mikdashi, Z. *The International Politics of Natural Resources*. Ithaca: Cornell University Press, 1976.

Nye, J.S. "Multinational Corporations in World Politics," *Foreign Affairs,* (October 1974).

Robinson, R.D. *National Control of Foreign Business Entry: A Survey of Fifteen Countries*. New York: Praeger, 1976.

Streng, W.P. *International Business Transactions Tax and Legal Handbook*. Englewood Cliffs, NJ: Prentice-Hall, 1978.

United Nations Centre on Transnational Corporations. *National Legislation and Regulations Relating to Transnational Corporations*. New York: United Nations, 1978.

United Nations Center on Transnational Corporations. *Transnational Corporations in World Development*. New York: United Nations, 1978.

Vagts, D.F. "The Multinational Enterprise: A New Challenge for Transnational Law," *Harvard Law Review,* (1970), pp. 739–792.

Forms of Involvement in International Business

Aharoni, Y. *The Foreign Investment Decision Process*. Boston: Division of Research, Graduate School of Business Administration, Harvard University, 1966.

Alexandrides, C.G., and G.P. Moschis. *Export Marketing Management*. New York: Praeger, 1977.

Behrman, J.N., and W.A. Fischer. *Overseas R&D Activities of Transnational Companies*. Cambridge: Oelgeschlager, Gunn and Hain, 1980.

Behrman, J.N., and H. Wallender. *Transfers of Manufacturing Technology within Multinational Enterprises*. Cambridge: Ballinger, 1976.

Buckley, P.J., and M. Casson. *The Future of Multinational Enterprise*. New York: Holmes and Meier, 1976.

Finnegan, M.B., and R. Goldscheider. *Current Trends in Domestic and International Licensing: Patents, Knowhow and Industrial Property.* New York: Practicing Law Institute, 1974.

Franko, L.G. "International Joint Ventures in Developing Countries: Mystique and Reality," *Law and Policy in International Business,* (Spring 1974), pp. 315–336.

Franko, L.G. *Joint Venture Survival in Multinational Corporations.* New York: Praeger, 1972.

Heskett, J.L., and P.F. Mathias, "The Management of Logistics in MNCs," *Columbia Journal of World Business,* (Spring 1976), pp. 52–62.

Hood, N., and S. Young. *The Economics of Multinational Enterprise.* London: Longman, 1979.

Leff, N. "International Sourcing Strategy," *Columbia Journal of World Business,* (Fall 1974), pp. 71–79.

Pomper, C. *International Investment Planning.* Amsterdam: North-Holland, 1976.

Robinson, R.D. *International Business Management: A Guide to Decision Making,* 2nd ed. Hinsdale, IL: Dryden Press, 1978.

Ronstadt, R. *Research and Development Abroad by United States Multinationals.* New York: Praeger, 1977.

Tornedon, R. *Foreign Disinvestment by U.S. Multinational Corporations.* New York: Praeger, 1975.

Global-Strategy Formulation

Ansoff, H.I., R.P. Declerk, and R.L. Hayes. *From Strategic Planning to Strategic Management.* New York: Wiley, 1976.

Brooke, M.Z., and H.L. Remmers. *The Strategy of Multinational Enterprise: Organization and Finance.* London: Pitman, 1978.

Doz, Y.L. *Government Control and Multinational Strategic Management: Power Systems and Telecommunication Equipment.* New York: Praeger, 1979.

Doz, Y.L. "Strategic Management in Multinational Companies," *Sloan Management Review,* (Winter 1980), pp. 27–46.

Fayerweather, J. *International Business Strategy and Administration.* Cambridge: Ballinger, 1978.

Hutzel, J.M. *Strategy Formulation in the Multinational Business Environment.* San Jose: San Jose State University, 1976.

Leroy, G. *Multinational Product Strategy: A Typology for Analysis of Worldwide Product Innovation and Diffusion.* New York: Praeger, 1976.

Porter, M.E. *Competitive Strategy: Techniques for Analyzing Industries and Competitors.* New York: The Free Press, 1980.

Prahalad, C.K. "The Strategic Process in a Multinational Corporation," D.B.A. dissertation, Harvard Business School (1975).

Prahalad, C.K., and Y. Doz, "Strategic Management of Diversified Multinational Corporations," in A.R. Negandhi, ed. *Functioning of the Multinational Corporation: A Global Comparative Study.* New York: Pergamon Press, 1980.

Rapp, W.V. "Strategy Formulation and International Competition," *Columbia Journal of World Business,* (Summer 1973), pp. 98–112.

Schendel, D.E. and C.W. Hofer, eds. *Strategic Management: A New View of Business Policy and Planning.* Boston: Little, Brown, 1979.

Tsurumi, Y. *Multinational Management: Text, Readings and Cases.* Cambridge: Ballinger, 1976.

Yoshino, M.Y. *Japan's Multinational Enterprises.* Cambridge, MA: Harvard University Press, 1976.

Walter, I., and T. Murray, eds. *Handbook of International Business.* New York: Wiley, 1982.

Multinational Corporate Planning

Abell, D.F., and J.S. Hammond. *Strategic Market Planning: Problems and Analytical Approaches.* Englewood Cliffs, NJ: Prentice-Hall, 1979.

Ansoff, H.I., and H.J. Thanheiser. "Corporate Planning: A Comparative View of the Evolution and Current Practice in the United States and Western Europe." Working Paper 78-10. Brussels: European Institute for Advanced Studies in Management, 1978.

Channon, D.F., and R.M. Jalland. *Multinational Strategic Planning.* New York: Macmillan, 1978.

Gladwin, T.N. *Environment, Planning and the Multinational Corporation.* Greenwich, CT: JAI Press, 1977.

Interfutures. *Facing the Future: Mastering the Probable and Managing the Unpredictable.* Paris: OECD, 1979.

Kilmann, R.H., and K.I. Ghymm. "The MAPS Design Technology: Designing Strategic Intelligence Systems for MNCs," *Columbia Journal of World Business,* (Summer 1976), pp. 35–47.

Lorange, P. *Corporate Planning: An Executive Viewpoint.* Englewood Cliffs, NJ: Prentice-Hall, 1980.

Lorange, P. "A Framework for Strategic Planning in Multinational Corporations," *Long Range Planning,* (June 1976), pp. 30–57.

Lorange, P., and R.F. Vancil, eds. *Strategic Planning Systems.* Englewood Cliffs, NJ: Prentice-Hall, 1977.

Murray, J.A. "Intelligence Systems of the MNCs," *Columbia Journal of World Business,* (September/October 1972), pp. 63–71.

Schwendiman, J.S. "International Strategic Planning: Still in its Infancy?" *Worldwide P&I Planning,* (September/October 1971), pp. 52–61.

Schwendiman, J.S. *Strategic and Long Range Planning for the Multinational Corporation.* New York: Praeger, 1974.

Steiner, G.A., and W.M. Cannon. *Multinational Corporate Planning.* New York: Macmillan, 1966.

Steiner, G.A., and H. Schollhammer. "Pitfalls in Multinational Long Range Planning," *Long Range Planning,* (April 1975), pp. 2 ff.

Multinational Organizational Design

Bartlett, C.A. Multinational Structural Evolution: The Changing Decision Environment in International Divisions, D.B.A. thesis, Graduate School of Business Administration, Harvard University (1979).

Beer, J.M., and S.M. Davis. "Creating a Global Organization: Failures Along the Way," *Columbia Journal of World Business,* (Summer 1976), pp. 35–47.

Davis, S.M. *Managing and Organizing Multinational Corporations.* New York: Pergamon, 1979.

Davis, S.M. "Trends in the Organization of Multinational Corporations," *Columbia Journal of World Business,* (Summer 1976), pp. 25–34.

Davis, S.M., and P.R. Lawrence. *Matrix.* Reading, MA: Addison-Wesley, 1977.

Duerr, M.G., and J.M. Roach. *Organization and Control of International Operations.* New York: Conference Board, 1973.

Fouraker, L.E., and J.M. Stopford. "Organizational Structure and the Multinational Strategy," *Administrative Science Quarterly,* (June 1968).

Franko, L.G. *The European Multinationals.* Stamford: Greylock Press, 1976.

Harari, E., and Y. Zeira. "Limitations and Prospects of Planned Change in Multinational Corporations," *Human Relations,* (No. 7, 1976), pp. 659–676.

Heenan, D.A., and H.V. Perlmutter. *Multinational Organization Development.* Reading, MA: Addison-Wesley, 1979.

Hornstein, H.A., and N.M. Tichy. "Developing Organization Development for Multinational Corporations," *Columbia Journal of World Business,* (Summer 1976).

Rutenberg, D.P. "Organizational Archetypes of a Multinational Company," *Management Science,* (February 1970), pp. 337–349.

Stopford, J.M., and L.T. Wells, Jr. *Managing the Multinational Enterprise.* New York: Basic Books, 1972.

Stopford, J.M., and K.O. Haberich. "Ownership and Control of Foreign Operations," *Journal of General Management,* (Summer 1976), pp. 3–20.

Williamson, H.F., ed. *Evolution of International Management Structures.* Newark: University of Delaware Press, 1975.

Accounting Management for Multinationals

Alltashim, D.D., and J.W. Robertson. *Accounting for Multinational Enterprises.* Indianapolis: Bobbs-Merrill, 1978.

Arpan, J.S. *International Intracorporate Pricing: Non-American Systems and Views.* New York: Praeger, 1972.

Arpan, J.S., and L.H. Radebaugh. *International Accounting and Multinational Enterprises.* Boston: Warren, Gorham & Lamont, 1981.

Baker, H.K., *et al.* "Disclosure of Material Information: A Cross-National Comparison," *International Journal of Accounting Education and Research,* (Fall 1977), pp. 1–18.

Baruch, H. "The Foreign Corrupt Practices Act," *Harvard Business Review,* (January/February 1979), pp. 32 ff.

Bischel, J.E., and R. Feinschreiber. *Fundamentals of International Taxation.* New York: Practicing Law Institute, 1977.

Choi, F.D.S. "Multinational Challenges for Managerial Accountants," *Journal of Contemporary Business,* (Fall 1975), pp. 51–68.

Choi, F.D.S. "Price Level Adjustments and Foreign Currency Translation: Are They Compatible," *International Journal of Accounting Education and Research,* (Fall 1975), pp. 121–143.

Choi, F.D.S., and G.G. Mueller. *An Introduction to Multinational Accounting.* Englewood Cliffs, NJ: Prentice-Hall, 1978.

Chown, J. *Taxation and Multinational Enterprises.* London: Longman, 1974.

Fantl, I.L. "Control and the Internal Audit in the Multinational Firm," *International Journal of Accounting,* (Fall 1975), pp. 57–65.

Price Waterhouse International. *A Survey in 46 Countries: Accounting Principles and Reporting Practices.* London: Price Waterhouse, 1975.

Radebaugh, L.H. "Accounting for Price Level and Exchange Rate Changes for U.S. International Firms: An Empirical Study," *Journal of International Business Studies,* (Fall 1974), pp. 41–56.

Rueschhoff, N.G. *International Accounting and Financial Reporting*. New York: Praeger, 1976.

Watt, G.C., R.M. Hammer, and M. Burge. *Accounting for the Multinational Corporation*. New York: Financial Executives Research Foundation, 1977.

Public-Affairs Management for Multinationals

Barnet, R.J., and R.E. Muller. *Global Reach: The Power of the Multinational Corporation*. New York: Simon & Schuster, 1974.

Behrman, J.N., J. Boddewyn and A. Kapoor. *International Business-Government Communication*. Lexington, MA: D.C. Heath, 1975.

Bergsten, C.F., T. Horst and T.H. Moran. *American Multinationals and American Interests*. Washington, D.C.: Brookings Institution, 1978.

Blake, D.H. *Managing the External Relations of Multinational Corporations*. New York: Fund for Multinational Management Education, 1977.

Boddewyn, J.J. *International External Affairs*. Geneva: Business International, 1975.

Corporate Public Policy Division, Business International. *Managing International Government Relations*. New York: Business International, 1980.

Dunn, S.W., M.F. Cahill, and J.J. Boddewyn. *How Fifteen Transnational Corporations Manage Public Affairs*. Chicago: Crain Books, 1979.

Fayerweather, J., ed. *International Business-Government Affairs: Toward An Era of Accomodation.* Cambridge: Ballinger, 1973.

Gladwin, T.N., and I. Walter. "Multinational Enterprise, Social Responsiveness and Pollution Control," *Journal of International Business Studies,* (Fall/Winter 1976), pp. 57–74.

Humble, J. *The Responsible Multinational Enterprise*. London: Foundation for Business Responsibilities, 1975.

International Business–Government Counsellors. *The International Organizations Regulatory Guidebook*. Washington, D.C.: International Business–Government Counsellors, 1981.

Litvak, I., and C. Maule. "Foreign Corporate Responsibility in Less Developed Economies," *Journal of World Trade Law,* (March/April 1975).

Madden, C.H., ed. *The Case for the Multinational Corporation: Six Scholarly Views*. New York: Praeger, 1977.

Sauvant, K.P., and F.G. Lavipour. *Controlling Multinational Enterprises: Problems, Strategies, Counterstrategies*. Boulder: Westview Press, 1976.

Walter, I. "A Guide to Social Responsibility of the Multinational Enterprise," In J. Backman, ed. *Social Responsibility and Accountability*. New York: New York University Press, 1975.

Human-Resource Management for Multinationals

Bass, B.M., and P.C. Burger. *Assessment of Managers: An International Comparison*. New York: Free Press, 1979.

Blue, J.L., and U. Haynes, Jr. "Preparation for the Overseas Assignment," *Business Horizons,* (June 1977), pp. 61–67.

Daniels, J. "The Non-American Manager, Especially as Third Country National, in U.S. Multinationals: A Separate but Equal Doctrine?" *Journal of International Business Studies,* (Fall 1974), pp. 25–40.

Galbraith, J., and A. Edstrom. "International Transfers of Managers: Some Important Policy Considerations," *Columbia Journal of World Business,* (Summer 1976), pp. 100–111.

Hays, R.D. "Expatriate Selection: Insuring Success and Avoiding Failure," *Journal of International Business Studies,* (Spring 1974), pp. 25–38.

Heenan, D.A. *Multinational Management of Human Resources: A Systems Approach.* Austin: Bureau of Business Research, University of Texas, 1975.

Heenan, D.A., and C. Reynolds. "RPO's: A Step Toward Global Human Resources Management," *California Management Review,* (Fall 1975), pp. 5–9.

Kraus, D., and S. Patrick. "International Executive Compensation—Unmanaged or Unmanageable?" *Business Horizons,* (December 1974), pp. 45–52.

Kujawa, D., ed. *International Labor and the Multinational Enterprise.* New York: Praeger, 1975.

Noer, D.M. *Multinational People Management.* Washington, D.C.: Bureau of National Affairs, 1975.

Perlmutter, H.V., and D.A. Heenan. "How Multinational Should Your Top Managers Be?" *Harvard Business Review,* (November/December 1974), pp. 121–132.

Reynolds, C. "Managing Human Resources on a Global Scale," *Business Horizons,* (December 1976), pp. 51–56.

Sirota, D., and J.M. Greenwood. "Understanding Your Overseas Work Force," *Harvard Business Review,* (January/February 1971), pp. 53–60.

Weinberg, P.J. *European Labor and Multinationals.* New York: Praeger, 1978.

Zeira, Y., and E. Harari. "Genuine Multinational Staffing Policy: Expectations and Realities," *Academy of Management Journal,* (June 1977), pp. 327–333.

Marketing Management for Multinationals

Ayal, I., and J. Zif. "Market Expansion Strategies in Multinational Marketing," *Journal of Marketing,* (Spring 1979), pp. 84–94.

Brandt, W.K., and J.M. Hulbert. "Headquarters Guidance in Market Strategy in the Multinational Subsidiary," *Columbia Journal of World Business,* (Winter 1977), pp. 7–14.

Buzzell, R. "Can You Standardize Multinational Marketing," *Harvard Business Review,* (November/December 1968).

Davidson, W.H., and R. Harrigan, "Key Decisions in International Marketing: Introducing New Products Abroad," *Columbia Journal of World Business,* (Winter 1977), pp. 15–23.

Keegan, W.J. *Multinational Marketing Management,* 2nd ed. Englewood Cliffs, NJ: Prentice-Hall, 1980.

Killough, J. "Improved Payoffs from Transnational Advertising," *Harvard Business Review,* (July/August 1978).

McIntyre, D.R. "Multinational Positioning Strategy," *Columbia Journal of World Business,* (Fall 1975), pp. 106–110.

Terpstra, V. "International Product Policy: The Role of Foreign R&D," *Columbia Journal of World Business,* (Winter 1977), pp. 24–32.

Terpstra, V. *International Marketing,* 2nd ed. New York: Dryden Press, 1978.

Thorelli, H., and H. Becker, eds. *International Marketing Strategy,* rev. ed. New York: Pergamon, 1980.

Weber, J.A. "Comparing Growth Opportunities in the International Marketplace," *Management International Review,* (November 1, 1979), pp. 47–56.

Wiechmann, U.E. *Marketing Management in Multinational Firms: The Consumer Packaged Goods Industry.* New York: Praeger, 1976.

Wiechmann, U.E., and L.G. Pringle. "Problems that Plague Multinational Marketers," *Harvard Business Review,* (July/August 1979), pp. 118–124.

Wind, Y., S. Douglas, and H. Perlmutter. "Guidelines for Developing International Marketing Strategies," *Journal of Marketing,* (April 1973), pp. 14–23.

Sorenson, R.Z., and U.E. Weichmann. "How Multinationals View Marketing Standardization," *Harvard Business Review,* (May/June 1978).

Financial Management for Multinationals

Bursk, E.C., *et al. Financial Control of Multinational Corporations.* New York: Financial Executives Research Foundation, 1971.

Davis, S.I. *The Management Function in International Banking.* London: Macmillan, 1979.

Dufey, G. "Corporate Finance and Exchange Rate Variations," *Financial Management,* (Summer 1972), pp. 51–57.

Dufey, G., and I.H. Giddy, "International Financial Planning," *California Management Review,* (Fall 1978).

Eiteman, D.K., and A.I. Stonehill. *Multinational Business Finance,* 2nd ed. Reading, MA: Addison-Wesley, 1979.

Greene, J., and M.G. Duerr. *Intercompany Transactions in the Multinational Firm.* New York: Conference Board, 1970.

Hagemann, H. "Anticipate Your Long Term Foreign Exchange Risks," *Harvard Business Review,* (March/April 1977), pp. 81–88.

Lessard, D.R., ed. *International Financial Management.* Boston: Warren, Gorham & Lamont, 1979.

Levich, R.M., and C.G. Wihlborg, eds. *Exchange Risk and Exposure: Current Developments in International Financial Management.* Lexington, MA: Lexington Books, 1980.

Prindl, A.R. "Guidelines for MNC Money Managers," *Harvard Business Review,* (January/February 1976), pp. 73–80.

Robbins, S.M., and R.B. Stobaugh. *Money in the Multinational Enterprise: A Study in Financial Policies.* New York: Basic Books, 1973.

Rodriguez, R.M., and E.E. Carter. *International Financial Management,* 2nd ed. Englewood Cliffs, NJ: Prentice-Hall, 1979.

Shapiro, A.C. "Capital Budgeting for the Multinational Corporation," *Financial Management,* (Spring 1978), pp. 7–16.

Shapiro, A.C., "Evaluating Financing Costs for Multinational Subsidiaries," *Journal of International Business Studies,* (Fall 1975), pp. 25–32.

Shapiro, A.C., and D.P. Rutenberg. "Managing Exchange Risks in a Floating World," *Financial Management,* (Summer 1976), pp. 48–58.

Political-Risk Management for Multinationals

Baglini, N. *Risk Management in International Corporations.* New York: Risk Studies Foundation, 1976.

Blank, S., with J. Basek, S.J. Kobrin, and J. LaPalombara. *Assessing the Political Environment: An Emerging Function in International Companies.* New York: Conference Board, 1980.

Bradley, D.G. "Managing Against Expropriation." *Harvard Business Review,* (July/August 1977), pp. 75–83.

Davis, S.I. "How Risky is International Lending?" *Harvard Business Review,* (January/February 1977), pp. 135–143.

Haendel, D. *Foreign Investments and the Management of Political Risk.* Boulder: Westview Press, 1979.

Haendel, D., G.T. West and R. Meadow. *Overseas Investment and Political Risk*. Philadelphia: Foreign Policy Research Institute, 1975.

Kobrin, S.J. "Political Risk: A Review and Reconsideration." *Journal of International Business Studies*, (Summer 1979), pp. 67–80.

Kobrin, S.J. "When Does Political Instability Result in Increased Investment Risk?" *Columbia Journal of World Business*, (Fall 1978).

Kobrin, S.J., J. Basek, S. Blank, and J. LaPalombara. "The Assessment and Evaluation of Non-economic Environments by American Firms: A Preliminary Report," *Journal of International Business Studies*, (Spring/Summer 1980), pp. 32–47.

Kraar, L. "The Multinationals Get Smarter About Political Risks," *Fortune*, (March 24, 1980), pp. 86 ff.

Moran, T.H. "Transnational Strategies of Protection and Defense by Multinational Corporations: Spreading the Risk and Raising the Cost for Nationalization in Natural Resources," *International Organization*, (Spring 1973), pp. 273–287.

Robock, S.H. "Political Risk: Identification and Assessment," *Columbia Journal of World Business*, (July/August 1971).

Rummel, R.J., and D.A. Heenan. "How Multinationals Analyze Political Risk," *Harvard Business Review*, (January/February 1978), pp. 67–76.

Thunell, L.H. *Political Risks in International Business*. New York: Praeger, 1977.

Conflict Management for Multinationals

American Arbitration Association. *New Strategies for Peaceful Resolution of International Business Disputes*. Dobbs Ferry, NY: Oceana Publications, 1972.

Behrman, J.N. *Conflicting Constraints on the Multinational Enterprise: Potential for Resolution*. New York: Council of the Americas, 1974.

Committee for Economic Development, Research and Policy Committee. *Transnational Corporations and Developing Countries: New Policies for a Changing World Economy*. New York: Committee for Economic Development, 1981.

Frank, F. *Foreign Enterprise in Developing Countries*. Baltimore: Johns Hopkins University Press, 1980.

Gladwin, T.N., and I. Walter. "How Multinationals Can Manage Social and Political Forces," *Journal of Business Strategy*, (Summer 1980), pp. 54–68.

Gladwin, T.N., and I. Walter. *Multinationals Under Fire: Lessons in the Management of Conflict*. New York: Wiley, 1980.

Harnett, D.C., and L.L. Cummings. *Bargaining Behavior: An International Study*. Houston: Dame Publications, 1980.

Kapoor, A. *Planning for International Business Negotiation*. Cambridge, MA: Ballinger, 1975.

LaPalombara, J., and S. Blank. *Multinational Corporations and National Elites: A Study in Tensions*. New York: Conference Board, 1976.

Litvak, I.A., and C.J. Maule. "The Multinational Firm and Conflicting National Interests," *Journal of World Trade Law*, (November 3, 1976), pp. 309–318.

Mikesell, R.F. ed. *Foreign Investment in the Petroleum and Mineral Industries: Case Studies of Investor-Host Country Relations*. Baltimore: John Hopkins Press, 1971.

Vernon, R. *Sovereignty at Bay: The Multinational Spread of U.S. Enterprises*. New York: Basic Books, 1971.

Vernon, R. *Storm Over the Multinationals: The Real Issues*. Cambridge, MA: Harvard University Press, 1977.

Wells, L.T., Jr., and D.N. Smith. *Negotiating Third World Mineral Agreements*. Cambridge, MA: Ballinger, 1975.

Selected International Business Periodicals

GENERAL INTERNATIONAL BUSINESS

Across the Board
Business International
Business Week
Commerce America
Columbia Journal of World Business
The Economist
The Financial Times
Fortune
The International Executive
Harvard Business Review
Journal of International Business Studies
Multinational Business
World Business Weekly

ECONOMIC/FINANCIAL ENVIRONMENT

Finance and Development
IMF Survey
Intereconomics
Inter-American Economic Affairs
International Development Review
Journal of Common Market Studies
Journal of Development Economics
Journal of International Economics
Journal of International Law and Economics
Journal of World Trade Law
Lloyds Bank Review
OECD Observer
The World Economy

POLITICAL/CULTURAL ENVIRONMENT

The Bridge: A Review of Cross-Cultural Affairs and International Training
Comparative Political Studies
Economic Development and Cultural Change
Foreign Affairs
Foreign Policy
Harvard International Law Journal
Human Organization
International Organization
International Studies Quarterly
Journal of International Affairs
Law and Policy in International Business

Orbis
World Politics

INTERNATIONAL MANAGEMENT

Academy of Management Review
British Journal of Industrial Relations
California Management Review
International Labor Review
International Management
Journal of Business Strategy
Journal of General Management
Long Range Planning
Management International Review
Management Today
Sloan Management Review
Worldwide Projects and Installations
Vision

INTERNATIONAL MARKETING AND PUBLIC AFFAIRS

Advertising Age
The Arbitration Journal
Business and Society Review
Conflict Resolution
The Corporate Examiner
European Journal of Marketing
The International Advertiser
Journal of Marketing
Journal of Marketing Research
Multinational Monitor
Public Relations Journal
Risk Management
World Marketing

INTERNATIONAL ACCOUNTING AND FINANCE

Banker
Euromoney
European Taxation
Financial Executive
Financial Management
International Currency Review
The International Journal of Accounting
The International Tax Journal
International Tax Review

Journal of Finance
Management Accouting
Tax Executive
World Financial Markets

AREA NEWS AND STUDIES

African Business
Australian Quarterly
Business Asia
Business Europe
Business Latin America
Comercio Exterior de Mexico
Eastern Europe Report
Europe
The Latin American Times
L'Expansion
New Africa
Oriental Economist
Soviet Studies

Selected Sources of Published International Business Data

Daniells, L.M. *Business Information Sources*. Berkeley: University of California Press, 1976.

Daniels, J.D., E.W. Ogram, Jr., and L.H. Radebaugh. *International Business: Environments and Operations*. Reading, MA: Addison-Wesley, 1979. See instructor's manual.

SOURCES OF INFORMATION FOR INTERNATIONAL BUSINESS

A problem for many executives in international business is simply finding the services that are available, and most appropriate, for their particular activities. The following lists are intended to provide names and addresses, and brief descriptions where appropriate, of major services that may be of use to those engaged in international business. In addition, a comprehensive international business intelligence and consulting capability is provided by *Business International, Inc.,* 1 Dag Hammarskjöld Plaza, New York, NY 10016, Telephone (212) 750-6300.

I.	GOVERNMENT INFORMATION SERVICES	3
II.	MAJOR U.S. AND FOREIGN MULTINATIONAL CORPORATIONS	8
III.	INTERNATIONAL ACCOUNTING SERVICES	8
IV.	INTERNATIONAL LEGAL SERVICES	10
V.	INTERNATIONAL TRANSPORT SERVICES	13
VI.	INTERNATIONAL INSURANCE INSURANCE SERVICES	14
VII.	INTERNATIONAL RESEARCH AND CONSULTING SERVICES	15
VIII.	INTERNATIONAL BANKING SERVICES	19
IX.	INTERNATIONAL ADVERTISING SERVICES	21

SOURCES OF INFORMATION FOR INTERNATIONAL BUSINESS

Betty Jane Punnett

I. GOVERNMENT INFORMATION SERVICES

The U.S. Department of Commerce provides a wide range of services to businesses and it has broadened its export support operations to provide greater assistance to American companies competing in world markets. The Domestic and International Business Administration is specifically charged with promoting exports, analyzing and encouraging East-West trade, and strengthening the international commercial position of the United States. Its mission is carried out by 5 bureaus and 43 District Offices in the United States and Puerto Rico, and by many overseas trade promotion facilities. The services and publications available through the U.S. Government are so numerous that it is impossible to list even the major ones. The following list serves rather as a sample of what is available.

Services and Programs

Expansion of Exports
Expansion of East-West Trade
Expansion of Trade in the Near East and North Africa
Export Control Administration
Federal Participation in International Expositions
International Economic Policy and Research
National Technical Information Service
National Oceanic and Atmospheric Administration
Office of Minority Business Enterprise
U.S. Travel Service

Publications

Foreign Economic Trends
Overseas Business Reports
Global Market Surveys
Country Market Sectoral Surveys
International Economic Indicators

Current Price Developments in the U.S. and Major Foreign Countries
Market Share Reports
Survey of Current Business
Data Service Publications
Dictionary of Economic and Statistical Terms

It is strongly recommended that a Department of Commerce District Office from the following directory be contacted for complete information on available services and publications.

U.S. DEPARTMENT OF COMMERCE DISTRICT OFFICE DIRECTORY

ALABAMA
Birmingham—Suite 200-201, 908 South 20th Street, 35205, Tel. 205-254-1331

ALASKA
Anchorage—701 C St., P.O. Box 32, 99513, Tel 907-271-5041

ARIZONA
Phoenix—Suite 2950 Valley Bank Center, 201 North Central Ave., 85073, Tel 602-261-3285

ARKANSAS
Little Rock—(Memphis, Tenn. District) 1100 North University, Suite 109, 77207, Tel 501-378-5157

CALIFORNIA
Los Angeles—Room 800, 11777 San Vincente Blvd., 90049 Tel 213-824-7591

San Diego—233 A Street, Suite 310 92101 Tel 714-293-5395

San Francisco—Federal Building, Box 36013, 450 Golden Gate Ave. 94102, Tel 415-556-5860

COLORADO
Denver—Room 165, New Custom House, 19th & Stout St, 80202, Tel 303-837-3246

CONNECTICUT
Hartford—Room 610B, Federal Office Building, 450 Main St 06103, Tel 203-244-3530

FLORIDA
Miami—Room 821, City National Bank Building, 25 West Flagler St 33130, Tel 305-350-5267

Clearwater—128 North Osceola Ave. 33515, Tel 813-461-0011

Jacksonville—815 S. Main St, Suite 100, 32207 Tel 904-791-2796

Tallahassee—Collins Bldg. Rm. G20 32303 Tel 904-488-6469

GEORGIA
Atlanta—Suite 600, 1365 Peachtree St, NE 30309, Tel 404-881-7000

Savannah—222 U.S. Courthouse & P.O. Box 9746, 135-29 Bull St, 31412, Tel 912-232-4321 Ext. 204

HAWAII
Honolulu—4106 Federal Bldg, P.O. Box 50026 300 Ala Moana Blvd. 96850, Tel 808-546-8694

ILLINOIS
Chicago—1406 Mid Continental Plaza Bldg, 55 East Monroe St. 60603, Tel 312-353-4450

INDIANA
Indianapolis—357 U.S. Courthouse & Federal Office Bldg. 46 East Ohio St, Tel 317-269-6214

IOWA
Des Moines—817 Federal Bldg. 210 Walnut St. 50309, Tel 515-284-4222

KENTUCKY
Franfort—(Cincinnati, Ohio District) Capitol Plaza Office Tower, Rm. 2425, 40601 Tel 502-875-4421

LOUISIANA
New Orleans—432 Intl. Trade Mart, No. 2 Canal St. 70130, Tel 504-598-6546

MAINE
Portland—(Boston, Massachusetts District) Maine State Pier, 40 Commercial St. 04111, Tel 207 773-5608

MARYLAND
Baltimore—415 U.S. Customhouse, Gay and Lombard Sts. 21202, Tel 301-962-3560

MASSACHUSETTS
Boston—10th Fl. 441 Stuart St. 02116 Tel 617-223-2312

MICHIGAN
Detroit—445 Federal Bldg. 231 W. Lafayette 48226, Tel 313-226-3650
Grand Rapids—350 Ottawa St. N.W. 49503, Tel 616-456-2411/33

MINNESOTA
Minneapolis—218 Federal Building, 110 South 4th St. 55401 Tel 612-725-2133

MISSISSIPPI
Jackson—(Birmingham, Alabama District) P.O. Box 849, 1202 Walter Sillers Bldg. 39205, Tel 601-969-4388

MISSOURI
St. Louis—120 South Central Ave. 63105 Tel 314-425-3302/4
Kansas City—Rm 1840, 601 E. 12th St. 64104, Tel 816-374-3142

MONTANA
Butte—(Cheyenne, Wyoming District) 225 S. Idaho St, Rm 101 P.O. Box 3809, 59701 Tel 406-723-6561 Ext. 2317

NEBRASKA
Omaha—Capitol Plaza, Suite 703A, 1815 Capitol Ave. 68102 Tel 402-221-3665

NEVADA
Reno—777 W. 2nd St. Rm 120 89502, Tel 702-784-5203

NEW JERSEY
Newark—4th Fl, Gateway Bldg. Market St. & Penn Plaza 07102, Tel 201-645-6214

NEW YORK
Buffalo—1312 Federal Bldg., 111 W. Huron St. 14202 Tel 716-846-4191
New York—Room 3718, Federal Office Bldg., 26 Federal Plaza, Foley Square, 10007, Tel 212-264-0834

NORTH CAROLINA
Greensboro—203 Federal Bldg., W. Market St., P.O. 1950, 27402, Tel 919-378-5345

OHIO
Cincinnati—10504 Federal Office Bldg., 550 Main St. 45202, Tel 513-684-2944
Cleveland—Room 600, 666 Euclid Ave., 44114, Tel 216-522-4750

OKLAHOMA
Oklahoma City—4024 Lincoln Blvd., 73105, Tel 405-231-5302

OREGON
Portland—Room 618, 1220 SW 3d Ave., 97204, Tel 503-221-3001

PENNSYLVANIA
Philadelphia—9448 Federal Bldg., 600 Arch St., 19106, Tel 215-597-2886
Pittsburgh—2002 Federal Bldg., 1000 Liberty Ave., 15222, Tel 412-644-2850

PUERTO RICO
San Juan—Room 659, Federal Bldg., 00918, Tel 809-753-4555

SOUTH CAROLINA
Columbia—Suite 172, Strom Thurmond Federal Bldg., 1835 Assembly St., 29201, Tel 803-765-5345

TENNESSEE
Memphis—Room 710, 147 Jefferson Ave., 38103, Tel 901-521-3213

TEXAS
Dallas—Room 7A5, 1100 Commerce St., 75242 Tel 214-767-0542
Houston—2625 Federal Bldg., Courthouse, 515 Rusk St., 77002, Tel 713-226-4231

UTAH
Salt Lake City—1201 Federal Bldg., 125 S. State St., 84138, Tel 801-524-5115

VIRGINIA
Richmond—8010 Federal Bldg., 400 N. 8th St., 23240, Tel 804-771-2246

WASHINGTON
Seattle—Rm 706, Lake Union Bldg., Westlake Ave North 98109, Tel 20 5615

WEST VIRGINIA
Charleston—3000 New Fed Quarrier St 25301 Tel 30

WISCONSIN
Milwaukee—Fede
517 East Wiscor
3473

WYOMIN 82001, Tel 307-778-2200
Cheyen
2120
Ex

THE [ ] LARGEST U.S. MULTINATIONAL CORPORATIONS 1979

Rank	Company	Foreign Revenue (millions)	Total Revenue (millions)	Foreign as Percent of Total	Total Operating Profit[a] (millions)	Total Operating Profit[a] (millions)	Foreign as Percent of Total	Foreign Assets (millions)	Total Assets (millions)	Foreign as Percent of Total
	...aco	$44,333	$60,335	73.5	$1,947	$3,434	56.7	$22,645	$41,531	54.5
	...ford	20,481	34,736	59.0	639	1,126	56.7	11,827	22,611	52.3
	General Motors	18,927	28,608	66.2	436	853	51.2	10,840	20,249	53.5
		14,985	42,784	35.0	780	1,589	49.1	10,730	22,085	48.6
		14,172	63,221	22.4	453	3,508	12.9	7,217	30,417	23.7
6	Standard Oil of Calif	14,150	23,232	60.9	563	1,106	50.9	8,321	16,754	49.7
7	Intl Business Machines	11,040	21,076	52.4	1,584	3,111	50.9	11,021	20,771	53.1
8	International Tel & Tel	10,023	19,399	51.7	799	1,461	54.7	10,394	23,342	44.5
9	Gulf Oil	9,229	18,069	51.1	277	791	35.0	5,861	15,036	39.0
10	Citicorp	5,157	7,556	68.3	645	827	78.0	50,931	78,952	64.5
11	Engelhard Min & Chem	5,103	10,174	50.2	110	254	43.2	1,252	2,853	43.9
12	General Electric	4,379	20,073	21.8	274	1,230	22.3	3,715	15,036	24.7
13	Standard Oil of Indiana	3,823	14,961	25.6	363	1,076	33.7	4,350	14,109	30.8
14	Continental Oil	3,456	9,834	35.1	153	451	33.9	2,803	7,445	37.7
15	BankAmerica	3,438	6,964	49.4	177	498	35.5	36,133	81,600	44.3
16	Dow Chemical	3,242	6,888	47.1	369	1,051	35.1	4,403	8,789	50.1
17	Sears, Roebuck	2,834	26,320	10.8	43	905	4.8	1,409	25,836	5.5
18	Xerox	2,787	5,902	47.2	172	465	37.0	2,597	5,578	46.6
19	Chase Manhattan	2,787	4,461	62.5	105	197	53.3	30,822	54,921	56.1
20	Goodyear	2,709	7,489	36.2	229	650	35.3	2,211	5,231	42.3
21	Eastman Kodak	2,687	7,013	38.3	411	1,646	25.0	2,150	6,793	31.7
22	Occidental Petroleum	2,623	6,316	41.5	409	476	86.1	1,864	4,609	40.5
23	E I Du Pont de Nemours	2,572	10,584	24.3	244	1,577	15.5	1,911	8,070	23.7
24	Chrysler	2,552	13,618	18.7	-14	-234	6.0	1,682	6,981	24.1
25	Union Carbide	2,534	7,870	32.2	242	868	27.9	2,242	7,866	28.5

#	Company								
26	Colgate-Palmolive	2,441	4,312	56.6	233	374	62.4	1,203	2,385	50.5
27	Procter & Gamble	2,222	8,100	27.4	80	523	15.3	1,088	4,984	21.8
28	Sun Co.	2,163	7,525	28.7	52	427	12.1	1,281	5,498	23.3
29	F W Woolworth	2,093	6,103	34.3	143	315	45.4	1,045	2,707	38.6
30	Pan American World Airways	2,036	2,205	92.3	176	150	117.4	NM	2,048	NM
31	CPC International	2,031	3,222	63.0	214	295	72.5	1,206	1,861	64.8
32	Coca-Cola	1,983	4,338	45.7	460	732	62.9	1,093	2,583	42.3
33	General Tel & Elec	1,922	8,723	22.0	85	627	13.6	3,299	16,269	20.3
34	International Harvester	1,828	6,664	27.4	180	601	30.0	1,278	4,316	29.6
35	Minnesota Mining & Mfg	1,775	4,662	38.1	356	1,041	34.2	1,288	4,088	31.5
36	Union Oil of Calif	1,767	6,490	27.2	149	750	19.8	720	5,525	13.0
37	Firestone Tire & Rubber	1,707	4,878	35.0	66	−23	PD	1,271	3,486	36.5
38	Atlantic Richfield	1,691	12,298	13.7	99	804	12.3	890	12,060	7.4
39	Tenneco	1,652	8,762	18.9	167	1,176	14.2	2,224	10,134	21.9
40	Kraft	1,575	5,670	27.8	81	389	20.8	628	2,301	27.3
41	Johnson & Johnson	1,506	3,497	43.1	285	546	52.2	1,072	2,382	45.0
42	J P Morgan & Co	1,493	2,448	61.0	136	267	50.8	NA	38,536	NA
43	American Brands	1,490	3,293	45.2	113	505	22.5	1,078	2,897	37.2
44	Halliburton	1,476	6,642	22.2	226	660	34.3	952	3,397	28.0
45	NCR	1,450	2,611	55.6	168	396	42.4	1,175	2,596	45.2
46	Phillips Petroleum	1,447	6,998	20.7	788	1,464	53.8	1,642	6,935	23.7
47	W R Grace	1,420	4,310	32.9	176	449	39.2	913	3,268	27.9
48	General Foods	1,399	5,376	26.0	28	392	7.1	682	2,433	28.0
49	Trans World	1,398	3,720	37.6	123	174	71.0	713	2,387	29.9
50	Monsanto	1,388	5,019	27.6	36	663	5.4	1,615	5,032	32.1

THE 25 LARGEST NON-U.S. MULTINATIONAL CORPORATIONS

Rank	Company/Country	Foreign Revenue (millions)	Total Revenue (millions)	Foreign as Percent of Total	Total Net Income (millions)	Total Assets (millions)
1	Royal Dutch/Shell Group/Neth-Britain	NA	$45,246	—	$2,085	$42,277
2	British Petroleum/Britain	$22,200	27,407	81.0	853	24,463
3	Philips Gloeilampenfabrieken/Neth	13,592	15,096	90.0	327	16,235
4	Unilever/Britain-Neth	NA	18,152	—	510	7,143
5	Nestlé/Switzerland	NA	11,798	—	413	9,095
6	Bayer/Germany	8,030	11,369	70.6	183	12,116
7	Volkswagenwerk/Germany	7,717	13,305	58.0	276	9,935
8	Siemens/Germany	7,294	14,443	50.5	335	15,809
9	Compagnie Française des Pétroles*/France	NA	10,876	—	27	9,881
10	B.A.T. Industries/Britain	6,469	7,751	83.5	411	7,050
11	Daimler-Benz/Germany	6,321	12,066	52.4	295	7,036
12	Renault/France	5,717	12,684	45.1	4†	7,526†
13	BASF/Germany	5,447	10,710	50.9	210	8,681
14	Imperial Chemical Industries/Britain	4,474	8,701	51.4	584	10,504
15	ENI/Italy	NA	12,576E	—	−415	15,405†
16	Hoechst/Germany	3,983	12,044	33.1	167	11,436
17	Saint-Gobain-Pont-à-Mousson/France	3,795	7,579	50.1	92	7,667
18	AEG-Telefunken/Germany	3,236	7,018	46.1	−147	5,124
19	P.S.A. Peugeot-Citroën/France	NA	10,526	—	310	6,204†
20	BL Ltd/Britain	2,607	5,898	44.2	−25	4,067
21	Elf Aquitaine/France	2,248	9,093	24.7	334	12,561
22	Thyssen/Germany	2,026	11,193	18.1	61	7,020
23	Mannesmann/Germany	1,591	6,308	25.2	119	4,622
24	Pechiney Ugine Kuhlmann/France	1,525	6,116	24.9	58	6,061†
25	Montedison/Italy	NA	6,805	—	−317	8,880

Source. *Forbes*, June 25, 1979.
*All figures for 1977; company would have ranked higher if 1978 results were available.
†1977 results
E Estimated.
NA Company does not report revenue outside home country; Forbes ranked company based on estimates for foreign revenue.
Note: Sales and net income are converted at an average rate of exchange for the period, assets are converted at year-end rate of exchange.

II. MAJOR U.S. AND FOREIGN MULTINATIONAL CORPORATIONS

Listed below are the 50 largest U.S.-based multinational corporations and the 25 largest foreign-based multinationals as of 1979. Updates of this listing may be found in periodic issues of *Fortune, Business Week,* and *Forbes*. Similar listings and detailed profiles of numerous multinational firms are maintained by the United Nations Centre on Transnational Corporation, 605 Third Avenue, New York, N.Y. 10016.

III. INTERNATIONAL ACCOUNTING SERVICES

The eight largest U.S. accounting firms, or the "big eight" as they are better known, all offer services for multinational companies. They operate branches throughout the world so that their services are locally available in a variety of foreign countries. Following is a list of these eight firms and a brief description of each.

1. Arthur Andersen, 1301 Avenue of the Americas, New York, NY; 212-956-7700. Operates a single worldwide organization, owned and managed by partners residing in many countries. Its Societé Cooperative operates out of Switzerland to coordinate international operations and assure multinational clients of uniformly high quality service. AA is not as well known outside the U.S. as some of its competitors, but is one of the fastest growing public accounting firms. They have over 125 offices and 17,000 employees.

2. Coopers and Lybrand, 1251 Avenue of the Americas, New York, NY; 212-489-1100. Through an awareness of marketing, and what is seen as price cutting by the competition, they have become one of the world's largest accounting firms. They operate 351 offices in 90 countries with a total of 21,720 partners and employees.

3. Deloitte, Haskins and Sells, 2 Broadway, New York, NY; 212-422-9600. Operates 263 offices in 58 countries with more than 16,000 employees, in addition they have correspondent firms in another 13 countries. Their offices are staffed mainly be nationals familiar with local customs and laws, backed up by professionals from other countries who work on international assignments to serve multinational clients and individuals.

4. Ernst and Ernst, 153 53rd Street, New York, NY; 212-752-8100. Worldwide operations are under the name of Ernst and Whinney International. They operate over 304 offices in 71 countries with 14,000 employees. They believe in a single partnership approach to coordinate activities around the world. They feel this approach offers important advantages in meeting clients' needs.

5. Peat, Marwick and Mitchell, 345 Park Avenue, New York, NY; 212-758-9700. Operates PMM International with partners in 54 countries, who subscribe to common goals to achieve highest professional standards worldwide. Offices are staffed mainly by local nationals, but each office has some non-nationals to provide specialized skills and knowledge.

6. Price Waterhouse, 153 East 53rd Street, New York, NY; 212-371-2000. Believes itself to be the premier public accounting firm dealing with clients who are considered "select." They see their clients' needs as specialized and have established an Industry and Special Services Program which assigns their resources to specific industries or services.

7. Touche, Ross, 1633 Broadway, New York, NY; 212-489-1600. Operates over 315 offices in 80 countries. They have recently enlarged worldwide services by bringing a number of distinguished international firms into Touche-Ross. They emphasize a standardized audit approach and strict quality controls, and they offer a wide range of services to small and medium-sized firms through their program of integrated services.

8. Arthur Young, 277 Park Avenue, New York, NY; 212-922-2000. Operates in 268 cities in 56 countries with over 18,000 employees. They recently formed a European Group (AMSA) which combines their European Client Services with several large European firms. They feel this will make them more effective in responding to economic and political changes and increase their ability to meet the needs of their U.S. based clients with European operations.

IV. INTERNATIONAL LEGAL SERVICES

Listed below are the 50 largest U.S. international law firms by 1980 rank in terms of overall size, their international presence, and the total number of lawyers employed by each.

Rank 1979	1980	Firm Name and Principal Office	Branches and Number of Lawyers	Total Lawyers 1980	1979
1	1	Baker & McKenzie Chicago	Amsterdam (17), Bangkok (12), Bogota (16), Brussels (16), Caracas (28), Frankfurt (19), Geneva (6), Hong Kong (20), London (28), Madrid (15), Manila (9), Mexico City (22), Milano (9), New York (33), Paris (10), Rio de Janeiro (12), Rome (6), San Francisco (12), Sao Paulo (14), Sydney (29), Taipei (6), Tokyo (16), Toronto (19), Washington, D.C. (26), Zurich (14).	544	512
2	2	Shearman & Sterling New York	Paris (14), London (5), San Francisco (3), Hong Kong (2), Abu Dhabi (2), Algiers (1)	312	288
3	3	Vinson & Elkins Houston	Washington, D.C. (13), London (4), Austin, Tex. (3)	288	278
7	4	Sidley & Austin Chicago	Washington, D.C. (31), Los Angeles (12), London (3)	273	231
5	5	Morgan, Lewis & Bockius Philadelphia	Washington, D.C. (74), New York (39), Los Angeles (13), Harrisburg (10), Miami (9)	268	257
4	6	Fulbright & Jaworski Houston	Washington, D.C. (33), London (3), Austin (3), San Antonio (2)	261	260
8	7	Squire, Sanders & Dempsey Cleveland	Washington, D.C. (41), Columbus (10), Miami (5), Brussels (3), Phoenix (1)	250	227
6	8	Pillsbury, Madison & Sutro San Francisco	Washington, D.C. (5), London (2), Los Angeles (1)	249	237
11	9	Kirkland & Ellis Chicago	Washington, D.C. (na)	243	205
10	10	Baker & Botts Houston	Washington, D.C. (17)	222	216

Rank 1979	1980	Firm Name and Principal Office	Branches and Number of Lawyers	Total Lawyers 1980	1979
9	11	O'Melveny & Meyers Los Angeles	Century City (32), Washington, D.C. (17), Newport Beach (6), Paris (5)	222	223
14	12	Gibson, Dunn & Crutcher Los Angeles	Washington, D.C. (15), San Jose (5), London (3), Paris (2), Newport Brach (33), Century City (49), San Diego (6)	221	195
16	13	Jones, Day, Reavis & Pogue Cleveland	Washington, D.C. (54), Los Angeles (25), Columbus, Oh. (9)	221	194
21	14	Fried, Frank, Harris, Shriver & Jacobson New York	Washington, D.C. (65), London (3)	207	191
13	15	Sullivan & Cromwell New York	Washington, D.C. (9), London (3), Paris (3)	206	191
22	16	Skadden, Arps, Slate, Meagher & Flom New York	Washington, D.C. (11), Boston (9), Wilmington, Del. (8)	205	189
17	17	Davis, Polk & Wardwell New York	Washington, D.C. (7), Paris (6), London (3)	203	193
19	18	Simpson, Thacher & Bartlett New York	New York (35), Washington, D.C. (2), Santa Fe (2), London (2), Hong Kong (2), Columbus, Oh. (1)	201	182
15	19	Dewey, Ballantine, Bushby, Palmer & Wood New York	Washington, D.C. (10), Paris (3)	199	194
42	20	Baker, Hostetler & Patterson Cleveland	Washington, D.C. (42), Orlando (15), Columbus, Oh. (28), Denver (6)	192	138
24	21	Cleary, Gottleib, Steen & Hamilton New York	Washington, D.C. (34), Paris (27), Brussels (23), London (4), Hong Kong (2)	191	185
18	22	Mayer, Brown & Platt Chicago	Washington, D.C. (13), London (3), New York (2)	191	193
34	23	Weil, Gotshal & Manges New York	Washington, D.C. (7)	191	164
25	24	Cravath, Swaine & Moore New York	Paris (3), London (2)	187	184
27	25	Paul, Weiss, Rifkind, Wharton & Gibson New York	Paris (2)	187	178
30	26	Cahill, Gordon & Reindel New York	Paris (4), Washington, D.C. (7)	185	169

Rank 1979	Rank 1980	Firm Name and Principal Office	Branches and Number of Lawyers	Total Lawyers 1980	Total Lawyers 1979
12	27	Covington & Burling Washington, D.C.	—	185	190
26	28	Donovan, Leisure, Norton & Irvine New York	London (2), Paris (1), Los Angeles (13), Washington, D.C. (12)	185	180
28	29	Reed, Smith, Shaw & McCloy Pittsburgh	Washington, D.C. (30), Philadelphia (19), Harrisburg (4)	185	168
23	30	Milbank, Tweed, Hadley & McCoy New York	Hong Kong (3), Tokyo (2), London (2), Washington, D.C. (2)	184	187
29	31	Coudert Brothers New York	Paris (33), Hong Kong (14), London (5), Brussels (4), San Francisco (4), Singapore (4), Washington, D.C. (4), Bahrein (1), Rio de Janeiro (1), Riyadh (1)	183	159
32	32	McDermott, Will & Emory Chicago	Washington, D.C. (13), Miami (7)	180	168
20	33	White & Case New York	Washington, D.C. (12), Paris (6), London (5), Hong Kong (4), Palm Beach (3)	179	192
56	34	Seyfarth, Shaw, Fairweather & Geraldson Chicago	Washington, D.C. (50), Los Angeles (15), New York (11), Miami (6)	176	128
40	35	Rogers & Wells New York	Washington, D.C. (17), Los Angeles (16), London (5), Paris (5), San Diego (4)	172	151
31	36	Kaye, Scholer, Fierman, Hayes & Handler New York	Washington, D.C. (8), Palm Beach (1)	164	165
36	37	Pepper, Hamilton & Scheetz Philadelphia	Washington, D.C. (25), Harrisburg (6), Detroit (2), L.A. (2), Allentown, Pa. (1)	160	164
35	38	Foley & Lardner Milwaukee	Madison (11), Washington, D.C. (18)	159	156
55	39	Hunton & Williams Richmond	Washington, D.C. (14), Norfolk (3), Raleigh (9)	157	129
39	40	Kutak, Rock & Huie Omaha	Atlanta (37), Denver (18), Washington, D.C. (13), Minneapolis (6)	157	149
53	41	Dechert, Price & Rhoads Philadelphia	New York (11), Washington, D.C. (10), Denver (2), London (3), Brussels (2), Harrisburg (3)	155	130

Rank 1979	1980	Firm Name and Principal Office	Branches and Number of Lawyers	Total Lawyers 1980	1979
38	42	Cadwalader, Wickersham & Taft New York	Washington, D.C. (30)	151	152
58	43	Stroock & Stroock & Lavan New York	Los Angeles (15), Washington, D.C. (13), Miami (9)	150	127
37	44	Morrison & Foerster San Francisco	Los Angeles (12), Washington, D.C. (6), Denver (5), London (3), Jeddah (2)	149	141
45	45	Proskauer, Rose, Goetz & Mendelsohn New York	Washington, D.C. (5), Los Angeles (2), Boca Raton (2), London (1)	149	137
48	46	Lord, Bissell & Brook Chicago	Los Angeles (5)	147	134
47	47	Hogan & Hartson Washington, D.C.	—	146	134
33	48	Mudge, Rose, Guthrie & Alexander New York	Washington, D.C. (5), Paris (4)	144	148
44	49	Dorsey, Windhorst, Hanna- ford, Whitney & Halladay Minneapolis	St. Paul (6), Rochester, Minn. (5), Great Falls, Mont. (1), Paris (1)	143	138
67	50	Akin, Gump, Hauer & Feld Dallas	Washington, D.C. (76), Austin (4), Houston (1)	142	123

V. INTERNATIONAL TRANSPORT SERVICES

The 25 largest U.S. transport companies:

1. Trans World Airlines, New York, New York
2. United Airlines, Elk, Grove, Illinois
3. Union Pacific, New York, New York
4. United Parcel Service, Greenwich, Connecticut
5. American Airlines, New York, New York
6. Burlington Northern, St. Paul, Minnesota
7. Southern Pacific, San Francisco, California
8. Eastern Airlines, Miami, Florida
9. Pan Am World Airways, New York, New York
10. Santa Fe Industries, Chicago, Illinois
11. Seaboard Coastline Industries, Jacksonville, Florida
12. Delta Airlines, Atlanta, Georgia
13. Missouri Pacific Corp., St. Louis, Missouri

14. Chessie System, Baltimore, Maryland
15. Norfolk and Western Railway, Washington, D.C.
16. Consolidated Freightways, San Francisco, California
17. Southern Railway, Washington, D.C.
18. Northwest Airlines, St. Paul, Minnesota
19. Roadway Express, Akron, Ohio
20. Braniff International, Dallas, Texas
21. Leaseway Transportation, Cleveland, Ohio
22. Western Airlines, Los Angeles, California
23. Illinois Central Gulf Railroad, Chicago, Illinois
24. Continental Airlines, Los Angeles, California
25. Yellow Freight System, Overland Park, Kansas

The cities listed for these companies indicate their central offices. Most of these companies have offices in other major cities as well.

VI.   INTERNATIONAL INSURANCE SERVICES

The following list briefly describes the services offered by the 10 major U.S. insurers in the International Insurance Market (see also pp. B. 16–17).

1. *Allendale Insurance.*   International operations are under the name of Factory Mutual International. The company offers services in almost all of the free countries of the world, specializing in fire insurance. They entered the international market in 1962 and operate through licensed subsidiaries or through local carriers.

2. *Allstate Insurance Companies.*   The company operates subsidiaries in Switzerland, the Netherlands, England, West Germany, Mexico and Japan; and offers personal and commercial property/casualty and life/health coverages. International operations began in 1959.

3. *American Foreign Insurance Association.*   Formed in 1918 by large insurers to act as their worldwide foreign department and underwrite risks on overseas business. AFIA is the largest U.S. worldwide insurance organization operating in 80 countries with 250 branches.

4. *American International Group.*   American International Underwriters is the marketing unit which underwrites nonlife risks for AIG in more than 100 foreign countries. They have about 230 subsidiaries that provide all types of business insurance as well as specialized types of coverage. In addition, life insurance is offered in about 70 countries.

5. *Chubb Corporation.*   Principal foreign operations are in Canada, Australia, the Caribbean, South America, Europe, Hong Kong, and Japan. Their business is conducted through the group's foreign agents, brokers, and branch offices.

6. *Combined Group of Companies.*   Foreign subsidiaries or company branches in Australia, New Zealand, Canada, Ireland, the UK, France, and West

Germany. Accident coverage in New Zealand, and medical and life insurance in Canada, Australia, and the United Kingdom.

7. *Continental Insurance Companies.*   Majority of the group's operations are in Canada, but they also offer insurance in 70 other countries including West Germany, Spain, and Saudi Arabia. They offer property/casualty, reinsurance, and life insurance through local partners or their own licensed branches.

8. *Kemper Insurance.*   The company entered the international market in 1969 and now does business in about 60 foreign countries, including Belgium, Australia, Brazil, Bermuda, and Japan. They operate through subsidiaries as well as through cooperative agreements with local companies, and they offer all types of property/casualty coverage on both a direct and reinsurance basis.

9. *INA International Corporation.*   Operations in 145 countries, mainly in Europe, the United Kingdom, Africa, Canada, Latin America, and the Far East. They have 55 branch offices and 18 subsidiaries, offering major types of property/casualty, marine, aviation, reinsurance, and accident/health coverage.

10. *The Travellers Companies.*   The company is licensed to do business in Canada, the Bahamas, and Japan. Coverage is also offered in Europe, Africa, Asia, Australia, Latin America, and the Caribbean through agreements with the Riunione Adriatica Di Sicurta Group of Milan, Guardian Royal Exchange Assurance of London, and other companies. They provide most types of property/casualty insurance and worldwide employee benefit programs for multinational companies.

VII. INTERNATIONAL RESEARCH AND CONSULTING SERVICES

Consulting is a largely unlicensed, unregulated profession, and as a result services vary widely in terms of the quality and type available. The Institute of Management Consultants offers the title of Certificate Management Consultant to consultants with 5 years experience, and plans to expand certification to include a course and a test. This will give potential clients a better basis for judging consulting firms. The recent emphasis in consulting has been on specialty fields—helping customers solve specific problems—as opposed to the more general approach of setting up new management organizations to oversee diverse operations. The Big Eight accounting firms have become very influential in the consulting field and they all offer "Management Advisory Services." Academicians also serve as an important body of independent consultants.

The following list includes a brief description of the services offered by the 10 largest U.S. consulting firms:

1. Arthur D. Little, 25 Acorn Pk., Cambridge, MA 02140; 617-864-5770. International consulting, research, product development, and engineering for commercial, institutional, and governmental organizations. A multidisciplinary approach combines functional, technical, and industrial and

50 LEADING PROPERTY-CASUALTY COMPANIES AND GROUPS
(1978 NET PREMIUMS WRITTEN IN THOUSANDS OF DOLLARS)

	Total Property-Casualty Companies Premiums	Rank	Total Property-Casualty Premiums Less A&H	A&H Premiums of Property-Casualty Companies	A&H Premiums of Life Companies	Life Insurance Premiums	Total Premium Volume	Rank
State Farm	6,258,003	1	6,178,921	79,082	....	502,827	6,760,830	2
Allstate	4,114,343	2	3,861,443	252,900	4,371	211,955	4,330,669	2
Aetna Life & Casualty	3,419,500	3	3,256,545	162,955	1,708,853	2,458,635	7,586,988	3
Continental Insurance	2,567,046	4	2,472,448	94,598	19,951	67,961	2,654,958	5
Liberty Mutual	2,553,417	5	2,422,914	130,503	3,347	27,065	2,583,829	7
Travelers	2,487,986	6	2,394,232	93,754	1,696,007	1,897,208	6,081,201	4
Hartford Fire	2,425,304	7	2,425,304	....	228,704	111,769	2,765,777	6
INA	2,303,670	8	2,295,703	7,967	277,132	326,814	2,907,616	8
Fireman's Fund	2,178,138	9	2,152,235	25,903	93,894	48,850	2,320,882	9
Farmers Insurance	2,084,045	10	2,084,045	....	27,524	123,098	2,234,667	10
U.S. Fidelity & Guaranty	1,882,287	11	1,864,498	17,789	1,945	43,129	1,927,361	11
Nationwide	1,545,199	12	1,469,045	76,154	126,963	254,156	1,926,318	13
Kemper	1,502,610	13	1,414,898	87,712	116	99,596	1,602,322	12
Crum & Forster	1,433,775	14	1,424,207	9,568	619	11,176	1,445,570	14
Home Insurance	1,427,622	15	1,414,354	13,268	71,793	41,816	1,541,231	15
St. Paul	1,217,010	16	1,216,968	42	55,545	61,720	1,334,275	16
CNA	1,154,068	17	1,128,022	26,046	562,599	365,944	2,082,611	17
American International	1,118,452	18	1,045,160	73,292	36,754	124,915	1,280,121	19
Chubb	996,998	19	991,288	5,710	36,697	81,447	1,115,142	18
Connecticut-General	971,868	20	872,326	99,542	1,386,060	921,000	3,278,928	20
Royal-Globe	903,784	21	899,627	4,157	....	10,868	914,652	22
Commercial Union	859,328	22	854,656	4,672	689	13,881	873,898	21
Prudential of America	820,432	23	746,658	73,774	2,255,272	5,426,261	8,501,965	25
Reliance	799,909	24	797,051	2,858	53,293	26,446	879,648	23
American Financial	724,728	25	720,237	4,491	3,561	77,550	805,839	24
Employers of Wausau	696,286	26	696,289	-3	76,071	18,308	790,665	26

Company							
Ohio Casualty	695,173	27	693,325	1,848	......	7,663	702,836	29
SAFECO	689,582	28	689,589	−7	45,545	63,767	798,894	28
USAA	686,415	29	686,415	......	......	37,936	724,351	30
General Reinsurance	674,818	30	674,818	......	16,873	94,787	786,478	31
American General	655,972	31	654,409	1,563	114,620	611,602	1,382,194	27
Transamerica	638,592	32	638,584	8	559,368	695,820	1,893,780	34
Sentry	620,450	33	602,697	17,753	70,318	98,431	789,199	33
Government Employees	606,710	34	606,710	......	3,500	25,562	635,772	32
General Accident	536,452	35	533,648	2,804	......	......	536,452	38
Lincoln National	519,486	36	506,725	12,761	510,223	794,691	1,824,400	36
American Family	451,209	37	406,821	44,388	1,201	45,069	497,479	39
General Motors	447,050	38	447,050	......	5,402	8,681	461,133	37
America	427,905	39	420,984	6,921	101,827	263,141	792,873	40
Auto-Owners	420,668	40	420,571	97	135	9,771	430,574	42
Teledyne	403,494	41	403,521	−27	109,681	160,645	673,820	38
Auto Club of Southern California	398,631	42	398,631	......	......	......	398,631	41
Auto Club of Michigan	388,677	43	388,145	532	......	3,610	392,287	43
ERC	361,998	44	299,086	62,912	27,206	84,349	473,553	46
American Re-Insurance	356,669	45	356,669	......	......	......	356,669	44
American Mutual Liability	345,321	46	330,162	15,159	52	11,027	356,400	48
Zurich	343,396	47	317,986	25,410	556	4,508	348,460	45
Texas Employers-Employers Casualty	339,700	48	339,454	246	5,066	4,755	349,521	49
Swiss Reinsurance	329,664	49	329,620	44	27,673	43,424	400,761	47
NN Corp.	328,051	50	321,810	6,241	8	1,170	329,229	51

marketing specialists for clients. Specializes in economics and the environment, management processes, project engineering, and applied technology.

2. Booz, Allen and Hamilton, 135 LaSalle St., Chicago, IL 60603; 312-346-1900.   Offers a complete range of management assistance services including counselling and implementation.

3. Arthur Andersen, 69 W. Washington St., Chicago, IL 60603; 312-346-6262.   Their aim is to offer the best professional accounting and related services, emphasizing a combined approach including auditing, tax, and administrative services.

4. Coopers and Lybrand, 1251 Avenue of Americas, New York, NY 10020; 212-489-1100.   Services in all areas relating to planning, organizing, operating, and measuring activities for profit and nonprofit organizations. Specialized teams are used in the areas of health care, banking, education, securities, and insurance.

5. McKinsey, 245 Park Ave., New York, NY 10017; 212-692-6000.   Specializes in top management problem solving and program implementation on priority issues. Their aim is to work in the forefront of advanced management thinking to bring about constructive change, improvement, and adaptation in management techniques.

6. Touche, Ross, 1633 Broadway, New York, NY 10019; 212-489-1600.   They offer studies of efficiency, cost control, new factory operations, agriculture, health services, and transportation services conducted by engineers, mathematicians, economists, statisticians, accountants, social scientists, and other professionals.

7. Peat, Marwick and Mitchell, 345 Park Ave., New York, NY 10022; 212-758-9700.   Services in information processing, management science, manufacturing techniques, accounting systems, marketing, and general management. Special fields include government and institutional management, acquisition advisory services, actuarial services, and environmental economics.

8. Towers, Perin, Forster and Crosby, 600 3rd Ave., New York, NY 10016; 212-661-5080.   Specializes in design and implementation of programs of compensation, organization, and employee development and communication. Emphasis is on the link between achievement of overall goals and objectives and utilization of organization resources.

9. Hay Associates, 1845 Walnut St., Philadelphia, PA 19103; 215-561-7000.   Specializes in top management planning and strategy/policy; organization design and development; management selection, development, and assessment; motivation, compensation, and total reward programs; and human resource management. Hay Huggins deals with pension planning and actuarial services.

10. Price Waterhouse, 1251 Avenue of the Americas, New York, NY 10020; 212-489-8900.   Emphasizes design and implementation of information systems and financial and operational information needed to set direction, shape policies, and guide operations.

VIII. INTERNATIONAL BANKING SERVICES

Listed below are the 100 largest U.S. and overseas commercial banks, ranked by size of deposits in 1978 (data from *American Banker*). Annual updates of this list are available in the *American Banker* and *The Banker* (U.K.) For investment banking services, see appropriate reference works cited in Appendix A.

World
Rank
12/31/78
(Exclusive of Mutual Savings Banks)

1.	Bank of America NT&SA, San Francisco	United States
2.	Deutsche Bank, Frankfurt	Germany
3.	Banque Nationale de Paris	France
4.	Credit Agricole Mutuel, Paris	France
5.	Credit Lyonnais, Paris	France
6.	Citibank NA, New York	United States
7.	Société Générale, Paris	France
8.	Dresdner Bank, Frankfurt	Germany
9.	Dai-Ichi Kangyo Bank Ltd., Tokyo	Japan
10.	Chase Manhattan Bank NA, New York	United States
11.	Westdeutsche Landesbank Girozentrale, Duesseldorf	Germany
12.	Fuji Bank Ltd., Tokyo	Japan
13.	Sumitomo Bank Ltd., Osaka	Japan
14.	Commerzbank, Duesseldorf	Germany
15.	Mitsubishi Bank Ltd., Tokyo	Japan
16.	Sanwa Bank Ltd., Osaka	Japan
17.	Industrial Bank of Japan, Ltd., Tokyo	Japan
18.	Barclays Bank Ltd., London	United Kingdom
19.	National Westminster Bank Ltd., London	United Kingdom
20.	Bayerische Vereinsbank, Munich	Germany
21.	Bayerische Landesbank Girozentrale, Munich	Germany
22.	Long-Term Credit Bank of Japan Ltd., Tokyo	Japan
23.	Cooperative Centrale Raiffeisen-Boerenleenbank, Utrecht	Netherlands
24.	Amsterdam-Rotterdam Bank, Amsterdam	Netherlands
25.	Swiss Bank Corp., Basle	Switzerland
26.	Algemene Bank Nederland, Amsterdam	Netherlands
27.	Bayerische Hypotheken- und Wechsel-Bank, Munich	Germany
28.	Tokai Bank Ltd., Nagoya	Japan
29.	Union Bank of Switzerland, Zurich	Switzerland

30.	Royal Bank of Canada, Montreal	Canada
31.	Banca Nazionale del Lavoro, Rome	Italy
32.	Manufacturers Hanover Trust Co., New York	United States
33.	Taiyo Kobe Bank, Ltd., Kobe	Japan
34.	Canadian Imperial Bank of Commerce, Toronto	Canada
35.	Bank of Tokyo, Ltd.	Japan
36.	Mitsubishi Trust & Banking Corp., Tokyo	Japan
37.	Mitsui Bank, Ltd., Tokyo	Japan
38.	Sumitomo Trust & Banking Co., Ltd., Osaka	Japan
39.	Morgan Guaranty Trust Co., New York	United States
40.	Daiwa Bank, Ltd., Osaka	Japan
41.	Midland Bank Ltd., London	United Kingdom
42.	Banca Commerciale Italiana, Milan	Italy
43.	Lloyds Bank Ltd., London	United Kingdom
44.	Mitsui Trust & Banking Co., Ltd., Tokyo	Japan
45.	Bank fuer Gemeinwirtschaft, Frankfurt	Germany
46.	Credit Suisse, Zurich	Switzerland
47.	Bank of Montreal	Canada
48.	Société Générale de Banque, Brussels	Belgium
49.	Chemical Bank, New York	United States
50.	Nippon Credit Bank, Ltd., Tokyo	Japan
51.	Banco do Brasil, Brasilia	Brazil
52.	Kyowa Bank, Ltd., Tokyo	Japan
53.	Bank of Nova Scotia, Toronto	Canada
54.	Barclays Bank International Ltd., London	United Kingdom
55.	Hessische Landesbank-Girozentrale, Frankfurt	Germany
56.	Continental Illinois National Bank and Trust Co., Chicago	United States
57.	Yasuda Trust & Banking Co. Ltd., Tokyo	Japan
58.	Norddeutsche Landesbank Girozentrale, Hanover	Germany
59.	Banco di Roma, Rome	Italy
60.	Deutsche Genossenschaftsbank, Frankfurt	Germany
61.	Credito Italiano, Milan	Italy
62.	Monte dei Paschi di Siena	Italy
63.	Bankers Trust Co., New York	United States
64.	Toronto Dominion Bank	Canada
65.	Saitama Bank Ltd., Urawa	Japan
66.	First National Bank, Chicago	United States
67.	Istituto Bancario San Paolo di Torino, Turin	Italy
68.	Toyo Trust & Banking Co. Ltd., Tokyo	Japan
69.	Security Pacific National Bank, Los Angeles	United States

70.	Banque Bruxelles Lambert, Brussels	Belgium
71.	Nederlandsche Middenstadsbank, Amsterdam	Netherlands
72.	Hongkong & Shanghai Banking Corp., Hong Kong	Hong Kong
73.	Standard Chartered Bank Ltd., London	United Kingdom
74.	Wells Fargo Bank NA, San Francisco	United States
75.	Kredietbank, Brussels	Belgium
76.	Hokkaido Takushoku Bank, Ltd., Sapporo	Japan
77.	Bank of Yokohama, Ltd.	Japan
78.	Banco Central, Madrid	Spain
79.	Post-Och Kreditbanken, Stockholm	Sweden
80.	Banco Espanol de Credito, Madrid	Spain
81.	Commonwealth Banking Corp., Sydney	Australia
82.	Creditanstalt-Bankverein, Vienna	Austria
83.	Banco di Napoli, Naples	Italy
84.	Wuerttemtergische Kommunale Landesbank-Giro., Stuttgart	Germany
85.	Svenska Handelsbanken, Stockholm	Sweden
86.	Banco Hispanico-Americano, Madrid	Spain
87.	Marine Midland Bank, Buffalo, N.Y.	United States
88.	Bank of New South Wales, Sydney	Australia
89.	Crocker National Bank, San Francisco	United States
90.	Skandinaviska Enskilda Banken, Stockholm	Sweden
91.	Landesbank Rheinland-Pfalz Girozentrale, Mainz	Germany
92.	State Bank of India, Bombay	India
93.	Deutsche Giro.-Deutsche Kommunalbank, Frankfurt	Germany
94.	Lloyds Bank International Ltd. London	United Kingdom
95.	Bank Leumi le-Israel, Tel-Aviv	Israel
96.	United California Bank, Los Angeles	United States
97.	International Westminster Bank, Ltd., London	United Kingdom
98.	Landesbank Schleswig-Holstein Girozentrale, Kiel	Germany
99.	Banco de Bilbao	Spain
100.	Banco di Sicilia, Palermo	Italy

IX. INTERNATIONAL ADVERTISING SERVICES

Fifteen Major Advertising Agencies:

1. J. Walter Thompson, 420 Lexington Ave., New York, NY 10022; 212-867-1000.

2. Ogilvy and Mather, 2 E. 48th St., New York, NY 10017; 212-688-6100.

3. Doyle, Dane, Bernbach International, 437 Madison Ave., New York, NY 10022; 212-826-2000.

4. Foote, Cone and Belding, 401 N. Michigan Ave., Chicago, IL 60611; 312-467-9700.

5. Grey Advertising, 777 3rd Ave., New York, NY 10017; 212-751-3500.

6. Needham, Harper and Steers, 909 3rd Ave., New York, NY 10022; 212-758-7600.

7. Wells, Rich, Green, 767 5th Ave., New York, NY 10022; 212-758-4300.

8. Interpublic Group Companies, 1271 Ave. of the Americas, New York, NY 10020; 212-399-8000.

9. Combined Communications, 1111 N. Central Ave., Phoenix, AZ 85002; 602-257-1333.

10. John Blair and Co., 717 5th Ave., New York, NY 10022; 212-752-0400.

11. Young and Rubicam, 285 Madison Ave., New York, NY 10017; 212-953-2000.

12. Leo Burnett Co., Prudential Plaza, Chicago, IL 60601; 312-565-5959.

13. Ted Bates and Co., 1515 Broadway, New York, NY 10036; 212-869-3131.

14. BBDO International, 383 Madison Ave., New York, NY 10017; 212-355-5800.

15. Compton Advertising, 625 Madison Ave., New York, NY 10022; 212-754-1100.

INDEX

Abuse
European Economic Community and, **25** ·
9–11
Acceleration of a loan, 27 · 9
Acceptance Financing, *see* Bankers Acceptances
Accommodation
Conflict management and, **41** · 18, **41** · 22–23,
41 · 24
Accounting
Bibliography, **A** · 8–9
Consolidated financial statements, **23** · 32–37
Double-entry and balance of payments, **2** · 7
Financial reporting, **23** · 41, **23** · 46–47
Foreign currency translation, **23** · 3–4
Current-noncurrent method, **23** · 8, **23** · 9,
23 · 11, **23** · 12
Foreign currency financial statements, **23** · 5,
23 · 7–8, **23** · 14–16
Forward exchange contracts, **23** · 16–18
Gains, **23** · 8, **23** · 13–14
Hedging, **23** · 16–18, **23** · 19–20
Income concept, **23** · 18
Inflation and, **23** · 20, **23** · 27
Methods, **23** · 8–12
Monetary-nonmonetary method, **23** · 8, **23** ·
9–10, **23** · 11, **23** · 12
Proposals for, **23** · 14–18
Reasons for, **23** · 3
Reporting and, **23** · 18
Single-rate method, **23** · 8–9, **23** · 10, **23** · 12
Single-transactions, **23** · 5–6, **23** · 14
Smoothing option, **23** · 18–19
Two-transaction perspective, **23** · 6–7, **23** · 14
Foreign-operations disclosure, **23** · 37–41, **23** ·
42–45
Inflation and, **23** · 20–21
Current-cost adjustments, **23** · 21, **23** · 22–24,
23 · 28, **23** · 29–30
General-price-level adjustments, **23** · 21–22,
23 · 22–23, **23** · 25, **23** · 26
International response to, **23** · 28–32
Translation and, **23** · 27–28
U.S. response to, **23** · 23–28
Losses, **23** · 6, **23** · 8, **23** · 13–14
Major U.S. firms, **B** · 8–9
Multiple-rate methods, **23** · 9–10, **23** · 12
Periodicals on, **A** · 14–15
Temporal method, **23** · 8, **23** · 10, **23** · 11, **23** · 12,
23 · 27

Accounting (*Continued*)
See also Inventory
Accounting Systems
Classification frameworks for, **22** · 4, **22** · 6–7
Descriptive comparisons of, **22** · 3–4, **22** · 5
Inflation accounting, **23** · 28–32
Multinational corporations and, **22** · 28, **22** · 29,
22 · 31–32
National comparisons
Argentina, **23** · 30
Australia, **23** · 30
Belgium, **23** · 31
Brazil, **23** · 31
Canada, **23** · 31
France, **23** · 31
Germany, **22** · 11–17, **23** · 32
Implications of differences in, **22** · 27–29
Japan, **23** · 31
Netherlands, **22** · 17–20, **23** · 31–32
New Zealand, **23** · 32
Poland, **22** · 20–27
South Africa, **23** · 32
Sweden, **22** · 20–23
United Kingdom, **23** · 29–30
Standardization efforts, **22** · 29–35, **23** · 28–32
Statistical classification schemes, **22** · 7–10
Acquisition
Foreign market entry through, **31** · 17–19
Active Corps of Executives (ACE), 10 · 13
Adjustable Peg, 1 · 9
Admitted Insurance, 12 · 19–21
Ad Valorem **Tariff, 9** · 7, **9** · 15, **9** · 19, **26** · 10,
38 · 17
Advertising, 33 · 22–24
Agencies, **33** · 24, **B** · 21–22
Communist countries and, **15** · 35
Marketing mix, **32** · 7–11
See also Promotion
**Advisory Committee for Trade Negotiations
(ACTN), 6** · 8
Africa
Economic integration in, **4** · 34–37
**African Trade Union Confederation (ATUC),
35** · 14
Agency
International commercial banking and, **19** · 9
**Agency for International Development (A.I.D.),
10** · 21, **13** · 28
Merchant marine and, **11** · 12

Agent
  Exporting, **31** · 9–10
  Insurance, **12** · 33
Agent Distributor Service (ADS), 10 · 8–9
Agent Location, 10 · 8–9
Agreement on the Implementation of Article VII
  of the General Agreement, 26 · 8–10
Agreement on Technical Barriers to Trade, 26 ·
  27–28
Agricultural Act of 1956, 26 · 16
Agricultural Adjustment Act of 1933, 26 · 16
Agricultural Products
  Commodity Credit Corporation, **15** · 31
  Common Agricultural Policy, **4** · 19–20
  Communist countries and, **15** · 18, **15** · 32
  Export-Import Bank and, **10** · 18
  Foreign Agricultural Service, **10** · 14, **10** · 15–16,
    10 · 25
  Import restraints, **26** · 16
  Intervention price for, **4** · 19
Agriculture Department, 6 · 11, **10** · 14–16
  Commodity Credit Corporation and, **13** · 28
  Merchant marine and, **11** · 12
  Product standards and, **26** · 28
  Publications, **10** · 25–26
Air Cargo Transportation, 11 · 14–17, **33** · 22
Air Transport Association, 11 · 14
Air Travel, 14 · 16–18
  Cargo transportation, **11** · 14–17, **33** · 22
  Passenger transportation, **14** · 16–18
Alcan
  International organization, **39** · 13–14
All-African Trade Union Federation (AATUF),
  35 · 14
All-Risk Insurance, 12 · 10, **12** · 18
Alternative Optional Gross-Income Method,
  24 · 14
"American Bookkeeping," 22 · 4
American Federation of Labor/Congress of In-
  dustrial Organizations (AFL/CIO), 35 · 17
American Selling Price, 9 · 19, **26** · 10
Andean Group, 7 · 6
  Exporting to, **8** · 9
  Multinational corporations and, **7** · 17
Annual Report on Exchange Arrangements and
  Exchange Restrictions, **17** · 24
Antidumping, *see* Dumping
Antidumping Act of 1916, 15 · 33
Antidumping Act of 1921, 15 · 33,
  26 · 5
Antisubsidy Legislation, 26 · 5
Antitax Haven, 24 · 19
Antitrust
  European Economic Community and, **25** · 8–11
  Laws, **32** · 18–19
AOIP/Beyrard Case, **25** · 26, **25** · 27
Appreciation, 1 · 9
Arab Council of Economic Unity (CAEU), 4 · 34,
  4 · 35
Arbitrage, 18 · 25
  Exchange rate forecasting, **17** · 5–9
Argentina
  Inflation accounting, **23** · 30
ARIMA, 17 · 21–22
Arm's Length Standard, 24 · 23, **24** · 24, **24** · 25
  Technology acquisition and, **37** · 8
  Transfer prices and, **33** · 10

Arms Trade
  State and, **15** · 4
Arusha Agreement, 4 · 23
Asia
  Economic integration, **4** · 37
Asian Currency Market, 18 · 67
Asian Currency Unit (ACU), 18 · 67
Asset-Market Approach
  Exchange-rate analysis through, **18** · 37
Assets, *see* Fixed Assets
Association of Southeast Asian Nations (ASEAN),
    4 · 37, **7** · 6
  Exporting to, **8** · 9
  Multinational corporations and, **7** · 7
Association Treaties
  European Economic Community and, **4** · 23
Atlas of Economic Development, **29** · 9
Atomic Energy Community (Euratom), 4 · 10
Ausfuhrkredit (AKA), 13 · 29
Australia
  Inflation accounting, **23** · 30
Auten v. Auten, **27** · 17
Authority to Purchase (A/P), 13 · 12
Automatic Events of Default, 27 · 9
Avoidance Paths
  Conflict management and, **41** · 18, **41** · 20, **41** · 23

Back-to-Back Letter of Credit, 13 · 11–12
Back Translation, 30 · 24
Badger Company, 35 · 23
Balance of Payments
  Closed economies and, **2** · 22
  Currency, **2** · 8
  Definition, **2** · 3–7
  Double-entry accounting and, **2** · 7
  Eurocurrency market and, **18** · 45, **18** · 48–49,
    18 · 57
  Exchange rates and, **2** · 8, **18** · 12, **18** · 34–35
  International commercial banking, **19** · 8
  International Monetary Fund presentation, **2** ·
    9–15, **2** · 16
  Monetary approach, **2** · 18–21
  Multinational corporations, **7** · 9, **7** · 11, **16** · 9,
    16 · 11
  Overall balances, **2** · 8
  Overall payments
    International Monetary Fund and, **2** · 13–15,
      2 · 16
    Macroeconomic policy, **2** · 15–16
    U.S. approaches, **2** · 16–21
  Reporting systems, **2** · 7
  Trade barriers and, **9** · 3, **9** · 5
  Use of statistics, **2** · 21–22
  Valuation and timing, **2** · 7–8
  See also Foreign-Exchange Market
Balance on Goods
  Services and Remittances, **2** · 11–12
Balance Sheet
  Germany, **22** · 12–15
  Hedging, **34** · 6
  Netherlands, **22** · 19
  Poland, **22** · 26–27
Balancing
  Corporate planning and, **40** · 16
Bankers Acceptances, 11 · 14, **13** · 10, **13** · 21
  Advantages, **13** · 24
  Market, **13** · 24–25

Bankers Acceptances (*Continued*)
Types, **13** · 21–24
Use of, **13** · 4–5
Bank for International Settlements (BIS), 5 ·
16–17, **18** · 40, **19** · 15
Banking
Communist countries and, **15** · 20
National, **19** · 3–4, **19** · 5
Risk, **19** · 15–17
Banking Corporations, 19 · 11, **20** · 4
Bank of England Quarterly, **17** · 24
Bank Secrecy Act of 1970, 24 · 29
Banque Française pour le Commerce Exterieur
(BFCE), **13** · 29
Barometric Analysis, 29 · 18–20
Barter Transactions, 15 · 38–39, **33** · 9
Basic Agreement
European Economic Community and, **25** · 17–19
Basic Balance
Balance of payments and, **2** · 12–13
Basic Guide to Exporting, **10** · 24
Basle Accord, 18 · 96
Bayer/Gist-Brocades Agreement, 25 · 17–20,
25 · 23
Beecham/Parke Davis Case, **25** · 14–16, **25** · 22
Behavioristic Segmentation, 33 · 6
Belgium
Inflation accounting, **23** · 31
Bermuda Agreement, 14 · 16–17
Berne Union, 15 · 31
Bias in Marketing Research
Culture and, **30** · 7
Response, **30** · 21–22
Scoring procedures, **30** · 28
Bid Bond, 12 · 13
Bilateralism
State trading and, **15** · 11, **15** · 13
Bilateral Payment Arrangements, 18 · 16
Bilateral Tax Treaties, 24 · 9
Borrowing through international finance sub-
sidiary and, **24** · 28–29
Bill of Exchange, 11 · 13
Bill of Lading, 11 · 13, **31** · 10
Bloc Arrangement, 3 · 3
See also specific blocs
Block-Exemption Regulation
European Economic Community patent
licensing agreements and, **25** · 25–26
Bonds
Eurobonds, **18** · 87, **18** · 90, **92** · 94
Foreign, **18** · 90, **18** · 94–95
Surety, **12** · 12–15
Yankee, **18** · 90
See also International Bond Market
Border Tax Adjustments
General Agreement on Tariffs and Trade and,
5 · 20
Boston Consulting Group Portfolio Model, 29 · 29,
29 · 30
Bottin Europe, **33** · 6–7
Bottin International, **33** · 6–7
Bottom-Up Planning, 40 · 5
Box-Jenkins Technique, 17 · 22
Boycott
Income related to, **24** · 20
Branch Banking Overseas, 19 · 9, **19** · 10, **19** · 11,
20 · 4

Branch Income
Taxation, **24** · 4
Brand Loyalty, 32 · 8
Brand Name
Protection and selection of, **33** · 13–14
Brazil
Inflation accounting, **23** · 31
Bremen v. Zapata Off-Shore Co., **27** · 20
Bretton Woods Agreement, 1 · 9, **3** · 10
See also International Monetary Fund;
World Bank
Bribery
Conflict issue, **41** · 4, **41** · 6–7
Taxation and, **24** · 20
Britain, *see* United Kingdom
Broadcast Media, 33 · 23
Brokers
Foreign-exchange trading, **18** · 26
Insurance, **12** · 23
Brussels Definition of Value, 9 · 19
Brussels Tariff Nomenclature (BTN), 9 · 19
Budget
Risk and, **12** · 3
Buffer-Stock Financing Facility, 5 · 15
Bulk Carriers, 11 · 6
Business America, **10** · 24
Business International, 29 · 4–5, **29** · 13
Business Law, *see* International Business Law
Business-Sponsored Promotions, 10 · 10
Business Unionism, 35 · 6
Buy-American Act of 1933, 9 · 18, **26** · 35
Buyer Behavior, 32 · 13–14
Buying Agent, 33 · 17

Cafe Hag Case, **25** · 31–32
Campari Case, **25** · 26
Canada
Inflation accounting, **23** · 31
Canadian-American Automobile Agreement, 9 · 6
Capital
Balance of payments and, **2** · 5–6, **2** · 7
Capital Budgeting, 34 · 10–11
Capital Controls, 18 · 16
Eurocurrency market and, **18** · 46–48
International commercial banking and, **19** · 8
Capital Gains
Taxation and, **24** · 7–8
Capital Losses
Taxation and, **24** · 8
Cargo Insurance, 12 · 20–21
Cargo Liners, 11 · 3–4
Cargo Transportation, *see* International
Transportation
Caribbean Community (CARICOM), 4 · 31, **4** · 33
Caribbean Free Trade Area (CARIFTA), 4 · 31
Carnet, 33 · 26
Cartel Organizations, 7 · 7
See also specific cartels, ie, Organization of
Petroleum Exporting Countries
Cash in Advance, 33 · 11
Catalog Exhibitions, 10 · 10–11
Centrafarm v. American Home Products, **25** ·
35–36
Centrafarm B. V. v. Winthrop B. V., **25** · 32
Centrafarm v. Sterling Drug, **25** · 31, **25** · 32–33
Central African Customs and Economic Union
(UDEAC), **4** · 34, **4** · 35, **4** · 36

Central American Common Market (CACM), 4 · 31, 4 · 32–34, 8 · 9
Central Banks
  Balance sheet, 2 · 9
  Intervention in foreign exchange markets, 3 · 4, 13 · 27
Centrally Planned Economies, *see* Communist Countries
Center on Transnational Corporations, 7 · 8
CEPAL, 4 · 31
Channel of Distribution, 32 · 11–12, 33 · 16–22
CHIPS System, 18 · 71–72
Choice-of-Law Clause
  Loan agreement and, 27 · 17–19
C.I.F. (Cost, Insurance, Freight) Quotation, 31 · 11, 33 · 8, 33 · 9, 33 · 10
Citibank
  International organization, 39 · 18
Clark Equipment
  International division, 39 · 8
Closed Economies
  Balance of payments and, 2 · 22
Codes of Conduct, 28 · 3–4
  Effects of, 28 · 7–8
  Elements of, 28 · 4–6
  Historical perspective, 28 · 8–12
  Need for, 28 · 4
  United Nations, 28 · 8, 28 · 9–11
    Commission on Transnational Corporations, 28 · 6, 28 · 12–15
    Organization for Economic Cooperation and Development, 28 · 5, 28 · 6, 28 · 8, 28 · 11–12, 28 · 20–22
    Conference on Trade and Development, 28 · 5, 28 · 6, 28 · 9–10, 28 · 11
Codetermination
  West Germany and, 35 · 7
Collaboration
  Conflict management and, 41 · 18, 41 · 20, 41 · 21–22, 41 · 24
Collective Farm, 15 · 18
Commerce, Department of (DOC), 6 · 11
  Commercial intelligence and marketing information, 10 · 7–9, 29 · 7–8
  Counseling and assistance, 10 · 5–6
  Countervailing duty and, 9 · 11, 26 · 21–24
  District office directory, B · 3–5
  Dumping and, 26 · 24–25
  Merchant marine and, 11 · 12
  Organization, 10 · 3–5
  Product standards, 26 · 28
  Promotion, 10 · 9–12
  Publications, 10 · 23–25, 17 · 24, 33 · 3, 33 · 4, 33 · 7, 33 · 19
  See also International Trade Administration; Multilateral Trade Negotiations
Commerce Business Daily, 10 · 12
Commercial Bank Guarantee Programs
  Export-Import Bank, 10 · 17
Commercial Banking, *see* International Commercial Banking; International Investment Banking
Commercial Discount Corporation v. Lincoln First Commercial Corporation, 27 · 17
Commercial Letters of Credit, *see* Letters of Credit

Commercial News USA, 10 · 12
Commercial Solvents Corp. v. Commission, 25 · 11–12
Commission Notice of 1968, 25 · 15
Commodity Credit Corporation (CCC), 10 · 16, 13 · 28, 15 · 31
Commodity Exchange (COMEX), 18 · 34
Commodity Inconvertibility, 4 · 26, 15 · 22
Common Agricultural Policy (CAP), 4 · 19–20
Common External Tariff (CET), 4 · 16, 9 · 6
Common Market, 9 · 6
  Establishment, 4 · 9
  Exporting to, 8 · 9
  Product liability, 32 · 19
  Uniform export price, 33 · 8
  See also Central American Common Market; European Economic Community
Communist Countries
  Accounting, 22 · 20–27
  Agriculture organization, 15 · 18
  Banking, 15 · 20
  Communist Party, 15 · 17
  Government, 15 · 17
  Industry organization, 15 · 17–18
  Joint venture, 31 · 19
  Money, 15 · 20
  Planning, 15 · 18–20, 15 · 23
  Prices, 15 · 20–21
  State Trading
    Council for Mutual Economic Assistance, 4 · 7, 4 · 25–30, 4 · 39, 4 · 42, 15 · 23–27
    Currency, 15 · 22–23
    Economic integration and, 4 · 7–8, 4 · 10, 4 · 39
    Exporting to, 32 · 8
    General Agreement on Tariffs and Trade, 15 · 16
    Imports from, 26 · 15–16, 38 · 17
    Most-favored-nation status and, 15 · 32, 38 · 17
    Organization, 15 · 21–22
    Trade flow planning, 15 · 23
    See also East-West Trade
Communist Party, 15 · 17
  See also Communist Countries
Community Institutions
  European Economic Community, 25 · 7
Compagnie Française pour l'Assurance du Commerce Extérieur (COFACE), 13 · 29
Company Performance, *see* Marketing Information
Comparative Advantage
  Law of, 1 · 3–4, 6 · 4
Compensatory Financing, 2 · 13–14, 5 · 15
  International Monetary Fund and, 3 · 9
"Compensatory Official Financing," 2 · 13–14
Competition
  Conflict management and, 41 · 17, 41 · 20, 41 · 23
  European Economic Community and, 25 · 8–11, 25 · 28
  Market and, 29 · 15
  Multinational corporations and, 7 · 9, 7 · 10, 7 · 13
Complementarity Agreements, 4 · 10
Composite of Currencies, 3 · 3
Composition
  International investment banking and, 20 · 17
Compound Tariff, 9 · 7

Compressibility Ratio, 21 · 8
Compromise Paths
  Conflict management and, **41** · 18–19, **41** · 20,
    41 · 23–25
Computed Value
  Customs valuation by, **26** · 9, **26** · 10
Conduct, *see* Codes of Conduct
Confirmed Irrevocable Letter of Credit, 13 · 11,
  31· 11
Confirming Houses, 33 · 11
Conflict Management, 41 · 3–4
  Bibliography, **A** · 12
  Consequences of, **41** · 8–9
  Incentive systems for, **41** · 25–26
  International division elimination and, **39** · 7–12
  Issues, **41** · 4, **41** · 6–7
  Locus, **41** · 4–5, **41** · 13
  Opponents, **41** · 5, **41** · 8
  Strategies for dealing with, **41** · 9–11, **41** · 16–17
    Accommodative-mode, **41** · 18, **41** · 22–23,
      41 · 24
    Avoidance paths, **41** · 18, **41** · 20, **41** · 21–23
    Collaboration-mode, **41** · 18, **41** · 20, **41** · 21–22
    Competitive paths, **41** · 17, **41** · 20, **41** · 23
    Compromise paths, **41** · 18–19, **41** · 20, **41**
      · 23–25
    Interests and, **41** · 14–15
    Power and, **41** · 13–14, **41** · 21
    Relations and, **41** · 15–16, **41** · 20–21
    Sequential-mode, **41** · 20–21, **41** · 22
    Simultaneous-mode, **41** · 19–20
    Single-mode, **41** · 17–19
    Stakes and, **41** · 11–13, **41** · 21
  Tactics, **41** · 8
  Task systems for, **41** · 25, **41** · 26–27
  Trends in, **41** · 27–28
Conoco
  International division, **39** · 13
Consignment, 13 · 5, **13** · 8
Consolidated Financial Statements, 23 · 32–37
Consolidated Goodwill
  German practices, **22** · 14–15
Consolidated Tax Returns, 24 · 8
Consortium Bank, 19 · 9, **19** · 11
Consulting Firms
  Major U.S., **B** · 15, **B** · 18
Consumer Markets
  Competition in, **29** · 15
  International market segment, **32** · 13–14, **33** · 6
Consumer Price Levels
  Purchasing power parity theory, **17** · 12–14
Containerization, 11 · 6–7
  Air cargo, **11** · 16–17
  Maritime, **11** · 6–7
Container Ships, 11 · 6–7
Contests
  Sales promotion and, **33** · 24–25
Continental Can v. *Commission,* **25** · 10, **25** · 11,
  25 · 12, **25** · 13
Contingency Planning, 40 · 4
Contingent Insurance, 33 · 22
Contract Manufacturing
  Foreign market entry through, **31** · 15
Contractors Guarantee Program, 10 · 18
Contracts
  International business through, **25** · 5

Contracts (*Continued*)
  Specialized agreements of European Economic
    Community, **25** · 16–20
  Manufacturer and sale agreements, **25** · 20–22,
    25 · 23
Contracts in East-West Trade, 15 · 36–38
Contractual Agreements
  Market entry through, **31** · 4–5, **31** · 5–6,
    31 · 12–16
  Technology transfer by, **37** · 6
Controlled Foreign Corporation (CFC), 24
  · 17–18, **24** · 19, **24** · 20, **24** · 21
Controlled Group, 24 · 23–25
Controlled Offshore Manufacturing, 38 · 4
Convenience Sampling, 30 · 17
Convenience Translations
  Financial reports, **23** · 46
Conversion, 23 · 3
Conversion Loss, 23 · 6
Convertibility
  Currency, **3** · 3
Convertible Bonds
  Eurobonds, **18** · 92
  Foreign bonds, **18** · 95
Convertible Premium, 18 · 92
Cooperator Program
  Agriculture Department, **10** · 14
Coordinating Committee (COCOM), 15 · 28, **15**
  · 29–30
Coproduction Agreement
  East-West trade, **15** · 40
  Market entry through, **31** · 15–16
Copyrights
  European Common Market and, **25** · 31
Corporate Planning
  Balancing, **40** · 16
  Bibliography, **A** · 7
  Bottom-up, **40** · 5
  Contingency, **40** · 4
  Criteria, **40** · 14–15
  Department for, **40** · 19–23
  Diversification, **40** · 6–7
  Future of, **40** · 23–25
  Information for, **40** · 16–19
  Linking, **40** · 16
  Long-term planning, **40** · 10–11, **40** · 12
  Medium-term planning, **40** · 11, **40** · 13
  Purposes, **40** · 3–6
  Role of, **40** · 14–16
  Route, *see* Market Entry
  Short-term planning, **40** · 13–14
  Top-down, **40** · 5
  See also Market Entry
Corporate Taxation, *see* Taxation
Correspondent Banking Relationships, 19 · 8–9
Costa v. *Enel,* **25** · 28
Cost, Insurance, Freight (C.I.F.) Quotation, 31 · 11,
  33 · 8, **33** · 9, **33** · 10
Cost-Plus Method, 24 · 25, **32** · 6
Council for Mutual Economic Assistance
  (COMECON), 4 · 7, **4** · 25–30, **4** · 39, **4** · 42,
  15 · 23–27
Counterpurchase Agreements, 15 · 38–39
Countervailing Duty, 1 · 8, **9** · 11, **9** · 13, **26** · 19–24
  General Agreement on Tariffs and Trade and,
    5 · 21

Country Risk, 1 · 13, 21 · 3−5
 External economic aspects, 21 · 6−8
 Financial management and, 34 · 8−10
 Internal rate of return and, 34 · 11
 International banking and, 19 · 16−17
 International business decisions and, 21 · 17−19
 Liquidity aspects, 21 · 8
 Monetary aspects, 21 · 6
 Political aspects, 21 · 8−10
 Rating system, 21 · 10−17
 Structural aspects, 21 · 5−6
 Syndicated loans, 18 · 82, 18 · 83
 See also Political Risk
Courtesy Bias, 30 · 22
Covenants
 International lending and, 27 · 7−9
Covered Interest Arbitrage, 18 · 25
 Eurocurrency market and, 18 · 66
 Exchange rate determination and, 18 · 37
Covered Investment, 1 · 13
Covering, 34 · 5
 Exchange rate forecasting and, 17 · 26−27
Crawling Peg, 1 · 9
Credit, *see* Financing; Letters of Credit
Creditable Foreign Taxes, 24 · 10−11, 24 · 12
Credit Risk, 13 · 5
 International commercial banking and, 19 · 16
 Syndicated loan and, 18 · 83
Credit Swap
 International investment banking and, 20 · 13−14
Credit Tranches, 5 · 14
 International Monetary Fund and, 3 · 8
Cross-Default Provision, 27 · 8
Cruise Business, 14 · 13
Cultural Self-Referent Bias, 30 · 28
Culture
 Bibliography, A · 4−5
  Periodicals, A · 13−14
 Marketing and, 29 · 10, 29 · 11, 32 · 17−18
 Marketing research, 30 · 7
Cumulative Revolving Credit, 13 · 11
Currency
 Composite, 3 · 3
 Convertibility, 19 · 7
 Multiple, 18 · 16
 See also Exchange Rates; Foreign Exchange;
  International Monetary System;
  International Payments
Currency of Quotation, 33 · 11
Currency Risk, 13 · 16, 13 · 25
 International banking and, 19 · 17
Currency Swap
 International investment banking and, 20 · 13
Current Account
 Balance of payments, 2 · 12
Current Balances
 Balance of payments, 2 · 11−12
Current-Cost Adjustments, 23 · 21, 23 · 22−24,
 23 · 28, 23 · 29−30
Current-Noncurrent Accounting Method, 23 · 8,
 23 · 9, 23 · 11, 23 · 12
Customs Bond, 12 · 12−13
Customs Classification and Valuation, 9 · 18−19,
 26 · 8−10
 See also Imports; Tariffs
Customs Union, 4 · 9, 9 · 6
 European Community and, 4 · 15−16, 4 · 17

Customs Union (*Continued*)
 Theory of, 4 · 3−5
 Treaty of Rome, 25 · 7

DaCosta-Bourgeois-Lawson Clusters, 22 · 7−9
Data Extrapolation Techniques, 29 · 17−22, 29 · 23,
 29 · 24
Debt-Service Ratio, 21 · 8
Deducted Value
 Customs valuation by, 26 · 9−10
Deemed Dividend, 34 · 7−8
Deemed-Paid Credit, 24 · 15
 Controlled foreign corporation and, 24 · 18
Deemed Tax, 34 · 6
Default
 Events, 27 · 8−9
Defense, Department of, 6 · 11
 Arms trade and, 15 · 4
 Merchant marine and, 11 · 12
Deferred Payment, 13 · 10
***DeLaval/Stork* Case, 25 · 13−14**
Delphi Techniques, 29 · 31
Demand
 Analysis techniques, 29 · 17−22, 29 · 23, 29 · 24
 Marketing research for estimating, 30 · 5
Demographic Segmentation, 33 · 6
Departments of U.S. Government, *see specific*
  departments, ie, Agriculture Department;
  Commerce, Department of; *etc.*
Depreciation, 1 · 9
 Exchange rate and, 17 · 15−16
 Germany, 22 · 14
 Keynesian approach to, 1 · 11
 Poland, 22 · 25−26
 Sweden, 22 · 21
 Taxation and, 24 · 7
Destabilizing
 Speculation as, 1 · 11
***Deutsche Grammophon* v.** *Metro SB Grössmarkte,*
 25 · 31
Devaluation, 1 · 9
 Hedging and, 33 · 11
Developing Countries
 Accounting systems, 22 · 28−29
 Conflict management and, 41 · 27
 Economic integration, 4 · 6−7, 4 · 9−10,
  4 · 30−37, 4 · 39, 4 · 41−42
 Economies, 32 · 21
 Exchange rates, 18 · 16
 Generalized System of Preferences and, 38 · 17
 Illiteracy, 30 · 23−24
 Insurance and, 12 · 22
 International banking and, 19 · 17−18
 International reserves and, 18 · 20
 International transportation and, 11 · 8−9
 Joint venture in, 31 · 19
 Macrosurvey for market potential in, 29 · 22,
  29 · 23, 29 · 24
 Multinational corporations and code of conduct
  for, 28 · 8−9
  Technology transfer and, 26 · 15, 37 · 5,
   37 · 6−7, 37 · 10−11
 New International Economic Order, 28 · 9
 OPEC surplus recycling and, 18 · 87
 Research and development, 36 · 21−22
 Tariff preferences for, 26 · 10−12
 Technology transfer to, 36 · 14−16

Developing Countries (*Continued*)
Technology transfer to (*Continued*)
Appropriateness of technology and, **37** · 9−11
Control of, **37** · 11−15
Cost of acquisition, **37** · 8−9
Eastern European countries, **36** · 10−11
International intervention in, **37** · 13−15
Japan and Western countries and, **36** · 15−16
Mechanisms of, **37** · 5−8
Patents and, **37** · 4−5
Technical cooperation among, **36** · 8−10
Trademarks and, **37** · 5
See also Offshore Sourcing
Differentiated Products, 1 · 5, **32** · 4
Dillon Round of Multilateral Trade Negotiations,
9 · 7
"Dingley" Tariff Act of 1897, 26 · 4
Direct Export Channels, 30 · 6, **31** · 8−9
Direct Exporting, 31 · 8−9, **33** · 17, **33** · 19
Direct Foreign-Tax Credit, 24 · 10−14
Direct Investment, *see* Investment
Directions of Trade, **17** · 24
Directory of British Importers, **33** · 7
Dirty Float, *see* Managed Float
Discount Loan Program, of Export-Import Bank,
10 · 17
Discriminant Analysis
Country risk assessment by, **34** · 9−10
Exchange rate forecasting by, **17** · 23
Discrimination
State trading and, **15** · 11
Disinvestment
Industrial relations and, **35** · 23−24
Distress Dumping, 9 · 10
Distribution, 32 · 11−12, **33** · 16−22
Legal aspects, **32** · 19
Marketing mix and, **32** · 11−12
See also International Transportation
Distributor
Exporting and, **31** · 9−10, **32** · 11−12
Diversification
Corporate planning, **40** · 6−7
Power and, **41** · 14
DOC-sponsored Missions, 10 · 11
Document Against Acceptance Draft (D/A), 13 · 8
Document Against Payment Draft (D/P), 13 · 8
Documentary Draft, 31 · 11
Documentary Draft for Collection, 13 · 8, **13** · 9
Dollar
Defense of, **18** · 42
Foreign exchange market and, **18** · 27
Shortage and international commercial banking,
19 · 7
Dollar bloc (U.S.), 1 · 10
Dollar Bond, 18 · 90
See also International Bond Market
Dollar-Exchange Acceptance, 13 · 24
Domestic and International Business Administra-
tion, B · 3
Domestic International Sales Corporation (DISC),
10 · 20−21, **24** · 25−27, **32** · 19, **33** · 10, **33** · 17,
34 · 8
Domestic Law, *see* National Law
Domestic Subsidies, 26 · 20, **26** · 21
Domestic Trade
Financing, **13** · 23−24
Subsidies, **26** · 20, **26** · 21

Dominance
European Economic Community and, **25** · 8−11
Dominant Position
European Economic Community and, **4** · 17
"Doomsday Tax," 34 · 8
Double Taxation, 24 · 3
Foreign tax credit and, *see* Taxation
Dow Chemical
International organization, **39** · 16−17
Dow Corning
International organization, **39** · 17
Draft
Documentary-draft collection, **13** · 8, **13** · 9, **31** · 11
Sight, **13** · 10, **13** · 14, **33** · 11
Time, **13** · 10, **13** · 11
See also Bankers Acceptances
Dual Adaptation, 32 · 5
Dumping
Antidumping Act of 1916, **15** · 33
Antidumping Act of 1921, **15** · 33, **26** · 15
Antidumping duties, **9** · 10−11, **9** · 12, **26** · 24−25
Communist countries and, **15** · 33−34
Less-than-fair value and, **15** · 33, **15** · 34
Predatory, **9** · 10

East, *see* Communist Countries
East African Common Services Organization
(EASCO), 4 · 35
East African Community (EAC), 4 · 34, **4** · 35−36
East African Development Bank (EADB), 4 · 35
East-West Trade (EWT), 10 · 5, **15** · 34−41
Contracts, **15** · 36−38
Convertible currency debt of Communist
countries, **15** · 32
Dumping, **15** · 33−34
Export Administration Act, **15** · 28−29
Export controls in, **15** · 28
Financing, **15** · 30−32
Foreign direct investment and, **15** · 41
Import restrictions, **15** · 32−33
Industrial cooperation, **15** · 40−41
Negotiations, **15** · 36
Payments in, **15** · 38−39
Policy objectives, **15** · 27
Technology transfer and, **15** · 39−40
Transactions, **15** · 34−36
Eaton
International division, **39** · 11−12
Econometric Forecasting Models, 29 · 21−23
Econometric Models
For Exchange Rates, **17** · 22
Economic Community of the Countries of the
Great Lakes (CEPGL), 4 · 35
Economic Community of West African States
(ECOWAS), 4 · 34, **4** · 35, **4** · 36
Economic Environment
Bibliography, **A** · 3
Marketing and, **29** · 9, **32** · 21, **33** · 4
Marketing mix and, **32** · 21
Economic Exposure, 34 · 4
Economic Growth, 1 · 12
Economic Integration, 4 · 3
Communist countries, **4** · 7−8, **4** · 10, **4** · 39
Council for Mutual Economic Assistance, **4** · 7,
4 · 25−30, **4** · 39, **4** · 42, **15** · 23−27
Developing countries, **4** · 6−7, **4** · 9−10, **4** · 30−37,
4 · 39, **4** · 41−42

Economic Integration (*Continued*)
Economic case for, **4** · 3–8
European Free Trade Area, **4** · 24–25, **4** · 41
Future of, **4** · 40–42
Levels of, **4** · 8–10
Negative, **4** · 8–9, **4** · 11, **4** · 41
Political, **4** · 9, **4** · 37–40
Positive, **4** · 8, **4** · 38
Trade barriers and, **9** · 6
See also European Community; European
Economic Community
Economic Policy, *see* Policy Foundation
Economic Recovery Act, 24 · 14
Economic and Social Council (ECOSOC), 7 · 19
Economic Union, 4 · 9
Economies of Scale, 1 · 4
Edge Act Corporations (EACs), 19 · 11–12, **20** ·
3–5, **20** · 6
Mergers and, **20** · 14
Education
Trade in, **14** · 6–7, **14** · 21
Effective Rate of Protection, 1 · 7, **9** · 7–8
"Effects Theory," 25 · 11–12
Efficient-Market Hypothesis, 18 · 37
Embargo, 9 · 8
EMI **v.** *CBS* **Cases, 25** · 36
Employee Insurance, 12 · 16–17
Employment
Multinational corporations, **16** · 10
Tourism, **14** · 11
Trade barriers and, **9** · 3, **9** · 5
Enlarged Access Policy
International Monetary Fund, **3** · 10
Entertainment
Trade in, **14** · 6–7, **14** · 21
Entrepôt Finance Services, 18 · 66
Entry into Foreign Markets, *see* Market Entry
Environment
Conflict issue, **41** · 4, **41** · 7
See also Economic Environment
Equalization Tax, 24 · 6, **24** · 7
Escape-Clause, 9 · 15, **9** · 16, **26** · 12–16
General Agreement on Tariffs and Trade and,
5 · 24, **5** · 25, **9** · 14–15, **26** · 14, **26** · 15
Ethnocentric Pricing, 33 · 7–8
Ethnocentrism
Conflict management, **41** · 16
Eurobonds, 18 · 87, **18** · 90, **18** · 92–94
See also International Bond Market
Eurocurrency, 1 · 13, **26** · 9–10
Eurodollar loan and, *see* International Lending
Eurocurrency Deposits, 18 · 43, **18** · 57
Eurocurrency Lending, *see* International Lending
Eurocurrency Market, 18 · 3–5
Balance of payments, **18** · 57
Balance-of-payments controls of U.S. and,
18 · 48–49
Characteristics, **18** · 49–54, **18** · 55–56
Controlling, **18** · 5, **18** · 95–99
Definition, **18** · 42–44, **18** · 49–50
Financial centers, **18** · 66–68
Foreign-exchange market and, **18** · 54, **18** · 57
Functions, **18** · 54, **18** · 60–61
Growth and development, **18** · 44–48
Interest parity, **18** · 23
Interest rates, **18** · 64–66
Payments system, **18** · 71–72

Eurocurrency Market (*Continued*)
Sources and uses of funds, **18** · 50, **18** · 58,–59
Theoretical interpretations, **18** · 61–64
Transformation conducted by, **18** · 57, **18** · 60–61,
18 · 63
See also Foreign Exchange Market; International
Bond Market; International Lending
Eurodollar Loan, 18 · 43
See also International Lending
Euromonitor Statistics, 29 · 5, **29** · 6
**European Agricultural Guidance and Guarantee
Fund (FEOGA), 4** · 20
European Coal and Steel Community (ECSC), 4 · 8,
4 · 10
European Common Market, *see* European
Economic Community
European Community (EC), 4 · 10, **4** · 39–40
Coal subsidies, **9** · 17
Communist countries' agricultural imports and,
15 · 32
Customs union development, **4** · 15–16, **4** · 17
Economic union in, **4** · 16–20
Economies, **4** · 13–15
European Coal and Steel Community, **4** · 8, **4** · 10
State trading, **15** · 16
See also European Economic Community
European Court of Justice, 25 · 5
European Currency Snake, 3 · 3, **3** · 4, **4** · 21
See also European Economic Community
European Currency Unit (ECU), 3 · 3–4, **3** · 13,
3 · 14, **4** · 19, **4** · 21, **4** · 22, **18** · 10
European Economic Community (EEC), 4 · 8, **4** · 9,
4 · 10–13, **4** · 41, **4** · 42, **7** · 6, **9** · 6
Accounting practices, **22** · 33–34, **23** · 29
Consolidated financial statements, **23** · 33,
23 · 36–37
Foreign operations disclosure, **23** · 38
Common Agricultural Policy, **4** · 19–20
Competition policy, **4** · 16–17, **25** · 8–11, **25** · 28
Economic integration progress in, **4** · 23–24, **25** · 7
European Currency Unit, **3** · 3–4, **3** · 13, **3** · 14,
4 · 19, **4** · 21, **4** · 22, **18** · 10
European Trade Unions Congress, **35** · 14, **35** · 15
Exchange rate fluctuations, **3** · 3–4
External relations of, **4** · 23
Fiscal harmonization, **4** · 22
Legal principles, **25** · 6–11
Antitrust, **25** · 8–11, **25** · 28
Extraterritorial application of, **25** · 11–12
Market entry into, **25** · 5–12
Industrial property rights and, **25** · 23–27
Joint ventures, **25** · 12–23
Manufacture and sales agreements, **25** · 20–22,
25 · 23
Mergers, **25** · 6, **25** · 10, **25** · 13
Research and development, **25** · 14–16, **25** · 22
Specialization agreements and, **25** · 16–20
Monetary union and, **4** · 20–22
Multinational corporations and, **7** · 17
Regional policy of, **4** · 17–19
Supranational law established by, **25** · 4–5,
25 · 27–28
Treaty of Rome establishing, **25** · 4, **25** · 5, **25** · 6,
25 · 7, **25** · 27–28
Variable levy and, **9** · 12
See also European Monetary System
European Economic Treaties, 4 · 10–11

European Free Trade Area (EFTA), 4 · 9, 4 · 24–25, 4 · 41, 9 · 6, 15 · 16
European Investment Bank, 4 · 13
European Metalworkers Federation, 7 · 7
European Monetary Cooperation Fund (EMCF), 3 · 3, 3 · 13, 4 · 21¬22, 18 · 10
European Monetary System (EMS), 1 · 10, 3 · 4, 3 · 12–14, 4 · 21, 18 · 9–10, 18 · 12, 18 · 40
   European Currency Unit, 3 · 3–4, 3 · 13, 3 · 14, 4 · 19, 4 · 21, 4 · 22, 18 · 10
European Monetary Union (EMU), 4 · 20–21
European Payments Union, 5 · 27
European Regional Development Fund (ERDF), 4 · 18
European Trade Unions Congress, 35 · 14, 35 · 15
European Unit of Account, 4 · 21
   See also European Currency Unit
Even Dates, 18 · 24
Events of Default, 27 · 8–9
Exceptional Financing
   Balance of payments and, 2 · 11–12
Exchange Contract, 26 · 4
Exchange Control, 1 · 9
   Trade barrier and, 9 · 14
Exchange Rate Risk, 1 · 10, 1 · 13, 13 · 26
   Purchasing Power Parity and, 17 · 4
Exchange Rates, 1 · 8–12, 17 · 12, 18 · 4, 18 · 11–16
   Balance of payments and, 2 · 8
   Changes, 1 · 9
   Controls, 1 · 9
   Current system, 1 · 9–10
   Definition, 1 · 8
   Depreciation, 17 · 15–16
   Forecasting, 17 · 3–4
     Evaluating, 17 · 25
     Information sources for, 17 · 24, 17 · 25
     Management intervention in, 18 · 39–42
     Methods, 17 · 19–20, 18 · 35–38
       Advisory services, 17 · 23–24
       Econometric models, 17 · 22
       Evaluation of, 17 · 19–20
       Forward rate, 17 · 20–21
       Leading variables, 17 · 22–23
       Time-series analysis, 17 · 21–22
     Need for, 17 · 4–9, 17 · 9–10
       Arbitrage and, 17 · 5–9, 17 · 10
       Financial markets and, 17 · 5
       Goods markets and, 17 · 4–5
     Risk and, 17 · 26–27
     Theory, 17 · 12
       Governments and, 17 · 13, 17 · 14, 17 · 17–19
       Purchasing power parity and, 17 · 12–14
       Short-run-real exchange rate changes and, 17 · 14–16
       Very short run and, 17 · 11–12, 17 · 16–17
     Uncertainty and, 17 · 25–27
   General Agreement on Tariffs and Trade and, 5 · 26
   Macroeconomy and, 1 · 11–12
   Multiple, 9 · 14, 18 · 12
   Speculation, 1 · 10–11
   Spot, 1 · 10
     Interest-rate differential and, 18 · 23, 18 · 24
     Bibliography, A · 3–4
   See also Fixed Exchange Rates; Floating Exchange Rates; Foreign Exchange; Forward

Exchange Rates (*Continued*)
   Exchange Rate; International Monetary Fund; International Payments
Exchange Regime, 18 · 3
Exchange Stabilization Fund (ESF), 18 · 40
Exclusive Jurisdiction
   Industrial relations and, 35 · 6
"Exhaustion of Rights" Doctrine, 25 · 32
Exhibitions, 33 · 24
   Agriculture Department, 10 · 14
   Commerce Department, 10 · 9–10
Exhibits Schedule, 33 · 24
Existence/Exercise Doctrine
   European Economic Community, 25 · 30
Ex Named Point of Origin, 31 · 11
Expectation Theory
   Exchange rate determination by, 18 · 37, 18 · 38
Expected Return on Investments
   Risk attitude of firm, 17 · 26
Exploratory Research, 30 · 29
Export Administration Act, 15 · 28–29
Export Agents, 33 · 17
Export Briefs, 10 · 15, 10 · 25
Export Contact List Service, 10 · 8
Export Credit Guarantee Department, 13 · 29
Export Development (ED), 10 · 4, 10 · 10
Export-Import Bank, 6 · 12, 10 · 6, 10 · 16–18, 13 · 27
   East-West trade, 15 · 30–31
   Publications, 10 · 26
Export-Information Reference Room, 10 · 6
Exporting to United States, 38 · 16
Export Letter of Credit, 13 · 10, 13 · 12–15
   Bankers acceptance and, 13 · 21–23
Export Mailing List Service (EMLS), 10 · 8
Export Management Company (EMC), 31 · 7–8
Export Marketing Guide for Smaller Firms, 10 · 26
Export Quotas, 9 · 9–10
Exports
   Communist countries, *see* East-West Trade
   Country risk assessment, 21 · 6–7
   Developing countries, 26 · 10–12
   Direct, 31 · 8–9, 33 · 17, 33 · 19
   Direct channels, 31 · 6, 31 · 8–9
   Documentary requirements, 31 · 10
   Domestic international sales corporation and, 24 · 25–27
   Export management company, 31 · 7–8
   Financing, 8 · 4, 8 · 7, 10 · 16–18, 31 · 11
   Indirect, 31 · 6–8
   Indirect channels, 31 · 6, 33 · 17
   Licensing, 9 · 10, 15 · 28–29
     Communist countries and, 15 · 37
   Market entry by, 31 · 4, 31 · 5–12, 40 · 9
   Marketing boards and, 15 · 8
   Offshore sourcing, 38 · 14–15
   Organization, 8 · 4, 8 · 6–7, 31 · 11–12
   Pricing, 31 · 10–11, 32 · 4–6, 33 · 7–12
   Program development, 8 · 3–5
     Desire to export, 8 · 4, 8 · 5–6
     Economic studies for, 8 · 4, 8 · 7
     Entrepreneurial community for, 8 · 4, 8 · 6
     Financing, 8 · 4, 8 · 7
     Incentives, 8 · 4, 8 · 8–9
     Organization, 8 · 4, 8 · 6–7
     Product development, 8 · 4, 8 · 9–10
     Promotion, 8 · 4, 8 · 10–12

Exports (*Continued*)
Program development (*Continued*)
Training, **8** · 5, **8** · 12−13
Restrictions, **26** · 26−28, **32** · 18
See also Trade Barriers
Sales personnel for, **33** · 26
Tax on, **9** · 7
Tax incentives for, **8** · 4, **8** · 8−9, **10** · 20
See also Commerce, Department of; Financing;
State Trading; Technology Transfer
Export Subsidy, 1 · 7−8, **26** · 20−21
Exposure, 34 · 3−4
Current-rate method of translation and, **23** · 10
Foreign currency translation and, **23** · 10, **23** · 11
Hedging and, **34** · 4−6
Expropriation, 41 · 14
Extended Facility, 5 · 15
International Monetary Fund and, **3** · 9
Extension
International investment banking and, **20** · 17
External Affairs, *see* Public Affairs
Extrapolation Techniques, 29 · 17−22, **29** · 23,
29 · 24
Extraterritoriality
European Economic Commission and,
25 · 11−12

Factor Analysis
Exchange Rate Forecasting, **17** · 23
Factor-Price Version of Purchasing Power Theory,
1 · 3
Factor Services, 14 · 3−4
Factors of Production, 14 · 3
Fairs, *see* Trade Fairs
Fair-Trading Rules of General Agreement on
Tariffs and Trade, 5 · 21−22
F.A.S.B. 14, 23 · 37−38, **23** · 40, **23** · 41
F.A.S.B. 33, 23 · 23−28
F.A.S. (Free Along Side) Quotation, 31 · 11, **33** · 10
Federal Open Market Committee (FOMC), 18 · 40
Federal Reserve Act of 1913, 13 · 6
Federal Reserve Bulletin, **17** · 24
Federal Reserve System
Eurocurrency market and, **18** · 46−48
Exchange rate intervention, **18** · 40, **18** · 41, **18** · 42
International banking facilities, **18** · 69−71
Regulation D, **18** · 46, **18** · 47, **18** · 48, **18** · 69, **18** · 70
Regulation Q, **18** · 46−47, **18** · 48, **18** · 69, **18** · 70
Reserves, **18** · 69, **18** · 70
Federal Trade Commission (FTC), 6 · 12
Fidan v. Austral American Trading Corp.,
27 · 19
Fidelity Insurance, 12 · 12
Finance
Periodicals, **A** · 13, **A** · 14−15
See also International Financial Market
Finance Subsidiary
Borrowing through international, **24** · 28−29
Financial Centers, 18 · 66−68
Financial Diversification, 40 · 7
Financial Investment, 1 · 12
See also Investment
Financial Management
Bibliography, **A** · 3−4, **A** · 11
Capital budgeting, **34** · 10−11
Conflict issue of, **41** · 7
Investment decision, **34** · 11−12

Financial Management (*Continued*)
Offshore sourcing, **38** · 18−19
See also Accounting; Country Risk; Financing;
Foreign-Exchange Risk; International
Financial Market; Taxation
Financial Reporting, 23 · 41, **23** · 46−47
Foreign operations disclosure, **23** · 37−41,
23 · 42−45
See also Accounting
Financial Reporting and Changing Prices,
23 · 23−28
Financial Reporting for Segments of a Business
Enterprise, **23** · 37−38
Financial Risk
European Economic Community market entry
and, **25** · 6
Financial Statements
Consolidated, **23** · 32−37
Corporate planning and, **40** · 18
Foreign currency, **23** · 5, **23** · 7−8
Proposals for, **23** · 14−16
Translation methods and, **23** · 10−12
Inflation and, *see* Accounting
Primary, **23** · 47
Secondary, **23** · 47
See also Accounting Systems
Financing
East-West trade and, **15** · 30−32
Evaluation of, **13** · 3−4
Foreign exchange and, **13** · 25−27
Growth and importance, **13** · 4−5
Official agencies, **13** · 27−29
Payment process, **13** · 6−10, **33** · 11
Cash in advance, **33** · 11
Consignment, **13** · 5, **13** · 8
Documentary draft for collection, **13** · 8, **13** · 9
Open account, **13** · 7−8, **33** · 11
Payment in advance, **13** · 7
See also Drafts; Letters of Credit
Strategy, **13** · 5−6
See also Bankers Acceptances
Financing Corporations, 19 · 11, **20** · 4−5
Fire Insurance, 12 · 18
Fiscal Policy, 1 · 11
Five Freedoms Air Traffic, 14 · 16−17
Fixed Assets Valuation
Poland, **22** · 25, **22** · 26
Sweden, **22** · 21
Fixed Exchange Rates, 1 · 9, **18** · 11−12
Bretton Woods Agreement and, **3** · 10−11
International Monetary Fund and, **3** · 3
Fixing Rate, 18 · 26
Flag Fleet
Government support for, **11** · 10
Flags of Convenience/Necessity, 11 · 11−12
Flexible Exchange Rates, *see* Floating Exchange
Rates
Floating Currencies, 18 · 6
Floating Exchange Rates, 1 · 8−9, **3** · 11, **18** · 12,
18 · 16
Financing and, **13** · 5−6
Foreign-exchange market and, **18** · 38−39
International Monetary Fund and, **5** · 12
Managed, **3** · 11
Floating-Rate Notes (FRNs), 18 · 93
Flow
Corporate planning information and, **40** · 16

F.O.B. (Free on Board) Quotation, 31 · 11, 33 · 7, 33 · 8, 33 · 9, 33 · 10, 38 · 17
Fondasol Case, 25 · 27
Food and Agricultural Export Director, 10 · 25
Food for Peace Program, 10 · 16
Force Majeure, 15 · 37
Forecasting
  Conflict management and, 41 · 26
  Market potential, 29 · 17–22, 29 · 23, 29 · 24
  See also Country Risk; Exchange Rates, Forecasting
Foreign Agricultural Reports, 10 · 25
Foreign Agricultural Service (FAS), 10 · 14, 10 · 15–16, 10 · 25
Foreign-Base-Company Income, 24 · 18–21
Foreign-Base-Company Sales Income, 24 · 19
Foreign-Base-Company Services Income, 24 · 19–20
Foreign-Base-Company Shipping Income, 24 · 20, 24 · 21
Foreign Bond, 18 · 90, 18 · 94–95
  See also International Bond Market
Foreign Business Practices: Materials on Practical Aspects of Exporting, International Licensing, and Investing, 10 · 24
Foreign Buyers
  Commerce Department, and, 10 · 12
Foreign Commercial Service (FCS), 10 · 4, 10 · 6, 10 · 7, 10 · 8, 10 · 12
Foreign Corrupt Practices Act, 7 · 10
Foreign Credit Insurance Association (FCIA), 10 · 16–17, 10 · 18, 13 · 27
  Publications, 10 · 26
Foreign-Currency Financial Statements, *see* Financial Statements
Foreign Currency Translation, *see* Accounting
Foreign Direct Investment, 1 · 13–14, 21 · 7
  Offshore, 16 · 9–10
  Vertical, 11 · 14
  See also Investment
Foreign Direct Investment Program (FDIP), 18 · 45, 18 · 46
Foreign Economic Trends (FETs), 10 · 24
Foreign Exchange
  Control, 13 · 26–27
  Financing and, 13 · 25–27
  Market, 1 · 8
  Reserves, 3 · 5
  Tourism and, 14 · 11, 14 · 14
  Translation, *see* Accounting
  See also Exchange Rates; International Payments
Foreign Exchange Market, 18 · 3, 18 · 4
  Eurocurrency market, 18 · 54, 18 · 57
  Exchange rate, 18 · 34–35
  Floating exchange rates, 18 · 38–39
  Forward, 18 · 22–23, 18 · 24, 18 · 27,18 · 29, 18 · 32–33, 18 · 34
  Functions, 18 · 26
  Futures trading and, 18 · 34
  Management and intervention in, 18 · 39–42
  Spot, 18 · 21–22, 18 · 27, 18 · 29, 18 · 32–33
  Swap, 18 · 23–25, 18 · 27, 18 · 29, 18 · 32–33
  Trading and, 18 · 25–34
  See also Eurocurrency Market; Exchange Rates; International Monetary System

Foreign Exchange Risk, 13 · 5–6
  Assessing, 29 · 8
  Exposure and, 34 · 3–4
  Hedging and, 34 · 4–6
  Reducing, 18 · 23
Foreign Government Procurement, 10 · 12
Foreign Leases
  Taxation, 24 · 8–9
Foreign Market Entry, *see* Market Entry
Foreign Nonbank Subsidiaries, 19 · 11
Foreign-Operations Disclosure, 23 · 37–41, 23 · 42–45
Foreign-Personal-Holding Company Income (FPHC), 24 · 18–19
Foreign Policy
  Multinational corporations and, 7 · 10
Foreign Representative
  Product distribution and, 33 · 19–21
Foreign-Source Income Taxation, 24 · 6
Foreign Sovereign Immunities Act, 15 · 14
Foreign State, 27 · 13–14
  Immunity of, 27 · 13–15
  Syndicated loans to, 18 · 73
  See also State Trading
Foreign-Tax Credit (FTC), *see* Taxation
Foreign-Trade Bank (FTB), 15 · 22
Foreign Trade Organizations (FTOs), 15 · 21–22, 15 · 23, 15 · 34, 15 · 35, 15 · 36, 15 · 37, 15 · 38
Foreign Trade Reference Room, 10 · 7
Foreign Traders Index, 10 · 8, 10 · 9
Foreign Traders Index and Trade Lists, 33 · 7
Foreign-Travel Expenditures (Tourism), 14 · 6, 14 · 8–15, 14 · 17
Forum Non Conveniens, 27 · 20
Forum-Selection Clause, 27 · 20–21
Forward Discount, 18 · 24
Forward Exchange Contracts, 23 · 16–18
Forward Exchange Rate, 1 · 10
  Exchange rate forecasting and, 17 · 20–21, 18 · 37, 18 · 38
  Hedging and, 34 · 5
  Speculation and, 1 · 10–11
Forward-Forward, 18 · 25
Forward Premium, 18 · 24
Forward Transactions, 18 · 22–23, 18 · 24, 18 · 27, 18 · 29, 18 · 32–33
France
  Inflation Accounting, 23 · 31
Franchising
  Market entry through, 31 · 14–15, 40 · 8
Free Along Side (F.A.S.) Quotation, 31 · 11, 33 · 10
Free on Board Price (F.O.B.), 31 · 11, 33 · 7, 33 · 8, 33 · 9, 33 · 10, 38 · 17
Free Riders
  General Agreement on Tariffs and Trade and, 5 · 23–24
Free Trade Area, 4 · 8–9, 9 · 6
  European, 4 · 9, 4 · 24–25, 4 · 41, 9 · 6, 15 · 16
  Industrial relations and, 35 · 22
  Latin American, 4 · 9, 4 · 31–32, 4 · 33, 4 · 34, 7 · 6, 8 · 9, 9 · 6
  Pricing, 33 · 9
  Treaty of Rome and, 25 · 5
Free Trade Lobbyists, 1 · 6–7
Freight Transportation, *see* International Transportation
Functional Offshore Center, 18 · 67

Functional Organizations, 7 · 7
See also specific organizations
Funding Risk
International banking and, **19** · 17
Funny Faces **Scale, 30** · 27
Futures
Foreign exchange trading, **18** · 34

Gains from Trade, 1 · 5
Geigy **v.** *Commission,* **25** · 12
General Agreements to Borrow (GAB), 3 · 8
General Agreement on Tariffs and Trade (GATT),
1 · 6, **5** · 17−18
Countervailing duties and, **26** · 20−21
Customs valuation, **26** · 8
Dispute settlements, 5 · 22
Dumping by Communist countries and,
15 · 33
Escape clause, **5** · 24, **5** · 25, **9** · 14−15, **26** · 14,
26 · 15
Exchange rates and, **5** · 26
Fair-trading rules of, **5** · 21−22
Government procurement practices and, **9** · 18
Industrial restructuring, **5** · 25−26
Most-favored-nation principle, **9** · 5−6
National security and, **26** · 17
Nondiscrimination, **5** · 18−20
Nontariff barriers, **5** · 24−25
Origins, **6** · 6, **26** · 5−6
Quantitative restrictions, **5** · 20−21
Reciprocity, **9** · 6
Safeguard measures, **9** · 4−15
State trading and, **15** · 15−16
Subsidies and, **9** · 17
Tariff conferences, **5** · 23−24
Trade barriers, **9** · 5−6
See also Multilateral Trade Negotiations
General Electric
International organization, **39** · 15, **39** · 18
Generalized System of Preferences (GSP), 4 · 23, **9**
· 6, **26** · 11−12, **38** · 17
General License, 9 · 10
General Motors **v.** *EEC Commission,* **25** · 9
General-Price-Level Change
Accounting for, **23** · 21−22, **23** · 22−23, **23** · 25,
23 · 26
Generic Products, 33 · 13
Geocentric Pricing Policy, 32 · 7
Geographic Segmentation, 33 · 5
Germany, *see* West Germany
Glass-Steagall Act, 19 · 14, **20** · 5
Global Market Surveys (GMS), **10** · 7, **10** · 24
Global Matrix Organization, 39 · 16−18
Global Quotas, 9 · 8
Global Reserves, *see* International Reserves
Global Strategy
Bibliography, **A** · 6−7
Global Tax System, 24 · 6, **24** · 8
Goals
Conflict management and, **41** · 14−15
Gold
International Monetary Fund and, **5** · 12
International monetary system and, **3** · 6−7, **18**
· 8−10
International reserves and, **18** · 17−21
Goods
Balance of payments and, **2** · 3, **2** · 4

Goodwill
German practices, **23** · 14−15
Netherlands practices, **22** · 20
Swedish practices, **22** · 23
Governing-Law Clauses
Loan agreement and, **27** · 17−19
Government
Exchange rate determination, **17** · 3, **17** · 4, **17**
· 17−19
Information services, **B** · 3−5
Loans to, **27** · 5, **27** · 13−15
Procurement, **10** · 8, **10** · 12, **15** · 4−5
Code for, **26** · 29−36
Subsidies, **9** · 17−18
See also Country Risk; Political Risk; *specific*
departments, i.e., Commerce, Depart-
ment of; State Trading
Grace Periods
Events of default, **27** · 8−9
Great Britain, *see* United Kingdom
Green Rates, 4 · 20
Gross-Income Method, 24 · 13−14
Gross-Up, 34 · 6−7
Group Account, *see* Consolidated Financial
Statements
Grundig Consten **Case, 25** · 29−31

Hart-Scott-Rodino Act, 20 · 16
Heckscher-Ohlin Theory, 1 · 4
Hedging, 1 · 10, **33** · 11, **34** · 4−6
Exchange rate forecasting and, **17** · 26−27
Exchange rate risk and, **1** · 10
Foreign currency translation and, **23** · 16−18,
23· 19−20
Foreign exchange and, **13** · 26
Hierarchical Aggregation Process, 22 · 24
High-Risk Items, 12 · 5−6
Historical-Cost/Constant-Dollar Model of
Accounting, 23 · 21−22, **23** · 22−23, **23** · 25,
23 · 26
Hoffman-LaRoche **v.** *Centrafarm,* **25** · 35
Hoffman-LaRoche **v.** *Commission,* **25** · 10, **25** · 11
Holding Companies
Treaty provisions and, **24** · 29
Horizontal Acquisition
Market entry through, **31** · 17−18
Horizontal Foreign Direct Investment, 1 · 4
Horizontal Operations of Multinational opera-
tions, 16 · 5
Hugin **v.** *EEC Commission,* **25** · 9
Human Resources
Bibliography, **A** · 9−10
See also Industrial Relations
Human Rights
Conflict issue of, **41** · 4, **41** · 6
Multinational corporations and, **16** · 10−11
Hunt Commission, 18 · 70

IBM
International organization, **39** · 9−10, **39** · 18
ICI **v.** *Commission,* **25** · 12
Immunity
Foreign state and, **27** · 13−15
Imperial Chemical Industries Ltd. **v.** *Commission,*
20 · 22−23
Imperialism
Multinational corporations and, **7** · 14

International Trade Law, *see* International Business Law
International Trade Organization (ITO), 26 · 5-6
International Trade Secretariats, 7 · 19-20
International Trade Union Secretariats (ITSs), 35 · 14-15
International Transportation
  Air cargo, 11 · 14-17, 33 · 22
  Costs, 1 · 5
  Insurance, 12 · 20-21
  Major U.S. companies, B · 13-14
  Maritime, 11 · 3, 33 · 22
    Bulk carriers, 11 · 6
    Cargo liners, 11 · 3-4
    Communist countries, 15 · 37
    Containerization, 11 · 6-7
    Future, 11 · 7-9
    Income, 24 · 20, 24 · 21
    Less-developed countries, 11 · 8-9
    Lighter-aboard ship, 11 · 7
    Liner rates, 11 · 4-5
    Mechanics of, 11 · 12-14
    Roll-on/roll-off ship, 10 · 7
    Tramp steamers, 11 · 5-6
    U.S. merchant marine, 11 · 9-11
  Passenger, 14 · 6, 14 · 15-18
    Tourism, *see* International Transportation
  Surface, 33 · 22
International Union of Credit and Investment Insurers, *see* Berne Union
Intervention, 1 · 8-9
Intervention Price
  Agricultural products, 4 · 19
Interviewing
  Personal, 30 · 31-32
  Telephone, 30 · 30-31
Intra-European Payments Scheme, 5 · 26-27
Intraindustry Trade, 1 · 5
Inventions
  Patent Licensing Agreements, 25 · 25-27
  See also Research and Development
Inventory
  Poland, 22 · 26
  Sweden, 22 · 21-22
  Valuation, 24 · 6-7
Investment, 1 · 13-14
  Balance of payments and, 2 · 13
  Commerce Department and, 10 · 13
  Country risk assessment by, 21 · 7, 34 · 10
  Covered, 1 · 13
  Decision regarding overseas, 34 · 11-12
  Disinvestment, 35 · 23-24
  East-West trade and, 15 · 41
  Economic growth and, 1 · 12
  Eurocurrency market, 1 · 13
  Foreign direct, 1 · 13-14, 21 · 7
    Offshore, 16 · 9-10
  Industrial relations and, 35 · 21-22
  Information on, *see* Marketing Information
  Market entry through, 31 · 5, 31 · 6, 31 · 16-20, 40 · 9-10
  National climate classified by, 29 · 12-15
  Portfolio, 1 · 13
  Risk in, 1 · 12-13
  Taxation on earnings of in U.S. property, 24 · 20-21
  See also Multinational Corporations

Investment Banking
  Domestic, 20 · 19
  See also International Investment Banking
Investment Reserves
  Sweden, 22 · 22-23
Investment Tax Credit, 24 · 7
Invest in the U.S.A., 10 · 13
Iron and Steel Community, 7 · 6
Irrevocable Letter of Credit
  Confirmed, 13 · 11, 31 · 11
  Unconfirmed, 13 · 11
Italy v. EEC Council, 25 · 8
Iure Gestiones, 6 · 5, 15 · 14
Iure Imperii, 6 · 5, 15 · 14

Japan
  Gold and, 18 · 10
  Industrial relations, 35 · 10
  Inflation accounting, 23 · 31
  Technology transfer from to developing countries, 31 · 16
  Unpackaging and, 37 · 7
Johnson Debt Default Act, 15 · 30
Joint Enterprises, 4 · 10
Joint Venture
  Communist countries, 15 · 41
  Consortium bank as, 19 · 9, 19 · 11
  Coproduction agreements, 31 · 15-16
  European Economic Community, 25 · 12-23
  Licensing and, 31 · 14
  Market entry through, 31 · 19-20
  Technology transfer and, 37 · 6, 37 · 7-8
Joint Venture Offshore Sourcing, 38 · 4, 38 · 9, 38 · 10, 38 · 18
Judgmental Sampling, 30 · 16
Judicial System, *see* International Business Law
Jure Gestionis, 6 · 5, 15 · 14
Jure Imperii, 6 · 5, 15 · 14
Jurisdiction, 6 · 5
  International loans and, 27 · 19-21
  Multinational corporations and, 7 · 11
  See also International Trade Law
Justice Department, 6 · 11-12

Kelly's Manufacturers and Merchants Directory, 30 · 12
Kennedy Round of Multilateral Trade Negotiations, 5 · 24, 9 · 7
Keynesian Approach, 1 · 11-12
  Exchange rate analysis through, 18 · 35
Know-How License, 36 · 11
Knowledge Arrangements, *see* Market Entry

Labels of Products, 33 · 14-15
Labor Costs
  Inflation and, 17 · 7
Labor Department, 6 · 11
Labor-Intensive Products
  Offshore sourcing for, 38 · 7-8
Labor Relations, *see* Industrial Relations
LASH (Lighter/Aboard Ship), 11 · 7
Last-In-First-Out (LIFO) Inventory Valuation, 24 · 6-7
Latin America
  Free Trade Area, 4 · 9, 4 · 31-32, 4 · 33, 4 · 34, 7 · 6, 8 · 9, 9 · 6

Implementation
  Short-term planning and, 40 · 13-14
Import Certificates and Delivery Verification (IC/DV), 15 · 29-30
Import Duty, *see* Tariff
Import Letters of Credit, 13 · 8, 13 · 10, 13 · 15-21
  Bankers acceptances and, 13 · 23
Import Licensing, 9 · 10
Imports
  Communist countries, 38 · 17
  Country-risk assessment and, 21 · 7
  East-West trade, 15 · 32-33
  Insurance and, 33 · 22
  Marketing boards and, 15 · 8
  Offshore sourcing and, 38 · 16-18
  Restraints on
    Agricultural imports, 26 · 16
    "Escape clause," 26 · 12-16
    National security and, 26 · 16-17
    See also Trade Barriers
  Unfair practices, 26 · 5
Imputation Systems, 24 · 5-6, 24 · 7
Income
  Balance of payments and, 2 · 3, 2 · 4
  Subpart F, 24 · 17, 24 · 18-21
  Taxation on earnings abroad, 34 · 6-8
Income-Expenditure Theory
  Exchange rate analysis by, 18 · 35
Income Statement
  Foreign currency translation and, 23 · 18
  Germany, 22 · 15-17
  Netherlands, 22 · 19
  Poland, 22 · 27
Independent Factory Price, 24 · 13
Indirect Channels of Distribution, 33 · 17
Indirect Export Channels, 31 · 6
Indirect Exporting, 31 · 6-8
Indirect Foreign-Tax Credit, 24 · 10, 24 · 14-17
In Dubio Pro Communitate, 25 · 37
Industrial Cooperation Agreements, 36 · 11
Industrial Markets, 32 · 15-16
  Competition, 29 · 15
  Identifying, 33 · 6-7
  International market segment and, 33 · 6
Industrial Property Rights
  European Economic Community, 25 · 23-37
Industrial Relations
  Bibliography, A · 9-10
  Business strategy, 35 · 21
    Disinvestment decision, 35 · 23-24
    Investment decisions, 35 · 21-22
    Production-allocation decision, 35 · 22-23
  Conflict issue, 41 · 4, 41 · 6-7
  Government exchange rates and, 17 · 18
  Insurance, 12 · 16-17
  International Institute for Labor Studies, 35 · 13
  International Labor Office, 35 · 12-13, 35 · 14
  Management of
    Decision making and, 35 · 17-19
    Headquarters-staff role and, 35 · 19-21
  Multinational corporations and, 7 · 12
  Offshore sourcing and, 38 · 11-13
  Organization for Economic Cooperation and Development and, 35 · 12, 35 · 13, 35 · 14
  Significance, 35 · 3-4
  Strikes
    Japan, 35 · 10

Industrial Relations (*Continued*)
  Strikes (*Continued*)
    United Kingdom, 35 · 9
    United States, 35 · 6
    West Germany, 35 · 8
  System, 35 · 4-5, 35 · 11
    Japan, 35 · 9-11
    United Kingdom, 35 · 8-9
    United States, 35 · 5-6
    West Germany, 35 · 6-8
  Technology transfer and, 37 · 10-11
  Trade unions
    Conflict management and, 41 · 19
    Global internationals, 35 · 13-14
    Industrial internationals, 35 · 14-15
    Japan, 35 · 10
    Multinational corporations and, 7 · 8-9, 7 · 12, 7 · 19
    Offshore sourcing and, 38 · 12-13
    Regional internationals, 35 · 14
    Specialized internationals, 35 · 14
    United Kingdom, 35 · 8-9
    United States, 35 · 6, 35 · 16-17
    West Germany, 35 · 7
  See also specific unions
Industrial Restructuring
  General Agreement on Tariffs and Trade and, 5 · 25-26
Industry
  Communist countries, 15 · 17-18
  Cooperation in East-West trade, 15 · 40-41
  Infant, 1 · 7, 4 · 6, 9 · 3, 9 · 4
  Integrated, 4 · 32
  Material injury to for countervailing duty, 26 · 23
  Multinational corporations and, 16 · 14-15
Industry Organized Government-Approved Trade Missions (IOGA), 10 · 11
Infant Industry, 1 · 7, 4 · 6, 9 · 3, 9 · 4
Inflation, 1 · 11
  Eurocurrency market and, 18 · 5
  Exchange rates and, 17 · 4-5, 17 · 6-7, 17 · 9-10
  Labor costs and, 17 · 7
  Pricing and, 33 · 10-11
  Trade barriers and, 9 · 3, 9 · 5
  See also Accounting
Ingersoll Rand
  International organization, 39 · 15
Innovations, *see* Inventions
Institutional Risk, 13 · 6
Insurance, 12 · 3, 12 · 10
  Admitted, 12 · 19-21
  Amounts to buy, 12 · 18-19
  Contingent, 33 · 22
  Fidelity, 12 · 12
  International markets, 12 · 21-24
  Liability, 12 · 12, 12 · 15-16, 12 · 18
  Low-risk items and, 12 · 5
  Major U.S. insurers, B · 14-15, B · 16-17
  Non-risk concerns, 12 · 15-16
  Personnel, 12 · 16-17
  Property, 12 · 10-12, 12 · 18
  Shipping and, 33 · 22
  Stakes reduced by, 41 · 12
  Surety bonds, 12 · 12-15
  U.S. risks and taxation and, 24 · 20
  See also Risk Management
Integration, *see* Economic Integration

Integration Industries, 4 · 32
Inter-American Export Promotion Center (CIPE), 8 · 3
Interbank Market, 18 · 27
Intercompany Dividends
  Taxation and, 24 · 7
Interest Arbitrage, 34 · 6
Interest Charges
  Controlled group and, 24 · 23−24
Interest Equalization Tax (IET), 18 · 45−46, 18 · 48, 19 · 8, 20 · 8
  International bond market and, 18 · 90−91
Interest Expense
  Allocation, 24 · 13−14
Interest Parity, 18 · 23
Interest-Rate Parity
  Forward markets, 17 · 9
Interest Rates
  Arbitraging, 18 · 25
  Country-risk assessment by, 34 · 10
  Covered interest-rate differential, 18 · 25
  Eurocurrency market and, 18 · 46−47, 18 · 64−66, 18 · 88−89
  Floating rate notes and, 18 · 93
  Interest parity, 18 · 23
  Syndicated loans and, 18 · 78, 18 · 83
Interests
  Conflict management and, 41 · 14−15
Intergovernmentalism, 4 · 38
Intermediated Lending, 20 · 9
Internal Rate of Return, 34 · 10−11
International Accounting Standards Committee (IASC), 22 · 29−31, 23 · 28−29, 23 · 35
  Consolidated financial statements, 23 · 35
  Foreign operations disclosure, 23 · 38
International Air Transport Association (IATA), 11 · 16, 14 · 16, 14 · 17
International Bank for Economic Co-operation and Development (IBEC), 15 · 26
International Banking
  Facilities in United States, 18 · 69−72
    Payments system, 18 · 71−72
  Offshore, 18 · 66, 18 · 67−68
  See also Banking; Central Banks; Eurocurrency Market; International Commerical Banking; International Investment Banking; International Lending
International Bank for Reconstruction and Development (IBRD), 3 · 7, 5 · 5−8, 13 · 28
  Johnson Debt Default Act and, 15 · 30
  Publications, 33 · 3−4
  See also World Bank
International Banking Act of 1978, 18 · 6, 19 · 11−12, 19 · 13, 20 · 6
International Banking Facilities (IBFs), 18 · 49, 18 · 69−71
International Bond Market, 18 · 3−4, 18 · 5
  Borrowing, 18 · 86, 24 · 29
  Definitions, 18 · 87, 18 · 90
  Emergence of, 18 · 90−92
  Eurobond, 18 · 87, 18 · 90, 18 · 92−94, 20 · 8−9
  Foreign bond, 18 · 90, 18 · 94−95
  Nature of, 18 · 74−78, 18 · 80−82, 18 · 84−86
    Currency composition, 18 · 86, 18 · 90
    Interest rates on, 18 · 88−89
    New issues, 18 · 77−78
  Yankee bond, 18 · 90
  Yields on, 18 · 86, 18 · 88−89, 18 · 94

International-Boycott Factor, 24 · 20
International Business Law, 25 · 3−4
  Bibliography, A · 5
  Domestic law and, 25 · 3
  Government procurement, 26 · 28−36
  Historical overview, 26 · 3−6
  Import-restraints, 26 · 12−17
  Marketing and, 29 · 8−9, 32 · 18−20
  Offshore sourcing and, 38 · 18−19
  Policy foundation and, 6 · 5
  Promotion, 32 · 19−20
  Risk and, 29 · 8−9
  State trading and, 15 · 13−17
  Supranational law, 25 · 4−5
    See also European Economic Community
  Tariffs, 26 · 3−12
  Unfair competitive practices in, 26 · 17−28
    Countervailing duties, 26 · 19−24
    Dumping, 26 · 24−25
    Standards, 26 · 26−28
  U.S. law firms, B · 9−13
  See also General Agreement on Tariffs and Trade
International Commercial Banking, 19 · 3
  Balance of payments and, 2 · 7
  Definition, 19 · 4, 19 · 6
  Development, 19 · 6
  Foreign-exchange trading participation and, 18 · 26, 18 · 27
  International investment competition with, 20 · 19
  Investment banking competition with, 20 · 5−6
  Largest U.S. and overseas banks, B · 18−21
  National banking systems and, 19 · 3−4
  Operations, 19 · 13−17
  Organization
    Forms, 19 · 8−12
    in United States, 19 · 12−13
  Regulation, 19 · 18−19
  Risk and, 19 · 15−17
  Third World and, 19 · 17−18
  See also International Investment Banking; International Lending
International Commercial Terms, 31 · 10
International Confederation of Free Trade Unions (ICFTU), 35 · 13, 35 · 14
International Development Association (IDA), 5 · 8−9, 13 · 28
International Development Cooperation Agency (IDCA), 10 · 19, 10 · 21
International Economic Indicators, 10 · 24
International Economic Organization (IEO), 15 · 25
International Enterprise, see Multinational Corporations
International Federation of Accountants (IFA), 22 · 31
International Federation of Christian Trade Unions (CISC), 35 · 13, 35 · 14
International Finance Corporation (IFC), 5 · 9−10, 13 · 28
International Financial Market, 18 · 3−6
  Financial centers, 18 · 66−68
  See also Eurocurrency Market; Foreign Exchange Market; International Bond Market; International Monetary System
International Financial Statistics, 17 · 24, 18 · 20
International Institute for Labor Studies, 35 · 13

International Investment, see Investment
International Investment Bank (IIB), 15 · 26−27
International Investment Banking
  Activities, 20 · 6−7
    Mergers, 20 · 14−17
    Parallel loans, 20 · 13−14
    Project financing, 20 · 10−14
    Reorganizations, 20 · 17−18
    Securities issues, 20 · 8−10
  Domestic investment, 20 · 19
  Information networks of, 20 · 7−8
  Organization of
    Branching, 20 · 4
    Commercial bank competition with, 20 · 5−6, 20 · 19
    Edge Act subsidiaries, 20 · 3−5, 20 · 6
    Financial vs. banking subsidiaries, 20 · 4−5
    Ownership provisions, 20 · 3
  Risk and, 19 · 15−17
  Trends in, 20 · 18−19
  See also Investment
International Labor Organization (ILO), 35 · 12−13, 35 · 14
  Accounting systems and, 22 · 29
  Multinational corporation code of conduct and, 7 · 19, 28 · 5, 28 · 6, 28 · 11, 28 · 19−20
International Law
  Multinational corporations and, 7 · 20
International Lending
  Concepts of
    Conditions of lending, 27 · 3−5
    Covenants of borrower, 27 · 7−9
    Events of default, 27 · 8−9
    Representations, 27 · 5−7
    Warranties and, 27 · 5
  Eurocurrency loans, 20 · 8−9, 27 · 9−10
    Bank lending in, 19 · 15, 19 · 17
    Communist countries and, 15 · 31−32
    Extensions, 20 · 17
    Foreign and multicurrency loans, 27 · 12−13
    Funding, 27 · 10−11, 27 · 12
    London Interbank Offered Rate and, 18 · 78, 18 · 79, 27 · 11
    Market size and characteristics, 18 · 72−73, 18 · 74−78, 18 · 80−82, 18 · 84−86, 18 · 88−89
    OPEC surpluses recycled by, 18 · 73, 18 · 87
    Payment place, 27 · 12
    Syndicated, 18 · 72−73, 18 · 78−79, 18 · 82−83, 18 · 87
    Third World and, 19 · 8
    Yield protection, 27 · 11
  Governing-law clauses in, 27 · 17−19
  International commerical banks and, 19 · 4−17
    Foreign states and, 27 · 15
    Risk evaluation and, 9 · 15−17
  Jurisdiction stipulation, 27 · 19−21
  Participations, 27 · 16, 27 · 17
  Risks and, 18 · 79, 18 · 82−83
  Sovereign borrowers, 27 · 5, 27 · 13−15
  Syndicated loans, 27 · 15−16, 27 · 17
  See also International Bond Market
International Market Segment, 33 · 6
International Monetary Fund (IMF), 3 · 7−8, 5 · 10−16, 13 · 28
  Balance of payments and, 2 · 9−15, 2 · 16
  Consultation procedure, 3 · 11, 5 · 16
  Credit facilities, 3 · 8−10, 5 · 13−16
  Development, 5 · 10−11

International Monetary Fund (IMF) (Continued)
  Drawings on, 3 · 8−9, 5 · 13−14
  Exchange contract and, 26 · 4
  Exchange rates and, 18 · 2, 18 · 7−8
  Floating and, 5 · 12
  Gold and, 3 · 6, 5 · 12
  International monetary system and, 18 · 6−7
  International payments and, 3 · 3, 3 · 10, 3 · 11−12
  Johnson Debt Default Act and, 15 · 30
  Publications, 17 · 24, 18 · 20
  Quota and, 3 · 8, 5 · 13−14
  Reserve tranche in, 3 · 6, 3 · 8
  Special Drawing Right, 3 · 5−6, 3 · 12, 5 · 11−12
  Structure, 5 · 13
  Surveillance, 3 · 11−12, 5 · 16
International Monetary Market (IMM), 18 · 34
International Monetary System, 18 · 4, 18 · 6−7
  Bibliography, A · 3−4
  Bilateral payment arrangements, 18 · 16
  Capital controls, 18 · 16
  Gold in, 18 · 8−10
  International Monetary Fund and, 18 · 7−8
  International reserves, 18 · 16−21
  Multiple currency practices, 18 · 16
  Special Drawing Rights and, 18 · 8, 18 · 9, 18 · 10−11
  See also Bretton Woods Agreement; European Monetary System; Exchange Rates; Foreign Exchange Market
International Organizations
  Law and, 25 · 5
International Payments, 3 · 3−4
  Development of, 3 · 10−12
  Intervention by central banks, 3 · 4
  International reserves and, 3 · 4−7
  See also Balance of Payments; European Monetary System; International Monetary Fund
International-Product-Portfolio Model, 29 · 29−31
International Public Affairs, see Public Affairs
International Reserves, 3 · 4−7, 18 · 16−21
International Security Assistance and Arms Export Control Act, 15 · 4
International Tenders, 33 · 11−12
International Trade, see Exports; Imports, Tariffs; Trade; Trade Barriers
International Trade Administration (ITA), 10 · 3−5, 10 · 12
International Trade Commission (ITC), 6 · 12, 8 ·
  Agricultural imports and, 26 · 16
  Countervailing duties and, 9 · 11, 26 · 22−23
  Dumping and, 9 · 11, 26 · 24, 26 · 25
  Escape clause action and, 9 · 15, 26 · 12−13, 26 · 14−15
  Market description, 26 · 15−16
  Unfair trade practices and, 26 · 25−26
International Trade in Services, 14 · 3−8
  Balance of payments and, 2 · 3, 2 · 4
  Causation, 14 · 7−8
  Entertainment and education, 14 · 6−7,
  Factor services, 14 · 3−4
  Nonfactor services, 14 · 4−5
  Technology, 14 · 6, 14 · 18−21
  Tourism, 14 · 6, 14 · 8−15, 14 · 17
    Balance of payments and, 2 · 7
    Political situation and, 21 · 9
  Transportation, 14 · 6, 14 · 15−18

Latin America (*Continued*)
Integration Association, **4** · 31, **4** · 32, **4** · 42
Latin American Free Trade Area (LAFTA), 4 · 9,
4 · 31–32, **4** · 33, **4** · 34, **7** · 6, **8** · 9, **9** · 6
Latin American Integration Association (LAIA),
4 · 31, **4** · 32, **4** · 42
Law, *see* International Business Law; International
Lending; *specific laws*
Law of Comparative Advantage, 1 · 3–4
Law Firms, Major U.S., **B** · 9–13
Law of Nations, 25 · 3–4
See also International Business Law
Leading Variables for Exchange Rate Forecasting,
17 · 22–23
Lead-Lag Analysis, 29 · 18, **29** · 19
Lease Rentals
Controlled Group and, **24** · 24
Leases
German accounting practices on, **22** · 17
Legal Environment, *see* Law
Legitimacy, *see* Public Affairs
Lending, *see* International Lending
Less-Developed Countries (LDCs), *see* Developing
Countries
Less Than Fair Value (LTFV)
Dumping and, **15** · 33, **15** · 34
Letter of Interest
Export-Import Bank, **10** · 18
Letters of Credit (L/C), 12 · 13–14, **13** · 8, **13** · 10,
33 · 11
Authority to purchase, **13** · 12
Back-to-back, **13** · 11–12
Confirmed irrevocable, **13** · 11, **31** · 11
Deferred-payment, **13** · 10
East-West trade and, **15** · 38
Export, **13** · 10, **13** · 12–15
Bankers acceptances and, **13** · 21–23
Financing third-country transactions, **13** · 12
Foreign currency, **13** · 25–26
Import, **13** · 8, **13** · 10, **13** · 15–21
Bankers acceptances and, **13** · 23
Red-clause, **13** · 12
Revocable, **13** · 11
Revolving, **13** · 11
Sight draft, **13** · 10, **13** · 14, **33** · 11
Time draft, **13** · 10, **33** · 11
Transferable, **13** · 11
Unconfirmed irrevocable, **13** · 11, **31** · 11
Liability Insurance, 12 · 12, **12** · 15–16, **12** · 18
Licensing, 36 · 12
Foreign exchange control and, **13** · 27
Market entry through, **31** · 12–14, **40** · 8
Technology transfer and, **14** · 18, **14** · 19, **36** · 11
Communist countries and, **15** · 40
See also Exports
Licensing Agreement
European Economic Community and, **25** · 17,
25 · 19
Lighter/Aboard Ship (LASH), 11 · 7
Linking
Corporate planning and, **40** · 18
Liquidity
International reserves, **18** · 16–21
Liquidity Assessment
Country risk and, **21** · 8
Liquidity Balance
Balance of payments and, **2** · 17

Lloyd's, 12 · 21–22
Loans, *see* International Lending
Lobbies
Corporate conflict and, **41** · 5
Locked-In Value, 17 · 26–27
Lo/Lo, *see* Container Ship
Lomé Conventions, 4 · 23
London Interbank Offered Rate (LIBOR), 18 · 61,
18 · 78, **18** · 79, **19** · 17, **19** · 18, **20** · 8–9,
27 · 11
Long-Term Planning, 40 · 10–11, **40** · 12
Losses
Capital, **24** · 8
Foreign, **24** · 8–9
Net Operating, **24** · 8
Low-Risk Items, 12 · 4–5

"McKinley" Tariff Act of 1890, 26 · 4
Macroindicators
Marking information from, **29** · 12–15
Macrosurvey, 29 · 22, **29** · 23, **29** · 24
Mail Order
Exports, **33** · 19
Mail Surveys, 30 · 30
Main Economic Indicators, **17** · 24
Maintenance Bond, 12 · 13
Managed Float, 1 · 9, **3** · 4, **3** · 11
Management
Periodicals, **A** · 14
Management-Consultant Firms, 14 · 19–20
Management Contracts
Market entry through, **31** · 15, **40** · 8, **40** · 9
Management Fees, 14 · 6
Management Objectives
Market entry and, **29** · 28
See also Corporate Planning
Mano River Union (MRU), 4 · 35, **4** · 36
Manufacture and Sale Agreement of European
Economic Community, 25 · 20–22, **25** · 23
Manufacturing
Technology and, **36** · 5
See also Offshore Sourcing
Maritime Administration (Marad), 11 · 12, **11** · 13
Maritime Transportation, *see* International
Transportation
Market Differentiated Pricing, 33 · 8
Price positions and, **33** · 9–10
Market Disruption, 26 · 15–16
Market Economies
Direct sales and purchases by state, **15** · 4–5
Procurement by government, **10** · 8, **10** · 12,
15 · 4–5, **26** · 29–36
Sales and purchases by state-owned companies,
15 · 6–7
State marketing boards, **15** · 7–8, **15** · 10, **15** · 13
See also East-West Trade
Market Entry, 31 · 3, **40** · 7–8
Bibliography, **A** · 5–6
Knowledge arrangements, **40** · 8–9
Franchising, **31** · 14–15, **40** · 8
Licensing, **31** · 12–14, **40** · 8
Management contracts, **31** · 15, **40** · 8, **40** · 9
Modes
Contractual, **31** · 4–5, **31** · 5–6, **31** · 12–16
Decision rules for, **31** · 20–21
Export, **31** · 4, **31** · 5–12, **40** · 9
Investment, **31** · 5, **31** · 6, **31** · 16–20, **40** · 9–10

Market Entry (*Continued*)
  Strategy
    Constituent product/market plans for, **31** · 4
    Information needed for, **29** · 8–15, **29** · 23–28
    Monitoring, **31** · 21
    Planning, **31** · 3
    See also European Economic Community;
      Marketing Mix; Market Potential
Market Indicators, 33 · 3–4
Marketing
  Bibliography, **A** · 10–11
    Periodicals, **A** · 14
  Conflict issue, **41** · 4, **41** · 6–7
  Consumer, **29** · 15, **32** · 13–14, **33** · 6
  Control, **33** · 30
  Costs, **29** · 10–12
  Distribution, **32** · 11–12, **33** · 16–22
    See also International Transportation
  Economic environment, **29** · 9, **29** · 11, **32** · 21,
    33 · 4
  Industrial, **29** · 15, **32** · 15–16, **33** · 6–7
  Legal environment and, **29** · 8–9, **32** · 18–20
  Operations evaluation, **29** · 28–31
  Organizing for, **33** · 27–28
  Planning, **32** · 22–25, **33** · 28–30, **40** · 18
  Political environment, **29** · 8, **32** · 20–21, **33** · 5
  Pricing, **32** · 4–6, **33** · 7–12
  Product considerations, **32** · 4–6, **33** · 12–16
  Product diversification, **40** · 7
  Promotion, **32** · 7–9, **33** · 22–27
    Advertising, **33** · 22–24
    Coordinating, **32** · 9–11
  Sociocultural conditions and, **29** · 10, **29** · 11,
    32 · 17–18
  Target market selection, **32** · 12–13, **33** · 3–5
  Technology and, **36** · 5–6, **36** · 7–8
  See also Marketing Information; Marketing
    Research; Market Segmentation
Marketing Boards, 15 · 7–8, **15** · 10, **15** · 13
Marketing In, **10** · 23
Marketing Information, 29 · 3–4
  National business and market environment
    secondary data
    Aggregate macroindicators, **29** · 12–15
    Costs of market operation, **29** · 10–15
    Foreign market entry and, **29** · 8–15
    Information sources for, **29** · 4–7
    Market potential indicators, **29** · 9–10
    Risk factors and, **29** · 8–9
  Product market and company performance
    Company sales, **29** · 15–17
    Market size and structure, **29** · 15, **29** · 16
    Product-market performance, **29** · 15–17
    Sales and demand projections, **29** · 17–22,
      29 · 23, **29** · 24
  Use of, **29** · 22–23
    Market entry decisions, **29** · 23–28
    Reallocation decisions, **29** · 28–31
  See also Marketing Research
Marketing Mix, 32 · 3
  See also Marketing
Marketing Research, 30 · 3–4, **30** · 34–35
  Commerce Department and, **10** · 7
  Cultural bias and, **30** · 7, **30** · 28
  Data collection
    Exploratory research, **30** · 29
    Survey nonresponse, **30** · 32–33

Marketing Research (*Continued*)
  Data collection (*Continued*)
    Survey research, **30** · 6, **30** · 29–34
  Data quality, **30** · 32–34
    Nonsampling error, **30** · 32
    Reliability, **30** · 33–34
    Sampling error, **30** · 32–34
  Designing, **30** · 6–7
  Instrument design, **30** · 19–20
    Category equivalence, **30** · 21
    Conceptual equivalence and, **30** · 20–21
    Demographic equivalence, **30** · 21
    Development, **30** · 23–26
    Functional equivalence and, **30** · 20
    Nonverbal stimuli, **30** · 23–24
    Question formulation, **30** · 23–26
    Response bias, **30** · 21–22
    Response format, **30** · 26–28
    Scoring procedures, **30** · 28
    Translation, **30** · 24–26
  Organizing, **30** · 7
    Centralization vs. decentralization, **30** · 7–8
    In-house vs. external research services,
      30 · 8–10
  Primary data for, **30** · 11–12
    Sample composition comparability, **30** · 18
    Sample size, **30** · 17–18
    Sampling frame, **30** · 12–14
    Sampling procedures, **30** · 14–15, **30** · 18–19
    Sampling techniques, **30** · 16–17
  Public affairs and, **42** · 8
  Purposes, **30** · 5–6
    Secondary data, **30** · 10–11
  Types, **34** · 4–5
Marketing Strategy
  Marketing research for, **30** · 5–6
Market Intensity, 29 · 13–14
Market Launch Service of Commerce Department,
  10 · 10
Market Potential
  Assessing, **29** · 12–15
    Current, **29** · 15–17
    Future, **29** · 17–22, **29** · 24, **29** · 33
    Indicators, **29** · 9–10
  Market entry decision and, **29** · 23–28
Market Profile, **10** · 23–24
Markets
  Communist countries, **15** · 35–36
  Definition, **39** · 14
  Organization based on, **39** · 14–16
Market Segmentation, 32 · 13, **33** · 5–7
  Marketing research for, **30** · 5
  Segment extrapolation method, **29** · 20–21,
    29 · 22
Market Selection, 32 · 12–13, **33** · 3–5
Market Share
  Information on, **29** · 17
  Objectives, **33** · 28–29
Market Share Reports, **33** · 3
Market Size
  Information on, **29** · 15, **29** · 16
Market-Size Index, 29 · 14
Master Policy of FCIA, 10 · 16–17
Material Adverse Change
  Loan agreement and, **27** · 6–7
Material Injury to Industry, 26 · 23
Mean Squared Error of Forecast, 17 · 20

Media
  Advertising and, **33** · 22−24
  Plan, **33** · 29
Media Mix, 33 · 22
Medium-Term Financial Assistance, 3 · 13
Medium-Term Planning, 40 · 11, **40** · 13
Merchant Marine (U.S.), 11 · 9−11
  See also International Transportation
Mergers
  European Economic Community and, **25** · 6,
    25 · 10, **25** · 13
  International investment banking and,
    20 · 14−17
  See also Joint Venture
"Microtables," 33 · 3
Middlemen
  Distribution and, **32** · 11−12
Ministry of Foreign Trade (MFT), 15 · 21, **15** · 22,
  15 · 23
Monetary Approach, 1 · 12
  Balance of payments and, **2** · 18−21
  Exchange rate analysis by, **18** · 35−37
Monetary Balance
  Balance of payments and, **2** · 19−21
  Reserve currency and, **2** · 20−21
Monetary Compensation Amounts (MCA),
  4 · 19−20
Monetary Control Act of 1980, 18 · 47, **18** · 70
Monetary-Nonmonetary Accounting Method,
  23 · 8, **23** · 9−10, **23** · 11, **23** · 12
Monetary Policy, 1 · 11
Monetary Union, 4 · 9
Money-and-Credit Multiplier Model
  Eurocurrency market and, **18** · 61−63
Money Market, 18 · 4
  Hedging and, **34** · 5−6
  See also Eurocurrency Market
Monopoly
  State trading and, **15** · 4, **15** · 13
Most-Favored-Nation Status, 38 · 17
  Communist countries, **15** · 32, **38** · 17
  European Economic Community, **4** · 23
  General Agreement on Tariffs and Trade and,
    5 · 18−19, **9** · 5−6
Movie Industry
  Advertising in, **33** · 23−24
  Trade and, **14** · 21
Multicountry Research, *see* Marketing Research
Multicurrency Eurodollar Loans, 27 · 12−13
Multifiber Arrangement Regarding International
  Trade and Textiles, 26 · 16
Multilateral Development Banks, 5 · 4−10
  See also World Bank
Multilateral Trade Negotiations, 10 · 12
  Developing countries and, **26** · 11
  Dillon Round, **9** · 7
  Government procurement and, **9** · 18, **26** ·
    29−36
  Kennedy Round, **5** · 24, **9** · 7
  Licensing procedures, **9** · 10
  Nontariff barriers and, **5** · 24−25
  Private sector representatives, **6** · 8
  Standards code, **26** · 27−28
  Subsidies code, **26** · 20−21
  Tariffs, **9** · 7, **26** · 6, **26** · 7, **26** · 8
  Technical trade barrier and, **9** · 17
  Tokyo Round, **5** · 23, **10** · 12

Multinational Corporations (MNCs), 1 · 13
  Buying office, **33** · 17
  Competitive strength, **16** · 7−9
  Control of, *see* Codes of Conduct
  Country-risk assessment and, **21** · 7
  Definition, **28** · 4
  Extent, **16** · 4−5
  Financial reports, **23** · 41, **23** · 46−47
  Flags of convenience and, **11** · 11
  Host states and, **7** · 5−6, **7** · 11−17, **16** · 11−15
  Intercompany transaction taxation and,
    24 · 22−25
  Major U.S. and foreign, **B** · 5−8
  Mergers and, **20** · 16−17
  Natural resources and, **7** · 13, **16** · 12
  Nature of, **16** · 3−6
  Offshore activities, **16** · 5, **16** · 6
  Organization, **16** · 6−7, **39** · 3, **39** · 18−19
    Bibliography, **A** · 7−8
    Functional dimension in global terms, **39** · 12
    Geography as basis, **39** · 6−7
    Global matrix organization, **39** · 16−18
    International division, **39** · 3−6
      Elimination, **39** · 7−12
    Market-based, **39** · 14−16
    Product as basis, **39** · 6−7
  Parent states and, **6** · 9−11, **7** · 4−5, **7** · 8−11
  Political environment, **7** · 20−21
    International, **7** · 7−8, **7** · 18−20
    Levels of, **7** · 4−8
    Nature of, **7** · 3−4
    Regional, **7** · 6−7
  Pricing policy of, **33** · 8
  Product service and, **33** · 16
  State trading company and, **15** · 7
  Technology and, **16** · 13
    Research and development and, **36** · 20−23
    Trade in, **14** · 19, **14** · 20
  Technology transfer and, **7** · 12−13, **16** · 8−9
    Developing countries, **36** · 15, **37** · 5, **37** · 6,
      37 · 6−7, **37** · 10−11
    Marketing, **29** · 9−10, **29** · 11, **36** · 5−6
  Trade unions and, **7** · 8−9, **7** · 12, **7** · 19
  See also Accounting; Conflict Management;
    Industrial Relations; Marketing; Public
    Affairs
Multiple Currency Practices, 18 · 16
Multiple Exchange Rates, 9 · 14, **18** · 12
Multiple-Factor Indexes, 29 · 19−20
  Marketing information from, **29** · 13−15
Multiple-Rate Accounting Methods, 23 · 9−10,
  23 · 12
Multiplier Model
  Eurocurrency market and, **18** · 61−63
Multiplier System
  Pricing and, **33** · 10
Mutual Supply Arrangements
  European Economic Community and, **25** · 16−17
Myers and Warner Colloquial and Formal Rating
  Scales, 30 · 28

Names
  Insurance and, **12** · 21
National Banking Systems, 19 · 3−4, **19** · 5
National Carriers, 14 · 17−18
National Enterprises
  Trade and, **15** · 6

National Enterprises (*Continued*)
  See also Communist Countries
National Equipment Rental, Ltd. v. Graphic Art
  Designers, Inc., 27 · 19
National Equipment Rental, Ltd. v. Szukhent,
  27 · 19
Nationalism
  Conflict management and, 41 · 16, 41 · 27
  Expropriation, 41 · 4
  Supranationalism, 4 · 38
National Law, 25 · 3
  Industrial and property rights and European
    Economic Community and, 25 · 27–37
  See also International Business Law
National Security
  State trading and, 15 · 10
  Trade barriers and, 1 · 7, 9 · 3, 9 · 4, 11 · 9,
    26 · 16–17
Natural Resources
  Multinational corporations and, 7 · 13, 16 · 12
Negative Covenants, 27 · 7–8
Negative Integration, 4 · 8, 4 · 11, 4 · 41
  Free trade area and, 4 · 8–9
Net Exports of Goods and Services, 2 · 11
Netherlands
  Accounting, 22 · 17–20, 23 · 31–32
Net Liquidity Balance
  Balance of payments and, 2 · 18
Net Operating Losses
  Taxation and, 24 · 8
Net Subsidy, 26 · 22
New International Economic Order, 28 · 9
New Product Information Service, 10 · 12
New Products Testing System, 10 · 15
New Zealand
  Inflation accounting, 23 · 32
Nominal Terms of Contracts, 17 · 4, 17 · 5
Nonbank Financial Intermediaries
  Eurocurrency market and, 18 · 61, 18 · 63
Nonbank Subsidiaries, 19 · 11
Noncumulative Revolving Letter of Credit, 13 · 11
Nonfactor Services, 14 · 4–5
Nonintermediated Lending, 20 · 9
Nonresidents
  Taxation of, 24 · 9
Nonscheduled Airlines, 14 · 18
Nontariff Barriers (NTBs), 1 · 5–6, 9 · 7
Normalization of Scoring, 30 · 28
Notice Requirements
  Events of default and, 27 · 8–9

Obsolescing Bargain, 7 · 16, 7 · 17, 41 · 21
Odd Dates, 18 · 24
Office of Export Administration (OEA), 15 · 28–29
Office of Foreign Direct Investment (OFDI),
  18 · 46, 18 · 48
Office of U.S. Trade Representative, *see* United
  States Trade Representative
Official Reserve Assets, 3 · 5
Official Reserve Transactions Balance, 2 · 14
Official Settlements Balance
  Balance of payments and, 2 · 17
Offshore Banking, 18 · 66, 18 · 67–68
Offshore Foreign Direct Investment, 16 · 9–10
Offshore Sourcing, 38 · 3
  Communications problems in, 38 · 19–20
  Edge Act corporations and, 19 · 11

Offshore Sourcing (*Continued*)
  Forms of, 38 · 3–4
    Selection criteria, 38 · 4–6
  Industrial relations and, 35 · 22
  International commercial banking and, 19 · 15,
    19 · 16
  Joint venture, 38 · 4, 38 · 9, 38 · 10, 38 · 18
  Legal and financial considerations, 38 · 18–19
  Multinational corporations and, 16 · 5, 16 · 6
  Organization links and, 38 · 20–21
  Partners for
    Availability and capabilities, 38 · 5–6
    Evaluating, 38 · 9–10
  Product evaluation for, 38 · 6–9
    Trends in, 38 · 8–9
  Production site evaluation factors, 38 · 10
    Economic instability and, 38 · 15
    Government, 38 · 13–15
    Information sources on, 38 · 16
    Infrastructure, 38 · 13
    Labor, 38 · 11–13
    Political risk and, 38 · 15
  Purchasing and, 38 · 3–4
  Sources for, 38 · 9, 38 · 10
    Political risk and, 38 · 15
  Subcontracting and, 38 · 4
  U.S. Customs regulations, 38 · 16–18
Oil Facility of International Monetary Fund, 3 · 9
Old-Age Pensions, 12 · 16
Open Account, 13 · 7–8, 33 · 11
"Open" Procedure
  Government procurement and, 26 · 30,
    26 · 31–32
Operating Differential Subsidy, 11 · 10
Operational Exposure, 34 · 4
Opportunity Cost
  Licensing foreign market mode and, 31 · 13
Optimum Tariff, 1 · 6, 9 · 5
Orderly Marketing Arrangements (OMAs), 1 · 6,
  9 · 9
Organization, *see* Multinational Corporations
Organization of American States (OAS),
  Exports, 8 · 3
Organization for Economic Cooperation and
  Development (OECD), 5 · 26–28, 7 · 7,
    35 · 12, 35 · 13, 35 · 14
  Accounting standards, 22 · 32, 23 · 29, 23 · 35
    Foreign operations disclosure and, 23 · 38
    Multinational corporations and, 23 · 24
  Industrial cooperation agreements and,
    36 · 11
  Multinational corporations and, 7 · 18
    Accounting and, 23 · 24
    Code of conduct and, 28 · 5, 28 · 6, 28 · 8,
      28 · 11–12, 28 · 20–22
  Publications, 17 · 24, 33 · 3
  Tourism and, 14 · 8
Organization for European Economic Cooperation
  (OEEC), 5 · 26–27
Organization for Petroleum Exporting Countries
  (OPEC), 7 · 7, 7 · 13
  Eurocurrency market and, 18 · 63
  International commercial banking and, 19 · 8
  Lending and, 19 · 15
  Reserves, 18 · 20, 18 · 21
  Surpluses recycled, 18 · 73, 18 · 87
Osgood's Semantic Differential, 30 · 28

Overall Balance, *see* Balance of Payments
Overall Foreign-Tax-Credit Limitation, 24 · 8
Overall Profit Percentage Limitation, 24 · 26
Overseas Business Reports, 10 · 23–24, 33 · 4
Overseas Export Promotions Calendar, 10 · 9
Overseas Private Investment Corporation (OPIC),
    7 · 10, 10 · 18–20, 13 · 28, 41 · 12
    East-West trade and, 15 · 31
    Publications, 10 · 26

Packaging, 33 · 14–15
Parallel Loans
    International Investment banking and, 12 · 20,
    13 · 14
Parallel Translation, 30 · 25–26
Parke, Davis & Co. v. Centrafarm, 25 · 24, 25 · 28,
    25 · 33–34
Participation Agreement, 26 · 16, 27 · 17
Passenger Transportation, 14 · 6, 14 · 15–18
    Tourism, 14 · 6, 14 · 8–15, 14 · 17
Patent Licensing Agreements
    European Economic Community, 25 · 23–27
Patents, 33 · 13, 36 · 11–12, 37 · 4–5
    European Economic Community, 25 · 32–34
Payment, *see* Financing
Payment in Advance, 13 · 7
Penetration Prices, 33 · 9
Pensions, 12 · 16, 12 · 17
    Sweden, 22 · 23
Per-Country Foreign-Tax Credit Limitation, 24 · 8

Performance Bond, 12 · 13
Perils, *see* Risk, Management
Periodicals, A · 13–15
Personal Interviewing, 30 · 31–32
Personal Selling, 33 · 25–26
Personnel Insurance, 12 · 16–17
Petrodollar
    International commercial banking and, 19 · 8
Pfizer
    International division, 39 · 10
Physical Distribution, 33 · 21–22
Piggyback System, 33 · 17
Planned Economies, *see* Communist Countries
Planning, *see* Corporate Planning
Plans
    Communist countries, 15 · 18–20, 15 · 23
Point Forecast, 17 · 19–20
Point-of-Purchase Advertising, 33 · 24
Poland
    Accounting, 22 · 20–27
Policy Foundation, 6 · 3–4
    Economic principles, 6 · 4–5
    Effects, 6 · 7
    Forum, 6 · 7–12
    Legal principles, 6 · 5
    Objectives, 6 · 5–7
Political Integration, 4 · 9, 4 · 37–40
Political Risk
    Bibliography, A · 11–12
    Information for assessing, 29 · 8
    Investment entry and, 31 · 17
    Marketing and, 32 · 20–21, 33 · 5
    Offshore sourcing and, 38 · 15
    Project financing and, 20 · 12
    See also Country Risk
Political Unionism, 35 · 6

Politics
    Bibliography, A · 13–14
    Periodicals, A · 5
    Conflict issue, 41 · 4, 41 · 5, 41 · 6, 41 · 8
Polycentric Pricing Policy, 32 · 7
Portfolio Capital
    Balance of payments and, 2 · 13
Portfolio Investment, 1 · 13
    Balance of payments and, 2 · 7
Portfolio Theory
    Exchange rate analysis by, 18 · 35, 18 · 37
Positive Integration, 4 · 8, 4 · 38
Possession Corporation, 24 · 28
Postcapitalist Political Economy, 6 · 5
Power
    Conflict management and, 41 · 13–14, 41 · 21
Preflex/Lipski, 25 · 27
Preliminary Commitments of Export-Import Bank,
    10 · 18
Premiums
    Sales promotion and, 33 · 24–25
Price Controls, 32 · 19
Price Positions, 33 · 9–10
Price Quotations
    Exporting and, 31 · 10–11
Pricing
    Agricultural products and, 4 · 19
    Exports, 31 · 10–11, 32 · 4–6, 33 · 7–12
    Intercompany transactions and, 24 · 22–25
    Marketing and, 32 · 4–6, 32 · 7–12
    Marketing mix and, 32 · 6–7
Primary Data, *see* Marketing Research
Primary Financial Statements, 23 · 47
Principal International Businesses, 33 · 7
Print Media, 33 · 22–23
Prior Import Deposits, 9 · 14
Private Brand, 33 · 13
Private Export Funding Corporation (PEFCO),
    13 · 27–28
Probability
    Risk and, 12 · 4
Probability-Tree Method
    Country risk assessment by, 34 · 9
Procurement, *see* Government
Product
    Decisions, 32 · 4–6
    Design, 33 · 12
    Development, 33 · 16
    Differentiation, 1 · 5, 32 · 4
    Diversification, 40 · 7
    Invention, 32 · 5
        See also Research and Development
    Liability, 32 · 19
    Performance information, 29 · 15–17
    Position, 30 · 6
    Quality, 33 · 12
    Standards and export restrictions, 26 · 27
    Strategy, 33 · 16
    Testing, 33 · 16
    Usage data, 29 · 15
    See also Marketing; Offshore Sourcing
Product Adaptation-Promotional Extension, 32 · 5
Product Extension-Promotional Adaptation, 32 · 5
Product-Life-Cycle, 32 · 4, 33 · 16
    Organizational design and, 39 · 4
    Theory of Trade and, 1 · 4
    Unpackaging and, 37 · 7

Product Line, 33 · 16
**Product-Marketing Service of Commerce
  Department, 10** · 12
Product-Promotional Extension, 32 · 4–5
Profit-and-Loss Statement
  Risk and, **12** · 3
Profit Planning, 33 · 29–30
Project Financing
  International Investment Banking and,
    20 · 10–14
Promotion, 32 · 7–9, **33** · 22–27
  Advertising, **33** · 22–24
  Agriculture Department and, **10** · 14–15
  Coordinating, **32** · 9–11
  Exports and, **8** · 4, **8** · 10–12, **10** · 9–12
  Legal aspects, **32** · 19–20
  Product and, **32** · 4–6
  See also Sales Promotion
Promotional Mix, 33 · 27
  Definition, **42** · 34
  Industry type and, **42** · 4, **42** · 6
  Patterns, **42** · 13, **42** · 20
    Advanced, **42** · 15–19
    Intermediate, **42** · 15
    Minimal, **42** · 13–15
  Planning
    Goals, timetables and budgets, **42** · 12
    Information sources, **42** · 10–12
    Organization, **42** · 7–8
    Resources inventoried, **42** · 12
    Targets, **42** · 8–10
  Reason for, **42** · 3–4, **42** · 5
  Reporting
    Control, **42** · 34–36
    Managerial, **42** · 31–36
    Socioeconomic, **42** · 36
    Timing, **42** · 33–34
  Staffing, **42** · 20–26
    Outsiders, **42** · 23–25
    Roles, **42** · 21–23
Property
  Controlled group and sale of, **24** · 24–25
  Taxation on earnings of investments in U.S.,
    24 · 20–21
  Transfer of as tax-free transaction, **24** · 21–22
Property Insurance, 12 · 10–12, **12** · 18
Proportionality
  European Economic Community's principle of,
    25 · 11
Proprietary Technology
  Transfer of, *see* Technology Transfer Agree-
    ments
Protectionism, *see* Trade Barriers
***Provident National Bank* v. *Frankfort Trust
  Company, 27** · 17
Psychographic Segmentation, 33 · 6
Public Affairs, 33 · 25
  Action, **42** · 26–31
    Philosophy on public affairs and, **42** · 28–31
    Profile of company and, **42** · 26, **42** · 28
    Response, **42** · 26, **42** · 27
  Bibliography, **A** · 9
  Company policy and, **42** · 7
  Company size, growth and evolution and,
    42 · 6–7
Publicity, 33 · 25
  See also Promotion

***Public Prosecutor* v. *Dassonville*, 25** · 28
Public Relations, *see* Public Affairs
Purchasing-Power Parity (PPP), 17 · 4, **17** · 5, **17** · 6,
    17 · 7, **17** · 8, **17** · 10–11, **18** · 36
  Deviations from, **17** · 11, **17** · 14–16, **17** · 21,
    17 · 25
  Factor-price version, **17** · 13
  Long-run, **17** · 12–14

Quantitative Restriction, *see* Quotas
Questionnaires
  Mail surveys, **30** · 30
  Personal interviews, **30** · 31–32
  Telephone interviews, **30** · 30–31
Quotas, 1 · 5–6, **9** · 8–10, **11** · 9
  Communist goods and, **15** · 28, **15** · 32–33
  Embargo, **9** · 8
  Export, **9** · 9
  Foreign exchange control and, **13** · 27
  General Agreement on Tariffs and Trade and,
    5 · 20
  Global, **9** · 8
  Impact of, **9** · 8–9
  International Monetary Fund and, **3** · 8
  Offshore sourcing and, **38** · 17–18
  Orderly marketing agreement, **9** · 9
  Tariff-quota, **9** · 14
  Voluntary export restraint, **9** · 9
Quota Sampling, 30 · 16–17, **30** · 18

Radio
  Advertising and, **33** · 23
Randall Presidential Commission, 26 · 13
Random Sampling, 30 · 16, **30** · 18, **30** · 19
Random Walk, 30 · 16
Range, 17 · 19
Real-Capital Formation, 1 · 12
Recapture Provision, 34 · 8
  Overall foreign loss and, **24** · 9
Reciprocal Trade Agreements Act of 1934, 26 · 4
Reciprocity
  General Agreement on Tariffs and Trade and,
    5 · 23
Red-Clause Letter of Credit, 13 · 12
**Regional Co-operation for Development (RCD),
    4** · 37
Regional Organizations, 7 · 6–7
  See also specific organizations
Regulation
  Corporate conflict and, **41** · 5
  State trading and, **15** · 14
Regulation D, 18 · 46, **18** · 47, **18** · 48, **18** · 69, **18** · 70
Regulation Q, 18 · 46–47, **18** · 48, **18** · 69, **18** · 70
Regulatory Risk
  Syndicated loan and, **18** · 83
Related Person, 24 · 19
Release-of-Attachment Bond, 12 · 13
Relevant Market
  European Economic Community and, **25** · 9
Reorganization
  International investment banking and,
    20 · 17–18
Replacement Value Theory, 22 · 17–19
Reporting, 23 · 41, **23** · 46–47
***Report of the President on Export Promotion
  Functions and Potential Export
  Disincentives, 10** · 23

Representations
Loan agreement and, **27** · 5–7
Representative Office of Bank, 19 · 9
Representatives
Communist countries, **15** · 35–36
Product distribution and, **33** · 19–21
Resale-Price Method, 24 · 24
Research and Development (R&D)
European Economic Community, **25** · 14–16, **25** · 22
Expense allocation, **24** · 14
Management, **36** · 7, **36** · 17–23
Developing countries, **36** · 21–22
Guidelines, **36** · 18–20
Overseas by multinational corporations, **36** · 20–21
Relocation, **36** · 22–23
Risks, **36** · 17
Time and cost overruns, **36** · 17–18
Marketing, **36** · 8
Reserve Assets
International payments and, **3** · 3
Reserve Currency
Monetary balance, **2** · 20–21
Reserve Position in International Monetary Fund,
see Reserve Tranche in International
Monetary Fund
Reserves
Balance of payments and, **2** · 6, **2** · 7, **2** · 14–15
Federal Reserve Board and, **18** · 70
Foreign exchange, **3** · 5
International, **3** · 4–7, **18** · 16–21
Reserve Tranche in International Monetary Fund,
3 · 6, **3** · 8, **5** · 14
Residency
Taxation and, **24** · 4
Nonresidents, **24** · 9
Resort Tourism, 14 · 9, **14** · 11
Resource Reallocation Methods, 29 · 28–31
Response Bias, 30 · 21–22
Response-Style Bias, 30 · 22
Restate-Translate Method, 23 · 26–27
Restrictive Business Practices
United Nations Conference on Trade and
Development and, **28** · 16–17
Return on Investment
Expected, **17** · 26
Goal, **33** · 29
Internal rate, **34** · 10–11
Reuter Monitor, 18 · 26
Revaluation, 1 · 9
Revenue Act of 1971, 24 · 25
Revised American Foreign Trade Definitions,
31 · 10
Revocable Letter of Credit, 13 · 11
Revolving-Credit Loan, 18 · 73
Revolving Letter of Credit, 13 · 11
Ricardo, David, 6 · 4
Richardson-Merrill
International organization, **39** · 14–15
Right of Priority Clause, 33 · 14
Ringfence Provisions, 24 · 8
Risk
Exchange rate forecasting and, **17** · 26–27
Financial, **13** · 5, **29** · 8
Funding, **19** · 17
Institutional, **13** · 6

Risk (*Continued*)
International banking and, **19** · 15–17
International lending and, **18** · 79, **18** · 82–83
Investment and, **1** · 12–13
Legal factors and, **29** · 8–9
Management, **12** · 3, **12** · 4, **12** · 9–10
High-risk, **12** · 5–6
Low-risk, **12** · 4–5
Perils, **12** · 4–9
Project financing and, **20** · 11–12, **20** · 13
Research and development and, **36** · 17
Risk-return portfolio model, **29** · 30–31
Stake-reduction techniques and, **41** · 11–13
See also Country Risk; Credit Risk; Currency
Risk; Exchange Rate Risk; Foreign-
Exchange Risk; Insurance; Political Risk
Risk-Averse Firm
Exchange rate forecasting and, **17** · 26–27
Risk-Neutral Firm
Exchange rate forecasting and, **17** · 26–27
Risk-Return Portfolio Model, 29 · 30–31
Roll-On/Roll-Off Shop (Ro/Ro), 11 · 7
Rollover, 18 · 25
Rollover Ratio, 21 · 8
Royalties, 14 · 6, **14** · 20
European Economic Community and joint
ventures and, **25** · 16
Patent Licensing Agreements and, **25** · 24–27
See also Licensing

Safeguard Mechanism, 9 · 14–15
of General Agreement on Tariffs and Trade,
5 · 25
Safe-Haven Rules, 24 · 23, **24** · 24, **24** · 26
Sales
Information on, **29** · 15–17
Method, **24** · 14
Personnel, **33** · 26
Sales Analysis Techniques, 29 · 17–22, **29** · 23,
29 · 24
Sales Promotion, 33 · 24–25
Contests, **33** · 24–25
Exhibitions, **10** · 9–10, **10** · 14, **33** · 24
Premiums, **33** · 24–25
Trade fairs, **10** · 9–10, **15** · 34, **33** · 24
Sample Size, 30 · 17–18
Sampling Error, 30 · 32–34
Sampling Frame Selection, 30 · 12–14
Sampling Procedures, 30 · 14–15, **30** · 18–19
Saudi Arabian Monetary Agency (SAMA), 3 · 8
Savings, 1 · 12
Scaling Instruments, 30 · 28
Scheduled Airlines, 14 · 8
Scientific Cooperation Agreements
Communist countries, **15** · 39
Secondary Financial Statements, 23 · 47
Secondary Market
Eurobonds and, **18** · 93
Section 482 Regulations, 24 · 23–25
Section 936 Tax Credit, 24 · 28
Securities Exchange Commission (SEC), 6 · 12
Security
Participation and syndication and, **27** · 17
See also National Security
Segmentation
Market, *see* Market Segmentation
Segment Extrapolation, 29 · 20–21, **29** · 22

"Selective" Procedure
 Government procurement and, 26 · 30–31
Self-Anchoring Scale, 30 · 27–28
Semantic Differential
 Osgood's, 30 · 28
Seminar Mission, 10 · 11
Sensitivity Analysis
 Market entry and, 29 · 28
Service Corps of Retired Executives (SCORE),
  10 · 13
Service Fees
 Controlled group and, 24 · 24
Service of Process
 Foreign state and, 27 · 15
Service on Products, 33 · 15
Services, see International Trade in Services
Shell Offshore Center, 18 · 67
Shipper
 Locating, 11 · 12–13
 See also International Transportation
Shipping, see International Transportation
Shipping Conferences, 11 · 4–5
Short-Term Comprehensive Policy of FCIA, 10 · 16
Short-Term Monetary Support, 3 · 13
Short-Term Planning, 40 · 13–14
Sight Draft, 13 · 10, 13 · 14, 33 · 11
Single-Buyer Policies of FCIA, 10 · 17
Single-Rate Accounting Method, 23 · 8–9, 23 · 10,
  23 · 12
"Single" Tendering
 Government procurement and, 26 · 31
Sirena Srl. v. Eda GmbH, 25 · 28, 25 · 30, 25 · 31
Small Business
 Export-Import Bank and, 10 · 18
Small Business Administration (SBA), 10 · 13–14
 Publications, 10 · 26
Small Business Institute (SBI), 10 · 13
Small Business Market in the World, The, 10 · 26
"Smoot-Hawley" Tariff Act of 1930, 26 · 14
Smoothing
 Foreign currency translation and, 23 · 18–19
Social Affairs, see Public Affairs
Socialism, 6 · 4–5
 See also Communist Countries
Social Security, 12 · 16, 12 · 17
Societa Europa (SE), 22 · 33
Sociocultural Environment
 Bibliography, A · 4–5
 Marketing and, 29 · 10, 32 · 17–18
Solo Fairs, 10 · 9
South Africa
 Inflation accounting, 23 · 32
Southern African Customs Union, 4 · 34, 4 · 35
Sovereign Immunity
 State trading, 15 · 14
 See also Foreign States
Sovereign Risk, see Country Risk
Sovereignty, 6 · 5
Spasm
 Corporate planning information and, 40 · 16
Special Drawing Rights (SDR), 3 · 5–6, 3 · 12,
  5 · 11–12, 18 · 4, 18 · 8, 18 · 9, 18 · 10–11
Specialization Agreements
 East-West trade, 15 · 40
 European Economic Community, 25 · 16–20
Specific Tariff, 9 · 7, 26 · 10
Speculation, 1 · 10–11

Speculative Theory
 Exchange rate determination by, 18 · 37, 18 · 38
Split-Rate Tax System, 24 · 5
Spot Against Forward Swap, 18 · 25
Spot Exchange Rate, 1 · 10–11
Spot Transaction, 18 · 21–22, 18 · 27, 18 · 29,
  18 · 32–33
STABEX, 4 · 23
Stabilizing
 Speculation as, 1 · 11
Stakes
 Conflict management and, 41 · 11–13, 41 · 21
Standard Deviation, 17 · 19
Standard Index of Japan, 33 · 7
Standards
 Products and, 33 · 12–13
 Trade barrier and, 9 · 15, 9 · 17, 26 · 26–28
Standby Arrangements of International Monetary
  Fund, 3 · 9
State, Department of, 6 · 11
State Farm, 15 · 18
State Marketing Boards, 15 · 7–8, 15 · 10, 15 · 13
State Planning Committee (SPC), 15 · 19
State Trading
 Definition, 15 · 3
 Economic consequences, 15 · 11–13
 Exports and, 15 · 9
 Extent, 15 · 3–4
 Legal aspects, 15 · 13–17
 Objectives, 15 · 8
  Domestic, 15 · 10
  External, 15 · 8–10
 See also Communist Countries; East-West
  Trade; Market Economies
State Trading Companies, 15 · 7, 15 · 9, 15 · 10,
  15 · 11
 State marketing boards, 15 · 7–8, 15 · 10,
  15 · 13
Statutory Tax Rates, 24 · 4–5
Storage
 Financing, 13 · 24
Straight Bonds
 Eurobonds, 18 · 92, 18 · 93
 Foreign bonds, 18 · 95
Strikes, see Industrial Relations
Subcontracting
 East-West trade and, 15 · 40
 Offshore sourcing and, 38 · 4
Subject-Matter Jurisdiction
 Loan agreement and, 27 · 20
Subpart F Income, 24 · 17, 24 · 18–21, 24 · 29
Subsidiaries
 European Economic Community, 25 · 11–12
 International commercial banking and, 19 · 9,
  19 · 11
 Netherlands accounting practices and,
  22 · 19–20
 See also Joint Venture
Subsidies, 1 · 7–8, 9 · 17–18, 26 · 19, 26 · 20
 Countervailing duty and, 26 · 19–24
 Domestic, 26 · 20, 26 · 21
 Export, 26 · 20–21
 Net, 26 · 22
Subsidy Account of International Monetary Fund,
  3 · 10
Supplementary Financing Facility of International
  Monetary Fund, 3 · 9–10, 5 · 15–16

Supply Bond, 12 · 13
Supply and Demand
Eurocurrency market and, 18 · 63–64
Supranationalism, 4 · 38
Supranational Law, 25 · 4–5, 25 · 27–28
See also European Economic Community;
International Business Law
Surety Bonds, 12 · 12–15
Surface Transportation, 33 · 22
Survey of Current Business, 17 · 24
Survey Research, 30 · 6, 30 · 29–34
Swap Network, 18 · 40, 18 · 41, 18 · 42
Swap Transaction, 18 · 23–25, 18 · 27, 18 · 29,
18 · 32–33
Sweden
Accounting, 22 · 20–23
SWIFT, 18 · 72
Switch Transactions, 15 · 38
Switzerland Committee on Banking Regulations
and Supervisory Practices, 18 · 96,
18 · 97–99
Syndicated Loan, 18 · 72–73, 18 · 78–79, 18 · 82–83,
18 · 87, 27 · 15–16, 27 · 17
Synergy
Corporate planning and, 40 · 15

Tailored Export Marketing Plans Services
(TEMPS), 10 · 5–6
Tangible Property
Controlled group sale of, 24 · 24–25
Target Market Selection, 32 · 12–13, 33 · 3–5
Target Price
Agricultural products, 4 · 19
Tariff Act of 1930, 26 · 5
Unfair trade practices and, 26 · 25–26
Tariff Conferences of General Agreement on
Tariffs and Trade, 5 · 23–24
Tariff-Quota, 9 · 14
Tariffs, 1 · 5–6, 9 · 7–8, 11 · 9
Ad valorem, 9 · 7, 9 · 15, 9 · 19, 26 · 10, 38 · 17
Common external, 9 · 6
Compensation authority of president and,
26 · 7–8
Compound, 9 · 7
Customs valuation, 28 · 8–10
Definition, 26 · 3
Effective rate of protection, 9 · 7–8
European Economic Community, 25 · 7
Export value, 38 · 17
Historical aspects, 26 · 3–5
Impact, 9 · 8–9
Offshore sourcing and, 38 · 16–17
Optimum, 1 · 6
Preferences for developing countries, 26 · 10–12
Presidential authority and, 26 · 6–8
Specific, 9 · 7, 26 · 10
Tariff-quota, 9 · 14
Trade Act of 1974 and, 24 · 6–8
Variable levy, 9 · 12
See also General Agreement on Tariffs and Trade
Tariff Schedules of the United States, 38 · 16–17,
38 · 18
Task Systems
Conflict management and, 41 · 25, 41 · 26–27
Taxation
Comparative systems
Bilateral tax treaties, 24 · 9

Taxation (*Continued*)
Comparative systems (*(Continued*)
Characteristics, 24 · 4–9
Problems, 24 · 3–4
Earnings abroad, 34 · 6–8
Foreign-tax credit, 24 · 3
Controlled foreign corporation and, 24 · 18
Deductions allocation, 24 · 13
Deemed-paid credit, 24 · 15, 24 · 18
Direct, 24 · 10–14
Election, 24 · 11
Foreign losses and, 24 · 8–9
Foreign-source income and, 24 · 6
Indirect, 24 · 10, 24 · 14–17
Interest expense allocation, 24 · 13–14
Limitation, 24 · 11–12
Research and development expense
allocation, 24 · 14
Source of income rules, 24 · 12–13
Intercompany-transactions and, 24 · 22–25
License agreement and, 36 · 12
Multinational corporations and, 16 · 10
Offshore sourcing and, 38 · 14
Property transfer, 24 · 21–22
Special opportunities
Borrowing through international finance
subsidiary, 24 · 28–29
Domestic international sales corporation
exporting, 24 · 25–27
Section 936 tax credit, 24 · 28
Tax havens, 24 · 29–30
State trading and, 15 · 13–14
Tax deferral, 24 · 3
Controlled foreign corporations and,
24 · 17–18, 24 · 19, 24 · 20, 24 · 21
Subpart F income and, 24 · 17, 24 · 18–21,
24 · 29
Tax Credit
Foreign, *see* Taxation
Section 936 and, 24 · 28
Tax Deferral, *see* Taxation
Tax-Free Transactions
Property transfer as, 24 · 21–22
Tax-Haven, 24 · 3, 24 · 29–30
Antitax havens, 24 · 9
Income taxation and, 34 · 7–8
Tax Reduction Act of 1975, 10 · 20
Tax Reform Act of 1976, 10 · 20–21, 24 · 28
Recapture provision in, 34 · 8
Tax Treaties, *see* Bilateral Tax Treaties
Technical Cooperation Among Developing
Countries (TCDC), 36 · 8–10
Technical Help to Exporters, 33 · 13
Technological-Gap Theory, 1 · 4
Technology
Availability differences, 1 · 4
Conflict issue, 41 · 4, 41 · 7
Corporate planning and, 40 · 18
Diversification and, 40 · 7
Innovation, 36 · 7–8
See also Research and Development
Management, 36 · 6–8
Manufacturing and, 36 · 5
Marketing and, 29 · 9–10, 29 · 11, 36 · 5–6,
36 · 7–8
Organization, 36 · 4
Patent licensing agreements and, 25 · 25–27

Technology (*Continued*)
Planning, **36** · 4
Production and concentration, **37** · 3–5
Significance, **36** · 3
Strategy, **36** · 4
Trade in, **14** · 6, **14** · 18–21
Communist countries, **15** · 39–40
See also Multinational Corporations
Technology Transfer Agreements, 36 · 11–12
Instruments of, **36** · 10–11
Managing, **36** · 12–13
National approaches, **36** · 13–14
Costs, **36** · 16–17
Developed-country concerns and, **36** · 14
See also Developing Countries
United Nations Conference on Trade and
Development, **28** · 5, **28** · 17–19
Value conflicts, **41** · 15
See also Multinational Corporations
Telephone Interviewing, 30 · 30–31
Television
Advertising, **33** · 23
Trade and, **14** · 21
Temporal Accounting Method, 23 · 8, **23** · 10,
23 · 11
Translation and, **23** · 27
Tenders
International, **33** · 11–12
Term Loan, 18 · 73
Terms of Trade, 1 · 5
Trade barriers, **9** · 3–4, **9** · 5
Terrapin v. Terranova, **25** · 34
Territoriality
Industrial property rights, **25** · 27
Territorial Tax System, 24 · 6
Terrorism, 41 · 4, **41** · 6
Third-Country Transactions
Letter of Credit for, **13** · 12
Third World, *see* Developing Countries
Threshold Price
Agricultural products, **4** · 19
Time Draft, 13 · 10, **33** · 11
See also Bankers Acceptances
Time Horizon
Exchange rate forecasting and, **17** · 25
Time-Series Analysis
Exchange rate forecasts and, **17** · 21–22
Tokyo Round of Multilateral Trade Negotiations,
see Multilateral Trade Negotiations
Toll Charges, 24 · 4, **24** · 22
Tomorrow-Next Swap, 18 · 25
Top-Down Planning, 40 · 5
Topic Bias, 30 · 22
Tourism, *see* International Trade in Services
Trade, 1 · 3–5
See also Exports; Imports; International Trade
in Services; Technology; Trade Barriers
Trade Act of 1974
Communist countries, **15** · 34
Dumping and, **15** · 33
Escape clause action and, **9** · 15, **9** · 16, **26** · 12,
26 · 15
Export-Import Bank and, **15** · 30
Generalized System of Preferences, **26** · 11–12
Market disruption and, **15** · 33, **20** · 15–16
Private-sector-advisory committee mechanism,
6 · 9

Trade Act of 1974 (*Continued*)
Tariffs and, **24** · 6–8
Trade Act of 1979, 26 · 10
Countervailing duty and, **26** · 21–24
Most-favored-nation status and, **15** · 32
National security and, **26** · 16–17
Unfair competitive practices and, **26** · 18–19
Trade Advisory Center, 10 · 5, **10** · 12
Trade Agreements Act of 1934, 26 · 4–5
Trade Agreements Act of 1979, 26 · 5
Antidumping and, **9** · 11
Buy-American Act and, **9** · 18
Executive reorganization and, **6** · 9–10
Government procurement and, **26** · 35–36
Standards code and, **26** · 27–28
Trade Balance
Balance of payments and, **2** · 9, **2** · 11
Trade Barriers
Arguments against, **9** · 4–5
Cost, **9** · 4
Countervailing duties, **1** · 8, **9** · 11, **9** · 13,
26 · 19–24
Direct, **9** · 6–7
Antidumping duties, **9** · 10–11, **9** · 12,
26 · 24–25
Escape clause, **9** · 14–15, **9** · 16, **26** · 12–16
Export taxes, **9** · 7
Import and export licensing, **9** · 10
Payments restrictions, **9** · 14
Safeguard actions, **9** · 14–15
See also Tariffs
Domestic politics, **1** · 6–7
Economic integration and, **9** · 6
Effective rate, **1** · 7, **9** · 7–8
Indirect, **9** · 15–19
Customs, **9** · 18–19
Government and, **9** · 17–18
Standards, **9** · 15, **9** · 17, **26** · 26–28
International agreements regarding, **9** · 5–6
Motivations for, **9** · 3–4
National security and, **1** · 7, **9** · 3, **9** · 4,
11 · 9, **26** · 16–17
Nontariff barriers, **1** · 5–6, **9** · 7
Standards, **26** · 26–28
State trading and, **15** · 10–11, **15** · 12
Subsidies, **1** · 7–8
Technical, **9** · 17
Transport costs, **1** · 5
Unfair competitive practices, **9** · 3, **26** · 17–28
See also General Agreement on Tariffs and
Trade; Quotas
Trade Channel, **33** · 22
Trade Creation, 4 · 3–4
Trade Diversion, 4 · 3–4
Trade Exhibitions, *see* Exhibitions
Trade Expansion Act of 1962, 26 · 13–14
Trade Fairs, 33 · 24
Commerce Department, **10** · 9–10
Communist countries, **15** · 34
Trade Lists, **33** · 19
Trademarks, 37 · 5
European Economic Community, **25** · 29–36
Protection and selection of, **33** · 13–14
Trade Missions, 10 · 11
Trade Opportunity Program (TOP), 10 · 7–8
Trade Opportunity Referral Service, 10 · 15
Trade Reference Room, 10 · 7

Trade Representative, Office of the U.S., *see* United States Trade Representative
Trade Union Internationals (TUIs), 35 · 14
Trade Unions, *see* Industrial Relations
Trading Blocs, 4 · 3
Economic integration and large, 4 · 5−6
See also Economic Integration
"Trading with the Enemy" Act, 7 · 10
Tramp Steamers, 11 · 5−6
Transaction Exposure, 34 · 4
Transaction Value
Customs valuation, 26 · 9
Transborder Data Flow, 14 · 6, 14 · 19, 14 · 20−21
Transferable Letter of Credit, 13 · 11
Transfer Pricing, 33 · 9−10
Transfer Tax, 4 · 35
Translate-Restate Method, 23 · 26−27
Translation Exposure, 34 · 4
Translation Gain, 23 · 8, 23 · 13−14
Translation Loss, 23 · 6, 23 · 8, 23 · 13−14
Translations
Financial reports and, 23 · 46
Foreign currency and, *see* Accounting
Medium-term planning and, 40 · 11, 40 · 13
Transnational Corporations, *see* Multinational Corporations
Transportation, *see* International Transportation
Transportation Insurance, 12 · 20−21
Treasury, Department of
Dumping and, 15 · 33−34
Exchange rate intervention and, 18 · 40, 18 · 42
Treaty of Rome, *see* European Economic Community
Treaty Shopping, 24 · 29
See also Bilateral Tax Treaties
Trigger-Price Mechanism, 9 · 11
Tripartite Joint Ventures
Communist countries, 15 · 41
Trust Fund of International Monetary Fund, 3 · 9
Turnkey Contract
Market entry through, 31 · 15
Turnkey Plus, 31 · 15
Turnkey Projects, 15 · 38, 15 · 40
Developing countries and, 36 · 8

Unconfirmed Irrevocable Letter of Credit, 13 · 11
Underwriters, 12 · 21
Unemployment, 1 · 11
Unfair Trade Practices
Trade barriers and, 9 · 3, 26 · 17−28
Uniform Accounting Plan
Poland, 22 · 24−25
Union Européene des Experts Comptables Economiques et Financiers (UEC), 22 · 34
Unions, *see* Customs Unions; Industrial Relations
United Brands v. Commission, 25 · 9, 25 · 10−11
United Kingdom
Industrial relations, 35 · 9
Inflation accounting, 23 · 29−30, 23 · 31
Insurance and, 12 · 21
International banking in, 18 · 70−71
United Nations
Accounting practices, 22 · 31−32, 23 · 29, 23 · 34
Exports and, 8 · 3
Marketing information, 29 · 5
Multinational corporations and, 7 · 8, 7 · 18−19

United Nations (*Continued*)
Multinational corporations and (*Continued*)
Codes of conduct, 28 · 5, 28 · 6, 28 · 18−19
Publications, 17 · 24, 33 · 3
United Nations Conference on Trade and Development (UNCTAD), 5 · 28−29, 7 · 7, 11 · 8−9
Multinational corporations and, 7 · 19
Codes of conduct and, 28 · 5, 28 · 6, 28 · 9−10, 28 · 11, 28 · 15−19
Technology transfer, 37 · 13−14
Trade preference for developing countries, 26 · 11
United Nations Economic Commission for Latin America (CEPAL), 4 · 31
United Nations Economic and Social Council (UNESCO)
Marketing information, 29 · 5
United Nations Group of Experts on International Standards of Accounting and Reporting (GEISAR), 23 · 29, 23 · 35, 23 · 38−39
United Nations Industrial Development Organization (UNIDO), 8 · 3
United Nations Monthly Bulletin of Statistics, 17 · 24
United States Commercial Service (USCS), 10 · 4, 10 · 5
United States Merchant Marine, 11 · 9−11
United States Sovereign Immunities Act of 1976, 27 · 13−15
United States Trade Representative (USTR), 6 · 11
Product standards and, 26 · 28
Unfair competitive practices and, 26 · 19
United States Treasury Bulletin, 17 · 21
Unpackaging
Technology transfer and, 37 · 6, 37 · 7
Unrequited Transfers
Balance of payments and, 2 · 3, 2 · 4
Utility Model, 37 · 4

Vaessen/Moris Case, 25 · 26
Validated Export License, 9 · 10
Valuation
Balance of payments and, 2 · 7−8
Customs, 9 · 18−19, 26 · 8−10
Poland, 22 · 25−26
Value-Added Tax (VAT), 4 · 40
European Economic Community, 4 · 22
Van Zuylen Freres v. Hag A.G., 25 · 31−32
Variable Import Levy, 4 · 19, 9 · 12
Vertical Agreements
Patent licensing agreements and, 25 · 24
Vertical Foreign Direct Investment, 11 · 14
Vertical Integration
Diversification and, 40 · 7
Vertical Operations of Multinational Corporations, 16 · 5
Very Short-Term Financing Facility, 3 · 13
Vicious Cycle of Depreciation, 1 · 12
Video/Catalog Exhibitions, 10 · 10−11
Virtuous Cycle of Appreciation, 1 · 12
Voluntarism
United Kingdom, 35 · 9
Voluntary Export Restraint (VER), 1 · 6, 9 · 9
Voluntary Foreign Credit Restraint (VFCR) Program, 18 · 45, 18 · 46, 18 · 48

Wanderlust Tourism, 14 · 9, 14 · 10, 14 · 11

Warehousing, 33 · 22
Warranties
    Loan agreement and, 27 · 5
Warranties on Products, 33 · 15
Warrants
    Eurobonds, 18 · 92
    Foreign bonds, 18 · 95
WASAG/ICI Agreement, 25 · 20–22
Werner Report, 4 · 20
West, see Market Economies
West African Economic Community (CEAO),
    4 · 34, 4 · 35, 4 · 36
West Germany
    Accounting, 22 · 11–17, 23 · 32
    Industrial relations, 35 · 8
Withholding Tax, 24 · 5
"Witteveen Facility," see Supplementary Financing
    Facility of International Monetary Fund
Workmen's Compensation, 12 · 16, 12 · 17
World Aviation Directory, 33 · 7
World Bank, 3 · 7
    International Development Association, 5 · 8–9,
        13 · 28
    International Finance Corporation, 5 · 9–10,
        13 · 28
    Marketing information, 29 · 5, 29 · 7

World Bank (Continued)
    See also International Bank for Reconstruction
        and Development
Worldcasts, 29 · 7
World Development, 33 · 3–4
World Federation of Trade Unions (WFTU), 35 · 13,
    35 · 14
World Financial Markets, 17 · 24
World Guide to Trade Associations, 30 · 12
World Health Organization (WHO)
    Infant-baby formula and, 7 · 19
World Intellectual Property Organization (WIPO)
    Multinational organizations and, 7 · 19
World Trade Directory Reports, 33 · 19
World Trade Outlook, 10 · 24
World Traders Data Report (WTDR), 10 · 9
Worldwide Information Trading System (WITS),
    10 · 9
Worldwide Projects, 33 · 22

Yale Express System, Inc., In re, 27 · 16
Yankee Bonds, 18 · 90
    See also International Bond Market
Yaounde Conventions, 4 · 23
Yield to Maturity
    Eurobond and, 18 · 94